T0214335

# Lecture Notes in Computer Science　9327

*Commenced Publication in 1973*
Founding and Former Series Editors:
Gerhard Goos, Juris Hartmanis, and Jan van Leeuwen

More information about this series at http://www.springer.com/series/7410

Günther Pernul · Peter Y A Ryan
Edgar Weippl (Eds.)

# Computer Security – ESORICS 2015

20th European Symposium on Research in Computer Security
Vienna, Austria, September 21–25, 2015
Proceedings, Part II

Springer

*Editors*
Günther Pernul
University of Regensburg
Regensburg
Germany

Edgar Weippl
SBA Research
Wien
Austria

Peter Y A Ryan
University of Luxembourg
Luxembourg
Luxembourg

ISSN 0302-9743          ISSN 1611-3349 (electronic)
Lecture Notes in Computer Science
ISBN 978-3-319-24176-0          ISBN 978-3-319-24177-7 (eBook)
DOI 10.1007/978-3-319-24177-7

Library of Congress Control Number: 2015948157

LNCS Sublibrary: SL4 – Security and Cryptology

Springer Cham Heidelberg New York Dordrecht London

Printed on acid-free paper

Springer International Publishing AG Switzerland is part of Springer Science+Business Media
(www.springer.com)

# Foreword

It is our great pleasure to welcome you to the 20th European Symposium on Research in Computer Security (ESORICS 2015).

This year's symposium continues its tradition of establishing a European forum for bringing together researchers in the area of computer security, by promoting the exchange of ideas with system developers and by encouraging links with researchers in related areas.

The call for papers attracted 293 submissions – a record in the ESORICS series – from 41 countries. The papers went through a careful review process and were evaluated on the basis of their significance, novelty, technical quality, as well as on their practical impact and/or their level of advancement of the field's foundations. Each paper received at least three independent reviews, followed by extensive discussion. We finally selected 59 papers for the final program, resulting in an acceptance rate of 20 %.

The program was completed with keynote speeches by Sushil Jajodia, George Mason University Fairfax, USA and Richard Clayton, University of Cambridge, UK.

Putting together ESORICS 2015 was a team effort. We first thank the authors for providing the content of the program. We are grateful to the Program Committee, who worked very hard in reviewing papers (more than 880 reviews were written) and providing feedback for authors. There is a long list of people who volunteered their time and energy to put together and organize the conference, and who deserve special thanks: the ESORICS Steering Committee, and its chair Pierangela Samarati in particular, for their support; Giovanni Livraga, for taking care of publicity; Javier Lopez, as workshop chair, and all workshop co-chairs, who organized workshops co-located with ESORICS; and Yvonne Poul for the local organization and the social events.

Finally, we would like to thank our sponsors, HUAWEI, for the financial support and SBA Research, for hosting and organizing ESORICS 2015.

A different country hosts the conference every year. ESORICS 2015 took place in Vienna, Austria at the Vienna University of Technology. We are very happy to have hosted the 20th edition of the symposium in Vienna and we tried to put together a special social program for you, giving you the opportunity to share ideas with other researchers and practitioners from institutions around the world and see all the beautiful sights of Vienna.

We hope that you found this program interesting and thought-provoking and that you enjoyed ESORICS 2015 and Vienna.

July 2015

Günther Pernul
Peter Y A Ryan
Edgar Weippl

# Organization

## General Chair

Günther Pernul          Universität Regensburg, Germany

## Program Chairs

Peter Y A Ryan        University of Luxembourg, Luxembourg
Edgar Weippl         SBA Research & Vienna University of Technology, Austria

## Workshops Chair

Javier Lopez           University of Malaga, Spain

## Program Committee

| | |
|---|---|
| Alessandro Armando | Università di Genova, Italy |
| Vijay Atluri | Rutgers University, USA |
| Michael Backes | Saarland University, Germany |
| Feng Bao | Security and Privacy Lab, Huawei, China |
| David A. Basin | ETH Zurich, Switzerland |
| Giampaolo Bella | Università di Catania, Italy |
| Carlo Blundo | Università degli Studi di Salerno, Italy |
| Stefan Brunthaler | SBA Research, Austria |
| Ran Canetti | Tel Aviv University, Israel |
| Liqun Chen | HP Labs, UK |
| Michael Clarkson | Cornell University, USA |
| Jason Crampton | University of London, UK |
| Cas Cremers | University of Oxford, UK |
| Frédéric Cuppens | Télécom Bretagne, France |
| Nora Cuppens-Boulahia | Télécom Bretagne, France |
| Sabrina De Capitani di Vimercati | Università degli Studi di Milano, Italy |
| Wenliang Du | Syracuse University, USA |
| Hannes Federrath | University of Hamburg, Germany |
| Simon Foley | University College Cork, Ireland |
| Sara Foresti | Università degli Studi di Milano, Italy |
| Felix Freiling | Friedrich-Alexander-Universität Erlangen-Nürnberg, Germany |
| Michael Goldsmith | University of Oxford, UK |

# Contents – Part II

## Authentication

## Policies

## Applied Security

# Contents – Part I

**Crypto Applications and Attacks**

**Risk Analysis**

# Privacy

# *FP-Block*: Usable Web Privacy by Controlling Browser Fingerprinting

Christof Ferreira Torres[1], Hugo Jonker[2(✉)], and Sjouke Mauw[1]

[1] CSC/SnT, University of Luxembourg, Luxembourg, Luxembourg
[2] Open University of the Netherlands, Heerlen, The Netherlands
hugo.jonker@ou.nl

**Abstract.** Online tracking of users is used for benign goals, such as detecting fraudulent logins, but also to invade user privacy. We posit that for non-oppressed users, tracking within one website does not have a substantial negative impact on privacy, while it enables legitimate benefits. In contrast, *cross-domain* tracking negatively impacts user privacy, while being of little benefit to the user.

Existing methods to counter fingerprint-based tracking treat cross-domain tracking and regular tracking the same. This often results in hampering or disabling desired functionality, such as embedded videos. By distinguishing between regular and cross-domain tracking, more desired functionality can be preserved. We have developed a prototype tool, *FP-Block*, that counters cross-domain fingerprint-based tracking while still allowing regular tracking. *FP-Block* ensures that any embedded party will see a different, unrelatable fingerprint for each site on which it is embedded. Thus, the user's fingerprint can no longer be tracked across the web, while desired functionality is better preserved compared to existing methods.

## 1  Introduction

Online activities play an ever-growing role in everyday life. Consequently, companies are increasingly tracking users online [14]. There may be various reasons for such tracking, such as fraud prevention by identifying illegitimate usage attempts [16], suggesting related content, and better targeting advertisements. Where such tracking remains confined to the tracker's own website, the balance between privacy and functionality is (arguably) satisfied: the website learns a user's browsing habits *on that particular website*, which helps to improve the website *for this user*. We will call this type of tracking *regular tracking*.

However, some companies offer online services that are embedded on a large number of websites. Examples of such services are social sharing buttons, popular JavaScript libraries, and popular web analytics services. Thanks to this ubiquitous embedding, such companies can track users over large portions of the web. According to various studies, plenty of different companies are embedded on a sizable[1] portion of the Web. For example, consider the Facebook "Like" button.

---

[1] E.g. penetration rates for top 1 million sites according to BuiltWith.com (October 2014): *DoubleClick*.net 18.5 %, *Facebook Like button* 15.6 %, *Google Analytics* 46.6 %.

© Springer International Publishing Switzerland 2015
G. Pernul et al. (Eds.): ESORICS 2015, Part II, LNCS 9327, pp. 3–19, 2015.
DOI: 10.1007/978-3-319-24177-7_1

The embedding site includes a piece of code that triggers the user's browser to contact the Facebook servers to download the button. As browsers are made to explain where a request originated (the HTTP `Referer` field), the browser will tell Facebook exactly which URL triggered this request each time. This enables Facebook to track the user across the web [15], irrespective of whether or not the user even has a Facebook account. We will call this type of tracking *third-party tracking*.

This tracking can be done using an HTTP cookie, but even if such (third party) cookies are blocked, it is possible to infer a set of attributes (screen resolution, HTTP user agent, time zone, etc.) that are often sufficient to uniquely identify the user [5]. Note that such attributes were intended to benefit the user, e.g. to present her the mobile version of a site when browsing from a phone, or to present the page in the user's preferred language. Yet even though personalia such as name or age are not explicitly revealed, the tracker can learn far more about the users than one realises[2].

Identifying users by such means is called "fingerprinting". Much like a fingerprint belongs to one unique individual, a fingerprint of communication with a server belongs to a unique browser.

Existing countermeasures combat such fingerprint-based tracking with little regard for the impact on the user experience. The goal is then to find an approach that ensures a better balance between user experience (that is: less impact on desired embedded contents) and tracking. We address this with the concept of *web identity*: the set of fingerprintable browser characteristics. A web identity is generated for the main site visited (e.g., bbc.com), and that identity is then also used for all interaction with embedded contents on that site (e.g. videos, social media buttons, etc.). If the user visits a different site (e.g., cnn.com), a different identity is used (the web identity for cnn.com). Thus, a party embedded on both sites will first see the web identity for bbc.com, and later the web identity for cnn.com. As we ensure that the generated identities are distinct, the two visits can no longer be linked by means of their fingerprint. We focus on fingerprinters that aim to re-identify as many users as possible. We do not target tools that are seeking to track any one specific individual.

*Contributions.* The main contributions of our research are the following:

1. We argue that a distinction be made between regular and cross-domain tracking; we observe that current anti-tracking tools do not make this distinction.
2. We introduce the notion of a web identity to generalize the rather dynamic notion of a fingerprint. We propose *separation of web identities* as an approach to fingerprint privacy that prevents cross-domain tracking, while allowing regular tracking.
3. We have developed a prototype browser extension, *FP-Block*, that supports the automatic generation and management of web identities. A user's web identity remains constant across all his visits to the same domain, while his

---

[2] E.g. by data aggregation, a supermarket can infer if a customer is pregnant, and estimate her due date (Forbes.com, 2012).

web identities for different domains are not related. The tool has a user interface that shows which third parties are embedded in the current page, which fingerprintable attributes are requested by the website and how these are spoofed by the tool. This allows the user to fine-tune the tool for individual sites.

4. By deobfuscating the code of the most relevant fingerprinters, we compiled an up-to-date list of the attributes used by current fingerprinters. Further, based on a literature study, we compiled a list of the attributes affected by the most relevant anti-tracking tools. These lists guided our design and helped us to compare our work to existing tools.

5. We have tested our tool against six fingerprinters in two different scenarios: first-party fingerprinting and third-party fingerprinting. In all cases, our tool was successful in affecting the computed fingerprint.

   As final validation, we tested our tool against a commercial fingerprinter's online tracking ID. Again the tool was successful: the tracking ID without the tool was different from the ID when running the tool.

## 2 Related Work

We distinguish related work between work on fingerprinting and work on countermeasures against tracking and fingerprinting.

### 2.1 Fingerprinting

The possibility of remotely inferring characteristics of devices has been known for some time. E.g. Kohno et al. [6] use TCP clock skew to remotely fingerprint devices. Eckersley [5] was the first to draw significant attention to the problem of fingerprinting web browsers. His fingerprinting algorithm returned a unique fingerprint for 83.6 % of the browsers considered. Subsequent papers established how to fingerprint other aspects such as the user-agent string and IP address [17], the HTML5 "canvas" element [10], the used Javascript engine [9,11], the fonts present [3], etc. Other work has suggested approaches to combine several fingerprintable attributes to arrive at unique fingerprints (e.g. [3,17]). Using such techniques only on one site does not constitute a large invasion of privacy. However, as Mayer and Mitchel [8] and Roosendaal [15] have pointed out, social plugins are embedded on many pages, which allows the social network to track users across the Internet. Thanks to fingerprinting, such tracking does not even require an account – anyone with a unique fingerprint can be traced.

Several recent studies have investigated the practice of fingerprinting in more detail. Acar et al. [2] introduced a framework to detect online fingerprinters by detecting activities typical of fingerprinters (e.g. requesting values of certain attributes, enumerating fonts, etc.). Their detection algorithm found several fingerprinting techniques in action. Many of these were by companies offering fingerprinting services to others: the fingerprinters were either embedded by the visited site, or by a third party such as inside a third-party advertisement.

In a followup study, Acar et al. [1] investigate the spread of three tracking mechanisms, amongst which HTML5 canvas fingerprinting. They propose three heuristics to estimate whether a canvas is being used to fingerprint; we adopt these criteria in our tool. This paper also shows that canvas fingerprinting is being used by a popular 3rd party service (AddThis.com). Nikiforakis et al. [13] provide a detailed study of the fingerprinting techniques of three online fingerprint services (BlueCava, Iovation and ThreatMetrix). They found that fingerprinting can be tailored to the detected browser, e.g. when detecting a browser as Internet Explorer, the fingerprint would include Internet Explorer-specific attributes. Moreover, Flash was used by all three to enrich the established fingerprint. Flash allows access to many similar attributes as JavaScript, but may give a more detailed response (e.g. including major and minor kernel version number). Moreover, Flash ignores a browser's proxy settings for client-server communication. This allows the fingerprint services to detect if the user is behind a proxy or not, and correlate the IP address of the proxy with that of the user.

### 2.2   Countermeasures

Several existing plugins directly aim to stop trackers, including commercially developed ones (e.g. Ghostery, AVG Do Not Track, etc.), and academically developed ones, such as FireGloves [3], ShareMeNot  [14], PriVaricator [12], etc. Some of these work by blocking trackers, either by using a predefined blacklist or by updating the blacklist on the fly using heuristic rules. Krishnamurthy and Wills [7] argue that blacklists are prone to being incomplete (not all trackers blocked), and therefore ultimately fail at blocking trackers. A similar argument holds against heuristically updated blacklists: the next tracker may well use tracking methods not covered by the heuristics, and so escape notice. More damning, however, Mowery et al. [9] show how an attacker can detect a blacklist and use its content as an additional fingerprintable attribute.

Other plugins work by faking attributes (FireGloves, PriVaricator). As [5,13] point out, such spoofing may lead to inconsistencies that paradoxically make the user stand out more. Indeed, Acar et al. [2] argue this is the case for FireGloves-equipped browsers. Even more strongly, Nikiforakis et al. [13] advice against the use of any user-agent-spoofing extension.

We add the following observations. First of all, fingerprinting can be done both passively and actively. Passive fingerprinting uses attributes inherent in the communication (e.g. the order of HTTP headers), while active fingerprinting executes attribute-gathering scripts on the client-side (e.g. determine JavaScript engine speed). Anti-tracking tools should take into account both mechanisms. Secondly, anti-tracking tools should consider "fingerprint consistency", i.e., the extent to which a fingerprint is perceived as genuine. By carefully tailoring the spoofing system to account for known fingerprinters, their consistency checks can be satisfied. Secondly, fingerprinting trackers take a fingerprint of each user, and aim to link a new fingerprint to an existing fingerprint. If the new fingerprint is sufficiently different, this link can*not* be made – irrespective of how unique this new fingerprint is. PriVaricator [12] uses similar ideas to these. In contrast, our approach addresses both active and passive fingerprinting, uses real-world browser statistics to generate consistently spoofed fingerprints, and works as a browser extension instead of modifying the browser itself.

The Tor Browser[3], widely recognised as providing the best privacy, uses another approach: it aims to keep one single set of attribute values across all its instances. In ideal circumstances, this means that no two Tor Browser instances can be distinguished from each other, however, users can install plugins or tweak settings which undo this protection.

The Tor browser is strongly focused on preserving privacy, providing a level of privacy believed to be sufficient for use under intense state scrutiny. This strong privacy comes at the expense of some usability, most notably, that all data is sent via an onion routing network. We posit that the strong privacy offered by the Tor Browser exceeds the needs of non-oppressed users. Therefore, we will focus on the prevention of third-party tracking.

# 3    Determining the Fingerprint Surface

In this section, we determine the relevant set of characteristics that are used to fingerprint a user. Determining the full set of characteristics, the *fingerprint surface*, is not practically possible. For example, as a plugin can change the browser's behaviour in ways that can be detected, constructing a complete set of characteristics necessarily requires examining all browser plugins. Therefore, we focus pragmatically on that part of the fingerprint surface that is being used by fingerprinters. This implies that we use their definition of identity. As fingerprinters equate a fingerprint of the device with a user identity, we will use this (somewhat imprecise) abstraction as well.

To establish the fingerprint surface, we determine for four major commercial fingerprinters which characteristics they use to fingerprint, i.e., their *fingerprint vector*. We also examine four major anti-fingerprint tools and determine which part of the fingerprint surface they consider. Together, this gives us a practical approximation of the fingerprint surface. *FP-Block* then is built to ensure no two fingerprints are fully coincide within this approximation.

## 3.1    Limitations of Preventing Fingerprint Tracking

There are two approaches to prevent fingerprint-based tracking: blocking trackers, and spoofing attribute values. However, neither by itself suffices to prevent tracking, while both impact user experience.

*Blocking Fingerprinters.* A naive solution is to block any third party content. However, many webpages embed such content, without which the webpage renders incorrectly (e.g. content delivery networks, embedded video). Other third party content helps to sustain and improve the site (counters, advertisers, analytics,...). The impact of blocking all third party content on usability will be

---

[3] https://www.torproject.org/projects/torbrowser.html.en.

far too great. Blocking known major trackers would provide some protection. However, such a list will remain incomplete [7], irrespective of updates. Thus, blocking by itself cannot fully address third party tracking without impacting on desired functionality.

*Spoofing Attribute Values.* The attribute values that make up the fingerprint may be faked. This changes the fingerprint, which in turn changes what the tracker infers as the identity. There are many browser plugins that randomise a (sub)set of attributes. However, not all attributes can be faked without substantially impacting user experience (e.g. JavaScript engine speed). Moreover, faked data often makes the user's fingerprint stand out *more* [5,13], making the fingerprint more easy to recognise. Finally, new fingerprintable characteristics keep on being discovered. Thus, it is impossible in practice to determine and spoof the full set of fingerprintable characteristics.

Thus, determining the entire fingerprint surface is impossible. As such, no anti-fingerprint tool can prevent all fingerprinting. This motivates a pragmatic approach: determine which characteristics are used by a set of fingerprinters, and focus on those.

### 3.2   Fingerprint Vectors

To determine which characteristics are commonly used to fingerprint users, we determine the fingerprint vectors of several widely-used fingerprinters. We analyze three commercial trackers: BlueCava (BC), IOvation (IO), and Threat-Metrix (TM). Note that this part of our analysis builds on and expands the results of [13]. We furthermore analyze one social plugin that fingerprints users: AddThis (Add). We complement this with characteristics gathered from Eckersley's seminal work [5] (Pan) and from an open source fingerprint library, FingerPrintJS (FPjs). The results are presented in the left part of Table 1 (legend and footnotes in Table 2).

In Table 1, each row denotes a fingerprintable characteristic. A $\sqrt{}$ sign indicates that the fingerprinter uses this characteristic in determining a fingerprint. Characteristics marked with $\checkmark$ were previously reported in [13]; those marked with — were reported, but are no longer used.

Recall that in this work we only target the HTTP and JavaScript layer of the communication stack. Fingerprinting can also occur at other layers, e.g. at the TCP/IP layer, or at the Flash layer.

For *FP-Block* we only address HTTP and JavaScript characteristics that are used by one ore more of the six analyzed fingerprinters.

### 3.3   Fingerprint Surface

To determine the minimum set of characteristics that needs to be protected, we investigate four popular anti-fingerprinting tools: FireGloves [3] (FG), the Tor Browser (Tor), PriVaricator [12] (PV), and Random Agent Spoofer[4] (RAS). For

---

[4] https://github.com/jmealo/random-ua.js.

**Table 1.** Comparison of attributes used by various fingerprinting libraries.

| Attribute | Fingerprinters | | | | | | Countermeasures | | | | | |
|---|---|---|---|---|---|---|---|---|---|---|---|---|
| | Pan | BC | IO | TM | Add | FPjs | FG | Tor | PV | RAS | FPB | |
| Plugin Enumeration | ✓ | ✓ | ✔ | ✓ | ✔ | ✔ | ✔ | ✔ | ✔ | | ✔ | |
| Font Detection | ✓ | ✓ | | ✓ | | | ✔ | ✔ | ✔ | ✔ | ✔ | |
| User-Agent | ✓ | ✓ | ✓ | ✓ | ✔ | ✔ | ✔ | ✔ | | ✔ | ✔ | 1 |
| HTTP Header Accept | ✓ | | | | | | | | | | | 1,5 |
| HTTP Header Accept-Charset | ✓ | | | | | | | ✔ | | | | 1,5 |
| HTTP Header Accept-Encoding | ✓ | | | | | | | | ✔ | ✔ | | 1 |
| HTTP Header Accept-Language | ✓ | | | | | | | ✔ | ✔ | ✔ | | 1 |
| Screen Resolution | ✓ | ✓ | ✓ | ✓ | ✔ | ✔ | ✔ | ✔ | | ✔ | ✔ | |
| Timezone | ✓ | ✓ | ✓ | ✓ | ✔ | ✔ | ✔ | ✔ | | ✔ | ✔ | |
| Browser Language | | ✓ | ✓ | — | ✔ | ✔ | ✔ | | | | ✔ | |
| OS & Kernel Version | | ✔ | ✔ | ✓ | ✔ | ✔ | ✔ | ✔ | | ✔ | ✔ | |
| DOM Storage | ✓ | ✔ | ✔ | ✔ | ✔ | ✔ | | | ✔ | | ✔ | |
| IE userData | ✓ | ✔ | | | | | | | | | | 2 |
| Java Enabled | ✔ | | | | ✔ | | | | | | ✔ | |
| DNT User Choice | — | | | | ✔ | ✔ | | | ✔ | ✔ | | 1 |
| Cookies Enabled | ✓ | | ✔ | | | | | | | | ✔ | 1 |
| JS detect: Flash Enabled | ✓ | ✓ | ✓ | ✓ | ✔ | ✔ | | | | | ✔ | |
| ActiveX + CLSIDs | ✓ | ✓ | | ✓ | ✔ | ✔ | | | | | | 2 |
| Date & Time | | ✔ | ✓ | ✔ | ✔ | | | | | | | 5 |
| CPU | | ✔ | ✔ | | ✔ | ✔ | | | ✔ | | ✔ | |
| System/User Language | | ✓ | ✔ | | ✔ | | | | | | ✔ | 2 |
| OpenDatabase | | | ✔ | | ✔ | ✔ | | | | | ✔ | |
| Canvas Fingerprinting | | | | | ✔ | ✔ | | ✔ | | ✔ | ✔ | |
| Mime-type Enumeration | ✓ | | | ✓ | | | ✔ | ✔ | ✔ | | ✔ | |
| HTTP Proxy Detection | | | ✓ | ✓ | | | | | | | | 4 |
| IndexedDB | | | | | ✔ | ✔ | | | | | ✔ | |
| Math Constants | | ✓ | | | ✔ | | | | | | | 5 |
| Windows Registry | | ✓ | ✓ | | | | | | | | | 3 |
| TCP/IP Parameters | | ✓ | ✓ | | | | | ✔ | | | | 1 |
| Google Gears Detection | | ✓ | | | | | | | | | | 4 |
| Flash Manufacturer | | | | ✓ | | | | | | | | 4 |
| MSIE Security Policy | | ✓ | | | | | | | | | | 2 |
| AJAX Implementation | | ✓ | | | | | | | | | | 5 |
| MSIE Product key | | | ✓ | | | | | | | | | 3 |
| Device Enumeration | | ✓ | | | | | | | | | | 3 |
| Device Identifiers | | | ✓ | | | | | | | | | 3 |
| IP address | | ✓ | | | | | | ✔ | | | | 1 |
| HTML Body Behavior | | | | | | ✔ | | | | | | 2 |
| Battery | | | | | ✔ | | | ✔ | | | ✔ | |
| WebGLRenderingContext | | | | | ✔ | | | ✔ | ✔ | | ✔ | |

✓: Attribute previously reported in [13].
— : Attribute previously reported, but no longer present.

**Table 2.** Legend and footnotes for Table 1

| **Fingerprinters** | | Updated from | | **Countermeasures** |
|---|---|---|---|---|
| Pan | Panopticlick [5] | [13] | FG | FireGloves [3] |
| BC | BlueCava | [13] | Tor | Tor [4] Browser Bundle |
| IO | Iovation | [13] | PV | PriVaricator [12] |
| TM | ThreatMetrix | [13] | RAS | Random Agent Spoofer |
| Add | AddThis | **new** | **FPB** | **FingerPrint-Block** |
| FPjs | FingerPrintJS | **new** | | |

[1] Property can be checked passively, i.e., no client-side technology required.
[2] Property specific to Internet Explorer.
[3] Property is determined using a Windows DLL created by the fingerprinting company.
[4] Out of scope – *FP-Block* only targets HTTP and Javascript layers.
[5] Blocking or spoofing this attribute would break or limit important functionality.

each, we determine which characteristics are considered. The results are listed on the right side of Table 1.

Not all characteristics are equal: some can be used by the fingerprinter without using JavaScript (e.g. HTTP headers), some are specific to Internet Explorer, others require additional client-side software (e.g. Windows DLL), etc. For the implementation, we do not focus on these characteristics. Furthermore, some characteristics are intrinsic to the communication or the user experience (HTTP accept header, date & time), and cannot be blocked or spoofed without adverse effects. Taken together, these considerations lead us to formulate the intended fingerprint surface of our tool *FP-Block* in the rightmost column of Table 1. Consequently, *FP-Block* only generates web identities which are distinct with respect to this fingerprint surface.

## 4   Design

Our goal is to prevent third-party fingerprint-based tracking. To this end, we generate distinct web identities (i.e., sets of fingerprintable characteristics) and then use these web identities in such a fashion as to be untraceable. More precisely, for each new site visited, we use a freshly generated web identity that is distinct from all previous web identities. This web identity is then used for all interactions due to this site, be they with the site itself or with any of its third parties.

### 4.1   Balancing Usability vs. Privacy

The approach of separating web identities is not meant to interfere with regular tracking (tracking by the main site itself). It even allows third parties to track a user on a particular site – but it prevents third parties from linking that user to another user on a *different* site. Thus, this approach has the advantage that it

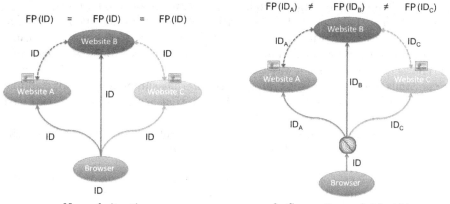

a. Normal situation.          b. Separating web identities.

**Fig. 1.** Third-party fingerprinting.

does not affect local login processes, nor is it affected by such a process. Moreover, third parties that embed site-specific codes (e.g. of the form http://facebook. com/FROM-SITE-A/) are free to do so. We remark that the defensive paradox, i.e. defenses make the user stand out more, strongly impacts regular tracking. With regards to third-party tracking, however, there is a great difference. Our approach focuses on linkability between different sites, not on distinguishing users on one site. A user that stands out on one website is not necessarily the same person as a user that stands out on another website, even if both stand out due to the defensive paradox. Hence, third-party tracking is affected less severely by the defensive paradox.

The approach of separating web identities thus stays very close to a normal user experience. However, when visiting a different site, a different web identity is used, and the user cannot be tracked to this new site by third-party fingerprint-based tracking. Figure 1a depicts the normal functioning of the web: embedded third parties (shown by the dashed arrows) can fingerprint the site's visitors and match a fingerprint on site A to a fingerprint on site B. Figure 1b depicts our approach: each website visited sees another fingerprint. Consider that sites A and C embed a social media plugin of site B. Then when the user visits site A, the web identity as seen by B is $ID_A$. When the user visits site C, however, the web identity as determined by B is $ID_C$. Finally, if the user visits B directly, yet another web identity is used. This allows B to track the user locally on site A and on C, but not *from* site A *to* C.

### 4.2 Generating Web Identities

To prevent fingerprint-based tracking, we need to ensure that two distinct web identities are seen as different by a fingerprinter. This is not necessarily as straightforward as it may seem: computers and browsers are regularly updated (changing their characteristics), and fingerprinters need to account for this. Thus, merely ensuring that the set of characteristics of one web identity do not coincide with any other web identity is not sufficient. Moreover, we recall the fingerprinting countermeasure paradox: the use of a countermeasure impacts fingerprintable characteristics in such a way that the resulting set of characteristics is more unique (thus, more traceable) than if no countermeasure was used. An example of this is a client that claims to be an iPhone 2, that is capable of running Flash (real iPhones do not run Flash).

This leads to two design requirements: web identities must be "enough" different, and a generated web identity must be "consistent".

*Ensuring Sufficient Difference.* Updating a browser affects browser-specific attributes, updating the operating system affects OS-specific attributes, etc. To ensure a freshly generated web identity is sufficiently different from previously generated web identities, accounting for anticipated updates, we group the attributes into the following classes:

- Browser, e.g. user agent, browser name, vendor, accept-encoding.
- Language, e.g. language, system language, user language.
- OS/CPU, e.g. platform, cpu class, oscpu.
- Screen, e.g. width, height, color depth.
- Timezone. i.e. time zone offset.

Ideally, a freshly generated web identity is different in all classes to all previous web identities. This impacts the time required to generate a new web identity. For *FP-Block*, we chose to require every newly generated web identity to have at least two different attributes from at least two different classes. This allows a decent trade off between time needed to generate a web identity and uniqueness. In future versions, the generation algorithm could be optimised to require more differences.

*Consistency of Web Identity.* A randomly generated web identity is unlikely to be consistent, that is, have no contradictory attributes (such as Flash running on an iPhone). To ensure consistency, web identities need to be generated using a realistic distribution of attribute values. For instance, the chance that a Firefox user is on a Linux computer is greater than the chance that an Internet Explorer user is. In effect, the process to generate a consistent web identity can be modelled as a Markov chain. As usage of different browsers and operating systems varies over time, such a Markov chain needs to be updatable to remain current. To this end, we identified classes of states (operating system, processor, screen properties, etc.). Any Markov chain for a web identity needs to contain these classes. Moreover, these can be ordered (operating system and processor are determined before the user agent is). In this way, we model a construction process for Markov chains generating web identities (see Fig. 2).

States and transition probabilities for Markov chains are derived from J. Mealo's data[5], based on actual usage statistics from Wikimedia. An excerpt

---

[5] https://github.com/jmealo/random-ua.js/commits/master/random_ua.js.

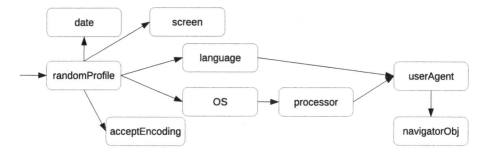

**Fig. 2.** Generic model of Markov chains for web identities.

of this data is shown in Table 3, and an example of how this translates into a Markov chain is shown in Fig. 3. In this figure, where no weights are indicated, the uniform distribution is implied. Remark that for windows operating systems, one of the attribute values for processor is the empty string ''.

**Table 3.** Example attribute distributions, due to J. Mealo

| | Win | Mac | Linux |
|---|---|---|---|
| chrome | .89 | .09 | .02 |
| firefox | .83 | .16 | .01 |
| opera | .91 | .03 | .06 |
| safari | | .04 | .96 |
| iexplorer | 1.00 | | |

| Platform | Processor string | probability |
|---|---|---|
| Linux | 'i686': | .5 |
| | 'x86_64': | .5 |
| Mac | 'Intel': | .48 |
| | 'PPC': | .01 |
| | 'U; Intel': | .48 |
| | 'U; PPC': | .01 |
| Windows | '': | .$\bar{3}$ |
| | 'WOW64': | .$\bar{3}$ |
| | 'Win64; x64': | .$\bar{3}$ |

## 5 Development and Implementation

### 5.1 Development

We developed *FP-Block* as a Firefox plugin. This ensures that *FP-Block* is publicly available and easy to install for a large group of users. To limit the scope of the project, *FP-Block* focuses on two communication layers: JavaScript, illustrating application of our approach to active fingerprinting, and HTTP, illustrating application to passive fingerprinting. In principle, tracking at other layers was not considered. An exception to this was made for Flash: all commercial fingerprinters use Flash to fingerprint and store information. To be effective, the tool hides Flash (i.e., removed from detected plugins). Another exception is made for ActiveX. As *FP-Block* does not include a full ActiveX implementation, it

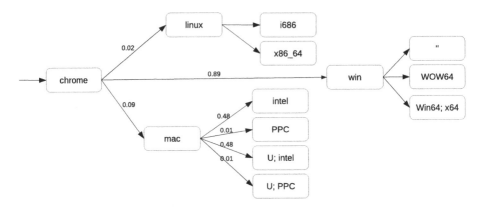

**Fig. 3.** Partial Markov chain for web identities for the Chrome profile.

cannot consistently pretend to be an Internet Explorer browser. Therefore, *FP-Block* never pretends to be Internet Explorer. Finally, *FP-Block* is designed for desktop browsers, and simulates only desktop browsers.

*FP-Block* is available from http://satoss.uni.lu/software/fp-block/, and is open source[6].

## 5.2  Implementation

*FP-Block* intercepts and modifies all outgoing requests and incoming responses. This is done by adding observers for the "topics" `http-on-modify-request` and `http-on-examine-{cached-}response`, respectively. For requests, first the existing web identity for the domain is retrieved, or, if none exists, a fresh web identity is generated and stored. Then HTTP headers like `Accept-Encoding` and `Accept-Language` are set according to the web identity. E-tag headers (which are intended to aid caching) can easily be exploited to track users, and are thus deleted (cf. Table 1). Finally, requests for social plugins that are explicitly blocked by user preference are cancelled. Currently, *FP-Block* can block the social plugins of Facebook, Twitter, Google Plus, LinkedIn, Tumblr, and Pinterest.

For incoming responses, the observer evaluates the fingerprint and constructs a Javascript script that enforces the fingerprint. Blocking access to blocked and spoofed attributes is handled by replacing the access functionality of Javascript using `navigator.__defineGetter__()`, for attributes such as `userAgent`, `app Name`, `cookieEnabled`, `battery`, `geolocation`, `oscpu`, etc. (cf. Table 1). Screen properties are protected analogously using `screen.__defineGetter__()`. Detection events are inserted in a similar way to detect when scripts use code that is typically used to fingerprint the user, such as enumerating mimetypes or plugins, using DOM storage, font detection, etc. Canvas fingerprinting is thwarted by adding random noise and the *FP-Block* logo to a random position on the

---

[6] Source available from GitHub repository FP-Block under the GPL v3 license.

canvas. This is then stored with the fingerprint to be reused in future visits. Finally, a few lines are added to remove the constructed script after execution, using `removeChild()` on the script's parent node. This ensures that the script cannot be found in the source by other scripts.

The thusly constructed script is then injected into the response at the very top, ensuring it is run before any other script sent by the server.

## 6    Experiments and Validation

We tested *FP-Block* in two different settings:

- *First-party fingerprinting*: the visited site uses fingerprinting, and
- *Third-party fingerprinting*: the visited site embeds a third-party fingerprinter.

We ran three main variations of the tests:

1. without *FP-Block*.
   This is to verify that the test setup is functioning correctly.
2. with *FP-Block*,
   a. with the test site using an open source fingerprinting script, `Finger PrintJS`.
      This allows us to verify that *FP-Block* affects fingerprinting.
   b. with the test sites using any one of the four commercial fingerprinting scripts.
      This is to test the effectiveness of *FP-Block* against real-life fingerprinters.

We updated each fingerprinting script to add the fingerprint it computed to the test page. This allows us to execute the tests as described by simply opening the test sites in a browser (see e.g. Fig. 4).

*Test 1: First-party Fingerprinting.* After successfully verifying that the test was set up correctly (Fig. 4a), we executed the test shown in Fig. 4b using Finger-PrintJS. The result was that *FP-Block* correctly ensures that a browser visiting the two sites has a different fingerprint on each site.

*Test 2: Embedded Fingerprinting.* We created a test page on site A which embeds fingerprinting content from site B, and vice versa (cf. Fig. 1). Both test sites also ran the same fingerprint scripts locally. We then visited each page with and without our tool. In both cases, we first tested this set up with the FingerPrintJS script.

Without *FP-Block*'s protection, the fingerprint is the same in all cases (cf. Fig. 1a). With *FP-Block*, however, this changes (Fig. 1b). The fingerprint script running on site A sees web identity $ID_A$ if the user visits A, but if the user visits B (which embeds the script from A), the same fingerprint script sees web identity $ID_B$. The script returns different fingerprints for these web identities.

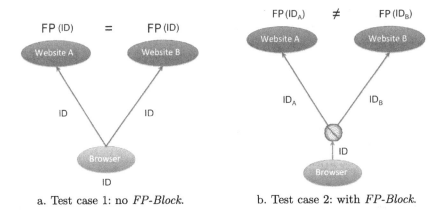

a. Test case 1: no *FP-Block*.     b. Test case 2: with *FP-Block*.

**Fig. 4.** First party fingerprinting tests.

*Testing Against Commercial Fingerprinters.* We then repeated tests, using the fingerprint scripts of the commercial fingerprinters (BlueCava, IOvation, Threat-Metrix, and AddThis). These scripts all compute a hash which seems to serve as the fingerprint. However, each of them also communicates the entire set of attributes and values used in this fingerprint back to the fingerprinter's servers. Our tests showed that, without *FP-Block*, the hash as computed by each script does not change – the behaviour is equivalent to that in Fig. 1a. With *FP-Block*, the hashes were different if they were computed by B's script embedded on site A, or by the same script of B computed when visiting site B. In short, the tests show that *FP-Block* successfully affects the fingerprint.

However, affecting the fingerprint does not necessarily mean that tracking is stopped. Given that commercial fingerprinters communicate the determined attribute values back to the fingerprinter, the fingerprinter may match such a set offline to previously seen sets. To test whether *FP-Block* is able to prevent such offline fingerprinting, we need to know the web identity which the fingerprinter attributes to us.

BlueCava provides such a service (the BlueCava advertising ID, available on BlueCava's "opt-out" page). Our final validation was to check our BlueCava advertising ID with and without *FP-Block*. The ID changed, which leads us to conclude that *FP-Block* successfully prevented BlueCava from tracking us. As can be seen in Table 1, BlueCava uses the most attributes for its fingerprint – they are by far the most advanced fingerprinters listed. As such, we believe that success against BlueCava provides a good estimate of success against other offline fingerprint algorithms.

*Update Frequency of Fingerprinters.* Finally, we monitored the rate of change of fingerprinters listed in Table 1. We downloaded each fingerprinter's script once an hour from September 2014 until June 2015. In this period, Panopticlick's script did not change. The open source script FingerPrintJS changed once, which turned out to be support for detecting screen orientation.

With respect to the commercial fingerprinters: the scripts of BlueCava and AddThis have not changed since we began monitoring them. The scripts for IOvation and ThreatMetrix include time and date of the download, ensuring that every downloaded script is different. Since both scripts are heavily obfuscated, verifying that there are no changes other than embedded time and date is difficult. However, the file size of IOvation's script remained constant since September 2014. We take this as an indication that the script has not changed. Finally, ThreatMetrix' script started changing on 27 October, 2014, and still continues to evolve swiftly. An initial analysis revealed that there are large changes to the code base. Once ThreatMetrix seems to be more stable, we intend to re-analyse the new code.

*Stability and Compatibility Testing.* To determine the robustness of our plugin, we have been using the plugin in our main browser since June 2014. Where early versions occasionally crashed or gave unexpected results, since October 2014 only Javascript-heavy and Flash pages are noticeably affected. *FP-Block* blocks Flash to prevent Flash side channels, but Flash can be enabled in *FP-Block*'s menu. Javascript-heavy pages are slow to load. A refresh solves this.

Lastly, we tested how the plugin cooperates with several popular privacy-focused plugins: AdBlock Plus, Privacy Badger, Ghostery, and Disconnect. *FP-Block* perfectly cooperates alongside all in default settings. We note two caveats to this. First, Disconnect blocks social media plugins, similar to *FP-Block*. This functionality is implemented similarly in the two plugins. When both are running, social media plugins are blocked by both. Enabling a social media plugin thus requires enabling it in both plugins. Second, AdBlock Plus is a generic blocking plugin, into which blocklists can be loaded. There exist blocklists for social plugins. Loading such a blocklist inherently causes interference between AdBlock Plus and *FP-Block*.

## 7  Conclusions

Ubiquitous tracking on the web is a reality, enabled by the proliferation of embedded content and effective fingerprinting techniques. Currently available countermeasures against fingerprinting work by either blocking embedded content or faking a web client's characteristics. Not only does this break benign applications of fingerprinting (such as detecting session hijacking), but it also reduces the user experience. In order to achieve a more practical balance between privacy and usability, we have introduced the notion of a web identity that allows for re-identification within a web site, while it prevents tracking across websites. Such a web identity is a set of fingerprintable characteristics that can be tweaked on the user side.

We have developed a prototype web browser extension that supports the use and management of web identities. In order to design our tool's capabilities, we investigated the *fingerprint vector*, i.e., the set of characteristics used for fingerprinting, of the major fingerprint tools. This led to an up-to-date overview of four major fingerprinters' abilities.

The web identities generated by our tool are *distinct* and *consistent*. This means that two generated web identities are sufficiently different to prevent being linked by current fingerprint tools and that the attributes are being spoofed in such a way that their combination doesn't stand out. Consistency is achieved by implementing a Markov model for the generating of attribute values.

Fingerprint tools will be able to re-identify users even after minor changes or regular updates of their computing environment. Therefore, our tool should not generate web identities that can be linked in this way. Our current approach, consisting of classifying attributes, is a rather crude heuristic. We consider a refinement of this approach as interesting future work. Thereto, we propose to collect data on the evolution of client side attributes, in order to build a Markov model that will decide if two generated web identities are sufficiently distinct.

Finally, our prototype implementation only addresses the HTTP and Java Script layers of communication. Given the focus of the current fingerprinting tools, this already provides a significant level of practical privacy. Nevertheless, the arms race between fingerprinters and anti-tracking tools will continue, so we consider extending the current fingerprint vector of our tool as an ongoing activity.

# References

1. Acar, G., Eubank, C., Englehardt, S., Juárez, M., Narayanan, A., Díaz, C.: The web never forgets: Persistent tracking mechanisms in the wild. In: Proceedings of 21st ACM Conference on Computer and Communications Security (CCS 2014), pp. 674–689. ACM Press (2014)
2. Acar, G., Juarez, M., Nikiforakis, N., Diaz, C., Gürses, S., Piessens, F., Preneel, B.: FPDetective: Dusting the web for fingerprinters. In: Proceedings of 20th ACM SIGSAC Conference on Computer and Communications Security (CCS 2013), pp. 1129–1140. ACM Press (2013)
3. Boda, K., Földes, Á.M., Gulyás, G.G., Imre, S.: User tracking on the web via cross-browser fingerprinting. In: Laud, P. (ed.) NordSec 2011. LNCS, vol. 7161, pp. 31–46. Springer, Heidelberg (2012)
4. Dingledine, R., Mathewson, N., Syverson, P.: Tor: The second-generation onion router. Technical report, Naval Research Lab Washington (2004)
5. Eckersley, P.: How unique is your web browser? In: Atallah, M.J., Hopper, N.J. (eds.) PETS 2010. LNCS, vol. 6205, pp. 1–18. Springer, Heidelberg (2010)
6. Kohno, T., Broido, A., Claffy, K.: Remote physical device fingerprinting. IEEE Trans. Dependable Secure Comput. **2**(2), 93–108 (2005)
7. Krishnamurthy, B., Wills, C.E.: Generating a privacy footprint on the internet. In: Proceedings of 6th ACM SIGCOMM Conference on Internet Measurement (ICM 2006), pp. 65–70. ACM Press (2006)
8. Mitchell, J.C., Mayer, J.R.: Third-party web tracking: Policy and technology. In: Proceedings of IEEE Symposium on Security and Privacy (S&P 2012), pp. 413–427 (2012)
9. Mowery, K., Bogenreif, D., Yilek, S., Shacham, H.: Fingerprinting information in JavaScript implementations. In: Proceedings of Web 2.0 Security & Privacy (W2SP 2011). IEEE Computer Society (2011)

10. Mowery, K., Shacham, H.: Pixel perfect: Fingerprinting canvas in HTML5. In: Proceedings of Web 2.0 Security & Privacy (W2SP 2012). IEEE Computer Society (2012)
11. Mulazzani, M., Reschl, P., Huber, M., Leithner, M., Schrittwieser, S., Weippl, E.R.: Fast and reliable browser identification with Javascript engine fingerprinting. In: Proceedings of Web 2.0 Security & Privacy (W2SP 2013), May 2013
12. Nikiforakis, N., Joosen, W., Livshits, B.: PriVaricator: Deceiving fingerprinters with little white lies. Technical report MSR-TR-2014-26, Microsoft Research, February 2014
13. Nikiforakis, N., Kapravelos, A., Joosen, W., Kruegel, C., Piessens, F., Vigna, G.: Cookieless monster: Exploring the ecosystem of web-based device fingerprinting. In: Proceedings of 34th IEEE Symposium on Security and Privacy (S&P 2013), pp. 541–555. IEEE Computer Society (2013)
14. Roesner, F., Kohno, T., Wetherall, D.: Detecting and defending against third-party tracking on the web. In: Proceedings of 9th USENIX Symposium on Networked Systems Design and Implementation (NSDI 2012), pp. 155–168. USENIX (2012)
15. Roosendaal, A.: We are all connected to facebook ... by facebook!. In: Gutwirth, S., Leenes, R., De Hert, P., Poullet, P. (eds.) European Data Protection: In Good Health, pp. 3–19. Springer, The Netherlands (2012)
16. Unger, T., Mulazzani, M., Fruhwirt, D., Huber, M., Schrittwieser, S., Weippl, E.R.: SHPF: Enhancing http(s) session security with browser fingerprinting. In: Proceedings of Eighth International Conference on Availability, Reliability and Security (ARES 2013), pp. 255–261. IEEE Computer Society (2013)
17. Yen, T.-F., Xie, Y., Yu, F., Yu, R.P., Abadi, M.: Host fingerprinting and tracking on the web: Privacy and security implications. In: Proceedings of 19th Annual Network & Distributed System Security Symposium (NDSS 2012). The Internet Society (2012)

# Mind-Reading: Privacy Attacks Exploiting Cross-App KeyEvent Injections

Wenrui Diao[1], Xiangyu Liu[1], Zhe Zhou[1], Kehuan Zhang[1(✉)], and Zhou Li[2]

[1] Department of Information Engineering, The Chinese University of Hong Kong,
Hong Kong, China
{dw013,lx012,zz113,khzhang}@ie.cuhk.edu.hk
[2] IEEE Member, Boston, MA, USA
lzcarl@gmail.com

**Abstract.** Input Method Editor (IME) has been widely installed on mobile devices to help user type non-Latin characters and reduce the number of key presses. To improve the user experience, popular IMEs integrate personalized features like reordering suggestion list of words based on user's input history, which inevitably turn them into the vaults of user's secret. In this paper, we make the first attempt to evaluate the security implications of IME personalization and the back-end infrastructure on Android devices. In the end, we identify a critical vulnerability lying under the Android KeyEvent processing framework, which can be exploited to launch cross-app KeyEvent injection (CAKI) attack and bypass the app-isolation mechanism. By abusing such design flaw, an adversary is able to harvest entries from the personalized user dictionary of IME through an ostensibly innocuous app only asking for common permissions. Our evaluation over a broad spectrum of Android OSes, devices, and IMEs suggests such issue should be fixed immediately. All Android versions and most IME apps are vulnerable and private information, like contact names, location, etc., can be easily exfiltrated. Up to hundreds of millions of mobile users are under this threat. To mitigate this security issue, we propose a practical defense mechanism which augments the existing KeyEvent processing framework without forcing any change to IME apps.

**Keywords:** Mobile security · Smart IME · Privacy leakage · System flaw

## 1 Introduction

Smartphone is becoming the major device for handling people's daily tasks like making calls, sending/receiving messages and surfing the Internet. Of particular importance in supporting these features are input devices. Among them,

---

Responsible disclosure: We have reported the CAKI vulnerability and the corresponding exploiting schemes to the Android Security Team on January 7th, 2015. The video demos can be found at https://sites.google.com/site/imedemo/.

© Springer International Publishing Switzerland 2015
G. Pernul et al. (Eds.): ESORICS 2015, Part II, LNCS 9327, pp. 20–39, 2015.
DOI: 10.1007/978-3-319-24177-7_2

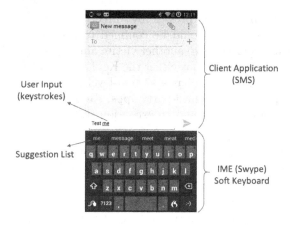

User Input
(keystrokes)

Client Application
(SMS)

Suggestion List

IME (Swype)
Soft Keyboard

**Fig. 1.** Smart IME on Android

**Fig. 2.** Warning message

keyboard, either hardware keyboard integrated within mobile phone or soft keyboard displayed on touch screen, receives a significant volume of users' input. These keyboards are mostly tailored to users speaking Latin languages. Users in other regions like Chinese and Japanese have to use Input Method Editor (or IME) to type non-Latin characters. In fact, a large number of IME apps[1] have emerged since the advent of smartphone and been installed by enormous population. The capabilities of IME are continuously extended to optimize users' typing experience. The present IME (see Fig. 1) is able to learn the words a user has inputted, customize the suggested words, and predict the words the user plans to type. These user-friendly features help the IME gain popularity even among Latin-language users.

The wide adoption of IME, however, does not come without cost. Previous research has raised the privacy concerns with **shady IMEs** which illegally spy on users' input [30,34,35,38]. Indeed, they could cause security and privacy issues if installed by common users, but their impact is limited as the majority of IMEs are well-behaved and there have been efforts in warning the risk of enabling a new IME (see Fig. 2). The question not yet answered is whether **legitimate IMEs** are bullet-proof. If the answer is negative, they can be exploited by adversary as stepping stones to breach the privacy of mobile users. In this work, we examine smart IMEs (the ones supporting optimization features) and the back-end framework in an attempt to verify their security implications. We choose Android as a target platform given its popularity and openness.

**KeyEvent Processing.** We first look into the underlying framework which handles input processing. In short, each key press on hardware keyboard triggers a sequence of KeyEvents [11] on Android. As for the purpose of automated

---

[1] We use IME and IME app interchangeably in this paper.

testing, a mobile app can also simulate key presses by directly injecting KeyEvents. Without a doubt, such behavior should be confined to prevent a malicious app from illegally injecting KeyEvents to another victim app. Android consolidates KeyEvent dispatching by ensuring that either the KeyEvent sender app and receiver app are identical or sender app has a system-level permission (INJECT_EVENTS) which cannot be possessed by third-party apps. Failing to pass such check will cause KeyEvent being discarded and an exception thrown.

**Our Findings.** Unfortunately, this seemingly invulnerable framework can be cracked. If a malicious app injects KeyEvents to its owned EditText widget with IME turning on, the KeyEvents will be redirected to the IME, resulting in **cross-app KeyEvent injection (CAKI)** attack. Following this trail, attacker can peep into IME dictionary (usually stored in the internal storage protected by app-isolation mechanisms) and know user's favorite words or even the words taken from other sensitive sources, like phone contact. The root cause of this vulnerability is that Android only performs security checks before KeyEvent is dispatched but misses such when KeyEvent is delivered. For this special case, because of the discrepancy between the point of checking and the point of delivering, IME is turned into the final receiver on the fly when KeyEvent is delivered, therefore the security check at the beginning is bypassed. Since this issue exists in the system layer, all IMEs are potentially under threat.

**Attack Against IME.** Even knowing this vulnerability, a successful attack against IME is not trivial. The challenges include how to efficiently extract words related to personal information or interest and how to hide the malicious activities from user. Towards solving the first challenge, we devise new technique to automatically enumerate the combinations of prefix letters and use differential analysis to infer the words private to user. This technique can be adapted to different language models and all achieve good results. To address the second challenge, we combine several well-founded techniques to make the attack context-aware and executed till user is absent.

We implemented a proof-of-concept malicious app named *DicThief* and evaluated it against 11 very popular IMEs and 7 Android OS versions. The result is quite alarming: all the Android versions we examined are vulnerable and most of the IMEs we surveyed are not immune. The population under threat is **at a scale of hundreds of millions** (see IME popularity in Table 3). Towards mitigating this urgent issue, we propose an origin-checking mechanism which augments the existing Android system without forcing any change to IME apps.

**Contributions.** We summarize this paper's contributions as below:

- *New Vulnerability.* We discovered a fundamental vulnerability in the Android KeyEvent processing framework leading to CAKI attack.
- *New Attack Surface.* We show by launching CAKI attack, an attacker can steal a variety of private information from IME dictionary. Differing with previous IME-based attacks, our attack is the first to exploit the innocent IMEs.
- *Implementation, Evaluation, and Defense.* We implemented the attack app DicThief and demonstrated the severeness of this problem by testing under different real-world settings. We also propose a defense scheme as a remedy.

## 2    Background and Adversary Model

### 2.1    IME and Personalized User Dictionary

IMEs have emerged to support users speaking different languages like English and Chinese. A smartphone is usually shipped with pre-installed IMEs, but alternatively, users could download and use other IME apps. IME have gained massive popularity: top IMEs like Sogou Mobile IME [16,17] has more than 200 million active users.

The IMEs used today have been evolved from solely soft keyboard to versatile input assistant with many new features to improve users' typing experience. The goals of these new features are to reduce the number of keys a user needs to type. For instance, current mainstream IMEs (such as SwiftKey [18], TouchPal [21], Sogou Mobile IME, etc.) implement features like dynamic suggestions order adjustment, contact names suggestions, next-word prediction and new word saving to provide suggestions for current or subsequent words. Hence, a user could select a word among them without typing the complete text. These features are called "optimization features" and we elaborate them below:

– **Dynamic Order Adjustment.** This feature adjusts the order of suggested words dynamically according to user's input history. For example, as shown in Fig. 3, two typed characters "ba" lead to different lists of suggested words. "bankruptcy" is the first suggestion in the upper picture while "banquet" is the first suggestion in the lower one.

**Fig. 3.** Dynamic order adjustment

– **Contact Names Suggestion.** IME can suggest a name from user's phone contact when part of the name is typed. In addition, suggestions also pop up when an unknown name is typed for correction. The READ_CONTACTS permission needs to be granted to support this feature.

– **Next-Word Prediction.** IME attempts to predict the next word user wants to input based on the previous words typed. Figure 4 shows an example that IME gives a prediction "Newcastle" based on the previous input "Fly to".

**Fig. 4.** Next-word prediction

– **New Word Saving.** When a word not existing in the dictionary is typed, IME automatically adds this word to its dictionary.

To summarize, all the above features are driven by user's personalized information, like user's input history. Furthermore, when the permissions shielding user's sensitive data are granted, IMEs can customize their dictionaries using various data sources, including SMS, Emails, and even social network data. It is very likely that the names of user's family members and friends and nearby locations are recorded by the IME after using for a while. We manually examined the settings and permissions of several IMEs and summarizes the data sources

**Table 1.** Data sources of mainstream IMEs for optimization features

| Production name | Version | Input history | Contacts | Emails/ SMS | Social network | Location |
|---|---|---|---|---|---|---|
| Go Keyboard [7] | 2.18 | √ | √ | | | |
| TouchPal [21] | 5.6 | √ | √ | √ | √ | |
| Adaptxt - Trial [1] | 3.1 | √ | √ | √ | √ | √ |
| Google Keyboard [8] | 4.0 | √ | √ | √ | √ | |
| SwiftKey Keyboard [18] | 5.0 | √ | √ | √ | √ | |
| Swype Keyboard Free [19] | 1.6 | √ | √ | | √ | |
| Fleksy Keyboard Free [5] | 3.3 | √ | √ | √ | √ | |
| Google Pinyin Input [9] | 4.0 | √ | √ | | | |
| Sogou Mobile IME [16] | 7.1 | √ | √ | | | √ |
| Baidu IME [3] | 5.1 | √ | √ | | | |
| QQ IME [14] | 4.7 | √ | √ | | | |

of mainstream IMEs (each of them has over 1 million installations) in Table 1. Apparently, the personalized dictionary should be considered private assets and protected in the safe vault. In fact, most of the IME apps we surveyed keep their dictionaries in the internal storage of mobile phone which is only accessible to the owner app.

## 2.2   Adversary Model

The adversary we envision here is interested in the dictionary entries of IME deemed private to the user, like contact names, and aims to steal and exfiltrate them to her side. We assume the user has installed a victim IME which is "**benign**" and "**smart**".

1. "Benign" means this IME exercises due diligence in protecting user's private data. The measures taken include keeping its dictionary in app's private folder (internal storage). This assumption differs fundamentally from previous IME-based attacks which assume IME itself is malicious.
2. "Smart" means this IME can learn unique word-using habits and build a personalized user dictionary based on user's input history, contacts, etc.

At the same time, we assume this user has downloaded and installed a malicious app named *DicThief* aiming to steal entries from victim IME. The default (enabled) IME on the device could be identified through the system class Settings.Secure [15]. This malware only claims two permissions: INTERNET and WAKE_LOCK. Both permissions are widely claimed by legitimate apps and unlikely to be rejected by users: nearly all apps declare the INTERNET permission, and WAKE_LOCK is also widely claimed by apps like alarm, instant messenger (e.g., WhatsApp and Facebook Messenger), etc. With the WAKE_LOCK permission, our

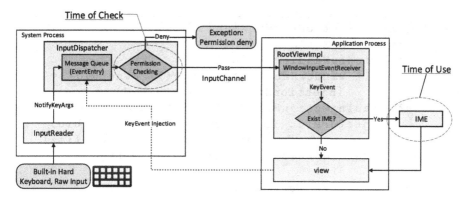

**Fig. 5.** Android KeyEvent processing framework and CAKI vulnerability

attack can be launched **when the phone is in sleep mode and locked with password**.

## 3   Vulnerability Analysis

While direct access to the dictionary of IME is prohibited if coming from a different and non-system app, our study shows this security guarantee can be violated. By revisiting the keystroke processing framework of Android, we discover a new vulnerability lying under Android OS, allowing us to launch **Cross-App KeyEvent Injection (CAKI)** attack. In essence, by exploiting such vulnerability, a malicious app can simulate user keystrokes on an IME, and read the suggested words. Below we describe the mechanism of keystroke processing in Android and the new vulnerability we identified.

### 3.1   Android KeyEvent Processing Flow

The internal mechanism of input processing in Android is quite sophisticated and here we only overview how KeyEvents[2] are processed. At a high level, when a key is pressed on hardware (built-in) keyboard, a sequence of KeyEvents will be generated by wrapping the raw input, and then sent to the corresponding handlers (e.g., IME). These two steps are called *KeyEvent pre-processing* and *KeyEvent dispatching*. We illustrate the process in Fig. 5 and then elaborate the details below[3]:

---

[2] IME accepts another kind of input event – MotionEvent [12], coming from soft keyboard (see Fig. 1). Its processing flow is different and not covered in this paper.

[3] Our descriptions are based on Android 4.4.4_r2.0.1 [2]. For other versions, the flows are mostly the same. Only the paths of source code could be different.

```
1  bool checkInjectionPermission(...) {
2    if (injectionState
3      && (windowHandle == NULL
4        || windowHandle->getInfo()->ownerUid !=
           injectionState->injectorUid)
5      && !hasInjectionPermission(injectionState->
         injectorPid, injectionState->injectorUid)) {
6        ...    // Code omitted due to space limit
7        return false; // Permission denied
8    }
9    return true; // Pass checking
10 }
```

**KeyEvent Pre-processing.** As soon as a hardware key (e.g., built-in keyboard) is pressed, a raw input event is sent to a system thread InputReader (initiated by WindowManagerService) and encapsulated into an object of type NotifyKeyArgs. Then, this object is passed to thread InputDispacher (also initiated by WindowManagerService) and a KeyEntry object is generated. Lastly, this object is converted to EventEntry object and posted to the message queue (InboundQueue) of InputDispacher to be distributed to right handlers. If a key press is simulated by an app, the corresponding KeyEvents are initiated directly and finally sent to the message queue (in the format of EventEntry).

**KeyEvent Dispatching.** Before event dispatching, there is a permission checking process on the corresponding EventEntry to ensure its legitimacy. The code undertaking such check is shown below (excerpted from the Android code repository [24]):

This routine first verifies whether the event is generated by a hardware device (checking injectionState). If injectionState is NULL, the check is passed and the event is directly sent to handlers. Otherwise (the event is generated by an app), this routine verifies whether the sender app owns the required permission or if it is identical to the receiver app (we fill in the details in Sect. 3.2).

An input event passing the above check will be dispatched via a system IPC mechanism InputChannel to the receiver app, which should run in the foreground and take the input focus. In particular, the WindowInputEventReceiver component belonging to the receiver app process will be notified and then forward the received KeyEvent to other components of ViewRootImpl, a native OS class handling GUI updates and input event processing, for further processing. When an IME is activated and also brought to the foreground (see Fig. 1), there exists a special policy: ViewRootImpl will redirect the KeyEvent to the IME, which absorbs the event and renders the resulting text (suggested word or the raw character) on the client app's view. This policy guarantees the KeyEvents are processed by IME with high priority.

## 3.2   Cross-App KeyEvent Injection Vulnerability

Since the simulated key-presses could come from a malicious app, Android enforces much stricter checking. Still, the checking routine is not flawless. Below, we elaborate a critical vulnerability in this routine:

**KeyEvent Injection.** An app can simulate various input events using the APIs provided by Android instrumentation library [10]. This is supposed to support automated app testing. For example, an app can invoke the function `Instrumentation.sendKeyDownUpSync()` to simulate user's keystrokes, such as "d", "7", "!", and the corresponding KeyEvents will be injected into the message queue subsequently.

**Verification.** Injected KeyEvent needs to be vetted. Otherwise, one app can easily manipulate the input to the app taking focus. If a KeyEvent is not originated from hardware keyboard, at least one of the security checks has to be passed (see the code block of `checkInjectionPermission` in Sect. 3.1):

1. The KeyEvent injector and receiver are the same.
2. The KeyEvent injector is granted with the `INJECT_EVENTS` permission.

As `INJECT_EVENTS` is a system-level permission, a non-system-level app (installed by user) simulating key-press has to meet the other requirement: the receiver app is itself.

**CAKI Vulnerability.** At first glance, the above verification process is sound. However, it fails when IME is in the picture, and as such, a malicious app can launch **Cross-App KeyEvent Injection (CAKI)** attack.

A non-system-level malicious app (named $app_x$) running in the foreground first activates IME (named $IME_y$) set as default by user, which could be achieved by setting the focus on an `EditText` widget [4] in $app_x$'s window. After $IME_y$ is ready and its virtual keyboard is displayed, $app_x$ injects a KeyEvent to the message queue. At this point (Time of Check), the KeyEvent receiver is also $app_x$ as it takes input focus (another party, IME, cannot take focus by design). The projected event flow turns out to be $\{app_x \rightarrow system \rightarrow app_x\}$ and clearly passes the check of routine `checkInjectionPermission`. Then (Time of Use), the KeyEvent is sent to `RootViewImpl` of $app_x$. Given $IME_y$ is activated at this moment, this KeyEvent is redirected to $IME_y$ (see Sect. 3.1), turning the actual event flow into $\{app_x \rightarrow system \rightarrow$ `RootViewImpl` of $app_x \rightarrow IME_y\}$. In this stage, no additional checks are enforced and $IME_y$ will respond to the KeyEvent. Obviously, the security guarantee is violated because $app_x$ and $IME_y$ are not identical. This vulnerability allows a malicious app to send arbitrary KeyEvents to IME.

This CAKI vulnerability can be attributed to a big class of software bugs, namely **time-of-check to time-of-use (TOCTTOU)** [31,39,41,44]. However, we are among the first to report such bugs in Android platform[4] and

---

[4] We found only one vulnerability disclosure by Palo Alto Networks' researchers [42] regarding TOCTTOU in Android, which was reported in March 2015.

our exploitation showcase indicates this CAKI vulnerability could cause serious consequences.

## 4    Attack

In this section, we describe the design and implementation of the proof-of-concept app *DicThief*, which exploits the CAKI vulnerability and steals dictionary entries.

After DicThief is run by the victim user, it starts to flood KeyEvents to an `EditText` widget which pops up the default IME when the owner app DicThief is in the foreground. IME will commit words to the `EditText` and they are captured by DicThief. When the number of stolen entries hit the threshold, DicThief will stop flooding KeyEvents and exfiltrate the result (compressed if necessary) to attacker's server. Since KeyEvent injection has been discussed in the previous section, here we elaborate how to harvest meaningful entries from the dictionary and our context inference technique in making the attack stealthy.

### 4.1    Enumerating Entries from Dictionary

Given the huge size of IME dictionary (hundreds of thousands of words), the biggest challenge is how to identify the entries comprehending user's private information efficiently. These entries could be added from user's typed words, imported from user's private data (e.g., contact names) or reordered according to user's type-in history. We refer to such entries as *private entries* here. Through manually testing several popular IME apps, we observed one important insight regarding these private entries: they usually show up after 2 or 3 letters/words typed and they are placed in 1st or 2nd position in the suggestion list. In other words, by enumerating a small number of letter/word combinations, a large number of private entries can be obtained. We design two attack modes based on such insight:

- **Attack Mode 1 – Word Completion:** For each round, DicThief injects 2 or 3 letters and then injects the space key or number "1" to obtain the first word from the suggestion list of IME, which is then appended to the list of collected results. After all the valid combinations are exhausted or the threshold is reached, the list is sent to attacker's server. This attack works based on the dynamic order adjustment feature of IME: e.g., if a user frequently chooses "bankruptcy" from suggestion list, when she types "ba", the suggestion list will become {bankruptcy | ban | bank | bad}, and the private entry can be easily determined.

- **Attack Mode 2 – Next-Word Prediction:** This time, DicThief injects a complete word (or several words) for each round and selects the first word prompted by IME. Similarly, the space key or number "1" is used to obtain the first suggestion, and the attack ends when a certain number of rounds is reached. This attack exploits IME's next-word prediction feature: e.g., the injected words "fly to" will trigger the list {Newcastle | the | be | get} if IME concludes that "Newcastle" is user's favorite choice.

The generated list comprehends both private entries and the entries irrelevant to customization. We need to filter out the latter ones. To this end, we carry out a differential analysis. We run DicThief against a freshly installed IME app which has not been used by anyone and compile all the first words in two modes. Next, we find the different words between the list collected from victim's phone with ours. The words left are deemed private entries. This procedure runs on attacker's server, but it can be executed on victim's phone instead to save the bandwidth.

## 4.2  Attack in Stealthy Mode

When DicThief is launched, it has to be displayed and run in the foreground in order to turn on IME. If user is using the phone at the same time, the malicious activities will be noticed easily. In this section, we propose several techniques to reduce the risks of notice.

**Context Inference.** DicThief is designed to run when user falls asleep. At that time, the phone should be placed on a flat platform (no acceleration observed), the screen should be dimmed, and the time should be at night. All of these information can be retrieved using APIs from system classes (`SensorManager` for accelerator metrics, `PowerManager` for screen status and `Calendar` for current time respectively) without any permission. These techniques are also exploited by other works [28, 36] to make their attacks stealthy.

When DicThief is opened by user, it stays in the background and is periodically awakened to infer the running context. DicThief will not start to inject key-presses until the current context meets the attack criteria.

**Circumventing Lock Screen.** Our attack has to be executed even if the phone is asleep and locked with password. To proceed the attack, DicThief requires the `WAKE_LOCK` permission being granted first. As discussed in Sect. 2.2, user will not reject such request in most cases. Besides, DicThief needs to add the `FLAG_SHOW_WHEN_LOCKED` flag in its window setting, making it take precedence over other lock screens [22].

Yet, common apps will not be brought to the top of foreground when phone is locked. Each app has a corresponding object `WindowState`, which stores Z-order regarding its order of layer in display. The window with the bigger Z-order will be shown in a higher layer. A general app window is set to 2 while key guard window (lock screen) is set to 13, therefore, key guard window will always display in front of other general apps. `WindowState` is managed by `WindowManagerService` and Z-order cannot be tweaked by app. Nevertheless, when an app invokes an IME, it will be brought to the top of the client app disregarding its assigned Z-order due to one policy of Android [25]. Hence, our attack can succeed even when the screen is securely locked with password.

## 4.3  Case Study of IMEs for Non-Latin Languages

Not only is our attack effective against IMEs for English, IMEs for non-Latin languages are vulnerable as well. Apart from English users, the users who type in

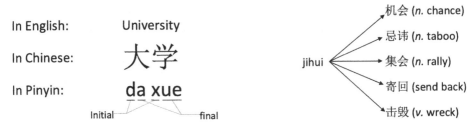

**Fig. 7.** One-to-many mapping

**Fig. 6.** Example of Chinese Pinyin

non-Latin words have to rely on alternative IMEs since the language characters are not directly mapped to English keys. In this section, we demonstrate a case study on attacking Chinese IMEs. It turns out just a few adjustments need to be applied to the enumeration algorithm and private entries can be effectively obtained, albeit the complexity of such language.

**Chinese and Pinyin.** Pinyin is the official phonetic system for transcribing the Mandarin pronunciations of Chinese characters into the Latin alphabet [13]. Pinyin-based IMEs are, in fact, the most popular IMEs used by Chinese users. Except for some special cases, every Chinese syllable can be spelled with exactly one *initial* followed by one *final* [13,23]. In total, there are 23 initials[5] and 37 finals. Figure 6 describes an example.

Each Chinese character has a unique syllable, but one syllable is associated with many distinct characters. Each Chinese word is composed of multiple characters (usually two to three). An example is shown in Fig. 7. The character combination poses a big challenge in harvesting meaningful Chinese entries: a prefix (e.g., "ji") might only reveal one Chinese character, far from meaningful words. On the other side, a prefix in English (e.g., "mis") can yield the the list of meaningful words with viable size.

**Attack.** Fortunately, Pinyin-based IME optimizes the input experience. By providing several syllable initials, the suggestion list of words with the same initials will be produced. For instance, typing "j'h" (initial j plus initial h) will yield the list of 5 Chinese words shown in Fig. 7. It motivates us to enumerate the combination of initials instead of the leading Pinyin letters. Here, we show the algorithm of attacking word-completion mode of Pinyin-based IME in Algorithm 1.

## 5  Evaluation

We analyzed the scope of attacks (the vulnerable Android versions and IMEs) and evaluated the effectiveness of the two attack modes described in Sect. 4.1.

---

[5] The initial set: $\{w, y, b, p, m, f, d, t, n, l, g, k, h, j, q, x, zh, ch, sh, r, z, c, s\}$.

---

**Algorithm 1.** Enumerating 2-character words of Pinyin-based IMEs

---

```
1  for Key_1=InitialSet.first; Key_1<=InitialSet.last; Key_1=Key_1.next() do
2      for Key_2=InitialSet.first; Key_2<=InitialSet.last; Key_2=Key_2.next() do
3          injectKeyEvent(Key_1) ;          // initial of the first character
4          injectKeyEvent(APOSTROPHE) ;     // divide two characters
5          injectKeyEvent(Key_2) ;          // initial of the second character
6          injectKeyEvent(KEYCODE_SPACE) ;  // commit the suggestion
7      end
8  end
```

---

## 5.1  Scope of Attack

The CAKI vulnerability discovered in this paper derives from the design flaw of Android framework. Thus, in theory, all Android devices should suffer from this vulnerability. We examined 7 different versions of Android OS on 4 physical Android phones and 2 Android images on an emulator, and it turns out all versions ranging from very old (2.3.7) to the latest (5.0) are vulnerable without exception. The list of vulnerable phones and OS versions is shown in Table 2.

Also, our attack is not limited to a specific language or a specific IME. All smart IMEs equipped with optimization features should be potentially vulnerable. We tested our attack on 11 popular IMEs and 8 among them are vulnerable, as shown in Table 3. Our attack does not succeed on 3 IMEs because they only respond to taps on soft keyboard, but ignore the key-presses simulated by app. These IMEs, however, may have compatibility issues since hardware keyboard is not supported well. We suspect such lucky escape is probably due to design flaw rather than protection enforced.

**Table 2.** Evaluation against Android OSes

| Phone model | Android version | Attack result |
|---|---|---|
| Nexus 6 (Genymotion Emulator [6]) | AOSP Android 5.0 | success |
| Sony Xperia Z3 | Sony official 4.4.4 | success |
| Samsung Galaxy S3 | CyanogenMod 4.4.4 | success |
|  | Samsung official 4.3 | success |
| Meizu MX2 | Meizu official 4.2.1 | success |
| Sony Xperia ion | Sony official 4.1.2 | success |
| Nexus S (Genymotion Emulator) | AOSP Android 2.3.7 | success |

## 5.2  Experiment on Word Completion Attack Mode

In this mode, DicThief injects 2 or 3 random letters and selects the first word suggested by IME. The victim IME we chose is Sogou Mobile IME [16], a dominant Pinyin-based IME in China with 200 million monthly active users [17]. The information leakage and overhead caused by DicThief are assessed separately:

**Information Leakage.** We conducted a user study[6] to portrait and quantify the leaked information. We recruited 5 Sogou Mobile IME users (labeled as $User_1$ – $User_5$) to participate in our experiments. All of them are native Chinese speakers (the mother tongue of $User_5$ is Cantonese, which is a dialect of Chinese). Their basic information and the final results are shown in Table 4.

All the participants installed a modified version of DicThief on their phones before the experiment. All 2-initial combinations are probed, counting up to 529 rounds (23 × 23 combinations, see Sect. 4.3). To address the privacy concerns of our human subjects, we did not collect any word entries from their phones. Instead, we asked them to report the type and quantity of personalized entries (calculated by DicThief). The detailed result is presented in two aspects:

1. **Intuition: Severity of Leaked Information.** DicThief shows the extracted words to the volunteers directly after the attack finishes and then the volunteers are asked to fill a survey. Questions include: how much sensitive information are extracted [*"Many"* / *"Some"* / *"None"*]? which categories can be used to summarize the leaked information [① *"Occupation"* / ② *"Contacts"* / ③ *"Location"* / ④ *"Hobby"* / ⑤ *"Other personalized information"*]? The result is shown in the 5th & 6th columns of Table 4.

2. **Quantification: Percentage of Personalized Entries.** For each volunteer, MD5 for all extracted words (529 entries total) are generated and compared with the MD5 of extracted words from the IME freshly installed. Personalized entry is counted if discrepancy identified. The result is shown in the last two columns of Table 4.

Apparently, a plenty of sensitive information will be leaked if the CAKI vulnerability is exploited by real attackers. On average, 58.8 % of the words

**Table 3.** Evaluation against IMEs

| Production name | Version | Language(s) | Vulnerable | Installations |
|---|---|---|---|---|
| Go Keyboard [7] | 2.18 | Multi-language | Yes | 50,000,000+ |
| TouchPal [21] | 5.6 | Multi-language | Yes | 10,000,000+ |
| SwiftKey Keyboard [18] | 5.0 | Multi-language | Yes | 10,000,000+ |
| Adaptxt - Trial [1] | 3.1 | Multi-language | Yes | 1,000,000+ |
| Google Pinyin Input [9] | 4.0 | Chinese, English | Yes | 10,000,000+ |
| Sogou Mobile IME [16,17] | 7.1 | Chinese, English | Yes | 200,000,000+ |
| Baidu IME [3] | 5.1 | Chinese, English | Yes | 1,000,000+ |
| QQ IME [14] | 4.7 | Chinese, English | Yes | 1,000,000+ |
| Swype Keyboard Free [19] | 1.6 | Multi-language | No | 1,000,000+ |
| Fleksy Keyboard Free [5] | 3.3 | Multi-language | No | 1,000,000+ |
| Google Keyboard [8] | 4.0 | Multi-language | No | 100,000,000+ |

[6] The experiments have followed the IRB rules, and all human subjects fully understood the privacy implication of the experiments and agreed to participate.

**Table 4.** User study – word completion attack mode

| User | Age | Gender | Installation time | Feeling of info leakage | Category of info leakage | Personalized entries | % of Personalization |
|------|-----|--------|-------------------|-------------------------|--------------------------|----------------------|----------------------|
| 1 | 25~30 | Male | 1 year+ | Many | ①②③⑤ | 416 | 78.6 % |
| 2 | 25~30 | Male | 8 months+ | Many | ①② | 239 | 45.2 % |
| 3 | 25~30 | Male | 1 year+ | Some | ②⑤ | 358 | 67.7 % |
| 4 | 18~25 | Male | 2 months+ | Many | ②③⑤ | 107 | 20.2 % |
| 5 | 18~25 | Male | 2 months+ | Some | ②⑤ | 436 | 82.4 % |

extracted are indeed personalized. Besides, all volunteers report that contact names are listed in the result, which are definitely sensitive to users.

**Time and Battery Consumption.** The time spent for KeyEvent injection is negligible, but DicThief has to pause for a while after a round of key injection till the IME renders its UI. The actual time overhead depends on the implementation of IME apps and the performance of phone's hardware. We measure it on Samsung Galaxy S3 and set the waiting period to 70 ms based on manual testing a priori. The total time consumed adds up to 221 s for all 2-initial combinations injections against Sogou Mobile IME. Meanwhile, the battery consumption is also slim, costing less than 1 % of total battery life. The whole attack process will hardly be detected by victim user if DicThief runs under the right context.

### 5.3   Experiment on Next-Word Prediction Attack Mode

In this mode, DicThief injects one or more words and choose the first word from the list of predictions provided by IME. The IME evaluated is TouchPal [21], an English IME with over 10 million installations worldwide. Since it is hard for us to recruit enough native English speakers as volunteers in our region, we decided to use public web resources to create virtual user profiles and customize IME dictionary with them. It brings the extra benefit that now we are allowed to look into what exact private entries are leaked. We document the steps for generating user profiles as below:

1. In a real-world scenario, an IME is customized by the text a user inputs or information left by the user. Likewise, for each virtual user, we compile the text she could enter and dump it to IME. In all, we create 5 users (labeled as $Sample_1$ – $Sample_5$) and use content scraped from 5 blogs to externalize them separately. The blogs are carefully chosen so that the topic focused on by each one is different. Table 5 shows statistics of the prepared data.
2. Since TouchPal is able to read messages and customize itself, we dump the collected blog content into the SMS sent box of the test phone (Samsung Galaxy S3) using an Android app developed by ourselves. We use one paragraph to fill one text message.
3. Now, TouchPal can proceed to customize its dictionary. We tick the options "*Learn messages automatically*" and "*Only learn sent messages*", and run the

**Table 5.** Simulation experiment – next-word prediction attack mode

| Sample | Crawled words | Author info & Blog topics | Personalized entries | % of personalization | Blog URL |
|---|---|---|---|---|---|
| 1 | 31581 | Female, professor, work experience | 273 | 63.3 % | http://ge\*\*\*hd.blogspot.com/ |
| 2 | 31661 | Male, cooking, food | 39 | 9.0 % | http://ff\*\*\*od.blogspot.com/ |
| 3 | 35606 | Male, American football | 73 | 17.0 % | http://fo\*\*\*og.blogspot.com/ |
| 4 | 40913 | Male, personal life | 54 | 12.5 % | http://li\*\*\*gy.blogspot.com/ |
| 5 | 32347 | Female, traveling | 208 | 48.3 % | http://www.st\*\*\*ls.com/ |

"*Learn from messages*" function of TouchPal. It takes one hour on average for the customization process to end.

When a predicted word is selected, TouchPal will prompt a new predicted word. Hence, a user can type one word and continuously choose the words provided by TouchPal to build a long phrase. We leverage this feature to carry out 3-level prediction attack. For example, DicThief injects one word "want" and then chooses three predicted words – "to", "go" and "shopping" – prompted consecutively (through injecting number "1"). A meaningful phrase "want to go shopping" will be revealed. Our empirical study suggests that starting from a verb, we have higher chances to capture a meaningful phrase. Therefore, we select 431 words from 1000 frequently used English verbs [20] (from "is" to "wrap") to bootstrap our attack. The remaining 569 words are not selected as they are either other tenses of the selected verbs or largely used as nouns.

**Information Leakage.** We followed the same leakage quantification method used in the last experiment and the result is shown in Table 5. Since the data comes from virtual users, we take a close look at the personalized words this time. We use $Sample_1$ as an example and show its leaked information in the list below. (Another example is described in Appendix).

For a sequence of injected keys, we compare the phrase generated from fresh IME (left-side of "→") and $Sample_1$'s IME (right-side of "→") (see Table 6). One can easily find words related to $Sample_1$'s occupation, such as "tenure", "professional editor", "advise", "university" and "recent talk". Expectedly, the privacy of a real-world user will be under severe threat if such attack is launched.

**Time and Battery Consumption.** The time overhead is also small. Injection of single key costs 35 ms (counting waiting time) and the whole attack takes around 401 s. The battery consumption is also negligible (less than 1 %).

**Table 6.** Examples of private entries – $Sample_1$

| – know what to do | $\rightarrow$ | know I always advise |
|---|---|---|
| – want to go to | $\rightarrow$ | want to publish an |
| – become a better place | $\rightarrow$ | become a professional editor |
| – relate to the gym and | $\rightarrow$ | relate to the New York |
| – create a new one | $\rightarrow$ | create a gmail account |
| – invest in a few days | $\rightarrow$ | invest in a recent talk |
| – rely on the way | $\rightarrow$ | rely on the tenure |
| – buy a new one | $\rightarrow$ | buy a new university |
| – wish I could have | $\rightarrow$ | wish I could write |

## 6  Defense

Our reported attack exploits a critical vulnerability of Android KeyEvent processing framework as the security checks fail to cover the complete execution path. However, it is not a trivial task to fix this vulnerability due to the highly sophisticated design of Android. Adding a new permission to limit such behavior is unhelpful. Injecting KeyEvent to the app itself should be permitted as usual for the purpose of automated testing unless IME is involved in the process. Yet, there is no way to ensure this when app installation. Simply modifying IME app code and rejecting all the injected KeyEvents is not a viable solution either, as the injections from system-level apps owning the INJECT_EVENTS permission should be allowed.

To mitigate such threat, we propose to augment the current KeyEvent processing framework. Currently, the information about KeyEvent sender is limited. It only tells whether KeyEvent is injected by one app or coming from hardware-keyboard, turning out to be too coarse-grained. We argue that the identity of the source app (i.e., package name, signature) should be enclosed in KeyEvent as well, which can be fulfilled by adding a new field to its data structure. Before a KeyEvent is dispatched, Android OS automatically attaches the sender's identity to it. Prior to forwarding KeyEvents to IME, Android OS verifies the sender and discard the injected KeyEvents if the sender is neither system app owning the INJECT_EVENTS permission nor hardware-keyboard. Attaching origin has also been explored by Wang et al. [40] to prevent one app from sending unauthorized intents to another app in Android. Their approach requires modifications to Android OS and app's code, and the policy setting process is delegated to the app side. In contrast, our approach only calls for modification to Android OS, as the policy should be identical to all IME apps, which protects them transparently.

Meanwhile, we examine other possible countermeasures, but they all come with the loss of usability or compatibility. One possible solution is to prohibit IME being invoked when the phone is securely locked, but this will disable the quick-reply feature of the default SMS app and third-party IM apps. We can also force IME to commit words to text controls only if the word displayed on touch screen is tapped, which, however, will block the input from hardware keyboard.

## 7    Related Works

**IME Security Issues.** All user typed text can be collected by IMEs, and user's privacy will be breached if an IME sends out the collected key presses out of malice. In fact, there have been questionable behaviors of IMEs observed in the wild [34,35]. Suenaga [38] and Mohsen et al. [30] also studied key-logging threats of malicious IMEs on Windows and Android platform respectively. In this work, we identify a totally different venue to abuse IME: rather than enticing users to install malicious IME, an adversary is able to exfiltrate the sensitive information through a new system design flaw and a novel IME probing technique.

**Key-Logging Attacks.** A non-system app on Android cannot obtain keystrokes directly. However, previous works show that it is possible to infer keystrokes through various side-channels. A touch on the phone surface, especially the soft keyboard will cause vibrations and touching on different positions will introduce distinctive vibration patterns. Previous works monitor the motion sensor like accelerometers to collect vibration statistics and infer what keys are pressed [26,27,33,43]. Besides, other sources are also exploited for keystrokes inference, including sound collected by microphone [32] and video camera [37]. On the other hand, our work steals user's input history in plain text and a large amount of typed text can be unveiled in a short time.

**Untrusted Input.** A plethora of key functionalities in mobile devices are driven by user's input and the modules handling such data are usually entailed with very high privileges. A natural path for a malicious app to elevate its privileges is impersonating human and injecting false input. Diao et al. [28] discovered that an adversary can inject prerecorded voice commands to the built-in voice assistant module (Google Voice Search) of Android and bypass permission checks. Jang et al. [29] investigated accessibility (a11y) support framework of popular desktop and mobile platforms and identified a number of system vulnerabilities in handling user's input. In this work, we identify a new channel to inject fake input and bypass permission checks. We believe this type of threats is not yet over and encourage future research in identifying other exploitable sources and building better input validation mechanisms.

## 8    Conclusion

In this paper, we identify a new cross-app KeyEvent injection vulnerability against IMEs installed on Android devices. By exploiting such flaw, an adversary can infer words frequently used by a user or coming from other sensitive sources. We implement DicThief, a prototype app and evaluate it under real-world settings. The result shows that all Android versions and most of popular IMEs are vulnerable, putting a large amount of users into danger. Such issue should be fixed immediately and we propose a solution only requiring changes to Android system. In the end, we believe this vulnerability is only the tip of the iceberg, and the security of input processing framework and IME needs to be further studied.

**Acknowledgments.** We thank anonymous reviewers for their insightful comments. This work was supported in part by Internal Grants C001-4055006 and C001-2050398 from The Chinese University of Hong Kong.

## Appendix: Additional Data for Experiments on Next-Word Prediction Attack Mode

For $Sample_5$, several terms related to traveling could be found. They reflect what topics the author often types. Especially, they point to a location – "Utah" and a type of transportation – "Sky train" which is the rapid transit railroad system operating in Bangkok, Thailand. After examining the blog content of $Sample_5$, we found the location was visited and the transportation was boarded before (Table 7).

**Table 7.** Examples of private entries – $Sample_5$

| | | |
|---|---|---|
| – see you soon then | → | see the stars and |
| – supply of the day | → | supply of our trip |
| – prepare for the first | → | prepare for the flight |
| – intend to do it again | → | intend to do in Utah |
| – behave like a good | → | behave like a packing |
| – rest of the day | → | rest of the city |
| – use the bathroom and | → | use the Sky train |
| – travel to the gym | → | travel tips for the |
| – search for the first | → | search for the flight |

## References

1. Adaptxt - Trial. https://play.google.com/store/apps/details?id=com.kpt.adaptxt. beta
2. Android Open Source Project: android-4.4.4_r2.0.1. https://android.googlesource. com/platform/frameworks/base/+/android-4.4.4_r2.0.1
3. Baidu IME. https://play.google.com/store/apps/details?id=com.baidu.input
4. EditText. http://developer.android.com/reference/android/widget/EditText.html
5. Fleksy Keyboard Free. https://play.google.com/store/apps/details?id=com. syntellia.fleksy.kb
6. Genymotion. http://www.genymotion.com/
7. GO Keyboard. https://play.google.com/store/apps/details?id=com.jb.gokeyboard
8. Google Keyboard. https://play.google.com/store/apps/details?id=com.google. android.inputmethod.latin
9. Google Pinyin Input. https://play.google.com/store/apps/details?id=com.google. android.inputmethod.pinyin

10. Instrumentation. http://developer.android.com/reference/android/app/Instrumentation.html
11. KeyEvent. http://developer.android.com/reference/android/view/KeyEvent.html
12. MotionEvent. https://developer.android.com/reference/android/view/MotionEvent.html
13. Pinyin. http://en.wikipedia.org/wiki/Pinyin
14. QQ, IME. https://play.google.com/store/apps/details?id=com.tencent.qqpinyin
15. Settings.Secure. http://developer.android.com/reference/android/provider/Settings.Secure.html
16. Sogou Mobile IME. https://play.google.com/store/apps/details?id=com.sohu.inputmethod.sogou
17. SOUHU.COM Annual Report. http://mfiles.sohu.com/corp/2013%20Annual%20Report.pdf
18. SwiftKey Keyboard. https://play.google.com/store/apps/details?id=com.touchtype.swiftkey
19. Swype Keyboard Free. https://play.google.com/store/apps/details?id=com.nuance.swype.trial
20. Top 1000 Verbs. http://www.talkenglish.com/Vocabulary/Top-1000-Verbs.aspx
21. TouchPal. https://play.google.com/store/apps/details?id=com.cootek.smartinputv5
22. WindowManager.LayoutParams. http://developer.android.com/reference/android/view/WindowManager.LayoutParams.html
23. ISO 7098:1991 Romanization of Chinese. ISO/TC 46 Information and Documentation (1991)
24. Android Open Source Project: InputDispatcher.cpp. https://android.googlesource.com/platform/frameworks/base/+/android-4.4.4_r2.0.1/services/input/InputDispatcher.cpp
25. Android Open Source Project: PhoneWindowManager.java. https://android.googlesource.com/platform/frameworks/base/+/android-4.4.4_r2.0.1/policy/src/com/android/internal/policy/impl/PhoneWindowManager.java
26. Aviv, A.J., Sapp, B., Blaze, M., Smith, J.M.: Practicality of accelerometer side channels on smartphones. In: Proceedings of the 28th Annual Computer Security Applications Conference (ACSAC) (2012)
27. Cai, L., Chen, H.: TouchLogger: inferring keystrokes on touch screen from smartphone motion. In: Proceedings of the 6th USENIX Workshop on Hot Topics in Security (HotSec) (2011)
28. Diao, W., Liu, X., Zhou, Z., Zhang, K.: Your voice assistant is mine: how to abuse speakers to steal information and control your phone. In: Proceedings of the 4th ACM Workshop on Security and Privacy in Smartphones & Mobile Devices (SPSM) (2014)
29. Jang, Y., Song, C., Chung, S.P., Wang, T., Lee, W.: A11y attacks: exploiting accessibility in operating systems. In: Proceedings of the 2014 ACM SIGSAC Conference on Computer and Communications Security (CCS) (2014)
30. Mohsen, F., Shehab, M.: Android keylogging threat. In: Proceedings of the 9th International Conference on Collaborative Computing: Networking, Applications and Worksharing (CollaborateCom) (2013)
31. Mulliner, C., Michéle, B.: Read it twice! a mass-storage-based TOCTTOU attack. In: Proceedings of the 6th USENIX Workshop on Offensive Technologies (WOOT) (2012)

32. Narain, S., Sanatinia, A., Noubir, G.: Single-stroke language-agnostic keylogging using stereo-microphones and domain specific machine learning. In: Proceedings of the 2014 ACM conference on Security and Privacy in Wireless and Mobile Networks (WiSec) (2014)

33. Owusu, E., Han, J., Das, S., Perrig, A., Zhang, J.: ACCessory: password inference using accelerometers on smartphones. In: Proceedings of the Twelfth Workshop on Mobile Computing Systems & Applications (HotMobile) (2012)

34. Rowe, I.: Chrome OS to warn users of privacy risks in alternate keyboard layouts, June 2014. http://www.linuxveda.com/2014/06/20/chrome-os-warn-users-privacy-risks-alternate-keyboard-layouts/

35. Sanders, J.: Japanese government warns Baidu IME is spying on users, January 2014. http://www.techrepublic.com/blog/asian-technology/japanese-government-warns-baidu-ime-is-spying-on-users/

36. Schlegel, R., Zhang, K., Zhou, X., Intwala, M., Kapadia, A., Wang, X.: Soundcomber: a stealthy and context-aware sound trojan for smartphones. In: Proceedings of the 18th Network and Distributed System Security Symposium (NDSS) (2011)

37. Simon, L., Anderson, R.: PIN skimmer: inferring PINs through the camera and microphone. In: Proceedings of the Third ACM Workshop on Security and Privacy in Smartphones & Mobile Devices (SPSM) (2013)

38. Suenaga, M.: IME as a possible keylogger. Virus Bull. 6–10 (2005)

39. Tsafrir, D., Hertz, T., Wagner, D., Silva, D.D.: Portably solving file TOCTTOU races with hardness amplification. In: Proceedings of the 6th USENIX Conference on File and Storage Technologies (FAST) (2008)

40. Wang, R., Xing, L., Wang, X., Chen, S.: Unauthorized origin crossing on mobile platforms: threats and mitigation. In: Proceedings of the 20th ACM Conference on Computer and Communications Security (CCS) (2013)

41. Wei, J., Pu, C.: TOCTTOU vulnerabilities in UNIX-style file systems: an anatomical study. In: Proceedings of the FAST 2005 Conference on File and Storage Technologies (FAST) (2005)

42. Xu, Z.: Android Installer Hijacking Vulnerability Could Expose Android Users to Malware (2015). http://researchcenter.paloaltonetworks.com/2015/03/android-installer-hijacking-vulnerability-could-expose-android-users-to-malware/

43. Xu, Z., Bai, K., Zhu, S.: TapLogger: inferring user inputs on smartphone touchscreens using on-board motion sensors. In: Proceedings of the Fifth ACM Conference on Security and Privacy in Wireless and Mobile Networks (WiSec) (2012)

44. Yang, J., Cui, A., Stolfo, S.J., Sethumadhavan, S.: Concurrency attacks. In: Proceedings of the 4th USENIX Workshop on Hot Topics in Parallelism (HotPar) (2012)

# Enabling Privacy-Assured Similarity Retrieval over Millions of Encrypted Records

Xingliang Yuan, Helei Cui, Xinyu Wang, and Cong Wang[(✉)]

City University of Hong Kong, Kowloon, Hong Kong
{xl.y,helei.cui}@my.cityu.edu.hk
{xinywang,congwang}@cityu.edu.hk

**Abstract.** Searchable symmetric encryption (SSE) has been studied extensively for its full potential in enabling exact-match queries on encrypted records. Yet, situations for similarity queries remain to be fully explored. In this paper, we design privacy-assured similarity search schemes over millions of encrypted high-dimensional records. Our design employs locality-sensitive hashing (LSH) and SSE, where the LSH hash values of records are treated as keywords fed into the framework of SSE. As direct combination of the two does not facilitate a scalable solution for large datasets, we then leverage a set of advanced hash-based algorithms including multiple-choice hashing, open addressing, and cuckoo hashing, and craft a high performance encrypted index from the ground up. It is not only space efficient, but supports secure and sufficiently accurate similarity search with constant time. Our designs are proved to be secure against adaptive adversaries. The experiment on 10 million encrypted records demonstrates that our designs function in a practical manner.

**Keywords:** Cloud security · Encrypted storage · Similarity retrieval

## 1 Introduction

Massive datasets are being outsourced to public clouds today, but outsourcing sensitive data without necessary protection raises acute privacy concerns. To address this problem, searchable encryption, as a promising technique that allows data encryption without compromising the search capability, has attracted wide-spread attention recently [2,5,6,9,12,14,22,24]. While these works provide solutions with different trade-offs among security, efficiency, data update, etc., most of them only support exact-match queries over encrypted data. Although useful in certain applications, they can be somewhat restrictive for situations where exact matches rarely exist, and approximate queries, particularly similarity queries are more desired. For instance, in multimedia databases or data mining applications, heterogeneous data like images, videos, and web pages are usually represented as high-dimensional records. In those contexts, finding similar records or nearest neighbors with respect to a given query record are much

© Springer International Publishing Switzerland 2015
G. Pernul et al. (Eds.): ESORICS 2015, Part II, LNCS 9327, pp. 40–60, 2015.
DOI: 10.1007/978-3-319-24177-7_3

more common and crucial to selectively retrieve the data of interest, especially in very large datasets [1, 10, 16, 19, 23].

In this work, we study the problem of privacy-assured similarity search over very large encrypted datasets. Essentially, we are interested in designing efficient search algorithms with sublinear time complexity. This requirement excludes all public key based approaches that usually demand linear search, and drives us to only focus on symmetric key based approaches, in particular, efficient encrypted searchable index designs. We first note that searchable symmetric encryption (SSE) has wide applicability as long as one can access the data via keywords. Thus, this problem could be theoretically handled by a direct combination of locality-sensitive hashing (LSH) [1] and SSE [13]. More technically, LSH, a well-studied algorithm for fast similarity search, hashes high-dimensional records such that the close ones collide with much higher probability than distant ones. Then by treating LSH hash value(s) as "keyword(s)", one may directly apply known SSE to realize private similarity search [15].

Such a straightforward solution, however, does not achieve practical efficiency as the sizes of datasets are continuously growing. Take the work in [15] for example: due to random padding, their proposed encrypted index needs to be augmented quadratically in the size of dataset. Even by combining LSH with one of the latest advancements of SSE [2] that achieves asymptotically optimal space complexity, the resulting index can still be prohibitively large due to the inherent issues from LSH [16] like its imbalanced structures and its demand of a large number of hash tables for accurate search. Besides, those issues will also readily turn most queries into a so-called "big query" [10, 16], where almost every query could comprise a large number of matched records, leading to substantial I/O resources and long search latency. Most of previous SSE constructions focused on exact keyword search for document retrieval. They are generic primitives without considering the above performance issues, and thus do not necessarily scale well in the context of similarity retrieval over large number of records.

Therefore, rather than just assembling off-the-shelf designs in a blackbox manner, we must consider security, space utilization, time efficiency, and search accuracy simultaneously, and build a new construction from the ground up. As an initial effort, we resort to recent advancements in high performance hash-based structures [10, 16, 18, 19] in the plaintext domain. Our goal is to intelligently incorporate their design philosophies into our encrypted index structure so as to make a practical design fully customized and thoroughly optimized. In particular, we explore multiple choice hashing, open addressing, and cuckoo hashing [18] to balance the index load, resolve the severe imbalance of LSH, and yield constant search time with a controllable trade-off on accuracy. Each query only requires $O(1)$ lookup and retrieves a small constant number of similar records with low latency. Such design also makes it possible that any form of post processing on retrieved records (e.g., distance ranking) can be efficiently completed at local.

For security, we apply pseudo-random functions to protect sensitive LSH hash values, use symmetric encryption to encrypt the index content, and implement the above hash-based optimizations in a random fashion. Through crafted algorithm designs, our proposed encrypted index can perform favorably even over a large number of data records. For completeness, we also propose a dynamic version of the index design to support secure updates of encrypted data records. We note that one trade-off of SSE is the compromise on security to pursue functionality and efficiency. Similar to previous definitions for SSE, our security strength is evaluated by capturing the controlled leakage in the context of LSH-based similarity search, and we formally prove the security against adaptive chosen keyword attacks. Our contributions are summarized as follows:

- We propose a novel encrypted index structure with optimal space complexity $O(n)$, where $n$ is the number of the data records. It supports secure similarity search with constant time while achieving good accuracy.
- We extend this index structure to enable the server to perform secure dynamic operations over the encrypted index, i.e., Insert and Delete.
- We formalize the leakage functions in the context of LSH-based similarity search, present the simulation-based security definition, and prove the security against adaptive chosen-keyword attacks.
- We implement our schemes with practical optimizations, and deploy them to Amazon cloud for 10 million 10, 000-dimensional records extracted from Common Crawl[1]. The evaluations show that our security designs are efficient in time and space, and the retrieved records are desired with good accuracy.

The rest of the paper is organized as follows. The related works are summarized in Sect. 2. The preliminaries are introduced in Sect. 3. The security definition is given in Sect. 4. Then we present the proposed schemes in Sect. 5. After that, we formally define the leakage functions and prove our schemes achieve the security against adaptive chosen-keyword attacks. Section 7 shows our experiment results. Finally, Sect. 8 makes the conclusion.

## 2   Related Works

Song et al. first introduce the notion of searchable encryption [21]. Then Goh develops a per-file index design via Bloom filter [7], and Chang et al. [4] also give a per-file index design. Curtmola et al. improve the security notions known as SSE and introduce new constructions against non-adaptive and adaptive chosen-keyword attacks [6]. Chase et al. generalize SSE by introducing the notion of structured encryption and give the first efficient scheme (i.e., sublinear time) with adaptive security [5]. Afterwards, Kamara et al. propose a dynamic SSE scheme with sublinear time and introduce the security framework that captures the leakage of dynamic operations [14]. Then Kamara et al. give the first dynamic SSE scheme supporting parallelizable search [12]. Meanwhile, several works extend SSE to support sophisticated functionalities. Cash et al. propose

---

[1] Common Crawl Corpus: an open repository of web crawl data, on line at http://commoncrawl.org/.

an SSE scheme for boolean queries that firstly achieves the asymptotically optimal search time [3], and Jarecki et al. extend that scheme in the multi-client scenario [11].

Very recently, Cash et al. implement a dynamic SSE for large databases when the index is stored in the hard disks [2]. The proposed hybrid packing approach considers the locality of documents, and improves I/O parallelism. Stefanov et al. propose a dynamic SSE that achieves *forward privacy* [22]. Yet, their design relies on an ORAM-like index with hierarchical structure. The search time complexity is polylogarithmic, and the client needs to rebuild the index periodically. Naveed et al. present a building block called *blind storage* as a sub-component of SSE for the privacy of document set, i.e., hiding the number of documents and the document sizes [17]. Their design splits each document into blocks and randomly inserts them into a huge array. The required storage cost is several times larger than the original document set. Besides, multiple round interactions are also needed when retrieving a large document. Hahn et al. propose an SSE scheme with secure and efficient updates, where the update operations leak no more information than the access pattern [9]. Specifically, an encrypted file index is built in advance, which stores encrypted keywords for each file. When one sends search queries, an inverted index will be built gradually. Because adding files only updates the file index, the server will not know whether those files contain the keywords searched before or not. The search cost is initially linear, then amortized over time.

SSE is applicable for any forms of private retrieval based on keywords [13]. Built on locality-sensitive hashing (LSH) or other distance embedding techniques, similarity search will be transformed to keyword search. Kuzu et al. [15] build an encrypted index from a LSH-based inverted index. Each distinct LSH hash value is associated with an $n$-bit vector, where $n$ is the total number of records in a dataset, and each bit indicates a matched record. In their encrypted index, a large amount of random padding is added to hide the number of distinct LSH hash values and the imbalance in the number of matched records. Consequently, the index has a quadratic space overhead as worst as $O(n^2)$.

# 3   Preliminaries

**Cuckoo Hashing:** Cuckoo hashing [18] is a variant of multiple choice hashing. It allows items moving between hash tables so as to achieve high load factors[2]. Let $\mathcal{X}$ be the universal domain, and cuckoo hashing is defined as:

**Definition 1 (Cuckoo Hashing).** *Given two hash tables $T_1$ and $T_2$ with $w$ capacity, two independent and random hash functions $u_1, u_2 : \mathcal{X} \to \{0, w - 1\}$ are associated to $T_1$ and $T_2$. Item $x \in \mathcal{X}$ can be placed either in bucket $T_1[u_1(x)]$ or in bucket $T_2[u_2(x)]$.*

---

[2] The load factor refers to the ratio between the number of items and the number of buckets in the index.

When inserting an item without a vacancy, the item in one of those two occupied buckets will be kicked out and moved to another hash table. We denote such operation as *cuckoo-kick*. *cuckoo-kick* will not stop until all "kicked" items are re-inserted within a threshold of iterations. When the number of such iterations exceeds the threshold, rehash will be activated such that all items are inserted again by newly selected hash functions. To reduce the probability of rehash, it is natural to extend cuckoo hashing from two hash tables to multiple ones so that each item has more buckets to place.

**Locality-Sensitive Hashing:** Locality-sensitive hashing (LSH) [1] is the state-of-the-art algorithm to solve the problem of approximate nearest neighbors in high-dimensional spaces. The functions in the LSH family project high-dimensional records such that the hashes of similar records collide with much higher probability than those of distant ones. From [1], the LSH family is defined in Appendix A.

**Cryptographic Primitives:** A private-key encryption scheme $\mathsf{SE}(\mathsf{Gen}, \mathsf{Enc}, \mathsf{Dec})$ consists of three algorithms: The probabilistic key generation algorithm $\mathsf{Gen}$ takes a security parameter $k$ to return a secret key $K$. The probabilistic encryption algorithm $\mathsf{Enc}$ takes a key $K$ and a plaintext $M \in \{0,1\}^*$ to return a ciphertext $C \in \{0,1\}^*$; The deterministic decryption algorithm $\mathsf{Dec}$ takes $k$ and $C \in \{0,1\}^*$ to return $M \in \{0,1\}^*$. Define a pseudo-random function (PRF) family is a family $\mathcal{F}$ of functions such that it is computationally infeasible to distinguish any function in $\mathcal{F}$ from a uniformly random function.

# 4    Notations and Definitions

This section gives the notations and the security definitions used throughout the paper. $D$ is defined as a $y$-dimensional record, and $D^*$ is the ciphertext of $D$. $A$ is the record identifier, which can also be its physical address. $\mathbf{D}$ is a record set $\{D_1, \cdots, D_n\}$, and $n$ is its cardinality. $V$ represents a vector, where $v_j$ is its $j$-th component. We denote $T$ as the hash table, $w$ as its capacity, and $T[i]$ as its $i$-th bucket, where $i \in [0, w)$. $0^{|a|}$ denotes a string with $|a|$ bits of '0'. Given two strings $x$ and $y$, their concatenation is written as $x||y$. $P$, $G$, and $F$ are the pseudo-random function (PRF). Our scheme contains the functions for key generation, index construction, and query operations. We give the definitions with specified inputs and outputs as follows:

$K \leftarrow \mathsf{GenKey}(1^k)$: takes as input a security parameter $k$, and outputs a secret key $K$.

$\mathcal{I} \leftarrow \mathsf{Build}(K, \mathbf{D})$: takes as input $K$ and a record set $\mathbf{D}$, and outputs an encrypted index $\mathcal{I}$.

$t \leftarrow \mathsf{GenTpdr}(K, D)$: takes as input $K$ and $D$, and outputs a trapdoor $t$.

$\mathbf{A} \leftarrow \mathsf{Search}(\mathcal{I}, t)$: takes as input $\mathcal{I}$ and $t$, and outputs a set of identifiers $\mathbf{A}$.

$\mathcal{I}' \leftarrow \mathsf{Insert}(\mathcal{I}, t, D)$: takes as input $\mathcal{I}$, $t$, and $D$ for insertion, and outputs the updated index $\mathcal{I}'$.

$\mathcal{I}' \leftarrow \mathsf{Delete}(\mathcal{I}, t, D)$: takes as input $\mathcal{I}$, $t$, and $D$ for deletion, and outputs the updated index $\mathcal{I}'$.

Our scheme follows the security notion of SSE stated in [6,14]: the server cannot infer any sensitive information of data records from the encrypted index before search; the server can only learn the limited information about the requested queries and the results. Like prior SSE schemes, there will be the leakage of access pattern and query pattern, for enabling search and updates over the encrypted index. Explicitly, the access pattern includes the results of queries; the query patten indicates not only the equality of query records but also the *similarity* between each other, where the latter is additional in contrast to other SSE schemes for exact keyword search (also recognized in [15]). Based on the simulation-based model [8] and the definition verbatim from [6,14], we give the formal security definition in Appendix B.

# 5   Our Proposed Schemes

## 5.1   Main Scheme

In this section, we present the main scheme for secure and scalable similarity search on encrypted high-dimensional records. Our core design is a high performance encrypted index built from the scratch. It supports secure and non-interactive search with constant time while preserving good accuracy of search results. Below, we give our design rationale before introducing the details.

**Design Rationale:** As mentioned, one can treat LSH hash values as keywords and employ any known SSE to make secure similarity search functionally correct [13,15]. However, directly applying existing SSE indices [2,6,12,14,15,22,24] will cause large space consumption and long query latency. First, the number of matched records varies for different LSH hash values. Such imbalance will make the space complexity as worst as quadratic in the size of dataset [15], because of random padding used in the inverted index based SSE schemes [6,14,24]. Second, the query latency scales with the number of matched records. It could be painfully long for large datasets. Third, multiple composite LSH functions are usually applied to each record for good accuracy. For $l$ composite LSH functions, each record will have $l$ hash values. Therefore, even the latest key-value pair based SSE indices [2,22] will result in an index with space complexity $O(ln)$, where $n$ is the number of the records. It might still be huge since $l$ can be as large as several hundred [16]. As analyzed, combining LSH and SSE directly appears to be neither practically efficient nor scalable for large datasets.

To address the above issues, we propose to build an advanced encrypted index, which aims to inherit the design benefits of LSH indices in the plaintext domain for performance while minimizing the extra overhead incurred by security. In particular, we resort to recent advancements on hash-based indices, which utilize high performance hashing algorithms such as multiple choice hashing [16,19], open addressing [16], and cuckoo hashing [10]. We also observe that most applications of similarity search suffice for an approximate result, e.g., high-value statistics such as nearest neighbors and Top-K analysis [1,15]. Besides, an appropriate approximation algorithm will improve search efficiency by orders of

---

Build($K, \mathbf{D}$):

CLIENT:

1. Setup stage:
   (a) call GenKey($1^k$) to generate the key set $K = (K_1, K_2, K_3)$;
   (b) set the index load factor $\tau$ and initiate $l$ hash tables: $\{T_1, \cdots, T_l\}$ with the capacity $w = \lceil \frac{n}{\tau l} \rceil$ for each;
   (c) assign a universal hash function $u_j : U \to \{0, w-1\}$ to $T_j$, $\forall j \in [1, l]$;
   (d) set the *cuckoo-kick* threshold $\alpha$ and the initial *random probing* step $d$;
   (e) $\forall D \in \mathbf{D}$, compute $lshV(D) = \{v_1, \cdots, v_l\}$, where $v_j = g_j(D)$.
2. Insertion stage, $\forall D \in \mathbf{D}$:
   (a) set $\beta = 0$ to mark the iterations of *cuckoo-kick*;
   (b) select $T_j$ randomly from $\{T_1, \cdots, T_l\}$ and compute $\{G(K_{v_j}^1, i)\}_d$, where $K_{v_j}^1 = P(K_1, v_j)$ and $i$ is from 1 to $d$;
   (c) scan $\{T_j[u_j(G(K_{v_j}^1, i))]\}_d$ from $T_j$ to the rest of tables incrementally and place $A$ to the very first vacant bucket;
   (d) if none of those buckets is empty, randomly select one of them and *cuckoo-kick* $A'$ inside by replacing it with $A$; increment $\beta$ and re-insert $A'$ via step b), c) and d) iteratively;
   (e) if $\beta$ reaches $\alpha$, randomly select $T_j$ and increment the cached $d$ of $v_j$. Place $A$ to $T_j[u_j(G(K_{v_j}^1, d))]$ if it is empty; iterate this step until $A$ is inserted.
3. Encryption stage:
   (a) encrypt occupied buckets: $B^* = A||0^{|a|} \oplus r$, where $|a|$ is the length of check tag, $r = F(K_{v_j}^2, b)$, $K_{v_j}^2 = P(K_2, v_j)$, and $b$ is the address offset of bucket.
   (b) fill empty buckets with random strings: $B^* = \mathsf{Enc}(K_3, 0^{|B^*|})$.

GenTpdr($K, D$):

CLIENT:

1. compute $\{v_j = g_j(D)\}_l$ for $j$ from 1 to $l$;
2. generate $t = (\{K_{v_j}^1\}_l, \{K_{v_j}^2\}_l)$, where $K_{v_j}^1 = P(K_1, v_j)$, and $K_{v_j}^2 = P(K_2, v_j)$.

Search($\mathcal{I}, t$): for each $K_{v_j}^1$ in $\{K_{v_j}^1\}_l$:

SERVER:

1. locate $\{T_j[u_j(G(K_{v_j}^1, i))]\}_{d_{max}}$ for $i$ from 1 to $d_{max}$;
2. compute $r = F(K_{v_j}^2, b)$ and $r \oplus B^*$ for each, where $B^* = T_j[u_j(G(K_{v_j}^1, i))]$;
3. if the least significant $|a|$ bits are all '0', push $A$ to $\mathbf{A}$.

**Fig. 1.** Index Build function and Search operation in the main scheme

magnitude while only introducing a small loss in accuracy [1,10,16]. Therefore, we incorporate this design philosophy into the framework of SSE and show how to build a provably secure and space efficient index with constant search time and good accuracy.

**Main Scheme in Detail:** Essentially, the client will build the index in three stages, i.e., setup, insertion, and encryption. The setup stage initializes the index structure and the prerequisite system parameters tuned on the input dataset; The insertion stage places all record identifiers to the buckets of index in a

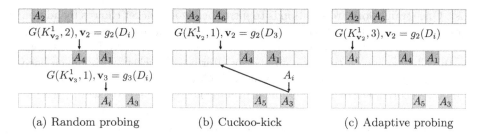

**Fig. 2.** The example illustrates three cases when inserting an identifier $A_i$. The number of hash functions $l$ is 3. The random probing step $d$ is 2. The one in purple is an adaptive probing bucket.

random manner; The encryption stage encrypts the identifiers inside and fills empty buckets with random padding. The Build function is presented in Fig. 1, and an example in Fig. 2 illustrates how an identifier is inserted. For easy presentation, we describe the insertion stage and the encryption stage, along which the system parameters are introduced.

In the insertion stage, the identifiers are sequentially inserted to the index buckets without loss of data confidentiality. We first introduce *secure multiple choice hashing* to balance the index load, and then combine it with *random open addressing* to handle the LSH imbalance. Moreover, we apply *cuckoo hashing* to build a very compact index. For security and correctness, those techniques are realized by utilizing different PRFs.

It is known that multiple choice hashing provides multiple positions for each inserted item so as to achieve load balance. It can be naturally extended in LSH indices [10,16,19], i.e., $l$ composite LSH functions $\{g_1, \cdots, g_l\}$ are associated with $l$ hash tables $\{T_1, \cdots, T_l\}$ respectively. The record identifiers are inserted into those hash tables which are indexable by LSH hash values. Given a record $D$, the bucket of its identifier $A$ is determined by $lshV(D) = \{v_1, \cdots, v_l\}$, where $v_j = g_j(D)$. Yet, such procedure does not consider security. Because LSH functions are not the cryptographic hash function, $D$ could be leaked from where it is stored. Thus, we use PRF to protect $lshV(D)$: $\{P(K_1, v_1), \cdots, P(K_1, v_l)\}$ shown at Stage 2.b of Build function in Fig. 1, where $P$ is PRF. The transformed hash values are now used to find available buckets. We note that such treatment is also seen in prior works [15,20]. Besides, multiple choice hashing can eliminate redundancy compared to the inverted index. It is not necessary to store all $l$ copies for each identifier to have good search accuracy. This advantage enables flexible approximate algorithms to make a trade-off between efficiency and accuracy [10,16,19]. In our case, we pursue practical efficiency at large scale and store a single copy of each identifier to achieve $O(n)$ space complexity. The size of index only scales with the number of data records.

*Secure multiple choice hashing* balances the load of index, but it might still not provide sufficient vacant buckets to handle the imbalance of LSH, i.e., a large number of records matched with the same LSH hash value could readily exist. One straightforward solution is to introduce more bucket choices by adding more hash tables, but accessing a large number of hash tables will degrade the performance. Therefore, we adopt open addressing to resolve LSH collisions [10, 16]. The key idea is to seek a number of alternative buckets within each hash table. But applying basic mechanisms of open addressing will disclose the locality of similar records. For example, if linear probing is used, the server will learn that similar records are placed next to each other. To hide such information, a probing sequence should be scrambled. Thus, we utilize *random probing* to generate a random probing sequence, $\{G(K^1_{v_j}, 1), \cdots, G(K^1_{v_j}, d)\}$, where $K^1_{v_j}$ denotes the transformed LSH hash value $P(K_1, v_j)$, $G$ is PRF, and $d$ is the probing step.

To compact our encrypted index, we further utilize the idea of cuckoo hashing, a variant of multiple choice hashing. It allows the identifiers to relocate, moving across different hash tables. In our design, when inserting a record $D$, if all $l * d$ probing buckets are occupied, one of them will be randomly selected. The identifier $A'$ inside will be kicked, and $A$ will be placed. Then $A'$ is re-inserted back. Such *cuckoo-kick* operation will loop until no identifier is not placed. We observe that *cuckoo-kick* will facilitate the refinement of clustering similar records and improve the search accuracy. Less similar records will be excluded via iterative *cuckoo-kick*. The empirical results will be shown later in Sect. 7.

It is worth noting that rehash may happen in cuckoo hashing when relocating items in an endless loop. Consequently, all identifiers should be re-inserted, which could be quite expensive for a large dataset. To sidestep this issue, we propose *adaptive probing* to seek more vacant buckets at each hash table in a heuristic way. When the number of *cuckoo-kick* reaches a given threshold $\alpha$, we start to randomly select $v_j \in lshV(D)$ and increment its probing step $d$ in $T_j$ so that one more bucket can be used for relocation. As a result, each $d$ for a given $v_j$ is cached, and the maximum probing step $d_{max}$ will be notified to the server after the index is built. It is used for search operations in such a way that each table will process constant $d_{max}$ buckets for a given query.

To achieve the security guarantees stated in Sect. 4, we have to encrypt the entire index and make each bucket indistinguishable. Considering security, efficiency, and correctness, we investigate the underlying data structure on bucket encryption. As introduced in Sect. 3, cuckoo hashing uses weak hash functions for a compact index. At Stage 1.c of Build function in Fig. 1, the output range of universal hash is $[0, w - 1]$, where $w$ is the hash table capacity. Because a weak hash function is not collision-resistant, two different LSH hash values might collide at the same bucket. To get correct results, one may append an encrypted LSH hash value with its identifier in the bucket, but it introduces additional storage overhead.

Tactfully, we embed LSH hash values into random masks for bucket encryption, so the matched results will be found on the fly. In particular, we concatenate the identifier with a check tag $A||0^{|a|}$, and encrypt the concatenated string by XORing a random mask $r$: $B^* = A||0^{|a|} \oplus r$, where $r = F(K^2_{v_j}, b)$, $K^2_{v_j} = P(K_2, v_j)$, and $b$ is the address offset of bucket from the base address of index. Only if $0^{|a|}$ is correctly recovered, the bucket will be the matched one. And because $b$ is unique for each bucket, each bucket is encrypted with different random mask even the same LSH hash value is embedded. Finally, the rest of empty buckets are filled with random padding to make all buckets indistinguishable.

**Search Operation:** Based on the index construction, the server can perform Search to return a constant number of encrypted similar records for a query record. In Search of Fig. 1, the client generates the trapdoor $t = (\{K^1_{v_j}\}_l, \{K^2_{v_j}\}_l)$ for a query $D$, which enables the server to locate and unmask the matched buckets. Upon receiving $\{K^1_{v_j}\}_l$, the server locates $d_{max}$ buckets in each hash table via PRF $G(K^1_{v_j}, i)$ for $i$ from 1 to $d_{max}$, where $d_{max}$ is the maximum probing step of all distinct LSH hash values. Then it computes random masks from $\{K^2_{v_j}\}_l$ via PRF $F(K^2_{v_j}, b)$, where $b$ is the bucket address offset. Only if the identifiers inside are associated with matched $v_j$, the check tag will be all "0" and the identifier will be considered as the correct result. Meanwhile, the server cannot unmask the identifiers inside if they have different LSH hash values to the query record's.

Regarding security, the random mask is generated from the unique address offset of bucket, and thus each bucket is encrypted via a different mask. Such design ensures that the server knows nothing before search. We also note that multiple choice hashing is designed for parallel search. The buckets in $l$ independent hash tables can be processed in parallel. Thus, the time complexity can achieve $O(c/min(p, l))$, where $p$ is the number of processors, and $c$ is a constant $l * d_{max}$. The number of retrieved ciphertext is bounded by $O(c)$.

## 5.2 Dynamic Scheme

To support secure dynamic operations, we design a variant of bucket construction. Accordingly, Insert and Delete are proposed to add and remove an identifier from the encrypted index, respectively. We note that updating a given record causes the change of its LSH hash values. As a result, its identifier will be relocated by first triggering Delete and then Insert.

Explicitly, we store the state information of ciphertext at the server, and ask the client to use fresh random masks generated from the state information to re-encrypt all the buckets which have been accessed in a given query. During the update, the bucket, whose underlying content is truly modified, is hidden due to the re-encryption. In particular, we design the bucket in the format such as: $B^* = (P(K_5, s) \oplus A||v_j, Enc(K_4, s))$, where $K_4$ and $K_5$ are private keys, $v_j$ is used to guarantee the correctness of Search, and the fresh random mask is generated by updating a random seed $s$. We note that the setup phase and the insertion phase remain unchanged when building the dynamic index. Only the encryption phase is different.

To insert a new record, one straightforward solution is to follow the insertion stage in Build. However, such procedure could trigger *cuckoo-kick* and cause many interactions between client and server. Besides, the client needs to re-encrypt all accessed buckets in each interaction, which will introduce computational burdens.

Alternatively, we employ a similar approach of *adaptive probing* to moderate the communication and computation overhead. To insert an identifier $A$ of given $D$, the client generates the trapdoor to enable the server to iteratively return $l$ buckets (one for each hash table) until $A$ finds a vacancy to stay. As we only notify $d_{max}$ to the server, it is required to use a map to record the latest probing step $\delta_{v_j}$ for each distinct $K_{v_j}^1$, where $\delta_{v_j}$ starts from $d_{max} + 1$. We also note that setting a less aggressive index load factor will help to insert $A$. As a result, the client can retrieve the latest probing buckets $\{T_j[u_j(G(K_{v_j}^1, \delta_{v_j}))]\}_l$ in each table. If no bucket is empty, the client will keep on asking the server to return $l$ new probing buckets by incrementing each $\delta_{v_j}$ for $j$ from 1 to $l$, i.e., one bucket in each of $l$ tables. To hide the location of $A$, the last $l$ buckets are re-encrypted via fresh random masks.

To delete $A$, the client generates the trapdoor to retrieve the corresponding $\sum_{j=1}^{l} \delta_{v_j}$ buckets, where one of them stores $A$. After decryption, the client locates the bucket of $A$ and replaces it with $\perp$. Likewise, it re-encrypts the accessed buckets with fresh random masks to hide the emptied one. Compared to our main scheme, Search now needs to return $\sum_{j=1}^{l} \delta_{v_j}$ encrypted buckets for a given trapdoor. The decryption is conducted at the local client. $v_j$ that matches the LSH hash value of the query record is considered as the correct result.

# 6  Security Analysis

In this section, we evaluate the security strength of main scheme $\Omega_1$ and dynamic scheme $\Omega_2$ under the security framework of SSE. We first define the leakage in search and update operations, and specifically discuss the security for LSH-based similarity search. Based on well-defined leakage functions, we prove that both schemes are secure against adaptive chosen-keyword attacks.

**Security on the Main Scheme:** Our scheme endows the server with an ability to find encrypted similar records by borrowing techniques from SSE. As a result, it does have the same limitation as prior SSE constructions. In particular, the server initially knows certain attributes of index without responding any Search query; that is, the capacity of encrypted index, the number of hash tables, and the bit length of encrypted bucket. As long as Search begins, the access pattern and the query pattern are subsequently revealed. Essentially, the access pattern for each query includes a set of identifiers of similar records and the accessed encrypted buckets of index. While for the query pattern, the notion in our scheme extends from the notion of SSE for keyword search, but it reveals more information, the similarity between each query. In keyword search, each query produces one single trapdoor. The query pattern is captured by recording those deterministic trapdoors, where the repeated ones indicate the keywords searched before. While in our scheme, each query generates a trapdoor that consists of multiple sub trapdoors. Therefore, if two trapdoors have an intersection, it will indicate that they are similar; that is, their underlying query records have matched LSH hash values. Accordingly, we quantify this similarity by $\theta$ defined as the size of the intersections between the two composite LSH hash values.

Formally, we define the leakage $\mathcal{L}^1_{\Omega_1}$ and $\mathcal{L}^2_{\Omega_1}$ as follows: $\mathcal{L}^1_{\Omega_1}(\mathbf{D}) = (N, l, |B^*|)$, where $N$ is the index capacity, $l$ is the number of hash tables, and $|B^*|$ is the length of encrypted bucket; $\mathcal{L}^2_{\Omega_1}(D) = (accp_{\Omega_1}(D), simp_{\Omega_1}(D))$. $accp_{\Omega_1}(D)$ is the access pattern for a query record $D$ defined as $(\{A\}_m, \{B^*\}_{ld_{max}})$, where $\{A\}_m$ is the identifiers of returned $m$ similar records, and $\{B^*\}_{ld_{max}}$ is the accessed buckets. $simp(D)_{\Omega_1}$ is the query pattern defined as $(\{\theta = |lshV(D) \cap lshV(D_i)|\}_q, i \in [1, q])$, where $D_i$ is one of $q$ queried records, and $\theta$ is the size of the intersections between $l$ composite hash values of $D$ and $D_i$.

Regarding the access pattern $accp_{\Omega_1}$, for a given query record $D$, the server decrypts $d_{max}$ buckets at each hash table, total $ld_{max}$ buckets for $l$ tables, to recover the result identifiers $\{A\}_m$, where $m \leq ld_{max}$. Therefore, the server knows where the identifiers are stored and how many identifiers are correctly recovered at each table. From the perspective of security, revealing $d_{max}$ does not appear to be harmful. It only informs the server when to stop random probing in each hash table. Regarding the query pattern $simp_{\Omega_1}$, the similarity of query records is known in addition to the equality. A trapdoor $t$ for a given $D$ contains $l$ sub trapdoors: $\{P(K_1, g_1(D)), \cdots, P(K_1, g_l(D))\}$. Considering another $D_i$, if $t_i = \{P(K_1, g_1(D_i)), \cdots, P(K_1, g_l(D_i))\}$ has at least one matched sub trapdoor as $t$, $D_i$ and $D$ are likely similar. From the definition of LSH [1], the $\theta$ between $D$ and $D_i$ will further tell their closeness. The bigger $\theta$ is, the closer they are.

We adopt the simulation-based definition in [6]. Given the leakage functions $\mathcal{L}^1_{\Omega_1}$ and $\mathcal{L}^2_{\Omega_1}$, a probabilistic polynomial time (P.P.T.) simulator $\mathcal{S}$ can simulate an index, respond a polynomial number of Search queries, and generate corresponding trapdoors. To prove the adaptive security defined in Appendix B, we show that any P.P.T. adversary $\mathcal{A}$ cannot differentiate: (1) the real index and the simulated index; (2) the real search results and the simulated results, the real trapdoors and the simulated trapdoors for a polynomial number of adaptive queries. We present Theorem 1 and the formal proof in Appendix C.

**Security on the Dynamic Scheme:** The dynamic scheme is built on the design of the main scheme. The underlying index structure is exactly the same, which does not show extra information. Thus, the leakage function $\mathcal{L}^1_{\Omega_2}$ is the same as $\mathcal{L}^1_{\Omega_1}$. Regarding $\mathcal{L}^2_{\Omega_2}$, the trapdoors for Search, Insert, and Delete are transformed via PRF from the LSH hash values of query records, so the similarity between inserted, deleted and searched records are also known. Therefore, the query pattern $simp_{\Omega_2}(D)$ is the same as $simp_{\Omega_1}(D)$. For the access pattern $accp_{\Omega_2}(D)$, the server needs to maintain the state information $\delta_{v_j}$ for each distinct LSH hash value to enable Insert and ensure the correctness of Delete and Search. We note that revealing $\delta_{v_j}$ does not compromise on security. Newly allocated probing sequences all start from $d_{max} + 1$ and each Insert interaction is a batch update on $l$ buckets. Thus, the server does not know which buckets are truly modified.

Most of efficient dynamic SSE schemes on exact keyword search leak the information such that: a keyword belongs to a newly added encrypted file if that keyword is searched before; a keyword belongs to a deleted encrypted file if that keyword is searched later. The former is defined as *forward leakage*, and the latter is defined as *backward leakage* in [22]. In our scheme, the server knows that the records are similar to a newly inserted $D$, if those records appear in search results before, since their LSH hash values have intersections with $D$; the server also knows that the records are similar to a deleted $D$, if those records appear in search results later. Formally, we define the leakage as $\mathcal{L}^3_{\Omega_2}(D) = (addp(D), delp(D))$, where $addp(D) = (\{\forall A_i : lshV(D) \cap lshV(D_i) \neq \emptyset\}_q, i \in [1, q])$ and $delp(D) = (\{\forall A_i : lshV(D) \cap lshV(D_i) \neq \emptyset\}_q, i \in [1, q])$. Given the leakage functions, we give Theorem 2 and prove it in Appendix C to demonstrate that our dynamic scheme is secure against an adaptive adversary.

# 7    Implementation and Evaluation

**Implementation:** Most of SSE schemes do not specifically address the cost for building the encrypted index when the size of dataset goes large. Such cost could be prohibitively expensive for the client with limited resources. To address this issue, we carefully select system parameters and optimize the implementation for Build. Given a dataset with $n$ records, the index load factor $\tau$ should be pre-set to determine the index capacity $N$. We set $\tau$ as 90 % based on empirical experience of cuckoo hashing based designs [10] to build a very compact index. Then we create $l$ arrays with continuous addresses as the underlying structure of hash tables, where $l$ is the number of composite LSH functions, trained via E2LSH package[3] on a sample dataset. The array capacity $w$ is set by $\lceil \frac{n}{\tau l} \rceil$.

We allocate a shared memory with total $|A| * N$ bits, excluding the check tag or the state information, so as to increase the capacity of index held in client's memory. We encrypt each bucket in memory, and dump it to the hard disk simultaneously or send it directly to the server as long as it is encrypted. Such method will avoid memory overflow at the clients with restricted physical memory. Meantime, we carefully set the *cuckoo-kick* threshold $\alpha$ and the initial *random probing* step $d$. If $\alpha$ is set as a large number, the chance of rehash can be reduced. As a trade-off, the insertion will take more time due to the expensive *cuckoo-kick*. Here, we pursue efficiency and set $\alpha = 50$ instead of hundreds. We note that the value of $d$ also has a trade-off on building efficiency and querying efficiency. If we set a large $d$, our index can have a large number of bucket choices to handle LSH collisions so as to reduce the iterations of *cuckoo-kick*, but search will process a large number of buckets and thus increase the latency.

**Experiment Setup:** we implement the main scheme and the dynamic scheme in *Java* to demonstrate the feasibility of our design at a large scale. We evaluate the performance and the search accuracy on a dataset with 10 million high-dimensional records. For cryptographic primitives, we use OpenSSL toolkit (version $1.0.1h$) to implement the symmetric encryption via *AES-128*, and pseudo-random function (PRF) via *HMAC-SHA1*. Our source code is available at Git[4]. To demonstrate the practicality, we deploy our implementation on a

---

[3] E2LSH package: online at http://web.mit.edu/andoni/www/LSH.

[4] SimSSE: on line available at https://github.com/harrycui/SimSSE.

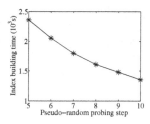
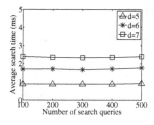
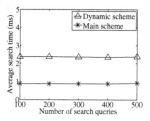

**Fig. 3.** Build time      **Fig. 4.** Search time in $\Omega_1$      **Fig. 5.** Search comparison

AWS EC2 large instance "r3.4xlarge". We generate 10 million records from a public dataset on AWS, "Common Crawl Corpus", which contains over billions of web pages. Because it is stored on Amazon S3, we directly launch map-reduce jobs on AWS Elastic MapReduce (EMR) to process these web pages on a cluster of EC2 instances. For each web page, we generate a $10,000$-dimensional Bag-of-Words (BoW) vector according to a dictionary with $10,000$ top frequent words, where such BoW model is commonly used in methods of web page clustering and similar web page detection. Here, we apply Euclidean distance as the distance metric and use the E2LSH package to train the parameters $l$ and $m$ defined in Appendix A. For training, $10\%$ vectors are randomly selected and the distance threshold $r$ is set to 0.5. Accordingly, tunable LSH parameters $l$ and $m$ are derived as 20 and 8 respectively.

**Performance Evaluation:** We evaluate our proposed schemes on index building cost, index space consumption, bandwidth cost, search and dynamic operation performance, and search accuracy. Figure 3 reports the index building time. For a fixed number of hash tables $l$, if the random probing sequence $d$ is small, few buckets can be used to resolve the imbalanced LSH collisions. Thus, more iterations of *cuckoo-kick* will be required. In fact, the building cost is proportional to the iterations of *cuckoo-kick*. As shown, increasing $d$ will reduce the iterations of *cuckoo-kick*, shortening the overall time, but it will introduce more bandwidth cost because the number of retrieved records is related to $d$ for fixed $l$. Although the building time is not moderate, over $2,000$ s in Fig. 1, it is a one-time cost, and we will improve it via concurrent programming in future.

Because we encrypt and dump the bucket simultaneously, the client only needs to allocate 4 bytes, the length of identifier, for each bucket in memory. In Table 1, for a dataset with 1 billion records, client only needs to allocate 4.4GB for our index with a load factor $90\%$. In our main scheme, an encrypted bucket is in the format as: $A||0^{|a|} \oplus r$. The mask $r$ is an output of *HMAC-SHA1*. Thus, each encrypted bucket is 20 bytes long. In our dynamic scheme, an encrypted bucket is in the format as: $A||v_j \oplus P(K_5, s), Enc(K_4, s)$, where the mask $P(K_5, s)$ is also 20 bytes long, and $Enc(K_4, s)$ is 16 bytes long with *AES-128*. We show the space consumption for different scales of datasets in Table 1. For datasets with 4 billions of records, our index consumes 160GB memory, which can fit into the main memory (244GB) of the largest Amazon EC2 instance. As mentioned, directly applying the implementations of prior SSE will consume much more

**Table 1.** Index space (GB) with a load factor $\tau = 90\%$.

| Schemes | $n = 10^7$ | $n = 10^8$ | $n = 10^9$ | $n = 4 * 10^9$ |
|---|---|---|---|---|
| $\Omega_1$, $\Omega_2$ at client | 0.04 | 0.4 | 4.4 | 17.8 |
| $\Omega_1$ at server | 0.22 | 2.2 | 22.2 | 88.9 |
| $\Omega_2$ at server | 0.40 | 4.0 | 40.0 | 160.0 |

space due to inherent issues of LSH. The comparison of space complexity is shown in Table 2 in Appendix E. Those indices will contain $ln$ key-identifier pairs at least, where $l$ is a tunable LSH parameter based on a predetermined distance threshold and selected training datasets, usually at scale of tens or hundreds. Such constant factor could result in an excessively huge index, e.g., more than 1000GB for $l = 20$ on 1 billion records. Our design is highly space efficient. The size of proposed index only scales with the size of dataset.

The bandwidth evaluation for Search is shown in Table 3 in Appendix D. For comparison, we build an inverted index with same LSH parameters. Then we randomly sample hundreds of search queries and calculate the average number of returned identifiers for each. In Table 3-(a), the statistics of LSH imbalance are reported for our selected 10 million records. We can see that the largest number of matched records is nearly 20 thousand. And most of LSH hash values have hundreds of matched records. In Table 3-(b), the size of results from the inverted index is over thousands which is huge and not scalable. In our design, Search costs a small sized bandwidth. For $l = 20$ and $d = 5$, the number of retrieved encrypted records is 100 at most. From Table 3-(b), comparing with an inverted index, our Search saves dozens of times of bandwidth cost. Because cuckoo hashing utilizes weak hash functions, records with different LSH hash values might be grouped. Recall that a specialized random mask and a check tag are used to enable the server to get the correct search results. Therefore, the number of result identifiers is less than 100 in Table 3-(b). From the parameter setting, 20 trapdoors (20 bytes for each) and 100 encrypted records (40 KB for each record) totally cost approximate 4 MB.

As proposed, Search only accesses a constant number of encrypted buckets, so our design can scale well when dealing with a "big query". Figure 4 reports Search performance of the main scheme. We randomly sample different numbers of queries and evaluate the average time for different probing step $d$. When the number of accessed buckets is equal to 100, it takes less than 1ms. Figure 5 compares Search performance of the main scheme and the dynamic scheme. Because Search in the dynamic scheme asks the client to perform the decryption of random masks, it needs more time than computing random masks directly at the cloud in the main scheme. Therefore, it is slower, but it still achieves millisecond latency, less than 3ms to process 100 encrypted buckets.

Multiple choice hashing is designed to enable lookup in each hash table concurrently. To measure the concurrency, we implement Search of our main scheme

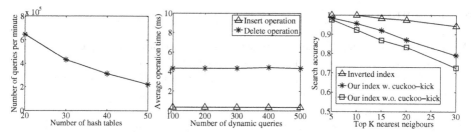

**Fig. 6.** Throughput          **Fig. 7.** Insert and Delete          **Fig. 8.** Search accuracy

in parallel threads. In particular, we create 16 threads simultaneously and measure the throughput for various number of hash tables in Fig. 6. It shows that our implementation can handle over 60 thousands of queries per minute. When the number of hash table increases, the throughputs will decrease. The reason is that accessing too many hash tables degrades the search performance. Therefore, the parameter $l$ should be kept relatively small for high concurrency.

The performance of Insert and Delete is shown in Fig. 7. The total time consists of the time for locating encrypted buckets at the server, and the time for decrypting and re-encrypting them at the client. For Insert, we conduct hundreds of Insert queries on the index with a load factor 90 %. Because it adopts *adaptive probing* to find available buckets by open addressing rather than expensive *cuckoo-kick*. The results show that even the index load is heavy, Insert can be fast. Insert succeeds in one interaction by only accessing 20 buckets for $l = 20$ and the average time is less than 1ms. Delete has to retrieve, decrypt, and re-encrypt all related $\sum_{j=1}^{l} \delta_{v_j}$ buckets. Therefore, the time is much longer. We do not perform Insert before Delete, so $\delta_{v_j}$ can be treated as $d_{max} + 1$, which is equal to 12 for this dataset. As shown in Fig. 7, the average time for Delete is around 4ms.

The search accuracy is measured based on the definition of $\frac{1}{K}\sum_{i=1}^{K} \frac{||D'_i - D_q||}{||D_i - D_q||}$ in [23], where $D_q$ is the query record and $D_i$ is the $i$-th closest record to $D_q$. This metric reflects a general quality of Top-$K$ neighbors. It quantifies the closeness between the Euclidean distances of Top-$K$ records from LSH-based indices and the ground truth nearest records via linear scan. For comparison, we also compute the accuracy of Top-$K$ results from an inverted index. Figure 8 shows that the results of inverted index are closer to the ground truth. We note that our design introduces a little loss in accuracy, because our index employs an approximation such that only one copy of each record identifier is stored and the search results do not include all the matched records. But we can see that *cuckoo-kick* improves accuracy a bit. The reason is that even if one of two similar records is kicked, it is probably still moved back to one of previous corresponding buckets. On the contrary, the less similar one might be kicked out since they have fewer matched LSH hash values. As a result, our design still achieves acceptable accuracy and saves dozens of times on the index space consumption, and the query latency and bandwidth.

## 8   Conclusion

We investigated secure and fast similarity search over large encrypted datasets. Our design starts from two building blocks, LSH and SSE. As we target for the high performance index design, we have explored practical hashing schemes, including multiple choice hashing, open addressing, and cuckoo hashing, to achieve a construction with superior space efficiency and low query latency. Adapting from the security framework of SSE, we carefully capture the information leakage and prove the security against adaptive chosen keyword attacks. We have implemented our schemes over 10 million encrypted high-dimensional data records at Amazon AWS. The experimental results are indeed promising.

**Acknowledgment.** This work was supported in part by Research Grants Council of Hong Kong (Project No. CityU 138513), grant from City University of Hong Kong (Project No. 7004279), and an AWS in Education Research Grant award.

## A   Definition of Locality-Sensitive Hashing

**Definition 2 (LSH Family $\mathcal{H}$).** *Given the distance $r$, $cr$, where $c > 1$, and the probability value $p_1$, $p_2$, where $p_1 > p_2$, a function family $\mathcal{H}$ is $(r, cr, p_1, p_2)$-sensitive if for any points $D, D' \in \mathcal{R}^d$ and any $h \in \mathcal{H}$: if distance $dist(D, D') \leq r$, $P[h(D) = h(D')] \geq p_1$; if distance $dist(D, D') > cr$, $P[h(D) = h(D')] \leq p_2$;*

In practice, the composite LSH function $\{g_1, \cdots, g_l\}$ is applied to enlarge the gap between $p_1$ and $p_2$. One explicit composite function $g_i$ contains $m$ independent LSH functions, which are randomly selected from $\mathcal{H}$: $g_i = (h_1, \ldots, h_m)$. As a result, for any $D, D' \in \mathcal{R}^d$: if $dist(D, D') \leq r$, $P[\exists i \in [1, l] : g_i(D) = g_i(D')] \geq 1 - (1 - p_1^m)^l$; $dist(D, D') > cr$, $P[\exists i \in [1, l] : g_i(D) = g_i(D')] \leq 1 - (1 - p_2^m)^l$.

## B   Simulation-Based Security Definition

**Definition 3.** *Let $\Omega = ($GenKey, Build, GenTpdr, Search, Insert, Delete$)$ be our scheme for secure similarity search, and let $\mathcal{L}^1_\Omega$, $\mathcal{L}^2_\Omega$, and $\mathcal{L}^3_\Omega$ be the stateful leakage function. Given an adversary $\mathcal{A}$ and a simulator $\mathcal{S}$, define the following probabilistic games $\mathbf{Real}_{\mathcal{A}}(k)$ and $\mathbf{Ideal}_{\mathcal{A},\mathcal{S}}(k)$:*

**Real$_{\mathcal{A}}(k)$:** *a challenger calls GenKey$(1^k)$ to output a key $K$. $\mathcal{A}$ selects $\mathbf{D}$ and asks the challenger to build $\mathcal{I}$ via Build. Then $\mathcal{A}$ adaptively performs a polynomial number of Search, Insert or Delete queries, and asks for the trapdoor $t$ of each query $q$ from the challenger. Finally, $\mathcal{A}$ returns a bit as the game's output.*

**Ideal$_{\mathcal{A},\mathcal{S}}(k)$:** *$\mathcal{A}$ selects $\mathbf{D}$, and $\mathcal{S}$ generates $\widetilde{\mathcal{I}}$ based on $\mathcal{L}^1_\Omega(\mathbf{D})$. Then $\mathcal{A}$ adaptively performs a polynomial number of queries. From $\mathcal{L}^2_\Omega(D)$ and $\mathcal{L}^3_\Omega(D)$ of each query $q$, $\mathcal{S}$ returns the ciphertext and generates the corresponding $\tilde{t}$. Finally, $\mathcal{A}$ returns a bit as the game's output.*

*Our proposed scheme $\Omega$ is $(\mathcal{L}_\Omega^1, \mathcal{L}_\Omega^2, \mathcal{L}_\Omega^3)$-secure against adaptive chosen-keyword attacks if for all probabilistic polynomial time adversaries $\mathcal{A}$, there exists a probabilistic polynomial time simulator $\mathcal{S}$ such that*

$$Pr[\mathbf{Real}_\mathcal{A}(k) = 1] - Pr[\mathbf{Ideal}_{\mathcal{A},\mathcal{S}}(k) = 1] \le \epsilon(k)$$

*where $\epsilon(k)$ is a negligible function in $k$.*

## C   Security Proofs

**Theorem 1.** *$\Omega_1$ is $(\mathcal{L}_{\Omega_1}^1, \mathcal{L}_{\Omega_1}^2)$-secure against adaptive chosen-keyword attacks in the random oracle model if SE is CPA-secure, and $F$, $P$, $G$ are PRF.*

*Proof.* We will demonstrate that, based on $\mathcal{L}_{\Omega_1}^1$, $\mathcal{S}$ can first simulate an index $\widetilde{\mathcal{I}}$, which is indistinguishable from $\mathcal{I}$. Then $\mathcal{S}$ can simulate result identifiers $\{\{\widetilde{A}\}_m\}_q$ and trapdoors $\{\widetilde{t}\}_q$ based on $\mathcal{L}_{\Omega_1}^2$ for $q$ adaptive queries, which are also indistinguishable from $\{\{A\}_m\}_q$ and $\{t\}_q$. To achieve the indistinguishability, $\{\widetilde{A}\}_m$ should be correctly recovered via $\widetilde{t}$ from $\widetilde{\mathcal{I}}$ for all $q$ queries. It means $\{\widetilde{t}\}_q$ should also be consistent with each other, which implicitly asks $\mathcal{S}$ to trace the dependencies between each query. The simulation is presented as follows:

- Simulate $\widetilde{\mathcal{I}}$: given $\mathcal{L}_{\Omega_1}^1(\mathbf{D}) = (N, l, |B^*|)$, $\mathcal{S}$ initializes an empty index $\widetilde{\mathcal{I}}$ with $l$ hash tables and total $N$ capacity, which are exactly the same as $\mathcal{I}$. After that, $\mathcal{S}$ generates $\widetilde{K_B}$ via $\mathsf{Gen}(1^k)$. Each bucket in $\widetilde{\mathcal{I}}$ is filled with $\mathsf{Enc}(\widetilde{K_B}, 0^{|B^*|})$, where $|B^*|$ is the bit length of bucket in $\mathcal{I}$.
- Simulate the first $\mathsf{Search}$ query: given $accp_{\Omega_1}(D)$ from $\mathcal{L}_{\Omega_1}^2(D)$, $\mathcal{S}$ outputs $\{\widetilde{A}\}_m$ which is identical to $\{A\}_m$, and then generates the trapdoor $\widetilde{t} = (\{\widetilde{K_j^1}\}_l, \{\widetilde{K_j^2}\}_l)$, where $\widetilde{K_j^1}$ and $\widetilde{K_j^2}$ are random strings with equal length of $K_{v_j}^1$ and $K_{v_j}^2$. By operating random oracles, $\mathcal{S}$ can use $\widetilde{t}$ to recover $\{A\}_m$. In particular, PRF $G$ and $F$ are replaced by two random oracles $H_1$ and $H_2$. We note that $\mathcal{L}_{\Omega_1}^2$ also tells $\mathcal{S}$ where the identifiers are stored and how many identifiers are correctly recovered at each table. Thus, on the input $\widetilde{t}$ and $\{\widetilde{A}\}_m$, $\mathcal{S}$ can locate the buckets $\{\widetilde{B^*}\}_{ld_{max}}$ with identical locations of $\widetilde{B^*}_{ld_{max}}$ via $\{H_1(\widetilde{K_j^1}||d)\}_{ld_{max}}$, where $d \in [1, d_{max}]$, and outputs $\{H_2(\widetilde{K_j^2}||b)\}_{ld_{max}}$ such that $H_2(\widetilde{K_j^2}||b) \oplus \widetilde{B^*} = A$ for buckets that can be correctly decrypted.
- Simulate subsequent $\mathsf{Search}$ queries: given $simp_{\Omega_1}(D)$ from $\mathcal{L}_{\Omega_1}^2(D)$, $\mathcal{S}$ can know whether there are similar query records that appear before or not. If $\{\theta\}_q$ are all 0, which means $D$ is a record which is distant to others, $\mathcal{S}$ follows

the same way for the first query to simulate trapdoors and search results. As long as there exists $\theta$ which is larger than 0, $\mathcal{S}$ uses the same random strings $K_j^1$ and $K_j^2$ of $D_i$ based on the intersection, and accesses the same buckets in $\widetilde{T}_j$. Meanwhile, $\mathcal{S}$ generates fresh random strings for sub trapdoors which did not appear before, and outputs the accessed buckets and the result identifiers from $\mathcal{L}_{\Omega_1}^2$ as described above.

We emphasize that $\mathcal{I}$ and $\widetilde{\mathcal{I}}$ have an identical structure with $N$ buckets and $l$ hash tables. The bucket $\mathcal{B}^*$ and $\widetilde{\mathcal{B}}^*$ are filled by ciphertext with equal length. Thus, $\mathcal{I}$ and $\widetilde{\mathcal{I}}$ are indistinguishable. For a given query, the result identifiers $\{A\}_m$ and $\{\widetilde{A}\}_m$ are identical, and the accessed buckets $\{\widetilde{B}^*\}_{ld_{max}}$ locates identically as $\{B^*\}_{ld_{max}}$. Due to the pseudo-randomness of $F$, $P$ and $G$, the trapdoors $t$ and $\widetilde{t}$ are indistinguishable. Meanwhile, the simulated $\{\widetilde{t}\}_q$ are consistent with each other, and the intersections among $\{\widetilde{t}\}_q$ are identical to the intersections $\{t\}_q$. Therefore, the outputs of $\mathbf{Real}_\mathcal{A}(k)$ and $\mathbf{Ideal}_{\mathcal{A},\mathcal{S}}(k)$ are computationally indistinguishable.

**Theorem 2.** $\Omega_2$ is $(\mathcal{L}_{\Omega_2}^1, \mathcal{L}_{\Omega_2}^2, \mathcal{L}_{\Omega_2}^3)$-secure against adaptive chosen-keyword attacks in random oracle model if SE is CPA-secure, and $P$, $G$ are PRF.

*Proof.* As stated in the proof of Theorem 1, simulator $\mathcal{S}$ can simulate an indistinguishable index $\widetilde{\mathcal{I}}$ from $\mathcal{L}_{\Omega_2}^1$. It can also generate consistent trapdoors, the access pattern and the query pattern from $\mathcal{L}_{\Omega_2}^2$, which are indistinguishable from real ones. For Search, Insert and Delete, $\mathcal{S}$ returns $\{\widetilde{B}^*\}_{\sum_{j=1}^l \delta_{v_j}}$ with identical locations of real buckets via operating random oracle $H_1(K_j^1, d_j)$, where $d_j \in [1, \delta_{v_j}]$. Meantime, $\mathcal{S}$ can operate random oracle $H_2(K_j^2, \widetilde{s})$ to recover the result identifier $A = H_2(\widetilde{K_j^2}, \widetilde{s}) \oplus B^*$, and update the encrypted bucket $B^* = H_2(\widetilde{K_j^2}, \widetilde{s}) \oplus A$ or $B^* = H_2(\widetilde{K_j^2}, \widetilde{s}) \oplus \bot$ so that the subsequent search results will be consistent. Note that for Insert and Delete, the buckets accessed by the server will be re-encrypted. $\mathcal{S}$ can generate new buckets via $\mathsf{Enc}(\widetilde{K_B}, 0^{|B^*|})$. From $\mathcal{L}_{\Omega_2}^3$, $addp(D)$ and $delp(D)$ show the identifiers in some of those updated buckets if they are searched either before or after, so $\mathcal{S}$ can generate the consistent trapdoors and masks via $H_2$ on the input of $B^*$, $A$ and $\bot$. Due to the CPA-secure of SE and the pseudo-randomness of $P$ and $G$, the adversary $\mathcal{A}$ cannot differentiate $\widetilde{\mathcal{I}}$ and $\mathcal{I}$, $\widetilde{t}$ and $t$, and $\widetilde{B}^*$ and $B^*$ respectively. Therefore, the outputs of $\mathbf{Real}_\mathcal{A}(k)$ and $\mathbf{Ideal}_{\mathcal{A},\mathcal{S}}(k)$ are indistinguishable (Table 2).

# D   Comparison with Prior Work

**Table 2.** We compare existing SSE schemes with our schemes by treating LSH hash values as keywords. $\#w$ is the number of keywords, $\#id_w$ is the number of matched identifiers for a given keyword $w$, $M_w$ is the maximum number of matched identifiers over all the keywords, $n$ is the number of records, $c$ is the retrieval constant, $(c \ll \#id_w$ shown in our experiment), $p$ is the number of used processors, and $l$ is the number of composite LSH functions.

| Scheme | Index size | Search time | Security | Index leak |
|---|---|---|---|---|
| CGKO'06 [6] | $O(\sum_w \#id_w + \#w)$ | $O(\#id_w)$ | NonAd | $\#w$ |
| CK'10 [5] | $O(\#wM_w)$ | $O(\#id_w)$ | Ad | $\#w$ |
| vLSDHJ'10 [24] | $O(\#wM_w)$ | $O(\log \#w)$ | Ad | $\#w$ |
| KPR'12 [14] | $O(\sum_w \#id_w + \#w)$ | $O(\#id_w)$ | Ad | $\#w$ |
| KIK'12 [15] | $O(ln^2)$ | $O(l)$ | Ad | - |
| KP'13 [12] | $O(\#wn)$ | $O((\#id_w \log n)/p)$ | Ad | $\#w$ |
| SPS'14 [22] | $O(\sum_w \#id_w)$ | $O(\#id_w + \log \sum_w \#id_w)$ | Ad | - |
| CJJJKRS'14 [2] | $O(\sum_w \#id_w)$ | $O(\#id_w/p)$ | Ad | $\sum_w \#id_w$ |
| Our scheme | $O(n)$ | $O(c/min(p,l))$ | Ad | - |

# E   Bandwidth Consumption Switch Appendix D with Appendix E

**Table 3.** Bandwidth evaluation.

| Matched IDs | $< 1K$ | $1K - 4K$ | $> 4K$ |
|---|---|---|---|
| $\# lshV$ | 15465K | 1861 | 68 |

(a) Statistics of LSH imbalance.

| #Samples | 100 | 200 | 300 | 400 | 500 |
|---|---|---|---|---|---|
| $\#A_{inv}$ | 2652 | 3730 | 4280 | 5285 | 3824 |
| $\#A$ | 95 | 96 | 93 | 90 | 95 |
| Saving | $27 \times$ | $38 \times$ | $45\times$ | $58 \times$ | $39 \times$ |

(b) Bandwidth comparison and saving.

# References

1. Andoni, A., Indyk, P.: Near-optimal hashing algorithms for approximate nearest neighbor in high dimensions. Commun. ACM **51**, 117–122 (2008)
2. Cash, D., Jaeger, J., Jarecki, S., Jutla, C., Krawczyk, H., Rosu, M.C., Steiner, M.: Dynamic searchable encryption in very large databases: Data structures and implementation. In: Proceedings of NDSS (2014)
3. Cash, D., Jarecki, S., Jutla, C., Krawczyk, H., Roşu, M.-C., Steiner, M.: Highly-scalable searchable symmetric encryption with support for boolean queries. In: Canetti, R., Garay, J.A. (eds.) CRYPTO 2013, Part I. LNCS, vol. 8042, pp. 353–373. Springer, Heidelberg (2013)

4. Chang, Y.-C., Mitzenmacher, M.: Privacy preserving keyword searches on remote encrypted data. In: Ioannidis, J., Keromytis, A.D., Yung, M. (eds.) ACNS 2005. LNCS, vol. 3531, pp. 442–455. Springer, Heidelberg (2005)

5. Chase, M., Kamara, S.: Structured encryption and controlled disclosure. In: Abe, M. (ed.) ASIACRYPT 2010. LNCS, vol. 6477, pp. 577–594. Springer, Heidelberg (2010)

6. Curtmola, R., Garay, J., Kamara, S., Ostrovsky, R.: Searchable symmetric encryption: improved definitions and efficient constructions. In: Proceedings of ACM CCS (2006)

7. Goh, E.J.: Secure indexes. Cryptology ePrint Archive (2003)

8. Goldreich, O.: Foundations of Cryptography: Volume 2, Basic Applications, vol. 2. Cambridge University Press, New York (2009)

9. Hahn, F., Kerschbaum, F.: Searchable encryption with secure and efficient updates. In: Proceedings of ACM CCS (2014)

10. Hua, Y., Xiao, B., Liu, X.: Nest: Locality-aware approximate query service for cloud computing. In: Proceedings of IEEE INFOCOM (2013)

11. Jarecki, S., Jutla, C., Krawczyk, H., Rosu, M., Steiner, M.: Outsourced symmetric private information retrieval. In: Proceedings of ACM CCS (2013)

12. Kamara, S., Papamanthou, C.: Parallel and dynamic searchable symmetric encryption. In: Proceedings of Financial Cryptography (2013)

13. Kamara, S., Papamanthou, C., Roeder, T.: CS2: A searchable cryptographic cloud storage system. Microsoft Research, Technical report MSR-TR-2011-58 (2011)

14. Kamara, S., Papamanthou, C., Roeder, T.: Dynamic searchable symmetric encryption. In: Proceedings of ACM CCS (2012)

15. Kuzu, M., Islam, M.S., Kantarcioglu, M.: Efficient similarity search over encrypted data. In: Proceedings of IEEE ICDE (2012)

16. Lv, Q., Josephson, W., Wang, Z., Charikar, M., Li, K.: Multi-probe lsh: Efficient indexing for high-dimensional similarity search. In: Proceedings of VLDB (2007)

17. Naveed, M., Prabhakaran, M., Gunter, C.: Dynamic searchable encryption via blind storage. In: Proceedings of IEEE S&P (2014)

18. Pagh, R., Rodler, F.F.: Cuckoo hashing. J. Algorithms 51(2), 122–144 (2004)

19. Panigrahy, R.: Entropy based nearest neighbor search in high dimensions. In: Proceedings of the 17th Annual ACM-SIAM Symposium on Discrete Algorithm (SODA) (2006)

20. Rane, S., Boufounos, P.T.: Privacy-preserving nearest neighbor methods: comparing signals without revealing them. IEEE Sig. Process. Mag. 30(2), 18–28 (2013)

21. Song, D., Wagner, D., Perrig, A.: Practical techniques for searches on encrypted data. In: Proceedings of IEEE S&P (2000)

22. Stefanov, E., Papamanthou, C., Shi, E.: Practical dynamic searchable symmetric encryption with small leakage. In: Proceedings of NDSS (2014)

23. Tao, Y., Yi, K., Sheng, C., Kalnis, P.: Quality and efficiency in high dimensional nearest neighbor search. In: Proceedings of ACM SIGMOD (2009)

24. van Liesdonk, P., Sedghi, S., Doumen, J., Hartel, P., Jonker, W.: Computationally efficient searchable symmetric encryption. In: Jonker, W., Petković, M. (eds.) SDM 2010. LNCS, vol. 6358, pp. 87–100. Springer, Heidelberg (2010)

# Privacy-Preserving Link Prediction in Decentralized Online Social Networks

Yao Zheng$^{(\boxtimes)}$, Bing Wang, Wenjing Lou, and Y. Thomas Hou

Virginia Polytechnic Institute and State University, Blacksburg, USA
{zhengyao,bingwang,wjlou,thou}@vt.edu

**Abstract.** We consider the privacy-preserving link prediction problem in decentralized online social network (OSNs). We formulate the problem as a sparse logistic regression problem and solve it with a novel decentralized two-tier method using alternating direction method of multipliers (ADMM). This method enables end users to collaborate with their online service providers without jeopardizing their data privacy. The method also grants end users fine-grained privacy control to their personal data by supporting arbitrary public/private data split. Using real-world data, we show that our method enjoys various advantages including high prediction accuracy, balanced workload, and limited communication overhead. Additionally, we demonstrate that our method copes well with link reconstruction attack.

**Keywords:** Distributed algorithms · ADMM · Mobile computing · Privacy · Social networks

## 1 Introduction

The last decade has witnessed the rise of online social network (OSNs). Starting from the late 2000s, OSNs have seen a rapid growth in their popularity. In 2014, two most profitable OSNs, Facebook ($140 billion) and Twitter ($35 billion) [1], jointly hold 1.3 billion active users worldwide [2]. These people conduct their personal lives and house their personal data via OSNs. They sync valuable information such as profiles, microblogs and photos with OSN websites every day. This situation raises serious privacy concerns among general public. The privacy control mechanisms provided by OSNs are cumbersome and ineffective [3]. It does not stop unauthorized parties from peeking into users' private data. More important, the OSNs privacy agreements state that the OSNs own the content that users upload. This allows OSNs to monetize users' personal information for commercial purposes such as advertising [4]. Such invasive act exacerbates the public distrust.

In order to address such concerns, a decentralized architecture for OSNs was recently proposed [5–7]. Instead of storing users' data in the OSNs' centralized database, the new architecture advocates decentralized data storage to avoid personal data monetization. In a decentralized OSN, users' data exists as a

© Springer International Publishing Switzerland 2015
G. Pernul et al. (Eds.): ESORICS 2015, Part II, LNCS 9327, pp. 61–80, 2015.
DOI: 10.1007/978-3-319-24177-7_4

collection of private files stored on their personal cloud storage service. Any action upon these files must be directed to the private repositories and consented by the users. This way, users retain full control of their personal data.

However, decentralized data storing precludes useful functionalities commonly seen in centralized OSNs. For instance, link prediction [8, chap. 1] is a common OSN analysis problem that helps to discover entities with whom a user might wish to connect. It operates by mining users' friendship and affiliation preferences from their personal data. The mining is usually done on powerful OSN servers. In decentralized OSNs, the mining functionality is difficult to provide due to the users' dilemma between privacy and usability. On the one hand, they wish to limit the personal data exposure. On the other hand, they lack the computing resources to analyze their personal data locally.

In this work, we study the link prediction problem in decentralized OSNs. We assume users' personal data can be split into two parts, private and public. The public part can be accessed directly whereas the private part must remain secret. For instance, consider a user who owns two twitter accounts, one is open for public and the other one has access restriction. The user wishes to determine how likely he will follow another user's tweets by correlating the target user's tweets with the textual materials in both of his accounts. Due to limited computing resources, the user can only process the materials in his private account and authorizes his online service provider to process the materials reside in the public account. Such split pose a challenge for training. On the one hand, the prediction accuracy will be poor if the user and his online service provider train their prediction models separately and try to merge the result together by voting. On the other hand, naive collaborative trainings reveal private information to online service providers.

We propose a novel privacy-preserving training method to solve the dilemma. The method allows users and their online service providers to collaboratively train link prediction models without revealing users' private data. We grant users fine-grained privacy control by supporting arbitrary public/private data split. We prove that the workload is properly balanced between users and their online service providers according to their computation capabilities. We apply our method to a real-world social network dataset to prove its validity. Additionally, we study the security risk of our method. We evaluate the possibility of the link reconstruction attack when adversaries can access users' public data.

## 2   Related Work

Our work is targeted on decentralized OSNs that allow users to maintain their data on their personal cloud server [9]. A typical decentralized OSN consists of independent servers that communicate with each other. Users can either register on an existing server or create their own. In the later case, users stay in control of their data because they are the administrators of their servers. The personal data initially resides on users' own servers. If friends from other servers request this information, it will be transfered to their servers through a server-to-server protocol. Ideally, a decentralized OSN can completely eliminate personal data monetization if different servers reside on different cloud platforms. In practice, a decentralized OSN may rely on additional cryptographic mechanisms to protect users' data since multiple servers may belong to the same cloud service provider.

There has been a substantial amount of work to enhance decentralized OSNs. The early researches use advanced cryptographic mechanisms to protect users' privacy. Two examples are Persona [10] and Safebook [11]. Persona combines attribute-based encryption (ABE) with traditional public key cryptography to offer flexible and fine-grained access control to data. Safebook combines a peer-to-peer architecture with a certification distribution system based on distributed hash table to avoid unauthorized access to users' data. These methods usually work at the cost of limiting OSN functionalities. Later works shift focus in adding new services to decentralized OSNs. Musubi [5], for instance, provides a toolkit for decentralized OSNs to support application development for multi-party interaction. Omlet [7] is a commercial decentralized OSN based on Musubi. Despite of their efforts, most functionalities that rely on data analysis are still not supported in decentralized OSNs.

Link prediction is a common OSN analysis problem that forms the basis of numerous OSN functional features. In [8, chap. 1], Aggarwal gives a comprehensive survey on the methods used for link prediction. These methods can be divided into two categories, *i.e.*, structured-based prediction methods and attributes-based prediction methods. The former is applicable to large scale networks consist millions of nodes [12]. The latter analyzes median, personal networks with detailed node descriptions [13]. Most of these methods must be redesigned to fit into the decentralized architecture. In this work, we mainly focus on users' personal social networks, a method commonly known as egocentric [14]. We use an attributes-based prediction method due to the nature of decentralization.

The method we use falls into the categories of privacy-preserving machine learning and distributed optimization. The most noteworthy idea for privacy-preserving machine learning is the $\epsilon$-differential privacy proposed by Dwork [15], in which carefully calibrated noise is injected into the dataset to achieve indistinguishability. However, $\epsilon$-differential privacy is unnecessary when data is owned by a single user. Perhaps the closest to our work is done by Yu *et al.* [16]. They use a distributed algorithm to train a support vector machine such that it preserves the privacy of different data blocks. But their method cannot protect the feature privacy within the same data block, which we address in Sect. 4.

## 3   System Model and Privacy Goals

Here we describe the link prediction problem. The set-up for this problem is a variation of Guha's framework [17]: We consider a decentralized OSN involving both positive and negative links. The positive links are formed due to friendship, support, or approval whereas the negative links are formed due to disapproval, disagreement, or distrust. We consider a privacy conscious user, Alice, who is unwilling to reveal part of her personal data. We are interested in predicting the link of Alice's personal social network. We consider an honest-but-curious system, Sara, that can only access Alice's public data. We allow Alice and Sara to jointly learn a prediction model. Alice's privacy is violated if Sara learns her private data or part of the prediction model that is associated with the private data.

### 3.1 Network Abstraction

Here we show how we model Alice's social network. We take an egocentric approach [14] and examine only Alice's immediate neighbors and associated interconnections that are commonly stored as part of Alice's personal data. We interpret this network as a directed graph $G = (V, E)$. The $i$th link is associated with two node vectors $t_i \in \mathbf{R}^n$ and $h_i \in \mathbf{R}^n$ that characterize the tail and head node of the link. These features are extracted from the materials shared through the group sharing services supported by decentralized OSNs [5]. The $i$th link is also associated with a label $q_i \in \{-1, 1\}$. We define the sign of $q_i$ to be positive or negative depending on whether the tail node expresses a positive or negative attitude toward the head node.

To facilitate the problem formulation, we use $K - 1$ scoring functions $f_k$ : $\mathbf{R}^n \times \mathbf{R}^n \to \mathbf{R}$ to construct the link vector. Let $p_{i,k} = f_k(t_i, h_i)$ be the score between the tail node $t_i$ and the head node $h_i$ calculated by the $k$th scoring function. Let $p_i = (p_{i,1}, p_{i,2}, \ldots, p_{i,K-1})$ be the link scores. We can represent each visible links in Alice's network with a vector $(p_i, q_i)$. For reasons we will show later, we define the link vector to be $a_i = (q_i p_i, q_i)$. We use a matrix $A \in \mathbf{R}^{|E| \times K}$ to represent all the link vectors in Alice's network.

Alice can define her privacy preferences by veiling part of $A$. For instance, Alice may regard certain scores or the link sign as private, which corresponds to cloaking a particular column of $A$. Alice may also choose to hide certain link entirely, which corresponds to cloaking a particular row of $A$. Without loss of generality, we divide $A$ into three parts[1]

$$A = \begin{pmatrix} \overleftarrow{A} & \overrightarrow{A} \\ A_{\downarrow} \end{pmatrix},$$

where the public features are within $\overleftarrow{A} \in \mathbf{R}^{|E|_{\uparrow} \times \overleftarrow{K}}$, the private features are within $\overrightarrow{A} \in \mathbf{R}^{|E|_{\uparrow} \times \overrightarrow{K}}$ and the private links are within $A_{\downarrow} \in \mathbf{R}^{|E|_{\downarrow} \times K}$. Note that $|E|_{\uparrow} + |E|_{\downarrow} = |E|$ and $\overleftarrow{K} + \overrightarrow{K} = K$. In practice, an implicit condition is $|E|_{\uparrow} \gg |E|_{\downarrow}$ and $\overleftarrow{K} \gg \overrightarrow{K}$, though our method can be applied to $\overleftarrow{A}$, $\overrightarrow{A}$ and $A_{\downarrow}$ with arbitrary sizes.

---

[1] We can rearrange the columns and rows of any $A$ to separate the public features from the private features and the private links.

## 3.2   Training Goal

Here we describe our training goal. We consider two learning modules, $\mathcal{A}$ and $\mathcal{S}$, owned by Alice and Sara. Assume that $\mathcal{A}$ only processes $\bar{A}$ and $A_\perp$ due to limited resources whereas $\mathcal{S}$ is powerful but is only allowed to access $\bar{A}$. Using $\mathcal{A}$ and $\mathcal{S}$, Alice and Sara jointly fit a sparse logistic regression model

$$\text{minimize } \frac{1}{|E|} \sum_{i=1}^{|E|} \log\left(1 + \exp\left(-q_i(p_i^T w + v)\right)\right) + \lambda\|w\|_1, \tag{1}$$

where $w \in \mathbf{R}^{K-1}$ is the weights for the link scores and $v \in \mathbf{R}$ is the intercept. Let $x \in \mathbf{R}^K$ equals $(w, v)$. The problem is equivalent to

$$\text{minimize } \frac{1}{|E|} \sum_{i=1}^{|E|} \log\left(1 + \exp\left(-Ax\right)\right) + \lambda r(x), \tag{2}$$

where $r(x) = \|w\|_1$. Let $x$ equals $(\overleftarrow{x}, \overrightarrow{x})$ where $\overleftarrow{x}$ is the weights of the public features and $\overrightarrow{x}$ is the weights of the private features. The method preserves Alice's privacy if Sara is oblivious of $\overrightarrow{A}$, $A_\perp$ and $\overrightarrow{x}$.

There exists a plethora of network link prediction models. The learning architectures range from shallow ones such as support vector machine [18] and statistical regressions [19] to deep ones such as graphical model [20] and deep neural networks [21]. The reason we choose a sparse logistic regression model are threefold: (1) The performances of all models are comparable given the appropriate feature set [8, chap. 1]. There is no clear and convincing evidence indicating that one model supersedes the others. (2) A sparse logistic regression model is representative of the types of shallow learning architectures that produce reliable and reproducible results [22, Sect. 4.4]. (3) More important, a sparse logistic regression model can be viewed as a regularized logistic neuron, which is the building block of deep learning architectures such as deep belief nets [23] and restricted Boltzmann machines [24]. Designing a privacy-preserving learning method for it opens the possibility of assembling more complicated privacy-preserving learning models.

## 3.3   Prediction Goal

Here we summarize our prediction goal. Once the model is jointly trained, we use it to predict the sign of any unknown link in which Alice is interested. Specifically, let $x^\star = (\overleftarrow{w}^\star, \overrightarrow{w}^\star, v^\star)$ where $\overleftarrow{w}^\star$ and $\overrightarrow{w}^\star$ are the optimal weights of the public and private link scores; $v^\star$ is the optimal intercept. Let $p_u = (\overleftarrow{p}_u, \overrightarrow{p}_u)$ be the link scores of the unknown link where $\overleftarrow{p}_u$ and $\overrightarrow{p}_u$ are the public and private scores. Let $\hat{q}_u$ be the predicted link sign. Alice and Sara should be able to assemble the logistic function

$$\mathbf{Prob}(\hat{q}_u = 1 \mid x^\star) = \frac{1}{1 + \exp\left(-(\overleftarrow{p}_u^T \overleftarrow{w}^\star + \overrightarrow{p}_u^T \overrightarrow{w}^\star + v^\star)\right)}, \tag{3}$$

without Sara knowing $\overrightarrow{p}_u$, $\overrightarrow{x}^\star$ and $\hat{q}_u$. To constitute a good prediction model, we also require $\hat{q}_u$ to equal the true link sign $q_u$ with high probability.

# 4  Methodology

We now present our method for the link prediction problem. We first give a short introduction of the core algorithm we use, $i.e.$, alternating direction method of multipliers (ADMM). Following that, we describe a two-tier training method. Specially, we show how we separate $\vec{A}$ and $A_\downarrow$ from $\overleftrightarrow{A}$ to protect Alice's privacy. We give a complexity analysis of the training method to show that the workload is properly divided base on the computation resources available for Alice and Sara. Finally, we show that our training method is capable of protecting Alice's prior knowledge about $x^\star$.

## 4.1  ADMM

ADMM, also known as the Douglas-Rachford splitting, is a *decomposition* procedure, in which the solutions to small local subproblems are coordinated to find a solution to a large global problem. It was first introduced in the mid-1970s by Glowinski and Marrocco [25] and Gabay and Mercier [26]. Originally, ADMM was designed to decouple the objective functionals to achieve better convergence. Later analyses [27] show that it is also well suited for large-scale distributed computing and massive optimization problems.

Let $f : \mathbf{R}^n \to \mathbf{R}$ and $g : \mathbf{R}^m \to \mathbf{R}$ be two functionals that are convex. The basic ADMM is an iterative method that solves problems in the form

$$\text{minimize}\quad f(x) + g(z)$$
$$\text{subject to}\quad Ax + Bz = c,$$

with variable $x \in \mathbf{R}^n$ and $z \in \mathbf{R}^m$, where $A \in \mathbf{R}^{p \times n}$, $B \in \mathbf{R}^{p \times m}$ and $c \in \mathbf{R}^p$. The augmented Lagrangian for the problem is

$$L_\rho(x, z, y) = f(x) + g(z) + y^T(Ax + Bz - c) + (\rho/2)\|Ax + Bz - c\|_2^2$$

where $y$ is the dual variable or Lagrange Multiplier, $\rho$ is the penalty parameter. Let $u = (1/\rho)y$ be the scaled dual variable. We can express each ADMM iteration as a full Gauss-Seidel iteration between $x$, $z$ and $u$

$$x^{k+1} := \underset{x}{\text{argmin}} \left( f(x) + (\rho/2)\|Ax + Bz^k - c + u^k\|_2^2 \right)$$
$$z^{k+1} := \underset{z}{\text{argmin}} \left( g(z) + (\rho/2)\|Ax^{k+1} + Bz - c + u^k\|_2^2 \right)$$
$$u^{k+1} := u^k + Ax^{k+1} + Bz^{k+1} - c.$$

The algorithm fully splits the objective into two terms, $i.e.$, the $x$-update and $z$-update, which involve evaluating the proximal operators [28] with respect to $f$ and $g$. If at least one of them is separable, we can run the algorithm in parallel fashion. Generally, evaluating such operators requires solving a convex optimization problem. But, depending on the nature of $f$ and $g$, simpler or faster specialized methods usually exist. Due to the smoothing of the proximal operators, ADMM can deal with the case when $f$ and $g$ are not differentiable. For a more detailed discussion on ADMM, we refer the readers to Boyd's work [27].

## 4.2   Two-Tier Training

Here we describe the two-tier training method for the link prediction problem. To protect Alice's privacy, we formulate problems into two specific canonical forms, *i.e.*, *consensus* and *sharing*, and solve them using ADMM. At the first tier, we split $A_\downarrow$ from $\overleftarrow{A}$ and $\overrightarrow{A}$ to protect the private links. At the second tier, we split $\overrightarrow{A}$ from $\overleftarrow{A}$ to protect the private features.

**Link Split.** At the first tier, we split $A$ by rows in order to protect the private links within $A_\downarrow$. Let $A_\uparrow \in \mathbf{R}^{|E|_\uparrow \times K}$ represents both $\overleftarrow{A}$ and $\overrightarrow{A}$. We first split $A$ into $A_\uparrow$ and $A_\downarrow$

$$ A \; = \; \begin{pmatrix} A_\uparrow \\ A_\downarrow \end{pmatrix}. $$

Define

$$ l_\uparrow\left(A_\uparrow x_\uparrow\right) = \frac{1}{|E|_\uparrow} \sum_{i=1}^{|E|_\uparrow} \log(1 + \exp(-A_\uparrow x_\uparrow)), $$

$$ l_\downarrow\left(A_\downarrow x_\downarrow\right) = \frac{1}{|E|_\downarrow} \sum_{i=1}^{|E|_\downarrow} \log(1 + \exp(-A_\downarrow x_\downarrow)). $$

We can explicitly convert the sparse logistic regression problem (Eq. 2) into consensus form [27]

$$ \begin{aligned} \text{minimize} \quad & l_\uparrow\left(A_\uparrow x_\uparrow\right) + l_\downarrow\left(A_\downarrow\right) + \lambda r(z_\updownarrow) \\ \text{subject to} \quad & x_\uparrow - z_\updownarrow = x_\downarrow - z_\updownarrow = 0, \end{aligned} $$

with local variable $x_\uparrow, x_\downarrow \in \mathbf{R}^K$ and global variable $z_\updownarrow \in \mathbf{R}^K$.

The problem can be solved using the following ADMM algorithm

$$ x_\uparrow^{k+1} := \underset{x_\uparrow}{\operatorname{argmin}}\left( l_\uparrow\left(A_\uparrow x_\uparrow\right) + (\rho/2)\|x_\uparrow - z_\updownarrow^k + u_\uparrow^k\|_2^2 \right) \tag{4} $$

$$ x_\downarrow^{k+1} := \underset{x_\downarrow}{\operatorname{argmin}}\left( l_\downarrow\left(A_\downarrow x_\downarrow\right) + (\rho/2)\|x_\downarrow - z_\updownarrow^k + u_\downarrow^k\|_2^2 \right) \tag{5} $$

$$ z_\updownarrow^{k+1} := \underset{z_\updownarrow}{\operatorname{argmin}}\left( r(z_\updownarrow) + (\rho/\lambda)\|z_\updownarrow - \overline{x}_\updownarrow^{k+1} - \overline{u}_\updownarrow^k\|_2^2 \right) \tag{6} $$

$$ u_\uparrow^{k+1} := u_\uparrow^k + x_\uparrow^{k+1} - z_\updownarrow^{k+1} \tag{7} $$

$$ u_\downarrow^{k+1} := u_\downarrow^k + x_\downarrow^{k+1} - z_\updownarrow^{k+1}, \tag{8} $$

where $u_\uparrow$ and $u_\downarrow$ are the scaled local dual variables correspond to $x_\uparrow$ and $x_\downarrow$; $\overline{x}_\updownarrow = (1/2)(x_\uparrow + x_\downarrow)$ and $\overline{u}_\updownarrow = (1/2)(u_\uparrow + u_\downarrow)$ are the averages of the local primal variables and scaled local dual variables. The termination criterion is that the primal and dual residuals must be small, *i.e.*,

$$\sqrt{\|x_\uparrow^k - \overline{x}_\updownarrow^k\|_2^2 + \|x_\downarrow^k - \overline{x}_\updownarrow^k\|_2^2} < \epsilon_\updownarrow^{\mathrm{pri}}$$

and

$$2\rho\|\overline{x}_\updownarrow^k - \overline{x}_\updownarrow^{k-1}\|_2 < \epsilon_\updownarrow^{\mathrm{dual}},$$

where $\epsilon_\updownarrow^{\mathrm{pri}} > 0$ and $\epsilon_\updownarrow^{\mathrm{dual}} > 0$ are feasibility tolerances for the primal and dual feasibility conditions [27].

The algorithm is very intuitive. The local primal variables, $x_\uparrow$ and $x_\downarrow$, and dual variables, $u_\uparrow$ and $u_\downarrow$, are separately updated through Eqs. 4, 5, 7 and 8. The local result are collected and brought into consensus through Eq. 6. When the algorithm terminates, $x_\uparrow$ and $x_\downarrow$ should both agree with $z_\updownarrow$.

Let $x_\uparrow$ equals $(\overleftarrow{x}_\uparrow, \overrightarrow{x}_\uparrow)$; $x_\downarrow$ equals $(\overleftarrow{x}_\downarrow, \overrightarrow{x}_\downarrow)$; $u_\uparrow$ equals $(\overleftarrow{u}_\uparrow, \overrightarrow{u}_\uparrow)$; $u_\downarrow$ equals $(\overleftarrow{u}_\downarrow, \overrightarrow{u}_\downarrow)$; $z_\updownarrow$ equals $(\overleftarrow{z}_\updownarrow, \overrightarrow{z}_\updownarrow)$. The variables that should be private to Alice are $\overrightarrow{x}_\uparrow$, $\overrightarrow{x}_\downarrow$, $\overrightarrow{u}_\uparrow$, $\overrightarrow{u}_\downarrow$ and $\overrightarrow{z}_\updownarrow$. To protect $A_\downarrow$, $\overrightarrow{x}_\downarrow$ and $\overrightarrow{u}_\downarrow$, we assign Eqs. 5 and 8 to $\mathcal{A}$ such that Alice can handle $A_\downarrow$, $x_\downarrow$ and $u_\downarrow$ exclusively. Equation 5 involves a $\ell_2$ regularized logistic regression problem that can be efficiently solved by Quasi-Newton methods like L-BFGS [29]. To further reduce her efforts, Alice can mandate the maximum L-BFGS iterations to be small and rely on the second tier for accuracy.

To protect $\overrightarrow{z}_\updownarrow$, we split Eq. 6. Since $r(z_\updownarrow)$ is essentially the proximal operator of a $\ell_1$ norm, we can calculate it using the *soft thresholding operator* [30]

$$S_\kappa(x) = (x - \kappa)_+ - (-x - \kappa)_-,$$

which is separable at the component level. We can split Eq. 6 into

$$\overleftarrow{z}_\updownarrow^{k+1} := (1/2)S_{\lambda/\rho}(\overleftarrow{x}_\uparrow^{k+1} + \overleftarrow{x}_\downarrow^{k+1} + \overleftarrow{u}_\uparrow^k + \overleftarrow{u}_\downarrow^k) \tag{9}$$

$$\overrightarrow{z}_\updownarrow^{k+1} := (1/2)S_{\lambda/\rho}(\overrightarrow{x}_\uparrow^{k+1} + \overrightarrow{x}_\downarrow^{k+1} + \overrightarrow{u}_\uparrow^k + \overrightarrow{u}_\downarrow^k), \tag{10}$$

We assign Eq. 9 to $\mathcal{S}$ but reserve and Eq. 10 to $\mathcal{A}$[2]. We allow Sara to send $\overleftarrow{z}_\updownarrow$ back to Alice since She need it to compute $x_\downarrow$ and $u_\downarrow$. To protect $\overrightarrow{u}_\uparrow$, we split Eq. 7 into

$$\overleftarrow{u}_\uparrow^{k+1} := \overleftarrow{u}_\uparrow^k + \overleftarrow{x}_\uparrow^{k+1} - \overleftarrow{z}_\updownarrow^{k+1} \tag{11}$$

$$\overrightarrow{u}_\uparrow^{k+1} := \overrightarrow{u}_\uparrow^k + \overrightarrow{x}_\uparrow^{k+1} - \overrightarrow{z}_\updownarrow^{k+1}. \tag{12}$$

We assign Eq. 11 to $\mathcal{S}$ but reserve and Eq. 12 to $\mathcal{A}$.

Finally, Eq. 4 contains data and variable that should be private to Alice, *i.e.*, $\overrightarrow{A}$ and $\overrightarrow{x}_\uparrow$, which we will handle at the second tier.

---

[2] Note that the intercept $v$ is not regularized. Equations 9 and 10 can be modified to incorporate the intercept by dropping the soft thresholding operator on the corresponding element in $z_\updownarrow$.

**Feature Split.** At the second tier, we split $A_\uparrow$ by columns in order to protect the private features within $\overleftarrow{A}$ and the corresponding weight $\overleftarrow{x}_\uparrow$. Recall that

Define

$$\overleftarrow{r}(\overleftarrow{x}_\uparrow) = (\rho/2)\|\overleftarrow{x}_\uparrow - \overleftarrow{z}_\uparrow^k + \overleftarrow{u}_\uparrow^k\|_2^2,$$
$$\overrightarrow{r}(\overrightarrow{x}_\uparrow) = (\rho/2)\|\overrightarrow{x}_\uparrow - \overrightarrow{z}_\uparrow^k + \overrightarrow{u}_\uparrow^k\|_2^2.$$

we can explicitly convert Eq. 4 into sharing form [27]

$$\text{minimize } l_\uparrow(\overleftarrow{z} + \overrightarrow{z}) + \overleftarrow{r}(\overleftarrow{x}_\uparrow) + \overrightarrow{r}(\overrightarrow{x}_\uparrow)$$
$$\text{subject to } \overleftarrow{A}\,\overleftarrow{x}_\uparrow - \overleftarrow{z} = \overrightarrow{A}\,\overrightarrow{x}_\uparrow - \overrightarrow{z} = 0,$$

with partial predictors $\overleftarrow{z}, \overrightarrow{z} \in \mathbf{R}_\uparrow^{|E|}$.

Let $\overleftrightarrow{u} \in \mathbf{R}_\uparrow^{|E|}$ be the single dual variable. The problem can be solved using the following ADMM algorithm

$$\overleftarrow{x}_\uparrow^{k'+1} := \underset{\overleftarrow{x}_\uparrow}{\text{argmin}} \left( \overleftarrow{r}(\overleftarrow{x}_\uparrow) + (\rho'/2)\|\overleftarrow{A}\,\overleftarrow{x}_\uparrow - \overleftarrow{A}\,\overleftarrow{x}_\uparrow^{k'} - \overleftrightarrow{z}^{k'} + \overline{A_\uparrow x_\uparrow}^{k'} + \overleftrightarrow{u}^{k'}\|_2^2 \right)$$

$$(13)$$

$$\overrightarrow{x}_\uparrow^{k'+1} := \underset{\overrightarrow{x}_\uparrow}{\text{argmin}} \left( \overrightarrow{r}(\overrightarrow{x}_\uparrow) + (\rho'/2)\|\overrightarrow{A}\,\overrightarrow{x}_\uparrow - \overrightarrow{A}\,\overrightarrow{x}_\uparrow^{k'} - \overleftrightarrow{z}^{k'} + \overline{A_\uparrow x_\uparrow}^{k'} + \overleftrightarrow{u}^{k'}\|_2^2 \right)$$

$$(14)$$

$$\overline{z}^{k'+1} := \underset{\overline{z}}{\text{argmin}} \left( l_\uparrow(2\overline{z}) + \rho'\|\overline{z} - \overline{A_\uparrow x_\uparrow}^{k'+1} - \overleftrightarrow{u}^{k'}\|_2^2 \right)$$

$$(15)$$

$$\overleftrightarrow{u}^{k'+1} := \overleftrightarrow{u}^{k'} + \overline{A_\uparrow x_\uparrow}^{k'+1} - \overline{z}^{k'+1},$$

$$(16)$$

where $\overline{A_\uparrow x_\uparrow} = (1/2)(\overleftarrow{A}\,\overleftarrow{x}_\uparrow + \overrightarrow{A}\,\overrightarrow{x}_\uparrow)$ and $\overline{z} = (1/2)(\overleftarrow{z} + \overrightarrow{z})$ are the averages of the partial predictors. The termination criterion is that the primal and dual residuals must be small, i.e.,

$$2\|\overline{A_\uparrow x_\uparrow}^{k'} - \overline{z}^{k'}\|_2 < \overleftrightarrow{\epsilon}^{\text{pri}}$$

and

$$\rho'\sqrt{\|\overleftarrow{A}^T(\overleftarrow{z}^{k'} - \overleftarrow{z}^{k'-1})\|_2^2 + \|\overrightarrow{A}^T(\overrightarrow{z}^{k'} - \overrightarrow{z}^{k'-1})\|_2^2} < \overleftrightarrow{\epsilon}^{\text{dual}}$$

where $\overleftrightarrow{\epsilon}^{\text{pri}} > 0$ and $\overleftrightarrow{\epsilon}^{\text{dual}} > 0$ are feasibility tolerances for the primal and dual feasibility conditions [27].

The algorithm is also intuitive. The local primal variables $\overline{x}_\uparrow$, and $\vec{x}_\uparrow$ and dual variable $\overleftrightarrow{u}$ are separately updated through Eqs. 13, 14 and 16. The partial predictors are collected, averaged then updated through a $\ell_2$ regularized logistic regression problem (Eq. 15).

To protect $\vec{A}$ and $\vec{x}_\uparrow$, we can assign all but Eq. 14 to $\mathcal{S}$. The reason is that only $\overleftrightarrow{z} = \overline{A}\,\overline{x}_\uparrow$ and $\vec{z} = \vec{A}\,\vec{x}_\uparrow$ are shared throughout the algorithm. From Eq. 1, we see that these partial predictors are in fact the *margin* of the training data, which is a monotonically decreasing function of the sub-optimality. Assuming the label $q$ is within $\vec{A}$, sharing these partial predictors reveals neither $\vec{A}$ nor $\vec{x}_\uparrow$.

Using this two-tier training method, Alice, who processes $A_\downarrow$ and $\vec{A}$, learns the entire model coefficient $x^\star$. Sara, who processes $\overline{A}$, only learns $\overline{x}^\star$ while remains oblivious about $A_\downarrow$, $\vec{A}$ and $\vec{x}^\star$. When predicting a link with unknown sign, Alice can either assemble Eq. 3 by herself, or outsource $\overleftarrow{p}_u^T \overline{w}^\star$ to Sara without jeopardizing her privacy.

### 4.3   Complexity Analysis

Here we analyze the complexities of the tasks assigned to $\mathcal{A}$ and $\mathcal{S}$. We show that the workload is properly divided between $\mathcal{A}$ and $\mathcal{S}$ such that Sara handles a majority of work.

For each training iteration, the dominate tasks for $\mathcal{A}$ are Eqs. 5 and 14. Equation 5 is a $\ell_2$ regularized logistic regression with a wide matrix $A_\downarrow$. Assuming we solve it with L-BFGS, the most expensive operations for each L-BFGS iteration are evaluating the function value, the gradient and approximating the Hessian matrix with a limited memory BFGS matrix [29]. The complexities for the first two are both $\mathcal{O}(|E|_\downarrow K)$. The complexity for the last one is $m^2|E|_\downarrow$, where $m$ is the number of BGFS corrections[3] [29]. Equation 5 is a $\ell_2$ regularized least squares problem with a tall matrix $\vec{A}$. The most expensive operations for that are forming and factoring the Gramian matrix $\vec{A}^T \vec{A}$. If we cache the factorization result, the total complexity for that is $\mathcal{O}(\vec{K}|E|_\uparrow)$ [31, Sect. 4.2].

For each training iteration, the dominate tasks for $\mathcal{S}$ are Eqs. 15 and 13. Equation 15 is essentially $|E|_\uparrow$s scalar $\ell_2$ regularized logistic regressions, which can be solved using a lookup table for the approximate value, followed by one or two Newton steps [27]. The overall complexity for that is $\mathcal{O}(|E|_\uparrow)$. Equation 13 is a $\ell_2$ least squares problem with a large matrix $\overline{A}$. If we cache the factorization result, the total complexity to solve that is $\mathcal{O}(\overline{K}|E|_\uparrow)$.

Assume the implicit condition that $|E|_\uparrow \gg |E|_\downarrow$ and $\overline{K} \gg \vec{K}$ holds, the workload ratio between $\mathcal{A}$ and $\mathcal{S}$ is approximately $c|E|_\downarrow / |E|_\uparrow$, where $c$ is the maximums L-BFGS iterations controlled by Alice.

---

[3] In practice, we assume $m$ to be small.

### 4.4 Protecting Prior Knowledge

Here we present two variations of the original learning model to incorporate Alice's prior knowledge. We assume that Alice knows *a priori* certain private features have higher influence on the link signs than the others within her network. To compensate that, we adjust the learning model by changing the regularization function. We show we can properly train the new model and protect Alice's prior knowledge using the same two-tier training method.

In practice, it is common to assume Alice vaguely knows the underlying reason of her link sign decisions. Although not wishing to reveal such reason, Alice would prefer a model that take her prior knowledge into account. Such preference can be expressed by swapping the $\ell_1$ regularization function for a generalized $\ell_1$ regularization function in Eq. 2,

$$\text{minimize} \ \frac{1}{|E|} \sum_{i=1}^{|E|} \log\left(1 + \exp\left(-Ax\right)\right) + \lambda \|Fx\|_1, \tag{17}$$

where $F \in \mathbf{R}^{|E| \times |E|}$ is an arbitrary linear transformation matrix. Alice can define different regularization strengths for different feature combinations through $F$. If $F$ is a diagonal matrix or a block diagonal matrix, *i.e.*,

Equations 6, 13 and 14 are separable. Therefore, we can still split the links and features through ADMM.

Another interesting variation is when Alice knows *a priori* that most private features affect her link sign decisions, *i.e.*, $\vec{w}$ is sparse but $\overline{w}$ is dense. Instead of $\ell_1$ regularization, Alice can apply $\ell_2$ regularization to $\overline{w}$. The problem becomes

$$\text{minimize} \ \frac{1}{|E|} \sum_{i=1}^{|E|} \log\left(1 + \exp\left(-Ax\right)\right) + \lambda \|\vec{w}\|_2^2 + \|\overline{w}\|_1, \tag{18}$$

where the $\ell_2$ regularization ensures that $\overline{w}$ is a dense vector. Since the regularizations are separable by $\vec{w}$ and $\overline{w}$, The $\ell_2$ regularization is not revealed to Sara during training. Therefore, Alice's prior knowledge privacy is still protected.

## 5 Experimentation and Evaluation

Here we evaluate the performance of our method with real-word OSN data. Our experiments is conducted on the Wikipedia Request for Adminiship (RfA) dataset [19,32], which contains a directed, signed network with rich textual features. We use it to assess the prediction accuracy, the privacy-preserving property, and the efficiency of our method.

## 5.1   Wikipedia RfA Dataset

Leskovec *et al.* [19] created the Wikipedia RfA dataset by crawling and parsing the Wikipedia RfA process webpages from 2003 to 2013. The dataset contains votes casted by Wikipedia members for promoting individual editors to the role of administrator. To apply for adminship, a *request for adminship* must be submitted either by the candidate or another community member [19]. Any Wikipedia member can cast a supporting, neutral, or opposing vote along with a short comment for the RfA. The comment explains the reason of the vote. For instance, A comment for a supporting vote may read, '*I have seen him around, a trustworthy editor with a good knowledge of policy*', whereas a comment for an opposing vote may read, '*This candidate's lack of experience in the en:Wikipedia administrative arena*'.

This induces a directed, signed network in which nodes represent Wikipedia members and links represent votes. The vote comments provide rich textual features, which makes the dataset well-suited for our experiments. West *et al.* [32] post-processed the dataset to exclude all neutral votes. The current dataset contains 10,835 nodes, 159,388 links (76 % positive). The average length of vote comments is 34 characters.

## 5.2   Experimental Setup

We follow the same training and testing paradigm in [32]. We randomly select 10 focal nodes. For each focal node we carry out a breadth-first search (following both in-link and out-link) until we have visited 350 nodes. This gives us 10 subgraphs, each has 350 nodes. For each subgraph, we randomly select 10 % links and mark them as unknown. We use the rest 90 % links to train a sparse logistic model and test its performance using the unknown links. Just to make a fair comparison about prediction accuracy, we also train a model for each subgraph $i$ and test it using subgraph $i + 1$ without any link masking, which follows the same setting in [32].

We use the term frequencies of the 10,000 most frequent words as link features, We excludes words that paraphrase link labels, *i.e.*, *support* or *oppose*, or words whose prefixes paraphrase link labels, *i.e.*, *support* or *oppos*. For feature split, we pre-train a regular sparse logistic model using a random sample of 10,000 comments without testing. We choose the 100 words that have highest weights and 900 random samples of the from the rest of the words as private features and the remaining 9000 words as public features. For link split, we choose half the opposing links as private links and the other half along with all supporting links as public links.

We train the model by solving a sparse logistic regression with different regularization parameters for $\bar{w}$ and $\vec{w}$, *i.e.*,

$$r(x) = \lambda_1 \|\bar{w}\|_1 + \lambda_2 \|\vec{w}\|_1,$$

where $\lambda_1 = 0.1$ and $\lambda_1 = 0.01$. We use a Python implementation to perform the two-tier training in parallel. The parallelism is provided by the IPython parallel engine. We use the `fmin_l_bfgs_b` in SciPy to update Eqs. 4, 5, and 15, which is essentially Nocedal's Fortran 77 implementation of L-BFGS [29]. We set the maximum L-BFGS iterations to 10 to limit Alice's effort. To verify the result, we also train the model without ADMM using a MATLAB implementation with CVX [33] and Gurobi [34]. All experiments are conducted on a Cray CS-300 cluster with 2.60 GHz octa-core Intel Sandy Bridge CPUs.

### 5.3 Evaluation Metrics

The metrics we use to evaluate the prediction accuracy are the areas under the curve (AUC) of the receiver operating characteristic (ROC) curves as well as the precision-recall (PR) curves. We only report the PR curve of the opposing links because it better describes the prediction accuracy [32]. The reason is because the class imbalance of 76 % supporting links. Even random guessing can achieve an AUC of 0.76 for supporting links comparing to an AUC of 0.24 for opposing links.

We show the privacy-preserving property by reporting the AUC/PR curves and the classification margins for the joint model, a model solely uses private features and a model solely uses public features. The last one represents the model Sara attains after the two-tier training. The differences between the three models signifies the information leakage due to exposing the public features.

The metrics we use to evaluate the algorithm efficiency and the communication overhead are the iteration versus suboptimality (IVS) curve and the cumulative runtime versus suboptimality (CRVS) curve. We consider one iteration as a complete cycle of both tiers. Due to parallelism, we report the cumulative runtime for both $\mathcal{A}$ and $\mathcal{S}$. The optimal value was verified using CVX [33] and Gurobi [34].

### 5.4 Results

We first verify that our training objective produces high quality prediction model. In Fig. 1, we compare our model with the sentiment model used in [32], which is trained through a $\ell_2$ regularized logistic regression. We randomly mask a set of links and train both models using the comments of the remaining links. Even with data rearrangement and splitting, the performance of our model is comparable to the sentiment model in terms of AUC/ROC curve and AUC/PR curve. The sentiment model slightly edges ours at the fourth decimal point, due to the sparsity constrain in our objective. The two models agree on 95 % of the signs among the top 100 weights. Interestingly, the improvement through increasing the visible link ratio is not significant for both models. This suggests that the kurtosis of the feature weights distributions is high. Most weights have small correlation with the link sign.

Our second experiment examines the privacy-preserving property of the two-tier training method. We compare the prediction accuracies of three models, the joint model that uses both public and private features, a private model that solely uses private features and a public model that solely uses public features.

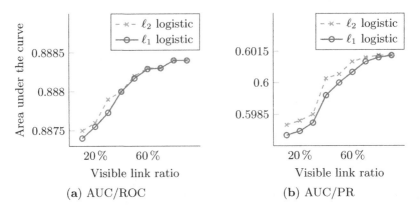

**Fig. 1.** Assess the model quality by comparing our model with the $\ell_2$ regularized logistic regression model used in [32]. **(a)** The AUC/ROC curves are comparable between the two models. **(b)** The AUC/PR curves are comparable between the two models.

Figure 2a shows the AUC/ROC curves of the three. Consider a baseline model that predicts link signs through random guess. The AUC/ROC for the baseline model is exactly 0.5. The public model's performance is 10 % better than the baseline model whereas the other two are 76 % and 50 % better than the baseline model. Since Sara only learns $\overleftarrow{x}^*$, her prediction accuracy is 86.8 % lower than Alice.

The public model does enjoy a slight performance bump when increasing the visible link ratio. That is because the corresponding increases of nonzero entities in $\overleftarrow{A}$, which enlarge the classification margin. But, such improvement is limited. Figure 2b shows the classification margin of the three models. We normalized the margins according to the largest one, *i.e.*, the margin of the joint model. The classification margin of the public model is the lowest among all three. It indicates that most predictions the public model makes are borderline cases with low confidence.

Finally, we report the training efficiency and workload for Alice and Sara. Using the experimental setup described earlier, the average number of links for each subgraph is 5000, among which 1000 are negative and 4000 are positive. This produces a matrix $A$ of size 5000 by 10,000, which divides into three parts, a matrix $A_\downarrow$ of size 500 by 10,000, a matrix $\overleftarrow{A}$ of size 4500 by 9900 and a matrix $\vec{A}$ of size 4500 by 100.

We measure the training process using the objective suboptimality. Let $\tilde{o}^k$ be the objective value at the $k$th iteration

$$\tilde{o}^k = \frac{1}{|E|} \sum_{i=1}^{|E|} \log\left(1 + \exp\left(-Az_\updownarrow^k\right)\right) + r(z_\updownarrow^k).$$

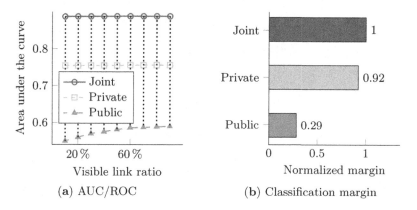

(a) AUC/ROC    (b) Classification margin

**Fig. 2.** Observe the private preserving property by comparing the prediction accuracies and the classification margins. (a) Using only public features, Sara's prediction accuracy is 86.8 % lower than Alice. (b) Using only public features, Sara's classification margins (prediction confident) is 71.0 % lower than Alice.

Let $o^\star$ be the optimal objective value

$$o^\star = \frac{1}{|E|} \sum_{i=1}^{|E|} \log\left(1 + \exp\left(-Ax^\star\right)\right) + r(x^\star).$$

The objective suboptimality is the difference between $\tilde{o}^k$ and $o^\star$, *i.e.*, $\tilde{o}^k - o^\star$. The optimal value $o^\star = 0.9752 \times 10^5$ is verified by our MATLAB implementation. Figure 3a shows the training progress by iteration. The dashed line marks the iteration when the stopping criterion is satisfied. The algorithm only takes 24 iterations to reach the optimal, which greatly reduces the communication overhead between Alice and Sara.

Figure 3b shows the CRVS curves for Alice and Sara. The dashed line marks convergence. The main task for Alice is to compute Eq. 5 using L-BFGS. We use L-BFGS with warm starting to reduce Alice's workload. This approach is effective in later iteration when the iterates approach consensus. The main task for Sara is to compute Eqs. 13, 15 and various matrix-vector multiplications. We cache the matrix factorization to reduce Sara's workload. However, Sara still need to compute large back-solves to produce the result. For both Alice and Sara, the runtime of early iterations is significantly longer than the latter ones. Overall, Sara's workload is approximately 10 times larger than Alice's workload.

To summarize, the experiments show three points: (1) Our decentralized method achieves equally high predication accuracy as the sentiment model used in [32]. Using data splitting to protect private data does not affect the modal quality. (2) Sara is oblivious of Alice's private data and their corresponding weights. Without Alice's help, Sara's prediction accuracy is fairly poor. Alice, on the other hand, enjoy the full benefit of the collaboration and is able to acquire high prediction accuracy with minimal efforts. (3) The data splitting

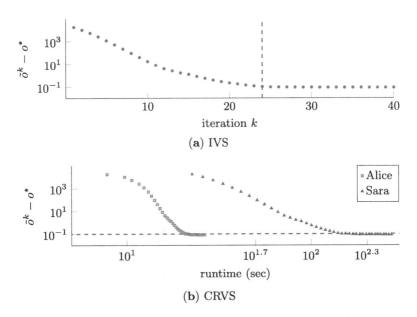

**Fig. 3.** Convergence analysis of the two-tier training method. The stopping criterion is satisfied at iteration 24, marked by the dashed lines. (**a**) X axis is the number of iterations, Y axis it the suboptimality measured by $\tilde{o}^k - o^\star$. (**b**) X axis is the cumulative runtime measured in seconds. The total runtime for Alice is 90.4 % lower than Sara.

assigns appropriate workload for Alice and Sara to fully utilize their computation resources.

## 6    Conclusion

In this paper, we studied the privacy-preserving link prediction problem in decentralized OSNs. We proposed a novel decentralized two-tier method that allows end users to collaborate with their online service providers without revealing their private data. Using a real-world social network dataset, we showed that our method produces high quality prediction model while eases users' computing burden. Additionally, we showed that our method can be secure against the link reconstruction attack. In the era of "Big Data", our method bridges the gap between the increasing volume of personal data and the insufficient analyzing resources of privacy conscious users in decentralized OSNs.

**Acknowledgment.** This work was supported by US National Science Foundation under grants CNS-1405747, CNS-1156318, CNS-1443889, and CSR-1217889.

## A    Appendix: Link Reconstruction Attack

Here we assess the possibility of link reconstruction attack. In a link reconstruction attack, we consider a passive adversary, Eve, tries to predict the link signs of Alice's network. Just like Sara, Eve can access the public data matrix $\overleftarrow{A}$. But, unlike Sara, Eve cannot collaborate with Alice. We assume Eve knows the training method Alice and Sara use. The goal for Eve is to build a model that has the same prediction power as the joint model. We evaluate the attack possibility by measuring Eve's prediction accuracy.

## A.1    Experimental Setup

Our previous experiments assume that Alice makes rational decision and protects features that have high correlation with the link sign. Although unlikely, Alice can split the data in such a way that all private features are irrelevant to the link sign. To consider different public/private splits, we shuffle the features of the matrix $A$ used in previous experiments.

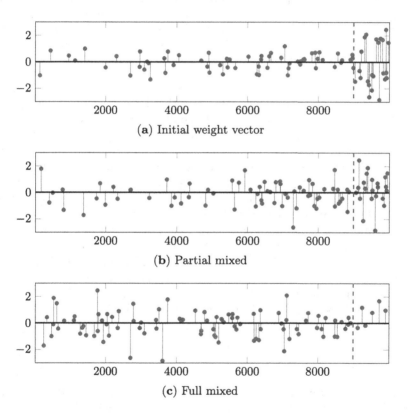

(a) Initial weight vector

(b) Partial mixed

(c) Full mixed

**Fig. 4.** Weight vectors generated by random walking the nonzero entries in the initial weight vector. The dashed line marks the feature split point. (a) The initial weight vector is the same as the optimal weight vector $w^\star$ learned from the Wikipedia RfA dataset. (b) Private features and public features are partially mixed. (c) Private features and public features are uniformly distributed.

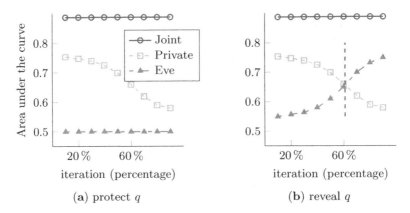

**Fig. 5.** AUC/ROCs of the public and private models versus shuffling iteration. The shuffling iterations is represented as the percentage of the maximum iterations. (a) Eve can not improve her prediction accuracy if Alice protect $q$. (b) Eve can improve her prediction accuracy if Alice reveal $q$. The dashed line marks the tipping point where Eve's model surpasses the private model.

The shuffle is done by rearranging features that have nonzero weights. We use a Monte Carlo random walk algorithm to shuffle matrix $A$. For each iteration, the algorithm moves the features that have nonzero weights randomly to the left or to the right. The resulting 'true' weight vectors are shown in Fig. 4. The initial weight vector represents the split that assigns top weighted features to the private data matrix $\vec{A}$. The random walk mixes the features in $\vec{A}$ with the features in $\overleftarrow{A}$. As the walking time increases, the 'true' weights approaches a steady state uniform distribution.

We use the total variation mixing time [35], $i.e.$, $t = n \log n$, where $n$ equals 10,000, as the maximum mixing iterations. For each $0.1t$, we record the shuffled matrix. This gives us 10 matrices whose 'true' weights gradually change from unevenly distributed to uniformly distributed. We split these matrices at a fixed index position. For each matrix, We train a prediction model for Eve solely using $\overleftarrow{A}$. We compare Eve's model with the private model and the joint model trained by Alice and Sara.

## A.2 Results

Figure 5 shows the prediction accuracy of Eve's model versus shuffling iteration. The results are distinct for two different scenarios. If the link sign column $q$ is within $\vec{A}$, shown in Fig. 5a, Eve is forced to train her model with random guesses. In that case, moving high weighted features into $\overleftarrow{A}$ does not improve Eve's model. Eve's prediction accuracy is exactly 0.5 regardless the features she uses.

If the link sign column $q$ is within $\overleftarrow{A}$, shown in Fig. 5b, Eve can properly train her model using the same sparse logistic regression. In that case, Eve's model can be improved if more high weighted features are within $\vec{A}$. In our experiment, Eve is able to increase her prediction accuracy by over 50 % when the weights are uniformly distributed.

Although the security properties are different, the impacts on Sara's prediction accuracy are the same. When the high weighted features are moved from $\vec{A}$ to $\overline{A}$, the predication accuracy of the private model decreases; the prediction accuracy of the public model increases; the prediction accuracy of the joint model remains the same. Sara, who benefits from collaborating with Alice, is able to make more accurate prediction using the public model.

To summarize, the experiments show: (1) that Alice can prevent the link reconstruction attack by marking the link sign ground truth as private. (2) Although not violating Alice's privacy, inappropriate data split could accidentally increases Sara's prediction power.

# References

1. Google finance. Accessed 19 June 2014. https://www.google.com/finance
2. Statistic brain. Accessed 20 June 2014. http://www.statisticbrain.com
3. Zheleva, E., Getoor, L.: To join or not to join: the illusion of privacy in social networks with mixed public and private user profiles. In: Proceedings of the 18th International Conference on World Wide Web, pp. 531–540 (2009)
4. Facebook. Data use policy. Accessed 25 June 2014. https://www.facebook.com/about/privacy
5. Dodson, B., Vo, I., Purtell, T., Cannon, A., Lam, M.: Musubi: disintermediated interactive social feeds for mobile devices. In: Proceedings of the 21st International Conference On World Wide Web, pp. 211–220 (2012)
6. Diaspora Inc. Accessed 28 May 2014. http://diasporaproject.org
7. Omlet Inc. Accessed 28 May 2014. http://www.omlet.me
8. Aggarwal, C.C.: Social Network Data Analytics. Springer, US (2011)
9. Datta, A., Buchegger, S., Vu, L.-H., Strufe, T., Rzadca, K.: Decentralized online social networks. In: Furht, B. (ed.) Handbook of Social Network Technologies and Applications, pp. 349–378. Springer, US (2010)
10. Baden, R., Bender, A., Spring, N., Bhattacharjee, B., Starin, D.: Persona: an online social network with user-defined privacy. ACM SIGCOMM Comput. Commun. Rev. **39**(4), 135–146 (2009)
11. Cutillo, L.A., Molva, R., Strufe, T.: Safebook: a privacy-preserving online social network leveraging on real-life trust. IEEE Commun. Mag. **47**(12), 94–101 (2009)
12. Backstrom, L., Leskovec, J.: Supervised random walks: predicting and recommending links in social networks. In: Proceedings of the Fourth ACM International Conference on Web Search and Data Mining, pp. 635–644 (2011)
13. Leskovec, J., Mcauley, J.J.: Learning to discover social circles in ego networks. Adv. Neural Inf. Process. Syst. **25**, 539–547 (2012)
14. Fisher, D.: Using egocentric networks to understand communication. IEEE Internet Comput. **9**(5), 20–28 (2005)
15. Dwork, C.: Differential privacy. In: Bugliesi, M., Preneel, B., Sassone, V., Wegener, I. (eds.) ICALP 2006. LNCS, vol. 4052, pp. 1–12. Springer, Heidelberg (2006)
16. Yu, H., Jiang, X., Vaidya, J.: Privacy-preserving svm using nonlinear kernels on horizontally partitioned data. In: Proceedings of the 2006 ACM Symposium on Applied Computing, pp. 603–610. ACM (2006)

17. Guha, R., Kumar, R., Raghavan, P., Tomkins, A.: Propagation of trust and distrust. In: Proceedings of the 13th International Conference on World Wide Web, pp. 403–412 (2004)
18. Al Hasan, M., Chaoji, V., Salem, S., Zaki, M.: Link prediction using supervised learning. In: Proceedings of SDM Workshop on Link Analysis, Counter-terrorism and Security (2006)
19. Leskovec, J., Huttenlocher, D., Kleinberg, J.: Predicting positive and negative links in online social networks. In: Proceedings of the 19th International Conference on World Wide Web, pp. 641–650 (2010)
20. Kim, M., Leskovec, J.: Latent multi-group membership graph model. In: Proceedings of the 29th International Conference on Machine Learning, pp. 1719–1726 (2012)
21. Salakhutdinov, R., Mnih, A., Hinton, G.: Restricted boltzmann machines for collaborative filtering. In: Proceedings of the 24th International Conference on Machine Learning, pp. 791–798 (2007)
22. Hastie, T., Tibshirani, R., Friedman, J.: The Elements of Statistical Learning: Data Mining, Inference, and Prediction, 2nd edn. Springer, Heidelberg (2009)
23. Hinton, G., Osindero, S., Teh, Y.-W.: A fast learning algorithm for deep belief nets. Neural Comput. **18**(7), 1527–1554 (2006)
24. Hinton, G.: A practical guide to training restricted boltzmann machines. Momentum **9**(1), 926 (2010)
25. Glowinski, R., Marroco, A.: Sur l'approximation, par éléments finis d'ordre un, et la résolution, par pénalisation-dualité d'une classe de problèmes de dirichlet non linéaires. ESAIM: Math. Model. Numer. Anal. Modélisation Math. Anal. Numérique **9**(R2), 41–76 (1975)
26. Gabay, D., Mercier, B.: A dual algorithm for the solution of nonlinear variational problems via finite element approximation. Comput. Math. Appl. **2**(1), 17–40 (1976)
27. Boyd, S., Parikh, N., Chu, E., Peleato, B., Eckstein, J.: Distributed optimization and statistical learning via the alternating direction method of multipliers. Found. Trends Mach. Learn. **3**(1), 1–122 (2011)
28. Parikh, N., Boyd, S.: Proximal algorithms. Found. Trends Optim. **1**(3), 123–231 (2013)
29. Byrd, R.H., Lu, P., Nocedal, J., Zhu, C.: A limited memory algorithm for bound constrained optimization. SIAM J. Sci. Comput. **16**(5), 1190–1208 (1995)
30. Donoho, D.L.: De-noising by soft-thresholding. IEEE Trans. Inf. Theory **41**(3), 613–627 (1995)
31. Golub, G.H., Van Loan, C.F.: Matrix Computations, 3rd edn. Johns Hopkins University Press, Baltimore (2013)
32. West, R., Paskov, H.S., Leskovec, J., Potts, C.: Exploiting social network structure for person-to-person sentiment analysis. Trans. Assoc. Comput. Linguist. **2**, 297–310 (2014)
33. Grant, M., Boyd, S.: CVX: Matlab software for disciplined convex programming, version 2.1 (2014). http://cvxr.com/cvx
34. Gurobi Optimization Inc., Gurobi optimizer reference manual, version 5.6 (2014). http://www.gurobi.com/documentation
35. Levin, D.A., Peres, Y., Wilmer, E.L.: Markov Chains and Mixing Times. American Mathematical Society, Providence (2009)

# Privacy-Preserving Observation in Public Spaces

Florian Kerschbaum[1]([✉]) and Hoon Wei Lim[2]

[1] SAP, Karlsruhe, Germany
florian.kerschbaum@sap.com
[2] Singtel R&D Laboratory, Singapore, Singapore
limhoonwei@singtel.com

**Abstract.** One method of privacy-preserving accounting or billing in cyber-physical systems, such as electronic toll collection or public transportation ticketing, is to have the user present an encrypted record of transactions and perform the accounting or billing computation securely on them. Honesty of the user is ensured by spot checking the record for some selected surveyed transactions. But how much privacy does that give the user, i.e. how many transactions need to be surveyed? It turns out that due to collusion in mass surveillance *all* transactions need to be observed, i.e. this method of spot checking provides no privacy at all. In this paper we present a cryptographic solution to the spot checking problem in cyber-physical systems. Users carry an authentication device that authenticates only based on fair random coins. The probability can be set high enough to allow for spot checking, but in all other cases privacy is perfectly preserved. We analyze our protocol for computational efficiency and show that it can be efficiently implemented even on platforms with limited computing resources, such as smart cards and smart phones.

## 1 Introduction

Cyber-physical systems are starting to permeate our daily lives. They record time and location information – together with sensory data – of ourselves and this data is, in turn, used to analyze our behavior in the physical world. A common application of such cyber-physical systems is billing, e.g. for toll collection [2, 22,26], public transportation [11,17,28], or electric vehicle charging [21]. The cyber-physical sensor records our identity, time, location and consumption. This data is then used to bill us based on the recorded transactions.

An obvious problem with this approach is privacy. All our transactions in the physical world are recorded and can be also analyzed for purposes other than billing. Every search engine or web-based e-mail user already gets displayed a huge amount of personalized ads.

Instead of centrally collecting all transactions they can be stored on user-owned devices. The user then presents its collected record of transactions and pays its bill. While this would remove the central data storage, the service provider observes all transactions during payment and could theoretically retain a copy. An approach for protecting privacy is to have the user present an

G. Pernul et al. (Eds.): ESORICS 2015, Part II, LNCS 9327, pp. 81–100, 2015.
DOI: 10.1007/978-3-319-24177-7_5

encrypted record of transactions. A computation on the encrypted transactions then results in the billing amount. No information – in the clear – is revealed during this process. This approach has been taken in [2,11,17,21,22,26,28]. Similar approaches can be realized using secure multi-party computation [4,5,13–16,18,19,30].

The problem is, of course, that the billed person could cheat and present an incomplete, tampered or even empty record of transactions. A solution is to record some transactions of the user in the physical world and spot check whether he honestly included them in the presented transactions during bill payment. Popa et al. [26] and Balasch et al. [2] recently presented systems for road toll pricing that follow this model. Yet, the problem is still not solved, since the users may collude in order to determine where and when they have been observed. Meiklejohn et al. [22] therefore proposed to keep the spots that are checked secret.

A problem that arises in the approach of [22] is that collusion among *dishonest* users is still possible, even if the spot checks are kept secret. A dishonest user may risk paying the penalty, if he gains from the information obtained. If this user is caught, he must be presented evidence that he cheated which reveals the observed spot. Dishonest users may therefore collude by submitting incomplete records of transactions and share the obtained information and the penalties for getting caught. We show in Sect. 3 that mass surveillance cannot prevent this collusion under reasonable penalties and *all* transactions need to be observed in order to prevent collusion. Clearly, this method then provides no privacy at all. Moreover, we argue that the proposal of [22] does not solve the problem of enforcing honesty vs. privacy. The question one has to ask is how many transactions need to be surveyed. Too few transactions may enable cheating and too many violate privacy. We investigate whether there is a privacy-compliant trade-off in public spot checking.

We propose a cryptographic solution to this problem. Particularly, we present a protocol for a privacy-preserving spot checking device. The basic idea is to run a randomized oblivious transfer of the trace of an authentication protocol and a random message. This device may authenticate the carrier (due to the authentication protocol) with a random probability that cannot be tweaked by the carrier (if the oblivious transfer sends the authentication trace). The observer learns nothing with a probability that cannot be tweaked by the reader (if the oblivious transfer sends the random message). The probability of authentication can be set high enough to allow for spot checking, but low enough to provide reasonable privacy. Since it is a personal device authenticating only its carrier, no information can be shared, and thus completely preventing collusion attacks.

We emphasize that the construction of our protocol is very efficient. We neither need any secure hardware nor verifiable encryption using zero-knowledge proofs. We achieve this by using a definition of fairness secure against one-sided malicious adversaries only restricting the attacks to incentive-compatible ones.

All our security objectives are provably achieved using efficient, established building blocks and assumptions. A secure device could be built from the specification by anyone – even suspicious citizens. Furthermore, we optimize the protocol for performance and present an implementation analysis of the optimized version for weak computation devices. We estimate that the protocol can be run in roughly half a second on very weak smart cards. As a conclusion it is likely that the protocol can be run even on flowing traffic without any disruptions.

In this paper we contribute

– an economic analysis of collusion in spot checked cyber-physical systems;
– a protocol for privacy-preserving spot checking;
– an implementation analysis of this protocol for weak computational devices.

The remainder of this paper is structured as follows. In the next section, we give a brief overview of related work on privacy-preserving electronic billing or accounting systems. In Sect. 3 we present our economic analysis of collusion in these systems. Then, we describe our privacy-preserving spot checking protocol in Sect. 4. We also give an implementation analysis and discuss the trade-off between privacy and enforcement of honesty. In Sect. 5 we give an example application and we present our conclusions in Sect. 6.

## 2   Related Work

### 2.1   Privacy-Preserving Billing

**Toll Collection.** Cryptographic privacy-preserving toll collection systems [2, 22, 26] have been proposed to resolve the tension between the desire for sophisticated road pricing schemes and drivers' interest in maintaining the privacy of their driving patterns. At the core of these systems is a monthly payment and an audit protocols performed between the driver, via an on-board unit (OBU), the toll service provider (operating the OBU) and the local government. Each driver commits to the road segments she traversed over the month and the cost associated with each segment. To ensure honest reporting, the systems rely on the audit protocol, which in turn, makes use of unpredictable spot checks by hidden roadside cameras. At month's end, the driver is challenged to show that her committed road segments include the segments in which she was observed, and that the corresponding prices are correct. (More description of such an audit protocol for privacy-preserving toll collection is given in Sect. 5.) As long as the spot checks are done unpredictably, any driver attempting to cheat will be caught with high probability. Meiklejohn et al. [22] proposed a system called Milo, which employs an oblivious transfer technique based on blind identity-based encryption [9] in its audit protocol, such that spot checks on a driver's committed road segments can be performed without revealing the checked locations. Nevertheless, privacy is preserved with respect to only the toll service provider. The cameras can actually observe *all* vehicles at all times, and thus, there is completely no privacy against the local government (audit authority), which can trace any vehicle and learn its driving patterns through the cameras.

**e-Ticketing in Public Transportation.** The use of contactless smart cards as electronic tickets (e-tickets) is popular in public transportation systems in many countries world-wide [11,17,28]. However, majority of existing e-ticketing systems are not designed to protect user privacy, i.e. travel records leak commuters' location information. In fact, transportation companies collect commuters' travel history in order to analyze traffic patterns and detect fraudulent transactions. However, this clearly is a privacy breach. Kerschbaum et al. [17] recently proposed a cryptographic solution for bill processing of travel records while allowing privacy-preserving data mining and analytics. However, privacy is achieved at the expense of high processing overhead of encrypted travel records and the need for an independent key management authority. Also, no notion of spot checking is used in their system.

**Electric Vehicle Charging.** Electric vehicles have been used as a more environmental-friendly alternative to traditional gasoline-based vehicles. However, electric vehicles require frequent recharging at dedicated locations. If not done properly, information of a driver's whereabouts can be leaked through the underlying payment system. Liu et al. [21] designed an anonymous payment protocol for enhancing the location privacy of electric vehicles. While a driver's location privacy is preserved against the power grid company, a malicious local government is still able to reveal any past transactions.

**Variants of Oblivious Transfer.** Oblivious transfer is a protocol between a sender and a receiver. In its most simple form, the sender has two messages and the receiver learns one without learning anything about the other one. Oblivious transfer has been introduced by Rabin [27] where the message received was a joint random choice between sender and receiver. Even et al. generalized this to a setting where the receiver could choose which message he receives [7].

Oblivious transfer is a very powerful primitive. Kilian showed that all cryptographic primitives can be based on oblivious transfer [20]. Also many variants of oblivious transfer exist. In priced oblivious transfer [1] a price is deducted from an encrypted account for each message received. In k-out-of-n oblivious transfer [3] $k$ messages can be chosen amongst $n$. We employ oblivious transfer in a new setting with authentication. Private information retrieval (PIR) is incompatible with our setting, since it may reveal information about the non-transferred message.

## 2.2   Threat Model

In privacy-preserving billing systems, the goal is to protect the location information of users while ensuring that the users behave in an honest manner.

We assume that there exist various *semi-honest* parties who may be interested in garnering information about users' travel patterns and location information; for example, service providers may do this for business reasons, local government for social or political reasons, and even users themselves may attempt to learn other users' whereabouts for malicious motives.

Moreover, there are *dishonest* users who may find every opportunity to cheat, including colluding with other users or deviating arbitrarily from the associated payment protocol. That is, they would attempt to avoid paying or paying less than they should for the services they have received.

# 3 Collusion Attack

Meiklejohn et al. [22] claim for their system Milo that it prevents collusion attacks, since it does not reveal the spot checked locations to an *honest* user. In this section we investigate the economic feasibility of a collusion attack for *dishonest* users. We consider a simplified model where the penalties and costs are linear in the number of transactions, but conjecture that similar solutions can be found in the non-linear case. Our conclusion is that in mass surveillance possible collusion leads to the need for observing all transactions.

## 3.1 Model

We divide *time* and *space* into discrete spots. Spots have a certain duration – usually as long as an observation period. Not all spots of a location must be observed, imagine, for example, mobile cameras.

A spot can be either observed, i.e. all transactions of users are recorded, or unobserved, i.e. no transaction is recorded. We assume that a fraction $\frac{1}{\alpha}$ of spots are to be observed. For the user the state of the spot may also be unknown, i.e. he does not know whether it is observed or unobserved.

During the duration of each spot *on average m* transactions of different users are observed. Imagine a camera that records the flowing car traffic and recognizes the license plates. In an hour on a busy street one can observe probably thousands of cars.

When the user reports his transactions, he has to pay cost $d$ for each reported transaction. He may also choose to cheat and not report some transactions. For every transaction where he gets caught doing so he has to pay penalty $p$ $(p > d)$.

## 3.2 Collusion Strategy

We consider the following strategy. For every spot where the user knows that he is unobserved, he does not report his transaction. For every spot where the user knows that he is observed, he, of course, reports, since $p > d$ and he will get caught. The question is whether he reports spots where the state is unknown to him.

For this we need to consider how a spot becomes known to be observed or unobserved. If a user does not report a spot and is charged with a penalty for that spot, the provider must present some evidence. From this evidence we can conclude that the spot is observed. If a user does not report a spot and is not charged with a penalty for that spot, he can likely conclude that the spot is unobserved.

We assume perfect information sharing about states of spots between all colluders, i.e. if one party is charged with a penalty all others know the spot is observed. We furthermore reward users for testing the states of the spots by not submitting transactions. If a user does not report a spot and is not charged with a penalty, he marks it as known unobserved and attaches his name to it. From now on, all other users also do not report this spot and pay a reward $e$ ($e < d$) to this user. Clearly, these users will save some money compared to being honest. For each known observed spot they pay $d$, for each known unobserved spot they pay $e$. Since $e < d$, this saves them some money.

### 3.3   Analysis

The utility of reporting a transaction for a spot whose state is unknown is

$$U = \frac{1}{\alpha}p - (1 - \frac{1}{\alpha})me. \tag{1}$$

If $U > 0$, then the user reports honestly (and will not learn any information). We can compute the necessary penalty for discouraging dishonesty as

$$d > e \wedge p > (\alpha - 1)md \Rightarrow U > 0.$$

If we consider mass surveillance (say $m$ on the order of thousands) and reasonable privacy (say $\alpha$ on the order of hundreds), the penalty $p$ needs to be significantly (on the order of several hundreds of thousands) higher than the cost $d$ for a transaction. Loosely speaking, this is roughly equivalent to a life sentence for getting caught riding on the bus without a ticket. Otherwise, it is rational to collude and cheat in our model.

Another solution to this problem is to observe every spot and transaction ($\alpha = 1$). This complete surveillance incentivizes honesty, but completely removes any privacy. The transactions of the user are known anyway, such that he does not need to report them in a privacy-preserving way, i.e. even the privacy-preserving measures are led ad absurdum. Our solution preserves privacy, but does single user privacy-preserving spot checking, i.e. $m = 1$. Surveillance monitors should still be at every spot, i.e. every spot is potentially observed, but the spot checking is random and cannot be forced.

Of course, the toll service provider could randomize spot checking by himself, but the user would have no guarantee and it is more economical for the provider to observe all spots. We eliminate this option of mass surveillance by proven privacy guarantees for the users.

$$\frac{P : s, SK, PK}{V : t} \xrightarrow{\;\Pi\;} \frac{P :}{V : z = s - t}$$
$$\text{if } z = 0 : PK$$

**Fig. 1.** Black-box protocol $\Pi$ for privacy-preserving spot checking

## 4 Privacy-Preserving Spot Checking

We have a user who needs to be randomly spot checked. In the spirit of zero-knowledge proofs[1] we call him prover $P$. We have a provider who needs to perform the spot checking. We call him the verifier $V$.

Privacy-preserving spot checking is a protocol $\Pi$ between $P$ and $V$. $P$'s inputs to $\Pi$ are a secret key $SK$, a public identifier $PK$ and a collection of random coins $s$. $V$'s inputs to $\Pi$ are random coins $t$. $V$'s outputs is whether $z = s - t = 0$. If $z = 0$, $V$ obtains the public identifier $PK$ of the prover; otherwise, he obtains nothing more. $P$ obtains no output – not even whether $z = 0$. Figure 1 displays the black-box input and output behavior of protocol $\Pi$.

### 4.1 Setup and Registration

There is a separate registration and verification phase. Each prover chooses a secret key $SK$ or has it chosen for him by some authority. He then computes the public identifier $PK$.

We operate in some finite group $\mathbb{G}$ of prime order. Let $v$ be the secret key. Then the public identifier is $g^v$. Clearly, we can assume that it is difficult to compute the secret key from the public identifier due to the hardness of the discrete logarithm problem. Since we only rely on the confidentiality of the secret key for authentication, we do not need any secure hardware in constructing our device.

The authority registers the personal identity of the prover along with public identifier $g^v$. Then, whenever presented with $g^v$ the authority can personally identify the prover. Moreover, the authority can detect forged spot checking devices, if there is no record for a presented public identifier.

Input $P$ :    (uniformly random) $r$, (secret key) $v$
Input $V$ :    (uniformly random) $a$
Output $P$ : –
Output $V$ : (public identifier) $g^v$, $accept/reject$

$$P \to V : g^v, g^r$$
$$V \to P : a$$
$$P \to V : r + av$$

**Fig. 2.** Protocol 1: standard schnorr identification

---

[1] Our protocol is not a full-fledged zero-knowledge protocol, but more efficient.

## 4.2  Security Properties

We demand a number of security properties from our privacy-preserving spot checking protocol.

*Authenticity:* In case $z = 0$, i.e. the verifier obtains public identifier $PK$, the prover cannot have produced $PK$ without knowing the corresponding secret key $SK$. Hence, the prover is authenticated. We formalize this security notion equivalent to the soundness notion of zero-knowledge protocols. Let $\mathcal{E}^{P(PK)}$ be an extractor that given rewinding access to $P$ extracts the secret key $SK$ from $P$ given that $z = 0$ and the public identifier $PK$ has been revealed. We say a protocol is *authentic*, if

$$P \xrightarrow{\Pi} V : z = 0, PK \Rightarrow 1 - \Pr[\mathcal{E}^{P(PK)} = SK] < 1/poly(\kappa).$$

*Privacy:* In case $z \neq 0$, i.e. the verifier does not obtain $PK$, the verifier cannot extract any information about the identity of the prover from the protocol. We formalize this security notion equivalent to zero-knowledge. Let $\mathcal{S}(s,t)^P$ be a simulator of the protocol view of the verifier – the messages of $P$ – in case $s - t \neq 0$. We denote computational indistinguishability as $\overset{cind}{\sim}$. We say a protocol is *private*, if

$$\mathcal{S}^P(s,t) \overset{cind}{\sim} \Pi^P_{s-t \neq 0}.$$

*Fairness:* Let $V(\Pi)$ denote the verifier's output from the protocol, i.e. whether the prover cheated. The verifier $V$ should only be able to force the case $z = 0$ with probability less than $\frac{1}{\alpha} + \frac{1}{poly(\kappa)}$. The prover $P$ should only be able to force the case $z \neq 0$ with probability less than $1 - \frac{1}{\alpha} + \frac{1}{poly(\kappa)}$ without being detected. Let $\mathcal{A}^V$ and $\mathcal{A}^P$ be the adversary taking the role of the verifier and prover, respectively. We say a protocol is *fair*, if

$$Pr[P \xrightarrow{\Pi} \mathcal{A}^V : z = 0] < \frac{1}{\alpha} + 1/poly(\kappa)$$

$$Pr[\mathcal{A}^P \xrightarrow{\Pi} V : z \neq 0, V(\Pi) = 1] < 1 - \frac{1}{\alpha} + 1/poly(\kappa).$$

*Reverse Unobservability:* The prover $P$ should not learn whether $z = 0$, i.e. whether he was observed or not. Let $\mathcal{S}^V$ be a simulator of the protocol view of the prover – the messages of $V$. We say a protocol is *reverse unobservable*, if

$$\mathcal{S}^V \overset{cind}{\sim} \Pi^V.$$

## 4.3  Protocol

We present the protocol in incremental steps in order to show the necessity and effect of individual messages. Let $g$ denote a group generator. We begin with a regular Schnorr identification protocol [29] in Fig. 2.

The verifier accepts if $g^{r+av} = (g^v)^a g^r$, else he rejects. Clearly, this already achieves authenticity, since it is a standard Schnorr identification protocol. We can construct an extractor in the usual way.

---

Input $P$ :    (uniformly random) $r$, (uniformly random) $s : 0 \leq s < \alpha$, (secret key) $v$
Input $V$ :    (uniformly random) $t : 0 \leq t < \alpha$
Output $P$ : $z = s - t$
Output $V$ : $z = s - t$, if $z = 0$ : (public identifier) $g^v$, $accept/reject$

$$P \rightarrow V : Commit(s), Commit(g^v), Commit(g^r), r + H(g^r)v$$
$$V \rightarrow P : t$$
$$P \rightarrow V : Open(s)$$
$$P \rightarrow V : \text{if } z = s - t = 0 : Open(g^v), Open(g^r)$$

---

**Fig. 3.** Protocol 2: schnorr identification with fair coin flip

**Theorem 1.** *Protocol 1 is* authentic.

*Proof.* The extractor proceeds as follows. It waits for the prover to send $g^r$. Then, it first sends $a_1$ and waits for $r + a_1 v$. Second, it rewinds $P$ to the second protocol step and sends $a_2$. From $r + a_1 v$ and $r + a_2 v$, it computes $v$. Since the probability of randomly choosing a valid public identifier is negligible, the verifier can also verify the authenticity.

The protocol can be made completely non-interactive using the weak Fiat-Shamir heuristic [8]. The challenge $a$ is then computed using a collision-resistant hash function $H(g^r)$.

Protocol 1 so far does not include a random choice, i.e. the identity of $P$ is always revealed. The verifier receives $g^v$ in the protocol. We now modify Protocol 1 to obtain Protocol 2. Here we incorporate a fair flip of a coin with probability $Pr[coin = 0] = 1/\alpha$ (and the Fiat-Shamir heuristic). Note that $r + av$ does not reveal the public identifier $g^v$, if also $g^r$ is unknown. Therefore the prover commits to $g^v$ and $g^r$ using a cryptographic commitment scheme and only opens if the coin turns up $z = 0$.

A cryptographic commitment scheme consists of two operations:

- $\gamma = Commit(x, c)$: A commitment $\gamma$ to $x$ using the random coins $c$.
- $Open(\gamma) = x, c$: An opening of the commitment revealing the value $x$ and the random coins $c$.

A cryptographic commitment scheme enjoys two properties:

- *Binding*: The probability that one can successfully open to a different $x'$ is negligible.
- *Blinding*: The probability to compute $x$ from $\gamma$ is negligible.

A possible commitment scheme is that by Pedersen [25], but in practical implementations one can use, e.g. HMAC (secure in the random oracle model). For clarity of the description we leave out the random coins in the description of the commitment of the protocol, i.e. we write $Commit(x)$ and $Open(x)$. The protocol proceeds as in Fig. 3.

**Theorem 2.** *Protocol 2 is* private.

*Proof.* In case $z \neq 0$, the verifier receives the following messages $Commit(s)$, $Commit(g^v)$, $Commit(g^r)$, $r + H(g^r)v$ and $Open(s)$. The simulator proceeds as follows. It chooses random $s$ and the corresponding coins and computes $Commit(s)$. It can already simulate two messages. It simulates $Commit(g^v)$ and $Commit(g^r)$ using two random commitments, since the commitments are never opened and blinding. It simulates $r + H(g^r)v$ using a random value, since $g^r$ is unknown and hence $H(g^r)$ is pseudo-random.

**Theorem 3.** *Protocol 2 is* fair.

*Proof.* The protocol embeds a regular fair coin flip. The prover first chooses and commits to its value $s$ and at the end of the protocol he opens the commitment. Due to the binding property of commitments, he must be honest or get caught, because either the commitment is not correctly opened or he chose an invalid value. He can only achieve $z \neq 0$ when $s \neq t$ or when he opens the commitment to a different value (in $[0, \alpha - 1]$). Hence the prover cannot force $z \neq 0$ with probability higher than $1 - \frac{1}{\alpha} + negl(\kappa)$.

The verifier chooses and sends his value $t$ after the choice of $s$. He must do so without knowledge of $s$, since the commitment is blinding. He can only achieve $z = 0$ when $t = s$ and he has no influence on $s$. Hence, he cannot force $z = 0$ with probability higher than $\frac{1}{\alpha}$.

Note that the previous statement also holds when $t$ is encrypted, since an invalid encryption of $t$ can only achieve $z \neq 0$.

The problem with this protocol is that the prover still learns the outcome of the fair coin flip, i.e. he knows whether he is being observed. In our scenario this leads to the problem that he can now easily choose which transactions to report, since he knows all observed spots. We therefore introduce a technique we call *blind decommitment* where the prover opens (decommits) his commitment without knowing whether he does that. The decommitment is probabilistic and opening occurs only with probability $\frac{1}{\alpha}$, but the prover cannot influence this probability nor can he determine the type of event – decommitment or not.

We use a semantically secure and additively homomorphic encryption scheme, e.g. Paillier's [24], for this purpose. Let $E_V()$ denote the encryption in this homomorphic scheme under the verifier's key and $D_V()$ the corresponding decryption. Then the following homomorphism properties hold:

$$D_V(E_V(x)E_V(y)) = x + y$$

$$D_V(E_V(x)^y) = xy.$$

The verifier sends its random value $t$ encrypted and the prover computes the decommitment homomorphically. We denote "$Open(x)$" as the encoding in $\mathbb{G}$ of the opening of $x$ for homomorphic encryption. The prover needs to ensure that in case $z \neq 0$ the decommitment is safely blinded, i.e. using sufficient randomness although $\alpha$ is small. In case $z = 0$, the verifier can check the validity of the

Input $P$ :    (uniformly random) $r$, (uniformly random) $u_1, u_2$
              (uniformly random) $s : 0 \leq s < \alpha$, (secret key) $v$
Input $V$ :    (uniformly random) $t : 0 \leq t < \alpha$
Output $P$ : −
Output $V$ : $z = s − t, z = 0$ : (public identifier) $g^v$, accept/reject

$P \to V : Commit(s), Commit(g^v), Commit(g^r), r + H(g^r)v$
$V \to P : E_V(−t)$
$P \to V : Open(s), E_V((s − t)u_1 + \text{``}Open(g^v)\text{''}), E_V((s − t)u_2 + \text{``}Open(g^r)\text{''})$

**Fig. 4.** Protocol 3: schnorr identification with fair coin flip and blind decommitment

authentication trace and hence the correctness of the homomorphic computation. As a consequence we do not need verifiable encryption by the prover. The protocol proceeds as in Fig. 4.

**Theorem 4.** *Protocol 3 is* reverse unobservable.

*Proof.* The prover only receives one message $E_V(−t)$. The simulator simulates this message using a random ciphertext due to the semantic security of the encryption scheme.

If $z \neq 0$, then the terms $(s − t)u_1$ and $(s − t)u_2$ are independently uniformly random, since $u_1$ and $u_2$ are independently uniformly random. Hence, we can simulate these messages using randomly chosen ciphertexts and the commitments are never opened. The other messages are as in the proof of Theorem 2. Note that we employ a weaker notion of fairness. The verifier could force $z \neq 0$, since he could choose $t > \alpha$, but that does not seem rational in our scenario and is hence not included in the security definitions. As a consequence we do not need verifiable encryption by the verifier.

The prover's ciphertext can be checked for correctness after decryption, if $z = 0$, since it then needs to contain a correct authentication trace. If $z \neq 0$, the plaintext is random and must not be checkable. Since the verifier receives $s$ and can check this against the commitment, he reliably knows $z$ and can hence decide whether to check the plaintext. Consequently, also the prover does not need use verifiable encryption.

## 4.4    Optimization

There are a few tricks we can use to make the protocol more efficient. First, we translate our Protocol 3 to the elliptic-curve (EC) setting and employ the EC-ElGamal additively homomorphic encryption scheme [6]. This way, we can avoid computationally expensive modular exponentiation (e.g. required by the Paillier scheme) on the prover-side, which potentially uses a device with limited computation resource. Let $\mathcal{P}$ be a point on an elliptic curve over a finite field and

$$P \to V : \mathrm{MAC}(s, K_1), \mathrm{MAC}(v\mathcal{P}, K_2), \mathrm{MAC}(r\mathcal{P}, K_3), r + H(r\mathcal{P})v$$
$$V \to P : w\mathcal{P}, -t\mathcal{P} + w\mathcal{V}$$
$$P \to V : s, K_1, u(w\mathcal{P} + y\mathcal{P}), u(-t\mathcal{P} + w\mathcal{V} + s\mathcal{P} + y\mathcal{V}) + \mathcal{K}_4, \mathrm{ENC}_{K_4}(v\mathcal{P}|K_2|r\mathcal{P}|K_3)$$

**Fig. 5.** Protocol 4: optimized protocol 3 in the EC setting

that generates the required cyclic subgroup. The prover's public identifier is then translated into $\mathcal{Q} = v\mathcal{P}$ for some random $v$ and $g^r$ is represented as $r\mathcal{P}$. Hence, let $\mathcal{V} = x\mathcal{P}$ be the public encryption key of $V$, where $x$ is the corresponding secret key, EC-ElGamal encryption of $-t$ is of the form $(w\mathcal{P}, -t\mathcal{P} + w\mathcal{V})$ for a randomly chosen $w$. In the last step of the protocol, $P$ encrypts $s$ in the form of $(y\mathcal{P}, s\mathcal{P} + y\mathcal{V})$ for a random $y$, homomorphically adds the ElGamal encryption of $s$ to the encryption of $-t$ from $V$, and blinds the sum with $u$ and adds an encoding $\mathcal{K}_4$ as a point on the elliptic curve of some random symmetric key $K_4$. This symmetric key is used to encrypt and protect the openings in a symmetric authenticated encryption mode like GCM. The complete protocol is illustrated in Fig. 5.

Moreover, we notice that $Commit(r\mathcal{P})$ does not need any random coins. It has sufficient entropy. Hence, $Open(r\mathcal{P})$ can be just $r\mathcal{P}$. Also, we do not need to encrypt $s$, but simply use a MAC that takes as input $s$ and a freshly chosen random seed $K$.

We note that although EC-ElGamal decryption can be very slow (on the orders of seconds and minutes) even for small messages [12], such an operation is not required in our protocol. Given $s$ (in the last step of the protocol), the verifier checks if $z = 0$. If so ($s = t$), $V$ recovers $\mathcal{K}$ using its secret key $v$ (to compute the term $uw\mathcal{V} + uy\mathcal{V}$). Otherwise, it simply does nothing and terminates the protocol.

### 4.5 Efficiency Analysis

We now analyze the computational and communication overhead of our EC-based protocol. We use a standard 160-bit elliptic curve `secp160r1`, which offers roughly the same security level as 1024-bit RSA. It is known that the dominant cost in EC-based cryptographic operations is point multiplications [10]. On the other hand, modular addition, modular multiplication, SHA-1 and AES operations are roughly three to four orders of magnitude faster than a point multiplication evaluation [31]. Hence, in our analysis, we consider only elliptic curve point multiplication (such as $r \cdot \mathcal{P}$) and elliptic curve double multiplication (such as $r \cdot \mathcal{P} + w \cdot \mathcal{V}$). Also, we believe that our analysis below represents a fairly conservative estimate for the amount of computational cost required by our protocol, since the actual processors used in real life would likely be more powerful.

**Table 1.** Estimated computation time (in ms) for the prover and the verifier

|  | Offline | | Online | | Total | |
| --- | --- | --- | --- | --- | --- | --- |
| **Prover** | | | | | | |
| – Smart card | 1075 | | 654 | | 1729 | |
| – Smart phone | 404 | | 246 | | 650 | |
| **Verifier** | $(z \neq 0)$ | $(z = 0)$ | $(z \neq 0)$ | $(z = 0)$ | $(z \neq 0)$ | $(z = 0)$ |
| – Auditor | 0.98 | 0.98 | 0 | 0.9 | 0.98 | 1.88 |

**Prover.** We consider two popular embedded microprocessors: 8-bit Atmel ATmega AVR and 32-bit ARM Cortex-M0+ microprocessors. The former represents a low-end contactless smart card (potentially used as an e-ticket in public transportation [17]), while the latter represents a low-end smart phone (potentially used as an OBU for toll collection [21]) in comparison with today's fast-evolving phone market with increasingly more powerful devices emerging.

According to recent implementations by Wenger et al. [32], the computation time required for a point multiplication is 327 ms with the 8-bit microprocessor and 123 ms with the 32-bit microprocessor; while a double multiplication takes roughly 421 ms and 158 ms, respectively. Their implementations are optimized based on set-instruction modification. The measurements are taken at a clock rate of 10 MHz. From these, we can estimate that the computation time required by the prover for one protocol run is roughly 1.7 s on a smart card and roughly 0.7 s on a smart phone. With (offline) pre-computation of some parameters used in the protocol, the computation time can be reduced by almost 60 % for both platforms. The computational cost of our protocol is summarized in Table 1.

In terms of communication cost, the prover sends two messages to the verifier during each protocol run. With our choice of elliptic curve, each message's length is only approximately $3 \times 160 = 480$ bits, and hence, the total bandwidth requirement is 960 bits per protocol run.

**Verifier.** We assume that the verifier is an auditor (local government), who will perform spot checks, and has much higher computational resources than the prover. A point multiplication and a double multiplication in the EC setting take 0.45 ms and 0.53 ms, respectively, using MIRACL compiled with GCC (with standard level-2 compiler optimization) and running on an Intel Single Core i5 520M 64-bit processor at 2.40 GHz. Given this, we estimate that in a protocol run, the computation time taken by the verifier is roughly 0.98 ms when $z \neq 0$, and 1.88 ms when $z = 0$.

On the other hand, the communication overhead incurred by the verifier is minimal. It sends out only one message of $2 \times 160 = 320$ bits.

In summary, our performance analysis shows that our protocol is very efficient using practical parameters. Using the toll collection scenario, assuming that the prover can pre-compute the necessary parameters before approaching a surveillance monitor[2], and without considering the communication latency between the verifier and the prover (via an OBU), our protocol can perform spot checks on up to roughly 4 vehicles in a second. We reiterate that our estimate is somewhat conservative. Newer ARM-based microprocessors and smart phones are likely to have even better computing speed.

Our protocol is designed to be lightweight. We omit verifying the recorded time and location by including a trustworthy GPS sensor and clock on the spot checking device. Hence, this information by the verifier is trusted. The verifier is not trusted to observe the privacy rights of the prover. Our protocol ensures this.

### 4.6   Rate Limiting

The frequency at which the spot checking identification device can be queried needs to be rate limited. Since we do not use any verifier authentication, anyone can query the device potentially tracking the user. If we assume a time $\tau$ between any two protocol initiations, we can estimate the average time $t_{id}$ until a successful identification in a non-stop querying attack as

$$t_{id} = \frac{\alpha}{2}\tau$$

This delay $\tau$ needs to be traded against potential denial-of-service attacks. A driver (in the toll collection example) can be delayed until the spot checking protocol has been completed. Hence, a malicious reader can read the device just before a spot checking point and delay the driver and traffic. We estimate values between 5 and 30 s to be good choices for $\tau$.

Another solution to this problem would be reader authentication. The reader could sign his message using a public key. The verification of the signature on the spot checking device would require at least one ECC multiplication for a fixed public key or at least two for public key certificates plus certificate handling. We opt against this design choice rather increasing the speed of our protocol.

### 4.7   Disposal

A simple idea of the prover to evade spot checking could be to remove or damage the spot checking device. Fortunately, this is very simple to detect: at any time, the verifier initiates a protocol, it is not completed by the prover. The security guarantees of our protocol design ensure that if the protocol is completed a valid public identifier is revealed with probability $1/\alpha$. Hence, a simple physical strategy can be employed to pursue provers without working spot checking devices. For example, a prover could not be allowed to proceed at a gate, photographed in flowing traffic as in many US toll collection sites or even chased by the police. Once caught, the police can even verify that the device is not working properly by re-running the protocol.

---

[2] The time required to travel from one spot to another spot, i.e. the distance between two surveillance monitors, would be abundant for our pre-computation purpose.

# 5   Example Application

For completeness, we give a sketch on how our privacy-preserving spot checking approach can be integrated with the Milo protocol for electronic toll collection [22].

We first describe a simplified version of the original Milo protocol[3] between the driver, toll service provider and the toll charger (local government):

**Setup**: The OBU generates the necessary key material and publishes the unique identifier $id$, including a signing key. The toll service provider and the toll charger each stores a copy of the OBU's verification key and its corresponding $id$. Hidden cameras are installed at random road segments and operated by the toll charger.

**Payment Protocol**: As the driver travels, the OBU picks up location ($where$) and time ($when$) information. The OBU then calculates the toll fare $d$ for each road segment based on the received information. It also computes a commitment to the $d$ value and encrypts the ($where, when, d$) tuple.[4] At the end of each billing month, the OBU transmits the billing information, which comprises its $id$ and a set of signed, encrypted and committed ($where, when, d$) tuples, to the toll service provider. The latter verifies the committed toll fares via zero-knowledge proofs; if the check succeeds, it forwards the billing information to the toll charger.

**Audit Protocol**: For each captured vehicle via a hidden camera, the toll charger identifies the corresponding $id$ and stores the ($id, where, when$) tuple. At month's end and upon receiving an audit request from the toll service provider (with the relevant encrypted billing information submitted by the driver), the toll charger randomly selects $n$ tuples where the corresponding $id$ matches the identifier for the driver to be audited. It then requests for the decryption keys corresponding to the selected ($id, where, when$) tuples in an oblivious manner (otherwise locations of the cameras would be revealed to the driver.) Upon decryption, the toll charger is convinced that the driver had behaved honestly only if the committed toll fares are correct for the checked road segments.

Using our privacy-preserving spot checking technique, some level of user privacy can be preserved,[5] while ensuring cheating drivers can be detected through the above described audit protocol. This requires the following small modification. Instead of using cameras, the surveillance monitors here are readers installed at gantries or booths setup along the roadside for all segments within an audit area. Moreover, we assume each vehicle uses an OBU to interact with the spot checking reader. Whenever the reader detects an approaching vehicle, it runs our proposed spot checking protocol. For each protocol run and if $z = 0$, the reader recovers and transmits the public identifier $PK$ of the interacted OBU

---

[3] Many details of the Milo protocol have been omitted. See [22] for a complete description.

[4] Anonymous identity-based encryption is used here. The encryption key for each record is based on the ($where, when$) tuple.

[5] We note that perfect privacy implies inability to detect dishonest users.

to a centralized server managed by the toll charger; otherwise, the reader sends nothing to the server. The rest of the Milo protocol remains the same.

There are two advantages for using our privacy-preserving spot checking mechanism. First, the toll charger provably sees only a fraction of the user's traveled road segments and spot checking is done randomly, i.e. the toll charger has no influence to which road segments it wants to check. That is our protocol actually preserves privacy and still discourages dishonest users from cheating by preventing any form of information sharing. Second, our approach potentially has lower operation cost. Particularly, the toll charger stores records associated with only a small fraction of the vehicles detected by the reader. Spot checking via cameras requires much higher storage and processing overhead. This is because each camera typically stores information of all vehicles that it captures.

## 6   Conclusions

In this paper we investigate collusion attacks on privacy-preserving billing or accounting systems. We show that in order to deter cheating all transactions in the cyber-physical world need to be observed or extreme penalties need to be imposed. This is not a sustainable choice for our society. We then present a privacy-preserving spot checking protocol that allows privacy-preserving observations in public spaces and can be used to enforce honesty in billing while still preserving privacy. For this we introduce a new variant of oblivious transfer: blind decommitment. We show that it can be efficiently implemented on weak computational devices such as smart cards or smart phones using a number of optimizations.

Our technique allows a socially acceptable trade-off between necessary observation (in public spaces) and privacy. We conclude that it is feasible to build cyber-physical billing systems that are economically dependable and privacy-preserving at the same time.

## A   Privacy vs. Penalty Analysis

We first analyze the probability of cheating detection with our spot checking mechanism. We then analyze how much privacy is achieved through our protocol and the required penalty to discourage users from cheating.

### A.1   Variables

Let us assume that an average user would commute for a distance that covers $k$ spots within a month. At each spot, only a fraction $\frac{1}{\alpha}$ of users are observed. Here we regard $\alpha$ as an "privacy indicator". The higher the value of $\alpha$, the higher the level of user (location) privacy can be preserved. Let also $C(k)$ denote the event when a cheating user is caught (or detected) *at least* once after having traveled $k$ spots. (For simplicity, we ignore the cases where a cheating user is detected more than once within a month.)

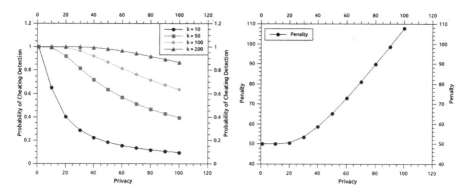

**Fig. 6.** (a) The relation between privacy parameter $\alpha$ and the probability $\Pr[\mathsf{C}(k)]$ of cheating detection at least once after $k$ spots. (b) The relation between privacy paramater $\alpha$ and the imposed penalty $p$ for any cheating user.

## A.2   Analysis

Using a probability analysis similar to that of [2,22], we have

$$\Pr[\mathsf{C}(k)] = 1 - (1 - \frac{1}{\alpha})^k \tag{2}$$

for $\alpha \geq 1$ and $k \geq 1$. Clearly, when $\alpha = 1$, there is no privacy; however, the relevant surveillance monitor will detect any cheating user with probability 1. On the contrary, the more user privacy we want to preserve, the harder it is for the surveillance monitor to detect any cheating user. Clearly, users who have traveled more spots (higher mileage) have higher chances of getting caught if they cheat. Figure 6(a) shows that for a user with very low monthly mileage ($k = 10$), $\alpha$ needs to be set very low (hence low privacy) between the range of 5 and 10, such that any cheating can be detected with probability 0.8. On the other extreme, a user with high monthly mileage ($k = 200$) can still be detected with high probability ($> 0.8$) if cheating, while enjoying a higher-level of privacy ($\alpha = 100$). For an average user (say $k = 100$), $\alpha$ needs to be set at most 60 in order to have probability of cheating detection of at least 0.8.

We now quantify how much penalty $p$ needs to be imposed for a cheating user to alleviate dishonest behavior. Let $d$ be the toll fare for each traveled spot. From Eq. (1), we have

$$p(\Pr[\mathsf{C}(k)]) - dk(1 - \Pr[\mathsf{C}(k)]) \geq \epsilon$$

where $\epsilon$ is the minimal net loss[6] that will incentivize a user to behave honestly. (Clearly, if the net loss is close to zero, there is little incentive for the user not

---

[6] Here net loss is assumed to be the difference between a fine (penalty) for being caught cheating and the amount of money that a cheating user would have saved should her dishonest behavior was not detected.

to cheat.) Setting $d = 0.50$ USD, $\epsilon = 50$ USD and $k = 100$, we can then define the relation between $p$ and $\alpha$ as

$$
\begin{aligned}
p &= \frac{\epsilon + dk(1 - \Pr[C(k)])}{\Pr[C(k)]} \\
&= \frac{50 + 0.5(100)(1 - \Pr[C(k)])}{\Pr[C(k)]} \\
&= 50 \left( \frac{1 + (1 - \frac{1}{\alpha})^{100}}{1 - (1 - \frac{1}{\alpha})^{100}} \right)
\end{aligned}
\tag{3}
$$

It is clear from Eq. (3) that $p$ increases when $\alpha$ grows. Figure 6(b) shows that for the case of an average user (say $k = 100$), $p$ grows at a lower rate for $\alpha < 30$, but at a much higher rate for $\alpha > 30$. To achieve a reasonable level of privacy while ensuring honesty for an average traveler (following our earlier probability analysis that infers $\alpha \leq 60$ and $\Pr[C(k)] \geq 0.8$ for $k = 100$), we must impose penalty of approximately \$70 for users who cheat at least once within a month.

We would like to point out how difficult it is to achieve a similar level of privacy using mobile cameras. One can think of the following hypothetical mobile camera. If we assume that a mobile camera (mounted on a special-purpose vehicle) moves in an unpredictable direction at a speed much higher than traffic and may stay at a specific spot for an unpredictably small amount of time, it is roughly saying that the camera is installed (fixed) at a location for a small fraction of time. Still, the mobile camera records a small fraction of users, but likely more than one as in our case who appear at the location where the camera is. Moreover, as analyzed by Meiklejohn et al. [22], the operational cost of even existing mobile cameras is much higher than that of fixed cameras. Their analysis shows that an audit vehicle costs at least $82{,}500$ US dollars per year. This includes the cost for employing a driver, as well as purchasing, operating and maintaining the audit vehicle. Our approach of spot checking offers more economical and fine-grained control (only one is observed) of the levels of cheating detection and user privacy by adjusting the relevant parameters.

## References

1. Aiello, W., Ishai, Y., Reingold, O.: Priced oblivious transfer: how to sell digital goods. In: Pfitzmann, B. (ed.) EUROCRYPT 2001. LNCS, vol. 2045, p. 119. Springer, Heidelberg (2001)
2. Balasch, J., Rial, A., Troncoso, C., Preneel, B., Verbauwhede, I., Geuens, C.: PrETP: privacy-preserving electronic toll pricing. In: Proceedings of the 19th USENIX Security Symposium (2010)
3. Brassard, G., Crépeau, C., Robert, J.M.: All-or-nothing disclosure of secrets. In: Odlyzko, A.M. (ed.) CRYPTO 1986. LNCS, vol. 263, pp. 234–238. Springer, Heidelberg (1987)
4. Catrina, O., Kerschbaum, F.: Fostering the uptake of secure multiparty computation in e-commerce. In: Proceedings of the International Workshop on Frontiers in Availability, Reliability and Security (FARES) (2008)

5. Dreier, J., Kerschbaum, F.: Practical privacy-preserving multiparty linear programming based on problem transformation. In: Proceedings of the 3rd IEEE International Conference on Privacy, Security, Risk and Trust (PASSAT) (2011)
6. El Gamal, T.: A public key cryptosystem and a signature scheme based on discrete logarithms. In: Blakely, G.R., Chaum, D. (eds.) CRYPTO 1984. LNCS, vol. 196, pp. 10–18. Springer, Heidelberg (1985)
7. Even, S., Goldreich, O., Lempel, A.: A randomized protocol for signing contracts. Commun. ACM **28**(6), 637–647 (1985)
8. Fiat, A., Shamir, A.: How to prove yourself: practical solutions to identification and signature problems. In: Odlyzko, A.M. (ed.) CRYPTO 1986. LNCS, vol. 263, pp. 186–194. Springer, Heidelberg (1987)
9. Green, M., Hohenberger, S.: Blind identity-based encryption and simulatable oblivious transfer. In: Kurosawa, K. (ed.) ASIACRYPT 2007. LNCS, vol. 4833, pp. 265–282. Springer, Heidelberg (2007)
10. Gura, N., Patel, A., Wander, A., Eberle, H., Shantz, S.C.: Comparing elliptic curve cryptography and RSA on 8-bit CPUs. In: Joye, M., Quisquater, J.-J. (eds.) CHES 2004. LNCS, vol. 3156, pp. 119–132. Springer, Heidelberg (2004)
11. Heydt-Benjamin, T.S., Chae, H.-J., Defend, B., Fu, K.: Privacy for public transportation. In: Danezis, G., Golle, P. (eds.) PET 2006. LNCS, vol. 4258, pp. 1–19. Springer, Heidelberg (2006)
12. Y. Hu.: Improving the efficiency of homomorphic encryption schemes. Ph.D thesis, Worcester Polytechnic Institute (2013)
13. Kerschbaum, F.: Building a privacy-preserving benchmarking enterprise system. Enterp. Inf. Syst. **2**(4), 421–441 (2008)
14. Kerschbaum, F.: A verifiable, centralized, coercion-free reputation system. In: Proceedings of the 8th ACM Workshop on Privacy in the Electronic Society (WPES) (2009)
15. Kerschbaum, F.: Outsourced private set intersection using homomorphic encryption. In: Proceedings of the 7th ACM Symposium on Information, Computer and Communication Security (ASIACCS) (2012)
16. Kerschbaum, F., Dahlmeier, D., Schrpfer, A., Biswas, D.: On the practical importance of communication complexity for secure multi-party computation protocols. In: Proceedings of the 24th ACM Symposium on Applied Computing (SAC) (2009)
17. Kerschbaum, F., Lim, H.W., Gudymenko, I.: Privacy-preserving billing for e-ticketing systems in public transportation. In: Proceedings of the 12th Annual ACM Workshop on Privacy in the Electronic Society (WPES) (2013)
18. Kerschbaum, F., Terzidis, O.: Filtering for private collaborative benchmarking. In: Müller, G. (ed.) ETRICS 2006. LNCS, vol. 3995, pp. 409–422. Springer, Heidelberg (2006)
19. Kerschbaum, F., Oertel, N.: Privacy-preserving pattern matching for anomaly detection in RFID anti-counterfeiting. In: Ors Yalcin, S.B. (ed.) RFIDSec 2010. LNCS, vol. 6370, pp. 124–137. Springer, Heidelberg (2010)
20. Kilian, J.: Founding crytpography on oblivious transfer. In: Proceedings of the 20th ACM Symposium on Theory of Computing (STOC) (1988)
21. Liu, J.K., Au, M.H., Susilo, W., Zhou, J.: Enhancing location privacy for electric vehicles (at the *Right* time). In: Foresti, S., Yung, M., Martinelli, F. (eds.) ESORICS 2012. LNCS, vol. 7459, pp. 397–414. Springer, Heidelberg (2012)
22. Meiklejohn, S., Mowery, K., Checkoway, S., Shacham, H.: The phantom tollbooth: privacy-preserving electronic toll collection in the presence of driver collusion. In: Proceedings of the 20th USENIX Security Symposium (2011)

23. MIRACL - Benchmarks and Subs. Certivox Developer Community (2014). https:// certivox.org/display/EXT/Benchmarks+and+Subs

24. Paillier, P.: Public-key cryptosystems based on composite degree residuosity classes. In: Stern, J. (ed.) EUROCRYPT 1999. LNCS, vol. 1592, p. 223. Springer, Heidelberg (1999)

25. Pedersen, T.P.: Non-interactive and information-theoretic secure verifiable secret sharing. In: Feigenbaum, J. (ed.) CRYPTO 1991. LNCS, vol. 576, pp. 129–140. Springer, Heidelberg (1992)

26. Popa, R.A., Balakrishnan, H., Blumberg, A.J.: VPriv: protecting privacy in location-based vehicular services. In: Proceedings of the 18th USENIX Security Symposium (2009)

27. Rabin, M.: How to exchange secrets by oblivious transfer. Technical Memo TR-81, Aiken Computation Laboratory (1981)

28. Sadeghi, A., Visconti, I., Wachsmann, C.: User privacy in transport systems based on RFID e-tickets. In: Proceedings of the 1st International Workshop on Privacy in Location-Based Applications (PilBA) (2008)

29. Schnorr, C.-P.: Efficient identification and signatures for smart cards. In: Brassard, G. (ed.) CRYPTO 1989. LNCS, vol. 435, pp. 239–252. Springer, Heidelberg (1990)

30. Schröpfer, A., Kerschbaum, F., Müller, G.: L1-an intermediate language for mixed-protocol secure computation. In: Proceedings of the 35th IEEE Computer Software and Applications Conference (COMPSAC) (2011)

31. Uhsadel, L., Poschmann, A., Paar, C.: Enabling full-size public-key algorithms on 8-bit sensor nodes. In: Stajano, F., Meadows, C., Capkun, S., Moore, T. (eds.) ESAS 2007. LNCS, vol. 4572, pp. 73–86. Springer, Heidelberg (2007)

32. Wenger, E., Unterluggauer, T., Werner, M.: 8/16/32 Shades of elliptic curve cryptography on embedded processors. In: Paul, G., Vaudenay, S. (eds.) INDOCRYPT 2013. LNCS, vol. 8250, pp. 244–261. Springer, Heidelberg (2013)

# Privacy-Preserving Context-Aware Recommender Systems: Analysis and New Solutions

Qiang Tang$^{(\boxtimes)}$ and Jun Wang

University of Luxembourg, Luxembourg, Luxembourg
{qiang.tang,jun.wang}@uni.lu

**Abstract.** Nowadays, recommender systems have become an indispensable part of our daily life and provide personalized services for almost everything. However, nothing is for free – such systems have also upset the society with severe privacy concerns because they accumulate a lot of personal information in order to provide recommendations. In this work, we construct privacy-preserving recommendation protocols by incorporating cryptographic techniques and the inherent data characteristics in recommender systems. We first revisit the protocols by Jeckmans et al. and show a number of security issues. Then, we propose two privacy-preserving protocols, which compute predicted ratings for a user based on inputs from both the user's friends and a set of randomly chosen strangers. A user has the flexibility to retrieve either a predicted rating for an unrated item or the Top-N unrated items. The proposed protocols prevent information leakage from both protocol executions and the protocol outputs. Finally, we use the well-known MovieLens 100k dataset to evaluate the performances for different parameter sizes.

## 1 Introduction

As e-commerce websites began to develop, users were finding it very difficult to make the most appropriate choices from the immense variety of items (products and services) that these websites were offering. Take an online book store as an example, going through the lengthy book catalogue not only wastes a lot of time but also frequently overwhelms users and leads them to make poor decisions. As such, the availability of choices, instead of producing a benefit, started to decrease users' well-being. Eventually, this need led to the development of recommender systems (or, recommendation systems). Informally, recommender systems are a subclass of information filtering systems that seek to predict the 'rating' or 'preference' that a user would give to an item (e.g. music, book, or movie) they had not yet considered, using a model built from the characteristics of items and/or users. Today, recommender systems play an important role in highly rated commercial websites such as Amazon, Facebook, Netflix, Yahoo, and YouTube. Netflix even awarded a million dollars prize to the team that

---

This paper is an extended abstract of the IACR report [32].

© Springer International Publishing Switzerland 2015
G. Pernul et al. (Eds.): ESORICS 2015, Part II, LNCS 9327, pp. 101–119, 2015.
DOI: 10.1007/978-3-319-24177-7_6

first succeeded in improving substantially the performance of its recommender system. Besides these well-known examples, recommender systems can also be found in every corner of our daily life.

In order to compute recommendations, the service provider needs to collect a lot of personal data from its users, e.g. ratings, transaction history, and location. This makes recommender systems a double-edged sword. On one side users get better recommendations when they reveal more personal data, but on the flip side they sacrifice more privacy if they do so. Privacy issues in recommender systems have been surveyed in [3,16,28]. The most widely-recognized privacy concern is about the fact the service provider has full access to all users' inputs (e.g. which items are rated and the corresponding ratings). Weinsberg et al. showed that what has been rated by a user can already breach his privacy [34]. The other less well-known yet equally serious privacy concern is that the outputs from a recommender system can also lead to privacy breaches against innocent users. Ten years ago, Kantarcioglu, Jin and Clifton expressed this concern for general data mining services [15]. Recently Calandrino et al. [6] showed inference attacks which allow an attacker with some auxiliary information to infer a user's transactions from temporal changes in the public outputs of a recommender system. In practice, advanced recommender systems collect a lot of personal information other than ratings, and they cause more privacy concerns.

## 1.1 State-of-the-Art

Broadly speaking, existing privacy-protection solutions for recommender systems can be divided into two categories. One category is cryptographic solutions, which heavily rely on cryptographic primitives (e.g. homomorphic encryption, zero knowledge proof, threshold encryption, commitment, private information retrieval, and a variety of two-party or multi-party cryptographic protocols). For example, the solutions from [2,7,8,11–14,19,23,24,27,31,36] fall into this category. More specifically, the solutions from [2,7,8,11,14,19,31] focus on distributed setting where every individual user is expected to participate in the recommendation computation, while those from [12,13,23,24,27,36] focus on partitioned dataset, where several organizations wish to compute recommendations for their own users by joining their private dataset. These solutions typically assume semi-honest attackers and apply existing cryptographic primitives to secure the procedures in standard recommender protocols. This approach has two advantages: rigorous security guarantee in the sense of secure computation (namely, every user only learns the recommendation results and the server learns nothing) can be achieved, and there is no degradation in accuracy. The disadvantage lies in the fact that these solutions are all computation-intensive so that they become impractical when user/item populations get large.

The other category is data obfuscation based solutions, which mainly rely on adding noise to the original data or computation results to achieve privacy. The solutions from [4,18,20–22,25,26,30,35] fall into this category. These solutions usually do not incur complicated manipulations on the users' inputs, so that they are much more efficient. The drawback is that they often lack rigorous privacy guarantees and downgrade the recommendation accuracy to some extent. With respect to privacy guarantees, an exception is the differential privacy based approach from [18] which does provide mathematically sound privacy notions. However, cryptographic primitives are required for all users to generate the accumulated data subjects (e.g. sums and covariance matrix).

## 1.2   Our Contribution

While most privacy-preserving solutions focus on recommender systems which only take into account users' ratings as inputs, Jeckmans, Peter, and Hartel [13] moved a step further to propose privacy-preserving recommendation protocols for context-aware recommender systems, which include social relationships as part of the inputs to compute recommendations. Generally the protocols are referred to as the JPH protocols, and more specifically they are referred to as JPH online protocol and JPH offline protocol respectively. Interestingly, the JPH protocols make use of the recent advances in somewhat homomorphic encryption schemes [5]. In this paper, our contribution is three-fold.

Firstly, we analyze the JPH protocols and identify a number of security issues. Secondly, we revise the prediction computation formula from [13] by incorporating inputs from both friends and strangers. This change not only aligns the formula with standard recommender algorithms [17] but also enables us to avoid the cold start problem of the JPH protocols. Security wise, it helps us prevent potential information leakages through the outputs of friends. We then propose two privacy preserving protocols. One enables a user to check whether a specific unrated item might be of his interest, and the other returns the Top-N unrated items. Therefore, we provide more flexible choices for users to discover their interests in practice. Both protocols are secure against envisioned threats in our threat model. Thirdly, we analyze accuracy performances of the new protocols, and show that for some parameters the accuracy is even better than some other well-known recommendation protocols, e.g. those from [17].

## 1.3   Organization

The rest of this paper is organized as follows. In Sect. 2, we demonstrate the security issues with the JPH protocols. In Sect. 3, we propose our new formulation and trust assumptions for recommender systems. In Sect. 4, we present two protocols for single prediction and Top-N recommendations respectively. In Sect. 5, we present security and accuracy analysis for the proposed protocols. In Sect. 6, we conclude the paper.

# 2   Analysis of JPH Protocols

When $X$ is a set, $x \xleftarrow{\$} X$ means that $x$ is chosen from $X$ uniformly at random, and $|X|$ means the size of $X$. If $\chi$ is a distribution, then $s \leftarrow \chi$ means that $s$ is sampled according to $\chi$. We use bold letter, such as $\boldsymbol{X}$, to denote a vector. Given two vector $\boldsymbol{X}$ and $\boldsymbol{Y}$, we use $\boldsymbol{X} \cdot \boldsymbol{Y}$ to denote their inner product. In a recommender system, the item set is denoted by $\mathbf{B} = (1, 2, \cdots, b, \cdots, |\mathbf{B}|)$, and a user $x$'s ratings are denoted by a vector $\mathbf{R}_x = (r_{x,1}, \cdots, r_{x,b}, \cdots, r_{x,|\mathbf{B}|})$. The rating value is often an integer from $\{0, 1, 2, 3, 4, 5\}$. If item $i$ has not been rated, then $r_{x,i}$ is set to be 0. With respect to $\mathbf{R}_x$, a binary vector $\mathbf{Q}_x = (q_{x,1}, \cdots, q_{x,b}, \cdots, q_{x,|\mathbf{B}|})$ is defined as follows: $q_{x,b} = 1$ iff $r_{x,b} \neq 0$ for every $1 \leq b \leq |\mathbf{B}|$. We use $\overline{r_x}$ to denote user $x$'s average rating, namely $\lceil \frac{\sum_{i \in \mathbf{B}} r_{x,i}}{\sum_{i \in \mathbf{B}} q_{x,i}} \rfloor$.

### 2.1 Preliminary of JPH Protocols

Let the active user, who wants to receive new recommendations, be denoted as user $u$. Let the friends of user $u$ be denoted by $\mathbf{F}_u$. Every friend $f \in \mathbf{F}_u$ and user $u$ assigns each other weights $w_{f,u}, w_{u,f}$ respectively, and these values can be regarded as the perceived importance to each other. Then, the predicted rating for an unrated item $b \in \mathbf{B}$ for user $u$ is computed as follows.

$$p_{u,b} = \frac{\sum_{f \in \mathbf{F}_u} q_{f,b} \cdot r_{f,b} \cdot (\frac{w_{u,f} + w_{f,u}}{2})}{\sum_{f \in \mathbf{F}_u} q_{f,b} \cdot (\frac{w_{u,f} + w_{f,u}}{2})} = \frac{\sum_{f \in \mathbf{F}_u} r_{f,b} \cdot (w_{u,f} + w_{f,u})}{\sum_{f \in \mathbf{F}_u} q_{f,b} \cdot (w_{u,f} + w_{f,u})} \tag{1}$$

The JPH protocols [13] and the new protocols from this paper rely on the Brakerski-Vaikuntanathan SWHE Scheme [5], which is recapped in the Appendix. In [13], Jeckmans et al. did not explicitly explain their notation $[x]_u + y$ and $[x]_u \cdot y$. We assume these operations are as $[x]_u + y = \mathsf{Eval}^*(+, [x]_u, y)$ and $[x]_u \cdot y = \mathsf{Eval}^*(\cdot, [x]_u, y)$. In any case, this assumption only affects the *Insecurity against Semi-honest Server* issue for the JPH online protocol. All other issues still exist even if this assumption is not true.

### 2.2 JPH Online Protocol

In the online scenario, the recommendation protocol is executed between the active user $u$, the server, and user $u$'s friends. In the *initialization phase*, user $u$ generates a public/private key pair for the Brakerski-Vaikuntanathan SWHE scheme, and all his friends and the server obtain a valid copy of his public key. The protocol runs in two stages as described in Fig. 1.

It is worth noting that the friends only need to be involved in the first stage. We observe the following security issues.

- *Hidden assumption.* Jeckmans et al. [13] did not mention any assumption on the communication channel between users and the server. In fact, if the communication channel between any user $f$ and the server does not provide confidentiality, then user $u$ can obtain $[n_{f,b}]_u, [d_{f,b}]_u$ by passive eavesdropping. Then, user $u$ can trivially recover $q_{f,b}$ and $r_{f,b}$.
- *Insecurity against Semi-honest Server.* With $[d_{f,b}]_u$, the server can trivially recover $q_{f,b}$, i.e. if $[d_{f,b}]_u = 0$ then $q_{f,b} = 0$; otherwise $q_{f,b} = 1$. After recovering

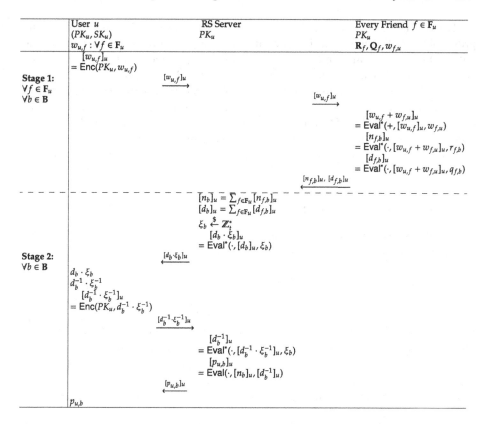

**Fig. 1.** JPH online protocol

$q_{f,b}$, the server can trivially recover $r_{f,b} = \frac{[n_{f,b}]_u}{[d_{f,b}]_u}$. The root of the problem is the homomorphic operations have been done in the naive way, with $\mathsf{Eval}^*(\cdot, , )$ and $\mathsf{Eval}^*(+, , )$.

- *Encrypted Division Problems.* The first concern is that it may not be able to determine the predicted rating $p_{u,b}$. As a toy example, let $t = 7$. In this case, both $\lfloor \frac{2}{3} \rfloor = 1$ and $\lfloor \frac{3}{1} \rfloor = 3$ link to the index $2 \cdot 3^{-1} = 3 \cdot 1^{-1} = 3 \mod 7$. If $p_{u,b} = 3$, then user $u$ will not be able to determine whether the predicted rating is $\lfloor \frac{2}{3} \rfloor = 1$ or $\lfloor \frac{3}{1} \rfloor = 3$. The second concern is that the representation of $p_{u,b}$ in the protocol may leak more information than the to-be predicted value $\lfloor \frac{n_b}{d_b} \rfloor$. As an example, $\lfloor \frac{2}{3} \rfloor = \lfloor \frac{3}{4} \rfloor = 1$. Clearly, giving $2 \cdot 3^{-1}$ or $3 \cdot 4^{-1}$ leaks more information than the to-be predicted value 1.

- *Potential Information Leakage through Friends.* For user $u$, his friends may not be friends with each other. For example, it may happen that some friend $f \in \mathbf{F}_u$ is not a friend of any other user from $\mathbf{F}_u$. Suppose that the users $\mathbf{F}_u \backslash f$ have learned the the value $p_{u,b}$ or some approximation of it (this is realistic as they are friends of user $u$). Then, they may be able to infer whether user $f$ has rated the item $b$ and the actual rating.

Besides the above security issues, there are some usability issues with the protocol as well. One issue is that, at the time of protocol execution, maybe only a few friends are online. In this case, the predicted rating may not be very accurate. It can also happen that $p_{u,b}$ cannot be computed, because none of user $u$'s friends has rated item $b$. This is the typical cold start problem in recommender systems [1]. The other issue is that the predicted rating needs to computed for every $b \in \mathbf{B}$ even if user $u$ has already rated this item. Otherwise, user $u$ may leak information to the server, e.g. which items have been rated. This not only leaks unnecessary information to user $u$, but also makes it very inefficient when user $u$ only wants a prediction for a certain unrated item.

### 2.3   JPH Offline Protocol

In the offline scenario, the friends $\mathbf{F}_u$ need to delegate their data to the server to enable user $u$ to run the recommendation protocol when they are offline. Inevitably, this leads to a more complex *initialization phase*. In this phase, both user $u$ and the server generate their own public/private key pair for the Brakerski-Vaikuntanathan SWHE scheme and they hold a copy of the valid public key of each other. Moreover, every friend $f \in \mathbf{F}_u$ needs to pre-process $\mathbf{R}_f$, $\mathbf{Q}_f$, and $w_{f,u}$. The rating vector $\mathbf{R}_f$ is additively split into two sets $\mathbf{S}_f$ and $\mathbf{T}_f$. The splitting for every rating $r_{f,b}$ is straightforward, namely choose $r \xleftarrow{\$} \mathbb{Z}_t^*$ and set $s_{f,b} = r$ and $t_{f,b} = r_{f,b} - r \mod t$. Similarly, the weight $w_{f,u}$ is split into $x_{f,u}$ and $y_{f,u}$. It is assumed that $\mathbf{T}_f$ and $\mathbf{Q}_f$ will be delivered to user $u$ through proxy re-encryption schemes. Running between user $u$ and the server, the two-stage protocol is described in Fig. 2.

This protocol has exactly the same *encrypted division, potential information leakage through friends* and usability issues, as stated in Sect. 2.2. In addition, we have the following new concerns.

– *Explicit Information Disclosure.* It is assumed that the $\mathbf{Q}_f$ values for all $f \in \mathbf{F}_u$ are obtained by user $u$ in clear. This is a direct violation of these users' privacy because it has shown that leaking what has been rated by a user can breach his privacy [34].
– *Key Recovery Attacks against the Server.* Chenal and Tang [9] have shown that given a certain number of decryption oracle queries an attacker can recover the private key of the Brakerski-Vaikuntanathan SWHE scheme. We show that user $u$ can manipulate the protocol and recover the server's private key $SK_u$. Before the attack, user $u$ sets up a fake account $u'$ and a set of fake friends $\mathbf{F}_{u'}$ (e.g. through Sybil attacks [10]). The key recovery attack relies on multiple executions of the protocol, and it works as follows in each execution.
  1. User $u'$ chooses a carefully-chosen ciphertext $c$ and replaces $[z_b + \xi_{1,b}]_s$ with $c$. He also sets $\xi_{1,b} = 0$ for $[-\xi_{1,b}]_u$.
  2. When receiving $[p_{u',b}]_{u'}$, user $u'$ can recover the constant in $\mathsf{Dec}(SK_s, c)$ because he knows $a_b$ and $d_b^{-1}$ (note that user $u'$ forged all his friends $\mathbf{F}_{u'}$).
  It is straightforward to verify that, if $c$ is chosen according to the specifics in [9] then user $u'$ (and user $u$) can recover $SK_s$ in a polynomial number of

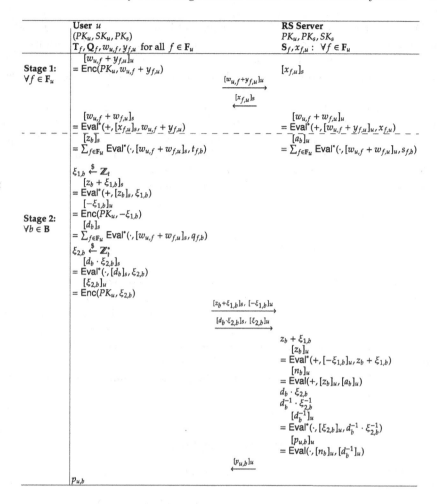

**Fig. 2.** JPH offline protocol

executions. With $SK_s$, user $u$ can recover the weights from his real friends in $\mathbf{F}_u$ and then infer their ratings. It is worth stressing that this attack does not violate the semi-honest assumption in [13].

# 3   New Formulation of Recommender System

## 3.1   Computing Predicted Ratings

In our solution, we compute the predicted rating for user $u$ based on inputs from both his friends and some strangers for both accuracy and security reasons. In reality friends like and consume similar items, but it might happen that very few friends have rated the item $b$. If this happens, the predicated value from

Eq. (1) may not be very accurate (cold start problem). In Sect. 2, we have shown that the private information of user $u$'s friends might be leaked through user $u$'s outputs. This is because the outputs are computed solely based on the inputs of user $u$'s friends. We hope that, by taking into account some randomly chosen strangers, we will mitigate both problems.

When factoring in the inputs from randomly chosen strangers, we will use the simple Bias From Mean (BFM) scheme for the purpose of simplicity. It is worth stressing that there are a lot of different choices for this task. Nevertheless, as to the accuracy, this scheme has similar performance to many other more sophisticated schemes, such as Slope One and Pearson/Cosine similarity-based collaborative filtering schemes [17]. Let the stranger set be $\mathbf{T}_u$, the predicted value $p^*_{u,b}$ for an unrated item $b$ is computed as follows.

$$p^*_{u,b} = \overline{r_u} + \frac{\sum_{t \in \mathbf{T}_u} q_{t,b} \cdot (r_{t,b} - \overline{r_t})}{\sum_{t \in \mathbf{T}_u} q_{t,b}} \tag{2}$$

When factoring in the inputs from the friends, we make two changes to Eq. (1) from Sect. 2.2. One is to only take into account the weight value from user $u$. This makes more sense because how important a friend means to user $u$ is a very subjective matter for $u$ only. Jeckmans et al. averaged the weights for the purpose of limiting information leakage [13]. The other is to compute the predication based on both $u$'s average rating and the weighted rating deviations from his friends. Let the friend set be $\mathbf{F}_u$, the predicted value $p^{**}_{u,b}$ for an unrated item $b$ is computed as follows.

$$p^{**}_{u,b} = \overline{r_u} + \frac{\sum_{f \in \mathbf{F}_u} q_{f,b} \cdot (r_{f,b} - \overline{r_f}) \cdot w_{u,f}}{\sum_{f \in \mathbf{F}_u} q_{f,b} \cdot w_{u,f}} \tag{3}$$

In practice, the similarity between friends means that they tend to prefer to similar items. However, this does not imply that they will assign very similar scores to the items. For example, a user Alice may be very mean and assign a score 3 to most of her favorite items while her friends may be very generous and assign a score 5 to their favorite items. Using the Eq. (1), we will likely generate a score 5 for an unrated item for Alice, who may just rate a score 3 for the item even if she likes it. In this regard, Eq. (3) is more appropriate because $\overline{r_u}$ reflects the user's rating style and $\frac{\sum_{f \in \mathbf{F}_u} q_{f,b} \cdot (r_{f,b} - \overline{r_f}) \cdot w_{f,u}}{\sum_{f \in \mathbf{F}_u} q_{f,b} \cdot w_{f,u}}$ reflects the user's preference based on inputs from his friends.

Based on the inputs from the strangers and friends, a combined predicted value $p_{u,b}$ for an unrated item $b$ can be computed as $p_{u,b} = \rho \cdot p^*_{u,b} + (1 - \rho) \cdot p^{**}_{u,b}$ for some $0 \leq \rho \leq 1$. Due to the fact that cryptographic primitives are normally designed for dealing with integers, we rephrase the formula as follows, where $\alpha, \beta$ are two integers.

$$p_{u,b} = \frac{\beta}{\alpha + \beta} \cdot p^*_{u,b} + \frac{\alpha}{\alpha + \beta} \cdot p^{**}_{u,b} \tag{4}$$

### 3.2    Threat Model

As to communication, we assume all communications are mediated by the RS server and the communication channels are integrity and confidentiality protected. Instead of making a general semi-honest assumption on all participants, we distinguish the following.

1. *Threat from Semi-honest RS Server.* In the view of all users, the RS server will follow the protocol specification but it may try to infer their private information from openly collected transaction records.
2. *Threat from a Semi-honest Friend.* In the view of a user, none of his friends will collude with the RS server or another party to breach his privacy. We believe the social norm deters such colluding attacks, and the deterrence comes from the fact that once such a collusion is known to the victim user then the friendship may be jeopardized. Nevertheless, we still need to consider possible privacy threats in two scenarios.
   - In the view of $f \in \mathbf{F}_u$, user $u$ may attempt to learn his private information when running the recommendation protocol. In the view of user $u$, his friend $f \in \mathbf{F}_u$ may also try to infer his information as well.
   - In the view of $f \in \mathbf{F}_u$, user $u$'s output (e.g. a new rated item and predicted rating value) may be leaked. If another party obtains such auxiliary information, then user $f$'s private information may be at risk. For example, the *Potential Information Leakage through Friends* security issue in Sect. 2.2 falls into this scenario.
3. *Threat from Strangers.* We consider the following two scenarios.
   - In the view of user $u$ and his friends, a stranger may try to learn their private information.
   - In the view of a stranger, who is involved in the protocol execution of user $u$, user $u$ may try to learn his private information.

## 4    New Privacy-Preserving Recommender Protocols

In this section, we propose two privacy-preserving protocols: one for the active user to learn the predicted rating for an unrated item, and the other is for the active user to learn Top-N unrated items. Both protocols share the same *initialization phase*.

In the initialization phase, user $u$ generates a public/private key pair $(PK_u, SK_u)$ for the Brakerski-Vaikuntanathan SWHE scheme and sends $PK_u$ to the server. For the purpose of enabling strangers to validate his public key, user $u$ asks his friends to certify his public key and puts the certification information on the server. In addition, user $u$ assigns a weight $w_{u,f}$ to each of his friend $f \in \mathbf{F}_u$. All other users perform the same operations in this phase. Besides the user-specific parameters, the global system parameters should also be established in the initialization phase. Such parameters should include $\alpha, \beta$ which determine how a predicated rating value for user $u$ is generated based on the inputs of friends and strangers, and they should also include the minimal sizes of friend set $\mathbf{F}_u$ and stranger set $\mathbf{T}_u$.

### 4.1  Recommendation Protocol for Single Prediction

When user $u$ wants to figure out whether the predicted rating for an unrated item $b$ is above a certain threshold $\tau$ in his mind, he initiates the protocol in Fig. 3. In more details, the protocol runs in three stages.

1. In the first stage, user $u$ generates a binary vector $\mathbf{I}_b$, which only has 1 for the $b$-th element, and sends the ciphertext $[\mathbf{I}_b]_u = \mathsf{Enc}(PK_u, \mathbf{I}_b)$ to the server. The server first sends $PK_u$ to some randomly chosen strangers who are the friends of user $u$'s friends in the system. Such a user $t$ can then validate $PK_u$ by checking whether their mutual friends have certified $PK_u$. After the server has successfully found a viable stranger set $\mathbf{T}_u$, it forwards $[\mathbf{I}_b]_u$ to every user in $\mathbf{T}_u$. With $PK_u$ and $(\mathbf{R}_t, \mathbf{Q}_t)$, user $t$ can compute the following based on the homomorphic properties. For notation purpose, assume $[\mathbf{I}_b]_u = ([\mathbf{I}_b^{(1)}]_u, \cdots, [\mathbf{I}_b^{(|B|)}]_u)$.

$$[q_{t,b}]_u = \sum_{1 \leq i \leq |B|} \mathsf{Eval}(\cdot, \mathsf{Enc}(PK_u, q_{t,i}), [\mathbf{I}_b^{(i)}]_u), \ [\mathbf{R}_t \cdot \mathbf{I}_b]_u$$

$$= \sum_{1 \leq i \leq |B|} \mathsf{Eval}(\cdot, \mathsf{Enc}(PK_u, r_{t,i}), [\mathbf{I}_b^{(i)}]_u)$$

$$temp = \sum_{1 \leq i \leq |B|} \mathsf{Eval}(\cdot, \mathsf{Enc}(PK_u, q_{t,i}), [\mathbf{I}_b^{(i)}]_u)$$

$$[q_{t,b} \cdot (\mathbf{R}_t \cdot \mathbf{I}_b - \overline{r_t})]_u = \mathsf{Eval}(\cdot, temp, \mathsf{Eval}(+, [\mathbf{R}_t \cdot \mathbf{I}_b]_u, -\mathsf{Enc}(PK_u, \overline{r_t})))$$

2. In the second stage, for every friend $f \in \mathbf{F}_u$, user $u$ sends the encrypted weight $[w_{u,f}]_u = \mathsf{Enc}(PK_u, w_{u,f})$ to the server, which then forwards $[w_{u,f}]_u$ and $[\mathbf{I}_b]_u$ to user $f$. With $PK_u$, $[\mathbf{I}_b]_u$, $[w_{u,f}]_u$ and $(\mathbf{R}_f, \mathbf{Q}_f)$, user $f$ can compute the following.

$$[q_{f,b}]_u = \sum_{1 \leq i \leq |B|} \mathsf{Eval}(\cdot, \mathsf{Enc}(PK_u, q_{f,i}), [\mathbf{I}_b^{(i)}]_u), \ [\mathbf{R}_f \cdot \mathbf{I}_b]_u$$

$$= \sum_{1 \leq i \leq |B|} \mathsf{Eval}(\cdot, \mathsf{Enc}(PK_u, r_{f,i}), [\mathbf{I}_b^{(i)}]_u)$$

$$temp = \sum_{1 \leq i \leq |B|} \mathsf{Eval}(\cdot, \mathsf{Enc}(PK_u, q_{f,i}), [\mathbf{I}_b^{(i)}]_u)$$

$$[q_{f,b} \cdot (\mathbf{R}_f \cdot \mathbf{I}_b - \overline{r_f}) \cdot w_{u,f}]_u$$
$$= \mathsf{Eval}(\cdot, \mathsf{Eval}(\cdot, temp, [w_{u,f}]_u), \mathsf{Eval}(+, [\mathbf{R}_f \cdot \mathbf{I}_b]_u, -\mathsf{Enc}(PK_u, \overline{r_f})))$$

3. In the third stage, user $u$ sends his encrypted average rating $[\overline{r_u}]_u = \mathsf{Enc}(PK_u, \overline{r_u})$ to the server. The server first computes $[n_T]_u$, $[d_T]_u$, $[n_F]_u$, $[d_F]_u$ as shown in Fig. 3, and then compute $[X]_u$, $[Y]_u$ as follows.

$$temp_1 = \mathsf{Eval}(\cdot, \mathsf{Eval}(\cdot, \mathsf{Eval}(\cdot, [d_F]_u, [\overline{r_u}]_u), [d_T]_u), \mathsf{Enc}(PK_u, \alpha + \beta))$$

$$temp_2 = \mathsf{Eval}(\cdot, \mathsf{Eval}(\cdot, [n_T]_u, [d_F]_u), \mathsf{Enc}(PK_u, \beta))$$

$$temp_3 = \mathsf{Eval}(\cdot, \mathsf{Eval}(\cdot, [n_F]_u, [d_T]_u), \mathsf{Enc}(PK_u, \alpha))$$

$$[X]_u = \mathsf{Eval}(+, \mathsf{Eval}(+, temp_1, temp_2), temp_3)$$

$$[Y]_u = \mathsf{Eval}(\cdot, \mathsf{Eval}(\cdot, [d_F]_u, [d_T]_u), \mathsf{Enc}(PK_u, \alpha + \beta))$$

Referring to Eqs. (2) and (3), we have $p^*_{u,b} = \overline{r_u} + \frac{n_T}{d_T}$ and $p^{**}_{u,b} = \overline{r_u} + \frac{n_F}{d_F}$. The ultimate prediction $p_{u,b}$ can be denoted as follows.

$$p_{u,b} = \frac{\beta}{\alpha+\beta} \cdot p^*_{u,b} + \frac{\alpha}{\alpha+\beta} \cdot p^{**}_{u,b} = \frac{(\alpha+\beta) \cdot d_T \cdot d_F \cdot \overline{r_u} + \beta \cdot n_T \cdot d_F + \alpha \cdot n_F \cdot d_T}{(\alpha+\beta) \cdot d_T \cdot d_F} = \frac{X}{Y}$$

Due to the fact that all values are encrypted under $PK_u$, user $u$ needs to run a comparison protocol COM with the server to learn whether $p_{u,b} \geq \tau$. Since $X, Y, \tau$ are integers, COM is indeed an encrypted integer comparison protocol: where user $u$ holds the private key $sk_u$ and $\tau$, the server holds $[X]_u, [Y]_u$, and the protocol outputs a bit to user $u$ indicating whether $X \geq \tau \cdot Y$. To this end, the protocol by Veugen [33] is the most efficient one.

## 4.2 Recommendation Protocol for Top-N Items

When the active user $u$ wants to figure out Top-N unrated items, he initiates the protocol in Fig. 4. In more details, the protocol runs in three stages.

1. In the first stage, the server sends $PK_u$ to some randomly chosen strangers who can then validate $PK_u$ as in the previous protocol. Suppose that the server has successfully found $\mathbf{T}_u$. With $PK_u$ and $(\mathbf{R}_t, \mathbf{Q}_t)$, user $t \in \mathbf{T}_u$ can compute $[q_{t,b} \cdot (r_{t,b} - \overline{r_t})]_u = \mathsf{Enc}(PK_u, q_{t,b} \cdot (r_{t,b} - \overline{r_t}))$ and $[q_{t,b}]_u = \mathsf{Enc}(PK_u, q_{t,b})$ for every $1 \leq b \leq |\mathbf{B}|$. All encrypted values are sent back to the server.
2. In the second stage, to every friend $f \in \mathbf{F}_u$, user $u$ sends the encrypted weight $[w_{u,f}]_u = \mathsf{Enc}(PK_u, w_{u,f})$. With $PK_u$, $[w_{u,f}]_u$ and $(\mathbf{R}_f, \mathbf{Q}_f)$, user $f$ can compute $[q_{f,b}]_u$ and

$$[q_{f,b} \cdot (r_{f,b} - \overline{r_f}) \cdot w_{u,f}]_u = \mathsf{Eval}(\cdot, \mathsf{Enc}(PK_u, q_{f,b} \cdot (r_{f,b} - \overline{r_f})), [w_{u,f}]_u)$$

for every $1 \leq b \leq |\mathbf{B}|$. All encrypted values are sent back to the server.
3. In the third stage, user $u$ generates two matrices $\mathbf{M}_X, \mathbf{M}_Y$ as follows: (1) generate a $|\mathbf{B}| \times |\mathbf{B}|$ identity matrix; (2) randomly permute the columns to obtain $\mathbf{M}_Y$; (3) to obtain $\mathbf{M}_X$, for every $b$, if item $b$ has been rated then replace the element 1 in $b$-th column with 0.

$$\begin{bmatrix} 1 & 0 & \cdots & 0 \\ 0 & 1 & \cdots & 0 \\ \cdots & \cdots & \cdots & \cdots \\ 0 & 0 & \cdots & 1 \end{bmatrix} \xrightarrow[\text{permutation}]{\text{column}} \mathbf{M}_Y = \begin{bmatrix} 0 & 1 & \cdots & 0 \\ 0 & 0 & \cdots & 1 \\ \cdots & \cdots & \cdots & \cdots \\ 1 & 0 & \cdots & 0 \end{bmatrix} \xrightarrow[\text{rated items}]{\text{zeroing}} \mathbf{M}_X = \begin{bmatrix} 0 & 1 & \cdots & 0 \\ 0 & 0 & \cdots & 0 \\ \cdots & \cdots & \cdots & \cdots \\ 1 & 0 & \cdots & 0 \end{bmatrix}$$

User $u$ encrypts the matrices (element by element) and sends $[\mathbf{M}_X]_u, [\mathbf{M}_Y]_u$ to the server, which then proceeds as follows.

| User $u$ | RS Server | Friends $\mathbf{F}_u$, Strangers $\mathbf{T}_u$ |
|---|---|---|
| $(PK_u, SK_u)$ | $PK_u$ | |
| $w_{u,f} : \forall f \in \mathbf{F}_u$ | $\alpha, \beta$ | |

$\mathbf{R}_t, \mathbf{Q}_t$

$[\mathbf{I}_b]_u$

$\xrightarrow{\quad [\mathbf{I}_b]_u \quad}$

$\xrightarrow{\quad PK_u \quad}$

Validate $PK_u$

$\xrightarrow{\quad [\mathbf{I}_b]_u \quad}$

$[q_{t,b}]_u$
$[q_{t,b} \cdot (\mathbf{R}_t \cdot \mathbf{I}_b - \overline{r_t})]_u$

$\xleftarrow{\quad [q_{t,b}\cdot(\mathbf{R}_t\cdot\mathbf{I}_b-\overline{r_t})]_u,\ [q_{t,b}]_u \quad}$

- - - - - - - - - - - - - - - - - - - - - - - - - - - - - - - - - -

$[\overline{w_{u,f}}]_u$

$\xrightarrow{\quad [w_{u,f}]_u \quad}$

$\xrightarrow{\quad [w_{u,f}]_u,\ [\mathbf{I}_b]_u \quad}$

$[q_{f,b}]_u$
$[q_{f,b} \cdot (\mathbf{R}_f \cdot \mathbf{I}_b - \overline{r_f}) \cdot w_{u,f}]_u$

$\xleftarrow{\quad [q_{f,b}\cdot(\mathbf{R}_f\cdot\mathbf{I}_b-\overline{r_f})\cdot w_{u,f}]_u \quad}$

$\xleftarrow{\quad [q_{f,b}]_u \quad}$

- - - - - - - - - - - - - - - - - - - - - - - - - - - - - - - - - -

$[\overline{r_u}]_u$

$\xrightarrow{\quad [\overline{r_u}]_u \quad}$

$[n_T]_u = \sum_{t \in \mathbf{T}_u} [q_{t,b} \cdot (\mathbf{R}_t \cdot \mathbf{I}_b - \overline{r_t})]_u$
$[d_T]_u = \sum_{t \in \mathbf{T}_u} [q_{t,b}]_u$
$[n_F]_u$
$= \sum_{f \in \mathbf{F}_u} [q_{f,b} \cdot (\mathbf{R}_f \cdot \mathbf{I}_b - \overline{r_f}) \cdot w_{u,f}]_u$
$[d_F]_u = \sum_{f \in \mathbf{F}_u} [q_{f,b}]_u$
$[X]_u = [(\alpha + \beta) \cdot d_T \cdot d_F \cdot \overline{r_u} +$
$\quad \alpha \cdot n_T \cdot d_F + \beta \cdot n_F \cdot d_T]_u$
$[Y]_u = [(\alpha + \beta) \cdot d_T \cdot d_F]_u$

$\xleftarrow{\quad COM([X]_u, [Y]_u, \tau) \quad}$

$p_{u,b} = \frac{X}{Y} \overset{?}{\geq} \tau$

**Fig. 3.** Single prediction protocol

(a) The server first computes $[n_{T,b}]_u$, $[d_{T,b}]_u$, $[n_{F,b}]_u$, $[d_{F,b}]_u$, $[X_b]_u$, $[Y_b]_u$ for every $1 \leq b \leq |\mathbf{B}|$ as shown in Fig. 4, in the same way as in the previous protocol. Referring to Eq. (4), we see that $\overline{r_u}$ appears in $p_{u,b}$ for every $b$. *For simplicity, we ignore this term when comparing the predictions for different unrated items.* With this simplification, the prediction $p_{u,b}$ can be denoted as follows.

$$p_{u,b} = \frac{\beta}{\alpha + \beta} \cdot \frac{n_{T,b}}{d_{T,b}} + \frac{\alpha}{\alpha + \beta} \cdot \frac{n_{F,b}}{d_{F,b}} = \frac{\beta \cdot n_{T,b} \cdot d_{F,b} + \alpha \cdot n_{F,b} \cdot d_{T,b}}{(\alpha + \beta) \cdot d_{T,b} \cdot d_{F,b}} = \frac{X_b}{Y_b}$$

(b) The server permutes the ciphertexts vector $(([X_1]_u, [Y_1]_u), ([X_2]_u, [Y_2]_u), \cdots, ([X_{|\mathbf{B}|}]_u, [Y_{|\mathbf{B}|}]_u))$ in an oblivious manner as follows.

$$([U_1]_u, [U_2]_u, \cdots, [U_{|\mathbf{B}|}]_u) = [\mathbf{M}_X]_u \cdot ([X_1]_u, [X_2]_u, \cdots, [X_{|\mathbf{B}|}]_u)^T$$
$$([V_1]_u, [V_2]_u, \cdots, [V_{|\mathbf{B}|}]_u) = [\mathbf{M}_Y]_u \cdot ([Y_1]_u, [Y_2]_u, \cdots, [Y_{|\mathbf{B}|}]_u)^T$$

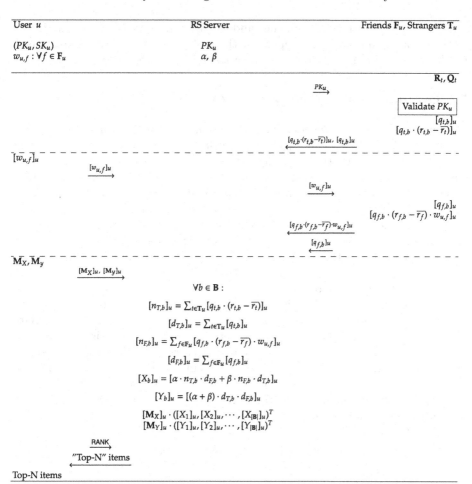

**Fig. 4.** Top-N protocol

The multiplication between the ciphertext matrix and ciphertext vector is done in the standard way, except that the multiplication between two elements is done with $\mathsf{Eval}(\cdot,,)$ and the addition is done with $\mathsf{Eval}(+,,)$. Suppose item $b$ has been rated before and $([X_b]_u, [Y_b]_u)$ is permuted to $([U_i]_u, [V_i]_u)$, then $U_i = 0$ because the element 1 in $b$-th column has been set to 0.

(c) Based on some COM protocol, e.g. that used in the previous protocol, the server ranks $\frac{U_i}{V_i}$ $(1 \leq i \leq |\mathbf{B}|)$ in the encrypted form using any standard ranking algorithm, where comparisons are done interactively with user $u$ through the encrypted integer comparison protocol COM.

(d) After the ranking, the server sends the "Top-N" indexes (e.g. the permuted Top-N indexes) to user $u$, who can then recover the real Top-N indexes.

The usage of matrix $\mathbf{M}_X$ in the random permutation of stage 3 guarantees that the rated items will all appear in the end of the list after ranking. As a result, the rated items will not appear in the recommended Top-N items.

## 5   Evaluating the Proposed Protocols

*Parameters and Performances.* The selection of the global parameters $\alpha, \beta$ and the sizes of $\mathbf{F}_u$ and $\mathbf{T}_u$ can affect the security, in particular when considering the threat from a semi-trusted friend. If $\frac{\alpha}{\alpha+\beta}$ gets larger or the size of $\mathbf{T}_u$ gets smaller, then the inputs from friends contribute more to the final outputs of user $u$. This will in turn make information reference attacks easier (for user $u$ to infer the inputs of his friends). However, if $\frac{\alpha}{\alpha+\beta}$ gets smaller and $\mathbf{T}_u$ gets larger, then we will lose the motivation of explicitly distinguishing friends and strangers in computing recommendations, namely the accuracy of recommendations may get worse. How to choose these parameters will depend on the application scenarios and the overall distributions of users' ratings.

In order to get some rough idea about how these parameters influence the accuracy of recommendation results. We choose the MovieLens 100k dataset[1] and define friends and strangers as follows. Given a user $u$, we first calculate the Cosine similarities with all other users and generate a neighborhood for user $u$. Then, we choose a certain number of users from the neighborhood as the friends, and randomly choose a certain number of users from the rest as strangers. For different parameters, the Mean Average Error (MAE) [29] of the proposed protocols is shown in Table 1. Note that lower MAE implies more accurate recommendations.

**Table 1.** MAE of experiments

| $\frac{\alpha}{\alpha+\beta}$ $(|\mathbf{F}_u|, |\mathbf{T}_u|)$ | 0.5 | 0.6 | 0.7 | 0.8 | 0.9 | 1.0 |
|---|---|---|---|---|---|---|
| (10, 10) | 0.8222 | 0.8168 | 0.8158 | 0.8193 | 0.8265 | 0.8444 |
| (30, 10) | 0.8033 | 0.7896 | 0.7819 | 0.7849 | 0.7871 | 0.7999 |
| (50, 10) | 0.7909 | 0.7762 | 0.7666 | 0.7623 | 0.7623 | 0.7684 |
| (70, 10) | 0.7824 | 0.7685 | 0.7538 | 0.7483 | 0.7460 | 0.7506 |
| (90, 10) | 0.7785 | 0.7598 | 0.7494 | 0.7419 | 0.7356 | 0.7378 |

From the numbers, it is clear that the more friends are involved the more accurate recommendation results user $u$ will obtain (i.e. the MAE is lower). There is also a trend that the MAE becomes smaller when the contribution factor $\frac{\alpha}{\alpha+\beta}$ becomes larger. According to the accuracy results by Lemire and Maclachlan (in Table 1 of [17] where the values are MAE divided by 4), their smallest MAE is $0.752 = 0.188 \times 4$. From the above Table 1, we can easily get lower MAE when $|F_u| \geq 70$ by adjusting $\frac{\alpha}{\alpha+\beta}$.

---

[1] http://grouplens.org/datasets/movielens/.

*Security Analysis.* Informally, the protocols are secure based on two facts: (1) all inputs are first freshly encrypted and then used in the computations; (2) all computations (e.g. computing predictions and ranking) done by the server and other users are in the encrypted form. As to the single prediction protocol in Sect. 4.1, we have the following arguments.

1. *Threat from Semi-honest RS Server.* Given the COM protocol is secure (namely, the server does not learn anything in the process). Then the server learns nothing about any user's private input information, e.g. $b, \tau, \mathbf{R}_u, \mathbf{Q}_u, \mathbf{R}_f, \mathbf{Q}_f, w_{u,f}, \mathbf{R}_t, \mathbf{Q}_t$ for all $f$ and $t$, because every element is freshly encrypted in the computation and all left computations are done homomorphically.

   Moreover, the server learns nothing about $p_{u,b} \overset{?}{\geq} \tau$ based on the security of COM.
2. *Threat from a Semi-honest Friend.* We consider two scenarios.
   - Informally, a friend $f$'s contribution to $p_{u,b}$ is protected by the inputs from users $\mathbf{F}_u \setminus f$ and the strangers $\mathbf{T}_u$. Given a randomly chosen unrated item for user $u$ and a randomly chosen friend $f \in \mathbf{F}_u$, we perform a simple experiment to show how $f$'s input influences the predicted rating. We set $\frac{\alpha}{\alpha+\beta} = 0.8$ and the $(|\mathbf{F}_u|, |\mathbf{T}_u|) = (30, 10)$ in all tests, and choose strangers randomly in every test.

**Table 2.** Influence of a single friend

| Tests<br>Rating Value | Test 1 | Test 2 | Test 3 | Test 4 | Test 5 |
|---|---|---|---|---|---|
| With $f$'s input ($r$) | 4.0351 | 3.7165 | 3.9125 | 3.9125 | 4.0667 |
| Without $f$'s input ($r'$) | 3.7014 | 4.0343 | 3.9125 | 3.9698 | 3.9556 |
| $r - r'$ | 0.3337 | -0.3178 | 0.0000 | -0.0573 | 0.1111 |

   The results in Table 2 imply that a friend $f$'s contribution to user $u$'s output is obfuscated by the inputs from the stranger set. Simply from the output of user $u$, it is hard to infer user $f$'s input. Furthermore, it should be clear that the larger the friend set is the less information of a single friend will be inferred. With encryption, the friends learn nothing about user $u$.
   - For similar reasons, it will be hard for $\mathbf{F}_u \setminus f$ to infer user $f$'s data even if they learned user $u$'s output at the end of a protocol execution.
3. *Threat from strangers.* We consider the following two scenarios.
   - In the view of strangers, all values are encrypted under user $u$'s public key, so that they will not be able to derive any information about the inputs and outputs of user $u$ and his friends.
   - For the strangers involved in a protocol execution, it does not leak much information for several reasons. Firstly, user $u$ does not know which stranger is involved in the protocol execution. Secondly, the inputs of a group strangers are blended in the output to user $u$. We perform a simple experiment to show how strangers' inputs influence the predicted ratings

**Table 3.** Influence of strangers

| Strangers \ Unrated Items | Item$_1$ | Item$_2$ | Item$_3$ | Item$_4$ | Item$_5$ |
|---|---|---|---|---|---|
| Stranger$_1$ | 0.0 | -0.0825 | 0.0 | 0.0 | 0.0 |
| Stranger$_2$ | 0.0 | 0.0 | 0.0 | 0.0 | 0.0 |
| Stranger$_3$ | 0.0 | 0.0211 | 0.0 | 0.0 | 0.0 |
| Stranger$_4$ | 0.0913, | 0.0 | 0.0 | 0.0 | 0.0 |
| Stranger$_5$ | 0.0 | 0.0134 | 0.0702 | 0.0 | 0.1375 |

for user $u$. We set $\frac{\alpha}{\alpha+\beta} = 0.8$ and the $(|\mathbf{F}_u|, |\mathbf{T}_u|) = (30, 10)$. Table 3 shows the rating differences for 5 unrated items, depending on whether a stranger is involved in the computation or not. It is clear that very little information about a stranger can be inferred from user $u$'s outputs.

Thirdly, the strangers are independently chosen in different protocol executions, so that it is difficult to leverage on the accumulated information.

Similar analysis applies to the Top-N protocol in Sect. 4.2. As to user $u$'s outputs, the matrices $[\mathbf{M}_X]_u, [\mathbf{M}_Y]_u$ randomly permuted the predictions so that the ranking does not leak any information about the Top-N items.

# 6    Conclusion

Recommender systems are complex in the sense that many users are involved and contributing to the outputs of each other. The privacy challenge is big because it is difficult to reach a realistic security model with efficient privacy-preserving protocols. This work, motivated by [13], tried to propose a realistic security model by leveraging on the similarity and trust between friends in digital communities. Compared to [13], we went a step further by introducing randomly selected strangers into the play and make it possible to protect users' privacy even if their friends' outputs are compromised. Moreover, we adjusted the recommendation formula and achieve better accuracy than some other well-known recommender protocols [17]. Following our work, many interesting topics remain open. One is to test our protocols on real dataset. Another is to implement the protocols and see how realistic the computational performances are. Another is to adjust the recommendation formula to reflect more advanced algorithms, such as Matrix Factorizations [19], which however will have different requirements on the involved user population. Another is to investigate stronger security models, e.g. assuming a malicious RS server. Yet another topic is to formally investigate the information leakages from the outputs. Our methodology, namely introducing randomly selected strangers, has some similarity with the differential privacy based approach [18]. A detailed comparative study will be very useful to understand their connections.

**Acknowledgements.** The authors are supported by a CORE (junior track) grant from the National Research Fund, Luxembourg.

# Appendix: Brakerski-Vaikuntanathan SWHE Scheme

Let $\lambda$ be the security parameter. The Brakerski-Vaikuntanathan public-key SWHE scheme [5] is parameterized by two primes $q, t \in \text{poly}(\lambda) \in \mathbb{N}$ where $t < q$, a degree $n$ polynomial $f(x) \in \mathbb{Z}[x]$, two error distributions $\chi$ and $\chi'$ over the ring $R_q = \mathbb{Z}_q[x]/\langle f(x) \rangle$. The message space is $\mathcal{M} = \mathbf{R}_t = \mathbb{Z}_t[x]/\langle f(x) \rangle$. An additional parameter is $D \in \mathbb{N}$, namely the maximal degree of homomorphism allowed (and to the maximal ciphertext length). The parameters $n, f, q, t, \chi, \chi', D$ are public.

- Keygen($\lambda$): (1) sample $s, e_0 \leftarrow \chi$ and $a_0 \in R_q$; (2) compute $\mathbf{s} = (1, s, s^2, \ldots, s^D) \in R_q^{D+1}$; (3) output $SK = \mathbf{s}$ and $PK = (a_0, b_0 = a_0 s + t e_0)$.
- Enc($PK, m$): (1) sample $v, e' \leftarrow \chi$ and $e'' \leftarrow \chi'$; (2) compute $c_0 = b_0 v + t e'' + m$, $c_1 = -(a_0 v + t e')$; (3) output $\mathbf{c} = (c_0, c_1)$.
- Dec($SK, \mathbf{c} = (c_0, \ldots, c_D) \in R_q^{D+1}$): output $m = (\mathbf{c} \cdot \mathbf{s} \mod q) \mod t$.

Since the scheme is somewhat homomorphic, it provides an evaluation algorithm Eval, which can multiply and add messages based on their ciphertexts only. For simplicity, we show how Eval works when the ciphertexts are freshly generated. Let $\mathbf{c}_\alpha = (c_{\alpha 0}, c_{\alpha 1})$ and $\mathbf{c}_\beta = (c_{\beta 0}, c_{\beta 1})$. Note that the multiplication operation will add an additional element for the ciphertext. This is why the Dec algorithm generally assumes the ciphertext to be a vector of $D + 1$ elements (if the ciphertext has less elements, simply pad 0s).

$$\text{Eval}(+, \mathbf{c}_\alpha, \mathbf{c}_\beta) = (c_{\alpha 0} + c_{\beta 0}, c_{\alpha 1} + c_{\beta 1}). \quad \text{Eval}(\cdot, \mathbf{c}_\alpha, \mathbf{c}_\beta)$$
$$= (c_{\alpha 0} \cdot c_{\beta 0}, c_{\alpha 0} \cdot c_{\beta 1} + c_{\alpha 1} \cdot c_{\beta 0}, c_{\alpha 1} \cdot c_{\beta 1}).$$

When the evaluations are done to a ciphertext and a plaintext message, there is a simpler form for the evaluation algorithm, denoted as Eval$^*$. This has been used in [13].

$$\text{Eval}^*(+, \mathbf{c}_\alpha, m') = (c_{\alpha 0} + m', c_{\alpha 1}). \quad \text{Eval}^*(\cdot, \mathbf{c}_\alpha, m') = (c_{\alpha 0} \cdot m', c_{\alpha 1} \cdot m').$$

Throughout the paper, given a public/private key pair $(PK_u, SK_u)$ for some user $u$, we use $[m]_u$ to denote a ciphertext of the message $m$ under public key $PK_u$. In comparison, Enc($PK_u, m$) represents the probabilistic output of running Enc for the message $m$. When $\mathbf{m}$ is a vector of messages, we use Enc($PK_u, \mathbf{m}$) to denote the vector of ciphertexts, where encryption is done for each element independently. We use the notation $\sum_{1 \le i \le N} [m_i]_u$ to denote the result of sequentially applying Eval($+, ,$) to the cipheretxts.

# References

1. Adomavicius, G., Tuzhilin, A.: Toward the next generation of recommender systems: a survey of the state-of-the-art and possible extensions. IEEE Trans. Knowl. Data Eng. **17**(6), 734–749 (2005)

2. Aïmeur, E., Brassard, G., Fernandez, J.M., Onana, F.S.M.: Alambic: a privacy-preserving recommender system for electronic commerce. Int. J. Inf. Secur. **7**, 307–334 (2008)

3. Beye, M., Jeckmans, A., Erkin, Z., Tang, Q., Hartel, P., Lagendijk, I.: Privacy in recommender systems. In: Zhou, S., Wu, Z. (eds.) ADMA 2012 Workshops. CCIS, vol. 387, pp. 263–281. Springer, Heidelberg (2013)

4. Bilge, A., Polat, H.: A scalable privacy-preserving recommendation scheme via bisecting k-means clustering. Inf. Process. Manag. **49**(4), 912–927 (2013)

5. Brakerski, Z., Vaikuntanathan, V.: Fully homomorphic encryption from Ring-LWE and security for key dependent messages. In: Rogaway, P. (ed.) CRYPTO 2011. LNCS, vol. 6841, pp. 505–524. Springer, Heidelberg (2011)

6. Calandrino, J.A., Kilzer, A., Narayanan, A., Felten, E.W., Shmatikov, V.: "You might also like:" privacy risks of collaborative filtering. In: 32nd IEEE Symposium on Security and Privacy, S & P 2011, pp. 231–246 (2011)

7. Canny, J.F.: Collaborative filtering with privacy. In: IEEE Symposium on Security and Privacy, pp. 45–57 (2002)

8. Canny, J.F.: Collaborative filtering with privacy via factor analysis. In: Proceedings of the 25th Annual International ACM SIGIR Conference on Research and Development in Information Retrieval, pp. 238–245 (2002)

9. Chenal, M., Tang, Q.: On key recovery attacks against existing somewhat homomorphic encryption schemes. In: Aranha, D.F., Menezes, A. (eds.) LATINCRYPT 2014. LNCS, vol. 8895, pp. 239–258. Springer, Heidelberg (2015)

10. Douceur, J.R.: The sybil attack. In: Druschel, P., Kaashoek, M.F., Rowstron, A. (eds.) IPTPS 2002. LNCS, vol. 2429, pp. 251–260. Springer, Heidelberg (2002)

11. Erkin, Z., Beye, M., Veugen, T., Lagendijk, R.L.: Efficiently computing private recommendations. In: International Conference on Acoustic, Speech and Signal Processing (2011)

12. Han, S., Ng, W.K., Yu, P.S.: Privacy-preserving singular value decomposition. In: Ioannidis, Y.E., Lee, D.L., Ng, R.T. (eds.) Proceedings of the 25th International Conference on Data Engineering, pp. 1267–1270. IEEE, Shanghai (2009)

13. Jeckmans, A., Peter, A., Hartel, P.: Efficient privacy-enhanced familiarity-based recommender system. In: Crampton, J., Jajodia, S., Mayes, K. (eds.) ESORICS 2013. LNCS, vol. 8134, pp. 400–417. Springer, Heidelberg (2013)

14. Jeckmans, A., Tang, Q., Hartel, P.: Privacy-preserving collaborative filtering based on horizontally partitioned dataset. In: 2012 International Symposium on Security in Collaboration Technologies and Systems (CTS 2012), pp. 439–446 (2012)

15. Kantarcioglu, M., Jin, J., Clifton, C.: When do data mining results violate privacy. In: The Tenth ACM SIGMOD International Conference on Knowledge Discovery and Data Mining, pp. 599–604. ACM (2004)

16. Lam, S.K.T., Frankowski, D., Riedl, J.: Do you trust your recommendations? An exploration of security and privacy issues in recommender systems. In: Müller, G. (ed.) ETRICS 2006. LNCS, vol. 3995, pp. 14–29. Springer, Heidelberg (2006)

17. Lemire, D., Maclachlan, A.: Slope one predictors for online rating-based collaborative filtering. In: Kargupta, H., Srivastava, J., Kamath, C., Goodman, A. (eds.) Proceedings of the 2005 SIAM International Conference on Data Mining, SDM 2005, pp. 471–475. SIAM, California (2005)

18. McSherry, F., Mironov, I.: Differentially private recommender systems: building privacy into the Netflix prize contenders. In: Proceedings of the 15th ACM SIGKDD International Conference on Knowledge Discovery and Data Mining, pp. 627–636 (2009)

19. Nikolaenko, V., Ioannidis, S., Weinsberg, U., Joye, M., Taft, N., Boneh, D.: Privacy-preserving matrix factorization. In: Proceedings of the 2013 ACM SIGSAC Conference on Computer and Communications Security, pp. 801–812 (2013)

20. Parameswaran, R.: A robust data obfuscation approach for privacy preserving collaborative filtering. Ph.D. thesis, Georgia Institute of Technology (2006)

21. Polat, H., Du, W.: Privacy-preserving collaborative filtering using randomized perturbation techniques. In: Proceedings of the Third IEEE International Conference on Data Mining, pp. 625–628 (2003)

22. Polat, H., Du, W.: Privacy-preserving collaborative filtering. Int. J. Electron. Commer. **9**, 9–36 (2005)

23. Polat, H., Du, W.: Privacy-preserving collaborative filtering on vertically partitioned data. In: Jorge, A.M., Torgo, L., Brazdil, P.B., Camacho, R., Gama, J. (eds.) PKDD 2005. LNCS (LNAI), vol. 3721, pp. 651–658. Springer, Heidelberg (2005)

24. Polat, H., Du, W.: Privacy-preserving top-n recommendation on horizontally partitioned data. In: 2005 IEEE/WIC/ACM International Conference on Web Intelligence (WI 2005), pp. 725–731. IEEE Computer Society (2005)

25. Polat, H., Du, W.: SVD-based collaborative filtering with privacy. In: Proceedings of the 2005 ACM Symposium on Applied Computing (SAC), pp. 791–795. ACM (2005)

26. Polat, H., Du, W.: Achieving private recommendations using randomized response techniques. In: Ng, W.-K., Kitsuregawa, M., Li, J., Chang, K. (eds.) PAKDD 2006. LNCS (LNAI), vol. 3918, pp. 637–646. Springer, Heidelberg (2006)

27. Polat, H., Du, W.: Privacy-preserving top-N recommendation on distributed data. J. Am. Soc. Inf. Sci. Technol. **59**, 1093–1108 (2008)

28. Ramakrishnan, N., Keller, B.J., Mirza, B.J., Grama, A.Y.: Privacy risks in recommender systems. IEEE Internet Comput. **5**, 54–63 (2001)

29. Shani, G., Gunawardana, A.: Evaluating recommendation systems. In: Ricci, F., Rokach, L., Shapira, B., Kantor, P.B. (eds.) Recommender Systems Handbook, pp. 257–297. Springer, USA (2011)

30. Shokri, R., Pedarsani, P., Theodorakopoulos, G., Hubaux, J.: Preserving privacy in collaborative filtering through distributed aggregation of offline profiles. In: Proceedings of the Third ACM Conference on Recommender Systems (RecSys 2009), pp. 157–164 (2009)

31. Tang, Q.: Cryptographic framework for analyzing the privacy of recommender algorithms. In: 2012 International Symposium on Security in Collaboration Technologies and Systems (CTS 2012), pp. 455–462 (2012)

32. Tang, Q., Wang, J.: Privacy-preserving context-aware recommender systems: analysis and new solutions (2015). http://eprint.iacr.org/2015/364

33. Veugen, T.: Comparing encrypted data (2011). http://bioinformatics.tudelft.nl/sites/default/files/Comparing

34. Weinsberg, U., Bhagat, S., Ioannidis, S., Taft, N.: BlurMe: inferring and obfuscating user gender based on ratings. In: Cunningham, P., Hurley, N.J., Guy, I., Anand, S.S. (eds.) Sixth ACM Conference on Recommender Systems, RecSys 2012, pp. 195–202. ACM, New York (2012)

35. Yakut, I., Polat, H.: Arbitrarily distributed data-based recommendations with privacy. Data Knowl. Eng. **72**, 239–256 (2012)

36. Zhan, J., Hsieh, C., Wang, I., Hsu, T., Liau, C., Wang, D.: Privacy-preserving collaborative recommender systems. Trans. Sys. Man Cyber Part C **40**, 472–476 (2010)

# Cloud Security

# Rich Queries on Encrypted Data: Beyond Exact Matches

Sky Faber, Stanislaw Jarecki, Hugo Krawczyk[(✉)], Quan Nguyen,
Marcel Rosu, and Michael Steiner

Yorktown, USA
hugo@ee.technion.ac.il

**Abstract.** We extend the searchable symmetric encryption (SSE) protocol of [Cash et al., Crypto'13] adding support for range, substring,
wildcard, and phrase queries, in addition to the Boolean queries supported in the original protocol. Our techniques apply to the basic single-
client scenario underlying the common SSE setting as well as to the
more complex Multi-Client and Outsourced Symmetric PIR extensions
of [Jarecki et al., CCS'13]. We provide performance information based on
our prototype implementation, showing the practicality and scalability of
our techniques to very large databases, thus extending the performance
results of [Cash et al., NDSS'14] to these rich and comprehensive query
types.

## 1 Introduction

*Searchable symmetric encryption (SSE)* addresses a setting where a client outsources an encrypted database (or document/file collection) to a remote server
$\mathcal{E}$ such that the client, which only stores a cryptographic key, can later search
the collection at $\mathcal{E}$ while hiding information about the database and queries
from $\mathcal{E}$. Leakage to $\mathcal{E}$ is to be confined to well-defined forms of data-access and
query patterns while preventing disclosure of explicit data and query plaintext
values. SSE has been extensively studied [4–7,9,11–14,16–19,24], particularly in
last years due to the popularity of clouds and data outsourcing, focusing almost
exclusively on single-keyword search.

Recently, Cash et al. [5] and Pappas et al. [19] presented the first SSE solutions that go well beyond single-keyword search by supporting Boolean queries on
multiple keywords in sublinear time. In particular, [4,5] build a very scalable system with demonstrated practical performance with databases containing indexes
in the order of tens of billions document-keyword pairs. In this work we extend
the search capabilities of the system from [5] (*referred to as the OXT protocol*) by
supporting range queries (e.g., return all records of people born between two given
dates), substring queries (e.g., return records with textual information containing
a given pattern, say 'crypt'), wildcard queries (combining substrings with one or
more single-character wildcards), and phrase queries (return records that contain
the phrase "searchable encryption"). Moreover, by preserving the overall system

© Springer International Publishing Switzerland 2015
G. Pernul et al. (Eds.): ESORICS 2015, Part II, LNCS 9327, pp. 123–145, 2015.
DOI: 10.1007/978-3-319-24177-7_7

design and optimized data structures of [4], we can run any of these new queries in combination with Boolean-search capabilities (e.g., combining a range and/or substring query with a conjunction of additional keywords/ranges/substrings) and we can do so while preserving the scalability of the system and additional properties such as support for *dynamic data*.

We also show how to extend our techniques to the more involved multi-client SSE scenarios studied by Jarecki et al. [12]. In the first scenario, denoted MC-SSE, the owner of the data, $\mathcal{D}$, outsources its data to a remote server $\mathcal{E}$ in encrypted form and later allows multiple clients to access the data via search queries and according to an authorization policy managed by $\mathcal{D}$. The system is intended to limit the information learned by clients beyond the result sets returned by authorized queries while also limiting information leakage to server $\mathcal{E}$. A second scenario, OSPIR-SSE or just OSPIR (for Outsourced Symmetric PIR), addresses the multi-client setting but adds a requirement that $\mathcal{D}$ can authorize queries to clients following a given policy, but without $\mathcal{D}$ learning the specific values being queried. That is, $\mathcal{D}$ learns minimal information needed to enforce policy, e.g., the query type or the field to which the keyword belongs, say last name, but not the actual last name being searched.

We present our solution for range queries in Sect. 3, showing how to reduce any such query to a *disjunction of exact keywords*, hence leveraging the Boolean query capabilities of the OXT protocol and its remarkable performance. In the OSPIR setting, we show how $\mathcal{D}$ can authorize range queries based on the total size of the queried range without learning the actual endpoints of the range. This is useful for authorization policies that limit the size of a range as a way of preventing a client from obtaining a large fraction of the database. Thus, $\mathcal{D}$ may learn that a query on a data field spans 7 days but not *which* 7 days the query is about. Achieving privacy from both $\mathcal{D}$ and $\mathcal{E}$ while ensuring that the authorized search interval does not exceed a size limit enforced by $\mathcal{D}$, is challenging. We propose solutions based on the notion of *universal tree covers* for which we present different instantiations trading performance and security depending on the SSE model that is being addressed.

The other queries we support, i.e. substrings, wildcards and phrases, are all derived from a novel technique that allows us to search on the basis of positioning information (where the data and the position information are encrypted). This technique can be used to implement any query type that can be reduced to Boolean formulas on queries of the form "are two data elements at distance $\Delta$?". For example, in the case of substring queries, the substring is tokenized (i.e., subdivided) into a sequence of possibly-overlapping k-grams (strings of $k$ characters) and the search is performed as a conjunction of such k-grams. However, to avoid false positives, i.e., returning documents where the k-grams appear but not at the right distances from each other, we use the relative positions of the tokens to ensure that the combined k-grams represent the searched substring. Wildcard queries are processed similarly, because $t$ consecutive wildcard positions (i.e., positions that can be occupied by any character) can be implemented by setting the distance between the two k-grams that bracket the string of $t$ wildcards to

$k + t$. Phrase queries are handled similarly, by storing whole words together with their encrypted positions in the text.

The crux of this technique is a homomorphic computation on encrypted position information that gives rise to a very efficient SSE protocol between client $\mathcal{C}$ and server $\mathcal{E}$ for computing relative distances between data elements while concealing this information from $\mathcal{E}$. This protocol meshes naturally with the homomorphic properties of OXT but in its general form it requires an additional round of interaction between client and server. In the SSE setting, the resulting protocol preserves most of the excellent performance of the OXT protocol (with the extra round incurring a moderate increase in query processing latency). Similar performance is achieved in the MC setting while for the OSPIR setting we resort to bilinear groups for some homomorphic operations, hence impacting performance in a more noticeable way which we are currently investigating.

We prove the security of our protocols in the SSE model of [5,7,9], and the extensions to the MC-SSE and OSPIR settings of [12], where security is defined in the real-vs-ideal model and is parametrized by a specified leakage function $\mathcal{L}(\mathsf{DB}, \mathbf{q})$. A protocol is said to be secure with leakage profile $\mathcal{L}(\mathsf{DB}, \mathbf{q})$ against adversary $\mathcal{A}$ if the actions of $\mathcal{A}$ on adversarially-chosen input $\mathsf{DB}$ and query set $\mathbf{q}$ can be simulated with access to the leakage information $\mathcal{L}(\mathsf{DB}, \mathbf{q})$ only (and not to $\mathsf{DB}$ or $\mathbf{q}$). This allows modeling and bounding the partial leakage incurred by SSE protocols. It means that even an adversary that has full information about the database and queries, or even chooses them at will, does not learn anything from the protocol execution other than what can be derived solely from the defined leakage profile. We achieve provable *adaptive* security against adversarial servers $\mathcal{E}$ and $\mathcal{D}$, and against malicious clients. Servers $\mathcal{E}$ and $\mathcal{D}$ are assumed to return correct results (e.g., server $\mathcal{E}$ returns all documents specified by the protocol) but can otherwise behave maliciously. However, in the OSPIR setting, query privacy from $\mathcal{D}$ is achieved as long as $\mathcal{D}$ does not collude with $\mathcal{E}$.

Practicality of our techniques was validated by a comprehensive implementation of: (i) the SSE protocols for range, substring and wildcard queries, and their combination with Boolean functions on exact keywords, and (ii) the OSPIR-SSE protocol for range queries. These implementations (extending those of [4,5,12]) were tested by an independent evaluator on DB's of varying size, up to 10 Terabytes with 100 million records and 25.6 billion record-keyword pairs. Performance was compared to MariaDB's (an open-source fork of MySQL) performance on the same databases running on *plaintext data and plaintext queries*. Due to the highly optimized protocols and careful I/O management, the performance of our protocols matched and often exceeded the performance of the plaintext system. These results are presented in Appendix A.

**Related Work.** The only work we are aware of that addresses substring search on symmetrically encrypted data is the work of Chase and Shen [8]. Their method, based on suffix trees, is very different than ours and the leakage profiles seem incomparable. This is a promising direction, although the applicability to (sublinear) search on large databases, and the integration with other query types, needs to be investigated. Its potential generalization to the multi-client or

OSPIR settings is another interesting open question. Range and Boolean queries are supported, also for the OSPIR setting, by Pappas et al. [19] (building on the work of Raykova et al [21]). Their design is similar to ours in reducing range queries to disjunctions (with similar data expansion cost) but their techniques are very different offering an alternative (and incomparable) leakage profile for the parties. The main advantages of our system are the support of the additional query types presented here and its scalability. The scalability of [19] is limited by their crucial reliance on Bloom filters that requires database sizes whose resultant Bloom filters can fit in RAM. A technique that has been suggested for resolving range queries in the SSE setting is *order-preserving encryption* (e.g., it is used in the CryptDB system [20]). However, it carries a significant intrinsic loss of privacy as the ordering of ciphertexts is visible to the holding server (and the encryption is deterministic). Range queries are supported in the multi-writer public key setting by Boneh-Waters [3] and Shi et al. [23] but at a significantly higher computational cost.

## 2   Preliminaries

Our work concerns itself with databases in a very general sense, including relational databases (with data arranged in "rows" and "columns"), document collections, textual data, etc. We use interchangeably the word 'document' and 'record'. We think of keywords as (attribute,value) pairs. The attribute can be structured data, such as name, age, SSN, etc., or it can refer to a textual field. We sometimes refer explicitly to the keyword's attribute but most of the time it remains implicit. We denote by $m$ the number of distinct attributes and use $I(w)$ to denote the attribute of keyword $w$.

**SSE Protocols and Formal Setting (following [5]).** Let $\tau$ be a security parameter. A database $\mathsf{DB} = (\mathsf{ind}_i, \mathsf{W}_i)_{i=1}^{d}$ is a list of identifier and keyword-set pairs, where $\mathsf{ind}_i \in \{0,1\}^{\tau}$ is a document identifier and $\mathsf{W}_i = \mathsf{DB}[\mathsf{ind}_i]$ is a list of its keywords. Let $\mathsf{W} = \bigcup_{i=1}^{d} \mathsf{W}_i$. A *query* $\psi$ is a predicate on $\mathsf{W}_i$ where $\mathsf{DB}(\psi)$ is the set of identifiers of document that satisfy $\psi$. E.g. for a single-keyword query we have $\mathsf{DB}(w) = \{\mathsf{ind}$ s.t. $w \in \mathsf{DB}[\mathsf{ind}]\}$.

A *searchable symmetric encryption (SSE) scheme* $\Pi$ consists of an algorithm Setup and a protocol Search fitting the following syntax. Setup takes as input a database $\mathsf{DB}$ and a list of document (or record) decryption keys $\mathsf{RDK}$, and outputs a secret key $K$ along with an encrypted database $\mathsf{EDB}$. The search protocol Search proceeds between a *client* $\mathcal{C}$ and *server* $\mathcal{E}$, where $\mathcal{C}$ takes as input the secret key $K$ and a query $\psi$ and $\mathcal{E}$ takes as input $\mathsf{EDB}$. At the end of the protocol, $\mathcal{C}$ outputs a set of $(\mathsf{ind}, \mathsf{rdk})$ pairs while $\mathcal{E}$ has no output. We say that an SSE scheme is *correct* for a family of queries $\Psi$ if for all $\mathsf{DB}, \mathsf{RDK}$ and all queries $\psi \in \Psi$, for $(K, \mathsf{EDB}) \leftarrow \mathsf{Setup}(\mathsf{DB}, \mathsf{RDK})$, after running Search with client input $(K, \psi)$ and server input $\mathsf{EDB}$, the client outputs $\mathsf{DB}(\psi)$ and $\mathsf{RDK}[\mathsf{DB}(\psi)]$ where $\mathsf{RDK}[S]$ denotes $\{\mathsf{RDK}[\mathsf{ind}] \,|\, \mathsf{ind} \in S\}$. Correctness can be statistical (allowing a negligible probability of error) or computational (ensured only against computationally bounded attackers - see [5]).

*Note (retrieval of matching encrypted records).* Above we define the output of the SSE protocol as the set of identifiers ind pointing to the encrypted documents matching the query (together with the set of associated record decryption keys rdk). The retrieval of the document payloads, which can be done in a variety of ways, is thus decoupled from the storage and processing of the metadata which is the focus of the SSE protocols.

**Multi-Client SSE Setting** [12]. The MC-SSE formalism extends the SSE syntax by an algorithm GenToken, which generates a search-enabling value token from the secret key $K$ generated by the data owner $\mathcal{D}$ in Setup, and query $\psi$ submitted by client $\mathcal{C}$. Protocol Search is then executed between server $\mathcal{E}$ and client $\mathcal{C}$ on resp. inputs EDB and token, and the protocol must assure that $\mathcal{C}$ outputs sets $DB(\psi)$ and $RDK[DB(\psi)]$.

**OSPIR SSE Setting** [12]. An OSPIR-SSE scheme replaces the GenToken procedure, which in MC-SSE is executed by the data owner $\mathcal{D}$ on the cleartext client's query $q$, with a two-party protocol between $\mathcal{C}$ and $\mathcal{D}$ that allows $\mathcal{C}$ to compute the search-enabling token without $\mathcal{D}$ learning $\psi$. However, $\mathcal{D}$ should be able to enforce a query-authorization policy on $\mathcal{C}$'s query. We consider attribute-based policies, where queries are authorized based on the attributes associated to keywords in the query (e.g., a client may be authorized to run a range query on attribute 'age' but not on 'income', or perform a substring query on the 'address' field but not on the 'name' field, etc.). Later, we will consider extensions where the policy can define further constraints, e.g., the total size of an allowed interval in a range query, or the minimal size of a pattern in a substring query. An attribute-based policy for any query type is represented by a set of attribute-sequences P s.t. a query $\psi$ involving keywords (or substrings, ranges, etc.) $(w_1, ..., w_n)$ is *allowed by policy* P if and only if the sequence of attributes $av(\psi) = (I(w_1), ..., I(w_n)) \in P$. Using this notation, the goal of the GenToken protocol is to let $\mathcal{C}$ compute token corresponding to its query on $\psi$ only if $av(\bar{w}) \in P$. Note that different query types will have different entries in P. Reflecting these goals, an OSPIR-SSE scheme is a tuple $\Sigma = ($Setup, GenToken, Search$)$ where Setup and Search are as in MC-SSE, but GenToken is a protocol run by $\mathcal{C}$ on input $\psi$ and by $\mathcal{D}$ on input $(P, K)$, with $\mathcal{C}$ outputting token if $av(\psi) \in P$, or $\perp$ otherwise, and $\mathcal{D}$ outputting $av(\psi)$.

## 3  Range Queries

Our solution for performing range queries on encrypted data reduces these queries to a disjunction of exact keywords and therefore can be integrated with SSE solutions that support such disjunctions. In particular, we use this solution to add range query support to the OXT protocol from [5,12] while keeping all the other properties of OXT intact. This includes OXT's remarkable scalability, its support for different models (SSE, MC, OSPIR), and its boolean search capability. Thus, we obtain a protocol where range queries can be run in isolation or in combination with boolean expressions on other terms, including conjunctive ranges such as $30 \leq \text{AGE} \leq 39$ and $50{,}000 \leq \text{INCOME} \leq 99{,}999$.

Range queries can be applied to any ordered set of elements; our description focuses on integer ranges for simplicity. We denote range queries with input an interval $[a, b]$, for integers $a \leq b$, by $RQ(a, b)$. We refer to $a$ and $b$ as the *endpoints* and to the number $b - a + 1$ as the *size of the range*. Inequality queries of the form $x \geq a$ are represented by the range $[a, b]$ where $b$ is an upper bound on all applicable values for the searched attribute; queries of the form $x \leq b$ are handled similarly.

We now describe the extensions to the OXT protocol (and its OSPIR version) for supporting range queries. Thanks to our generic reduction of range queries to disjunctions of exact keywords, our range-query presentation does not require a detailed knowledge of the OXT protocol and basic familiarity with OXT suffices (the interested reader can find more details on OXT in the above papers and also in Sect. 4.1).

**Pre-Processing (Setup).** For concreteness, consider a database table with an attribute (or column) $A$ over which range queries are enabled. The values in the column are mapped to integer values between 0 and $2^t - 1$ for some number $t$. To support range queries on attribute $A$ we augment the given cleartext database DB with $t$ *virtual* columns which are populated at Setup as follows. Consider a full binary tree with $t + 1$ levels and $2^t$ leaves. Each node in the tree is labeled with a binary string describing the path from the root to the node: The root is labeled with the empty string, its children with strings 0 and 1, its grandchildren with 00, 01, 10, 11, and so on. A node at depth $d$ is labeled with a string of length $d$, and the leaves are labeled with $t$-long strings that correspond to the binary representation of the integer value in that leaf, i.e. a $t$-bit binary representation padded with leading zeros.

Each of the $t$ added columns correspond to a level in the tree, denoted $A'(1), A'(2), \ldots, A'(t)$ ($A'$ indicates that this is a "virtual attribute" derived from attribute $A$). A record (or row) whose value for attribute $A$ has binary representation $v_{t-1}, \ldots, v_1, v_0$ will have the string $(v_{t-1}, \ldots, v_1, v_0)$ in column $A'(t)$, the string $(v_{t-1}, \ldots v_1)$ in column $A'(t-1)$, and so on till column $A'(1)$ which will have the string $v_{t-1}$. Once the above plaintext columns $A'(1), \ldots, A'(t-1)$ are added to DB (note that $A'(t)$ is identical to the original attribute $A$), they are processed by the regular OXT pre-processing as any other original DB column, but they will be used exclusively for processing range queries.

**Client Processing.** To query for a range $RQ(a, b)$, the client selects a set of nodes in the tree that form a *cover* of the required range, namely, a set of tree nodes for which the set of descendant leaves corresponds exactly to all elements in the range $[a, b]$ (e.g. a cover for range 3 to 9 in a tree of depth 4 will contain cover nodes 0011, 01, 100). Let $c_1, \ldots, c_\ell$ be the string representation of the nodes in the cover and assume these nodes are at depths $d_1, \ldots, d_\ell$, respectively (not all depths have to be different). The query then is formed as a *disjunction of the $\ell$ exact-match queries "column $A'(d_i)$ has value $c_i$", for $i = 1, \ldots, \ell$.* Note that we assume that the client knows how nodes in the tree are represented; in particular it needs to know the total depth of the tree. We stress that *this reduction to a disjunctive query works with any strategy for selecting* *the cover set.* This is important since different covers present different trade-offs between performance and leakage. Moreover, since the pre-processing of data is independent of the choice of cover, one can allow multiple cover strategies to co-exist to suit different leakage-performance trade-offs. Later, we will describe specific strategies for cover selection.

**Interaction of Client $C$ with Server $\mathcal{E}$.** The search at $\mathcal{E}$ is carried exactly as in the Search phase of OXT as with any other disjunction. In particular, $\mathcal{E}$ does not need to know whether this disjunction comes from a range query.

**Server $\mathcal{D}'s$ Token Generation and Authorization.** For the case of single-client and multi-client) SSE, token generation and authorization work as with any disjunction in the original OXT protocol. However, in the OSPIR setting, $\mathcal{D}$ needs to authorize the query without learning the queried values. Specifically, in the scenario addressed by our implementation, authorization of range queries is based on the searched attribute (e.g., age) and the total size of the range (i.e., policy attaches to each client an upper bound on the size of a range the client is allowed to query for the given attribute). To enforce this policy, we allow $\mathcal{D}$ to learn the searched attribute and the total size of the range, i.e., $b - a + 1$, but not the actual end-point values $a, b$. This is accomplished as follows.

Client $C$ computes a cover corresponding to his range query and maps each node in the cover to a keyword $(d, c)$, where $d$ is the depth of the node in the tree and $c$ the corresponding string. It then generates a disjunction of the resultant keywords $(d_i, c_i), i = 1, \ldots, \ell$, where $\ell$ is the size of the cover, $d_i$ acts as the keyword's attribute and $c_i$ as its value. $C$ provides $\mathcal{D}$ with the attributes $d_1, \ldots, d_\ell$ thus allowing $\mathcal{D}$ to provide the required search tokens to $C$ as specified by the OXT protocol for the OSPIR setting [12] (OXT requires the keyword attribute to generate such token). However, before providing these tokens, $\mathcal{D}$ needs to verify that the total size of the range is under the bound that $C$ is authorized for. $\mathcal{D}$ computes this size using her knowledge of the depths $d_1, \ldots, d_\ell$ by the formula $\sum_{i=1}^{\ell} 2^{t-d_i}$ which gives the number of leaves covered by these depths. This ensures the total size of the range to be under a given bound but the range can be formed of non-consecutive intervals. Importantly, this authorization approach works with any cover selection strategy used by the client.

**Cover Selection.** There remains one *crucial* element to take care of: Making sure that the knowledge of the cover depths $d_1, \ldots, d_\ell$ does not reveal to $\mathcal{D}$ any information other than the total size of the range. Note that the way clients select covers is essentially independent of the mechanisms for processing of range queries described above. Here we analyze some choices for cover selection. The considerations for these choices are both *performance* (e.g. size of the cover) and *privacy.* Privacy-wise the goal is to limit the leakage to server $\mathcal{E}$ and, in the OSPIR case, also to $\mathcal{D}$. In the latter case, the goal is to avoid leakage beyond the size of the range that $\mathcal{D}$ needs to learn in order to check policy compliance. These goals raise general questions regarding *canonical covers* and *minimal over-covers* which we outline below.

A natural cover selection for a given range is one that minimizes the number of nodes in the cover (hence minimizes the number of disjuncts in the search expression). Unfortunately, such cover leaks information beyond the size of a range, namely, it allows to distinguish between ranges of the same size. E.g., ranges $[0, 3]$ and $[1, 4]$ are both of size 4 but the first has a single node as its minimal cover while the latter requires 3 nodes. Clearly, if $\mathcal{C}$ uses such a cover, $\mathcal{D}$ (and possibly $\mathcal{E}$) will be able to distinguish between the two cases.

**Canonical Profiles and Universal Covers.** The above example raises the following question: Given that authorization allows $\mathcal{D}$ to learn the depths of nodes in a cover, is there a way of choosing a cover that only discloses the total size of the range (i.e., does not allow to distinguish between two different ranges of the same size even when the depths are disclosed)? In other words, we want a procedure that given a range produces a cover with a number of nodes and depths that is the same for any two ranges of the same size. We call such covers universal. The existence of universal covers is demonstrated by the cover that uses each leaf in the range as a singleton node in the cover. Can we have a *minimal universal cover*? Next, we answer this question in the affirmative.

**Definition 1.** *The* profile *of a range cover is the multi-set of integers representing the heights of the nodes in the cover. (The* height *of a tree node is its distance from a leaf, i.e., leaves have height 0, their parents height 1, and so on up to the root which has height $t - 1$.) A profile for a range of size $n$ is* universal *if any range of size $n$ has a cover with this profile. A* universal cover *is one whose profile is universal. A universal profile for $n$ is* minimal *if there is a range of size $n$ for which all covers have that profile. (For example, for $n > 2$ the all-leaves cover is universal but not minimal.)*

**Definition 2 (Canonical Profile).** *A profile for ranges of size $n$ is called* canonical *if it is composed of the heights $0, 1, 2, \ldots, L-1$, where $L = \lfloor \log(n + 1) \rfloor$, plus the set of powers ('1' positions) in the binary representation of $n' = n - 2^L + 1$. A* canonical cover *is one whose profile is canonical.*

Example: for $n = 20$ we have $L = 4, n' = 5$, and the canonical profile is $\{0, 1, 2, 3, 0, 2\}$ where the last $0, 2$ correspond to the binary representation 101 of 5 (note that $20 = 2^0 + 2^1 + 2^2 + 2^3 + 2^0 + 2^2$).

**Lemma 1.** *For every integer $n > 0$ the canonical profile of ranges of size $n$ is universal and minimal (and the only such profile).*

The proof of this lemma is presented in the full version [10] where we also present a simple procedure to compute a canonical cover for any range. (A similar notion has been used, independently and in a different context, in [15]).

**3-node Universal Over-Covers.** The canonical cover has the important property of not leaking any information to $\mathcal{D}$ beyond the size of the range (that $\mathcal{D}$ needs to learn anyway to authorize a query). However, the number of nodes in a canonical cover can leak information on the range size to server $\mathcal{E}$ (assuming that $\mathcal{E}$ knows that a given disjunction corresponds to a range query). Another drawback is that canonical covers may include $2 \log n$ nodes. Ideally, we would like to use covers with a small and fixed number of nodes that also have *universal profiles*, i.e., any two ranges of a given size will always be represented by covers with the same depths profile. While we show this to be impossible for exact covers, we obtain covers with the above properties by allowing false-positives, i.e., covers that may include elements outside the requested range, hence we call them *over-covers*. In the full version [10] we instantiate this approach for 3-node universal over-covers.

# 4 Substring Queries

Our substring-search capable SSE scheme is based on the conjunctive-search SSE protocol OXT of [5], and it extends that protocol as follows: Whereas the OXT scheme of [5] supported efficient retrieval of records containing several required keywords at once (i.e. satisfying a *conjunction* of several keyword-equality search terms), our extension supports efficient retrieval of records containing the required keywords *at required relative positions to one another*. This extension of conjunctive search with positional distance criteria allows us to handle several query types common in text-based information retrieval. To simplify the description, and using the notation from Sect. 2, consider a database $\mathsf{DB} = (\mathsf{ind}_i, T_i)$ containing records with just one free text attribute, i.e. where each record $T_i$ is a text string. We support the following types of queries $q$:

**Substring Query.** Here $q$ is a text string, and $\mathsf{DB}(q)$ returns all $\mathsf{ind}_i$ s.t. $T_i$ contains $q$ as a substring.

**Wildcard Query.** Here $q$ is a text string which can contain wildcard characters $'?'$ (matching any single character), and $\mathsf{DB}(q)$ returns all $\mathsf{ind}_i$ s.t. $T_i$ contains a substring $q'$ s.t. for all $j$ from 1 to $|q|$, $q_j =' ?' \lor q_j = q'_j$, where $q_j$ and $q'_j$ denote $j$-th characters in strings $q$ and $q'$. If the query should match only prefixes (suffixes) of $T_i$, the query can be prefixed (suffixed) with a $'^\wedge'$ ($'\$'$).

**Phrase Query.** Here $q$ is a sequence of words, i.e. text strings, $q = (q^1, \ldots, q^l)$, where each $q^i$ can equal to a wildcard character $'?'$. Records $T_i$ in $\mathsf{DB}$ are also represented as sequences of words, $T_i = (T_i^1, \ldots, T_i^n)$. $\mathsf{DB}(q)$ returns all $\mathsf{ind}_i$ s.t. for some $k$ and for all $j$ from 1 to $l$, it holds that $q^j =' ?' \lor q^j = T_i^{k+j}$. (Note that phrase queries allow a match of a single wildcard with a whole word of any size, while in a wildcard query a single wildcard can match only a single character).

All these query types utilize the same crypto machinery that we describe next for the substring case. In Sect. 4.2 we explain briefly how to adapt the techniques to these queries too.

## 4.1   Basic SSE Substring Search

Here we present protocol SUB-SSE-OXT that supports substring search in the basic SSE model (i.e., a single client $\mathcal{C}$ outsources its encrypted database to server $\mathcal{E}$) and where the query consists of a single substring. This simpler case allows us to explain and highlight the basic ideas that we also use for addressing the general case of boolean expressions that admit substrings as the expression terms as well as for extending these solutions to the more involved MC and OSPIR settings.

Figure 1 describes the protocol where shadowed text highlights the changes with respect to the original OXT protocol from [5] for resolving conjunctive queries in the SSE model (the reader can visualize the underlying OXT protocol by omitting the shadowed text). We first explain the basic rationale and functioning of the conjunctive-search OXT protocol, and then we explain how we extend it by imposing additional constraints on *relative positions* of the searched terms, and how this translates into support for substring-search SSE.

**The Conjunctive SSE Scheme OXT.** Let $q = (w_1, \ldots, w_n)$ be a conjunctive query where $\mathsf{DB}(q) = \cap_{i=1}^n \mathsf{DB}(w_i)$. Let $F_G$ be a Pseudorandom Function (PRF) with key $K_G$. (This PRF will map onto a cyclic group $G$, hence the name). Let the setup algorithm create as metadata a set of (keyed) hashes XSet, named for "cross-check set", containing the hash values $\mathsf{xtag}_{w,\mathsf{ind}} = F_G(K_G, (w, \mathsf{ind}))$ for all keywords $w \in \mathsf{W}$ and records $\mathsf{ind} \in \mathsf{DB}(w)$. Let the setup also create the metadata needed to quickly retrieve the set of record indexes $\mathsf{DB}(w)$ matching any given *single* keyword $w \in \mathsf{W}$. The OXT protocol is based on a simple conjunctive *plaintext* search algorithm which identifies all records corresponding to a conjunctive query $q = (w_1, \ldots, w_n)$ as follows: It first identifies the set of indexes $\mathsf{DB}(w_1)$ satisfying the first term $w_1$, called an *s-term*, and then for each $\mathsf{ind} \in \mathsf{DB}(w_1)$ it returns ind as part of $\mathsf{DB}(q)$ if and only if hash value $\mathsf{xtag}_{w_i,\mathsf{ind}} = F_G(K_G, (w_i, \mathsf{ind}))$ is in XSet for all *x-terms* (i.e. "cross-check terms") $w_2, \ldots, w_n$. If group $G$ is sufficiently large then except for negligible collision probability, if $\mathsf{xtag}_{w_i,\mathsf{ind}} \in \mathsf{XSet}$ for $i \geq 2$ then $\mathsf{ind} \in \cap_{i=2}^n \mathsf{DB}(w_i)$, and since ind was taken from $\mathsf{DB}(w_1)$ it follows that $\mathsf{ind} \in \mathsf{DB}(q)$. Since this algorithm runs in $O(|\mathsf{DB}(w_1)|)$ time $w_1$ should be chosen as the least frequent keyword in $q$.

To implement the above protocol over *encrypted* data the OXT protocol modifies it in three ways: First, the metadata supporting retrieval of $\mathsf{DB}(w)$ is implemented using single-keyword SSE techniques, specifically the *Oblivious Storage* data structure TSet [4,5], named for "tuples set", which reveals to server $\mathcal{E}$ only the total number of keyword occurrences in the database, $\sum_{w \in \mathsf{W}} |\mathsf{DB}(w)|$, but hides all other information about individual sets $\mathsf{DB}(w)$ except those actually retrieved during search. (A TSet can be implemented very efficiently as a hash table using PRF $F$ whose key $K_T$ is held by client $\mathcal{C}$, see [4,5]). Secondly, the information stored for each $w$ in the TSet datastructure, denoted $\mathsf{TSet}(w)$, which $\mathcal{E}$ can recover from TSet given $F(K_T, w)$, is not the plaintext set of indexes $\mathsf{DB}(w)$ but the encrypted version of these indexes using a special-purpose encryption. Namely, a tuple corresponding to the $c$-th index $\mathsf{ind}_c$ in $\mathsf{DB}(w)$ (arbitrarily ordered) contains value $y_c = F_p(K_I, \mathsf{ind}_c) \cdot F_p(K_z, c)^{-1}$, an element in a prime-order group $Z_p$ where $F_p$ is a PRF onto $Z_p$, and $K_I, K_z$ are two PRF keys where $K_I$ is global and $K_z$ is specific to keyword $w$. This encryption enables fast secure computation of hash $\mathsf{xtag}_{w_i, \mathsf{ind}_c}$ between client $\mathcal{C}$ and server $\mathcal{E}$, where $\mathcal{E}$ holds ciphertext $y_c = F_p(K_I, \mathsf{ind}_c) \cdot F_p(K_z, c)^{-1}$ of $c$-th index $\mathsf{ind}_c$ taken from $\mathsf{TSet}(w_1)$ and $\mathcal{C}$ holds keyword $w_i$ and keys $K_I, K_z$. Let $F_G(K_G, (w, \mathsf{ind})) = g^{F_p(K_X, w) \cdot F_p(K_I, \mathsf{ind})}$ where $g$ generates group $G$ and $K_G = (K_X, K_I)$ where $K_X$ is a PRF key. $\mathcal{C}$ then sends to $\mathcal{E}$:

$$\mathsf{xtoken}[c, i] = g^{F_p(K_X, w_i) \cdot F_p(K_z, c)}$$

for $i = 2, \ldots, h$ and $c = 1, \ldots, |\mathsf{TSet}(w_1)|$, and $\mathcal{E}$ computes $F_G(K_G, (w_i, \mathsf{ind}_c))$ for each $c, i$ as:

$$(\mathsf{xtoken}[c, i])^{y_c} = (\mathsf{xtoken}[c, i])^{F_p(K_I, \mathsf{ind}_c) \cdot F_p(K_z, c)^{-1}}$$

Since $K_z$ is specific to $w_1$ mask $z_c = F_p(K_z, c)$ applied to $\mathsf{ind}_c$ in $y_c$ is a one-time pad, hence this protocol reveals only the intended values $F_G(K_G, (w_i, \mathsf{ind}_c))$ for all $\mathsf{ind}_c \in \mathsf{DB}(w_1)$ and $w_2, \ldots, w_n$.

**Extending OXT to Substring SSE.** The basic idea for supporting substring search is first to represent a substring query as a conjunction of k-grams (strings of length $k$) at given relative distances from each other (e.g., a substring query *'yptosys'* can be represented as a conjunction of a 3-gram *'tos'* and 3-grams *'ypt'* and *'sys'* at relative distances $-2$ and $2$ from the first 3-gram, respectively), and then to extend the conjunctive search protocol OXT of [5] so that it verifies not only whether the conjunctive terms all occur within the same document, but also that they occur at positions whose relative distances are specified by the query terms. We call representation of a substring $q$ as a set of k-grams with relative distances a *tokenization* of $q$. We denote the *tokenizer* algorithm as $T$, and we denote its results as $T(q) = (\mathsf{kg}_1, (\Delta_2, \mathsf{kg}_2), \ldots, (\Delta_h, \mathsf{kg}_h))$ where $\Delta_i$ are any non-zero integer values, including negatives, e.g. $T(\text{'yptosys'})$ can output $(\text{'tos'}, (-2, \text{'ypt'}), (2, \text{'sys'}))$, but many other tokenizations of the same string are possible. We call k-gram $\mathsf{kg}_1$ an *s-gram* and the remaining k-grams *x-grams*, in parallel to the s-term and x-term terminology of OXT, and as in OXT the s-gram should be chosen as the least frequent k-gram in the tokenization of $q$. Let KG be a list of k-grams which occur in DB. Let $\mathsf{DB}(\mathsf{kg})$ be the set of $(\mathsf{ind}, \mathsf{pos})$ pairs s.t. $\mathsf{DB}[\mathsf{ind}]$ contains k-gram $\mathsf{kg}$ at position $\mathsf{pos}$, and let $\mathsf{DB}(\mathsf{ind}, \mathsf{kg})$ be the set of $\mathsf{pos}$'s s.t. $(\mathsf{ind}, \mathsf{pos}) \in \mathsf{DB}(\mathsf{kg})$.

The basic idea of the above conjuctive-search protocol to handling substrings is that the hashes $\mathsf{xtag}$ inserted into the XSet will use PRF $F_G$ applied to a *triple* $(\mathsf{kg}, \mathsf{ind}, \mathsf{pos})$ for each $\mathsf{kg} \in \mathsf{KG}$ and $(\mathsf{ind}, \mathsf{pos}) \in \mathsf{DB}(\mathsf{kg})$, and when processing search query $q$ where $T(q) = (\mathsf{kg}_1, (\Delta_2, \mathsf{kg}_2), \ldots, (\Delta_h, \mathsf{kg}_h))$, server $\mathcal{E}$ will return (encrypted) index $\mathsf{ind}$ corresponding to some $(\mathsf{ind}_c, \mathsf{pos}_c)$ *pair* in $\mathsf{DB}(\mathsf{kg}_1)$ if and only if

$$F_G(K_G, (\mathsf{kg}_i, \mathsf{ind}_c, \mathsf{pos}_c + \Delta_i)) \in \mathsf{XSet} \text{ for } i = 2, \ldots, h$$

---

**Setup(DB, RDK)**

- Select keys $K_S$, $K_T$ for PRF $F_\tau$ and $K_I, K_X$ for PRF $F_p$, and parse DB as $(\text{ind}_i, \mathbf{pos}_i, \text{kg}_i)_{i=1}^d$. (PRF $F_\tau$ maps onto $\{0,1\}^\tau$ and $F_p$ onto $Z_p$.)
- Initialize **T** to an empty array and XSet to an empty set. For each **k-gram kg $\in$ KG** do the following:
  - Set strap $\leftarrow F_\tau(K_S, \text{kg})$, $(K_z, K_e, K_u) \leftarrow (F_\tau(\text{strap}, 1), F_\tau(\text{strap}, 2), F_\tau(\text{strap}, 3))$.
  - For $c = 1, \ldots, |\text{DB(kg)}|$, for $(\text{ind}, \mathbf{pos})$ a $c$-th tuple in DB(kg) (randomly permuted) do:
    - Set rdk $\leftarrow$ RDK(ind), $e \leftarrow \text{Enc}(K_e, (\text{ind}|\text{rdk}))$, xind $\leftarrow F_p(K_I, \text{ind})$.
    - Set xtag $\leftarrow g^{F_p(K_X, \text{kg}) \cdot \text{xind}^{\mathbf{pos}}}$ and add xtag to XSet.
    - Set $z \leftarrow F_p(K_z, c)$, $u \leftarrow F_p(K_u, c)$, $y \leftarrow \text{xind} \cdot z^{-1}$, $v \leftarrow \text{xind}^{\mathbf{pos}} \cdot u^{-1}$.
    - Append $(e, y, v)$ to **T**[kg].
- Set TSet $\leftarrow$ TSetSetup(**T**, $\langle F_\tau \rangle, K_T$). Output $K = (K_S, K_X, K_T)$ and EDB $= (\text{TSet}, \text{XSet})$.

**Search protocol**

Client $\mathcal{C}$, on input $K = (K_S, K_X, K_T)$ defined above and query $q$ s.t. $T(q) = (\text{kg}_1, (\Delta_2, \text{kg}_2), \ldots, (\Delta_h, \text{kg}_h))$:

- Set stag $\leftarrow F_\tau(K_T, \text{kg}_1)$, strap $\leftarrow F_\tau(K_S, \text{kg}_1)$.
- $(K_z, K_e, K_u) \leftarrow (F_\tau(\text{strap}, 1), F_\tau(\text{strap}, 2), F_\tau(\text{strap}, 3))$, and $\{\text{xtrap}_i \leftarrow g^{F_p(K_X, \text{kg}_i)}\}_{i=2}^h$.
- Send (stag, $\Delta_2, \ldots, \Delta_h$) to $\mathcal{E}$, and for $c = 1, 2, \ldots,$ until $\mathcal{E}$ sends stop, do the following:
  - Set $z_c \leftarrow F_p(K_z, c)$, $u_c \leftarrow F_p(K_u, c)$, and $\{\text{xtoken}[c, i] \leftarrow (\text{xtrap}_i)^{((z_c)^{\Delta_i} \cdot (u_c))}\}_{i=2}^h$.
  - Send xtoken$[c] = (\text{xtoken}[c, 2], \ldots, \text{xtoken}[c, h])$ to $\mathcal{E}$.

Server $\mathcal{E}$, on input EDB $= (\text{TSet}, \text{XSet})$, responds with a set ESet formed as follows:

- On message (stag, $\Delta_2, \ldots, \Delta_n$) from $\mathcal{C}$, retrieve $t \leftarrow$ TSetRetrieve(TSet, stag) from TSet.
- For $c = 1, \ldots, |t|$, retrieve $c$-th tuple $(e, y, v)$ in **t**.
- On xtoken$[c]$ from $\mathcal{C}$, add $e$ to ESet if $\forall i = 2, \ldots, h : (\text{xtoken}[c, i])^{(y^{\Delta_i} \cdot v)} \in$ XSet. When $c = |t|$ send stop to $\mathcal{C}$.

Client $\mathcal{C}$ computes $(\text{ind}|\text{rdk}) \leftarrow \text{Dec}(K_e, e)$ for each $e$ in ESet and adds $(\text{ind}, \text{rdk})$ to its output.

---

**Fig. 1.** SUB-SSE-OXT: SSE Protocol for Substring Search (shadowed text indicates additions to the basic OXT protocol for supporting substring queries)

To support this modified search over encrypted data the setup procedure Setup(DB, RDK) forms EDB as a pair of data structures TSet and XSet as in OXT, except that keywords are replaced by k-grams and both the encrypted tuples in TSet and the hashes xtag in XSet will be modified by the position-related information as follows. First, the tuple corresponding to the $c$-th (index,position) pair $(\text{ind}_c, \text{pos}_c)$ in DB(kg) will contain value $y_c = F_p(K_I, \text{ind}_c) \cdot F_p(K_z, c)^{-1}$ together with a new position-related value $v_c = F_p(K_I, \text{ind}_c)^{\text{pos}_c} \cdot F_p(K_u, c)^{-1}$, where $K_z, K_u$ are independent PRF keys specific to kg. Secondly, XSet will contain values computed as:

$$F_G((K_X, K_I), (\text{kg}, \text{ind}, \text{pos})) = g^{F_p(K_X, \text{kg}) \cdot F_p(K_I, \text{ind})^{\text{pos}}} \tag{1}$$

In the Search protocol, client $\mathcal{C}$ will tokenize its query $q$ as $T(q) = (\text{kg}_1, (\Delta_2, \text{kg}_2), \ldots, (\Delta_h, \text{kg}_h))$, send $\text{stag}_{\text{kg}_1} = F_T(K_T, \text{kg}_1)$ to server $\mathcal{E}$, who uses it to retrieve $\text{TSet}(\text{kg}_1)$ from $\text{TSet}$, send the position-shift vectors $(\Delta_2, \ldots, \Delta_h)$ to $\mathcal{E}$, and then, in order for $\mathcal{E}$ to compute $F_G(K_G, (\text{kg}_i, \text{ind}_c, \text{pos}_c + \Delta_i))$ for all $c, i$ pairs, client $\mathcal{C}$ sends to $\mathcal{E}$:

$$\text{xtoken}[c, i] = g^{F_p(K_X, \text{kg}_i) \cdot (F_p(K_z, c))^{\Delta_i} \cdot F_p(K_u, c)}$$

which lets $\mathcal{E}$ compute $F_G(\text{kg}_i, \text{ind}_c, \text{pos}_c + \Delta_i)$ as $(\text{xtoken}[c, i])$ exponentiated to power $(y_c)^{\Delta_i} \cdot v_c$ for $(y_c, v_c)$ in the $c$-th tuple in $\text{TSet}(\text{kg}_1)$, which computes correctly because

$$y_c^{\Delta_i} \cdot v_c = F_p(K_I, \text{ind}_c)^{\Delta_i + \text{pos}_c} \cdot F_p(K_z, c)^{-\Delta_i} \cdot F_p(K_u, c)^{-1}$$

## 4.2 Wildcards and Phrase Queries

Any sequence of single character wildcards within regular substring queries can be handled by changing tokenization to allow gaps in the query string covered by the computed tokens, e.g. $T('ypt??yst')$ would output $('ypt', (5, 'yst'))$.

In addition to support *wildcard queries* matching prefixes and/or suffixes, we add special "anchor" tokens at the beginning $('\hat{\ }')$ and end $('\$')$ of every record to mark the text boundaries. These anchors are then added during tokenization. This allows searching for substrings at fixed positions within a record. For these queries $T('ypt??yst')$ would output $('\hat{\ }yp', (1, 'ypt'), (6, 'yst'), (7, 'st\$'))$.

Still, this simple change limits us to queries which contain $k$ consecutive characters in-between every substring of wildcards. However, we can remove this restriction if we add to the XSet all unigrams (i.e. $k = 1$) occurring in a text in addition to the original k-grams.

Adding support for phrase queries is another simple change to the way we parse DB. Instead of parsing by (k-gram, position) pairs, we parse each record by (word, position). Tokenization of $q$ then becomes splitting $q$ into its component words and relative position of each word to the s-term word. As with substrings, wildcards in $q$ result in a gap in the returned $\Delta$'s.

## 4.3 Substring Protocol Extensions

Due to space limitations (this material is available from the authors upon request), we only discuss briefly the extensions to the above SUB-SSE-OXT protocol needed to support richer functionality as well as the MC and OSPIR settings. A first extension extends the single-substring of SUB-SSE-OXT to any Boolean query where atomic terms can be formed by any number of substring search terms and/or exact keyword terms. Moreover, the user can specify as an s-term either one of the exact keyword terms or a k-gram in one of the substring terms. We call the resulting protocol MIXED-SSE-OXT, so named because it freely *mixes* substring and exact keyword search terms. The ability to handle Boolean formulas on exact keywords together with substring terms comes from the similarities between substring-handling SUB-SSE-OXT and Boolean-formula-handling OXT of [5]. However, one significant adjustment needed to put the two together is to disassociate the position-related information $v_c$ in the tuples in $\mathsf{TSet(kg)}$ from the index-related information $y_c$ in these tuples. This is because when all k-gram terms are x-terms (as would be the case e.g. when an exact keyword is chosen as an s-term) then $\mathcal{E}$ must identify the position-related information pertaining to a particular $(\mathsf{kg}, \mathsf{ind})$ pair given the $(\mathsf{kg}, \mathsf{ind})$-related xtoken value. Our MIXED-SSE-OXT protocol supports this by adding another oblivious $\mathsf{TSet}$-like datastructure which uses $\mathsf{xtag_{kg,ind}}$ to retrieve the position-related information, i.e. the $v_c$'s, for all $\mathsf{pos} \in \mathsf{DB(ind, kg)}$.

A second extension generalizes the SUB-SSE-OXT protocol to the OSPIR setting [12] where $\mathcal{D}$ can *obliviously* enable third-party clients $\mathcal{C}$ to compute the search-enabling tokens (see Sect. 2). The main ingredient in this extension is the usage of Oblivious PRF (OPRF) evaluation for several PRF functions used in MIXED-SSE-OXT for computing search tokens. Another important component is a novel protocol which securely computes the $\mathsf{xtag_{kg,ind,pos}}$ values given these obliviously-generated trapdoors, in a way which avoids leaking any partial-match information to $\mathcal{C}$. This protocol uses bilinear maps which results in a significant slowdown compared to the MIXED-SSE-OXT in the Client-Server setting. Fortunately, for the Multi-Client (MC) setting where the third-party clients' queries are not hidden from the database owner $\mathcal{D}$, we can simplify this xtag-computation protocol, in particular eliminating the usage of bilinear maps, and making the resulting protocol MIXED-MC-OXT almost equal in cost to the underlying MIXED-SSE-OXT protocol.

## 5    Security Analysis

Privacy of an SSE scheme, in the SSE, Multi-Client, or OSPIR settings, is quantified by a *leakage profile* $\mathcal{L}$, which is a function of the database $\mathsf{DB}$ and the sequence of client's queries $\mathbf{q}$. We call an SSE scheme $\mathcal{L}$-*semantically-secure* against party $P$ (which can be $\mathcal{C}$, $\mathcal{E}$, or $\mathcal{D}$) if for all $\mathsf{DB}$ and $\mathbf{q}$, the entirety of $P$'s view of an execution of the SSE scheme on database $\mathsf{DB}$ and $\mathcal{C}$'s sequence of queries $\mathbf{q}$ is efficiently *simulatable* given only $\mathcal{L}(\mathsf{DB}, \mathbf{q})$. We say that the scheme is *adaptively* secure if the queries in $\mathbf{q}$ can be set adaptively by the adversary based on their current view of the protocol execution. An efficient simulation of a party's view in the protocol means that everything that the protocol exposes to this party carries no more information than what is revealed by the $\mathcal{L}(\mathsf{DB}, \mathbf{q})$ function. Therefore specification of the $\mathcal{L}$ function fully characterizes the privacy quality of the solution: What it reveals about data $\mathsf{DB}$ and queries $\mathbf{q}$, and thus also what it hides. (See [5,12] for a more formal exposition.)

**Security of Range Queries.** Below we state the security of the range query protocol for stand-alone range queries and we informally comment on the case of range queries that are parts of composite (e.g., Boolean) queries. See full version [10] for a more complete security treatment of range queries. We consider adaptive security against honest-but-curious and non-colluding servers $\mathcal{E}, \mathcal{D}$, and against fully malicious clients. For query $q^j = \mathsf{RQ}(a^j, b^j)$, let $((d_1^j, c_1^j), \ldots,$ $(d_t^j, c_t^j))$ be the tree cover of interval $[a^j, b^j]$ and let $w_i^j = (d_i^j, c_i^j)$. We define three leakage functions for $\mathcal{D}, \mathcal{E}, \mathcal{C}$, respectively:

- $\mathcal{L}_{\mathcal{D}}(\mathsf{DB}, (q^1, \ldots, q^m))$ includes the query type ("range" in this case), the attribute to which $q^j$ pertains, and the size of the range $b^j - a^j + 1$, for each $q^j$.
- $\mathcal{L}_{\mathcal{E}}(\mathsf{DB}, (q^1, \ldots, q^m)) = \mathcal{L}_{\mathsf{OXT}}(\mathsf{DB}, (w_1^1, \ldots, w_t^m))$ where the latter function represents the leakage to server $\mathcal{E}$ in the OXT protocol for a query series that includes all $w_i^j$'s. By the analysis of [5], this leakage contains the TSet leakage (which in our TSet implementation is just the total number of document-keyword pairs in DB), the sequence $\{(|\mathsf{DB}(w_i^j)| : (i, j) = (1, 1), \ldots, (t, m)\}$, i.e., the number of elements in each $\mathsf{DB}(w_i^j)$, and the result set returned by the query (in the form of encrypted records).
- $\mathcal{L}_{\mathcal{C}}(\mathsf{DB}, (q^1, \ldots, q^m)) = \emptyset$.

**Theorem 1.** *The range protocol from Sect. 3 is secure in the OSPIR model with respect to $\mathcal{D}, \mathcal{E}, \mathcal{C}$ with leakage profiles $\mathcal{L}_{\mathcal{D}}, \mathcal{L}_{\mathcal{E}}, \mathcal{L}_{\mathcal{C}}$, respectively.*

The leakage functions for $\mathcal{D}$ and $\mathcal{C}$ are as good as possible: $\mathcal{D}$ only learns the information needed to enforce authorization, namely the attribute and size of the range, while there is no leakage at all to the client. The only non-trivial leakage is $\mathcal{E}$'s which leaks the number of documents matching each disjunct or, equivalently, the size of each sub-range in the range cover. The leakage to $\mathcal{D}$ remains the same also when the range query is part of a composite query. For the client this is also the case except that when the range query is the s-term of a Boolean expression, the client also learns an upper bound on the sizes $|\mathsf{DB}(w_i^j)|$ for all $i, j$. For $\mathcal{E}$, a composite query having range as its s-term is equivalent to $tm$ separate expressions $w_i^j$ as in [5] (with reduced leakage due to disjoint s-terms), and if the range term is an x-term in a composite query then $w_i^j$'s leak the same as if they were x-terms in a conjunction.

**Security of Substring Queries.** Here we state the security of protocol SUB-SSE-OXT against server $\mathcal{E}$. Our security arguments are based on the following assumptions: the T-set implementation is secure against adaptive adversaries [4,5]; $F_p$ and $F_\tau$ are secure pseudorandom functions; the hash function $H$ is modeled as a random oracle; and the q-DDH assumption [1] holds in $G$.[1]

The security analysis follows the corresponding argument in [5] adapting the leakage profile to the substring case.

*Leakage to Server $\mathcal{E}$.* We represent a sequence of $Q$ non-adaptive substring queries by $\mathbf{q} = (\mathbf{s}, \mathbf{x}, \boldsymbol{\Delta})$ s.t. $(\mathbf{s}[i], (\mathbf{x}[i], \boldsymbol{\Delta}[i]))$ is the tokenization $T(\mathbf{q}[i])$ of the $i$-th substring query $\mathbf{q}[i]$, where $\mathbf{s}[i], \mathbf{x}[i]$ are k-grams, and $\boldsymbol{\Delta}[i]$ is an integer between $-k+1$ and $k-1$. For notation simplicity we assume that vector $\mathbf{q}$ does not contain repeated queries, although $\mathcal{E}$ would learn that a repeated query has been made.

---

[1] Our extension to the OSPIR model relies on the One-More Gap Diffie-Hellman assumption and the linear DH assumption [2,22] on bilinear groups.

Function $\mathcal{L}_{\mathcal{E}}(\mathsf{DB}, \mathbf{q})$ which specifies leakage to $\mathcal{E}$ outputs $(N, \bar{\mathbf{s}}, \mathsf{SP}, \mathsf{RP}, \mathsf{DP}, \mathsf{IP})$, defined as follows:

- The $(N, \bar{\mathbf{s}}, \mathsf{SP}, \mathsf{RP})$ part of this leakage is exactly the same as in the conjunctive SSE protocol SSE-OXT of [5] on which our substring-search SUB-SSE-OXT protocol is based. $N = \sum_{i=1}^{d} |\mathsf{W}_i|$ is the total number of appearances of all k-grams in all the documents, and it is revealed simply by the size of the EDB metadata. $\bar{\mathbf{s}} \in [m]^Q$ is the *equality pattern* of $\mathbf{s} \in \mathsf{KG}^Q$ indicating which queries have the equal s-terms. For example, if $\mathbf{s} = (abc, abc, xyz, pqr, abc, pqr, def, xyz, pqr)$ then $\bar{\mathbf{s}} = (1, 1, 2, 3, 1, 3, 4, 2, 3)$. $\mathsf{SP}$ is the *s-term support size* which is the number of occurrences of the s-term k-gram in the database, i.e. $\mathsf{SP}[i] = |\mathsf{DB}(\mathbf{s}[i])|$. Finally, $\mathsf{RP}$ is the *results pattern*, i.e. $\mathsf{RP}[i]$ is the set of $(\mathsf{ind}, \mathsf{pos})$ pairs where $\mathsf{ind}$ is an identifier of document which matches the query $q$, and $\mathsf{pos}$ is a position of the s-term k-gram $\mathbf{s}[i]$ in that document.
- $\mathsf{DP}$ is the *Delta pattern* $\boldsymbol{\Delta}[i]$ of the queries, i.e. the shifts between k-grams in a query which result from the tokenization of the queries.
- $\mathsf{IP}$ is the *conditional intersection pattern*, which is a $Q$ by $Q$ table $\mathsf{IP}$ defined as follows: $\mathsf{IP}[i, j] = \emptyset$ if $i = j$ or $\mathbf{x}[i] \neq \mathbf{x}[j]$. Otherwise, $\mathsf{IP}[i, j]$ is the set of all triples $(\mathsf{ind}, \mathsf{pos}, \mathsf{pos}')$ (possibly empty) s.t. $(\mathsf{ind}, \mathsf{pos}) \in \mathsf{DB}(\mathbf{s}[i])$, $(\mathsf{ind}, \mathsf{pos}') \in \mathsf{DB}(\mathbf{s}[j])$, and $\mathsf{pos}' = \mathsf{pos} + (\boldsymbol{\Delta}[i] - \boldsymbol{\Delta}[j])$.

*Understanding Leakage Components.* Parameter $N$ is the size of the meta-data, and leaking such a bound is unavoidable. The equality pattern $\bar{\mathbf{s}}$, which leaks repetitions in the s-term k-gram of different substring queries, and the s-term support size $\mathsf{SP}$, which leaks the total number of occurrences of this s-term in the database, are both a consequence of the optimized search that singles out the s-term in the query, which we adopt from the conjunctive SSE search solution of [5]. $\mathsf{RP}$ is the result of the query and therefore no real leakage in the context of SSE. Note also that the $\mathsf{RP}$ over-estimates the information $\mathcal{E}$ observes, because $\mathcal{E}$ observes only a pointer to the encrypted document, and a pointer to the encrypted tuple storing a unique $(\mathsf{ind}, \mathsf{pos})$ pair, but not the pair $(\mathsf{ind}, \mathsf{pos})$ itself. $\mathsf{DP}$ reflects the fact that our protocols leak the relative shifts $\Delta$ between k-grams which result from tokenization of the searched string. If tokenization was canonical, and divided a substring into k-grams based only on the substring length, the shifts $\Delta$ would reveal only the substring length. (Otherwise, see below for how $\Delta$'s can be hidden from $\mathcal{E}$).

The $\mathsf{IP}$ component is the most subtle. It is a consequence of the fact that when processing the $\mathbf{q}[i]$ query $\mathcal{E}$ computes the (pseudo)random function $F_G(\mathbf{x}[i], \mathsf{ind}, \mathsf{pos} + \boldsymbol{\Delta}[i])$ for all $(\mathsf{ind}, \mathsf{pos}) \in \mathsf{DB}(\mathbf{s}[i])$, and hence can see collisions in it. Consequently, if two queries $\mathbf{q}[i]$ and $\mathbf{q}[j]$ have the same x-gram then for any document $\mathsf{ind}$ which contains the s-grams $\mathbf{s}[i]$ and $\mathbf{s}[j]$ in positions, respectively, $\mathsf{pos}$ and $\mathsf{pos}' = \mathsf{pos} + (\boldsymbol{\Delta}[i] - \boldsymbol{\Delta}[j])$, server $\mathcal{E}$ can observe a collision in $F_G$ and triple $(\mathsf{ind}, \mathsf{pos}, \mathsf{pos}')$ will be included in the $\mathsf{IP}$ leakage. Note, however, that $\mathsf{IP}[i, j]$ defined above overstates this leakage, because $\mathcal{E}$ does not learn the $\mathsf{ind}, pos_i, pos_j$ values themselves, but only establishes a link between two *encrypted* tuples, the one containing $(\mathsf{ind}, \mathsf{pos})$ in $\mathsf{TSet}(\mathbf{s}[i])$ and the one containing $(\mathsf{ind}, \mathsf{pos}')$ in $\mathsf{TSet}(\mathbf{s}[j])$. To visualize the type of queries which will trigger this leakage, take $k = 3$, $\mathbf{q}[i]$ = *MOTHER*, $\mathbf{q}[j]$ = *OTHER*, and let $\mathbf{q}[i]$ and $\mathbf{q}[j]$ tokenize with a common x-gram, e.g. $T(\mathbf{q}[i]) = (\text{MOT}, (\text{HER}, 3))$ and $T(\mathbf{q}[j]) = (\text{OTH}, (\text{HER}, 2))$. The $\mathsf{IP}[i, j]$ leakage will contain tuple $(\mathsf{ind}, \mathsf{pos}, \mathsf{pos}')$ for $\mathsf{pos}' = \mathsf{pos} + (\Delta[i] - \Delta[j]) = \mathsf{pos} + 1$ iff record DB[ind] contains 3-gram $\mathbf{s}[i] = \text{MOT}$ at position $\mathsf{pos}$ and 3-gram $\mathbf{s}[j] = \text{OTH}$ at position $\mathsf{pos} + 1$, i.e. iff it contains substring MOTH.

**Theorem 2.** *Protocol SUB-SSE-OXT (restricted to substrings which tokenize into two k-grams) is adaptively $\mathcal{L}_{\mathcal{E}}$-semantically-secure against malicious server $\mathcal{E}$, assuming the security of the PRF's, the encryption scheme* Enc, *and the* TSet *scheme, the random oracle model for hash functions, and the q-DDH assumption on the group $G$ of prime order.*

The proof of Theorem 2 is presented in the full version [10].

# A   Implementation and Performance

Here we provide testing and performance information for our prototype implementation of the range and SUB-SSE-OXT protocols described in Sects. 3 and 4.1. The results confirm the scalability of our solutions to very large databases and complex queries. The prototype is an extension of the OXT implementation of [4]. Both the description of the changes and performance information are limited, to the extent possible, to the protocols introduced in this paper. An extensive evaluation of the prototype is outside of the scope of this paper as it would be highly dependent on previous work.

**Prototype Summary.** The three components of our system are the preprocessor, the server, and the client. The preprocessor generates the encrypted database from the cleartext data. The client, which implements a representative set of SQL commands, 'encrypts' end-user requests and 'decrypts' server responses. The server uses the encrypted database to answer client SELECT-type queries or expands the encrypted database on UPDATE, INSERT, and (even) DELETE queries [4].

To support range queries (see Sect. 3) the Boolean-query OXT prototype was augmented with generation of range-specific TSet's at pre-processing, and with range-specific authorization and range-cover computation at the client. Support for substring and wildcard queries required redesigning pre-processing to take into account the k-gram position information, adding support for 'k-gram'-based record tokenization to the client, and changing the Search protocol to support *position-enhanced* computation (see Sect. 4) and authorization. A few other changes were necessary in order to continue handling UPDATE, INSERT and DELETE queries. These extensions largely follow the update mechanics outlined in [4], with the addition of a new PSet$^+$ data structure.

To match the SQL standard, our implementation uses the LIKE operator syntax for substring and wildcard queries: '_' ('%') represent single-character (variable-length) wildcards and the query must match the complete field, i.e., unless a query must match the prefix (suffix) of fields, it should begin (end) with a '%'.

**Experimental Platform.** The experiments described in the remainder of this section were run on two Dell PowerEdge R710 systems, each one of them equipped with two Intel Xeon X5650 processors, 96 GB RAM (12x8 1066 MHz), an embedded Broadcom 1 GB Ethernet with TOE and a PERC H700 RAID controller with a 1 GB Non-Volatile Cache and 1 or 2 daisy-chained MD1200 disk controllers each with 12 2 TB 7.2 k RPM Near-Line SAS hard drives configured for Raid 6 (19 TB and 38 TB total storage per machine).

An automated test harness, written by an independent evaluator [25], drives the evaluation, including the set of queries and the dataset used in the experiments.

**Dataset.** The synthetic dataset used in the reported experiments is a US census-like table with twenty one columns of standard personal information, such as name (first, last), address (street, city, state, zipcode), SSN, etc. The values in each column are generated according to the distributions in the most recent US census. In addition, the table has one XML column with at most 10000 characters, four text columns with varying average lengths (a total of at most 12300 characters or ≈ 2000 words), and a binary column (payload) with a maximum size of 100 KB. Our system can perform structured queries on data in all but the XML and binary columns. The size of (number of records in) the table is a parameter of the dataset generator. We tested on a wide variety of database sizes, but we focus our results on a table with 100 million records or 10 TBytes.

**Cryptographic Algorithms.** Our implementation uses AES-128 for all symmetric key operations (including data encryption), SHA-256 for hashing, and NIST's Elliptic Curve p224 for group operations.

**Experimental Methodology.** In the initial step, the encrypted database is created from the cleartext data stored in a MariaDB (a variant of open-source MySQL RDBMS) table. Then, a per-protocol collection of SQL queries, generated by the harness to test its features, is run against the MariaDB sever and against our system. The queries are issued sequentially by the harness, which also records the results and the execution times of each query. Finally, the harness validates the test results by comparing the result sets from our system and from the MariaDB server. Not only does this step validate the correctness of our system, it also ensures our system meets our theoretical false positive threshold over large, automatically generated, collections of queries.

**Encrypted Index.** We built a searchable index on all personal information columns (twenty one) in the plaintext database but we only use a small subset of these indexes for the following experiments. Note that we support substring and wildcard queries simultaneously over a given column using a single shared index. We built a substring-wildcard index for four columns (average length of 12 characters) and a range index for five columns of varying types (one 64 bit integer, one date, one 32 bit integer, and one enum). Each substring-wildcard index was constructed with a single $k$ value of 4. Each range index has a granularity of one. For the date type, this equates to a day. We support date queries between 0-01-01 and 9999-12-31, and integer queries between 0 and integer max ($2^{32} - 1$ or $2^{64} - 1$).

On average each record generates 256.6 document-keyword pairs (tuples) among all indexes. This equates to a total encrypted index for our largest database of $\approx 20\,\text{TB}$. We back our XSet by an in memory Bloom filter with a false positive rate of $2^{-12}$; this allows us to save unnecessary disk accesses and it does not influence the false positive rate of the system.

**Query Flexibility.** While many queries can be formed by using substring or wildcard queries independently, many queries are not computable. We can greatly increase the number of available queries by combining the two query types. This allows us to answer any query $q$ s.t. all non-wildcard characters in $q$ are part of at least one $k$ length substring containing no wildcards and $q$ starts and ends with a non-wildcard character. This may require a sufficiently large $k$ (a performance benefit) but limit the type of queries supported. To further increase flexibility we can index fields with multiple values for $k$ or with a different $k$ for each data structure: $k_x$ for XSet and $k_s$ for TSet. The result is a very flexible policy that we can support any query $q$ that meets the following: (1) there exists at least one consecutive $k_s$ length sequence of non-wildcards in $q$, (2) all non-wildcard characters in $q$ are part of at least one $k_x$ length substring containing no wildcards, and (3) $q$ starts and ends with a non-wildcard character.

**Performance Costs by Query Type.** Our complex query types have both increased storage overhead and query time costs as compared to the keyword only implementation of [4]. In order to support substring and wildcard queries on a column, we must store additional tuples: for a record of length $l$ (for the indexed field) we must store $(l - k) + 3$ tuples. Note that we must pay this cost for each $k$ we chose to create the index for. The choice of $k$ also affects query time performance. For a query $q$, it's performance is linearly dependent on the number of tokens generated by the tokenization $T(q)$. A smaller $k$ results in a larger number of tokens. Specifically for subsequence queries there will be $\lceil |q|/k \rceil - 1$ xtokens[2]. $k$ also impacts the number of matching documents returned by the s-term. A larger $k$ results in a higher entropy s-term. The choice of $k$ is a careful trade-off between efficiency and flexibility.

Range queries incur storage costs linear in their bit depth. Specifically, $log_2(max\_value)$ tuples are stored for a record for each range field. Notably for date fields this value is 22. In addition we implemented the *canonical cover* from Sect. 3, which results in up to $2 * log_2(max\_value)$ disjunctions.

Phrase queries incur storage costs linear in the total number of words in a column. Specifically for every record with $n$ free-text words, the index stores $n$ tuples. Although phrase queries and free-text queries can be supported via the

---

[2] Wildcard queries pay a similar overhead, related to the size of each contiguous substring within the query.

same index, we have to pay the marginally higher price of the phrase index in which we must store even repeated words.

**Encrypted Search Performance.** We illustrate the performance of our system using the latency (i.e., total time from query issuing to completion) of a large number of representative SELECT queries. The independent evaluator selected a representative set of queries to test the correctness and performance of the range, substring and wildcard queries (phrase queries were not implemented). The two leftmost columns in Table 1 show how many unique queries were selected for each query type. The third, fourth and fifth columns characterize the 95 % fastest queries of each type. Finally, the rightmost column shows the percentage of queries that complete in less than two minutes.

All queries follow the pattern SELECT id FROM CensusTable WHERE ..., with each query having a specific WHERE clause. Range-type queries use the BETWEEN operator to implement two-sided comparison on numerical fields as well as date and enum fields. Specific queries were chosen to assess the performance effect of differing result set sizes and range covers. In particular, in order to assess the effect of cover size, queries with moderate result sets (of size under 10,000) were chosen while the size of cover sets range from a handful to several dozens. The results show relatively homogeneous latencies (all under 0.8 s) in spite of the large variations in cover size, highlighting the moderate effect of cover sizes.

Our instantiation of SUB-SSE-OXT includes extensions for supporting substring and wildcard searches simultaneously. However, to evaluate the effects of each specific extension we measure them individually. Both query types use the LIKE operator in the WHERE clause.

Substring queries use the variable-length wildcard '%' at the beginning, at the end, or at both ends of the LIKE operand, as in WHERE city LIKE '%ttle Falls%'. Wildcard queries use the single-character wildcard ('_') anywhere in the LIKE operand, provided the query criteria dictated by $k$ is still met.

In addition, we noticed that the choice of s-gram dominates the latency of the substring queries. Our analysis shows that low performing queries can often be tied to high-frequency s-terms (e.g., "ing" or "gton"), which are associated with large Tsets. By default, the current implementation uses the first $k$ characters in the pattern string as s-gram. Thus, implementing a tokenization strategy guided by the text statistics (which we leave for future work) can significantly reduce query latency for many of the slow performers. To estimate the potential benefits of such a strategy, we added the STARTAT 'n' option to the LIKE 'pattern' operator, where 'n' is the starting position of the s-gram. Experiments using the '%gton Colle%' pattern show latency improvements of up to 32 times when the s-gram starts at the third or fourth character in the pattern string.

**Comparison to Cleartext Search.** Here we include the most relevant aspects of the performance comparison between our prototype and MariaDB. In the case of the 100 million record database, for ≈ 45 % of the range queries, the two systems have very similar performance. For the remaining 55 %, our system is increasingly (up to 500 times!) faster, admittedly due to MariaDB's lack of support for indexed substring search. The large variations in MariaDB performance

**Table 1.** Latency (in secs) for 10 TByte DB, 100 M records, 25.6 billion record-keyword pairs

| Query type | # of queries | Fastest 95 % | | | % ≤ 120 s |
|---|---|---|---|---|---|
| | | Avg | Min | Max | |
| Range | 197 | .37 | .19 | .61 | 100 |
| Substring | 939 | 40 | 0.22 | 166 | 93 |
| Wildcard | 511 | 31.22 | 6.7 | 224 | 93 |

seem to arise from its reliance on data (and index) caching, which is hindered by large DBs. In contrast, our system issues between $\log_2 s$ and $2 \log_2 s$ disk accesses *in parallel* (where $s$ is the size of the cover). On smaller census databases (with fewer records) that fit in RAM, MariaDB outperforms our system, sometimes by more than one order of magnitude, although in this case all query latencies (ours and MariaDB's) are under a second. For substring and wildcard queries and the largest, 100 million records database, our system outperforms MariaDB by such a large factor largely because MariaDB does not use any index for these queries. Instead, it scans the full database to resolve queries involving the LIKE operator.

# References

1. Boneh, D., Boyen, X.: Efficient selective-id secure identity-based encryption without random oracles. In: Cachin, C., Camenisch, J.L. (eds.) EUROCRYPT 2004. LNCS, vol. 3027, pp. 223–238. Springer, Heidelberg (2004)
2. Boneh, D., Boyen, X., Shacham, H.: Short group signatures. In: Franklin, M. (ed.) CRYPTO 2004. LNCS, vol. 3152, pp. 41–55. Springer, Heidelberg (2004)
3. Boneh, D., Waters, B.: Conjunctive, subset, and range queries on encrypted data. In: Vadhan, S.P. (ed.) TCC 2007. LNCS, vol. 4392, pp. 535–554. Springer, Heidelberg (2007)
4. Cash, D., Jaeger, J., Jarecki, S., Jutla, C., Krawczyk, H., Rosu, M.C., Steiner, M.: Dynamic searchable encryption in very large databases: data structures and implementation. In: Symposium on Network and Distributed Systems Security (NDSS 2014) (2014)
5. Cash, D., Jarecki, S., Jutla, C., Krawczyk, H., Roşu, M.-C., Steiner, M.: Highly-scalable searchable symmetric encryption with support for boolean queries. In: Canetti, R., Garay, J.A. (eds.) CRYPTO 2013, Part I. LNCS, vol. 8042, pp. 353–373. Springer, Heidelberg (2013)
6. Chang, Y.-C., Mitzenmacher, M.: Privacy preserving keyword searches on remote encrypted data. In: Ioannidis, J., Keromytis, A.D., Yung, M. (eds.) ACNS 2005. LNCS, vol. 3531, pp. 442–455. Springer, Heidelberg (2005)
7. Chase, M., Kamara, S.: Structured encryption and controlled disclosure. In: Abe, M. (ed.) ASIACRYPT 2010. LNCS, vol. 6477, pp. 577–594. Springer, Heidelberg (2010)

8. Chase, M., Shen, E.: Pattern matching encryption. Cryptology ePrint Archive, Report 2014/638 (2014). http://eprint.iacr.org/
9. Curtmola, R., Garay, J.A., Kamara, S., Ostrovsky, R.: Searchable symmetric encryption: improved definitions and efficient constructions. In: Juels, A., Wright, R.N., Vimercati, S. (eds.) ACM CCS 06: 13th Conference on Computer and Communications Security, pp. 79–88. ACM Press, Alexandria (2006)
10. Faber, S., Jarecki, S., Krawczyk, H., Nguyen, Q., Rosu, M.C., Steiner, M.: Rich queries on encrypted data: Beyond exact matches. Cryptology ePrint Archive (2015). http://eprint.iacr.org/2015
11. Goh, E.J.: Secure indexes. Cryptology ePrint Archive, Report 2003/216 (2003). http://eprint.iacr.org/
12. Jarecki, S., Jutla, C., Krawczyk, H., Rosu, M., Steiner, M.: Outsourced symmetric private information retrieval. In: Proceedings of the 2013 ACM SIGSAC conference on Computer & communications security, pp. 875–888. ACM (2013)
13. Kamara, S., Papamanthou, C.: Parallel and dynamic searchable symmetric encryption. In: Sadeghi, A.-R. (ed.) FC 2013. LNCS, vol. 7859, pp. 258–274. Springer, Heidelberg (2013)
14. Kamara, S., Papamanthou, C., Roeder, T.: Dynamic searchable symmetric encryption. In: Yu, T., Danezis, G., Gligor, V.D. (eds.) ACM CCS 12: 19th Conference on Computer and Communications Security, pp. 965–976. ACM Press, Raleigh (2012)
15. Kiayias, A., Tang, Q.: How to keep a secret: leakage deterring public-key cryptosystems. In: Proceedings of the 2013 ACM SIGSAC Conference on Computer & Communications Security, pp. 943–954. ACM (2013)
16. Kurosawa, K., Ohtaki, Y.: UC-secure searchable symmetric encryption. In: Keromytis, A.D. (ed.) FC 2012. LNCS, vol. 7397, pp. 285–298. Springer, Heidelberg (2012)
17. van Liesdonk, P., Sedghi, S., Doumen, J., Hartel, P., Jonker, W.: Computationally efficient searchable symmetric encryption. In: Jonker, W., Petković, M. (eds.) SDM 2010. LNCS, vol. 6358, pp. 87–100. Springer, Heidelberg (2010)
18. Naveed, M., Prabhakaran, M., Gunter, C.A.: Dynamic searchable encryption via blind storage. In: 35th IEEE Symposium on Security and Privacy, pp. 639–654. IEEE Computer Society Press (2014)
19. Pappas, V., Vo, B., Krell, F., Choi, S., Kolesnikov, V., Keromytis, A., Malkin, T.: Blind seer: a scalable private DBMS. In: 35th IEEE Symposium on Security and Privacy, pp. 359–374. IEEE Computer Society Press (2014)
20. Popa, R.A., Redfield, C.M.S., Zeldovich, N., Balakrishnan, H.: CryptDB: protecting confidentiality with encrypted query processing. In: Proceedings of the 23rd ACM Symposium on Operating Systems Principles (SOSP 2011). ACM, October 2011
21. Raykova, M., Vo, B., Bellovin, S.M., Malkin, T.: Secure anonymous database search. In: Proceedings of the 2009 ACM Workshop on Cloud computing security, pp. 115–126. ACM (2009)
22. Shacham, H.: A cramer-shoup encryption scheme from the linear assumption and from progressively weaker linear variants. Cryptology ePrint Archive, Report 2007/074 (2007). http://eprint.iacr.org/
23. Shi, E., Bethencourt, J., Chan, T.H., Song, D., Perrig, A.: Multi-dimensional range query over encrypted data. In: IEEE Symposium on Security and Privacy, SP 2007, pp. 350–364. IEEE (2007)

24. Song, D.X., Wagner, D., Perrig, A.: Practical techniques for searches on encrypted data. In: 2000 IEEE Symposium on Security and Privacy, pp. 44–55. IEEE Computer Society Press, Oakland, May 2000
25. Varia, M., Price, B., Hwang, N., Hamlin, A., Herzog, J., Poland, J., Reschly, M., Yakoubov, S., Cunningham, R.K.: Automated assesment of secure search systems. Operating Syst. Rev. **49**(1), 22–30 (2015)

# Extended Proxy-Assisted Approach: Achieving Revocable Fine-Grained Encryption of Cloud Data

Yanjiang Yang[1]([⊠]), Joseph K. Liu[2], Kaitai Liang[3],
Kim-Kwang Raymond Choo[4], and Jianying Zhou[1]

[1] Institute for Infocomm Research, Singapore, Singapore
{yyang,jyzhou}@i2r.a-star.edu.sg
[2] Faculty of Information Technology, Monash University, Melbourne, Australia
joseph.liu@monash.edu
[3] Department of Computer Science, Aalto University, Greater Helsinki, Finland
kaitai.liang@aalto.fi
[4] University of South Australia, Adelaide, Australia
raymond.choo@fulbrightmail.org

**Abstract.** Attribute-based encryption has the potential to be deployed in a cloud computing environment to provide scalable and fine-grained data sharing. However, user revocation within ABE deployment remains a challenging issue to overcome, particularly when there is a large number of users. In this work, we introduce an extended proxy-assisted approach, which weakens the trust required of the cloud server. Based on an all-or-nothing principle, our approach is designed to discourage a cloud server from colluding with a third party to hinder the user revocation functionality. We demonstrate the utility of our approach by presenting a construction of the proposed approach, designed to provide efficient cloud data sharing and user revocation. A prototype was then implemented to demonstrate the practicality of our proposed construction.

## 1 Introduction

Cloud storage services (e.g. Dropbox, Microsoft's Azure storage, and Amazon's S3) enable users to upload and store their data remotely in the cloud environment as well as accessing and downloading the remotely stored data in real-time using a web browser or a mobile application [24]. To ensure the security and privacy of user data [9], particularly against an untrusted cloud service provider, one could encrypt the data prior to uploading and storing the data in the cloud [8,10,11,15,16,18,35]. In practice, data encryption often serves as an access control mechanism in cloud data sharing, where end users' decryption capabilities are defined based on a specified access control policy. For instance, a scientific research team may choose to share their research data and findings (that are stored in a cloud server) in real-time with their team workers [19], based on some pre-determined attributes or roles. To provide the scalability and flexibility of real-time data sharing, a fine-grained access control is required.

© Springer International Publishing Switzerland 2015
G. Pernul et al. (Eds.): ESORICS 2015, Part II, LNCS 9327, pp. 146–166, 2015.
DOI: 10.1007/978-3-319-24177-7_8

Attribute-based encryption (ABE) [4,13,14,20,28] has been identified as a suitable solution to enforce fine-grained decryption rights.

ABE can be broadly categorized into key policy ABE (KP-ABE) and ciphertext policy ABE (CP-ABE). KP-ABE allows data to be encrypted with a set of *attributes*, and each decryption key is associated with an *access policy* (defined in terms of attributes); while CP-ABE is complementary – data are encrypted and tagged with the pre-determined access policy, and a decryption key is associated with the set of *attributes*. In either type, a ciphertext can be decrypted using the corresponding decryption key only if the attributes satisfy the access policy. ABE has been shown to be an effective and scalable access control mechanism for encrypted data, but one key limiting factor is *user revocation* in an environment where there are many users (e.g. in a cloud storage environment).

There are several possible approaches to address this challenge. For example, one could implement an authentication based revocation mechanism in a conventional access control system. However, such an approach requires the cloud server to be fully trusted. This approach also imposes additional computational requirements on both the users and the cloud server – the users are required to possess another authentication secret and the cloud server needs to deal with the additional authentication. Another potential approach is the key-update based revocation, such as those proposed in [17,29,34], where key materials will be updated to exclude a revoked user. This approach, however, suffers from limited scalability as all data must be re-encrypted, and all non-revoked legitimate user keys need to be either updated or re-distributed. This is prohibitive in a data-intensive and high user volume environment, such as cloud storage. Although in [17,29,34] the majority of data re-encryption workload is often performed by the cloud server, it remains an attractive option to reduce the computational requirements in a real-world implementation.

Several researchers have introduced an alternative approach for user revocation by introducing an "expiry time" attribute such that a decryption key is effective only for a period of time [4,13]. The shortcoming of this method is that it is not possible to do real-time user revocation. Ostrovsky et al. [23] employ *negative* constrains in access policy, such that a revocation of certain attributes amounts to negating the attributes. The system does not scale well in the revoking of individual users, because each encryption requires the information of all revoked users and each of which is treated as a distinctive attribute. Attrapadung et al. [1] aim to solve the revocation problem by incorporating the broadcast encryption revocation mechanism [22] into ABE. The resulting scheme, however, generates the public system key in size proportional to the total number of users. Consequently, such a scheme has limited scalability. The scheme introduced in [21] attempts to leverage revocation and traceability to ABE in real-world applications, such as Pay-TV, where a decryption key is contained in a black-box. The scheme is, unfortunately, not practical as the size of each of public key, private key and ciphertext is $O(n)$, where $n$ is the total number of users.

More recently, proxy-assisted user revocation was introduced in [32,33,35] as a potential solution. In this approach, a cloud server acts as a proxy, and each user's decryption capability is split and represented by two parts, namely: the first part is held by the cloud server (i.e. cloud-side key), and the other is held by the user (i.e. user-side key). A decryption requires a partial decryption using the cloud-side key by the cloud server, and a final/full decryption using the user-side key by the user. In user revocation, the cloud server will erase the key associated with the user to be revoked. This method is particularly promising, as it supports immediate revocation, without compromising efficiency as it does not require data re-encryption or key update. The idea of recurring to a third party for *immediate user revocation* could be traced back to mediated cryptography, where a mediator is introduced for the purpose of user revocation (e.g. [3]). The difference between proxy-assisted user revocation (e.g. [32,33,35]) and mediated cryptography will be clarified in Sect. 2.

However, we observe that both proxy-assisted and mediated cryptography approaches require the cloud server to be trusted, which as pointed out in [5] that 'there are legitimate concerns about cloud service providers being compelled to hand over user data that reside in the cloud to government agencies without the user's knowledge or consent due to territorial jurisdiction by a foreign government'. In the aftermath of the revelations by Edward Snowden that the National Security Agency has been conducting wide-scale government surveillance, including those targeting cloud users - see http://masssurveillance. info/, the requirement of a honest cloud server (in this context, the cloud server is assumed not to disclose users' cloud-side keys) may limit the adoption of the proxy-assisted approach or the mediated cryptography approach. Key disclosure could also be due to unscrupulous employees of the cloud service provider or an attacker who has successfully compromised the cloud system.

**Our Contributions.** We are, thus, motivated to address this problem; extending the proxy/mediator assisted user revocation approach (based on an 'all-or-nothing' principle) to mitigate the risk due to a dishonest cloud server. More specifically, the private key of the cloud server is also required for the cloud-side partial decryption. Consequently, in order for the cloud server to collude with another user to disclose a user's cloud-side key, the cloud server would also have to reveal its private key in order to perform a partial decryption. We coin this approach as an *extended proxy-assisted user revocation*. We regard the contributions of this work to be three-fold: (1) We formulate the definition and threat model for cloud data encryption using the extended proxy-assisted user revocation; (2) We propose a concrete construction instantiating our extended proxy-assisted approach, which demonstrates the utility of this approach; and (3) We implement a prototype of our construction, which demonstrates the practicality of our proposed construction.

## 2   Related Work

**Cloud Data Encryption with ABE.** Over the last decade, a large number of cloud data encryption schemes have been proposed in the literature. Of particular relevance are those that utilize ABE. As an one-to-many encryption scheme, ABE is required to provide user revocation. However, the various proposed *attribute revocation* mechanisms for ABE, such as "expiry time" attributes and negative attributes [1,4,13,21,23], are generally not suitable for cloud data encryption deployment as discussed below and in the preceding section.

Yu *et al.* [34] suggested adopting KP-ABE to achieve fine-grained data sharing. To support user revocation, they proposed using proxy re-encryption (PRE) [2] in the updating of user's decryption key. In this approach, the bulk of the computationally expensive operations (e.g. re-generation of encrypted cloud data due to user revocation) are performed by the cloud server. Although a cloud generally has significantly more computational resources, each user's quota is cost-based. Similar limitation is observed in the scheme proposed by Wang *et al.* [29]. Sahai *et al.* [26] proposed an attribute revocable CP-ABE scheme, using ciphertext delegation and the piecewise property of private keys. In particular, the system proceeds in epochs, and in each epoch, the attribute authority generates a set of update keys (as the other piece of each private key) according to the revocation list. All the ciphertexts are then re-encrypted with a new access policy (the principal access policy remains unchanged, but the extra access policy changes in each epoch). A similar attribute revocation method has also been explored in the multi-authority setting [30,31], where users' attributes are issued by multiple independent attribute authorities. Similar to other ABE schemes with built-in attribute revocation support (such as expiry time and negative attributes), these schemes face the challenge of transforming attribute revocation into efficient revocation for individual users. In addition, the overheads introduced by these schemes in the re-generation of encrypted data should be addressed. In our extended proxy-assisted approach, however, the overhead imposed upon both the cloud server and users due to user revocation is relatively less.

**Mediated Cryptography.** Boneh *et al.* proposed "mediated RSA" to split the private key of RSA into two shares; one share is delegated to an online "mediator" and the other is given to the user [3]. As RSA decryption and signing require the collaboration of both parties, the user's cryptographic capabilities are immediately revoked if the mediator does not cooperate. Recently, Chen *et al.* [7] presented a mediated CP-ABE scheme, where the mediator's key is issued over a set of attributes. The scheme in [12] can also be viewed as mediated ABE, although its purpose is to outsource the costly ABE decryption to the mediator. This does now result in immediate revocation. A common issue associated with existing mediated cryptographic schemes is *key escrow*. In other words, there is a party responsible for generating the key shares such that the party knows both shares. Similar to our proposed extended proxy-assisted approach, mediated cryptography is intended to provide immediate user revocation (we remark that mediator and proxy are essentially the same concept). However, a key difference between the (extended) proxy-assisted approach and the mediated cryptography is that the former approach does not suffer from the key escrow problem, since the shares are generated by different parties and no single party knows both shares. This is a particularly attractive option in the current privacy conscious landscape.

Unlike other mediated schemes, the mediated certificateless encryption [6] avoids key escrow by employing a combination of identity-based encryption and conventional public key encryption; the private key corresponding to the identity-based encryption held by the mediator is generated by a key generation authority, and the private key of public key encryption can be generated by the user. Unfortunately, such an approach cannot be straightforwardly used in the (extended) proxy-assisted approach by simply replacing identity based encryption with ABE. This is due to the fact that using ABE for data encryption, the encryptor does not have any particular recipients. Both the mediated certificateless encryption (as well as other mediated cryptographic schemes) and the proxy-assisted approach (such as those in [32,35]) require the mediator/proxy to be honest in maintaining user's key shares. As mentioned earlier, this may not be a realistic assumption to privacy conscious (or paranoid) users. Our extended proxy-assisted approach exactly is designed to address this issue.

# 3    Proposed Revocable Cloud Data Encryption Model

## 3.1    System Overview

A cloud storage system allows an owner to remotely store the data at a cloud storage server, and the data can be accessed by a group of users authorized by the data owner. As an example, the data owner could be an organization and the authorized users are the organization employees. Without fully trusting the cloud server, the data owner encrypts the data to ensure the security and privacy of the data. Here, data encryption serves as a measure of fine-grained access control, and users have different decryption capabilities based on the specified need-to-know basis. In particular, a user's decryption capability is delineated by a set of attributes according to the user's functional role. Each data encryption is associated with an access control policy (specified with respect to attributes), such that a user can successfully decipher the encrypted record, if, and only if, the user's attributes satisfy the access policy. As the system is in a multiuser setting, user revocation is a critical requirement (e.g. when a user leaves the organization or is no longer involved in the project). User revocation would allow the data owner to revoke a user's ability to decipher the data.

## 3.2    Notations

We use the definitions of "attribute" and "access structure" from [4,13].

**Attributes.** Let $\Lambda$ denotes the dictionary of descriptive attributes used in the system. Each authorized cloud storage user, $u$, is assigned with a set of attributes

$\mathbb{A}_u \subseteq \Lambda$, which defines the user's functional role. The attribute assignment procedure is application specific and is beyond the scope of this paper.

**Access Policy.** In the system, an access control policy is expressed by an *access tree*, where each leaf node represents an attribute and we use $\mathsf{att}(\ell)$ to denote the attribute associated with leaf node $\ell$. Each non-leaf node of the tree represents a threshold gate, described by its children and a threshold value. Let $num_n$ be the number of children of a non-leaf node $n$, and $t_n$ be its threshold value, where $1 \leq t_n \leq num_n$. When $t_n = 1$, the threshold gate is an OR gate, and when $t_n = num_n$, it is an AND gate. The parent of a node $n$ in the tree is denoted by $\mathsf{parent}(n)$. The tree also defines an ordering among the children of a node – i.e. the child nodes of a node $n$ are numbered from 1 to $num_n$. The function $\mathsf{index}(n)$ calculates the unique number associated with a node $n$. The access tree can express any access policy in the form of monotonic formula.

**Satisfying an Access Tree.** Let $\mathcal{T}$ be an access tree with root $rt$. The subtree of $\mathcal{T}$ rooted at node $n$ is denoted as $\mathcal{T}_n$; hence, $\mathcal{T} = \mathcal{T}_{rt}$. When a set $\mathbb{A}$ of attributes satisfy the access tree $\mathcal{T}_n$, it is denoted as $\mathcal{T}_n(\mathbb{A}) = 1$. $\mathcal{T}_n(\mathbb{A})$ is computed in a recursive way as follows: if $n$ is a non-leaf node, then compute $\mathcal{T}_{n'}(\mathbb{A})$ for all child nodes $n'$; $\mathcal{T}_n(\mathbb{A})$ returns 1 if, and only if, at least $t_n$ children return 1; if $n$ is a leaf node, then $\mathcal{T}_n(\mathbb{A})$ returns 1 if and only if $\mathsf{att}(n) \in \mathbb{A}$.

### 3.3 Extended Proxy-Assisted User Revocation Approach

To strengthen key revocation and to reduce the possibility of a dishonest cloud server, our approach requires the cloud server to use its own private key in the partial decryption phase. In other words, unless the cloud server is willing to disclose its private key, the exposure of a user's cloud-side key (referred to as proxy key in this paper) to a third party (e.g. a foreign government agency) does not help in deciphering the encrypted cloud data. As our approach is an extension of the proxy-assisted approach, it inherits the advanced features of the latter, such as immediate user revocation, small amount of overhead for revocation, light computation cost for user side, and key escrow-free.

### 3.4 Formulation of Revocable Cloud Data Encryption

A revocable cloud data encryption system involves three types of entities, namely: data owner (denoted as DO), a set of users, and a cloud server (denoted as CS). Each user and CS have their respective public/private key pairs. To authorize a user, DO generates a proxy key based on the user's attributes, the user's public key, and CS's public key; the proxy key is given to and held by CS. Therefore, CS maintains a Proxy Key list, with each entry containing a user's identity and the corresponding proxy key. When a user requests to retrieve a data record from the cloud, CS executes a *proxy decryption* operation over the data with the user's proxy key and its own private key to generate an intermediate value. The value is then returned to the user, who is able to obtain the underlying plain data by running a *user decryption* operation with his/her private key. Specifically, the system consists of the following algorithms.

**Definition 1.** *Let $\Lambda$ denote the universe of attributes. A revocable cloud data encryption system (RCDE) is defined as a collection of the following algorithms.*

**Setup**$(1^\kappa) \rightarrow (params, msk)$: *Taking as input a security parameter $1^\kappa$, DO executes the algorithm to set up public parameters, params, and a master secret key, msk. Below, we assume that params is implicit in the input of the rest algorithms unless stated otherwise.*

**UKGen**$(u) \rightarrow (pk_u, sk_u)$: *The user key generation algorithm takes as input a user identity, $u$, and outputs a pair of public/private keys, $(pk_u, sk_u)$, for $u$. Note that $(pk_u, sk_u)$ is a pair for a standard public key cryptosystem.*

Each system entity (including users and CS) runs this algorithm to generate a key pair. As $(pk_{CS}, sk_{CS})$ – the key pair of CS –is a standard public key cryptosystem, we assume that $(pk_{CS}, sk_{CS})$ is for long term use, and CS does not expose the private key, $sk_{CS}$.

**PxKGen**$(msk, pk_{CS}, pk_u, \mathbb{A}_u) \rightarrow PxK_u$: *The proxy key generation algorithm takes as input msk, the server's public key, $pk_{CS}$, a user $u$'s public key, $pk_u$, and the user's attributes, $\mathbb{A}_u \subset \Lambda$, and outputs a proxy key, $PxK_u$, for $u$.*

DO runs this algorithm to authorize a user based on the user's attributes. The proxy key, $PxK_u$, will be given to CS who adds a new entry in its Proxy Key list $\mathcal{L}_{PxK}$ – i.e. $\mathcal{L}_{PxK} = \mathcal{L}_{PxK} \cup \{u, PxK_u\}$.

**Encrypt**$(m, \mathcal{T}) \rightarrow c$: *The encryption algorithm takes as input a message, $m$, and an access tree, $\mathcal{T}$, specifying an access policy, and outputs a ciphertext, $c$, under $\mathcal{T}$.*

DO runs this algorithm to encrypt data to be uploaded to CS.

**PxDec**$(sk_{CS}, PxK_u, c) \rightarrow v$: *The proxy decryption algorithm takes as input CS's private key, $sk_{CS}$, a user's proxy key, $PxK_u$, and a ciphertext, $c$, and outputs an intermediate value, $v$.*

The CS runs this algorithm to help a user, $u$, partially decrypt an encrypted record requested by the user with the corresponding proxy key.

**UDec**$(sk_u, v) \rightarrow m$: *The user decryption algorithm takes as input a user private key, $sk_u$, and an intermediate value, $v$, and outputs a message, $m$.*

An authorized user runs this algorithm to obtain the data with the intermediate value returned by CS and his/her private key.

**Revoke**$(u, \mathcal{L}_{PxK}) \rightarrow \mathcal{L}'_{PxK}$: *Taking as input a user identity, $u$, and the Proxy Key list, $\mathcal{L}_{PxK}$, the algorithm revokes $u$'s decryption capability by updating and outputting an updated Proxy Key list, $\mathcal{L}'_{PxK}$.*

**Correctness.** Correctness of the system stipulates that UDec$(sk_u,$ PxDec$(sk_{CS}, PxK_u, c)) = m$ if $\mathcal{T}(\mathbb{A}) = 1$, for all $(pk_u, sk_u) \leftarrow$ UKGen$(u)$, $PxK_u \leftarrow$ PxKGen $(msk, pk_{CS}, pk_u, \mathbb{A})$ and $c \leftarrow$ Encrypt$(m, \mathcal{T})$, where $(params, msk) \leftarrow$ Setup$(1^\kappa)$.

**Remark.** The separation of the algorithms, UKGen and PxKGen, highlights the distinction between our key-escrow-free approach and the mediated cryptography with key escrow. For the latter, the two algorithms are combined into one, which is executed by a single party (e.g., DO in our case).

**Security Requirements.** We define the security requirements for our system.

*Data Privacy Against Cloud Server.* The primary purpose of data encryption is to protect data privacy against CS. It guarantees that CS cannot learn any useful information about the data in its storage system even with the knowledge of all users' proxy keys (as well as its own private key).

**Definition 2.** *[Data Privacy Against Cloud Server] A revocable cloud data encryption system (RCDE) achieves data privacy against the cloud server if for any probabilistic polynomial time (PPT) adversary, the probability of the following game returns 1 is $1/2 + \epsilon(\kappa)$, where $\epsilon(.)$ is a negligible function with respect to the security parameter, $\kappa$.*

**Setup.** *The game challenger runs the Setup algorithm, and returns params to the adversary.*

**Phase 1.** *The adversary generates its own pair of public/private keys, and gives the public key to the challenger. It then makes repeated queries to the proxy key generation oracle by querying sets of attributes $\mathbb{A}_1, ..., \mathbb{A}_{q_1}$. For each query $i$, (1) the challenger runs the UKGen algorithm to get a user public/private key pair; (2) with the adversary's public key, the user public key, and the attribute set $\mathbb{A}_i$, the challenger runs the PxKGen algorithm to get a proxy key; (3) the challenger returns the proxy key along with the user public key to the adversary.*

**Challenge.** *The adversary submits two equal-length messages, $m_0$ and $m_1$, along with a challenge access tree, $T^*$. The challenger flips a random coin, $b$, runs the Encrypt algorithm on $m_b$ and $T^*$, and returns the ciphertext, $c^*$, to the adversary.*

**Phase 2.** *The adversary continues to make proxy key generation queries, and the challenger responds as in Phase 1.*

**Guess.** *The adversary outputs a guess, $b'$, on $b$. If $b' = b$, then the challenger returns 1; otherwise returns 0.*

*Data Privacy Against Users.* From the perspective of access control over cloud data, a user should not be able to decrypt data beyond the user's authorized access rights issued by DO. In particular, a collusion of a set of malicious users will not afford these users' decryption capabilities beyond those authorized.

**Definition 3.** *[Data Privacy against Users] A revocable cloud data encryption system (RCDE) achieves data privacy against users if for any PPT adversary, the probability of the following game returns 1 is $1/2 + \epsilon(\kappa)$.*

**Setup.** *The challenger runs the Setup algorithm, and returns params to the adversary.*

**Phase 1.** *The adversary makes repeated queries to the proxy key generation oracle (PxKGen) by issuing sets of attributes, $\mathbb{A}_1, ..., \mathbb{A}_{q_1}$. To respond the queries, the challenger first generates a public/private key pair as the CS's key by executing the UKGen algorithm, and gives the key pair to the adversary; then for each* *query i, the challenger (1) first generates a user public/private key by executing the UKGen algorithm and gives the key pair to the adversary; (2) then generates a proxy key by executing the PxKGen algorithm upon the CS's public key, and the user public key and $\mathbb{A}_i$, and returns the resulting proxy key to the adversary.*

**Challenge.** *The adversary submits two equal-length messages, $m_0$ and $m_1$, along with an access tree, $\mathcal{T}^*$, subjecting to a restriction that none of the $\mathbb{A}$'s satisfies $\mathcal{T}^*$. The challenger flips a random coin, b, runs the Encrypt algorithm on $m_b$ and $\mathcal{T}^*$, and returns the ciphertext, $c^*$, to the adversary.*

**Phase 2.** *The adversary continues to make proxy key generation queries by submitting attribute sets as in Phase 1, with the restriction that none of the attribute sets satisfies $\mathcal{T}^*$.*

**Guess.** *The adversary outputs a guess, $b'$, on b. If $b' = b$, then the challenger returns 1; otherwise returns 0.*

Remark. This definition depicts a stronger adversarial capability as it allows users to gain access to the cloud server's key and the proxy keys.

*User Revocation Support.* The extended proxy-assisted user revocation approach guarantees that without knowing CS's private key, any user cannot decipher encrypted data even given the corresponding proxy key (in addition to the user key pair).

**Definition 4.** *[User Revocation Support] A revocable cloud data encryption system (RCDE) supports user revocation if for any PPT adversary, the probability of the following game returns 1 is $1/2 + \epsilon(\kappa)$.*

**Setup.** *The challenger runs the Setup algorithm, and returns params to the adversary.*

**Phase 1.** *The challenger generates a public/private key pair as CS's key by executing the UKGen algorithm, and gives the public key to the adversary. The adversary makes repeated queries to the proxy key generation oracle by issuing a set of attributes $\mathbb{A}_1, ..., \mathbb{A}_{q_1}$. For each query i, the challenger (1) generates a user public/private key pair and gives the key pair to the adversary; (2) generates a proxy key by executing the PxKGen algorithm upon the CS's public key, the user public key and $\mathbb{A}_i$, and returns the resulting proxy key to the adversary.*

**Challenge.** *The adversary submits two equal-length messages, $m_0$ and $m_1$, along with an access tree, $\mathcal{T}^*$. The challenger flips a random coin, b, runs the Encrypt algorithm on $m_b$ and $\mathcal{T}^*$, and returns the ciphertext, $c^*$, to the adversary.*

**Phase 2.** *The adversary continues to make proxy key generation queries, as in Phase 1.*

**Guess.** *The adversary outputs a guess, $b'$, on b. If $b' = b$, the challenger returns 1; otherwise returns 0.*

# 4   Our Construction

In this section, we present a concrete construction of our novel extended proxy-assisted user revocation approach described in Sect. 3. The construction is adapted from the CP-ABE scheme in [4], and it achieves the same expressiveness for access policy as in [4,13]. We state that it is not difficult to extend the following construction idea to other ABE schemes with more expressive attributes, such as the scheme in [28].

## 4.1   Construction Details

The main challenge in our construction is the generation of a user's proxy key by seamlessly incorporating the cloud server's public key and the user's public key into the decryption key generation algorithm of the CP-ABE scheme in [4]. Let $s \in_R S$ denotes an element $s$ randomly chosen from a set $S$. The details of our construction are described as follow.

**Setup**($1^\kappa$): On input a security parameter $1^\kappa$, the algorithm: determines a bilinear map, $e : G_0 \times G_0 \rightarrow G_T$, where $G_0$ and $G_T$ are cyclic groups of $\kappa$-bit prime order $p$. Selects $g$, which is a generator of $G_0$. Selects a cryptographic hash function, $H : \{0,1\}^* \rightarrow G_0$. Picks $\alpha, \beta \in_R Z_p$, and sets $params = (e, G_0, g, h = g^\beta, \mathcal{G}_\alpha = e(g,g)^\alpha)$ and $msk = (\alpha, \beta)$.

**UKGen**($u$): On input a user identity $u$, the algorithm chooses $x_u \in_R Z_p$, and sets $(pk_u = g^{x_u}, sk_u = x_u)$. It can be seen that $(pk_u, sk_u)$ is a standard ElGamal type key pair. CS also uses this algorithm to generate a key pair, $(pk_{\mathsf{CS}} = g^{x_{\mathsf{CS}}}, sk_{\mathsf{CS}} = x_{\mathsf{CS}})$.

**PxKGen**($msk, pk_{\mathsf{CS}}, pk_u, \mathbb{A}_u$): On input $msk = (\alpha, \beta), pk_{\mathsf{CS}} = g^{x_{\mathsf{CS}}}, pk_u = g^{x_u}$ and $\mathbb{A}_u$, the algorithm chooses $r_1, r_2, r_i \in_R Z_p, \forall i \in \mathbb{A}_u$, and sets $PxK_u = (k = (pk_{\mathsf{CS}}^{r_1} pk_u^\alpha g^{r_2})^{\frac{1}{\beta}}, k' = g^{r_1}$ and $\forall i \in \mathbb{A}_u : \{k_{i1} = g^{r_2} H(i)^{r_i}, k_{i2} = g^{r_i}\})$.

**Encrypt**($m, \mathcal{T}$): Taking as input a message, $m$, and $\mathcal{T}$, the algorithm works as follows: Firstly, it selects a polynomial, $q_n$, for each node, $n$, (including the leaf nodes) in $\mathcal{T}$. These polynomials are chosen in a top-down manner starting from the root node, $rt$. For each node $n$, set the degree $d_n$ of the polynomial $q_n$ to be $d_n = t_n - 1$, where $t_n$ is the threshold value of node $n$. Starting with the root node, $rt$, the algorithm chooses an $s \in_R Z_p$, and sets $q_{rt}(0) = s$. It next selects $d_{rt}$ other random points to define $q_{rt}$ completely. For any other node $n$, it sets $q_n(0) = q_{\mathsf{parent}(n)}(\mathsf{index}(n))$, and chooses $d_n$ other points to define $q_n$. Let $L$ be the set of leaf nodes in $\mathcal{T}$. The algorithm sets the ciphertext, $c$, as $c = (\mathcal{T}, C = m \cdot \mathcal{G}_\alpha^s, C' = h^s, C'' = g^s, \forall \ell \in L : \{C_{\ell 1} = g^{q_\ell(0)}, C_{\ell 2} = H(\mathsf{att}(\ell))^{q_\ell(0)}\})$.

**PxDec**($sk_{\mathsf{CS}}, PxK_u, c$): On input $sk_{\mathsf{CS}} = x_{\mathsf{CS}}$, and $PxK_u = (k, k', \forall i \in \mathbb{A}_u : \{k_{i1}, k_{i2}\})$ associating with a set of attributes, $\mathbb{A}_u$, and a ciphertext, $c = (\mathcal{T}, C, C', C'', \forall \ell \in L : \{C_{\ell 1}, C_{\ell 2}\})$, the algorithm outputs an intermediate value, $v$ if $\mathcal{T}(\mathbb{A}_u) = 1$, and $\perp$ otherwise. Specifically, the algorithm is recursive. We first define an algorithm, $\mathsf{DecNd}_n(PxK_u, c)$, on a node, $n$, of $\mathcal{T}$. If node, $n$, is a leaf node, we let $z = \mathsf{att}(n)$ and define as follows:

$z \notin \mathbb{A}_u$, $\mathsf{DecNd}_n(PxK_u, c) = \perp$; otherwise $\mathsf{DecNd}_n(PxK_u, c) = F_n$, where $F_n = \frac{e(k_{z1}, C_{n1})}{e(k_{z2}, C_{n2})} = \frac{e(g^{r_2}H(z)^{r_z}, g^{q_n(0)})}{e(g^{r_z}, H(z)^{q_n(0)})} = e(g, g)^{r_2 \cdot q_n(0)}$.

We now consider the recursive case when $n$ is a non-leaf node. The algorithm, $\mathsf{DecNd}_n(PxK_u, c)$, then works as follows. For each child node $ch$ of $n$, it calls $\mathsf{DecNd}_{ch}(PxK_u, c)$, and stores the output as $F_{ch}$. Let $S_n$ be an arbitrary $t_n$-sized set of child nodes, $ch$, such that $F_{ch} \neq \perp$. If such a set does not exist, then the node is not satisfied and $\mathsf{DecNd}_n(PxK_u, c) = F_n = \perp$. Otherwise, we let the Lagrange coefficient, $\triangle_{i,S}$ for $i \in Z_p$, and a set $S$ of elements in $Z_p$ be $\triangle_{i,S}(x) = \prod_{j \in S, j \neq i} \frac{x-j}{i-j}$. We next compute

$$
\begin{aligned}
F_n &= \prod_{ch \in S_n} F_{ch}^{\triangle_{i,S_n'}(0)}, \text{ where } \begin{array}{l} i = \mathrm{index}(ch), \\ S_n' = \{\mathrm{index}(ch) : ch \in S_n\} \end{array} \\
&= \prod_{ch \in S_n} (e(g, g)^{r_2 \cdot q_{ch}(0)})^{\triangle_{i,S_n'}(0)} = \prod_{ch \in S_n} (e(g, g)^{r_2 \cdot q_{\mathrm{parent}(ch)}(\mathrm{index}(ch))})^{\triangle_{i,S_n'}(0)} \\
&= \prod_{ch \in S_n} (e(g, g)^{r_2 \cdot q_n(i)})^{\triangle_{i,S_n'}(0)} = e(g, g)^{r_2 \cdot q_n(0)}
\end{aligned}
$$

In this way, $\mathsf{DecNd}_{rt}(PxK_u, c)$ for the root node $rt$ can be computed if $\mathcal{T}_{rt}(\mathbb{A}_u) = 1$, where $\mathsf{DecNd}_{rt}(PxK_u, c) = e(g, g)^{r_2 \cdot q_{rt}(0)} = e(g, g)^{r_2 \cdot s} = F_{rt}$. Next, the proxy decryption algorithm computes

$$
\frac{e(k, C')}{e(k', C'')^{x_{\mathrm{CS}}} F_{rt}} = \frac{e((pk_{\mathrm{CS}}^{r_1} pk_u^\alpha g^{r_2})^{\frac{1}{\beta}}, h^s)}{e(g^{r_1}, g^s)^{x_{\mathrm{CS}}} e(g, g)^{r_2 \cdot s}} = e(pk_u, g)^{s \cdot \alpha}.
$$

Finally, it sets $v = (C = m \cdot \mathcal{G}_\alpha^s, e(pk_u, g)^{s \cdot \alpha})$.

**UDec**$(sk_u, v)$: On input a user private key, $sk_u = x_u$, and an intermediate value, $v = (C = m \cdot \mathcal{G}_\alpha^s, e(pk_u, g)^{s \cdot \alpha})$, the user decryption algorithm computes $\frac{m \cdot \mathcal{G}_\alpha^s}{(e(pk_u, g)^{s \cdot \alpha})^{x_u^{-1}}} = m$.

**Revoke**$(u, \mathcal{L}_{PxK})$: On input a user identity, $u$, and the Proxy Key list, $\mathcal{L}_{PxK}$, the user revoking algorithm deletes the entry corresponding to $u$ from the list – i.e. $\mathcal{L}_{PxK}' = \mathcal{L}_{PxK} \setminus \{u, PxK_u\}$. In a real world application, an interface should be provided to DO for DO to perform the updating in real-time.

### 4.2   Functional Analysis – Features

Our construction enjoys a number of features as described below.

*Efficient and Immediate User Revocation.* The only overhead incurred due to user revocation is the deletion of the revoked user's proxy key from the cloud server. Once the proxy key of a user is eliminated, the cloud server is no longer able to perform the proxy decryption for the revoked user.

*Mitigation against Cloud-User Collusion.* The primary purpose of the extended proxy-assisted user revocation is to reduce the likelihood of proxy keys disclosure (e.g. the cloud server may collude with some revoked users to reveal their proxy keys). In our construction, the leakage of a proxy key does not lead to the success of proxy decryption.

We note that there exists another way of colluding to invalidate user revocation. More specifically, the cloud server keeps a copy of a revoked user's proxy key before it is deleted by the data owner, and then continues to service the revoked user's data access with the retained proxy key. Unfortunately, such collusion cannot be prevented by any proxy/mediator based system. However, it is not difficult to detect collusion of this nature in practice (compared to the proxy keys disclosure collusion), as it requires ongoing engagement of the cloud server.

*Free of Key Escrow.* Each user generates its own key pair, and the data owner generating each authorized user's proxy key does not need to know the user's private key.

*Cloud Transparency.* Although the cloud server's key is involved in the authorized users' proxy keys, encrypting data only needs the access policy associated with the data to be encrypted, without the need to involve the cloud server. In other words, data encryption works as a regular CP-ABE encryption algorithm.

*Minimal User Side Overhead.* The bit-length of an intermediate value, $v$, output by the algorithm, PxDec, is $2|G_T|$, independent of the complexity of access policy. In addition, the main computation overhead of the algorithm, UDec, includes just a single exponentiation in $G_T$ (unlike $G_0$, $G_T$ is a regular finite field) without any bilinear pairing operation. Thus, the complexity overhead at the user side is relatively low in terms of both communication and computation.

*No User Authentication.* The cloud server is not require to check the authenticity of a requesting user, as the intermediate value output by the proxy decryption algorithm can only be decrypted by the user being impersonated (i.e. the impersonator will not be able to decrypt the intermediate value output).

### 4.3   Security Analysis

We have the following theorem asserting the security of our construction, and the security proof is deferred to the Appendix.

**Theorem 1.** *Our construction is a revocable cloud data encryption system achieving Data Privacy Against Cloud Server (in the sense of Definition 2), Data Privacy Against Users (in the sense of Definition 3), and User Revocation Support (in the sense of Definition 4), in the generic group model [25].*

## 5   Implementation of Our Construction

### 5.1   Proof-of-Concept

To demonstrate the practicality of the construction described in Sect. 4, we present a Web-based proof-of-concept.

**Architecture.** The prototype consists of a Web application representing a cloud server (running the algorithm PxDec), a data owner application, and a user application running the algorithm UDec. The data owner application takes charge of the algorithms Setup, PxKGen and Encrypt. A cloud-data-owner interface is provided, allowing the data owner application to upload encrypted data to the Web server. A cloud-user interface is also provided for the user to access and download data from the Web server. The Web server runs on a desktop with 2.66 GHz Intel Core2Duo and 3.25 GB RAM, the data owner application runs on a laptop with 2.10 GHz Intel Core i3-5010U Processor and 4 GB RAM, and the user application runs on a smartphone configured with a 1.2 GHz CPU and 2 GB RAM.

The implementation is based on the Pairing-Based Cryptography (PBC) library (https://crypto.stanford.edu/pbc/). The bilinear map in our construction is instantiated with a 512-bit supersingular curve of embedding degree 2, with $|p| = 160$. For the cryptographic hash function $H : \{0, 1\}^* \to G_0$, a simplified realization of choosing random values from $G_0$ is used, as there is no off-the-shelf hash function of this nature. The data encryption follows the common practice of *data encapsulation + key encapsulation*, namely, an encryption of a message, $m$, is of the form $(\mathrm{AES}_k(m), \mathsf{Encrypt}(k, \mathcal{T}))$, where $k$ is a random encryption key. To achieve the security level guaranteed by the 512-bit supersingular curve, 128-bit AES is chosen. Since $G_T$ is an ordinary finite field, the AES keys can be directly encrypted by the algorithm $\mathsf{Encrypt}$.

**Reducing Storage Overhead.** In the prototype, we are concerned with reducing the storage overhead. Recall that the ciphertext size in our construction is linear with the number of leaf nodes in a given access tree - for a payload message $m \in G_T$, a ciphertext introduces an extra storage overhead of $2 + 2\ell$ group of elements in $G_0$, where $\ell$ is the total number of leaf nodes of the access tree. When $\ell$ is large, the complexity overhead dominates the storage cost.

The mode of hybrid data/key encapsulation offers us a possibility to amortize the above complexity overhead. Specifically, all data sharing the same access policy are encrypted with the same encryption key. The high ciphertext overhead resulting from the encapsulation of the encryption key by the algorithm $\mathsf{Encrypt}$ is amortized by all these data. Note that the data owner is not necessarily involved in the management of the encryption keys. Instead, the data owner can obtain the key by retrieving and decrypting the corresponding ciphertext from the cloud server, if the access policy has already been used. We also remark that the decryption process by the data owner is very simple. With $\alpha$, the data owner only needs to retrieve the $C, C''$ elements of the ciphertext, and computes $\frac{C}{e(g^\alpha, C'')}$ to recover the encryption key. If the data owner chooses to keep $g^\alpha$ as a part of the master secret key, $msk$, the computation overhead is a single pairing operation. Figure 1 illustrates the logical structure of encrypted data records, where each ciphertext of the algorithm $\mathsf{Encrypt}$ serves as an index, pointing to all encrypted payload data that are governed by the same access policy.

The role played by this overhead amortization mechanism in user revocation is as follows. Once a user is revoked, the data owner will use a new key for every access policy when encrypting new data. This guarantees that the newly generated cloud data cannot be decrypted by the revoked user even if it is given the corresponding payload part. In practice, it is usually not a concern that a revoked user can decrypt the data it has been entitled to before its revocation.

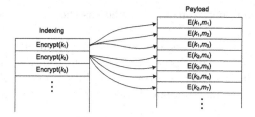

**Fig. 1.** A snapshot of the encrypted cloud data structure

## 5.2  Performance Results

We evaluated the performance of PxKGen, Encrypt, PxDec, and UDec, respectively, on their corresponding platforms. The experimental results are shown in Fig. 2. As observed in Fig. 2(a) and (b), the runtimes of the algorithms, PxKGen and Encrypt, are linear to the number of attributes. In our implementation, we had not undertaken any optimization on multi-exponentiation operations; therefore, the runtime of PxKGen is slightly more costly than that of Encrypt given the same number of attributes.

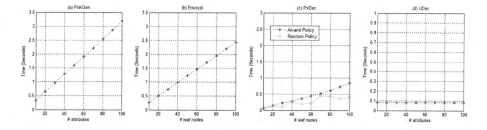

**Fig. 2.** Experimental results

We experiment the algorithm, PxDec, with two types of access policies. The first type consists of access trees whose non-leaf nodes are all "and" gates (we call them all-and access trees). Access trees in such a form ensure that all attributes (leaf nodes) are needed in PxDec. Thus, the access trees are expected to impose the heaviest workload, among access trees with the same number of leaf nodes. The second type includes access trees that are constructed randomly (we call them random access trees). It is clear that for a random access tree whose non-leaf nodes are "or" or "threshold" gates, not all of the leaf nodes are necessary in order to satisfy the tree. The actual leaf nodes needed in PxDec are tree-specific. Figure 2(c) corroborates this fact. In the case of all-and access trees, the computation overhead is basically linear with the number of leaf nodes. It can also be seen that PxDec is more efficient than Encrypt given the same number of attributes (i.e. the same access tree). This is because the former is dominated by the exponentiation operations in $G_T$, whereas the latter is dominated by the exponentiations in $G_0$.

Figure 2(d) shows that a UDec operation costs about 80 milliseconds on the experimenting smartphone platform. Considering in addition that the communication overhead for user is merely $2|G_T| = 1\,\mathrm{K}$ bits in our implementation, this could be deployed on a smart mobile device (e.g. Android or iOS device).

## 6    Conclusion

In this paper, we presented an extended proxy-assisted approach in order to overcome the limitation of needing to trust the cloud server not to disclose users' proxy keys inherent in proxy/mediator assisted user revocation approaches. In our approach, we bind the cloud server's private key to the data decryption operation, which requires the cloud server to reveal its private key should the cloud server decide to collude with revoked users. We then formulated a primitive, 'revocable cloud data encryption', under the approach. We presented a concrete construction of the primitive and implemented the construction using a proof-of-concept. The experimental results suggested that our construction is suitable for deployment even on smart mobile devices.

**Acknowledgment.** Joseph K. Liu is supported by National Natural Science Foundation of China (61472083). Kaitai Liang is supported by privacy-aware retrieval and modelling of genomic data (PRIGENDA, No. 13283250), the Academy of Finland.

## Appendix: Security Proof for Theorem 1

*Proof.* We prove that our construction satisfies the three security requirements.

**Lemma 1.** *The construction satisfies Data Privacy Against Cloud, as defined in Definition 2 in the generic group model.*

*Proof.* In the definition, the attributes, $\mathbb{A}_i$, submitted by the adversary could or could not satisfy the challenge access tree $\mathcal{T}^*$. To consider the strongest adversary possible, we assume every $\mathbb{A}_i$ satisfy $\mathcal{T}^*$. We then prove under the generic group model, no efficient adversary can output $b' = b$ in the security game defined in Definition 2 noticeably better than a random guess. Note that a random guess, $b'$, by the adversary equals $b$ with probability $1/2$, thus we often call $\epsilon$ the advantage of the adversary if $b' = b$ with probability $1/2 + \epsilon$.

In the generic group model [25], each element of groups, $G_0, G_T$, is encoded as a unique random string; thus, the adversary can directly test no properties other than equality. The opaque encoding of the elements in $G_0$ is defined as the function $\xi_0 : Z_p \rightarrow \{0,1\}^*$, which maps all $a \in Z_p$ to the string representation $\xi_0(a)$ of $g^a \in G$. Likewise, $\xi_T : Z_p \rightarrow \{0,1\}^*$ maps $a \in Z_p$ to the string representation $\xi_T(a)$ of $e(g,g)^a \in G_T$. The adversary communicates with the oracles to perform group action on $G_0, G_T$ and bilinear map $e : G_0 \times G_0 \rightarrow G_T$, by way of the $\xi_0$-representation and $\xi_T$-representation only.

For simplicity, the original game is slightly modified: in the challenge phase of the original security game, the adversary is given a challenge ciphertext, whose $C$ component is either $m_0 \cdot e(g,g)^{\alpha \cdot s}$ or $m_1 \cdot e(g,g)^{\alpha \cdot s}$. We modify $C$ to be either $e(g,g)^{\alpha \cdot s}$ or $e(g,g)^{\vartheta}$, for a random $\vartheta$ in $Z_p$. Indeed, any adversary that has a advantage $\epsilon$ in the original game can be transformed into an adversary having advantage $\epsilon/2$ in the modified game (consider two hybrids: one in which the adversary is to distinguish between $m_0 \cdot e(g,g)^{\alpha \cdot s}, e(g,g)^{\vartheta})$, and the other in which the adversary is to distinguish between $m_1 \cdot e(g,g)^{\alpha \cdot s}$ and $e(g,g)^{\vartheta}$.

Hereafter, we consider the adversary in the modified game. In the Setup phase, the challenger sends the public parameters $\xi_0(1), \xi_0(\beta), \xi_T(\alpha)$ to the adversary. To simulate the hash function $H$, the challenger maintains a table, which is initially empty. Whenever a query $i$ is asked on $H$, if $i$ has never been asked before, the challenger selects a random value $t_i \in_R Z_p$, and adds an entry $(i, t_i, \xi_0(t_i))$ to the table and returns $\xi_0(t_i)$; otherwise, returns the already defined $\xi_0(t_i)$.

In Phase 1, the adversary starts by selecting $x \in_R Z_p$ and getting $\xi_0(x)$ from the challenger. Then, the adversary makes a set of proxy key generation queries. For a $j$th query $\mathbb{A}_j$, the challenger first picks $x_j \in_R Z_p$ and computes $\xi_0(x_j)$. Then the challenger picks $r_1, r_2, r_i \in_R Z_p$ for all $i \in \mathbb{A}_j$, and sets $PxK_j = (k = \xi_0(\frac{r_1 \cdot x + x_j \cdot \alpha + r_2}{\beta}), k' = \xi_0(r_i), \forall i \in \mathbb{A}_j : \{k_{i1} = \xi_0(r_2 + t_i \cdot r_i), k_{i2} = \xi_0(r_i)\})$, where $t_i$ is obtained by querying $i$ upon the random oracle $H$ as described above. Finally, the challenger gives $\xi_0(t_i), \xi_0(x_j)$ and $PxK_j$ to the adversary.

In the Challenge phase, the adversary submits two equal-length challenge messages $m_0, m_1$ and a challenge access tree $T^*$. The challenger responds as follows. Select $s \in_R Z_p$, and compute shares $\varsigma_i$ of $s$ for each attribute $i$ contained in $T^*$ (represented by $T$'s leaf nodes) along the tree as described in the Encryp algorithm. Note that $\varsigma_i$'s are random values subject to the underlying secret sharing induced by $T^*$. Finally, the challenger chooses $\vartheta \in_R Z_p$, and returns to the adversary the challenge ciphertext $c^*$ as $C = \xi_T(\vartheta), C' = \xi_0(\beta \cdot s), C'' = \xi_0(s)$, and $C_{i1} = \xi_0(\varsigma_i), C_{i2} = \xi_0(t_i \cdot \varsigma_i)$ for each attribute $i$ in $T^*$.

In Phase 2, the challenger responds to the proxy key generation queries from the adversary, just as in Phase 1.

**Analysis of the Simulated Game.** Let $q$ bound the total number of group elements the adversary receives during the game from the queries it makes to the oracles for $G_0, G_T$, the bilinear map, and the hash function (including the hash function queries implicitly invoked by the proxy key generation and the challenge ciphertext generation). We will show that with probability $1 - \mathcal{O}(q^2/p)$, the adversary's view in this simulated game is identically distributed to what its view could be if it has been given $C = \xi_T(\alpha \cdot s)$ in the game. Note that in the current game, the adversary's advantage is 0, as $\xi_T(\vartheta)$ is independent of the encryption of the challenge messages. We thus conclude that the advantage of the adversary, when given $C = \xi_T(\alpha \cdot s)$, is at most $\mathcal{O}(q^2/p)$, which proves the theorem if $q^2/p$ is negligible.

**Table 1.** Rational functions in $G_0$

| System setup | $\beta$ | | | |
|---|---|---|---|---|
| Proxy key queries | $x$ | $x^{[j]}$ | $\frac{r_1^{[j]} \cdot x + x^{[j]} \cdot \alpha + r_2^{[j]}}{\beta}$ | $r_1^{[j]}$ |
| | $t_i$ | $r_2^{[j]} + t_i \cdot r_i^{[j]}$ | $r_i^{[j]}$ | |
| Challenge ciphertext | $\beta \cdot s$ | $s$ | $\varsigma_{i'}$ | $t_{i'}$ |
| | $t_{i'} \cdot \varsigma_{i'}$ | | | |

We assume that the adversary communicates with group oracles, only with values it has already received from the oracles. Note that each query the adversary makes is of the form of a rational function $\pi = \chi/\gamma$ in the variables of $\alpha, \beta, x, x^{[j]}, r_1^{[j]}, r_2^{[j]}, t_i, r_i^{[j]}, s$, and $\varsigma_i$, where the subscript variable $i$ denotes the attribute strings and the superscript variable $[j]$ is the index of the proxy key queries. We now place a condition on the event that no "unexpected collisions" occur in either $G_0$ and $G_T$. An unexpected collision is one when two queries of two distinct rational functions $\chi/\gamma \neq \chi'/\gamma'$ coincide in value, due to the random choices of the values of the involved variables. For any pair of queries corresponding to $\chi/\gamma$ and $\chi'/\gamma'$, a collision occurs only if the non-zero polynomial $\chi/\gamma - \chi'/\gamma'$ evaluates to be zero. In our case, the degree of $\chi/\gamma - \chi'/\gamma'$ is a small number; thus, the probability of a collision is $\mathcal{O}(1/p)$ [27,36]. By a union bound, the probability of any unexpected collision happens is at most $\mathcal{O}(q^2/p)$ for $q$ queries. As a result, we have probability $1 - \mathcal{O}(q^2/p)$ that no unexpected collisions happen.

Subject to the condition of no unexpected collisions, we need to show that the adversary's view is identically distributed if the challenger has set $\vartheta = \alpha \cdot s$. The view of the adversary can differ in the case of $\vartheta = \alpha \cdot s$ only if there are two queries $\pi, \pi'$ into $G_T$, such that $\pi \neq \pi'$ but $\pi \mid_{\vartheta = \alpha \cdot s} = \pi' \mid_{\vartheta = \alpha \cdot s}$. We will show that this will not happen.

Recall that $\vartheta$ only occurs as $\xi_T(\vartheta)$, which is an element of $G_T$. Thus, the only difference that $\pi$ and $\pi'$ can have on $\vartheta$ is such that $\pi - \pi' = \eta \vartheta - \eta \alpha \cdot s$, for a constant $\eta$. It suffices to show that the adversary can never construct a query for $\xi_T(\eta \alpha \cdot s = \pi - \pi' + \eta \vartheta)$, given that no unexpected collisions occur. This reaches a contradiction and establishes the theorem.

This follows from the following analysis, based on the information given to the adversary during the game. For ease of reference, Table 1 enumerates all rational functions in $G_0$ known to the adversary by means of the system setup, proxy key generation queries and challenge ciphertext query ($i, i'$ are possible attribute strings, and $j$ is the index of the proxy key generation queries). In addition, the adversary also knows the value of $x$ (which represents the cloud server's key). Any query in $G_T$ is a linear combination of products of pairs of these rational functions (of course, $x$ or $\frac{1}{x}$ can be the coefficients, as the adversary knows the value of $x$). Observe from the table that the only rational function containing $\alpha$ is $\frac{r_1^{[j]} \cdot x + x^{[j]} \cdot \alpha + r_2^{[j]}}{\beta}$. In order for the adversary to produce a rational function containing $\eta\alpha \cdot s$, while at the same time canceling out other elements as much as possible, the only choice is multiplying $\frac{r_1^{[j]}\cdot x + x^{[j]}\cdot \alpha + r_2^{[j]}}{\beta}$ and $\beta \cdot s$. This will create a polynomial of the form $r_1^{[j]} \cdot x \cdot s + x^{[j]} \cdot \alpha \cdot s + r_2^{[j]} \cdot s$ (for simplicity, we always omit constant coefficients whenever possible). It is easy to cancel out the term $r_1^{[j]} \cdot x \cdot s$ by multiplying $r_1^{[j]}$ and $s$, together with the knowledge of $x$. Now, we have a polynomial $x^{[j]} \cdot \alpha \cdot s + r_2^{[j]} \cdot s$, and we need to eliminate the term $r_2^{[j]} \cdot s$. There are two options: (1) Multiplying $r_2^{[j]} + t_i \cdot r_i^{[j]}$ and $s$ introduces an additional term $t_i \cdot r_i^{[j]} \cdot s$. This additional term can be canceled out only by an appropriate combination of the products of $t_{i'} \cdot \varsigma_{i'}$ and $s$, following the secret sharing induced by $\mathcal{T}^*$. We are eventually left with the term $x^{[j]} \cdot \alpha \cdot s$. To construct a query for $\xi_T(\eta\alpha \cdot s)$ where $\eta$ is a constant known to the adversary, we must cancel out $x^{[j]}$ from $x^{[j]} \cdot \alpha \cdot s$. This is not possible using any combination of the rational functions in Table 1, as long as the adversary does not know $x^{[j]}$ and $\frac{1}{x^{[j]}}$. (2) Multiplying $r_2^{[j]} + t_i \cdot r_i^{[j]}$ and $\varsigma_{i'}$, which eventually leads to the canceling out of $r_2^{[j]} \cdot s$ and other introduced terms (following the secret sharing induced by $\mathcal{T}^*$) as desired. But again, we need to cancel out $x^{[j]}$ from $x^{[j]} \cdot \alpha \cdot s$, as in the first case. This completes the proof.     □

**Lemma 2.** *The construction satisfies Data Privacy Against Users as defined in Definition 3, if the CP-ABE scheme in [4] is CPA secure.*

*Proof.* We prove that an adversary $\mathcal{A}$ to our scheme can be transformed to an adversary $\mathcal{B}$ to the CP-ABE scheme [4] which is proven secure in the generic group model. The construction of $\mathcal{B}$ is by means of invoking $\mathcal{A}$, with the help of its own chosen plaintext attack (CPA) game in terms of the CP-ABE scheme. In particular, $\mathcal{B}$ has to answer $\mathcal{A}$'s proxy key generation queries. We show that within the context of the CPA game between $\mathcal{B}$ and its own challenger, $\mathcal{B}$ can answer $\mathcal{A}$'s proxy key generation queries, simulating $\mathcal{A}$'s challenger.

Specifically, when the CPA game between $\mathcal{B}$ and its challenger starts, $\mathcal{B}$ starts the Setup phase with $\mathcal{A}$ by passing the public system parameters it gets from its own challenger (we do not consider the delegate functionality in [4]). In Phase 1, $\mathcal{B}$ first generates $(g^x, x \in_R Z_p)$ as the cloud server's key pair. When receiving an attribute set $\mathbb{A}$ from $\mathcal{A}$ as $j$th proxy key generation query, $\mathcal{B}$ first makes a key generation (KeyGen in [4]) query on $\mathbb{A}$ to its own challenger, and upon it, $\mathcal{B}$ gets a decryption key of the form $(k = g^{\frac{\alpha + r_2}{\beta}}, \{k_{i1} = g^{r_2}H(i)^{r_i}, k_{i2} = g^{r_i}\}_{i \in \mathbb{A}})$ (having been collated with the notations in our construction). The challenge of the simulation is how to derive a valid proxy key for $\mathcal{A}$ from the decryption key. To this end, $\mathcal{B}$ generates $(g^{x_j}, x_j \in_R Z_p)$ as the user key pair; then picks $r_1 \in_R Z_p$, and computes $k = k^{x_j} = g^{\frac{\alpha \cdot x_j + r_2 \cdot x_j}{\beta}}, k' = g^{r_1}, \forall i \in \mathbb{A} : k_{i1} = k_{i1}^{x_j} \cdot g^{-xr_1} = g^{r_2 \cdot x_j - xr_1}H(i)^{r_i \cdot x_j}, k_{i2} = k_{i2}^{x_j} = g^{r_i \cdot x_j}$, and the proxy key is set to be $(k, k', \{k_{i1}, k_{i2}\}_{i \in \mathbb{A}})$. It remains to see that this is a valid proxy key. Note that $k = g^{\frac{\alpha \cdot x_j + r_2 \cdot x_j}{\beta}} = g^{\frac{xr_1 + \alpha \cdot x_j + r_2 \cdot x_j - xr_1}{\beta}} = ((g^x)^{r_1}(g^{x_j})^{\alpha}g^{r_2 \cdot x_j - xr_1})^{\frac{1}{\beta}}$. Hence $(k, k', \{k_{i1}, k_{i2}\}_{i \in \mathbb{A}})$ is indeed a valid proxy key, with "$r_2$" being $r_2 \cdot x_j - xr_1$ and "$r_i$" being $r_i \cdot x_j$.

In Challenge phase, when $\mathcal{A}$ submits $m_0, m_1$ and $\mathcal{T}^*$, $\mathcal{B}$ submits them to its own challenger. As a response, $\mathcal{B}$ gets a challenge ciphertext of the form $(\mathcal{T}^*, C = m_b \cdot \mathcal{G}_\alpha^s, C' = h^s, \forall \ell \in L : \{C_{\ell 1} = g^{q_\ell(0)}, C_{\ell 2} = H(\mathsf{att}(\ell))^{q_\ell(0)}\})$ according to the encryption algorithm (i.e. Encrypt) in [4]. Note that this ciphertext is of the same format as in our construction, except that it does not have the $C'' = g^s$ element in our construction. Fortunately, $g^s$ actually can be computed from $\forall \ell \in L : \{C_{\ell 1} = g^{q_\ell(0)}\}$, following the secret sharing induced by $\mathcal{T}^*$.

In Phase 2, $\mathcal{B}$ answers $\mathcal{A}$'s proxy key generation queries as in Phase 1. Finally, $\mathcal{B}$ outputs whatever bit $\mathcal{A}$ outputs. It can be seen that the simulation by $\mathcal{B}$ is perfect. This completes the proof.                              □

**Lemma 3.** *The construction satisfies User Revocation Support as defined in Definition 4.*

*Proof.* The proof will in general proceed in a similar way as in the proof for Lemma 1. The main difference is that in this proof, the adversary knows the value of $x^{[j]}$'s, instead of $x$. This results in the effect that it cannot cancel out the term $r_1^{[j]} \cdot x \cdot s$ from the polynomial $r_1^{[j]} \cdot x \cdot s + x^{[j]} \cdot \alpha \cdot s + r_2^{[j]} \cdot s$. To avoid repetition, we omit the details.                              □

Combining the proofs for the above three lemmas, we complete the proof of Theorem 1.                              ■

# References

1. Attrapadung, N., Imai, H.: Attribute-based encryption supporting direct/indirect revocation modes. In: Parker, M.G. (ed.) Cryptography and Coding 2009. LNCS, vol. 5921, pp. 278–300. Springer, Heidelberg (2009)
2. Blaze, M., Bleumer, G., Strauss, M.: Divertible protocols and atomic proxy cryptography. In: Nyberg, K. (ed.) EUROCRYPT 1998. LNCS, vol. 1403, pp. 127–144. Springer, Heidelberg (1998)
3. Boneh, D., Ding, X., Tsudik, G., Wong, C.M.: A method for fast revocation of public key certificates and security capabilities. In: Proceedings of USENIX Security (2001)
4. Bethencourt, J., Sahai, A., Waters, B.: Ciphertext-policy attribute-based encryption. In: Proceedings of IEEE S&P, pp. 321–334 (2007)
5. Choo, K.K.R.: Legal issues in the cloud. IEEE Cloud Comput. **1**(1), 94–96 (2014)
6. Chow, S.S.M., Boyd, C., González Nieto, J.M.: Security-mediated certificateless cryptography. In: Yung, M., Dodis, Y., Kiayias, A., Malkin, T. (eds.) PKC 2006. LNCS, vol. 3958, pp. 508–524. Springer, Heidelberg (2006)
7. Chen, Y., Jiang, L., Yiu, S., Au, M., Xuan, W.: Fully-RCCA-CCA-Secure ciphertext-policy attribute based encryption with security mediator. In: Proceedings of ICICS 2014 (2014)
8. Cloud Security Alliance: Security guidance for critical areas of focus in cloud computing (2009). http://www.cloudsecurityalliance.org
9. Chu, C.-K., Zhu, W.T., Han, J., Liu, J.K., Xu, J., Zhou, J.: Security concerns in popular cloud storage services. IEEE Pervasive Comput. **12**(4), 50–57 (2013)
10. European Network and Information Security Agency: Cloud computing risk assessment (2009). http://www.enisa.europa.eu/act/rm/files/deliverables/cloud-computing-risk-assessment

11. Gartner: Don't trust cloud provider to protect your corporate assets, 28 May 2012. http://www.mis-asia.com/resource/cloud-computing/gartner-dont-trust-cloud-provider-to-protect-your-corporate-assets
12. Green, M., Hohenberger, S., Waters, B.: Outsourcing the decryption of ABE ciphertexts. In: Proceedings of USENIX Security (2011)
13. Goyal, V., Pandy, O., Sahai, A., Waters, B.: Attribute-based encryption for fine-grained access control of encrypted data. In: Proceedings of ACM CCS 2006, pp. 89–98 (2006)
14. Hohenberger, S., Waters, B.: Online/offline attribute-based encryption. In: Krawczyk, H. (ed.) PKC 2014. LNCS, vol. 8383, pp. 293–310. Springer, Heidelberg (2014)
15. Jiang, T., Chen, X., Li, J., Wong, D.S., Ma, J., Liu, J.: TIMER: secure and reliable cloud storage against data re-outsourcing. In: Huang, X., Zhou, J. (eds.) ISPEC 2014. LNCS, vol. 8434, pp. 346–358. Springer, Heidelberg (2014)
16. Liang, K., Au, M.H., Liu, J.K., Susilo, W., Wong, D.S., Yang, G., Phuong, T.V.X., Xie, Q.: A DFA-based functional proxy pe-encryption scheme for secure public cloud data sharing. IEEE Trans. Inf. Forensics Secur. **9**(10), 1667–1680 (2014)
17. Liang, K., Liu, J.K., Wong, D.S., Susilo, W.: GO-ABE: an efficient cloud-based revocable identity-based proxy re-encryption scheme for public clouds data sharing. In: Proceedings of ESORICS 2014, pp. 257-272 (2014)
18. Liang, K., Susilo, W., Liu, J.K.: Privacy-preserving ciphertext multi-sharing control for big data storage. IEEE Trans. Inf. Forensics Secur. **10**(8), 1578–1589 (2015)
19. Liu, J.K., Au, M.H., Susilo, W., Liang, K., Lu, R., Srinivasan, B.: Secure sharing and searching for real-time video data in mobile cloud. IEEE Netw. **29**(2), 46–50 (2015)
20. Li, M., Huang, X., Liu, J.K., Xu, L.: GO-ABE: group-oriented attribute-based encryption. In: Au, M.H., Carminati, B., Kuo, C.-C.J. (eds.) NSS 2014. LNCS, vol. 8792, pp. 260–270. Springer, Heidelberg (2014)
21. Liu, Z., Wong, D.S.: Practical attribute based encryption: traitor tracing, revocation, and large universe. https://eprint.iacr.org/2014/616.pdf
22. Naor, D., Naor, M., Lotspiech, J.: Revocation and tracing schemes for stateless receivers. In: Kilian, J. (ed.) CRYPTO 2001. LNCS, vol. 2139, pp. 41–62. Springer, Heidelberg (2001)
23. Ostrovsky, R., Sahai, A., Waters, B.: Attribute-based encryption with non-monotonic access structures. In: Proceedings of ACM CCS 2007, pp. 195–203 (2007)
24. Quick, D., Martini, B., Choo, K.K.R.: Cloud Storage Forensics. Syngress/Elsevier, Amsterdam (2014)
25. Shoup, V.: Lower bounds for discrete logarithms and related problems. In: Fumy, W. (ed.) EUROCRYPT 1997. LNCS, vol. 1233, pp. 256–266. Springer, Heidelberg (1997)
26. Sahai, A., Seyalioglu, H., Waters, B.: Dynamic credentials and ciphertext delegation for attribute-based encryption. In: Safavi-Naini, R., Canetti, R. (eds.) CRYPTO 2012. LNCS, vol. 7417, pp. 199–217. Springer, Heidelberg (2012)
27. Schwartz, J.T.: Fast probabilistic algorithms for verification of polynomial identities. J. ACM **27**(4), 701–717 (1980)
28. Waters, B.: Ciphertext-policy attribute-based encryption: an expressive, efficient, and provably secure realization. In: Catalano, D., Fazio, N., Gennaro, R., Nicolosi, A. (eds.) PKC 2011. LNCS, vol. 6571, pp. 53–70. Springer, Heidelberg (2011)

29. Wang, G., Liu, Q., Wu, J.: Hierarhical attribute-based encryption for fine-grained access control in cloud storage services. In: Proceedings of ACM CCS 2010, pp. 735–737 (2010)
30. Yang, K., Jia, X.: Expressive, efficient, and revocable data access control for multi-authority cloud storage. IEEE Trans. Parallel Distrib. Syst. **25**(7), 1735–1744 (2014)
31. Yang, K., Jia, X., Ren, K., Zhang, B., Xie, R.: DAC-MACS: effective data access control for multiauthority cloud storage systems. IEEE Trans. Inf. Forensics Secur. **8**(11), 1790–1801 (2013)
32. Yang, Y., Ding, X., Lu, H., Wan, Z., Zhou, J.: Achieving revocable fine-grained cryptographic access control over cloud data. In: Proceedings of ISC 2013 (2013)
33. Yang, Y., Lu, H., Weng, J., Zhang, Y., Sakurai, K.: Fine-grained conditional proxy re-encryption and application. In: Chow, S.S.M., Liu, J.K., Hui, L.C.K., Yiu, S.M. (eds.) ProvSec 2014. LNCS, vol. 8782, pp. 206–222. Springer, Heidelberg (2014). Extended version to appear: Pervasive and Mobile Computing, ELSEVIER
34. Yu, S., Wang, C., Ren, K., Lou, W.: Achieving secure, scalable, and fine-grained aata access control in cloud computing. In: Proceedings of IEEE INFOCOM 2010 (2010)
35. Yuen, T.H., Zhang, Y., Yiu, S.M., Liu, J.K.: Identity-based encryption with post-challenge auxiliary inputs for secure cloud applications and sensor networks. In: Kutyłowski, M., Vaidya, J. (eds.) ICAIS 2014, Part I. LNCS, vol. 8712, pp. 130–147. Springer, Heidelberg (2014)
36. Zippel, R.: Probabilistic algorithms for sparse polynomials. In: Ng, K.W. (ed.) EUROSAM/ISSAC 1979. LNCS, vol. 72, pp. 216–226. Springer, Heidelberg (1979)

# Batch Verifiable Computation of Polynomials on Outsourced Data

Liang Feng Zhang[1](✉) and Reihaneh Safavi-Naini[2]

[1] ShanghaiTech University, Shanghai, China
zhanglf@shanghaitech.edu.cn
[2] University of Calgary, Calgary, Canada

**Abstract.** Secure outsourcing of computation to cloud servers has attracted much attention in recent years. In a typical outsourcing scenario, the client stores its data on a cloud server and later asks the server to perform computations on the stored data. The verifiable computation (VC) of Gennaro, Gentry, Parno (Crypto 2010) and the homomorphic MAC (HomMAC) of Backes, Fiore, Reischuk (CCS 2013) allow the client to verify the server's computation with substantially less computational cost than performing the outsourced computation. The existing VC and HomMAC schemes that can be considered practical (do not required heavy computations such as computing fully homomorphic encryptions), are limited to compute linear and quadratic polynomials on the outsourced data. In this paper, we introduce a *batch verifiable computation* (BVC) model that can be used when the computation of the same function on multiple datasets is required, and construct two schemes for computing polynomials of high degree on the outsourced data. Our schemes allow *efficient client verification*, *efficient server computation*, and *composition* of computation results. Both schemes allow new elements to be added to each outsourced dataset. The second scheme also allows new datasets to be added. A unique feature of our schemes is that the storage required at the server for storing the authentication information, stays the same as the number of outsourced datasets is increased, and so the *server storage overhead* (the ratio of the server storage to the total size of the datasets) approaches 1. In all existing schemes this ratio is $\geq 2$. Hence, our BVC can effectively halve the required server storage.

## 1 Introduction

Cloud computing provides an attractive solution for computationally weak clients that need to outsource data and perform large-scale computations on the outsourced data. This however raises the important security requirement of enabling the client to verify the correctness of the outsourced computation. A cloud server may return an incorrect result, accidentally or intentionally, and the ability to verify the result is a basic requirement. This requirement has motivated the research on the verifiability of outsourced computation in two directions: exploring the theoretical foundation of what computations can be

© Springer International Publishing Switzerland 2015
G. Pernul et al. (Eds.): ESORICS 2015, Part II, LNCS 9327, pp. 167–185, 2015.
DOI: 10.1007/978-3-319-24177-7_9

securely outsourced, and proposing secure solutions for specific problems with emphasis on practicality. Our work follows the latter direction.

**Verifiable Computation.** Several models have been proposed for secure outsourcing of computation. In the verifiable computation (VC) model of Gennaro, Gentry and Parno [14], the client's data defines a function and a computation is equivalent to evaluating this function that is computationally expensive. To outsource this computation, the client computes a one-time encoding of the function and stores it at the server. This enables the server to not only evaluate the function on any input, but also provide a proof that the evaluation has been done correctly. The client's verification must be substantially less time-consuming than evaluating the original function. The effort of generating the one-time encoding will be amortized over multiple evaluations of the function and so is considered acceptable.

Following [14] a number of VC schemes [2,10,11,14,21] to delegate generic functions have been proposed. These schemes are based on fully homomorphic encryption (FHE) and so with today's constructions of FHE, cannot be considered practical. Benabbas et al. [5] initiated a line of research [5,9,13,20] on *practical* VC for specific functions such as polynomials, which do not require heavy cryptographic computations such as FHE. In a VC for polynomials, the client's data consists of the coefficients of a polynomial. The client stores an encoding of the coefficients on a cloud server; this encoding allows the server to evaluates the polynomial on any requested point; the client can efficiently verify the server's computation. These schemes are secure against a malicious server which is allowed to make a polynomial (in the security parameter) number of attempts to deceive the client into accepting a wrong computation result, with each attempt being told successful or not.

Practical VC schemes however are limited to the computation of linear functions on the outsourced data (e.g., evaluating a polynomial at a point $x$ is equivalent to computing the inner product of a vector defined by the coefficients with a vector defined by $x$ and linear in the coefficients). This means that even simple statistical functions such as variance, cannot be computed. Also, the encoding of the function doubles the cloud storage needed by the function itself. Evaluating polynomials arise in applications such as proof of retrievability and verifiable keyword search [13], where the number of polynomial coefficients is roughly equal to the number of data elements in a file or database. In those scenarios doubling the cloud storage will result in a substantial increase of the client's expense and will become increasingly problematic as more and more data is outsourced.

**Homomorphic MAC.** Homomorphic MAC (HomMAC) [16] allows a client to store a *dataset* (a set of data elements) on a cloud server, and later request the computation of some specified functions, referred to as the *admissible function family*, on the dataset. The dataset may consist of employee records of an institution and a possible computation could be evaluating a function of the records. One can add elements to, or remove elements from, the dataset as needed. The encoding of the dataset consists of all data elements and a special MAC tag for each data element. The tags allow the server to produce a MAC tag for the computation of any admissible function.

HomMACs for admissible linear functions [1] and admissible nonlinear functions [4,8,16] have been proposed. Some of these schemes require heavy cryptographic computations, such as FHE [16]. Catalano and Fiore [8] proposed an elegant HomMAC for high degree polynomials with efficient server computations (including PRF computations and polynomial evaluations over relatively small finite fields). The client verification cost however is effectively the same as performing the outsourced computation. Backes, Fiore and Reischuk [4] removed this drawback by restricting the class of admissible functions to polynomials of degree 2. They considered the computations of the same function on multiple datasets. The verification of the computations requires an expensive preprocessing which is done only once and amortized over all verifications. Restriction on the degree of the polynomials however limits their applicability. For example an important task in data analysis is to determine if a dataset is normally distributed. Two commonly used statistical measures for symmetry and flatness of a distribution relative to normal distribution, are skewness and kurtosis, which require computation of degree 3 and 4 polynomials of the data elements, respectively.

Compared to the VC model of [5,14], the security model of HomMAC is more demanding. Here the server is allowed to learn the MAC tags of arbitrary data elements of its choice and also make a polynomial (in the security parameter) number of attempts to deceive the client into accepting a wrong computation result, with each attempt being told successful or not. This stronger security property means that the HomMACs can be straightforwardly translated into VC schemes but the converse may not be true in general. In a HomMAC based VC scheme the server has to store both the data elements and the MAC tags. This usually doubles the cloud storage consumed by the data elements.

An additional desirable property of HomMACs is that they allow *composition*. That is, given multiple computation results and their MAC tags, one can perform a high level computation on these results and also generate a corresponding MAC tag for this high level computation.

**Motivation.** The existing VC schemes satisfy a subset of the following desirable properties: (p1) *Large admissible function family*: enabling the computation of high degree polynomials (not limited to the linear and quadratic ones) on the outsourced data; (p2) *Efficient client verification*: the client's verification is substantially less expensive than computing the delegated computation; (p3) *Efficient server computation*: the server does not need to do heavy cryptographic computations (such as FHE); (p4) *Efficient server storage*: the server stores an encoding of the client's data and the encoding consumes almost no extra storage than the data itself. (p5) *Unbounded data*: the client can freely update the outsourced data by adding new elements to every dataset and also adding new datasets. Our goal is to construct schemes that provide *all* the above properties.

## 1.1   Our Contributions

We introduce *batch verifiable computation (BVC)*, and construct two BVC schemes that satisfy properties (p1)–(p5). Similar to Backes et al. [4], we also consider outsourcing of multiple datasets with two labels. The outsourced data $m$ defines an $N \times s$ matrix $(m_{i,j})_{N \times s}$, where each column is called a *dataset*, and each entry $m_{i,j}$ is labeled by a pair $(i,j) \in [N] \times [s]$. However, the similarity ends here: Backes et al. allow computation of different functions on each dataset with the restriction that the polynomials are of degree at most two. Our main observation is that by batching computation of the same function on all datasets, an impressive set of properties can be achieved. In particular one can save storage at the server, and this saving will be significant when the computation on more datasets are outsourced. In BVC the client computes a tag $t_i$ for the $i$th row of $m$ for every $i \in [N]$, and stores $\mathbf{t} = (t_1, \ldots, t_N)$ as an extra column at the cloud server. A computation is specified by a program $\mathcal{P} = (f, I)$, where $f(x_1, \ldots, x_n)$ is a function and $I = \{i_1, \ldots, i_n\} \subseteq [N]$ specifies the subset of elements of each dataset which will be used in the computation of $f$. Given the program $\mathcal{P}$, the server returns $s$ results $\rho_1 = f(m_{i_1,1}, \ldots, m_{i_n,1}), \ldots, \rho_s = f(m_{i_1,s}, \ldots, m_{i_n,s})$ and a single *batch proof* $\pi$; the client accepts the $s$ results only if they successfully pass the client's verification. A BVC scheme is secure if no malicious cloud server can deceive the client into accepting wrong results. We consider the computation of any polynomial function (i.e., arithmetic circuit) on the outsourced data, and construct two BVC schemes with the following properties.

**Large Admissible Function Family.** The first scheme admits polynomials of degree as high as any polynomial in the security parameter. The second scheme admits any constant degree polynomials. The only other known practical schemes that can compute the same class of functions is from [8] in which the client's verification is effectively as heavy as the outsourced computation.

**Efficient Client Verification.** In our BVC schemes the client can verify the computation results on the $s$ datasets using a single batch proof that is computed from the tag column. In both schemes verifying the computation result of each dataset is by evaluating the batch proof (which is a polynomial) at a specific point. The batch proof in the first scheme is a univariate polynomial of bounded degree, and in the second scheme is a multivariate polynomial of bounded degree. Compared with the naive construction where the scheme in [8] is used on each dataset, the client's average verification cost in our schemes is substantially less than what is required by the original computation as long as $s$ is large enough.

**Efficient Server Computation.** The server computation in our schemes consists of PRF computations and polynomial evaluations over relatively small finite fields (such as $\mathbb{Z}_p$ for $p \approx 2^{128}$ when the security parameter $\lambda = 128$). This is similar to [8] and more efficient than [4] where the server must compute a large number of exponentiations and pairings over significantly larger groups.

**Efficient Server Storage.** In a VC (or BVC) scheme the client stores an encoding of its data on the cloud server. We define the *storage overhead* of a VC (or BVC) scheme as the ratio of the size of the encoding to the size of data. It is easy to see that the storage overhead is lower bounded by 1. In both schemes a tag has size equal to an element of $m$, resulting in a storage overhead of $1 + 1/s$ which approaches 1 as $s$ increases. In all existing practical VC schemes [4,5,8,9,13] the storage overhead is $\geq 2$.

**Unbounded Data.** In our BVC schemes the outsourced data $m$ consists of $s$ datasets, each consisting of $N$ elements. Our schemes allow the client to add an arbitrary number of new rows and/or columns to $m$, and efficiently update the tag column without downloading $m$. While adding new rows to $m$ is straightforward, adding new datasets to $m$ without performing the tag computation from scratch (and so downloading the already outsourced data) is highly non-trivial. This is because in our schemes each row of $m$ is authenticated using a single tag, and so adding a new dataset (a new data element to each row) could destroy the well-formed tag of the row, requiring the tag of the updated row to be computed from scratch. We show that our second scheme allows the client to add new datasets and efficiently update the tag column, *without downloading* $m$.

In summary our BVC schemes provide all the desirable properties of a VC scheme in practice, together with the unique property that the storage overhead reduces with the number of datasets. The storage efficiency however comes at a somewhat higher cost of computing the proofs by the server. In Sect. 4 we give comparisons of our schemes with [8] that supports the same functionality, when applied to the $s$ datasets individually.

**Composition.** Our BVC schemes support composition. Let $m = (m_{i,j})_{N \times s}$ be the client's outsourced data, and $\mathcal{P}_1 = (f_1, I_1), \ldots, \mathcal{P}_n = (f_n, I_n)$ be $n$ programs, where $f_i$ is a function and $I_i \subseteq [N]$ for every $i \in [n]$. Computing the $n$ programs on the datasets gives a matrix $\rho = (\rho_{i,j})_{n \times s}$ of computation results and $n$ proofs $\pi_1, \ldots, \pi_n$, where $\rho_{i,j}$ is the result of computing $f_i$ on the $j$th dataset and $\pi_i$ is a proof of the correctness of the $i$th row of $\rho$. Our schemes allow composition in the sense that there is a polynomial time algorithm Comb that takes $(\rho, (\pi_1, \ldots, \pi_n))$ and any program $\mathcal{P} = (f(x_1, \ldots, x_n), I = [n])$ as input, and outputs $\xi_1 = f(\rho_{1,1}, \ldots, \rho_{n,1}), \ldots, \xi_s = f(\rho_{1,s}, \ldots, \rho_{n,s})$ along with a batch proof $\pi$. Moreover, the client's cost to verify $\xi_1, \ldots, \xi_s$ is substantially less than what is required by computing $\xi_1, \ldots, \xi_s$.

## 1.2 Overview of the Constructions

We use a novel interpretation of the technique in [8] when applied to multiple datasets to design schemes that satisfy properties (p1)–(p5). Let $m = (m_{i,j})_{N \times s}$ be a collection of $s$ datasets that are to be outsourced. We shall authenticate the $s$ elements in each row of $m$ using a single authentication tag that has size equal to an entry of $m$. This immediately results in a storage overhead of $1 + 1/s$. The $N$ tags are generated such that the cloud server can compute any program $\mathcal{P} = (f, I)$ on the $s$ datasets, and also produce a single proof that verifies the correctness of *all* $s$ computation results. The main idea is a generalization of the technique of [8] to $s$ elements. We pick a *curve* (or a *plane*)

$\sigma_i$ that passes through the $s$ points determined by the $s$ elements in the $i$th row of $m$ and also a point determined by a pseudorandom value $F_k(i)$, where $F$ is a pseudorandom function; the stored tag is a single field element that can be used by the server to determine $\sigma_i$; the computations of any program $\mathcal{P} = (f, I)$ on all the $s$ outsourced datasets can be efficiently verified using the once computation of $f$ on the pseudorandom values $\{F_k(i) : i \in I\}$.

In the first scheme, the client picks a secret key $sk = (k, a) \leftarrow \mathcal{K} \times (\mathbb{Z}_p \setminus \{0, 1, \ldots, s\})$ and determines a univariate polynomial $\sigma_i(x)$ of degree $\leq s$ that passes through the $s + 1$ points $(1, m_{i,1}), \ldots, (s, m_{i,s})$ and $(a, F_k(i))$, for every $i \in [N]$. The client takes the coefficient of $x^s$ in $\sigma_i(x)$ as the tag $t_i$ that authenticates all data elements in the $i$th row of $m$, i.e., $m_{i,1}, \ldots, m_{i,s}$. The client stores $pk = (m, \mathbf{t} = (t_1, \ldots, t_N))$ on the cloud server. Let $\mathcal{P} = (f, I)$ be a program where $f(x_1, \ldots, x_n)$ is a polynomial, and $I = \{i_1, \ldots, i_n\} \subseteq [N]$ specifies the elements of each dataset that are used in the computation of $f$. Given the program $\mathcal{P}$, the server returns both the $s$ computation results $\rho_1 = f(m_{i_1,1}, \ldots, m_{i_n,1}), \ldots, \rho_s = f(m_{i_1,s}, \ldots, m_{i_n,s})$ and a proof $\pi = f(\sigma_{i_1}(x), \ldots, \sigma_{i_n}(x))$. The client accepts all $s$ results only if $\pi(j) = \rho_j$ for every $j \in [s]$ and $\pi(a) = f(F_k(i_1), \ldots, F_k(i_n))$. In the second scheme, the client picks a secret key $sk = (k, \mathbf{a} = (a_0, a_1, \ldots, a_s)) \leftarrow \mathcal{K} \times (\mathbb{Z}_p^*)^{s+1}$ and determines an $(s+1)$-variate polynomial $\sigma_i(\mathbf{y}) = \sigma_i(y_0, y_1, \ldots, y_s) = t_i \cdot y_0 + m_{i,1} \cdot y_1 + \cdots + m_{i,s} \cdot y_s$ that passes through the $s+1$ points $(\mathbf{e}_2, m_{i,1}), \ldots, (\mathbf{e}_{s+1}, m_{i,s})$ and $(\mathbf{a}, F_k(i))$ for every $i \in [N]$, where $\mathbf{e}_j \in \mathbb{Z}_p^{s+1}$ is a 0–1 vector whose $j$th entry is equal to 1 and all other entries are equal to 0. The client stores $pk = (m, \mathbf{t} = (t_1, \ldots, t_N))$ on the cloud server. Given the program $\mathcal{P} = (f, I)$, the server returns both the $s$ computation results $\rho_1, \ldots, \rho_s$ and a proof $\pi = f(\sigma_{i_1}(\mathbf{y}), \ldots, \sigma_{i_n}(\mathbf{y}))$. The client accepts all $s$ results only if $\pi(\mathbf{e}_{j+1}) = \rho_j$ for every $j \in [s]$ and $\pi(\mathbf{a}) = f(F_k(i_1), \ldots, F_k(i_n))$.

In both schemes the server's computation consists of PRF computations and polynomial evaluations over a relatively small finite field $\mathbb{Z}_p$. In Sect. 4 we will show that the first scheme admits computation of polynomials of degree as high as any polynomial in the security parameter $\lambda$, and the second scheme admits computation of any constant-degree polynomials where the constant however can be much larger than two. In both schemes, the client's complexity of verifying all $s$ computation results is dominated by the once computation of $f$ on the $n$ pseudorandom values $F_k(i_1), \ldots, F_k(i_n)$. In particular, this complexity becomes substantially less than the complexity incurred by the $s$ outsourced computations on datasets when the number $s$ is large enough. In both of our schemes the $s$ datasets of size $N$ contained in $m$ are authenticated using a single vector $\mathbf{t}$ of $N$ tags, where each tag is a single field element. As a consequence, the storage overheads of our schemes are both equal to $(|m| + |\mathbf{t}|)/|m| = (Ns + N)/(Ns) = 1 + 1/s$, which can be arbitrarily close to the lower bound 1 as long as $s$ is large enough. Hence, our schemes achieve the properties (p1)–(p4).

In our schemes, a malicious cloud server may want to deceive the client into accepting some wrong results $(\bar{\rho}_1, \ldots, \bar{\rho}_s) \neq (\rho_1, \ldots, \rho_s)$ with a forged proof $\bar{\pi}$. In the first scheme, the forged proof $\bar{\pi}$, as the correct proof $\pi$, is a univariate polynomial of degree $\leq d_1 = s \cdot \deg(f)$. The malicious server succeeds only if $(\bar{\pi}(1), \ldots, \bar{\pi}(s)) = (\bar{\rho}_1, \ldots, \bar{\rho}_s) \neq (\rho_1, \ldots, \rho_s) = (\pi(1), \ldots, \pi(s))$ and $\bar{\pi}(a) = f(F_k(i_1), \ldots, F_k(i_n)) = \pi(a)$. Let $\bar{\pi} - \pi = u_0 + u_1 x + \cdots + u_{d_1} x^{d_1}$ and $\mathbf{a} = (1, a, \ldots, a^{d_1})$. Then breaking the security of our first scheme is equivalent to finding a non-zero vector $\mathbf{u} = (u_0, \ldots, u_{d_1})$ such that the inner product $\mathbf{u} \cdot \mathbf{a} = 0$. In the second scheme, the forged proof $\bar{\pi}$, as the correct proof $\pi$, is an $(s + 1)$-variate polynomial of degree $\leq d_2 = \deg(f)$. The malicious server succeeds only if $(\bar{\pi}(\mathbf{e}_2), \ldots, \bar{\pi}(\mathbf{e}_{s+1})) = (\bar{\rho}_1, \ldots, \bar{\rho}_s) \neq (\rho_1, \ldots, \rho_s) = (\pi(\mathbf{e}_2), \ldots, \pi(\mathbf{e}_{s+1}))$ and $\bar{\pi}(\mathbf{a}) = f(F_k(i_1), \ldots, F_k(i_n)) = \pi(\mathbf{a})$, where $\mathbf{a} = (a_0, \ldots, a_s)$. Let $\bar{\pi} - \pi$ have coefficient vector $\mathbf{u} \in \mathbb{Z}_p^h$ and let $\boldsymbol{\alpha} = \langle \mathbf{a}^{\mathbf{i}} : \mathrm{wt}(\mathbf{i}) \leq d_2 \rangle \in \mathbb{Z}_p^h$, where $h = \binom{s+1+d_2}{d_2}$ and $\mathbf{a}^{\mathbf{i}} = a_0^{i_0} a_1^{i_1} \cdots a_s^{i_s}$ for every $\mathbf{i} = (i_0, i_1, \ldots, i_s)$. Then breaking the security of our second scheme is equivalent to finding a non-zero vector $\mathbf{u}$ such that $\mathbf{u} \cdot \boldsymbol{\alpha} = 0$. In Sect. 2, we provide a technical lemma that shows the probability that any adversary finds such a vector $\mathbf{u}$ in both schemes is negligible in $\lambda$ and thus the security proofs follow.

In both schemes, client can easily authenticate an arbitrary number of new rows using the same secret key and thus extend the size of all datasets. The second scheme also allows the number of datasets to be increased. To add a new dataset $(m_{1,s+1}, \ldots, m_{N,s+1})$, the client picks $(k', a_{s+1}) \leftarrow \mathcal{K} \times \mathbb{Z}_p^*$, and sends both $(m_{1,s+1}, \ldots, m_{N,s+1})$ and $(\Delta_1, \ldots, \Delta_N)$ to the cloud server, where $\Delta_i = a_0^{-1}(F_k(i) - F_{k'}(i) + a_{s+1} \cdot m_{i,s+1})$ for every $i \in [N]$. The cloud server will update $m$ to $(m_{i,j})_{N \times (s+1)}$ and update $\mathbf{t}$ to $\mathbf{t}' = (t_1', \ldots, t_N')$, where $t_i' = t_i - \Delta_i$ for every $i \in [N]$. Intuitively, doing so reveals no information about $\mathbf{a}' = (a_0, \ldots, a_s, a_{s+1})$ to the cloud server. The $t_i'$ is computed such that $\sigma_i'(y_0, \ldots, y_{s+1}) = t_i' \cdot y_0 + m_{i,1} \cdot y_1 + \cdots + m_{i,s+1} \cdot y_{s+1}$ passes through $(\mathbf{a}', F_k(i)), (\mathbf{e}_2, m_{i,1}), \ldots, (\mathbf{e}_{s+2}, m_{i,s+1})$. Thus, all the algorithms of the second scheme will work well with the new secret key $sk' = (k', \mathbf{a}')$. We show that breaking the security of this extended scheme is equivalent to finding a non-zero vector $\mathbf{u}$ such that $\mathbf{u} \cdot \boldsymbol{\alpha}' = 0$, where $\boldsymbol{\alpha}' = \langle (\mathbf{a}')^{\mathbf{i}} : \mathrm{wt}(\mathbf{i}) \leq d_2 \rangle$. We show that this cannot be done except with negligible probability. Thus the second scheme also satisfies (p5).

In both schemes, the composition property follows from the intrinsic structure of the constructions. Let $\mathcal{P}_1 = (f_1, I_1), \ldots, \mathcal{P}_n = (f_n, I_n)$ be $n$ programs. In the first scheme the cloud server would compute these programs on $pk = (m, \mathbf{t})$ and then obtain a matrix $(\rho_{i,j})_{n \times s}$ of results and $n$ proofs $(\pi_1, \ldots, \pi_n)$. Given any high level program $\mathcal{P} = (f(x_1, \ldots, x_n), I = [n])$, the cloud server would be able to compute $\mathcal{P}$ on $(\rho_{i,j})_{n \times s}$ to obtain $s$ results $\xi_1, \ldots, \xi_s$ and also compute $\mathcal{P}$ on $(\pi_1, \ldots, \pi_n)$ to obtain a proof $\pi = f(\pi_1, \ldots, \pi_n)$.

## 1.3   Related Work

The problem of securely outsourcing computation has a long history. We refer the readers to [5,14] for the solutions that require strong assumptions on adversaries, and the theoretical solutions [19] that require interaction. We are only interested in the non-interactive solutions in the standard model.

**Verifiable Computation.** The verifiable computation of Gennaro et al. [14] gave a non-interactive solution for securely outsourcing computation in the standard model. The VC schemes of [2,11,14] can delegate any generic functions but have limited practical relevance due to their use of fully homomorphic encryption (FHE). The memory delegation [10] can delegate computations on an arbitrary portion of the outsourced data. However, the client must be stateful and suffer from the impracticality of PCP techniques. Benabbas et al. [5] initiated the study of practical (private) VC schemes for delegating specific functions such as polynomials. Parno et al. [21] initiated the study of public VC schemes. Fiore et al. [13] generalized the constructions of [5] and obtained public VC schemes for delegating polynomials and matrices. Papamanthou et al. [20] constructed a public VC scheme for delegating polynomials that allows efficient update. The storage overhead of all these schemes is $\geq 2$. Furthermore, they only admit linear computations on the outsourced data. In particular, the multi-function VC [13] has similar setting as ours but only admits linear computations and has storage overhead $\geq 2$.

**Homomorphic MACs and Signatures.** A homomorphic MAC or signature scheme [7,16] allows one to freely authenticate data and then verify computations on the authenticated data. Such schemes give VC: the client can store data elements and their MAC tags (or signatures) with a server such that the server can compute some admissible functions on an arbitrary subset of the data elements; the server provides both the answer and a MAC tag (or signature) vouching for the correctness of its answer. The storage overhead of the resulting VC scheme is $\geq 2$. Catalano and Fiore [8] proposed a practical HomMAC that admits polynomials of degree as high as a polynomial in the security parameter. However, the client's verification requires as much time as the delegated computation. Backes, Fiore and Reischuk [4] proposed a HomMAC that has amortized efficient verification but only admits polynomials of degree $\leq 2$.

**Non-interactive Proofs.** Goldwasser et al. [18] gave a non-interactive scheme for delegating NC computations. However, for any circuit of size $n$, the server's running time may be a high degree polynomial of $n$ and thus not practical. The SNARGs/SNARKs of [3,6,15] give non-interactive schemes for delegating computations. However, they must rely on the non-falsifiable assumptions [17] which are not standard and much stronger than the common assumptions such as the existence of secure PRFs we use in this paper.

### 1.4 Organization

In Sect. 2 we provide a formal definition of batch verifiable computation and its security; we also develop a lemma which will be used in our security proofs; In Sect. 3 we present our BVC schemes; In Sect. 4, we give a detailed analysis of the proposed schemes and compare them with the solutions based on [4,8]; we also discuss extra properties of our schemes such as composition; Sect. 5 contains some concluding remarks.

## 2    Preliminaries

Let $\lambda$ be a security parameter. We say that a function $q(\lambda)$ is a polynomial function of $\lambda$, denoted as $q(\lambda) = \mathsf{poly}(\lambda)$, if there is a real number $c > 0$ such that $q(\lambda) = O(\lambda^c)$; we say that a function $\epsilon(\lambda)$ is a negligible function of $\lambda$, denoted as $\epsilon(\lambda) = \mathsf{neg}(\lambda)$, if $\epsilon(\lambda) = o(\lambda^{-c})$ for any real number $c > 0$. Let $\mathcal{A}(\cdot)$ be a probabilistic polynomial time (PPT) algorithm. The symbol "$y \leftarrow \mathcal{A}(x)$" means that $y$ is the output distribution of running algorithm $\mathcal{A}$ on the input $x$. We denote by $\mathbf{u} = \langle u_x : x \in X \rangle$ any vector whose entries are labeled by elements of the finite set $X$.

### 2.1    Batch Verifiable Computation on Outsourced Data

In this section we formally define the notion of batch verifiable computation on outsourced data. In our model, the client has a set of data elements and stores them on the cloud server. The set is organized as a matrix $m = (m_{i,j})_{N \times s}$, where each element $m_{i,j}$ is labeled with a pair $(i,j) \in [N] \times [s]$. Each column of $m$ is called a *dataset*. Let $\mathcal{F}$ be any admissible function family. The client is interested in delegating the computation of some function $f(x_1, \ldots, x_n) \in \mathcal{F}$ on the $n$ elements labeled by $I = \{i_1, \ldots, i_n\} \subseteq [N]$, of every dataset. In other words, the client is interested in learning $\rho_1 = f(m_{i_1,1}, \ldots, m_{i_n,1}), \rho_2 = f(m_{i_1,2}, \ldots, m_{i_n,2}), \ldots, \rho_s = f(m_{i_1,s}, \ldots, m_{i_n,s})$. We say that such a batch of computations is defined by a *program* $\mathcal{P} = (f, I) \in \mathcal{F} \times 2^{[N]}$.

**Definition 1** (Batch Verifiable Computation). *A BVC scheme for $\mathcal{F}$ is a tuple $\Pi = (\mathsf{KeyGen}, \mathsf{ProbGen}, \mathsf{Compute}, \mathsf{Verify})$ of four polynomial-time algorithms, where*

- *$(sk, pk) \leftarrow \mathsf{KeyGen}(1^\lambda, m)$ is a key generation algorithm that takes as input the security parameter $\lambda$ and a set $m = (m_{i,j})_{N \times s}$ of data elements and outputs a secret key $sk$ and a public key $pk$;*
- *$vk \leftarrow \mathsf{ProbGen}(sk, \mathcal{P})$ is a problem generation algorithm that takes as input $sk$, a program $\mathcal{P} = (f, I) \in \mathcal{F} \times 2^{[N]}$ and outputs a verification key $vk$;*
- *$(\rho, \pi) \leftarrow \mathsf{Compute}(pk, \mathcal{P})$ is a computation algorithm that takes as input $pk$ and a program $\mathcal{P} = (f, I) \in \mathcal{F} \times 2^{[N]}$ and outputs an answer $\rho = (\rho_1, \ldots, \rho_s)$ and a proof $\pi$; and*
- *$\{0,1\} \leftarrow \mathsf{Verify}(sk, vk, (\rho, \pi))$ is a verification algorithm that verifies $\rho$ with $(sk, vk, \pi)$; it outputs 1 (to indicate acceptance) or 0 (to indicate rejection).*

In our BVC model, the client generates $(sk, pk) \leftarrow \mathsf{KeyGen}(1^\lambda, m)$ and gives $pk$ to the server. To compute some program $\mathcal{P} = (f, I)$ on the outsourced data, the client generates $vk \leftarrow \mathsf{ProbGen}(sk, \mathcal{P})$ and gives $\mathcal{P}$ to the server. Given $(pk, \mathcal{P})$, the server computes and replies with $(\rho, \pi) \leftarrow \mathsf{Compute}(pk, \mathcal{P})$. At last, the client accepts $\rho$ only if $\mathsf{Verify}(sk, vk, (\rho, \pi)) = 1$.

**Correctness.** This property requires that the client always accepts the results computed by an honest server (using the algorithm $\mathsf{Compute}$). Formally, the

- SETUP. Given $m$, the challenger computes $(sk, pk) \leftarrow \mathsf{KeyGen}(1^\lambda, m)$ and gives $pk$ to $\mathcal{A}$;
- QUERIES. The adversary $\mathcal{A}$ adaptively makes a polynomial number of queries:
  For every $\ell = 1$ to $q = \mathsf{poly}(\lambda)$,
    • The adversary $\mathcal{A}$ picks a program $\mathcal{P}_\ell$ and gives it to the challenger;
    • The challenger computes $vk_\ell \leftarrow \mathsf{ProbGen}(sk, \mathcal{P}_\ell)$;
    • The adversary $\mathcal{A}$ constructs a response $(\bar{\rho}_\ell, \bar{\pi}_\ell)$ to the challenger;
    • The challenger gives the output $b_\ell = \mathsf{Verify}(sk, vk, (\bar{\rho}_\ell, \bar{\pi}_\ell))$ to $\mathcal{A}$.
- FORGERY. The adversary $\mathcal{A}$ picks a program $\mathcal{P}^*$ and gives it to the challenger. The challenger computes $vk^* \leftarrow \mathsf{ProbGen}(sk, \mathcal{P}^*)$. At last, $\mathcal{A}$ constructs a response $(\bar{\rho}^*, \bar{\pi}^*)$ to the challenger.
- OUTPUT. The challenger computes $(\rho^*, \pi^*) \leftarrow \mathsf{Compute}(pk, \mathcal{P}^*)$. The adversary wins the security game if $\mathsf{Verify}(sk, vk, (\bar{\rho}^*, \bar{\pi}^*)) = 1$ but $\bar{\rho}^* \neq \rho^*$.

**Fig. 1.** Security game

scheme $\Pi$ is *correct* if for any data $m = (m_{i,j})$, any $(sk, pk) \leftarrow \mathsf{KeyGen}(1^\lambda, m)$, any program $\mathcal{P}$, any $vk \leftarrow \mathsf{ProbGen}(sk, \mathcal{P})$ and any $(\rho, \pi) \leftarrow \mathsf{Compute}(pk, \mathcal{P})$, it holds that $\mathsf{Verify}(sk, vk, (\rho, \pi)) = 1$.

**Security.** This property requires that no malicious server can deceive the client into accepting any incorrect results. Formally, the scheme $\Pi$ is said to be *secure* if any PPT adversary $\mathcal{A}$ wins with probability $< \mathsf{neg}(\lambda)$ in the security game of Fig. 1.

REMARKS: (1) In the FORGERY phase the adversary $\mathcal{A}$ behaves just like it has done in any one of the $q$ queries. Without loss of generality, we can suppose $(\mathcal{P}^*, \bar{\rho}^*, \bar{\pi}^*) = (\mathcal{P}_{\ell^*}, \bar{\rho}_{\ell^*}, \bar{\pi}_{\ell^*})$ for some $\ell^* \in [q]$, i.e., $\mathcal{A}$ picks one of its $q$ queries as the final forgery. (2) In the literature, many VC schemes such as [2,11,14] are not immune to the "rejection problem": if the malicious server knows whether the client has accepted or rejected its answer, then the algorithm $\mathsf{KeyGen}$ (requiring heavy computation effort) must be run again to refresh both $sk$ and $pk$; otherwise, the VC scheme becomes no longer secure. In our security definition, the adversary $\mathcal{A}$ is allowed to make a polynomial number of queries and learns whether some adaptively chosen answers in each query will be accepted by the client. Therefore, the BVC schemes secure under our definition will be immune to the "rejection problem". (3) Our definition of BVC is different from the VC [5] in the sense that we neither consider the outsourced data as a function nor consider the client's input to $\mathsf{ProbGen}$ as an input from that function's domain. In our definition, the client's input to $\mathsf{ProbGen}$ is a program $\mathcal{P} = (f, I) \in \mathcal{F} \times 2^{[N]}$ that specifies the computations of an admissible function $f$ on the portion labeled by $I$ of every dataset. Clearly our definition captures more general scenarios than [5]. In particular, the VC model of [5] can be captured by our BVC as below. Let $m(x)$ be the client's function which will be delegated to the cloud server (e.g.,

$m(x)$ may be a polynomial $m_1 + m_2x + \cdots + m_Nx^{N-1}$ in [5]); from our point of view, the coefficients $(m_1, \ldots, m_N)$ of the polynomial $m(x)$ is a dataset; and furthermore, any input $\alpha$ to the polynomial $m(x)$ specifies a program $\mathcal{P} = (f_\alpha, [N])$, where $f_\alpha(m_1, \ldots, m_N) = m(\alpha)$. Therefore, the polynomial evaluations considered in [5] can be captured by some specific linear computations in our BVC model. (4) In our BVC, the client's verification requires the secret key $sk$. Thus, our BVC schemes are *privately verifiable*. (5) A critical efficiency measure of the BVC scheme in Definition 1 is to what extent the client's verification requires less computing time (resources) than the delegated computations. The client's verification in [5,9,13,14,20,21] is efficient in the sense that it requires substantially less time than performing the delegated computation. In our BVC, the client performs verification by generating a verification key $vk \leftarrow \mathsf{ProbGen}(sk, \mathcal{P})$ and then running the verification algorithm $\mathsf{Verify}(sk, vk, (\rho, \pi))$. The client's verification time is equal to the total time required for running both algorithms. Let $t_\mathcal{P}$ be the time required for computing the program $\mathcal{P}$ on the outsourced data. We say that a BVC scheme is *outsourceable* if the client's verification time is of the order $o(t_\mathcal{P})$. In this paper, we shall construct BVC schemes that are outsourceable.

## 2.2    A Lemma

In this section we present a lemma (Lemma 1) that underlies the security proofs of our BVC schemes. Let $\lambda$ be a security parameter. Let $p$ be a $\lambda$-bit prime and let $\mathbb{Z}_p$ be the finite field of $p$ elements. Let $h \geq 0$ be an integer. We define an equivalence relation $\sim$ over $\mathbb{Z}_p^{h+1} \setminus \{\mathbf{0}\}$ as below: two vectors $\mathbf{u}, \mathbf{v} \in \mathbb{Z}_p^{h+1} \setminus \{\mathbf{0}\}$ are said to be *equivalent* if there exists $\xi \in \mathbb{Z}_p \setminus \{0\}$ such that $\mathbf{u} = \xi \cdot \mathbf{v}$. Let $\Omega_{p,h} = (\mathbb{Z}_p^{h+1} \setminus \{\mathbf{0}\})/\sim$ be the set of all equivalence classes. We represent each equivalence class with a vector in that class. Without loss of generality, we agree that the representative of each class in $\Omega_{p,h}$ is chosen such that its first non-zero element is 1. For any $\mathbf{u}, \mathbf{v} \in \Omega_{p,h}$, we define $\mathbf{u} \odot \mathbf{v} = 0$ if the inner product of $\mathbf{u}$ and $\mathbf{v}$ is equal to 0 modulo $p$ and define $\mathbf{u} \odot \mathbf{v} = 1$ otherwise. The following game models the malicious server's attack in our BVC schemes.

**Game$_\mathcal{V}$.** Let $\mathcal{A}$ be any algorithm. Let $\mathcal{V} \subseteq \Omega_{p,h}$ and let $q = \mathsf{poly}(\lambda)$. In this problem, a vector $\mathbf{v}^* \leftarrow \mathcal{V}$ is chosen and hidden from $\mathcal{A}$; for $i = 1$ to $q$, $\mathcal{A}$ adaptively picks a query $\mathbf{u}_i \in \Omega_{p,h}$ and learns $b_i = \mathbf{u}_i \odot \mathbf{v}^* \in \{0,1\}$; $\mathcal{A}$ *wins* the game if there exists an index $i^* \in [q]$ such that $b_{i^*} = 0$.

In Appendix A, we show the following technical lemma:

**Lemma 1.** *Let $p$ be a prime and let $d, h, s > 0$ be integers.*

*(1) Let $A \subseteq \mathbb{Z}_p$ be a non-empty subset of $\mathbb{Z}_p$. Let $\mathcal{V}_{\mathrm{up}} = \{(1, a, \ldots, a^h) : a \in A\}$. Then any adversary $\mathcal{A}$ wins in **Game$_{\mathcal{V}_{\mathrm{up}}}$** with probability $\leq hq/|A|$.*

*(2) Let $\mathcal{V}_{\mathrm{mp}} = \{\langle \mathbf{a}^\mathbf{i} : \mathrm{wt}(\mathbf{i}) \leq d \rangle : \mathbf{a} \in A^{s+1}\}$, where $h = \binom{s+1+d}{d} - 1$. Then any adversary $\mathcal{A}$ wins in **Game$_{\mathcal{V}_{\mathrm{mp}}}$** with probability $\leq dq/|A|$.*

## 3   Constructions

In this section we propose two BVC schemes for delegating polynomial computations on outsourced data. Our schemes use curves and planes to authenticate the outsourced data, respectively.

### 3.1   The First Construction

Let $p$ be a $\lambda$-bit prime and let $F : \mathcal{K} \times \{0,1\}^* \to \mathbb{Z}_p$ be a PRF with key space $\mathcal{K}$, domain $\{0,1\}^*$ and range $\mathbb{Z}_p$. Let $s > 0$ be an integer. Let $m = (m_{i,j}) \in \mathbb{Z}_p^{N \times s}$ be a matrix that models the client's data. We consider $1, 2, \ldots, s$ as elements of $\mathbb{Z}_p$. Below is our first construction $\Pi_1$.

- $(sk, pk) \leftarrow \mathsf{KeyGen}(1^\lambda, m)$: Pick $k \leftarrow \mathcal{K}$ and $a \leftarrow \mathbb{Z}_p \setminus \{0, 1, 2, \ldots, s\}$. For every $i \in [N]$, compute the coefficients of a polynomial $\sigma_i(x) = \sigma_{i,1} + \sigma_{i,2} \cdot x + \cdots + \sigma_{i,s} \cdot x^{s-1} + t_i \cdot x^s$ such that $\sigma_i(j) = m_{i,j}$ for every $j \in [s]$ and $\sigma_i(a) = F_k(i)$. This can be done by solving the following equation system

$$
\begin{pmatrix}
1 & 1 & 1 & \cdots & 1 \\
1 & 2 & 2^2 & \cdots & 2^s \\
\vdots & \vdots & \vdots & \cdots & \vdots \\
1 & s & s^2 & \cdots & s^s \\
1 & a & a^2 & \cdots & a^s
\end{pmatrix}
\begin{pmatrix}
\sigma_{i,1} \\
\sigma_{i,2} \\
\vdots \\
\sigma_{i,s} \\
t_i
\end{pmatrix}
=
\begin{pmatrix}
m_{i,1} \\
m_{i,2} \\
\vdots \\
m_{i,s} \\
F_k(i)
\end{pmatrix}
\tag{1}
$$

for every $i \in [N]$. The algorithm outputs $pk = (m, \mathbf{t})$ and $sk = (k, a)$, where $\mathbf{t} = (t_1, \ldots, t_N)$.

- $vk \leftarrow \mathsf{ProbGen}(sk, \mathcal{P})$: Let $\mathcal{P} = (f, I)$ be a program, where $f(x_1, \ldots, x_n)$ is a polynomial of degree $d$ over $\mathbb{Z}_p$ and $I = \{i_1, \ldots, i_n\} \subseteq [N]$ specifies the data elements on which $f$ should be computed. This algorithm computes and outputs a verification key $vk = f(F_k(i_1), \ldots, F_k(i_n))$.

- $(\rho, \pi) \leftarrow \mathsf{Compute}(pk, \mathcal{P})$: Let $\mathcal{P} = (f, I)$ be a program, where $f(x_1, \ldots, x_n)$ is a polynomial of degree $d$ over $\mathbb{Z}_p$ and $I = \{i_1, \ldots, i_n\} \subseteq [N]$ specifies the data elements on which $f$ should be computed. This algorithm computes $\rho_j = f(m_{i_1,j}, \ldots, m_{i_n,j})$ for every $j \in [s]$. It solves the following equation system

$$
\begin{pmatrix}
1 & 1 & 1 & \cdots & 1 \\
1 & 2 & 2^2 & \cdots & 2^{s-1} \\
\vdots & \vdots & \vdots & \cdots & \vdots \\
1 & s & s^2 & \cdots & s^{s-1}
\end{pmatrix}
\begin{pmatrix}
\sigma_{i,1} \\
\sigma_{i,2} \\
\vdots \\
\sigma_{i,s}
\end{pmatrix}
=
\begin{pmatrix}
m_{i,1} - t_i \\
m_{i,2} - 2^s t_i \\
\vdots \\
m_{i,s} - s^s t_i
\end{pmatrix}
\tag{2}
$$

to determine $s$ coefficients $\sigma_{i,1}, \ldots, \sigma_{i,s}$ for every $i \in I$. Let $\sigma_i(x) = \sigma_{i,1} + \sigma_{i,2} \cdot x + \cdots + \sigma_{i,s} \cdot x^{s-1} + t_i \cdot x^s$. This algorithm outputs $\rho = (\rho_1, \ldots, \rho_s)$ and $\pi = f(\sigma_{i_1}(x), \ldots, \sigma_{i_n}(x))$.

- $\{0,1\} \leftarrow \mathsf{Verify}(sk, vk, (\rho, \pi))$: This algorithm accepts $\rho$ and outputs 1 only if $\pi(a) = vk$ and $\pi(j) = \rho_j$ for every $j \in [s]$.

It is easy to see $\Pi_1$ is correct. In the full version we show that no PPT adversary can win in the standard security game (Fig. 1) for $\Pi_1$ except with negligible probability. So we have

**Theorem 1.** *If $F$ is a secure PRF, then $\Pi_1$ is a secure BVC scheme.*

### 3.2 The Second Construction

Let $p$ be a $\lambda$-bit prime and let $F : \mathcal{K} \times \{0,1\}^* \to \mathbb{Z}_p$ be a PRF with key space $\mathcal{K}$, domain $\{0,1\}^*$ and range $\mathbb{Z}_p$. Let $s > 0$ be an integer. Let $m = (m_{i,j}) \in \mathbb{Z}_p^{N \times s}$ be a matrix that models the client's data. We consider $1, 2, \ldots, s$ as elements of $\mathbb{Z}_p$. Below is our second construction $\Pi_2$.

- $(sk, pk) \leftarrow \mathsf{KeyGen}(1^\lambda, m)$: Pick $k \leftarrow \mathcal{K}$ and $a_0, a_1, \ldots, a_s \leftarrow \mathbb{Z}_p^*$; for every $i \in [N]$, compute

$$t_i = a_0^{-1}(F_k(i) - a_1 \cdot m_{i,1} - \cdots - a_s \cdot m_{i,s}). \tag{3}$$

  This algorithm outputs $pk = (m, \mathbf{t})$ and $sk = (k, \mathbf{a})$, where $\mathbf{t} = (t_1, \ldots, t_N)$ and $\mathbf{a} = (a_0, a_1, \ldots, a_s)$.
- $vk \leftarrow \mathsf{ProbGen}(sk, \mathcal{P})$: Let $\mathcal{P} = (f, I)$ be a program, where $f(x_1, \ldots, x_n)$ is a polynomial of degree $d$ over $\mathbb{Z}_p$ and $I = \{i_1, \ldots, i_n\} \subseteq [N]$ specifies the data elements on which $f$ should be computed. This algorithm computes and outputs a verification key $vk = f(F_k(i_1), \ldots, F_k(i_n))$.
- $(\rho, \pi) \leftarrow \mathsf{Compute}(pk, \mathcal{P})$: Let $\mathcal{P} = (f, I)$ be a program, where $f(x_1, \ldots, x_n)$ is a polynomial of degree $d$ over $\mathbb{Z}_p$ and $I = \{i_1, \ldots, i_n\} \subseteq [N]$ specifies the data elements on which $f$ should be computed. This algorithm computes $\rho_j = f(m_{i_1,j}, \ldots, m_{i_n,j})$ for every $j \in [s]$. Let $\sigma_i(\mathbf{y}) = t_i \cdot y_0 + m_{i,1} \cdot y_1 + \cdots + m_{i,s} \cdot y_s$ for every $i \in I$, where $\mathbf{y} = (y_0, y_1, \ldots, y_s)$. This algorithm outputs $s$ results $\rho = (\rho_1, \ldots, \rho_s)$ and a proof $\pi = f(\sigma_{i_1}(\mathbf{y}), \ldots, \sigma_{i_n}(\mathbf{y}))$.
- $\mathsf{Verify}(sk, vk, (\rho, \pi))$: This algorithm accepts $\rho$ and outputs 1 only if $\pi(\mathbf{a}) = vk$ and $\pi(\mathbf{e}_{j+1}) = \rho_j$ for every $j \in [s]$, where $\mathbf{e}_{j+1} \in \mathbb{Z}_p^{s+1}$ is a 0–1 vector whose $j + 1$st component is 1 and all other components are 0.

It is easy to see $\Pi_2$ is correct. In the full version we show that no PPT adversary can win the standard security game (Fig. 1) for $\Pi_2$ except with negligible probability. So we have

**Theorem 2.** *If $F$ is a secure PRF, then $\Pi_2$ is a secure BVC scheme.*

## 4 Analysis

In this section we analyze our BVC schemes and compare them with several (naive) solutions based on the existing works [4,8].

**Admissible Function Family.** In both of our schemes the integer $s$ is allowed to be $O(\lambda)$ to capture the scenario that a large enough number of datasets are outsourced. In $\Pi_1$ the cloud server's computation consists of computing $f$ on $s$ points, solving $n$ equation systems of the form (2) and also computing a proof $\pi = f(\sigma_{i_1}(x), \ldots, \sigma_{i_n}(x))$. On one hand, the first two computations are light for the powerful server. On the other hand, computing the proof $\pi$ involves some symbolic computation and seems heavy. However, $\pi$ is a univariate polynomial of degree $\leq sd$. So $\pi$ can be interpolated given $D = sd+1$ evaluations of $\pi$, which requires the computations of $f$ on $O(D) = O(ds)$ points. This work is acceptable for the cloud server even if $d = \text{poly}(\lambda)$. Therefore, $\Pi_1$ allows the computation of polynomials of degree $d$ as high as a polynomial in the security parameter. In $\Pi_2$ the cloud server's computation consists of computing $f$ on $s$ points and also computing a proof $\pi = f(\sigma_{i_1}(\mathbf{y}), \ldots, \sigma_{i_n}(\mathbf{y}))$. On one hand, the first computation is light for the powerful cloud server. On the other hand, computing the proof $\pi$ involves some symbolic computation. Note that $f(x_1, \ldots, x_n)$ is of degree $d$ and each of the $(s+1)$-variate polynomials $\sigma_{i_1}(\mathbf{y}), \ldots, \sigma_{i_n}(\mathbf{y})$ is of degree 1. The cost required by computing $\pi$ is roughly equal to that required by computing $f$ on $(s+1)^d$ points. Furthermore, the server needs to send a representation of $\pi$ that consists of $\binom{s+1+d}{d}$ field elements. If we allow $s = O(\lambda)$, then degree $d$ must be restricted to $O(1)$ such that the server's computation and communication are not too costly. So $\Pi_2$ allows the computation of any $O(1)$-degree polynomials. This admissible function family of $O(1)$-degree polynomials can be significantly larger than the admissible function family of quadratic polynomials in [4].

**Efficient Client Verification.** Let $\mathcal{P} = (f, I)$ be a program, where $f(x_1, \ldots, x_n)$ is a polynomial function and $I = \{i_1, \ldots, i_n\} \subseteq [N]$. Let $(\rho, \pi)$ be the results and proof generated by Compute. The verification complexity is measured by the time complexity of running two algorithms: ProbGen$(sk, \mathcal{P})$ and Verify$(sk, vk, (\rho, \pi))$. In our schemes, the time complexity of running Verify is independent of $n$. As we always consider large enough $n$, the verification complexity in both of our schemes will be dominated by the time complexity of running ProbGen$(sk, \mathcal{P})$. This is the complexity of computing $f$ on $n$ pseudorandom values $F_k(i_1), \ldots, F_k(i_n)$ once. Note that this computation requires roughly $1/s$ times as much time as that required by the $s$ delegated computations of $f$ on the outsourced data. Whenever $s$ is large enough, the client's verification per each dataset uses substantially less time than computing $f$ on each dataset. Hence, our schemes are outsourceable.

**Efficient Server Computation.** In our schemes, the cloud server's computation only involves PRF computations and polynomial evaluations over the finite field $\mathbb{Z}_p$. Note that we never need any number-theoretic assumptions. As a result, the size of the finite field $\mathbb{Z}_p$ can be chosen as small as $p \approx 2^{128}$ when the security parameter $\lambda = 128$. In particular, the PRF $F$ in our both constructions can be chosen as some heuristic PRFs such as AES block ciphers in practical implementations. In Sect. 4.3 we shall see that our server's computation is significantly more efficient than [4].

**Efficient Server Storage.** The storage overheads of our schemes are equal to $|pk|/|m|$, where $|pk|$ and $|m|$ denote the numbers of field elements contained in $pk$ and $m$ respectively. Recall that the number $|pk|/|m|$ is always $\geq 1$ and our objective is making it as close to 1 as possible. It is trivial to see that $|pk|/|m| = (|m| + |\mathbf{t}|)/|m| = (Ns + N)/Ns = 1 + 1/s$ in our schemes. Therefore, the storage overheads of our schemes can be made arbitrarily close to 1 as long as $s$ is large enough.

**Extending the Size of Datasets.** In our schemes the client's outsourced data is a collection $m = (m_{i,j})_{N \times s}$ of $s$ datasets, each containing $N$ elements. In practice, the client may add new data elements to the outsourced datasets. Let $\Pi = \Pi_1$ or $\Pi_2$. Let $(pk, sk)$ be any public key and secret key generated by $\Pi.\mathsf{KeyGen}(1^\lambda, m)$. Note that $pk$ takes the form $(m, \mathbf{t} = (t_1, \ldots, t_N))$, where $t_i$ is a tag authenticating the elements $(m_{i,1}, \ldots, m_{i,s})$ for every $i \in [N]$. In particular, the tag $t_i$ is computed using (1) when $\Pi = \Pi_1$ and using (3) when $\Pi = \Pi_2$, respectively. Let $N' = N + 1$. To add $s$ new elements $(m_{N',1}, \ldots, m_{N',s})$ to the $s$ datasets, the client can simply compute a tag $t_{N'}$ authenticating these elements and instruct the cloud server to change $pk = (m, \mathbf{t})$ to $pk' = (m', \mathbf{t}')$, where $m' = (m_{i,j})_{N' \times s}$ and $\mathbf{t}' = (t_1, \ldots, t_{N'})$. In particular, when $\Pi = \Pi_1$, the tag $t_{N'}$ will computed by solving the equation system (1) for $i = N'$; and when $\Pi = \Pi_2$, the tag $t_{N'}$ will be computed using the equation (3) for $i = N'$. Extending the size of all datasets in this way will never compromise the security of the underlying schemes.

**Extending the Number of Datasets in $\Pi_2$.** In practice, the client may also want to extend the number of datasets. Let $s' = s + 1$. We consider the scenario of the client updating $m$ to $m' = (m_{i,j})_{N \times s'}$, where $(m_{1,s'}, \ldots, m_{N,s'})$ is a new dataset. The general case for adding more than one new datasets can be done by adding one after the other. In a naive way of updating $m$ to $m'$, the client may simply download $pk = (m, \mathbf{t})$, verify the integrity of $m$ and then run our schemes on $m'$. However, this method will be quite inefficient when the size of $m$ is large. Here we show how the client in $\Pi_2$ can authenticate $m'$ without downloading $m$.

Let $F : \mathcal{K} \times \{0,1\}^* \to \mathbb{Z}_p$ be the PRF and let $sk = (k, \mathbf{a}) \leftarrow \mathcal{K} \times (\mathbb{Z}_p^*)^{s+1}$ be the secret key used to outsource $m = (m_{i,j})_{N \times s}$ in $\Pi_2$. Let $pk = (m, \mathbf{t})$, where $t_i = a_0^{-1}(F_k(i) - a_1 \cdot m_{i,1} - \cdots - a_s \cdot m_{i,s})$ for every $i \in [N]$. Let $(m_{1,s+1}, \ldots, m_{N,s+1})$ be a new dataset. To authenticate $m' = (m_{i,j})_{N \times s'}$, the client picks $(k', a_{s+1}) \leftarrow \mathcal{K} \times \mathbb{Z}_p^*$, updates $sk$ to $sk' = (k', \mathbf{a}' = (a_0, \ldots, a_s, a_{s+1}))$ and instructs the server to change $pk$ to $pk' = (m', \mathbf{t}' = (t_1', \ldots, t_N'))$, where $t_i' = a_0^{-1}(F_{k'}(i) - a_1 \cdot m_{i,1} - \cdots - a_{s+1} \cdot m_{i,s+1}) = t_i - a_0^{-1} \cdot (F_k(i) - F_{k'}(i) + a_{s+1} \cdot m_{i,s+1})$. To do so, the client only needs to send the new dataset $(m_{1,s+1}, \ldots, m_{N,s+1})$ together with $\Delta_i = a_0^{-1}(F_k(i) - F_{k'}(i) + a_{s+1} \cdot m_{i,s+1}), 1 \leq i \leq N$, to the cloud server such that the server can update $t_i$ to $t_i'$ by computing $t_i' = t_i - \Delta_i$ for every $i \in [N]$. All the other algorithms will be changed as below to work with $(sk', pk')$:

- $vk \leftarrow \mathsf{ProbGen}(sk', \mathcal{P})$: Let $\mathcal{P} = (f, I)$ be a program, where $f(x_1, \ldots, x_n)$ is a polynomial of degree $d$ over $\mathbb{Z}_p$ and $I = \{i_1, \ldots, i_n\} \subseteq [N]$ specifies on which elements of each dataset $f$ should be computed. This algorithm computes and outputs a verification key $vk = f(F_{k'}(i_1), \ldots, F_{k'}(i_n))$.

- $(\rho, \pi) \leftarrow \mathsf{Compute}(pk', \mathcal{P})$: Let $\mathcal{P} = (f, I)$ be a program, where $f(x_1, \ldots, x_n)$ is a polynomial of degree $d$ over $\mathbb{Z}_p$ and $I = \{i_1, \ldots, i_n\} \subseteq [N]$ specifies on which elements of each dataset $f$ should be computed. This algorithm computes $\rho_j = f(m_{i_1,j}, \ldots, m_{i_n,j})$ for every $j \in [s+1]$. Let $\sigma_i(\mathbf{y}) = t'_i \cdot y_0 + m_{i,1} \cdot y_1 + \cdots + m_{i,s} \cdot y_s + m_{i,s+1} \cdot y_{s+1}$ for every $i \in I$, where $\mathbf{y} = (y_0, y_1, \ldots, y_s, y_{s+1})$. This algorithm outputs $\rho = (\rho_1, \ldots, \rho_{s+1})$ and a proof $\pi = f(\sigma_{i_1}(\mathbf{y}), \ldots, \sigma_{i_n}(\mathbf{y}))$.
- $\mathsf{Verify}(sk', vk, (\rho, \pi))$: This algorithm accepts $\rho$ and outputs 1 only if $\pi(\mathbf{a}') = vk$ and $\pi(\mathbf{e}_{j+1}) = \rho_j$ for every $j \in [s+1]$.

We say that these modifications resulting in an extended scheme $\Pi'_2$. It is trivial to verify the correctness of $\Pi'_2$. In the full version we show that no PPT adversary can win a slight modification of the standard security game (Fig. 1) for $\Pi'_2$ except with negligible probability, where the modification means that the adversary is allowed to know two tag vectors $\mathbf{t}$ and $\mathbf{t}'$ instead of one.

**Theorem 3.** *If $F$ is a secure PRF, then $\Pi'_2$ is a secure BVC scheme.*

**Composition.** We now show that our BVC schemes allow composition and the composed computations can be efficiently verified as well. Let $\Pi = \Pi_1$ or $\Pi_2$. Let $m = (m_{i,j})_{N \times s} \in \mathbb{Z}_p^{N \times s}$ be a collection of $s$ datasets. Let $pk$ and $sk$ be any public key and secret key generated by $\Pi.\mathsf{KeyGen}(1^\lambda, m)$. Let $\mathcal{P}_1 = (f_1, I_1), \ldots, \mathcal{P}_n = (f_n, I_n)$ be $n$ programs, where $f_i \in \mathcal{F}$ and $I_i \subseteq [N]$. Let $vk_i = f_i(\langle F_k(j) : j \in I_i \rangle)$ be generated by $\Pi.\mathsf{ProbGen}(sk, \mathcal{P}_i)$ for every $i \in [n]$. Let $((\rho_{i,1}, \ldots, \rho_{i,s}), \pi_i) \leftarrow \Pi.\mathsf{Compute}(pk, \mathcal{P}_i)$ be the results and proof generated by the computing algorithm. We can consider $\rho = (\rho_{i,\ell})_{n \times s}$ as a collection of $s$ new datasets and consider $(\rho, \{\pi_i\}_{i=1}^n)$ as an encoding of $\rho$. Let $\mathcal{P} = (f(x_1, \ldots, x_n), I = [n])$ be a program that defines a computation on $\rho$.

If $\Pi = \Pi_1$, we have that $sk = (k, a) \in \mathcal{K} \times (\mathbb{Z}_p \setminus \{0, 1, \ldots, s\})$ and $pk = (m, \mathbf{t})$. Due to the correctness of $\Pi_1$, we have that $\mathsf{Verify}(sk, vk_i, \{\rho_{i,\ell}\}_{\ell \in [s]}, \pi_i) = 1$ for every $i \in [n]$, that is, $\pi_i(1) = \rho_{i,1}, \pi_i(2) = \rho_{i,2}, \ldots, \pi_i(s) = \rho_{i,s}$ and $\pi_i(a) = vk_i$. Below is the combing algorithm:

- $((\xi_1, \ldots, \xi_s), \pi) \leftarrow \mathsf{Comb}(f, (\rho_{i,\ell})_{n \times s}, \{\pi_i\}_{i \in [n]})$: computes $\xi_\ell = f(\rho_{1,\ell}, \ldots, \rho_{n,\ell})$ for every $\ell \in [s]$ and $\pi = f(\pi_1(x), \ldots, \pi_n(x))$. Outputs $\xi_1, \ldots, \xi_s$ and $\pi$.

If $\Pi = \Pi_2$, we have that $sk = (k, \mathbf{a}) \in \mathcal{K} \times (\mathbb{Z}_p^*)^{s+1}$ and $pk = (m, \mathbf{t})$. Due to the correctness of $\Pi_2$, we have $\mathsf{Verify}(sk, vk_i, \{\rho_{i,\ell}\}_{\ell \in [s]}, \pi_i) = 1$ for every $i \in [n]$, that is, $\pi_i(\mathbf{e}_2) = \rho_{i,1}, \pi_i(\mathbf{e}_3) = \rho_{i,2}, \ldots, \pi_i(\mathbf{e}_{s+1}) = \rho_{i,s}$ and $\pi_i(\mathbf{a}) = vk_i$. Below is the combing algorithm:

- $((\xi_1, \ldots, \xi_s), \pi) \leftarrow \mathsf{Comb}(f, (\rho_{i,\ell})_{n \times s}, \{\pi_i\}_{i \in [n]})$: computes $\xi_\ell = f(\rho_{1,\ell}, \ldots, \rho_{n,\ell})$ for every $\ell \in [s]$ and $\pi = f(\pi_1(\mathbf{y}), \ldots, \pi_n(\mathbf{y}))$. Outputs $\xi_1, \ldots, \xi_s$ and $\pi$.

# 5   Concluding Remarks

We introduced a model for batch verifiable computation and constructed two BVC schemes with attractive properties. Extending the first scheme to support efficient outsourcing of new datasets, expanding the admissible function family of the second scheme, and constructing publicly verifiable batch computation schemes are interesting open problems that follow from this work.

**Acknowledgement.** Liang Feng Zhang's research is currently supported by Shang-haiTech University's start-up funding (No. F-0203-15-001). This work was done when the author was a postdoctoral fellow at the University of Calgary. Reihaneh Safavi-Naini's research is supported in part by Alberta Innovates Technology Futures, in the Province of Alberta, Canada.

# A    Proof of Lemma 1

Our proof of Lemma 1 begins with the following lemma from [22].

**Lemma 2** (Zhang and Safavi-Naini [22]). *If there is a number $0 < \epsilon < 1$ such that $|\{\mathbf{v} \in \mathcal{V} : \mathbf{u} \odot \mathbf{v} = 0\}| \leq \epsilon \cdot |\mathcal{V}|$ for every $\mathbf{u} \in \Omega_{p,h}$, then $\mathcal{A}$ wins in the* **Game**$_\mathcal{V}$ *with probability $\leq \epsilon q$.*

**Example 1.** Let $A \subseteq \mathbb{Z}_p$ be a non-empty subset of $\mathbb{Z}_p$. Let $\mathcal{V}_{\mathrm{up}} = \{(1, a, \ldots, a^h) : a \in A\} \subseteq \Omega_{p,h}$. For any $\mathbf{u} = (u_0, u_1, \ldots, u_h) \in \Omega_{p,h}$ and $\mathbf{v} = (1, a, \ldots, a^h) \in \mathcal{V}_{\mathrm{up}}$, $\mathbf{u} \odot \mathbf{v} = 0$ if and only if $a$ is a root of the polynomial $u_0 + u_1 x + \cdots + u_h x^h$. Note that any non-zero univariate polynomial of degree $\leq h$ has $\leq h$ roots in $\mathbb{Z}_p$ (and thus has $\leq h$ roots in $A$). For any $\mathbf{u} \in \Omega_{p,h}$, there are $\leq h$ elements $\mathbf{v} \in \mathcal{V}_{\mathrm{up}}$ such that $\mathbf{u} \odot \mathbf{v} = 0$. It follows that $\epsilon \triangleq \max_{\mathbf{u}} \frac{|\{\mathbf{v} \in \mathcal{V}_{\mathrm{up}} : \mathbf{u} \odot \mathbf{v} = 0\}|}{|\mathcal{V}_{\mathrm{up}}|} \leq \frac{h}{|A|}$.

Let $s > 0$ be an integer. Let $\mathbb{Z}_p[\mathbf{y}]$ be the ring of polynomials in $\mathbf{y} = (y_0, y_1, \ldots, y_s)$ with coefficients from $\mathbb{Z}_p$. For any vector $\mathbf{i} = (i_0, i_1, \ldots, i_s)$ of non-negative integers, we denote $\mathbf{y}^{\mathbf{i}} = y_0^{i_0} y_1^{i_1} \cdots y_s^{i_s}$. We define the weight of $\mathbf{i}$ to be $\mathrm{wt}(\mathbf{i}) = i_0 + i_1 + \cdots + i_s$. Then $\mathbf{y}^{\mathbf{i}}$ is a monomial of total degree $\mathrm{wt}(\mathbf{i})$.

**Definition 2** (Hasse Derivative). *For any polynomial $P(\mathbf{y}) \in \mathbb{Z}_p[\mathbf{y}]$ and any vector $\mathbf{i} = (i_0, i_1, \ldots, i_s)$ of non-negative integers, the $\mathbf{i}$-th Hasse Derivative of $P(\mathbf{y})$, denoted as $P^{(\mathbf{i})}(\mathbf{y})$, is the coefficient of $\mathbf{w}^{\mathbf{i}}$ in the polynomial $P(\mathbf{y} + \mathbf{w}) \in \mathbb{Z}_p[\mathbf{y}, \mathbf{w}]$, where $\mathbf{w} = (w_0, w_1, \ldots, w_s)$.*

**Definition 3** (Multiplicity). *For any polynomial $P(\mathbf{y}) \in \mathbb{Z}_p[\mathbf{y}]$ and any point $\mathbf{a} \in \mathbb{Z}_p^{s+1}$, the multiplicity of $P$ at $\mathbf{a}$, denoted as $\mathrm{mult}(P, \mathbf{a})$, is the largest integer $M$ such that for any non-negative integer vector $\mathbf{i} = (i_0, i_1, \ldots, i_s)$ with $\mathrm{wt}(\mathbf{i}) < M$, we have $P^{(\mathbf{i})}(\mathbf{a}) = 0$ (if $M$ may be taken arbitrarily large, then we set $\mathrm{mult}(P, \mathbf{a}) = \infty$).*

It is trivial to see that $\mathrm{mult}(P, \mathbf{a}) \geq 0$ for any polynomial $P(\mathbf{y})$ and any point $\mathbf{a}$. Furthermore, $P(\mathbf{a}) = 0$ if and only if $\mathrm{mult}(P, \mathbf{a}) \geq 1$. The following lemma is from [12] and shows an interesting property of multiplicity.

**Lemma 3.** *Let $P(\mathbf{y}) \in \mathbb{Z}_p[\mathbf{y}]$ be any non-zero polynomial of total degree at most $d$. Then for any finite set $A \subseteq \mathbb{Z}_p$, it holds that $\sum_{\mathbf{a} \in A^{s+1}} \mathrm{mult}(P, \mathbf{a}) \leq d \cdot |A|^s$.*

Let $\mathcal{N}_A(P)$ be the number of roots of $P(\mathbf{y})$ in the set $A^{s+1}$. Recall that any root $\mathbf{a} \in \mathbb{Z}_p^{s+1}$ of $P(\mathbf{y})$ must satisfies the property that $\mathrm{mult}(P, \mathbf{a}) \geq 1$. Then $\mathcal{N}_A(P) \leq \sum_{\mathbf{a} \in A^{s+1}} \mathrm{mult}(P, \mathbf{a})$. Lemma 3 in particular implies that $\mathcal{N}_A(P) \leq d \cdot |A|^s$ whenever $P(\mathbf{y})$ has total degree at most $d$. As a generalization of Example 1, we have the following Example related to multivariate polynomials.

**Example 2.** Let $\mathcal{V}_{\mathrm{mp}} = \{\langle \mathbf{a}^{\mathbf{i}} : \mathrm{wt}(\mathbf{i}) \leq d \rangle : \mathbf{a} \in A^{s+1}\} \subseteq \Omega_{p,h}$, where $h = \binom{s+1+d}{d} - 1$. For any two vectors $\mathbf{u} = \langle u_{\mathbf{i}} : \mathrm{wt}(\mathbf{i}) \leq d \rangle \in \Omega_{p,h}$ and $\mathbf{v} = \langle \mathbf{a}^{\mathbf{i}} : \mathrm{wt}(\mathbf{i}) \leq d \rangle \in \mathcal{V}_{\mathrm{mp}}$, $\mathbf{u} \odot \mathbf{v} = 0$ if and only if $\mathbf{a}$ is a root of the $s$-variate polynomial $P(\mathbf{y}) = \sum_{\mathrm{wt}(\mathbf{i}) \leq d} u_{\mathbf{i}} \cdot \mathbf{y}^{\mathbf{i}}$. Note that $|\{\mathbf{v} \in \mathcal{V}_{\mathrm{mp}} : \mathbf{u} \odot \mathbf{v} = 0\}| = \mathcal{N}_A(P) \leq d \cdot |A|^s$ and $|\mathcal{V}_{\mathrm{mp}}| = |A|^{s+1}$. Thus, $\epsilon \triangleq \max_{\mathbf{u}} \frac{|\{\mathbf{v} \in \mathcal{V}_{\mathrm{mp}} : \mathbf{u} \odot \mathbf{v} = 0\}|}{|\mathcal{V}_{\mathrm{mp}}|} \leq \frac{d}{|A|}$.

Lemma 2 together with Examples 1 and 2 gives us the technical Lemma 1.

# References

1. Agrawal, S., Boneh, D.: Homomorphic MACs: MAC-based integrity for network coding. In: Abdalla, M., Pointcheval, D., Fouque, P.-A., Vergnaud, D. (eds.) ACNS 2009. LNCS, vol. 5536, pp. 292–305. Springer, Heidelberg (2009)
2. Applebaum, B., Ishai, Y., Kushilevitz, E.: From secrecy to soundness: efficient verification via secure computation. In: Abramsky, S., Gavoille, C., Kirchner, C., Meyer auf der Heide, F., Spirakis, P.G. (eds.) ICALP 2010. LNCS, vol. 6198, pp. 152–163. Springer, Heidelberg (2010)
3. Backes, M., Barbosa, M., Fiore, D., Reischuk, R.M.: ADSNARK: nearly practical and privacy-preserving proofs on authenticated data. In: 2015 IEEE Symposium on Security and Privacy (2012)
4. Backes, M., Fiore, D., Reischuk, R.M.: Verifiable delegation of computation on outsourced data. In: 2013 ACM Conference on Computer and Communication Security. ACM Press, November 2013
5. Benabbas, S., Gennaro, R., Vahlis, Y.: Verifiable delegation of computation over large datasets. In: Rogaway, P. (ed.) CRYPTO 2011. LNCS, vol. 6841, pp. 111–131. Springer, Heidelberg (2011)
6. Bitansky, N., Canetti, R., Chiesa, A., Tromer, E.: From extractable collision resistance to succinct non-interactive arguments of knowledge, and back again. In: ITCS 2012: Proceedings of the 3rd Symposium on Innovations in Theoretical Computer Science (2012)
7. Boneh, D., Freeman, D.M.: Homomorphic signatures for polynomial functions. In: Paterson, K.G. (ed.) EUROCRYPT 2011. LNCS, vol. 6632, pp. 149–168. Springer, Heidelberg (2011)
8. Catalano, D., Fiore, D.: Practical homomorphic MACs for arithmetic circuits. In: Johansson, T., Nguyen, P.Q. (eds.) EUROCRYPT 2013. LNCS, vol. 7881, pp. 336–352. Springer, Heidelberg (2013)
9. Catalano, D., Fiore, D., Gennaro, R., Vamvourellis, K.: Algebraic (trapdoor) one-way functions and their applications. In: Sahai, A. (ed.) TCC 2013. LNCS, vol. 7785, pp. 680–699. Springer, Heidelberg (2013)
10. Chung, K.-M., Kalai, Y.T., Liu, F.-H., Raz, R.: Memory delegation. In: Rogaway, P. (ed.) CRYPTO 2011. LNCS, vol. 6841, pp. 151–168. Springer, Heidelberg (2011)

11. Chung, K.-M., Kalai, Y., Vadhan, S.: Improved delegation of computation using fully homomorphic encryption. In: Rabin, T. (ed.) CRYPTO 2010. LNCS, vol. 6223, pp. 483–501. Springer, Heidelberg (2010)
12. Dvir, Z., Kopparty, S., Saraf, S., Sudan, M.: Extensions to the method of multiplicities, with applications to kakeya sets and mergers. In: FOCS 2009, pp. 181–190 (2009)
13. Fiore, D., Gennaro, R.: Publicly verifiable delegation of large polynomials and matrix computations, with applications. In: 2012 ACM Conference on Computer and Communication Security. ACM Press, October 2012
14. Gennaro, R., Gentry, C., Parno, B.: Non-interactive verifiable computing: outsourcing computation to untrusted workers. In: Rabin, T. (ed.) CRYPTO 2010. LNCS, vol. 6223, pp. 465–482. Springer, Heidelberg (2010)
15. Gennaro, R., Gentry, C., Parno, B., Raykova, M.: Quadratic span programs and succinct NIZKs without PCPs. In: Johansson, T., Nguyen, P.Q. (eds.) EURO-CRYPT 2013. LNCS, vol. 7881, pp. 626–645. Springer, Heidelberg (2013)
16. Gennaro, R., Wichs, D.: Fully homomorphic message authenticators. In: Sako, K., Sarkar, P. (eds.) ASIACRYPT 2013, Part II. LNCS, vol. 8270, pp. 301–320. Springer, Heidelberg (2013)
17. Gentry, C., Wichs, D.: Separating succinct non-interactive arguments from all falsifiable assumptions. In: Fortnow, L., Vadhan, S.P. (eds.) 43rd ACM STOC, pp. 99–108. ACM Press, June 2011
18. Goldwasser, S., Kalai, Y.T., Rothblum, G.N.: Delegating computation: interactive proofs for muggles. In: Ladner, R.E., Dwork, C. (eds.) 40th ACM STOC, pp. 113–122. ACM Press, May 2008
19. Goldwasser, S., Micali, S., Rackoff, C.: The knowledge complexity of interactive proof systems. SIAM J. Comput. 18(1), 186–208 (1989)
20. Papamanthou, C., Shi, E., Tamassia, R.: Signatures of correct computation. In: Sahai, A. (ed.) TCC 2013. LNCS, vol. 7785, pp. 222–242. Springer, Heidelberg (2013)
21. Parno, B., Raykova, M., Vaikuntanathan, V.: How to delegate and verify in public: verifiable computation from attribute-based encryption. In: Cramer, R. (ed.) TCC 2012. LNCS, vol. 7194, pp. 422–439. Springer, Heidelberg (2012)
22. Zhang, L.F., Safavi-Naini, R.: Verifiable delegation of computations with storage-verification trade-off. In: Kutyłowski, M., Vaidya, J. (eds.) ESORICS 2014, Part I. LNCS, vol. 8712, pp. 112–129. Springer, Heidelberg (2014)

# CloudBI: Practical Privacy-Preserving Outsourcing of Biometric Identification in the Cloud

Qian Wang[1], Shengshan Hu[1], Kui Ren[2], Meiqi He[1], Minxin Du[1], and Zhibo Wang[1]([✉])

[1] State Key Lab of Software Engineering, School of CS, Wuhan University, Wuhan, China
{qianwang,zbwang}@whu.edu.cn
[2] Department of CSE, University at Buffalo, Suny, Buffalo, USA
kuiren@buffalo.edu

**Abstract.** Biometric identification has been incredibly useful in the law enforcement to authenticate an individual's identity and/or to figure out who someone is, typically by scanning a database of records for a close enough match. In this work, we investigate the privacy-preserving biometric identification outsourcing problem, where the database owner outsources both the large-scale encrypted database and the computationally intensive identification job to the semi-honest cloud, relieving itself from data storage and computation burden. We present new privacy-preserving biometric identification protocols, which substantially reduce the computation burden on the database owner. Our protocols build on new biometric data encryption, distance-computation and matching algorithms that novelly exploit inherent structures of biometric data and properties of identification operations. A thorough security analysis shows that our solutions are practically-secure, and the ultimate solution offers a higher level of privacy protection than the-state-of-the-art on biometric identification outsourcing. We evaluate our protocols by implementing an efficient privacy-preserving fingerprint-identification system, showing that our protocols meet both the security and efficiency needs well, and they are appropriate for use in various privacy-preserving biometric identification applications.

**Keywords:** Biometric identification · Data outsourcing · Privacy · Cloud computing

## 1 Introduction

Biometric data, which include fingerprints, DNA, irises, voice patterns, palmprints, and facial patterns etc., are the measurable biological or behavioral characteristics widely-used for identification of individuals [9]. Matching biometric data or biometric identification has been incredibly useful in the law enforcement to authenticate an individual's identity and/or to figure out who someone

© Springer International Publishing Switzerland 2015
G. Pernul et al. (Eds.): ESORICS 2015, Part II, LNCS 9327, pp. 186–205, 2015.
DOI: 10.1007/978-3-319-24177-7_10

is, typically by scanning a database of records for a *good* match. A typical biometric identification system consists of a server-side database owner and users who submit candidate biometric records to the database owner for profile identification. Formally, the database owner holds a large set of biometric records $\mathcal{D} = \langle \mathbf{b}_i, p_i \rangle_{i=1}^{m}$, where $\mathbf{b}_i$ denotes the biometric data corresponding to its identity profile $p_i$. A user who has a candidate biometric record $\mathbf{b}_c$ wants to learn the target profile $p_{i*}$ for which $\mathbf{b}_{i*}$ matches the query $\mathbf{b}_c$ closely enough according to a certain metric.

Nowadays with the increasing development and popularity of cloud computing, individuals, companies and governments are highly motivated to outsource their data onto remote cloud servers to get rid of expensive local storage and computation costs [14]. As far as the biometric identification system is concerned, the database owner (*e.g.*, the FBI is responsible for managing the national fingerprint collection) may desire to outsource the extremely large size of biometric data records to the cloud, readily enjoying the biometric data matching service from the cloud service provider (*e.g.*, Amazon). However, to protect the privacy of sensitive biometric data, the database owner should *encrypt* the database before outsourcing. Whenever a government agency (*e.g.*, the FBI's partner) wants to authenticate an individual's identity or to figure out who someone is (by a fingerprint left on a murder weapon or a bomb, for example), he will turn to the FBI and issue an identification query. After receiving the query from the user, the FBI also generates the encrypted query, which allows the cloud server to execute it over the encrypted database, *i.e.*, scanning the encrypted database for a close match. Now the challenging problem is *how to enable privacy-preserving biometric identification over the encrypted database while apparently relieving the database owner of its high computation burden and relying on the cloud for providing fast and reliable biometric identification service.*

Privacy-preserving biometric identification has been extensively investigated in the secure two-party computation model, where the database owner and the user interactively execute the identification protocol without revealing the self-biometric data information to each other [1,6,15,17]. These works, however, either have efficiency issues (heavily rely on homomorphic encryption) [6] or fail to support the computation of a global minimum [15], which limits their applications. To enable efficient identification for a large-scale database, recently Huang *et al.* [8] and Blanton *et al.* [3] proposed privacy-preserving biometric identification protocols by combining both homomorphic encryption and garbled circuits [12]. Still, the biometric identification problem is essentially formulated as a secure two-party computation problem, their solutions cannot be directly applied to the identification outsourcing model. This is because the semi-trusted cloud server cannot know any private inputs/data except for the encrypted biometric database in the outsourcing computation model. The direct extensions of the above approaches, if applied to our model, (i) will lead to extremely high communication overhead and (ii) cannot relieve the database owner of a high computation burden, *i.e.*, for each identification query, the database owner has to traverse the database to compute the Euclidean distances without taking advantage of the cloud for undertaking heavy computations.

Recently, the biometric identification problem has been explored in the outsourced environment [2,4]. In [2], its single-server solution is far from practical for a large database while its multi-server solution requires that the database is shared among (at least three) servers in a split form. In [4], the authors developed a new outsourceable approach that secures the database and the candidate biometric. But it is assumed that two non-colluding servers cooperate to run the protocol and one of them knows the secret key. Moreover, its protocol requires frequent interactions between two servers which will lead to too much communication overhead. Another line of work similar to privacy-preserving identification is the kNN search problem over the encrypted database. Most of them, however, such as [16], considered the kNN problem in the two-party computation model. In [19], the authors proposed a new "encryption" scheme that achieves privacy-preserving outsourcing, but the scheme can be cracked when there exist collusions between the cloud server and the user. As a following work, [5] proposed a secure kNN query protocol which achieves a higher security level than [19]. But it also assumes the cloud to be two non-colluding servers and has the same drawbacks (*i.e.*, leakage of key secret and low efficiency) as [4], due to the use of the same techniques to compute Euclidean distance. The most similar work to ours is the biometric identification scheme proposed by Yuan *et al.* [20], which also considered the cloud-based identification outsourcing model. It appears that very high identification efficiency can be obtained as compared to [8]. They claimed their scheme is secure under the known-plaintext attack (KPA) model or even the chosen-plaintext attack (CPA) model. We show that, however, the security arguments given for their work do not hold, and the scheme can be completely broken once we manipulate the ciphertexts to remove the introduced randomness in the presence of collusion.

In this work, we, for the first time, identify the deficiencies and security weaknesses of previous privacy-preserving biometric identification protocols in the computation outsourcing model. We propose new schemes that support privacy-preserving biometric identification outsourcing in cloud computing. Our design is carefully tuned to meet the security and efficiency requirements under a three-party outsourcing computation model, where one or two parties may be semi-honest. We exploit inherent structures of biometric data and properties of biometric identification operations and use similarity transformation, trace computation by eigenvalues, and triangular matrix to design effective biometric data encryption algorithms (on the database owner side) while enabling privacy-preserving and correct distance-computation and matching over encrypted biometric data (on the cloud server side). Our main contributions can be summarized as follows.

- We formulate the problem of privacy-preserving biometric data identification outsourcing, establish a well-defined threat model by carefully characterizing attack-specific capabilities in various scenarios. We examine the state-of-the-art solutions and show their insufficiencies and security weaknesses when

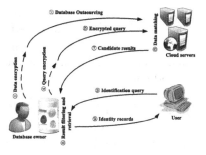

**Fig. 1.** An overview of cloud-based biometric-matching system.

meeting the practical needs under the biometric identification outsourcing model.

- We present a suite of privacy-preserving biometric identification protocols, which achieve different levels of security strength and substantially reduce the computation burden on the database owner side. Our protocols build on new and secure biometric data encryption and matching algorithms that novelly exploit inherent structures of biometric data and properties of biometric identification. A thorough security analysis shows that our solutions are practically-secure in different attack models.

- We have implemented our protocols to build an efficient privacy-preserving fingerprint-identification system. The system performance is carefully evaluated for each phase of the protocol, in terms of preparation time, communication cost and identification time. Our protocols meet both the security and efficiency needs well, and they are appropriate for use in various privacy-preserving biometric identification applications.

## 2  Problem Formulation: Outsourcing Computation of Biometric Identification

### 2.1  System Model and Assumptions

In our work, we consider a cloud-based biometric-matching system involving three parties: the *database owner*, the *user*, the *cloud server* (as illustrated in Fig. 1). In this application scenario, we assume a database owner holding a database $\mathcal{D}$ that contains a collection of biometric data $\langle \mathbf{b}_i \rangle_{i=1}^{m}$ (*e.g.*, fingerprints, voice patterns, palmprints, and facial patterns etc.), which are associated with certain profile information $\langle p_i \rangle_{i=1}^{m}$ (e.g., name, age and criminal record etc.). Before outsouring $\mathcal{D}$ to the remote cloud server, the database owner first pre-processes $\mathcal{D}$ to generate its encrypted form $\mathcal{C}$ and sends it to the cloud for storage. With a candidate biometric image, a user first locally derives its corresponding feature vector and sends the identification query to the database owner. After receiving the query, the database server generates an encrypted query and sends it to the cloud server. Subsequently, the cloud server executes the encrypted identification query over the encrypted database $\mathcal{C}$ and finally returns all the candidate matching results (*i.e.*, hitting encrypted FingerCodes and profiles) to the database owner. Finally, the database owner filters the results based on certain similarity threshold and compute the final output for the user.

More specifically, we assume that both the database owner's biometric data and the user's candidate biometric reading (*e.g.*, fingerprint images) have been processed such that the representations are suitable for biometric matching, *i.e.*, each raw biometric image is pre-processed by some widely-used feature extraction algorithms. Without loss of generality, we follow [8,20] and target fingerprint identification using FingerCodes [10] in our work. In our system, a FingerCode of a fingerprint consists of $n$ elements with size $l$-bit (typically $n = 640$ and $l = 8$). For two FingerCodes $\mathbf{x} = (x_1, \ldots, x_n)$ and $\mathbf{y} = (y_1, \ldots, y_n)$, they are considered a good match if the *Euclidean distance* between them is below a pre-defined threshold $\varepsilon$, which means that the fingerprints can be considered good candidates from the same person if

$$\|\mathbf{x} - \mathbf{y}\| < \varepsilon. \tag{1}$$

Therefore, the process of identifying a candidate (encrypted) fingerprint and its corresponding profile from a (encrypted) database of fingerprints can be divided into three steps: *secure Euclidian-distance computation, top-matching fingerprint determination* and *result filtering and retrieval*. The first and the second steps are executed on the cloud server side, and the third step is executed on the database owner side.

In the cloud-based biometric identification system, the encrypted database and the time-consuming biometric identification tasks are outsourced to the cloud. The system is expected to provide privacy-preserving biometric identification without disclosing any information about the database owner's biometric data to the cloud server and/or the user, and without disclosing any information about the user's biometric data (*i.e.*, query feature vectors) to the cloud (if no collusion exists between the cloud server and the user). We assume the cloud server and the user are semi-trusted, *i.e.*, they will execute the protocol as specified but may try to learn additional information from the encrypted biometric data and all the intermediate results generated during the protocol execution. In particular, under certain circumstances, we assume that the cloud server and the user may collude with each other and try to uncover the encrypted database.

## 2.2   Threat Model

In our model, we assume that the adversary knows the encryption scheme except the secret key. From a practical point of view, real-life adversaries have different level of background information and capabilities. To this end, we carefully define the threat model and characterize the attack-specific capabilities of adversary in three different scenarios. The *Attack Scenario 1* reflects the very practical case. In the *Attack Scenario 2*, the cloud server knows a set of plaintexts of the database but he does not know the corresponding encrypted values. In the *Attack Scenario 3*, the cloud server may collude with the user. Obviously, attackers in *Attack Scenario 2* and *Attack Scenario 3* are more powerful than that in *Attack Scenario 1*, but there is no higher or lower form of security level between *Scenario 2* and *Scenario 3*.

*Attack Scenario 1:* The cloud server is semi-trusted and can be seen as the adversary. It observes only the encrypted database $C$ and all encrypted biometric identification queries. This model is similar to the well-known ciphertext-only attack (COA) model [11] used in the security evaluation of data encryption protocols. In practice, there are applications only accessed by secluded users but others can hardly observe any information other than the encrypted data.

*Attack Scenario 2:* On the basis of *Attack Scenario 1*, we assume that the adversary has some samples of the database in plaintext but he does not know the corresponding encrypted values. This corresponds to the known-sample attack in database literature [13]. For example, the attacker observes the encrypted database and some of his sources are clients who have been collected fingerprints by the government, it then knows the values of several records in the plaintext database.

*Attack Scenario 3:* On the basis of *Attack Scenario 1*, we assume that the cloud server and the user may collude with each other. Thus, in addition to the encrypted biometric database the adversary can arbitrarily choose the user's biometric identification query of interest for encryption and execute the encrypted query over $C$. Considering this attack model is also necessary in some application cases. For example, it is possible for the cloud service provider to act as a user to submit fingerprint information for identification, so it can observe and even control the content of users' candidate FingerCode.

**Definition 1.** *A biometric identification outsourcing scheme is secure under Attack Scenario $\alpha$ ($\alpha \in \{1, 2, 3\}$) if no adversary can learn any other information from the encrypted biometric database $C$ and the encrypted identification queries besides what it has already known.*

*Remarks.* The above security definition takes both collusion and no-collusion cases into account. The cloud server can observe the encrypted biometric database and the encrypted identification queries. It should be noted that if a scheme is secure under both *Attack Scenario 2* and *Attack Scenario 3*, it does not mean that the cloud server can both collude with the user and simultaneously observe some plaintexts of the database. This attack is too strong that as far as we know there exist no effective schemes that can defend against this sophisticated attack. In the following discussion, we show that our scheme achieves a well balance between efficiency and security requirements.

# 3    Privacy-Preserving Biometric Identification: An Examination of the State-of-the-Art

In this section, we provide an examination of two most closely-related works, which reflect the most recent progress and results in privacy-preserving biometric identification. A careful analysis of these solutions (in terms of both the model and the security strength) motivates us to seek new solutions.

## 3.1    The Biometric Identification Scheme of Huang et al.

Huang et al. [8] explored the privacy-preserving biometric identification problem in the secure two-party computation model, where the database owner holds the biometric database locally, and the database owner and the user carry the burden of expensive identification jobs. This is completely different from our outsourcing computation model, where we propose to take full advantage of cloud to take away the burden of storing, maintaining and performing computations over the extremely large database (*e.g.*, billions of biometric data and profiles). In particular, the biometric identification outsourcing model assumes the semi-trusted cloud server and users, from which the privacy of biometric database should be protected while enabling effective identification over the encrypted database. This makes the privacy-preserving biometric identification approach in [8] unsuitable for our application model.

Firstly, as reported from the experiment in [8], for a biometric database with one million FingerCodes (a vector of 16 8-bit integers), the corresponding profile size (including photos and other personal information) is around 2 TB (assuming each profile is 2 MB approximately). By using a local machine with an Intel Xeon CPU running at 2.0 GHz and a memory of 4 GB as the database owner, it then requires 1.88 h to run the protocol for each identification query (besides the preparation time of more than 100 h). When the database expands to 1 billion FingerCodes with 2000 TB profiles (the setting is also practical in the real world), the identification time that linearly increases with the database size will be about 78 days. This is apparently unbearable for both the database owner and the user.

Secondly, the entire encrypted biometric database should be transmitted to the user for each identification query, which leads to extremely large communication overhead. For a database of size 5 GB (including the encrypted profiles), according to the experimental results in [8], it will take about 3.5 GB bandwidth to complete the transmission when 100 queries are arriving simultaneously. Finally, we show that even if there is a powerful semi-trusted cloud server the database owner can cooperate with, Huang et al.'s [8] encryption method is still not applicable in the outsourcing computation model due to its ineffective use of cloud. Specifically speaking, in the Euclidean-Distance Protocol of [8], the squared Euclidean distance $d_i$ between $\mathbf{v}_i$ (one of the vectors in the database) and $\mathbf{v}'$ (candidate vector) is computed as follows

$$d_i = ||\mathbf{v}_i - \mathbf{v}'||^2 = \sum_{j=1}^{N}(v_{i,j} - v_j')^2$$

$$= \sum_{j=1}^{N} v_{i,j}^2 + \sum_{j=1}^{N}(-2v_{i,j}v_j') + \sum_{j=1}^{N} v_j'^2.$$

Let $S_{i,1} = \sum_{j=1}^{N} v_{i,j}^2$, $S_{i,2} = \sum_{j=1}^{N}(-2v_{i,j}v_j')$ and $S_{i,3} = \sum_{j=1}^{N} v_j'^2$. Obviously, the encrypted $S_{i,1}$, denoted by $[S_{i,1}]$, can be outsourced to the cloud server for storage space savings and free of data maintenance. By homomorphic encryption, we have

$$[S_{i,2}] = [\sum_{j=1}^{N}(-2v_{i,j}v_j')] = \prod_{j=1}^{N}[-2v_{i,j}]^{v_j'}. \qquad (2)$$

Then, the database owner can outsource $[-2v_{i,j}]$ for $1 \leq j \leq N$ and $1 \leq i \leq M$ to the cloud, where $M$ denotes the database size. These are one-time executions and can be done in the preparation phase. However, when the database owner receives the plaintext identificatrion query $v'$ from the user, he has to download all $[-2v_{i,j}]$ from the cloud server because $v'$ appears in the plaintext form in the computation of $[S_{i,2}]$ (as shown in Eq. (2)) and cannot be encrypted and outsourced to the cloud. Then the database owner has to traverse the database to compute $[S_{i,2}]$ for each $1 \leq i \leq M$ according to Eq. (2). It is obvious that the cloud server cannot free the database owner from the burden of heavy computations. Therefore, we claim that Huang et al. scheme cannot be directly extended to our biometric identification outsourcing model.

### 3.2   The Biometric Identification Scheme of Yuan et al.

Yuan et al. [20] investigated the biometric identification outsourcing problem under the same system model as ours, and they claimed that their scheme is highly efficient and secure under the chosen message attack model. Roughly, their main idea is to encrypt each extended FingerCode by multiplying randomly-selected matrices and exploit properties embedded in these matrices for Euclidian distance computations. Yuan et al. claimed their scheme is resilient to the *Attack Scenario 3* when the unknowns (associated with the secret keys and data) are less than the system of equations built by the adversary. However, we show that this is not the case at all!

We first describe their scheme in further detail. Let the $i$-th ($i \in [1, m]$) fingerprint in the database be a $n$-dimensional feature vector, the database owner generates its FingerCode as $\mathbf{b}_i = [b_{i1}, b_{i2}, \ldots, b_{in}]$, where $b_{ik}$ ($k \in [1, n]$) is an 8-bit integer. To facilitate identification, each feature vector is extended to $\mathbf{B}_i = [b_{i1}, b_{i2}, \ldots, b_{in}, b_{i(n+1)}]$, where $b_{i(n+1)} = -\frac{1}{2}(b_{i1}^2 + b_{i2}^2 + \ldots + b_{in}^2)$. Then, $\mathbf{B}_i$ is used to generate matrix $\mathbf{B}_i'$ as

$$\mathbf{B}_i' = \begin{pmatrix} b_{i1} & 0 & \cdots & 0 \\ 0 & b_{i2} & \cdots & 0 \\ \vdots & \vdots & \cdots & \vdots \\ 0 & \cdots & 0 & b_{i(n+1)} \end{pmatrix}. \qquad (3)$$

The database owner randomly generates two $(n + 1)$-dimensional vectors $\mathbf{H} = [h_1, h_2, \ldots, h_{n+1}]$ and $\mathbf{R} = [r_1, r_2, \ldots, r_{n+1}]$, and it also randomly generates three $(n + 1) \times (n + 1)$ invertible matrices $\mathbf{M}_1, \mathbf{M}_2$ and $\mathbf{M}_3$ as secret keys. For each $\mathbf{B}'_i$, a random $(n + 1) \times (n + 1)$ matrix $\mathbf{A}_i$ is generated to hide $\mathbf{B}'_i$ by

$$\mathbf{D}_i = \mathbf{A}_i^T \mathbf{B}'_i, \tag{4}$$

where $\mathbf{A}_{ik} = [a_{ik1}, a_{ik2}, \ldots, a_{ik(n+1)}]$ is the row vector of $\mathbf{A}_i$ ($k \in [1, n + 1]$). It has the property $\mathbf{H}\mathbf{A}_{ik}^T = \sum_{j=1}^{n+1} h_j a_{ikj} = 1$. This implies

$$\mathbf{H}\mathbf{A}_i^T = (1, 1, \ldots, 1). \tag{5}$$

The database owner further encrypts $\mathbf{H}$, $\mathbf{R}$ and $\mathbf{D}_i$ with $\mathbf{M}_1$, $\mathbf{M}_2$ and $\mathbf{M}_3$ as

$$\begin{aligned} \mathbf{C}_i &= \mathbf{M}_1 \mathbf{D}_i \mathbf{M}_2, \\ \mathbf{C_H} &= \mathbf{H}\mathbf{M}_1^{-1}, \\ \mathbf{C_R} &= \mathbf{M}_3^{-1} \mathbf{R}^T. \end{aligned} \tag{6}$$

After encryption, a *Index* $I_i$ is built for each FingerCode $\langle \mathbf{b}_i, \mathbf{C}_i \rangle$. Finally, $(I_i, \mathbf{C}_i, \mathbf{C_H}, \mathbf{C_R})$ is uploaded to the cloud.

When the user has a candidate fingerprint to be identified, it extends its corresponding FingerCode $\mathbf{b}_c = [b_{c1}, b_{c2}, \ldots, b_{cn}]$ to a $(n+1)$-dimensional vector $\mathbf{B}_c = [b_{c1}, b_{c2}, \ldots, b_{cn}, 1]$. Then $\mathbf{B}_c$ is transferred to $\mathbf{B}'_c$ as in Eq. (3). Finally, the database owner disguises $\mathbf{B}'_c$ by multiplying a $(n+1) \times (n+1)$ random matrix $\mathbf{E}_c$

$$\mathbf{F}_c = \mathbf{B}'_c \mathbf{E}_c,$$

where $\mathbf{E}_{ck} = [e_{ck1}, e_{ck2}, \ldots, e_{ck(n+1)}]$ ($k \in [1, n + 1]$). Similar to $\mathbf{A}_{ik}$, it also has the property $\mathbf{E}_{ck}\mathbf{R}^T = \sum_{j=1}^{n+1} r_j e_{ckj} = 1$, which implies that $\mathbf{E}_c \mathbf{R}^T = (1, 1, \ldots, 1)^T$. The database owner further blinds $\mathbf{F}_c$ with secret keys $\mathbf{M}_2$ and $\mathbf{M}_3$ to generate the encrypted identification query $\mathbf{C_F}$ as

$$\mathbf{C_F} = \mathbf{M}_2^{-1} \mathbf{F}_c \mathbf{M}_3.$$

Then, $\mathbf{C_F}$ is submitted to the cloud for identification. Finally, on receiving $\mathbf{C_F}$, the cloud server compares Euclidean distance between $\mathbf{b}_i$ and $\mathbf{b}_c$ by computing $P_i = \mathbf{C_H}\mathbf{C}_i\mathbf{C_F}\mathbf{C_R}$ (We eliminate other details since they are irrelevant for the attacks we will describe).

In the following analysis, we show that there exist inherent flaws in the above design. The cloud server can exploit these flaws to figure out $\mathbf{M}_2$, and further to recover the database owner's FingerCodes $\mathbf{b}_i$ or $\mathbf{B}_i$ ($i = 1, \ldots, m$).

Our attacks rely on the knowledge of a set of plaintext-ciphertext pairs $(\mathbf{B}_i, \mathbf{C}_i)$, *i.e.*, the known-plaintext attack model. Yuan et al. [20] even claimed that a number of users can collude with the cloud server to choose arbitrary plaintexts of candidate queries and obtain the corresponding ciphertexts (*i.e.*, the known-candidate attack defined in [20]). However, we show this is not true.

**Attack on the Encrypted Biometric Database by Eliminating Randomness.** See Appendix A.

**Attack on the Encrypted Biometric Database by Exploiting Euclidian Distance Results.** See Appendix B.

# 4 Our Construction: The New and Improved Solutions

In this work, our ultimate goal is to enable privacy-preserving biometric identification of the encrypted biometric database stored in the cloud, finding the top matching identities for users. We have the following specifical goals. First, correctness, *i.e.*, the correctness of the identification results should be guaranteed. Second, privacy assurance, *i.e.*, the privacy of biometric data should be protected from the adversary. Third, efficiency, *i.e.*, the computation efficiency of the privacy-preserving biometric identification protocol should be practically high.

Keep the above design goals in mind, in this section we first present a cloud-based privacy-preserving biometric matching scheme secure under the *Attack Scenario 2*. We named this basic scheme as CloudBI-I. Then, we propose an enhanced version named CloudBI-II, which achieves security under both the *Attack Scenario 2* and *Attack Scenario 3* and show how it effectively avoids flaws of [20].

## 4.1 CloudBI-I: The Basic Scheme

**Database Encryption Phase.** The database owner pre-processes each fingerprint image for which a feature vector FingerCode $\mathbf{b}_i$ is generated. For each $n$-dimensional FingerCode $\mathbf{b}_i = [b_{i1}, b_{i2}, \ldots, b_{in}]$ ($\mathbf{b}_i \in \langle \mathbf{b}_i \rangle_{i=1}^{m}$ and typically $n = 640$), it is extended to a $(n+2)$-dimensional vector $\mathbf{B}_i = [b_{i1}, b_{i2}, \ldots, b_{in}, b_{i(n+1)}, 1]$, where $b_{i(n+1)} = -\frac{1}{2}(b_{i1}^2 + b_{i2}^2 + \ldots + b_{in}^2)$. Then $\mathbf{B}_i$ is transferred to a $(n+2) \times (n+2)$ matrix $\mathbf{B}_i'$ with the similar form in Eq. (3). To encrypt the biometric data, the database owner randomly generates two $(n+2) \times (n+2)$ invertible matrices $\mathbf{M}_1$ and $\mathbf{M}_2$. Then for each $\mathbf{B}_i'$, it computes

$$\mathbf{C}_i = \mathbf{M}_1 \mathbf{B}_i' \mathbf{M}_2$$

Given a security parameter $k$, call $sk \leftarrow$ SKE.KeyGen($1^k, r$), where $r$ is a random number and SKE is a PCPA-secure symmetric encryption scheme. Let $\mathbf{c_p} \leftarrow$ Enc($sk, \mathbf{p}$), where $\mathbf{p} = \langle p_i \rangle_{i=1}^{m}$ is the set of profiles.

After encryption, the tuple $\langle \mathbf{C}_i, \mathbf{c}_{\mathbf{p}_i} \rangle_{i=1}^{m}$ is uploaded to the cloud.

**Biometric Data Matching Phase.** The user has a candidate fingerprint (image) to be identified. To this end, it sends the corresponding FingerCode $\mathbf{b}_c = [b_{c1}, b_{c2}, \ldots, b_{cn}]$ to the database owner, who will extend the FingerCode to $\mathbf{B}_c = [b_{c1}, b_{c2}, \dots, b_{cn}, 1, r_c]$, where $r_c$ is a random value generated by the database owner. Note that $r_c$ is chosen independently for each $\mathbf{b}_c$. Similarly, $\mathbf{B}_c$ is extended to the matrix $\mathbf{B}'_c$ with the form in Eq. (3). To encrypt the identification query, the database server computes

$$\mathbf{C_F} = \mathbf{M}_2^{-1}\mathbf{B}'_c\mathbf{M}_1^{-1}.$$

The encrypted query $\mathbf{C_F}$ is then sent to the cloud server for identification.

To compare the Euclidean distances between each encrypted FingerCode $\mathbf{C}_i$ ($i = 1, \dots, m$) and $\mathbf{C_F}$, the cloud server first computes

$$\mathbf{P}_i = \mathbf{C}_i\mathbf{C_F} = \mathbf{M}_1\mathbf{B}'_i\mathbf{B}'_c\mathbf{M}_1^{-1}.$$

Then the cloud server computes the eigenvalues of $\mathbf{P}_i$, denoted by $\lambda_j$ ($j = 1, \dots, n + 2$), by solving the equations $|\lambda I_{(n+2)} - P_i| = 0$, where $I_{(n+2)}$ is the $(n + 2) \times (n + 2)$ identity matrix. Let $T_i$ denote the *trace* of $\mathbf{P}_i$, we have

$$T_i = \mathrm{tr}(\mathbf{P}_i) = \sum_{j=1}^{n+2} \lambda_j.$$

Finally, the cloud server only needs to rank $T_i$ ($i = 1, \dots, m$) to find out the minimum $k$ traces or the minimum one (*i.e.*, $k = 1$). For ease of exposition, we consider the $k = 1$ case in the following discussion. Assume $\mathbf{C}_{i*}$ is the encrypted biometric data that achieves the minimum, and its corresponding profile is denoted by $p_{i*}$. Finally, the cloud server sends $(\mathbf{C}_{i*}, \mathbf{c_{p_{i*}}})$ back to the database owner.

**Result Filtering and Retrieval Phase.** After receiving $(\mathbf{C}_{i*}, \mathbf{c_{p_{i*}}})$, the database owner decrypts $\mathbf{C}_{i*}$ to have $\mathbf{B}'_{i*} = \mathbf{M}_1^{-1}\mathbf{C}_{i*}\mathbf{M}_2^{-1}$. Then it transform $\mathbf{B}'_{i*}$ to $\mathbf{B}_{i*}$ and the plaintext FingerCode $\mathbf{b}_{i*}$. Finally, it computes the actual Euclidean distance between $\mathbf{b}_{i*}$ and $\mathbf{b}_c$. By checking $\|\mathbf{b}_{i*} - \mathbf{b}_c\| < \varepsilon$, the database owner decrypts $\mathbf{c_{p_{i*}}}$ to have $p_{i*}$ and sends it to the user if it holds. Otherwise, it outputs $\perp$.

**Correctness Analysis.** In linear algebra, the transformation $\mathbf{B}'_i\mathbf{B}'_c \mapsto \mathbf{M}_1$ $(\mathbf{B}'_i\mathbf{B}'_c)\mathbf{M}_1^{-1}$ is called a *similarity transformation*. Based on the properties of *similar matrices*, the *trace* is *similarity-invariant*, which means that two similar matrices have the same *trace*, *i.e.*, $\mathrm{tr}(\mathbf{P}_i) = \mathrm{tr}(\mathbf{B}'_i\mathbf{B}'_c)$. We now compute the trace of $\mathbf{B}'_i\mathbf{B}'_c$, denoted by $\mathrm{tr}(\mathbf{B}'_i\mathbf{B}'_c)$. As can be seen, $\mathbf{B}'_i\mathbf{B}'_c$ has the following structure

$$\mathbf{B}'_i\mathbf{B}'_c = \begin{pmatrix} b_{i1}b_{c1} & 0 & 0 & \cdots & 0 & 0 \\ 0 & b_{i2}b_{c2} & 0 & \cdots & 0 & 0 \\ \cdots & \cdots & \cdots & \cdots & \cdots & \cdots \\ 0 & \cdots & 0 & b_{in}b_{cn} & 0 & 0 \\ 0 & 0 & \cdots & 0 & -0.5\sum_{j=1}^n b_{ij}^2 & 0 \\ 0 & 0 & \cdots & 0 & 0 & r_c \end{pmatrix}. \tag{7}$$

By the definition of *trace* and *similarity-invariance* property we have

$$T_i = \text{tr}(\mathbf{B}'_i \mathbf{B}'_c) = \sum_{j=1}^{n} b_{ij} b_{cj} - 0.5 \sum_{j=1}^{n} b_{ij}^2 + r_c. \tag{8}$$

Let $\text{dist}_{ic}$ and $\text{dist}_{zc}$ denote the Euclidean distance between FingerCode $\mathbf{b}_i$ and query $\mathbf{b}_c$, the Euclidean distance between FingerCode $\mathbf{b}_z$ and query $\mathbf{b}_c$, respectively. Then we have

$$\text{dist}_{ic}^2 - \text{dist}_{zc}^2 = \sum_{j=1}^{n} (b_{ij} - b_{cj})^2 - \sum_{j=1}^{n} (b_{zj} - b_{cj})^2.$$

We expand the above expression and re-arrange them to have

$$\begin{aligned}
\text{dist}_{ic}^2 - \text{dist}_{zc}^2 &= 2(\sum_{j=1}^{n} b_{zj} b_{cj} - 0.5 \sum_{j=1}^{n} b_{zj}^2 + r_c) \\
&\quad - 2(\sum_{j=1}^{n} b_{ij} b_{cj} - 0.5 \sum_{j=1}^{n} b_{ij}^2 + r_c) \\
&= 2(\text{tr}(\mathbf{B}'_z \mathbf{B}'_c) - \text{tr}(\mathbf{B}'_i \mathbf{B}'_c)) \\
&= 2(T_z - T_i)
\end{aligned} \tag{9}$$

Based on Eq. (9), the cloud server can determine $\text{dist}_{ic} \geq \text{dist}_{zc}$ if $T_z \geq T_i$; otherwise $\text{dist}_{zc} < \text{dist}_{ic}$. After repeating this checking process for all the encrypted FingerCode $\mathbf{C}_i$'s, the cloud server is able to find out $\mathbf{b}_{i*}$ (in encrypted form) that has the minimum distance to $\mathbf{b}_c$ (in encrypted form).

### Security Analysis

**Theorem 1.** *Our CloudBI-I scheme is secure under the Attack Scenario 2.*

*Proof.* Due to the space limitation, please refer to our technical report [18] for the full proof.

### 4.2 CloudBI-II: The Enhanced Scheme

In the previous section, we have proved that CloudBI-I is secure under the *Attack Scenario 2*. However, it can be broken under the *Attack Scenario 3*. Specifically, in the equation $\mathbf{P}_i = \mathbf{C}_i \mathbf{C}_\mathbf{F} = \mathbf{M}_1 \mathbf{B}'_i \mathbf{B}'_c \mathbf{M}_1^{-1}$, as $\mathbf{B}'_i \mathbf{B}'_c$ is a diagonal matrix and the eigenvalues of a diagonal matrix is equal to its main diagonal elements, the cloud server can establish equation $\lambda_j = b_{ij} b_{cj}$. When there exists the collusion between the cloud server and the user, which means $b_{cj}$ can be obtained by the cloud server, it then can work out $b_{ij}$ and thus get all $B_i$'s. Therefore CloudBI-I is not secure under *Attack Scenario 3*. Besides, some approximate information may be leaked to the adversary. For example, an attacker may formulate a system of equations as a simultaneous Diophantine approximate problem [7] and will find some approximate values corresponding to $q'_{11}$ and $p'_{1k}$ $(k = 1, \ldots, n+2)$. To solve the above problems and achieve higher security strength, we further propose an improved privacy-preserving biometric identification outsourcing scheme. The main idea of the enhanced scheme is to introduce more randomness in the encryptions of the biometric data and the biometric identification query. Consequently, it is impossible to derive any information about $\mathbf{M}_1$ and $\mathbf{M}_2$.

The key difference between CloudBI-II and CloudBI-I is that the database owner will multiply $\mathbf{B}'_i$ and $\mathbf{B}'_c$ each by an additional random triangular matrix during the encryption process. In the *database encryption phase*, for each $\mathbf{B}'_i$ $(i = 1, \ldots, m)$, the database owner encrypts it as

$$\mathbf{C}_i = \mathbf{M}_1 \mathbf{Q}_i \mathbf{B}'_i \mathbf{M}_2,$$

where $\mathbf{Q}_i$ is a randomly-generated *lower triangular matrix* with diagonal entries set to 1.

In the *biometric data matching phase*, for each identification query $\mathbf{B}_c$ the database owner randomly generates a *lower triangular matrix* $\mathbf{Q}_c$ with diagonal entries set to 1, and it encrypts the plaintext query as

$$\mathbf{C_F} = \mathbf{M}_2^{-1} \mathbf{B}'_c \mathbf{Q}_c \mathbf{M}_1^{-1}.$$

The remaining operations for the *result filtering and retrieval phase* are the same as the basic scheme.

**Correctness Analysis.** We show that the new probabilistic encryption algorithm will not affect the correctness of the final results. After receiving $\mathbf{C}_i$ and $\mathbf{C_F}$, the cloud server computes

$$\mathbf{P}_i = \mathbf{C}_i \mathbf{C_F} = \mathbf{M}_1 \mathbf{Q}_i \mathbf{B}'_i \mathbf{M}_2 \mathbf{M}_2^{-1} \mathbf{B}'_c \mathbf{Q}_c \mathbf{M}_1^{-1}$$
$$= \mathbf{M}_1 \mathbf{Q}_i \mathbf{B}'_i \mathbf{B}'_c \mathbf{Q}_c \mathbf{M}_1^{-1}.$$

Due to the property of *similarity transformation*, $T_i = \mathrm{tr}(\mathbf{P}_i) = \mathrm{tr}(\mathbf{Q}_i \mathbf{B}'_i \mathbf{B}'_c \mathbf{Q}_c)$. In linear algebra, the product of a *diagonal matrix* and a *lower triangular matrix* is also *lower triangular*. Thus, we have

$$\mathbf{Q}_i \mathbf{B}'_i = \begin{pmatrix} b_{i1} & 0 & 0 & \ldots & 0 & 0 \\ t_{21} & b_{i2} & 0 & \ldots & 0 & 0 \\ \ldots & \ldots & \ldots & \ldots & \ldots & \ldots \\ t_{n1} & \ldots & t_{n(n-1)} & b_{in} & 0 & \ldots \\ t_{(n+1)1} & t_{(n+1)2} & \cdots & t_{(n+1)n} & -\frac{1}{2}\sum_{j=1}^{n} b_{ij}^2 & 0 \\ t_{(n+2)1} & t_{(n+2)2} & \cdots & t_{(n+2)n} & t_{(n+2)(n+1)} & 1 \end{pmatrix}, \qquad (10)$$

where $t_{ij}$ are random values. It shows that the multiplication of $\mathbf{B}'_i$ by $\mathbf{Q}_i$ does not change its main diagonal entries.

Following the same reason, the multiplication of $\mathbf{B}'_i \mathbf{B}'_c$ by $\mathbf{Q}_i$ and $\mathbf{Q}_c$ respectively will not change the main diagonal entries of $\mathbf{B}'_i \mathbf{B}'_c$ (as shown in Eq. (7)). It indicates that $\mathrm{tr}(\mathbf{Q}_i \mathbf{B}'_i \mathbf{B}'_c \mathbf{Q}_c)$ is also equal to $\sum_{j=1}^{n} b_{ij} b_{cj} - 0.5 \sum_{j=1}^{n} b_{ij}^2 + r_c$. Thus, Eq. (9) still holds. So, the cloud server can return the target $(\mathbf{C}_{i*}, \mathbf{c}_{\mathbf{p}_{i*}})$ to the database owner.

**Table 1.** A summary of complexity costs. Here, $m$ denotes the number of ⟨*FingerCode, profile*⟩ pairs in the database; $k$ denotes the number of closest fingerprints required to be returned, *e.g.*, $k = 1$ if the closest one is returned; $n \ll m$.

|  |  | Phases | Yuan et al. scheme [20] | CloudBI-I | CloudBI-II |
|---|---|---|---|---|---|
| Comp. | Database owner | **Prep.** | $\mathcal{O}(mn^3)$ | $\mathcal{O}(mn^3)$ | $\mathcal{O}(mn^3)$ |
|  |  | **Iden.** | $\mathcal{O}(n^3)$ | $\mathcal{O}(n^3)$ | $\mathcal{O}(n^3)$ |
|  |  | **Retr.** | $\mathcal{O}(n)$ | $\mathcal{O}(n)$ | $\mathcal{O}(n)$ |
|  | User | **Iden.** |  |  |  |
|  | Cloud server | **Iden.** | $\mathcal{O}(mn^2 + m\log m)$ | $\mathcal{O}(mn^3 + m\log m)$ | $\mathcal{O}(mn^3 + m\log m)$ |
| Comm. | Database owner | **Prep.** | $\mathcal{O}(mn^2)$ | $\mathcal{O}(mn^2)$ | $\mathcal{O}(mn^2)$ |
|  |  | **Iden.** | $\mathcal{O}(n^2)$ | $\mathcal{O}(n^2)$ | $\mathcal{O}(n^2)$ |
|  |  | **Retr.** | $\mathcal{O}(k)$ | $\mathcal{O}(k)$ | $\mathcal{O}(k)$ |
|  | User | **Iden.** | $\mathcal{O}(1)$ | $\mathcal{O}(1)$ | $\mathcal{O}(1)$ |
|  | Cloud server | **Iden.** | / | / | / |
|  |  | **Retr.** | $\mathcal{O}(k)$ | $\mathcal{O}(k)$ | $\mathcal{O}(k)$ |
| Security | *Attack Scenario 2* |  | Yes | Yes | Yes |
|  | *Attack Scenario 3* |  | No | No | Yes |

**Security Analysis.** Apparently, the multiplication of random matrices will not compromise the security of CloudBI-I, thus the enhanced scheme CloudBI-II is also secure under the *Attack Scenario 2*. For the *Attack Scenario 3*, we have the following theorem.

**Theorem 2.** *Our CloudBI-II scheme is secure under the Attack Scenario 3.*

*Proof.* Due to the space limitation, please refer to our technical report [18] for the full proof.

*Remarks.* By the introduction of random matrices $\mathbf{Q}_i$ and $\mathbf{Q}_c$, CloudBI-II makes it impossible for the adversary to apply simultaneous Diophantine approximation attack. Specifically, according to CloudBI-II, all the relevant equations that involves $p_{11}$ can be listed by the adversary are

$$\begin{cases} p_{11}q_{11} + t_{21}p_{12}q_{11}, \ldots + t_{(n+2)1}p_{1(n+2)}q_{11} = \mathbf{C}_{i1(11)} \\ p_{11}q_{12} + t_{21}p_{12}q_{12}, \ldots + t_{(n+2)1}p_{1(n+2)}q_{12} = \mathbf{C}_{i1(12)} \\ \ldots \\ p_{11}q_{1(n+2)} + t_{21}p_{12}q_{1(n+2)}, \ldots + t_{(n+2)1}p_{1(n+2)}q_{1(n+2)} \\ \quad = \mathbf{C}_{i1(1(n+2))}. \end{cases} \quad (11)$$

However, in Eq. (11), there are $n + 2$ equations with $3n + 5$ unknowns in total such that $p_{11}$ cannot be determined or even approximately solved.

## 5    Implementation and Evaluation

We evaluate the performance of our protocols by implementing a privacy-preserving fingerprint identification system. We set up the cloud with 1000 nodes, each with an Intel Core i5-4440M 2.80 GHz CPU and 16 GB memory. We set up the database owner on a separate machine with the same hardware configuration. We randomly generate 640-entry vectors to construct the FingerCode database following [8,20], and the database size ranges from one million to ten million $\langle FingerCode, profile \rangle$ pairs. We also randomly select a sequence of feature vectors as the query FingerCodes.

### 5.1    Complexity Analysis

Before delving into the experimental results, we first provide an overview of the complexity of the privacy-preserving fingerprint identification execution on all three participating parties, in terms of computation and communication overheads. Table 1 summarizes the complexities for our system (including CloudBI-I and CloudBI-II) and for the biometric identification system proposed in [20]. Here, we eliminate the discussion of Huang et al. [8], who essentially considered the two-party secure computation model (see Sect. 3.1 for further details of its extension to the computation outsourcing model). The *preparation phase*, the *identification phase* and the *retrieval phase* are corresponding to the three phases (as described before) during the protocol execution. Note that, we assume each matrix multiplication has time complexity of $\mathcal{O}(n^3)$, where $n$ is the dimension of a FingerCode. $\mathcal{O}(m \log m)$ is the sorting cost of fuzzy Euclidian distances. It is worth noting that although the computation and communication complexities grow linearly with the database size, these are one-time costs that will not influence the real-time performance of the biometric identification process. Our system focuses on outsourcing of the storage and computation workloads to the cloud for utilizing its high storage and computation capacity. In practice, our privacy-preserving fingerprint identification protocol allows the identification process to be performed in parallel on multiple cloud instances, which can ensure the efficiency of the identification process even with a very large-scale fingerprint database.

### 5.2    Experimental Evaluation

*Preparation Phase.* Figure 2 shows the time cost and the bandwidth cost in the preparation phase. Note that, both costs are one-time startup costs. Not surprisingly, the database encryption time and the communication cost for outsourcing to the cloud increase linearly with the database size (*i.e.*, the number of FingerCodes contained in the database). The experimental results conform to the theoretical results in Table 1, which shows that CloudBI-I and CloudBI-II have the same computation complexity with [20]. As CloudBI-I has less matrix multiplication operations than [20], it can save about 33 % time cost for biometric database encryption. The bandwidth consumptions of three schemes, as shown

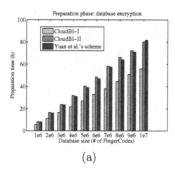
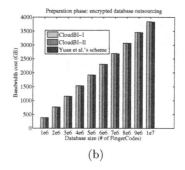

(a)                                          (b)

**Fig. 2.** Preparation phase: (a) Time costs for different sizes of database; (b) Bandwidth costs for different sizes of database.

in Fig. 2(b), are almost the same. As suggested in practical applications, hard disks can be used to drive the outsourced encrypted data transmission services offered by cloud service provider (*e.g.*, Amazon) to save bandwidth consumption.

*Identification Phase.* Figure 3 shows the time cost and the bandwidth cost in the identification phase. As demonstrated in Fig. 3(a), for a single query, with the increase of database size, the biometric data matching time of our schemes and [20] are linear functions of the database size. In the identification phase, the computation cost of [20] are far less than CloudBI-II (*i.e.*, $mn^2$ vs. $mn^3$). However, we **emphasize** that Yuan et al. [20] have not noticed that substantial security is sacrificed for achieving such fast computation of $\mathbf{P}_i$ in [20], where matrix multiplications are transformed to vector-matrix multiplications. As discussed in Sect. 3.2, we launch successful attacks on [20] by leveraging this weakness (see Eq. (12)). For bandwidth consumption of a single query, the cost is constant (*e.g.*, 400 KB in our experimental setting) as shown in Fig. 3(b). In our system, a query request can be processed in parallel on the cloud side. A set of computing instances in the cloud can be used to handle biometric data matching on distinct small portions of database in parallel, and each of them can find out a candidate result. Finally, by comparing these candidate results, a cloud instance can figure out the final result. If simultaneous queries come, as shown in Fig. 4(a), the identification time increases linearly with the number of queries without putting additional workload. The above results clearly validate the scalability of our cloud-based privacy-preserving biometric identification system. To demonstrate the computation savings on the database owner, we show the comparison of time costs of biometric identification on the database owner with and without identification outsourcing in Fig. 4(b). As can be seen, our schemes achieves constant time cost on the database owner, while the time cost of performing identification locally (over plaintext biometric database without outsourcing) increases linearly with the database size. The larger the database size (*e.g.*, with 10 million FingerCodes) is, the higher efficiency gain can be achieved.

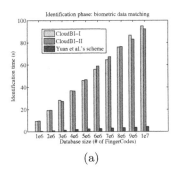
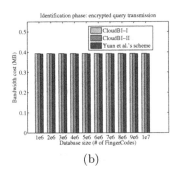

**Fig. 3.** Identification phase: (a) Time costs for different sizes of database; (b) Bandwidth costs for different sizes of database.

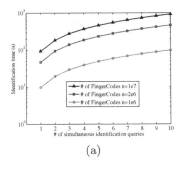
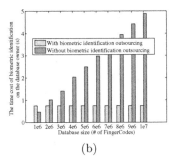

**Fig. 4.** a) Time costs under different number of simultaneous identification queries; (b) Comparison of time costs of biometric identification on the database owner.

## 6    Concluding Remarks

In this work, we investigated the privacy-preserving biometric identification outsourcing problem by developing new privacy-preserving biometric identification protocols. Our approaches enable efficient and privacy-preserving biometric matching with minimum database owner's involvement. Our experimental results show that the cloud-based biometric identification system is appropriate for use in various privacy-preserving biometric identification applications.

**Acknowledgments.** Kui's research is supported in part by US National Science Foundation under grant CNS-1262277. Qian's research is supported in part by National Natural Science Foundation of China (Grant No. 61373167), Natural Science Foundation of Hubei Province (Grant No. 2013CFB297), Wuhan Science and Technology Bureau (Grant No. 2015010101010020), National Basic Research Program of China (973 Program, Grant No. 2014CB340600) and National High Technology Research and Development Program of China (863 Program, Grant No. 2015AA016004). Zhibo's research is supported in part by Fundamental Research Funds for the Central Universities (No. 2042015kf0016).

# A  Attack on Yuan et al. [20] by Eliminating Randomness

We begin by describing an attack on the scheme as described above to recover $\mathbf{B}_i$ by eliminating the randomness in the encrypted biometric database.

Based on $(\mathbf{C}_i, \mathbf{C_H})$, the server can eliminate the random matrix $\mathbf{A}_i$ and then derive the secret matrix $\mathbf{M}_2$ by computing

$$
\begin{aligned}
\mathbf{C_H}\mathbf{C}_i &= (\mathbf{HM}_1^{-1})(\mathbf{M}_1\mathbf{D}_i\mathbf{M}_2) \\
&= \mathbf{HD}_i\mathbf{M}_2 = \mathbf{H}(\mathbf{A}_i^T\mathbf{B}_i')\mathbf{M}_2 = (\mathbf{HA}_i^T)\mathbf{B}_i'\mathbf{M}_2 \\
&= (1,1,\ldots,1)\cdot\mathbf{B}_i'\mathbf{M}_2 = \mathbf{B}_i\mathbf{M}_2.
\end{aligned} \tag{12}
$$

Here, note that $(1,1,\ldots,1)\cdot\mathbf{B}_i' = \mathbf{B}_i$. In Eq. (12), since $\mathbf{M}_2$ is a $(n+1)\times(n+1)$ constant matrix, if the cloud server possesses $(n+1)$ *linearly independent* $\mathbf{B}_i$ and constructs $(n+1)$ equations, then $\mathbf{M}_2$ can be recovered. Once $\mathbf{M}_2$ is known, the cloud server can recover all $\mathbf{B}_i$'s $(i = 1,\ldots,m)$ according to Eq. (12). Next we give an illustrating example of this attack.

Assume that $n = 2$ and the database owner has $\mathbf{B}_i$ $(i = 1,\ldots,m)$, $\mathbf{H} = [1,2,3]$ and $\mathbf{R} = [1,1,2]$. The three randomly-generated secret matrices $\mathbf{M}_1, \mathbf{M}_2, \mathbf{M}_3$ are

$$
\mathbf{M}_1 = \begin{pmatrix} 1 & 2 & 0 \\ 1 & 1 & 0 \\ 0 & 0 & 1 \end{pmatrix}, \mathbf{M}_2 = \begin{pmatrix} 1 & 0 & 1 \\ 0 & 2 & 1 \\ 0 & 3 & 1 \end{pmatrix}, \mathbf{M}_3 = \begin{pmatrix} 2 & 0 & 0 \\ 1 & 0 & 1 \\ 0 & 1 & 2 \end{pmatrix}.
$$

Correspondingly, $\mathbf{A}_1, \mathbf{A}_2$ and $\mathbf{A}_3$ are generated to satisfy $\mathbf{HA}_i^T = (1,1,\ldots,1)$ as

$$
\mathbf{A}_1 = \begin{pmatrix} 1 & 0 & 0 \\ -1 & 1 & 0 \\ 0 & -1 & 1 \end{pmatrix}, \mathbf{A}_2 = \begin{pmatrix} 0 & 2 & -1 \\ 1 & 0 & 0 \\ -1 & 1 & 0 \end{pmatrix},
$$

$$
\mathbf{A}_3 = \begin{pmatrix} -1 & -2 & 2 \\ 1 & 0 & 0 \\ 0 & -1 & 1 \end{pmatrix}.
$$

Then we have

$$
\mathbf{C_H} = \mathbf{HM}_1^{-1} = [1,0,3], \text{ where } \mathbf{M}_1^{-1} = \begin{pmatrix} -1 & 2 & 0 \\ 1 & -1 & 0 \\ 0 & 0 & 1 \end{pmatrix}
$$

Without loss of generality, we assume $\mathbf{B}_1 = [1,3,-5], \mathbf{B}_2 = [0,2,-2]$ and $\mathbf{B}_3 = [2,2,-4]$. According to Eq. (4), we can compute $\mathbf{D}_i$. Based on Eq. (6), we have $\mathbf{C}_i$ $(i = 1,2,3)$

$$
\mathbf{C}_1 = \begin{pmatrix} 1 & 36 & 14 \\ 1 & 15 & 6 \\ 0 & -15 & -5 \end{pmatrix}, \mathbf{C}_2 = \begin{pmatrix} 0 & -2 & 0 \\ 0 & 4 & 2 \\ 0 & 0 & 0 \end{pmatrix},
$$

$$
\mathbf{C}_3 = \begin{pmatrix} -10 & 28 & 0 \\ -6 & 16 & 0 \\ 4 & -12 & 0 \end{pmatrix}.
$$

Then $(\mathbf{C}_1, \mathbf{C}_2, \mathbf{C}_3, \mathbf{C_H})$ are sent to the cloud server (*i.e.*, the adversary in our model), who can construct the following equations using Eq. (12)

$$
\begin{aligned}
\mathbf{B}_1\mathbf{M}_2' &= \mathbf{C_H}\mathbf{C}_1 = (1,-9,-1), \\
\mathbf{B}_2\mathbf{M}_2' &= \mathbf{C_H}\mathbf{C}_2 = (0,-2,0), \\
\mathbf{B}_3\mathbf{M}_2' &= \mathbf{C_H}\mathbf{C}_3 = (2,-8,0).
\end{aligned}
$$

According to the known-plaintext attack model (or the extension to the chosen-plaintext attack model) defined in [20], if we let the adversary (*i.e.*, the cloud server) observe $\mathbf{B}_1, \mathbf{B}_2, \mathbf{B}_3$, it can solve for

$$\mathbf{M}_2' = \begin{pmatrix} 1 & 0 & 1 \\ 0 & 2 & 1 \\ 0 & 3 & 1 \end{pmatrix} = \mathbf{M}_2.$$

By plugging $\mathbf{M}_2$ into Eq. (12), then the cloud server can solve for all unknown $\mathbf{B}_i$ $(i = 4, \ldots, m)$!

*Remarks.* The above attack works due to the elimination of the randomness introduced by $\mathbf{A}_i$. When applying the property Eq. (5) in Eq. (12), the number of secret unknowns will be equal to the number of equations. In fact, we can also show that by knowing a set of $(\mathbf{B}_c, \mathbf{C_F})$'s, any plaintext query can be recovered by eliminating the random matrix $\mathbf{E}_c$ with the property $\mathbf{E}_c \mathbf{R}^T = (1, 1, \ldots, 1)^T$. This implies that by knowing a sequence of users' queries and their encrypted versions, the cloud can reveal any other plaintext queries (submitted by other users) even if they have been encrypted. So, the biometric identification scheme in [20] is also insecure under the *Attack Scenario 3*. Due to the space limitation, we omit the analysis here.

## B    Attack on Yuan et al. [20] by Exploiting Euclidian Distance Results

We next describe another attack on the scheme to recover $\mathbf{B}_i$ by exploiting the Euclidian distance results.

In the scheme of Yuan et al. [20], the cloud server compares Euclidean distance between $\mathbf{b}_i$ and $\mathbf{b}_c$ by computing

$$\mathbf{P}_i = \mathbf{C_H} \mathbf{C}_i \mathbf{C_F} \mathbf{C_R} = \sum_{j=1}^{n+1} b_{ij} b_{cj} = \sum_{j=1}^{n} b_{ij} b_{cj} - \frac{1}{2} \sum_{j=1}^{n} b_{ij}^2. \qquad (13)$$

We show that it is easy to construct enough equations to recover $\mathbf{B}_i$. Similarly, we give an illustrating example. Assume that $n = 2$ and $\mathbf{B}_i = [0, 2, -2]$ ($i \in [1, m]$). Yuan et al. [20] claimed that their scheme allows the collusion between the cloud server and a number of users. Based on this fact, the adversary can select query plaintexts of his interest for encryption. Therefore, assume that two *linear independent* FingerCodes $\mathbf{B}_{c1} = [7, 8, 1]$ and $\mathbf{B}_{c2} = [1, 2, 1]$ are chosen for query, and their corresponding encrypted queries $\mathbf{C_{F1}}$ and $\mathbf{C_{F2}}$ are also known by the cloud server. After performing the Euclidian distance comparison using Eq. (13), the cloud server has $\mathbf{P}_1 = 14$ and $\mathbf{P}_2 = 2$. By using two equations $\mathbf{P}_i = \sum_{j=1}^{2} b_{i'j} b_{cj} - \frac{1}{2} \sum_{j=1}^{2} b_{i'j}^2$ ($i = 1, 2$), the cloud server can solve $\mathbf{B}_{i'} = [0, 2, -2] = \mathbf{B}_i$. The success of this attack further demonstrates that Yuan's scheme is vulnerable in the *Attack Scenario 3*. This attack works due to the lack of randomness in the Euclidian distance results $\mathbf{P}_i$. It tells us that besides the biometric data, $\mathbf{P}_i$ should also be well-protected while not affecting result correctness.

# References

1. Barni, M., Bianchi, T., Catalano, D., Raimondo, M.D., Labati, R.D., Failla, P., Fiore, D., Lazzeretti, R., Piuri, V., Scotti, F. et al.: Privacy-preserving fingercode authentication. In: Proceedings of MMSec 2010, pp. 231–240. ACM (2010)
2. Blanton, M., Aliasgari, M.: Secure outsourced computation of iris matching. J. Comput. Secur. **20**(2), 259–305 (2012)
3. Blanton, M., Gasti, P.: Secure and efficient protocols for iris and fingerprint identification. In: Atluri, V., Diaz, C. (eds.) ESORICS 2011. LNCS, vol. 6879, pp. 190–209. Springer, Heidelberg (2011)
4. Chun, H., Elmehdwi, Y., Li, F., Bhattacharya, P., Jiang, W.: Outsourceable two-party privacy-preserving biometric authentication. In: Proceedings of ASIACCS 2014, pp. 401–412. ACM (2014)
5. Elmehdwi, Y., Samanthula, B.K., Jiang, W.: Secure k-nearest neighbor query over encrypted data in outsourced environments. In: Proceedings of ICDE 2014, pp. 664–675. IEEE (2014)
6. Erkin, Z., Franz, M., Guajardo, J., Katzenbeisser, S., Lagendijk, I., Toft, T.: Privacy-preserving face recognition. In: Goldberg, I., Atallah, M.J. (eds.) PETS 2009. LNCS, vol. 5672, pp. 235–253. Springer, Heidelberg (2009)
7. Galbraith, S.D.: Mathematics of Public Key Cryptography. Cambridge University Press, New York (2012)
8. Huang, Y., Malka, L., Evans, D., Katz, J.: Efficient privacy-preserving biometric identification. In: Proceedings of NDSS 2011 (2011)
9. Jain, A.K., Hong, L., Pankanti, S.: Biometric identification. Commun. ACM **43**(2), 90–98 (2000)
10. Jain, A.K., Prabhakar, S., Hong, L., Pankanti, S.: Filterbank-based fingerprint matching. IEEE Trans. Image Process. **9**(5), 846–859 (2000)
11. Katz, J., Lindell, Y.: Introduction to Modern Cryptography: Principles and Protocols. CRC Press, Boca Raton (2007)
12. Lindell, Y., Pinkas, B.: A proof of security of yaos protocol for two-party computation. J. Cryptology **22**(2), 161–188 (2009)
13. Liu, K., Giannella, C.M., Kargupta, H.: An attacker's view of distance preserving maps for privacy preserving data mining. In: Fürnkranz, J., Scheffer, T., Spiliopoulou, M. (eds.) PKDD 2006. LNCS (LNAI), vol. 4213, pp. 297–308. Springer, Heidelberg (2006)
14. Mell, P., Grance, T.: Draft nist working definition of cloud computing. Referenced June 3rd **15**, 32 (2009)
15. Osadchy, M., Pinkas, B., Jarrous, A., Moskovich, B.: Scifi-a system for secure face identification. In: Proceedings of the S&P 2010, pp. 239–254. IEEE (2010)
16. Qi, Y., Atallah, M.J.: Efficient privacy-preserving k-nearest neighbor search. In: Proceedings of ICDCS 2008, pp. 311–319. IEEE (2008)
17. Sadeghi, A.-R., Schneider, T., Wehrenberg, I.: Efficient privacy-preserving face recognition. In: Lee, D., Hong, S. (eds.) ICISC 2009. LNCS, vol. 5984, pp. 229–244. Springer, Heidelberg (2010)
18. Wang, Q., Hu, S.S., Ren, K., He, M.Q., Du, M.X., Wang, Z.B.: CloudBI: Practical privacy-preserving outsourcing of biometric identification in the cloud. Technical report (2015). http://web.eecs.utk.edu/~zwang32/publications/CloudBI.pdf
19. Wong, W.K., Cheung, D.W-L., Kao, B., Mamoulis, N.: Secure knn computation on encrypted databases. In: Proceedings of SIGMOD 2009, pp. 139–152. ACM (2009)
20. Yuan, J., Yu, S.: Efficient privacy-preserving biometric identification in cloud computing. In: Proceedings of INFOCOM 2013, pp. 2652–2660. IEEE (2013)

# Protocols and Attribute-based Encryption

# Typing and Compositionality for Security Protocols: A Generalization to the Geometric Fragment

Omar Almousa[1], Sebastian Mödersheim[1(✉)], Paolo Modesti[2],
and Luca Viganò[3]

[1] DTU Compute, Lyngby, Denmark
samo@dtu.dk
[2] School of Computing Science, Newcastle University, Newcastle upon Tyne, UK
[3] Department of Informatics, King's College London, London, UK

**Abstract.** We integrate, and improve upon, prior relative soundness results of two kinds. The first kind are typing results showing that any security protocol that fulfils a number of sufficient conditions has an attack if it has a well-typed attack. The second kind considers the parallel composition of protocols, showing that when running two protocols in parallel allows for an attack, then at least one of the protocols has an attack in isolation. The most important generalization over previous work is the support for all security properties of the geometric fragment.

## 1 Introduction

**Context and Motivation.** Relative soundness results have proved helpful in the automated verification of security protocols as they allow for the reduction of a complex verification problem into a simpler one, if the protocol in question satisfies sufficient conditions. These conditions are of a syntactic nature, i.e., can be established without an exploration of the state space of the protocol.

A first kind of such results are *typing results* [4,6,13,18]. In this paper, we consider a *typed model*, a restriction of the standard protocol model in which honest agents do not accept any ill-typed messages. This may seem unreasonable at first sight, since in the real-world agents have no way to tell the type of a random bitstring, let alone distinguish it from the result of a cryptographic operation; yet in the model, they "magically" accept only well-typed messages. The relative soundness of such a typed model means that if the protocol has an attack, then it also has a well-typed attack. This does not mean that the intruder cannot send ill-typed messages, but rather that this does not give him any advantage as he could perform a "similar" attack with only well-typed messages. Thus, if we are able to verify that a protocol is secure in the typed model,

This work was partially supported by the EU FP7 Projects no. 318424, "FutureID: Shaping the Future of Electronic Identity" (futureid.eu), and by the PRIN 2010–2011 Project "Security Horizons". We thank Thomas Groß for many useful discussions.

© Springer International Publishing Switzerland 2015
G. Pernul et al. (Eds.): ESORICS 2015, Part II, LNCS 9327, pp. 209–229, 2015.
DOI: 10.1007/978-3-319-24177-7_11

then it is secure also in an untyped model. Typically, the conditions sufficient to achieve such a result are that all composed message patterns of the protocol have a different (intended) type that can somehow be distinguished, e.g., by a tag. The restriction to a typed model in some cases yields a decidable verification problem, allows for the application of more tools and often significantly reduces verification time in practice [5,6].

A similar kind of relative soundness results appears in *compositional reasoning*. We consider in this paper the *parallel composition* of protocols, i.e., running two protocols over the same communication medium, and these protocols may use, e.g., the same long-term public keys. (In the case of disjoint cryptographic material, compositional reasoning is relatively straightforward.) The compositionality result means to show that if two protocols satisfy their security goals in isolation, then their parallel composition is secure, provided the protocols meet certain sufficient conditions. Thus, it suffices to verify the protocols in isolation. The sufficient conditions in this case are similar to the typing result: every composed message can be uniquely attributed to one of the two protocols, which again may be achieved, e.g., by tags.

**Contributions.** Our contributions are twofold. First, we unify and thereby simplify existing typing and compositionality results: we recast them as an instance of the same basic principle and of the same proof technique. In brief, this technique is to reduce the search for attacks to solving constraint reduction in a symbolic model. For protocols that satisfy the respective sufficient conditions, constraint reduction will never make an ill-typed substitution, where for compositionality "ill-typed" means to unify messages from two different protocols.

Second, this systematic approach also allows us to significantly generalize existing results to a larger set of protocols and security properties. For what concerns protocols, our soundness results do not require a particular fixed tagging scheme like most previous works, but use more liberal requirements that are satisfied by many existing real-world protocols like TLS.

While many existing results are limited to simple secrecy goals, we prove our results for the entire geometric fragment suggested by Guttman [11]. We even augment this fragment with the ability to directly refer to the intruder knowledge in the antecedent of goals; while this does not increase expressiveness, it is very convenient in specifications. In fact, handling the geometric fragment also constitutes a slight generalization of existing constraint-reduction approaches.

**Organization.** In Sects. 2 and 3, we introduce a symbolic protocol model based on strands and properties in the geometric fragment. In Sect. 4, we reduce verification of the security properties to solving constraints. In Sects. 5 and 6, we give our typing and parallel compositionality results. In Sect. 7, we introduce a tool that checks if protocols are parallel-composable and report about first experimental results. In Sect. 8, we conclude and discuss related work. Proof sketches are in the appendix.

# 2    Messages, Formats and the Intruder Model

## 2.1    Messages

Let $\Sigma$ be a finite set of *operators* (also referred to as *function symbols*); as a concrete example, Table 1 shows a $\Sigma$ that is representative for a wide range of security protocols. Further, let $\mathcal{C}$ be a countable set of *constants* and $\mathcal{V}$ a countable set of *variables*, such that $\Sigma$, $\mathcal{V}$ and $\mathcal{C}$ are pairwise disjoint. We write $\mathcal{T}_{\Sigma \cup \mathcal{C}}(\mathcal{V})$ for the set of *terms* built with these constants, variables and operators, and $\mathcal{T}_{\Sigma \cup \mathcal{C}}$ for the set of *ground terms*. We call a term $t$ *atomic* (and write $atomic(t)$) if $t \in \mathcal{V} \cup \mathcal{C}$, and *composed* otherwise. We use also other standard notions such as *subterm*, denoted by $\sqsubseteq$, and *substitution*, denoted by $\sigma$.

The set of constants $\mathcal{C}$ is partitioned into three countable and pairwise disjoint subsets: (i) the set $\mathcal{C}_{P_i}$ of *short-term constants* for each protocol $P_i$, denoting the constants that honest agents freshly generate in $P_i$; (ii) the set $\mathcal{C}_{priv}$ of *long-term secret constants*; and (iii) the set $\mathcal{C}_{pub}$ of *long-term public constants*. This partitioning will be useful for compositional reasoning: roughly speaking, we will allow the intruder to obtain all public constants, and define that it is an attack if the intruder finds out any of the secret constants.

## 2.2    Formats

We use in this paper a notion of *formats* that is crucial to make our typing and compositionality results applicable to real-world protocols like TLS. Here, we break with the formal-methods tradition of representing clear-text structures of data by a *pair* operator $(\cdot, \cdot)$. For instance, a typical specification may contain expressions like $(A, NA)$ and $(NB, (KB, A))$. This representation neglects the details of a protocol implementation that may employ various mechanisms to enable a receiver to decompose a message in a unique way (e.g., field-lengths or XML-tags). The abstraction has the disadvantage that it may easily lead to false positives and false negatives. For example, the two messages above have a unifier $A \mapsto NB$ and $NA \mapsto (KB, NA)$, meaning that a message meant as $(A, NA)$ may accidentally be parsed as $(NB, (KB, A))$, which could lead to a "type-flaw" attack. This attack may, however, be completely unrealistic in reality.

To handle this, previous typing results have used particular *tagging schemes*, e.g., requiring that each message field starts with a tag identifying the type of that field. Similarly, compositionality results have often required that each encrypted message of a protocol starts with a tag identifying the protocol that this message was meant for. Besides the fact that this does not really solve the problem of false positives and false negatives due to the abstraction, practically no existing protocol uses exactly this schema. Moreover, it is completely unrealistic to think that a widely used protocol like TLS would be changed just to make it compatible with the assumptions of an academic paper — the only chance to have it changed is to point out a vulnerability that can be fixed by the change.

Formats are a means to have a faithful yet abstract model. We define formats as functions from data-packets to concrete strings. For example, a format from

**Table 1.** Example Operators $\Sigma$

| Description | Operator | Analysis rule |
|---|---|---|
| Symmetric encryption | $\mathsf{scrypt}(\cdot,\cdot)$ | $\mathsf{Ana}(\mathsf{scrypt}(k,m)) = (\{k\},\{m\})$ |
| Asymmetric encryption | $\mathsf{crypt}(\cdot,\cdot)$ | $\mathsf{Ana}(\mathsf{crypt}(\mathsf{pub}(t),m)) = (\{t\},\{m\})$ |
| Signature | $\mathsf{sign}(\cdot,\cdot)$ | $\mathsf{Ana}(\mathsf{sign}(t,m)) = (\{\emptyset\},\{m\})$ |
| Formats, e.g., $\mathsf{f}_1$ | $\mathsf{f}_1(t_1,\cdots,t_n)$ | $\mathsf{Ana}(\mathsf{f}_1(t_1,\cdots,t_n)) = (\emptyset,\{t_1,\cdots,t_n\})$ |
| One-way functions, e.g., hash | $\mathsf{hash}(\cdot)$ | $\mathsf{Ana}(\mathsf{hash}(t)) = (\{\emptyset\},\{\emptyset\})$ |
| Public key of a given private key | $\mathsf{pub}(\cdot)$ | $\mathsf{Ana}(\mathsf{pub}(t)) = (\{\emptyset\},\{\emptyset\})$ |
| All other terms | | $\mathsf{Ana}(t) = (\{\emptyset\},\{\emptyset\})$ |

TLS is **client_hello(time, random, session_id, cipher_suites, comp_ methods)** = $\mathsf{byte}(1) \cdot \mathsf{off}_3(\mathsf{byte}(3) \cdot \mathsf{byte}(3) \cdot time \cdot random \cdot \mathsf{off}_1(session\_id) \cdot \mathsf{off}_2(cipher\_suites) \cdot \mathsf{off}_1(comp\_methods))$, where $\mathsf{byte}(n)$ means one concrete byte of value $n$, $\mathsf{off}_k(m)$ means that $m$ is a message of variable length followed by a field of $k$ bytes, and $\cdot$ represents string concatenation.

In the abstract model, we are going to use only abstract terms like the part in bold in the above example. It is shown in [19] that under certain conditions on formats this abstraction introduces neither false positives nor false negatives. The conditions are essentially that formats must be parsed in an unambiguous way and must be pairwise disjoint; then every attack on the concrete bytestring model can be simulated in the model based on abstract format symbols (in the free algebra). Both in typing and compositionality, these conditions allow us to apply our results to real world protocols no matter what formatting scheme they actually use (e.g., a TLS message cannot be accidentally be parsed as an EAC message). In fact, these reasonable conditions are satisfied by many protocols in practice, and whenever they are violated, typically we have a good chance to find actual vulnerabilities.

We will model formats as *transparent* in the sense that if the intruder learns $\mathsf{f}(t_1,\ldots,t_n)$, then he also obtains the $t_i$.

### 2.3   Intruder Knowledge and Deduction Rules

We specify how the intruder can compose and decompose messages in the style of the Dolev-Yao intruder model.

**Definition 1.** *An intruder knowledge $M$ is a finite set of ground terms $t \in \mathcal{T}_{\Sigma \cup \mathcal{C}}$. Let $\mathsf{Ana}(t) = (K,T)$ be a function that returns for every term $t$ a pair $(K,T)$ of finite sets of subterms of $t$. We define $\vdash$ to be the least relation between a knowledge $M$ and a term $t$ that satisfies the following intruder deduction rules:*

$$\frac{}{M \vdash t} \; \text{(Axiom)}, \quad t \in M \qquad \frac{}{M \vdash c} \; \text{(Public)}, \quad c \in \mathcal{C}_{pub} \qquad \frac{M \vdash t_1 \quad \cdots \quad M \vdash t_n}{M \vdash f(t_1,\cdots,t_n)} \; \text{(Compose)}, \quad f \in \Sigma^n$$

$$\frac{M \vdash t \quad M \vdash k_1 \quad \cdots \quad M \vdash k_n}{M \vdash t_i} \; \text{(Decompose)}, \quad \mathsf{Ana}(t) = (K,T), \; K = \{k_1,\cdots,k_n\}, \; t_i \in T$$

The rules *(Axiom)* and *(Public)* formalize that the intruder can derive any term $t \in M$ that is in his knowledge and every long-term public constant $c \in \mathcal{C}_{pub}$, respectively, and the *(Compose)* rule formalizes that he can use compose known terms with any operator in $\Sigma$ (where $n$ denotes the arity of $f$). Table 1 provides an example $\Sigma$ for standard cryptographic operators, along with the Ana function defined for each of them, which are available to all agents, including the intruder.

For message decomposition, we namely rely on analysis rules for terms in the form of $\mathsf{Ana}(t) = (K, T)$, which intuitively says that if the intruder knows the keys in set $K$, then he can analyze the term $t$ and obtain the set of messages $T$. We require that all elements of $K$ and $T$ are subterms of $t$ (without any restriction, the relation $\vdash$ would be undecidable). Consider, e.g., the analysis rule for symmetric encryption given in Table 1: $\mathsf{Ana}(\mathsf{scrypt}(k, m)) = (\{k\}, \{m\})$ says that given a term $\mathsf{scrypt}(k, m)$ one needs the key $\{k\}$ to derive $\{m\}$. By default, atomic terms cannot be analyzed, i.e., $\mathsf{Ana}(t) = (\emptyset, \emptyset)$. The generic *(Decompose)* deduction rule then formalizes that for any term with an Ana rule, if the intruder can derive the keys in $K$, he can also derive all the subterms of $t$ in $T$.

# 3    Protocol Semantics

We define the following notions. A protocol consists of a set of *operational strands* (an extension of the strands of [12]) and a set of *goal predicates* that the protocol is supposed to achieve. The semantics of a protocol is an infinite-state transition system over symbolic states and security means that all reachable states satisfy the goal predicates. A *symbolic state* $(\mathcal{S}; M; E; \phi)$ consists of a set $\mathcal{S}$ of operational strands (representing the honest agents), the intruder knowledge $M$, a set $E$ of events that have occurred, and a symbolic constraint $\phi$ on the free variables occurring in the state. We first define constraints, then operational strands, the transition relation on symbolic states, and finally the goal predicates.

## 3.1    Symbolic Constraints

The syntax of *symbolic constraints* is

$$\phi := M \vdash t \mid \phi_\sigma \mid \neg \exists \bar{x}. \phi_\sigma \mid \phi \wedge \phi \mid \underbrace{\phi \vee \phi \mid \exists \bar{x}. \phi}_{\star} \quad \text{with} \quad \phi_\sigma := s \doteq t \mid \phi_\sigma \wedge \phi_\sigma$$

where $s, t$ range over terms in $\mathcal{T}_{\Sigma \cup \mathcal{C}}(\mathcal{V})$, $M$ is a finite set of terms (not necessarily ground) and $\bar{x}$ is list of variables. The sublanguage $\phi_\sigma$ defines *equations* on messages, and we can existentially quantify variables in them, e.g., consider a $\phi$ of the form $\exists x. y \doteq f(x)$. We refer to equations also as *substitutions* since the application of the standard most general unifier on a conjunction of equations results in a set of substitutions. The constraints can contain such substitutions in positive and negative form (excluding all instances of a particular substitution).

$M \vdash t$ is an *intruder constraint*: the intruder must be able to derive term $t$ from knowledge $M$. Note that we have no negation at this level, i.e., we cannot write negated intruder constraints. A *base constraint* is a constraint built according to this grammar without the two cases marked $\star$, i.e., disjunction $\phi \vee \phi$ and existential quantification $\exists \bar{x}. \phi$, which may only occur in negative substitutions.

For ease of writing, we define the semantics of the constraint language as standard for each construct (rather than following strictly the grammar of $\phi$).

**Definition 2.** *Given an interpretation $\mathcal{I}$, which maps each variable in $\mathcal{V}$ to a ground term in $\mathcal{T}_\Sigma$, and a symbolic constraint $\phi$, the model relation $\mathcal{I} \models \phi$ is:*

$$\mathcal{I} \models M \vdash t \ \text{iff} \ \mathcal{I}(M) \vdash \mathcal{I}(t) \quad \mathcal{I} \models s \doteq t \ \text{iff} \ \mathcal{I}(s) = \mathcal{I}(t) \quad \mathcal{I} \models \neg \phi \ \text{iff} \ \text{not} \ \mathcal{I} \models \phi$$
$$\mathcal{I} \models \phi_1 \wedge \phi_2 \ \text{iff} \ \mathcal{I} \models \phi_1 \ \text{and} \ \mathcal{I} \models \phi_2 \quad \mathcal{I} \models \phi_1 \vee \phi_2 \ \text{iff} \ \mathcal{I} \models \phi_1 \ \text{or} \ \mathcal{I} \models \phi_2$$
$$\mathcal{I} \models \exists x. \phi \ \text{iff} \ \text{there is a term} \ t \in \mathcal{T}_\Sigma \ \text{such that} \ \mathcal{I}[x \mapsto t] \models \phi$$

*We say that $\mathcal{I}$ is a* model *of $\phi$ iff $\mathcal{I} \models \phi$, and that $\phi$ is* satisfiable *iff it has a model. Two constraints are* equivalent, *denoted by $\equiv$, iff they have the same models. We define as standard the* variables, *denoted by $var(\cdot)$, and the* free variables, *denoted by $fv(\cdot)$, of terms, sets of terms, equations, and constraints. A constraint $\phi$ is* closed, *in symbols $closed(\phi)$, iff $fv(\phi) = \emptyset$.*

Every constraint $\phi$ can be quite straightforwardly transformed into an equivalent constraint of the form

$$\phi \equiv \exists \bar{x}. \phi_1 \vee \ldots \vee \phi_n,$$

where the $\phi_i$ are base constraints. Unless noted otherwise, in the following we will assume that constraints are in this form.

**Definition 3.** *A constraint is* well-formed *if each of its base constraints $\phi_i$ satisfies the following condition: we can order the conjuncts of $\phi_i$ such that $\phi_i = M_1 \vdash t_1 \wedge \ldots \wedge M_n \vdash t_n \wedge \phi_i'$, where $\phi_i'$ contains no further $\vdash$ constraints and such that $M_j \subseteq M_{j+1}$ (for $1 \le j < n$) and $fv(M_j) \subseteq fv(t_1) \cup \ldots \cup fv(t_{j-1})$.*

Intuitively, this condition expresses that the intruder knowledge grows monotonically and all variables that occur in an intruder knowledge occur in a term that the intruder sent earlier in the protocol execution. We will ensure that all constraints that we deal with are well-formed.

## 3.2 Operational Strands

In the original definition of [21], a strand denotes a part of a concrete protocol execution, namely, a sequence of ground messages that an agent sends and receives. We introduce here an extension that we call *operational strands*, where terms may contain variables, there may be positive and negative equations on messages, and agents may create events over which we can formulate the goals:

$$S := \mathsf{send}(t).S \mid \mathsf{receive}(t).S \mid \mathsf{event}(t).S \mid (\exists \bar{x}. \phi_\sigma).S \mid (\neg \exists \bar{x}. \phi_\sigma).S \mid 0$$

where $\phi_\sigma$ is as defined above; we will omit the parentheses when there is no risk of confusing the dots. *fv* and *closed* extend to operational strands as expected, with the exception of the receiving step, which can bind variables: we set $fv(\text{receive}(t).S) = fv(S) \setminus fv(t)$. According to the semantics that we define below, in $\text{receive}(x).\text{receive}(f(x)).\text{send}(x).0$ the variable $x$ is bound actually in the first receive, i.e., the strand is equivalent to $\text{receive}(x).\text{receive}(y).(y \doteq f(x)).\text{send}(x).0$.

A *symbolic state* $(S; M; E; \phi)$ consists of a (finite or countable) set[1] $S$ of closed operational strands, a finite set $M$ of terms representing the intruder knowledge, a finite set $E$ of events, and a formula $\phi$. $fv(\cdot)$ and *closed* extend to symbolic states again as expected. We ensure that $fv(S) \cup fv(M) \cup fv(E) \subseteq fv(\phi)$ for all reachable states $(S; M; E; \phi)$, and that $\phi$ is well-formed. This is so since in the transition system shown shortly, the operational strands of the initial state are closed and the transition relation only adds new variables in the case of $\text{receive}(t)$, but in this case $\phi$ is updated with $M \vdash t$.

A *protocol specification* $(S_0, G)$ (or simply *protocol*) consists of a set $S_0$ of closed operational strands and a set $G$ of goal predicates (defined below). For simplicity, we assume that the bound variables of any two different strands in $S_0$ are disjoint (which can be achieved by $\alpha$-renaming). The strands in $S_0$ induce an *infinite-state transition system* with *initial state* $(S_0; \emptyset; \emptyset; \top)$ and a transition relation $\Rightarrow$ defined as the least relation closed under six transition rules:

T1 $(\{\text{send}(t).S\} \cup S; M; E; \phi) \Rightarrow (\{S\} \cup S; M \cup \{t\}; E; \phi)$
T2 $(\{\text{receive}(t).S\} \cup S; M; E; \phi) \Rightarrow (\{S\} \cup S; M; E; \phi \wedge M \vdash t)$
T3 $(\{\text{event}(t).S\} \cup S; M; E; \phi) \Rightarrow (\{S\} \cup S; M; E \cup \text{event}(t); \phi)$
T4 $(\{\phi'.S\} \cup S; M; E; \phi) \Rightarrow (\{S\} \cup S; M; E; \phi \wedge \phi')$
T5 $(\{0\} \cup S; M; E; \phi) \Rightarrow (S; M; E; \phi)$
T6 $(S; M; E; \phi) \Rightarrow (S; M; E \cup \{\mathit{lts}(c)\}; \phi)$ for every $c \in \mathcal{C}_{priv}$

The rule T1 formalizes that sent messages are added to the intruder knowledge $M$. T2 formalizes that an honest agent receives a message of the form $t$, and that the intruder must be able to create that message from his current knowledge, expressed by the new constraint $M \vdash t$; this indirectly binds the free variables of the rest of the strand in the sense that they are now governed by the constraints of the state. (In a non-symbolic model, one would at this point instead need to consider all ground instances of $t$ that the intruder can generate.) T3 formalizes that we add events to the set $E$. T4 simply adds the constraint $\phi'$ to the constraint $\phi$. T5 says that if a strand reaches $\{0\}$, then we remove it. Finally, for every secret constant $c$ in $\mathcal{C}_{priv}$, T6 adds the event $\mathit{lts}(c)$ to the set $E$. (We define later as a goal that the intruder never obtains any $c$ for which $\mathit{lts}(c) \in E$.) We cannot have this in the initial set $E$ as we need it to be finite; this construction is later crucial in the parallel composition proof as we can at any time blame a protocol (in isolation) that leaks a secret constant. We discuss below that in practice this semantic rule does not cause trouble to the verification of the individual protocols.

---

[1] Some approaches instead use multi-sets as we may have several identical strands, but since one can always make a strand unique, using sets is without loss of generality.

## 3.3    Goal Predicates in the Geometric Fragment

We express goals by *state formulas in the geometric fragment* [11]. Here, we also allow to directly talk about the intruder knowledge, but in a restricted manner so that we obtain constraints of the form $\phi$. Security then means: every reachable state in the transition system induced by $\mathcal{S}_0$ satisfies each state formula, and thus an *attack* is a reachable state where at least one goal does not hold.

The constraints $\phi$ we have defined above are interpreted only with respect to an interpretation of the free variables, whereas the state formulas are evaluated with respect to a symbolic state, including the current intruder knowledge and events that have occurred (as before, we define the semantics for each construct).

**Definition 4.** State formulas $\Psi$ in the geometric fragment *are defined as:*

$$\Psi := \forall \bar{x}.(\psi \implies \psi_0) \ with \ \begin{cases} \psi := \mathsf{ik}(t) \mid \mathsf{event}(t) \mid t \doteq t' \mid \psi \wedge \psi' \mid \psi \vee \psi' \mid \exists \bar{x}.\psi \\ \psi_0 := \mathsf{event}(t) \mid t \doteq t' \mid \psi_0 \wedge \psi_0' \mid \psi_0 \vee \psi_0' \mid \exists \bar{x}.\psi_0 \end{cases}$$

*where* $\mathsf{ik}(t)$ *denotes that the intruder knows the term* $t$. $fv(\cdot)$ *and closed extend to state formulas as expected. Given a state formula* $\Psi$, *an interpretation* $\mathcal{I}$, *and a state* $\mathfrak{S} = (\mathcal{S}; M; E; \phi)$, *we define* $\mathcal{I}, M, E \models_{\mathfrak{S}} \Psi$ *as:*

$$
\begin{array}{llll}
\mathcal{I}, M, E \models_{\mathfrak{S}} \mathsf{event}(t) & \textit{iff} & \mathcal{I}(\mathsf{event}(t)) \in \mathcal{I}(E) \\
\mathcal{I}, M, E \models_{\mathfrak{S}} \mathsf{ik}(t) & \textit{iff} & \mathcal{I}(M) \vdash \mathcal{I}(t) \\
\mathcal{I}, M, E \models_{\mathfrak{S}} s \doteq t & \textit{iff} & \mathcal{I}(s) = \mathcal{I}(t) \\
\mathcal{I}, M, E \models_{\mathfrak{S}} \Psi \wedge \Psi' & \textit{iff} & \mathcal{I}, M, E \models_{\mathfrak{S}} \Psi \text{ and } \mathcal{I}, M, E \models_{\mathfrak{S}} \Psi' \\
\mathcal{I}, M, E \models_{\mathfrak{S}} \Psi \vee \Psi' & \textit{iff} & \mathcal{I}, M, E \models_{\mathfrak{S}} \Psi \text{ or } \mathcal{I}, M, E \models_{\mathfrak{S}} \Psi' \\
\mathcal{I}, M, E \models_{\mathfrak{S}} \neg \Psi & \textit{iff} & \text{not } \mathcal{I}, M, E \models_{\mathfrak{S}} \Psi \\
\mathcal{I}, M, E \models_{\mathfrak{S}} \exists x.\Psi & \textit{iff} & \text{there exists } t \in \mathcal{T}_{\Sigma} \text{ and } \mathcal{I}[x \mapsto t] \models_{\mathfrak{S}} \Psi.
\end{array}
$$

**Definition 5.** *A protocol* $P = (\mathcal{S}_0, \{\Psi_0, \cdots, \Psi_n\})$, *where the* $\Psi_i$ *are closed state formulas, has an attack against goal* $\Psi_i$ *iff there exist a reachable state* $\mathfrak{S} = (\mathcal{S}; M; E; \phi)$ *in the transition system induced by* $\mathcal{S}_0$ *and an interpretation* $\mathcal{I}$ *such that* $\mathcal{I}, M, E \models_{\mathfrak{S}} \neg \Psi_i$ *and* $\mathcal{I} \models_{\mathfrak{S}} \phi$. *We also call* $\mathfrak{S}$ *an attack state in this case.*

Note that in this definition the interpretation $\mathcal{I}$ does not matter in $\mathcal{I}, M, E \models_{\mathfrak{S}} \neg \Psi_i$ because $\Psi_i$ is closed.

*Example 1.* If a protocol generates the event[2] $\mathsf{secret}(x_A, x_B, x_m)$ to denote that the message $x_m$ is supposed to be a secret between agents $x_A$ and $x_B$, and—optionally—the event $\mathsf{release}(x_m)$ to denote that $x_m$ is no longer a secret, then we can formalize *secrecy* via the state formula $\forall x_A x_B x_m.(\mathsf{secret}(x_A, x_B, x_m) \wedge \mathsf{ik}(x_m) \implies x_A = \mathsf{i} \vee x_B = \mathsf{i} \vee \mathsf{release}(x_m))$, where $\mathsf{i}$ denotes the intruder. The release event can be used to model declassification of secrets as needed

---

[2] Strictly speaking, we should write $\mathsf{event}(\mathsf{secret}(x_A, x_B, x_m))$ but, for readability, here and below we will omit the outer $\mathsf{event}(\cdot)$ when it is clear from context.

to verify perfect forward secrecy (when other data should remain secret even under the release of temporary secrets). We note that previous compositionality approaches do not support such goals. A typical formulation of *non-injective agreement* [15] uses the two events $\mathsf{commit}(x_A, x_B, x_m)$, which represents that $x_A$ intends to send message $x_m$ to $x_B$), and $\mathsf{running}(x_A, x_B, x_m, x_C)$, which represents that $x_B$ believes to have received $x_m$ from $x_A$, with $x_C$ a unique identifier: $\forall x_A x_B x_m x_C. (\mathsf{running}(x_A, x_B, x_m, x_C) \implies \mathsf{commit}(x_A, x_B, x_m) \lor x_A = \mathsf{i} \lor x_B = \mathsf{i})$, and *injective agreement* would additionally require: $\forall x_A x_B x_m x_C x_C'. \mathsf{running}(x_A, x_B, x_m, x_C) \land \mathsf{running}(x_A, x_B, x_m, x_C') \implies x_A = \mathsf{i} \lor x_B = \mathsf{i} \lor x_C = x_C'$. □

## 4  Constraint Solving

We first show how to translate every state formula $\Psi$ in the geometric fragment for a given symbolic state $\mathfrak{S} = (\mathcal{S}; M; E; \phi)$ into a constraint $\phi'$ (in the fragment defined in Sect. 3.1) so that the models of $\phi \land \phi'$ represent exactly all concrete instances of $\mathfrak{S}$ that violate $\Psi$. Then, we extend a rule-based procedure to solve $\phi$-style constraints (getting them into an equivalent simple form). This procedure provides the basis for our typing and parallel composition results.

### 4.1  From Geometric Fragment to Symbolic Constraints

Consider a reachable symbolic state $(\mathcal{S}; M; E; \phi)$ and a goal formula $\Psi$. As mentioned earlier, we require that $\Psi$ is closed. Let us further assume that the bound variables of $\Psi$ are disjoint from the variables (bound or free) of $\mathcal{S}$, $M$, $E$, and $\phi$. We now define a *translation function* $tr_{M,E}(\Psi) = \phi'$ where $\phi'$ represents the negation of $\Psi$ with respect to intruder knowledge $M$ and events $E$. The negation is actually manifested in the first line of the definition:

$$tr_{M,E}(\forall \bar{x}. \psi \Rightarrow \psi_0) = \exists \bar{x}. tr'_{M,E}(\psi) \land tr'_{M,E}(\neg \psi_0)$$
$$tr'_{M,E}(\mathsf{ik}(t)) = M \vdash t$$
$$tr'_{M,E}(\mathsf{event}(t)) = \bigvee\nolimits_{\mathsf{event}(s) \in E} s \doteq t$$
$$tr'_{M,E}(s \doteq t) = s \doteq t$$
$$tr'_{M,E}(\psi_1 \lor \psi_2) = tr'_{M,E}(\psi_1) \lor tr'_{M,E}(\psi_2)$$
$$tr'_{M,E}(\psi_1 \land \psi_2) = tr'_{M,E}(\psi_1) \land tr'_{M,E}(\psi_2)$$
$$tr'_{M,E}(\exists \bar{x}. \psi) = \exists \bar{x}. tr'_{M,E}(\psi)$$
$$tr'_{M,E}(\neg \mathsf{event}(t)) = \bigwedge\nolimits_{\mathsf{event}(s) \in E} \neg s \doteq t$$
$$tr'_{M,E}(\neg s \doteq t) = \neg s \doteq t$$
$$tr'_{M,E}(\neg(\exists \bar{x}. \psi_1 \lor \psi_2)) = tr'_{M,E}(\neg \exists \bar{x}. \psi_1) \land tr'_{M,E}(\neg \exists \bar{x}. \psi_2)$$
$$tr'_{M,E}(\neg \neg \phi) = tr'_{M,E}(\phi)$$
$$tr'_{M,E}(\neg \exists \bar{x}. \mathsf{event}(t_1) \land \cdots \land \mathsf{event}(t_n) \land u_1 \doteq v_1 \land \cdots u_m \doteq v_m) =$$
$$\bigwedge\nolimits_{\mathsf{event}(s_1) \in E \ldots \mathsf{event}(s_n) \in} \neg \exists \bar{x}. (s_1 \doteq t_1 \land \cdots \land t_n \doteq s_n \land u_1 \doteq v_1 \land \cdots u_m \doteq v_m)$$

**Theorem 1.** *Let $\mathfrak{S} = (\mathcal{S}; M; E; \phi)$ be a symbolic state and $\Psi$ a formula in the geometric fragment such that $fv(\Psi) = \emptyset$ and $var(\Psi) \cap var(\phi) = \emptyset$. For all $\mathcal{I} \models \phi$, we have $\mathcal{I}, M, E \models_{\mathfrak{S}} \neg \Psi$ iff $\mathcal{I} \models tr_{M,E}(\Psi)$. Moreover, if $\phi$ is well-formed, then so is $\phi \land tr_{M,E}(\Psi)$.*

## 4.2   Constraint Reduction

As mentioned before, we can transform any well-formed constraint into the form $\phi \equiv \exists \bar{x}.\phi_0 \vee \ldots \vee \phi_n$, where $\phi_i$ are base constraints, i.e., without disjunction and existential quantification (except in negative substitutions). We now discuss how to find the solutions of such well-formed base constraints. Solving intruder constraints has been studied quite extensively, e.g., in [7,16,18,20], where the main application of constraints was for efficient protocol verification for a bounded number of sessions of honest agents. Here, we use constraints rather as a proof argument for the shape of attacks. Our result is of course not restricted to a bounded number of sessions as we do not rely on an exploration of reachable symbolic states (that are indeed infinite) but rather make an argument about the constraints in each of these states.

We consider *constraint reduction rules* of the form $\dfrac{\phi'}{\phi}$ expressing that $\phi'$ entails $\phi$ (if the side condition *cond* holds). However, we will usually read the rule backwards, i.e., as: one way to solve $\phi$ is $\phi'$.

**Definition 6.** *The* satisfiability calculus for the symbolic intruder *comprises the following constraint reduction rules:*

$$\frac{eq(\sigma) \wedge \sigma(\phi)}{M \vdash t \wedge \phi} \; (Unify), \; s,t \notin \mathcal{V}, s \in M, \qquad \frac{eq(\sigma) \wedge \sigma(\phi)}{s \doteq t \wedge \phi} \; (Equation), \; \sigma \in mgu(s \doteq t),$$
$$\sigma \in mgu(s \doteq t) \qquad \qquad s \notin \mathcal{V} \text{ or } s \in fv(t) \cup fv(\phi)$$

$$\frac{\phi}{M \vdash c \wedge \phi} \; (PubConsts), \; c \in \mathcal{C}_{pub} \qquad \frac{M \vdash t_1, \cdots, M \vdash t_n}{M \vdash f(t_1, \cdots, t_n)} \; (Compose), \; f \in \Sigma^n$$

$$\frac{\bigwedge_{k \in K} M \vdash k \wedge (M \vdash t \wedge \phi)^{T \gg M}}{M \vdash t \wedge \phi} \; \begin{array}{l} (Decompose), \; s \in M, \mathbf{Ana}(s) = (K,T), T \not\subseteq M, \\ \text{and } (Decompose) \text{ has not been applied with} \\ \text{the same } M \text{ and } s \text{ before} \end{array}$$

*where* $(M' \vdash t)^{T \gg M}$ *is* $M' \cup T \vdash t$ *if* $M \subseteq M'$ *and* $M' \vdash t$ *otherwise,* $(\cdot)^{T \gg M}$ *extends as expected,* $eq(\sigma) = x_1 \doteq t_1 \wedge \ldots \wedge x_n \doteq t_n$ *is the constraint corresponding to a substitution* $\sigma = [x_1 \mapsto t_1, \ldots, x_n \mapsto t_n]$, *and* $mgu(s \doteq t)$ *is the standard most general unifier for the pair of terms* $t$ *and* $s$ *(in the free-algebra).*

Recall that the *mgu*, if it exists, is unique modulo renaming (*mgu* extends as expected). Let us now explain the rules. (*Unify*) expresses that one way to generate a term $t$ from knowledge $M$ is to use any term $s \in M$ that can be unified with $t$, but one commits in this case to the unifier $\sigma$; this is done by applying $\sigma$ to the rest of the constraint and recording its equations. (*Unify*) cannot be applied when $s$ or $t$ are variables; intuitively: when $t$ is a variable, the solution is an arbitrary term, so we consider this a solved state (until elsewhere a substitution is required that substitutes $t$); when $s$ is variable, then it is a subterm of a message that the intruder created earlier. If the earlier constraint is already solved (i.e., a variable) then $s$ is something the intruder could generate from an earlier knowledge and thus redundant.

(*Equation*), which similarly allows us to solve an equation, can be applied if $s$ or $t$ are variables, provided the conditions are satisfied, but later we will have to prevent vacuous application of this rule to its previous result, i.e., the equations $eq(\sigma)$. (*PubConsts*) says that the intruder can generate all public constants.

(*Compose*) expresses that one way to generate a composed term $f(t_1, \ldots, t_n)$ is to generate the subterms $t_1, \ldots, t_n$ (because then $f$ can be applied to them). (*Decompose*) expresses that we can attempt decryption of any term in the intruder knowledge according to the **Ana** function. Recall that Table 1 provides examples of **Ana**, and note that for variables or constants Table 1 will yield $(\emptyset, \emptyset)$, i.e., there is nothing to analyze. However, if there is a set $T$ of messages that can potentially be obtained if we can derive the keys $K$, and $T$ is not yet a subset of the knowledge $M$ anyway, then one way to proceed is to add $M \vdash k$ for each $k \in K$ to the constraint store, i.e., committing to finding the keys, and under this assumption we may add $T$ to $M$ and in fact to any knowledge $M'$ that is a superset of $M$. Also for this rule we must prevent vacuous repeated application, such as applying analysis directly to the newly generated $M \vdash k$ constraints.

The reduction of constraints deals with conjuncts of the form $M \vdash t$ and $s \doteq t$. However, we also have to handle negative substitutions, i.e., conjuncts of the form $\neg \exists \bar{x}.\phi_\sigma$. We show that we can easily check them for satisfiability.

**Definition 7.** *A constraint $\phi$ is* simple, *written simple$(\phi)$, iff $\phi = \phi_1 \wedge \ldots \wedge \phi_n$ such that for each $\phi_i$ $(1 \leq i \leq n)$:*

- *if $\phi_i = M \vdash t$, then $t \in \mathcal{V}$;*
- *if $\phi_i = s \doteq t$, then $s \in \mathcal{V}$ and $s$ does not appear elsewhere in $\phi$;*
- *if $\phi_i = \neg \exists \bar{x}.\phi_\sigma$, then $mgu(\theta(\phi_\sigma)) = \emptyset$ for $\theta = [\bar{y} \mapsto \bar{c}]$ where $\bar{y}$ are the free variables of $\phi_i$ and $\bar{c}$ fresh constants that do not appear in $\phi$.*

**Theorem 2.** *If simple$(\phi)$, then $\phi$ is satisfiable.*

**Theorem 3 (Adaption of [18, 20]).** *The satisfiability calculus for the symbolic intruder is sound, complete, and terminating on well-formed constraints.*

## 5  Typed Model

In our typed model, the *set of all possible types for terms* is denoted by $\mathcal{T}_{\Sigma \cup \mathfrak{T}_a}$, where $\mathfrak{T}_a$ is a finite set of *atomic types*, e.g., $\mathfrak{T}_a = \{Number, Agent, PublicKey, PrivateKey, SymmetricKey\}$. We call all other types *composed types*. Each atomic term (each element of $\mathcal{V} \cup \mathcal{C}$) is given a type; constants are given an *atomic type* and variables are given either an atomic or a composed type (any element of $\mathcal{T}_{\Sigma \cup \mathfrak{T}_a}$). We write $t : \tau$ to denote that a term $t$ has the type $\tau$. Based on the type information of atomic terms, we define the *typing function* $\Gamma$ as follows:

**Definition 8.** *Given $\Gamma(\cdot) : \mathcal{V} \to \mathcal{T}_{\Sigma \cup \mathfrak{T}_a}$ for variables and $\Gamma(\cdot) : \mathcal{C} \to \mathfrak{T}_a$ for constants, we extend $\Gamma$ to map all terms to a type, i.e., $\Gamma(\cdot) : \mathcal{T}_{\Sigma \cup \mathcal{C}}(\mathcal{V}) \to \mathcal{T}_{\Sigma \cup \mathfrak{T}_a}$, as follows: $\Gamma(t) = f(\Gamma(t_1), \cdots, \Gamma(t_n))$ if $t = f(t_1, \cdots, t_n)$ and $f \in \Sigma^n$. We say that a substitution $\sigma$ is* well-typed *iff $\Gamma(x) = \Gamma(\sigma(x))$ for all $x \in dom(\sigma)$.*

For example, if $\Gamma(k) = PrivateKey$ and $\Gamma(x) = Number$ then $\Gamma(\mathsf{crypt}(\mathsf{pub}(k), x)) = \mathsf{crypt}(\mathsf{pub}(PrivateKey), Number)$.

As we require that all constants be typed, we further partition $\mathcal{C}$ into disjoint countable subsets according to different types in $\mathfrak{T}_a$. This models the intruder's ability to access infinite reservoirs of public fresh constants. For example, for protocols $P_1, P_2$ and $\mathfrak{T}_a = \{\beta_1, \ldots, \beta_n\}$, we have the disjoint subsets $\mathcal{C}_{pub}^{\beta_i}$, $\mathcal{C}_{priv}^{\beta_i}$, $\mathcal{C}_{P_1}^{\beta_i}$ and $\mathcal{C}_{P_2}^{\beta_i}$, where $i \in \{1, \ldots, n\}$ and, e.g., $\mathcal{C}_{pub}^{\beta_i}$ contains all $\mathcal{C}_{pub}$ elements of type $\beta_i$. $\mathcal{C}_{P_1}^{\beta_i}$ and $\mathcal{C}_{P_2}^{\beta_i}$ are short-term constants, whereas $\mathcal{C}_{pub}^{\beta_i}$ and $\mathcal{C}_{priv}^{\beta_i}$ are long-term, and we consider it an attack if the intruder learns any of $\mathcal{C}_{priv}^{\beta_i}$.

By an easy induction on the structure of terms, we have:

**Lemma 1.** *If a substitution $\sigma$ is well-typed, then $\Gamma(t) = \Gamma(\sigma(t))$ for all terms $t \in \mathcal{T}_{\Sigma \cup \mathcal{C}}(\mathcal{V})$.*

According to this typed model, $\mathcal{I}$ is a *well-typed interpretation* iff $\Gamma(x) = \Gamma(\mathcal{I}(x))$ for all $x \in \mathcal{V}$. Moreover, we require for the typed model that $\Gamma(s) = \Gamma(t)$ for each $s \doteq t$. This is a restriction only on the strands of the honest agents (as they are supposed to act honestly), not on the intruder: he can send ill-typed messages freely. We later show that sending ill-typed messages does not help the intruder in introducing new attacks in protocols that satisfy certain conditions.

### 5.1    Message Patterns

In order to prevent the intruder from using messages of a protocol to attack a second protocol, we need to guarantee the disjointness of the messages between both protocols. Thus, we use formats to wrap raw data, as discussed in Sect. 2.2. In particular, all submessages of all operators (except formats and public key operator) must be "wrapped" with a format, e.g., $\mathsf{scrypt}(k, \mathsf{f}_a(Na))$ and $\mathsf{scrypt}(k, \mathsf{f}_b(Nb))$ should be used instead of $\mathsf{scrypt}(k, Na)$ and $\mathsf{scrypt}(k_1, Nb)$.

We define the set of protocol message patterns, where we need to ensure that each pair of terms has disjoint variables: we thus define a well-typed $\alpha$-renaming $\alpha(t)$ that replaces the variables in $t$ with completely new variable names.

**Definition 9.** *The* message pattern *of a message $t$ is $MP(t) = \{\alpha(t)\}$. We extend MP to strands, goals and protocols as follows: The set $MP(S)$ of message patterns of a strand $S$ and the set $MP(\Psi)$ of message patterns of a goal $\Psi$ are defined as follows:*

$$
\begin{aligned}
MP(\mathsf{send}(t).S) &= MP(t) \cup MP(S) & MP(\forall x.\psi \Rightarrow \psi_0) &= MP(\psi) \cup MP(\psi_0) \\
MP(\mathsf{event}(t).S) &= MP(t) \cup MP(S) & MP(\mathsf{ik}(t)) &= MP(t) \\
MP(\mathsf{receive}(t).S) &= MP(t) \cup MP(S) & MP(\mathsf{event}(t)) &= MP(t) \\
MP(s \doteq t.S) &= MP(\sigma(S)), & MP(\psi_1 \vee \psi_2) &= MP(\psi_1) \cup MP(\psi_2) \\
&\quad \text{for } \sigma \in mgu(s \doteq t) & MP(\psi_1 \wedge \psi_2) &= MP(\psi_1) \cup MP(\psi_2) \\
MP(s \doteq t.S) &= \emptyset \text{ if } mgu(s \doteq t) = \emptyset & MP(s \doteq t) &= MP(s) \cup MP(t) \\
MP((\neg \exists \bar{x}.\phi_\sigma).S) &= MP(\phi_\sigma) \cup MP(S) & MP(\neg \phi) &= MP(\phi) \\
MP(0) &= \emptyset
\end{aligned}
$$

*The* set of message patterns *of a protocol $P = (\{S_1, \cdots, S_m\}; \{\Psi_0, \cdots, \Psi_n\})$ is $MP(P) = \bigcup_{i=1}^{m} MP(S_i) \cup \bigcup_{i=1}^{n} MP(\Psi_i)$, and the set of sub-message patterns of a protocol $P$ is $SMP(P) = \{\alpha(s) \mid t \in MP(P) \wedge s \sqsubseteq t \wedge \neg atomic(s)\} \setminus \{u \mid u = pub(v) \text{ for some term } v\}$. SMP applies to messages, strands, goals as expected.*

*Example 2.* If $S = \mathsf{receive}(\mathsf{scrypt}(k, (\mathsf{f_1}(x, y)))).\mathsf{send}(\mathsf{scrypt}(k, y))$, then $SMP(S)$ = $\{\mathsf{scrypt}(k, \mathsf{f_1}(x_1, y_1)), \mathsf{scrypt}(k, y_2), \mathsf{f_1}(x_3, y_3)\}$. □

**Definition 10.** *A protocol $P = (\mathcal{S}_0, G)$ is type-flaw-resistant iff the following conditions hold:*

- *$MP(P)$ and $\mathcal{V}$ are disjoint, i.e., $MP(P) \cap \mathcal{V} = \emptyset$ (which ensures that none of the messages of $P$ is sent as raw data).*
- *If two non-atomic sub-terms are unifiable, then they have the same type, i.e., for all $t_1, t_2 \in SMP(P)$, if $\sigma(t_1) = \sigma(t_2)$ for some $\sigma$, then $\Gamma(t_1) = \Gamma(t_2)$.*
- *For any equation $s \doteq t$ that occurs in strands or goals of $P$ (also under a negation), $\Gamma(s) = \Gamma(t)$.*
- *For any variable $x$ that occurs in equations or events of $G$, $\Gamma(x) \in \mathfrak{T}_a$.*
- *For any variable $x$ that occurs in inequalities or events of strands, $\Gamma(x) \in \mathfrak{T}_a$.*

Intuitively, the second condition means that we cannot unify two terms unless their types match. Note that this match is a restriction on honest agents only, the intruder is still able to send ill-typed messages.

*Example 3.* Example 2 included a potential type-flaw vulnerability as $\mathsf{scrypt}(k, \mathsf{f_1}(x_1, y_1))$ and $\mathsf{scrypt}(k, y_2)$ have the unifier $[y_2 \mapsto \mathsf{f_1}(x_1, y_1)]$. Here $y_1$ and $y_2$ must have the same type since they have been obtained by a well-typed variable renaming in the construction of $SMP$. Thus, the two messages have different types. The problem is that the second message encrypts raw data without any information on who it is meant for and it may thus be mistaken for the first message. Let us thus change the second message to $\mathsf{scrypt}(k, \mathsf{f_2}(y_2))$. Then $SMP$ also includes $\mathsf{f_2}(y_4)$ for a further variable $y_4$, and now no two different elements of $SMP$ have a unifier. $\mathsf{f_2}$ is not necessarily inserting a tag: if the type of $y$ in the implementation is a fixed-length type, this is already sufficient for distinction. □

**Theorem 4.** *If a type-flaw-resistant protocol $P$ has an attack, then $P$ has a well-typed attack.*

Note that this theorem does not exclude that type-flaw attacks are possible, but rather says that for every type-flaw attack there is also a (similar) well-typed attack, so it is safe to verify the protocol only in the typed model.

# 6   Parallel Composition

In this section, we consider the parallel composition of protocols, which we often abbreviate simply to "composition". We define the set of operational strands for the composition of a pair of protocols as the union of the sets of the operational strands of the two protocols; this allows all possible transitions in the composition. The goals for the composition are also the union of the goals of the pair, since any attack on any of them is an attack on the whole composition (i.e., the composition must achieve the goals of the pair).

**Definition 11.** *The* parallel composition $P_1 \parallel P_2$ *of* $P_1 = (S_0^{P_1}; \Psi_0^{P_1})$ *and* $P_2 = (S_0^{P_2}; \Psi_0^{P_2})$ *is* $P_1 \parallel P_2 = (S_0^{P_1} \cup S_0^{P_2}; \Psi_0^{P_1} \cup \Psi_0^{P_2})$.

Our parallel composition result relies on the following key idea. Similar to the typing result, we look at the constraints produced by an attack trace against $P_1 \parallel P_2$, violating a goal of $P_1$, and show that we can obtain an attack against $P_1$ alone, or a violation of a long-term secret by $P_2$. Again, the core of this proof is the observation that the unification steps of the symbolic intruder never produce an "ill-typed" substitution in the sense that a $P_1$-variable is never instantiated with a $P_2$ message and vice versa. For that to work, we have a similar condition as before, namely that the non-atomic subterms of the two protocols (the SMPs) are disjoint, i.e., each non-atomic message uniquely says to which protocol it belongs. This is more liberal than the requirements in previous parallel compositionality results in that we do not require a particular tagging scheme: any way to make the protocol messages distinguishable is allowed. Further, we carefully set up the use of constants in the protocol as explained at the beginning of Sect. 5, namely that all constants used in the protocol are: long-term public values that the intruder initially knows; long-term secret values that, if the intruder obtains them, count as a secrecy violation in *both* protocols; or short-term values of $P_1$ or of $P_2$.

The only limitation of our model is that long-term secrets cannot be "declassified": we require that all constants of type private key are either part of the long-term secrets or long-term public constants. Moreover, the intruder can obtain all public keys, i.e., $\mathsf{pub}(c)$ for every $c$ of type private key. This does not prevent honest agents from creating fresh key-pairs (the private key shall be chosen from the long-term constants as well) but it dictates that each private key is either a perpetual secret (it is an attack if the intruder obtains it) or it is public right from the start (as all public keys are). This only excludes protocols in which a private key is a secret at first and later revealed to the intruder, or where some public keys are initially kept secret.

**Definition 12.** *Two protocols $P_1$ and $P_2$ are* parallel-composable *iff the following conditions hold:*

*(1)* $P_1$ *and* $P_2$ *are SMP-disjoint, i.e., for every* $s \in SMP(P_1)$ *and* $t \in SMP(P_2)$, *either* $s$ *and* $t$ *have no unifier (*$mgu(s \doteq t) = \emptyset$*) or* $s = \mathsf{pub}(s_0)$ *and* $t = \mathsf{pub}(t_0)$ *for some* $s_0, t_0$ *of type private key.*

*(2)* *All constants of type private key that occur in* $MP(P_1) \cup MP(P_2)$ *are part of the long-term constants in* $\mathcal{C}_{pub} \cup \mathcal{C}_{priv}$.

*(3)* *All constants that occur in* $MP(P_i)$ *are in* $\mathcal{C}_{pub} \cup \mathcal{C}_{priv} \cup \mathcal{C}_{P_i}$, *i.e., are either long term or belong to the short-term constants of the respective protocol.*

*(4)* *For every* $c \in \mathcal{C}_{P_i}^{PrivateKey}$, $P_i$ *also contains the strand* $\mathsf{send}(\mathsf{pub}(c)).0$.

*(5)* *For each secret constant* $c \in \mathcal{C}_{priv}^{\beta_i}$, *for each type* $\beta_i$, *each* $P_i$ *contains the strands* $\mathsf{event}(lts_{\beta_i, P_i}(c)).0$ *and the goal* $\forall x : \beta_i. \, \mathsf{ik}(x) \implies \neg lts_{\beta, P_i}(x)$.

*(6)* *Both* $P_1$ *and* $P_2$ *are type-flaw resistant.*

Some remarks on the conditions: (1) is the core of the compositionality result, as it helps to avoid confusion between messages of the two protocols; (2) ensures that every private key is either initially known to the intruder or is part of the long-term secrets (and thus prevents "declassification" of private keys as we discussed above). (3) means that the two protocols will draw from disjoint sets of constants for their short-term values. (4) ensures that public keys are known to the intruder. Note that typically the goals on long-term secrets, like private keys and shared symmetric keys, are very easy to prove as they are normally not transmitted. The fact that we do not put all public keys into the knowledge of the intruder in the initial state is because the intruder knowledge must be a finite set of terms for the constraint reduction to work. Putting it into strands means they are available at any time, but the intruder knowledge in every reachable state (and thus constraint) is finite. Similarly, for the goals on long-term secrets: the set of events in every reachable state is still finite, but for every leaked secret, we can in one transition reach the corresponding predicate that triggers the secrecy violation goal. (5) ensures that when either protocol $P_i$ leaks any constant of $\mathcal{C}_{priv}^{\beta_i}$, it is a violation of its secrecy goals. (6) ensures that for both protocols, we cannot unify terms unless their types match.

**Theorem 5.** *If two protocols $P_1$ and $P_2$ are parallel-composable and both $P_1$ and $P_2$ are secure in isolation in the typed model, then $P_1 \parallel P_2$ is secure (also in the untyped model).*

We can then apply this theorem successively to any number of protocols that satisfy the conditions, in order to prove that they are all parallel composable.

This compositionality result entails an interesting observation about parallel composition with insecure protocols: unless one of the protocols leaks a long-term secret, the intruder never needs to use one protocol to attack another protocol. This means actually: even if a protocol is flawed, it does not endanger the security of the other protocols as long as it at least manages not to leak the long-term secrets. For instance, the Needham-Schroeder Public Key protocol has a well-known attack, but the intruder can never obtain the private keys of any honest agent. Thus, another protocol relying on the same public-key infrastructure is completely unaffected. This is a crucial point because it permits us to even allow for security statements in presence of flawed protocols:

**Corollary 1.** *Consider two protocols $P_1$ and $P_2$ that are parallel-composable (and thus satisfy all the conditions in Definition 12). If $P_1$ is secure in isolation and $P_2$, even though it may have an attack in isolation, does not leak a long-term secret, then all goals of $P_1$ hold also in $P_1 \parallel P_2$.*

## 7 Tool Support

We have developed the *Automated Protocol Composition Checker* APCC (available at http://www2.compute.dtu.dk/~samo/APCC.zip), a tool that verifies the two main syntactic conditions of our results: it checks both if a given protocol is type-flaw-resistant and if the protocols in a given set are pairwise parallel-composable. In our preliminary experiments, we considered a suite that includes widely used protocols like TLS, Kerberos (PKINIT and Basic) and protocols defined by the ISO/IEC 9798 standard, along with well-known academic protocols (variants of Needham-Schroeder-Lowe, Denning-Sacco, etc.). Although we worked with abstract and simplified models, we were able to verify that TLS and Kerberos are parallel-composable. In contrast, since some protocols of the ISO/IEC 9798 standard share common formats, they are not *SMP*-disjoint.

Another result is that many academic protocols are not pairwise parallel-composable. This was largely expected because they do not have a standardized implementation, and thus the format of messages at the wire level is not part of the specification. In fact, in these protocols there are several terms that may be confused with terms of other protocols, whereas a concrete implementation may avoid this by choosing carefully disjoint messages formats that can prevent the unification. Hence, our tool APCC can also support developers in the integration of new protocols (or new implementations of them) in an existing system.

## 8   Conclusions and Related Work

This paper unifies research on the soundness of typed models (e.g., [4,6,13, 18]) and on parallel protocol composition (e.g., [2,8–10,12]) by using a proof technique that has been employed in both areas: attack reduction based on a symbolic constraint systems. For typing, the idea is that the constraint solving never needs to apply ill-typed substitutions if the protocol satisfies some sufficient conditions; hence, for every attack there exists a well-typed variant and it is thus without loss of generality to restrict the model to well-typed execution. For the parallel composition of $P_1$ and $P_2$ that again satisfy some sufficient conditions, the constraint solving never needs to use a message that the intruder learned from $P_1$ to construct a message of $P_2$; thus, the attack will work in $P_1$ alone or in $P_2$ alone, and from verifying them in isolation, we can conclude that their composition is secure.

We also make several generalizations over previous results. First, we are not limited to a fixed set of properties like secrecy [3,6]. Instead, we consider the entire geometric fragment proposed by Guttman [11] that we believe is the most expressive language that can work with the given constraint-solving argument that is at the core of handling typing and compositionality results uniformly. Other expressive property languages have been considered, e.g., PS-LTL for typing results [4]; an in-depth comparison of the various existing property languages and their relative expressiveness is yet outstanding. Another common limitation is to rely on a fixed public key infrastructure, e.g., [3,4,8]. Our approach in contrast allows for the exchange of public keys (including freshly generated ones). Moreover, early works on typing and parallel composition used a fixed tagging scheme, whereas we use the more general notion of non-unifiable subterms for messages that have different meaning. Using the notion of formats, our results are applicable to existing real-world protocols like TLS with their actual formats.

Our work considered so far protocols only in the initial term algebra without any algebraic properties. There are some promising results for such properties (e.g., [9,14,17]) that we would like to combine with our approach. The same holds for other types of protocol composition, e.g., the sequential composition considered in [9], where one protocol establishes a key that is used by another protocol as input.

# A    Appendix: Proofs of the Technical Results

For space reasons, we only outline the proofs to convey the main ideas. The detailed proofs are in [1].

*Proof Sketch of Theorem 1.* We prove by induction a corresponding property for $tr'$ that is invoked by the $tr$ function, i.e., that $\mathcal{I}, M, E \models_\mathfrak{S} \psi$ iff $\mathcal{I} \models tr'_{M,E}(\psi)$ for all suitable $\mathcal{I}, M, E$ and $\psi$. Here we use the fact that in all reachable states, $E$ is finite, i.e., $\mathsf{event}(t) \in E$ is equivalent to a finite enumeration $t = e_1 \vee \ldots \vee t = e_n$. All other cases and the extension to $tr$ are straightforward. The well-formedness follows from the fact that in each state, the knowledge $M$ is a superset of all $M'$ that occur in a deduction constraint $M' \vdash t$ in $\phi$.    □

*Proof Sketch of Theorem 2.* Since $\phi$ is simple, it is a conjunction of intruder deduction constraints of the form $M \vdash x$ with $x \in \mathcal{V}$, equations $x \doteq t$ where $x \in \mathcal{V}$ and where $x$ does not occur elsewhere in $\phi$, as well as inequalities. Let $\bar{y}$ be all variables that occur freely in intruder deduction constraints and inequalities, and let $\theta = [\bar{y} \mapsto \bar{c}]$ for new constants $\bar{c} \in \mathcal{C}_{pub}$ (that do not occur in $\phi$ and are pairwise different). We show that $\theta(\phi)$ is satisfiable: all intruder deduction constraints are satisfiable since the constants are in $\mathcal{C}_{pub}$, and the equations are obviously satisfiable. It remains to show that the inequalities are satisfiable under $\theta$. Let $\phi_0 = \neg \exists \bar{x}. \phi_\sigma$ with $\phi_\sigma = \bigwedge s_i \doteq t_i$ be any inequality. $\theta(\phi_0)$ is closed, and since $\phi$ is simple we have $mgu(\theta(\phi_\sigma)) = \emptyset$. Thus, $\theta(\phi_0)$ holds.    □

The completeness of the symbolic intruder constraint reduction is similar to existing results on symbolic intruder constraints; what is particular is our generalization to constraints with quantified inequalities. To that end, we show:

**Lemma 2.** *Let* $\phi = \neg \exists \bar{x}. \phi_\sigma$ *where* $\phi_\sigma = \bigwedge s_i \doteq t_i$, *and let* $\theta = [\bar{y} \mapsto \bar{c}]$ *where* $\bar{y} = fv(\phi)$ *and* $\bar{c}$ *are fresh public constants that do not occur in* $\phi$. *Then* $\phi$ *is satisfiable iff* $\theta(\phi)$ *is satisfiable. Moreover,* $\phi$ *is satisfiable iff* $mgu(\theta(\phi_\sigma)) = \emptyset$.

*Proof Sketch.* If $\theta(\phi)$ is unsatisfiable, then also $\phi$ is unsatisfiable. For the other direction, we show that the following two formulas are a contradiction: (1) $\exists \bar{y}. \forall \bar{x}. \bigvee_{i=1}^n s_i \neq t_i$ and (2) $\exists \bar{x}. \bigwedge_{i=1}^n \theta(s_i) = \theta(t_i)$. By (2), we can find a substitution $\xi = [\bar{x} \mapsto \bar{u}]$ where $\bar{u}$ are ground terms such that $\bigwedge_{i=1}^n \xi(\theta(s_i)) = \xi(\theta(t_i))$. Since $\theta$ and $\xi$ are substitutions with disjoint domain and grounding, we have $\theta(\xi(\cdot)) = \xi(\theta(\cdot))$, and thus we obtain (2') $\bigwedge_{i=1}^n \theta(\xi(s_i)) = \theta(\xi(t_i))$. By (1), choosing a particular value for the $\bar{x}$, we obtain (1') $\exists \bar{y}. \bigvee_{i=1}^n \xi(s_i) \neq \xi(t_i)$. Then we can find an $i \in \{1, ..., n\}$ such that $\exists \bar{y}. \xi(s_i) \neq \xi(t_i)$. Thus, taking $s := \xi(s_i)$

and $t := \xi(t_i)$, we have (1") $\exists \bar{y}. s \neq t$ and (2") $\theta(s) = \theta(t)$. By case distinction on whether $s$ and $t$ are atomic or not, follows immediately that (1") and (2") are a contradiction. Now we can decide the satisfiability of $\phi$ with the *mgu*-algorithm since $\theta(\phi)$ is a closed formula and the remaining variables of $\theta(\phi_\sigma)$ are the $\bar{x}$. $\square$

*Proof Sketch of Theorem 3.* As this is building on standard results [18,20], we only describe the basic idea and highlight the particularities of our adaption. Let us write $\phi \rightsquigarrow \phi'$ if $\frac{\phi'}{\phi}$ is an instance of a reduction rule, i.e., representing one solution step. It is straightforward that the rules are sound, i.e., that $\mathcal{I} \models \phi'$ and $\phi \rightsquigarrow \phi'$ imply $\mathcal{I} \models \phi$. The hard part is the completeness, i.e., when $\mathcal{I} \models \phi$, then either $\phi$ is already simple or we can apply some rule, obtaining $\phi \rightsquigarrow \phi'$ for some $\phi'$ with $\mathcal{I} \models \phi'$. Thus, we show that every solution $\mathcal{I}$ of a constraint is preserved by at least one applicable reduction rule until we obtain a simple constraint (that we already know is satisfiable by Theorem 2). The core idea is as follows. Since $\mathcal{I}$ satisfies $\phi$, for every intruder deduction $M \vdash t$ in $\phi$, there exists a proof $\mathcal{I}(M) \vdash \mathcal{I}(t)$ according to Definition 1. This proof has a tree shape with $\mathcal{I}(M) \vdash \mathcal{I}(t)$ at the root and axioms as leaves for members of $\mathcal{I}(M)$. We label each $M \vdash t$ with such a proof for $\mathcal{I}(M) \vdash \mathcal{I}(t)$. We now proceed from the first (in the order induced by the well-formedness of $\phi$) intruder constraint $M \vdash t$ where $t \notin \mathcal{V}$ (i.e., not yet simple) and show: depending on the form of the derivation tree, we can pick a rule so that we can label all new deduction constraints in the resulting constraint $\phi'$ again with matching proof trees, i.e., so that they support still the solution. In particular, we will apply the (*Unify*) rule only with substitutions of which $\mathcal{I}$ is an instance.

For the equalities $s \doteq t$ that are not yet simple (i.e., where neither $s$ nor $t$ is a variable that occurs only once in the constraint), we can at any time in the reduction apply (*Equation*), if the equation actually *has* a unifier. If not, obviously the entire constraint is satisfiable. For the inequalities, suppose we have a non-simple inequality $\phi_0 = \neg \exists \bar{x}.\phi_\sigma$, i.e., $mgu(\theta(\phi_\sigma)) \neq \emptyset$ for a substitution $\theta$ from the free variables of $\phi_0$ to fresh constants. Then, by Lemma 2, $\phi_0$ is not satisfiable, contradicting that $\mathcal{I} \models \phi$. This concludes the completeness proof.

For termination, it is standard to define a *weight* $(n, m, l)$ for a constraint $\phi$, where $n$ is the number of free variables in $\phi$, $m$ is the number of unanalyzed subterms in the intruder knowledges of constraints; and $l$ is the size of the constraint (in symbols). Ordering these three components lexicographically, every $\rightsquigarrow$ step reduces the weight. $\square$

*Proof Sketch of Theorem 4.* The key idea is to consider a satisfiable constraint $\Phi = \phi \wedge tr_{M,E}(\Psi)$ that represents an attack against $P$, i.e., where $\phi$ is the constraint of a reachable state of $P$ and $tr_{M,E}(\Psi)$ is the translation of the violated goal in that state. We have to show that the constraint has also a well-typed solution. By Theorem 3 and since $\Phi$ is satisfiable, we can use the symbolic intruder reduction rules to obtain a simple constraint $\Phi'$, i.e., $\Phi \rightsquigarrow^* \Phi'$. The point is now that for a type-flaw resistant protocol, all substitutions in this reduction must be well-typed! To see that, first observe that by construction, all equations $s \doteq t$ (including inequalities) of $\Phi$ have $\Gamma(s) = \Gamma(t)$ and for inequalities, we have that all variables of $s$ and $t$ are of atomic type. Further, all terms that occur are either instances of terms in $SMP(P)$ or atomic. We have to show also that during all reduction steps, this property is preserved. Now note that we cannot apply the (*Unify*) rule on a pair of terms $s$ and $t$ that are variables. So, they are either both the same constant (which trivially preserves our invariants) or they are composed and thus instances of terms in $SMP(P)$. That in turn means that $s$ and $t$ can only have a unifier if $\Gamma(s) = \Gamma(t)$ by the type-flaw resistance property. Thus, the resulting unifier is well-typed. For the (*Equation*) rule, we can obtain only well-typed unifiers since all equations have to be well-typed. Finally, with a similar construction as in Theorem 2 and using the fact that inequalities cannot have composed variables, we can show that, when reaching a simple constraint (in which all equations are well-typed), it has a well-typed solution.    □

*Proof Sketch of Theorem 5.* Consider an attack against $P_1 \parallel P_2$ violating a goal $\Psi$ of $P_1$. By Theorem 4, there must be a well-typed attack against $P_1 \parallel P_2$, so we consider only a well-typed attack. We show that this attack works also in $P_1$ isolation, or one of the $P_i$ in isolation leaks one of the long-term secret constants. We use again a similar argument as in Theorem 4: let $\phi$ be a constraint that represents the attack against $P_1 \parallel P_2$ and thus has a well-typed model $\mathcal{I}$; we can then extract a constraint that represents an attack against $P_1$ or $P_2$ in isolation. First, it does thus not change satisfiability of $\phi$ if we substitute each variable of a composed type $f(\tau_1, \ldots, \tau_n)$ by an expression $f(x_1, \ldots, x_n)$ where $x_i$ are new variables of types $\tau_i$, and repeat this process until we have only variables of atomic types. We substitute every variable $x$ of type private key with $\mathcal{I}(x)$. Thus we have no variables of type private key anymore, and for every $\mathsf{pub}(t)$, $t$ is a public or secret long-term constant of type private key.

For every constraint $M \vdash t$ in $\phi$, $t$ is a message that was received by a strand of either $P_1$ or $P_2$ and each $s \in M$ is a message sent by a strand of either $P_1$ or $P_2$. It is thus just a matter of book keeping to label $t$ and each element of $M$ with either $P_1$ or $P_2$ accordingly. The property of parallel-composable requires that all public constants of $\mathcal{C}_{pub}$ and all public keys $\mathsf{pub}(c)$ for $c$ of type private key are available to the intruder in each of the protocols; so when they occur in the knowledge $M$ of a constraint, we shall label them with $\star$ instead, as they are not protocol-specific. By construction, no variable can occur both in a $P_1$-labeled term and in a $P_2$-labeled term (and this property is preserved over all reductions); we can thus also label variables uniquely as being either $P_1$-variables or $P_2$-variables. By construction, in all $s \doteq t$, both $s$ and $t$ are labeled the same.

Next, we can attack one of the two protocols without a unification between a $P_1$ and a $P_2$ message. In the constraint system, this means that a constraint $M \vdash t$ where $t$ is labeled $P_1$ can always be solved when removing all $P_2$-labeled messages from $M$. Following the reductions for a given well-typed solution $\mathcal{I}$, the only critical rule is (*Unify*), solving $M \vdash t$ by unifying $t$ with some term $s \in M$. Suppose $t$ is labeled $P_1$; $s$ may be labeled $P_1$, $P_2$ or $\star$. We show that there is a solution without using a $P_2$ message. Since (*Unify*) requires that $s, t \notin \mathcal{V}$, they either are both the same constant or they are both composed. In case of a constant, it cannot belong to the protocol-specific constants $\mathcal{C}_{P_1}$ or $\mathcal{C}_{P_2}$ (since they are disjoint by construction labeled for the respective protocol), so it must be a long-term constant, belonging either to $\mathcal{C}_{pub}$ (then we can solve this constraint instead with the (*PubConsts*) rule), or to $\mathcal{C}_{priv}$. In the latter case, we have that one of the two protocols has leaked a long-term secret, and we can extract the constraints up to this point as a witness that we have already an attack for one protocol in isolation. It remains the case of composed messages $s$ and $t$ being unified. One special case is that $s = t = \mathsf{pub}(c)$, in which case we have that $\mathsf{pub}(c)$ is available in both protocols by parallel-composable. In all other cases, we can use again that all non-atomic messages are instances of terms in $SMP(P_1)$ or $SMP(P_2)$ and that the protocols are SMP-disjoint, so if $s$ and $t$ have a unifier, they must belong to the same $SMP(P_i)$. Thus the attack never relies on the unification between a $P_1$ and a $P_2$ message, and we can extract a pure $P_1$ or a pure $P_2$ constraint that violates a goal of the respective protocol. Note that it is either a violation of a long-term secrecy goal or violating the goal $\Psi$ of $P_1$ that the initial attack against $P_1 \parallel P_2$ violates.    □

# References

1. Almousa, O., Mödersheim, S., Modesti, P., Viganò, L.: Typing and compositionality for security protocols: a generalization to the geometric fragment (extended version). DTU Compute Technical report-2015-03 (2015). http://www.imm.dtu.dk/~samo/
2. Andova, S., Cremers, C.J.F., Gjøsteen, K., Mauw, S., Mjølsnes, S.F., Radomirovic, S.: A framework for compositional verification of security protocols. Inf. Comput. **206**(2–4), 425–459 (2008)
3. Arapinis, M., Duflot, M.: Bounding messages for free in security protocols. In: Arvind, V., Prasad, S. (eds.) FSTTCS 2007. LNCS, vol. 4855, pp. 376–387. Springer, Heidelberg (2007)
4. Arapinis, M., Duflot, M.: Bounding messages for free in security protocols - extension to various security properties. Inf. Comput. **239**, 182–215 (2014)
5. Armando, A., Compagna, L.: SATMC: a sat-based model checker for security protocols. In: Alferes, J.J., Leite, J. (eds.) JELIA 2004. LNCS (LNAI), vol. 3229, pp. 730–733. Springer, Heidelberg (2004)
6. Blanchet, B., Podelski, A.: Verification of cryptographic protocols: tagging enforces termination. Theor. Comput. Sci. **333**(1–2), 67–90 (2005)
7. Comon-Lundh, H., Delaune, S., Millen, J.K.: Constraint solving techniques and enriching the model with equational theories. In: Formal Models and Techniques for Analyzing Security Protocols, pp. 35–61. IOS Press (2011)
8. Cortier, V., Delaune, S.: Safely composing security protocols. Form. Methods Syst. Des. **34**, 1–36 (2009)
9. Ciobâcă, Ş., Cortier, V.: Protocol composition for arbitrary primitives. In: CSF, pp. 322–336. IEEE (2010)
10. Guttman, J.D.: Cryptographic protocol composition via the authentication tests. In: de Alfaro, L. (ed.) FOSSACS 2009. LNCS, vol. 5504, pp. 303–317. Springer, Heidelberg (2009)
11. Guttman, J.D.: Establishing and preserving protocol security goals. J. Comput. Secur. **22**(2), 203–267 (2014)
12. Guttman, J.D., Thayer, F.J.: Protocol independence through disjoint encryption. In: CSFW, pp. 24–34. IEEE (2000)

13. Heather, J., Lowe, G., Schneider, S.: How to prevent type flaw attacks on security protocols. J. Comput. Secur. **11**(2), 217–244 (2003)
14. Küsters, R., Truderung, T.: Using ProVerif to analyze protocols with Diffie-Hellman exponentiation. In: CSF, pp. 157–171. IEEE (2009)
15. Lowe, G.: A hierarchy of authentication specifications. In: CSFW, pp. 31–44 (1997)
16. Millen, J.K., Shmatikov, V.: Constraint solving for bounded-process cryptographic protocol analysis. In: CCS, pp. 166–175. ACM (2001)
17. Mödersheim, S.: Diffie-Hellman without difficulty. In: Barthe, G., Datta, A., Etalle, S. (eds.) FAST 2011. LNCS, vol. 7140, pp. 214–229. Springer, Heidelberg (2012)
18. Mödersheim, S.: Deciding security for a fragment of ASLan. In: Foresti, S., Yung, M., Martinelli, F. (eds.) ESORICS 2012. LNCS, vol. 7459, pp. 127–144. Springer, Heidelberg (2012)
19. Mödersheim, S., Katsoris, G.: A sound abstraction of the parsing problem. In: CSF, pp. 259–273. IEEE (2014)
20. Rusinowitch, M., Turuani, M.: Protocol insecurity with a finite number of sessions and composed keys is NP-complete. Theor. Comput. Sci. **299**(1–3), 451–475 (2003)
21. Thayer, F.J., Herzog, J.C., Guttman, J.D.: Strand spaces: proving security protocols correct. J. Comput. Secur. **7**(1), 191–230 (1999)

# Checking Trace Equivalence: How to Get Rid of Nonces?

Rémy Chrétien[1,2]([⊠]), Véronique Cortier[1], and Stéphanie Delaune[2]

[1] LORIA, INRIA Nancy - Grand-Est, Villers-lès-Nancy, France
chretien@lsv.ens-cachan.fr
[2] LSV, ENS Cachan & CNRS, Cachan Cedex, France

**Abstract.** Security protocols can be successfully analysed using formal methods. When proving security in symbolic settings for an unbounded number of sessions, a typical technique consists in abstracting away fresh nonces and keys by a bounded set of constants. While this abstraction is clearly sound in the context of secrecy properties (for protocols without else branches), this is no longer the case for equivalence properties.

In this paper, we study how to soundly get rid of nonces in the context of equivalence properties. We show that nonces can be replaced by constants provided that each nonce is associated to two constants (instead of typically one constant for secrecy properties). Our result holds for deterministic (simple) protocols and a large class of primitives that includes *e.g.* standard primitives, blind signatures, and zero-knowledge proofs.

## 1  Introduction

Security protocols are notoriously difficult to design as exemplified by a long history of attacks. For example, the TLS protocol has been shown once again to be vulnerable to a new attack called FREAK [4]. Formal methods offer symbolic models to carefully analyse security protocols, together with a set of proof techniques and efficient tools such as ProVerif [5], Scyther [17], Maude-NPA [21], or Avispa [3]. Security properties can be divided into two main categories.

- Trace properties are used to express secrecy or various forms of authentication properties. They ensure that a certain statement holds for any execution.
- Equivalence properties are typically used to state privacy properties like anonymity, unlinkability [8], or vote privacy [18]. More generally, equivalence properties may state indistinguishability properties, such as game-based definitions inherited from models used in cryptography [15,22].

When proving security properties, it is important to obtain guarantees for an unlimited number of sessions. Unfortunately, it is well known that even secrecy

---

The research leading to these results has received funding from the European Research Council under the European Union's Seventh Framework Programme (FP7/2007–2013)/ERC grant agreement n° 258865, project ProSecure, and the ANR project JCJC VIP n° 11 JS02 006 01.

G. Pernul et al. (Eds.): ESORICS 2015, Part II, LNCS 9327, pp. 230–251, 2015.
DOI: 10.1007/978-3-319-24177-7_12

is undecidable [20] in this context. Undecidability comes from two main factors. First, messages may grow arbitrarily during an execution. Second, even when considering messages of fixed size, it has been shown that nonces still cause undecidability [2]. Intuitively, nonce freshness may be used to create pointers that are used in turns to build chained lists and thus again arbitrarily large data. Therefore, a standard restriction consists in bounding the number of nonces (and keys). Under this assumption, several decidability results have been established for secrecy [7,13,20], as well as for trace equivalence [9,10].

Replacing nonces by constants is sound in the context of secrecy properties. More precisely, assuming that $\overline{P}$ is obtained from the security protocol $P$ by replacing nonces (and keys) by constants, whenever $\overline{P}$ is secure (w.r.t. a trace property such as secrecy) then $P$ is secure as well. Indeed, replacing nonces by constants may only introduce more attacks, since it may only create more equalities, as long as the protocol $P$ under study does not have else branches. Therefore, the decidability results developed for secrecy (*e.g.* [7,13,20]) may be seen as proof techniques: if $\overline{P}$ falls in a decidable class and can be shown to be secure then the protocol $P$ is secure as well. Unfortunately, such an approach is no longer valid in the context of equivalence properties. Indeed, consider the processes:

$$P = \,! \text{ new } n.\text{out}(c, \{n\}_k) \quad \text{and} \quad Q = \,! \text{ out}(c, \{n\}_k).$$

The ! operator denotes the replication. Intuitively, both processes send out an arbitrary number of messages on the public channel $c$. The process $P$ sends out each time a fresh nonce $n$ encrypted by a (secret) key $k$ while $Q$ always sends the same message. We assume here that encryption is not randomised. Clearly, the processes $P$ and $Q$ are not in equivalence (denoted $P \not\approx Q$) since an attacker can easily notice that $P$ sends distinct messages while $Q$ sends identical messages. However, abstracting away fresh names with constants, the resulting equivalence holds (denoted $\overline{P} \approx \overline{Q}$). Indeed, the two resulting processes are actually identical: $\overline{P} = \overline{Q} =\,! \text{ out}(c, \{n\}_k)$. This illustrates that $\overline{P} \approx \overline{Q} \not\Rightarrow P \approx Q$.

**Main Contribution.** We identify a technique to (soundly) get rid of freshly generated data (*e.g.* nonces, keys). The main idea consists in introducing an additional copy of each replicated nonce. More precisely, we show that:

$$!\overline{P} \mid P^\star \approx\,!\overline{Q} \mid Q^\star \quad \Rightarrow \quad !P \approx\,!Q$$

where $P^\star$ is obtained from $P$ by renaming all fresh nonces and keys to distinct (fresh) constants. Our result holds for simple processes, a notion that has been introduced in [15] and used in several subsequent works (*e.g.* [10]). Roughly, each process communicates on a distinct channel. This corresponds to the fact that in practice each machine has its own IP address and each session is characterised by some session identifier. We consider a large family of primitives, provided that they can be described by a destructor/constructor theory with no critical pair. In particular, our technique allows one to deal with standard primitives (asymmetric and symmetric encryption, hash, signatures, MACs) as well as *e.g.* blind signatures and zero-knowledge proofs. As an application, we deduce that the decidability result developed in [10] for tagged protocols without nonces can be applied to study the security of protocols *with* nonces. The full proofs of the results presented in this paper can be found in [11].

**Related Work.** Abstracting nonces and keys by constants is known to be sound for secrecy properties as part of the "folklore". We did not find a precise reference for this result. A related result is a reduction to two agents [14] for trace properties. Reducing the number of nonces can be obtained in a similar way.

The tool ProVerif [5,6] also makes use of an abstraction for fresh data. In case of secrecy, nonces are abstracted by functions applied to the process inputs. In case of equivalence properties, nonces are additionally given a counter (termination is of course not guaranteed). The abstraction technique is therefore more precise than using only constants but seems dedicated to the internal behaviour of the ProVerif tool.

The only decidability result for equivalence *with* nonces (for an unbounded number of sessions) has been recently presented in [12]. For protocols that fall in the class of [12], it is therefore more direct to use this decidability result than applying our simplification. However, the class of protocols we consider here is more general: we do not need protocols to be tagged nor to induce an "acyclic dependency graph" and we cover a much wider class of cryptographic primitives.

## 2　Model for Security Protocols

Security protocols are modelled through a process algebra inspired from [1] that manipulates terms.

### 2.1　Term Algebra

We assume an infinite set $\mathcal{N}$ of *names*, which are used to represent keys and nonces and an infinite set $\mathcal{X}$ of variables. We assume a signature $\Sigma$, *i.e.* a set of function symbols together with their arity, and we make a distinction between *constructor* symbols and *destructor* symbols: $\Sigma = \Sigma_c \uplus \Sigma_d$. Given a signature $\Sigma$, we denote by $\mathcal{T}(\Sigma, \mathsf{A})$ the set of terms built from symbols in $\Sigma$ and atomic data in $\mathsf{A}$. Terms without variables are called *ground*. The set $\mathcal{T}(\Sigma_c, \mathcal{X} \cup \mathcal{N})$ is the set of *constructor terms*. Then among the terms in $\mathcal{T}(\Sigma_c, \mathcal{N})$ we distinguish a special subset of terms called *messages* and noted $\mathcal{M}_\Sigma$, and that is stable under renaming of names: a message does *not* contain any destructor symbol, and $m \in \mathcal{M}_\Sigma$ implies that $m\rho \in \mathcal{M}_\Sigma$ for any renaming $\rho$ (not necessarily a bijective one).

In addition to the set of variables $\mathcal{X}$, we consider an infinite disjoint set of variables $\mathcal{W}$. Variables in $\mathcal{W}$ intuitively refer to variables used to store messages learnt by the attacker. We denote $vars(u)$ the set of variables that occur in a term $u$. The application of a substitution $\sigma$ to a term $u$ is written $u\sigma$, and we denote $dom(\sigma)$ its *domain*. The *positions* of a term are defined as usual. Two terms $u$ and $v$ are *unifiable* if there is a substitution $\sigma$ such that $u\sigma = v\sigma$.

The properties of the primitives are expressed using rewriting rules of the form $g(t_1, \ldots, t_n) \rightarrow t$ where $g$ is a destructor, that is $g \in \Sigma_d$, and $t_1, \ldots, t_n, t$ are constructor terms. A rewriting rule can only be applied to constructor terms. Formally, we say that $u$ can be *rewritten into* $v$ if there is a position $p$ and a rule $g(t_1, \ldots, t_n) \rightarrow t$ such that $u$ at position $p$ is equal to $g(t_1, \ldots, t_n)\theta$ and $v = u[t\theta]_p$ (that is $u$ where the term at position $p$ has been replaced by $t\theta$) for some substitution $\theta$ such that $t_1\theta, \ldots, t_n\theta, t\theta$ are messages. We only consider sets of rewriting rules that yield convergent rewrite systems. We denote by $u\downarrow$ the *normal form* of a given term $u$. We refer the reader to [19] for the precise definitions of rewriting systems, convergence, and normal forms.

*Example 1.* A typical signature for representing symmetric encryption and pair is

$$\Sigma = \{\mathsf{senc}, \mathsf{sdec}, \langle \, \rangle, \mathsf{proj}_1, \mathsf{proj}_2\} \uplus \Sigma_0$$

where $\Sigma_0$ is a set of atomic data. The set $\Sigma_0$ typically contains the public constants known to the attacker (*e.g.* agent names a, b, ...). The symbols senc and sdec of arity 2 represent symmetric encryption and decryption. Pairing is modelled using $\langle \, \rangle$ of arity 2, whereas projection functions are denoted $\mathsf{proj}_1$ and $\mathsf{proj}_2$ (both of arity 1). The relations between encryption/decryption and pairing/projections are represented through the following convergent rewrite system:

$$\mathsf{sdec}(\mathsf{senc}(x, y), y) \rightarrow x, \quad \text{and} \quad \mathsf{proj}_i(\langle x_1, x_2 \rangle) \rightarrow x_i \text{ with } i \in \{1, 2\}.$$

We have that $\mathsf{proj}_1(\mathsf{sdec}(\mathsf{senc}(\langle s_1, s_2 \rangle, k), k))\downarrow = s_1$. Note that, since a destructor can only be applied on messages, no rewriting rule can be applied on the term $\mathsf{sdec}(\mathsf{senc}(s, \mathsf{proj}_1(s)), \mathsf{proj}_2(s))$ which is thus in normal form (but not a message). This signature $\Sigma$ is split into two parts as follows: $\Sigma_c = \{\mathsf{senc}, \langle \, \rangle\} \uplus \Sigma_0$ and $\Sigma_d = \{\mathsf{sdec}, \mathsf{proj}_1, \mathsf{proj}_2\}$. Then, we may consider $\mathcal{M}_\Sigma$ to be $\mathcal{M}_c = \mathcal{T}(\Sigma_c, \mathcal{N})$ the set of all ground constructor terms. We may also restrict $\mathcal{M}_\Sigma$ to be $\mathcal{M}_{\mathsf{atomic}}$, the set of ground constructor terms that only use atomic data in key position.

Finally, we assume $\Sigma$ to be split into two parts, and this distinction is orthogonal the one made between destructor and constructor symbols. We denote by $\Sigma_{\mathsf{pub}}$ the set of function symbols that are public, *i.e.* available to the attacker, and $\Sigma_{\mathsf{priv}}$ for those that are private. Actually, an attacker builds his own messages by applying public function symbols to terms he already knows. Formally, a computation done by the attacker is modelled by a term in $\mathcal{T}(\Sigma_{\mathsf{pub}}, \mathcal{W})$, called a *recipe*. Note that such a term does not contain any name. Indeed, all names are initially unknown to the attacker.

## 2.2   Process Algebra

Let $\mathcal{Ch}$ be an infinite set of *channels*. We consider processes built using the grammar below where $u \in \mathcal{T}(\Sigma_c, \mathcal{N} \cup \mathcal{X})$, $v \in \mathcal{T}(\Sigma, \mathcal{N} \cup \mathcal{X})$, $n \in \mathcal{N}$, and $c, c' \in \mathcal{Ch}$:

$$
\begin{array}{llll}
P, Q := 0 & null & | \; (P \mid Q) & parallel \\
\quad | \;\; \text{in}(c, u).P & input & | \; !P & replication \\
\quad | \;\; \text{out}(c, u).P & output & | \; \text{new } n.P & restriction \\
\quad | \;\; \text{let } x = v \text{ in } P & evaluation & | \; \text{new } c'.\text{out}(c, c').P & channel\ generation
\end{array}
$$

The process $0$ does nothing. The process "$\text{in}(c, u).P$" expects a message $m$ of the form $u$ on channel $c$ and then behaves like $P\sigma$ where $\sigma$ is a substitution such that $m = u\sigma$. The process "$\text{out}(c, u).P$" emits $u$ on channel $c$, and then behaves like $P$. The variables that occur in $u$ are instantiated when the evaluation takes place. The process "$\text{let } x = v \text{ in } P$" tries to evaluate $v$ and in case of success the process $P$ is executed; otherwise the process is blocked. The process "$P \mid Q$" runs $P$ and $Q$ in parallel. The process "$!P$" executes $P$ some arbitrary number of times. The restriction "$\text{new } n$" is used to model the creation of a fresh random number (e.g., a nonce or a key) whereas channel generation "$\text{new } c'.\text{out}(c, c').P$" is used to model the creation of a fresh channel name that shall immediately be made public. Note that we consider only public channels. It is still useful to generate fresh channel names to let the attacker identify the different sessions (as it is often the case in practice through sessions identifiers).

Note that our calculus allows both message filtering as well as explicit application of destructor symbols. For example, to represent a process that waits for a message, decrypts it with a key $k$, and sends the plaintext in clear, we may write $P = \text{in}(c, \text{senc}(x, k)).\text{out}(c, x)$ as well as $Q = \text{in}(c, y).\text{let } x = \text{sdec}(y, k) \text{ in out}(c, x)$. However, the choice of filtering or let yields a slightly different behaviour since a message will be received in $P$ only if it matches the expected format while any message will be received in $Q$ (and then the format is checked).

We write $fv(P)$ for the set of *free variables* that occur in $P$, i.e. the set of variables that are not in the scope of an input or a let construction. We assume $Ch = Ch_0 \uplus Ch^{\text{fresh}}$ where $Ch_0$ and $Ch^{\text{fresh}}$ are two infinite sets of channels. Intuitively, channels of $Ch^{\text{fresh}}$, denoted $ch_1, \ldots, ch_i, \ldots$ will be used in the semantics to *instantiate* the channels generated during the execution of a protocol. They shall not be part of its specification.

**Definition 1.** *A protocol $P$ is a process such that $P$ is ground, i.e. $fv(P) = \emptyset$; and $P$ does not use channel names from $Ch^{\text{fresh}}$.*

*Example 2.* The Yahalom protocol [23] is a key distribution protocol using symmetric encryption and a trusted server. The Paulson's version of this protocol can be described informally as follows:

1. $A \to B : A, N_a$
2. $B \to S : B, N_b, \{A, N_a\}_{K_{bs}}$
3. $S \to A : N_b, \{B, K_{ab}, N_a\}_{K_{as}}, \{A, B, K_{ab}, N_b\}_{K_{bs}}$
4. $A \to B : \{A, B, K_{ab}, N_b\}_{K_{bs}}, \{N_b\}_{K_{ab}}$

where $\{m\}_k$ denotes the symmetric encryption of a message $m$ with key $k$, $A$ and $B$ are agents trying to authenticate each other, $S$ is a trusted server, $K_{as}$ (resp. $K_{bs}$) is a long term key shared between $A$ and $S$ (resp. $B$ and $S$), $N_a$ and $N_b$ are nonces generated by $A$ and $B$, whereas $K_{ab}$ is a key generated by $S$.

We propose a modelling of the Yahalom protocol in our formalism using the signature given in Example 1. We use restricted channels to model the use of unique session identifiers used along an execution of the protocol. Below, $k_{as}$, $k_{bs}$, $n_a$, $n_b$, $k_{ab}$ are names, whereas a and b are constants from $\Sigma_0$ and $c_A$, $c_B$, and $c_S$ are (public) channel names for respectively the role of $A$, $B$, and $S$. We denote by $\langle x_1, \ldots, x_{n-1}, x_n \rangle$ the term $\langle x_1, \langle \ldots \langle x_{n-1}, x_n \rangle \rangle \rangle$.

$$P_{\mathsf{Yah}} = !\, \mathsf{new}\ c_1.\mathsf{out}(c_A, c_1).P_A \mid !\, \mathsf{new}\ c_2.\mathsf{out}(c_B, c_2).P_B \mid !\, \mathsf{new}\ c_3.\mathsf{out}(c_S, c_3).P_S$$

where the processes $P_A$, $P_B$, and $P_S$ are given below:

$$
\begin{aligned}
P_A =\ & \mathsf{new}\ n_a.\ \mathsf{out}(c_1, \langle a, n_a \rangle).\ \mathsf{in}(c_1, \langle x_{nb}, \mathsf{senc}(\langle b, x_{ab}, n_a \rangle, k_{as}), x_{bs} \rangle).\\
& \mathsf{out}(c_1, \langle x_{bs}, \mathsf{senc}(x_{nb}, x_{ab}) \rangle);\\
P_B =\ & \mathsf{in}(c_2, \langle a, y_{na} \rangle).\ \mathsf{new}\ n_b.\ \mathsf{out}(c_2, \langle b, n_b, \mathsf{senc}(\langle a, y_{na} \rangle, k_{bs}) \rangle).\\
& \mathsf{in}(c_2, \langle \mathsf{senc}(\langle a, b, y_{ab}, n_b \rangle, k_{bs}), \mathsf{senc}(n_b, y_{ab}) \rangle);\\
P_S =\ & \mathsf{in}(c_3, \langle b, z_{nb}, \mathsf{senc}(\langle a, z_{na} \rangle, k_{bs}) \rangle).\ \mathsf{new}\ k_{ab}.\\
& \mathsf{out}(c_3, \langle n_b, \mathsf{senc}(\langle b, k_{ab}, z_{na} \rangle, k_{as}), \mathsf{senc}(\langle a, b, k_{ab}, z_{nb} \rangle, k_{bs}) \rangle).
\end{aligned}
$$

## 2.3 Semantics

The operational semantics of a process is defined using a relation over configurations. A *configuration* is a pair $(\mathcal{P}; \phi)$ where:

- $\mathcal{P}$ is a multiset of ground processes.
- $\phi = \{\mathsf{w}_1 \triangleright m_1, \ldots, \mathsf{w}_n \triangleright m_n\}$ is a *frame*, *i.e.* a substitution where $\mathsf{w}_1, \ldots, \mathsf{w}_n$ are variables in $\mathcal{W}$, and $m_1, \ldots, m_n$ are messages, *i.e.* terms in $\mathcal{M}_\Sigma$.

We often write $P$ instead of $(\{P\}; \emptyset)$, and $P \cup \mathcal{P}$ or $P \mid \mathcal{P}$ instead of $\{P\} \cup \mathcal{P}$. The terms in $\phi$ represent the messages that are known by the attacker. The operational semantics of a process is induced by the relation $\xrightarrow{\alpha}$ as defined below.

$(\mathsf{in}(c, u).P \cup \mathcal{P}; \phi) \xrightarrow{\mathsf{in}(c, R)} (P\sigma \cup \mathcal{P}; \phi)$ where $R$ is a recipe such that $R\phi{\downarrow}$ is a message and $R\phi{\downarrow} = u\sigma$ for some $\sigma$ with $dom(\sigma) = vars(u)(\mathsf{out}(c, u).P \cup \mathcal{P}; \phi)$
$\xrightarrow{\mathsf{out}(c, \mathsf{w}_{i+1})} (P \cup \mathcal{P}; \phi \cup \{\mathsf{w}_{i+1} \triangleright u\})$ where $u$ is a message and $i$ is the number of elements in $\phi(\mathsf{new}\ c'.\mathsf{out}(c, c').P \cup \mathcal{P}; \phi) \xrightarrow{\mathsf{out}(c, ch_i)} (P\{^{ch_i}/_{c'}\} \cup \mathcal{P}; \phi)$ where $ch_i$ is the "next" fresh channel name available in $Ch^{\mathsf{fresh}}$(let $x = v$ in $P \cup \mathcal{P}; \phi) \xrightarrow{\tau}$ $(P\{^{v\downarrow}/_x\} \cup \mathcal{P}\ \phi)$ where $v{\downarrow}$ is a message (new $n.P \cup \mathcal{P}; \phi) \xrightarrow{\tau} (P\{^{n'}/_n\} \cup \mathcal{P}; \phi)$ where $n'$ is a fresh name in $\mathcal{N}(!P \cup \mathcal{P}; \phi) \xrightarrow{\tau} (P \cup !P \cup \mathcal{P}; \phi)$.

The first rule allows the attacker to send to some process a term built from publicly available terms and symbols. The second rule corresponds to the output of a term: the corresponding term is added to the frame of the current configuration, which means that the attacker can now access the sent term. Note that the term is outputted provided that it is a message. The third rule corresponds to the special case of an output of a freshly generated channel name. In such a case, the channel is not added to the frame but it is implicitly assumed known to the attacker, as all the channel names. These three rules are the only observable actions. The fourth rule corresponds to the evaluation of the term $v$; if this succeeds, *i.e.* if $v\downarrow$ is a message then $x$ is bound to the result and $P$ is executed; otherwise the process is blocked. The two remaining rules are quite standard and are unobservable by the attacker.

The relation $\xrightarrow{\alpha_1...\alpha_n}$ between configurations (where $\alpha_1...\alpha_n$ is a sequence of actions) is defined as the transitive closure of $\xrightarrow{\alpha}$. Given a sequence of observable actions tr, we write $K \xRightarrow{\text{tr}} K'$ when there exists a sequence $\alpha_1...\alpha_n$ such that $K \xrightarrow{\alpha_1...\alpha_n} K'$ and tr is obtained from $\alpha_1...\alpha_n$ by erasing all occurrences of $\tau$. For every protocol $P$, we define its *set of traces* as follows:

$$\text{trace}(P) = \{(\text{tr}, \phi) \mid P \xRightarrow{\text{tr}} (\mathcal{P}; \phi) \text{ for some configuration } (\mathcal{P}; \phi)\}.$$

*Example 3.* The Yahalom protocol as presented in Example 2 is known to be flawed as informally described below.

> *(i)* 1. $I(A) \to B : A, N_i$
> *(i)* 2. $B \to I(S) : B, N_b, \{A, N_i\}_{K_{bs}}$
> $\qquad$ *(ii)* 1. $I(A) \to B : A, B, K_i, N_b$
> $\qquad$ *(ii)* 2. $B \to I(S) : B, N'_b, \{A, B, K_i, N_b\}_{K_{bs}}$
> *(i)* 4. $I(A) \to B : \{A, B, K_i, N_b\}_{K_{bs}}, \{N_b\}_{K_i}$

Intuitively, the attacker opens two sessions with $B$. In the second session *(ii)*, the attacker uses $B$ as an encryption oracle. This attack can be reflected by the following sequence tr.

$$\text{tr} = \text{out}(c_B, ch_1).\text{in}(ch_1, \langle \mathsf{a}, \mathsf{n}_i \rangle).\text{out}(ch_1, \mathsf{w}_1).\text{out}(c_B, ch_2).\text{in}(ch_2, \langle \mathsf{a},\mathsf{b}, \mathsf{k}_i, R_b \rangle).$$
$$\text{out}(ch_2, \mathsf{w}_2).\text{in}(ch_1, \langle \text{proj}_2(\text{proj}_2(\mathsf{w}_2)), \text{senc}(R_b, \mathsf{k}_i) \rangle)$$

where $\mathsf{k}_i$ and $\mathsf{n}_i$ are public constants from $\Sigma_0$, and $R_b = \text{proj}_1(\text{proj}_2(\mathsf{w}_1))$. This sequence tr allows one to reach the frame:

$$\phi = \{\mathsf{w}_1 \triangleright \langle \mathsf{b}, n_b, \text{senc}(\langle \mathsf{a}, n_i \rangle, k_{bs}) \rangle, \ \mathsf{w}_2 \triangleright \langle \mathsf{b}, n'_b, \text{senc}(\langle \mathsf{a}, \langle \mathsf{b}, \mathsf{k}_i, n_b \rangle \rangle, k_{bs}) \rangle \}.$$

We have that $(\text{tr}, \phi) \in \text{trace}(P_{\text{Yah}})$. Roughly, agent $\mathsf{b}$ has completed a session apparently with agent $\mathsf{a}$, and has established a session key $\mathsf{k}_i$. However, the agent $\mathsf{a}$ has never participated to this execution, and $\mathsf{k}_i$ is actually a key known to the attacker.

## 2.4 Trace Equivalence

Intuitively, two protocols are equivalent if they cannot be distinguished by any attacker. Trace equivalence can be used to formalise many interesting security properties, in particular privacy-type properties, such as those studied for instance in [8,18]. We first define symbolic indistinguishability of sequences of messages, called *static equivalence*.

**Definition 2.** *Two frames $\phi_1$ and $\phi_2$ are statically equivalent, $\phi_1 \sim \phi_2$, when we have that $dom(\phi_1) = dom(\phi_2)$, and:*

– *for any recipe $R$, $R\phi_1\downarrow \in \mathcal{M}_\Sigma$ if, and only if, $R\phi_2\downarrow \in \mathcal{M}_\Sigma$; and*
– *for all recipes $R_1$ and $R_2$ such that $R_1\phi_1\downarrow, R_2\phi_1\downarrow \in \mathcal{M}_\Sigma$, we have that $R_1\phi_1\downarrow = R_2\phi_1\downarrow$ if, and only if, $R_1\phi_2\downarrow = R_2\phi_2\downarrow$.*

Intuitively, two frames are equivalent if an attacker cannot see the difference between the two situations they represent. If some computation fails in $\phi_1$ for some recipe $R$, *i.e.* $R\phi_1\downarrow$ is not a message, it should fail in $\phi_2$ as well. Moreover, the frames $\phi_1$ and $\phi_2$ should satisfy the same equalities. In other words, the ability of the attacker to distinguish whether a recipe $R$ produces a message, or whether two recipes $R_1, R_2$ produce the same message should not depend on the frame. The choice of $\mathcal{M}_\Sigma$ as well as the choice of public symbols allow to fine-tune what an attacker can observe. The set of public function symbols tell exactly which functions the attacker may use. Then the choice $\mathcal{M}_\Sigma$ defines when computations fail. For example, if $\mathcal{M}_\Sigma$ represents the set of terms with atomic keys only, then an attacker may potentially observe that some computation fails because he was able to inject a non atomic key.

*Example 4.* Consider $\phi_1 = \{w_1 \rhd \mathsf{senc}(m_1, k_i)\}$, and $\phi_2 = \{w_1 \rhd \mathsf{senc}(m_2, k_i)\}$. Assuming that $m_1$, $m_2$ are public constants from $\Sigma_0$, we have that $\phi_1 \not\sim \phi_2$. An attacker can observe that decrypting the message of $\phi_1$ with the public constant $k_i$ leads to the public constant $m_1$. This is not the case in $\phi_2$. Consider the recipes $R_1 = \mathsf{sdec}(w_1, k_i)$ and $R_2 = m_1$. We have that $R_1\phi_1\downarrow = R_2\phi_1\downarrow$ whereas $R_1\phi_2\downarrow \neq R_2\phi_2\downarrow$.

Intuitively, two protocols are *trace equivalent* if, however they behave, the resulting sequences of messages observed by the attacker are in static equivalence.

**Definition 3.** *Let $P$ and $Q$ be two protocols. We have that $P \sqsubseteq Q$ if for every $(\mathsf{tr}, \phi) \in \mathsf{trace}(P)$, there exists $(\mathsf{tr}', \phi') \in \mathsf{trace}(Q)$ such that $\mathsf{tr} = \mathsf{tr}'$ and $\phi \sim \phi'$. They are in* trace equivalence, *written $P \approx Q$, if $P \sqsubseteq Q$ and $Q \sqsubseteq P$.*

*Example 5.* We wish to check strong secrecy of the key received by $B$ for the Yahalom protocol. A way of doing so is to check that $P^1_{\mathsf{Yah}} \approx P^2_{\mathsf{Yah}}$ where $P^i_{\mathsf{Yah}}$ (with $i \in \{1, 2\}$) is as $P_{\mathsf{Yah}}$ but we add the instruction $\mathsf{out}(c_2, \mathsf{senc}(m_i, y_{ab}))$ at the end of the process $P_B$. The terms $m_1$ and $m_2$ are two distinct public constants from $\Sigma_0$. The idea is to check whether an attacker can see the difference when the key that has been established is used to encrypt different public constants. Actually, this equivalence does not hold.

Let $\mathsf{tr}' = \mathsf{tr}.\mathsf{out}(ch_1, w_3)$, and $\phi'_j = \phi \cup \{w_3 \rhd \mathsf{senc}(m_j, k_i)\}$ (with $j \in \{1, 2\}$) where $(\mathsf{tr}, \phi)$ is as described in Example 3. We have that $(\mathsf{tr}', \phi'_1) \in \mathsf{trace}(P^1_{\mathsf{Yah}})$ and $(\mathsf{tr}', \phi'_2) \in \mathsf{trace}(P^2_{\mathsf{Yah}})$. However, we have that $\phi'_1 \not\sim \phi'_2$ (as explained in Example 4). Thus, $P^1_{\mathsf{Yah}}$ and $P^2_{\mathsf{Yah}}$ are not in trace equivalence. An attacker can observe the encrypted message sent at the end of the execution and see which constant has been encrypted since he knows the key $k_i$.

# 3   Main Contribution: Getting Rid of Nonces

As explained in introduction, our main contribution is to provide a transformation that soundly abstracts nonces. Informally, we prove an implication of the following form:

$$!\overline{P} \mid P^\star \approx !\overline{Q} \mid Q^\star \quad \Rightarrow \quad !P \approx !Q$$

where $\overline{P}$ is obtained from $P$ by replacing nonces by constants, and $P^\star$ is a copy of $P$. Before defining formally this transformation in Sect. 3.2, we introduce in Sect. 3.1 which hypotheses are required for the soundness of our transformation.

## 3.1   Our Hypotheses

Our technique soundly abstracts nonces and keys for trace equivalence, for *simple protocols* and for a large family of security primitives, namely *adequate theories*, that we define in this section. We first introduce the class of simple protocols, similar to the one introduced *e.g.* in [10, 15].

**Definition 4.** *A simple protocol $P$ is a protocol of the form:*

$$!new\ c_1'.out(c_1, c_1').B_1 \mid \ldots \mid !new\ c_m'.out(c_m, c_m').B_m \mid B_{m+1} \mid \ldots \mid B_{m+p}$$

*where each $B_i$ with $1 \le i \le m + p$ is a* basic process on $c_i$, *that is a ground process built using the following grammar:*

$$B := 0 \mid in(c_i, u).B \mid out(c_i, u).B \mid let\ x = v\ in\ B \mid new\ n.\ B$$

*where $u \in \mathcal{T}(\Sigma_c, \mathcal{N} \cup \mathcal{X})$, $v \in \mathcal{T}(\Sigma, \mathcal{N} \cup \mathcal{X})$, and $n \in \mathcal{N}$. Moreover, we assume that $c_1, \ldots, c_m, c_{m+1}, \ldots, c_{m+p}$ are pairwise distinct.*

Even if considering simple processes may seem to be restricted, in practice it is often the case that an attacker may identify processes through *e.g.* IP addresses and even sessions using sessions identifiers. Therefore, encoding protocols in such a class may be considered as a good practice since it allows to potentially discover more flaws. Indeed, it gives more power to the attacker and allows him to know from which agent he receives a message.

*Example 6.* The protocol $P_{Yah}$ (see Example 2), as well as $P_{Yah}^1$ and $P_{Yah}^2$ as described in Example 5, are simple protocols.

In order to establish our result, we have to ensure that considering two distinct constants instead of fresh nonces is sufficient. We need this property to hold on terms first. Intuitively, when a term cannot be reduced further, it should be possible to isolate two nonces that cause the reduction to fail. This is indeed the case for a large class of primitives. We formalise this notion as follows:

**Definition 5.** *Given a signature $\Sigma = \Sigma_c \uplus \Sigma_d$, a convergent rewriting system $\mathcal{R}$, and a set of messages $\mathcal{M}_\Sigma$, we say that the theory $(\Sigma, \mathcal{R})$ is* adequate *w.r.t. $\mathcal{M}_\Sigma$ when for any term $t \in \mathcal{T}(\Sigma, \mathcal{N}) \setminus \mathcal{M}_\Sigma$ in normal form, there exist $n_1, n_2 \in \mathcal{N}$ such that for any renaming $\rho$ with $\rho(n_1) \ne \rho(n_2)$ then $t\rho\!\downarrow \notin \mathcal{M}_\Sigma$.*

Intuitively, we require that whenever a term $t$ is not a message, it is possible to fix two names of $t$ such that any renaming of $t$ (preserving these two names) is still not a message. We could generalise our criterion to $n$-adequate theories where the number of names that need to fixed is bounded by $n$ but two names are actually sufficient to deal with most of the theories.

*Example 7.* The theory described in Example 1 is adequate w.r.t. to the two notions of messages $\mathcal{M}_c$ and $\mathcal{M}_{\mathsf{atomic}}$ that have been introduced. Intuitively, when a term is not a message, either this property is actually stable for any renaming (*e.g.* $\mathsf{sdec}(n, k)$) or is due to the failure of a decryption (*e.g.* $\mathsf{sdec}(\mathsf{senc}(n, k), k')$). In such a case, maintaining the disequality between the terms modelling the encryption and the decryption keys is sufficient to ensure that the resulting term will not become a message.

Since proving a theory to be adequate may be a bit tedious, we develop in Sect. 4.2 a criterion that allows us to conclude for the theory given above and many others.

## 3.2 Our Transformation

We now explain how to formally get rid of nonces. Our transformation is actually modular w.r.t. which nonces shall be abstracted. Let $P$ be a simple process in which any name is bound at most once. This means that any name that does not occur explicitly in the scope of a restriction is distinct from those introduced by the new operator. Moreover, a same name can not be introduced twice by the operator new. Our transformation is parametrised by a set of names N which correspond to the new instructions that we want to remove (typically those under a replication).

We denote by $\overline{P}^{\mathsf{N}}$ (or simply $\overline{P}$ when N is clear from the context) the process obtained from $P$ by removing every instruction new $n$ for any $n \in \mathsf{N}$. Given $B(c)$ a basic process built on channel $c$, we denote by $B^\star(c^\star)$ the process obtained from $B$ by applying a bijective alpha-renaming on each name bound by a new instruction and replacing each occurrence of the channel $c$ with the channel $c^\star$ (that is assumed to be fresh).

*Example 8.* Consider the process $P = !\mathsf{new}\ c'.\mathsf{out}(c, c').B$ where $B$ is a basic process built on channel $c'$. Let $B = \mathsf{new}\ n.\mathsf{out}(c', \mathsf{senc}(n, k))$, and $\mathsf{N} = \{n\}$. We have that:

1. $\overline{P} = !\mathsf{new}\ c'.\mathsf{out}(c, c').\mathsf{out}(c', \mathsf{senc}(n, k))$, and
2. $B^\star(c^\star) = \mathsf{new}\ n^\star.\mathsf{out}(c^\star, \mathsf{senc}(n^\star, k))$.

Note that $B$ and $B^\star(c^\star)$ are identical up to the fact that they proceed on different channel. The transformation $\star$ applied on the basic process is just here to emphasise the fact that bound names are renamed to avoid some confusion due to name clashes.

Now, our transformation consists of combining these two building blocks. When removing fresh names from a process $P$, we keep a copy of one of the replicated basic processes of $P$, identified by its channel $c$. More formally, given a simple process $P$ of the form $P = !\,\text{new}\,c'.\text{out}(c, c').B \mid P'$, and a set of names N, the resulting process $\overline{P}^{N,c}$ is defined as follows:

$$\overline{P}^{N,c} \stackrel{\text{def}}{=} \overline{P}^{N} \mid B^{\star}(c^{\star}).$$

Sometimes we simply write $\overline{P}^{c}$ instead of $\overline{P}^{N,c}$ when N is clear from the context.

*Example 9.* Continuing Example 8, we have that:

$$\overline{P}^{N,c} = !\,\text{new}\,c'.\text{out}(c, c').\text{out}(c', \text{senc}(n, k)) \mid \text{new}\,n^{\star}.\text{out}(c^{\star}, \text{senc}(n^{\star}, k)).$$

### 3.3 Main Result

We are now able to state our main result. We consider a signature $\Sigma = \Sigma_c \uplus \Sigma_d$ together with a convergent rewriting system $\mathcal{R}$, and a notion of messages $\mathcal{M}_\Sigma$ such that the theory $(\Sigma, \mathcal{R})$ is adequate w.r.t. $\mathcal{M}_\Sigma$. Given a simple process $P$, we note $\text{Ch}(P)$ the set of public channel names occurring under a replication in $P$.

**Theorem 1.** *Let $P$ and $Q$ be two simple protocols such that $\text{Ch}(P) = \text{Ch}(Q)$, and N be a set of names (intuitively those that we want to abstract away). We have that:*

$$[\forall c \in \text{Ch}(P).\ \overline{P}^{N,c} \approx \overline{Q}^{N,c}] \Rightarrow P \approx Q$$

Note that, in case $\text{Ch}(P) \neq \text{Ch}(Q)$, we trivially have that $P \not\approx Q$ since one process is able to emit on a channel whereas the other is not.

This theorem shows that whenever two processes are not in trace equivalence, then it is possible to find a witness of non-equivalence when nonces are replaced by constants provided that one basic process under a replication has been duplicated.

*Example 10.* Continuing the example developed in introduction and pursued in Sect. 3.2, we consider

1. $P = !\text{new}\,c'.\text{out}(c, c').\text{new}\,n_P.\text{out}(c', \text{senc}(n_P, k))$, and
2. $Q = !\text{new}\,c'.\text{out}(c, c').\text{out}(c', \text{senc}(n_Q, k))$.

Let $N = \{n_P\}$. We have that:

1. $\overline{P}^{c} = !\text{new}\,c'.\text{out}(c, c').\text{out}(c', \text{senc}(n_P, k)) \mid \text{new}\,n_P^{\star}.\text{out}(c^{\star}, \text{senc}(n_P^{\star}, k))$, and
2. $\overline{Q}^{c} = !\text{new}\,c'.\text{out}(c, c').\text{out}(c', \text{senc}(n_Q, k)) \mid \text{out}(c^{\star}, \text{senc}(n_Q, k))$.

Clearly $\overline{P}^{c} \not\approx \overline{Q}^{c}$ since an attacker can observe that $\overline{P}^{c}$ may send two distinct messages while $\overline{Q}^{c}$ cannot. Intuitively, the attack reflecting that $P \not\approx Q$ can be reflected in $\overline{P}^{c} \not\approx \overline{Q}^{c}$. Another choice for N is to consider the set $\{n_P, n_Q\}$ but this would lead exactly to the same result.

## 3.4   Sketch of Proof

To establish our result, we first establish how to map traces from $P$ to $\overline{P}^{\mathsf{N}}$. Given a simple process $P$, and a trace $(\mathsf{tr}, \phi) \in \mathsf{trace}(P)$, we denote by $\rho^{P,\mathsf{N}}_{(\mathsf{tr},\phi)}$ the replacement that associates to each name $r \in \mathcal{N}$ generated during the execution under study and occurring in the frame $\phi$, the name $n \in \mathsf{N}$ that occurs in the instruction new $n$ of $P$ and that is responsible of the generation of this fresh name. This amounts in losing freshness of all the new $n$ instructions with $n \in \mathsf{N}$. Indeed all nonces induced by such an instruction are collapsed into a single nonce $n$. Our transformation is parametric in $\mathsf{N}$: we may replace all new instructions or simply part of them. Note that, for simple processes, once $(\mathsf{tr}, \phi)$ is fixed, this replacement is uniquely defined.

**Lemma 1.** *Let $P$ be a simple protocol, $\mathsf{N}$ be a set of names, and $(\mathsf{tr}, \phi) \in$ $\mathsf{trace}(P)$. We have that $(\mathsf{tr}, \phi\rho^{P,\mathsf{N}}_{(\mathsf{tr},\phi)}) \in \mathsf{trace}(\overline{P}^{\mathsf{N}})$.*

This proposition is shown by induction on the length of the trace under study and by case analysis on the rule of the semantics that is applied to allow the process to evolve. The crucial point is that the lack of freshness induced by considering $\overline{P}^{\mathsf{N}}$ instead of $P$ only generates more equalities between terms, and thus more behaviours. Now, it remains to ensure that the disequality that is needed to witness the non-equivalence still remains, and this is the purpose of considering a fresh copy, namely $B^{\star}(c^{\star})$.

*Sketch of proof of Theorem* 1. The idea is to show that a witness of non-equivalence for $P \not\approx Q$ can be converted into a witness of non-equivalence for $\overline{P}^{c} \not\approx \overline{Q}^{c}$ for at least one $c \in \mathsf{Ch}(P) = \mathsf{Ch}(Q)$. Due to the fact that we consider simple processes, three main cases may occur (the three other symmetric cases can be handled similarly). We have that $(\mathsf{tr}, \phi) \in \mathsf{trace}(P)$, and

1. there exists $\psi$ such that $(\mathsf{tr}, \psi) \in \mathsf{trace}(Q)$ and two recipes $R_1, R_2$ such that $R_1\phi{\downarrow}$, $R_2\phi{\downarrow}$, $R_1\psi{\downarrow}$ and $R_2\psi{\downarrow}$ are messages; $R_1\phi{\downarrow} = R_2\phi{\downarrow}$ and $R_1\psi{\downarrow} \neq R_2\psi{\downarrow}$; or
2. there exists $\psi$ such that $(\mathsf{tr}, \psi) \in \mathsf{trace}(Q)$ and a recipe $R$ such that $R\phi{\downarrow}$ is a message but $R\psi{\downarrow}$ is not; or
3. there exists no frame $\psi$ such that $(\mathsf{tr}, \psi) \in \mathsf{trace}(Q)$.

Each case is proved separately, following the same lines. First, thanks to Lemma 1, in case $(\mathsf{tr}, \phi\rho^{P,\mathsf{N}}_{(\mathsf{tr},\phi)})$ is still a witness of non-equivalence, we easily conclude. This roughly means that we do not even need the fresh copy to exhibit the non-equivalence. Otherwise, we need to maintain a disequality to ensure that the distinguishing test will not hold on the $Q$ side. Since we consider adequate theories, we know that this disequality can be maintained through the use of two distinct names. This is exactly why a fresh copy is needed. The other cases can be handled similarly.

## 4    Scope of Our Result

In this section, we explain why we need to assume simple processes and adequate theories and we discuss which class of protocols and primitives can be covered.

### 4.1    Simple Processes

Simple processes are really necessary for our simplification result to hold. We provide below a small counter example to our result for non simple processes.

*Example 11.* We consider symmetric encryption and pairs as in Example 1 with $\mathsf{ok} \in \Sigma_0$. We define the two following processes.

$$
\begin{aligned}
P = \; & ! \, \mathsf{new}\, c.\mathsf{out}(c_1, c).\mathsf{new}\, n.\mathsf{out}(c, \mathsf{senc}(n, k)) && (1)\\
& | \; ! \, \mathsf{new}\, c.\mathsf{out}(c_2, c).\mathsf{in}(c, \langle \mathsf{senc}(x, k), \mathsf{senc}(x, k), \mathsf{senc}(y, k)\rangle).\mathsf{out}(c, \mathsf{ok}) && (2)\\
& | \; ! \, \mathsf{new}\, c.\mathsf{out}(c_2, c).\mathsf{in}(c, \langle \mathsf{senc}(x, k), \mathsf{senc}(y, k), \mathsf{senc}(x, k)\rangle).\mathsf{out}(c, \mathsf{ok}) && (3)\\
& | \; ! \, \mathsf{new}\, c.\mathsf{out}(c_2, c).\mathsf{in}(c, \langle \mathsf{senc}(y, k), \mathsf{senc}(x, k), \mathsf{senc}(x, k)\rangle).\mathsf{out}(c, \mathsf{ok}) && (4)\\
Q = \; & ! \, \mathsf{new}\, c.\mathsf{out}(c_1, c).\mathsf{new}\, n.\mathsf{out}(c, \mathsf{senc}(n, k)) \\
& | \; ! \, \mathsf{new}\, c.\mathsf{out}(c_2, c).\mathsf{in}(c, \langle \mathsf{senc}(x, k), \mathsf{senc}(y, k), \mathsf{senc}(z, k)\rangle).\mathsf{out}(c, \mathsf{ok}).
\end{aligned}
$$

Intuitively $P$ expects a list of three ciphertexts among which two must be identical, while $Q$ expects any three ciphertexts. The process $Q$ is simple but $P$ is *not* since several processes in parallel proceed on channel $c_2$. We have that $P \not\approx Q$: it is possible using (1) to generate distinct ciphertexts, concatenate them, and send the resulting message on $c_2$. This message will not be accepted in $P$, but it will be accepted in $Q$.

Now, consider the process $\overline{P}^{c_1}$ and $\overline{Q}^{c_1}$ with $\mathsf{N} = \{n\}$, that is the processes obtained by applying our transformation on channel $c_1$ (the only branch that contains nonce generation) with the goal of getting rid of the instruction $\mathsf{new}\, n$ on both sides. We obtain:

$$
\begin{aligned}
\overline{P}^{c_1} = \; & ! \, \mathsf{new}\, c.\mathsf{out}(c_1, c).\mathsf{out}(c, \mathsf{senc}(n, k)) \\
& | \;\; \mathsf{new}\, n^\star.\, \mathsf{out}(c^\star, \mathsf{senc}(n^\star, k)) \\
& | \; ! \, \mathsf{new}\, c.\mathsf{out}(c_2, c).\mathsf{in}(c, \langle \mathsf{senc}(x, k), \mathsf{senc}(x, k), \mathsf{senc}(y, k)\rangle).\mathsf{out}(c, \mathsf{ok}) \\
& | \; ! \, \mathsf{new}\, c.\mathsf{out}(c_2, c).\mathsf{in}(c, \langle \mathsf{senc}(x, k), \mathsf{senc}(y, k), \mathsf{senc}(x, k)\rangle).\mathsf{out}(c, \mathsf{ok}) \\
& | \; ! \, \mathsf{new}\, c.\mathsf{out}(c_2, c).\mathsf{in}(c, \langle \mathsf{senc}(y, k), \mathsf{senc}(x, k), \mathsf{senc}(x, k)\rangle).\mathsf{out}(c, \mathsf{ok}) \\
\overline{Q}^{c_1} = \; & ! \, \mathsf{new}\, c.\mathsf{out}(c_1, c).\mathsf{out}(c, \mathsf{senc}(n, k)) \\
& | \;\; \mathsf{new}\, n^\star.\, \mathsf{out}(c^\star, \mathsf{senc}(n^\star, k)) \\
& | \; ! \, \mathsf{new}\, c.\mathsf{out}(c_2, c).\mathsf{in}(c, \langle \mathsf{senc}(x, k), \mathsf{senc}(y, k), \mathsf{senc}(z, k)\rangle).\mathsf{out}(c, \mathsf{ok}).
\end{aligned}
$$

It is quite easy to see that the witness of non-equivalence given above is not a valid one anymore. Actually, we have that $\overline{P}^{c_1}$ and $\overline{Q}^{c_1}$ are in trace equivalence since only two distinct ciphertexts may be produced.

Note that it is easy to express standard protocols as simple processes. As explained previously, encoding security protocols as simple processes is a good practice, and gives power to the attacker. However, it prevents the modeling of unlinkability properties.

## 4.2   Adequate Theories

The fact that we consider adequate theories may seem to be a proof artefact. We could probably go beyond adequate theories, but this would be at the price of considering a more complex transformation, and in particular additional constants. We provide below an example of a theory that reflects the same kind of issues than the ones illustrated by the processes presented in Example 11.

*Example 12.* In addition to the signature introduced in Example 1, we consider an additional destructor symbol g together with the following rewriting rules:

$$g((\langle senc(x, z), senc(x, z), senc(y, z)\rangle)) \rightarrow ok$$
$$g((\langle senc(x, z), senc(y, z), senc(x, z)\rangle)) \rightarrow ok$$
$$g((\langle senc(y, z), senc(x, z), senc(x, z)\rangle)) \rightarrow ok$$

Assume for instance that $\mathcal{M}_\Sigma$ is $\mathcal{M}_c = \mathcal{T}(\Sigma_c, \mathcal{N})$ the set of all ground constructor terms. The resulting theory is not adequate. For instance, we have that the term $t = g((\langle senc(n_1, k), senc(n_2, k), senc(n_3, k)\rangle))$ is in normal form and not a message. However, any renaming $\rho$ that preserves distinctness between only two names among $n_1, n_2, n_3$, will be such that $t\rho\downarrow \in \mathcal{M}_\Sigma$. This yields a counter-example to our result, illustrated by the two following processes.

$$P' = \, ! \, new \, c.out(c_1, c).new \, n.out(c, senc(n, k))$$
$$\mid \quad in(c_2, \langle senc(x_1, k), senc(x_2, k), senc(x_3, k)\rangle).$$
$$let \, y = g((\langle senc(x_1, k), senc(x_2, k), senc(x_3, k)\rangle)) \, in \, out(c_2, y).$$
$$Q' = \, ! \, new \, c.out(c_1, c).new \, n.out(c, senc(n, k))$$
$$\mid \quad in(c_2, \langle senc(x_1, k), senc(x_2, k), senc(x_3, k)\rangle).out(c_2, ok).$$

The process $P'$ expects three ciphertexts and returns the result of applying g to them while $Q'$ directly returns ok. For the same reasons as those explained in Example 11, we have that $P' \not\approx Q'$ whereas $\overline{P'}^{c_1} \approx \overline{Q'}^{c_1}$.

The equational theory above is contrived, and actually most of the equational theories useful to model cryptographic protocols can be shown to be adequate. An example of a non-adequate theory is tdcommit as described in [18] which does not fit the structure of our rules. Since the adequacy hypothesis might be cumbersome to prove by hand for each theory, we exhibit a simple criterion that ensures adequacy: the absence of critical pair.

**Definition 6.** *Given a signature* $\Sigma = \Sigma_c \uplus \Sigma_d$, *and a convergent rewriting system* $\mathcal{R}$, *we say that the theory* $(\Sigma, \mathcal{R})$ *has* no critical pair *if* $\ell_1$ *and* $\ell_2$ *are not unifiable for any distinct rules* $\ell_1 \rightarrow r_1$, *and* $\ell_2 \rightarrow r_2$ *in* $\mathcal{R}$.

Our notion of critical pairs actually coincide with the usual one for the theories we consider. Indeed, rewrite rules are all of the form $\ell \rightarrow r$ such that the head symbol of $\ell$ is a destructor symbol and destructors may not appear anywhere else in $\ell$ nor $r$. Theories without critical pairs are convergent and adequate.

**Lemma 2.** *Given a signature* $\Sigma = \Sigma_c \uplus \Sigma_d$, *a convergent rewriting system* $\mathcal{R}$, *and a set of messages* $\mathcal{M}_\Sigma$ *such that* $\mathcal{T}(\Sigma_c, \mathcal{N}) \smallsetminus \mathcal{M}_\Sigma$ *is stable by renaming. If the theory* $(\Sigma, \mathcal{R})$ *has no critical pair, then* $(\Sigma, \mathcal{R})$ *is convergent and adequate* w.r.t. $\mathcal{M}_\Sigma$.

This lemma allows us to conclude that many theories used in practice to model security protocols are actually adequate. This is the case of the theory given in Example 1, and the theories that are presented below.

*Standard Cryptographic Primitives.* We may enrich the theory described in Example 1 with function symbols to model asymmetric encryption, and digital signatures.

$$\Sigma^+ = \Sigma \cup \{\mathsf{aenc}, \mathsf{adec}, \mathsf{sign}, \mathsf{checksign}, \mathsf{getmsg}, \mathsf{pub}, \mathsf{priv}, \mathsf{ok}\}.$$

Symbols adec/aenc and sign/checksign of arity 2 are used to model asymmetric encryption and signature, whereas pub/priv of arity 1 will be used to model key pairs, and the symbol priv will be part of the signature $\Sigma_{\mathsf{priv}}$. The symbol getmsg may be used in case we want to consider a signature algorithm that does not protect the signed message. The corresponding rewrite rules are defined as follows:

$$\mathsf{checksign}(\mathsf{sign}(x, \mathsf{priv}(y)), \mathsf{pub}(y)) \to \mathsf{ok} \qquad \mathsf{adec}(\mathsf{aenc}(x, \mathsf{pub}(y)), \mathsf{priv}(y)) \to x$$
$$\mathsf{getmsg}(\mathsf{sign}(x, \mathsf{priv}(y))) \to x$$

Regarding the notion of messages, a reasonable choice for $\mathcal{M}_{\Sigma^+}$ is to consider $\mathcal{M}_c^+ = \mathcal{T}(\Sigma_c \uplus \{\mathsf{aenc}, \mathsf{sign}, \mathsf{pub}, \mathsf{priv}, \mathsf{ok}\}, \mathcal{N})$ the set of all ground constructor terms. We may also restrict $\mathcal{M}_{\Sigma_+}$ in various ways to only allow some specific terms in key positions.

*Blind Signatures.* The following theory is often used to model blind signatures (see *e.g.* [18]), checksign and unblind are the only destructor symbols.

$$\mathsf{checksign}(\mathsf{sign}(x, \mathsf{priv}(y)), \mathsf{pub}(y)) \to x$$
$$\mathsf{unblind}(\mathsf{blind}(x, y), y) \to x$$
$$\mathsf{unblind}(\mathsf{sign}(\mathsf{blind}(x, y), \mathsf{priv}(z)), y) \to \mathsf{sign}(x, \mathsf{priv}(z))$$

*Zero-Knowledge Proofs.* A typical signature for representing zero-knowledge proofs is $\Sigma_{\mathsf{ZKP}} = \{\mathsf{Verify}, \mathsf{ZKP}, \mathsf{ok}\}$ where ZKP represents a zero-knowledge proof and Verify models the verification of the proof. To ease the presentation, we present how to model the proof of a particular statement, namely the fact that a ciphertext is the encryption of either 0 or 1. Such proofs are thoroughly used for example in the context of e-voting protocols such as Helios. In particular, the theory we consider here has been introduced in [16]. Specifically, let $\Sigma_{\mathsf{ZKP}}^+ = \Sigma_{\mathsf{ZKP}} \uplus \{\mathsf{raenc}, \mathsf{radec}, \mathsf{pub}, \mathsf{priv}, 0, 1\}$ and consider the following rewrite rules.

$$\mathsf{radec}(\mathsf{raenc}(x, z, \mathsf{pub}(y)), \mathsf{priv}(y)) \to x$$
$$\mathsf{Verify}(\mathsf{ZKP}(x, \mathsf{raenc}(0, x, \mathsf{pub}(y)), \mathsf{pub}(y)), \mathsf{raenc}(0, x, \mathsf{pub}(y)), \mathsf{pub}(y)) \to \mathsf{ok}$$
$$\mathsf{Verify}(\mathsf{ZKP}(x, \mathsf{raenc}(1, x, \mathsf{pub}(y)), \mathsf{pub}(y)), \mathsf{raenc}(1, x, \mathsf{pub}(y)), \mathsf{pub}(y)) \to \mathsf{ok}$$

The symbol raenc represents randomised asymmetric encryption as reflected by the first rewrite rule. The two last rules ensure that a proof is valid only if the corresponding ciphertext contains either 0 or 1 and nothing else. Many variants of zero-knowledge proofs can be modelled in a very similar way.

## 5    Application of Our Result

Abstracting nonces with constants (as done in Theorem 1) may introduce false attacks. A typical case is when protocols make use of temporary secrets.

*Example 13.* Consider the signature described in Example 1. Let $P$ and $Q$ be:

$$P = \text{! new } c'.\text{out}(c, c').\text{in}(c', x).\text{new } n.\text{out}(c', \text{senc}(\text{ok}, n)).$$
$$\text{let } y = \text{sdec}(x, n) \text{ in out}(c', y);$$
$$Q = \text{! new } c'.\text{out}(c, c').\text{in}(c', x).\text{new } n.\text{out}(c', n).$$

The two processes are in equivalence: $P \approx Q$. Now, consider the processes $\overline{P}^c$ and $\overline{Q}^c$ with $N = \{n\}$, that is, the processes obtained by applying our transformation on channel $c$ to get rid of the fresh nonces.

$$\overline{P}^c = \text{! new } c'.\text{out}(c, c').\text{in}(c', x).\text{out}(c', \text{senc}(\text{ok}, n)).\text{let } y = \text{sdec}(x, n) \text{ in out}(c', y)$$
$$| \text{ in}(c^\star, x).\text{out}(c^\star, \text{senc}(\text{ok}, n^\star)).\text{let } y = \text{sdec}(x, n^\star) \text{ in out}(c^\star, y)$$

$\overline{Q}^c$ is defined similarly. It is easy to notice that the output of the constant ok is now reachable, yielding $\overline{P}^c \not\approx \overline{Q}^c$.

### 5.1    Is Our Abstraction Precise Enough?

Our transformation may in theory also introduce false attacks for protocols without temporary secrets. In this section, we review several (secure) protocols of the literature and study whether a false attack is introduced by our transformation. To perform this analysis we rely on the ProVerif tool. For each protocol, we first consider a scenario with honest agents only as for the Yahalom protocol (Sect. 2). We then consider a richer scenario where honest agents are also willing to engage communications with a dishonest agent. In each case, we check whether ProVerif is able to establish:

1. the equivalence between the original processes (left column);
2. all the equivalences obtained after getting rid of all the nonces using our transformation (right column).

The results are reported on the table below: a ✓ means that ProVerif succeeded and a ✗ means that it failed. Actually, on most of the protocols/scenarios we have considered, our abstraction does not introduce any false attack. ProVerif models of our experiments are available online at http://www.lsv.ens-cachan.fr/~chretien/prot.tar.

| Protocol name | Original (with nonces) | Our transformation (no nonce) |
|---|---|---|
| YAHALOM (corrected version) | | |
| - simple scenario | ✓ | ✓ |
| - with a dishonest agent | ✓ | ✓ |
| OTWAY-REES | | |
| - simple scenario | ✓ | ✓ |
| - with a dishonest agent | ✓ | ✓ |
| KAO-CHOW (tagged version) | | |
| - simple scenario | ✓ | ✓ |
| - with a dishonest agent | ✓ | ✓ |
| NEEDHAM-SCHROEDER-LOWE | | |
| - simple scenario (secrecy of $N_a$) | ✓ | ✗ |
| - simple scenario (secrecy of $N_b$) | ✓ | ✓ |
| - with a dishonest agent (secrecy of $N_b$) | ✓ | ✓ |
| DENNING-SACCO (asymmetric) | | |
| - simple scenario | ✓ | ✓ |
| - with a dishonest agent | ✓ | ✓ |

*Needham Schroeder Lowe Protocol.* We briefly comment on the false attack introduced by our transformation on the Needham Schroeder Lowe protocol.

1. $A \to B : \{A, N_a\}_{\mathsf{pub}(B)}$      1. $I(A) \to B : \{A, N_i\}_{\mathsf{pub}(B)}$
2. $B \to A : \{N_a, N_b, B\}_{\mathsf{pub}(A)}$      2. $B \to I(A) : \{N_i, N_b, B\}_{\mathsf{pub}(A)}$
3. $A \to B : \{N_b\}_{\mathsf{pub}(B)}$      3. $I(A) \to B : \{N_b\}_{\mathsf{pub}(B)}$

The protocol is given on the left, and the (false) attack depicted on the right. This attack scenario (and more precisely step 3 of this scenario) is only possible when nonces are abstracted away with constants. Indeed, the attacker will not be able to decrypt the message $\{N_i, N_b, B\}_{\mathsf{pub}(A)}$ he has received to retrieve the nonce $N_b$. Instead he will simply replay an old message coming from a previous honest session between $A$ and $B$. Since nonces have been replaced by constants, $B$ will accept this old message, and will assume that $N_i$ is a secret shared between $A$ and $B$, while $N_i$ is known by the attacker. Unfortunately, this abstraction does not seem to help ProVerif prove the security of new protocols. Nonetheless it can still be used as a proof technique to prove the security of protocols in classes defined in [9,10].

## 5.2    Proof Technique

Our result can be used as a proof technique to show that two simple protocols are in trace equivalence. In particular, we have that the decidability result developed in [10] for tagged protocols without nonces can now, thanks to our transformation, be applied to study the security of protocols *with nonces*.

The decidability result given in [10] applies on *type-compliant* protocols. This roughly means that ciphertexts cannot be confused and this can be achieved by adding some identifier (a tag that is re-used in all sessions) in each ciphertext.

Applying our transformation to a simple, type-compliant protocol yields a process that belongs to the decidable class of [10].

**Proposition 1.** *Let* $(\Sigma, \mathcal{R})$ *be the theory given in Example 1 with* $\mathcal{M}_\Sigma = \mathcal{M}_{\mathsf{atomic}}$. *Let* $P$ *and* $Q$ *be two simple and type-compliant protocols built on* $(\Sigma, \mathcal{R})$, *and such that* $\mathsf{Ch}(P) = \mathsf{Ch}(Q)$. *Let* $\mathsf{N}$ *be the set of names that occur in* $P$ *or* $Q$.

*The problem of deciding whether* $\overline{P}^{\mathsf{N},c}$ *and* $\overline{Q}^{\mathsf{N},c}$ *are in trace equivalence is decidable (for any* $c \in \mathsf{Ch}(P)$).

## 6    Conclusion

Our simplification result allows to soundly reduce the equivalence of processes with nonces to the equivalence of processes without nonce. This can be seen as a proof technique. For example for tagged simple protocols with symmetric encryption, the resulting protocols fall in the decidable class of [10]. Similarly, we could use the decidability result of [9] for ping-pong protocols with one variable per transition.

Our result assumes protocols to be simple processes. Otherwise, to prevent some transition, it could be necessary to maintain several disequalities. We plan to go slightly beyond simple processes and simply require some form of determinacy. More generally, we plan to study whether such a reduction result can be obtained for arbitrary processes, that is, study whether it is possible to compute a bound on the number of fresh copies from the structure of the processes.

Regarding adequate theories, we believe that our criterion is general enough to capture even more theories like exclusive or, or other theories with an associative and commutative operator. This would however require to extend our formalism to arbitrary terms (not just destructor/constructor theories).

## A    Appendix

Lemma 1 is a direct corollary of Lemma 3 which we state below. In the following, we will only consider theories adequate w.r.t. $\mathcal{M}_\Sigma$. Given a frame $\phi$ (resp. $\psi$) and a name $r$ in $\phi$ (resp. $\psi$), let $n(r)$ be the nonce in $P$ (resp. $Q$) such that $r$ is an instance of $n(r)$ and let $c(r)$ be the channel of the protocol's branch which generated it. Actually, it can be computed as the channel on which $r$ appeared first in $\mathsf{tr}\phi{\downarrow}$ (resp. $\mathsf{tr}\psi{\downarrow}$). We note $\mathcal{D}_\phi = \{r \in \phi \mid n(r) \in \mathsf{N}\}$ and for any $A \subseteq \mathcal{D}_\phi$, we denote $n(A)$ the application having $A$ as domain, and such that $n(A)(r) = n(r)$ for any $r \in A$. To each nonce $n \in \mathsf{N}$, we can associate a new name $n^\star$: we can then define the function $n^\star(\cdot)$ to be the function mapping any $r \in \mathcal{D}_\phi$ to $(n(r))^\star$. Similarly, for any $A \subseteq \mathcal{D}_\phi$, we denote $n^\star(A)$ the function mapping any $r \in A$ to $(n(r))^\star$.

**Lemma 3.** *We have the two following properties.*

1. *Let* $(\mathsf{tr}, \phi) \in \mathsf{trace}(P)$, $\mathcal{D}_\phi = \{r \in \phi \mid n(r) \in \mathsf{N}\}$ *and* $\rho_0 = n(\mathcal{D}_\phi)$. *Then* $(\mathsf{tr}, \phi\rho_0) \in \mathsf{trace}(\overline{P}^{\mathsf{N}})$.
2. *Moreover, let* $ch$ *be a channel such that* $\mathsf{tr} = \mathsf{tr}_1.\mathsf{out}(c, ch).\mathsf{tr}_2$, $\tilde{\mathcal{D}}_\phi = \{r \in \phi \mid n(r) \in \mathsf{N} \wedge c(r) = ch\}$ *and* $\rho = n(\mathcal{D}_\phi \setminus \tilde{\mathcal{D}}_\phi) \cup n^\star(\tilde{\mathcal{D}}_\phi)$. *Then* $(\mathsf{tr}^\star, \phi\rho) \in \mathsf{trace}(\overline{P}^{\mathsf{N},c})$, *where* $\mathsf{tr}^\star = \mathsf{tr}_1.\mathsf{tr}_2\{^{c^\star}/_{ch}\}$.

*Proof.* The proof of case 2 is done by induction on the length of the execution of $\mathsf{tr}$ in $P$. For any rule in our semantics, we prove that the renaming $\rho$ does not prevent the action from being executed as it only introduces new equalities and that the resulting multiset of processes and frame are similar, up to application of $\rho$. Finally, case 1 can be seen as a special instance of case 2.   □

**Theorem 1.** *Let $P$ and $Q$ be two simple protocols such that* $\mathsf{Ch}(P) = \mathsf{Ch}(Q)$, *and $\mathsf{N}$ be a set of names (intuitively those that we want to abstract away). We have that:*

$$[\forall c \in \mathsf{Ch}(P).\ \overline{P}^{\mathsf{N},c} \approx \overline{Q}^{\mathsf{N},c}] \Rightarrow P \approx Q.$$

*Proof.* Let us assume there exists a witness of non-equivalence $(\mathsf{tr}, \phi) \in \mathsf{trace}(P)$. Three main cases can occur:

1. there exists $\psi$ such that $(\mathsf{tr}, \psi) \in \mathsf{trace}(Q)$ and two recipes $R_1, R_2$ such that $R_1\phi{\downarrow}, R_2\phi{\downarrow}, R_1\psi{\downarrow}$ and $R_2\psi{\downarrow}$ are messages; $R_1\phi{\downarrow} = R_2\phi{\downarrow}$ and $R_1\psi{\downarrow} \neq R_2\psi{\downarrow}$;
2. or there exists $\psi$ such that $(\mathsf{tr}, \psi) \in \mathsf{trace}(Q)$ and a recipe $R$ such that $R\phi{\downarrow}$ is a message but $R\psi{\downarrow}$ is not;
3. or, finally, there exists no frame $\psi$ such that $(\mathsf{tr}, \psi) \in \mathsf{trace}(Q)$.

Note that the remaining symmetric cases are handled by considering a witness $(\mathsf{tr}, \psi) \in \mathsf{trace}(Q)$ instead, as $P$ and $Q$ are both simple. We will deal with each case separately, with the same intermediate goal: define a renaming $\rho$ on $\mathcal{D}_\psi$ such that any test failing in $\psi$ still fails in $\psi\rho$ while the successful tests in $\phi$ remain so; then translate it into a valid trace of $\overline{P}^{\mathsf{N},c}$ for some $c \in \mathsf{Ch}(P)$.

*Case 1:* Let us examine $R_1\psi{\downarrow}$ and $R_2\psi{\downarrow}$. If the two terms do not share the same constructors, then for any renaming $\rho$, $R_1(\psi\rho){\downarrow} \neq R_2(\psi\rho){\downarrow}$, while for any renaming $\rho'$, $R_1(\phi\rho'){\downarrow} = R_2(\phi\rho'){\downarrow}$ (as the constructors are left unchanged, because every term is a message). Now, if the two terms share the same constructors, there must exist a leaf position $p$ in them such that $R_1\psi{\downarrow}|_p \neq R_2\psi{\downarrow}|_p$. Let us call $t$ and $s$ these terms respectively. If $s$ or $t$ is *not* an element of $\mathcal{D}_\psi$, then $s\rho \neq t\rho$ for any $\rho$ with $dom(\rho) = \mathcal{D}_\psi$. As in the previous case, we get that $R_1(\psi\rho){\downarrow} \neq R_2(\psi\rho){\downarrow}$, while $R_1(\phi\rho'){\downarrow} = R_2(\phi\rho'){\downarrow}$ for any renaming $\rho'$. Else, assume $s = r_1$ and $t = r_2$ are two nonces of $\mathcal{D}_\psi$ such that $n(r_1) = n_1 \in \mathsf{N}$ (resp. $n(r_2) = n_2 \in \mathsf{N}$). If $n_1 \neq n_2$, consider the renaming $\rho_0^Q$ mapping any $r \in \mathcal{D}_\psi$ to $n(r)$. Then $s\rho_0^Q \neq t\rho_0^Q$ and we get that $R_1(\psi\rho_0^Q){\downarrow} \neq R_2(\psi\rho_0^Q){\downarrow}$. By Lemma 3, $(\mathsf{tr}, \psi\rho_0^Q) \in \mathsf{trace}(\overline{Q}^{\mathsf{N}})$.

Similarly, by defining $\rho_0^P$ as the function mapping any name $r \in \mathcal{D}_\phi$ to $n(r)$, we have that $(\mathsf{tr}, \phi\rho_0^P) \in \mathsf{trace}(\overline{P}^{\mathsf{N}})$. and $R_1(\phi\rho_0^P)\!\downarrow = R_2(\phi\rho_0^P)\!\downarrow$. Hence we get a witness of non-equivalence between $\overline{P}^{\mathsf{N}}$ and $\overline{Q}^{\mathsf{N}}$, which can translate into a witness between $\overline{P}^{\mathsf{N},c}$ and $\overline{Q}^{\mathsf{N},c}$ for any $c \in \mathsf{Ch}(P)$.

Else, if $n(r_1) = n(r_2) = n$, we need to be more precise to define a proper $\rho$. Let $\mathsf{out}(c, ch)$ be the action of $\mathsf{tr}$ such that $\mathsf{tr} = \mathsf{tr}_1.\mathsf{out}(c, ch).\mathsf{tr}_2$ and $c(r_2) = ch$. Let $\tilde{\mathcal{D}}_\psi = \{r \in \psi \mid n(r) \in \mathsf{N} \wedge c(r) = ch\}$ and $\tilde{\mathcal{D}}_\phi = \{r \in \phi \mid n(r) \in \mathsf{N} \wedge c(r) = ch\}$. $r_1 \in \mathcal{D}_\psi \setminus \tilde{\mathcal{D}}_\psi$ but $r_2 \in \tilde{\mathcal{D}}_\psi$. Consider now $\rho_Q = n(\mathcal{D}_\psi \setminus \tilde{\mathcal{D}}_\psi) \cup n^\star(\tilde{\mathcal{D}}_\psi)$. In particular, $r_1\rho_Q = n$ while $r_2\rho_Q = n^\star$. Then $s\rho_Q \neq t\rho_Q$ and we get that $R_1(\psi\rho_Q)\!\downarrow \neq R_2(\psi\rho_Q)\!\downarrow$ and Lemma 3 ensures $(\mathsf{tr}^\star, \psi\rho_Q) \in \mathsf{trace}(\overline{Q}^{\mathsf{N},c})$. Similarly, by defining $\rho_P = n(\mathcal{D}_\phi \setminus \tilde{\mathcal{D}}_\phi) \cup n^\star(\tilde{\mathcal{D}}_\phi)$, Lemma 3 ensures $(\mathsf{tr}^\star, \phi\rho_P) \in \mathsf{trace}(\overline{P}^{\mathsf{N},c})$ and $R_1(\phi\rho_P)\!\downarrow = R_2(\phi\rho_P)\!\downarrow$ (only equalities have been introduced by removing the name restriction in $P$). Hence we get a witness of non-equivalence between $\overline{P}^{\mathsf{N},c}$ and $\overline{Q}^{\mathsf{N},c}$

*Case 2:* Because $R\psi\!\downarrow$ is not a message and our signature is adequate (see Definition 5), there must exist $a, b \in \mathcal{N}$ such that $a \neq b$ and for any renaming $\sigma : \mathcal{N} \to \mathcal{N}$, $a\sigma \neq b\sigma \Rightarrow t\sigma\!\downarrow \notin \mathcal{M}_\Sigma$. If $a \notin \mathcal{D}_\psi$ or $b \notin \mathcal{D}_\psi$, consider the renaming $\rho_0^Q$ mapping any name $r \in \mathcal{D}_\psi$ to $n(r)$: as $a\rho_0^Q = a$ and $n(r) \neq a$ for any $r \in \mathcal{D}_\psi$, $R(\psi\rho_0^Q)\!\downarrow$ is still not a message. On the other hand, if $\rho_0^P = n(\mathcal{D}_\phi)$, as $R\phi\!\downarrow$ is a message, $R\phi\!\downarrow\rho_0^P = R(\phi\rho_0^P)\!\downarrow$ is a message. Hence, Lemma 3 ensures $(\mathsf{tr}, \phi\rho_0^P) \in \mathsf{trace}(\overline{P}^{\mathsf{N}})$ while $(\mathsf{tr}, \psi\rho_0^Q) \notin \mathsf{trace}(\overline{Q}^{\mathsf{N}})$, leading to a witness of non-equivalence between $\overline{P}^{\mathsf{N}}$ and $\overline{Q}^{\mathsf{N}}$.

Else, assume $a = r_1$ and $b = r_2$ are two nonces in $\mathcal{D}_\psi$. If $n(r_1) \neq n(r_2)$, $r_1\rho_0^Q \neq r_2\rho_0^Q$ and we can apply the same exact reasoning as before. So let us consider the case where $n(r_1) = n(r_2) = n$. Let $\mathsf{out}(c, ch)$ be the action of $\mathsf{tr}$ such that $\mathsf{tr} = \mathsf{tr}_1.\mathsf{out}(c, ch).\mathsf{tr}_2$ and $c(r_2) = ch$. Let $\tilde{\mathcal{D}}_\psi = \{r \in \psi \mid n(r) \in \mathsf{N} \wedge c(r) = ch\}$ and $\tilde{\mathcal{D}}_\phi = \{r \in \phi \mid n(r) \in \mathsf{N} \wedge c(r) = ch\}$. $r_1 \in \mathcal{D}_\psi \setminus \tilde{\mathcal{D}}_\psi$ but $r_2 \in \tilde{\mathcal{D}}_\psi$. Consider now $\rho_Q = n(\mathcal{D}_\psi \setminus \tilde{\mathcal{D}}_\psi) \cup n^\star(\tilde{\mathcal{D}}_\psi)$. In particular, $r_1\rho_Q = n$ while $r_2\rho_Q = n^\star$. Definition 5 ensures $R(\psi\rho_Q)\!\downarrow$ is still not a message. On the other hand, if $\rho_P = n(\mathcal{D}_\phi \setminus \tilde{\mathcal{D}}_\phi) \cup n^\star(\tilde{\mathcal{D}}_\phi)$, as $R\phi\!\downarrow$ is a message, $R\phi\!\downarrow\rho_P = R(\phi\rho_P)\!\downarrow$ is a message. Hence, Lemma 3 ensures $(\mathsf{tr}^\star, \phi\rho_P) \in \mathsf{trace}(\overline{P}^{\mathsf{N},c})$ while $(\mathsf{tr}^\star, \psi\rho_Q) \in \mathsf{trace}(\overline{Q}^{\mathsf{N},c})$, leading to a witness of non-equivalence between $\overline{P}^{\mathsf{N},c}$ and $\overline{Q}^{\mathsf{N},c}$.

*Case 3:* if $\mathsf{tr}$ ends with an output $\mathsf{out}(c, w)$ such that $w\psi$ is not a message, we can define $\rho_Q$ and $\rho_P$ as in case 2 and obtain a witness of non-equivalence. Similarly, if $\mathsf{tr}$ ends with an input or output $\mathsf{out}(c, w)$ which cannot be executed in $Q$ because a let action did not reduce to a message, we can define $\rho_Q$ and $\rho_P$ as in case 2 and obtain a witness of non-equivalence. Consider now the subcase where $\mathsf{tr} = \mathsf{tr}'.\mathsf{in}(c, R)$ for some $\mathsf{tr}'$ such that $(\mathsf{tr}', \phi) \in \mathsf{trace}(P)$ and $(\mathsf{tr}', \psi) \in \mathsf{trace}(Q)$ for some frame $\psi$. Because $P$ and $Q$ are both simple protocols, there exists a unique term $u_P$ (resp. at most one term $u_Q$) in the multiset $\mathcal{P}$ (resp. $\mathcal{Q}$) of processes from the execution of $\mathsf{tr}'$ in $P$ (resp. in $Q$) such that $\mathsf{in}(c, u_P).M \in \mathcal{P}$ for some $M$ (resp. $\mathsf{in}(c, u_Q).N \in \mathcal{Q}$ for some $N$). Moreover, there exists $\sigma_P$ such that $R\phi\downarrow = u_P\sigma_P$ while there is no $\sigma$ such that $R\psi\downarrow = u_Q\sigma$. As before, we consider the renamings $\rho_0^Q = n(\mathcal{D}_\psi)$ and $\rho_0^P = n(\mathcal{D}_\phi)$. As $(\mathsf{tr}, \phi\rho_0^P) \in \mathsf{trace}(\overline{P}^N)$ and $(\mathsf{tr}, \psi\rho_0^Q) \in \mathsf{trace}(\overline{Q}^N)$ by Lemma 3, if there exists no $\sigma$ such that $u_Q\rho_0^Q\sigma = R\psi\downarrow\rho_0^Q$, $\mathsf{tr}$ is a witness of non-equivalence between $\overline{P}^N$ and $\overline{Q}^N$ and we are done. So let us then assume there exists $\sigma_0$ such that $u_Q\rho_0^Q\sigma_0 = R\psi\downarrow\rho_0^Q$ while $u_Q\sigma \neq R\psi\downarrow$ for every $\sigma$. There exist two leaves with positions $p_1$ and $p_2$ in $R\psi\downarrow$ which corresponds to positions below variables in $u_Q$ such that $R\psi\downarrow|_{p_1} \neq R\psi\downarrow|_{p_2}$ but $R(\psi\rho_0^Q)\downarrow|_{p_1} = R(\psi\rho_0^Q)\downarrow|_{p_2}$ and $R\psi\downarrow|_{p_1} = r_1$ and $R\psi\downarrow|_{p_2} = r_2$ such that $n(r_1) = n(r_2) = n \in \mathsf{N}$. As repeatedly before, let $\mathsf{out}(c, ch)$ be the action of $\mathsf{tr}$ such that $\mathsf{tr} = \mathsf{tr}_1.\mathsf{out}(c, ch).\mathsf{tr}_2$ and $c(r_2) = ch$. Let $\tilde{\mathcal{D}}_\psi = \{r \in \psi \mid n(r) \in \mathsf{N} \wedge c(r) = ch\}$ and $\tilde{\mathcal{D}}_\phi = \{r \in \phi \mid n(r) \in \mathsf{N} \wedge c(r) = ch\}$. We have that $r_1 \in \mathcal{D}_\psi \smallsetminus \tilde{\mathcal{D}}_\psi$ but $r_2 \in \tilde{\mathcal{D}}_\psi$. Consider now $\rho_Q = n(\mathcal{D}_\psi \smallsetminus \tilde{\mathcal{D}}_\psi) \cup n^\star(\tilde{\mathcal{D}}_\psi)$. In particular, $r_1\rho_Q = n$ while $r_2\rho_Q = n^\star$. As $R\psi\downarrow$ is a message (by virtue of our semantics), $R\psi\downarrow\rho_Q = R(\psi\rho_Q)\downarrow$ and now $R(\psi\rho_Q)\downarrow|_{p_1} \neq R(\psi\rho_Q)\downarrow|_{p_2}$. As such, $u_Q\rho_Q\sigma \neq R\psi\rho_Q\downarrow$ for any $\sigma$. By defining $\rho_P = n(\mathcal{D}_\phi \smallsetminus \tilde{\mathcal{D}}_\phi) \cup n^\star(\tilde{\mathcal{D}}_\phi)$, as $R\phi\downarrow$ is a message, $R\phi\downarrow\rho_P = R(\phi\rho_P)\downarrow$ is a message. Hence, Lemma 3 ensures $(\mathsf{tr}^\star, \phi\rho_P) \in \mathsf{trace}(\overline{P}^{N,c})$ while $(\mathsf{tr}^\star, \psi) \notin \mathsf{trace}(\overline{Q}^{N,c})$ for any $\psi$, leading to a witness of non-equivalence between $\overline{P}^{N,c}$ and $\overline{Q}^{N,c}$.                    $\square$

# References

1. Abadi, M., Fournet, C.: Mobile values, new names, and secure communication. In: 28th Symposium on Principles of Programming Languages (POPL 2001). ACM Press (2001)

2. Amadio, R.M., Charatonik, W.: On name generation and set-based analysis in the dolev-yao model. In: Brim, L., Jančar, P., Křetínský, M., Kučera, A. (eds.) CONCUR 2002. LNCS, vol. 2421, pp. 499–514. Springer, Heidelberg (2002)

3. Armando, A., et al.: The AVISPA tool for the automated validation of internet security protocols and applications. In: Etessami, K., Rajamani, S.K. (eds.) CAV 2005. LNCS, vol. 3576, pp. 281–285. Springer, Heidelberg (2005)

4. Beurdouche, B., et al.: A messy state of the union: Taming the composite state machines of tls. In: IEEE Symposium on Security & Privacy 2015 (Oakland 2015). IEEE (2015)

5. Blanchet, B.: An efficient cryptographic protocol verifier based on prolog rules. In: 14th Computer Security Foundations Workshop (CSFW 2001). IEEE Computer Society Press (2001)

6. Blanchet, B., Abadi, M., Fournet, C.: Automated verification of selected equivalences for security protocols. In: 20th Symposium on Logic in Computer Science (2005)

7. Blanchet, B., Podelski, A.: Verification of cryptographic protocols: tagging enforces termination. In: Gordon, A.D. (ed.) FOSSACS 2003. LNCS, vol. 2620, pp. 136–152. Springer, Heidelberg (2003)

8. Bruso, M., Chatzikokolakis, K., den Hartog, J.: Formal verification of privacy for RFID systems. In: 23rd Computer Security Foundations Symposium (CSF 2010) (2010)

9. Chrétien, R., Cortier, V., Delaune, S.: From security protocols to pushdown automata. In: Fomin, F.V., Freivalds, R., Kwiatkowska, M., Peleg, D. (eds.) ICALP 2013, Part II. LNCS, vol. 7966, pp. 137–149. Springer, Heidelberg (2013)

10. Delaune, S., Chrétien, R., Cortier, V.: Typing messages for free in security protocols: the case of equivalence properties. In: Baldan, P., Gorla, D. (eds.) CONCUR 2014. LNCS, vol. 8704, pp. 372–386. Springer, Heidelberg (2014)

11. Chrétien, R., Cortier, V., Delaune, S.: Checking trace equivalence: how to get rid of nonces? Research report LSV-15-07. Laboratoire Spécification et Vérification, ENS Cachan, France (2015)

12. Chrétien, R., Cortier, V., Delaune, S.: Decidability of trace equivalence for protocols with nonces. In: Proceedings of the 28th IEEE Computer Security Foundations Symposium (CSF 2015). IEEE Computer Society Press (June 2015, to appear)

13. Comon-Lundh, H., Cortier, V.: New decidability results for fragments of first-order logic and application to cryptographic protocols. In: Nieuwenhuis, R. (ed.) RTA 2003. LNCS, vol. 2706, pp. 148–164. Springer, Heidelberg (2003)

14. Comon-Lundh, H., Cortier, V.: Security properties: two agents are sufficient. In: Degano, P. (ed.) ESOP 2003. LNCS, vol. 2618, pp. 99–113. Springer, Heidelberg (2003)

15. Comon-Lundh, H., Cortier, V.: Computational soundness of observational equivalence. In: 15th ACM Conference on Computer and Communications Security (CCS 2008). ACM Press (2008)

16. Cortier, V., Smyth, B.: Attacking and fixing helios: an analysis of ballot secrecy. J. Comput. Secur. **21**(1), 89–148 (2013)

17. Cremers, C.J.F.: The scyther tool: verification, falsification, and analysis of security protocols. In: Gupta, A., Malik, S. (eds.) CAV 2008. LNCS, vol. 5123, pp. 414–418. Springer, Heidelberg (2008)

18. Delaune, S., Kremer, S., Ryan, M.D.: Verifying privacy-type properties of electronic voting protocols. J. Comput. Secur. **4**, 435–487 (2008)

19. Dershowitz, N., Jouannaud, J.-P.: Rewrite systems. In: van Leeuwen, J. (ed.) Handbook of Theoretical Computer Science. Elsevier, The Netherlands (1990)

20. Durgin, N., Lincoln, P., Mitchell, J., Scedrov, A.: Undecidability of bounded security protocols. In: Workshop on Formal Methods and Security Protocols, Trento, Italia (1999)

21. Escobar, S., Meadows, C., Meseguer, J.: A rewriting-based inference system for the NRL protocol analyzer and its meta-logical properties. Theor. Comput. Sci. **367**(1–2), 162–202 (2006)

22. Bellare, M., Desai, A., Pointcheval, D., Rogaway, P.: Relations among notions of security for public-key encryption schemes. In: Krawczyk, H. (ed.) CRYPTO 1998. LNCS, vol. 1462, pp. 26–45. Springer, Heidelberg (1998)

23. SPORE: Security protocols open repository. http://www.lsv.ens-cachan.fr/spore/index.html

# Attribute Based Broadcast Encryption with Short Ciphertext and Decryption Key

Tran Viet Xuan Phuong[1]($\boxtimes$), Guomin Yang[1], Willy Susilo[1],
and Xiaofeng Chen[2]

[1] Centre for Computer and Information Security Research, School of Computing
and Information Technology, University of Wollongong, Wollongong, Australia
tvxp750@uowmail.edu.au, {gyang,wsusilo}@uow.edu.au
[2] State Key Laboratory of Integrated Service Networks, Xidian University,
Xi'an, People's Republic of China
xfchen@xidian.edu.cn

**Abstract.** Attribute Based Broadcast Encryption (ABBE) is a combination of Attribute Based Encryption (ABE) and Broadcast Encryption (BE). It allows a broadcaster (or encrypter) to broadcast an encrypted message that can only be decrypted by the receivers who are within a predefined user set *and* satisfy the access policy specified by the broadcaster. Compared with normal ABE, ABBE allows direct revocation, which is important in many real-time broadcasting applications such as Pay TV. In this paper, we propose two novel ABBE schemes that have distinguishing features: the first scheme is key-policy based and has short ciphertext and constant size decryption key; and the second one is ciphertext-policy based and has constant size ciphertext and short decryption key. Both of our schemes allow access policies to be expressed using AND-gate with positive, negative, and wildcard symbols, and are proven secure under the Decision $n$-BDHE assumption without random oracles.

**Keywords:** Attribute based encryption · Broadcast encryption · AND-gate · Wildcard

## 1 Introduction

Broadcast encryption (BE), introduced by Berkovits [1] and Fiat and Naor [2], is a very useful tool for securing a broadcast channel. In a traditional BE scheme, a broadcaster can specify a subset of privileged users (out of the user universe) as the legitimate receivers of a message. Due to the practicality of broadcast encryption in real-world applications, many BE schemes have been proposed in various settings since its introduction (e.g., [3–9]).

Attribute Based Encryption (ABE), first introduced by Sahai and Waters [10], allows an encrypter to embed a fine-grained access policy into the ciphertext when encrypting a message. There are two types of ABE. In a Ciphertext Policy (CP) ABE system, each user secret key is associated with a set of user attributes, and every ciphertext is associated with an access policy. A ciphertext can be

© Springer International Publishing Switzerland 2015
G. Pernul et al. (Eds.): ESORICS 2015, Part II, LNCS 9327, pp. 252–269, 2015.
DOI: 10.1007/978-3-319-24177-7_13

decrypted by a secret key if and only if the attributes associated with the secret key satisfy the access policy in the ciphertext. Key Policy (KP) ABE is the dual form of CP-ABE, where attributes are used in the encryption process, and access policies are used in the user secret key generation. ABE systems can provide fine-grained access control of encrypted data, and has been extensively studied in recent years (e.g., [11–16]).

Since ABE gives a one-to-many relationship between a ciphertext and the corresponding valid decryption keys, it can be considered as a natural broadcast encryption where the legitimate decryptors are defined by the access policies (CP-ABE) or the attributes (KP-ABE) associated with the ciphertext. As pointed out in [11,17], ABE is useful in some broadcasting systems, such as Pay TV, which require dynamic and flexible access control. For example, the broadcasting company can specify an access policy ((Location: City A) AND (Age: >18)) when generating an encrypted data stream for a TV program, and the access policy may be changed to ((Location: City A) AND (Age: *)) (here '*' denotes the wildcard symbol, meaning "don't care") for the next program. However, one drawback of using ABE for broadcasting is that the cost of revoking a user (e.g., those fail to pay the subscription fee for Pay TV) is very high, since the secret keys of all the other non-revoked users must be updated.

Attribute Based Broadcast Encryption (ABBE) is a combination of ABE and BE. Specifically, in a CP-ABBE scheme, a user secret key $SK$ is associated with a user identity (or index) $ID$ and a set of user attributes $L$, and a ciphertext $CT$ generated by the broadcaster is associated with a user list $S$ and an access policy $W$. The ciphertext $CT$ can be decrypted using $SK$ if and only if $L$ satisfies $W$ (denoted by $L \models W$) and $ID \in S$. KP-ABBE is the dual form of CP-ABBE where the positions of the attributes and the access policy are swapped. We can see that similar to normal ABE, ABBE also allows fine-grained and flexible access control. On the other hand, ABBE can provide *direct revocation*, which is difficult or expensive to achieve in normal ABE systems. Direct revocation means the broadcaster can directly exclude some revoked users without affecting any non-revoked users, and ABBE can easily achieve this by removing the revoked users from the receiver set $S$. As highlighted in [17,18], direct revocation is important for real-time broadcasting applications such as Pay TV.

**Existing ABBE Constructions.** Several ABBE schemes [17–19] have been proposed in the literature. In [19], Lubicz and Sirvent proposed a CP-ABBE scheme which allows access policies to be expressed in disjunctive normal form, with the OR function provided by ciphertext concatenation. Attrapadung and Imai [18] proposed two KP-ABBE and two CP-ABBE schemes, which are constructed by algebraically combining some existing BE schemes (namely, the Boneh-Gentry-Waters BE scheme [5] and the Sahai-Waters BE scheme [20]) with some existing ABE schemes (namely, the KP-ABE scheme by Goyal et al. [11] and the CP-ABE scheme by Waters [14]). Junod and Karlov [17] also proposed a CP-ABBE scheme that supports boolean access policies with AND, OR and NOT gates. Junod and Karlov's scheme achieved direct revocation by simply treating each user's identity as a unique attribute in the attribute universe.

**This Work.** In order to use ABBE in real-time applications such as Pay TV, the bandwidth requirement and the decryption cost are the most important factors to be considered. Unfortunately, the ciphertext size of the existing ABBE schemes reviewed above is quite high (See Table 1). The motivation of this work is to construct efficient ABBE schemes in terms of ciphertext and key size, as well as decryption cost.

The contribution of this paper are two efficient ABBE schemes allowing access policies to be expressed using AND-gate with positive $(+)$, negative $(-)$, and wildcard $(*)$ symbols. To give a high-level picture of our constructions, we use the *positions* of different symbols (i.e., positive, negative, and wildcard) to do the matching between the access structure (containing wildcards) and the attribute list (containing no wildcard) in the ABE underlying ABBE schemes. We put the indices of all the positive, negative and wildcard attributes defined in an access structure into three sets. By using the Viète's formulas [21], based on the wildcard set, the decryptor can remove all the wildcard positions, and obtain the correct message if and only if the remaining positive and negative attributes have a perfect position match. We then incorporate the technique of Boneh-Gentry-Waters broadcast encryption scheme [5] into our ABE scheme to enable direct revocation.

Our first ABBE scheme is key policy based, and achieves constant key size and short ciphertext size. The second scheme is ciphertext policy based, achieving constant ciphertext size[1] and short key size. Both schemes require only constant number of pairing operations in decryption. A comparison between our ABBE schemes and the previous ones is given in Table 1.

**Table 1.** Performance comparison among different ABBE schemes

| CP-ABBE | Ciphertext | Private Key | Dec. (Pairing) | Access Structure | Assumption |
|---------|-----------|-------------|----------------|------------------|------------|
| [19] | $O(r)|\mathbb{G}| + 1|\mathbb{G}_T|$ | $O(t)|\mathbb{G}|$ | $O(1)$ | DNF | GDHE |
| [18] | $O(n)|\mathbb{G}| + 1|\mathbb{G}_T|$ | $O(t)|\mathbb{G}|$ | $O(t)$ | LSSS | $n$-BDHE, MEBDH |
| [17] | $O(n)|\mathbb{G}| + 1|\mathbb{G}_T|$ | $O(m+t)|\mathbb{G}|$ | $O(1)$ | DNF, CNF | GDHE |
| Ours | $O(1)|\mathbb{G}| + 1|\mathbb{G}_T|$ | $O(N)|\mathbb{G}|$ | $O(1)$ | AND Gates + wildcard | $n$-BDHE |
| KP-ABBE | Ciphertext Size | Private Key | Dec. (Pairing) | Access Structure | Assumption |
| [18] | $O(t)|\mathbb{G}| + 1|\mathbb{G}_T|$ | $O(n)|\mathbb{G}|$ | $O(t)$ | LSSS | $n$-BDHE, MEBDH |
| Ours | $O(N)|\mathbb{G}| + 1|\mathbb{G}_T|$ | $O(1)|\mathbb{G}|$ | $O(1)$ | AND Gates + wildcard | $n$-BDHE |

In the table, we compare our ABBE schemes with the previous ones in terms of ciphertext and private key size, decryption cost, access structure, and security assumption. We use "p" to denote the pairing operation, "$n$" the number of

---

[1] We should note that in our CP-ABBE scheme the wildcard positions should be attached with the ciphertext. A naive way to do this is to include an $n$-bit string where a bit "1" indicates wildcard at that position. Similar to the previous works on BE [5] and ABBE [18], this information together with the target receiver set $S$ are not counted when measuring the ciphertext size in Table 1.

attributes in an access structure, "$t$" the number of attributes in an attribute list, "$m$" and total number of attributes in the system, "$r$" the number of revoked users in the system, and "$N$" the maximum number of wildcard in an access structure in our proposed ABBE schemes.

**Paper Organisation.** In the next section, we review some primitives that will be used in our constructions, and the formal definition and security model of KP- and CP-ABBE. We then present our KP- and CP-ABBE schemes in Sects. 3 and 4, respectively. We give the formal security proofs for our proposed schemes in Sect. 5, and conclude the paper in Sect. 6.

## 2 Preliminaries

### 2.1 Bilinear Map on Prime Order Groups

Let $\mathbb{G}$ and $\mathbb{G}_T$ be two multiplicative cyclic groups of same prime order $p$, and $g$ a generator of $\mathbb{G}$. Let $e : \mathbb{G} \times \mathbb{G} \to \mathbb{G}_T$ be a bilinear map with the following properties:

1. Bilinearity: $e(u^a, v^b) = e(u^b, v^a) = e(u, v)^{ab}$ for all $u, v \in \mathbb{G}$ and $a, b \in \mathbb{Z}_p$.
2. Non-degeneracy: $e(g, g) \neq 1$.

Notice that the map $e$ is symmetric since $e(g^a, g^b) = e(g, g)^{ab} = e(g^b, g^a)$.

**Decision $n$-BDHE Assumption.** The Decision $n$-BDHE problem in $\mathbb{G}$ is defined as follows: Let $\mathbb{G}$ be a bilinear group of prime order $p$, and $g, h$ two independent generators of $\mathbb{G}$. Denote $\overrightarrow{y}_{g,\alpha,n} = (g_1, g_2, \ldots, g_n, g_{n+2}, \ldots, g_{2n}) \in \mathbb{G}^{2n-1}$ where $g_i = g^{\alpha^i}$ for some unknown $\alpha \in \mathbb{Z}_p^*$. We say that the $n$-BDHE assumption holds in $\mathbb{G}$ if for any probabilistic polynomial-time algorithm $A$

$$|\Pr[A(g, h, \overrightarrow{y}_{g,\alpha,n}, e(g_{n+1}, h)) = 1] - \Pr[A(g, h, \overrightarrow{y}_{g,\alpha,n}, T) = 1]| \leq \epsilon(k)$$

where the probability is over the random choive of $g, h$ in $\mathbb{G}$, the random choice $\alpha \in \mathbb{Z}_p^*$, the random choice $T \in \mathbb{G}_T$, and $\epsilon(k)$ is negligible in the security parameter $k$.

### 2.2 The Viète's formulas

Both of our schemes introduced in this paper are based on the Viète's formulas [21] which is reviewed below. Consider two vectors $\overrightarrow{v} = (v_1, v_2, \ldots, v_L)$ and $\overrightarrow{z} = (z_1, z_2, \ldots, z_L)$. Vector $v$ contains both alphabets and wildcards, and vector $z$ only contains alphabets. Let $J = \{j_1, \ldots, j_n\} \subset \{1, \ldots, L\}$ denote the positions of the wildcards in vector $\overrightarrow{v}$. Then the following two statements are equal:

$$v_i = z_i \lor v_i = * \text{ for } i = 1 \ldots L$$

$$\sum_{i=1, i \notin J}^{L} v_i \prod_{j \in J} (i - j) = \sum_{i=1}^{L} z_i \prod_{j \in J} (i - j). \tag{1}$$

Expand $\prod_{j \in J} (i - j) = \sum_{k=0}^{n} a_k i^k$, where $a_k$ are the coefficients dependent on $J$, then (1) becomes:

$$\sum_{i=1, i \notin J}^{L} v_i \prod_{j \in J} (i - j) = \sum_{k=0}^{n} a_k \sum_{i=1}^{L} z_i i^k \tag{2}$$

To hide the computations, we choose random group elemen $H_i$ and put $v_i, z_i$ as the exponents of group elements: $H_i^{v_i}, H_i^{z_i}$. Then (2) becomes:

$$\prod_{i=1, i \notin J}^{L} H_i^{v_i \prod_{j \in J} (i - j)} = \prod_{k=0}^{n} (\prod_{i=1}^{L} H_i^{z_i i^k})^{a_k} \tag{3}$$

Using Viète's formulas we can construct the coefficient $a_k$ in (2) by:

$$a_{n-k} = (-1)^k \sum_{1 \leq i_1 < i_2 < \ldots < i_k \leq n} j_{i_1} j_{i_2} \cdots j_{i_k}, \ 0 \leq k \leq n. \tag{4}$$

where $n = |J|$. If we have $J = \{j_1, j_2, j_3\}$, the polynomial is $(x - j_1)(x - j_2)(x - j_3)$, then:

$$a_3 = 1$$
$$a_2 = -(j_1 + j_2 + j_3)$$
$$a_1 = (j_1 j_2 + j_1 j_3 + j_2 j_3)$$
$$a_0 = -j_1 j_2 j_3.$$

### 2.3 Access Structure

Let $U = \{Att_1, Att_2, ..., Att_L\}$ be the universe of attributes in the system. Each attribute $Att_i$ has two possible values: positive and negative. Let $W = \{Att_1, Att_2, ..., Att_L\}$ be an AND-gates access policy with wildcards. A wildcard '*' means "don't care" (i.e., both positive and negative attributes are accepted). We use the notation $S \models W$ to denote that the attribute list $S$ of a user satisfies $W$.

For example, suppose $U = \{Att_1 = \text{CS}, Att_2 = \text{EE}, Att_3 = \text{Faculty}, Att_4 = \text{Student}\}$. Alice is a student in the CS department; Bob is a faculty in the EE department; Carol is a faculty holding a joint position in the EE and CS department. Their attribute lists are illustrated in Table 2. The access structure $W_1$ can be satisfied by all the CS students, while $W_2$ can be satisfied by all CS people.

### 2.4 KP-ABBE Definition

Let $U$ denote the set of all user indices, and $N$ the set of all user attributes. A key-policy attribute based broadcast encryption scheme consists of four algorithms:

– **Setup**$(1^\lambda)$: The setup algorithm takes the security parameter $1^\lambda$ as input and outputs the public parameters $PK$ and a master key $MSK$.

**Table 2.** List of attributes and policies

| Attributes | $Att_1$ | $Att_2$ | $Att_3$ | $Att_4$ |
|---|---|---|---|---|
| Description | CS | EE | Faculty | Student |
| Alice | + | − | − | + |
| Bob | − | + | + | − |
| Carol | + | + | + | − |
| $W_1$ | + | − | − | + |
| $W_2$ | + | − | * | * |

- **Encrypt**$(S, L, M, PK)$: The encryption algorithm takes as input the public parameters $PK$, a message $M$, a set of user index $S \subseteq U$ and a set of attributes $L \subseteq N$, and outputs a ciphertext $CT$.
- **Key Generation**$(ID, W, MSK, PK)$: The key generation algorithm takes as input the master key $MSK$, public parameters $PK$, a user index $ID \in U$, and an access structure $W$, and outputs a private key $SK$.
- **Decrypt**$(PK, CT, SK)$: The decryption algorithm takes as input the public parameters $PK$, a ciphertext $CT$, and a private key $SK$, and outputs a message $M$ or a special symbol '$\perp$'.

**Security Definition for KP-ABBE.** We define the Selective IND-CPA security for KP-ABBE via the following game.

- **Init:** The adversary commits to the challenge user indices $S^*$ and target attribute set $L^*$.
- **Setup:** The challenger runs the Setup algorithm and gives $PK$ to the adversary.
- **Phase 1:** The adversary queries for private keys with pairs of user index and access structure $(ID, W)$ such that $L^* \not\models W$ or $ID \notin S^*$.
- **Challenge:** The adversary submits messages $M_0, M_1$ to the challenger. The challenger flips a random coin $\beta$ and passes the ciphertext $ct^* = Encrypt(PK, M_\beta, L^*, S^*)$ to the adversary.
- **Phase 2:** Phase 1 is repeated.
- **Guess:** The adversary outputs a guess $\beta'$ of $\beta$.

**Definition 1.** *We say a KP-ABBE scheme is selective IND-CPA secure if for any probabilistic polynomial time adversary*

$$Adv_{kp}^{s\text{-}ind\text{-}cpa}(\lambda) = |\Pr[\beta' = \beta] - 1/2|$$

*is a negligible function of $\lambda$.*

## 2.5 CP-ABBE Definition

A ciphertext-policy attribute based broadcast encryption scheme consists of four algorithms:

- **Setup($1^\lambda$):** The setup algorithm takes the security parameter $1^\lambda$ as input and outputs the public parameters $PK$ and a master key $MSK$.
- **Encrypt($S, W, M, PK$):** The encryption algorithm takes as input the public parameters $PK$, a message $M$, an access structure $W$, a set of user index $S \subseteq U$, and outputs a ciphertext $CT$.
- **Key Generation($ID, L, MSK, PK$):** The key generation algorithm takes as input the master key $MSK$, public parameters $PK$, a user index $ID \in U$, and a set of attributes $L \subseteq N$, and outputs a private key $SK$.
- **Decrypt($PK$, $CT$, $SK$):** The decryption algorithm takes as input the public parameters $PK$, a ciphertext $CT$, and a private key $SK$, and outputs a message $M$ or a special symbol '$\perp$'.

**Security Definition for CP-ABBE.** We define the Selective IND-CPA security for CP-ABBE via the following game.

- **Init:** The adversary commits to the challenge user indices $S^*$ and target access structure $W^*$.
- **Setup:** The challenger runs the Setup algorithm and gives $PK$ to the adversary.
- **Phase 1:** The adversary queries for private keys with pairs of user index and a user attribute list $(ID, L)$ such that $L^* \not\models W$ or $ID \notin S^*$.
- **Challenge:** The adversary submits messages $M_0, M_1$ to the challenger. The challenger flips a random coin $\beta$ and passes the ciphertext $ct^* = Encrypt(PK, M_\beta, W^*, S^*)$ to the adversary.
- **Phase 2:** Phase 1 is repeated.
- **Guess:** The adversary outputs a guess $\beta'$ of $\beta$.

**Definition 2.** *We say a CP-ABBE scheme is selective IND-CPA secure if for any probabilistic polynomial time adversary*

$$Adv_{cp}^{s\text{-}ind\text{-}cpa}(\lambda) = |\Pr[\beta' = \beta] - 1/2|$$

*is a negligible function of $\lambda$.*

## 3   KP-ABBE Scheme

In our KP-ABBE scheme, we assume that $|U| \le n$ and $|N| \le n$ where $n$ is a system parameter. Let $N_1, N_2, N_3$ be three upper bounds for the user attributes:

- $N_1$: the maximum number of wildcard in an access structure.
- $N_2$: the maximum number of positive attribute in an attribute list $L$.
- $N_3$: the maximum number of negative attribute in an attribute list $L$.

▶ **Setup($1^\lambda$):** The setup algorithm first generates bilinear groups $\mathbb{G}, \mathbb{G}_T$ with order $p$, and selects random generators $g, h_1, \ldots, h_N \in_R \mathbb{G}$, and $\alpha \in_R \mathbb{Z}_p$. Then compute $g_i = g^{\alpha^i} \in \mathbb{G}$ for $i = 1, 2, \ldots, n, n+2, \ldots, 2n$, randomly choose $\gamma, \delta, \theta, x_1, \ldots, x_{N_1} \in_R \mathbb{Z}_p$, and set:

$$\nu = g^\gamma, V_0 = g^\delta, V_1 = g^\theta,$$

$$V_{01} = (g^\delta)^{x_1}, \ldots, V_{0N_1} = (g^\delta)^{x_{N_1}},$$

$$V_{11} = (g^\theta)^{x_1}, \ldots, V_{1N_1} = (g^\theta)^{x_{N_1}},$$

The public key and master secret key are defined as:

$$
\begin{aligned}
PK &= (g, g_1, \ldots, g_n, g_{n+2}, \ldots, g_{2n}, h_1, \ldots, h_N, \nu, V_0, V_1, V_{01}, \ldots, V_{0N_1}, \\
& \quad V_{11}, \ldots, V_{1N_1}) \\
MSK &= (\alpha, \gamma, \delta, \theta, x_1, \ldots, x_{N_1}).
\end{aligned}
$$

▶ **Encrypt**$(S, L, M, PK)$: Given a user index set $S \subseteq U$, an attribute list $L$ which contains:

- $n_2 \leq N_2$ positive attributes at positions $V = \{v_1, \ldots, v_{n_2}\}$;
- $n_3 \leq N_3$ negative attributes at positions $Z = \{z_1, \ldots, z_{n_3}\}$;

the algorithm randomly chooses $r \in \mathbb{Z}_p$ and computes:

$$C_0 = M \cdot e(g_n, g_1)^r, C_1 = g^r, C_2 = (\nu \prod_{j \in S} g_{n+1-j})^r,$$

$$
\left(
\begin{array}{l}
C_{3,0} = (V_0 \prod_{i \in V} h_i)^r \\
C_{3,1} = (V_{01} \prod_{i \in V} h_i^i)^r \\
\cdots \\
C_{3,N_1} = (V_{0N_1} \prod_{i \in V} h_i^{i^{N_1}})^r
\end{array}
\right)
,
\left(
\begin{array}{l}
C_{4,0} = (V_1 \prod_{i \in Z} h_i)^r \\
C_{4,1} = (V_{11} \prod_{i \in Z} h_i^i)^r \\
\cdots \\
C_{4,N_1} = (V_{1N_1} \prod_{i \in Z} h_i^{i^{N_1}})^r
\end{array}
\right).
$$

The ciphertext is $CT = (C_0, C_1, C_2, C_{3,0}, \ldots, C_{3,N_1}, C_{4,0}, \ldots, C_{4,N_1})$.

▶ **Key Generation**$(ID, W, MSK, PK)$: Suppose that the access structure $W$ contains:

- $n_1 \leq N_1$ wildcards at positions $J = \{w_1, \ldots, w_{n_1}\}$.
- $n_2 \leq N_2$ positive attributes at positions $V' = \{v'_1, \ldots, v'_{n_2}\}$.
- $n_3 \leq N_3$ negative attributes at positions $Z' = \{z'_1, \ldots, z'_{n_3}\}$.

Randomly choose $s_1, s_2 \in \mathbb{Z}_p$, and apply the Viete formulas on $J$ to compute $a_k(0 \leq k \leq n_1)$ and set $t = \sum_{k=0}^{n_1} x_k a_k$ where $x_0 = 1$. Then compute

$$D_1 = g^{\alpha^{ID}\gamma + \delta s_1 + \theta s_2}, D_2 = g^{\frac{s_1}{t}}, D_3 = g^{\frac{s_2}{t}},$$

$$D_4 = (\prod_{i \in V'} h_i^{\prod_{j=0}^{n_1}(i-w_j)})^{\frac{s_1}{t}}, D_5 = (\prod_{i \in Z'} h_i^{\prod_{j=0}^{n_1}(i-w_j)})^{\frac{s_2}{t}}.$$

and set the secret key $SK = (D_1, D_2, D_3, D_4, D_5)$.

▶ **Decrypt**$(PK, CT, SK)$: The decryption algorithm first applies the Viete formulas on $J$ included in the secret key to compute $a_k$ for $0 \leq k \leq n_1$, and

$$e(D_1, C_1) = e(g^{\alpha^{ID}\gamma + \delta s_1 + \theta s_2}, g^r)$$
$$= e(g^{\alpha^{ID}\gamma}, g^r)e(g,g)^{\delta s_1 r}e(g,g)^{\theta s_2 r}$$

$$e(D_4, C_1) = e((\prod_{i \in V'} h_i^{\prod_{j=0}^{n_1}(i-w_j)})^{s_1/t}, g^r)$$

$$e(D_5, C_1) = e((\prod_{i \in Z'} h_i^{\prod_{j=0}^{n_1}(i-w_j)})^{s_2/t}, g^r)$$

---

$$e(g_{ID}, C_2) = e(g^{\alpha^{ID}}, (\nu \prod_{j \in S} g_{n+1-j})^r)$$
$$= e(g^{\alpha^{ID}}, \nu)^r e(g^{\alpha^{ID}}, \prod_{j \in S} g_{n+1-j})^r$$

$$e(\prod_{j \in S, j \neq ID} g_{n+1-j+ID}, C_1) = e(\prod_{j \in S, j \neq ID} g_{n+1-j+ID}, g^r)$$

$$\Rightarrow e(g_{ID}, C_2)/e(\prod_{j \in S, j \neq ID} g_{n+1-j+ID}, C_1) = e(g^{\alpha^{ID}}, \nu)^r \cdot e(g_n, g_1)^r$$

$$e(D_2, \prod_{k=0}^{n_1} C_{3,k}^{a_k}) = e(g^{s_1/t}, V_0^{r \sum_{k=0}^{n_1} x_k a_k} \prod_{i \in V} h_i^{\sum_{k=0}^{n_1} i^k a_k r})$$
$$= e(g, V_0)^{s_1 r} e(\prod_{i \in V} h_i^{\prod_{j=0}^{n_1}(i-w_j)r}, g^{s_1/t})$$

$$e(D_3, \prod_{k=0}^{n_1} C_{4,k}^{a_k}) = e(g^{s_2/t}, V_1^{r \sum_{k=0}^{n_1} x_k a_k} \prod_{i \in Z} h_i^{\sum_{k=0}^{n_1} i^k a_k r})$$
$$= e(g, V_1)^{s_2 r} e(\prod_{i \in Z} h_i^{\prod_{j=0}^{n_1}(i-w_j)r}, g^{s_2/t})$$

If $L \models W$ and $ID \in S$, then we have:

$$M = \frac{C_0 \cdot e(g^{\alpha^{ID}\gamma}, g^r)e(g,g)^{\delta s_1 r}e(g,g)^{\theta s_2 r}e((\prod_{i \in V'} h_i^{\prod_{j=0}^{n_1}(i-w_j)})^{s_1/t}, g^r)e((\prod_{i \in Z'} h_i^{\prod_{j=0}^{n_1}(i-w_j)})^{s_2/t}, g^r)}{e(g^{\alpha^{ID}}, \nu)^r \cdot e(g_n, g_1)^r e(g, V_0)^{s_1 r} e(\prod_{i \in V} h_i^{\prod_{j=0}^{n_1}(i-w_j)r}, g^{s_1/t})e(g, V_1)^{s_2 r} e(\prod_{i \in Z} h_i^{\prod_{j=0}^{n_1}(i-w_j)r}, g^{s_2/t})}.$$

## 4    CP-ABBE Scheme

Our CP-ABBE scheme is the dual-form of our KP-ABBE scheme.

▶ **Setup**$(1^\lambda)$: The setup algorithm first generates bilinear groups $\mathbb{G}, \mathbb{G}_T$ with order $p$, and selects random generators $g, h_1, \ldots, h_N \in_R \mathbb{G}$, and $\alpha \in_R \mathbb{Z}_p$.

Then compute $g_i = g^{\alpha^i} \in \mathbb{G}$ for $i = 1, 2, \ldots, n, n+2, \ldots, 2n$, randomly choose $\gamma, \delta, \theta \in_R \mathbb{Z}_p$, and set:

$$\nu = g^\gamma, V_0 = g^\delta, V_1 = g^\theta.$$

The public key and master secret key are defined as:

$$PK = (g, g_1, \ldots, g_n, g_{n+2}, \ldots, g_{2n}, h_1, \ldots, h_N, \nu, V_0, V_1)$$
$$MSK = (\alpha, \gamma, \delta, \theta).$$

▶ **Encrypt**$(S, W, M, PK)$: Given a user index set $S \subseteq U$, and an access structure $W$ containing:
- $n_1 \leq N_1$ wildcards at positions $J = \{w_1, \ldots, w_{n_1}\}$;
- $n_2 \leq N_2$ positive attributes at positions $V = \{v_1, \ldots, v_{n_2}\}$;
- $n_3 \leq N_3$ negative attributes at positions $Z = \{z_1, \ldots, z_{n_3}\}$;
the algorithm randomly chooses $r \in \mathbb{Z}_p$ and computes:

$$C_0 = M \cdot e(g_n, g_1)^r, C_1 = g^r, C_2 = (\nu \prod_{j \in S} g_{n+1-j})^r,$$

$$C_3 = (V_0 \prod_{i \in V} h_i^{\prod\limits_{j=0}^{n_1}(i-w_j)})^r, C_4 = (V_1 \prod_{i \in Z} h_i^{\prod\limits_{j=0}^{n_1}(i-w_j)})^r.$$

The ciphertext is $CT = (J, C_0, C_1, C_2, C_3, C_4)$.

▶ **Key Generation**$(ID, L, MSK, PK)$: Given a user identity $ID$ and an attribute list $L$ which contains:
- $n_2 \leq N_2$ positive attributes at positions $V' = \{v'_1, \ldots, v'_{n_2}\}$;
- $n_3 \leq N_3$ negative attributes at positions $Z' = \{z'_1, \ldots, z'_{n_3}\}$;
randomly choose $s_1, s_2 \in \mathbb{Z}_p$ and compute:

$$D_1 = g^{\alpha^{ID}\gamma + \delta s_1 + \theta s_2}, D_2 = g^{s_1}, D_3 = g^{s_2}$$

$$\begin{pmatrix} D_{4,0} = (\prod\limits_{i \in V'} h_i)^{s_1} \\ D_{4,1} = (\prod\limits_{i \in V'} h_i^i)^{s_1} \\ \ldots \\ D_{4,N_1} = (\prod\limits_{i \in V'} h_i^{i^{N_1}})^{s_1} \end{pmatrix}, \begin{pmatrix} D_{5,0} = (\prod\limits_{i \in Z'} h_i)^{s_2} \\ D_{5,1} = (\prod\limits_{i \in Z'} h_i^i)^{s_2} \\ \ldots \\ D_{5,N_1} = (\prod\limits_{i \in Z'} h_i^{i^{N_1}})^{s_2} \end{pmatrix},$$

and set the secret key $SK = (D_1, D_2, D_3, D_{4,0}, \ldots, D_{4,N_1}, D_{5,0}, \ldots, D_{5,N_1})$.

▶ **Decrypt**$(PK, CT, SK)$: The decryption algorithm first applies the Viete formulas on $J$ included in the ciphertext to compute $a_k$ for $0 \leq k \leq n_1$:

$$e(D_1, C_1) = e(g^{\alpha^{ID}\gamma + \delta s_1 + \theta s_2}, g^r)$$
$$= e(g^{\alpha^{ID}\gamma}, g^r)e(g,g)^{\delta s_1 r}e(g,g)^{\theta s_2 r}$$

$$e((\prod_{k=0}^{n_1} D_{4,k}^{a_k}), C_1) = e(\prod_{i \in V'} h_i^{\sum_{k=0}^{n_1} i^k a_k s_1}, g^r)$$
$$= e(\prod_{i \in V'} h_i^{\prod_{j=0}^{n_1}(i-w_j)s_1}, g^r)$$

$$e((\prod_{k=0}^{n_1} D_{5,k}^{a_k}), C_1) = e(\prod_{i \in Z'} h_i^{\sum_{k=0}^{n_1} i^k a_k s_2}, g^r)$$
$$= e(\prod_{i \in Z'} h_i^{\prod_{j=0}^{n_1}(i-w_j)s_2}, g^r)$$

---

$$e(g_{ID}, C_2) = e(g^{\alpha^{ID}}, (\nu \prod_{j \in S} g_{n+1-j})^r)$$
$$= e(g^{\alpha^{ID}}, \nu)^r e(g^{\alpha^{ID}}, \prod_{j \in S} g_{n+1-j})^r$$

$$e(\prod_{j \in S, j \neq ID} g_{n+1-j+ID}, C_1) = e(\prod_{j \in S, j \neq ID} g_{n+1-j+ID}, g^r)$$

$$\Rightarrow e(g_{ID}, C_2)/e(\prod_{j \in S, j \neq ID} g_{n+1-j+ID}, C_1) = e(g^{\alpha^{ID}}, \nu)^r \cdot e(g_n, g_1)^r$$

$$e(D_2, C_3) = e(g^{s_1}, (V_0 \prod_{i \in V} h_i^{\prod_{j=0}^{n_1}(i-w_j)})^r)$$
$$= e(g^{s_1}, V_0^r)e(g^{s_1}, \prod_{i \in V} h_i^{\prod_{j=0}^{n_1}(i-w_j)})^r$$

$$e(D_3, C_4) = e(g^{s_2}, (V_1 \prod_{i \in Z} h_i^{\prod_{j=0}^{n_1}(i-w_j)})^r)$$
$$= e(g^{s_2}, V_1^r)e(g^{s_2}, \prod_{i \in Z} h_i^{\prod_{j=0}^{n_1}(i-w_j)})^r$$

If $L \models W$ and $ID \in S$, then we have

$$M = \frac{C_0 \cdot e(g^{\alpha^{ID}\gamma}, g^r)e(g,g)^{\delta s_1 r}e(g,g)^{\theta s_2 r} \cdot e(\prod_{i \in V'} h_i^{\prod_{j=0}^{n_1}(i-w_j)s_1}, g^r)e(\prod_{i \in Z'} h_i^{\prod_{j=0}^{n_1}(i-w_j)s_2}, g^r)}{e(g^{\alpha^{ID}}, \nu)^r \cdot e(g_n, g_1)^r e(g^{s_1}, V_0^r)e(g^{s_1}, \prod_{i \in V} h_i^{\prod_{j=0}^{n_1}(i-w_j)})^r e(g^{s_2}, V_1^r)e(g^{s_2}, \prod_{i \in Z} h_i^{\prod_{j=0}^{n_1}(i-w_j)})^r}.$$

## 5   Security Analysis

We prove that the proposed KP-ABBE and CP-ABBE schemes are selectively secure under the Decision $n$-BDHE assumption.

**Theorem 1.** *Assume that the Decision n-BDHE assumption holds, then no polynomial-time adversary against our KP-ABBE scheme can have a non-negligible advantage over random guess in the Selective IND-CPA security game.*

**Proof:** Suppose that there exists an adversary $\mathcal{A}$ which can attack our scheme with non-negligible advantage $\epsilon$, we construct another algorithm $\mathcal{B}$ which uses $\mathcal{A}$ to solve the Decision $n$-BDHE problem. On input $(g, h, \overrightarrow{y}_{g,\alpha,n} = (g_1, g_2, \ldots, g_n, g_{n+2}, \ldots, g_{2n}), T)$, where $g_i = g^{\alpha^i}$ and for some unknown $\alpha \in \mathbb{Z}_p^*$, the goal of $\mathcal{B}$ is to determine whether $T = e(g_{n+1}, h)$ or a random element of $\mathbb{G}_T$.

**Init:** $\mathcal{A}$ gives $\mathcal{B}$ the challenge user indices $S^*$ and the target attribute set $L^*$ with $n_2 \leq N_2$ positive attributes which occur at positions $V^* = \{v_1^*, \ldots, v_{n_2}^*\}$, and $n_3 \leq N_3$ negative attributes which occur at positions $Z^* = \{z_1^*, \ldots, z_{n_3}^*\}$ at the beginning of the game.

**Setup:** $\mathcal{B}$ chooses $d, v_0, v_1, u_1, \ldots, u_n, x_1, \ldots, x_{N_1} \in \mathbb{Z}_p$ and generates:

$$\nu = g^d\left(\prod_{j \in S^*} g_{n+1-j}^{-1}\right) = g^{d - \sum_{j \in S^*} \alpha^{n+1-j}} = g^\gamma,$$

$$V_{0j} = (g^{v_0})^{x_j} \prod_{i \in V^*} g^{\alpha^{n+1-i}i^j} = (g^{v_0})^{x_j} g^{\sum_{i \in V^*} \alpha^{n+1-i}i^j}, \text{ for } j = 0, \ldots, N_1$$

$$V_{1j} = (g^{v_1})^{x_j} \prod_{i \in Z^*} g^{\alpha^{n+1-i}i^j} = (g^{v_1})^{x_j} g^{\sum_{i \in Z^*} \alpha^{n+1-i}i^j}, \text{ for } j = 0, \ldots, N_1$$

where $x_0 = 1$, and $h_i = g^{u_i - \alpha^{n+1-i}}$, then $\mathcal{B}$ sets public key as:

$$PK = (g, g_1, \ldots, g_n, g_{n+2}, \ldots, g_{2n}, h_1, \ldots, h_N, \nu, V_0, V_1, V_{01}, \ldots, V_{0N_1}, V_{11}, \ldots, V_{1N_1}).$$

**Phase 1:** $\mathcal{A}$ submits a pair of user index and access structure $(ID, W)$ in a secret key query, which satisfies $L^* \not\models W$ or $ID \notin S^*$. Assume $W$ consists of $n_1 \leq N_1$ wildcards which occur at positions $J = \{w_1, \ldots, w_{n_1}\}$, $n_2 \leq N_2$ positive attributes which occur at positions $V = \{v_1, \ldots, v_{n_2}\}$, and $n_3 \leq N_3$ negative attributes which occur at positions $Z = \{z_1, \ldots, z_{n_3}\}$. $\mathcal{B}$ applies the Viete formulas on $J = \{j_1, \ldots, j_{n_1}\}$ to get $a_k$ and set $t = \sum_{k=0}^{n_1} x_k a_k$. Consider the following two cases in Phase 1:

– **Case 1:** $ID \notin S^*$. $\mathcal{B}$ first selects a random number $s_1, s_2 \in \mathbb{Z}_p$, then computes:

$$D_1 = g_{ID}^d \prod_{j \in S^*} (g_{n+1-j+ID})^{-1} g^{v_0 s_1} \prod_{i \in V^*} (g_{n+1-i})^{s_1} g^{v_1 s_2} \prod_{i \in Z^*} (g_{n+1-i})^{s_2}$$

$$= g^{\alpha^{ID}(d - \sum_{j \in S^*} \alpha^{n+1-j})} (g^{v_0 + \sum_{i \in V^*} \alpha^{n+1-i}})^{s_1} (g^{v_1 + \sum_{i \in Z^*} \alpha^{n+1-i}})^{s_2}$$

$$= g^{\alpha^{ID}\gamma + \delta s_1 + \theta s_2}.$$

$$D_2 = g^{\frac{s_1}{t}},$$
$$D_3 = g^{\frac{s_2}{t}},$$

$$D_4 = (\prod_{i \in V} (g^{u_i - \alpha^{n+1-i}})^{\prod_{j \in J}(i - w_j)})^{\frac{s_1}{t}} = (\prod_{i \in V} h_i^{\prod_{j \in J}(i - w_j)})^{\frac{s_1}{t}},$$

$$D_5 = (\prod_{i \in Z} (g^{u_i - \alpha^{n+1-i}})^{\prod_{j \in J}(i - w_j)})^{\frac{s_2}{t}} = (\prod_{i \in Z} h_i^{\prod_{j \in J}(i - w_j)})^{\frac{s_2}{t}}.$$

- **Case 2:** $ID \in S^*$. In this case, due to the constraint $L^* \not\models W$, $W$ has at least one position $i^*$ which has a different attribute value from $L^*$, which means $\{V \cup Z^*\} \neq \emptyset$ or $\{Z \cup V^*\} \neq \emptyset$.

  ⋄ If there exists an $i^* \in \{V \cup Z^*\} \neq \emptyset$:

  $\mathcal{B}$ selects two random numbers $s_1', s_2' \in \mathbb{Z}_p$ and implicitly sets $s_1, s_2$ as:

$$\begin{cases} s_1 = s_1' \\ s_2 = s_2' + \alpha^{i^*} \end{cases} \text{ by setting } D_2 = g^{s_1'} = g^{s_1}, D_3 = g^{s_2' + \alpha^{i^*}} = g^{s_2}. \text{ Then } \mathcal{B}$$

  can compute $D_1, D_4, D_5$ as follows:

$$D_1 = g^{\alpha^{ID}\gamma + \delta s_1 + \theta s_2}.$$
$$= g^{\alpha^{ID}(d - \sum_{j \in S^*} \alpha^{n+1-j})} g^{v_0 s_1} \prod_{i \in V^*} (g_{n+1-i})^{s_1} g^{v_1 s_2} \prod_{i \in Z^*} (g_{n+1-i})^{s_2}$$
$$= g_{ID}^d \prod_{j \in S^*} (g_{n+1-j+ID})^{-1}$$
$$(g^{v_0})^{s_1'} (g^{\sum_{i \in V^*} \alpha^{n+1-i}})^{s_1'} (g^{v_1})^{s_2' + \alpha^{i^*}} (g^{\sum_{i \in Z^*} \alpha^{n+1-i}})^{s_2' + \alpha^{i^*}}$$
$$= g_{ID}^d \prod_{j \in S^*, j \neq ID} (g_{n+1-j+ID})^{-1} \cdot g^{-\alpha^{n+1}}$$
$$(g^{v_0})^{s_1'} (g^{\sum_{i \in V^*} \alpha^{n+1-i}})^{s_1'}$$
$$(g^{v_1})^{s_2' + \alpha^{i^*}} (g^{\sum_{i \in Z^*} \alpha^{n+1-i}})^{s_2'} (g^{\sum_{i \in Z^*, i \neq i^*} \alpha^{n+1-i+i^*}}) g^{\alpha^{n+1}}$$
$$= g_{ID}^d \prod_{j \in S^*, j \neq ID} (g_{n+1-j+ID})^{-1} (g^{v_0})^{s_1'} (g^{\sum_{i \in V^*} \alpha^{n+1-i}})^{s_1'}$$
$$(g^{v_1})^{s_2' + \alpha^{i^*}} (g^{\sum_{i \in Z^*} \alpha^{n+1-i}})^{s_2'} (g^{\sum_{i \in Z^*, i \neq i^*} \alpha^{n+1-i+i^*}}),$$

$$D_4 = (\prod_{i \in V} (g^{u_i - \alpha^{n+1-i}})^{\prod_{j \in J}(i - w_j)})^{s_1'/t} = (\prod_{i \in V} h_i^{\prod_{j \in J}(i - w_j)})^{s_1'/t},$$

$$D_5 = (\prod_{i \in Z} (g^{u_i - \alpha^{n+1-i}})^{\prod_{j \in J}(i - w_j)})^{(s_2' + \alpha^{i^*})/t} = (\prod_{i \in Z} h_i^{\prod_{j \in J}(i - w_j)})^{s_2'/t}.$$

  We should note that since $i^* \notin Z$, the item $g^{\alpha^{n+1}}$ will not occur in the calculation of $D_5$.

  ⋄ If there exists an $i^* \in \{Z \cup V^*\} \neq \emptyset$:

  the simulation can be performed in a similar way by choosing two random numbers $s_1', s_2' \in \mathbb{Z}_p$ and implicitly setting $s_1, s_2$ as: $\begin{cases} s_1 = s_1' + \alpha^{i^*} \\ s_2 = s_2' \end{cases}$. We omit the details here.

$\mathcal{B}$ returns to $\mathcal{A}$ the secret key $SK = (D_1, D_2, D_3, D_4, D_5)$.

**Challenge:** The adversary gives two messages $M_0$ and $M_1$ to $\mathcal{B}$. Then $\mathcal{B}$ flips a coin $b$ and generate the challenge ciphertext by setting $C_1 = g^\tau = h$ for some unknown $\tau$ and

$$
\begin{aligned}
C_2 &= h^d = (g^d)^\tau \\
&= (g^d \prod_{j \in S^*} (g_{n+1-j})^{-1} \prod_{j \in S^*} (g_{n+1-j}))^\tau = (\nu \prod_{j \in S^*} (g_{n+1-j}))^\tau \\
C_{3,k} &= h^{v_0 x_k + \sum\limits_{i \in V^*} u_i i^k} = (g^{v_0 x_k + \sum\limits_{i \in V^*} u_i i^k})^\tau, \\
C_{4,k} &= h^{v_1 x_k + \sum\limits_{i \in Z^*} u_i i^k} = (g^{v_1 x_k + \sum\limits_{i \in Z^*} u_i i^k})^\tau.
\end{aligned}
$$

$\mathcal{B}$ then sends the following challenge ciphertext to $\mathcal{A}$

$$
CT^* = (M_b T, C_1, C_2, \{C_{3,k}\}, \{C_{4,k}\}).
$$

**Phase II:** Same as Phase I.

**Guess:** $\mathcal{A}$ output $b' \in \{0, 1\}$. If $b' = b$ then $\mathcal{B}$ outputs 1, otherwise outputs 0.

**Analysis:** If $T = e(g_{n+1}, h)$, then the simulation is the same as in the real game. Hence, $\mathcal{A}$ will have the probability $\frac{1}{2} + \epsilon$ to guess $b$ correctly. If $T$ is a random element of $\mathbb{G}_T$, then $\mathcal{A}$ will have probability $\frac{1}{2}$ to guess $b$ correctly. Therefore, $\mathcal{B}$ can solve the Decision $n$-BDHE assumption also with advantage $\epsilon$.  □

**Theorem 2.** *Assume that the Decision $n$-BDHE assumption holds, then no polynomial-time adversary against our CP-ABBE scheme can have a non-negligible advantage over random guess in the Selective IND-CPA security game.*

**Proof:** Suppose that there exists an adversary $\mathcal{A}$ which can attack our scheme with non-negligible advantage $\epsilon$, we construct another algorithm $\mathcal{B}$ which uses $\mathcal{A}$ to solve the Decision $n$-BDHE problem. On input $(g, h, \overrightarrow{y}_{g,\alpha,n} = (g_1, g_2, \ldots, g_n, g_{n+2}, \ldots, g_{2n}), T)$, where $g_i = g^{\alpha^i}$ and for some unknown $\alpha \in \mathbb{Z}_p^*$, the goal of $\mathcal{B}$ is to determine whether $T = e(g_{n+1}, h)$ or a random element of $\mathbb{G}_T$.

**Init:** $\mathcal{A}$ gives $\mathcal{B}$ the challenge user indexes $S^*$ and the challenge access structure $W^*$ with $n_1 \le N_1$ wildcards which occur at positions $J^* = \{w_1^*, \ldots, w_{n_1}^*\}$, $n_2 \le N_2$ positive attributes which occur at positions $V^* = \{v_1^*, \ldots, v_{n_2}^*\}$, $n_3 \le N_3$ negative attributes which occur at positions $Z^* = \{z_1^*, \ldots, z_{n_3}^*\}$ at the beginning of the game.

**Setup:** $\mathcal{B}$ chooses $d, v_0, v_1, u_1, \ldots, u_n \in \mathbb{Z}_p$ and generates:

$$
\nu = g^d (\prod_{j \in S^*} g_{n+1-j}^{-1}) = g^{d - \sum_{j \in S^*} \alpha^{n+1-j}} = g^\gamma,
$$

$$
V_0 = g^{v_0} \prod_{i \in V^*} g^{\alpha^{n+1-i} \prod_{j \in J^*}(i - w_j^*)} = g^{v_0 + \sum_{i \in V^*} \alpha^{n+1-i} \prod_{j \in J^*}(i - w_j^*)} = g^\delta,
$$

$$
V_1 = g^{v_1} \prod_{i \in Z^*} g^{\alpha^{n+1-i} \prod_{j \in J^*}(i - w_j^*)} = g^{v_1 + \sum_{i \in Z^*} \alpha^{n+1-i} \prod_{j \in J^*}(i - w_j^*)} = g^\theta,
$$

and $h_i = g^{u_i - \alpha^{n+1-i}}$, then $\mathcal{B}$ sets public key as:

$$PK = (g, g_1, \ldots, g_n, g_{n+2}, \ldots, g_{2n}, h_1, \ldots, h_N, \nu, V_0, V_1).$$

**Phase 1:** $\mathcal{A}$ submits $(ID, L)$ in a secret key query, where $L^* \not\models W$ "or" $ID \notin S^*$. Suppose the attribute set $L$ contains $n_2 \leq N_2$ positive attributes which occur at positions $V = \{v_1, \ldots, v_{n_2}\}$, and $n_3 \leq N_3$ negative attributes which occur at positions $Z = \{z_1, \ldots, z_{n_3}\}$. We consider two cases in Phase 1:

- **Case 1:** $ID \notin S^*$. $\mathcal{B}$ first selects random numbers $s_1, s_2 \in \mathbb{Z}_p$ and computes:

$$
\begin{aligned}
D_1 &= g_{ID}^d \prod_{j \in S^*} (g_{n+1-j+ID})^{-1} g^{v_0 s_1} \prod_{i \in V^*} (g_{n+1-i}^{\prod_{j \in J^*}(i-w_j^*)})^{s_1} g^{v_1 s_2} \prod_{i \in Z^*} (g_{n+1-i}^{\prod_{j \in J^*}(i-w_j^*)})^{s_2} \\
&= g^{\alpha^{ID}(d - \sum_{j \in S^*} \alpha^{n+1-j})} \\
&\quad (g^{v_0 + \sum_{i \in V^*} \alpha^{n+1-i} \prod_{j \in J^*}(i-w_j^*)})^{s_1} (g^{v_1 + \sum_{i \in Z^*} \alpha^{n+1-i} \prod_{j \in J^*}(i-w_j^*)})^{s_2} \\
&= g^{\alpha^{ID} \gamma + \delta s_1 + \theta s_2}, \\
D_2 &= g^{s_1}, \\
D_3 &= g^{s_2}, \\
D_{4,k} &= \prod_{i \in V} (g^{u_i - \alpha^{n+1-i}})^{i^k s_1} = \prod_{i \in V} h_i^{i^k s_1}, \\
D_{5,k} &= \prod_{i \in Z} (g^{u_i - \alpha^{n+1-i}})^{i^k s_2} = \prod_{i \in Z} h_i^{i^k s_2}.
\end{aligned}
$$

- **Case 2:** $ID \in S^*$. In this case, due to the constraint $L^* \not\models W$, $L$ has at least one position $i^*$ which has a different attribute value from $W^*$, which means $\{V \cup Z^*\} \neq \emptyset$ or $\{Z \cup V^*\} \neq \emptyset$.
  ◇ If there exists $i^* \in \{V \cup Z^*\} \neq \emptyset$:
  $\mathcal{B}$ selects two random numbers $s_1', s_2' \in \mathbb{Z}_p$ and implicitly sets $s_1, s_2$ as:

$$
\begin{cases}
s_1 = s_1' \\
s_2 = s_2' + \dfrac{\alpha^{i^*}}{\prod_{j \in J^*}(i^* - w_j^*)}
\end{cases}
\quad \text{by setting } D_2 = g^{s_1'} = g^{s_1}, D_3 =
$$

$$
g^{s_2' + \frac{\alpha^{i^*}}{\prod_{j \in J^*}(i^* - w_j^*)}} = g^{s_2}. \text{ Then } \mathcal{B} \text{ can compute } D_1, D_{4,k}, D_{5,k} \text{ as follows:}
$$

$$
\begin{aligned}
D_1 &= g^{\alpha^{ID} \gamma + \delta s_1 + \theta s_2}. \\
&= g^{\alpha^{ID}(d - \sum_{j \in S^*} \alpha^{n+1-j})} g^{v_0 s_1} \prod_{i \in V^*} (g_{n+1-i}^{\prod_{j \in J^*}(i-w_j^*)})^{s_1} g^{v_1 s_2} \prod_{i \in Z^*} (g_{n+1-i}^{\prod_{j \in J^*}(i-w_j^*)})^{s_2} \\
&= g_{ID}^d \prod_{j \in S^*} (g_{n+1-j+ID})^{-1} (g^{v_0})^{s_1'} (g^{\sum_{i \in V^*} \alpha^{n+1-i} \prod_{j \in J^*}(i-w_j^*)})^{s_1'} \\
&\quad (g^{v_1})^{s_2' + \frac{\alpha^{i^*}}{\prod_{j \in J^*}(i^* - w_j^*)}} (g^{\sum_{i \in Z^*} \alpha^{n+1-i} \prod_{j \in J^*}(i-w_j^*)})^{s_2' + \frac{\alpha^{i^*}}{\prod_{j \in J^*}(i^* - w_j^*)}} \\
&= g_{ID}^d \prod_{j \in S^*, j \neq ID} (g_{n+1-j+ID})^{-1} g^{-\alpha^{n+1}} \\
&\quad (g^{v_0})^{s_1'} (g^{\sum_{i \in V^*} \alpha^{n+1-i} \prod_{j \in J^*}(i-w_j^*)})^{s_1'} \\
&\quad (g^{v_1})^{s_2' + \frac{\alpha^{i^*}}{\prod_{j \in J^*}(i^* - w_j^*)}} (g^{\sum_{i \in Z^*} \alpha^{n+1-i} \prod_{j \in J^*}(i-w_j^*)})^{s_2'}
\end{aligned}
$$

$$(g^{\frac{\sum_{i\in Z^*,i\neq i^*} \alpha^{n+1-i+i^*} \prod_{j\in J^*}(i-w_j^*)}{\prod_{j\in J^*}(i^*-w_j^*)}})g^{\alpha^{n+1}}$$

$$= g_{ID}^d \prod_{j\in S^*,j\neq ID}(g_{n+1-j+ID})^{-1}$$

$$(g^{v_0})^{s_1'}(g^{\sum_{i\in V^*}\alpha^{n+1-i}\prod_{j\in J^*}(i-w_j^*)})^{s_1'}$$

$$(g^{v_1})^{s_2'+\frac{\alpha^{i^*}}{\prod_{j\in J^*}(i^*-w_j^*)}}(g^{\sum_{i\in Z^*}\alpha^{n+1-i}\prod_{j\in J^*}(i-w_j^*)})^{s_2'}$$

$$(g^{\frac{\sum_{i\in Z^*,i\neq i^*}\alpha^{n+1-i+i^*}\prod_{j\in J^*}(i-w_j^*)}{\prod_{j\in J^*}(i^*-w_j^*)}})$$

$$D_{4,k} = \prod_{i\in V}(g^{u_i-\alpha^{n+1-i}})^{i^k s_1'} = \prod_{i\in V}h_i^{i^k s_1}$$

$$D_{5,k} = \prod_{i\in Z}(g^{u_i-\alpha^{n+1-i}})^{i^k(s_2'+\frac{\alpha^{i^*}}{\prod_{j\in J^*}(i^*-w_j^*)})} = \prod_{i\in Z}h_i^{i^k s_2}$$

◇ If there exists an $i^* \in \{Z\cup V^*\} \neq \emptyset$:
the simulation can be performed in a similar way by choosing two random numbers

$s_1', s_2' \in \mathbb{Z}_p$ and implicitly setting $s_1, s_2$ as: $\begin{cases} s_1 = s_1' + \dfrac{\alpha^{i^*}}{\prod_{j\in J^*}(i^*-w_j^*)} \\ s_2 = s_2' \end{cases}$ . We omit the

details here.

$\mathcal{B}$ returns to $\mathcal{A}$ the secret key $SK = (D_1, D_2, D_3, \{D_{4,k}\}, \{D_{5,k}\})$.

**Challenge:** The adversary gives two messages $M_0$ and $M_1$ to $\mathcal{B}$. Then $\mathcal{B}$ flips a coin $b$ and generates the challenge ciphertext by setting $C_1 = g^\tau = h$ for some unknown $\tau$ and

$$C_2 = h^d = (g^d)^\tau$$
$$= (g^d \prod_{j\in S^*}(g_{n+1-j})^{-1}\prod_{j\in S^*}(g_{n+1-j}))^\tau$$
$$= (\nu \prod_{j\in S^*}(g_{n+1-j}))^\tau$$

$$C_3 = h^{v_0+\sum_{i\in V^*}u_i\prod_{j\in J^*}(i-w_j^*)} = (g^{v_0+\sum_{i\in V^*}u_i\prod_{j\in J^*}(i-w_j^*)})^\tau$$
$$C_4 = h^{v_1+\sum_{i\in Z^*}u_i\prod_{j\in J^*}(i-w_j^*)} = (g^{v_1+\sum_{i\in Z^*}u_i\prod_{j\in J^*}(i-w_j^*)})^\tau$$

$\mathcal{B}$ sends the following challenge ciphertext to $\mathcal{A}$:

$$CT^* = (M_b T, C_1, C_2, C_3, C_4).$$

**Phase II:** Same as Phase I.

**Guess:** $\mathcal{A}$ outputs $b' \in \{0,1\}$. If $b' = b$ then $\mathcal{B}$ outputs 1, otherwise outputs 0.

**Analysis:** If $T = e(g_{n+1}, h)$, then the simulation is the same as in the real game. Hence, $\mathcal{A}$ will have the probability $\frac{1}{2} + \epsilon$ to guess $b$ correctly. If $T$ is a random element of $\mathbb{G}_T$, then $\mathcal{A}$ will have probability $\frac{1}{2}$ to guess $b$ correctly. Therefore, $\mathcal{B}$ can solve the Decision $n$-BDHE assumption also with advantage $\epsilon$. □

## 6   Conclusion

We proposed two efficient Attribute Based Broadcast Encryption (ABBE) schemes allowing access policies to be expressed using AND-gate with positive, negative, and wildcard symbols. Our first key policy ABBE scheme achieves constant secret key size, while the second ciphertext policy ABBE scheme achieves constant ciphertext size, and both schemes require only constant number of pairing operations in decryption. We also proved the security of our schemes under the Decision $n$-BDHE assumption. One open problem is to construct an ABBE scheme that has constant ciphertext and secret key, and we leave it as our future work.

## References

1. Berkovits, S.: How to broadcast a secret. In: Davies, D.W. (ed.) EUROCRYPT 1991. LNCS, vol. 547, pp. 535–541. Springer, Heidelberg (1991)
2. Fiat, A., Naor, M.: Broadcast encryption. In: Stinson, D.R. (ed.) CRYPTO 1993. LNCS, vol. 773, pp. 480–491. Springer, Heidelberg (1994)
3. Naor, D., Naor, M., Lotspiech, J.: Revocation and tracing schemes for stateless receivers. In: Kilian, J. (ed.) CRYPTO 2001. LNCS, vol. 2139, p. 41. Springer, Heidelberg (2001)
4. Dodis, Y., Fazio, N.: Public key trace and revoke scheme secure against adaptive chosen ciphertext attack. In: Desmedt, Y.G. (ed.) PKC 2003. LNCS, vol. 2567, pp. 100–115. Springer, Heidelberg (2002)
5. Boneh, D., Gentry, C., Waters, B.: Collusion resistant broadcast encryption with short ciphertexts and private keys. In: Shoup, V. (ed.) CRYPTO 2005. LNCS, vol. 3621, pp. 258–275. Springer, Heidelberg (2005)
6. Boneh, D., Waters, B.: A fully collusion resistant broadcast, trace, and revoke system. In: ACM CCS, pp. 211–220 (2006)
7. Delerablée, C., Paillier, P., Pointcheval, D.: Fully collusion secure dynamic broadcast encryption with constant-size ciphertexts or decryption keys. In: Takagi, T., Okamoto, T., Okamoto, E., Okamoto, T. (eds.) Pairing 2007. LNCS, vol. 4575, pp. 39–59. Springer, Heidelberg (2007)
8. Gentry, C., Waters, B.: Adaptive security in broadcast encryption systems (with short ciphertexts). In: Joux, A. (ed.) EUROCRYPT 2009. LNCS, vol. 5479, pp. 171–188. Springer, Heidelberg (2009)
9. Phan, D.-H., Pointcheval, D., Shahandashti, S.F., Strefler, M.: Adaptive CCA broadcast encryption with constant-size secret keys and ciphertexts. In: Susilo, W., Mu, Y., Seberry, J. (eds.) ACISP 2012. LNCS, vol. 7372, pp. 308–321. Springer, Heidelberg (2012)
10. Sahai, A., Waters, B.: Fuzzy identity-based encryption. In: Cramer, R. (ed.) EUROCRYPT 2005. LNCS, vol. 3494, pp. 457–473. Springer, Heidelberg (2005)
11. Goyal, V., Pandey, O., Sahai, A., Waters, B.: Attribute-based encryption for fine-grained access control of encrypted data. In: ACM CCS, pp. 89–98 (2006)
12. Bethencourt, J., Sahai, A., Waters, B.: Ciphertext-policy attribute-based encryption. In: IEEE S&P, pp. 321–334 (2007)
13. Cheung, L., Newport, C.: Provably secure ciphertext policy ABE. In: ACM CCS, pp. 456–465 (2007)

14. Waters, B.: Ciphertext-policy attribute-based encryption: an expressive, efficient, and provably secure realization. In: Catalano, D., Fazio, N., Gennaro, R., Nicolosi, A. (eds.) PKC 2011. LNCS, vol. 6571, pp. 53–70. Springer, Heidelberg (2011)

15. Attrapadung, N., Libert, B., de Panafieu, E.: Expressive key-policy attribute-based encryption with constant-size ciphertexts. In: Catalano, D., Fazio, N., Gennaro, R., Nicolosi, A. (eds.) PKC 2011. LNCS, vol. 6571, pp. 90–108. Springer, Heidelberg (2011)

16. Lewko, A., Waters, B.: New proof methods for attribute-based encryption: achieving full security through selective techniques. In: Safavi-Naini, R., Canetti, R. (eds.) CRYPTO 2012. LNCS, vol. 7417, pp. 180–198. Springer, Heidelberg (2012)

17. Junod, P., Karlov, A.: An efficient public-key attribute-based broadcast encryption scheme allowing arbitrary access policies. In: ACM Workshop on Digital Rights Management, pp. 13–24 (2010)

18. Attrapadung, N., Imai, H.: Conjunctive broadcast and attribute-based encryption. In: Shacham, H., Waters, B. (eds.) Pairing 2009. LNCS, vol. 5671, pp. 248–265. Springer, Heidelberg (2009)

19. Lubicz, D., Sirvent, T.: Attribute-based broadcast encryption scheme made efficient. In: Vaudenay, S. (ed.) AFRICACRYPT 2008. LNCS, vol. 5023, pp. 325–342. Springer, Heidelberg (2008)

20. Sahai, A., Waters, B.: Revocation systems with very small private keys. IACR Cryptology ePrint Archive 2008/309

21. Sedghi, S., van Liesdonk, P., Nikova, S., Hartel, P., Jonker, W.: Searching keywords with wildcards on encrypted data. In: Garay, J.A., De Prisco, R. (eds.) SCN 2010. LNCS, vol. 6280, pp. 138–153. Springer, Heidelberg (2010)

# Accountable Authority Ciphertext-Policy Attribute-Based Encryption with White-Box Traceability and Public Auditing in the Cloud

Jianting Ning[1], Xiaolei Dong[2]($\boxtimes$), Zhenfu Cao[2]($\boxtimes$), and Lifei Wei[3]

[1] Department of Computer Science and Engineering, Shanghai Jiao Tong University,
Shanghai 200240, China
jtning@sjtu.edu.cn
[2] Shanghai Key Lab for Trustworthy Computing, East China Normal University,
Shanghai 200062, China
{dongxiaolei,zfcao}@sei.ecnu.edu.cn
[3] College of Information Technology,
Shanghai Ocean University, Shanghai 201306, China
Lfwei@shou.edu.cn

**Abstract.** As a sophisticated mechanism for secure fine-grained access control, ciphertext-policy attribute-based encryption (CP-ABE) is a highly promising solution for commercial applications such as cloud computing. However, there still exists one major issue awaiting to be solved, that is, the prevention of key abuse. Most of the existing CP-ABE systems missed this critical functionality, hindering the wide utilization and commercial application of CP-ABE systems to date. In this paper, we address two practical problems about the key abuse of CP-ABE: (1) The key escrow problem of the semi-trusted authority; and, (2) The malicious key delegation problem of the users. For the semi-trusted authority, its misbehavior (i.e., illegal key (re-)distribution) should be caught and prosecuted. And for a user, his/her malicious behavior (i.e., illegal key sharing) need be traced. We affirmatively solve these two key abuse problems by proposing the first accountable authority CP-ABE with white-box traceability that supports policies expressed in any monotone access structures. Moreover, we provide an auditor to judge publicly whether a suspected user is guilty or is framed by the authority.

**Keywords:** Attribute-based encryption · Ciphertext-policy · Key abuse · White-box traceablity · Public auditing

## 1 Introduction

As a new commercial and exciting paradigm, cloud computing has attracted much attention from both industrial and academic world. Due to the advantage of cloud computing, plenty of enterprises and individuals can share and outsource their data to cloud servers instead of building and maintaining data centers of their own, and themselves or other authorized users can access the outsorced data anywhere

© Springer International Publishing Switzerland 2015
G. Pernul et al. (Eds.): ESORICS 2015, Part II, LNCS 9327, pp. 270–289, 2015.
DOI: 10.1007/978-3-319-24177-7_14

and anytime [1]. Despite lots of benefits provided by cloud computing, the concerns on data security are probably the main obstacles hindering the wide usage of cloud services. To address the data security concerns, encryption has been applied on the data of enterprises and individuals before outsourcing. Nevertheless, in some practical applications of cloud computing, data is often shared with some potential users without knowing who will receive it, thus a fine-grained access control over data is desired. Attribute-Based Encryption (ABE, [13]) is a promising approach to protect the confidentiality of sensitive data and express fine-grained access control for cloud computing. In a CP-ABE system, enterprises and individuals can specify access policies over attributes that the potential users possess. And the data customers whose attributes satisfy the specified access policy can decrypt successfully and get access to the outsourced data.

**A Motivating Story.** Consider a company employs a cloud storage system to outsource its data after encrypting the data under some access policies. Each employee is assigned with several attributes (such as "manager", "engineer", etc.). And those whose attributes satisfy the access policy over the outsourced data could decrypt the ciphertext and get access to the sensitive data stored in the cloud. As a versatile one-to-many encryption mechanism, CP-ABE system is quite suitable in this cloud storage scenario. If it happens to exist an employee from the company's competitor who is not authorized but could get access to the sensitive data stored in the cloud, as such, the company will suffer severe financial loss. Then, who leaks the decryption key to him? In addition, if an employee from the company named Bob is traced as the traitor (who leaks the decryption key) but claims to be innocent and framed by the system, then how to judge whether Bob is indeed innocent or not? Does Bob have an opportunity to argue for himself?

The problems, as described above, are the main obstacles when CP-ABE is implemented in cloud storage service. In a CP-ABE system, a user's decryption key is issued by a trusted authority according to the attributes the user possesses. The authority is able to generate and (re-)distribute decryption keys for any user without any risk of being caught and confronted in a court of law. Thus the security of a CP-ABE system relies heavily on trusting the authority. It is actually the key escrow problem in CP-ABE. One approach to reduce this trust is to employ multiple authorities [8,16,19]. However, this approach inevitably causes additional communication and infrastructure cost, and the problem of collusion among collaborating authorities remains. It is better to adopt the accountable authority approach to mitigate the key escrow problem in CP-ABE. The problem described above is the key abuse problem of authority. There exists another kind of key abuse problem: the key abuse problem of users. In a CP-ABE system, the decryption keys are defined over sets of attributes shared by multiple users. The misbehavior users may illegally share their decryption keys with others for profits without being detected. It is actually the malicious key delegation problem. It is necessary to trace the malicious users who leak their decryption keys illegally. Moreover, if a user is traced to be malicious (for leaking the decryption key) but claims to be innocent and framed by the system, it is necessary to enable an auditor to judge whether the user is indeed innocent or is framed by the system.

## 1.1 Our Contribution

In this paper, we address the key abuse and the auditing problems of CP-ABE and affirmatively solve these by proposing an accountable authority CP-ABE system with white-box traceability and public auditing. To the best of our knowledge, this is the first CP-ABE scheme that supports the following properties: traceability of malicious users, accountable authority, almost no storage for tracing, public auditing and high expressiveness (i.e. supporting access policies expressed in any monotone access structures). Also, we prove that our new system is fully secure in the standard model.

We solve the obstacles of CP-ABE implementation in cloud storage scenario as follows:

1. Traceability of malicious users. Anyone who may leak their decryption keys to others for profits can be traced.
2. Accountable authority. The semi-trusted authority could be caught if it illegally generates and distributes legitimate keys to any unauthorized users.
3. Public auditing. We provide an auditor to judge whether a suspected user (for leaking his/her decryption key) is guilty or is framed by the authority. In addition, the auditability of our system is public, that is, anyone can run the Audit algorithm to make a judgement with no additional secret needed.
4. Almost no storage for tracing. We use a Paillier-style encryption as an extractable commitment in tracing the malicious users. And we do not need to maintain an identity table of users for tracing as used in [21]. As a result, we need almost no storage for tracing.

Table 1 gives the comparison between our work and some other related work.

**Table 1.** Comparison with other related work

|  | [18] | [17] | [21] | [20] | [22] | Ours |
|---|---|---|---|---|---|---|
| Traceability of malicious users | × | × | × | √ | √ | √ |
| Accountable authority | √ | × | × | × | × | √ |
| Storage for tracing[a] | none | none | linear | none | constant | none |
| Supporting any monotone access structures | × | × | √ | √ | √ | √ |
| Public auditing | × | × | × | × | × | √ |
| Fully secure | × | × | √ | √ | × | √ |
| Standard model | × | √ | √ | √ | √ | √ |

[a] In [17,18,20] and this paper, the systems need almost no storage for tracing, for simplicity, we use *none* stands for almost no storage for tracing.

## 1.2   Our Technique

In this subsection, we briefly introduce the main idea we utilize to realize the properties of traceability of malicious users, accountable authority and public auditing before giving the full details in Sect. 4.

To trace malicious users who may leak their decryption keys to others for profits, we use a Paillier-style encryption as an extractable commitment to achieve white-box traceability. Specifically, we use a Paillier-style extractable commitment to make a commitment to a user's identity when the user queries for his decryption key. The commitment is further inserted into the user's decryption key as a necessary part for successful decryption. Due to the hiding and binding properties of the Paillier-style extractable commitment, the user does not know what is inserted into his decryption key and even cannot change the identity insert into his decryption key. When it comes to the Trace algorithm, the algorithm uses a trapdoor for the commitment to recover the identity of the user from his decryption key. Note that the decryption key needs to take a *key sanity check* algorithm to see whether it is *well-formed* or not prior to the tracing step. Take the advantage of the Paillier-style extractable commitment, we do not have to maintain the identity table as used in [21], as a result, we need almost no storage for tracing.

To achieve accountable authority, the main idea is to let the user's decryption key be jointly determined by both of the authority and the user himself, hence the authority does not have complete control over the decryption key. We let a user get his decryption key $sk$ corresponding to his attributes and identity from the authority using a secure key generation protocol. The protocol allows the user to obtain a decryption key $sk$ for his attributes and identity without letting the authority know which key he obtained. Now if the authority (re-)distribute a decryption key $\tilde{sk}$ (corresponding to a user's attributes and identity) for malicious usage, with all but negligible probability, it will be different from the key $sk$ which the user obtained. Hence the key pair $(sk, \tilde{sk})$ is a cryptographic proof of malicious behavior of the authority.

Furthermore, the difference between the user's decryption key $sk$ and the decryption key $\tilde{sk}$ (re-)distributed by the authority allows the auditor to judge publicly whether the malicious user is guilty or is framed by the system. And note that the auditor is assumed to be fair and credible.

## 1.3   Related Work

Attribute-Based Encryption, first introduced by Sahai and Waters [27], generalizes the notion of fuzzy Identity-Based Encryption (IBE) [6,28]. Goyal et al. [13] formalized two complementary forms of Attribute-Based Encryption (ABE): Key-Policy Attribute-Based Encryption (KP-ABE) and Ciphertext-Policy Attribute-Based Encryption (CP-ABE). In a CP-ABE system, every user's decryption key is associated with a set of attributes she/he possesses, and every ciphertext is associated with an access policy defined over attributes. KP-ABE is reversed in that every ciphertext is associated with a set of attributes and every user's decryption key is associated with an access policy. ABE (especially CP-ABE) is envisioned as a highly promising public key primitive for implementing scalable and fine-grained access control over encrypted data, and has attracted much attention in the research community. A series of ABE (including CP-ABE and KP-ABE) systems have been proposed [4,11,14,15,20–22,24–26,29], aiming at better efficiency, expressiveness or security.

Li et al. first introduced the notion of accountable CP-ABE [18] to prevent illegal key sharing among colluding users. Then a user accountable multi-authority CP-ABE scheme was proposed in [17] which only supported AND gates with wildcard. White-box [21] and black-box [20] traceability CP-ABE systems which supported policies expressed in any monotone access structures were later proposed by Liu et al. Recently, Ning et al. [22] proposed a practical large universe CP-ABE system with white-box traceability. Deng et al. [9] provided a tracing mechanism of CP-ABE to find the leaked access credentials in cloud storage systems. Unfortunately, the above work either only support less expressive access policy, or do not consider the misbehavior of the authority, or do not address the auditing issue.

### 1.4 Organization

Section 2 introduces the background, including the notation, the access policy, the linear secret sharing scheme, the composite order bilinear groups, the assumptions and the zero-knowledge proof of knowledge of discrete log. Section 3 gives the formal definition of accountable authority CP-ABE with white-box traceability and public auditing (AAT-CP-ABE) and its security model. Section 4 presents the construction of our AAT-CP-ABE system as well as the security proof. Finally, Sect. 5 presents a brief conclusion and foresees our future work.

## 2  Background

### 2.1  Notation

We define $[l] = \{1, 2, ..., l\}$ for $l \in \mathbb{N}$. We denote by $s \xleftarrow{R} S$ the fact that $s$ is picked uniformly at random from the finite set $S$. By PPT we denote probabilistic polynomial-time. We denote $(v_1, v_2, ..., v_n)$ be a row vector and $(v_1, v_2, ..., v_n)^{\perp}$ be a column vector. By $v_i$ we denote the $i$-th element in a vector $v$. And by $Mv$ we denote the product of matrix $M$ with vector $v$. We denote $\mathbb{Z}_p^{l \times n}$ be the set of matrices of size $l \times n$ with elements in $\mathbb{Z}_N$. The set of column vectors of length $n$ (i.e. $\mathbb{Z}_N^{n \times 1}$) are the two special subsets and the set of row vectors of length $n$ (i.e. $\mathbb{Z}_N^{1 \times n}$).

### 2.2  Access Policy

**Definition 1.** *(Access Structure [2]): Let $S$ be the attribute universe. A collection (respectively, monotone collection) $\mathbb{A} \subseteq 2^S$ of non-empty sets of attributes is*

*an access structure (respectively, monotone access structure) on S. A collection*
$\mathbb{A} \subseteq 2^S$ *is called monotone if* $\forall B, C \in \mathbb{A} : if\ B \in \mathbb{A}\ and\ B \subseteq C,\ then\ C \in \mathbb{A}.$
*The sets in* $\mathbb{A}$ *are called the authorized sets, and the sets not in* $\mathbb{A}$ *are called the unauthorized sets.*

For CP-ABE, if a user of the system possess an authorized set of attributes then he can decrypt the ciphertext. Otherwise, the set he possed is unauthorized and he can't get any information from ciphertext. In our construction, we restrict our attention to monotone access structure.

### 2.3   Linear Secret-Sharing Schemes

**Definition 2.** *(Linear Secret-Sharing Schemes (LSSS) [2,22]). Let S denote the attribute universe and p denote a prime. A secret-sharing scheme* $\prod$ *with domain of secrets* $\mathbb{Z}_p$ *realizing access structure on S in called linear (over* $\mathbb{Z}_p$*) if*

1. *The shares of a secret* $s \in \mathbb{Z}_p$ *for each attribute form a vector over* $\mathbb{Z}_p$.
2. *For each access structure* $\mathbb{A}$ *on S, there exists a matrix M with l rows and n columns called the share-generating matrix for* $\prod$*. For* $i = 1, ..., l$*, we define a function* $\rho$ *labels row i of M with attribute* $\rho(i)$ *from the attribute universe S. When we consider the column vector* $\boldsymbol{v} = (s, r_2, ..., r_n)$*, where* $s \in \mathbb{Z}_p$ *is the secret to be shared and* $r_2, ..., r_n \in \mathbb{Z}_p$ *are randomly chosen. Then* $M\boldsymbol{v} \in \mathbb{Z}_p^{l \times 1}$ *is the vector of l shares of the secret s according to* $\prod$*. The share* $(M\boldsymbol{v})_j$ *"belongs" to attribute* $\rho(j)$*, where* $j \in [l]$*.*

As shown in [2], every linear secret-sharing scheme according to the above definition also enjoys the linear reconstruction property, defined as follows: we suppose that $\prod$ is an LSSS for the access structure $\mathbb{A}$, $S' \in \mathbb{A}$ is an authorized set and let $I \subset \{1, 2, ..., l\}$ be defined as $I = \{i \in [l] \land \rho(i) \in S'\}$. Then, there exist constants $\{\omega_i \in \mathbb{Z}_p\}_{i \in I}$ such that for any valid shares $\{\lambda_i = (M\boldsymbol{v})_i\}_{i \in I}$ of a secret $s$ according to $\prod$, then $\sum_{i \in I} \omega_i \lambda_i = s$. Additionally, it is shown in [2] that these constants $\{\omega_i\}_{i \in I}$ can be found in time polynomial in the size of the share-generating matrix $M$. On the other hand, for any unauthorized set $S''$, no such constants $\{\omega_i\}$ exist.

Note that if we encode the access structure as a monotonic Boolean formula over attributes, there exists a generic algorithm by which we can generate the corresponding access policy in polynomial time [2].

In our construction, an LSSS matrix $(M, \rho)$ will be used to express an access policy associated to a ciphertext.

### 2.4   Composite Order Bilinear Groups

Composite order bilinear groups are widely used in IBE and ABE systems, which are first introduced in [7]. We let $\mathcal{G}$ denote a group generator, which takes a security parameter $\lambda$ as input and outputs a description of a bilinear group $G$. We define the output of $\mathcal{G}$ as $(p_1, p_2, p_3, G, G_T, e)$, where $p_1, p_2, p_3$ are distinct primes, $G$ and $G_T$ are cyclic groups of order $N = p_1 p_2 p_3$, and $e : G^2 \to G_T$ is a map such that:

1. Bilinearity: $\forall u, v \in G$ and $a, b \in \mathbb{Z}_p$, we have $e(u^a, v^b) = e(u, v)^{ab}$.
2. Non-degeneracy: $\exists g \in G$ such that $e(g, g)$ has order $N$ in $G_T$.

We assume that group operations in $G$ and $G_T$ as well as the bilinear map $e$ are computable in polynomial time with respect to $\lambda$. We refer to $G$ as the *source group* and $G_T$ as the *target group*, and assume the group descriptions of $G$ and $G_T$ include a generator of each group. Let $G_{p_1}$, $G_{p_2}$, and $G_{p_3}$ be the subgroups of order $p_1$, $p_2$, and $p_3$ in $G$, respectively. Note that these subgroups are "orthogonal" to each other under the bilinear map $e$: for any $u_i \in G_{p_i}$ and $u_j \in G_{p_j}$ where $i \neq j$, $e(u_i, u_j) = 1$. Any element $E_N \in G$ can (uniquely) be expressed as $g_1^{r_1} g_2^{r_2} g_3^{r_3}$ for some values $r_1, r_2, r_3 \in \mathbb{Z}_N$, where $g_1, g_2, g_3$ are the generators of $G_{p_1}, G_{p_2}, G_{p_3}$ respectively. And we will refer to $g_1^{r_1}, g_2^{r_2}, g_3^{r_3}$ as the "$G_{p_1}$ part of $E_N$", "$G_{p_2}$ part of $E_N$" and "$G_{p_3}$ part of $E_N$", respectively. Assume $G_{p_1 p_2}$ be the subgroups of order $p_1 p_2$ in $G$. Similarly, any element $E_{p_1 p_2} \in G_{p_1 p_2}$ can be expressed as the product of an element from $G_{p_1}$ and an element from $G_{p_2}$.

## 2.5   Complexity Assumptions

**Assumption 1.** *(Subgroup Decision Problem for 3 Primes): [14] Given a group generator $\mathcal{G}$, define the following distribution:*

$$\mathbb{G} = (N = p_1 p_2 p_3, G, G_T, e) \xleftarrow{R} \mathcal{G},$$
$$g \xleftarrow{R} G_{p_1}, X_3 \xleftarrow{R} G_{p_3},$$
$$D = (\mathbb{G}, g, X_3),$$
$$T_1 \xleftarrow{R} G_{p_1 p_2}, T_2 \xleftarrow{R} G_{p_1}.$$

The advantage of an algorithm $\mathcal{A}$ in breaking this assumption is defined to be: $Adv1_{\mathcal{G},\mathcal{A}}(\lambda) = |Pr[\mathcal{A}(D, T_1) = 1] - Pr[\mathcal{A}(D, T_2) = 1]|$.

**Definition 3.** *We say that $\mathcal{G}$ satisfies Assumption 1 if $Adv1_{\mathcal{G},\mathcal{A}}(\lambda)$ is a negligible function of $\lambda$ for any polynomial time algorithm $\mathcal{A}$.*

**Assumption 2.** *[14] Given a group generator $\mathcal{G}$, define the following distribution:*

$$\mathbb{G} = (N = p_1 p_2 p_3, G, G_T, e) \xleftarrow{R} \mathcal{G},$$
$$g, X_1 \xleftarrow{R} G_{p_1}, X_2, Y_2 \xleftarrow{R} G_{p_2}, X_3, Y_3 \xleftarrow{R} G_{p_3}$$
$$D = (\mathbb{G}, g, X_1 X_2, X_3, Y_2 Y_3),$$
$$T_1 \xleftarrow{R} G, T_2 \xleftarrow{R} G_{p_1 p_3}.$$

The advantage of an algorithm $\mathcal{A}$ in breaking this assumption is defined to be: $Adv2_{\mathcal{G},\mathcal{A}}(\lambda) = |Pr[\mathcal{A}(D, T_1) = 1] - Pr[\mathcal{A}(D, T_2) = 1]|$.

**Definition 4.** *We say that $\mathcal{G}$ satisfies Assumption 2 if $Adv2_{\mathcal{G},\mathcal{A}}(\lambda)$ is a negligible function of $\lambda$ for any polynomial time algorithm $\mathcal{A}$.*

**Assumption 3.** *[14] Given a group generator $\mathcal{G}$, define the following distribution:*

$$\mathbb{G} = (N = p_1 p_2 p_3, G, G_T, e) \xleftarrow{R} \mathcal{G}, \alpha, s \xleftarrow{R} \mathbb{Z}_N,$$
$$g \xleftarrow{R} G_{p_1}, X_2, Y_2, Z_2 \xleftarrow{R} G_{p_2}, X_3 \xleftarrow{R} G_{p_3}$$
$$D = (\mathbb{G}, g, g^\alpha X_2, X_3, g^s Y_2, Z_2),$$
$$T_1 = e(g,g)^{\alpha s}, T_2 \xleftarrow{R} G_T.$$

The advantage of an algorithm $\mathcal{A}$ in breaking this assumption is defined to be: $Adv3_{\mathcal{G},\mathcal{A}}(\lambda) = |Pr[\mathcal{A}(D,T_1) = 1] - Pr[\mathcal{A}(D,T_2) = 1]|$.

**Definition 5.** *We say that $\mathcal{G}$ satisfies Assumption 3 if $Adv3_{\mathcal{G},\mathcal{A}}(\lambda)$ is a negligible function of $\lambda$ for any polynomial time algorithm $\mathcal{A}$.*

**Assumption 4.** *(l-SDH assumption [5, 10]): Let $\mathbb{G}$ be a bilinear group of prime order $p$ and $g$ be a generator of $\mathbb{G}$, the l-Strong Diffie-Hellman (l-SDH) problem in $\mathbb{G}$ is defined as follows: given a $(l+1)$-tuple $(g, g^x, g^{x^2}, ..., g^{x^l})$ as inputs, output a pair $(c, g^{1/(c+x)}) \in \mathbb{Z}_p \times \mathbb{G}$. An algorithm $\mathcal{A}$ has advantage $\epsilon$ in solving l-SDH in $\mathbb{G}$ if $Pr[\mathcal{A}(g, g^x, g^{x^2}, ..., g^{x^l}) = (c, g^{1/(c+x)})] \geq \epsilon$, where the probability is over the random choice of $x$ in $\mathbb{Z}_p^*$ and the random bits consumed by $\mathcal{A}$.*

**Definition 6.** *We say that the $(l, t, \epsilon)$-SDH assumption holds in $\mathbb{G}$ if no t-time algorithm has advantage at least in solving the l-SDH problem in $\mathbb{G}$.*

### 2.6   Zero-Knowledge Proof of Knowledge of Discrete Log

Informally, a zero-knowledge proof of knowledge (ZK-POK) of discrete log protocol enables a prover to prove that it possesses the discrete log $t$ of a given group element $T$ in question to a verifier.

A ZK-POK protocol has two distinct properties: the zero-knowledge property and the proof of knowledge property. The property of zero-knowledge implies that there exists a simulator $S$ which is able to simulate the view of a verifier in the protocol without being given the witness as input. The proof of knowledge property implies there exists a knowledge-extractor $Ext$ which interacts with the prover and extracts the witness using rewinding techniques [10]. We refer the reader to [3] for more details about ZK-POK.

## 3   Accountable Authority CP-ABE with White-Box Traceability and Public Auditing

### 3.1   Definition

An Accountable Authority CP-ABE with White-Box Traceability and Public Auditing (AAT-CP-ABE) is a CP-ABE system which could hold the misbehaved authority accountable, trace the malicious user by his/her decryption key and judge whether the suspected a user is indeed innocent or not. An AAT-CP-ABE system consists of seven algorithms as follows:

- $\text{Setup}(1^\lambda, \mathcal{U}) \to (pp, msk)$: The algorithm takes as input a security parameter $\lambda \in \mathbb{N}$ encoded in unary and the attribute universe description $\mathcal{U}$. It outputs the public parameters $pp$ and the master secret key $msk$.

- $\text{KeyGen}(pp, msk, id, S) \to sk_{id,S}$: This is an interactive protocol between the authority $AT$ and a user $U$. The public parameters $pp$ and a set of attributes $S$ for a user with identity $id$ are the common input to the $AT$ and $U$. The master secret key $msk$ is the private input to the $AT$. Additionally, the $AT$ and $U$ may use a sequence of random coin tosses as private input. At the end of the protocol, $U$ is issued a secret key $sk_{id,S}$ corresponding to $S$.

- $\text{Encrypt}(pp, m, \mathbb{A}) \to ct$: The encryption algorithm takes as input the public parameters $pp$, a plaintext message $m$, and an access structure $\mathbb{A}$ over the universe of attributes. It outputs the ciphertext $ct$[1].

- $\text{Decrypt}(pp, sk_{id,S}, ct) \to m$ or $\perp$: The decryption algorithm takes as input the public parameters $pp$, a secret key $sk_{id,S}$, and a ciphertext $ct$. If the set of attributes of the private key satisfies the access structure of the ciphertext, the algorithm outputs the plaintext $m$. Otherwise, it outputs $\perp$.

- $\text{KeySanityCheck}(pp, sk) \to 1$ or $0$: The key sanity check algorithm takes as input the public parameters $pp$ and a secret key $sk$. If $sk$ passes the key sanity check, it outputs 1. Otherwise, it outputs 0. The key sanity check is a deterministic algorithm [10,12], which is used to guarantee the secret key to be well-formed in the decryption process.

- $\text{Trace}(pp, msk, sk) \to id$ or $\top$: The tracing algorithm takes as input the public parameters $pp$, the master secret key $msk$ and a secret key $sk$. The algorithm first checks whether $sk$ is *well-formed* or not so as to determine whether $sk$ needs to be traced. A secret key $sk$ is defined as *well-formed* which means that $\text{KeySanityCheck}(pp, sk) \to 1$. If $sk$ is well-formed, the system extracts the identity $id$ from $sk$. Then it outputs an identity $id$ with which the $sk$ associates. Otherwise, it outputs a special symbol $\top$ indicates that $sk$ does not need to be traced.

- $\text{Audit}(pp, sk_{id}, sk_{id}^*) \to$ *guilty* or *innocent*. This is an interactive protocol between a user $U$ and a public auditor $PA$. It judges whether a user is *guilty* or *innocent*.

### 3.2   Security

An AAT-CP-ABE system is deemed secure if the following three requirements are satisfied. First, it must satisfy the standard semantic security notion for CP-ABE system: ciphertext indistinguishability under chosen plaintext attacks (IND-CPA). Second, it is intractable for the authority to create a decryption key such that the Trace algorithm outputs a user and the Audit algorithm outputs the user is guilty. Finally, it is infeasible for a user to create a decryption key such that the Audit algorithm implicates the user is innocent. To define security for AAT-CP-ABE system satisfies the above three requirements, we define the following three games, respectively.

---

[1] We assume that $\mathbb{A}$ is implicitly in the ciphertext $ct$.

**The IND-CPA game.** The IND-CPA game for AAT-CP-ABE system is similar to that of the CP-ABE system [15], excepting every key query is companied with an explicit identity. The game proceeds as follows:

- **Setup:** The challenger runs the Setup$(1^\lambda, \mathcal{U})$ algorithm and sends the public parameters $pp$ to the attacker.
- **Query Phase 1:** In this phase the attacker can adaptively query the challenger for secret keys corresponding to sets of attributes $(id_1, S_1), (id_2, S_2), ...,$ $(id_{Q_1}, S_{Q_1})$. For each $(id_i, S_i)$ the challenger calls KeyGen$(pp, msk, id, S_i) \rightarrow sk_{id,S_i}$ and sends $sk_{id,S_i}$ to the attacker.
- **Challenge:** The attacker declares two equal length messages $m_0$ and $m_1$ and an access structure $\mathbb{A}^*$. Note that this access structure cannot be satisfied by any of the queried attributes sets $(id_1, S_1), (id_2, S_2), ..., (id_{Q_1}, S_{Q_1})$. The challenge flips a random coin $\delta \in \{0, 1\}$ and calls Encrypt$(pp, m_\delta, \mathbb{A}^*) \rightarrow ct$. It sends $ct$ to the attacker.
- **Query Phase 2:** The attacker adaptively queries the challenger for the secret keys corresponding to sets of attributes $(id_{Q_1+1}, S_{Q_1+1}), ..., (id_Q, S_Q)$ with the added restriction that none of these satisfy $\mathbb{A}^*$. For each $(id_i, S_i)$ the challenger calls KeyGen$(pp, msk, id, S_i) \rightarrow sk_{id,S_i}$ and sends $sk_{id,S_i}$ to the attacker.
- **Guess:** The attacker outputs a guess $\delta' \in \{0, 1\}$ for $\delta$.

An attacker's advantage in this game is defined to be $Adv = |\Pr[\delta' = \delta] - 1/2|$.

**Definition 7.** *An AAT-CP-ABE system is fully secure if all probabilistic polynomial time (PPT) attackers have at most a negligible advantage in the above game.*

**The DishonestAuthority Game.** The DishonestAuthority game for the AAT-CP-ABE system is defined as follows. The intuition behind this game is that an adversarial authority attempts to create a decryption key which will frame a user. It is described by a game between a challenger and an attacker.

- **Setup:** The attacker (acting as a malicious authority) generates public parameters $pp$, and sends $pp$, a user's $(id, S)$ to the challenger. The challenger runs a sanity check on $pp$ and $(id, S)$ aborts if the check fails.
- **Key Generation:** The attacker and the challenger engage in the key generation protocol KeyGen to generate a decryption key $sk_{id}^*$ corresponding to the user's $id$ and $S$. The challenger gets the decryption key $sk_{id}^*$ as input and runs a sanity check on it to ensure that it is well-formed. It aborts if the check fails.
- **Output:** The attacker outputs a decryption key $sk_{id}^*$ and succeeds if Trace$(pp, msk, sk_{id}^*) \rightarrow id$, and Audit$(pp, sk_{id}, sk_{id}^*) \rightarrow guilty$.

The attacker's advantage in this game is defined to be $Adv = |\Pr[\mathcal{A} \ succeeds]|$ where the probability is taken over the random coins of Trace, Audit, the attacker and the challenger.

**Definition 8.** *An AAT-CP-ABE system is DishonestAuthority secure if all PPT attackers have at most a negligible advantage in the above security game.*

**The DishonestUser Game.** The DishonestUser game for the AAT-CP-ABE system is defined as follows. The intuition behind this game is that a malicious user attempts to create new decryption key which will frame the authority. It is described by a game between a challenger and an attacker.

- **Setup:** The challenger runs the $\texttt{Setup}(1^\lambda, \mathcal{U})$ algorithm and sends the public parameters $pp$ to the attacker.
- **Key Query:** The attacker submits the sets of attributes $(id_1, S_1), ..., (id_q, S_q)$ to request the corresponding decryption keys. The challenger calls $\texttt{KeyGen}(pp, msk, id, S_i) \to sk_{id,S_i}$ and returns $sk_{id,S_i}$ to the attacker.
- **Key Forgery:** The attacker will output a decryption key $sk_*$. If $\{\texttt{Trace}(pp, msk, sk_*) \neq \top$ and $\texttt{Trace}(pp, msk, sk_*) \notin \{id_1, ..., id_q\}\}$ or $\{\texttt{Trace}(pp, msk, sk_*) = id$ and $\texttt{Audit}(pp, sk_{id}, sk_{id}^*) \to innocent\}$, the attacker wins the game.

An attacker's advantage in this game is defined to be $Adv = |\Pr[\mathcal{A}\ succeeds]|$ where the probability is taken over the random coins of $\texttt{Trace}$, $\texttt{Audit}$, the attacker and the challenger.

**Definition 9.** *An AAT-CP-ABE system is fully traceable if all PPT attackers have at most a negligible advantage in the above security game.*

**The Key Sanity Check Game.** According to [23], the Key Sanity Check game for the AAT-CP-ABE system is defined as follows. It is described by the following game between an attacker and a simulator. On input a security parameter $1^\lambda$ ($\lambda \in \mathbb{N}$), a simulator invokes an attacker $\mathcal{A}$ on $1^\lambda$. $\mathcal{A}$ returns the public parameters $pp$, a ciphertext $ct$ and two different secret keys $sk_{id,S}$ and $\tilde{sk}_{id,S}$ corresponding to the same set of attributes $S$ for a user with identity $id$. $\mathcal{A}$ wins the game if

(1) $\texttt{KeySanityCheck}(pp, sk_{id,S}) \to 1$.
(2) $\texttt{KeySanityCheck}(pp, \tilde{sk}_{id,S}) \to 1$.
(3) $\texttt{Decrypt}(pp, sk_{id,S}, ct) \neq \bot$.
(4) $\texttt{Decrypt}(pp, \tilde{sk}_{id,S}, ct) \neq \bot$.
(5) $\texttt{Decrypt}(pp, sk_{id,S}, ct) \neq \texttt{Decrypt}(pp, \tilde{sk}_{id,S}, ct)$.

$\mathcal{A}$'s advantage in the above game is defined as $\Pr[\mathcal{A}\ wins]$. And it is easy to see that the intuition of "Key Sanity Check" is captured combining the notion captured in the above game and the related algorithms ($\texttt{KeySanityCheck}$ and $\texttt{Decrypt}$) defined in this section [23].

# 4    Our System

## 4.1    Construction

- $\texttt{Setup}(\lambda, \mathcal{U}) \to (pp, msk)$: The algorithm calls the group generator $\mathcal{G}$ with $\lambda$ as input and gets a bilinear group $G$ of order $N = p_1 p_2 p_3$ (3 distinct primes), $G_{p_i}$ the subgroup of order $p_i$ in $G$, and $g, g_3$ the generator of the subgroup

$G_{p_1}, G_{p_3}$ respectively. It then chooses exponents $\alpha, a, \kappa, \mu \in \mathbb{Z}_N$ and a group element $v \in G_{p_1}$ randomly. For each attribute $i \in \mathcal{U}$, the algorithm chooses a random value $u_i \in \mathbb{Z}_N$. Also, the algorithm chooses two random primes $p$ and $q$ for which it holds $p \neq q$, $|p| = |q|$ and $gcd(pq, (p-1)(q-1)) = 1$, and then let $n = pq$, $\pi = lcm(p-1, q-1)$, $Q = \pi^{-1} \bmod n$ and $g_1 = (1+n)$. The public parameters are set to $pp = (N, n, g_1, v, g, g^a, g^\kappa, g^\mu, e(g,g)^\alpha, \{\mathcal{U}_i = g^{u_i}\}_{i \in \mathcal{U}})$. And the master secret key $msk$ is set to $msk = (p, q, \alpha, g_3)$.

- KeyGen$(pp, msk, id, S) \rightarrow sk_{id,S}$: The authority $AT$ and a user $U$ (with the identity $id^2$) interact in the key generation protocol as follows.
  1. $U$ first chooses $t \in \mathbb{Z}_N$ randomly and computes $R_U = g^t$. Next, it sends $g^t$, the identity $id$ and a set of attributes $S$ to $AT$. Then, it runs an interactive ZK-POK of the discrete log of $R_U$ with respect to $g$ with $AT$.
  2. $AT$ first checks whether the ZK-POK is valid or not. If the check fails, $AT$ aborts the interaction. Otherwise, it chooses a random $c \in \mathbb{Z}_N$, a random $r \in \mathbb{Z}_n^*$ and random elements $R, R_0, R_0', \{R_i\}_{i \in S} \in G_{p_3}$. Then, it computes the primary secret key $sk_{pri}$ as follows:

$$\langle S, \overline{K} = g^{\frac{\alpha}{a+T}}(g^t)^{\frac{\kappa}{a+T}} v^c R, \ \overline{T} = g_1^{id} r^n \bmod n^2,$$

$$\overline{L} = g^c R_0, \ \overline{L'} = g^{ac} R_0', \ \{\overline{K}_i = \mathcal{U}_i^{(a+\overline{T})c} R_i\}_{i \in S}\rangle.$$

  And it sends $(c, sk_{pri})$ to $U$.
  3. $U$ checks whether the following equalities hold or not:
    (1) $e(\overline{L'}, g) = e(\overline{L}, g^a) = e(g^a, (g)^c)$.
    (2) $e(\overline{K}, g^a g^T) = e(g,g)^\alpha e(\overline{L'}(\overline{L})^T, v) e(R_U, g^\kappa)$.
    (3) $\exists x \in S$ s.t. $e(\mathcal{U}_x, \overline{L'}(\overline{L})^T) = e(\overline{K}_x, g)$.
  If no, $U$ aborts the interaction. Otherwise, $U$ computes $t_{id} = \frac{c}{t}$ and sets his decryption key $sk_{id,S}$ as follows:

$$\langle S, K = \overline{K}(g^\mu)^{t_{id}}, T = \overline{T}, L = \overline{L}, L' = \overline{L'}, R_U, t_{id}, \{K_i = \overline{K}_i\}_{i \in S}\rangle.$$

- Encrypt$(pp, m, (A, \rho)) \rightarrow ct$: The algorithm takes the access structure encoded in an LSSS policy[3], the public parameters $pp$ and a plaintext message $m$. The algorithm chooses $\overrightarrow{y} = (s, y_2, ..., y_n)^\perp \in \mathbb{Z}_N^{n \times 1}$ randomly, where $s$ is the random secret to be shared among the shares according to Subsect. 2.3. Then it chooses $r_j \in \mathbb{Z}_N$ for each row $A_j$ of $A$ randomly. The ciphertext $ct$ is set as follows:

$$\langle C = m \cdot e(g,g)^{\alpha s}, C_0 = g^s, C_1 = (g^a)^s, C_2 = (g^\kappa)^s, C_3 = (g^\mu)^s,$$

$$\{C_{j,1} = v^{A_j \overrightarrow{y}} \mathcal{U}_{\rho(j)}^{-r_j}, C_{j,2} = g^{r_j}\}_{j \in [l]}, (A, \rho)\rangle.$$

---

[2] We assume that the identity $id$ is an element in $\mathbb{Z}_n$. One can extend the construction to arbitrary identities in $\{0,1\}^*$ easily by adopting a collision-resistant hash $H : \{0,1\}^* \rightarrow \mathbb{Z}_n$.

[3] where $A$ is an $l \times n$ matrix and $\rho$ is a map from each row $A_j$ of $A$ to an attribute $\rho(j)$.

– $\text{Decrypt}(pp, sk_{id,S}, ct) \rightarrow m$ or $\perp$: The algorithm first parses the $sk_{id,S}$ to $(S, K, T, L, L', R_U, t_{id}, \{K_i\}_{i \in S})$ and $ct$ to $(C, C_0, C_1, C_2, C_3, \{C_{j,1}, C_{j,2}\}_{j \in [l]}, (A, \rho))$. The algorithm will output $\perp$ if the attribute set $S$ cannot satisfy the access structure $(A, \rho)$ of $ct$. Otherwise, the algorithm first computes constants $\omega_j \in \mathbb{Z}_N$ such that $\sum_{\rho(j) \in S} \omega_j A_j = (1, 0, ..., 0)$. It then computes:

$$D = e((C_0)^T C_1, K)(e(C_2, R_u)e(C_3, (g^T g^a)^{t_{id}}))^{-1}$$

$$E = \Pi_{\rho(j) \in S}(e(C_{j,1}, (L)^T L')e(C_{j,2}, K_{\rho(j)}))^{\omega_j}$$

$$F = D/E = e(g, g)^{\alpha s}, m = C/F$$

– $\text{KeySanityCheck}(pp, sk) \rightarrow 1$ or 0: The algorithm takes as input the public parameters $pp$ and a secret key $sk$. The secret key $sk$ passes the key sanity check if
  (1) $sk$ is in the form of $(S, K, T, L, L', R_U, t_{id}, \{K_i\}_{i \in S})$ and $T \in \mathbb{Z}_{n^2}^*$, $K, L, L', R_U, \{K_i\}_{i \in S} \in G$.
  (2) $e(L', g) = e(L, g^a)$.
  (3) $e(K, g^a g^T) = e(g, g)^\alpha e(L'(L)^T, v)e(R_U, g^\kappa)e((g^a g^T)^{t_{id}}, g^\mu)$.
  (4) $\exists x \in S$ s.t. $e(\mathcal{U}_x, L'(L)^T) = e(K_x, g)$.
  If $sk$ passes the key sanity check, the algorithm outputs 1. Otherwise, it outputs 0.
– $\text{Trace}(pp, msk, sk) \rightarrow id$ or $\top$: If $\text{KeySanityCheck}(pp, sk) \rightarrow 0$, the algorithm outputs $\top$. Otherwise, it is a well-formed decryption key[4], and the algorithm will extract the identity $id$ from $T = g_1^{id} r^n \bmod n^2$ in $sk$ as follows: note that $Q = \pi^{-1} \bmod n$ and observe that $T^{\pi Q} = g_1^{id \cdot \pi Q} \cdot r^{n \cdot \pi Q} = g_1^{id} = 1 + id \cdot n \bmod n^2$. Thus, it recovers $id = \frac{((T)^{\pi Q} \bmod n^2) - 1}{n} \bmod n$ and outputs the identity $id$.
– $\text{Audit}(pp, sk_{id}, sk_{id}^*) \rightarrow guilty$ or $innocent$: Suppose a user $U$ (with identity $id$ and decryption key $sk_{id}$) is identified as a malicious user by the system (through the traced key $sk_{id}^*$), but claims to be innocent and framed by the system. $U$ will interact with the public auditor $PA$ in the following protocol.
  (1) $U$ sends its decryption key $sk_{id}$ to $PA$. If $\text{KeySanityCheck}(pp, sk) \rightarrow 0$, $PA$ aborts. Otherwise, go to (2).
  (2) $PA$ tests whether the equality $t_{id} = t_{id}^*$ hold or not. If no, it outputs $innocent$ indicates that $U$ is innocent and is framed by the system. Otherwise, it outputs $guilty$ indicates that $U$ is malicious and $sk_{id}^*$ is leaked by $U$.

## 4.2   IND-CPA Security

Since our construction of accountable authority traceable CP-ABE system is based on the CP-ABE system in [14], for simplicity, we will reduce the IND-CPA security proof of our construction to that of the system in [14]. We denote by $\Sigma_{cpabe}$, $\Sigma_{aatcpabe}$ the CP-ABE system in [14] and our system respectively.

---

[4] i.e. the decryption privilege of the key is described by attribute set $S_\top = \{x | x \in S \wedge e(K_x, g) = e(\mathcal{U}_x, L'(L)^T) \neq 1\}$.

The security model of $\Sigma_{cpabe}$ in [14] is almost the same with the IND-CPA security model of our system $\Sigma_{aatcpabe}$ in Subsection in 3.2, excepting every key query is companied with an identity and the decryption key is jointly determined by a user and the authority.

**Lemma 1.** *[14] If Assumptions 1,2,3 hold, then the CP-ABE system $\Sigma_{cpabe}$ in [14] is secure.*

*(2) IND-CPA Security of our AAT-CP-ABE system:*

**Lemma 2.** *[14] If the CP-ABE system $\Sigma_{cpabe}$ in [14] is secure, then our AAT-CP-ABE system $\Sigma_{aatcpabe}$ in is secure in the IND-CPA security game of Subsect. 3.2.*

Due to space, we refer the reader to Appendix A for the proof of this lemma.

**Theorem 1.** *If Assumptions 1,2,3 hold, then our AAT-CP-ABE system $\Sigma_{aatcpabe}$ is secure.*

**Proof.** It follows directly from Lemmas 1 and 2.

### 4.3   DishonestAuthority Security

**Theorem 2.** *If computing discrete log is hard in $G_{p_1}$, the advantage of an adversary in the DishonestAuthority game is negligible for our AAT-CP-ABE system.*

Due to space, we refer the reader to Appendix B for the proof of this theorem.

### 4.4   DishonestUser Security

In this subsection, we prove the DishonestUser secure of our AAT-CP-ABE system based on $q$-SDH assumption and Assumption 2. We adopt a similar method from [5] and [21].

**Theorem 3.** *If $q$-SDH assumption and Assumption 2 hold, then our AAT-CP-ABE system is DishonestUser secure provided that $q' < q$.*

Due to space, we refer the reader to Appendix C for the proof of this theorem.

### 4.5   Key Sanity Check Proof

In this subsection, we will give the key sanity check proof of our AAT-CP-ABE system. We use the proof method from [23].

**Theorem 4.** *The advantage of an attacker in the key sanity check game (in Subsect. 3.2) is negligible for our AAT-CP-ABE system.*

Due to space, we refer the reader to Appendix D for the proof of this theorem.

## 5   Conclusion and Future Work

In this work, we addressed two practical problems about the key abuse of CP-ABE in the cloud, and have presented an accountable authority CP-ABE system supporting white-box traceability and public auditing. Specifically, the proposed system could trace the malicious users for illegal key sharing. And for the semi-trusted authority, its illegal key (re-)distributing misbehavior could be caught and prosecuted. Furthermore, we have provided an auditor to judge whether a malicious user is innocent or framed by the authority. As far as we known, this is the first CP-ABE system that simultaneously supports white-box traceability, accountable authority and public auditing. We have also proved that the new system is fully secure in the standard model.

Note that there exists a stronger notion for traceability called black-box traceability. In black-box scenario, the malicious user could hide the decryption algorithm by tweaking it, as well as the decryption key. And in this case, the proposed system with white-box traceability in this paper will fail since both the decryption key and decryption algorithm are not well-formed. In our future work, we will focus on constructing an accountable authority CP-ABE system which is black-box traceability and public auditing.

**Acknowledgements.** We are grateful to the anonymous reviewers for their invaluable suggestions. This work is supported in part by the National Natural Science Foundation of China under Grant 61321064, Grant 61371083, Grant 61373154, Grant 61402282, and Grant 61411146001, in part by the Specialized Research Fund for the Doctoral Program of Higher Education of China through the Prioritized Development Projects under Grant 20130073130004, and in part by the Natural Science Foundation of Shanghai of Yang-Fan Plan under Grant 14YF1410400.

## A   Proof of Lemma 2

*Proof.* Suppose there exists a PPT attacker $\mathcal{A}$ that has advantage $Adv_{\mathcal{A}}\Sigma_{aatcpabe}$ in breaking $\Sigma_{aatcpabe}$. We construct a PPT algorithm $\mathcal{B}$ that has advantage $Adv_{\mathcal{B}}\Sigma_{cpabe}$ in breaking the underlying CP-ABE system $\Sigma_{cpabe}$, which equals to $Adv_{\mathcal{A}}\Sigma_{aatcpabe}$.

- **Setup:** $\Sigma_{cpabe}$ gives $\mathcal{B}$ the public parameters $pp_{cpabe} = (N, g, g^{\beta}, e(g,g)^{\alpha}, \{\mathcal{U}_i = g^{u_i}\}_{i \in \mathcal{U}})$. $\mathcal{B}$ randomly chooses $a, \kappa \in \mathbb{Z}_N$, it also chooses two random primes $p$ and $q$ for which it holds $p \neq q$, $|p| = |q|$ and $gcd(pq, (p-1)(q-1)) = 1$, and then let $n = pq$, $\pi = lcm(p-1, q-1)$, $Q = \pi^{-1} \ mod \ n$ and $g_1 = (1 + n)$. $\mathcal{B}$ gives $\mathcal{A}$ the public parameters $(N, n, g_1, v = g^{\beta}, g, g^{a}, g^{\kappa}, g^{\mu}, e(g,g)^{\alpha}, \{\mathcal{U}_i = g^{u_i}\}_{i \in \mathcal{U}})$.
- **Query Phase 1:** The attacker $\mathcal{A}$ will submit $(id, S)$ to $\mathcal{B}$ to query a decryption key, then $\mathcal{B}$ submits $S$ to $\Sigma_{cpabe}$ and gets the corresponding decryption key in the form of $\tilde{sk} = \langle \tilde{K} = g^{\alpha}g^{\beta\tilde{c}}R, \tilde{L} = g^{\tilde{c}}R_0, \{\tilde{K}_i = \mathcal{U}_i^{\tilde{c}}R_i\}_{i \in S}\rangle$. Note that in the proof of [14], the authority is free to choose a decryption key on its own and passes it on to the user. In our setting, however, the authority and the user

engage in a key generation protocol where the decryption key is jointly determined by both of them (via the choice of numbers $t$ and $c$). Hence the authority does not have complete control over the decryption key. The problem can be solved as follows. The authority generates a primary secret key $sk_{pri}$ on its own and then "forces" the output of a user during key generation. Recall that during the key generation protocol, a user first chooses a random $t \in \mathbb{Z}_N$ and sends $R_U = g^t$ to the authority. The user gives to the authority a zero-knowledge proof of knowledge of the discrete log of $R_U$. The proof of knowledge property of the proof system implies the existence of a *knowledge extractor* **Extr** (see Sect. 2.6). Using **Extr** on the user during the proof of knowledge protocol, the authority can extract the discrete log $t$ (by rewinding the user during protocol execution) with all but negligible probability. Thus, in the IND-CPA security game, $\mathcal{B}$ could extract the discrete log $t$ of $R_U$ (which was sent by the attacker $\mathcal{A}$). Then $\mathcal{B}$ chooses a random $r \in \mathbb{Z}_N^*$. It computes $T = \tilde{T} = g_1^{id} r^n \bmod n^2$ and $1/(a+T) \bmod N$. Then $\mathcal{B}$ sets $c = \tilde{c}/(a+T)$, $t_{id} = c/t$ implicitly and randomly chooses $R_0' \in G_{p3}$ by using $g_3$, then computes $\bar{K} = (\tilde{K})^{\frac{1}{a+T}}(g^t)^{\frac{1}{a+T}} = (g^\alpha g^{\beta \tilde{c}} R)^{\frac{1}{a+T}} g^{\frac{\kappa t}{a+T}} = g^{\frac{\alpha}{a+T}} v^c g^{\frac{\kappa t}{a+T}} R^{\frac{1}{a+T}}$, $K = \bar{K}(g^\mu)^{t_{id}}$, $\bar{L} = (\tilde{L})^{\frac{1}{a+T}} = (g^{\tilde{c}} R_0)^{\frac{1}{a+T}} = g^c R_0^{\frac{1}{a+T}}$, $L = \bar{L}$, $\bar{L}' = (\tilde{L})^{\frac{1}{a+T}} = (g^{\tilde{c}} R_0)^{\frac{a}{a+T}} = g^{ac} R_0^{\frac{a}{a+T}} R_0'$, $L' = \bar{L}'$, $\{\bar{K}_i = \tilde{K}_i = \mathcal{U}_i^{\tilde{c}} R_i = \mathcal{U}_i^{(a+T)c} R_i\}_{i \in S}$, $\{K_i = \tilde{K}_i\}_{i \in S}$. $\mathcal{B}$ gives $\mathcal{A}$ the decryption key $sk_{id,S} = \langle S, K, T, L, L', R_U, t_{id}, \{K_i\}_{i \in S} \rangle$.[5]

- **Challenge:** The attacker $\mathcal{A}$ submits to $\mathcal{B}$ two equal length messages $(m_0, m_1)$ and an LSSS matrix $(A^*, \rho)$. Then $\mathcal{B}$ submits $(m_0, m_1)$ and $(A^*, \rho)$ to $\Sigma_{cpabe}$, and obtains the challenge ciphertext as follows: $\tilde{ct} = \langle \tilde{C} = m_\delta \cdot e(g,g)^{\alpha s}, \tilde{C}_0 = g^s, \{\tilde{C}_{j,1} = g^{\beta A_j \vec{y}} \mathcal{U}_{\rho(j)}^{-r_j}, \tilde{C}_{j,2} = g^{r_j}\}_{j \in [l]}, (A^*, \rho) \rangle$. $\mathcal{B}$ sets $C = \tilde{C}, C_0 = \tilde{C}_0, C_1 = (\tilde{C}_0)^a = g^{as}, C_2 = (\tilde{C}_0)^\kappa = g^{\kappa s}, C_3 = (\tilde{C}_0)^\mu = g^{\mu s}, C_{j,1} = \tilde{C}_{j,1} = v^{A_j \vec{y}} \mathcal{U}_{\rho(j)}^{-r_j}$, $C_{j,2} = \tilde{C}_{j,2}$. Then, $\mathcal{B}$ gives the challenge ciphertext $ct = \langle C, C_0, C_1, C_2, C_3, \{C_{j,1}, C_{j,2}\}_{j \in [l]}, (A^*, \rho) \rangle$ to $\mathcal{A}$.
- **Query Phase 2:** This phase is the same with Phase 1.
- **Guess:** $\mathcal{A}$ outputs and gives his guess $\delta'$ to $\mathcal{B}$. Then $\mathcal{B}$ gives $\delta'$ to $\Sigma_{cpabe}$.
  Since the distributions of the public parameters, decryption keys and challenge ciphertext in the above game are the same as that in the real system, we have $Adv_{\mathcal{B}} \Sigma_{cpabe} = Adv_{\mathcal{A}} \Sigma_{aatcpabe}$.

# B    Proof of Theorem 2

*Proof.* Suppose there exists a PPT attacker $\mathcal{A}$ that has non-negligible advantage in winning the DishonestAuthority game for our AAT-CP-ABE system. We construct a PPT algorithm $\mathcal{B}$ that has non-negligible advantage in solving discrete log in $G_{p1}$.

$\mathcal{B}$ proceeds as follows. $\mathcal{B}$ runs the algorithm $\mathcal{A}$ and gets the public parameters $pp = (N, n, g_1, v, g, g^a, g^\kappa, g^\mu, e(g,g)^\alpha, \{\mathcal{U}_i = g^{u_i}\}_{i \in \mathcal{U}})$ and a user's $(id, S)$ from

---

[5] Note that $R_0'$ makes the $G_{p3}$ part of $L'$ uncorrelated to the $G_{p3}$ part of $L$, this is why our simulator needs $g_3$.

$\mathcal{A}$. It then invokes the challenger and passes on $g$ to it, and gets a challenge $R_U = g^t$. The goal of $\mathcal{B}$ is to makes use of $\mathcal{A}$ to get the discrete log $t$ of $R_U$ with respect to $g$.

$\mathcal{B}$ will engage in the key generation protocol with $\mathcal{A}$ to get a decryption key for the user with $(id, S)$ as follows. It sends $R_U$ to the attacker $\mathcal{A}$ and has to give a zero-knowledge proof of knowledge of the discrete log of $R_U$. The zero-knowledge property of the proof system implies the existence of a simulator $S$ which is able to successfully simulate the view of $\mathcal{A}$ in the protocol (by rewinding $\mathcal{A}$) with all but negligible probability. $\mathcal{B}$ will use the simulator $S$ to simulate the required proof even without of knowledge of $t$. And $\mathcal{B}$ receives $c$ and the primary secret key $sk_{pri}$ as follows: $\langle S, \overline{K} = g^{\frac{\alpha}{a+\overline{T}}} g^{\frac{\kappa t}{a+\overline{T}}} v^c R, \overline{T} = g_1^{id} r^n \bmod n^2, \overline{L} = g^c R_0, \overline{L'} = g^{ac} R_0', \{\overline{K_i} = \mathcal{U}_i^{(a+\overline{T})c} R_i\}_{i \in S} \rangle$. As before, $\mathcal{B}$ checks whether the following equalities hold or not: $(1) e(\overline{L'}, g) = e(\overline{L}, g^a) = e(g^a, (g)^c)$; $(2)$ $e(\overline{K}, g^a g^{\overline{T}}) = e(g, g)^{\alpha} e(\overline{L'}(\overline{L})^{\overline{T}}, v) e(R_U, g^{\kappa})$; $(3)$ $\exists x \in S$ s.t. $e(\mathcal{U}_x, \overline{L'}(\overline{L})^{\overline{T}}) = e(\overline{K_x}, g)$.

If any of these checks fail, $\mathcal{B}$ aborts as would an honest user in the key generation protocol.

Now with non-negligible advantage, the attacker $\mathcal{A}$ outputs a decryption key $sk_{id}^*$ such that $\texttt{Trace}(pp, msk, sk_{id}^*) \to id$, $\texttt{Audit}(pp, sk_{id}, sk_{id}^*) \to guilty$ and $t_{id}^*$ equals $t_{id}$ (which is unknown to $\mathcal{B}$). The decryption key $sk_{id}^*$ is set as follows: $\langle S, K = \overline{K}(g^{\mu})^{t_{id}}, T = \overline{T}, L = \overline{L}, L' = \overline{L'}, R_U, t_{id}^*, \{K_i = \overline{K_i}\}_{i \in S} \rangle$. Then $\mathcal{B}$ computes $t = c/t_{id}^*$ and outputs $t$ as the discrete log (with respect to $g$) of the challenge $R_U$ and halts.

## C    Proof Sketch of Theorem 3

**Proof Sketch.** Suppose there exists a PPT attacker $\mathcal{A}$ that has non-negligible advantage $\epsilon$ in winning the traceability game after making $q'$ key queries, w.l.o.g., assuming $q = q' + 1$, we construct a PPT algorithm that has non-negligible advantage in breaking $q$-SDH assumption or Assumption 2. $\mathcal{B}$ is given an instance of $q$-SDH problem and an instance of Assumption 2 problem as follows[6].

- $\mathcal{B}$ is given an instance of $q$-SDH problem: Let $G$ be a bilinear group of order $N = p_1 p_2 p_3$ (three distinct primes), $G_i$ be the subgroup of order $p_i$ in $G$ (where $1 \leq i \leq 3$), $e : G \times G \to G_T$ be a bilinear map, $a \in \mathbb{Z}_{p_1}^*$ and $\tilde{g} \in G_{p_1}$. $\mathcal{B}$ is given an instance of $q$-SDH problem $\mathcal{INS}_{SDH} = (G, G_T, N, e, \tilde{g}, \tilde{g}^a, ..., \tilde{g}^{a^q}, p_1, p_2, p_3)$.
- $\mathcal{B}$ is given an instance of Assumption 2 problem: Let $G$ be a bilinear group of order $N = p_1 p_2 p_3$ (three distinct primes), $G_i$ be the subgroup of order $p_i$ in $G$ (where $1 \leq i \leq 3$), $e : G \times G \to G_T$ be a bilinear map, $\tilde{g}, X_1 \in G_{p_1}$, $X_2, Y_2 \in G_{p_2}$, $X_3, Y_3 \in G_{p_3}$, $\delta \in \{0, 1\}$ and if $\delta = 0$, $T' \in G$, if $\delta = 1$, $T' \in G_{p_1 p_3}$. $\mathcal{B}$ is given an instance of Assumption 2 problem $\mathcal{INS}_{Ass2} = (G, G_T, N, e, \tilde{g}, X_1 X_2, X_3, Y_2 Y_3, T')$.

---

[6] Note that this two instances are independent from each other.

The goal of $\mathcal{B}$ is to output a bit $\delta' \in \{0,1\}$ to determine $T' \in G$ or $T' \in G_{p_1 p_3}$ for solving the Assumption 2 problem, and a tuple $(T_i, w_i) \in \mathbb{Z}_{p_1} \times G_{p_1}$ satisfying $w_i = \tilde{g}^{1/(a+T_i)}$ for solving the $q$-SDH problem. $\mathcal{B}$ will make use of $\mathcal{A}$ to break at least one of the above assumptions.

Note that the structure of our system is similar to that of [21], and both of the two systems use a Boneh-Boyen-style signature to achieve the unforgeability property of decryption key. Correspondingly, the proof of the DishonestUser game in our system is also similar to the proof of white-box traceability in [21]. And using a similar proof method from [21], it is easy to give a proof that $\mathcal{B}$ will make use of $\mathcal{A}$ to break at least one of the above assumptions in our system. Due to space limitations, we refer the interested reader to the full version of this paper for the proof of this theorem.

## D    Proof of Theorem 4

*Proof.* Let the output of an attacker $\mathcal{A}$ be the public parameters $pp$, two different secret keys $sk_{id,S} = \langle S, K, T, L, L', R_U, t_{id}, \{K_i\}_{i \in S} \rangle$ and $\tilde{sk}_{id,S} = \langle S, \tilde{K}, \tilde{T}, \tilde{L}, \tilde{L}', \tilde{R}_U, \tilde{t}_{id}, \{\tilde{K}_i\}_{i \in S} \rangle$, and a ciphertext $ct = \langle C, C_0, C_1, C_2, C_3, \{C_{j,1}, C_{j,2}\}_{j \in [l]}, (A, \rho) \rangle$. $\mathcal{A}$ wins implies that the following conditions (as defined in the key sanity check game in Subsect. 3.2) are all fulfilled.

Conditions $(1) - (5)$:
(1) $\texttt{KeySanityCheck}(pp, sk_{id,S}) \to 1$; (2) $\texttt{KeySanityCheck}(pp, \tilde{sk}_{id,S}) \to 1$;
(3) $\texttt{Decrypt}(pp, sk_{id,S}, ct) \neq \bot$; (4) $\texttt{Decrypt}(pp, \tilde{sk}_{id,S}, ct) \neq \bot$;
(5) $\texttt{Decrypt}(pp, sk_{id,S}, ct) \neq \texttt{Decrypt}(pp, \tilde{sk}_{id,S}, ct)$.
Condition (1) implies

(1) $sk$ is in the form of $(S, K, T, L, L', R_U, t_{id}, \{K_i\}_{i \in S})$ and $T \in \mathbb{Z}_{n^2}^*, K, L, L',$ $R_U, \{K_i\}_{i \in S} \in G$.
(2) $e(L', g) = e(L, g^a)$.
(3) $e(K, g^a g^T) = e(g, g)^\alpha e(L'(L)^T, v) e(R_U, g^\kappa) e((g^a g^T)^{t_{id}}, g^\mu)$.
(4) $\exists x \in S$ s.t. $e(\mathcal{U}_x, L'(L)^T) = e(K_x, g)$.

Similarly, condition (2) implies

(1) $sk$ is in the form of $(S, \tilde{K}, \tilde{T}, \tilde{L}, \tilde{L}', \tilde{R}_U, \tilde{t}_{id}, \{\tilde{K}_i\}_{i \in S})$ and $\tilde{T} \in \mathbb{Z}_{n^2}^*,$ $\tilde{K}, \tilde{L}, \tilde{L}', \tilde{R}_U, \{\tilde{K}_i\}_{i \in S} \in G$.
(2) $e(\tilde{L}', g) = e(\tilde{L}, g^a)$.
(3) $e(\tilde{K}, g^a g^{\tilde{T}}) = e(g, g)^\alpha e(\tilde{L}'(\tilde{L})^{\tilde{T}}, v) e(\tilde{R}_U, g^\kappa) e((g^a g^{\tilde{T}})^{\tilde{t}_{id}}, g^\mu)$.
(4) $\exists x \in S$ s.t. $e(\mathcal{U}_x, \tilde{L}'(\tilde{L})^{\tilde{T}}) = e(\tilde{K}_x, g)$.

From conditions (1) and (3), we have $D = e((C_0)^T C_1, K)(e(C_2, R_u) e(C_3, (g^T g^a)^{t_{id}}))^{-1}$, $E = \Pi_{\rho(j) \in S}(e(C_{j,1}, (L)^T L') e(C_{j,2}, K_{\rho(j)}))^{\omega_j}$, $F = D/E = e(g,g)^{\alpha s}, m = C/F$. And from conditions (2) and (4), we have $\tilde{D} = e((C_0)^{\tilde{T}} C_1, \tilde{K})(e(C_2, \tilde{R}_u) e(C_3, (g^{\tilde{T}} g^a)^{\tilde{t}_{id}}))^{-1}$, $\tilde{E} = \Pi_{\rho(j) \in S}(e(C_{j,1}, (\tilde{L})^{\tilde{T}} \tilde{L}') e(C_{j,2}, \tilde{K}_{\rho(j)}))^{\omega_j}, \tilde{F} = \tilde{D}/\tilde{E} = e(g,g)^{\alpha s}, m = C/\tilde{F}$.

From conditions $(1) - (4)$, we have $F = D/E = e(g,g)^{\alpha s} = \tilde{F} = \tilde{D}/\tilde{E}, m = C/F = C/\tilde{F}$ $(*)$. However, condition $(5)$ implies that $C/F \neq C/\tilde{F}$, where $F = D/E, \tilde{F} = \tilde{D}/\tilde{E}$, which contradicts to $(*)$. Thus $\mathcal{A}$ wins the game only with negligible probability.

# References

1. Armbrust, M., Fox, A., Griffith, R., Joseph, A.D., Katz, R., Konwinski, A., Lee, G., Patterson, D., Rabkin, A., Stoica, I., et al.: A view of cloud computing. Commun. ACM **53**(4), 50–58 (2010)
2. Beimel, A.: Secure schemes for secret sharing and key distribution. Ph.D. thesis, Israel Institute of Technology, Technion, Haifa, Israel (1996)
3. Bellare, M., Goldreich, O.: On defining proofs of knowledge. In: Brickell, E.F. (ed.) CRYPTO 1992. LNCS, vol. 740, pp. 390–420. Springer, Heidelberg (1993)
4. Bethencourt, J., Sahai, A., Waters, B.: Ciphertext-policy attribute-based encryption. In: IEEE Symposium on Security and Privacy. SP 2007, pp. 321–334. IEEE (2007)
5. Boneh, D., Boyen, X.: Short signatures without random oracles. In: Cachin, C., Camenisch, J.L. (eds.) EUROCRYPT 2004. LNCS, vol. 3027, pp. 56–73. Springer, Heidelberg (2004)
6. Boneh, D., Franklin, M.: Identity-based encryption from the weil pairing. In: Kilian, J. (ed.) CRYPTO 2001. LNCS, vol. 2139, p. 213. Springer, Heidelberg (2001)
7. Boneh, D., Goh, E.-J., Nissim, K.: Evaluating 2-DNF formulas on ciphertexts. In: Kilian, J. (ed.) TCC 2005. LNCS, vol. 3378, pp. 325–341. Springer, Heidelberg (2005)
8. Chase, M.: Multi-authority attribute based encryption. In: Vadhan, S.P. (ed.) TCC 2007. LNCS, vol. 4392, pp. 515–534. Springer, Heidelberg (2007)
9. Deng, H., Wu, Q., Qin, B., Mao, J., Liu, X., Zhang, L., Shi, W.: Who Is touching my cloud. In: Kutyłowski, M., Vaidya, J. (eds.) ESORICS 2014, Part I. LNCS, vol. 8712, pp. 362–379. Springer, Heidelberg (2014)
10. Goyal, V.: Reducing trust in the PKG in identity based cryptosystems. In: Menezes, A. (ed.) CRYPTO 2007. LNCS, vol. 4622, pp. 430–447. Springer, Heidelberg (2007)
11. Goyal, V., Jain, A., Pandey, O., Sahai, A.: Bounded ciphertext policy attribute based encryption. In: Aceto, L., Damgård, I., Goldberg, L.A., Halldórsson, M.M., Ingólfsdóttir, A., Walukiewicz, I. (eds.) ICALP 2008, Part II. LNCS, vol. 5126, pp. 579–591. Springer, Heidelberg (2008)
12. Goyal, V., Lu, S., Sahai, A., Waters, B.: Black-box accountable authority identity-based encryption. In: Proceedings of the 15th ACM Conference on Computer and Communications Security, pp. 427–436. ACM (2008)
13. Goyal, V., Pandey, O., Sahai, A., Waters, B.: Attribute-based encryption for fine-grained access control of encrypted data. In: Proceedings of the 13th ACM Conference on Computer and Communications Security, pp. 89–98. ACM (2006)
14. Lewko, A., Okamoto, T., Sahai, A., Takashima, K., Waters, B.: Fully secure functional encryption: attribute-based encryption and (hierarchical) inner product encryption. In: Gilbert, H. (ed.) EUROCRYPT 2010. LNCS, vol. 6110, pp. 62–91. Springer, Heidelberg (2010)
15. Lewko, A., Waters, B.: New proof methods for attribute-based encryption: achieving full security through selective techniques. In: Safavi-Naini, R., Canetti, R. (eds.) CRYPTO 2012. LNCS, vol. 7417, pp. 180–198. Springer, Heidelberg (2012)

16. Lewko, A., Waters, B.: Decentralizing attribute-based encryption. In: Paterson, K.G. (ed.) EUROCRYPT 2011. LNCS, vol. 6632, pp. 568–588. Springer, Heidelberg (2011)
17. Li, J., Huang, Q., Chen, X., Chow, S.S.M., Wong, D.S., Xie, D.: Multi-authority ciphertext-policy attribute-based encryption with accountability. In: Proceedings of the 6th ACM Symposium on Information, Computer and Communications Security, pp. 386–390. ACM (2011)
18. Li, J., Ren, K., Kim, K.: A2be: Accountable attribute-based encryption for abuse free access control. IACR Cryptology ePrint Arch. 2009, 118 (2009)
19. Liu, Z., Cao, Z., Huang, Q., Wong, D.S., Yuen, T.H.: Fully secure multi-authority ciphertext-policy attribute-based encryption without random oracles. In: Atluri, V., Diaz, C. (eds.) ESORICS 2011. LNCS, vol. 6879, pp. 278–297. Springer, Heidelberg (2011)
20. Liu, Z., Cao, Z., Wong, D.S.: Blackbox traceable cp-abe: how to catch people leaking their keys by selling decryption devices on ebay. In: Proceedings of the 2013 ACM SIGSAC Conference on Computer & Communications Security, pp. 475–486. ACM (2013)
21. Liu, Z., Cao, Z., Wong, D.S.: White-box traceable ciphertext-policy attribute-based encryption supporting any monotone access structures. IEEE Trans. Inf. Forensics Secur. 8(1), 76–88 (2013)
22. Ning, J., Cao, Z., Dong, X., Wei, L., Lin, X.: Large universe ciphertext-policy attribute-based encryption with white-box traceability. In: Kutyłowski, M., Vaidya, J. (eds.) ESORICS 2014, Part II. LNCS, vol. 8713, pp. 55–72. Springer, Heidelberg (2014)
23. Ning, J., Dong, X., Cao, Z., Wei, L., Lin, X.: White-box traceable ciphertext-policy attribute-based encryption supporting flexible attributes. IEEE Trans. Inf. Forensics Secur. 10(6), 1274–1288 (2015)
24. Okamoto, T., Takashima, K.: Fully secure functional encryption with general relations from the decisional linear assumption. In: Rabin, T. (ed.) CRYPTO 2010. LNCS, vol. 6223, pp. 191–208. Springer, Heidelberg (2010)
25. Ostrovsky, R., Sahai, A., Waters, B.: Attribute-based encryption with non-monotonic access structures. In: Proceedings of the 14th ACM Conference on Computer and Communications Security, pp. 195–203. ACM (2007)
26. Sahai, A., Seyalioglu, H., Waters, B.: Dynamic credentials and ciphertext delegation for attribute-based encryption. In: Safavi-Naini, R., Canetti, R. (eds.) CRYPTO 2012. LNCS, vol. 7417, pp. 199–217. Springer, Heidelberg (2012)
27. Sahai, A., Waters, B.: Fuzzy identity-based encryption. In: Cramer, R. (ed.) EURO-CRYPT 2005. LNCS, vol. 3494, pp. 457–473. Springer, Heidelberg (2005)
28. Shamir, A.: Identity-based cryptosystems and signature schemes. In: Blakely, G.R., Chaum, D. (eds.) CRYPTO 1984. LNCS, vol. 196, pp. 47–53. Springer, Heidelberg (1985)
29. Waters, B.: Ciphertext-policy attribute-based encryption: an expressive, efficient, and provably secure realization. In: Catalano, D., Fazio, N., Gennaro, R., Nicolosi, A. (eds.) PKC 2011. LNCS, vol. 6571, pp. 53–70. Springer, Heidelberg (2011)

# Code Analysis and Side-Channels

# DexHunter: Toward Extracting Hidden Code from Packed Android Applications

Yueqian Zhang, Xiapu Luo$^{(\boxtimes)}$, and Haoyang Yin

Department of Computing, The Hong Kong Polytechnic University Shenzhen Research Institute, The Hong Kong Polytechnic University, Kowloon, Hong Kong {csyzhang,csxluo}@comp.polyu.edu.hk, yin.haoyang@connect.polyu.hk

**Abstract.** The rapid growth of mobile application (or simply app) economy provides lucrative and profitable targets for hackers. Among OWASP's top ten mobile risks for 2014, the lack of binary protections makes it easy to reverse, modify, and repackage Android apps. Recently, a number of packing services have been proposed to protect Android apps by hiding the original executable file (i.e., dex file). However, little is known about their effectiveness and efficiency. In this paper, we perform the first systematic investigation on such services by answering two questions: (1) what are the major techniques used by these services and their effects on apps? (2) can the original dex file in a packed app be recovered? If yes, how? We not only reveal their techniques and evaluate their effects, but also propose and develop a novel system, named *DexHunter*, to extract dex files protected by these services. It is worth noting that *DexHunter* supports both the Dalvik virtual machine (DVM) and the new Android Runtime (ART). The experimental results show that *DexHunter* can extract dex files from packed apps effectively and efficiently.

## 1 Introduction

Being the most popular mobile operating system [29], Android has attracted around 60 % more app downloads than iOS, and made nearly \$3 billion in revenue from Google Play last year [18], not to mention many other third-party Android markets. The massive success of Android apps poses lucrative and profitable targets for attackers. For example, it was recently reported that 98 % of mobile malware targeted on Android devices [21]. In particular, attackers usually disassemble popular apps, insert malicious components, and then upload the repackaged apps to various markets for compromising victims' smartphones [13,15,16,45,51,53]. Moreover, attackers can make profits by changing the client IDs of ad components in apps created by others or adding new ad libraries to these apps [23]. These attacks are due to the lack of binary protections, which is among OWASP's top ten mobile risks for 2014 [4].

Recently, a number of packing services (or simply packers) have been proposed to protect Android apps from being reversed, modified, and repackaged [10,22]. The packers usually adopt various approaches to hide the original executable file (i.e., dex file) and impede the attempt of dumping the dex file. They

© Springer International Publishing Switzerland 2015
G. Pernul et al. (Eds.): ESORICS 2015, Part II, LNCS 9327, pp. 293–311, 2015.
DOI: 10.1007/978-3-319-24177-7_15

also employ code obfuscation techniques to raise the bar of understanding the internal logics. Note that attackers also use packers to harden malware so that they could evade signature-based detection and make it very difficult for security analysts to understand malware [9].

However, little is known about these packers, such as their effectiveness and efficiency. In this paper, we conduct the *first* systematic investigation on Android packers by answering two questions:

- What are the major techniques used by these packers and their effects on apps?
- Can the original **dex** file in a packed app be extracted? If yes, how?

We inspect six packing services that provide web portals to allow users to upload apps for hardening [8,11,12,30,39,50]. Our analysis in Sect. 2 reveals that these packing services usually employ one or more techniques to protect apps, including code obfuscation, dynamic code modification, dynamic loading, and anti-debugging. Moreover, we quantify their overhead, in terms of app's size and launch time, in Sect. 5.1.

Then, we examine whether the original **dex** file in a packed app can be extracted. We propose and develop a novel system, named *DexHunter*, which provides a general approach to recover the **dex** files from packed apps. *DexHunter* exploits the class loading process of Android's virtual machine, including both the Dalvik virtual machine (DVM) and the new Android Runtime (ART) [25]. It is non-trivial to design and develop *DexHunter* because of many challenging issues, such as handling dynamic code modification through a general approach, avoiding anti-debugging techniques, etc. By applying *DexHunter* to packed apps, we found that the packers under examination cannot effectively protect apps and the original **dex** files can be recovered. Note that in this paper we focus on how to extract hidden **dex** files from packed apps *without* touching on how the packers obfuscate the code [14], because obtaining the **dex** files is the prerequisite of deobfuscating the code, and we will investigate the latter in future work.

In summary, our major contributions include:

- We perform the *first* systematic examination on Android packers. We examine their techniques, assess their effectiveness in protecting apps, and evaluate their overhead introduced to apps. Our findings shed light on the research of Android apps protection.
- We propose *DexHunter*, a novel system for recovering the **dex** files from packed apps in both ART and DVM. To our best knowledge, *DexHunter* is the first system that can handle packed apps running on both Android runtimes. We implement *DexHunter* by modifying ART and DVM, and conduct careful evaluation on its effectiveness and efficiency.
- By applying *DexHunter* to real apps packed by six packers, we observe that it can automatically recover most **dex** files. The results indicate that existing packing services are *not* as secure as expected. We also share lessons learnt when dealing with these packers.

The rest of this paper is organized as follows. We examine the techniques used by existing packers in Sect. 2. Section 3 describes the goal and the basic idea of *DexHunter* and Sect. 4 details the design and implementation of *Dex-Hunter*. Section 5 reports the evaluation result. Section 6 discusses the limitations of *DexHunter* and our future work. After introducing related work in Sect. 7, we conclude the paper in Sect. 8.

# 2   Analysis of Packing Services

In this section, we analyze six app packers, including, Ali [8], Baidu [11], Bangcle [12], Tencent [50], Qihoo 360 Mobile [39], and ijiami [30]. The reasons of selecting them are twofold. First, these packers allow users to upload apps through web portals and then return packed apps. Hence, attackers can easily use such services to pack malware. In contrast, other packers, such as Arxan[1] and Apperian[2], do not provide such services, thus having few samples for analysis. Although it was reported that malware used ApkProtect to evade the detection [9], we cannot access the web page of ApkProtect. Second, China is one of a few countries that have very high Android malware encounter rates [32] and these packers are the major packing services in China, which are developed by professional security companies or big IT companies. We introduce the major techniques used by these packers in Sect. 2.1 and report the evaluation result of the overhead introduced by packers on apps in Sect. 5.1.

## 2.1   Common Techniques Used by Packing Services

**Obfuscation.** Obfuscation aims at preventing analysts from understanding the code [14]. Android provides ProGuard to obfuscate apps through modifying the names of classes, fields, and methods [24]. Advanced techniques to obfuscate Android apps, such as reordering control flow graphs, encrypting constant strings, etc., have been recently proposed [40,52]. Developers can also manually conduct obfuscation, such as, using Java reflection to call methods and access fields, implementing major functions in native code and then invoking them through Java native interface(JNI), etc. They can further obfuscate the correlation between Java code and native code by registering JNI methods with semantically meaningless names in the JNI_OnLoad function.

**Dynamic Code Modification.** Android apps are mostly written in Java and then turned into Dalvik bytecode. Note that it is not easy for apps in Dalvik bytecode to arbitrarily modify itself in DVM in a dynamic manner. Instead, they can invoke native code through JNI to modify bytecode in DVM [37], because the native code is running in the same context as the app's DVM so that the native code can access and manipulate the memory storing the bytecodes. As

---

[1] https://www.arxan.com/.

[2] http://www.apperian.com/.

an example, malware can employ native code to generate malicious bytecodes dynamically and then execute them in DVM [44].

Before executing the dex file in the new Android runtime (i.e., ART), ART will compile the dex file into oat file in the ELF format. The native codes in so files can not only change instructions in dex and oat files, but also modify key data structures in the memory, such as DexHeader, ClassDef, ArtMethod, etc., in order to assure that the contents are correct only when they are used, and the contents will be wiped out after they have been used.

**Dynamic Loading.** Android allows apps to load codes from external sources (in dex or jar format) at runtime. Leveraging this feature, packers usually encrypt the original dex file, decrypt and load it before running the app.

**Anti-debugging.** Since Linux allows a process to attach to another process for debugging, to thwart the debugging through *gdb*, packed apps usually attach to themselves using *ptrace*[1]. The rationale is that only one process can attach to a target process at the same time. In other words, if an app (target process) attaches to itself at runtime, gdb cannot attach to it, thus further debugging operations are prohibited. Some packers will also check whether special threads, such as the JDWP (Java Debug Wire Protocol) thread, have been attached. Moreover, advanced packers can check whether the apps are running in an emulator or the underlying system has been rooted.

**Table 1.** A summary of the six packers' features.

| Packing service | Obfuscation | Dynamic code mod- ification | Dynamic loading | Anti- debugging | Add shared libraries | Insert classes | Support ART |
|---|---|---|---|---|---|---|---|
| Bangcle | YES | NO | YES | YES | YES | YES | YES |
| Tencent | YES | YES | NO | YES | YES | YES | YES |
| 360 Mobile | YES | NO | YES | YES | YES | YES | YES |
| ijiami | YES | NO | YES | YES | YES | YES | YES |
| Ali | YES | YES | YES | YES | YES | YES | NO |
| Baidu | YES | YES | YES | YES | YES | YES | YES |

## 2.2 Packers Under Investigation

We identify the major techniques used in the six packers through manual analysis. Since these packers are evolving and do not provide version number, our examination is based on the packed apps whose original versions were uploaded those packers' web portals on March-15-2015. As shown in Table 1, all of them add extra shared libraries (i.e., 6th column) and new instructions to the original app (i.e., 7th column). Moreover, they adopt obfuscation (i.e., 2nd column) and anti-debugging techniques (i.e., 5th column). While only half of them use dynamic code modification (i.e., 3rd column), all except Tecent packer employ dynamic loading approach. As Google introduced the new runtime (i.e., ART) to replace DVM, all except Ali packer support ART.

# 3  DexHunter: Goal and Basic Idea

*DexHunter* aims at extracting dex files from packed apps through a unified approach. It first launches the packed app in a real smartphone, and then locates and dumps the unpacked content when the app is running. We will also correct some fields corrupted by packers if necessary. Note that *DexHunter* does not handle code obfuscation and junk instructions. Moreover, it only considers the dynamic loading conducted when an app is executed, because most packers do so to shorten launch time. We discuss how to extend *DexHunter* to deal with arbitrary dynamic loading in Sect. 6.

## 3.1  Basic Idea

Android apps are compiled to dex files, which are in turn zipped into a single apk file together with other resources. If DVM is utilized, when a newly installed app is started for the first time, DVM converts the dex file extracted from the apk file to the odex format. If ART is used, it will turn the dex file into the oat file upon the installation [20].

An intuitive approach to realize *DexHunter* is to first locate the odex header or the oat header in the memory by searching for their magic numbers, and then dump the corresponding memory by parsing the headers. However, this approach has several limitations. First, accessing the packed app's memory requires such approach to attach to the app's process, such as using ptrace[1]. Unfortunately, packed apps usually employ anti-debugging techniques as described in Sect. 2 to prevent itself from being attached. Second, this approach will miss the real content resulted from dynamic code modification that happens when a class is being initialized. Note that a class may be loaded without being initialized. Third, this approach may miss dex files due to corrupted dex headers caused by packed apps. Fourth, this approach may dump fake odex or oat files because packed apps can create fake headers.

To tackle these issues, we propose a novel and unified approach that exploits the class loading process of Android runtime, including both DVM and ART, to locate and dump the desired files. The rationale behind the basic idea is that Android runtime can locate and parse the dex file in order to execute it. While the following analysis is based on the source code of Android 4.4.3, we believe the basic idea can be applied to future versions.

Since each class should be loaded before it can be used, Android provides three approaches [28] to load classes: (1) the implicit procedure of loading classes,

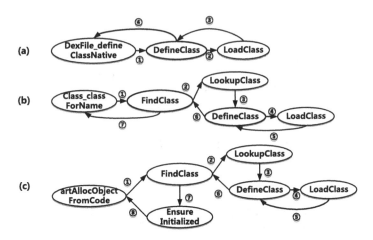

**Fig. 1.** The three approaches of loading classes and their invocation graphs in ART. The numbers indicate the invocation order.

such as the **new** operation, which happens if the corresponding class has never been used before; (2) the explicit invocation of `Class.forName`; (3) the explicit invocation of `ClassLoader.loadClass`. Although DVM and ART have different implementations for these class loading approaches, we observe that for a given virtual machine these three approaches share a few key common functions, which will be elaborated in Sects. 3.2 and 3.3 for ART and DVM, respectively.

Leveraging this observation, *DexHunter* inserts codes into a selected key function to locate the required files and trigger the invocation of <clinit>. Moreover, we propose novel approaches (Sect. 4.3) to pro-actively load and initialize classes. To overcome anti-debugging and anti-emulating techniques, we integrate *Dex-Hunter* with DVM and ART, and execute packed apps in a real smartphone running modified DVM and ART as described in Sect. 4.2.

## 3.2   ART

In KitKat (Android 4.4), the new Android runtime, ART, was introduced to replace DVM for better performance by compiling an app's bytecode into native instructions. Adopting the ahead-of-time compilation *(AOT)* technology, ART performs the compilation when an app is being installed. More precisely, the **dex** file will be compiled into **oat** file that adopts the ELF format.

To load a class, ART reads the **dex** or **jar** file using a native method called `DexFile_openDexFileNative` in *libart.so*. If the corresponding **oat** file does not exist, ART invokes a tool named **dex2oat** to compile the **dex** or **jar** file into an **oat** file. If the **oat** file exists but has not been loaded, ART reads it and puts it into a memory cache map to avoid opening the file repeatedly. After successfully accessing the **oat** file, ART creates a structure named `OatFile` to record important information of this file. We will detail it when describing how to dump the **dex** file in Sect. 4.2.

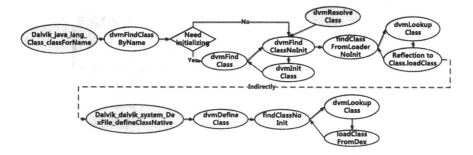

**Fig. 2.** The three approaches of loading classes and their invocation graphs in DVM.

Then, ART can use different methods to load the class, whose invocation graphs are shown in Fig. 1. More precisely, the explicit invocation of `ClassLoader.loadClass` will call the native method `DexFile_define ClassNative` (i.e., Fig. 1(a)). The invocation of `Class.forName` will call the native method `Class_classForName` (i.e., Fig. 1(a)). The new operation will eventually call the native method `artAllocObjectFromCode` (i.e., Fig. 1(c)). By comparing the two sub-figures in Fig. 1, we can locate the common functions called by these three approaches. More precisely, we select `DefineClass` as the key function for inserting *DexHunter*'s code, because it creates the `Class` object and is responsible for loading and linking classes.

### 3.3 DVM

Figure 2 illustrates the three approaches of loading classes and their invocation graphs in DVM. The invocation of `Class.forName` will call `Dalvik_java_lang_Class_classForName`. Calling `ClassLoader.loadClass` will eventually invoke `Dalvik_dalvik_system_DexFile_defineClassNative`. The implicit class loading will result in the invocation of `dvmResolveClass`. Moreover, `dvmInitClass` is responsible for initializing a class. Before invoking it, the initialization status is checked through `dvmIsClassInitialized`. The *Reflection to Class.loadClass* in Fig. 2 means that there is a reflection invoking procedure that invokes the related class loader's `loadClass` method at Java level. By analyzing Fig. 2, we select `Dalvik_dalvik_system_DexFile _defineClassNative` as the key function for injecting *DexHunter*'s code, because it creates the `Class` object and loads the class from the dex file directly.

## 4 DexHunter: Design and Implementation

### 4.1 Architecture

Figure 3 depicts the major procedure of *DexHunter*. Given a packed app, *Dex-Hunter* first determines whether it is packed by known packing services (i.e., those in Table 1) through the signatures to be described in Sect. 4.4. Moreover,

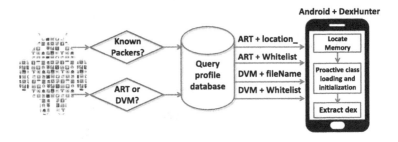

**Fig. 3.** Using DexHunter in smartphone to recover **dex** files from packed apps.

we will check which runtime can run this app. If the app supports both DVM and ART, we will use the ART version *DexHunter* to recover the **dex** file. If the app is packed by known packers, we will obtain the corresponding parameters from the profile database, including **location_** for ART and **fileName** for DVM, which will be detailed in Sect. 4.2. Otherwise, *DexHunter* will dump the target memory but exclude system libraries listed in a while list.

Depending on the selected runtime, the packed app will be installed and executed in a smartphone with modified libart.so or libdvm.so for ART or DVM, respectively. If DVM is used, *DexHunter* will first dump the optimized **dex** file from the smartphone and then combine it and its dependent files to reconstruct the **dex** file. If ART is adopted, *DexHunter* will generate the **dex** file directly.

## 4.2   Locating and Dumping Dex Files

**ART.**  Note that each **oat** file contains the information of the original **dex** file in its **oatdata** section [43]. Therefore, after ART opens and reads an **oat** file, it will create an **OatFile** structure to record important information of the file and a **DexFile** object containing information related to the original **dex** file. In particular, there are three important values in the **DexFile** object, through which we can locate the **dex** file, including:

- **begin_**, which depicts the start address of the memory region containing the original dex file;
- **size_**, which represents the length;
- **location_**, which indicates the **oat** file's location.

We add codes in the **DefineClass** function to check the value of **location_** when a class is being loaded. Section 4.5 describes how to decide the packed app's **location_** and the system libraries' **location_**. Therefore, by specifying the value of **location_**, we can recognize all classes in the original **dex** file and then create a thread to accomplish the dumping operation. In this thread, the **DexFile** object, which is also a parameter of the **DefineClass** function, is passed in and then the thread can get the memory region to which the **DexFile** object refers. By invoking the methods **DexFile::Begin()** and **DexFile::Size()**, we can obtain the start address and the length of the memory region containing the original dex file. As a result, we can recover the original **dex** file.

**DVM.** After loading a `dex` or `jar` file, DVM will create a structure named `DexOrJar`, which records the information of the file. One member named `fileName` refers to the location of the file. Moreover, a `DvmDex` object, which represents an open `odex` file, is associated with the corresponding `DexOrJar` object. The `DvmDex` object has a member named `memMap` that maintains the corresponding memory region of the opened dex file. Its `addr` member stores the start address while the `length` member denotes the length of the memory region.

To dump the desired `dex` file, we add codes to the selected function `Dalvik_dalvik_system_DexFile_defineClassNative` and specify the value of `fileName`. Once the `dex` file we expect is located through `fileName`, the memory region of the targeted `odex` file can also be figured out through the related `DvmDex` object. More precisely, the member `memMap` in the `DvmDex` object records the specified memory region. The member `addr` of `memMap` indicates the start address while the member `length` stores the length. As a result, we can obtain the `odex` file.

The `odex` file format was designed to let DVM work more efficiently and it is usually much smaller than the original `dex` file, because it only includes critical information. For instance, in an `odex` file, references to framework APIs are replaced by indexes of a pre-loaded *vtable* and therefore methods can be quickly invoked. Therefore, `odex` files rely on dependence files, which are device-specific and can be found in the directory `/system/framework`.

`Odex` files cannot be converted into `dex` format directly because they rely on dependencies. Since dependencies are device-specific, they must be copied from the same device that runs the packed app. Finally, *DexHunter* uses smali/backsmali to recover the `dex` file from the `odex` file and its dependencies [2].

### 4.3   Proactive Class Loading and Initialization

For each newly loaded class, its class initializer (i.e. <clinit>) may not be invoked yet. Since this method is invoked before any other method in the same class, packers can add codes in <clinit> to perform dynamic code modification.

To deal with this potential issue, we propose a novel approach that turns ART's lazy initialization into proactive class loading and initialization. Note that ART calls <clinit> only after the `Class` object is used for the first time, such as invoking static method member, etc. Our approach loads all classes in the same `dex` file and initializes them as shown in Algorithm 1. More precisely, in ART, before the dumper thread is created, *DexHunter* traverses all classes in the same `dex` file in `DefineClass` function, and then invokes the `FindClass` function along with every class's descriptor for loading them. Note that invoking `FindClass` can avoid loading the same class repeatedly in the same class loader. After that, each class is initialized by invoking `EnsureInitialized`. All these operations are done in the same loop.

The algorithm for DVM is similar except that `FindClass` is changed to `dvmDefineClass` and `EnsureInitialized` is replaced with `dvmIsClass Initialized` and `dvmInitClass`.

**Algorithm 1.** Traversing and Initializing Classes

---

**input**  : A "DexFile" pointer $dex\_file$ and the number of classes in this dex file $n$
**output**: All initialized "Class" objects belonging to the dex file

> **for** $i \leftarrow 0$ **to** $n - 1$ **do**
> | ClassDef $\leftarrow$ GetClassDef($dex\_file,i$);
> | Descriptor $\leftarrow$ GetClassDescriptor(ClassDef);
> | ClassObject $\leftarrow$ FindClass(Descriptor);
> | ClassObject $\leftarrow$ EnsureInitialized(ClassObject);
> **end**

---

### 4.4 Identifying Packers

**Known Packers.** *DexHunter* identifies known packers using (1) changes in files, (2) inserted classes, and (3) location_ for ART and fileName for DVM. We observe that all packers add new files, especially native codes (i.e., so files), as shown in Table 2. Moreover, they modify the original AndroidManifest.xml and classes.dex. After inspecting packed apps, we find that all packers insert their own classes into the app, as shown in Table 3. We will describe how to extract location_ or fileName in Sect. 4.5. Since it is easy to recognize and differentiate these inserted files and classes, we use them as features to recognize known packers. In future work, we will investigate advanced features, such as Software bertillonage [17], if packers try to hide current features.

**Unknown Packers.** For unknown packers, we observe that they usually adopt dynamic code modification with the following common steps. First, they load packed dex files dynamically into memory, which will be converted to oat files by ART. Then, they employ memory manipulation functions (e.g., *"memcpy"*) to modify the code. Before that, they may call *"mprotect"* to alter the accessing attributes of corresponding memory regions, for example, changing a memory fragment from read-only (r--) to readable and writable (rw-). We can hook aforementioned functions to capture this behavior patten. If such behavior pattern is observed, *DexHunter* regards the app as a packed app.

### 4.5 Extracting the Values of location_ and fileName

location_ and fileName provide hints to dump the desired dex files in ART and DVM, respectively. To examine their values set by different packers and those used by system libraries, we modify ART and DVM to collect these values.

In ART, we add a function named GetUid to obtain the current process's user id by invoking system calls directly instead of using getuid in bionic library due to the limit of the configuration for compiling Android. Moreover, we modify DefineClass function to record all location_ values if the current process's user id is equal to that of the target app. Therefore, when DefineClass is used to generate the Class object for the opened oat file, we can obtain the names

**Table 2.** New files introduced by the packers. "xxx" denotes the app's original package name.

| Packers | New files |
|---------|-----------|
| 360 | assets/libprotectClass.so, assets/libprotectClass_x86.so, assets/libqupc.so |
| ALi | lib/armeabi/libmobisec.so, lib/armeabi/libmobisecx.so,lib/armeabi/libmobisecy.so, |
| | lib/armeabi/libmobisecz.so |
| Baidu | assets/baiduprotect.jar,assets/libbaiduprotect_x86.so,lib/armeabi/ libbaiduprotect.so, |
| | lib/x86/libbaiduprotect.so |
| Bangcle | assets/bangcleplugin/container.apk,assets/bangcleplugin/dgc,assets/meta-data/manifest.mf |
| | assets/meta-data/rsa.pub,assets/meta-data/rsa.sig,assets/bangcle_classes.jar |
| | assets/libsecexe.so,assets/libsecexe.x86.so,assets/libsecmain.so |
| | assets/libsecmain.x86.so,assets/libsecpreload.so,assets/libsecpreload.x86.so |
| | assets/xxx,assets/xxx.art,assets/xxx.L |
| | assets/xxx.x86,assets/xxx.x86.L |
| ijiami | assets/ijm_lib/armeabi/libexec.so,assets/ijm_lib/armeabi/libexecmain.so, |
| | assets/ijm_lib/x86/libexec.so |
| | assets/ijm_lib/x86/libexecmain.so,assets/ijiami.dat |
| | META_INF/af.bin, META_INF/sdata.bin,META_INF/signed.bin |
| Tencent | assets/lib/armeabi/libmain.so,assets/lib/armeabi/libshell.so |

**Table 3.** Inserted classes. The classes in parentheses will only appear if the original dex file has an Application class. Otherwise, they will not be inserted.

| Packers | Inserted classes |
|---------|------------------|
| 360 | com.qihoo.util.StubApplication, com.qihoo.util.DefenceReport |
| ALi | com.ali.mobisecenhance.StubApplication |
| Baidu | com.baidu.protect.A, com.baidu.protect.StubApplication, com.baidu.protect.StubProvider |
| Bangcle | com.bangcle.protect.Acall,com.bangcle.protect.MyClassLoader, com.bangcle.protect.Util |
| | neo.proxy.DistributeReceiver |
| | (com.bangcle.protect.FirstApplication), (com.bangcle.protect.ApplicationWrapper) |
| ijiami | com.shell.NativeApplication |
| | (com.shell.SuperApplication) |
| Tencent | com.tencent.StubShell.ProxyShell, com.tencent.StubShell.ShellHelper |

**Table 4.** The values of `location_` or `fileName` in apps packed by six packers.

| Packers | String |
|---------|--------|
| Bangcle | /data/data/package_name/.cache/classes.jar |
| Baidu | /data/data/package_name/.1/classes.jar |
| Tencent | /data/app/installed_apk_name |
| 360 | internal.dex (/data/local/tmp/fake@apk.dex) |
| ijiami | /data/data/package_name/cache/.0000 |
| ALi | /data/app-lib/installed_apk_name/libmobisecy.so (i.e., the path of libmobisecy.so, which is located in the app's native library directory) |

of all `dex` files related to the classes being loaded. We first filter out all known system libraries and then decide which names should be kept according to the features of different packers. For instance, some packers load the original `dex` file dynamically and the `oat` file bound to the name of installed apk is only a stub. Hence, such names should be removed.

In DVM, we follow the similar steps to collect the values of `file Name`. More precisely, we modify the function `Dalvik_dalvik_system_DexFile_defineClassNative` to locate the `DexOrJar` object and get the value of `fileName` in this object.

Table 4 lists the `location_` or `fileName` from six packers we examine. For apps packed by 360 packer, the value is "/data/local/tmp/fake@apk.dex" when the apps are executed for the first time. Then, the value is changed to "internal.dex".

## 5    Evaluation

We downloaded 40 open source apps from F-Droid [6] and uploaded them to the web portals of the six packers. Then, we execute the packed apps and *DexHunter* on a Nexus 4 smartphone running Android 4.4.3 with Qualcomm Snapdragon S4 Pro 1.5 GHz CPU and 2G RAM. Table 5 shows that not all apps can be successfully packed by those packers and some packed apps cannot be run.

### 5.1    Overhead Introduced by Packers

We evaluate the overhead introduced by different packers in terms of increased file size and prolonged launch time. By subtracting the original file size from the size of packed app, we obtain the increased file size. Figure 4 illustrates that most packed apps are larger than the original apps and Bangcle introduces more than 600 KB data. A few packed apps are smaller than the original ones. The reason is some packers will compress the original dex file.

To measure the prolonged launch time, we randomly select 17 apps and run each original app and the packed one 30 times in the smartphone. We collect

**Table 5.** Creating packed apps.

| Packers | Number of apps | Number of packed apps | Numbers of packed apps that can run |
|---|---|---|---|
| 360 | 40 | 39 | 37 |
| ALi | 40 | 39 | 37 |
| Baidu | 40 | 37 | 36 |
| Bangcle | 40 | 40 | 40 |
| ijiami | 40 | 40 | 40 |
| Tencent | 40 | 40 | 38 |

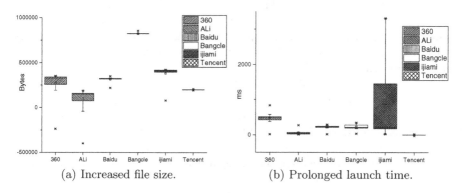

(a) Increased file size.          (b) Prolonged launch time.

**Fig. 4.** Overhead introduced by packers in terms of increased file size and launch time.

the samples of launch time (i.e. from its start to the end of its main activity's initialization) measured by executing "am start -n -W MainActivity", and then compute the inflated launch time. Figure 4(b) demonstrates that all packers introduce obvious additional delays. The minimal delay brought by Tencent packer may be due to the fact that it does not load external dex files.

## 5.2 DexHunter's Effectiveness

We apply *DexHunter* to all packed apps that can run in the smartphone. In fact, *DexHunter* can bypass all anti-debugging methods used by these packers. Since it becomes part of the process created by Zygote, all anti-debugging methods mentioned in Sect. 2.1 will not stop *DexHunter*.

For apps packed by 360 packer and ijiami packer, *DexHunter* can recover the dex files in both ART and DVM. Moreover, the extracted dex files can be parsed by de-compilers (e.g., smali/baksmali, IDA, etc.).

For apps packed by Bangle, *DexHunter* can successfully extract the dex files in both ART and DVM. The dex files dumped from DVM can be parsed by de-compilers. However, the dex files recovered from ART have some instructions that cannot be parsed by baksmali. The reason is that the dex files are extracted from the oat files prepared by Bangcle packer that has used some new Dalvik opcodes [5]. The developer of baksmali said that this issue will be fixed soon.

For apps packed by Tencent packer, we found that the dex files dumped by *DexHunter* are incomplete in both ART and DVM, because the method objects in the heap, which represent hidden methods, are modified dynamically but the dex file in memory is not changed. However, since the valid data is still in the dex file's data section, we can manually correct the attributes and the related pointers of the hidden methods in the dex file.

For apps packed by Baidu packer, we observe that the dex file's header will be wiped if any class's initializer is executed. Hence, we perform the dumping operations without pro-actively initializing the classes. Moreover, we found that the dumped dex files are incomplete. More precisely, in dex files, for each class, there is a class_data_item object to describe the members of the class. However, some class_data_item objects of the dumped dex file are wiped by Baidu packer. In order to capture the positions of the class_data_item objects, we modified the runtime to record the addresses of class_data_item objects. When the application runs, the wiped class_data_item objects in so files will be released to the heap and the pointers, which are in the dex file, to the class_data_item objects will also be corrected. After filling in the correct data in the class_data_item objects, we can obtain complete dex files.

Since Ali packer only supports DVM, *DexHunter* recovers the dex files in DVM. In a dex file, each code_item object describes a method and maintains a pointer to it. But some pointers to code_item objects are invalid in the dumped dex files. We modified DVM to obtain the addresses of code_item objects and the corresponding instructions. Combining the process's memory layout, we found that the lost code_item objects and instructions are located in a memory region allocated by the packed app. To repair the dex files, we could also dump this memory region and record the addresses of the lost code_item objects.

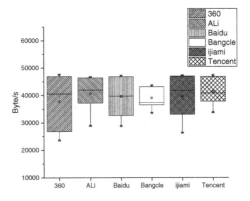

**Fig. 5.** Dumping speed of *DexHunter*.

## 5.3    DexHunter's Efficiency

We also evaluate *DexHunter*'s efficiency on the same Nexus 4 device. We randomly select 15 apps that can be packed by all six packers. For each sample, *DexHunter* performs the dumping operation for 30 times. Note that the time complexity of the dumping procedure is $O(n)$ ($n$ represents size of the target memory region in bytes). Figure 5 shows *DexHunter*'s dumping speed which is around 40 KB/s and does not change much among different packers.

# 6    Discussion

Although *DexHunter* can recover the dex files from apps packed by existing packers, it has the following limitations and we will tackle them in future work. First, some packers will wreck some fields in the dumped dex files as mentioned in Sect. 5.2. Currently, we repair them through semi-automatic or manual approach. In future work, we will enhance *DexHunter* to automate this process.

Second, if an app dynamically loads components from other places after waiting for a long period or certain conditions, *DexHunter* cannot dump this dex file, because *DexHunter* does not know when the component will be loaded. We will extend DexHunter to handle it by hooking all methods for dynamic class loading in future work. Alternatively, we can first conduct static analysis [38] to determine how to trigger the app's dynamic class loading and then perform it.

# 7    Related Work

Hardening Android apps has attracted great attention from the industry [9,26]. Although there are a few simultaneous work from the industry, there lacks of a systematic study on it yet. In a recent article and presentation [9,34], Apvrille and Nigam reported the results of manually unpacking apps packed by a few packers, such as APKProtect and Bangcle. Strazzere and Sawyer reported their tool, named android-unpacker, to defeat four packers including APKProtect, Bangcle, 360 Mobile, and LIAPP [48,49]. Since it will attach to the last thread of an app, we observed that it failed in several scenarios, such as, the thread has already been attached by a ptrace, the thread is killed, etc. Note that *DexHunter* will not be affected by this issue because it is integrated into the runtime. We developed *DexDumper* for extracting the dex files of apps running on Android 2.3 or older versions [45]. Note that *DexDumper* lacks of the functions provided by *DexHunter*, including handling apps running on Android with version newer than 2.3, dealing with anti-debugging, processing odex files, etc.

ZjDroid was released by Baidu Inc. [7] for unpacking packed apps. It relies on Xposed [3] and locates the dex files by hooking `BaseDexClassLoader` to obtain `DexOrJar`. There are several significant differences between ZjDroid and *DexHunter*. First, *DexHunter* supports both ART and DVM while ZjDroid only works in DVM. Second, ZjDroid cannot pro-actively load and initialize classes and therefore it may miss the real content resulted from dynamic code modification that happens when a Class object is being initialized. *DexHunter* can overcome this issue because it conducts pro-active class loading and initialization. Third, since ZjDroid waits for user commands to dump the dex files, it may be evaded by packers that destroy some key data which is used only once. *DexHunter* can handle this issue because it extracts the dex files *before* the first class in the dex file is used. Fourth, since ZjDroid relies on Xposed and obtains the information at Java level, it can be easily detected and interrupted by advanced packed. In contrast, *DexHunter* will not be affected.

Park described one general unpacking method for packed apps [35]. It is quite different from *DexHunter* because it needs to insert codes to packed apps (i.e., repackage the packed app). This approach can be easily detected by packed apps. Moreover, compared to *DexHunter*, its functionality is quite limited.

Since packing is widely used by malware to evade the signature-based detection, many studies have investigated how to unpack such malware [19]. However, all of them focus on packers for Windows/Linux native codes [41]. It is worth noting that unpacking techniques for x86 binaries cannot be applied to Android because of two reasons. First, Android and x86 have different execution model. Second, techniques for x86 unpacking only need to examine x86 instructions in memory while dumping odex files need to investigate both the memory of Android runtime (e.g., DVM) and that of the underlying Linux because packers usually use native codes running on Linux to modify the byte codes in DVM.

We review some representative work of automatically dumping packed native executables because an app's native codes can be packed through traditional approaches. PolyUnpack is the first general approach to automatically identify and dump packed codes [42]. It first statically analyzes an executable and then uses debugging APIs to check each instruction. If an instruction sequence does not exist in the disassembly of the executable, PolyUnpack identifies the packed codes and then extracts them. Renovo runs a packed executable in QEMU and monitors each instruction [31]. If new codes are written to memory and then executed, Renovo regards it as one layer of unpacking conducted by the packed program. Instead of tracking each instruction, OmniUnpack [33] and Eureka [46] adopt coarse-grained execution monitoring to improve the performance. The former uses OllyBone [47] to track executed pages and the latter monitors selected system calls. Justin employs a set of heuristics to improve the detection of the end of unpacking and adopts several countermeasures to defeat some evasion techniques used by malware [27]. Although dynamic approaches could effectively extract packed code, they suffer from some common limitations, such as, higher overhead compared to static analysis, limited time of executing packed program, etc. Perdisci et al. developed a classification system for determining whether an executable is packed or not before sending it to unpacking systems, thus significantly saving the processing time [36].

# 8 Conclusion

We conduct the first systemic investigation on existing Android packers by examining their major techniques, evaluating their effects on apps, and assessing their effectiveness. We propose and develop *DexHunter*, a novel system for recovering dex files from packed apps in both ART and DVM. To our best knowledge, it is the first unpacking system that supports both ART and DVM. The experimental results based on real packed apps demonstrate the effectiveness and efficiency of *DexHunter*. This research reveals important issues in existing Android packers and sheds light on the future research of Android apps protection.

**Acknowledgments.** We thank the anonymous reviewers for their quality reviews. We thank Yuru Shao and Xian Zhan for their contributions to the preliminary study of this research. This work is supported in part by the Hong Kong GRF (No. PolyU 5389/13E), the National Natural Science Foundation of China (No. 61202396), the PolyU Research Grant (G-UA3X), and the Open Fund of Key Lab of Digital Signal and Image Processing of Guangdong Province (2013GDDSIPL-04).

# References

1. ptrace. http://linux.die.net/man/2/ptrace
2. Smali. https://code.google.com/p/smali/
3. Xposed. http://forum.xda-developers.com/xposed/xposed-installer-versions-chan gelog-t2714053
4. Owasp mobile top 10 risks (2014). http://bit.ly/1FAIJiv
5. Dalvik opcode changes in art (2015). https://github.com/anestisb/oatdump_plus# dalvik-opcode-changes-in-art
6. F-droid (2015). https://f-droid.org/
7. Zjdroid (2015). http://safe.baidu.com/opensec_detail_2.html
8. Alibaba Inc.: http://jaq.alibaba.com/
9. Apvrille, A., Nigam, R.: Obfuscation in android malware, and how to fight back. In: Virus Bulletin, July 2014
10. Arxan Tech., Inc.: Securing mobile apps in the wild with app hardening and runtime protection (2014). http://bit.ly/1aliJil
11. Baidu Inc.: http://apkprotect.baidu.com/
12. Bangcle Inc.: http://www.bangcle.com/
13. Chen, K., Liu, P., Zhang, Y.: Achieving accuracy and scalability simultaneously in detecting application clones on android markets. In: Proceedings of the ACM ICSE (2014)
14. Collberg, C., Nagra, J.: Surreptitious Software: Obfuscation, Watermarking, and Tamperproofing for Software Protection. Addison-Wesley, Upper Saddle River (2009)
15. Crussell, J., Gibler, C., Chen, H.: Attack of the clones: detecting cloned applications on android markets. In: Foresti, S., Yung, M., Martinelli, F. (eds.) ESORICS 2012. LNCS, vol. 7459, pp. 37–54. Springer, Heidelberg (2012)
16. Crussell, J., Gibler, C., Chen, H.: Scalable semantics-based detection of similar android applications. In: Proceedings of the ESORICS (2013)

17. Davies, J., German, D., Godfrey, M., Hindle, A.: Software bertillonage - determining the provenance of software development artifacts. Empirical Softw. Eng. **18**(6), 1195–1237 (2013)
18. Dredge, S.: Android beats IOS for app downloads, but revenues are still a different story (2015). http://bit.ly/1A2conk
19. Egele, M., Scholte, T., Kirda, E., Kruegel, C.: A survey on automated dynamic malware-analysis techniques and tools. ACM Comput. Surv. **44**(2), 1–42 (2012)
20. Frumusanu, A.: A closer look at android runtime (ART) in android L
21. Fung, B.: The time a major financial institution was hacked in under 15 minutes (2015). http://wapo.st/1zcKNj0
22. Gartner Inc.: Debunking six myths of app wrapping (2015). http://gtnr.it/1aGJizc
23. Gibler, C., Stevens, R., Crussell, J., Chen, H., Zang, H., Choi, H.: Adrob: examining the landscape and impact of android application plagiarism. In: Proceedings of the ACM MobiSys (2013)
24. Google: Proguard. http://goo.gl/CLBIkD
25. Google Inc.: ART and Dalvik
26. Grassi, M.: Reverse engineering, pentesting, and hardening of android apps
27. Guo, F., Ferrie, P., Chiueh, T.: A study of the packer problem and its solutions. In: Lippmann, R., Kirda, E., Trachtenberg, A. (eds.) RAID 2008. LNCS, vol. 5230, pp. 98–115. Springer, Heidelberg (2008)
28. Halloway, S.: Component Development for the Java Platform. Addison-Wesley, Boston (2002)
29. IDC.: Android and IOS squeeze the competition (2015). http://bit.ly/17wYoFF
30. Ijiami Inc.: http://www.ijiami.cn/
31. Kang, M., Poosankam, P., Yin, H.: Renovo: a hidden code extractor for packed executables. In: Proceedings of WORM (2007)
32. Lookout Inc.: Mobile threats, made to measure (2014). http://goo.gl/EhJzdt
33. Martignoni, L., Christodorescu, M., Jha, S.: Omniunpack: fast, generic, and safe unpacking of malware. In: Proceedings of the ACSAC (2007)
34. Nigam, R.: Android packers: separating from the pack, June 2014. http://goo.gl/YiULcy
35. Park, Y.: We can still crack you! general unpacking method for android packer (no root). In: Proceedings of the Blackhat Asia (2015)
36. Perdisci, R., Lanzi, A., Lee, W.: Classification of packed executables for accurate computer virus detection. Pattern Recogn. Lett. **29**(14), 1941–1946 (2008)
37. Qian, C., Luo, X., Shao, Y., Chan, A.: On tracking information flows through JNI in android applications. In: Proceedings of the IEEE/IFIP DSN (2014)
38. Qian, C., Luo, X., Yu, L., Gu, G.: Vulhunter: towards discovering vulnerabilities in android applications. IEEE Micro **35**(1), 44–53 (2015)
39. Qihoo360 Inc.: http://dev.360.cn/protect/welcome
40. Rastogi, V., Chen, Y., Jiang, X.: Droidchameleon: evaluating android anti-malware against transformation attacks. In: Proceedings of the ACM ASIACCS (2013)
41. Roundy, K., Miller, B.: Binary-code obfuscations in prevalent packer tools. ACM Comput. Surv. **46**(1), 1–32 (2013)
42. Royal, P., Halpin, M., Dagon, D., Edmonds, R., Lee, W.: Polyunpack: automating the hidden-code extraction of unpack-executing malware. In: Proceedings of the ACSAC (2006)
43. Sabanal, P.: State of the art: exploring the new android kitkat runtime
44. Schulz, P.: Android security analysis challenge: tampering dalvik bytecode during runtime (2013). http://goo.gl/eIszsj

45. Shao, Y., Luo, X., Qian, C., Zhu, P., Zhang, L.: Towards a scalable resource-driven approach for detecting repackaged android applications. In: Proceedings of the ACSAC (2014)
46. Sharif, M., Yegneswaran, V., Saidi, H., Porras, P.A., Lee, W.: Eureka: a framework for enabling static malware analysis. In: Jajodia, S., Lopez, J. (eds.) ESORICS 2008. LNCS, vol. 5283, pp. 481–500. Springer, Heidelberg (2008)
47. Stewart, J.: Ollybone: semi-automatic unpacking on ia-32 (2006). http://goo.gl/LbQYiN
48. Strazzere, T.: android-unpacker (2014). https://github.com/strazzere/android-unpacker
49. Strazzere, T., Sawyer, J.: Android hacker protection level 0 (2014). http://goo.gl/BSKEop
50. Tencent Inc.: http://www.qcloud.com/product/product.php?item=appup
51. Zhang, F., Huang, H., Zhu, S., Wu, D., Liu, P.: Viewdroid: towards obfuscation-resilient mobile application repackaging detection. In: Proceedings of the ACM WiSec (2014)
52. Zheng, M., Lee, P.P.C., Lui, J.C.S.: ADAM: an automatic and extensible platform to stress test android anti-virus systems. In: Flegel, U., Markatos, E., Robertson, W. (eds.) DIMVA 2012. LNCS, vol. 7591, pp. 82–101. Springer, Heidelberg (2013)
53. Zhou, W., Zhou, Y., Jiang, X., Ning, P.: Detecting repackaged smartphone applications in third-party android marketplaces. In: Proceedings of the ACM CODASPY (2012)

# Identifying Arbitrary Memory Access Vulnerabilities in Privilege-Separated Software

Hong Hu[✉], Zheng Leong Chua, Zhenkai Liang, and Prateek Saxena

Department of Computer Science, National University of Singapore,
Singapore, Singapore
{huhong,chuazl,liangzk,prateeks}@comp.nus.edu.sg

**Abstract.** Privilege separation is a widely used technique to secure complex software systems. With privilege separation, software components are divided into several partitions and these partitions can only communicate through limited interfaces. However, the interfaces still provide a channel for one partition to influence code in other partitions. As a result, certain memory access patterns can be leveraged by attackers to perform arbitrary memory access. We refer to this type of memory access errors by the acronym *DUI (Dereference Under the Influence)*. In this paper, we present a systematic method to detect vulnerabilities leading to DUI through binary analysis, and to estimate the capability attackers can obtain through DUI exploits. The evaluation shows that our approach can accurately identify vulnerable code that leads to arbitrary memory access in real-world software components and programs, when they are transformed to privilege-separated designs.

## 1 Introduction

Privilege separation is widely used to secure complex software systems. With this method, software components are divided into several partitions. Each partition only has a reduced set of privileges and inter-partition communication is only possible via clearly defined interfaces. To protect legacy programs using privilege separation, developers need to transform the monolithic legacy programs. For example, the OpenSSH server was originally implemented as a monolithic program, where a single vulnerability will expose all critical resources to attackers. To mitigate the threat, part of OpenSSH code without access to high-privileged resources (e.g., password) was separated from other code and isolated as a slave process [39]. In addition, Qmail [4], Postfix [7] and Google Chrome [3,46] are also designed (or re-designed) with privilege separation.

To facilitate retrofitting legacy code into privilege-separation designs, many solutions have been proposed to partition software and assign each partition a different set of privileges, such as Wedge [6], Privtrans [11], and Privman [27]. The deployed techniques include sandboxing [44–46] and process-based isolation [6,11,27]. When the monolithic code is divided into several partitions, some program behaviors inside the original code (e.g., function calls or direct memory access) need to be transformed into inter-partition communications (e.g., via

© Springer International Publishing Switzerland 2015
G. Pernul et al. (Eds.): ESORICS 2015, Part II, LNCS 9327, pp. 312–331, 2015.
DOI: 10.1007/978-3-319-24177-7_16

socket and shared memory). As a result, program logic ensuring the correctness of program semantics, such as valid ranges of variables, may be separated into different partitions and fail to enforce the correctness. Therefore, additional checking code is often needed, especially in the high-privileged partitions, to make sure that data from other partitions is valid. However, if the transformation process fails to include checking code in a high-privileged partition, or the added checking code is inadequate, attackers can use specially-crafted inputs to compromise the high-privileged partitions and carry out malicious actions with escalated privileges.

Memory errors such as buffer overflow can be exploited in such cross-partition attacks. There are more subtle memory errors with which attackers can perform arbitrary memory access inside the high-privileged partition, if the victim partition has certain memory access patterns. For example, if a partition uses an input from an untrusted interface as the array index, writing to the array inside the partition is an arbitrary memory access under the influence of the input provider. If attackers provide the input, they can utilize this memory access behavior to modify critical data or retrieve secrets of the partition in a targeted manner.

In this paper, we refer to this type of memory access errors by the acronym *DUI (Dereference Under the Influence)*. It stems from the memory access pattern in the vulnerable partition: The address used in memory read or memory write is influenced by malicious data from other partitions. Through DUI exploits, attackers can corrupt discrete memory locations, instead of a continuous memory block, significantly improving the stability of the attacks.

**Challenges.** DUI exploits can be prevented through sufficient checks on interface inputs. Unfortunately, it is non-trivial to ensure that adequate checking code has been added at correct locations. The checking code in legacy programs is often scattered across many program locations in the monolithic code base, which is split during the privilege-separation transformation, it is necessary to guarantee that each of these program locations are checked correctly. However, to achieve this goal, manual modification usually takes a long time to fully understand the requirement of checking operations, while automatic separation methods often miss important checks. Therefore, we need a systematic method to detect such DUI vulnerabilities resulting from privilege-separation transformations.

**Our Approach.** To address these challenges, we develop an approach, DUI Detector, to automatically detect code suspicious to DUI exploits in the binary of trusted partitions. Specifically, through binary program analysis, we identify the suspicious instructions that use data from other partitions to dereference memories. Then we use symbolic analysis to identify code with the DUI vulnerability and assess the attackers' capabilities in exploiting them. DUI Detector helps to identify concrete code instances that are easily influenced by attackers among a large code base.

We applied our approach on several real-world software systems retrofitted with different types of isolation schemes. DUI Detector successfully detected

DUI vulnerabilities inside them. We present four case studies where attackers can perform DUI attacks. Furthermore, our approach reports the attackers' capability to the developers, providing a comprehensive understanding of the vulnerability.

In summary, this paper makes the following contributions:

- We study the problem of arbitrary memory access (DUI) in privilege-separation transformations, and identify several general memory access patterns leading to DUI vulnerabilities in binary instruction level.
- We design a novel mechanism to automatically detect DUI vulnerabilities, and to estimate attackers' capability in controlling user memory spaces. It helps developers add sufficient checking.
- We prototype an automated tool and evaluate it on several real-world software. Our tool automatically detects and comprehensively analyzes DUIs in these software programs when they are gone through privilege-separation transformation.

## 2  Problem Overview

In this section, we motivate the problem by a concrete example. Then we provide the problem definition of DUI detection and discuss two DUI types: The write DUI and the read DUI. At the end we discuss the memory access patterns used to detect DUI vulnerabilities.

```
1    struct subobj { ... } * p_sub;
2    struct object { ...
3        struct subobj * sub;
4    } * p_obj;
5
6    int main()  {
7        p_obj = create_object();
8        p_sub = create_subobj();
9        p_obj->sub = p_sub;
10   }
11
12   // create an object instance and return its pointer
13   struct object * create_object()
14   { ... }
15
16   // create a subobj instance and return its pointer
17   struct subobj * create_subobj()
18   { ... }
```

Listing 1.1. Example code to illustrate DUI problem.

### 2.1  Motivating Example

We use the example in Listing 1.1 to illustrate the memory access problem during the program transformation. In this example, the structure object has

one pointer of structure subobj. Functions create_object and create_subobj
return pointers of new structure instances. The statement on line 9 in function main assigns the pointer p_sub of a subobj instance to the subobj field
of a object instance. Originally function create_object and create_subobj
are in the same partition with the function main, and there are checking code
inside them to make sure that the return values are correct. During the transformation, these two functions are separated into a low-privileged partition since
they are not trusted any more. In this case, the return values could be malicious. To protect the high-privileged main function, we can use memory isolation to prevent the direct memory access from low-privileged code to main's
memory, in which case function create_object and create_subobj just manage main's memory. However, this is inadequate to protect the high-privileged
main: The statement on line 9 contains a memory access vulnerability. When
the low-privileged partition is malicious, it allows writing a malicious p_obj to a
memory location p_sub inside the protected one. The statement on line 9 is an
instance of DUI vulnerability.

## 2.2   Problem Definition

We give the definition of the problem solved in this paper.

*DUI Detection:* Given a partition of a privilege-separated program, we detect
whether the partition's memory access behaviors can be influenced by data from
its interfaces. In particular, the memory addresses or the data are derived from
the interface inputs, giving attackers the ability to read or write to a large range
of memory inside the partition.

Attackers use the DUI vulnerability as a memory access service to mount
attacks. They specify the address and the data through specially-crafted inputs.
DUI vulnerability then finishes the memory operation on behalf of attackers. In
real-world programs, the logics used to derive the address from the interface
inputs could be complicated, thus subtle and hard to spot. However, the final
result is that the attacker can exercise certain levels of influence over the address
of the memory operation. It is worthwhile to note that only controlling the
memory address is inadequate to corrupt the memory or to steal the sensitive
information. Corresponding data flows are necessary to provide the malicious
data or send the confidential data out. Based on the direction of the memory
access, there are two types of DUI, the write DUI and the read DUI.

```
1    v1 = API_recv();
2    v2 = API_recv();
3    array[v1] = v2;
```

Listing 1.2. An example of write DUI

**Write DUI.** We call a memory write operation the *write DUI* if both the memory address and the value to be written in the operation are derived from the
interface inputs. Take the code in Listing 1.2 as an example. The *API_recv()* is

an interface through which the code can receive data from other partitions. The memory write operation on line 3 has the address $array + v1$ and the data $v2$ derived from the interface inputs, which allows the input provider to write the selected data to any address in its memory space. We can relax the requirement of the data to be written to a value predictable by attackers. An example is that if $v2$ in Listing 1.2 is a constant 0, attackers can use $v2$ to reset important flags, or terminate a C-style string. With the write DUI, attackers can corrupt the memory of the vulnerable program. Not only can they mount control flow hijacking attacks by corrupting code pointers or return addresses, they can also change critical data in memory to mount non-control-data attacks [16,26].

```
1   v1   = API_recv ();
2   data = *(base + v1);
3   API_send(data);
```

**Listing 1.3.** An example of read DUI

***Read DUI.*** We call a memory read operation the *read DUI* if the memory address in the operation is derived from the interface inputs and the retrieved data are eventually passed to the output interface of the partition. Consider the example in Listing 1.3. *API_recv()* and *API_send()* are APIs used by the code to receive data from other partitions and send data to other partitions, respectively. This code snippet retrieves data from a local buffer and sends it out. Since the data retrieving address $base + v1$ is under the control of attackers via the interface input $v1$, attackers can steal sensitive information from the partition. For read DUI, it is insufficient to control the memory read address. The data being read has to reach an output interface for it to complete. In real-world programs, the web client may have secret keys or high-privileged files on the server client. Attackers can use read DUI vulnerability to steal the secret key or file. Another exploit is to leak the randomized address of the loaded modules, leading to bypassing address randomization protections [5,37].

### 2.3   Memory Access Patterns to Detect DUIs

Although attackers can use various ways to control the memory access, one DUI vulnerability is inevitably represented as attacker-controllable memory address and data in memory access instructions, i.e., the address is derived from the input, and the data also comes from the input (for the write DUI) or is sent out (for the read DUI). This observation inspires us to use instruction-level memory access patterns to detect DUI vulnerabilities. We summarize the memory access patterns used in DUI exploits below.

– *Write DUI Pattern 1.* The memory write address and the data are derived from the interface inputs. In this case, attackers control both the value and the address in memory write operation.

- *Write DUI Pattern 2.* The memory write address is derived from the interface inputs. The data value is predictable to attackers. Attackers can exploit this code to set the predictable value to any memory address.
- *Read DUI Pattern.* The memory read address is calculated from the interface inputs. The retrieved data are then passed to output interfaces (e.g., via network, file operation or standard printing).

# 3  Design

## 3.1  Overview

Figure 1 shows the design of our DUI detection tool, DUI Detector. It takes two inputs: The program binary containing the partition to be checked and a normal input to the program. It detects DUI vulnerabilities during the binary execution for the given input and estimates the capability of attackers obtained by DUI exploits. There are three phases in the process: Execution state collection, suspicious instruction shortlisting and dereference behavior analysis.

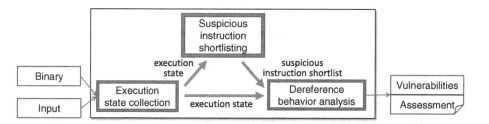

**Fig. 1.** Design of the DUI Detector. There are two inputs to the system. One is the program binary, containing the partition to be checked. Another one is a normal input to the program. The output is the list of DUI vulnerabilities and the assessment of attackers' capabilities.

**Execution State Collection.** First we run the program binary in an emulated environment with the given input and record all the execution states of the checked partition, including instructions, operands, processor states and memory states. We also log system-level information such as module loading and unloading behaviors.

**Suspicious Instruction Shortlisting.** From the execution states, our tool identifies instructions potentially vulnerable to DUI exploits. We use data dependency analysis to find the source of the memory address and the data used in memory access instructions. For a memory read operation, we also search forward to check whether the retrieved data is sent to other partitions through output interfaces. If the address is derived from the interface inputs and the data is derived or used in an attacker-controllable manner, we report this memory operation as a suspicious DUI vulnerability.

**Dereference Behavior Analysis.** Our tool generates the symbolic formula, called the *access formula*, to capture all the constraints from the interface inputs to the suspicious instruction. Then it analyzes the access formula to verify the DUI vulnerability and to assess the capability of attackers in controlling the memory space of the vulnerable partition.

DUI Detector reports the verified DUI vulnerabilities together with their severity to developers, helping them to fix the vulnerable code. Next, we introduce the key phases of the DUI Detector.

## 3.2    Suspicious Instruction Shortlisting

From the collected execution states, we use data dependency analysis to track the data flow of the memory address and the data used in memory access instructions. The methods used to detect DUIs are given below.

To detect write DUIs, we check for the following conditions for each instruction. (1) It is a memory write instruction, i.e., instructions that write the data into memory, like mov, add, push and successful conditional move cmov. (2) The source operand is derived from the interface inputs, or predictable to attackers. (3) The address of the destination operand is also derived from the interface inputs.

To detect read DUIs, it is insufficient to check just one single instruction. Other than the actual memory read operation, it is also necessary to identify the data flow from the read operation to output interfaces, as we discuss in Sect. 2. Hence, we use a two-step approach to identify a read DUI.

1. A memory read instruction is selected for further checking if it matches the following two conditions: (1) The instruction reads data from memory and saves the data into registers. Instructions reading from registers or without saving the data into registers are ignored. (2) The memory address is derived from the interface inputs.
2. For an instruction selected above, we perform forward slicing on the data flow of the destination operand (the retrieved data). If the data reaches an output interface, we report it as a potential read DUI.

Our tool generates a list of the suspicious instructions potential vulnerable to DUIs. However, strong constraints on the interface inputs could significantly limits the attackers' capability, even making the instruction unexploitable. Hence we need to analyze each suspicious instruction to confirm the vulnerability and assess attackers' capability.

## 3.3    Dereference Behavior Analysis

Given a suspicious instruction identified in the previous step, our tool extracts an access formula to represent the relationship between the interface inputs and the address or data used in the instruction. The access formula captures all the constraints in the execution states with respect to the interface inputs. There are four types of constraints in the access formula as follows.

- **Data-Flow Constraints.** Data-flow constraints describe the arithmetic relations between the address and the data in the DUI instruction and the interface inputs. They are presented as a sequence of arithmetic operations.
- **Control-Flow Constraints.** Control-flow constraints ensure that the attacked partition follows the same path as the one recorded in the execution states. We only consider the path constraints related to the interface inputs. Other path constraints are out of the attacker's control and are assumed to be satisfied.
- **Memory Space Constraints.** To reach the suspicious instruction, all the memory accesses should be legitimate. Specifically, the code must have the correct write or read permission of the accessed page. Otherwise, page fault exceptions will be raised and divert the execution path. This constraint limits the attacker's capability since only a subset of memory space is accessible.
- **Data Life-Cycle Constraints.** To create an effective attack, the malicious data (written data or retrieved data) must be used within its life-cycle. Otherwise, the suspicious instruction cannot be exploited. For example, if the malicious data written to a selected location is immediately overwritten by a benign value, the attack does not have any effect on the victim partition. To capture this constraint, our tool considers subsequent instructions in order to track the aliveness of the data.

The generated access formula captures all the constraints on the interface inputs to reach the suspicious instruction and continue the execution. By assessing the attacker's capability by exploiting the instruction, we can determine if the suspicious instruction is indeed a DUI vulnerability. If so, we report the suspicious instruction and the attackers' capability to developers.

**Attackers' Capability Assessment.** Attackers' capability is represented as the ability to control the address and the value in the memory operation. A larger memory range controllable by attackers indicates a stronger attackers' capability. However, due to the constraints on the interface inputs, not all the malicious inputs lead to a successful attack. The working inputs form a valid data space, and the attacker's capability is determined by the size of this space. Our tool constructs constraint queries to estimate this space size. Specifically, we assign concrete values or a memory range to the operands of the suspicious instruction, i.e., the address or the data. Then these assignments are added to the access formula as new constraints to form a query. By solving the query using a constraint solver, we get the answer to the following questions: **Q1:** Is there any input making the partition follow the same path to the suspicious instruction when the address or the data in the address have to be a given value? **Q2:** Is there any input making the partition follow the same path to the suspicious instruction when the address or the data have to be within a given range? **Q3:** Is it true that for any address or any data in the given range there is an input making the partition follow the same path to the suspicious instruction? The answer to the question **Q1** indicates attackers' capability on controlling specific addresses. This is useful to build real exploits, for example, writing the ROP gadget address to a function pointer. A negative answer to the question **Q2** helps filter out a memory range from attackers' capability. While a positive answer to the question **Q3** adds the queried range into attackers' capability.

We take several query strategies to efficiently answer these questions. These strategies are based on the bit-pattern analysis and the range analysis [33, 35]. Through these methods, we can estimate the valid memory space controllable by attackers for each of the suspicious instruction.

- **Initial Target Analysis.** We first consider the memory page permission to initialize the memory range. For a memory read operation, the target memory location has to be readable. For a memory write operation, the target memory location has to be writable. Using this method, the queried memory range is limited to the readable or writable memory space.
- **Bit-Pattern Analysis.** Bit pattern analysis uses queries that specify concrete values on particular bits (or all bits) of the target value [33, 35]. An example of the query is whether the last two bits of the address have to be 10. This gives the answer to question **Q1**.
- **Range Analysis.** The range query identifies whether the values inside a particular range are valid [35] or not. If all values are valid, we conclude that the queried range is a valid range. If no value is valid, we remove the range from the valid memory space. If only some values are valid, the query solver will give a concrete valid value. We use this value to divide the range to two subranges. Then we use the range query to query both subranges. This query answers question **Q2** and **Q3**.

Finally the report given by DUI Detector includes the identified DUI vulnerabilities, together with the attackers' capability obtained by exploiting such vulnerabilities. It points out all the vulnerable-prone code in the checked partition. This enables security analysts to focus their efforts on a particular portion of the code.

## 4    Implementation

We built a prototype of DUI Detector on a 32-bit Ubuntu 10.04 system by extending the BitBlaze [42] platform. The prototype uses STP [22] as the SMT solver to query the access formula.

### 4.1    Taint Propagation

DUI Detector uses taint analysis to track the data flow of the interface inputs. Data from the interfaces are bound with the taint information of the source. Taint information has two aspects: One aspect is the taint attribute, a flag indicating whether a particular memory byte is tainted or not. Another aspect is the taint record, which contains the sources of the taint attribute. We use TEMU, the dynamic analysis engine of BitBlaze, as the base of taint propagation. However, there are several problems when we use TEMU to build our tool. Next we discuss these problems and present our solutions.

**Finer-Gained Taint Record Propagation.** Since we need to capture all the execution constraints, the taint propagation has to be accurate to permit the identification of all data sources. The normal taint propagation focuses on taint attribute propagation, and pays less attention on the taint record propagation. For example, for a given instruction, TEMU checks all its operands, and copies the taint records of the first tainted operand to the destination operand. This propagation method loses some taint sources. For example, in the instruction add %ebx, %eax, if eax and ebx are tainted by different data sources, the taint sources of ebx get lost. To solve this problem, we instead identify all the tainted source operands and copy all distinct taint records to the destination operand. As a result, the taint records for each operand capture all the data sources used to derive the operand.

**1-Level Table Lookup.** If a memory read address is tainted, taint analysis has to decide to propagate the taint to the destination operand or not. Table lookup is a method to propagate the taint. However, table lookup results in over-tainting problem, leading to a high false positive. A better tainting method for table lookup is necessary to capture the read DUI and avoid the over-tainting problem. We observe that as more table lookups are performed, attackers likely have increasingly less influence over the destination. As such, we propose the 1-level table lookup: Only propagating the taint for a single level of memory indexing. When the tainted data retrieved from table lookup are used as an index again, we will not propagate the taint. Our implementation uses the most significant bit of the taint attribute to indicate whether it is tainted through table lookup or not. Note that 1-level table lookup will miss attacks that utilize high-level table lookup to corrupt memory locations. However, we believe that the benefit on false positive reduction overweighs the false negative introduced since attacks with high-level lookup are rare in real-world attacks. With 1-level table lookup, our tool captures memory read operations that are strongly controlled by attackers, and skips the weakly-controlled operations.

**Taint Propagation for XMM Registers.** XMM (eXtended Multi-Media) registers are used to speed up the memory operation (e.g., memcpy), by joining several 4-byte copies into a single 16-byte operation. TEMU does not support the taint propagation through XMM registers. When tainted data are copied into an XMM register, the taint information gets lost. To support the taint propagation, we extend TEMU to correctly propagate taint to XMM registers and read taint information from XMM registers.

### 4.2 Access Formula Generation

We use VINE [42], the static analysis component of BitBlaze, to generate the formula for memory access from the trace. As discussed in Sect. 3.3, there are four types of constraints affecting memory access. However, VINE only generates two constraints, the data-flow constraint and the control-flow constraint. To bridge this gap, we develop tools to add additional two constraints into the formula. There are two steps to generate the memory space constraints.

1. In the guest OS, we insert a kernel module to detect the module loading and unloading behaviors. The kernel module sends the update information of the loaded and unloaded module to TEMU. We log such information together with the number of traced instructions when a behavior happens.
2. Using the log file, we can construct the readable and writable memory ranges for each instruction. Specifically, we collect all the modules that are still loaded in the memory for a given instruction. The union of their readable and writable memory ranges is the valid memory space. We add the memory range as a memory space constraint to the access formula.

To generate the data life-cycle constraints for a particular instruction, we search forward from the given instruction in the trace to find the first memory write instruction that overwrites the data at the same address. We call this instruction the update instruction. The data life-cycle of the data starts from the given instruction, and ends at its update instruction.

## 5   Evaluation

We evaluated our approach in the following system: The host OS is a 32 bit Ubuntu 10.04 system, running on Openstack Cloud with two 2.4 GHz vCPUs and 4 GB RAM. The guest OS in TEMU is a 32 bit Ubuntu 9.10 system. Next, we present our evaluation results and then discuss the security implication of our findings.

### 5.1   Efficacy

We applied DUI Detector on privilege-isolated programs to detect DUI vulnerabilities in protected partitions. We focus on two particular isolation schemes: The isolation between malicious OS kernels and user space programs [17,25,32,41,48], and the isolation between malicious libraries and main programs [19,21,44–46]. We ran several programs on Linux system to get the execution trace, which were written to drive the execution through communications between different partitions. DUI Detector successfully detected read DUI and write DUI vulnerabilities in the protected user space code and the protected program main code. Further, DUI Detector assesses the attackers' capability obtained by exploiting such vulnerabilities. Next we present the details of these DUI vulnerabilities.

**User-Kernel Isolation.** A few proposals remove the OS kernel from the trusted base of the program execution, like hardware-based isolation (e.g., Flicker [31]) and hypervisor-based isolation (e.g., Overshadow [17]). These isolation schemes are designed to protect the sensitive data in user-space programs from the malicious kernel, so the kernel have no direct access to program memory space. Our goal is to detect DUI vulnerabilities inside protected user-space programs that allow the malicious kernel to corrupt programs' private user-space memory.

— *Glibc code exploitable by* brk. A write DUI was detected in the malloc function, which manages the heap memory for programs. The malloc calls the brk system call to request a new heap memory and takes the return value as the break value (the upper bound of data segment). Before looking into the detected DUI, we first illustrate the logic in malloc handling the return values of brk.

```
1   addr1 = brk(0);                    // get the current brk value
2   addr2 = brk(argument);             // request more space
3   *(addr1 + 4) = addr2 - addr1;      // store the size as metadata
```

This code snippet calls brk twice to create a heap memory region. The first brk call on line 1 is used to get the current break value (saved in $addr1$), which is the start address of the heap. The second brk call on line 2 is used to request more memory space and the new break value is stored in $addr2$. The memory location $addr1 + 4$ is used to store the size of the allocated data chunk, which is $addr2 - addr1$ in this case. The code on line 3 stores the size value into the metadata address. One of our tested programs invokes the malloc library call to call brk. In the recorded execution states, we found two instructions that match the write DUI Pattern 1, as listed below.

```
1   mov %eax, 0x4(%edx)
2   ...
3   mov %eax, 0x4(%edi)
```

For each instruction, both the value and the memory address are derived from the return values of brk system calls. By manipulating the system call return values, the malicious kernel can write any value into an arbitrary address in the victim process, even if the process is protected by encryption. We analyzed the capability of attackers and found that only the second instruction is exploitable. For the mov instruction on line 1, the data life-cycle constraints show that the value is immediately overwritten by another benign value. For the instruction on line 2, the first return value has to be a multiple of 8. We show the constraints on the return value generated by our tool below, where the $brkn$ is the $nth$ return value. DUI Detector generated the payloads in order to exploit this DUI vulnerability. The generated payloads successfully wrote the given address to the selected stack address.

```
1   condition( brk1%8 == 0 && brk2>brk1 )
2   address = brk1 + 0x2718;
3   data    = (brk2 - brk1 - 0x2718) | 0x1;
```

To explore other paths, we changed the condition to invalidate one of the constraints. The following are two conditions that lead to the write DUIs in other paths. The last one is the scenario of the Iago attack [15]. Note that DUI

Detector accurately identified the constraints of Iago attack: The address has to be non-multiple of 8 and the data write to the memory has to be congruent to 1 modulo 8.

```
1   condition(brk1%8 != 0 && brk1<brk2<brk3)
2   address : relies on brk1;
3   data    : relies on brk1 and brk2;
```

```
1   condition(brk1%8 != 0 && brk1<brk2>brk3)
2   address : relies on brk1;
3   data    : relies on brk1 and brk3;
```

— *Glibc code exploitable by* mmap2. The second DUI vulnerability in Glibc is in the code handling the mmap2 system call. The mmap2 system call on Linux is used to map files or devices into memory in the Linux system. It is widely used by programs to map large files into memory. From the execution trace, we identified a total of 1,653 suspicious instructions matching write DUI patterns. We further reduced them to 302 based on the attackers' capability analysis. Analysis of the remaining 302 instructions reveals that all of them use values derived from the first 3 mmap2 return values. Here we show the very first instruction among them. This is a write DUI, where the memory address and the data are derived from the first and the third mmap2 return values.

```
1   mov %eax, 0x1ac(%edi)
```

Using the queries we discuss in Sect. 3.3, we identified the valid memory space which the attacker can write values to. For a stack memory range over 0x0BFFF000 to 0x0BFFF2FF, we found that the attacker has no control over addresses whose last four bits are 1100 or 0100.

— cat *exploitable by* read *and* write. The UNIX utility program cat reads data from the given files, concatenates the content and writes them out to the standard output file. This behavior results in consecutive file read and write operations. The cat program we used is a derivative of the BSD cat program[1]. We identified read DUIs in the cat code, which can be exploited by malicious kernel to steal program's private information. To illustrate the read DUI, we present the pseudo code below.

```
1   nr = read(rfd, buf, size);
2   for(off = 0; nr; nr -= nw, off += nw)
3   {
4     nw = write(wfd, buf + off, nr);
5     if (nw == 0 || nw == -1)
6       goto error;
7   }
```

The loop condition *nr* is fully controlled by the malicious kernel. First, it is initialized by the return value of the read system call on line 1. For each loop,

---

[1] http://www.opensource.apple.com/source/text_cmds/text_cmds-87/cat/cat.c.

it is updated by the return value nw of the write call on line 2. nw is also used to advance the buffer for the next write call. When the kernel is changed to be untrusted, isolation mechanisms use deep copy to duplicate all system call parameters to a shared memory between kernel and process [41]. In this case, by manipulating the return value nw, the malicious kernel drives the process to copy its private data into shared memory space. With further capability analysis, we find that the attacker has full control over the value, i.e., the attacker is able to access any memory with the values ranging from 0x00000000 to 0xFFFFFFFF.

**Library Isolation.** Dynamic shared libraries are linked to software process at the runtime. Since the dynamic library lives in the same memory space with the program's main code, any vulnerability in the library is inherited by the program. Memory separation designs [44–46] provide transparent memory isolation between the main code and libraries. The goal is to prevent the untrusted libraries from directly accessing the main memory. However, attackers can still leverage the DUIs in the main code to indirectly access the main memory.

— *Programs Using* libsdl. The Simple DirectMedia Layer (SDL) library provides programming interfaces to access low lever hardware, like keyboard, screen, audio and so on. The main program requests an SDL object and performs operation through the SDL object. For example, the main program can request a screen object, and then invoke the screen object methods to set display attributes, like colors and fonts. When the library isolation technique Codejail [45] is used, the SDL library code cannot directly access the memory of the main code. A monitor module will selectively commit the memory changes from the library to the main code. However, the memory isolation provided by Codejail cannot prevent the memory access from the library to the main memory through DUIs in the main code. We write a simple program that requests a screen object from the SDL library and then sets the color attribute. The pseudo code of the simple program is shown below.

```
1   screen = SDL_SetVideoMode (...);   // get framebuffer surface
2   color = SDL_MapRGB (...);          // get a pixel value
3   pixmem16 = screen->pixels + x + y * pixelsperline ;
4                                      // get pixel address
5   *pixmem16 = color;                 // set the color
```

Our tool detected the write DUI in the main code (on line 5) of this simple program. A malicious SDL library can exploit this DUI vulnerability to corrupt any memory location of the main code, even if the main program is protected by memory isolation schemes. Using attackers' capability estimation, our tool reports that there is no limitation on the address or value, which means that attackers have full control of the main code memory through the DUI exploit.

## 5.2    Performance

Table 1 shows the performance details of each experiment conducted using our tool. We can see that our tool is able to analyze and detect a DUI vulnerability

**Table 1.** Performance of DUI Detector. T1 is the time for trace generation; T2 is the time to get the access formula; T3 is the time to solve the formula. "Inst. #" is the number of executed instruction, while "Infl. #" is the number of tainted instructions. All times are measured in second.

| Trusted part | Untrusted part | APIs | DUI | Inst. # | Infl. # | T1 | T2 | T3 |
|---|---|---|---|---|---|---|---|---|
| User space | Linux kernel | brk | write | 168,089 | 103 | 21.79 | 1.70 | 0.18 |
| User space | Linux kernel | mmap2 | write | 167,644 | 69,486 | 21.19 | 2.94 | 3.11 |
| Cat code | Linux kernel | read, write | read | 2,288,914 | 684 | 104.76 | 16.58 | 0.16 |
| Main code | SDL library | SDL APIs | write | 100,424,507 | 68 | 7574.23 | 1.52 | 0.10 |

in a few minutes. The time required for the generation of the trace is largely dependent on the number of instructions that are generated and logged in the trace. On the other hand, the amount of time required for the generation of the STP formula is very small. For the STP formula solving, the time required highly varies due to its dependence on the query inputs, formula and how quickly the STP solver can obtain a solution for us.

### 5.3   Security Implications

Our tool detected DUI vulnerabilities in different program transformation scenarios, including untrusted kernel isolation and untrusted libraries isolation. In this part, we discuss the security implications of our findings.

– *Simple memory isolation is inadequate to prevent unauthorized memory access.* Although a lot of designs aim to prevent the malicious partition from accessing the protected memory, our result shows that simple memory isolation cannot completely stop the unauthorized memory access. DUI vulnerabilities inside the protected partition still allow other partitions to access arbitrary protected memory.
– *API-review is necessary to provide a secure environment.* Since DUI vulnerabilities can be leveraged to mount attacks through interfaces, developers need to pay special attention to the checking code on interface inputs when the legacy code is retrofitted into a memory isolation model. More specifically, there is a need to review the interfaces between trusted and untrusted partitions.

## 6   Discussion

In this section we present the limitation of our work and discuss the possible defense against the DUI exploits.

***Code Coverage.*** Our analysis only considers one particular code path executed during the trace generation. However, it is possible for the program to have other DUI vulnerabilities in other paths. We employ an iterative process to detect other DUI vulnerabilities. Specifically, after the analysis for one execution path, we invalidate the path condition in the control-flow constraints and require the solver to provide an input that satisfies the invalidated condition [23]. The given input makes the program follow a new code path. The same analysis is performed on it and this process is repeated until no additional new path can be generated. This may lead to the path explosion problem [1]. To mitigate the problem, we only invalidate the conditional branches that are affected by untrusted input to generate the new path. Existing methods to mitigate path explosion, like [30,43] can also be considered.

*Defense.* Once a DUI vulnerability has been identified, developers can mitigate the consequences of the vulnerability by introducing proper checks to the vulnerable code. Different checks should be used accordingly based on the type of the interface inputs. For the Glibc `brk` attack, where the interface inputs are addresses, the sanitization code needs to make sure that the returned address either equals to the requested one or points to a newly allocated memory region. For operation counters (e.g., the return value of the `read` system call), sanitization code should perform strict checks on the length, like comparing it with the file size or the buffer size.

# 7 Related Works

*Vulnerability Detection.* Symbolic execution and dynamic taint analysis are two techniques that are commonly used for vulnerability detection. In symbolic execution, the program is executed with symbols rather than concrete values. Operations on the inputs are represented as an expression of the symbols, naturally providing constraints on possible values of the input after each operation. As a result, symbolic execution [28] has been extensively used in program testing and vulnerability analysis [8,12,13,34,40]. Dynamic taint analysis is another technique frequently used to detect vulnerabilities. In taint analysis, attacker-controlled inputs are usually marked with a tag. This tag is propagated whenever the data is derived from the input. This enables the analyst to determine the data flow and the attackers' influence. A series of work has utilized taint analysis to detect and analyze vulnerabilities [9,14,49] and malware [18,47]. Newsome *et al.* [36] proposed using dynamic taint analysis to find bugs. In these methods, attacks are detected when the tainted data are used in a dangerous way, like jump address or system call parameters. Our approach differs in application of these techniques. In order to detect DUI vulnerabilities, our focus is on detecting certain access pattern while at the same time considering implicit constraints such as memory constraints. As such, our approach aims to obtain a better understanding of the vulnerability in addition to detection.

*Automatic Exploit Generation.* The goal of the automatic exploit generation is to generate a working payload that successfully compromises the vulnerable program. Heelan *et al.* [24] discussed algorithms to automatically generate exploits to hijack the control flow for a given vulnerable path. Brumley *et al.* [10]

proposed the automatic patch-based exploit generation for a given vulnerable program together with security patches. A followup work [2] presents an automatic exploit generation tool for buffer overflow and format string vulnerabilities. Felmetsger *et al.* [20] proposed AEG on web applications. In another work [26] we present an automatic method to generate data-oriented attacks. Different from these AEG-style approaches, our goal is to estimate the attackers' capability. Hence, rather than obtaining the payload for a vulnerable program, we quantify the potential severity of the vulnerability.

***Privilege Separation in Software Systems.*** Privilege separation is a way to realize the principle of least privilege in software designs. It is often achieved by using memory isolation to protect resources of high-privileged partitions from low-privileged ones. For examples, Provos [39] retrofitted OpenSSH with a privilege-separated design and other methods [6,11,27] automatically separate and isolate components within monolithic legacy programs. Other security solutions proposed new threat models. For example, some [17,29,31] treat the kernel as potentially untrusted and remove it from the trusted computing base. However, the work [15,38] shows that just isolating the components is insufficient as attackers might be able to leverage on poorly designed legacy interfaces to compromise the isolated components. Our solution complements this work with a systematic method to detect DUI vulnerabilities when adopting new isolation schemes.

## 8   Conclusion

In this paper, we present a systematic solution to detect arbitrary memory access vulnerability in binary programs. Our approach builds access formula for a binary using program analysis techniques. The formula is then utilized to detect the memory access patterns that can be leveraged by attackers to perform arbitrary memory accesses. Detailed analysis is also performed to assess the capability of attackers using such vulnerabilities. We demonstrate the effectiveness and accuracy of our approach in the evaluation, where we present four case studies of DUI vulnerabilities in programs utilizing isolation schemes. Finally, we provide the security implications based on the results of the evaluation.

**Acknowledgments.** We thank Xinshu Dong and the anonymous reviewers for their insightful comments. This research is supported in part by the National Research Foundation, Prime Minister's Office, Singapore under its National Cybersecurity R&D Program (Award No. NRF2014NCR-NCR001-21) and administered by the National Cybersecurity R&D Directorate, and by a research grant from Symantec.

## References

1. Anand, S., Godefroid, P., Tillmann, N.: Demand-driven compositional symbolic execution. In: Ramakrishnan, C.R., Rehof, J. (eds.) TACAS 2008. LNCS, vol. 4963, pp. 367–381. Springer, Heidelberg (2008)

2. Avgerinos, T., Cha, S.K., Hao, B.L.T., Brumley., D.: AEG: automatic exploit generation. In: Proceedings of the 18th Annual Network and Distributed System Security Symposium (2011)
3. Barth, A., Jackson, C., Reis, C., Team, T.G.C.: The Security Architecture of the Chromium Browser. Technical report (2008)
4. Bernstein, D.J.: Some thoughts on security after ten years of Qmail 1.0. In: Proceedings of the 14th ACM Workshop on Computer Security Architecture (2007)
5. Bhatkar, E., Duvarney, D.C., Sekar, R.: Address obfuscation: An efficient approach to combat a broad range of memory error exploits. In: Proceedings of the 12th USENIX Security Symposium (2003)
6. Bittau, A., Marchenko, P., Handley, M., Karp, B.: Wedge: splitting applications into reduced-privilege compartments. In: Proceedings of the 5th USENIX Symposium on Networked Systems Design and Implementation (2008)
7. Blum, R.: Postfix. Sams, Indianapolis (2001)
8. Brumley, D., Caballero, J., Liang, Z., Newsome, J., Song, D.: Towards automatic discovery of deviations in binary implementations with applications to error detection and fingerprint generation. In: Proceedings of 16th USENIX Security Symposium (2007)
9. Brumley, D., Newsome, J., Song, D., Wang, H., Jha, S.: Towards automatic generation of vulnerability-based signatures. In: Proceedings of the 27th IEEE Symposium on Security and Privacy (2006)
10. Brumley, D., Poosankam, P., Song, D., Zheng, J.: Automatic patch-based exploit generation is possible: Techniques and implications. In: Proceedings of the 2008 IEEE Symposium on Security and Privacy (2008)
11. Brumley, D., Song, D.: Privtrans: automatically partitioning programs for privilege separation. In: Proceedings of the 13th USENIX Security Symposium (2004)
12. Cadar, C., Dunbar, D., Engler, D.: KLEE: unassisted and automatic generation of high-coverage tests for complex systems programs. In: Proceedings of the 8th USENIX Conference on Operating Systems Design and Implementation (2008)
13. Cadar, C., Ganesh, V., Pawlowski, P.M., Dill, D.L., Engler, D.R.: EXE: automatically generating inputs of death. In: Proceedings of the 13th ACM Conference on Computer and Communications Security (2006)
14. Caselden, D., Bazhanyuk, A., Payer, M., McCamant, S., Song, D.: HI-CFG: construction by binary analysis and application to attack polymorphism. In: Crampton, J., Jajodia, S., Mayes, K. (eds.) ESORICS 2013. LNCS, vol. 8134, pp. 164–181. Springer, Heidelberg (2013)
15. Checkoway, S., Shacham, H.: Iago attacks: why the system call API is a bad untrusted RPC interface. In: Proceedings of the 18th International Conference on Architectural Support for Programming Languages and Operating Systems (2013)
16. Chen, S., Xu, J., Sezer, E.C., Gauriar, P., Iyer, R.K.: Non-control-data attacks are realistic threats. In: Proceedings of the 14th USENIX Security Symposium (2005)
17. Chen, X., Garfinkel, T., Lewis, E.C., Subrahmanyam, P., Waldspurger, C.A., Boneh, D., Dwoskin, J., Ports, D.R.: Overshadow: a virtualization-based approach to retrofitting protection in commodity operating systems. In: Proceedings of the 13th International Conference on Architectural Support for Programming Languages and Operating Systems (2008)
18. Egele, M., Kruegel, C., Kirda, E., Yin, H., Song, D.: Dynamic spyware analysis. In: Proceedings of USENIX Annual Technical Conference (2007)
19. Erlingsson, U., Abadi, M., Vrable, M., Budiu, M., Necula, G.C.: XFI: Software guards for system address spaces. In: Proceedings of the 7th Symposium on Operating Systems Design and Implementation (2006)

20. Felmetsger, V., Cavedon, L., Kruegel, C., Vigna, G.: Toward automated detection of logic vulnerabilities in web applications. In: Proceedings of the 19th USENIX Security Symposium (2010)
21. Ford, B., Cox, R.: Vx32: lightweight user-level sandboxing on the x86. In: Proceedings of USENIX Annual Technical Conference (2008)
22. Ganesh, V., Dill, D.L.: A decision procedure for bit-vectors and arrays. In: Damm, W., Hermanns, H. (eds.) CAV 2007. LNCS, vol. 4590, pp. 519–531. Springer, Heidelberg (2007)
23. Godefroid, P., Klarlund, N., Sen, K.: DART: directed automated random testing. In: Proceedings of the 26th ACM SIGPLAN Conference on Programming Language Design and Implementation (2005)
24. Heelan, S.: Automatic Generation of Control Flow Hijacking Exploits for Software Vulnerabilities. Technical report, Computing Laboratory, University of Oxford, September 2009
25. Hofmann, O.S., Kim, S., Dunn, A.M., Lee, M.Z., Witchel, E.: InkTag: secure applications on an untrusted operating system. In: Proceedings of the 18th International Conference on Architectural Support for Programming Languages and Operating Systems (2013)
26. Hu, H., Chua, Z.L., Adrian, S., Saxena, P., Liang, Z.: Automatic generation of data-oriented exploits. In: 24th USENIX Security Symposium (2015)
27. Kilpatrick, D.: Privman: a library for partitioning applications. In: Proceedings of USENIX Annual Technical Conference (2003)
28. King, J.C.: Symbolic execution and program testing. Commun. ACM **19**(7), 385–394 (1976)
29. Lie, D., Thekkath, C.A., Horowitz, M.: Implementing an untrusted operating system on trusted hardware. In: Proceedings of the 19th ACM Symposium on Operating Systems Principles (2003)
30. Ma, K.-K., Yit Phang, K., Foster, J.S., Hicks, M.: Directed symbolic execution. In: Yahav, E. (ed.) Static Analysis. LNCS, vol. 6887, pp. 95–111. Springer, Heidelberg (2011)
31. McCune, J.M., Parno, B.J., Perrig, A., Reiter, M.K., Isozaki, H.: Flicker: an execution infrastructure for tcb minimization. In: Proceedings of the 3rd ACM SIGOPS/EuroSys European Conference on Computer Systems (2008)
32. McKeen, F., Alexandrovich, I., Berenzon, A., Rozas, C.V., Shafi, H., Shanbhogue, V., Savagaonkar, U.R.: Innovative instructions and software model for isolated execution. In: Proceedings of the 2nd International Workshop on Hardware and Architectural Support for Security and Privacy (2013)
33. Meng, Z., Smith, G.: Calculating bounds on information leakage using two-bit patterns. In: Proceedings of the ACM SIGPLAN 6th Workshop on Programming Languages and Analysis for Security (2011)
34. Molnar, D.A., Molnar, D., Wagner, D., Wagner, D.: Catchconv: Symbolic Execution and Run-Time Type Inference for Integer Conversion Errors. Technical report, UC Berkeley EECS (2007)
35. Newsome, J., McCamant, S., Song, D.: Measuring channel capacity to distinguish undue influence. In: Proceedings of the ACM SIGPLAN 4th Workshop on Programming Languages and Analysis for Security (2009)
36. Newsome, J., Song, D.: Dynamic taint analysis for automatic detection, analysis, and signature generation of exploits on commodity software. In: Proceedings of the 12th Annual Network and Distributed System Security Symposium (2005)
37. PaX Team. PaX Address Space Layout Randomization (ASLR) (2003). http://pax.grsecurity.net/docs/aslr.txt

38. Ports, D.R.K., Garfinkel, T.: Towards application security on untrusted operating systems. In: Proceedings of the 3rd Conference on Hot Topics in Security (2008)
39. Provos, N., Friedl, M., Honeyman, P.: Preventing privilege escalation. In: Proceedings of the 12th USENIX Security Symposium (2003)
40. Qi, D., Roychoudhury, A., Liang, Z., Vaswani, K.: Darwin: an approach for debugging evolving programs. In: Proceedings of the the 7th Joint Meeting of the European Software Engineering Conference and the ACM SIGSOFT Symposium on The Foundations of Software Engineering (2009)
41. Shinde, S., Tople, S., Kathayat, D., Saxena, P.: PODARCH: Protecting Legacy Applications with a Purely Hardware TCB. Technical Report NUS-SL-TR-15-01, School of Computing, National University of Singapore, February 2015
42. Song, D., Brumley, D., Yin, H., Caballero, J., Jager, I., Kang, M.G., Liang, Z., Newsome, J., Poosankam, P., Saxena, P.: BitBlaze: a new approach to computer security via binary analysis. In: Sekar, R., Pujari, A.K. (eds.) ICISS 2008. LNCS, vol. 5352, pp. 1–25. Springer, Heidelberg (2008)
43. Staats, M., Păsăreanu, C.: Parallel symbolic execution for structural test generation. In: Proceedings of the 19th International Symposium on Software Testing and Analysis (2010)
44. Wahbe, R., Lucco, S., Anderson, T.E., Graham, S.L.: Efficient software-based fault isolation. In: Proceedings of the 14th ACM Symposium on Operating Systems Principles (1993)
45. Wu, Y., Sathyanarayan, S., Yap, R.H.C., Liang, Z.: Codejail: application-transparent isolation of libraries with tight program interactions. In: Foresti, S., Yung, M., Martinelli, F. (eds.) ESORICS 2012. LNCS, vol. 7459, pp. 859–876. Springer, Heidelberg (2012)
46. Yee, B., Sehr, D., Dardyk, G., Chen, J.B., Muth, R., Ormandy, T., Okasaka, S., Narula, N., Fullagar, N.: Native client: a sandbox for portable, untrusted x86 native code. In: Proceedings of the 30th IEEE Symposium on Security and Privacy (2009)
47. Yin, H., Song, D., Egele, M., Kruegel, C., Kirda, E.: Panorama: capturing system-wide information flow for malware detection and analysis. In: Proceedings of the 14th ACM Conference on Computer and Communications Security (2007)
48. Zhang, F., Chen, J., Chen, H., Zang, B.: CloudVisor: retrofitting protection of virtual machines in multi-tenant cloud with nested virtualization. In: Proceedings of the 23rd ACM Symposium on Operating Systems Principles (2011)
49. Zhang, M., Yin, H.: AppSealer: automatic generation of vulnerability-specific patches for preventing component hijacking attacks in android applications. In: Proceedings of the 21st Network and Distributed System Security Symposium (2014)

# vBox: Proactively Establishing Secure Channels Between Wireless Devices Without Prior Knowledge

Wei Wang[1,2,3], Jingqiang Lin[1,2], Zhan Wang[1,2(✉)], Ze Wang[1,2],
and Luning Xia[1,2]

[1] Data Assurance and Communication Security Research Center,
Chinese Academy of Sciences, Beijing 100093, China
wangzhan@iie.ac.cn
[2] State Key Laboratory of Information Security, Institute of Information
Engineering, Chinese Academy of Sciences, Beijing, China
[3] University of Chinese Academy of Sciences, Beijing, China

**Abstract.** Establishing secure channels between two wireless devices without any prior knowledge is challenging, especially when such devices only have very simple user interface. Most existing authentication and key negotiation solutions leverage the received signal strength (RSS) of wireless signals, and the security guarantees depend on the environments too much; in a static environment of less motion, the adversaries could control or predict the RSS of legitimate devices. We propose *vBox* in this paper, a *proactive* method to establish secure channels between wireless devices, without the assumption on environments. By holding and waving two devices to communicate, the owner creates a virtual "shield box". The adversaries outside the box cannot send signals with stable RSS into the box, so the legitimate devices can easily be authenticated based on the variation of RSS. At the same time, the adversaries cannot correctly measure or detect the RSS of wireless signals transmitted between the in-box devices, and then they can directly transmit secret keys in plaintext. Then, after the simple operation by the owner for a few seconds, the authenticated nodes will securely communicate using the shared secret key. We implement the vBox prototype on commercial-off-the-shelf ZigBee devices, and evaluate it with extensive experiments under the normal case and several attack scenarios. The experiment results and security analysis show that, vBox establishes secure channels handily against various attacks and is suitable for different environments.

**Keywords:** Authentication · Key establishment · Received signal strength · Wireless personal area network

Z. Wang—This work was partially supported by the National 973 Program under award No. 2013CB338001 and the National Natural Science Foundation of China under Grant 61272479.

G. Pernul et al. (Eds.): ESORICS 2015, Part II, LNCS 9327, pp. 332–351, 2015.
DOI: 10.1007/978-3-319-24177-7_17

# 1  Introduction

With the proliferation of wireless personal devices, wireless personal area networks (WPANs) have experienced great development in recent years. A WPAN involves a variety of lightweight, small-size and low-power wireless devices, which are held or carried by the owner. For example, around an owner, a mobile phone receives daily fitness data from an associated smart bracelet and exchanges voices with the Bluetooth headset. Other typical WPAN nodes include intelligent watches, wearable sensors and so on.

Because the wireless personal devices inevitably transmit private information in WPANs, the communications need to be secured; however, conventional solutions are unsuitable for the wireless devices to establish secure channels. First of all, there is no "mobile" trusted third server to facilitate the wireless nodes to authenticate each other or negotiate secret keys, which hardly allows the owner to connect two WPAN devices anytime and anywhere. Secondly, because the small-size WPAN devices are equipped with very limited input and output interfaces, it is difficult to type some characters as prior knowledge or display a passcode to verify the communication peer, before they establish secure channels. For example, the Xiaomi smart bracelet has only three LED lights as its output interface to users. Finally, although the owner could connect wireless devices by wires and then set up prior associations securely, it is very inconvenient and harms the benefits of wireless communications.

To establish secure channels between a WPAN device and another device, both of which are carried by the owner, we need to ensure that, (a) the wireless communication peer is held or controlled by the owner, i.e., *authentication*; and (b) the messages exchanged are not leaked to other entities, i.e., *confidentiality*. To authenticate a wireless device without prior knowledge, existing proximity-based authentication solutions [4,6,13] employ the received signal strength (RSS) feature of nearby wireless devices, to distinguish a legitimate node from distant (or illegitimate) ones in real time. Therefore, the proximity-based authentication can be finished without requiring the owner's explicit operations. As for the confidentiality issue, existing solutions usually leverage the reciprocity of wireless communication to negotiate secret keys, so that the eavesdroppers cannot extract the same key as the pair of WPAN nodes.

In this paper, we propose *vBox*, a simple but effective RSS-based solution to establish secure channels between two wireless devices without any prior knowledge. vBox follows distinct principles from the existing solutions: it requires *explicit* operations executed by the owner so as to *proactively* prevent threats from adversaries. By holding and simultaneously waving two WPAN devices that need to establish secure channels, the owner easily "builds" a virtual shield box, so that (a) the adversaries at distance cannot send wireless signals with stable RSS to the shielded devices; and (b) the strength of wireless signals sent between these shielded devices, cannot be measured accurately by the adversaries at distance. Different from existing solutions, vBox follows a proactive philosophy. In particular, the owner explicitly creates a special environment that is static to the legitimate nodes but unpredictable to the adversaries, and deliberately tunes the strength of the signal for the key establishment.

vBox consists of two phases, one of which is for authentication; and the second phase is to transmit secret keys. In the first phase, one node (called the *initiator* in this paper) sends signals with stable RSS for a certain period of time, and the other node (called the *listener*) verifies the stableness to authenticate the initiator. In the key transmission phase, the initiator tunes its transmitting power level based on a random number, i.e., transmits a session key in plaintext; and the listener obtains the secret key based on RSS. Note that these two phases are performed, as the owner waves them together in an unpredictable way. Then, the listener replies with a message generated by the secret key (e.g., a message authentication code) to acknowledge the integrity of the received secret key. The subsequent communications will be secured by such secret key. In addition, the above operations can be triggered after the owner presses a special button on the devices (and waves them), or when the devices detect the wave and automatically start the process of authentication and key transmission because more and more WPAN devices are configured with motion sensors.

While vBox takes advantage of RSS to complete the authentication and key transmission, the statistics of RSS is greatly affected by the relative distance and direction between the sender and the receiver. When the initiator and the listener devices are being held together and waved by the owner, the relative distance and direction between two devices remains unchanged. In contrast, it is extremely difficult to predict such relative distance and direction between the initiator (or the listener) and any other wireless devices not being held by the owner. In this way, the RSS detected by the listener can be synchronized by the initiator so that the authentication and key transmission succeed. Meanwhile, the listener node being waved cannot receive wireless signals with stable strength from any other wireless devices, so no adversarial wireless device would be authenticated successfully by the listener. Finally, no wireless device except the listener can detect the signal strength (i.e., the secret key) tuned by the initiator.

We implemented vBox on commercial-off-the-shelf ZigBee devices. Through extensive experiments under the normal case and several attack scenarios, we demonstrate that, by choosing suitable parameters including the authentication threshold and the power level difference for key transmission, vBox successfully establishes secure channels between wireless devices against various attacks.

The rest of this paper is organized as follows. Section 2 introduces preliminary knowledge on wireless propagation and related works. Section 3 illustrates the main idea of vBox. Section 4 presents the complete vBox protocol and discusses the parameters. Section 5 depicts the extensive experiments we have conducted for validating the properties of vBox. Section 6 evaluates the proposed scheme from the security and usability aspects. Section 7 concludes the paper.

## 2    Preliminaries and Related Work

### 2.1    Wireless Signal Propagation

The strength of a wireless signal fades, when it propagates over the air. The received signal strength (RSS), i.e., the receiver's measurement of the wireless signals, is determined by two factors: ($a$) the initial strength of the wireless signal, or the transmitting power at the transmitter, and ($b$) the path loss, which depicts how the signal is fading through the wireless channel. So, the RSS can be expressed as Eq. 1 as follows,

$$P_R = P_0 - P_L \tag{1}$$

where $P_R$ is the strength (or power) of wireless signals at the receiver, and $P_0$ is the initial strength. $P_0$ and $P_R$ are usually measured in $dBm$, and the path loss $P_L$ is represented in $dB$, representing the ratio between the strengths at the transmitter and the receiver.

The path loss mainly consists of two factors, called the *slow fading* and the *fast fading*. The slow fading is caused by events such as shadowing, where a hill or large building obscures the main signal path between the transmitter and the receiver. The two main causes of fast fading are (1) the multipath effect, where the wireless signal reaches the receiver through two or more paths; (2) *Doppler* shift, where the relative motion between the transmitter and the receiver causes frequency shifts of the signal. Fast fading is reflected by the tremendous fluctuations of the instantaneous RSS values.

The path loss of wireless signals inside a building or densely populated area, is modeled as a log-distance formula [11] as follows:

$$P_L = C + 10\alpha \lg(d) + F_g \tag{2}$$

The first part $C$ is a constant which accounts for system losses. The second part $10\alpha log(d)$ is related to the slow fading, where $\alpha$ is called the path loss exponent, $d$ is the distance between the transmitter and the receiver. The values of $\alpha$ range from 1.2 to 8 [9], depending on the certain propagation environment. In the free space, the value of $\alpha$ is 2.

The fast fading is mainly expressed in the third part $F_g$, which is a variable reflecting the channel fading. In an indoor environment, the channel fading is mainly fast fading caused by the multipath effect. Particularly, for a receiver that is moving rapidly, the fading is aggravated by Doppler shift, which results in great fluctuations in its RSS measurements of received wireless signals. In this case, $F_g$ is a variable with Rician distribution [1].

## 2.2   RSS-based Authentication and Key Establishment

Since the RSS is highly related to the wireless channels from the transmitter to the receiver, RSS-based approaches are proposed for proximity authentication [10] and key establishment. RSS measurement is a generally available feature for most commercial-off-the-shelf wireless devices, so such approaches outrange many hardware-based solutions in terms of usability.

In temporal RSS variation authentication (TRVA) [16], one node sends a list of RSS variations of acknowledgment frames that it has ever received, and then the other node authenticates the sender if the list is consistent to its own observation. TRVA is based on the reciprocity principle of wireless channels, but it requires that the two nodes authenticate each other a priori by other means. On the other hand, in proximity-based authentication solutions, the receiver collects the RSS statistics to determine their proximity, and decide a proximate applicant as legitimate; so they eliminate the necessary prior knowledge in traditional authentication systems. Good Neighbor [4] is a wireless device pairing scheme, and it requires neither shared secrets nor out-of-band channels as vBox. However, Good Neighbor assumes that the receiver device has at least two antennas separated by a reasonable distance (e.g., 10 cm), so it is not always suitable for small-size WPAN devices. The authentication design of vBox shares the same spirit with BANA [13], which employs the distinct RSS variation to authenticate legitimate nodes. In BANA, the unique on-body channel characteristic arises from the multipath fading in the surroundings, while vBox requires the owner to explicitly build such an environment (i.e., wave the WPAN devices).

RSS-based key establishment leverages the reciprocity of wireless communication, i.e., the wireless channels between two communicating parties affect both the parties *equally* and causes *identical* RSS variations on each of them. Moreover, these variations are distinct from other channels between any communicating party and attackers, especially in dynamic environments. Therefore, a shared key can be generated secretly based on the observed RSS variations. Radio-telepathy [7] establishes a shared secret key between 802.11 nodes by exploiting the reciprocity property. R. Wilson *et al.* discussed such key establishment approaches in ultrawideband channels and analyzed the approximation and upper bound on the key size [15].

However, the difference of the RSS variations between the channels of legitimate nodes and those of adversaries, becomes insignificant in static environments. S. Jana *et al.* evaluated the effectiveness of key extraction based on the reciprocity principle in different wireless scenarios, and showed that, in *static* environments the eavesdropper could predict the "secret" key between two nodes [5]. Then, an adaptive approach was proposed to generate secret keys [5] at a high rate and high entropy, in both static and dynamic environments. In fact, the similar risk is also notified by the designers of BANA [13], that is, when the owner is not in motion, the legitimate on-body channel characteristic is not so distinct from that of the attack channels.

## 3    vBox Design

### 3.1    Design Goal and Threat Model

The goal of vBox is to establish secure channels between two small-size wireless devices, without any prior association. After the two phases of vBox, these two devices called the *initiator* and the *listener*[1], authenticate each other and share a secret session key used for the confidentiality, authenticity and integrity of

---

[1] The terms "initiator" and "listener", are used to emphasize their roles in the authentication and key transmission phases; however, in the following secure communications, these nodes can play different roles according to the applications.

the following wireless communication. Designed for small-size mobile wireless nodes, vBox requires no extra hardware or human interface, and it leverages the RSS measurement for authentication and key transmission, which is a standard function of wireless devices. No computationally-expensive or time-consuming processing (e.g., public-key cryptographic computations) is involved in vBox, so this lightweight solution is very suitable for resource-constrained devices.

In vBox, the two wireless devices are picked up by the owner, so we assume that the owner has the ability and caution to distinguish his own devices from any other malicious devices, not belonging to him. We do not consider the social engineering attacks on the owner; for example, replace the owner's Bluetooth headset by another one with embedded malicious codes. The detailed parameters and steps of the vBox protocol are publicly known. At the same time, adversaries could eavesdrop and send wireless signals, attempting to be authenticated as a legitimate device or obtain the secret key. In particular, an attacker would receive and measure all wireless signals from the initiator or the listener, or send signals to them arbitrarily. Moreover, we assume that, the adversaries might be a place very close to the owner, e.g., only 1 m, but not be detected physically.

### 3.2  Basic Insight

**Building a Virtual Box over the Wireless Channels.** As mentioned in the preliminaries, the wireless signal prorogation between two devices is highly related to their relative position. For two nearby devices that are relatively static to each other, the wireless channel between them is very stable. On the contrary, for two devices that are in rapid relative motion, the wireless signal prorogation between them experiences tremendous fluctuations. When two devices are held together and waved randomly in the air: the wireless channel between the two relatively static devices remains stable, while any channel between a third device and either of these two devices is fluctuated remarkably. Based on this fact, the owner can build a shielded environment for the legitimate initiator and listener in terms of signal stability, by holding and randomly waving them together. We name the virtual shield environment *vBox*.

Figure 1 illustrates the functionality of vBox in a typical indoor environment in the presence of an adversary. The initiator and the listener are held together and waved by the owner, while the adversary hides behind the wall. The solid-arrowed line indicates the direct path between the legitimate nodes, while the dashed-arrowed lines indicate the multiple paths between the legitimate devices and the adversary. We recognize three wireless channels in this scenario:

- *The initiator-listener channel.* Because the initiator and the listener are kept very close, the direct path (DP) is the dominant path [12], which suffers little from the environment changes. In other words, the RSS variation is very small.
- *The adversary-listener channel.* This channel exists when the adversary tries to send data to the listener to be authenticated as a legitimate device. The signal propagates through multiple paths. Meanwhile, the rapid relative motion between the adversary and the listener causes the Doppler shift. So the channel is filled with fluctuations, leading to large RSS variations at the listener.

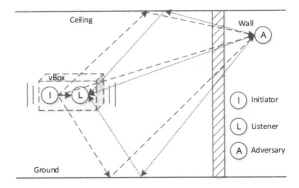

**Fig. 1.** Signal propagation of the in-box channel and the off-box channel

– *The initiator-adversary channel.* This channel exists when the adversary tries to eavesdrop data sent between the legitimate nodes. This channel is also fluctuated due to the rapid movement of the initiator and filled with fluctuations that lead to large RSS variations at the adversary.

In the remainder, the stable channel between the initiator and the listener is also called the *in-box* channel, and sometimes the *off-box* channel is used to represent both the initiator-adversary and adversary-listener channels.

**Proximity-Based Authentication Within vBox.** In the first phase, the initiator is authenticated as follows. This phase can be triggered by the user by pressing buttons on the devices, or automatically by the device themselves if they are configured with motion sensors.

(a) The initiator sends a sequence of packets at a fixed TX power level for a predetermined period of time, as an authentication request;
(b) On receiving the authentication request, the listener calculates the standard deviation of the sequence's RSS;
(c) If the calculated standard deviation is lower than a threshold, the listener accepts the authentication request; otherwise, it is rejected and the vBox protocol terminates.

vBox ensures that, only the initiator that is held and waved together with the listener, will be authenticated successfully. As is illustrated above, the RSS variation of the in-box channel is very small, while that of off-box channel is much greater. So, this security goal is achieved by determining the threshold of RSS standard deviation.

**Tuned-RSS as Secret Keys Within vBox.** After being successfully authenticated, the initiator sends a *plaintext* secret key to the listener, by tuning the RSS of another sequence of packets. We name this key transmission method *active RSS tuning*. The method is as follows:

(a) The initiator generates an $m$-bit random key on its own. Then, it sends the key as a sequence of packets, where the TX power of each packet is tuned by one key bit: if the bit is '1', the packet is transmitted at the power level of $P_{0H}$; if it is '0', the packet is transmitted at $P_{0L}$.

(b) The listener receives the $m$ packets, and extracts the secret key based on its RSS measurements.

vBox ensures that, the secret key recovered by listener is identical to the one generated by the initiator, and adversaries cannot recover these random bits. The in-box channel is very stable and suffers little noise, while the secret information (i.e., the initial TX power) is mixed with the noise in the off-box channel. So, the security goals are achieved by determining $P_{0H}$ and $P_{0L}$ as well as the key recovery rule at the listener.

### 3.3 The RSS Analysis of vBox

**RSS Variation of the Channels.** We analyze the RSS (or the strength at the receiver) of the three channels, to show the practicability of vBox and find the suitable parameters in the protocols. For the in-box channel, the distance $d$ between the two devices is almost kept unchanged; and the fading between the two closely-located devices (i.e., $F_g$) is expressed as a Gaussian variable $X_{\sigma_X}$ related to the static environment. From Eqs. 1 and 2, we have

$$P_R = P_0 - (C + 10\alpha \lg(d) + F_g) \approx P_0 + X_{\sigma_X} + C' \tag{3}$$

where $C'$ is a constant. The RSS variation is mainly determined by $\sigma_X$, the standard deviation of $X$, which is typical very small if there is not malicious wireless jamming.

As for the off-box channel, the rapid relative motion between the communicating peers aggravates the fast fading phenomenon substantially, and it follows the Rician distribution. When the adversary is relatively distant from the legitimate devices and the owner waves the nodes around his body, the change of the distance between the initiator (or the listener) and the adversary is very small, compared with the effect of fast fading. From Eqs. 1 and 2, we have

$$P_R = P_0 - (C + 10\alpha \lg(d) + F_g) \approx P_0 + R_{\sigma_R} + C'' \tag{4}$$

where $C''$ is another constant and $R$ is a variable of Rician distribution with standard deviation $\sigma_R$. Note the RSS variation of the initiator-adversary channel is identical to that of the adversary-listener channel.

**RSS Analysis on Authentication.** The authentication of vBox requires that, the RSS variation through the in-box channel is much smaller than the RSS variation through the off-box channel, and there is a clear gap between them. From Eqs. 3 and 4, it is required that: $\sigma_X \ll \sigma_R$.

Figure 2 shows the elementary experiment results in these different channels. In the experiment, the initiator and the adversary send packets to the listener

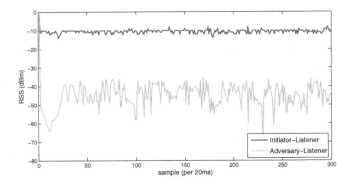

**Fig. 2.** RSS at Listener, sent by Initiator and Adversary with fixed TX power

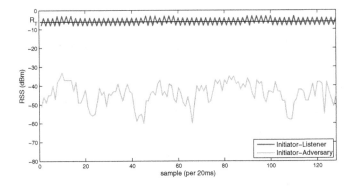

**Fig. 3.** RSS at Listener and Adversary, of a tuned key sent by Initiator

with fixed power at a rate of 50 packet/s, respectively; the RSS measured at the listener is also shown. The legitimate nodes are held and waved rapidly together, while the adversary is placed 3 m away from them. The experiment took place in an office room for 6 s. From Fig. 2, it is found that, the RSS through the in-box channel is very stable, almost fixed at −10 dBm. In contrast, the RSS of the adversary-listener channel is filled with fluctuations, varying dramatically in the range of [−70 dBm, −35 dBm]. It is verified that there exists a clear gap between the RSS variation of the in-box channel and that of the off-box channel, i.e. the RSS variation of the initiator-listener channel is restricted in a small range, while that of the adversary-listener channel is much more significant.

**RSS Analysis on Key Transmission.** Firstly at all, to transmit key bits correctly, the difference between $P_{0H}$ and $P_{0L}$, i.e. $\Delta P_0 = P_{0H} - P_{0L}$, shall be great enough to eliminate the interference of the RSS variation through the in-box channel; at the same time, to transmit key bits secretly, $\Delta P_0$ shall be smaller enough, to prevent the adversary from recovering the random bits through the off-box channel. Basically, we have: $\sigma_X \ll \Delta P_0/2 \ll \sigma_R$.

Figure 3 is the experiment result of the key bit tuning in vBox. This experiment configuration is the same as that in Fig. 2, except that the initiator sends 128 bits by tuning the signal strength of 128 consecutive packets in 3 s, and $\Delta P_0$ is 4 dBm. The sequence of bits consists of '0' and '1' alternatingly, i.e., 010101...0101. It is shown that, by choosing a reasonable threshold $R_T$ (the dashed line in Fig. 3), the listener is able to recover the bit sequence from its RSS measurements correctly: if the RSS is higher than $R_T$, the bit is '1'; if lower, it is '0'. In contrast, adversaries cannot recover the correct bit sequence from its RSS measurements, as the original tuning is overwhelmed by the inherent fluctuations in the initiator-adversary channel.

# 4    The Detailed vBox Protocol

In this section, we describe the detailed authentication and key transmission steps, and then present the parameters in this protocol.

## 4.1    The Initiator-Listener Protocol

The secure communication between the two devices is composed of three phases. In the first stage, the listener authenticates the initiator, following the proximity-based authentication; in the second stage, the initiator transmits the secret key to the listener, by actively tuning the RSS. These two phases shall be performed, as the owner waves the virtual box. Then, in the third phase, all data are protected by the negotiated secret key; e.g., each data packet is encrypted and appended with a message authentication code.

In vBox, the secure channel is established by the owner explicitly. Sometimes, the owner needs to be responsible for two issues: ($a$) appoint the roles (i.e., the initiator or the listener); and ($b$) trigger the vBox protocol. These inputs can be set by simple interface. For example, a long press on the button means the listener, and a normal press means the initiator; then, the devices will start the protocol. However, these issues may be solved automatically, too. For example, a mobile phone always acts as the listener, and a smart bracelets or Bluetooth headset always acts as the initiator; or, if the devices are configured with motion sensors, the protocol can be triggered as they are waved. In the following description, $I$ and $L$ stand for the initiator and the listener, respectively.

### Phase 1: Initiator Authentication

(a) $I \rightarrow L$: $AuthReq(j)$, where $j = 1, ..., N$ and $N$ is the packet number for $I$ to send. $I$ sends $N$ consecutive $AuthReq$ using the fixed TX power level $P_{0I}$.

(b) $L \rightarrow I$: $AuthResp(AuthResult)$. $L$ receives $N$ $AuthReq$ from $I$ and measures the RSS values. Upon receiving the $N$ $AuthReq$, $L$ calculates the mean value and the standard deviation of the $N$ values, denoted as $R_T$ and $\sigma$, respectively. Then $\sigma$ is compared against a predetermined threshold $\sigma_T$. If $\sigma < \sigma_T$, $L$ replies $I$ with a "success" message; otherwise, replies with a "fail" message.

**Phase 2: Key Transmission and Listener Authentication**

(c) $I \rightarrow L$: $BitCarrierMsg(i)$, where $i = 1, ..., M$ and $M$ is the length of the key. $I$ decides its two transmitting power levels as $P_{0H} = P_{0I} + \Delta P_0/2$, $P_{0L} = P_{0I} - \Delta P_0/2$. $I$ successively sends $M$ key bit messages to $L$ with transmitting power level $P_{0H}$ or $P_{0L}$. The transmitting power of the $i$th message is decided by the $k^{th}$ key bit $k_i$. If $k_i = 1$, it is transmitted at power level $P_{0H}$; if $k_i = 0$, it is done at $P_{0L}$.

(d) $L \rightarrow I$: $AuthBack(E_{K'}(OK))$. $L$ receives the $M$ $BitCarrierMsg$ from $I$ and records the $M$ corresponding RSS values. $L$ firstly verifies that all the RSS values fall into the range $[R_T - \Delta P_0/2 - 3\sigma_X, R_T + \Delta P_0/2 + 3\sigma_X]$, where $R_T$ is the mean of the RSS values of $AuthReq$ in (b). Then $L$ starts to recover the key from the $M$ RSS values. $L$ interprets each RSS value above $R_T$ into bit '1' and each RSS value below $R_T$ into bit '0', orderly. The key recovered by $L$ is denoted as $K'$. $L$ replies $I$ with an "OK" message encrypted by $K'$.

(e) $I \rightarrow L$: $Success()$. $I$ decrypts the encrypted "OK" message with the original key $K$, to verify the correctness of $K'$ and authenticates $L$. If $K' = K$ is verified, $I$ replies $L$ with a success message.

(f) $L$: On receiving the $Success$ message, $L$ blinks its LED to inform the user. Till now, a common secret key $K$ has been established between $I$ and $L$ after they authenticate each other.

**Phase 3: Encrypted Communication**

(g) $I \leftrightarrow L$: $I$ and $L$ protect the following communication with the established symmetric key.

### 4.2    Parameters

The following parameters are used in the prototype. A more detailed discussion on the parameters is given in Appendix A. We use a 128-bit key for key transmission, and configure $T$ as 20 ms, i.e. 50 packets are transmitted per second for authentication and key transmission. The authentication time is 4 s in Phase 1.

**The Power Level Difference $\Delta P_0$.** To deliver a 128-bit key correctly with a probability of 0.99, $\Delta P_0$ should satisfy: $\Delta P_0 \geq 5 \cdot \sigma_X$. At the same time, $\Delta P_0$ should be as small as possible on the premise of ensuring the reliability of the key transmission.

**The Valid RSS Range for Key Transmission.** We determine a valid RSS range for key transmission, which is $[R_T - \Delta P_0/2 - 3\sigma_X, R_T + \Delta P_0/2 + 3\sigma_X]$, according to the empirical *3-sigma* rule for Gaussian distribution [2]. The protocol requires that all the RSS values of the $BitCarrierMsg$ should fall in to the valid range.

## 5    Experiments

We carry out extensive experiments in real world scenarios on three aspects: (1) Estimation of the RSS variation of the in-box channel and the off-box channel; (2) Verification of the effectiveness of the vBox protocol, including both authentication and key establishment; (3) Verification of the security of vBox.

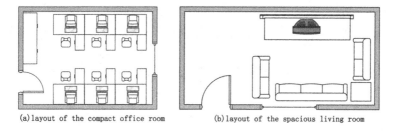

(a) layout of the compact office room          (b) layout of the spacious living room

**Fig. 4.** Layout of the rooms in Scenario A and Scenario B

## 5.1 Setup

The experimental system involves three wireless nodes: the initiator, the listener, and the adversary. Each wireless node in our experiment is a SmartRF05 evaluation board from Texas Instruments, which is a popular ZigBee application tester in home automation development. The node works at the radio frequency of 2.4 GHz and is capable of varying its transmission power. Each node is equipped with a 2 dBi omni-directional SMA antenna.

The initiator and the listener are held together by a researcher in his hand and kept relatively stationary to each other during the experiment. The researcher waves initiator and the listener simultaneously rapidly in front of himself. The adversary is placed at a distance away from the researcher, which can be as near as 1 m and as far as 8 m. The experiments are carried out in three scenarios:

- *Scenario A.* Compact office room. The office room is 4 m × 3.5 m × 3.5 m in size. The layout is shown by Fig. 4(a).
- *Scenario B.* Spacious living room. The living room is 8 m × 4 m × 3.5 m in size. The layout is shown by Fig. 4(b).
- *Scenario C.* Large dining hall. The dining hall is as large as 20 m × 15 m and the ceiling is 6 m high. A clean area of 50 m² in the hall is selected for the experiment.

## 5.2 Real World Estimation of the RSS Variation $\sigma_X$ and $\sigma_R$

The experiments show that $\sigma_X \ll \sigma_R$ holds in real world environment. We evaluate the approximation of $\sigma_X$ and $\sigma_R$ by performing the authentication phase of the vBox protocol 50 times in each experimental scenario and calculating the RSS variations of the initiator-listener channel and the initiator-adversary channel, respectively. The results for the initiator-listener channel is independent of the scenario, so they are shown in Fig. 5 as "Legitimate"; the results for the initiator-adversary channel are shown in Fig. 5 as "Scenario A", "Scenario B", and "Scenario C", respectively. From the experimental results, we expect the real world RSS Variation $\sigma_X$ and $\sigma_R$ to be around 0.67 dBm and 6.21 dBm, respectively. A detailed description of the process is given in Appendix B.

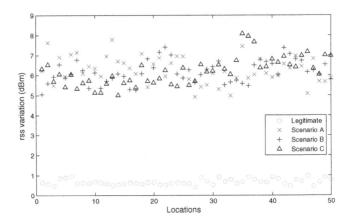

**Fig. 5.** $\sigma$ values in different scenarios

### 5.3 On the Effectiveness of the vBox Protocol

We conducted a series of experiments to verify the effectiveness of vBox. The protocol parameters are determined based on the experiment results and the principles in Sect. 4.2, and are used throughout the following experiments.

**The Accuracy of Authentication.** We verify the accuracy of the proximity-based authentication in the vBox protocol by testing it against the initiator and the adversary at the same time. In this experiment, both the initiator and the adversary try to authenticate themselves to the listener following the protocol. The difference is that, the initiator is held and waved together with the listener, while the adversary is placed at a distance away. The experiment is conducted for 50 times in each scenario, and the adversary is located at a different spot each time. The authentication threshold, i.e. $\sigma_T$, is set to 1.5 dBm, according to the results of Sect. 5.2. The authentication time is set to 4s, i.e. 200 packets are transmitted for authentication. The experimental results show that the authentication achieves 100 % accuracy through all the scenarios, with no false positive or false negative.

**The Reliability of Key Transmission.** We verify the reliability of the key transmission of the vBox protocol by making the initiator deliver a known 128-bit key to the listener with active RSS tuning following the protocol, and validating whether listener can restore the key correctly from the RSS measurements. According to Eq. 7, $\Delta P_0$ is set to 4 dBm. The packet rate is $50/s$. The key is a random 128-bit sequence generated by the initiator, denoted as $K$. The experiment is conducted 50 times in each scenario, and the adversary is located at a different spot each time. The experimental results show that the success ratio of key transmission reaches 100 % through all the scenarios.

**The Resistance Against Eavesdropping.** When the initiator transmits the key, the adversary might be placed at a distance away and eavesdrops on the

**Table 1.** Correlation coefficient for eavesdropping

|  | $\rho$ (average) | $\rho$ (min) | $\rho$ (max) |
|---|---|---|---|
| *Scenario A* | 0.06 | 0.002 | 0.17 |
| *Scenario B* | 0.06 | 0.002 | 0.20 |
| *Scenario C* | 0.08 | 0.002 | 0.21 |
| *Overall* | 0.07 |  |  |

key transmission process. The experiment is conducted for 50 times in each scenario, and the adversary is located at a different spot each time. The key is the same random key generated by the initiator in the above section. We evaluate the resistance against eavesdropping of the key transmission method by calculating the Pearson correlation coefficient between the key derived by the adversary $(K')$ and the original key $(K)$, both in the form of bit sequence. The smaller the correlation coefficient is, the greater resistance the method has against eavesdropping. The Pearson correlation coefficient is calculated as:

$$\rho_{K,K'} = \frac{E(KK') - E(K)E(K')}{\sqrt{E(K^2) - E(K)^2}\sqrt{E(K'^2) - E(K')^2}} \tag{5}$$

The results are shown in Table 1. The overall correlation coefficient of the eavesdropped key and the original key throughout all the scenarios is 0.07. Even in the worst case, which actually only occurred twice among 150 trials, the coefficient is no larger than 0.21. The small correlation coefficient indicates that little information can the adversary get from the eavesdropped RSS values. In addition, the adversary himself has no idea which bits of the key are incorrect. The result implies that recovering the key correctly by eavesdropping is infeasible, even when performed at a distance as near as 1 m from the initiator.

**The Resistance Against False Key Attack.** We simulate the effect of a false key attack using the same $\Delta P_0$ as the initiator. As analyzed in Sect. 6.1, such attacks will be detected and failed by the valid range check. On this premise, we still want to test the distortion effect that the channel fluctuation causes on the false key. We assume that the listener recovers the key bits from the RSS measurements of the adversary regardless of the valid RSS range: interpreting any RSS above the mean value as '1', and any RSS below the mean value as '0'. Then we calculate the correlation coefficient between the recovered key and the original false key. We let the adversary send a false key to the moving listener from 50 random spots in each scenario, with other experimental settings unchanged. The results regarding the detection ratio of the attack and the correlation between the recovered key and the original false key are shown in Table 2: The detection ratio column clearly shows that all of the false key attack attempts are detected by the valid range check. On this premise, the results on the correlation coefficient in the rest columns is similar to those in Table 1, which is a proof of the distortion effect of the channel fluctuations.

**Table 2.** Detection ratio and correlation coefficients

|            | Detect Ratio | $\rho$ (average) | $\rho$ (min) | $\rho$ (max) |
|------------|--------------|------------------|--------------|--------------|
| *Scenario A* | 100 %       | 0.06             | 0.02         | 0.16         |
| *Scenario B* | 100 %       | 0.07             | 0.02         | 0.20         |
| *Scenario C* | 100 %       | 0.07             | 0.03         | 0.19         |
| *Overall*    | 100 %       | 0.07             |              |              |

## 6    Evaluation and Analysis

In this section, we analyze vBox in terms of security and usability.

### 6.1    Security

**Eavesdropping.** The security of the scheme against eavesdropping is well guaranteed by the RSS fluctuations on the adversary's side which are introduced by the movements. The key transmission SNR for the initiator-adversary channel is too low for the adversary to recover the key bits. As shown in Table 1, the adversaries cannot obtain enough information on the key bits, even when they are very close (1 m) to the initiator. We can even choose a smaller $\Delta P_0$ to ensure more protections against eavesdropping, for the value of $\Delta P_0$ in our experiments is more than sufficient for reliable key transmission in the in-box channel.

**False Key Attacks.** In extreme cases, if the initiator suddenly loses the connection with the listener right after being authenticated successfully (e.g., out of battery), the adversary might launch a *false key attack* by sending a key to the listener in the name of the initiator. The false key in this attack is also delivered in the RSS tuning way as required by the protocol. However, the attack will be detected and prevented in the vBox protocol. For an attacker that uses a very large $\Delta P_0$ parameter to overcome the great fluctuation of the adversary-listener channel, the attempt will be thwarted by the valid range check in Step (d) of the protocol. For an attacker that uses the same $\Delta P_0$ parameter as the initiator, the situation is worse, because: (1) he can not pass the valid range check, either; (2) the key is greatly distorted by the great fluctuation of the adversary-listener channel (similar to the case of eavesdropping), so the listener will shared a "fake" key with the adversary and the adversary cannot decrypt packets.

**LOS (line-of-sight) Attacks.** LOS attacks refer to the scenarios where the attacker can getting relatively close to the user and a direct signal propagation path exists between them. For some RSS-based authentication or key establishment schemes whose security heavily rely on a multipath environment [5,13], such attacks can be very threatening. However, vBox has strong resistance against LOS attacks, because the fast relative motion between the legitimate devices and the attacker leads to tremendous Doppler shift in the off-box channel [11], which contributes largely to the fast fading of the channel. Even if the attacker launch attacks in a very near proximity (1 m as described in the experiment section) with no obstacle, the security is still well guaranteed. In the same spirit, the nature of vBox also makes it more resistant to attacks using directional antennas, where the attacker tries to eliminate the multipath effect by using directional antennas that provide a narrower main lobe of the radio wave.

**Channel Prediction Attacks.** The proposed scheme is also secure against channel prediction attacks. In such attacks, the attacker might leverage his knowledge of the environment to predict the wireless channel between himself and the target device. However, this attack is usually effective against stationary targets only. In our scheme, the random movement of the initiator makes the realtime channel prediction impractical. Note that this random entropy comes from the wave by the owner but also the greatly aggravated fast fading of the wireless channel due to the wave.

### 6.2 Usability

**Operation Time.** The vBox protocol is very efficient in terms of time consumption. The experiment results show an operation time of about 6.5 s (4 s for authentication, and 2.5 for key transmission). The time efficiency is remarkably high compared with existing works, which averagely takes more than 10s to finish the authentication [4, 13].

**Secret Bit Rate.** The secret bit rate (as defined in [5]) of vBox is approximately 1, meaning that each RSS measurement can contribute nearly 1 secret bit. This can be seen as an advantage over existing key extraction approaches, whose secret bit rates are mostly around 0.3 [3,5,7,14]. At a sending speed of 50 packet/s, vBox can finish the establishment of a 128-bit key within 3 s.

**Computation Overhead.** vBox is lightweight in terms of computation overhead. Unlike approaches that leverage public key cryptography, there is no computationally expensive operations involved in vBox. This lightweight feature makes it a good choice for low-end WPAN nodes.

**Versatility.** vBox does not rely on any pre-shared secrets between the devices or additional hardware support such as special biometric sensors, NFC transceivers, or multiple antennas. vBox is applicable for almost all off-the-shelf small-size wireless devices.

**Ease of Use.** The users of vBox do not need any special training. The human interaction involved is very simple: pressing a button and waving for a short period of time. For devices that are equipped with motion sensor (which has already been widely adopted), the operation can be even simpler by detecting the motion of the user and starting the protocol automatically.

## 7  Conclusion

In this paper, we proposed vBox, a method to proactively establish secure channels between wireless devices without any prior knowledge. By requiring the owner to simply waving the devices together, vBox builds a virtually shielded environment for RSS-based authentication and secret key transmission in plaintext. vBox eliminates the dependence on dynamic environments of existing RSS-based authentication and key negotiation approaches. We presented the detailed vBox protocol and implemented it on commercial-off-the-shelf ZigBee devices. The experiment results and security analysis demonstrate that vBox is lightweight, easy-of-use, efficient and secure against various attacks.

# A    Detailed Discussion of the Parameters

**Key Length.** We recommend that the symmetric key delivered in Phase 2 use a length of 128. The time cost of Phase 2 is proportional to the length of the key, so the key material should not be too lengthy. 128-bit key is security enough for a symmetric encryption algorithm such as AES.

**The Packet Interval $T$.** The packet interval $T$ in the protocol is the time interval between the transmission of two successive *AuthReq* or *BitCarrierMsg*, which are used by the initiator for authentication or key transmission, respectively. To eliminate the correlation between the measured RSS values, $T$ should be greater than the coherence time of the adversary-listener channel. The coherence time is estimated with the formula $t_c = c/2fv$, where $c$ denotes the speed of light, $f$ denotes the radio frequency, and $v$ denotes the moving speed of the listener. In our protocol, the listener is held by the user and waved rapidly in the air, the speed of which is around $3\,\mathrm{m/s}$. The radio frequency is $2.4\,\mathrm{GHz}$. The resulting coherence time is about $20\,\mathrm{ms}$.

**The Authentication Time.** In the protocol, the initiator is required to send $N$ consecutive *AuthReq* packets to the listener for authentication with the time interval $T$. The listener measures and records the RSS of the $N$ packets to calculate the standard deviation $\sigma$. $N$ should be large enough to provide the listener with sufficient samples for the evaluation. Particularly, the amount of RSS measurements should be sufficient for the listener to detect and evaluate the fluctuations in the adversary-listener channel, so as to defeat the malicious authentication trials by the adversary. As a matter of fact, our protocol can detect the existence of the adversary in several seconds, because the intentional movements of listener makes the adversary-listener channel fluctuates tremendously.

**The Power Level Difference $\Delta P_0$.** In our protocol, the process of delivering an $m$-bit key is composed by the consecutive transmissions of $m$ data packets. The transmitting power of each packet is either $P_{0H}$ (representing bit '1') or $P_{0L}$ (representing bit '0'), in consistency with the key bits orderly. As the *Active RSS Tuning* method can be deemed as a form of baseband transmission of digital signal through an AWGN (Additive White Gaussian Noise) channel, the level difference $\Delta P_0$ directly affects the reliability of the key transmission by affecting the SNR (signal-to-noise ratio). The SNR (in dB) can be estimated using the formula:

$$S/N = 10 \lg(\sigma_P^2/\sigma_X^2) \tag{6}$$

where $\sigma_P = \Delta P_0/2$, $\sigma_X$ is the standard deviation of the Gaussian noise as defined in Eq. 3. By consulting the theoretical BER-SNR curve in [8], we can figure out that, to deliver a 128-bit key correctly with a probability of 0.99, the SNR should be greater than $8dB$. According to Eq. 6, we can derive:

$$\Delta P_0 \geq 5 \cdot \sigma_X \tag{7}$$

At the same time, $\Delta P_0$ should be as small as possible on the premise of ensuring the reliability of the key transmission. A low $\Delta P_0$ relative to the RSS variation of the initiator-adversary channel, $\sigma_R$, helps prevent the adversary from retrieving the key bits from the channel fluctuations.

**The Valid RSS Range for Key Transmission.** We use $R_T$ to denote the mean value of the RSS measurements on the listener during the authentication phase. If the initiator-listener channel is noiseless, when $P_{0I}$ (TX power) produces $R_T$ (RSS), $P_{0H}$ should produce $R_T + \Delta P_0/2$, and $P_{0L}$ should produce $R_T - \Delta P_0/2$. However, the actually measured RSS values might be a little deviated from $RSS_H$ and $RSS_L$ due to the existence of the Gaussian noise. So we determine a valid RSS range for key transmission, which is $[R_T - \Delta P_0/2 - 3\sigma_X, R_T + \Delta P_0/2 + 3\sigma_X]$. The measured RSS is likely to fall into this range with a probability higher than $99.7\%$, according to the empirical *3-sigma* rule for Gaussian distribution [2]. The protocol requires that all the RSS values of the *BitCarrierMsg* should fall in to the valid range, so as to resist the *False Key Attack* as described in Sect. 6.1. The listener restores the key by interpreting a RSS among $[R_T, R_T + \Delta P_0/2 + 3\sigma_X]$ into bit '1', and a RSS among $[R_T - \Delta P_0/2 - 3\sigma_X, R_T]$ into bit '0'.

# B    Real World Estimation of $\sigma_X$ and $\sigma_R$

The initiator and the listener is held together within the researcher's hand, and their antennas are in parallel with a distance of about 3 cm. During the experiment, the researcher waves the two devices rapidly in front of himself as described in the protocol. The initiator consecutively sends 200 repetitive packets to the listener at a rate of 50/s with a fixed TX power, 0 dBm. The listener records the 200 RSS values and calculates their standard deviation $\sigma$, as an estimation of the initiator-listener channel RSS variation. The experiment is carried out for 50 times. Note that the initiator-listener channel is a near field channel which suffers little influence from the environment, so we did not change the location of this experiment intentionally. The results are shown in Fig. 5 as "legitimate". All of the 50 $\sigma$ values fall into the range [0.40 dBm, 0.97 dBm], and the average is 0.67 dBm. We expect the initiator-listener channel RSS variation to be around 0.67 dBm.

We measure the RSS variation of the initiator-adversary channel in three different scenarios as described above: a compact office room, a spacious living room, and a large dining hall, respectively. In this experiment, the adversary is placed a distance away from the initiator, at a different location for each trial. Again, the initiator consecutively sends 200 repetitive packets to the adversary at a rate of $50/s$ with a fixed TX power, 0 dBm. The adversary records the 200 RSS values and calculates their standard deviation $\sigma$, as an estimation of the initiator-adversary channel RSS variation. In each scenario, the experiment is carried out for 50 times. In each trial, adversary is located at a random spot of the current scenario. The distance between the two nodes ranges from 1m to 8m. We believe that $1m$ is the minimum distance that an attacker can launch attacks near the user without being noticed. The results are shown in Fig. 5 as "scenario A", "scenario B", and "scenario C", respectively. All of the 150 $\sigma$ values fall into the range [5 dBm, 8 dBm]. The overall mean of $\sigma$ of the three scenarios is 6.21 dBm. As an approximation, we expect the initiator-listener channel RSS variation to be around 6.21 dBm, which is far larger than that of the initiator-listener channel as estimated above (0.67 dBm).

# References

1. Wireless Propagation. http://people.seas.harvard.edu/jones/es151/prop_models/propagation.html
2. Normal Distribution. http://en.wikipedia.org/wiki/Normal_distribution
3. Aono, T., Higuchi, K., Ohira, T., Komiyama, B., Sasaoka, H.: Wireless secret key generation exploiting reactance-domain scalar response of multipath fading channels. IEEE Trans. Antennas Propag. **53**, 3776–3784 (2005)
4. Cai, L., Zeng, K., Chen, H., Mohapatra, P.: Good neighbor: Ad hoc pairing of nearby wireless devices by multiple antennas. In: Proceedings of the Network and Distributed System Security Symposium, NDSS 2011 (2011)
5. Jana, S., Premnath, S.N., Clark, M., Kasera, S.K., Patwari, N., Krishnamurthy, S.V.: On the effectiveness of secret key extraction from wireless signal strength in real environments. In: Proceedings of the 15th Annual International Conference on Mobile Computing and Networking, MOBICOM 2009, pp. 321–332 (2009)
6. Kalamandeen, A., Scannell, A., de Lara, E., Sheth, A., LaMarca, A.: Ensemble: cooperative proximity-based authentication. In: Proceedings of the 8th International Conference on Mobile Systems, Applications, and Services (MobiSys 2010), pp. 331–344 (2010)
7. Mathur, S., Trappe, W., Mandayam, N.B., Ye, C., Reznik, A.: Radio-telepathy: extracting a secret key from an unauthenticated wireless channel. In: Proceedings of the 14th Annual International Conference on Mobile Computing and Networking, MOBICOM 2008, pp. 128–139 (2008)
8. Divya, M.: Bit error rate performance of bpsk modulation and ofdm-bpsk with rayleigh multipath channel. Int. J. Eng. Adv. Technol. (IJEAT) **2**(4), 623–626 (2013). ISSN: 2249-8958
9. Neskovic, A., Neskovic, N., Paunovic, G.: Modern approaches in modeling of mobile radio systems propagation environment. IEEE Commun. Surv. Tutorials **3**(3), 2–12 (2000)

10. Patwari, N., Kasera, S.K.: Robust location distinction using temporal link signatures. In: Proceedings of the 13th Annual International Conference on Mobile Computing and Networking, MOBICOM 2007, pp. 111–122 (2007)
11. Rappaport, T.S.: Wireless communications - principles and practice. Prentice Hall, Upper Saddle River (1996)
12. Rappaport, T., Milstein, L.: Effects of radio propagation path loss on ds-cdma cellular frequency reuse efficiency for the reverse channel. IEEE Trans. Veh. Technol. **41**(3), 231–242 (1992)
13. Shi, L., Li, M., Yu, S., Yuan, J.: BANA: body area network authentication exploiting channel characteristics. In: Proceedings of the Fifth ACM Conference on Security and Privacy in Wireless and Mobile Networks, WiSec 2012, pp. 27–38 (2012)
14. Tope, M.A., McEachen, J.C.: Unconditionally secure communications over fading channels. In: MILCOM, Military Communications Conference (2001)
15. Wilson, R.D., Tse, D., Scholtz, R.A.: Channel identification: Secret sharing using reciprocity in ultrawideband channels. IEEE Trans. Inf. Forensics Secur. **2**, 364–375 (2007)
16. Zeng, K., Govindan, K., Mohapatra, P.: Non-cryptographic authentication and identification in wireless networks. IEEE Wireless Commun. **17**(5), 56–62 (2010)

# Detection and Monitoring

# Accurate Specification for Robust Detection of Malicious Behavior in Mobile Environments

Sufatrio[✉], Tong-Wei Chua, Darell J.J. Tan, and Vrizlynn L.L. Thing

Institute for Infocomm Research, 1 Fusionopolis Way, #21-01, Connexis, Singapore
{sufatrio,twchua,jjdtan,vriz}@i2r.a-star.edu.sg

**Abstract.** The need to accurately specify and detect malicious behavior is widely known. This paper presents a novel and convenient way of accurately specifying malicious behavior in mobile environments by taking Android as a representative platform of analysis and implementation. Our specification takes a sequence-based approach in declaratively formulating a malicious action, whereby any two consecutive security-sensitive operations are connected by either a control or taint flow. It also captures the invocation context of an operation within an app's component type and lifecycle/callback method. Additionally, exclusion of operations that are invoked from UI-related callback methods can be specified to indicate an action's stealthy execution portions. We show how the specification is sufficiently expressive to describe malicious patterns that are commonly exhibited by mobile malware. To show the usefulness of the specification, and to demonstrate that it can derive stable and distinctive patterns of existing Android malware, we develop a static analyzer that can automatically check an app for numerous security-sensitive actions written using the specification. Given a target app's uncovered behavior, the analyzer associates it with a collection of known malware families. Experiments show that our obfuscation-resistant analyzer can associate malware samples with their correct family with an accuracy of 97.2%, while retaining the ability to differentiate benign apps from the profiled malware families with an accuracy of 97.6%. These results positively show how the specification can lend to robust mobile malware detection.

**Keywords:** Behavior specification · Mobile security · Malware detection

## 1 Introduction

Recent years have seen smart mobile devices becoming increasingly pervasive in our world. The threat posed by malicious mobile applications (apps), however, seriously undermines the security and privacy of mobile users [16], who are usually not even aware of any incidents occurring on their own devices. To deal with this, a mechanism that can accurately specify malicious behavior of mobile malware is important and necessary. Using such a specification, malware detectors can subsequently be built to help ascertain the presence of malicious apps.

G. Pernul et al. (Eds.): ESORICS 2015, Part II, LNCS 9327, pp. 355–375, 2015.
DOI: 10.1007/978-3-319-24177-7_18

This paper presents a novel way of accurately specifying malicious behavior in mobile environments. The specification is concise, convenient to write, and sufficiently expressive to capture a wide range of malicious behavior patterns that are commonly exhibited by mobile malware. Our specification declaratively expresses a malicious behavioral action as a sequence of security-sensitive operations, where any two consecutive operations are connected by either a control or taint flow. It also captures the invocation context of an operation, including the one that intercepts a broadcast-based system event, within its Android app-component type and lifecycle/callback method. Additionally, exclusion of operations that are invoked from UI-related callback methods can be specified on selective parts of a malicious action to indicate the absence of user involvement. We show how our specification is at least as expressive as existing specification schemes in describing malicious behavior in mobile environments.

To demonstrate the usefulness of our specification, we use it to compile an initial list of malicious and security-relevant behavior patterns in Android, which serves as a representative platform of our analysis and implementation. We then develop a static analyzer to utilize the pattern base and characterize apps in terms of their applicable pattern entries. Based on the uncovered entries of target apps, the analyzer associates the apps with a set of known malware families. Our goal here is to empirically demonstrate that the specification can facilitate a compilation of malicious pattern base, which can be used by an analyzer to derive stable, distinctive and obfuscation-resistant behavior patterns of existing malware families. Experiments show that the analyzer can associate malware samples with their correct family with an accuracy of 97.2 %. When tested on presumably-benign top free apps from Google Play, it can differentiate the apps from profiled malware with an accuracy of 97.6 %. App similarity techniques [7, 19,20] can additionally be employed for a higher combined association accuracy.

In summary, our work makes the following contributions to mobile security:

- We propose a novel malware specification language, which can handily capture a wide range of malicious behavior in mobile environments (see Sect. 2).
- We analyze and compare the scheme's expressiveness and usage convenience with other existing specification techniques (see Sect. 3).
- We build a static analyzer that utilizes a database of malicious and security-sensitive patterns, which are declaratively written using the specification, to characterize an app and correlate it with known malware families (see Sect. 4).
- Using a set of experiments, we demonstrate how the analyzer can perform an association of malware samples with their correct family with a high accuracy of 97.2 % (see Sect. 5). Benign apps are deemed different from the profiled malware families with an accuracy of 97.6 %. We additionally show how the analyzer is robust against various code obfuscation attacks, which significantly reduce the average detection rate of 55 other anti-malware systems connected to VirusTotal from 70.8 % to 34.4 %.

The remainder of this paper is organized as follows. Section 2 elaborates our specification scheme. Section 3 analyzes and compares it with other schemes. Section 4 explains the design and implementation of our static analyzer, while

Sect. 5 reports its experiments. Section 6 gives additional discussions on our specification and analyzer. Section 7 mentions related work and Sect. 8 concludes this paper.

# 2  Malicious Behavior Specification for Mobile Environments

## 2.1  Goals, Rules and Notation of Specification Scheme

In Android, operations that access protected resources are invoked through permission-guarded API calls. To accomplish a certain security-sensitive action, multiple security-sensitive operations may be required. For instance, to record audio, an app needs to successively invoke the following methods of an object of `android.media.MediaRecorder` class: `setAudioSource()`, `setOutputFormat()`, `setOutputFile()`, and `start()`. Throughout its execution, an untrusted Android app may execute a number of possibly independent security-sensitive actions.

In this work, we call a sequence of API calls that can independently realize a security-sensitive action as a *malicious behavior pattern*. Our proposed specification scheme, called *Sequence-based Malicious Behavior Specification (SeqMalSpec)*, declaratively specifies malicious behavior patterns that are commonly or potentially exhibited by mobile malware in an accurate and convenient manner. Although we specifically target the Android platform[1], our specification scheme in principle can be easily adapted to other systems employing permission-guarded API calls for accessing protected resources.

We specifically take a sequence-based specification approach in order to yield a semantically-aware scheme that is both convenient for formulation and interpretation by human analysts, and is amenable to processing by automated analyzers. The specification intentionally avoids referring to any user-supplied identifiers so that it is robust against identifier renaming attacks [14]. App behavior characterization using *SeqMalSpec* is defined in a top-down fashion as follows.

- A *malicious app* (*maliciousApp*) is defined in terms of a set of its applicable malicious behavior patterns.
- A *malicious behavior pattern* (*maliciousPattern*) represents a path (sequence) of security sensitive operations, where any two consecutive operations in the path are connected by either:
  $\rightsquigarrow$: a control-flow based sub-path of length $\geq 1$, which may contain non security-sensitive operations in between;
  $\rightarrow$: a control-flow based sub-path of length 1;
  $\appro>$: a taint-flow based sub-path of length $\geq 1$, which may contain non security-sensitive operations;
  $\Rightarrow$: a taint-flow based sub-path of length 1.

---

[1] We limit the scope of our behavior specification in this paper to operations at the Java/Dalvik code level. Operations that are performed by native code are thus beyond the scope of this paper, and may be addressed by future work.

As can be seen above, our specification allows multiple occurrences of a taint-flow based sub-path. Based on analyzing the attack threat in Android, we however observe that taint-flow related behavior of Android malware is mostly pertinent to private information leakage. Hence, in practice, only one taint-flow based sub-path is present at the end of a malicious pattern. It links up a private-information access operation with the corresponding exfiltration operation. Notice that this taint-flow sub-path, however, can be part of a longer pattern containing multiple preceding control-flow based sub-paths.

- A *security-sensitive operation* (*sensitiveOp*) is defined as a tuple $\langle x, y, z \rangle$, with:

  $x$: a non-empty element of the set of all possible combinations of Android app-component types from which operation $z$ is invoked. We can thus write $x \in \mathcal{P}(\mathbb{X}) - \{\varnothing\}$, where $\mathbb{X} = \{activity, service, broadcastReceiver\}$. When $x = \mathbb{X}$, we can write a notational shorthand "*" instead.

  $y$: a non-empty element of the set of all possible combinations of lifecycle and callback methods. That is, $y \in \mathcal{P}(\mathbb{Y}) - \{\varnothing\}$, where $\mathbb{Y}$ is the set of all lifecycle and callback methods. When $y = \mathbb{Y}$, we can write "*". For convenience, we can also specify the set of lifecycle or callback methods $m$ that should not be present as $!m$. In other words, $y = \mathbb{Y} - m$. This shorthand is useful, for instance, to exclude API invocations from a particular set of methods, such as UI-related callback methods.

  $z$: either an API call (*APICall*), a similar API call set (*similarAPICallSet*), or a system-event interception (*eventInterception*) operation.

- An *API call* (*APICall*) is defined based on its class type, method signature, and possible argument values to match. It is expressed as the following tuple:

$$APICall = \langle className, returnType, APICallName$$
$$(parameterType_1 = value_1, \ldots, parameterType_n = value_n) \rangle.$$

For $value_i$, where $1 \leq i \leq n$, we can specify a special generic value "*any*" if the corresponding parameter does not need to be matched. An example of a security-sensitive operation of *APICall* type is $\langle \{service, broadcastReceiver\}, *, \langle \mathtt{android.telephony.TelephonyManager}, \mathtt{java.lang.String}, \mathtt{getDevice\text{-}Id()} \rangle \rangle$. This corresponds to an invocation of $\mathtt{getDeviceId()}$ from any lifecycle method of a service or broadcast receiver, which runs in the background.

- A *similar API-call set* (*similarAPICallSet*) is a set of API calls sharing the same functionality, or an API call that has different argument signatures. Multiple API calls can have the same functionality in Android, for instance, when a new API call is used to replace deprecated one(s). An API can have different argument signatures when it is overloaded with different arguments.

- A *system-event interception operation* (*eventInterception*) is defined for each broadcast intent that is related to a system event, such as for $\mathtt{android.provider.Telephony.SMS\_RECEIVED}$ intent. Since such an event interception occurs within the $\mathtt{onReceive()}$ method of a broadcast receiver, the tuple of a system-event interception operation is set with $x = \{broadcastReceiver\}$ and $y = \{\mathtt{onReceive()}\}$. In an analyzed app, the presence of a system-event interception operation is assumed whenever:

1. There exists a broadcast receiver that is registered, either statically in `AndroidManifest.xml` or dynamically by invoking `registerReceiver()`, to receive the corresponding system intent in its intent filters.
2. The `onReceive()` lifecycle method is present (i.e. overridden) within that broadcast receiver.

A static analyzer that analyzes an app for malicious behavior patterns, such as ours described in Sect. 4, may assume these system-event interception operations at the beginning of the pertinent `onReceive()` methods.

- A *method-exclusion constraint* (*methodExclusionConstraint*) can be defined on a control- or taint-flow based sub-path of length $\geq 2$ by specifying a set of methods to be excluded along the sub-path. That is, along the sub-path, the constraint disallows the presence of *any* operations that are invoked from within any methods in the set.[2] While we can specify any methods to be excluded in a sub-path, in practice we are concerned only with UI callback methods, such as `onClick()`, `onLongClick()` or `onKey()`. By specifying a set of all UI callback methods, referred to as *UICallbackSet*, on a sub-path, we thus require the sub-path to consist of operations that are performed without any user interactions. Notationally, we can write a method-exclusion constraint $c$ with its excluded method set $m$ by putting $!m$ on top of the control-flow based sub-path (i.e. $\overset{!m}{\rightsquigarrow}$) or taint-flow based sub-path (i.e. $\overset{!m}{\approx\!\!\!>}$).

*SeqMalSpec* can be described in the Extended Backus-Naur Form (EBNF) notation as shown in Table 1 of Appendix A.

## 2.2 Sample Specified Malicious Patterns

The following are two commonly-exhibited malicious behavior patterns in Android environment that are expressed using *SeqMalSpec*. For easier reading, we omit the parameters of some API calls (denoted as "...") in these patterns:

- An automatic opening of the camera that is followed by the trigger of an image capture within the `onReceive()` method of a broadcast receiver, without any user interaction in between:
  
  $\langle\{broadcastReceiver\}, \{$`onReceive()`$\}, \langle$`android.hardware.Camera, android.hardware.Camera, open()`$\rangle\rangle \overset{!UICallbackSet}{\rightsquigarrow} \langle\{broadcastReceiver\}, \{$`onReceive()`$\}, \langle$`android.hardware.Camera, void, takePicture(...)`$\rangle\rangle$.

- A sending of the phone's IMEI number to the Internet upon receipt of an SMS without any user interaction, which represents a behavior pattern of GoldDream malware that is previously specified using predicates in [8]:
  
  $\langle\{broadcastReceiver\}, \{$`onReceive()`$\},$ `SMS_RECEIVED_INTERCEPTION()`$\rangle$

---

[2] If desired, one can define variations of exclusion constraint depending on which part of a sub-path that must satisfy the exclusion. That is, we may have $!prefix(n, m)$ and $!suffix(n, m)$, which disallow operations that are invoked from methods in set $m$ within the first and last $n$ operations of the sub-path, respectively. Our constraint that disallows all operations throughout a sub-path can be renamed as $!all(m)$.

$\overset{!UICallbackSet}{\rightsquigarrow}$ $\langle\{broadcastReceiver\},\{\texttt{onReceive()}\},\langle\texttt{android.content.Con-}$
$\texttt{text},\texttt{android.content.ComponentName},\texttt{startService}(\dots)\rangle\rangle^{!UICallbackSet}_{\rightsquigarrow}$
$\langle\{service\},\{\texttt{onStartCommand()}\},\langle\texttt{android.telephony.TelephonyManager},$
$\texttt{java.lang.String},\texttt{getDeviceId()}\rangle\rangle\overset{!UICallbackSet}{\approx\!\!>}$ $\langle\{service\},\{\texttt{onStartCom-}$
$\texttt{mand()},\langle\texttt{org.apache.http.client.HttpClient},\texttt{org.apache.http.HttpRes-}$
$\texttt{ponse},\texttt{execute}(\dots)\rangle\rangle\rangle.$

## 3    Expressiveness of *SeqMalSpec* and Its Comparison

### 3.1    Expressiveness of *SeqMalSpec*

We give an analysis of the expressiveness of *SeqMalSpec* by asserting the following two claims, whose (sketch of) proof is given in Appendix B.

**Claim 1.** In a system where accesses to protected resources are invoked through a finite set of well-defined API calls, *SeqMalSpec* is able to express the following types of malicious action[3]:

1. A finite series of API calls that realizes an action to a protected resource;
2. A finite series of API calls that obtains a piece of information from a protected resource and subsequently performs other operations on it, including ultimately releasing it out of the system via a communication channel.

Defining a malicious action in terms of the Android-level API calls as in our specification allows us to express a more accurate semantic description than that based on the OS-level API/system calls in the traditional desktop environment. This is because the Android-level API calls are defined with more relevant operational semantics, which are directly pertinent to the protected resources on a mobile device and their access permission models. As a result, our specification can yield a more accurate and clearer behavior specification of Android malware compared to schemes that operate on the OS-level API calls.

**Claim 2.** Suppose we have an event-driven system, where each user interaction with an app raises a UI event. For each raised UI event, the system invokes a registered UI callback method, which is either an overridden correspondingly-named method of a registered event-handler object, or other arbitrarily-named handler method that is registered to process the event. On such a system model, on which Android is based, *SeqMalSpec* is able to express variants of malicious action described in Claim 1, whose any two API calls are executed through a series of operations that involve no user interaction.

---

[3] We remark that the use of Java reflection, together with string encryption, in Android may hinder static malware detectors in determining an invoked API call. As such, they may not be able to match a pattern whose series of API calls are explicitly named, thus apparently limiting the use of the specification. This is, in fact, a widely known limitation of static analyzers. To deal with it, one can incorporate a dynamic analyzer to uncover the invoked API calls. A static analyzer with such a runtime information feedback then would be able to inspect the app and match the pattern.

With regard to Claim 2, we would like to make the following important remarks. A pattern in *SeqMalSpec* whose all API calls are invoked from non UI-related callback methods, and also specifies UI-related method exclusion constraint, means that no user interaction should appear along the pattern. This is used to specify stealthy actions. An execution path *involving* a user interaction, however, does not necessarily mean that the action is *intended* or *consented* by the user. This is because a malware may perform malicious actions while the user is legitimately interacting with its activities. This subtle point highlights that a flow connector with an added UI-related exclusion constraint is a stricter version of its unconstrained one. It is to be specified when we know that a particular malware sample performs the pertinent patterns in a totally stealthy manner.

### 3.2 Comparison with Other Malware Specification Schemes

We now compare *SeqMalSpec* with other existing malware specification schemes. There exist various ways of specifying malicious behavior. Most of them [2,4–6,9,12,13], however, pre-date modern mobile OSes and are designed primarily for desktop security. As such, they work mostly at the native code level, where the higher-level operational semantics at the mobile OS level cannot be fully utilized. Below, we compare *SeqMalSpec* with other schemes that are specifically proposed for mobile setting with respect to expressiveness power and usage convenience.

**Predicate Based Specification.** Feng et al. [8] recently proposed Apposcopy, which specifies the signatures of Android malware in Horn-clause based Datalog language. For this purpose, a number of unary and binary predicates are introduced. A malicious pattern is considered present in an app if all its specified predicates evaluate to true, possibly through a unification process. While Datalog-based predicates are suitable to identify relations, usually between two API operations, our sequence-based specification allows us to naturally express a chain of *any number* consecutive operations, together with the context of each operation invocation. As a result, we can easily specify multiple context-based operations that must appear in order, including affixing possible UI-exclusion constraints on selective parts of a sequence. Since Apposcopy can define new predicates, it can extend its specification to mimic our newly-proposed invocation context and constraints. Yet *SeqMalSpec*, in our view, look more natural to human analysts since a pattern's operations are expressed using the original Android API calls rather than newly-defined predicate-based expressions. Section 7 additionally mentions further differences between our work and [8] with respect to the signature derivation and static analyzer implementation.

**Temporal-Logic Based Specification.** Model checking systems use a behavior signature expressed as a temporal logic formula. This formula can be based on Computational Tree Logic (CTL) or Linear Temporal Logic (LTL); or their extensions, such as CTPL [12] or SCTPL/SLTPL [15]. While previous model-checking based detectors work at the native code level [12] or on a generic platform [2], a recent work [15] applies model checking to Android apps.

Although a temporal logic formula can describe various temporal-based correlation of events, its usage in specifying malicious behavior, including the one in [12,15], is typically limited to describing the existence of a sequence of related operations. Consequently, the relevant formulae employ linear-time temporal operators $\mathbf{F}$ (*finally/eventually*) and $\mathbf{U}$ (*until*); or appear as a CTL-based formula in the form of $\mathbf{EF}(\phi_1, \mathbf{EF}(\phi_2))$ or $\mathbf{E}(\phi_1 \ \mathbf{U} \ \phi_2)$. As reasoned above, *SeqMalSpec* is able to express such formulae using a more intuitive notation. While the extended temporal logic used in [15] can deal with variables to identify the reading of a private information and its subsequent exfiltration, we instead use the notion of taint-flow relationship between a set of source and sink API calls as in [1]. The use of API call sequence in *SeqMalSpec* additionally allows us to selectively encode the context of an API call invocation (i.e. using *sensitiveOp*) and to impose the exclusion of UI-related operations (i.e. using *methodExclusionConstraint*), which are both lacking in the existing logic-based specifications.

## 4   Static Analyzer Utilizing *SeqMalSpec*

### 4.1   Goal and Approach

To demonstrate the usefulness of *SeqMalSpec* and how one can leverage on it, we have developed a static analyzer that uncovers the presence of behavior patterns within Android apps by taking a list of *SeqMalSpec*-based specifications as an input. Unlike the static analyzer in [8], which determines if an app exhibits the behavior patterns of a particular malware family that are manually-specified by human experts, we instead devise our analyzer to automatically derive behavior patterns of each existing malware family. To this end, using *SeqMalSpec*, we compile a list of security-sensitive behavior patterns that are commonly exhibited by Android malware. We also include other behaviors that are potentially relevant from the security analysis viewpoint, such as inter-component activation operations. Given this compiled pattern database, our static analyzer inspects an app and reports the presence/absence of each pattern entry in the database.

Following this app characterization, the analyzer then associates an app with a set of known malware families by reporting the app's similarity distance to

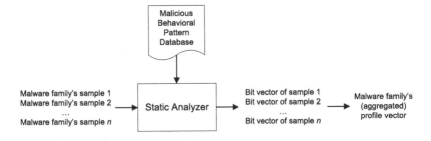

**Fig. 1.** Profiling a malware family for its malicious behavior pattern profile.

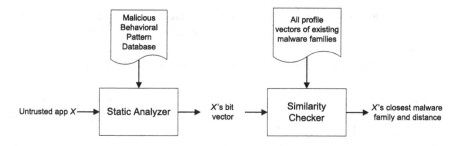

**Fig. 2.** Analysis of an untrusted app to determine its closest existing malware family.

the closest profiled malware family. This association is carried out to empirically show that the proposed specification, which is our main contribution in this work, allows for a derivation of stable, distinctive and obfuscation-resistant behavior profile of existing malware families. Figure 1 illustrates the process workflow of profiling an existing malware family. Figure 2 depicts how an association of an untrusted app is performed. The details of all these steps are elaborated below.

### 4.2   System Design and Implementation

**Compilation of Malicious Pattern Database.** We compile a behavior pattern database by examining how Android malware can launch various attack modalities on a device. For this, we analyze numerous existing security advisories on existing Android malware, as well as examine Android permissions to see how they can possibly be abused by apps. Our approach to identifying these patterns is thus a human-determined one. We take this approach since we specifically want the patterns to be accurate, accountable and explainable.

While this compilation effort requires the enumeration of all potentially relevant sensitive operations, we argue that producing a relatively comprehensive pattern database for Android is feasible owing to the following reasons:

- Android permissions, which guard a device's protected resources, are limited.
- Apps invoke a known set of API calls to access these permission-guarded resources. While malware writers may craft their samples to perform various processing steps, including for obfuscation purposes, the API calls represent a well-guarded gateway to performing the samples' payloads.

We remark that once such a pattern database is compiled, it can be shared with the security community for a crowd-sourcing based extension or refinement.[4]

The database used in our experiments includes patterns that perform the following types of operations: system-event interception, broadcast-intent related processing   (e.g. `android.content.BroadcastReceiver:abortBroadcast()`),

---

[4] Correspondingly, we do not assume that the uncovered patterns of a malware family in our experimentation give a complete specification of the family. This is because the completeness level depends on the employed pattern database.

incoming message processing (e.g. `android.os.Bundle:get("pdus")`), app component activation, audio/video/camera processing, access of private information, information release through SMS and data network, network management operations (e.g. reconnecting a WiFi network), and alarm-related operations.

**Detection of Behavior Patterns.** To uncover the presence of entries of the compiled behavior pattern database, we leverage on FlowDroid [1], which is built on top of the Soot framework. FlowDroid is a precise static analysis for Android apps, which finds potential privacy leaks between a list of source and sink API calls. We use FlowDroid to obtain the callgraph and all intra-procedural graphs of an Android app, as well as to perform a taint-flow analysis between a given source and sink method within a behavior pattern.

Note that by making use of our expressive behavior specification, which covers both control- and data-flow aspects of an app, our analyzer can characterize malware behavior more precisely than FlowDroid. In addition, we also made the following enhancements to FlowDroid in order to detect the compiled patterns:

- Identification of system-event interception operations of an app by scanning both its statically- and dynamically-registered broadcast receivers. All identified dynamic broadcast receivers are added as the app's entry points.
- Control-flow based, i.e. $\leadsto$ sub-path, reachability analysis of a pattern entry.
- Utilization of control-flow based reachability to filter out any source and sink pairs that are known to be unconnected. This avoids extra taint-flow checking by FlowDroid, which is computationally more expensive.
- Argument value determination of a number of parameterized API calls, possibly through a number of preceding intermediary assignment statements.

Our current prototype does not impose any method-exclusion constraints. Yet, it can be extended to apply the constraints as discussed in Sect. 6.

**Profiling of Existing Malware Families.** As can be seen in Fig. 1, we profile a malware family by having the static analyzer check all the samples within the family. For each sample, we generate its bit vector $v$ of length $\ell$, where $\ell$ is the number of pattern entries in the database. An entry at index $i$, i.e. $v[i]$, is set to 1 if the $i$-th pattern is present in the analyzed sample; or it is set to 0 otherwise.

Once we produce the bit vectors for all the samples of a malware family, we can derive the profile vector for that family, whose entries are real numbers between 0 and 1 (inclusive), as follows. Let us denote $k$ as the number of samples in the family; and $v_i$ as the bit vector of the $i$-th sample in the family, with $1 \leq i \leq k$. The malware family's profile vector $p$ is derived by setting its entry at index $j$, for all $1 \leq j \leq \ell$, as follows:

$$p[j] = \frac{1}{k} \cdot \sum_{i=1}^{k} v_i[j]. \tag{1}$$

An entry $p[j]$ thus quantifies the *presence rate* of a malicious behavior pattern $j$ across all the samples within the malware family.[5]

**Association of Apps with Profiled Malware.** Figure 2 shows how an association of an untrusted app is performed by comparing its bit vector against the profile vectors of all known malware families. Its detailed steps are as follows.

First, we want to associate each behavior pattern entry with a weight that indicates its usage prevalence for solely malicious purposes. The more a pattern is used more exclusively by malicious apps, the higher its weight is to be set. To achieve this, we take an automated weight-generation approach to determine $b_i$, with $0 \leq b_i \leq 1$, as the occurrence rate of pattern $i$ among (presumably) benign apps. Then, we can derive a vector $w$ of length $\ell$, where $w[i] = 1 - b_i$, for $1 \leq i \leq \ell$.

Let us now denote $f$ as the number of all known malware families. The profile vectors of all malware families can be considered as a real-valued matrix $M$ of dimension $f \times \ell$. A cell entry $M[i][j]$ represents the index $j$ (with $1 \leq j \leq \ell$) of the profile vector belonging to malware family $i$ (with $1 \leq i \leq f$).

We calculate the *weighted Euclidean distance* between the input app (with its bit vector $a$) and malware family $i$ (with its profile vector $M[i]$) as follows:

$$distance_{ai} = \sqrt{\sum_{j=1}^{\ell} w[j] \cdot (a[j] - M[i][j])^2} . \tag{2}$$

Once we have calculated the target app's distance scores against all malware families, which form a multiset $\{distance_{ai}, 1 \leq i \leq f\}$, we can determine the set of the closest malware families for the app, called $closestFamilySet_a$, as follows:

$$closestFamilySet_a = \{x, 1 \leq x \leq f \mid \forall y, 1 \leq y \leq f : distance_{ax} \leq distance_{ay}\}. \tag{3}$$

Note that while we define $closestFamilySet_a$ as a set, which may have multiple elements that all share a common similarity score, we however expect it to be a singleton, i.e. $|closestFamilySet_a| = 1$. In the case where $distance_{ax} > \tau$, with $\tau$ serving as a distance threshold, we then view the app to be sufficiently different from all the profiled malware families. Note, however, that we only compare apps and known malware solely based on their exhibited malicious patterns. Our similarity checking thus can be complemented by other app similarity techniques [7,11,19,20], which analyze different app modalities, to further ascertain if an app is really similar to a known malware family. Section 7 further discusses this point.

We build our analyzer module that generates the profiles of existing malware as in (1) and associates app with the profiled malware as in (2–3) in Python.

---

[5] In the case where a malware family actually consist of a few sub-families with significantly different behavior (see our empirical findings in Sect. 5.1), we may thus want to first perform a clustering on the family to partition it into several sub-families. Hence, each sub-family will have its own more accurate profile vector. The similarity checking step is then done against the profile vectors of the formed sub-families.

# 5    Experimentation Results

This section reports the experimentation results of our analyzer with regards to its association results. In the following, we successively explain the used malware dataset, experimentation objectives, taken methodology, and obtained results.

## 5.1    Used Malware Dataset

We evaluate our static analyzer using real-world malware samples from the Android Malware Genome Project [21], which in its entirely consists of 1,260 malware samples from 49 families. The distribution of malware samples among the families are, however, unequal. There are families that contain very few samples. Since we need to evaluate the analyzer by dividing each family's samples into profiling and testing samples, we thus omit malware families that have only six or less samples. We also exclude BaseBridge and Asroot, which perform an update attack and a root exploit with no observable payload execution within its Java code, respectively [21]. The following 22 families constitute our experimental dataset: ADRD, AnserverBot, BeanBot, Bgserv, DroidDream, DroidDreamLight, DroidKungFu1, DroidKungFu2, DroidKungFu3, DroidKungFu4, Geinimi, GoldDream, Gone60, jSMSHider, KMin, Pjapps, Plankton, RogueSPPush, SndApps, YZHC, zHash and Zsone. Out of 1,083 total samples from these 22 families, 125 (11.5 %) samples apparently did not run to completion during the taint-flow analysis using FlowDroid (see additional discussion in Sect. 6). Hence, 958 samples, or 76 % of the total samples in the Android Malware Genome Project, form our analyzed malware samples.

When we characterized the listed families to build their profile vectors, we observed that some families seem to consist of different sub-families. From [21], we learn that among the 1,260 malware samples in the Android Malware Genome Project, 1,083 (86.0 %) of them are repackaged. Thus, while the samples under the same family share a common payload, they may actually stem from a few variants of repackaged apps. The carrier apps may have other additional operations, including those security-sensitive ones. We, however, cannot fully ascertain this inference since the information of the exact mechanisms used to classify the samples into families is unavailable to us. To capture the existence of sub-families, we thus performed a clustering on the bit vectors of malware samples within a family. Based on our experimentation with the employed parameterized clustering technique, we empirically formed a cluster for each five samples within a family.[6] We found that the performed clustering on the families gave well-partitioned sub-families, thus supporting our hypothesis of the existence of sub-families.

---

[6] Notice that, for our purpose of associating an app with a set of profiled malware sub-families, separating samples belonging to the same malware sub-family into two different clusters will not affect the association result. This is because the derivation of the set *closestFamilySet$_a$* in (3) will yield either a single sub-family or multiple (possibly separated) sub-families with the same smallest distance score.

## 5.2   Experimentation Objectives and Obtained Results

We aim to evaluate our developed analyzer with the following three objectives:

1. To test the association of malware samples with their correct families;
2. To test the association of presumably benign apps with the malware families;
3. To test the robustness of the analyzer against code obfuscation.

**Objective 1 (Associating Malware Samples into Correct Families).** For each malware family in the dataset, we randomly select 80 % of the samples to derive the profile of the family, and leave the remaining 20 % to form the testing set. Since we form sub-families of malware, we compare each test sample against all sub-families, and report the family whose sub-family produces the smallest distance. We empirically set $\tau = 2.45$ as an approximate midpoint that separates the results of malicious samples (objective 1) and benign apps (objective 2). Using this threshold value, our analyzer can correctly associate the test samples with an accuracy of 97.18 %. The weighted Euclidean distances of the test samples range from 0.00 to 7.03, with an average distance of 0.64.

**Objective 2 (Association of Benign Apps with Profiled Families).** We also test if presumably benign apps listed as the top free apps on Google Play can be sufficiently similar to any of the profiled malware families. Analyzing 546 apps using the same threshold value gives an accuracy of 97.62 %. In other words, only 2.38 % of the tested benign apps is inaccurately determined to be similar to one of the profiled malware families. Upon inspection, we find that these apps are all inaccurately associated with Gone60 malware family. The generated profile vectors reveal that Gone60 exhibits only a few applicable patterns. A malware characterization in [21] lists Gone60 to perform only an SMS-based personal information stealing. This may explain why a number of benign apps can share similar patterns with Gone60. The weighted Euclidean distances of the tested benign apps range from 2.42 to 25.47, with an average distance of 7.03.

**Objective 3 (Robustness Against Transformation Attacks).** To show the robustness of our analyzer against malware transformation attacks, we compare the bit vectors of original malware samples with those of the transformed ones. If each vector pair always matches, that means our analyzer is resistant against the applied transformations. For this, we select 8 families from our dataset (i.e. Bean-Bot, Bgserv, DroidDream, Geinimi, GoldDream, Pjapps, Sndapps, Zsone), each with 4 random samples, for variant generation and detection. We use apktool to produce an app's disassembled smali code, and then modify the code to apply a sequence of transformations as listed in Table 2 of Appendix C.

The results show that our analyzer *always* produces the same bit vector for each transformed and original sample pair. The robustness of our analyzer stems from the following two important features of *SeqMalSpec*:

- Its avoidance of using any developer-supplied identifiers.
- The control- or taint-flow reachability property between two operations, which is robust against possible control-flow based obfuscation.

While the applied obfuscation methods are still limited, they are sufficient to deceive many anti-malware systems connected to VirusTotal (https://www.virustotal.com). Table 3 in Appendix D shows the results of transforming randomly-selected 5 malware families, with 2 samples in each family.

## 6   Discussions

### 6.1   Threats to Validity

We now address possible threats to the validity of our analyzer evaluation:

- *The used features of SeqMalSpec:* Our compiled pattern database exercises a simplified usage of *SeqMalSpec* in that only a single taint-flow connector ($\approx\!\!>$) is present to link a source and sink API call. We can implement a more expressive usage of the taint-flow connector by allowing a successive occurrences of taint-flow connected operations, where: (i) its beginning and end API calls represent the source and sink operations, respectively; and (ii) the intermediary API calls represents the 'pass-through' operations along the taint flow. In our implementation, we however choose to see how the simplified scheme can work in profiling and associating malware samples.
- *Malicious behavior database compilation:* Our compiled pattern database might not be sufficiently comprehensive. In fact, generating a sufficiently complete database may require a collective and cumulative effort. We however believe that a sufficiently good database is feasible to be constructed, which can then be refined over time, preferably in a crowd-sourced manner.
- *The developed analyzer:* Our analyzer relies on FlowDroid to perform its taint-flow analysis. While FlowDroid represents a state-of-the-art tool in performing taint analysis for Android apps, we encountered some apps that took a rather long time (i.e. hours or even a few days) of taint analysis processing on our machine. A number of apps throwed exceptions, including the memory-insufficiency related ones. In addition, the FlowDroid's option to output multiple paths between a detected source and sink pair seems to be very time- and memory-consuming. Any extensible tools that can give the same or even higher level of analysis precision as FlowDroid's, but with lower processing and memory footprint, will thus be useful. Since our specification and app association technique are independent of any implementation platforms, they can be realized using other tools as they become available.
- *Testing methodology:* For the experimentation, there is always a concern of not having sufficient samples in the dataset. We have tested our analyzer against most malware samples in the Android Malware Genome Project as well as more than five hundreds widely-used top free apps from Google Play. Further testing with more samples, especially recent ones, however will always be good to be carried out. We also assume that the top free apps downloaded from Google Play are benign, which may not always be the case. As mentioned in Sect. 5.1, the observed need for partitioning malware families into their

sub-families may warrant manual inspection to ascertain the presence of sub-families in the dataset. Lastly, we set the distance threshold value $\tau$ as an approximate midpoint that gives almost equal distance separation on both the malicious samples (objective 1) and benign apps (objective 2). Deciding a more fitting threshold value warrants further investigation, and is ideally to be done on a large number of analyzed apps.

- *Known challenges to static analysis:* Lastly, we also mention the widely-known challenges that may hinder any static analysis systems, namely the use of native code and Java reflection. Our system currently does not deal with these challenges, which may be best handled by dynamic analysis or other security techniques.

## 6.2   Future Work

Our experiments show that our specification and analyzer can derive patterns that form a stable and distinctive profile of a malware family. Nonetheless, they are less useful in profiling malware families that perform update attacks or dynamic code loading, such as BaseBridge. They also cannot effectively characterize malware families that do not execute their malicious payloads at the Java-based Android code, such as Asroot. To deal with this issue, our association can be complemented by another round of similarity checking that examines app structure similarity. Our app association, however, are useful in establishing app similarity with respect to the compiled pattern base, with an added benefit of being able to report explainable and comprehensible uncovered patterns.

Other possible future work that can improve our prototype system include:

- Our current prototype does not implement the UI-method exclusion constraints yet. We can implement the defined $!m$ (i.e. $!all(m)$) constraint rather easily by removing all excluded methods in the callgraph of an analyzed app. To implement $!prefix(n, m)$ and $!suffix(n, m)$, however, we need to ensure that a constructed path must avoid using any operations in the excluded methods, either in the beginning or ending part of the path as desired.
- As mentioned earlier, we can implement an analyzer that detects a pattern with multiple occurrences of the taint-flow connector ($\approx\!\triangleright$). For this, we need to ensure that a taint-flow must pass a number of intermediary operations.
- We can further measure the robustness of our prototype system against obfuscation attacks by applying and testing more app transformations.

## 7   Related Work

The comparison of *SeqMalSpec* with other existing mobile malware specification schemes is given in Sect. 3.2. Below, we highlight further differences with other specification work with regard to the associated detector implementation.

The design and implementation of our static analyzer differs from that in Apposcopy [8] in the two following aspects:

1. Apposcopy implements its own custom static analyzer, with a significant effort spent on developing its taint-flow tracker. In contrast, we leverage on Flow-Droid [1], which is known to perform a highly precise static taint analysis for Android apps. We additionally perform a number of enhancements to FlowDroid as described in Sect. 4.2.
2. Apposcopy requires its authors to manually inspect malware samples and craft the signature for each malware family. Its experimentation was then carried out to check whether a set of existing malware samples and benign apps match all the predicates in the manually-crafted signatures. In contrast, we need to compile a generic pattern base only once, from which our analyzer then automatically profiles all existing malware families. Hence, our analyzer not only checks the existence of certain behavior patterns within target apps, but also profiles all existing malware families and then associates a sample with its correct family in an automated manner as reported in Sect. 5.

DroidMiner [17] generates a behavior graph in order to mine segments of the graph that might correspond to known suspicious behavior, which are called *modalities* in the work. While our specification makes use of declarative, human-formulated operation sequences to be searched on samples from the control- and taint-flow viewpoints, DroidMiner extracts graph-reduction based modalities to be further processed by a classifier or associated with the rule mining process. Due to this, our approach in specifying malicious behavior is thus more in line with how human analysts work in analyzing a malicious app.

RiskRanker [10] detects malware samples, including possible zero-day ones, that invoke known root exploit, illegal cost creation and privacy-violation exploit patterns. DroidRanger [22] analyzes apps based on their permission-based behavioral footprint. While the two systems describe and scan for behavior patterns, they however lack a generic declarative behavior model that can concisely specify behavior patterns, and is also robust against transformation attacks.

FlowDroid [1] is a highly precise static taint analysis tool for Android apps, which is context, flow, field and object sensitive. Our work extends FlowDroid, which implicitly detects only privacy-leakage operations involving a pair of source and sink, to deal with any general sequence-based operations. Our improved analyzer not only reports privacy leakages, but also analyzes and characterizes an untrusted app, and then associates it with a known malware family.

Pegasus [3] detects malicious behavior that violates the temporal properties of safe interactions between an app and the Android event system. It thus can detect, for instance, if an operation is invoked without the prerequisite GUI-based interaction that indicates the user's consent. Meanwhile, AppIntent [18] checks if a data transmission in an app is intended by the user. Similar to these two systems, our work considers operations that are invoked without user involvement. Our analyzer can implement a feature that looks for a sequence of operations, whose sub-path(s) exclude any operations from within UI-related callback methods. The presence of these patterns, which are declaratively specified, are used by our analyzer to characterize and classify a malware sample.

# 8    Conclusion

We have presented our sequence-based specification scheme called *SeqMalSpec*, which is concise, convenient and sufficiently expressive to capture malicious behavior in mobile environments. We have also demonstrated how *SeqMalSpec* can be utilized by a static analyzer to characterize apps in terms of their malicious behavior patterns. Experiments have shown that the analyzer can associate a malicious app with its correct malware family with a high accuracy of 97.2 %, while still being able to differentiate benign apps from the profiled malware families with an accuracy of 97.6 %. Lastly, we have also demonstrated the analyzer's robustness against various code obfuscation attacks. The proposed *SeqMalSpec*, as we foresee it, will thus open up various other effective approaches to mitigating malware in mobile environments, including the malware-plagued Android platform that commands a huge user base.

## Appendix A: *SeqMalSpec* Scheme in Extended BNF

Malicious behavior specification using *SeqMalSpec* can be described in the EBNF notation as shown in Table 1. In the notation, we take the liberty of expressing the terminals belonging to a defined set using a natural language description (written within "[ ]") instead of explicitly listing all the set elements.

## Appendix B: Sketch of Proof of *SeqMalSpec* Expressiveness

The sketch of proof for the two expressiveness claims in Sect. 3 is as follows.

*Proof of Claim 1:* Suppose there exists a malicious action that is inexpressible using *SeqMalSpec*. Due to the assumed system, where all protected resources are guarded by a set of well-defined API calls, the malicious action must manifest itself as a series, i.e. sequence, of security-sensitive API calls:

- If the action involves no taint flow: *SeqMalSpec* is able to express that action using all control-flow based connectors. This leads to a contradiction.
- If it involves a taint flow from one operation to the other(s): *SeqMalSpec* is also able to express that action using a combination of control- and taint-flow based connectors. This also leads to a contradiction.

Hence, *SeqMalSpec* is able to express the actions described in Claim 1.    □

*Proof of Claim 2:* Suppose there is an action that involves no user interaction. We will show that *SeqMalSpec* is able to describe this action. Based on Claim 1, we know that the action is expressible with a sequence of API calls that are connected with the defined connectors. We can then add a non-UI method exclusion constraint on each of the used control- or taint-flow based connector. We additionally specify that all the security-sensitive API calls are not invoked from any UI-related callback methods. This means that *no* operation of the action is ever

**Table 1.** The notation of *SeqMalSpec* in Extended Backus-Naur Form (EBNF).

---

$maliciousApp ::= \{maliciousPattern+\},$

$maliciousPattern ::= sensitiveOp \mid (sensitiveOp\ connector)+\ sensitiveOp,$

$connector ::= \rightarrow \mid \overset{!methodExclusionSet}{\rightsquigarrow} \mid \Rightarrow \mid \overset{!methodExclusionSet}{\Rrightarrow},$

$methodExclusionSet ::= \{excludedMethod+\},$

$excludedMethod ::=$ "[all context methods from which an invocation is to be excluded]",

$sensitiveOp ::=$

$\quad\quad \langle appComponentTypeSet, invocationMethodSet, similarAPICallSet \rangle \mid$

$\quad\quad \langle appComponentTypeSet, invocationMethodSet, APICall \rangle \mid$

$\quad\quad \langle \{broadcastReceiver\}, \{\texttt{onReceive}()\}, eventInterception \rangle,$

$appComponentTypeSet ::= \{appComponentType+\},$

$appComponentType ::=$ "*activity*" $\mid$ "*service*" $\mid$ "*broadcastReceiver*",

$invocationMethodSet ::= \{lifecycleOrUICallbackMethod+\},$

$lifecycleOrUICallbackMethod ::= lifecycleMethod \mid UICallbackMethod,$

$lifecycleMethod ::=$ "[all lifecycle methods belonging to elements of *appComponentType*]",

$UICallbackMethod ::=$ "[all recognized UI callback methods]",

$similarAPICallSet ::= \{APICall+\},$

$APICall ::= \langle className, returnType, APICallName(valuedParameters) \rangle,$

$className ::=$ "[all Android classes containing elements of *APICallName* ]",

$returnType ::=$ "[all possible return types]",

$APICallName ::=$ "[all security-sensitive API calls]",

$valuedParameters ::= paramType = value \mid (paramType = value,)+ paramType = value,$

$paramType ::=$ "[all possible parameter types]",

$value ::=$ "[all possible values to parameter types, including a special value called 'any']",

$eventInterception ::=$ "[all system-event interception operations]".

---

invoked from UI-related callback methods, which are triggered by the assumed event-driven system in the event of user interaction with the app. If the action runs automatically upon a broadcast system event, *SeqMalSpec* is also able to describe a system event interception in its pattern. This shows that *SeqMalSpec* is able to express the stealthy action.                                                    □

## Appendix C: Applied App Obfuscation Attacks

Table 2 lists a sequence of app obfuscations that are applied to malware samples as discussed in Sect. 5.2.

**Table 2.** The sequence of app obfuscations that are applied to a malicious sample in order to generate its new variants.

| Step | Transformation | Transformation details |
|---|---|---|
| 1 | Package name renaming | Replace a sample's package name, which can be found in its `AndroidManifest.xml`, with random English words found in the dictionary |
| 2 | Identifier renaming | Replace all method names and strings with random English words found in the dictionary. We however do not rename identifiers with a single and dual characters (e.g. 'a', 'b', 'aa', 'ab'), which could have been subject to previous obfuscation by ProGuard |
| 3 | Junk code insertion | Insert junk code following arithmetical-operation based opaque predicates |
| 4 | Control-flow obfuscation | Relocate the invocation points of sensitive Android API calls by using an indirect method invocation |
| 5 | Reassembling and repacking | Reassemble the transformed smali code into an APK file using `apktool`, and then sign the file with a new custom key |

# Appendix D: Evaluation Results of Obfuscation Attacks on Other Anti-Malware Systems

Table 3 shows the results of evaluating 55 anti-malware systems that are connected to VirusTotal (https://www.virustotal.com) as explained in Sect. 5.2.

**Table 3.** Detection comparison between the transformed and their original samples on 55 anti-malware systems connected to VirusTotal.

| Malware family | Average detection rate | | Detection rate reduction |
|---|---|---|---|
| | Original samples | Transformed samples | |
| BeanBot | 66 % | 35 % | 31 % |
| Bgserv | 70 % | 35 % | 35 % |
| GoldDream | 73 % | 45 % | 28 % |
| Sndapps | 70 % | 27 % | 43 % |
| Zsone | 75 % | 30 % | 45 % |
| Average | 70.8 % | 34.4 % | 36.4 % |

# References

1. Arzt, S., Rasthofer, S., Fritz, C., Bodden, E., Bartel, A., Klein, J., Le Traon, Y., Octeau, D., McDaniel, P.: Flowdroid: Precise context, flow, field, object-sensitive and lifecycle-aware taint analysis for Android apps. In: 35th Conference on Programming Language Design and Implementation (2014)
2. Beaucamps, P., Gnaedig, I., Marion, J.-Y.: Abstraction-based malware analysis using rewriting and model checking. In: Foresti, S., Yung, M., Martinelli, F. (eds.) ESORICS 2012. LNCS, vol. 7459, pp. 806–823. Springer, Heidelberg (2012)
3. Chen, K.Z., Johnson, N., D'Silva, V., Dai, S., MacNamara, K., Magrino, T., Wu, E., Rinard, M., Song, D.: Contextual policy enforcement in Android applications with permission event graphs. In: 20th Network and Distributed System Security Symposium (2013)
4. Christodorescu, M., Jha, S.: Static analysis of executables to detect malicious patterns. In: 12th USENIX Security Symposium (2003)
5. Christodorescu, M., Jha, S., Kruegel, C.: Mining specifications of malicious behavior. In: 6th Joint Meeting of the European Software Engineering Conference and the ACM SIGSOFT Symposium on the Foundations of Software Engineering (2007)
6. Christodorescu, M., Jha, S., Seshia, S.A., Song, D., Bryant, R.E.: Semantics-aware malware detection. In: 2005 IEEE Symposium on Security and Privacy (2005)
7. Crussell, J., Gibler, C., Chen, H.: Attack of the clones: Detecting cloned applications on Android markets. In: Foresti, S., Yung, M., Martinelli, F. (eds.) ESORICS 2012. LNCS, vol. 7459, pp. 37–54. Springer, Heidelberg (2012)
8. Feng, Y., Anand, S., Dillig, I., Aiken, A.: Apposcopy: Semantics-based detection of Android malware through static analysis. In: 22nd ACM SIGSOFT International Symposium on Foundations of Software Engineering (2014)
9. Fredrikson, M., Jha, S., Christodorescu, M., Sailer, R., Yan, X.: Synthesizing near-optimal malware specifications from suspicious behaviors. In: 31st IEEE Symposium on Security and Privacy (2010)
10. Grace, M., Zhou, Y., Zhang, Q., Zou, S., Jiang, X.: Riskranker: Scalable and accurate zero-day Android malware detection. In: 10th International Conference on Mobile Systems, Applications, and Services (2012)
11. Hanna, S., Huang, L., Wu, E., Li, S., Chen, C., Song, D.: Juxtapp: A scalable system for detecting code reuse among Android applications. In: Flegel, U., Markatos, E., Robertson, W. (eds.) DIMVA 2012. LNCS, vol. 7591, pp. 62–81. Springer, Heidelberg (2012)
12. Kinder, J., Katzenbeisser, S., Schallhart, C., Veith, H.: Detecting malicious code by model checking. In: Julisch, K., Kruegel, C. (eds.) DIMVA 2005. LNCS, vol. 3548, pp. 174–187. Springer, Heidelberg (2005)
13. Kruegel, C., Kirda, E., Mutz, D., Robertson, W., Vigna, G.: Polymorphic worm detection using structural information of executables. In: Valdes, A., Zamboni, D. (eds.) RAID 2005. LNCS, vol. 3858, pp. 207–226. Springer, Heidelberg (2006)
14. Rastogi, V., Chen, Y., Jiang, X.: DroidChameleon: Evaluating Android anti-malware against transformation attacks. In: 8th ACM Symposium on Information, Computer and Communications Security (2013)
15. Song, F., Touili, T.: Model-checking for Android malware detection. In: Garrigue, J. (ed.) APLAS 2014. LNCS, vol. 8858, pp. 216–235. Springer, Heidelberg (2014)
16. Sufatrio, Tan, D.J.J., Chua, T.W., Thing, V.L.L.: Securing Android: a survey, taxonomy, and challenges. ACM Comput. Surv. **47**(4), 45 (2015). Article 58

17. Yang, C., Xu, Z., Gu, G., Yegneswaran, V., Porras, P.: DroidMiner: Automated mining and characterization of fine-grained malicious behaviors in Android applications. In: Kutyłowski, M., Vaidya, J. (eds.) ESORICS 2014, Part I. LNCS, vol. 8712, pp. 163–182. Springer, Heidelberg (2014)

18. Yang, Z., Yang, M., Zhang, Y., Gu, G., Ning, P., Wang, X.S.: Appintent: Analyzing sensitive data transmission in Android for privacy leakage detection. In: 20th ACM Conference on Computer and Communications Security (2013)

19. Zhou, W., Zhou, Y., Grace, M., Jiang, X., Zou, S.: Fast, scalable detection of 'piggybacked' mobile applications. In: 3rd ACM Conference on Data and Application Security and Privacy (2013)

20. Zhou, W., Zhou, Y., Jiang, X., Ning, P.: Detecting repackaged smartphone applications in third-party Android marketplaces. In: 2nd ACM Conference on Data and Application Security and Privacy (2012)

21. Zhou, Y., Jiang, X.: Dissecting Android malware: Characterization and evolution. In: 33rd IEEE Symposium on Security and Privacy (2012)

22. Zhou, Y., Wang, Z., Zhou, W., Jiang, X.: Hey, you, get off of my market: Detecting malicious apps in official and alternative Android markets. In: 19th Network and Distributed System Security Symposium (2012)

# A Bytecode Interpreter for Secure Program Execution in Untrusted Main Memory

Maximilian Seitzer, Michael Gruhn$^{(\boxtimes)}$, and Tilo Müller

Department of Computer Science, Friedrich-Alexander University
Erlangen-Nürnberg, Erlangen, Germany
{maximilian.seitzer,michael.gruhn,tilo.mueller}@fau.de

**Abstract.** Physical access to a system allows attackers to read out RAM through cold boot and DMA attacks. Thus far, counter measures protect only against attacks targeting disk encryption keys, while the remaining memory content is left vulnerable. We present a bytecode interpreter that protects code and data of programs against memory attacks by executing them without using RAM for sensitive content. Any program content within memory is encrypted, for which the interpreter utilizes TRESOR [1], a cold boot resistant implementation of the AES cipher. The interpreter was developed as a Linux kernel module, taking advantage of the CPU instruction sets AVX for additional registers, and AES-NI for fast encryption. We show that the interpreter is secure against memory attacks, and that the overall performance is only a factor of 4 times slower than the performance of Python. Moreover, the performance penalty is mostly induced by the encryption.

**Keywords:** Coldboot · Secure computation · Encrypted bytecode

## 1 Introduction

Physical security has often been a weak point in the defense of computer systems, especially mobile ones. Against physical access, software protection methods are often no longer effective. Even though methods such as full disk encryption can protect parts of the system, namely the hard disk, encryption keys still reside in RAM. As it stands, encryption is not applied to RAM, which makes memory attacks feasible today. A memory attack is a physical attack that lets an adversary obtain a memory contents of the targeted running system. One type of memory attack is known as the *cold boot attack* [2,3]. Cold boot attacks exploit the *data remanence effect* [4] which says that data in RAM gradually fades away and can be accessed for a short period of time after powering off [5–7]. Another threat are *DMA attacks*. DMA attacks exploit the fact that *direct memory access* allows external devices to directly interface with RAM, without the operating system being involved [8,9].

© Springer International Publishing Switzerland 2015
G. Pernul et al. (Eds.): ESORICS 2015, Part II, LNCS 9327, pp. 376–395, 2015.
DOI: 10.1007/978-3-319-24177-7_19

## 1.1  Motivation

As the spread of full disk encryption extends, and devices become more and more mobile, the importance of memory attacks increases. Persons who use encryption rely on their data to be protected against physical access, which hard disk encryption alone cannot provide. Main memory can no longer be regarded as a trusted resource because of cold boot and DMA attacks. Consequently, multiple counter measures have been developed to make disk encryption withstand memory attacks. One approach is to run the encryption algorithm only on the CPU without using memory [1,10,11]. Another solution are hard disks encrypting their data with a built-in crypto-module that stores keys securely in the disk itself. However, all these solutions have in common that they protect only the disk encryption key against main memory attacks. The memory contents of any program currently executed rests unprotected in RAM. An attacker can exploit this fact to obtain information about both, programs running on the target system, and the data they are operating on. Therefore, solutions are required to overcome the issue of sensitive data being openly accessible in RAM. Special software solutions already exist to protect private keys [12,13] during computations. However, these solutions are limited to computations with private keys. Hardware solutions such as Intel's software guard extensions (SGX) [14] could be used to protect RAM contents more generically. However, SGX has not been released by Intel. Hence, we provide a software only solution to protecting RAM contents during computations.

## 1.2  Contributions

To protect program code and data in RAM during computations, our contributions are as follows:

- We provide a Turing complete execution environment running on x86 commodity hardware, which allows program execution to treat RAM as untrusted. To this end, we use a bytecode interpreter executing programs without directly using RAM for code and data. This interpreter stores its state in CPU registers and uses RAM only to store encrypted data, effectively securing it against memory attacks.
- We provide a proof-of-concept implementation of the interpreter targeting the x86 architecture. It is delivered in form of a loadable kernel module compatible with recent Linux kernels. The interpreter can be used as the central part of a software-only trusted computing base.
- We evaluate the interpreter with regard to several attack types. Concerning memory attacks, we show that the interpreter fulfills our goals and is fully secure against those kind of attacks. Against attacks on the software level, the interpreter provides a considerable security add-on that can protect the confidentiality of executed programs even against attackers with root privileges.

– We benchmarked the interpreter against three other programming languages, namely C, Java, and Python. The results show that C and Java are both between one or two magnitudes faster than both Python and our interpreter, which is not surprising considering that these languages utilize native code execution. Between our interpreter and Python, the difference in performance is much smaller, with Python being faster than the interpreter by an average factor of 4.

### 1.3  Outline

In Sect. 2, the design and implementation of our interpreter is described. Subsect. 2.1 introduces different parts the interpreter consists of, and how they interact with each other. Subsect. 2.2 depicts where and how the interpreter manages the state of an executed program. In Subsect. 2.3, we discuss how the encryption algorithm of TRESOR [1] was adapted to fit our needs, and how encryption is applied to the interpreter data. Subsect. 2.4 shows the steps the interpreter goes through while executing a program. Our implementation is evaluated in regards to several aspects of performance and security in Sect. 3. In chapter Sect. 4 we review other solutions to protecting RAM contents during computation. Last, Sect. 5 contains a discussion about limitations and ideas for further developments.

## 2  Implementation

In the following we describe the design and implementation of our interpreter. While implementing the interpreter, we have to keep two security policies in mind. First, we are not allowed to use main memory for any sensitive data, as memory is considered untrusted. Second, we should not weaken the given security of the system provided by TRESOR [1]. We solve the first challenge by enforcing that any data is encrypted before it hits memory. The second task is fulfilled by ensuring the confidentiality of the TRESOR key during interpreter runtime.

### 2.1  General Interpreter Composition

In this section, we show what the different parts the interpreter consists of are, what their purpose is, and how they interact. We do this by walking through a program's life cycle from being programmed over compilation and execution to termination. The interpreter consists of three parts: the front-end, running in user-mode, which takes encrypted binary programs as input and outputs the results of the calculations, and the back-end, running in kernel mode, which does the actual interpretation of the given encrypted program. Additionally, a compiler tool is provided. It compiles programs from a simplified C dialect to interpreter bytecode, and encrypts them afterwards. A general overview of the layout is given by Fig. 1.

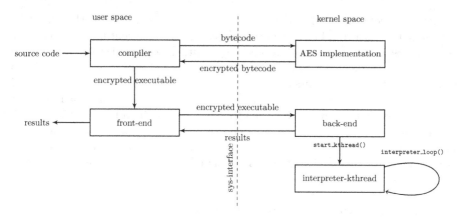

**Fig. 1.** The interpreter is separated into a compiler and front-end in user space, and a back-end with the AES implementation in kernel space. The different parts communicate over the kernel's sys-interface. On program execution, the back-end starts a kernel thread running the interpreter loop.

At first, the Linux kernel has to be booted up. At this point, TRESOR asks for a password which is used to derive the encryption key. During the system's life time, every program created will be encrypted with this key, and every program the interpreter executes will be decrypted with this key. After a password is entered, a program to be executed can be created. For this task, a simple programming language was devised to avoid having to program directly in bytecode. This programming language is called *"secure C-like language"*. Its files are called .scll. It is based on a reduced subset of C that lacks features such as arrays and global variables. The grammar of SCLL is given in Appendix A.1.

A finished program is passed to the compiler to translate into bytecode. After compilation, the bytecode is not yet ready for execution; to meet our goal of secure execution, it has to be encrypted first. Encryption needs the key which is stored in debug registers by TRESOR. Therefore the interpreter back-end runs in kernel space and provides the necessary encryption facilities; these are made accessible to user space programs through the kernel sys-interface /sys/kernel/bispe/crypto. The compiler utilizes this and sends the unencrypted bytecode through the sys-interface to kernel space, where it gets encrypted with the currently set key. After getting back the encrypted bytecode, the program is outputted as an encrypted executable file, now with the extension .scle (for *"secure C-like executable"*).

In order to execute our encrypted program, the interpreter front-end is used. The front-end acts as a user mode wrapper to the functionalities exported by the back-end. After its call, the front-end invokes interpretation of the program by passing the program to the back-end, again through the sys-interface. The sys-entry for this is /sys/kernel/bispe/invoke. Alongside the program, additional information is passed to the back-end, e.g. command line arguments and buffers providing space for execution results. The front-end then blocks until the back-end has finished execution of the program.

Before execution begins, the back-end first has to initialize the execution environment. Most notably, this means allocating the different memory segments the interpreter uses. These are the code segment, the operand stack, and the call stack. The just allocated code segment gets pre-filled with the encrypted program. The different segments and their usage are described in detail in Sect. 2.2. After initialization, the back-end creates a new kernel thread which runs the interpretation. There are two reasons to use a kernel thread instead of starting the interpretation directly in the back-end thread. First, it allows for clean signal handling. If the user gets impatient and stops the front-end before the execution is fully done, for instance with a SIGINT signal, the back-end must ensure that all kernel memory is freed before returning back to user space. With a kernel thread running the interpretation, the back-end thread just sleeps until execution is done, and if the sleep is interrupted by a signal, the kernel thread is issued to stop execution. The kernel thread notices that it should stop, and releases all allocated kernel memory. The second reason are future extensions: Currently, only one interpretation can be run at a time. If the interpretation is executed as a separate thread, it is easier to extend the program to allow multiple concurrent interpretations in the future.

To begin execution, the kernel thread repeats the interpreter loop. The interpreter loop is described in detail in Sect. 2.4. If the program is either finished, an error occurred, or the interpreter is ordered to cancel by the user, the loop is stopped. The kernel thread wakes up the sleeping back-end, reports the execution results, and finally terminates. Back in the main thread, the execution results get copied back to the front-end. Last, all allocated kernel resources are released, and control flow returns to user space. The front-end unblocks, reads out the execution results and potential output data is presented to the user.

## 2.2    Interpreter Memory Layout

This section details how the interpreter organizes the executed program's memory, and in which way the encryption interacts with the data. The interpreter is simulating a simple *stack machine*. This means that arithmetic and logical instructions always take their operands from top of a stack structure, on which they also put their computation results. The reason why a stack based interpreter is chosen over a register based one is that the bytecode instruction set is simplified, even though register based interpreters have been found to offer better performance [15].

The interpreter uses a unified word size of four byte for every instruction and every data element, which simplifies data accesses. An instruction consists of a four byte opcode and a four byte argument, if the instruction specifies one. The unit by which the interpreter accesses memory is per row consisting of 16 byte. Every time the interpreter reads from memory, it reads in a full row, even though the requested data is only of word size, because in memory, there is only *encrypted* data. The AES algorithm, by which this data is en- and decrypted, uses a block size of 16 byte. A program uses three memory segments during its execution: the code segment, the operand stack segment, and the call stack segment. Each segment's start address is aligned to 16 byte.

The *code segment* stores the code of the program. Before execution starts, the encrypted bytecode is relocated to this segment. The interpreters instruction pointer pointing into the code segment can be padded with random data before encryption so an adversary can not deduce program flow from it.

Intermediate data is stored in the *operand stack segment*, with a stack pointer pointing to the top of the stack. Every instruction that works on data expects its arguments and leaves its result on the operand stack. The only exceptions are load and store instructions which can transfer data between the operand stack and variables. Subroutines leave their result on this stack.

The *call stack segment* stores function related data. Every time a subroutine is called, a new stack frame is generated on top of the call stack. This frame contains subroutine arguments, local variables, and the return address, which is the address where execution is resumed after the subroutine ends. Like the operand stack, the call stack has a pointer pointing to its top.

We now take a look at how data from the segments can be used by the interpreter, although it rests encrypted in memory. To this end, throughout runtime, a decrypted 16 byte slice of each segment is held in a so-called *row register*, that is one of the 16 byte SSE registers. In case of the code and operand stack segments, this slice is always the row the instruction or stack pointer currently points to. For the call stack segment, it is the row which contains the data element currently processed. Instructions can now process their required data, because this data is always present in decrypted form.

When an element is requested from memory, the base address of the containing row is calculated from which 16 byte are copied from memory to the corresponding row register. The register gets decrypted and the data is almost ready to be accessed. Before a bytecode instruction can actually use it, the element needs to be extracted from the register row to a general purpose register.

Let us suppose an instruction has altered an element in some way and wants to push that element on top of the operand stack. The element now takes the inverse way back to memory. First, the stack pointer gets increased by four bytes to make space for the new element. Second, the element gets inserted in the stack row register at the four byte offset specified by the stack pointer, relative to the base address of the row. Further instructions are processed until eventually the stack pointer is increased so far that it exceeds the current row and points into a new row. To make space for the new stack row, the current row register must then be moved away to memory. This happens by encrypting the stack row register, and saving it to the corresponding memory location. New data elements can then be inserted in the empty stack row register. This procedure is largely the same for the code and the call stack segment.

## 2.3   Encryption Scheme

The interpreter utilizes the AES-256 encryption and decryption routines provided by TRESOR. TRESOR uses the SSE registers to store the AES round keys. However, this leaves no space for the interpreter state inside the SSE registers. Fortunately, with the introduction of the Advanced Vector Extensions

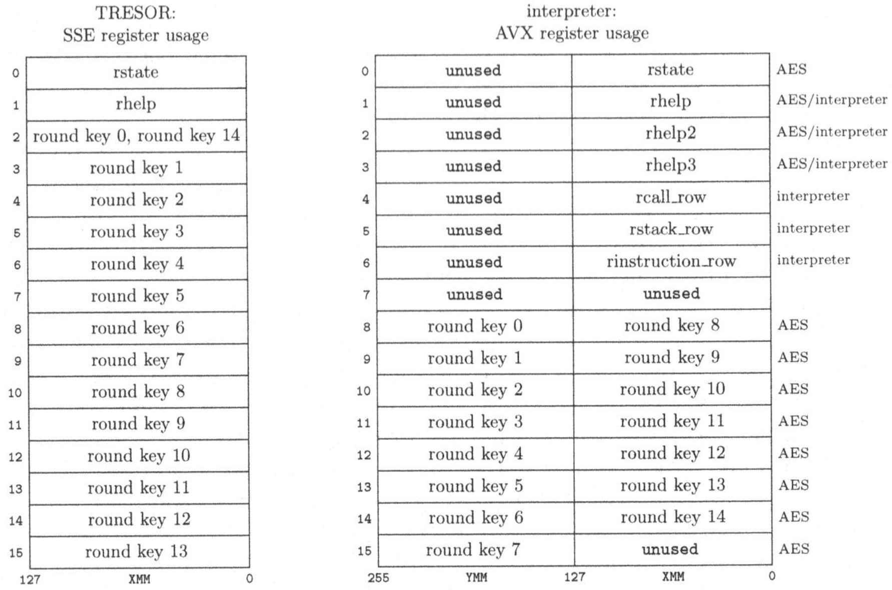

TRESOR: SSE register usage | interpreter: AVX register usage

| # | TRESOR (XMM) | # | YMM | XMM | |
|---|---|---|---|---|---|
| 0 | rstate | 0 | unused | rstate | AES |
| 1 | rhelp | 1 | unused | rhelp | AES/interpreter |
| 2 | round key 0, round key 14 | 2 | unused | rhelp2 | AES/interpreter |
| 3 | round key 1 | 3 | unused | rhelp3 | AES/interpreter |
| 4 | round key 2 | 4 | unused | rcall_row | interpreter |
| 5 | round key 3 | 5 | unused | rstack_row | interpreter |
| 6 | round key 4 | 6 | unused | rinstruction_row | interpreter |
| 7 | round key 5 | 7 | unused | unused | |
| 8 | round key 6 | 8 | round key 0 | round key 8 | AES |
| 9 | round key 7 | 9 | round key 1 | round key 9 | AES |
| 10 | round key 8 | 10 | round key 2 | round key 10 | AES |
| 11 | round key 9 | 11 | round key 3 | round key 11 | AES |
| 12 | round key 10 | 12 | round key 4 | round key 12 | AES |
| 13 | round key 11 | 13 | round key 5 | round key 13 | AES |
| 14 | round key 12 | 14 | round key 6 | round key 14 | AES |
| 15 | round key 13 | 15 | round key 7 | unused | AES |

127     XMM     0       255     YMM     127     XMM     0

**Fig. 2.** Modification of TRESOR's register allocation to host the interpreter state.

(AVX), the size of the SSE registers was increased from 128 bits to 256 bits [16]. This allows us to place two round keys in each of the 256 bit registers, cutting the amount of registers needed for round keys in half. Figure 2 displays how the register distribution was changed from TRESOR to the interpreter, and also which registers are used for encryption, and which for the interpreter.

The interpreter uses *cipher block chaining* (CBC) [17] as its cipher mode. For both stack segments, the IV is created at runtime, directly after the segments were allocated, before execution start. The interpreter writes 128 random bits to the beginning of the segment, obtained from the kernel function `get_random_bytes`, which uses the Linux kernel's internal pseudo random number generator (PRNG). For the code segment, the IV is determined at compile time, from `/dev/urandom`, and it stays the same for the executable until a recompilation occurs.

The crypto-routines of the interpreter are in `backend/bispe_crypto_asm.S`. Programmatically, most of TRESOR's code could be carried over, but a few changes were made. Those changes mostly address access to the AVX registers instead of SSE for key material. Further, the crypto module of the interpreter was extended with routines to encrypt memory in CBC mode (`bispe_encblk_mem_cbc`), as well as encrypting a register in place (`bispe_encblk`).

The implementation of the CBC mode for memory segments during runtime is, in all but one case, trivial. The non-trivial case occurs because the call stack segment allows writing to arbitrary elements; a saving of the call stack row register to memory triggers a re-encryption from the changed block up to the end of the segment. As writes to the stack segment only target the frame of the current function, however, the chain to be encrypted is short.

## 2.4   The Interpreter Loop

When executing a program, the interpreter has to repeat the same set of steps for every instruction. The instruction specified by the instruction pointer is fetched from memory and the interpreter performs the appropriate actions to execute the instructions, based on the fetched opcode. Afterwards, the instruction pointer is changed to point to the next instruction. These steps basically get repeated in a loop until the program is finished.

Figure 3 lists the individual steps taken during the interpreter loop in a textual manner. Figure 4 shows a flowchart version of the process. The interpreter splits up this loop in individual cycles – which are not to be confused with the above mentioned fetch-execute cycle.

1. Begin atomic CPU section by disabling scheduling and interrupts.
2. Generate AES round keys in AVX registers.
3. Load program state to registers.
4. Repeat until cycle has ended or halt flag is set:
    4.1. Extract opcode of current instruction from instruction row.
    4.2. Jump to instruction routine specified by opcode.
    4.3. Execute instruction routine.
    4.4. Increase instruction pointer. If new instruction is not present in current instruction row, load and decrypt next instruction row from memory.
5. Save program state encrypted to memory, clear AVX registers.
6. End atomic CPU section by enabling interrupts and scheduling.
7. If halt flag is set or execution was stopped by the user, break interpreter loop. Otherwise, go back to step 1.

**Fig. 3.** Individual steps the interpreter repeats during a cycle.

A cycle consists of multiple instructions executed subsequently. The amount of instructions executed in one cycle is not fixed but user configurable. From the outside, a cycle represents an atomic unit. Therefore, one cycle always runs uninterruptible and even the kernel is not able to interrupt execution. This is necessary to protect the integrity of both the program and the cipher key, as during the cycle, the AVX registers hold decrypted program- and encryption state, and these registers are principally free to access for any process.

Since the interpreter runs in kernel mode, it has access to kernel functions which can create an atomic section. Preemptive kernel scheduling can be disabled with the function preempt_disable. To provide true atomicity, local_irq_save has to be called for disabling interrupts.

At the beginning of a cycle, after an atomic section has been started, the interpreter first derives the round keys from the cipher key and places them in the round key registers. The next step is to load the program state into registers, so that the interpreter instructions can operate properly. This means that

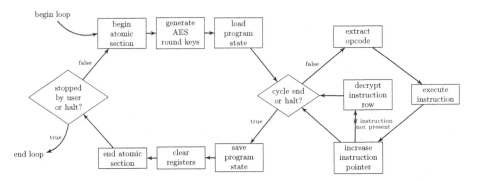

**Fig. 4.** The different steps the interpreter repeats in the interpreter loop. One pass represents an atomic cycle, in which program data and encryption state are protected from leaking to memory.

for each segment, a row gets decrypted to the corresponding row register, as described in Sect. 2.2. Internally, every segment pointer in memory is mapped to a general purpose CPU register, e.g. the instruction pointer to register r11, because these pointers have to be accessed often during program execution. In the "load program state step", the state pointers get loaded from memory in their respective register. Then the interpreter is ready to process bytecode instructions. The used technique is *indirect threading*; each bytecode instruction is represented by a single routine in backend/asm_instructions.S. When one of these routines gets executed, it simulates the bytecode instruction it represents on the programs state. The addresses of each of those routines are stored in a jump table. To execute a bytecode instruction, the interpreter extracts the opcode of the current instruction from the instruction row and calls the appropriate routine to process the instruction. In Appendix A.3, the functionality of each bytecode instruction is explained.

After the instruction is finished, the instruction pointer gets updated to point to the instruction to be executed next. Before a new instruction is executed, however, it is checked if the amount of instructions executed in this cycle exceed the specified maximum amount of instructions in one cycle or the halt flag was set, e.g. by the special finish instruction, or due to the occurrence of a runtime error, e.g. a division through zero, or a stack overflow. If either of this is the case, the next instruction is not executed. Instead, the interpreter saves the current program state to memory. This is done by encrypting the row registers and saving them to memory. Additionally, the values of the state pointer registers are written to their counterpart in memory again. Before the atomic section is left again, it is important to reset the content of the AVX registers, before anyone else can have access to them. At last, the atomic section is ended by activating scheduling and interrupts again.

As the interpreter code itself is only executed during an atomic section, an adversary has no way to observe and infer any knowledge from the rip instruction pointer pointing to interpreter code execution.

However, when a subroutine within the interpreter code is called, the *return address* is pushed on the stack. The leaked information about a single instruction causes nearly no actual damage, but it is desirable to thwart even theoretical attacks. The solution is to not use the `call` instruction directly but rather store the current position in a register (`%r9`) and jump into the function. For returning, instead of calling `ret` an indirect jump to an address stored in a register (`jmp *%r9`) is used.

## 3   Evaluation

We evaluate our interpreter concept and its implementation with respect to two criteria. In Subsect. 3.1, we discuss benchmarks comparing the performance of the interpreter against other programming languages. And in Subsect. 3.2, we deliver an analysis of the interpreter's security against memory attacks, software attacks, and hardware attacks.

### 3.1   Performance

In this section, we investigate the performance of our interpreter. Given the interpreter's design, a performance drop-off compared to other execution environments must be expected due to encryption. The interesting question is how big the difference in performance compared to other programming languages is. To test this, benchmarks with four different language environments were performed, one of them being our own bytecode interpreter. All benchmarks were performed on an Intel Core i5-3570K CPU which supports AVX as well as AES-NI. The operating system is Xubuntu Linux 14.04 with kernel version 3.8.2 and TRESOR patch applied.

The other three languages (C, Java and Python) were selected to fit into different kinds of execution types. As C compiles to machine code which can be executed natively by the CPU, C should run the fastest among the tested languages. The C programs have been compiled with GCC version 4.8.2. The second language chosen is the Java language. Java represents the class of JIT-compiled interpreted languages. Therefore, we expected Java to perform quite well albeit a bit slower than C. The Java version used was OpenJDK 1.7.0_65. The third and last language choice is the Python language, using the default Python implementation in version 2.7.6. Python represents a simpler kind of interpreter implementation. It uses no JIT compilation, and the source code is parsed to bytecode just before execution. This makes Python a slower type of interpreter, which makes its performance results closest to our interpreter's performance.

We benchmarked the following mathematical algorithms:

- the $n$th *Fibonacci numbers*
- the first $n$ *Prime numbers*
- the *Pascal triangle* with $n$ rows.

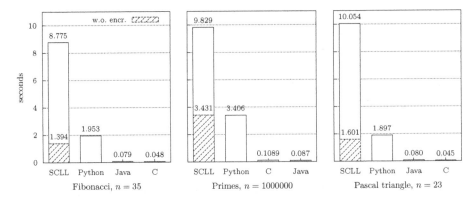

**Fig. 5.** The results of the language benchmark show that the interpreter is vastly slower than C and Java, but still within performance reach of Python.

The implementation of the three algorithms in the interpreter's language. It can be found in Appendix A.2. The elapsed time of a program run has been measured with the built-in `time` shell command of the Bash shell.

An additional property of the interpreter is that execution is divided in atomic cycles. Each of these cycles creates a performance overhead. We tested the exact influence of this setting on performance and have chosen the default instructions per cycle value of the interpreter to be 2000. This was also the value used for performance tests.

The benchmark results are listed in Fig. 5, with the results averaged out from 50 program runs. The column labeled "SCLL" contains the benchmark results of our interpreter. A first overview shows roughly the same picture for all three programs. As expected, the interpreter is slower than Python, and C and Java perform both much faster than Python and SCLL. C and Java are between one or two magnitudes faster – their bars in the figure are only barely visible. This is owed to the power of native code execution, for Java enabled through JIT. If we compare our interpreter to Python, we see that the interpreter performs reasonably well. On average, SCLL is about a factor 4 slower than Python.

The influence of encryption on the interpreter's performance is interesting, and we decided to measure it explicitly. In Fig. 5, the results of this benchmark are shown as striped bars within the SCLL bar. It is easy to see that encryption takes up a major part of the interpreter's runtime. On average, the interpreter spends four fifth of the overall runtime with encryption.

If we contrast the individual programs, we can see that in respect to the other languages, the interpreter performs best on the Primes program. Whereas performance for Fibonacci and Pascal is similar, the ratio to the other languages is the best for Primes. Looking for the reasons, we have to take a look at the source codes of the programs (see Appendix A.2). We can see that Primes is implemented purely iterative, Fibonacci recursive, and Pascal uses both iteration and recursion. This indicates that recursive programs affect the interpreter's performance negatively. Recursion requires the repetitive use of function calls.

Within each function call, a stack frame has to be allocated and freed which creates encryption overhead at the interpreter. In the Primes program, encryption takes up two thirds of the running time, whereas for Fibonacci and Pascal, the overall execution time is composed of five sixths of encryption time.

Summarizing, we have benchmarked the interpreter against three other popular programming languages: C, Java, and Python. The interpreter is slowed down considerably by the overhead caused by encryption, and without it, the performance of the implementation is on par with Python.

## 3.2   Security

The most important property of our interpreter is the security it can provide. In Sect. 3.2, we show that the interpreter holds its designated goal and is secure against attacks on memory such as cold boot attacks. We also discuss how far the interpreter is protected against software attacks in Sect. 3.2 and investigate possible weaknesses of the interpreter against hardware attacks in Sect. 3.2.

**Protection Against Memory Attacks.** As outlined in Sect. 2, great care has been taken to ensure that no sensitive interpreter state or even encryption keys are leaked into RAM. However, we now like to practically uphold this fact. To this end, we perform memory scans of a system running the interpreter. We used a Qemu/KVM virtual machine running Debian Linux with kernel version 3.8.2 (TRESOR patched) to obtain memory images.

Three memory dumps were taken at different times. The first without running the interpreter at all, to compare if running the interpreter influenced the scan results. Afterwards, the interpreter kernel module was loaded, and the interpreter ran the program calculating the Fibonacci numbers from the previous section. The second memory dump was taken during the interpreter running the program, and a third one after the Fibonacci program was executed a hundred times. We searched the memory dump for both AES key schedule patterns as well as cleartext patterns of bytecode programs that are decrypted by the interpreter. Only small matches could be found that can be attributed to coincidence, because searching for any random pattern also yields matches of the same length.

These results indicate that neither debug registers nor AVX registers get leaked to memory, which confirms the adherence of the interpreter's security goal to leak no sensitive data in memory. In sum, we can state that the interpreter's implementation protects executed programs against memory attacks.

**Protection Against Software Attacks.** Another interesting topic is the level of protection the interpreter can provide for executed programs against attacks on the software level. That is, the attacker model now switches from physical access to logical access to the system the interpreter is running on.

One idea is to pick off the data during interpreter runtime when the interpreter is processing it in decrypted form. The interpreter holds decrypted data in the segment row registers. If an attacker can continuously copy the content of those row registers, while the interpreter is running the program, a complete picture of the program's code can be reconstructed, as well as the data the program is working with. This would, however, require outside access to the row registers at the time they contain decrypted data. Since the row registers hold decrypted data only within the atomic CPU section, this is not easily possible. The atomic section prevents any other process that could read out the registers from running on that CPU, and the atomic section can only be ended by the interpreter itself – even the kernel can not interrupt it. Attackers with system privileges can change the code of our kernel module such that no atomic section is entered before interpretation.

Attackers with system privileges, however, also have another attack surface. The encryption key is stored in the CPU debug registers at all times. Debug registers are a privileged resource which means that ring 0, the kernel, can access them. The debug registers are accessible for user space applications only through the `ptrace` system call. TRESOR patches certain kernel code to make the debug register inaccessible – the `ptrace` system call is patched to not return the debug register content.

It is impossible for a non-privileged attacker to read out the debug registers. Only an attacker with root privileges has more possibilities. By using a loadable kernel module (LKM), or `/dev/kmem`, arbitrary code can be inserted into the kernel and executed from within ring 0. In its current form, the interpreter is vulnerable to attacks of this kind. To protect against this security flaw, the TRESOR authors advise to compile the kernel without support for LKM and `/dev/kmem`, as then even root attackers are unable to access the cipher key. For now, the interpreter is designed as a LKM itself, but it would be possible to change the module into a kernel patch, which would allow hard compiling the interpreter into the kernel, while disabling support for LKMs. An attacker would then be required to use some kind of kernel exploit that allows to execute code. All in all, this would make the interpreter also resistant against most attacks on the software level.

**Protection Against Hardware Attacks.** A simple hardware attack would succeed if CPU registers keep their content after rebooting of the system. Fortunately, according to the authors of TRESOR, this is not the case.

In our discussion of the interpreter's resistance against attacks on memory, we mostly had the cold boot scenario in mind. DMA attacks, however, are also viable. Blass and Robertson [18] introduce an attack on CPU based encryption systems, exploiting DMA to write malicious code to kernel memory. In fact, the attack is named "TRESOR-Hunt" explicitly targeting TRESOR. Through patching the interrupt descriptor table, the kernel is issued to execute a payload, which is essentially a piece of code that dumps the debug registers to memory. After the cipher key is in memory, the attacker can obtain it via DMA. This attack, however, can be defended by device whitelisting, to only allow known devices to use DMA, or using a input/output memory management unit (IOMMU) to block critical memory regions from DMA access.

Physical access to the CPU also enables other kinds of attacks. The JTAG interface of a microprocessor allows an engineer to debug the running processor by connecting with the JTAG ports on the physical device. Some modern Intel CPUs also expose JTAG ports on their surface, which can be used to read out the debug registers. However, we are not aware of anyone successfully carrying out such an attack.

## 4  Related Work

Different solutions for CPU bound encryption on x86 exist such as TRESOR [1] and LoopAmnesia [11]. Also for ARM, a cold boot resistant implementation named ARMORED [19] has been developed. However, CPU bound encryption alone can only protect single encryption keys, which are mostly used as disk encryption keys as explained above. In contrast, we want to protect entire programs and their data against memory attacks. One solution which comes into mind for supporting the execution of encrypted programs is *Frozen cache* [10]. Frozen cache, however, must reserve the entire CPU cache which renders this approach unfeasible as it slows down the overall system performance too much.

In the past, encrypted program execution has already been worked at in different ways: Brenner et al. [20] have shown that secure program execution would be possible with a fully homomorphic encryption scheme [21]. They focus on securing programs in an untrusted environment, e.g. in cloud computing, which is not the primary goal of this work. Another approach is to use full memory encryption [22,23], which would indeed protect programs against memory attacks. However, software-based full memory encryption suffers from considerable performance drawbacks, while hardware-based full memory encryption is not available for end-users. Duc and Keryell [22], for example, rely on their own, special hardware architecture. [23] is restricted to ARM processors equipped with security hardware, while [22] relies on its own, special hardware architecture. Another memory encryption solution explicitly designed to mitigate cold boot attacks is Cryptkeeper [24]. Unfortunately, on its own, Cryptkeeper poses no viable solution because the encryption key itself is stored in clear in RAM.

Working special solutions are PRIME [12] and Copker [13]. However, they are restricted to computations with private keys.

A possible future technology to solve the issues surrounding secure program execution is Intel's Software Guard Extensions (SGX) [14]. SGX allows applications to run in so-called *enclaves*, which are secure memory containers inaccessible by anyone but the application itself. To achieve this, enclave memory is encrypted in hardware, with the encryption key stored securely in hardware. The system is explicitly designed to both protect programs against memory attacks and to enable running them securely in an untrusted environment. While being announced by Intel in 2013, it is still unknown when the first CPUs supporting SGX are released to the public.

Last but not least, this work was partially inspired by Breuer and Bowen [25]. They propose a "crypto-processor unit" (KPU) which instructions and data enter and leave encrypted only. While the concept is not practically feasible yet, the underlying idea was useful to us in providing a generic software only protection mechanism for code and data during computations.

## 5  Conclusion and Future Work

In this chapter, we draw conclusions about our developed bytecode interpreter for secure program execution. In the previous chapters, we evaluated the interpreter regarding performance and security. We summarize the found limitations in Sect. 5.1. In Sect. 5.2, we present future tasks and investigations that can be pursued to further extend the interpreter's scope of applicability. Finally, in Sect. 5.3, we summarize the work done in this thesis and draw a conclusion about the overall applicability of our interpreter concept.

### 5.1  Limitations

Currently, the developed bytecode language supports only a narrow set of features. However, we have not yet found any obstacles caused by the interpreter's design which will impede future integration of common programming language features.

### 5.2  Future Work

In this section, we present some possible future developments. A certainly worthwhile goal is to extend the bytecode language to be fully compatible with the C language. This would make encrypted program execution through the interpreter widely applicable, as many programs are written in C, and several other programming languages can be compiled to C. The longterm goal is to be able to securely run everyday software, like text editors, browsers, and mail-, or office programs through the interpreter.

Usability must also be increased. Currently, a program can be executed and encrypted only with a single key; and for changing the key, the system has to be rebooted, which is quite inconvenient. It would be desirable, that the user is able to specify a password to use for encryption at compilation, and to enter that password again for execution. To implement this, the user password must be scrambled with the master key set by TRESOR.

Advances in performance can be gained by Intel's AVX-512 instruction set. AVX-512 increases the amount of SIMD registers to 32, and the register width to 512 bits, which yields four times more available register space than AVX has. The interpreter can use the additional space for caching. AVX-512 also brings many new assembler instructions, which may allow simplifying the code of the current implementation, yielding performance gains as well.

There are further cipher modes that also guarantee authenticity of the encrypted data, but that can be more complex to implement, so the interpreter currently limits itself to CBC. If it turns out that other cipher modes are needed, they can be integrated in the future.

## 5.3  Conclusion

Physical security has always been a weak point in the defenses of computer systems, especially mobile systems. Regardless of software protection measures, the data of a stolen laptop can easily be obtained by reading out the hard disk. As full disk encryption became common and closed a simple attack vector, attacks moved a level lower, targeting the disk encryption keys within the unencrypted RAM instead. Several kind of attacks on memory have been shown viable. Executing programs outside memory, using memory only for encrypted data, would protect sensitive user data against memory attacks.

In this work, we have shown how encrypted program execution is feasible when treating main memory as untrusted. The design consists of an interpreter which executes encrypted bytecode programs without using RAM for sensitive data. The program's bytecode and data is held decrypted only within CPU registers that are processed by the interpreter.

We provide a working proof-of-concept implementation for the x86 architecture, in form of a kernel module for the Linux kernel. Our proof-of-concept implementation supports a simple bytecode language, but we have shown that the concept can be extended to include more features soon.

To analyze the interpreter's resistance against memory attacks, several memory dumps were taken and scanned for patterns of encryption keys, round keys as well as code and data of executed programs. A significantly long byte pattern, that would indicate the interpreter leaking to memory, could not be found in any case. Furthermore, this result is strengthened by the fact that the interpreter uses the same protection approach as TRESOR which was thoroughly controlled before. The interpreter resists attacks on the software level as long as the attacker has no ring 0 privileges, as then the debug registers are no longer a secure storage for cryptographic keys. Without further measures, the interpreter is vulnerable to a special DMA attack [18], which inserts malicious code into the kernel to obtain keys. This attack can be mitigated by restricting DMA, as supported by recent Linux kernels.

**Acknowledgement.** This work was supported by the German Research Foundation (DFG) as part of the Transregional Collaborative Research Centre "Invasive Computing" (SFB/TR 89).

# A    Appendix

## A.1    SCLL Grammar

**Listing 1.1.** Grammar of SCLL in Extended Backus-Naur Form.

```
integer        =  digit , {digit} ;
identifier     =  (letter | '_'), { (letter | digit | '_') } ;
type           =  'void' | 'int' ;
num_op         =  '+' | '-' | '*' | '/' | '%';
bool_op        =  '==' | '!=' | '>' | '<' | '<=' | '>=' ;
fcall_arglist  =  [expression, ',', [fcall_arglist]] ;
fcall          =  identifier , '(', fcall_arg_arglist , ')' ;
```

```
expression     =  ( fcall
                  | identifier
                  | ['-'], integer
                  | '(', expression, ')'), [num_op, expression] ;
var_def        =  type, identifier, ['=', expression] ;
var_assign     =  identifier '=' expression ;
print          =  'print', expression ;
return         =  'return', [expression] ;
cond           =  expression, bool_op, expression ;
branch         =  'if', '(', cond, ')', '{', sequence, '}',
                  ['else', '{', sequence, '}'] ;
loop_head      =  (var_def | var_assign), cond, var_assign ;
loop           =  'while', '(', cond, ')', '{', sequence, '}'
                  | 'for', '(', loop_head, ')', '{', sequence, '}'
                  | 'do', '{', sequence, '}', 'while', '(', cond, ')', ';' ;
statement      =  (var_def | var_assign | fcall | print | return) ';' ;
sequence       =  (statement | branch | loop), [sequence] ;
argdefnce      =  type | identifier ;
arglist        =  argdef, [',', arglist] | 'void' ;
func           =  type, identifier, '(', arglist, ')', ('{', sequence, '}' | ';') ;
program        =  [func, program] ;
```

## A.2   Source Codes

In this section, the SCLL source codes of programs that were used to evaluate our work are listed. In particular, the programs 1.2, 1.3, and 1.4 were used in benchmarking (Fig. 6).

**Listing 1.2.** Program calculating the n'th Fibonacci number.

```
int fib(int i);

int fib(int i) {
        if(i == 1) return 1;
        if(i == 2) return 1;
        return fib(i-1) + fib(i-2);
}

void main(int n) {
        print fib(n);
}
```

**Listing 1.3.** Program calculating the primes to `primes`.

```
void print_prime(int p) {
        if(p % 2 == 0) return;

        for(int i = 3; i * i <= p; i = i + 2) {
                if(p % i == 0) return;
        }
        print p;
}

void main(int primes) {
        for(int i = 2; i <= primes; i = i + 1)
                print_prime(i);
}
```

**Listing 1.4.** Program calculating the pascal triangle with `max_row` rows.

```
int binom(int n, int k);

int binom(int n, int k) {
        if(k == 0) return 1;
        if(n == k) return 1;
        return binom(n-1, k-1) + binom(n-1, k);
}

void main(int max_row) {
        for(int n = 0; n < max_row; n = n + 1) {
                for(int k = 0; k < n+1; k = k + 1)
                        print binom(n, k);
        }
}
```

## A.3  Bytecode Language

| opcode | mnemonic | argument | operand stack: before → after | description |
|---|---|---|---|---|
| 0 | nop | | | perform no operation |
| 1 | finish | | | halt execution |
| 2 | push | value | → value | push integer *value* on the stack |
| 3 | print | | value → | write *value* to output buffer |
| 4 | load | index | → value | load *value* from local variable at *index* |
| 5 | store | index | value → | save *value* to local variable at *index* |
| 6 | add | | value1, value2 → result | add two integers, r = v2 + v1 |
| 7 | sub | | value1, value2 → result | subtract two integers, r = v2 - v1 |
| 8 | mul | | value1, value2 → result | multiply two integers, r = v2 * v1 |
| 9 | div | | value1, value2 → result | divide two integers, r = v2 / v1 |
| 10 | mod | | value1, value2 → result | remainder of two integers, r = v2 % v1 |
| 11 | jmp | address | | jump to instruction at *address* |
| 12 | jeq | address | value1, value2 → | if *value2* is equal to *value1*, jump to instruction at *address* |
| 13 | jne | address | value1, value2 → | if *value2* is not equal to *value1*, jump to instruction at *address* |
| 14 | jl | address | value1, value2 → | if *value2* is less than *value1*, jump to instruction at *address* |
| 15 | jle | address | value1, value2 → | if *value2* is less than or equal to *value1*, jump to instruction at *address* |
| 16 | jg | address | value1, value2 → | if *value2* is greater than *value1*, jump to instruction at *address* |
| 17 | jge | address | value1, value2 → | if *value2* is greater or equal to *value1*, jump to instruction at *address* |
| 18 | call | address | | call subroutine at *address* |
| 19 | ret | | | return from subroutine |
| 20 | prolog | amount | | allocate space for *amount* elements on the call stack (subroutine prolog) |
| 21 | epilog | amount | | free space of *amount* elements on the call stack (subroutine epilog) |
| 22 | argload | index | | save command line argument *index* to local variable at *index* |

**Fig. 6.** Complete listing of all bytecode instructions.

# References

1. Müller, T., Freiling, F.C., Dewald, A.: Tresor runs encryption securely outside ram. In: Proceedings of the 20th USENIX Conference on Security (SEC 2011), pp. 17–17. USENIX Association, Berkeley (2011)
2. Alex Halderman, J., Schoen, S.D., Clarkson, W., Heninger, N., Paul, W., Calandrino, J.A., Feldman, A.J., Appelbaum, J., Felten, E.W.: Lest we remember: cold-boot attacks on encryption keys. Commun. ACM **52**(5), 91–98 (2009). doi:10.1145/1506409.1506429
3. Gruhn, M., Müller, T.: On the practicability of cold boot attacks. In IEEE Conference Publications, editor, Eighth International Conference on Availability, Reliability and Security (ARES), pp. 390–397 (2013)
4. A Guide to Understanding Data Remanence in Automated Information Systems. NCSC-TG-025, National Computer Security Centre, Sep 1991
5. Gutmann, P.: Data remanence in semiconductor devices. In: Proceedings of the 10th Conference on USENIX Security Symposium, SSYM 2001, vol. 10. USENIX Association, Berkeley (2001)
6. Skorobogatov, S.: Low temperature data remanence in static RAM. Technical report UCAM-CL-TR-536, University of Cambridge, Computer Laboratory, Jun 2002

7. Wyns, P., Anderson, R.L.: Low-temperature operation of silicon dynamic random-access memories. IEEE Trans. Electron. Devices **36**(8), 1423–1428 (1989). doi:10. 1109/16.30954, ISSN 0018–9383

8. Becher, M., Dornseif, M., Klein, C.N.: FireWire: all your memory are belong to us. In: Proceedings of CanSecWest Applied Security Conference, Vancouver, British Columbia, Canada (2005)

9. Carrier, B.D., Grand, J.: A hardware-based memory acquisition procedure for digital investigations. Digital Invest. **1**(1), 50–60 (2004)

10. Pabel, J.: Frozen cache, Jan 2009. http://frozenchache.blogspot.com

11. Simmons, P.: Security through amnesia: a software-based solution to the cold boot attack on disk encryption. In: Proceedings of the 27th Annual Computer Security Applications Conference, ACSAC 2011, pp. 73–82. ACM, New York (2011). ISBN 978-1-4503-0672-0

12. Garmany, B., Müller, T.: PRIME: private RSA infrastructure for memory-less encryption (best paper award). In: Applied Computer Security Associates (ACSA) and ACM (eds.) Proceedings of the 29th Annual Computer Security Applications Conference (2013)

13. Guan, L., Lin, J., Luo, B., Jing, J.: Copker: Computing with private keys without ram. In: Network and Distributed System Security Symposium (NDSS) (2014)

14. McKeen, F., Alexandrovich, I., Berenzon, A., Rozas, C.V., Shafi, H., Shanbhogue, V., Savagaonkar, U.R.: Innovative instructions and software model for isolated execution. In: Proceedings of the 2nd International Workshop on Hardware and Architectural Support for Security and Privacy, HASP 2013, pp. 10:1–10:1. ACM, New York (2013). doi:10.1145/2487726.2488368, ISBN 978-1-4503-2118-1

15. Shi, Y., Casey, K., Anton Ertl, M., Gregg, D.: Virtual machine showdown: stack versus registers. ACM Trans. Archit. Code Optim. **4**(4), 2:1–2:36 (2008). doi:10. 1145/1328195.1328197, ISSN 1544–3566

16. Lomont, C.: Introduction to Intel Advanced Vector Extensions. Intel Corporation, Jun 2011

17. National Institute for Standards and Technology. Recommendation for Block Cipher Modes of Operation, NIST Special Publication 800–38A edition, Dec 2001

18. Blass, E.-O., Robertson, W.: TRESOR-HUNT: attacking CPU-bound encryption. In: Proceedings of the 28th Annual Computer Security Applications Conference, ACSAC 2012, pp. 71–78. ACM, New York (2012). doi:10.1145/2420950.2420961, ISBN 978-1-4503-1312-4

19. Götzfried, J., Müller, T.: ARMORED: CPU-bound encryption for android-driven ARM devices. In: Proceedings of the 2013 International Conference on Availability, Reliability and Security, ARES 2013, pp. 161–168. IEEE Computer Society, Washington, DC (2013). doi:10.1109/ARES.2013.23, ISBN 978-0-7695-5008-4

20. Brenner, M., Wiebelitz, J., von Voigt, G., Smith, M.: Secret program execution in the cloud applying homomorphic encryption. In: 2011 Proceedings of the 5th IEEE International Conference on Digital Ecosystems and Technologies Conference (DEST), pp. 114–119, May 2011. doi:10.1109/DEST.2011.5936608

21. Gentry, C.: A fully homomorphic encryption scheme. Ph.D. thesis, Stanford University (2009). http://crypto.stanford.edu/craig

22. Duc, G., Keryell, R.: CryptoPage: an efficient secure architecture with memory encryption, integrity and information leakage protection. In: 22nd Annual Computer Security Applications Conference, ACSAC 2006, pp. 483–492, Dec 2006. doi:10.1109/ACSAC.2006.21

23. Henson, M., Taylor, S.: Beyond full disk encryption: protection on security-enhanced commodity processors. In: Jacobson, M., Locasto, M., Mohassel, P., Safavi-Naini, R. (eds.) ACNS 2013. LNCS, vol. 7954, pp. 307–321. Springer, Heidelberg (2013)
24. Peterson, P.A.H.: Cryptkeeper: Improving security with encrypted RAM. In: 2010 IEEE International Conference on Technologies for Homeland Security (HST), pp. 120–126, Nov 2010. doi:10.1109/THS.2010.5655081
25. Breuer, P.T., Bowen, J.P.: A fully homomorphic crypto-processor design: correctness of a secret computer. In: Jürjens, J., Livshits, B., Scandariato, R. (eds.) ESSoS 2013. LNCS, vol. 7781, pp. 123–138. Springer, Heidelberg (2013)

# Learning from Others: User Anomaly Detection Using Anomalous Samples from Other Users

Youngja Park[1]([✉]), Ian M. Molloy[1], Suresh N. Chari[1], Zenglin Xu[2], Chris Gates[2], and Ninghi Li[2]

[1] IBM T.J. Watson Research Center, Yorktown Heights, NY 10598, USA
{young_park,molloyim,schari}@us.ibm.com
[2] Purdue University, West Lafayette, IN, USA
{xu218,gates,ninghui}@cs.purdue.edu

**Abstract.** Machine learning is increasingly used as a key technique in solving many security problems such as botnet detection, transactional fraud, insider threat, etc. One of the key challenges to the widespread application of ML in security is the lack of labeled samples from real applications. For known or common attacks, labeled samples are available, and, therefore, supervised techniques such as multi-class classification can be used. However, in many security applications, it is difficult to obtain labeled samples as each attack can be unique. In order to detect novel, unseen attacks, researchers used unsupervised outlier detection or one-class classification approaches, where they treat existing samples as benign samples. These methods, however, yield high false positive rates, preventing their adoption in real applications.

This paper presents a local outlier factor (LOF)-based method to automatically generate both benign and malicious training samples from unlabeled data. Our method is designed for applications with multiple users such as insider threat, fraud detection, and social network analysis. For each target user, we compute LOF scores of all samples with respect to the target user's samples. This allows us to identify (1) other users' samples that lie in the boundary regions and (2) outliers from the target user's samples that can distort the decision boundary. We use the samples from other users as malicious samples, and use the target user's samples as benign samples after removing the outliers.

We validate the effectiveness of our method using several datasets including access logs for valuable corporate resources, DBLP paper titles, and behavioral biometrics of user typing behavior. The evaluation of our method on these datasets confirms that, in almost all cases, our technique performs significantly better than both one-class classification methods and prior two-class classification methods. Further, our method is a general technique that can be used for many security applications.

## 1 Introduction

Driven by an almost endless stream of well publicized cases of information theft by malicious insiders, such as *Wikileaks* and *Snowden*, there is increased interest

© Springer International Publishing Switzerland 2015
G. Pernul et al. (Eds.): ESORICS 2015, Part II, LNCS 9327, pp. 396–414, 2015.
DOI: 10.1007/978-3-319-24177-7_20

for monitoring systems to detect anomalous user behavior. Today, in addition to traditional access control and other security controls, organizations actively deploy activity monitoring mechanisms to detect such attacks. Activity monitoring is done through enforced rules as well as anomaly detection using ML techniques. To best apply ML techniques, it is ideal if we can train a model with lots of both anomalous and benign samples. This is very difficult for security applications: it is often unrealistic to expect to gather enough anomalous samples for labeling. The lack of anomalous samples prohibits the applicability of more accurate classification techniques, and, thus, most monitoring applications have adopted anomaly detection or one-class classification techniques. These methods construct a profile of a subject's normal behavior using the subject's past behavior by treating them as benign sample and compare a new observed behavior with the normal profile resulting in high false positive cases. The lack of labeled data can also extend to samples of normal activity. In some situations, there may be a small number of samples to learn a user's normal behavior, or the sample contain anomalous cases. This makes it difficult to learn an accurate model for the data. Another problem of existing approaches is that they treat the samples in the training period as benign. However, the training data can contain anomalies, and, thus, training with this data can result in high false negative rates.

Prior work has addressed the issue of mapping such one class classification problems into two class classification problems [1–5]. However, earlier approaches generate samples for the second class randomly [1,2] or by following a predefined distribution such as uniform or Gaussian distribution [3–5]. While these data points are generated from the data, they do not represent actual behavior in most real-world problems.

In contrast, we observe that multiple users share the system and exhibit distinct behavioral patterns in many monitoring applications. Examples of such scenarios include user authentication determining the authenticity of a user based on users' keystroke patterns, insider threat detection identifying deviation of a user's access patterns from past behavior, and social network analysis detecting anomaly in a user's collaboration patterns. In these scenarios, we expect other users' behavioral pattern to be distinct from the target user's behavior. Thus, we can utilize other users' samples to estimate a target user's possible abnormal behavioral patterns. We leverage these "abnormal" samples to help the classifier learn a boundary between a user's expected behavior and unexpected behavior. There are no assumptions made about the distribution of anomalous samples, no manual labeling is necessary, and it is independent of the underlying learning algorithms.

The basic idea of our algorithm lies in the concept of a local density and is built on the Local Outlier Factor algorithm [6]. LOF is a density-based anomaly detection algorithm and finds anomalous data points based on their deviation with respect to their neighbours. The locality of a data point is defined by its $k$-nearest neighbors, and the distance to the $k$-neighbors is used to estimate the density. If the density of a data point has much lower density than its neighbors, the data point is considered as an outlier.

We extend the idea of LOF and propose a new local density-based method for selecting a good set of anomalous samples from the other users' sample set. For a given target user, we compute the Local Outlier Factor (LOF) value for all data points with respect to the target user's data points and choose data points from other users' samples that are distant from the target user's data as anomalous samples. Our method, named as *reference points-based LOF*, gives us an estimate of the degree of "outlier-ness" of the other data points with respect to the target user's behavior. Given this measure of LOF, we have explored two broad strategies to select abnormal samples: use the points with the highest LOF, which deviate the most from the target user's data points, or use the points with the lowest LOF above a certain threshold, which are just "slightly different" from the target user's data. Further, we use the reference points-based LOF to remove outliers from the target user's sample set and produce more coherent benign sample set.

We evaluate these approaches using four different data sets: keystroke dynamics data for user authentication, typing patterns for user recognition, user access patterns for a source code repository, and, finally, paper titles from the DBLP bibliography. For each test user, we generate both benign data points and abnormal data points using the LOF-based strategies. We then train two-class classifiers—Decision Tree, Logistic Regression and Random Forest—for evaluation. In each case, our evaluation has shown that the strategy of providing abnormal data points for users using the *Reference Points-based LOF* provides uniformly better results compared to the one class classifier approach and binary-class approach using synthetically constructed distributions of abnormal samples for training. Our methods produce better AUC (Area Under the ROC Curve) across all users in the various data sets. Our technique is promising and applicable to a large number of problems in security relying on anomaly detection and user profiling.

## 2    Approach

This paper addresses the critical problem of detecting anomalous user behavior, targeting use cases such as continuous user authentication and insider threat detection. The key challenge we aim to address is the difficulty in obtaining labeled anomalous samples. The primary goal is to detect anomalous behavior of a user, i.e., when a user's behavior deviates significantly from his/her own historical behavior. While user-specific modeling can provide higher accuracy and adaptability to changing environments, obtaining known anomalous samples for each individual user is made even more challenging.

Standard anomaly detection techniques, such as statistical analysis or one-class classification, aim to rank new samples based on their similarity to the model of the negative samples, assuming that all previously known samples are negative (benign). Many approaches use distance or density of the points as a measurement for the similarity, in which data points with the lowest density or the longest average distance to the previously known (negative) samples are considered most anomalous.

In contrast, our approach makes no assumption on the underlying data distribution. We assume that data samples in these applications are generated independently by many users with different underlying distributions. Consider, for example, the case of detecting anomalous user access to a source code repository shared by many employees. In this case, we expect that users' access patterns will depend on their role in the organization or project and will, in general, be different from each other. For instance, we expect software developers to exhibit similar access patterns e.g. access the repository regularly during business hours, and to be significantly different from the access patterns of testers, business managers, backup administrators etc. Further, we assume that, in these multi-user applications, malicious actors often change their behaviors subtly or try to impersonate another person to hide their malicious intention. Thus, an anomalous point of a user's behavior can look perfectly normal in the global view, and, anomaly detection per user can detect these stealth attacks better than a global anomaly detection. However, while user-specific modeling can produce more accurate detection, the data sparseness problem becomes even worse. In this case, in addition to the lack of anomalous cases, we may not have enough benign cases for some users, such as new users or not active users.

We address the lack of labeled samples by exploiting data samples from the other users in the target application. Our intuition is that, when there are many users, other users' behavior can provide additional insights on potential anomalies. We assume that a user's actions are similar each other and tend to form a few clusters occupying a small area in the data space. However, when we combine data samples from many users, they provide more accurate projection of the entire data space and help to estimate accurate boundaries between different users.

The main focus of this study is on how to generate anomalous samples automatically from other users' behaviors. To identify possibly anomalous samples for a target user, we adopt a common definition of anomaly which considers the data points in low density areas as anomalous [7]. We examine all the samples of all users in the data set and identify the samples that are considered different from a target user's data samples. We apply Local Outlier Factor (LOF) [6] to estimate the degree of "outlier-ness" and select anomalous samples for the target user from other users' data samples which have high LOF with respect to the target user's data samples. We call the target user's data points the *reference points*, and call the LOF computed based on the reference points as the *reference points-based LOF*. Figure 1 illustrates the difference between outliers based on the standard LOF and outliers based on the *reference points-based LOF*. Standard anomaly detection methods will identify two clusters of dense area and detect only the two data points $p_1$ and $p_2$ as outliers as shown in Fig. 1(a). However, the reference points-based outlier detection method will measure the density of all the points with respect to their distance to the reference points $(C_1)$, and thus will consider all the data points in $C_2$ as outliers as well. The main differences of our approach from other density-based anomaly detection methods are in that we measure the outlier-ness of a data point with respect to

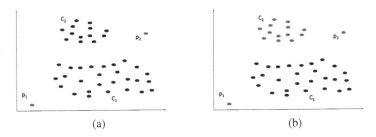

(a)                                    (b)

**Fig. 1.** Comparison of standard outlier detection (a) and reference points-based outlier detection (b). The data points in $C_1$ are the reference points, and the red points represent outliers (Color figure online).

a fixed set of existing data points in the space, and, we use low density samples as anomalous samples to build a binary classifier.

Apparently, if the data points of a user (i.e., reference points) are dispersed over a wide area in the data space and mingled with other users' samples, this method would not work well. To validate our assumption that one user's actions tend to form close clusters, we analyzed a data set of 51 distinct users containing 200 cases for each user (10,200 cases in total) from the dynamic keystroke analysis study [8]. We considered the 200 instances of the first user as the reference points, and computed the LOF scores for all 10,200 samples with respect to the 200 reference points. Figure 2 shows the LOF scores of the data points of all the users. The x-axis represents the 51 users, and each cross point in the chart represents a keystroke instance.

As we can see, all samples belonging to the first user have very low LOF scores, while other users' data points have much higher LOF scores, indicating that the data points belonging to a user are close each other, while data points from other users are separated. The analysis result supports our hypothesis on exploiting other users' data points to generate anomalous samples for the target user.

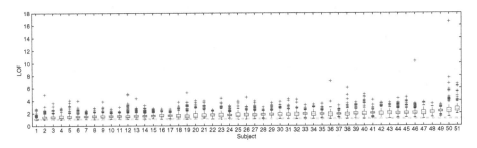

**Fig. 2.** The reference points-based LOF scores for the 51 users in the Keystroke Data Set [8] using the data points of the first user as the reference points. The dashed red line is the 95 % confidence interval for the target user (Color figure online).

# 3    Reference Points-Based LOF

In this section, we explain the reference points-based LOF method in detail. The task is to build an anomaly detection model for each user with both normal and anomalous samples. In the absence of labeled anomalous samples, we explore other users' samples as potential anomalous points for a target user. We find possible anomalous samples for each user from the other users' normal samples. The basic idea is to measure the degree of "outlier-ness" of all the training samples and identify the data points that deviate from the target user's samples.

In density-based anomaly detection, a data point is considered as an outlier if the local density of the point is substantially lower than its neighbors. In this work, we use the Local Outlier Factor (LOF) for local density estimation [6], where the local area is determined by its $k$ nearest neighbors from the target user. LOF is computed as defined in Eqs. 1 and 2.

$$LOF(p) = \frac{\sum_{q \in kNN(p)} \frac{LRD(q)}{LRD(p)}}{|kNN(p)|} \tag{1}$$

The local reachability distance (LRD) is defined as in Eq. 2.

$$LRD(p) = \frac{|kNN(p)|}{\sum_{q \in kNN(p)} \max\{k\text{-}distance(q), dist(p,q)\}} \tag{2}$$

where $k\text{-}distance(q)$ be the distance of the point $q$ to its $k$-th nearest neighbor.

Let $\mathcal{U}$ be the set of users, $\mathcal{D}$ be the set of training samples for all the users, $\mathcal{D}_u$ be the samples of a target user $u$, and $\overline{\mathcal{D}_u}$ be the samples from all other users except $u$, i.e., $\mathcal{D} = \mathcal{D}_u \cup \overline{\mathcal{D}_u}$. Unlike the standard LOF, where $k$-nearest neighbors are found from the entire data set, we compute the LOF values of all data points $p \in \mathcal{D}$ based on their distance to the $k$-nearest neighbors from the target user's data points, $\mathcal{D}_u$. Figure 3 shows a high level sketch of the reference points-based LOF.

---

**Reference Points based LOF($\mathcal{D}, U, K$)**

---

$\mathcal{D}_u$ = extract samples of user $u$ from $\mathcal{D}$
**for** ($p \in \mathcal{D}$) **do**
    **for** ($q \in \mathcal{D}_u$) **do**
        compute the distance between $p$ and $q$, $dist(p,q)$
    **end for**
**end for**
**for** ($p \in \overline{\mathcal{D}_u}$) **do**
    $kNN(p)$ = $K$ nearest neighbors of p in $\mathcal{D}_u$
    compute $LOF(p)$ using Equation 1
**end for**

---

**Fig. 3.** Algorithm for computing LOF based on a set of reference points

In this work, we compute the distance between two data points $p$ and $q$ using a normalized Manhattan distance.

$$dist(p, q) = \sum_i \frac{|p_i - q_i|}{max(i) - min(i)} \tag{3}$$

where $max(i)$ and $min(i)$ denote the maximum and minimum value for the $i$-th features respectively. Alternative to the $k$-nearest neighbors, one can use the $\epsilon$-neighborhood as described in the DBSCAN clustering algorithm [9]. In this case, the degree of outlier-ness of a sample $p$ can be computed as the average distance to the data points in its directly reachable neighbors.

## 4    Abnormal Behavior Detection

In this section, we explore several strategies to generate a labeled training set based on the reference points-based LOF. Sections 4.1 and 4.2 describe strategies for choosing normal samples and anomalous samples respectively. Note that the algorithm in Fig. 3 computes the LOF scores for all data points including both the target user's data points and other users' data points. We use the LOF scores to select both normal and abnormal samples to train a two-class classification model for each user.

### 4.1    Normal Sample Selection

We apply the following 2 different strategies for generating normal samples for training.

1. All Self Samples (Self): This method uses all the samples from the target user during the training period as normal samples, similarly to unsupervised anomaly detection or one-class classification approach.
2. No Outlier Samples (LowLOF): Note that we compute LOF values for the target user's own samples as well. The data points with relatively high LOF scores are outliers in the target user's samples. We discard these outlier samples from the target user's sample set and use the remaining samples as normal samples for training. This strategy can handle noisy data.

### 4.2    Abnormal Sample Selection

For anomalous training sample generation, we apply the following four strategies to extract anomalous samples for the target user. These strategies aim to find other users' samples that are outside of the target user's samples, i.e., outliers from the perspective of the target user.

1. Boundary Sampling (LowLOFAll): Out of all other users' samples that have LOF higher than a threshold, we choose the samples with lowest LOF scores. This method finds anomalous samples that are located close to the boundaries. These samples would have higher LOF scores than most of the target user's samples, but have lower LOF scores than most of the other users' samples.

2. Boundary Sampling Per User (LowLOFUser): This method is also intended to choose boundary samples. However, this method selects low LOF samples from each of the other users. If we want to generate $N$ anomalous samples, and there are $m$ other users, we generate approximately $\frac{N}{m}$ samples from each user.

3. Outlier Sampling (HighLOFAll): This method generates anomalous samples which deviate mostly from the target users' samples, i.e., samples with highest LOF scores from the sample set from all the other users as in LowLOFAll.

4. Outlier Sampling per User (HighLOFUser): This method is similar to LowLOFUser. The difference is that it chooses samples with highest LOF scores from each of the other users.

We note that our algorithm chooses anomalous samples which have an LOF score higher than a threshold to exclude other users' samples that are inside of or too close to the target user's region. Further, the LowLOF method for generating normal samples (Sect. 4.1) can also discard a few normal samples. Thus, for very small data sets like the Typist data set, we can generate a smaller number of samples than requested.

## 4.3  Training Sample Generation

By combining the two methods for normal sample generation and the four for abnormal samples, we have eight methods for generating training samples. We label the methods as 'Normal Sampling Method'-'Abnormal Sampling Method' (e.g., Self-LowLOFAll and LowLOF-HighLOWUser). Figure 4 illustrates the differences of the sampling methods. Here, the circle points are the data samples of the target user, and the triangle, square and diamond points belong to the other three users, $U_1$, $U_2$, and $U_3$ respectively. Figure 4(a) shows the LowLOF method and Fig. 4(b) the Self method for selecting normal samples respectively. With Self, all circle points are selected as normal, while the two white circles are discarded because their LOF scores are high and considered as outlier with the LowLOF method. Suppose we plan to include nine anomalous samples in the training data set: Fig. 4(a) shows per-user basis sampling methods, LowLOFUser and HighLOFUser, and chooses three samples from each user. The points enclosed by dashed lines are selected by LowLOFUser, while the points enclosed by solid lines are chosen by HighLOFUser. Figure 4(b) shows anomalous samples selected by LowLOFAll (dashed line) and HighLOFAll (solid line).

## 4.4  Binary Classification

Having both normal and anomalous samples in the training data allows us to cast the anomaly detection task as a two-class classification problem, and learn a classifier that can discriminate the abnormal samples from the normal samples. Any classification algorithm can be applied and may be chosen based on the application. We use classification algorithms that produce the class probability as an output, rather than a binary decision. The advantage of having class

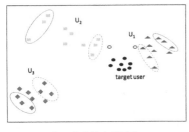     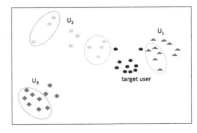

(a) LowLOF–LOFUser                (b) Self–LOFAll

**Fig. 4.** Illustrations of the reference points-based LOF sampling methods. The circles are the instances of the target user. (a) depicts LowLOF-LowLOFUser and LowLOF-HighLOFUser methods, and (b) depicts Self-LowLOFAll and Self-HighLOFAll methods. The points enclosed with dashed lines have low LOF values, and those enclosed with solid lines have high LOF values.

probability estimation over a binary decision of *normal* versus *abnormal* is that the system administrators can adjust the ratio of alarms according to available resources and costs. In this work, we conduct experiments with three classification algorithms: Decision Tree, Logistic Regression, and Random Forest. We use the implementations in RapidMiner [10] for all the experiments described in Sect. 5.

## 5   Experiments

We validated the proposed sampling methods with three publicly available data sets and one private data set from information security application. This section decribes the four data sets and the evaluation methods in details.

### 5.1   Data

We validate our algorithms for anomalous sample generation using the following four data sets: *Keystroke Dynamics Benchmark Data*; *Typist Recognition Data*; *DBLP Collaboration Network Data*; and *Access Log Data*. The first three data sets are publicly available and the last data set is private.

**Keystroke Dynamics Benchmark Data:** Killourhy and Maxion [8] collected keystroke data from 51 users typing the same strong password 400 times, broken into eight equal-length sessions[1]. They collected various timing features such as the length of time between each keystroke, and the time each key was depressed. They used this data set to compare the accuracy of fourteen one-class classifiers at identifying impostors.

**Typist Recognition Data:** Hempstalk, Frank and Witten [5] collected data on the typing patterns of ten different users and build a classifier to identify

---

[1] http://www.cs.cmu.edu/afs/cs/Web/People/keystroke/.

individual typists. The typing pattern are represented by eight features such as typing speed and error rate (backspace)[2]. The typing behavior of the users is broken into units, approximately one paragraph's worth of typing. Each user contains between 24 and 75 records with an average of 53.3.

**DBLP Collaboration Network Data:** DBLP[3] is a large database of publications from computer science journals, conferences, and workshops. We extracted DBLP records of "inproceedings" and "incollection" publications, and authors with publication records between 25 and 150 papers in the data set. We then randomly selected 200 authors from the extracted data and generated a corpus containing the publication records of the selected 200 authors. The paper titles are preprocessed by removing stop words and performing lemmatization on the remaining words, and each publication record is converted to a vector of term:count pairs found in the title. We build models to learn what a "normal" paper title is for an author.

**Access Log Data:** The access log data set comes from a source code repository used in a large IT company. The logs were collected over 5 years and consist of 2,623 unique users, 298,365 unique directories, 1,162,259 unique files, and 68,736,222 total accesses. Each log contains a timestamp, a user ID, a resource name, and the action performed on the resource. We process these logs down to individual periods per user which represent the user's behavior in a given week. The features include the number of total accesses, the number of unique accesses in that period, new unique accesses given a user's history, counts for the actions performed, counts for the file extensions accessed, and similarity scores to the target user as discussed in [11]. The similarity scores represent how similar a user is to the other users given the user's current access pattern and the other users' past access patterns.

## 5.2   Evaluation Method

While we assume that most of a target user's activity is benign, we need to prevent our training data from containing samples of malicious behavior to be detected. For example, if the target user's account is compromised by an adversary, the classifier should not have been trained on the activity of the adversary. For this reason, we train and test a classifier on different user groups. For each target user, we perform $K$-fold cross validation by dividing the user population into $K$ disjoint sets of training and testing user groups. For example, suppose there are three users $U_1$, $U_2$ and $U_3$, and $U_1$ is the target user. We train a classifier on $U_1$ and $U_2$ and test on $U_1$ and $U_3$, and train a second classifier on $U_1$ and $U_3$, and test on $U_1$ and $U_2$. The user actions are also split into training and testing samples using a pivot point in time when applicable, that is, all training actions occur strictly prior to all testing actions. We choose anomalous samples only from the training user group and measure the performance on the evaluation user group. The training user group and the evaluation user group for each

---

[2] http://www.cs.waikato.ac.nz/ml/data/typist.arff.
[3] http://snap.stanford.edu/data/com-DBLP.html.

**Table 1.** Sizes of the four experiment data sets both for training and testing. The number of samples denote the mean values for each cross-validation set.

| Data Set | Num. Users | Training | | Testing | |
|---|---|---|---|---|---|
| | | Normal | Abnormal | Normal | Abnormal |
| Keystroke | 51 | 200 | 200 | 200 | 54 |
| Typist | 10 | 47 | 45 | 5 | 45 |
| DBLP | 28 | 91 | 85 | 23 | 34 |
| Access Log | 202 | 125 | 151 | 37 | 201 |

fold are mutually exclusive, so no evaluation user is seen during training. Table 1 shows the average size of the training and test data sets.

To ease comparison with some prior work, we evaluate the performance of a two-class classifier versus a one-class classifier for detecting changes in user behavior. Further, for all experiments, we report the average results over the cross-validation splits and compare the algorithms based on AUC (Area Under Curve), as it is the metric used in all previous work.

### 5.3  Baseline Methods

We use two baseline methods for evaluation. The first baseline method is a two-class classification using randomly selected anomalous samples from other users. We use all training samples from the target user as normal samples (i.e., Self), and apply a standard random sampling strategy (Random) on the other users' sample set. We call this baseline Self-Random, and compare this method with the eight different combinations of sampling methods described in the previous section.

We also compare two-class classification with one-class classification based on one-class SVM using all samples of a target user as normal samples. We use the SVM implementation from SVM KMToolbox [12][4] with RBF kernel and the upper bound on the number of errors $\nu$ was set to 0.1.

## 6  Results

### 6.1  Keystroke Dynamics Benchmark Data

Killourhy and Maxion [8] collected the Keystroke data to build one-class classifiers to detect imposters. There are 51 users in the data, where each user contributed 400 samples. They evaluated fourteen scoring methods, one of which is a one-class SVM. Each method is trained using normal samples obtained only from the target user and is not exposed to malicious samples during training. However, our methods need anomalous samples from other users. To make the

---

[4] Download available at http://asi.insa-rouen.fr/enseignants/~arakoto/toolbox/.

**Table 2.** AUC comparison for the Keystroke Dynamics Data. Our Algorithm (LOF) reports the best result obtained from the LOF-based strategies.

| Cross validation | LOF | Self-Random | One-Class SVM |
|---|---|---|---|
| 1 | **0.979** | 0.934 | 0.927 |
| 2 | **0.967** | 0.939 | 0.908 |
| 3 | **0.971** | 0.905 | 0.905 |
| 4 | **0.945** | 0.933 | 0.800 |
| 5 | **0.968** | 0.957 | 0.844 |
| Avg. | **0.966** | 0.934 | 0.877 |

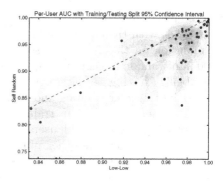

**Fig. 5.** AUC values of the classifiers for individual target users, and the variance across the five training-testing folds.

comparison objective, we divided the 51 users into 5-fold cross validation sets comprising a training user group and an evaluation user group as described in Sect. 5.2. Each training and testing group contains approximately 41 users and 10 users respectively.

Following Killourhy et al.'s convention, we considered one user from a training user group as the target user, and treat all remaining users in the training user group as malicious users. For each target user, we use the user's first 200 samples to select the benign training samples and extract five samples randomly from each malicious user as anomalous samples for training. Therefore, the training data set contains 200 benign cases and 200 anomalous cases. For testing, we use the remaining 200 samples from the target user and extract five samples randomly from each user in the testing user group as anomalous samples. The performance is measured using the average AUC over all 51 users. Table 2 shows the average AUC of the 5-fold cross validation results. As we can see from the table, the LOF-based method produces a higher AUC than the Self-Random baseline method and the one-class SVM for all folds.

Next, we evaluate how well the individual classifiers compare across each target user. Figure 5 compares the classifiers for individual target users and the error rates of the AUC across the five splits. Here, the x-axis is the AUC score of the LowLOF-LowLOFUser method, and the y-axis is the AUC for the random baseline method, Self-Random. The red error ellipse around each point has a diameter of one standard deviation for the AUC scores over the five splits. Points below the $y$-equal-$x$ line (red-dashed) are classifiers where our LOF method produced strictly better results.

## 6.2   Typist Recognition Data

Hempstalk et al. [5] proposed a technique for combining density and class probability estimation for continuous typist recognition. They collected a dataset of

15 emails from each of ten participants to validate their method. To compare our methods with theirs, we conducted experiments using a stratified 10-fold cross validation on the same data set as described in [5]. For each user, we choose 90 % of randomly chosen samples as training samples and the remaining 10 % for benign testing samples. Due to the small user population, we don't split the users into disjoint training and evaluation groups.

To generate anomalous training samples for each target user, we first merge the training samples for all users, assuming the target user's samples as "normal" and samples from the other nine users as "abnormal". We then compute the reference points-based LOF scores all the samples in the training data, and generate abnormal samples as described in Sect. 3. To replicate the experiments by Hempstalk et al. as close as we can, we set the number of anomalous samples to the number of normal samples for the target users. However, our method often produces a smaller number of samples than requested as we noted in Sect. 4.2, because LowLOF normal sampling method discards outliers from the target user's sample set.

Table 3 compares the results of our algorithm, random sampling-based method, and two density estimation-based methods from [5]. The table shows the average AUC over the 10-fold cross validation for each user. As we can see, our method outperforms both of the density estimation methods, and is slightly better than the random sampling method for this data set. However, as we noted

**Table 3.** AUC results for the Typist Recognition Data. Our Algorithm (LOF) reports the best result obtained from the LOF-based strategies. The results of Gaussian and EM methods are obtained by the density and class probability estimation described in [5].

| Participant | LOF | Self-Random | Density* | | One-Class SVM |
|---|---|---|---|---|---|
| | | | Gaussian | EM | |
| A | **0.946** | 0.923 | 0.924 | 0.923 | 0.894 |
| B | 0.965 | **0.984** | 0.934 | 0.929 | 0.725 |
| C | **0.852** | 0.825 | 0.707 | 0.786 | 0.769 |
| D | 0.903 | 0.922 | **0.924** | 0.902 | 0.918 |
| E | 0.977 | **0.982** | 0.973 | 0.971 | 0.932 |
| F | **0.902** | 0.872 | 0.852 | 0.867 | 0.749 |
| G | **0.960** | 0.949 | 0.942 | 0.952 | 0.856 |
| H | 0.909 | 0.877 | 0.909 | **0.914** | 0.822 |
| I | **0.976** | 0.974 | 0.956 | 0.950 | 0.913 |
| J | **1.000** | 0.989 | **1.000** | **1.000** | 0.982 |
| Avg. | **0.939** | 0.930 | 0.912 | 0.919 | 0.856 |
| Std. | **0.046** | 0.056 | 0.082 | 0.060 | 0.087 |

**Table 4.** AUC results for the DBLP data set.

| Authors | LOF | *Self-Random* | One-Class SVM | Authors | LOF | *Self-Random* | One-Class SVM |
|---|---|---|---|---|---|---|---|
| 1 | **0.783** | 0.664 | 0.59 | 16 | 0.846 | **0.852** | 0.54 |
| 2 | 0.810 | **0.859** | 0.74 | 17 | **0.750** | 0.696 | 0.71 |
| 3 | **0.926** | 0.909 | 0.72 | 18 | **0.760** | 0.756 | 0.62 |
| 4 | **0.805** | 0.718 | 0.78 | 19 | 0.734 | **0.824** | 0.46 |
| 5 | **0.837** | 0.765 | 0.71 | 20 | **0.659** | 0.625 | 0.58 |
| 6 | 0.760 | **0.821** | 0.48 | 21 | **0.890** | 0.883 | 0.75 |
| 7 | 0.694 | **0.760** | 0.33 | 22 | 0.603 | **0.607** | 0.48 |
| 8 | **0.845** | 0.825 | 0.79 | 23 | **0.814** | 0.642 | 0.67 |
| 9 | **0.918** | 0.896 | 0.75 | 24 | **0.735** | 0.676 | 0.72 |
| 10 | 0.802 | 0.720 | **0.84** | 25 | 0.849 | **0.865** | 0.63 |
| 11 | **0.807** | 0.779 | 0.59 | 26 | 0.779 | **0.858** | 0.49 |
| 12 | **0.810** | 0.730 | 0.74 | 27 | 0.685 | **0.686** | 0.61 |
| 13 | 0.547 | **0.630** | 0.35 | 28 | **0.628** | 0.552 | 0.51 |
| 14 | 0.835 | **0.868** | 0.76 | Avg. | **0.770** | 0.760 | 0.621 |
| 15 | 0.658 | **0.822** | 0.47 | Std. | **0.093** | 0.100 | 0.137 |

earlier, the results demonstrate our algorithm's advantage, as it used a smaller number of training samples than the other three methods in most testing cases.

### 6.3 DBLP Collaboration Network Data

While the DBLP data contain publication information about many authors, each user has a small number of publications. Many authors do not have enough data points for training a reliable model. In this experiments, we selected authors with at least 50 publications in the data set, resulting in 28 distinct authors. We used the words in the publication titles as the features and represent each user with a bag of word vector after removing stop words and converting words to their base form, resulting in 9,670 unique features. We ran PCA (Principal Component Analysis) on the entire samples, and reduced the dimension to 200. Then, we conducted a 5-fold cross validation test similar to the password data sets. Table 4 summarizes the average AUC of each user over the 5-fold splits.

### 6.4 Access Log Data

The access log data contains a mixture of real user IDs and system IDs which periodically run batch processes. These system processes perform tasks such as nightly builds of source code and exhibit vastly different behavioral patterns from real users. We discarded these system IDs from the logs. Further, we eliminated any user that is active in fewer than 150 weeks (not active users) or more than 250 weeks (very active) out of 260 weeks during which the logs were collected. The final data set contain 202 unique users. The samples are then split by time into 80 % for training and 20 % for testing.

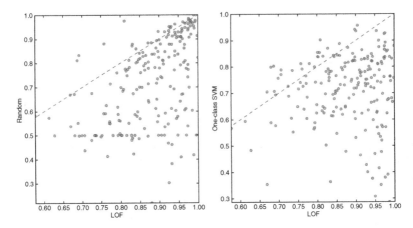

**Fig. 6.** Comparison of AUC scores for LOF, Random, and One-Class SVM across the 202 per-user classifiers.

Figure 6 shows the comparison of the three sampling methods in terms of the AUC scores for the individual classifiers per target user, and Table 5 shows the mean and standard deviation of the AUC scores of the 202 users.

In both scatter plots, the AUC scores of LOF  are given on the x-axis, and the AUC scores for the competing methods, Self-Random for the left plot and one-class SVM for the right, are given on the y-axis. The dashed red-line is the *y-equals-x* line. For any points below the line, our LOF method outperformed the other methods for the given target user, producing better results across the majority of target users (89.1 % compared to Self-Random and 87.1 % compared to one-class SVM). Further, the improvement in AUC scores is significant: 0.155 (stdev 0.155) higher compared to Self-Random, and 0.163 (stdev 0.155) compared to one-class SVM. We also note that the biggest impediment to the use of analytics for insider threat detection is the high false positive rates. As shown above, our approach significantly reduces false positive rates, thus improving the applicability of anomaly detection mechanisms.

### 6.5   Comparison of Sampling Methods

Lastly, we compare the performance of the eight LOF-based sampling methods and the Self-Random baseline. The comparison was conducted using the Keystroke Data and the three binary classifiers—Decision Tree, Logistic Regression, and Random Forest—over a 5-fold cross validation, resulting in 6,885 experiments in total (51 *users* × 9 *sampling methods* × 3 *classifiers* × 5 *folds*). We counted how many times a sampling method preformed the best for each of the user and classifier combinations. When multiple sampling algorithms made a tie, we considered all the methods as the best performing one.

The comparison results are shown in Fig. 7. The x-axis denotes the five methods for generating anomalous samples—four LOF-based methods and the

**Table 5.** Mean and Standard Deviation for AUC scores of the 202 users in the Access Log data.

| Method | Mean AUC | Stdev AUC |
|---|---|---|
| LOF | **0.877** | 0.089 |
| Self-Random | 0.722 | 0.176 |
| One-Class SVM | 0.714 | 0.134 |

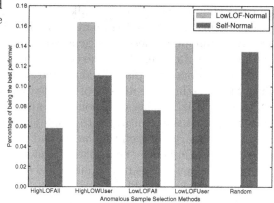

**Fig. 7.** The percentage of each sampling method being the best performer.

Random method. The blue bars represent the LowLOF method for generating normal samples, and the pink bars indicate that all samples of the target user were used as normal (Self). We can see that LowLOF-HighLOFUser was the best performing method most of the time, closely followed by LowLOF-LowLOFUser. The results confirm two findings. First, discarding outlier cases from the normal sample significantly increase the detection accuracy, as indicated by all blue bars (LowLOF outperforming red bards (Self). Second, sampling from each user is more beneficial than from the merged sample set (LOFUser vs. LOFAll for anomalous samples). The reason that there is no significant difference between High-LOFUser and LowLOFUser methods for anomalous sample generation is because the sample size was relatively small, and many of the selected anomalous samples appear in both training sets.

# 7  Related Work

Anomaly detection has been an important research problem in security analysis [13,14]. Various techniques based on domain knowledge/statistics [15–19] or on data mining algorithms [20–22], haven been proposed for anomaly detection for a number of application domains. Due to the absence or insufficiency of labeled examples, most of the techniques have modeled anomaly detection as a unsupervised learning problem. However, unsupervised modeling suffers from a number of problems, e.g., the incapability of discriminative modeling and the difficulty of tuning parameters, leading to high false-positive rates.

To solve this problem, several anomaly detection methods tried to artificially generate samples as a second class based on some heuristics, posing a one-class classification task as a binary classification problem. For example, in a word spotting application, Chang and Lippmann [1] presented a method to artificially enlarge the number of training talkers to increase variabilities of training samples. They transformed one talker's speech pattern to that of a new talker by generating more varied training examples of keywords. Theiler and Cai [2] applied a resampling method to generate a random sample by choosing each of its coordinates randomly from the coordinate values that are in the data. Later, Fan et al. [3] proposed a distribution-based artificial anomaly generation method, which first measures the density of each feature value in the original data set $D$ and then artificially generates anomaly points near to the normal data points by replacing low-density features with a different value in $D$. This method assumes that the boundary between the known and anomalous instances is very close to the existing data, hence "near misses" can be safely assumed to be anomalous. However, this methods is not applicable to data with a very high dimensionality or with continuous variables.

Further, Hastie et al. [4] summarized techniques for transforming the density estimation (unsupervised learning) problem into one of supervised learning using artificially generated data in the context of association rule learning. A reference model, such as uniform or Gaussian, can be used to generate artificial training samples as "contrast" statistics that provide information concerning departures of the data density from the chosen reference density. Following this principle, Hempstalk et al. [5] further proposed to employ the training data from the target class to generate artificial data based on a known reference distribution. But it restrict the underlying classification algorithm to produce class probability estimates rather than a binary decision.

Despite the success of the above methods, they suffer either from strong restrictions, which made them not applicable to problems with high dimensional data other application domains, or from the requirement of estimating the reference data distribution, which is usually not accurate and may lead to suboptimal performance. Our method addresses both limitations: (1) artificially generated samples do not reflect real cases, (2) assuming an underlying data distribution is unrealistic in multi-user environments. Instead, our LOF-based sampling provides a unified mechanism to filter out bad normal samples and generate potential anomalous samples for each target user.

## 8   Conclusion

This study focused on abnormal behavior detection for applications where multiple users share the system or application. Many applications exist in computer security such as user authentication, insider threat detection, and network security, and anomalous user activity detection in social network. In each case, we learn a target user's normal behavior from the user's training samples, and estimate the user's possible abnormal behavioral patterns from other users' training samples, who exhibit quite different behavioral patterns from the target user.

We proposed the reference points based LOF method which measures outlierness of a data point with respect to a set of known data points, and showed, through empirical evaluations, that reference points-based LOF methods find good anomalous samples from the behavior of other users. Our evaluation has shown that the our methods provide uniformly better results compared to the one class classifier approach and the approach of providing synthetically constructed distributions of abnormal samples for training. Our technique is promising and seems to be applicable to a large number of problems in security relying on anomaly detection and user profiling.

# References

1. Chang, E.I., Lippmann, R.P.: Using voice transformations to create additional training talkers for word spotting. In: Advances in Neural Information Processing Systems, pp. 875–882 (1995)
2. Theiler, J., Cai, D.M.: Resampling approach for anomaly detection in multispectral images. In: Proceedings of the SPIE, pp. 230–240 (2003)
3. Fan, W., Miller, M., Stolfo, S., Lee, W., Chan, P.: Using artificial anomalies to detect unknown and known network intrusions. Knowl. Inf. Syst. **6**(5), 507–527 (2004)
4. Hastie, T., Tibshirani, R., Friedman, J., Franklin, J.: The elements of statistical learning: data mining, inference and prediction. The Math. Intelligencer **27**(2), 83–85 (2005)
5. Hempstalk, K., Frank, E., Witten, I.H.: One-class classification by combining density and class probability estimation. In: Daelemans, W., Goethals, B., Morik, K. (eds.) ECML PKDD 2008, Part I. LNCS (LNAI), vol. 5211, pp. 505–519. Springer, Heidelberg (2008)
6. Breunig, M.M., Kriegel, H.-P., Ng, R.T., Sander, J.: LOF: Identifying density-based local outliers. In: ACM Sigmod Record, vol. 29, no. 2, pp. 93–104. ACM (2000)
7. Bishop, C.M.: Novelty detection and neural network validation. In: IEE Proceedings Vision, Image and Signal Processing, vol. 141, no. 4, pp. 217–222. IET (1994)
8. Killourhy, K.S., Maxion, R.A.: Comparing anomaly-detection algorithms forkeystroke dynamics. In: IEEE/IFIP International Conference on Dependable Systems and Networks, DSN 2009, pp. 125–134 (2009)
9. Ester, M., Kriegel, H.-P., Sander, J., Xu, X.: A density-based algorithm for discovering clusters in large spatial databases with noise. In: Kdd, vol. 96, pp. 226–231 (1996)
10. Hofmann, M., Klinkenberg, R.: RapidMiner: Data Mining Use Cases and Business Analytics Applications. CRC Press, Boca Raton (2013)
11. Gates, C., Li, N., Xu, Z., Chari, S.N., Molloy, I., Park, Y.: Detecting insider information theft using features from file access logs. In: Kutyłowski, M., Vaidya, J. (eds.) ICAIS 2014, Part II. LNCS, vol. 8713, pp. 383–400. Springer, Heidelberg (2014)
12. Canu, S., Grandvalet, Y., Guigue, V., Rakotomamonjy, A.: Svm and kernel methods matlab toolbox. Perception Systmes et Information, INSA de Rouen, Rouen, France (2005)
13. Salem, M., Hershkop, S., Stolfo, S.: A survey of insider attack detection research. In: Insider Attack and Cyber Security, pp. 69–90 (2008)
14. Chandola, V., Banerjee, A., Kumar, V.: Anomaly detection: A survey. ACM Comput. Surv. (CSUR) **41**(3), 15 (2009)
15. Denning, D.E.: An intrusion-detection model. IEEE Trans. Softw. Eng. **SE–13**(2), 222–232 (1987)

16. Javitz, H.S., Valdes, A.: The SRI IDES statistical anomaly detector. In: Research in Security and Privacy (1991)

17. Apap, F., Honig, A., Hershkop, S., Eskin, E., Stolfo, S.J.: Detecting malicious software by monitoring anomalous windows registry accesses. In: Wespi, A., Vigna, G., Deri, L. (eds.) RAID 2002. LNCS, vol. 2516, pp. 36–53. Springer, Heidelberg (2002)

18. Stolfo, S.J., Hershkop, S., Bui, L.H., Ferster, R., Wang, K.: Anomaly detection in computer security and an application to file system accesses. In: Hacid, M.-S., Murray, N.V., Raś, Z.W., Tsumoto, S. (eds.) ISMIS 2005. LNCS (LNAI), vol. 3488, pp. 14–28. Springer, Heidelberg (2005). http://dx.doi.org/10.1007/11425274_2

19. Chen, Y., Malin, B.: Detection of anomalous insiders in collaborative environments via relational analysis of access logs. In: CODASPY 2011: Proceedings of the First ACM Conference on Data and Application Security and Privacy, Feb 2011

20. Papadimitriou, S., Kitagawa, H., Gibbons, P.B., Faloutsos, C.: Loci: Fast outlier detection using the local correlation integral. In: Dayal, U., Ramamritham, K., Vijayaraman, T.M. (eds.) ICDE, pp. 315–326. IEEE Computer Society (2003)

21. Wang, Y., Parthasarathy, S., Tatikonda, S.: Locality sensitive outlier detection: A ranking driven approach. In: Abiteboul, S., Bhm, K., Koch, C., Tan, K.-L. (eds.) ICDE, pp. 410–421. IEEE Computer Society (2011)

22. Senator, T.E., Goldberg, H.G., Memory, A., Young, W.T., Rees, B., Pierce, R., Huang, D., Reardon, M., Bader, D.A., Chow, E., Essa, I., Jones, J., Bettadapura, V., Chau, D.H., Green, O., Kaya, O., Zakrzewska, A., Briscoe, E., Mappus, R.I.L., McColl, R., Weiss, L., Dietterich, T.G., Fern, A., Wong, W.-K., Das, S., Emmott, A., Irvine, J., Lee, J.-Y., Koutra, D., Faloutsos, C., Corkill, D., Friedland, L., Gentzel, A., Jensen, D.: Detecting insider threats in a real corporate database of computer usage activity. In: KDD 2013: Proceedings of the 19th ACM SIGKDD International Conference on Knowledge Discovery and Data Mining. ACM Request Permissions, Aug 2013

# Authentication

# Towards Attack-Resistant Peer-Assisted Indoor Localization

Jingyu Hua[⊠], Shaoyong Du, and Sheng Zhong

State Key Laboratory for Novel Software Technology,
Department of Computer Science and Technology,
Nanjing University, Nanjing, China
{huajingyu,zhongsheng}@nju.edu.cn, shaoyong.du.cs@gmail.com

**Abstract.** Peer-assisted smartphone localization, which leverages pairwise acoustic ranging among nearby peer phones to refine location estimation, significantly pushes the accuracy limit of WiFi-based indoor localization. Unfortunately, this technique is designed for non-adversarial settings. Dishonest peers may cheat in their distance measurements. Outside attackers may interfere with the acoustic ranging by continually broadcasting interference signals. In this paper, we propose countermeasures against each of these attacks. We first present an algorithm that can identify peers that are not cheating in the current localization, by searching for devices that can be embedded into the same plane according to their pairwise distances. We also design a robust acoustic ranging method exploiting signal modulation, which can defend effectively against intentional interference of outside attackers. Experimental results demonstrate that our countermeasures can greatly improve the robustness of peer-assisted localization.

**Keywords:** Peer-assisted localization · Acoustic ranging · Attack resistance · Smartphone

## 1 Introduction

Outdoor localization with smartphones is being widely used in our daily life. Indoor localization, however, remains in the elementary stage. Although there do exist many accurate indoor location mechanisms [3, 8, 16], they require either special hardware not yet supported by smartphones, or infrastructures expensive to deploy. Compared with them, WiFi-based localization, which leverages radio signals of existing WiFi access points, is much cheaper to implement on smartphones. Whereas current proposals [1, 17, 21, 23, 24] can only achieve room-level accuracy. For example, according to the experiments of Liu et al. [13], the errors of Fingerprinting Based Localization [2, 17, 23], which is one of the most

This work was supported by NSFC-61321491, NSFC-61425024, and NSFC-61300235. The extended version of this paper is available at http://cl.ly/3d3V1z0D2d45.

G. Pernul et al. (Eds.): ESORICS 2015, Part II, LNCS 9327, pp. 417–437, 2015.
DOI: 10.1007/978-3-319-24177-7_21

popular WiFi localization technologies, may exceed 8 m. This is far from enough for indoor localization.

Targeting this problem, Liu et al. [13] propose an interesting approach of peer-phone assisted acoustic ranging to push the accuracy limit of WiFi based localization on smartphones. This proposal mainly takes advantage of the high accuracy of acoustic ranging (Measurement error can be confined below 5 cm [15]) to eliminate large WiFi localization errors. Specifically, when a target phone wants to improve its location accuracy, a group of nearby peer phones (including itself) are made to emit sound signals according to the schedule of a central server. They also make recordings in this process, and all the recorded sound files are sent back to the server. The server analyzes these files to calculate pairwise distances among these peers based on the Time of Flight (ToF) approach, and then uses the obtained relative positions of nearby phones as physical constraints to refine the WiFi-based location estimation of the target phone. Their experiments show that this approach can reduce the maximum and 80 % errors to 2 m and 1 m, respectively.

While such peer-phone assisted localization (PAL) is effective for non-adversarial settings, it is vulnerable to various attacks that can significantly reduce its high accuracy or even prevent it from working properly. First, PAL relies on a group of peers that are not under the control of the server. It is hard to guarantee that all of them are honest. Instead, they may cheat by emitting their signals without following the server's schedule (which we call *emission attacks* – see Sect. 2.2), or by directly manipulating the uploaded sound files (which we call *tampering attacks* – see Sect. 2.2), thus altering the distance measurements, and so disrupt the final location estimation of the target phone. In addition, current acoustic ranging can be easily interfered with by even outsider attacks: The server in PAL has no ability to associate ranging signals detected from the recorded data to their emitters except based on their present order. As a result, if an attacker continuously broadcasts his interference signals during the ranging process, the server may mistake the interference signals for legitimate ones and then obtain false distance measurements. We call these attacks *saturation attacks* (please see Sect. 2.2).

Location information is a critical input to a wide variety of high-level location-based applications. Compromised localization results are a serious threat because of their impacts on applications [4]. For example, indoor navigation application may bring users to wrong ways and advertising applications may deliver unmatched ads to users if localization results are compromised. So, in this paper, we aim to achieve a secure PAL resistant to the three attacks we mentioned above. Specifically, we make the following contributions:

We first study emission attacks. We show that when a peer launches this kind of attack, all the distance measurements between him and other phones are increased or decreased by the same value, which in theory makes this peer no longer embeddable in the same plane with any three honest ones. We leverage this observation to identify those peers having not performed emission attacks. In particular, we prove that if we find greater than or equal to $k + 3$ peers (here, $k$ is the number of dishonest peers) embeddable in the same plane according to their distance measurements, we can guarantee that none of them is launching emission attacks.

Next, we consider the scenario involving tampering attacks. Dishonest peers launch this kind of attack could manipulate any distance measurement involving them to arbitrary values. We show that so long as we synchronize the clocks of peers in advance, the above result for emission attacks also applies to this scenario and the distance measurements among the $k + 3$ or more peers, which can be embedded into the same plane, do not suffer from any emission attacks.

We thus present an algorithm in search of no fewer than $k + 3$ peers that can be embedded in the same plane if they really exist. These phones are considered not cheating in the current localization. This algorithm has a worst-case computational complexity polynomial in $n$ – the total number of peers. Since $n$ is usually very small due to the limitation of the transmission range of beep signals, this algorithm is extremely fast. In addition, to apply this algorithm to the real world, we take ranging errors into consideration. We propose additional mechanisms to reduce false positives and false negatives due to these errors.

After that, we propose a new correlation-based beep detection approach that can well defend against saturation attacks during acoustic ranging. In this approach, beep signals assigned to peers are produced by modulating distinct pseudonoise (PN) codes on a sine carrier wave. Such modulations guarantee that these signals are poorly cross-correlated. The server can then precisely identify a specific beep from a recorded signal by searching for the earliest sharp peak of the cross-correlation function between them. If attackers have no knowledge of the PN codes, they have small chance of producing highly correlated beeps to interfere with the beep detection.

We finally perform extensive experiments to demonstrate the real effects of the above countermeasures. For the algorithm against dishonest peers, we show that it can achieve a high detection rate of honest peers while produce very few false positives. For the new correlation-based acoustic ranging method, we show that it confines the ranging errors to the same level (below 20 cm) before and after we introduce the saturation attack. By contrast, the errors of the existing energy-based method may exceed 1 m facing this attack.

## 2    Peer Assisted Localization and Attacks

### 2.1    Review of Peer Assisted Localization

Peer Assisted Localization (PAL) proposed by Liu et al. [13] uses nearby phones as reference anchors to push the limit of WiFi-based indoor localization. It exploits the high accuracy of acoustic ranging. There can be many possible designs of PAL protocols. To be specific, we use [13] as an example in this subsection and present attacks against it in Sect. 2.2. This technique includes the following four steps:

(1) WiFi-Based Localization: Smartphones use traditional WiFi-based localization techniques to roughly estimate their locations.

(2) Peer Recruitment: When a target phone wants to refine his location, he has to first broadcast a special audio signal to recruit a group of nearby peers. All the phones receiving this signal will report themselves to a central server.

(3) Relative Acoustic Ranging Among Peers: The server creates a time schedule to specify which device should emit a beep signal for ranging at what time. Involved devices send beeps accordingly while also turn on their recording function at the outset. All the recorded sound files are uploaded to the server, which will compute the relative distances among peers by estimating the sound travel time among them, and then construct a graph based these distances.

(4) Location Refining: the server then refines the location estimation of the target by superimposing the graph based on the relative distances among peers onto the graph base on the WiFi localization. The final result is sent back to the target.

We now review more details on the third step since most of our work below focuses on the acoustic ranging process in this step. We first want to mention that peer phones in this system are only responsible for emitting and recording beeps, and all the signal processing and computation are carried out on the server. This could avoid the inconvenient peer-to-peer communication among smartphones. Next, the high accuracy of the acoustic ranging is based on an assumption that the server could precisely detect the earliest position of each beep signal in the recorded sound files of peer phones, which is corresponding to the arrival time of each beep signal on these phones. The server uses the difference between the specified emission time and the detected arrival time to estimate the distances between two phones.

There exist two methods to detect beep signals hidden in the sound files [13, 22]. The first one is correlation-based. It computes the cross-correlation (CC) function of an emitted beep signal and a recorded signal. The first sharp peak in this function is considered with a high probability to be corresponding to the arrival time. The second method is energy-based. It generates beep signals with stronger energy than the background noises. Thereby, the point before and after which the energy distribution differs significantly is regarded as the arrival point of a beep signal. Through extensive experiments, Liu et al. [13] employ the second method due to its higher accuracy.

## 2.2 Attacks Against Peer Assisted Localization

As the current PAL system is designed for non-adversarial settings, it is highly vulnerable to both insider and outsider attacks. We now analyze the possible vulnerabilities of PAL and present the details of the attacks this research aims to address.

**Insider Attacks.** As peers in PAL are recruited randomly from the neighbors of the target and are beyond the control of the system, their behaviors are hard to predict. We mentioned earlier in this section that peer devices in PAL are mainly responsible for signal emitting and recording. Dishonest peers may launch attacks by cheating in either of them.

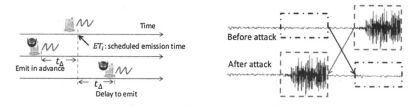

(a) An example of emission attacks    (b) An example of tampering attacks

**Fig. 1.** Attacks from dishonest peers

In the emission task, they may intentionally bring forward or delay their beep emissions rather than follow the schedule of the server. The server computes the distance between two devices by estimating the sound travel time between them. Suppose that the server schedules peer $P_i$ to emit his beep signal $b_i$ at time $ET_i$. Then, if $P_i$ follows this schedule and really emits $b_i$ at time $ET_i$, the server can learn the true distance between $P_i$ and $P_j$ by computing $d_{ij} = c(RT_{ij} - ET_i)$ provided that their clocks are synchronized. Here, $c$ is the sound speed, and $RT_{ij}$ is the arrival time of $b_i$ at $P_j$, which is obtained by analyzing the audio record uploaded by $P_j$. However, if $P_i$ sends his beep (ranging) signal $t_\delta$ earlier or later than $ET_i$ as we show in Fig. 1(a), all the values of $RT_{ij}(j = 1, 2, \cdots, n)$ will be $t_\delta$ smaller or larger than the true value, respectively. As a result, all the distances $d_{ij}$ from $P_i$ to other peers are decreased or increased by the same value $ct_\delta$.

In the recording task, dishonest peers may manipulate their recorded signals before sending them back to the server. Since the server learns $RT_{ij}$ based on the detected position of the related beep signal in the recorded data uploaded by $P_j$, if $P_j$ intentionally modifies the position of this signal (e.g., swaps the positions of this signal and a nearby noise window as we show in Fig. 1(b)), $RT_{ij}$ will diverge from its real value and the obtained distance will also be changed. We name such kind of attacks *tampering attacks*. Compared with emission attacks, tampering attacks are relatively more flexible: a dishonest peer could freely choose one or several phones to change his distances to them without affecting other distances.

In addition, we assume that dishonest peers know their own locations in advance and may collude with each other.

**Outsider Attacks.** Outsider attacks are mainly caused by another vulnerability exists in the energy-based beep detection approach employed in acoustic-ranging. As we show in Fig. 2, the arrival of a beep signal will significantly change

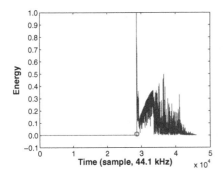

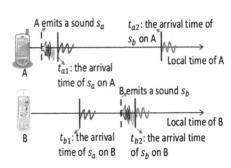

**Fig. 2.** Detecting the arrival time of a signal by identifying the energy saltation point (circled in red) (Color figure online)

**Fig. 3.** Event sequence in the acoustic ranging algorithm of Beepbeep

the energy distribution of the recorded signal. This approach then locates ranging beeps in the recorded signal by identifying the earliest saltation points (marked by a red circle in Fig. 2) from where the energy distribution changes severely. It has no way to tell the difference between beep signals emitted by different devices but based on the assumption that the server's schedule makes these beep signals touch every device in a pre-defined order. Consequently, this technique can be easily fooled by interference signals from attackers even outside the system. For example, if an attacker in the proximity emits a strong signal at the same time when a peer emits his beeps, other peers may mistake the arrival of the interference signal for the legitimate one.

We may alleviate this problem by encrypting the communications between the server and the peers with individualized keys to prevent them and outside attackers from knowing the emission time of other devices. However, attackers may still obstruct the normal ranging with *saturation attacks*, i.e., constantly emitting interference signals. Such attacks will make the audio files recorded by peers full of energy saturation points. It is hard for the server to tell which one of them is due to the arrival of a real ranging signal. In this research, we focus on improving the PAL system to resist the above three attacks.

## 3   Countermeasure Against Insider Attacks

In this section, we first present countermeasures against insider attacks in an ideal scenario without measurement errors in the acoustic ranging. We then consider measurement errors to make our countermeasures more practical.

### 3.1   Countermeasure Against Emission Attacks

We first consider emission attacks, in which dishonest peers violate the server's schedule to bring forward or delay their beep emissions. We temporarily assume that dishonest peers do not perform tampering attacks except those altering distance measurements among themselves.

A naive way to defeat emission attacks is to employ the acoustic ranging algorithm of Beepbeep [15], which can reach an accuracy of 5 cm when there are *unintentional faults* in the timing of emitting signals. Below we briefly explain why this naive approach does not work when there are *intentional attacks*.

In this algorithm, the distance between two peers $P_1$ and $P_2$ is computed by

$$d_{P_1 P_2} = \frac{c}{2} \cdot (t_{b1} - t_{a1} + t_{a2} - t_{b2}) + \frac{d_{AA} + d_{BB}}{2}, \tag{1}$$

where $c$ is the speed of sound and $d_{xy}$ is the distance between device x's speaker and device y's microphone. Other notations are illustrated in Fig. 3. If $P_1$ delays his emission for $t_\Delta$ due to unintentional faults, then both $t_{a1}$, the arrival time of his beep on $P_1$, and $t_{b1}$, the arrival time of the same beep on $P_2$, are increased by $t_\Delta$. These two increments will cancel each other out in Eq. 1, and we will obtain the correct distance measurement between $P_1$ and $P_2$. In fact, the biggest advantage of this mechanism is that many uncertainties including those due to the lack of clock synchronization between devices can be eliminated in the calculation.

Nevertheless, if $P_1$ is an intentional attacker, he can easily bypass this countermeasure by manipulating his recorded sound file to change the value of $t_{a1}$ before uploading it. For instance, $P_1$ can move a noise window of length $t_\Delta$ after the position of his ranging signal to its front in his recorded data, which will result in an error of $c/2 \cdot t_\Delta$ in every distance measurement involving $P_1$. Thus, we require a more advanced mechanism to defend against this type of attack.

Our new mechanism aims to filter out false distance measurements due to emission attacks. For simplicity, we present our theoretical analysis in a two-dimensional scenario. This is reasonable because the peers in PAL are on the same floor. In addition, we first assume the estimated distances among honest peers are exactly equal to their real values and we will consider measurement errors in the final algorithm design. Under these assumptions, we have the following lemma:

**Lemma 1.** *For four peers in the same plane but not in the same line, if one of them launches the emission attack while the other three keep honest, these four peers cannot be embedded in the same plane according to their distance measurements.*

Please find the proof in the extended version. This leads to our first theorem:

**Theorem 1.** *Let $k$ be the maximum possible number of dishonest peers. Assume that the target phone is not in the same line with any three peers, and there are only emission attacks and no other attacks. If we can find $m \geq k + 3$ peers (including the target phone) that can be embedded into the same plane according to distance measurements among them, none of them performs emission attacks.*

Please find the proof in the extended version. We may design an algorithm based on Theorem 1 to identify a group of peers that do not launch emission attacks. However, Theorem 1 does not consider tampering attacks. If dishonest peers are allowed to perform tampering attacks, Theorem 1 is valid only when $k < 3$. We explain the reasons below.

### 3.2    Countermeasure Against Tampering Attacks

In PAL, the emission schedule in PAL guarantees that the arrival sequence of beep signals on each peer is exactly the same as the emission sequence. The server leverages this property to distinguish among different beep signals. Unfortunately, this property may also be exploited by dishonest peers. Two of them with synchronized clocks could associate their recorded data to calculate the time difference that the same beep touched them. Therefore, if there exist three or more dishonest peers that know their own locations, they could cooperate with each other to precisely locate every honest peer with TDoA localization technique.

Once the dishonest peers know the exact locations of the honest peers, they can further invalidate Lemma 1 and Theorem 1 by tampering with their recorded sound signals. For instance, if $P_4$ knows the positions of $P_1, P_2$ and $P_3$, he can easily predict the false distance measurements between him and these peers due to his emission attack. He can then adjust these measurements by altering the positions of corresponding beep signals in his recorded data to make them consistent in the same plane again. Therefore, due to the presence of tampering attacks, even if a peer can be embedded into the same plane with three honest peers, he may still perform emission attacks without being detected. Lemma 1 works iff $k < 3$ in the presence of tampering attacks. When $k < 3$, since the number of dishonest peers is not enough to position honest peers, they do not know how to adjust their distance measurements to make them consistent in the same plane.

We now present countermeasures against tampering attacks. Our proposal requires that all the peers synchronize their clocks before the localization. A possible solution is to use NTP (Network Time Protocol). There exists a free Android application, ClockSync, which can synchronize system clocks of Android devices with atomic time from local or remote NTP servers. If the user can use the root mode, the accuracy can reach milliseconds based on the NTP server.

Since the server knows the scheduled emission time of every peer, he can derive two distance estimations for each pair of peers ($P_i$ and $P_j$): $d_{ij} = c \cdot (t_{ij} - t_{eP_i})$ and $d_{ji} = c \cdot (t_{ji} - t_{eP_j})$, where $t_{ij}$ is the detected arrival time of $P_i$'s ranging signal on $P_j$, and $t_{eP_i}$ is the emission time of $P_i$. Once all the peers' clocks are synchronized, the two estimations for the same pair should be very close: if not exactly the same because of other local uncertainties of smartphones, the difference will, at least, be much less than the error due to attacks. If they are inconsistent (i.e. the difference between them is beyond some predefined threshold $\epsilon$), we can conclude that at least one peer has lied. On the other hands, however, if the two values are consistent, we cannot simply claim that both phones are honest because they may have colluded with each other. Under this assumption, we have the following theorem:

**Theorem 2.** *Let $k$ be the maximum possible number of dishonest peers. Assume that there are Tampering Attacks in addition to Emission Attacks, but no other attacks. If we can find $m \geq k + 3$ peers (including the target phone) that can be embedded into the same plane according to the distance measurements among them, and if any three involved peers are not in the same line, then none of them has performed any attack that affects the distance measurements among them.*

Please find the proof in the extended version.

We design an algorithm based on Theorem 2 to identify a group of peers that do not lie about the distances among them. This algorithm can always succeed when the total number of peers (including the target phone) $n \geq 2k+3$. Its basic idea is to transverse triangles including the target phone (The total number of such triangles is $C(n-1, 2)$) until we find one that can be embedded into the same plane with at least additional $k$ peers. Specifically, for each triangle, we first test whether it can be embedded into the same planes with $R > k$ peers (We name them candidate peers) separately. If so, we place this triangle into a two-dimensional coordinate system by assigning the three peers coordinates consistent with their distance measurements. Once we do like this, the coordinates of the $R$ candidate peers are also determined based on their distances to the triangle vertexes. We compute the required lengths of edges between each pair of the candidate peers and then remove those peers that the derived distance measurements based on their uploaded sound files are contradicting to the corresponding edge lengths. Afterwards, if the number of remained candidate peers is greater than $k$, the algorithm succeeds. Otherwise, it tries the next triangle. Due to the space limit, please find the pseudocode of this algorithm in Appendix.

It is easy to find that the worst-case time complexity of Algorithm 1 is $O(n^4)$. Since $n$ is very small in PAL (usually below 10), this algorithm can be fast enough as you can see in Sect. 5. Once we identify these correct distance measurements, we can execute the last step of PAL to precisely locate the target phone.

Our discussion has assumed that there is no measurement error in acoustic ranging, which is obviously too ideal for the real world. Thus, to apply Algorithm 1 into the real world, we have to consider how to tolerate measurement errors. Due to the space limit, please find this part in Appendix.

# 4 Countermeasure Against Saturation Attacks

So far we have presented the countermeasures against insider attacks. We now consider countermeasures against Saturation Attacks.

As we pointed out in Sect. 2.2, the energy-based beep detection technique in current PAL is a major reason for the existence of saturation attacks. Beepbeep [15] uses a correlation-based technique, which is completely different from the energy-based method, to detect the location of a specific beep signal within a recorded signal. This technique has the potential to be extended to defend against saturation attacks: so long as we can prevent attackers from producing interference beeps that are highly correlated with ranging signals, they cannot affect the normal beep detection in theory because non-correlated interferences will not introduce noisy sharp peaks in the correlation functions with ranging signals.

Beepbeep does not fully solve this challenge since security is not its major focus. It makes all the ranging participants simply share the same ranging signal, which leads to that even if we prevent the outside attackers from knowing this signal, malicious peers inside can still launch saturations attacks to interfere with the server. In this section, we aim to present a new correlation-based method that can better resist saturation attacks.

### 4.1  Modulation-Based Beep Generation

Specifically, to resist the saturation attacks, we need beep signals that satisfy the following requirements:

- Each beep signal is only assigned to one peer. Aside from this peer and the server, it is infeasible for others to guess it in a short time.
- Beep signals have bad cross-correlation with each other or background noises. It is also hard to create a signal that is highly cross-correlated with a beep signal without knowing it.
- Each beep signal has a good auto-correlation property, which is critical for countering multi-path effects.

We find that the modulation technique in Direct Sequence Spread Spectrum (DSSS) [20], which is widely used in digital radio communication systems, can help us generate our required signals. The basic idea is to produce beep signals by using pseudonoise (PN) codes to modulate a sine sound-wave. For simplicity, we use Binary Phase Shifting Key (BPSK) as our modulation strategy. The correlation properties of the obtained signals are completely determined by PN codes (i.e., binary sequences in BPSK). If we can find a family of PN codes that satisfy the requirements above, the resulting signals hold similar properties.

We find that Maximum Length Sequences (M-Sequences) [20], which is a special class of pseudo-random binary sequences generated with maximal linear feedback shift registers, are ideal for such PN codes. An M-Sequence has a good autocorrelation property: the autocorrelation function $R_A(\tau)$ reaches its peak when $\tau = 0$, and as $\tau$ deviates from 0, $R_A(\tau)$ drops quickly. As a result, if we choose non-overlapped subsequences from the same M-Sequence as our PN codes for modulation, they must satisfy the requirements of R2 and R3. In addition,

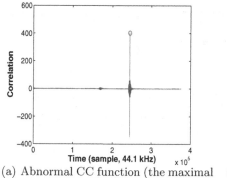

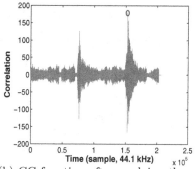

(a) Abnormal CC function (the maximal peak is due to a strong noise or interference signal)

(b) CC function after applying the normalization

**Fig. 4.** An illustration of the effects of random signal attenuation on the results of CC functions (the peaks in red circles are due to the presence of ranging signals) (Color figure online)

to guarantee R1, we can use an extremely long M-Sequence that can produce a huge number of PN codes. For instance, if we use an M-Sequence of length $2^{48} - 1$ and suppose the length of the final PN codes is 256 bits (this length is long enough according to our experiments), we can obtain a family of $2^{40}$ PN codes. Given such a huge space, it is infeasible for an attacker to guess a specific code assigned to a peer.

## 4.2  Beep Detection

To detect a specific ranging signal from a recorded signal, we have to compute their CC function and then search for the sharp peak of this function. This task is not trivial due to the possible existence of some noise peaks, which are mainly caused by the correlation noises of the ranging signal with background noises, interference signals and the same signals due to the multi-path effect.

Because of the careful design of ranging signals, noise peaks due to background noises and interference signals are usually much lower than the desired peaks due to real ranging signals. However, there are abnormal cases where noise peaks suppress the true one when the strength of a ranging signal has become very weak when it arrives at another peer. We show an example in Fig. 4(a). We solve this problem by normalizing recorded signals before correlation. Specifically, when we compute the CC value of a recorded signal $\chi$ at time $t$ with a ranging beep, we first find the maximal signal power of $\chi$ within a window of length $2d$ around $t$. Here, $d$ is the length of the ranging beep. We then use this maximum value to normalize the signal segment involved in computing the CC value at $t$. Figure 4(b) shows the CC function after applying such normalization for the abnormal case in Fig. 4(a). We see that its maximum peak now becomes the one we desire.

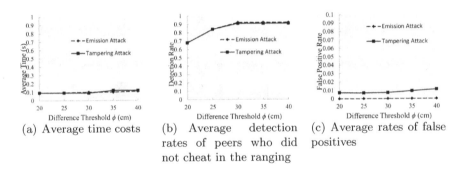

**Fig. 5.** Performance of Algorithm 1 in experiments with real smartphones ($\phi$ is the difference threshold to etermine whether two distance values between the same pair of peers are consistent in the presence of measurement errors.)

Due to the existence of multi-path effects, the maximum peak we identify now may still not correspond to the earliest time that a ranging signal touches a phone. We deal with this problem with a simple method. We first locate the maximum peak whose correlation value is $C_m$. We then compute all the correlation values in a small window (500 samples) before the maximum peak and the first one whose value is larger than $85\%C_m$ is regarded as the earliest presence point of the ranging signal.

## 5   Evaluation

We have performed extensive experiments to evaluate the effects of our proposed countermeasures against the three attacks. We develop an Android application responsible for the beep emission and recording, and deploy it on five different Android smartphones: HTC G14, HTC G7, Motome 600 , HTC G12 and Coolpad 7260. All of them are equipped with two built-in speakers and one microphone that support 44.1 kHz sampling rate. In all the experiments, we use the back speaker and the microphone on every phone. We generate distinct beep signals for each device based on the design in Sect. 4.1. Due to the space limit, we have to put the detailed parameters for this process in the extended version.

To measure the distance between two phones, we make them emit their beep signals at a random order. All their recorded files are then manually copied to a desktop for analysis with a MatLab application that implements the automatic beep detection and distance calculation. We do not implement the last step of PAL because it depends on what WiFi localization technique that the peers use and is also beyond the scope of this paper. We only aim to verify whether our proposals can guarantee that all the distance measurements input into the last step are true.

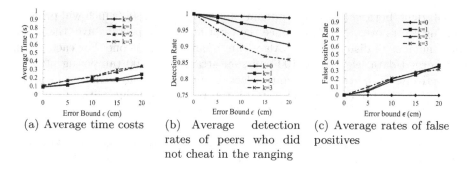

(a) Average time costs  (b) Average detection rates of peers who did not cheat in the ranging  (c) Average rates of false positives

**Fig. 6.** Performance of Algorithm 1 in simulations with different numbers of dishonest peers (the measurement error is uniformly distributed over $[-\epsilon, \epsilon]$ and $\phi = 3\epsilon$)

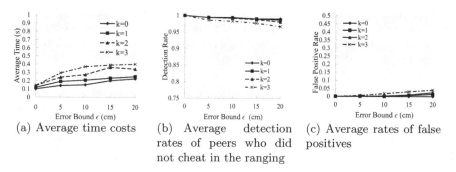

(a) Average time costs  (b) Average detection rates of peers who did not cheat in the ranging  (c) Average rates of false positives

**Fig. 7.** Performance of Algorithm 1 (employing the patch in Appendix to filter false positives) in simulations with different number of dishonest peers (The measurement error is uniformly distributed over $[-\epsilon, \epsilon]$ and $\phi = 3\epsilon$)

## 5.1  Evaluation of Algorithm 1

We first evaluate the real performance of Algorithm 1 against dishonest peers. We conduct experiments in an empty room that is about 10 m × 6 m. We make five students carrying smartphones stand inside a circle of 2 m radius. Their topology is random but ensures line-of-sight between any two devices. Due to the limitation of the penetrating power of the used ranging signal, we do not consider the scenarios where some students stand in the corridor and some students stand in the room. We make phones emit their assigned ranging signals in a random order, and all their recorded data are uploaded to a desktop for analysis. We repeat this process for five times and each time all the students change their positions (i.e. topology). Therefore, we will obtain five groups of recorded signals.

Since we use Formula (1) to calculate distances, both emission and tampering attacks are carried out by manipulating dishonest peers' recorded signals, which are collected earlier. For emission attacks, we move the signal window containing the dishonest peer's ranging signal $m$ samples ahead. For tampering attacks, we simply insert a noise window of $n$ samples immediately after the ranging signal. Here, both $m$ and $n$ are random values over $[260, 780]$, which will produce ranging errors over $[1\,m, 3\,m]$. Since the total number of peers is five, the maximum number of dishonest peer Algorithm 1 can tolerate is one. For each group of recorded data, we launch 100 emission attacks and 100 tampering attacks, respectively. Each attack randomly selects one device as the dishonest peer and another as the target peer. We perform the pairwise ranging with our matlab application and can get 500 inputs for Algorithm 1 for each kind of attack.

We then run Algorithm 1 for each input and each value of $\phi$, which is the threshold for determining whether two distances are consistent, from 20 cm to 40 cm in steps of 5 cm. We have applied the patches for reducing FPs and FNs. To filter out FPs, we use 2.6 m as the upper bound for the average distance of an honest peer. The average detection rate of peers who did not cheat in the ranging, and the average rate of false positives are plotted in Fig. 5(b) and (c), respectively. We can see that the average detection rate exceeds 90 % in both two attacks when $\phi$ is larger than 30 cm. The false positive rates are always small enough to ignore. In addition, the average time cost is below 0.15 s and increases slightly in $\phi$.

Due to the limited number of smartphones available for experiments, the above experiments only consider the scenario with three honest peers and one dishonest peer. To better evaluate the performance of Algorithm 1 with more peers, especially more dishonest ones, we do further simulations using Java language programs. We assume that there are 10 peer phones within an area of $4\,m \times 4\,m$ and one of them is the target phone. We think it is difficult and also meaningless to employ more peers in the real world. The positions of each node is selected uniformly over the $4\,m \times 4\,m$ area. Since the total number of nodes is fixed to ten, the maximum number of dishonest nodes this algorithm can tolerate is three. These dishonest peers are uniformly selected, and they are made to perform emission attacks and tampering attacks concurrently: bidirectional distance measurements between dishonest and honest nodes are enlarged by the same value $\delta$, which is a random value over $[1\,m, 3\,m]$. We also assume the measurement error is uniformly distributed over $[-\epsilon, \epsilon]$, and two distances measurements between the same pair of nodes are thought consistent if and only if their difference is within $[-3\epsilon, 3\epsilon]$. We make Algorithm 1 try all the possible coordinate combinations of nodes in $S_1$ to reduce false negatives.

We run this algorithm 1000 times for each value of $\epsilon$ from 0 cm to 20 cm in steps of 4 cm and each possible value of $k$. In each run, all the nodes are assigned new positions. Figure 6(a) shows that the average simulation time increases in both $k$ and $\epsilon$. The reason for the first observation is obvious: a larger number of dishonest peers makes the algorithm harder to find enough number of nodes that can be embedded into the same plane. The reason for the second observation, however, is not so straightforward. According to our analysis, the increase is due to the fact that larger ranging errors usually bring more ambiguous nodes as Fig. 9(a) shows, which are extremely time consuming to deal with.

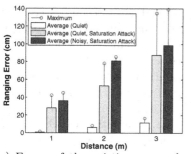

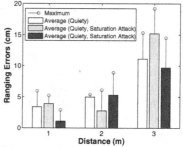

(a) Errors of the existing energy-based acoustic ranging approach

(b) Errors of the proposed correlation-based acoustic ranging approach

**Fig. 8.** Comparing the errors of the existing acoustic ranging approach in PAL and our proposal under different environments

We plot the average detection rate, and the average false positive rate in Fig. 6(b) and (c), respectively. We can see that Algorithm 1 works exactly the same as we expect in the cases without measurement errors: it can identify all the nodes that did not cheat in the ranging without bringing about any false positives. However, when we introduce measurement errors, Algorithm 1 produces both FNs and FPs. As we have applied our measure for avoiding FNs, the detection rate exceeds 90 % for all the cases except the one with three dishonest peers and $\epsilon = 20\,\text{cm}$. The rate of FPs, however, is a little bit too high.

We then apply the patch mentioned in Appendix to reduce false positives: we consider a node to be malicious if its average distance to other nodes exceeds 3.7 m. We determine this threshold with extensive experiments. The new result is plotted in Fig. 7. The false positive rates are now confined below 4 %, which are much smaller that those in Fig. 6(c).

## 5.2 Evaluation of Countermeasures Against Saturation Attacks

We next evaluate the real effects of our acoustic ranging mechanism against saturation attacks. We conduct ranging between HTC G7 and Coolpad 7260 in the three indoor environments: (1) quiet, (2) quiet with Saturation Attack and (3) Noisy with Saturation Attack. Please find the detailed information about these environments in the extended version.

In all the experiments, we place two phones parallel to each other and back to back. For each environment, we vary the distance between two phones among 1 m, 2 m and 3 m, and repeat each experiment for four times. Besides our proposed correlation-based acoustic ranging, we also implement the energy-based method proposed in [13] as the reference. We present the average and the maximum ranging errors of these two methods in Fig. 8(b) and (a), respectively. We see that the ranging errors of the existing energy-based method could exceed 1 m in the latter two cases when two phones are placed 3 m apart. For our proposal, however, we do not observe any big difference in the ranging errors between the environments with and without saturation attacks or noises. All the measurement errors are below 20 cm. We obtain similar results among other smartphones. This well demonstrates that our modulation-based acoustic ranging could well defend against the saturation attack.

In addition, the total signal processing time (i.e., compute the TOAs of the two ranging signals within the two recorded signals) in our proposal is 0.73 s on average. Although this value is much higher than 0.24 s in the energy-based approach, it is still acceptable. According to our analysis, most of the time is spent on the computations of the cross-correlation values. We may leverage the emission time of each ranging signal to reduce this time.

## 6    Related Work

Our work is towards robust peer-assisted indoor localization by defending against different kinds of attacks. Although PAL is novel, robust localization and ranging are not new. Related theory and systems have been developed for a long time, especially in the context of wireless sensor networks.

Most of current robust localization algorithms are designed for beacon-based localization systems. These systems require the presence of special nodes, so-called beacons or anchors, that know their own locations. Other nodes estimate their locations by measuring their distances to a set of beacons. Robust localization algorithms [10–12,18,25] then aims to enable a node to locate himself precisely even if some beacons are malicious. However, these algorithms have a premise that most of the beacons are still honest. For instance, Misra et al. [14] prove that the minimum number of honest beacons required for exact localization of the target in the presence of dishonest beacons is $\lceil n/2 \rceil + 2$, where $n$ is the total number beacons. In our work, if we regard peer nodes as beacons, since the errors of their rough locations from WiFi localization reach 4 m on average, all of them can be regarded to have lied about their locations considering the strict requirement of indoor localization on the accuracy. As a result, we cannot directly use robust localization algorithms in this area. Compared with beacon-based localization, the scenario of beacon-less localization [5,9,19] is much closer to our problem. However, few of them consider security issues.

The last attack that we focus on is due to vulnerabilities in acoustic ranging. Girod et al. [6,7] propose a robust acoustic ranging mechanism that cleverly exploits signal modulation. Specially, the system is composed by a transmitter and a receiver. The transmitter produces a distinct sound by modulating a sine sound-wave with some special PN code. After the transmitter plays this sound, the receiver detects the arrival time of this sound by searching for the first sharp peak in the cross-correlation function between this sound and the recorded signal. Using a known sound speed and the emission time, the distance travelling from the transmitter and the receiver can be computed. While their work can work very well even in very obstructed or noisy environments, they only consider the interference from background noises and reflections, and do not consider intentional interference from attackers.

# 7   Conclusion

Peer-assisted localization (PAL) through acoustic ranging could significantly improve the accuracy of WiFi localization. In this paper, we have studied the problem of robust PAL in the presence of dishonest peers and outside attackers. We first show that so long as the number of peers that can be embedded in the same plane according to their distance measurements exceeds some threshold, we can guarantee that none of them lies on these distances. We then present an algorithm based on this principle to identify peers having not cheated in the current localization, which can finish in polynomial time even in the worst case. We also present a robust acoustic ranging mechanism that leverages signal modulation to resist saturating interference from outside attackers. Extensive experiment on real smartphones have demonstrated that our countermeasures can greatly improve the robustness of peer-assisted localization.

# Appendix

### Practical Consideration of Measurement Errors

Our discussion has assumed that there is no measurement error in acoustic ranging, which is obviously too ideal for the real world. Thus, to apply Algorithm 1 into the real world, we consider how to tolerate measurement errors in this subsection.

Our solution is straightforward: facing measurement errors, Algorithm 1 regards two different distance measurements between the same pair of peers, or a distance measurement and its expected value, as consistent so long as their difference is below some pre-defined threshold $\phi$. We empirically set $\phi = 3\epsilon$, where $\epsilon$ is the upper bound of the measurement error. Nevertheless, this mechanism has a side effect that it can produce both false negatives and false positives.

(a) Source of false negatives          (b) Source of false positives

**Fig. 9.** False positives and negatives of Algorithm 1

False negatives (FNs) refer to that some peers which did not cheat in the ranging are falsely classified as dishonest by Algorithm 1. They mainly occur

---

**Input:** $P_{1,2,\cdots,n}$: $n$ peer points
$P_t$: the target point
$\{d_{ij}|i,j \in \{1,\cdots,n,t\}\}$: $d_{ij}$ is the distance between $P_i$ and $P_j$ based on the recorded data of $P_j$

1  **for** $i = 0, \cdots, n$ **do**
2  |  **if** $d_{it}$ *is conflicting with* $d_{ti}$ **then** continue;
3  |  **for** $j = i+1, \cdots, n$ **do**
4  |  |  **if** $j - i > Malicous_{max} + 1$ **then** break ;
5  |  |  **if** $d_{jt}$ *is conflicting with* $d_{tj}$ *or* $d_{ij}$ *is conflicting with* $d_{ji}$ **then** continue;
6  |  |  Assign $P_t$, $P_i$ and $P_j$ two-dimension coordinates that meet their side-length requirements ;
7  |  |  $failCount = 0$;
8  |  |  Define an empty set $S_1$;
9  |  |  **foreach** $P_k(k \notin \{i,j\})$ **do**
10 |  |  |  **if** $P_k$ *can be embedded in the plane of* $\triangle P_t P_i P_j$ **then**
11 |  |  |  |  compute the coordinates of $P_k$;
12 |  |  |  |  $S_1 = S_1 \cup \{P_k\}$;
13 |  |  |  **end**
14 |  |  |  **else**
15 |  |  |  |  $failCount + +$;
16 |  |  |  |  **if** $failCount > n - 2 - Malicious_{max}$ **then** break;
17 |  |  |  **end**
18 |  |  **end**
19 |  |  **if** $Size(S_1) < Malicious_{max}$ **then** continue;
20 |  |  Define another empty set $S_2$;
21 |  |  **foreach** $P_a \in S_1$ **do**
22 |  |  |  **if** $S_2$ *is empty* **then**
23 |  |  |  |  $S_2 \cup \{P_a\}$;
24 |  |  |  |  Continue;
25 |  |  |  **end**
26 |  |  |  **foreach** $P_b \in S_2$ **do**
27 |  |  |  |  Compute $d'_{ab} = \sqrt{(P_a.x - P_b.x)^2 + (P_a.y - P_b.y)^2}$;
28 |  |  |  |  **if** $d_{ba}$ *is consistent with* $d'_{ab}$ **then** $S_2 \cup \{P_a\}$;
29 |  |  |  |  **if** $d_{ab}$ *is conflicting with* $d'_{ab}$ **then** $S_2 - \{P_b\}$;
30 |  |  |  **end**
31 |  |  **end**
32 |  |  **if** $Size(S_2) >= Malicious_{max}$ **then**
33 |  |  |  Output $S_2 \cup \{P_i, P_j\}$;
34 |  |  |  Stop the Algorithm;
35 |  |  **end**
36 |  **end**
37 **end**

**Algorithm 1.** Algorithm to identify true distances in the presence of emission attacks and tampering attacks in the special cases that the three vertices of the winning triangle $\triangle P_i P_j P_t$ in Algorithm 1 are either too close to each other or approximately in the same straight line, which makes the algorithm determine false positions for some nodes in the presence of measurement errors. We show an example in Fig. 9(a). Suppose $\triangle P_1 P_2 P_3$ is the winning triangle and the algorithm is computing the coordinates of $P_4$ at line 11. We also assume that another node $P_4'$ satisfies the condition: $d_{P_4 P_1} = d_{P_4' P_1}$ and $d_{P_4 P_2} = d_{P_4' P_2}$. Then, since $P_1, P_2, P_3$ are almost collinear, the distance measurement between $P_4'$ and $P_3$ can be even closer to $d_{P_4 P_3}$ than the measurement between $P_4$ and $P_3$ in the presence of measurement errors. As a result, the algorithm may assign the coordinates of $P_4'$ to $P_4$, which will lead to contradictories at line 25 or 26 and then falsely classify $P_4$ as a dishonest node. We can solve this problem by recording both coordinates of such special nodes, and then executing Line 21–31 for each possible coordinate combination of the nodes in $S_1$.

False positives (FPs) refer to that some dishonest peers which launched attacks are falsely reported as honest by Algorithm 1. They are mainly caused by dishonest nodes that are located on one side of the other nodes (i.e., not surrounded by any triangles formed by other nodes), launching emission attacks. We show a typical example in Fig. 9(b). Suppose $P_1$, $P_2$ and $P_3$ are honest, while $P_4$ is dishonest and delayed his emission for some time. So, the three distance measurements between $P_4$ and the other three nodes are increased by the same value, which is impossible in theory. However, when we move $P_4$ further from $\triangle P_1 P_2 P_3$, for example to the new position of $P_4'$, the real increments of the three distances are very close even if their absolute values are very large. Thus, in the presence of measurement errors, these different changes may be approximated to be equal, which leads to the fact that $P_4$ can be accepted to be at some position in the same plane of $\triangle P_1 P_2 P_3$.

We find that dishonest nodes causing FPs usually do not choose to shorten their distance measurements. This is because the peer phones in PAL should be in the vicinity in order to receive each other's ranging signals. If the dishonest peers not surrounded by other nodes shorten their distance measurements, they are very likely to be falsely positioned at a place surrounded by some honest peers, and so they can be captured. In addition, some distance measurements in this case may even become minus, which is obviously ridiculous. Therefore, these dishonest peers usually choose to enlarge their distance measurements. However, since they are located on one side of the other nodes, their real average distances to other nodes are already larger than those of normal nodes. If they further enlarge their distance measurements, they will expose a larger anomaly. We leverage this observation to add a patch to Algorithm 1 to reduce false positives: before we check the size of $S_2$ at Line 32, we first remove each node whose average distance measurement to other nodes exceeds some threshold.

# References

1. Azizyan, M., Constandache, I., Choudhury, R.R.: Surroundsense: mobile phone localization via ambience fingerprinting. In: Proceedings of the 15th MOBICOM, pp. 261–272. ACM (2009)
2. Bahl, P., Padmanabhan, V.: Radar: an in-building RF-based user location and tracking system. In: Proceedings of the 19th INFOCOM, pp. 775–784. IEEE (2000)
3. Borriello, G., Liu, A., Offer, T., Palistrant, C., Sharp, R.: WALRUS: wireless acoustic location with room-level resolution using ultrasound. In: Proceedings of the 3rd MobiSys, pp. 191–203. ACM (2005)
4. Chen, Y., Trappe, W., Martin, R.P.: Attack detection in wireless localization. In: Proceedings of the 26th INFOCOM, pp. 1964–1972. IEEE (2007)
5. Fang, L., Du, W., Ning, P.: A beacon-less location discovery scheme for wireless sensor networks. In: Proceedings of the 24th INFOCOM, vol. 1, pp. 161–171. IEEE (2005)
6. Girod, L., Estrin, D.: Robust range estimation using acoustic and multimodal sensing. In: Proceedings of the 2001 IROS, vol. 3, pp. 1312–1320. IEEE (2001)
7. Girod, L.: A self-calibrating system of distributed acoustic arrays. Ph.D. thesis, University of California Los Angeles (2005)
8. Hazas, M., Kray, C., Gellersen, H., Agbota, H., Kortuem, G., Krohn, A.: A relative positioning system for co-located mobile devices. In: Proceedings of the 3rd MobiSys, pp. 177–190. ACM (2005)
9. Ji, X., Zha, H.: Sensor positioning in wireless ad-hoc sensor networks using multidimensional scaling. In: Proceedings of the 23rd INFOCOM, vol. 4, pp. 2652–2661. IEEE (2004)
10. Li, Z., Trappe, W., Zhang, Y., Nath, B.: Robust statistical methods for securing wireless localization in sensor networks. In: Proceedings of the 4th IPSN, pp. 91–98. IEEE (2005)
11. Liu, D., Ning, P., Du, W.: Detecting malicious beacon nodes for secure location discovery in wireless sensor networks. In: Proceedings of the 25th ICDCS, pp. 609–619. IEEE (2005)
12. Liu, D., Ning, P., Liu, A., Wang, C., Du, W.: Attack-resistant location estimation in wireless sensor networks. ACM Trans. Inf. Syst. Secur. (TISSEC) 11(4), 22 (2008)
13. Liu, H., Gan, Y., Yang, J., Sidhom, S., Wang, Y., Chen, Y., Ye, F.: Push the limit of WiFi based localization for smartphones. In: Proceedings of the 18th MOBICOM, pp. 305–316. ACM (2012)
14. Misra, S., Bhardwaj, S., Xue, G.: Rosetta: robust and secure mobile target tracking in a wireless ad hoc environment. In: Proceedings of the 2006 MILCOM, pp. 1–7. IEEE (2006)
15. Peng, C., Shen, G., Zhang, Y., Li, Y., Tan, K.: Beepbeep: a high accuracy acoustic ranging system using cots mobile devices. In: Proceedings of the 5th SenSys, pp. 1–14. ACM (2007)
16. Priyantha, N., Chakraborty, A., Balakrishnan, H.: The cricket location-support system. In: Proceedings of the 6th MOBICOM, pp. 32–43. ACM (2000)
17. Rai, A., Chintalapudi, K., Padmanabhan, V., Sen, R.: Zee: zero-effort crowdsourcing for indoor localization. In: Proceedings of the 18th MOBICOM, pp. 293–304. ACM (2012)
18. Ray, S., Ungrangsi, R., Pellegrini, D., Trachtenberg, A., Starobinski, D.: Robust location detection in emergency sensor networks. In: Proceedings of the 22nd INFOCOM, vol. 2, pp. 1044–1053. IEEE (2003)

19. Shang, Y., Rumi, W., Zhang, Y., Fromherz, M.: Localization from connectivity in sensor networks. IEEE Trans. Parallel Distrib. Syst. **15**(11), 961–974 (2004)
20. Simon, M., Omura, J., Scholtz, R., Levitt, B.: Spread Spectrum Communications Handbook, vol. 2. McGraw-Hill, New York (1994)
21. Wu, C., Yang, Z., Liu, Y., Xi, W.: Will: wireless indoor localization without site survey. In: Proceedings of the 31st INFOCOM, pp. 64–72. IEEE (2012)
22. Yang, J., Sidhom, S., Chandrasekaran, G., Vu, T., Liu, H., Cecan, N., Chen, Y., Gruteser, M., Martin, R.: Detecting driver phone use leveraging car speakers. In: Proceedings of the 17th MOBICOM, pp. 97–108. ACM (2011)
23. Yang, Z., Wu, C., Liu, Y.: Locating in fingerprint space: wireless indoor localization with little human intervention. In: Proceedings of the 18th MOBICOM, pp. 269–280. ACM (2012)
24. Ye, H., Gu, T., Zhu, X., Xu, J., Tao, X., Lu, J., Jin, N.: Ftrack: infrastructure-free floor localization via mobile phone sensing. In: Proceedings of the 10th PerCom, pp. 2–10. IEEE (2012)
25. Zhong, S., Jadliwala, M., Upadhyaya, S., Qiao, C.: Towards a theory of robust localization against malicious beacon nodes. In: Proceedings of the 27th INFOCOM, pp. 1391–1399. IEEE (2008)

# Leveraging Real-Life Facts to Make Random Passwords More Memorable

Mahdi Nasrullah Al-Ameen[1]($\boxtimes$), Kanis Fatema[1], Matthew Wright[1], and Shannon Scielzo[2]

[1] Department of Computer Science and Engineering,
The University of Texas at Arlington, Arlington, TX, USA
{mahdi.al-ameen,kanis.fatema}@mavs.uta.edu, mwright@cse.uta.edu
[2] Department of Psychology, The University of Texas at Arlington,
Arlington, TX, USA
scielzo@uta.edu

**Abstract.** User-chosen passwords fail to provide adequate security. System-assigned random passwords are more secure but suffer from memorability problems. We argue that the system should remove this burden from users by assisting with the memorization of randomly assigned passwords. To meet this need, we aim to apply the scientific understanding of long-term memory. In particular, we examine the efficacy of augmenting a system-assigned password scheme based on textual recognition by providing users with *verbal cues*—real-life facts corresponding to the assigned keywords. In addition, we explore the usability gain of including images related to the keywords along with the verbal cues. We conducted a multi-session in-lab user study with 52 participants, where each participant was assigned three different passwords, each representing one study condition. Our results show that the textual recognition-based scheme offering verbal cues had a significantly higher login success rate (94 %) as compared to the control condition, i.e., textual recognition without verbal cues (61 %). The comparison between textual and graphical recognition reveals that when users were provided with verbal cues, adding images did not significantly improve the login success rate, but it did lead to faster recognition of the assigned keywords. We believe that our findings make an important contribution to understanding the extent to which different types of cues impact the usability of system-assigned passwords.

**Keywords:** Usable security · System-assigned passwords · Memorability · Verbal cues

## 1 Introduction

Traditional user-chosen textual passwords suffer from security problems because of password reuse and predictable patterns [13,38]. Users are tasked with creating a password that should be both secure and memorable, but they typically

© Springer International Publishing Switzerland 2015
G. Pernul et al. (Eds.): ESORICS 2015, Part II, LNCS 9327, pp. 438–455, 2015.
DOI: 10.1007/978-3-319-24177-7_22

lack information about what is secure in the face of modern cracking and attacks tools, as well as how to construct memorable strings, memorize them quickly, and accurately recall them later. Faced with this challenge, users often compromise on security and create a weak but memorable password. While policies have been deployed to get users to create stronger passwords [19,38], such policies do not necessarily lead to more secure passwords but do adversely affect memorability [33,38].

Studies in psychology have shown that recognition, such as identifying an assigned picture from a set, is an easier memory task than recall, such as traditional textual passwords [6,42,43]. Inspired by these findings, researchers have proposed and examined recognition-based authentication schemes as alternatives to pure recall-based schemes in hopes that by reducing the memory burden on users, more secure passwords can be generated. Wright et al. [45] implemented the concept of recognition for a text-based scheme, where users are shown several portfolios of keywords (e.g., "Cheetah", "Mango", "Camera", etc.), and one keyword per portfolio serves as the authentication secret that they have to recognize during login. Passfaces [1] is an example of a graphical recognition-based scheme, which is now commercially available and deployed by a number of large websites.[1]

To ensure security, the commercial Passfaces [1] product assigns a random image for each portfolio instead of allowing users to choose. With system-assigned passwords, the user does not have to guess whether a password is secure, and the system can ensure that all passwords offer the desired level of security. Additionally, while password reuse could pose a serious security threat [13], using system-assigned passwords ensures that users do not reuse a password (or modification thereof) already used on another account. Unfortunately, it is difficult for most people to memorize system-assigned passwords for both textual [45] and graphical recognition [17]. Thus, it still remains a critical challenge to design an authentication scheme that offers satisfactory memorability for system-assigned random passwords.

## 1.1   Contributions

To this end, we draw upon several prominent theories of cognitive psychology to enhance the memorability of system-assigned recognition-based passwords. In particular, we examine the impact of offering *verbal cues*, i.e., real-life facts related to the system-assigned keywords. For example, "Cheetah is faster than any other land animal" is a verbal cue for the keyword "Cheetah". The use of cues facilitates a detailed encoding that helps to transfer the authentication information (e.g., assigned keywords) from the working memory to long-term memory at registration [7], helping users recognize their keywords when logging in later. We provide a detailed discussion on these memorization processes in Sect. 3.

The study of Wright et al. [45] found insufficient memorability for textual recognition, where the keywords in a portfolio remained same but were shown at

---

[1] http://www.realuser.com/ shows testimonials about Passfaces from customers.

different positions each time that portfolio was loaded. The authors anticipated that showing the keywords in the same position each time would improve the memorability for recognition-based schemes and suggested the approach to be examined in future work. We adopt suggestion of Wright et al. [45] to design our study conditions by showing the keywords in a portfolio in the same position each time that a portfolio is loaded. We also accommodate the *variant response* feature in our schemes to gain resilience against observation attacks like shoulder surfing (see Sect. 3.5 for details).

To examine the impact of verbal cues in improving the memorability for textual recognition, we design a scheme, *TextV*: **Text**ual Recognition with **V**erbal cues, and compare it with the *Control* condition that requires users remembering the assigned keywords without the help of verbal cue. In addition, we aim to understand whether adding images related to the keywords contributes to higher memorability than when users are provided with just verbal cues. To achieve the goal, we design another scheme, *GraphicV*: **Graphic**al Recognition with **V**erbal cues, and compare it with the TextV scheme. To the best of our knowledge, no study yet has compared textual and graphical recognition-based schemes in terms of usability.

In our within-group study with 52 participants, every participant was assigned three different passwords, each representing one study condition. The major findings from our study include:

- In contrast to the suggestion of Wright et al. [45], keeping the position of keywords fixed in a portfolio did not provide a satisfactory login success rate (61.5%).
- Verbal cues made a significant contribution in improving the login success rate for textual recognition (94.2%).
- Despite the *picture superiority effect* (see Sect. 3), we found no significant difference between textual and graphical recognition in terms of login success rate when both conditions included verbal cues.
- We did find, however, a significant improvement in login time for graphical recognition as compared to textual recognition, even though the number of attempts for successful logins did not differ significantly between these conditions.

We organize the rest of this paper as follows: In Sect. 2, we give an overview of notable authentication schemes with a discussion on their limitations and the respective scopes of possible improvements. In Sect. 3, we explain from the perspective of cognitive psychology how the design choices for our study conditions are set up. We then describe our study procedure in Sect. 4 and present the results in Sect. 5. In Sect. 6, we discuss the findings from our study and highlight the possible directions for future research, followed by a conclusion in Sect. 7.

## 2    Related Work

In this section, we give a brief overview of notable textual and graphical password schemes in which we highlight why existing schemes are insufficient.

## 2.1  Textual Password Schemes

**Traditional Passwords.** Traditional user-chosen textual passwords are fraught with security problems because of password reuse and predictable patterns [13, 38]. Different password restriction policies (e.g., increasing the minimum password length, requiring a combination of different types of characters, and using password strength meters) have been deployed to get users to create stronger passwords [19,38]. However, in separate studies, Proctor et al. [33] and Shay et al. [38] report that such policies do not necessarily lead to more secure passwords but do adversely affect memorability in some cases.

**Mnemonic Passwords.** Kuo et al. [28] studied passwords based on mnemonic phrases, in which the user chooses a memorable phrase and uses a character (often the first letter) to represent each word in the phrase. Results [28] show that user-selected mnemonic passwords are slightly more resistant to brute-force attacks than traditional passwords. However, mnemonic passwords are found to be more predictable when users choose common phrases to create their passwords. A properly chosen dictionary may further increase the success rate in guessing mnemonic passwords [28].

**System-Assigned Passwords.** System-assigned random textual password schemes are more secure but fail to provide sufficient memorability, even when natural-language words are used [37,45]. Wright et al. [45] compared the usability of three different system-assigned textual password schemes: Word Recall, Word Recognition, and Letter Recall. None of these schemes had sufficient memorability rates.

**PTP.** Forget et al. [20,22] proposed the Persuasive Text Passwords (PTP) scheme, in which the user first creates a password, and PTP improves its security by placing randomly-chosen characters at random positions into the password. PTP is resilient against attacks exploiting password reuse and predictable patterns. Unfortunately, the memorability for PTP is just 25 % when two random characters are inserted at random positions [20].

**Cognitive Questions.** Furnell et al. [23] revealed the potential of cognitive questions and reported a high level of user satisfaction in using that for primary authentication. However, Just and Aspinall [27] identified the usability and security problems of using cognitive questions for authentication, and several other studies [34,36] reported the vulnerability of this approach to targeted guessing attacks.

## 2.2  Graphical Password Schemes

Graphical password schemes can be divided into three categories [8], based on the kind of memory leveraged by the systems: (i) Drawmetric (recall-based), (ii) Locimetric (cued-recall-based), and (iii) Cognometric (recognition-based).

**Drawmetric.** The user is asked to reproduce a drawing in this category of graphical passwords. In *Draw-a-Secret (DAS)* [26], a user draws on top of a grid, and the password is represented as the sequence of grid squares. Nali and Thorpe [29] have shown that users choose predictable patterns in DAS that include drawing symmetric images with 1–3 pen strokes, using grid cell corners and lines (presumably as points of reference) and placing their drawing approximately in the center of the grid.

*BDAS* [16] intends to reduce the amount of symmetry in the user's drawing by adding background images, but this may introduce other predictable behaviors such as targeting similar areas of the images or image-specific patterns [8]. DAS and BDAS have recall rates of no higher than 80 %.

**Locimetric.** The password schemes in this category present users with one or more images as a memory cue to assist them selecting their particular points on the image(s). In the *Passpoints* [9] scheme, users select a sequence of click-points on a single image as their password. *Cued Click-Points (CCP)* [11] is a modified version of Passpoints, where users sequentially choose one click-point on each of five images. Dirik et al. [15] developed a model that can predict 70–80 % of users' click positions in Passpoints. To address this issue, Chiasson et al. proposed *Persuasive Cued Click-Points (PCCP)* [12,21], in which a randomly-positioned viewport is shown on top of the image during password creation, and users select their click-point within this viewport. The memorability for PCCP was found to be 83–94 %.

In a follow-up study, Chiasson et al. [10] found predictability in users' click points, showing that in Passpoints, the click points are roughly evenly spaced across the image, in straight lines starting from left to right, and either completely horizontal or sloping from top to bottom. The authors [10] indicate that predictability is still a security concern for PCCP.

**Cognometric.** In this recognition-based category of graphical passwords, the user is asked to recognize and identify their password images from a set of distractor images. *Passfaces* [1] is the most studied cognometric scheme as it is commercially deployed by a number of large websites. The commercial Passfaces [1] product assigns a random set of faces instead of allowing users to choose, since the research [14] has found that users select predictable faces, biased by race, gender, and attractiveness of faces. However, Everitt et al. [17] show that users have difficulty in remembering system-assigned Passfaces.

Davis et al. [14] proposed the *Story* scheme, in which users select a sequence of images as their password and, to aid memorability, are encouraged to mentally construct a story to connect those images. During login, users have to identify their images in accurate order from a panel of decoy images. Though the user choices in Story are found to be more varied than the face-recognition-based scheme, the results still display some exploitable patterns, and the user study showed a memorability rate of about 85 % [14].

In a recent study [5], Al-Ameen et al. found satisfactory memorability by combining various cues for graphical recognition, which suggests that the use of cues is very promising and motivates further study. In their experiment [5], the authors did not examine the impact of different cues, nor they studied textual recognition. Our deeper investigation on this issue helps to understand how humans' cognitive abilities could be leveraged through verbal cues for enhanced memorability in system-assigned textual recognition-based passwords. We also compare textual and graphical recognition to explore the usability gain of accommodating images, when users are provided with verbal cues.

## 3   System Design

Hlywa et al. [25] provide a guideline to design recognition-based authentication schemes with password-level security. We follow this guideline to design our study conditions, where the user is assigned five keywords at registration and has to recognize each of the assigned keywords from a distinct portfolio of 16 keywords during login. A successful authentication requires the user to recognize all five keywords correctly. For an unsuccessful login, the user is shown an error message at the end of the login attempt but not informed on which portfolio the mistake was made.

In our study, we implement three different recognition-based schemes. In Control condition, users remember and recognize the assigned keywords without the help of verbal cues (see Fig. 1). In TextV scheme, the system offers verbal cues to help users with the memorization and recognition of the assigned keywords, where cues are shown both at registration and login (see Fig. 2). In GraphicV scheme, the system provides users with images corresponding to the keywords along with the verbal cues (see Fig. 3). In this section, we explain our design choices from the perspective of cognitive psychology and existing password literature.

### 3.1   Memory Retrieval

Users are required to perform a recognition task in our study. Researchers in psychology have found that recognition (identifying the correct item among a set of distractors) is easier than recall (reproducing the item from memory) [42] and have developed two main theories to explain this: *Generate-recognize theory* [6] and *Strength theory* [43].

Generate-recognize theory [6] speculates that recall is a two-phase process. In the generate phase, a list of candidate words is formed by searching longterm memory. Then, in the recognize phase, the list of words is evaluated to see if they can be recognized as the sought-out memory. According to this theory, recognition tasks do not utilize the generation phase and are thus faster and easier to perform. Strength theory [43] states that although recall and recognition involve the same memory task, recognition requires a lower threshold of strength that makes it easier. The point is commonly illustrated in examples from everyday life. For example, multiple choice questions are frequently easier than essay questions since the correct answer is available for recognition.

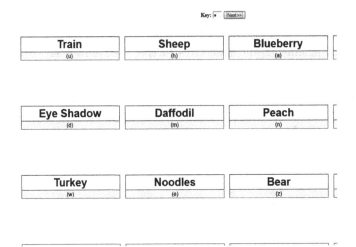

**Fig. 1.** A partial screen shot of the *Control* condition during login. Users enter the key, a lowercase letter shown in parentheses, in the password field (on top) to select the corresponding keyword. The keys are randomly assigned to keyword each time the portfolio is loaded, where no two keywords share the same key. During login, users are shown five such portfolios, where each presents a distinct set of 16 keywords including one of the five assigned keywords.

## 3.2   Semantic Priming

Having a fixed set of objects in a certain place aids to augment *semantic priming*, which refers to recognizing an object through its relationship with other objects around it [1]. Semantic priming thus eases the recognition task [1]. For example, in Fig. 3, the clock is not only in the upper-left-hand corner each time, but it is always next to the mango and above the dining table. This establishes a relationship between the objects and reinforces semantic priming. Thus, in each of our study conditions, the keywords in a portfolio remain same and presented at a fixed position whenever that a portfolio is loaded.

## 3.3   Verbal Cues

We incorporate the scientific understanding of long-term memory to advance the usability properties of recognition-based authentication. According to the cognitive memory model proposed by Atkinson and Shiffrin [7], any new information is transferred to short-term memory (STM) through the sensory organs, where STM holds the information as *memory codes*, or mental representations of selected parts of the information. The information is transferred from STM to long-term memory (LTM), but only if it can be further processed and encoded. This encoding helps people to remember and retrieve the processed information efficiently over an extended period of time. To motivate such encoding, we examine the efficacy of providing verbal cues with the keywords.

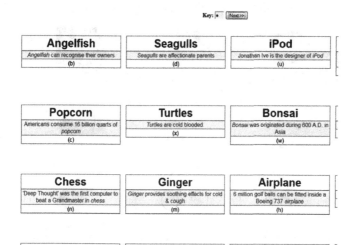

**Fig. 2.** A partial screen shot of *TextV* scheme during login. The facts corresponding to each keyword appear below that keyword.

If the system provides verbal cues, i.e., real-life facts related to the keywords, then users may focus their attention on associating the keywords with the corresponding cues, which should help to process and encode the information in memory and store them in the long-term memory. For example, the keyword "Turtles" is associated with the verbal cue "Turtles are cold blooded". The cues would also assist users to recognize the keywords in the future and thus enhance their memorability.

Psychology research [6,42] has shown that it is difficult to remember information spontaneously without memory cues, and this suggests that authentication schemes should provide users with cues to aid memory retrieval. *Encoding specificity theory* [41] postulates that the most effective cues are those that are present at the time of remembering. In TextV and GraphicV schemes, verbal cues are provided during registration, i.e., the learning period, and also at login.

### 3.4   Visual Memory

In GraphicV scheme, we leverage users' visual memory, in addition to offering verbal cues. Psychology research shows that the human brain is better at memorizing graphical information as compared to textual information [30,32]. This is known as the *picture superiority effect*. Several explanations for the picture superiority effect have been proposed. The most widely accepted is *dual-coding theory* [32], which postulates that in human memory, images are encoded not only visually and remembered as images, but they are also translated into a verbal form (as in a description) and remembered semantically. Another explanation of picture superiority effect is the *sensory-semantic model* [30], which states that images are accompanied by more distinct sensory codes that allow them to be more easily accessed than the textual information.

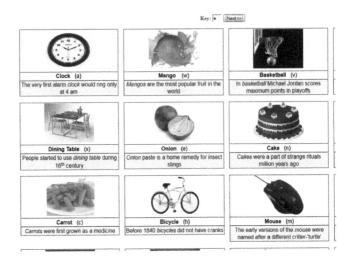

**Fig. 3.** A partial screen shot of GraphicV scheme during login. Each keyword is accommodated with the corresponding image.

### 3.5 Variant Response

In the existing recognition-based schemes [1,25,45], mouse input is used to select a keyword or image, where the keywords/images in a portfolio remain the same but are positioned randomly each time that a portfolio is loaded to compensate for shoulder surfing risk during login. However, the shoulder-surfing study of Tari et al. [39] reveals that recognition-based schemes with keyboard input provide higher resilience to shoulder surfing than schemes with mouse input, since the keyboard input associated with a particular keyword/image changes across the user's login sessions. This feature is called *variant response*, i.e., varying the user's responses across the login sessions [8].

For a recognition-based scheme providing variant response through varying keyboard inputs, the shoulder surfer needs to learn both the user's keystrokes and the corresponding keywords/images by looking at the keyboard and monitor. Tari et al.'s study [39] shows that observing both the monitor and keyboard at the same time is difficult.[2] Thus, the schemes in our study provide users with variant response feature, where each time a portfolio is loaded, a distinct lowercase letter a-z is assigned randomly as a *key* to one keyword on the page, and the user inputs the key letter corresponding to her assigned keyword into a single-character password field to move on to the next portfolio (see Figs. 1, 2 and 3).

## 4 User Study

We now present the design of our user study, where we used a within-subjects design consisting of three experimental conditions. Using a within-subjects design

---

[2] Though we note that videotaping could overcome this.

controls for individual differences and permits the use of statistically stronger hypothesis tests. The study procedures were approved by our university's Institutional Review Board (IRB) for human subjects research.

## 4.1 Participants, Apparatus and Environment

For this experiment, we recruited 52 students (34 women, 18 men) through our university's Psychology Research Pool. Participants came from diverse backgrounds, including majors from Nursing, Psychology, Business, Environmental Science, Biochemistry, and Spanish Language. The age of the participants varied between 18 to 48 with a mean age of 22. Each participant was compensated with course credit for participation and was aware that her performance or feedback in this study would not affect the amount of compensation.

The lab studies were conducted with one participant at a time to allow the researchers to observe the users' interactions with the system. We created three realistic and distinct websites, including sites for banking, email, and social networking. The sites used the images and layouts from familiar commercial sites, and each of them was equipped with one of our three password schemes.

In our study, each of the five portfolios in a scheme consists of unique set of keywords and images that are not repeated in any other portfolio nor in any other scheme. In other words, we did not reuse any keywords or images. We collected the images and real-life facts (verbal cues) from free online resources.

## 4.2 Procedure

We conducted the experiment in two sessions, each lasting around 30 min. The second session took place one week after the first one to test users' memorization of the assigned passwords. A one-week delay is larger than the maximum average interval for a user between subsequent logins to any of her important accounts [24] and is also a common interval used in authentication studies (e.g., [2,4,5, 16,31,45]).

**Session 1.** After signing a consent form, the participants were given an overview of our study. Then they performed registration for each of the three sites, each outfitted with a distinct scheme. The sites were shown to the participants at random order during registration. After registering with each scheme, participants performed a practice login with that scheme. They performed another practice login with each scheme after completing registration for all of the three sites. We did not collect data for these practice trials. They were asked to not record (e.g., write down or take a picture) their authentication secrets.

**Session 2.** The participants returned one week after registration and logged into each of the three sites using the assigned passwords. The sites were shown to the participants in random order, and they could make a maximum of five attempts for a successful login. After they had finished, we conducted an anonymous survey. Participants were then compensated and thanked for their time.

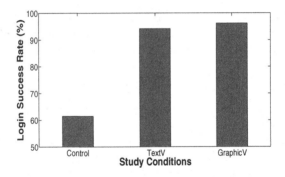

**Fig. 4.** Login success rates for the study conditions [Number of participants = 52]

### 4.3  Ecological Validity

Most of our participants were young and all of them were university educated, which represents a large number of frequent Web users, but may not generalize to the entire population. They came from diverse majors. As the study was performed in a lab setting, we were only able to gather data from 52 participants. However, lab studies have been preferred to examine brain-powered memorability of passwords [18]. Since lab studies take place in a controlled setting, it helps to establish performance bounds and figure out whether field tests are worthwhile in future research. We believe that 52 provides a suitable sample size for a lab study as compared to the prior studies on password memorability [2, 4, 5, 11, 12, 40, 44].

## 5  Results

We now discuss the results of our user study. To analyze our results, we use statistical tests and consider results comparing two conditions to be significantly different when we find $p < 0.05$. When comparing two conditions where the variable is at least ordinal, we use a Wilcoxon signed-rank test for the matched pairs of subjects and a Wilcoxon-Mann-Whitney test for unpaired results. Wilcoxon tests are similar to t-tests, but make no assumption about the distributions of the compared samples, which is appropriate to the datasets in our conditions. Whether or not a participant successfully authenticated is a binary measure, and so we use either a McNemar's test (for matched pairs of subjects) or a chi-squared test (for unpaired results) to compare login success rates between two conditions. Here, we tested the following hypotheses:

**Hypothesis 1.** $H_1$: *The login success rate for TextV would be significantly higher than that for the Control condition.*

The TextV scheme offers verbal cues (i.e., real-life facts related to the keyword), where cues are shown both at registration and login. So, the users could memorize their keywords through associating them with the corresponding cues, which should help to process and encode the information to store them in long-term memory (see Sect. 3 for detailed discussion). Moreover, the cues would assist

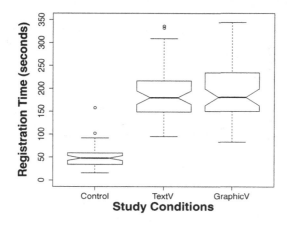

**Fig. 5.** Registration time for the study conditions

users to recognize the keywords in the future, which should enhance their memorability. Thus, we hypothesized that TextV scheme would have significantly higher login success rate than the Control condition.

Our results show that out of 52 participants in our study, 49 participants (94.2 %) succeeded to log in using TextV, while 32 participants (61.5 %) logged in successfully with the Control condition (see Fig. 4). Whether or not a participant successfully authenticated is a binary measure, so we compare login success rates between conditions using McNemar's test. We found that the login success rate for TextV scheme was significantly higher than that for the Control condition, $\mathcal{X}^2(1, N = 52) = 12.2$, $p < 0.01$. Thus, $H_1$ is supported by these results.

**Hypothesis 2.** $H_1$: *The login success rate for GraphicV would be significantly higher than that for the TextV scheme.*

In GraphicV scheme, we accommodate images corresponding to the keywords, in addition to offering verbal cues. Psychology research reveals *picture superiority effect* showing that the human brain is better at memorizing graphical information as compared to textual information [30,32]. Thus, we hypothesized that the login success rate for GraphicV would be significantly higher than that for the TextV scheme.

We found that out of 52 participants in our study, 50 participants (96.2 %) succeeded to log in using GraphicV scheme, and 49 participants (94.2 %) logged in successfully with the TextV scheme. The results for McNemar's test show that there was no significant difference between TextV and GraphicV schemes in terms of login success rate, $\mathcal{X}^2(1, N = 52) = 0$, $p = 1$. Hence, $H_2$ is not supported by these results.

### 5.1 Registration Time

We illustrate the results for registration time in Fig. 5. We found that the median registration times for Control, TextV, and GraphicV schemes were 48 s, 180 s,

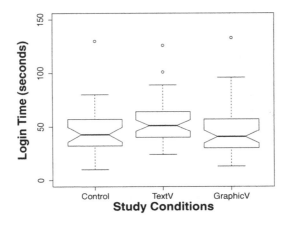

**Fig. 6.** Login time for the study conditions

and 181 s, respectively. We use a Wilcoxon signed-rank test (appropriate for matched pairs of subjects) to evaluate two schemes in terms of registration time. The results show that the registration time for TextV ($V = 0$, $p < 0.01$) and GraphicV ($V = 1$, $p < 0.01$) were significantly less than that for the Control condition. We did not find a significant difference in registration time between TextV and GraphicV schemes ($V = 633.5$, $p = 0.62$).

### 5.2  Login Time and Number of Attempts

In this paper, *number of attempts* and *login time* respectively refer to the required attempts and time for successful logins only, unless otherwise specified. We do not get matched pairs of subjects while comparing two schemes in terms of login time or number of attempts for successful logins, since some participants who logged in successfully for one scheme failed in the other scheme. So, we use a Wilcoxon-Mann-Whitney test (appropriate for unpaired results) to evaluate two schemes in terms of login time and the number of attempts for successful logins.

**Login Time.** We illustrate our results for login time in Fig. 6. We found that the median login time for Control, TextV, and GraphicV were 43 s, 51 s, and 41 s, respectively. The results for Wilcoxon-Mann-Whitney tests show that the

**Table 1.** Number of attempts for successful logins [SD: Standard Deviation]

| Study Conditions | Mean | Median | SD |
|---|---|---|---|
| Control | 1.3 | 1 | 0.8 |
| TextV | 1.4 | 1 | 0.9 |
| GraphicV | 1.3 | 1 | 0.6 |

**Table 2.** Questionnaire responses for the usability of each of the three schemes. Scores are out of 10. * indicates that scale was reversed. *Med*: Median, *Mo*: Mode

| Questions | Control | | TextV | | GraphicV | |
|---|---|---|---|---|---|---|
| | *Med* | *Mo* | *Med* | *Mo* | *Med* | *Mo* |
| I could easily sign up with this scheme | 5 | 1 | 7.5 | 10 | 9 | 10 |
| Logging in using this scheme was easy | 5.5 | 1 | 7.5 | 10 | 9 | 10 |
| Passwords in this scheme are easy to remember | 5 | 1 | 7 | 10 | 8 | 10 |
| I could easily use this scheme every day | 5 | 4 | 7 | 10 | 8 | 10 |

login time for Control ($W = 569.5$, $p < 0.05$) and GraphicV ($W = 878.5$, $p < 0.05$) were significantly less than that for the TextV scheme. We did not find a significant difference in login time between Control and GraphicV ($W = 790$, $p = 0.93$).

**Number of Attempts.** The mean number of attempts for a successful login was less than two for each of the three study conditions, while the median was one in each case (see Table 1). The results for Wilcoxon-Mann-Whitney tests found no significant difference between any pair of study conditions in terms of the number of attempts for a successful login.

### 5.3   User Feedback

We asked the participants to answer a set of 10-point Likert-scale questions (1: *strong disagreement*, 10: *strong agreement*) at the end of the second session, where a higher score indicates a more positive result for a scheme. We illustrate the results in Table 2. Since Likert scale data are ordinal, it is most appropriate to calculate mode and median for Likert-scale responses [35].

   The feedback of the participants were overall positive (mode and median higher than neutral) for TextV and GraphicV schemes, however, the majority of participants reported concern about the usability of Control condition. The results for Wilcoxon signed-rank tests (appropriate for matched pairs of subjects) show that the user feedback was significantly better for TextV and GraphicV schemes in comparison to the Control condition; for *ease of registration*: TextV-Control ($V = 500$, $p < 0.05$), GraphicV-Control ($V = 118$, $p < 0.05$), *ease of login*: TextV-Control ($V = 567$, $p < 0.05$), GraphicV-Control ($V = 124$, $p < 0.05$), *memorability*: TextV-Control ($V = 577$, $p < 0.05$), GraphicV-Control ($V = 108.5$, $p < 0.05$), and *ease of everyday use*: TextV-Control ($V = 672$, $p < 0.05$), GraphicV-Control ($V = 27$, $p < 0.05$).

## 6   Discussion

System-assigned recognition-based passwords (e.g., Passfaces [1]) are now commercially available and deployed by a number of large websites. They fail, however, to gain satisfactory memorability [17], since it is difficult for most people to memorize system-assigned passwords. Our study explores a promising direction to improve memorability for these passwords by leveraging humans' cognitive abilities through verbal cues, and presents a comparison between textual and graphical recognition to understand the underlying usability gain of adding images, when users are provided with such memory cues.

We accommodate the scientific understanding of long-term memory to improve the memorability of system-assigned recognition-based passwords. As noted by Atkinson and Shiffrin [7], any new information is transferred from short-term memory to long-term memory, when it is duly processed and encoded. In our study, we explored the impact of verbal cues for an elaborate encoding of authentication information to ease recognition during login. As we compared TextV scheme with the Control condition, our results showed a significant improvement in login success rate when users were provided with verbal cues to aid textual recognition.

We design GraphicV scheme to examine the *picture superiority effect* when users are provided with verbal cues. As we compared TextV with GraphicV scheme, our results found no significant difference in login success rate. The login time for GraphicV was significantly less than that for TextV scheme, although we found no significant difference in number of attempts for successful logins. Thus, we infer that when verbal cues are provided, accommodating images with the keywords might not contribute to gain a significant improvement in login success rate, however, aids users with a faster recognition of the keywords, and so on, reduces the login time.

During registration with TextV and GraphicV schemes, the participants may have learned the assigned keywords by correlating them with the verbal cues. This then assisted them with the elaborate processing of the authentication information, but also contributed to the higher registration time compared to the Control condition. No significant difference was found between TextV and GraphicV schemes in terms of registration time.

*Future Work.* Now that lab-study results show promise for implementing verbal cues, it would be interesting to evaluate the approaches through a long-term field study with larger and more diverse populations, where we would explore the training effects on login performances over time. A recent field study [3] reveals that login time significantly decreases with the frequent use of a scheme due to training effects.

In future work, we would explore the efficacy of verbal cues for the people from different age groups. We would also make a deeper investigation to understand the impact of cues in improving the memorability of passwords for the people with different cognitive limitations.

## 7   Conclusion

In our study, we aimed to understand the impact of verbal cues on system-assigned recognition-based passwords, and designed three different study conditions to achieve this goal. In a study with 52 participants, we had a 94.2 % login success rate for a textual recognition-based scheme offering verbal cues (TextV), which was significantly higher than that for the Control condition. To understand the usability gain of accommodating images for a scheme providing verbal cues, we compared TextV and GraphicV schemes, and found no significant difference in login success rate, although users required less time to recognize the keywords when they were accommodated with images. These findings shed light on a promising research direction to leverage humans' cognitive ability through verbal cues in gaining high memorability for system-assigned random passwords.

**Acknowledgement.** This material is based upon work supported by the National Science Foundation under Grant No. CNS-1423163 and CAREER Grant No. CNS-0954133.

# References

1. Passfaces corporation. The science behind Passfaces. White paper. http://www.passfaces.com/enterprise/resources/white_papers.htm
2. Al-Ameen, M.N., Haque, S.M.T., Wright, M.: Q-A: Towards the solution of usability-security tension in user authentication. Technical report (2014). arXiv:1407.7277 [cs.HC]
3. Al-Ameen, M.N., Wright, M.: A comprehensive study of the GeoPass user authentication scheme. Technical report (2014). arXiv:1408.2852 [cs.HC]
4. Al-Ameen, M.N., Wright, M.: Multiple-password interference in the GeoPass user authentication scheme. In: USEC (2015)
5. Al-Ameen, M.N., Wright, M., Scielzo, S.: Towards making random passwords memorable: leveraging users' cognitive ability through multiple cues. In: CHI (2015)
6. Anderson, J.R., Bower, G.H.: Recognition and recall processes in free recall. Psychol. Rev. **79**(2), 97–123 (1972)
7. Atinkson, C.R., Shiffrin, M.R.: Human memory: a proposed system and its control processes. In: Spence, K.W., Spence, J.T. (eds.) Advances in the Psychology of Learning and Motivation. Academic press, New York (1968)
8. Biddle, R., Chiasson, S., van Oorschot, P.: Graphical passwords: learning from the first twelve years. ACM Comput. Surv. **44**(4), 19 (2012)
9. Chiasson, S., Biddle, R., van Oorschot, P.C.: A second look at the usability of click-based graphical passwords. In: SOUPS (2007)
10. Chiasson, S., Forget, A., Biddle, R., van Oorschot, P.: User interface design affects security: patterns in click-based graphical passwords. Int. J. Inf. Secur. **8**(6), 387–398 (2009)
11. Chiasson, S., van Oorschot, P.C., Biddle, R.: Graphical password authentication using cued click points. In: Biskup, J., López, J. (eds.) ESORICS 2007. LNCS, vol. 4734, pp. 359–374. Springer, Heidelberg (2007)
12. Chiasson, S., Stobert, E., Biddle, R., van Oorschot, P.: Persuasive cued click-points: design, implementation, and evaluation of a knowledge- based authentication mechanism. IEEE TDSC **9**, 222–235 (2012)
13. Das, A., Bonneau, J., Caesar, M., Borisov, N., Wangz, X.: The tangled web of password reuse. In: NDSS (2014)

14. Davis, D., Monrose, F., Reiter, M.: On user choice in graphical password schemes. In: USENIX Security (2004)
15. Dirik, A.E., Memon, N., Birget, J.C.: Modeling user choice in the passpoints graphical password scheme. In: SOUPS (2007)
16. Dunphy, P., Yan, J.: Do background images improve "Draw a Secret" graphical passwords? In: CCS (2007)
17. Everitt, K., Bragin, T., Fogarty, J., Kohno, T.: A comprehensive study of frequency, interference, and training of multiple graphical passwords. In: CHI (2009)
18. Fahl, S., Harbach, M., Acar, Y., Smith, M.: On the ecological validity of a password study. In: SOUPS (2013)
19. Florencio, D., Herley, C.: Where do security policies come from? In: SOUPS (2010)
20. Forget, A.: A World with Many Authentication Schemes. Ph.D. thesis, Carleton University (2012)
21. Forget, A., Chiasson, S., van Oorschot, P.C., Biddle, R.: Persuasion for stronger passwords: motivation and pilot study. In: Oinas-Kukkonen, H., Hasle, P., Harjumaa, M., Segerståhl, K., Øhrstrøm, P. (eds.) PERSUASIVE 2008. LNCS, vol. 5033, pp. 140–150. Springer, Heidelberg (2008)
22. Forget, A., Chiasson, S., van Oorschot, P., Biddle, R.: Improving text passwords through persuasion. In: SOUPS (2008)
23. Furnell, S., Papadopoulos, I., Dowland, P.: A long-term trial of alternative user authentication technologies. Inf. Manag. Comput. Secur. 12(2), 178–190 (2004)
24. Hayashi, E., Hong, J.I.: A diary study of password usage in daily life. In: CHI (2011)
25. Hlywa, M., Biddle, R., Patrick, A.S.: Facing the facts about image type in recognition-based graphical passwords. In: ACSAC (2011)
26. Jermyn, I., Mayer, A., Monrose, F., Reiter, M., Rubin, A.: The design and analysis of graphical passwords. In: USENIX Security (1999)
27. Just, M., Aspinall, D.: Personal choice and challenge questions a security and usability assessment. In: SOUPS (2009)
28. Kuo, C., Romanosky, S., Cranor, L.F.: Human selection of mnemonic phrase-based passwords. In: SOUPS (2006)
29. Nali, D., Thorpe, J.: Analyzing user choice in graphical passwords. Technical report TR-04-01, School of Computer Science, Carleton University (2004)
30. Nelson, D.L., Reed, V.S., McEvoy, C.L.: Learning to order pictures and words: a model of sensory and semantic encoding. J. Exp. Psychol. Hum. Learn. Mem. 3(5), 485–497 (1977)
31. Nicholson, J., Coventry, L., Briggs, P.: Age-related performance issues for PIN and face-based authentication systems. In: CHI (2013)
32. Paivio, A.: Mind and Its Evolution: A Dual Coding Theoretical Approach. Lawrence Erlbaum, Mahwah, NJ (2006)
33. Proctor, R.W., Lien, M.C., Vu, K.P.L., Schultz, E.E., Salvendy, G.: Improving computer security for authentication of users: influence of proactive password restrictions. Behav. Res. Meth. Instrum. Comput. 34(2), 163–169 (2002)
34. Rabkin, A.: Personal knowledge questions for fallback authentication: security questions in the era of Facebook. In: SOUPS (2008)
35. Robertson, J.: Stats: we're doing it wrong, April 2011. http://cacm.acm.org/blogs/blog-cacm/107125-stats-were-doing-it-wrong/fulltext
36. Schechter, S., Brush, A.J.B., Egelman, S.: It's no secret: measuring the security and reliability of authentication via 'secret' questions. In: IEEE S&P (2009)

37. Shay, R., Kelley, P.G., Komanduri, S., Mazurek, M.L., Ur, B., Vidas, T., Bauer, L., Christin, N., Cranor, L.F.: Correct horse battery staple: exploring the usability of system-assigned passphrases. In: SOUPS (2012)
38. Shay, R., Komanduri, S., Kelley, P.G., Leon, P.G., Mazurek, M.L., Bauer, L., Christin, N., Cranor, L.F.: Encountering stronger password requirements: user attitudes and behaviors. In: SOUPS (2010)
39. Tari, F., Ozok, A., Holden, S.: A comparison of perceived and real shoulder-surfing risks between alphanumeric and graphical passwords. In: SOUPS (2006)
40. Thorpe, J., MacRae, B., Salehi-Abari, A.: Usability and security evaluation of GeoPass: a geographic location-password scheme. In: SOUPS (2013)
41. Tulving, E., Thompson, D.M.: Encoding specificity and retrieval processes in episodic memory. Psychol. Rev. 80(5), 352–373 (1973)
42. Tulving, E., Watkins, M.: Continuity between recall and recognition. Am. J. Psychol. 86(4), 739–748 (1973)
43. Wickelgren, W.A., Norman, D.A.: Strength models and serial position in short-term recognition memory. J. Math. Psychol. 3, 316–347 (1966)
44. Wiedenbeck, S., Waters, J., Birget, J., Brodskiy, A., Memon, N.: Authentication using graphical passwords: effects of tolerance and image choice. In: SOUPS (2005)
45. Wright, N., Patrick, A.S., Biddle, R.: Do you see your password? applying recognition to textual passwords. In: SOUPS (2012)

# The Emperor's New Password Creation Policies:

## An Evaluation of Leading Web Services and the Effect of Role in Resisting Against Online Guessing

Ding Wang[1,2(✉)] and Ping Wang[2,3]

[1] School of EECS, Peking University, Beijing 100871, China
[2] National Engineering Research Center for Software Engineering, Beijing, China
{wangdingg,pwang}@pku.edu.cn
[3] School of Software and Microelectronics, Peking University, Beijing 100260, China

**Abstract.** While much has changed in Internet security over the past decades, textual passwords remain as the dominant method to secure user web accounts and they are proliferating in nearly every new web services. Nearly every web services, no matter new or aged, now enforce some form of password creation policy. In this work, we conduct an extensive empirical study of 50 password creation policies that are currently imposed on high-profile web services, including 20 policies mainly from US and 30 ones from mainland China. We observe that no two sites enforce the same password creation policy, there is little rationale under their choices of policies when changing policies, and Chinese sites generally enforce more lenient policies than their English counterparts.

We proceed to investigate the effectiveness of these 50 policies in resisting against the primary threat to password accounts (i.e. online guessing) by testing each policy against two types of weak passwords which represent two types of online guessing. Our results show that among the total 800 test instances, 541 ones are accepted: 218 ones come from trawling online guessing attempts and 323 ones come from targeted online guessing attempts. This implies that, currently, the policies enforced in leading sites largely fail to serve their purposes, especially vulnerable to targeted online guessing attacks.

**Keywords:** User authentication · Password creation policy · Password cracking · Online trawling guessing · Online targeted guessing

## 1 Introduction

Textual passwords are perhaps the most prevalent mechanism for access control in a broad spectrum of today's web services, ranging from low value news portals and ftp transfers, moderate value social communities, gaming forums and emails to extremely sensitive financial transactions and genomic data protection [25]. Though its weaknesses (e.g., vulnerable to online and offline guessing [38]) have been articulated as early as about forty years ago and various alternative authentication schemes (e.g., multi-factor authentication protocols [24,47]

© Springer International Publishing Switzerland 2015
G. Pernul et al. (Eds.): ESORICS 2015, Part II, LNCS 9327, pp. 456–477, 2015.
DOI: 10.1007/978-3-319-24177-7_23

and graphical passwords [51]) have been successively suggested, password-based authentication firmly stays as the dominant form of user authentication over the Internet. Due to both economical and technical reasons [23], it will probably still take the lead on web authentication in the foreseeable future.

It has long been recognised that system-assigned passwords are hardly usable [1,4], yet when users are allowed to select passwords by themselves, they tend to prefer passwords that are easily memorable, short strings but not arbitrarily long, random character sequences, rendering the accounts protected by user-generated passwords at high risk of compromise [5,16,49]. It is a rare bit of good news from recent password studies [15,42,45] that, if properly designed, password creation policies do help user select memorable yet secure passwords, alleviating this usability-security tension. Unsurprisingly, nearly every web service, no matter new or aged, follows the fashion and now enforces some form of password creation policy. Generally, a password creation policy[1] is composed of *some password composition rules* and *a password strength meter* (see Fig. 1). The former requires user-generated passwords to comply with some complexity (e.g., a combination of both letters and numbers) and nudges users towards selecting strong passwords [9,36], while the latter provides users with a visual (or verbal) feedback [15,45] about the password strength during registration.

**Fig. 1.** A typical example of password creation policy

However, to what extent can the widely-deployed password creation policies on the Internet be relied upon has long been an open issue. In 2007, Furnell [18] initiated an investigation into the password practices on 10 popular websites and found that, password rules and meters are vastly variable among the examined sites and none of them can perform ideally across all of the evaluated criteria.

In 2010, Bonneau and Preibush [7] conducted the first large-scale empirical study of password policy implementation issues in practice. By examining 150 different websites, they observed that bad password practices were commonplace and particularly, highly inconsistent policies were adopted by individual sites, which suggests that there is a lack of widely accepted industry standards for password implementations. At the meantime, Florêncio and Herley [17] investigated

---

[1] In this work, we use "password policy" and "password creation policy" interchangeably, and don't consider other password policies like expiration and storage [3,11].

the rationale underlying the choices of password policies among 75 high-profile websites and found that, greater security demands (e.g., the site scale, the value protected and the level of severity of security threats) generally do not constitute the dominant factor for selecting more stringent password rules. Instead, these Internet-scale, high value web services (e.g., e-commerce sites like Paypal and online banking sites like Citibank) accept relatively weak passwords and these sites bearing no consequences from poor usability (e.g., government and university sites) usually implement restrictive password rules.

To figure out whether leading websites are improving their password management policies as time goes on, in 2011 Furnell [19] made an investigation into 10 worldwide top-ranking sites and compared the results with those of the study [18] he performed in 2007. Disappointingly, he reported that, during the four-year intervening period there has been hardly any improvement in password practices while the number of web services and security breaches has increased greatly. In 2014, Carnavalet and Mannan [10] investigated the problem of to what extent the currently deployed password strength meters are lack of sound design choices and consistent strength outcomes. They systematically evaluated 13 meters from 11 high-profile web services by testing about 4 million passwords that are leaked from popular online services as well as specifically composed passwords. It is found that most meters in their study are "quite simplistic in nature and apparently designed in an ad-hoc manner, and bear no indication of any serious efforts from these service providers" [10]. Fortunately, most meters can correctly assign sensible scores to highly weak popular passwords, e.g., at least 98.4 % of the top 500 passwords [8], such as `password, 123456, iloveyou` and `qwerty`, are considered "weak" or "very weak" by every meter.

**Motivations.** However, most of the existing works [7,17–19] were conducted five years ago, while the online world has evolved rapidly during the intervening period. In early 2010, Twitter had 26 million monthly active Users, now this figure has increased tenfold;[2] In Nov. 2010, Gmail had 193 million active users, now this figure reaches 500 million;[3] In April 2010, Xiaomi, a privately owned smartphone company headquartered in Beijing, China, just started up, now it has become the world's 3rd largest smartphone maker (ranked after Apple and Samsung) and there are 100 million Xiaomi users worldwide who rely on its cloud service.[4] All these three sites have recently been the victims of hacking and leaked large amounts of user credentials [34,37,39]. As we will demonstrate, they all (as well eight other sites examined in this work) have changed their policies at least once during the past five years. Moreover, at that time how to accurately measure password strength was an open problem and there were few real-life password datasets publicly available, and thus the methodologies used in these earlier works are far from systematic (mature) and satisfactory.

The sole recent work by Carnavalet and Mannan [10] mainly focuses on examining password meters from 13 sites, paying little attention to the other

---

[2] http://www.statista.com/statistics/282087/.

[3] http://thefusejoplin.com/2015/01/choose-google-gmail-yahoo-mail/.

[4] https://www.techinasia.com/xiaomi-miui-100-million-users/.

part of password policies (i.e., password composition rules). Due to the fact that a password (e.g., `Wanglei123`) measured "strong" by the password meter of a site (e.g., AOL) may violate the password rule of this site, finally it is still rejected by the site. In addition, many sites (e.g., Edas, AOL and Sohu) enforce *mandatory* password rules but *suggestive* meters, a password metered "weak" might pass the password rule of these sites, and finally this "weak" password is still accepted. Consequently, the question of how well these sites *actually* reject weak passwords and withstand online guessing remains unanswered.

Another limitation of existing works is that little attention has been given to non-English web services. As typical hieroglyphics, Chinese has been the main language used in a total of over 3.64 million web services until 2014 and about 0.95 million new web services that started up in 2014 (which means 0.95M new password policies come out and impact on common users.) [22]. What's more, Chinese web users, who have reached 649 million by the end of 2014 [12], have been the largest Internet population in the world and account for a quarter of the world's total netizens. Therefore, it is important (and interesting) to investigate what's the strengths and weaknesses of the current password policies in Chinese web services as compared to their English counterparts.

**Our Contributions.** The main contributions of this work are as follows:

(1) First, we propose a systematic, evidence-grounded methodology for measuring password creation policies and investigate the status quo of policies enforced by 50 leading web services (with special emphasis on Chinese web services) with a total of ten application domains. We find that, generally, gaming sites, email sites, e-commerce sites and non-profit organizations manage with the least restrictive password rules, while the sites of IT manufacturers impose the most stringent ones; Web portals, email sites, e-commerce sites and technical forums tend to provide explicit feedbacks of the password strength to users, while sites of security companies, IT manufacturers and academic services, ironically, often do not bother to provide users with any piece of information about password strength.

(2) Second, we explore the differences in password policy choices between English sites and Chinese sites. Compared to their English counterparts, Chinese sites, in general, are more undaunted (audacious) in their password rule choices, while there is no significant difference between these two groups of sites with regard to the password meter choices.

(3) Third, we employ state-of-the-art password cracking techniques (including the probabilistic-context-free-grammar (PCFG) based and Markov-Chain-based) to measure the strength of the 16 testing passwords that are used to represent two primary types of online password guessing attempts. This provides a reliable benchmark (ordering) of the actual strength of these testing passwords beyond intuitive (heuristic) estimates as opposed to previous works like [10,19]. We observe that most of the meters overestimate the strength of at least some of these 16 passwords, rendering the corresponding web services vulnerable to online guessing.

## 2  Our Methodology

As there is little research on studying password practices and the approaches used in the few pioneering works [7,10,17,19] are far from systematic and may be demoded over the past five years, in the following we take advantage of state-of-the-art techniques and elaborate on a systematic methodology for measuring password policies. As far as we know, for the first time several new approaches (e.g., the use of large-scale real-life passwords as corroborative evidence, the use of targeted online guessing to measure password strength, and the classification and selection of testing passwords) are introduced into this domain.

### 2.1  Selecting Representative Sites

To investigate the status quo of password creation policies deployed in today's Internet (with special emphasis on Chinese web services), first of all we selected ten themes of web services that we are most interested in and that are also highly relevant to our daily online lives: web portal, IT corporation, email, security corporation, e-commerce, gaming, technical forum, social forum, academic service and non-profit organization. Then, for each theme we choose its top 5 sites according to the Alexa Global Top 500 sites list based on their traffic ranking (http://www.alexa.com/topsites). Some companies (e.g., Microsoft and Google) may offer various services (e.g., email, search, news, product support) and have a few affiliated sites, fortunately they generally rely on the same authentication system (e.g., Windows Live and Google Account) to manage all consumer credentials and we can consider all the affiliated sites as one. Similarly, for each theme we also choose its top 10 sites that are among the Alexa Top 500 Chinese sites rank list. In this way, there are 15 leading sites selected for each theme: 5 from English sites and 10 from Chinese sites. Further, we randomly selected 5 sites out of these 15 sites for each theme, resulting in 50 sites used in this work (see Table 5): 20 from English sites and 30 from Chinese sites.

We note that though our selected websites have a wide coverage, yet many other themes are still left unexplored, such as e-banking, e-health and e-government. The primary reason why we does not include them is that, they rely heavily on multi-factor authentication techniques in which passwords play a much less critical role. In addition, the number of sites allocated for each theme is also limited. Nonetheless, our sample characterizes the current most recognised and leading portion of the online web services, which attract the majority of the visit traffic [26,28]. Therefore, the password practices used by these sites will impact on the major fraction of end-users and may also became a model for other less leading sites (which generally are with less technical, capital and human resources). Further considering the amount of work incurred for one site, an inspection of 50 sites is really not an easy task, let alone an initial study like ours (as there is no sophisticated procedure to follow, we have to carry out an iterative process of data collection). In the future work, we are considering to increase the number of sites for each theme to 10 or possibly 20, and the investigation results as well as a set of evidence-supported, practicable policy recommendations will be made available at the companion site http://wangdingg.weebly.com/password-policy.html.

## 2.2 Measuring Password Policy Strength

The task of measuring strength of *a policy* is generally accomplished by evaluating strength of *the password dataset* generated under this policy, and a number of methods for tackling the latter issue have been proposed, including statistical-based ones (e.g., guessing entropy and $\alpha$-guesswork [5]) and cracking-based ones (e.g., [31,48]). However, these methods all require access to a real password dataset with sufficient size. Fortunately, we note that Florêncio and Herley [17]'s simple metric $-N_{min} \cdot log_2 C_{min}-$ is not subject to this restriction and sufficient for our purpose, where $N_{min}$ is the minimum length allowed and $C_{min}$ is the cardinality of the minimum charset imposed.[5] For instance, the strength of a policy that requires a user's password to be no short than 6 and must contain a letter and a number is 31.02($=6 \cdot log_2 36$) bits. This metric well characterizes the minimum strength of passwords allowed by the policy, providing a lower bound of the policy strength. We adopt this metric in our work.

**Table 1.** Basic information about the seven password datasets used in this work

| Dataset | Services | Location | Language | When leaked | How leaked | Total passwords |
|---------|----------|----------|----------|-------------|------------|-----------------|
| Rockyou | Social | USA | Englsih | Dec. 14, 2009 | SQL injection | 32,603,387 |
| Tianya | Social | China | Chinese | Dec. 4, 2011 | Hacker breached | 30,233,633 |
| 7k7k | Gaming | China | Chinese | Dec. 2, 2011 | Hacker breached | 19,138,452 |
| Dodonew | Ecommerce | China | Chinese | Dec. 3, 2011 | Hacker breached | 16,231,271 |
| CSDN | Programming | China | Chinese | Dec. 2, 2011 | Hacker breached | 6,428,287 |
| Duowan | Gaming | China | Chinese | Dec. 1, 2011 | Insider disclosed | 4,982,740 |
| Yahoo | Portal | USA | English | July 12, 2012 | SQL injection | 453,491 |

## 2.3 Exploiting Real-Life Password Datasets

Our work relies on seven password datasets, a total of 124.9 million real-life passwords (see Table 1), to train the cracking algorithms and learn some basic statistics about user password behaviors in practice. Five datasets of Chinese web passwords, namely Tianya (31.7 million), 7k7k (19.1 million), Dodonew (16.3 million), Duowan (8.3 million) and CSDN (6.4 million), were all leaked during Dec. 2011 in a series of security breaches [33]. Tianya is the largest social forum in China, 7k7k, Dodonew and Duowan are all popular gaming forums in China, and CSDN is a well-known technical forum for Chinese programmers.

Two datasets of English web passwords, namely Rockyou (32.6 million) and Yahoo (0.5 million), were among the most famous datasets in password research [32,48]. Rockyou is one of the world's largest in-game video and platform for premium brands located in US, and its passwords were disclosed by a hacker

---

[5] This implicitly assumes that users are least-effort ones.

using a SQL injection in Dec. 2009 [2]. This dataset is the first source of large-scale real-life passwords that are publicly available. Yahoo is one of the most popular sites in the world known for its Web portal, search engine and related services like Yahoo Mail, Yahoo News and Yahoo Finance. It attracts "more than half a billion consumers every month in more than 30 languages". Its passwords were hacked by the hacker group named D33Ds in July 2012 [50]. We will pay special attention to this site because it has changed its password policy, as far as we can confirm, at least three times during the past five years.

### 2.4   Measuring Password Strength

Essentially, the strength of a password is its guessing resistance against the *assumed* attacker. This equals the uncertainty this attacker has to get rid of, and naturally the idea of shannon entropy was suggested to measure password strength, called NIST entropy [9]. Later, NIST entropy was found to correlates poorly with guess resistance and can at best serve as a "rough rule of thumb" [31, 48]. In contrast, the *guess-number* metric, which is based on password cracking algorithms (e.g., PCFG-based and Markov-based [32]), was shown to be much more effective, and it has been used in a number of following works like [35,42].

However, we note that the traditional use of guess-number metric generally implicitly assumes that the attacker is a random, trawling attacker $\mathcal{A}_{tra}$ (i.e., not targeting a selected user). In many cases this is evidently not realistic. For a targeted attacker $\mathcal{A}_{tar}$, with the knowledge of the name of the target user, she can drastically reduce the guess number required to find the right password. In this work, we consider these two kinds of attacker and suppose that the targeted attacker knows of the user's name. This assumption is reasonable because, for $\mathcal{A}_{tar}$ to launch a targeted attack, he must know some specific information about the victim user $\mathcal{U}_v$, and $\mathcal{U}_v$'s name is no-doubt the most publicly available data.

To take advantage of name information in cracking, we slightly modify the PCFG-based and Markov-based algorithms by specially increasing the probability of the name-related letter segments. This can be easily achieved in PCFG-based attacks [32]. For instance, assuming the victim's name is "wanglei", after the PCFG-based training phase, one can increase the probability of the item "$L_4 \rightarrow wang$" in the PCFG grammars to that of the most popular $L_4$ segment and similarly, the item "$L_7 \rightarrow wanglei$" to that of the most popular $L_7$ segment.

However, for Markov-based attacks since there is no concrete instantiation of "letter segments" during training, we substitute all the name segments (including full, sur- and first names) in training passwords (we use 2M Duowan passwords and 2M CSDN passwords together as training sets) with the victim's corresponding name segments before training. For instance, "zhangwei0327" is replaced with "wanglei01", "zhao@123" is replaced with "wang@123", and "pingpku@123" is replaced with "leipku@123", where "wang" and "lei" is $U_v$'s surname and first name in Chinese Pinyin, respectively. Our basic idea is that *the popularity of name-based passwords in the training sets largely reflects the probability of the targeted user to use a name-based password, and the clever attacker* $\mathcal{A}_{tar}$ *will base on this probability to exploit* $U_v$'s *name.* Our Markov-based algorithm for targeted online guessing is shown as Algorithm 1. One can easily see that, based on our idea, besides Chinese Pinyin names, this algorithm can be readily extended to incorporate names in any other language (e.g., "James Smith" in English), and to incorporate other user-specific data (such as account name and birthdate) to model a more knowledgeable targeted attacker.

---

**Algorithm 1.** Our Markov-Chain-based generation of targeted guesses

---

**Input**: A training set $\mathcal{TS}$; A name list *nameList*; The victim user's name *victimName*; The size $k$ of the guess list to be generated (e.g., $k = 10^7$)

**Output**: A guess list $L$ with the $k$ highest ranked items

1  **Pre-Training**:
2      **for** *name* $\in$ *nameList* **do**
3           $trieTree.insert(name)$
4      **for** *password* $\in$ $\mathcal{TS}$ **do**
5          **for** *letterSegment* $\in$ *splitToLetterSegments(password)* **do**
6              **if** *InTrieTree(letterSegment)* **then**
7                  **if** *isFullName(letterSegment)* **then**
8                      $password.replace(letterSegment, victimName.fullName)$
9                  **if** *isSurName(letterSegment)* **then**
10                     $password.replace(letterSegment, victimName.surName)$
11                 **if** *isFirstName(letterSegment)* **then**
12                     $password.replace(letterSegment, victimName.firstName)$
13 **Ordinary Markov-Chain-based training on the pre-trained set** $\mathcal{TS}$ **using Good-Turing smoothing and End-Symbol normalization (for more details see [46]);**
14 **Produce a list** $L$ **with top-$k$ guesses in decreasing order of probability.**

---

To avoid ambiguity, we only consider name segments no shorter than 4. To determine whether a password picked from the training set includes a name or not, we first build a name-based Trie-tree by using the 20 million hotel reservation data leaked in Dec., 2013 [21]. This name dataset consists of 2.73 million unique Chinese full names and thus is adequate for our purpose. We also add 504 Chinese surnames which are officially recognized in China into the Trie-tree. These surnames are adequate for us to identify the first names of Chinese users in the Trie-tree to be used in Markov-based targeted guess generation.

## 2.5  Selecting Testing Passwords

As we have mentioned in Sect. 2.3, we measure how the 50 password policies we are interested in are resistant to two types of guessing attacker, i.e., a trawling attacker $\mathcal{A}_{tra}$ and a targeted attacker $\mathcal{A}_{tar}$ (with the victim's name). The aim of $\mathcal{A}_{tra}$ is to break *as many accounts as possible* with a few password trials [5], while $\mathcal{A}_{tar}$ intends to break *the single account* of the given victim user $\mathcal{U}_v$.

To be effective, $\mathcal{A}_{tra}$ would try the most popular passwords in decreasing order of probability with regard to *the targeting population*, while $\mathcal{A}_{tar}$ would

**Table 2.** Two types of passwords modeling two kinds of guessing attacks ('Guess rank' is the order in which the corresponding attacker will try that guess; '–' = not exist)

| User password | | Guess rank in trawling PCFG | Guess rank in trawling Markov | Guess rank in targeted PCFG | Guess rank in targeted Markov |
|---|---|---|---|---|---|
| Type A (Hotspot) | 123456 | 1 | 1 | 3 | 2 |
| | 123456789 | 3 | 2 | 1 | 3 |
| | 5201314 | 6 | 8 | 9 | 10 |
| | woaini | 12 | 19 | 30 | 423 |
| | iloveyou | 43 | 347 | 24 | 359 |
| | password | 84 | 164 | 34 | 194 |
| | woaini1314 | 737 | 116 | 1501 | 32736 |
| | password123 | 17002 | 36834 | 6572 | 36679 |
| Type B (Name-based) | wanglei | 281 | 595 | 64 | 1 |
| | wanglei123 | 13929 | 35852 | 324 | 7 |
| | wanglei1 | 42627 | 86999 | 3450 | 16 |
| | wanglei12 | 169546 | 235971 | 11205 | 58 |
| | Wanglei123 | 3020809 | 6222672 | 323 | 392 |
| | wang.lei | 301547 | 7856239 | 2287915 | 379205 |
| | wanglei@123 | 5291970 | – | 1927185 | 5109 |
| | Wanglei@123 | – | – | 1927186 | 206144 |

**Table 3.** Popularity of Type A passwords in real-life password datasets

| Hotspot password | Tianya (31.7M,2011) | | Dodonew (16.3M,2011) | | 7k7k (19.1M,2011) | | Duowan (8.3M,2011) | | Rockyou (32.6M,2009) | | Yahoo (0.5M,2012) | |
|---|---|---|---|---|---|---|---|---|---|---|---|---|
| | Rank | Freq. | Rank | Freq. | Rank | Freq. | Rank | Freq. | Rank | Freq. | Rank | Freq. |
| 123456 | 1 | 3.98 % | 1 | 1.45 % | 1 | 3.79 % | 1 | 3.43 % | 1 | 0.89 % | 1 | 0.38 % |
| 123456789 | 4 | 0.59 % | 3 | 0.32 % | 4 | 0.63 % | 3 | 0.62 % | 3 | 0.24 % | 6 | 0.05 % |
| **5201314** | 7 | 0.19 % | 5 | 0.19 % | 6 | 0.34 % | 6 | 0.28 % | 415 | 0.01 % | 5090 | 0.00 % |
| **woaini** | 17 | 0.09 % | 26 | 0.04 % | 15 | 0.09 % | 18 | 0.07 % | 3626 | 0.00 % | – | 0.00 % |
| iloveyou | 49 | 0.04 % | 106 | 0.01 % | 53 | 0.03 % | 45 | 0.03 % | 5 | 0.15 % | 16 | 0.03 % |
| password | 86 | 0.02 % | 23 | 0.04 % | 98 | 0.02 % | 87 | 0.02 % | 4 | 0.18 % | 2 | 0.18 % |
| **woaini1314** | 295 | 0.01 % | 18 | 0.05 % | 72 | 0.02 % | 57 | 0.03 % | 87348 | 0.00 % | – | 0.00 % |
| password123 | 20045 | 0.00 % | 8004 | 0.00 % | 22462 | 0.00 % | 14382 | 0.00 % | 1384 | 0.00 % | 153 | 0.01 % |

**Table 4.** Popularity of Type B passwords in real-life datasets

| Name dictionary | Tianya | Dodonew | 7k7k | Duowan | Average Chinese | Rockyou | Yahoo | Average English |
|---|---|---|---|---|---|---|---|---|
| Pinyin_surname (len $\geq$ 4) | 6.34 % | 10.04 % | 7.14 % | 8.44 % | 7.99 % | 1.38 % | 1.29 % | 1.34 % |
| Pinyin_fullname (len $\geq$ 4) | 9.87 % | 15.90 % | 11.42 % | 13.42 % | 12.65 % | 5.37 % | 3.61 % | 4.49 % |
| Pinyin_name_total (len $\geq$ 4) | 10.91 % | 18.06 % | 14.81 % | 14.92 % | 14.68 % | 5.36 % | 4.21 % | 4.78 % |

try the most popular passwords in decreasing order of probability with regard to *the specific user*. As shown in Table 2, we use Type A passwords (we call hotspot passwords) to represent the attempts $\mathcal{A}_{tra}$ will try and Type B passwords (we call Chinese-Pinyin-name-based passwords) to represent the attempts $\mathcal{A}_{tar}$ will try, respectively. As revealed in [46], Chinese web users create a new type of passwords, named "Chinese-style passwords", such as woaini, 5201314 and wanglei123 based on their language. Note that, "wanglei" is not a random string of length 7 but a highly popular Chinese name, among the top-20 list of Chinese full names [44]; "520" sounds as "woaini" in Chinese, equivalent to "i love you" in English; "1314" sounds as "for ever and ever" in Chinese. Thus, both "woaini1314" and "5201314" mean "I love you for ever and ever". Such passwords are extremely popular among Chinese users (see Table 3) and thus are as dangerous as internationally bad passwords like iloveyou and password123.

In the following we show why these two types of passwords are weak and can really serve as representatives of password attempts that the aforementioned two types of attacker would try. Table 3 reveals that, all the eight Type A passwords are among the top-200 rank list in at least one web services. More specifically, all the Type A passwords (except woaini1314 and password123) are among the top-100 rank list in the four Chinese web services, while woaini1314 is only slightly less popular (i.e., with a rank 295) in Tianya and English services, and password123 is comparatively much more popular in English services, i.e., with a rank 153 in Yahoo and a rank 1384 in Rockyou, respectively. Besides popularity, these eight Type A passwords are also different in length, culture (language) and composition of charsets. Therefore, they well represent the characteristics of potential passwords that a trawling attacker $\mathcal{A}_{tra}$ would try.

As stated in Sect. 2.4, to model a targeted guessing attacker $\mathcal{A}_{tar}$, we mainly focus on the case that $\mathcal{A}_{tar}$ knows of the victim's name. Without loss of much generality, we assume the victim is a Chinese web user, named "wanglei". From Table 4 (and see more data in [46]) we can see that Chinese users really love to include their (Pinyin) names into passwords: an average of 14.68 % of Chinese users have this habit. That is, given a targeted user, it is confident to predict that there is a chance of 14.68 % that she includes her name into her password, and $\mathcal{A}_{tar}$ would gain great advantage by making use of this fact. We conservatively deal with the ambiguities during the name matching. For instance, there are some English surnames (e.g., Lina) may coincide with a Chinese full name, and we take no account of such names when processing English datasets. Well, how does a user uses her name, which can be seen as a word, to build a password? There are a dozen of mangling rules to accomplish this aim, and the most popular ones [13,27] include appending digits and/or symbols, capitalizing the first letter, leet etc. This results in our eight Type B passwords. One can see that the guess rank in Markov-based targeted attack (see the last column in Table 2) quite accords with the rank of general user behaviors as surveyed in [13]. This implies the effectiveness of our Markov-based targeted attacking algorithm.

## 2.6 Collecting Data from Sites

To obtain first-hand data on password policy practices, we create real accounts on each site, read the html/PHP/Javascript source code of the registration page, and test sample passwords to see the reaction of the meter when available. We note that there are many unexpected behaviors of sites. For example, in some sites (e.g., Edas, Easychar and Yahoo) the descriptions of password policies are not explicitly given (or the information explicitly given are not complete), and additional data about policies can only be extracted from the feedbacks of the server after one have actually clicked the "submit" button. Consequently, for all sites and every password testing instance, we press the "submit" button down and take note of the response to avoid missing anything important.

Initially, considering the great amount of manual workload involved, we attempt to automate the collection of data from each site by using PHP/Python scripts or web spiders. However, we have to abandon this idea mainly due to four reasons: (1) A large portion of sites (38 %) prevent automated registration by requiring users to solve CAPTCHA puzzles when registration; (2) 18 % sites need to input the verification code received by user's mobile phone to accomplish the registration; (3) 8 % sites involve a verification code to be received by the user's email before the user can input the password; (4) Information displayed on each site is highly heterogeneous, as demonstrated in Sect. 3, no two sites share the same password policy, and thus batch processing hardly works. As a result, the whole data collection process is manually handled. To assure accuracy, every process is conducted at least twice (at intervals of more than one week) and the collected data all has been cross validated by the authors.

## 3   Our Results

In this section, we first present the status quo of the password policies employed in the 50 web services that we are interested in, and then examine the effectiveness of these policies in resisting against online guessing attacks. All of the data were collected from these services between the months of Jan. to Feb. in 2015.

### 3.1   Password Composition Rules in the Wild

For each password composition rule, we investigate the following six common requirements: length limits, charset requirement, whether rules are explicitly stated, whether allowing symbols, whether using a blacklist and whether deterring the use of personal data. The results are summarized in Table 5.

**Length Limits.** All sites but one impose a minimum length limit. 60 % sites require passwords to be no shorter than 6, 30 % sites require passwords to be no shorter than 8, with the remaining 8 % sites raging from 5, 7 to 9. It is interesting to see that, all sites from the IT corporation category enforce a minimum-8 length limit. Is this because that these services care the security of user account more than other services examined? We will explore this question later.

At the meantime, 72 % sites impose a maximum length limit no larger than 64, as far as they can be identified. Surprisingly, 22 % sites do not allow passwords to be longer than 16. As it is cognitively impossible for common users to remember complex non-linguistic strings yet attack vectors are increasing, passphrases have recently received much interest and shown to be more useable than passwords [30,43], and actually, they have been used successfully and gain popularity (see an example http://correcthorsebatterystaple.net/). However, passphrases are highly likely to exceed such maximum length limits (e.g.,

**Table 5.** An overview of the password composition rules in the selected web services ('-' means a length limit of larger than 64; '∅' means no charset requirement; 'Blacklist' means a list of banned popular passwords or structures (e.g., repetition); 'User info' considers two types of a user's personal information, i.e. name and account name.)

| Web services | | Len. limits | | Charset requirement | Rules explicit | Accept symbol | Using blacklist | Checking user info |
|---|---|---|---|---|---|---|---|---|
| | | Min | Max | | | | | |
| Web portal | Sina | 6 | 16 | ∅ | Yes | Yes | No | No |
| | China.com | 6 | - | $1^+$lower, $1^+$upper, $1^+$digit | No[a] | Yes | No | No |
| | Tecent | 6 | 16 | Not a number with len<9 | Yes | Yes | No | No |
| | Ifeng | 6 | 20 | ∅ | Yes | Yes | No | Account |
| | Yahoo | 7 | 30 | ∅ | No | Yes | No | Both[b] |
| IT corp. | Microsoft | 8 | 16 | Any 2 charsets | Yes | Yes | No | Both |
| | Intel | 8 | 15 | $1^+$letter, $1^+$digit, $1^+$symbol | Yes | Yes | No | Account |
| | Apple | 8 | 32 | $1^+$lower, $1^+$upper, $1^+$digit | Yes | Yes | No | Account |
| | Lenovo | 8 | 20 | Any 2 of letter, digit, symbol | No | Yes | No | No |
| | Huawei | 8 | 60 | $1^+$letter, $1^+$digit, $1^+$symbol | Yes | Yes | No | Account |
| Email | 139 | 6 | 16 | Not a number with len<8 | No[a] | Yes[c] | Yes | No |
| | 163 | 6 | 16 | ∅ | Yes | Yes | Yes | Account |
| | AOL | 8 | 16 | ∅ | Yes | Yes | Yes | Both |
| | Sohu | 6 | 16 | ∅ | Yes | Yes | Yes | No |
| | Gmail | 8 | - | ∅ | Yes | Yes | Yes | Both |
| | Rsing | 6 | - | ∅ | Yes | Yes | No | NO |
| Security corp. | Symantec | 8 | 25 | $1^+$letter, $1^+$digit | Yes | Yes | No | Account |
| | Kaspersky | 6 | 16 | ∅ | Yes | Yes | No | NO |
| | McAfee | 8 | 32 | $1^+$letter, $1^+$digit, no symbol | Yes | No | No | No |
| Ecommerce | 360 | 6 | 20 | ∅ | Yes | Yes | Yes | No |
| | Taobao | 6 | 20 | Any 2 of letter, digit, symbol | Yes | Yes | No | Account |
| | Jd.com | 6 | 20 | ∅ | Yes | Yes | Yes | Account |
| | Dangdang | 6 | 20 | ∅ | Yes | Yes | No | No |
| | Amazon | 6 | - | ∅ | Yes | Yes | No | No |
| | Meituan | 6 | 32 | ∅ | Yes | Yes | No | No |
| Gaming | 17173 | 6 | 20 | Not digits only | No[a] | Yes | Yes | No |
| | Duowan | 8 | 20 | Not a number with len<9 | Yes | Yes | No | No |
| | 4399.com | 6 | 20 | ∅ | Yes | Yes | No | No |
| | Sdo.com | 6 | 30 | Only letter and digit | Yes | No | Yes | No |
| | Wanmei | 6 | 16 | Only letter and digit | Yes | No | No | No |
| Technical forum | CSDN | 6 | 20 | ∅ | Yes | Yes | No | No |
| | 51CTO | 8 | 20 | ∅ | Yes | Yes | No | No |
| | ChinaUnix | 6 | 24 | Any 2 of letter, digit, symbol[d] | Yes | Yes | No | Account |
| | Hack80 | 9 | - | ∅ | Yes | Yes | No | No |
| | Pediy.com | 5 | - | ∅ | No[e] | Yes | Yes | No |
| Social forum | Tianya | 6 | - | $1^+$letter, $1^+$digit | Yes | Yes | Yes | No |
| | BBS.xiaomi | 8 | 16 | Any 2 of letter, digit, symbol | Yes | Yes | No | No |
| | Renren | 6 | 20 | ∅ | Yes | Yes | No | No |
| | Twitter | 6 | - | ∅ | Yes | Yes | Yes | Account |
| | Facebook | 6 | - | ∅ | Yes | Yes | Yes | No |
| Academic service | WoS | 8 | - | $1^+$letter, $1^+$digit, $1^+$special | Yes | Yes | No | No |
| | CNKI | 6 | 20 | No symbol(except '_') | Yes | No | Yes | No |
| | Cjc.ac.cn | 1 | - | ∅ | Yes | Yes | No | No |
| | Easychair | 6 | 40 | Not digits only | No | Yes | No | No |
| | Edas | 7 | - | $1^+$letter, $1^+$digit | No | Yes | Yes | No |
| Non-profit Org. | IEEE | 8 | 64 | $1^+$digit | Yes | Yes | Yes[f] | No |
| | ACM | 6 | 26 | ∅ | Yes | Yes | No | No |
| | W3C | 8 | - | ∅ | Yes | Yes | No | No |
| | CCF | 6 | 32 | ∅ | No | Yes | No | No |
| | CACR | 6 | - | ∅ | Yes | Yes | No | No |

[a]China.com, 139 and 17173 only explicitly require that password must be no shorter than 6, yet when one submits a password that do not fulfill the charset requirement, they prompt that more type(s) of character(s) is(are) needed.

[b]Yahoo checks whether user's personal name are incorporated in the password yet it is case sensitive, e.g., "wanglei123" will not be blocked if we input the surname 'Wang' instead of 'wang'.

[c]139 only accepts six kinds of symbols (i.e., _~@#$^).

[d]ChinaUnix explicitly states that a password must contain two types of characters, yet it accepts passwords (e.g., "123456789" and "qwertasdfg") that are measured as "medium" or "strong".

[e]There is no explicit rule in Pediy.com, yet when one submits a password shorter than 5, it prompts that an accepted password must be no shorter than 5.

[f]IEEE's blacklist only includes one item (i.e., "password"), which is explicitly stated.

16 and 20) and thus are prohibited from use. This may impair both security and usability.

Further considering that, increasing the password length is generally more effective in enhancing password security than extending the charsets [40], it is more advisable to set a maximum length limit that is large enough (e.g., 64).

**Charset Requirement.** Among the 50 sites, 23 sites (46 %) implement some charset requirements. Once again, all sites from the IT corp. category enforce a charset requirement, while other categories do not show this feature. Remarkably, 3 Chinese sites require that a digit-only password cannot be shorter than some minimum length (e.g., 9). This may be due to their insight into the fact that Chinese users highly love to use digit-only passwords—according to one of our earlier works [46], an average of 52.93 % Chinese users use digit-only passwords.

**Symbol Acceptance.** It is perhaps surprising to note that four sites (including both English and Chinese sites) prevent symbols to be included into passwords. Theoretically, among the 95 printable ASCII characters, 33 ones are symbols, excluding which would largely reduce an attacker's search space. It has also been established empirically that passwords with symbol(s) are generally much secure than passwords with no symbol [35,48]. The only plausible reason for forbidding symbols that we can imagine is to prevent SQL injection attacks, yet such attacks can be well prevented by properly handling the escape characters. It is really beyond comprehension why these four sites forbid symbols.

**Using Blacklist.** As recommended in NIST-800-63 [9], a blacklist of sufficient size (e.g., at least 50,000) is highly desirable in prevent popular passwords which are particularly vulnerable to statistical attacks [41]. US-CERT also suggest the use of blacklist [36]. However, only 16 sites (32 %) impose a blacklist and none of their blacklists are adequate. For instance, the blacklist of Twitter only contains 370 bad passwords and ironically, the blacklist of IEEE only consists of the famous "password". Also note that, all email sites impose a blacklist; 33 % Chinese services impose a blacklist, and this figure for English services is 30 %.

**Checking User Info.** As highlighted in both NIST-800-63 [9] and NIST-800-118 [40], uses tend to use their personal data (e.g., account name and personal name) to build passwords for better memorization, and accordingly, preventing the use of personal data in a password can raise the min-entropy of this password. However, only 14 sites (28 %) disallow account name and/or personal name to be included into passwords. Among these 14 sites, 9 come from English sites.

**Explicit Rules.** Despite the long-standing use of and familiarity with passwords, good password practices have not become "an established part of our security culture", and "even basic provision of guidance can help to deliver a tangible improvement" [20]. Consequently, it is crucial for sites to provide users with explicit advice and guidance, otherwise the implicit rules would only provide users with frustration and fatigue. However, there are still 9 sites (including 3 sites from English sites and 6 from Chinese sites) that do not make the password rules explicit, leaving the users to try their luck to comply with the required rules.

**Summary.** Despite the long-standing use of passwords and long-recognised importance of the provision of sound password practices, many leading web services seem to lose their lead in enforcing sensible password rules. As no two services examined share the same password rule, there seems to be no generally agreed-upon practice. In 2010, Bonneau and Preibusch [7] found "many aspects of password implementation are not standardised", while our results suggest that after five years of development, basic password practices are still highly diversified. What's worse, policy recommendations from major authorities are also quite different from each other (e.g., US-CERT [36] vs. NIST [40] vs. DISA [14]) and often far from practicable (e.g., "use different passwords on different systems" [36,40] and "users must not be able to reuse any of their previous 10 passwords." [14]). This greatly impairs their authoritativeness. Unsurprisingly, a large fraction of high-profile sites (e.g., Yahoo, Apple, Microsoft and Kaspersky) each maintains their own, even unnecessary, illogical rules. Security background or abundant capital, engineering resources do not correlate with noticeable advantages in policy strength (see Fig. 2). In addition, generally English sites implement more demanding rules than their Chinese counterparts.

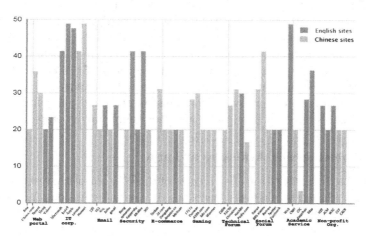

**Fig. 2.** Strength (in bits) of the 50 password composition rules

## 3.2   Password Strength Meters in the Tangle

To give users a feedback about the goodness of their selected passwords, password strength meters are employed to accomplish this aim. Recent research has shown that password meters, especially those with a timely [42], easily comprehensible [15] and accurate [45] feedback, can lead to tangible improvements in password security. Table 6 shows that 26 sites (10 English and 16 Chinese) employ a meter.

Among these 26 sites with a meter, 5 sites (including 3 from English sites and 2 from Chinese sites) only verbally show the password strength, and a mere 9 sites (including 5 from English sites and 4 from Chinese sites) impose mandatory strength requirements. Further considering that there are only 20 English sites out of 50 sites investigated, this suggests that, generally, English sites are more stringent in ensuring password security. It is also worth noting that, some sites (i.e., 139, IEEE and Hack80) provides strength feedback to a user only when the user's password meets with their password composition rules first.

According to Furnell's 2007 investigation [18], only two of the 10 sites studied provide a meter, while his 2011 investigation [19] saw a great advancement: 6 out of 10 sites provide a meter during user registration. However, our results show no advancement in password meter adoption during the past five years.

It is interesting to note that, most sites from the categories of web portal, email, e-commerce and technical forum employ a password meter, while most sites from the categories of IT corp., security corp. and academic service do not provide thus feature. Further considering that the later categories of sites typically employ more restrictive password rules (see Fig. 2), one would really be confused about what's their ultimate purpose of imposing a password creation policy from the user prospective. From the site prospective, as composition rules is highly more easy to be implemented and maintained than a password meter, and thus different choices mean different engineering cost involved. Consequently, one plausible (yet ironical) reason may be that, IT corp. sites, security corp. sites and academic service sites do not provide a meter due to engineering cost. Another reason may be that, due to the "failure of the academic literature to provide approaches that are convincingly better than current practices" [6], these technically-savvy sites are aware of the ineffectiveness of the current password meters, yet there is no adequate, concrete and well-grounded knowledge (e.g., about architectures, frameworks, algorithms, metrics and guidelines) available for them to get things (towards) right, and they simply do not employ any meter.

### 3.3   Online Guessing Attackers at Large

We proceed to investigate the effectiveness of these 50 policies in resisting against the primary threat to password accounts, i.e. online guessing. As detailed in Sect. 2.5, we specially select two types of weak passwords to model the two different types of online guessing (i.e., trawling and targeted) attacks, respectively. Each type is composed of 8 testing passwords, and each password is tested against every service, meaning a total of $800(=2*8*50)$ testing instances.

Our results (see Table 7) show that among the 800 testing instances, 541 ones are accepted, where 257 ones are accepted without providing any strength information, 83 ones are accepted while they are metered "weak/low", and each site accepts at least two instances (passwords). Among these 259 rejected instances, 221 ones are rejected by password rules, 17 ones are rejected by password meters, and 21 ones are rejected by both the password rule and meter.

This has at least two important implications. First, considering that at least 2 (and an average of 10.8) weak passwords are allowed by every site and that, ironically, 15 leading sites, including many technically savvy services (e.g., Kaspersky, Rsing and ACM) and financially sound services (e.g., Amazon and Dangdang), accept all the 16 weak passwords like "123456", "woaini" and "wanglei", it is really difficult to refuse the implication that the password policies imposed by

**Table 6.** An overview of the password strength meters in the selected web services ('∅' stands for no strength scale; '-' stands for non-existence; 'Monotonicity' stands for whether an additional character contributes to a better score)

| Web Services | | Strength score scale | Verbal or visual | Monotonicity | Least score enforcement |
|---|---|---|---|---|---|
| Web portal | Sina | Very weak, Weak, Medium, High | Both | Yes | Weak |
| | China.com | Weak, Medium, Strong | Both | Yes | Medium |
| | Tecent | Weak, Medium, Strong | Both | Yes | ∅ |
| | Ifeng | Low, Medium, High | Both | Yes | ∅ |
| | Yahoo | 1(Easy to guess), 2(weak), 3(Medium), 4(Strong), 5(Very Strong)[a] | Visual[b] | Yes | 3(Medium) |
| IT Corp. | Microsoft | ∅ | None | - | ∅ |
| | Intel | ∅ | None | - | ∅ |
| | Apple | Weak, Medium, Strong | Verbal | No | Medium |
| | Lenovo | ∅ | None | - | ∅ |
| | Huawei | ∅ | None | - | ∅ |
| Email | 139 | ∅ | None | No | ∅ |
| | 163 | Weak, Medium, Strong | Both | Yes | ∅ |
| | AOL | Weak, Strong, Brilliant | Both | Yes | ∅ |
| | Sohu | Weak, Medium, Strong | Both | Yes | ∅ |
| | Gmail | Too short, Weak, Fair, Slightly strong, Strong | Both | No | Fair |
| Security Corp. | Rsing | ∅ | None | - | ∅ |
| | Symantec | ∅ | None | - | ∅ |
| | Kaspersky | ∅ | None | - | ∅ |
| | McAfee | ∅ | None | - | ∅ |
| | 360 | ∅ | None | - | ∅ |
| Ecommerce | Taobao | Low, Medium, High | Both | Yes | Medium |
| | Jd.com | Weak, Medium, Strong | Both | Yes | ∅ |
| | Dangdang | Weak, Medium, Strong | Both | Yes | ∅ |
| | Amazon | ∅ | None | - | ∅ |
| | Meituan | Weak, Medium, Strong | Both | - | ∅ |
| Gaming | 17173 | Weak, Medium, Strong | Verbal | - | ∅ |
| | Duowan | ∅ | None | - | ∅ |
| | 4399.com | ∅ | None | - | ∅ |
| | Sdo.com | Weak, Medium, Strong | Both | - | ∅ |
| | Wanmei | Low, Medium, High | Both | - | ∅ |
| Technical Forum | CSDN | Low, Medium, High | Both | Yes | ∅ |
| | 51CTO | Weak, Medium, Strong | Both | Yes | ∅ |
| | ChinaUnix | Weak, Medium, Strong | Both | Yes | Medium |
| | Hack80 | Weak, Medium, Strong | Both | Yes | ∅ |
| | Pediy.com | ∅ | None | - | ∅ |
| Social Forum | Tianya | ∅ | None | - | ∅ |
| | BBS.xiaomi | ∅ | None | - | ∅ |
| | Renren | Weak, Fair, Very brilliant | Verbal | Yes | ∅ |
| | Twitter | Too obvious/short, NSE, Can be more secure, Ok, Medium, Strong, Perfect | Visual[b] | No | Not secure enough (NSE) |
| | Facebook | ∅ | None | - | ∅ |
| Academic Service | WoS | ∅ | None | - | ∅ |
| | CNKI | ∅ | None | - | ∅ |
| | Cjc.ac.cn | ∅ | None | - | ∅ |
| | Easychair | ∅ | None | - | ∅ |
| | Edas | Weak, Medium, Strong | Verbal | No | ∅ |
| Non-profit Org. | IEEE | Should be stronger, Good, Great | Both | No | ∅ |
| | ACM | ∅ | None | - | ∅ |
| | W3C | Very weak, Weak, Sufficient, Strong, Very strong | Verbal | Yes | Sufficient |
| | CCF | ∅ | None | - | ∅ |
| | CACR | ∅ | None | - | ∅ |

[a] According to the results obtained in 2013 [10], the password meter of Yahoo was "Weak, Strong, Very strong". Yet, at the time of this writing Yahoo has changed its policy and divides its strength bar into five scales. Although Yahoo's meter only verbally displays the strength score when the password is "1 (Easy to guess)" or "2 (Weak)", and for the other cases, only a visual progress bar is in place, fortunately one can identify the total number of such cases (i.e., three). In line with its scores in 2013, we suppose the three scores corresponding to these three scales that are not verbally displayed are "3(Medium)", "4(Strong)" and "5(Very Strong)", respectively.

[b] The password meters of Yahoo and Twitter only verbally displays the strength score when a password can not be accepted. When a password can be accepted, *only* a visual progress bar is in place. Consequently, their meters is deemed to be visually displayed.

**Table 7.** An overview of the evaluation results of 16 passwords on 50 web services

| | 123456 | 123456789 | 5201314 | woaini | iloveyou | password | woainil314 | password123 | wanglei | wanglei123 | wangleil | wanglei2 | Wanglei123 | wang.lei | wanglei@123 | Wanglei@123 |
|---|---|---|---|---|---|---|---|---|---|---|---|---|---|---|---|---|
| Sina | ✓,VW | ✓,W | ✓,VW | ✓,W | ✓,VW | ✓,VW | ✓,VW | ✓,S | ✓,S | ✓,W | ✓,S | ✓,M | ✓,M | ✓,S | ✓,M | ✓,S |
| China.com | ⊗,W | ⊗,W | ⊗,W | ⊗,W | ⊗,W | ⊗,W | ⊗,W | ⊗,M | ⊗,M | ⊗,W | ⊗,M | ⊗,M | ⊗,M | ✓,M | ⊗,M | ✓,S |
| Tecent | ⊗,W | ✓,W | ⊗,W | ⊗,W | ✓,W | ✓,W | ✓,W | ✓,M | ✓,M | ✓,W | ✓,M | ✓,W | ✓,M | ✓,S | ✓,M | ✓,S |
| Ifeng | ✓,L | ✓,L | ✓,L | ✓,L | ✓,L | ✓,L | ✓,L | ✓,M | ✓,M | ✓,L | ✓,M | ✓,M | ✓,M | ✓,H | ✓,M | ✓,H |
| Yahoo | ⊗,W | ✓,M | ⊗,W | ⊗,W | ⊗,W | ⊗,W | ⊗,W | ✓,M | ✓,S | ⊗,W | ✓,M | ✓,M | ✓,M | ⊗,W | ✓,M | ⊗,W |
| Microsoft | ® | ® | ® | ® | ® | ® | ® | ✓ | ✓ | ® | ® | ✓ | ✓ | ® | ® | ✓ |
| Intel | ® | ® | ® | ® | ® | ® | ® | ✓ | ✓ | ® | ® | ✓ | ✓ | ® | ® | ✓ |
| Apple | ®,W | ®,W | ⊗,W | ®,W | ®,W | ®,W | ®,M | ®,M | | ®,W | ®,M | ®,W | ✓,W | | ®,M | ✓,S |
| Lenovo | ® | ® | ® | ® | ® | ® | ® | ✓ | ✓ | ® | ® | ✓ | ✓ | ® | ® | ✓ |
| Huawei | ® | ® | ® | ® | ® | ® | ® | ✓ | ✓ | ® | ® | ✓ | ✓ | ® | ® | ✓ |
| 139 | ®,W | ®,W | ®,W | ®,W | ✓,W | ✓,W | ✓,W | ✓,M | ✓,M | ✓,W | ✓,M | ✓,M | ✓,M | ✓,S | | ✓,S |
| 163 | ®,W | ®,W | ®,W | ®,W | ✓,W | ✓,W | ✓,W | ✓,M | ✓,M | ✓,W | ®,S | ®,S | ®,S | ®,S | ✓,M | ®,S |
| AOL | ®,W | ®,W | ®,W | ®,W | ✓,W | ✓,W | ✓,W | ✓,S | ✓,S | ® | ®,M | ✓,M | ✓,M | ✓,M | ✓,W | ®,B |
| Sohu | ®,W | ®,W | ®,W | ®,W | ✓,W | ✓,W | ✓,W | ✓,M | ✓,M | ✓,W | ✓,M | ✓,M | ✓,M | ✓,M | ✓,M | ✓,M |
| Gmail | ®,TS | ®,W | ®,TS | ⊗,W | ®,TS | ✓,W | ✓,W | ✓,M | ✓,W | ✓,W | ✓,F | ✓,F | ✓,SS | ✓,SS | ✓,F | ✓,S |
| Rsing | ® | ® | ®, | ® | ® | ® | ✓ | ✓ | ✓ | ® | ✓ | ✓ | ✓ | ✓ | ® | ® |
| Symantec | ® | ® | ® | ® | ® | ® | ✓ | ✓ | ✓ | ® | ✓ | ✓ | ✓ | ✓ | ® | ® |
| kaspersky | ® | ® | ® | ® | ® | ® | ✓ | ✓ | ✓ | ® | ✓ | ✓ | ✓ | ✓ | ® | ® |
| McAfee | ® | ® | ® | ® | ® | ® | ✓ | ✓ | ✓ | ® | ✓ | ✓ | ✓ | ✓ | ® | ® |
| 360 | ® | ® | ® | ® | ® | ® | ✓ | ✓ | ✓ | ® | ✓ | ✓ | ✓ | ✓ | ® | ® |
| Taobao | ®,L | ®,M | ®,M | ®,L | ®,M | ®,M | ®,M | ✓,M | ✓,M | ®,L | ✓,M | ✓,M | ✓,M | ✓,M | ✓,M | ✓,H |
| Jd.com | ®,W | ®,W | ®,W | ®,W | ®,W | ®,W | ®,W | ✓,M | ✓,S | ✓,W | ✓,M | ✓,M | ✓,M | ✓,M | ✓,S | ✓,S |
| Dangdang | ✓,W | ✓,W | ✓,W | ✓,W | ✓,W | ✓,W | ✓,W | ✓,M | ✓,M | ✓,W | ✓,M | ✓,M | ✓,M | ✓,S | ✓,S | ✓,S |
| Amazon | | | | | | | | | | | | | | | | |
| Meituan | ✓,W | ✓,W | ✓,W | ✓,W | ✓,W | ✓,W | ✓,W | ✓,M | ✓,M | ✓,W | ✓,M | ✓,W | ✓,M | ✓,S | ✓,W | ✓,S |
| 17173 | ®,W | ®,W | ®,W | ®,W | ®,W | ®,W | ✓,W | ✓,M | ✓,M | ®,W | ✓,M | ✓,M | ✓,M | ✓,S | ✓,S | ✓,S |
| Duowan | ® | ® | ® | ® | ® | ® | ✓ | ✓ | ✓ | ® | ✓ | ✓ | ✓ | ✓ | ® | ® |
| 4399.com | ® | ® | ® | ® | ® | ® | ✓ | ✓ | ✓ | ® | ✓ | ✓ | ✓ | ✓ | ® | ® |
| Sdo.com | ®,W | ®,M | ✓,M | ✓,M | ✓,W | ✓,M | ✓,M | ✓,M | ✓,S | ✓,M | ✓,M | ✓,M | ✓,M | ✓,M | | |
| Wanmei | ®,L | ✓,L | ✓,L | ✓,L | ✓,L | ✓,L | ✓,L | ✓,M | ✓,M | ✓,L | ✓,M | ✓,L | ✓,M | ✓,H | ® | ® |
| CSDN | ✓,L | ✓,L | ✓,L | ✓,L | ✓,L | ✓,L | ✓,L | ✓,H | ✓,H | ✓,L | ✓,H | ✓,M | ✓,M | ✓,H | ✓,H | ✓,H |
| 51CTO | ✓,W | ✓,W | ✓,W | ✓,W | ✓,W | ✓,W | ✓,W | ✓,M | ✓,M | ✓,W | ✓,M | ✓,M | ✓,M | ✓,M | ✓,S | ✓,S |
| Chinaunix | ®,W | ✓,M | ®,W | ®,W | ®,W | ®,W | ®,W | ✓,M | ✓,M | ®,W | ✓,M | ® | ✓,M | ✓,M | ✓,S | ✓,S |
| Hack80 | ✓,W | ✓,W | | | | | | ✓,M | ✓,M | ✓,M | ✓,M | | | | | |
| Pediy.com | ® | | ® | ® | ® | ® | ✓ | ✓ | ✓ | ® | ✓ | ✓ | ✓ | ✓ | ® | ® |
| Xiaomi | ® | ® | ✓ | ✓ | ® | ✓ | ✓ | ✓ | ✓ | ® | ✓ | ✓ | ✓ | ✓ | ® | ® |
| Tianya | ® | ® | ® | ® | ® | ® | ✓ | ✓ | ✓ | ® | ✓ | ✓ | ✓ | ✓ | ® | ® |
| Renren | ®,W | ®,W | ✓,W | ✓,W | ®,W | ✓,W | ✓,M | ✓,M | ®,W | ✓,M | ✓,M | ✓,M | ✓,S | ✓,M | ✓,S | ✓,S |
| Twitter | ®,TO | ®,TO | ✓,CMS | ✓,NSE | ® | ®,TO | ✓,OK | ®,TO | ✓,NSE | ✓,OK | ✓,NSE | ✓,CMS | ✓,M | ✓,CMS | ✓,S | ✓,P |
| Facebook | ® | ® | ® | ® | ® | ® | ® | ® | ® | ® | ® | ® | ® | ® | ® | ® |
| WoS | ® | ® | ® | ® | ® | ® | ® | ✓ | ✓ | ® | ✓ | ✓ | ✓ | ✓ | ✓ | ✓ |
| CNKI | ® | ® | ® | ® | ® | ® | ✓ | ✓ | ✓ | ® | ✓ | ✓ | ✓ | ✓ | ✓ | ✓ |
| CJC | ® | ® | ® | ® | ® | ® | ✓ | ✓ | ✓ | ® | ✓ | ✓ | ✓ | ✓ | ✓ | ✓ |
| Easychair | ® | ® | ® | ® | ® | ® | ✓ | ✓ | ✓ | ® | ✓ | ✓ | ✓ | ✓ | ✓ | ✓ |
| Edas | ®,W | ®,W | ®,W | ®,W | ®,W | ®,W | ✓,W | ✓,W | ✓,W | ®,W | ✓,W | ✓,W | ✓,W | ✓,M | ✓,W | ✓,S |
| IEEE | ® | ® | ® | ® | ® | ® | ✓,G | ® | ✓,G | ✓,SBS | ✓,G | ✓,G | ® | ✓,G | ✓,G | |
| ACM | ® | ® | ® | ® | ® | ® | ® | ® | ® | ® | ® | ® | ® | ® | ® | ® |
| W3C | ⊗,VW | Ⓜ,VW | ⊗,VW | ⊗,VW | Ⓜ,VW | Ⓜ,VW | ✓,Suf | ✓,Suf | ⊗,VW | ✓,Suf | Ⓜ,W | ✓,W | ✓,S | Ⓜ,W | ✓,Suf | ✓,VS |
| CCF | ® | ® | ® | ® | ® | ® | ✓ | ✓ | ® | ✓ | ✓ | ✓ | ✓ | ✓ | ✓ | ✓ |
| CACR | ® | ® | ® | ® | ® | ® | ✓ | ✓ | ® | ✓ | ✓ | ✓ | ✓ | ✓ | ✓ | ✓ |

1° **Notations:** ✓: Accepted; ®: Rejected by password composition rules; Ⓜ: Rejected by password strength meter; ⊗: Rejected by both the password rule and meter.

2° **Abbreviations:** B = Brilliant; G = Good; H = High; L = Low; M = Medium; P = Perfect; S= Strong; W = Weak; SS = Slightly strong; ; TO = Too obvious; TS = Too short; TW = Too weak; VS = Very strong; VW = Very weak; CMS = Can be more secure; NSE = Not secure enough; SBS= Should be stronger, Suf = Sufficient.

3° The evaluation result for password $A$ vs. site $B$ is in the "X,Y" format, where "X" indicates whether $A$ is accepted or rejected by $B$, and "Y" indicates $A$'s strength score given by $B$'s password meter. If $B$ is with no meter, "Y" is naturally absent. We note that for three sites with meters (i.e., AOL, Twitter and Hack80), the strength score "Y" is also absent in cases where the password $A$ does not comply with $B$'s password rules.

the 50 sites largely fail to serve their purpose—resisting online guessing. Second, currently, password rules are overwhelmingly dominant in the filtering of bad passwords, and password meters should have played a more important role.

Perhaps unsurprisingly, password strength scores of the 50 selected sites are highly inconsistent, which accords with previous work [10]. Very often, inherently weak passwords (e.g., "password123" and "wangleil") pass the check of password rules and is labeled as strong by password meters, and they are accepted by sites of significant value (e.g., all of the five e-commerce sites); the same password receives highly inconsistent strength outcomes from different password meters and is accepted or rejected for unintelligible reason. For instance, "Wanglei@123" is measured as "weak" by Yahoo, "medium" by Sohu and "strong" by Gmail; It is rejected by McAfee (which accepts "wanglei123"). These *inaccuracies* provide users with a false sense of security, and what's worse, these *inconsistencies* cause user confusion in selecting a stronger password, both of which would lead the "weakest link" (i.e., common users) in the security chain to be weaker.

Particularly, among the 541 accepted instances, 323 ones (i.e., 59.7%) are used for the test against targeted online guessing, which suggests that web services on today's Internet are comparatively more vulnerable to targeted attacks (at least, against Chinese users). The right part of Table 7, further shows that, most of the meters largely overestimate the strength of Type B passwords and Chinese sites show no better performance, which renders such kind of passwords at large over the Internet and also provides a false sense of security to users.

**Some Remarks.** To the best of our knowledge, 15 web services studied in this work have been the victims of hacking and leaked large amounts of user credentials (see some shivery news [33,34,37,39]). As far as can be confirmed, among these 15 leaked sites, 9 ones have changed their password policies during the past five years. More specifically, Yahoo has changed its length limits from 6–32 to 7–30 in the last year as compared to the data reported in 2014 by [10]; Apple changed its some lenient charset requirement to the current "$1^+$lower, $1^+$upper, $1^+$digit" in 2012 according to [29]; As compared to the data reported in 2011 by [19], Microsoft has changed its length limits from 6–16 to 8–16 and its meter ratings from {Weak, Medium, Strong} to {∅}, Gmail has changed its meter ratings from {Weak, Fair, Good, Strong} to the current {Too short, Weak, Fair, ⋯ }, Twitter has changed its meter ratings from {⋯ , Weak, Good, Strong, Very strong} to the current {⋯ , Medium, Strong, Perfect}, Facebook has changed its meter ratings from {Weak, Medium, Strong} to {∅}; As victims of the 2011 catastrophic hacking event [33], Duowan changed its length limits from 6–20 to 8–20, CSDN changed its length limits from 8–20 to 6–20, and Tianya added the current charset requirement. In addition, we can identify that AOL has changed its length limits from 6–16 to 8–16 as compared to the data we collected in Mar. 2014, and Taobao changed its length limits from 6–16 to 6–20.

In all, during the past five years, as far as we know, 6 sites have adopted more complex and stringent rules, 1 sites have relaxed its rules, 2 sites have changed their rating scores and 2 sites have chosen not to provide meters at all. While 8 of the 11 changed sites may be towards seemingly more stringent or usable policies, 3 sites are highly going against the trend of good password practices, bearing no serious efforts from these 3 service providers. In a nutshell, as shown in Table 7, all these 11 "new" password policies still largely fail to serve their purposes and are virtually equivalent to '*the emperor's new password policies*'.

At least, new services or existing ones that wish to establish/change a password policy, should not start the development of yet another policy, but rather consider using or extending the pacemakers' policies to be more consistent with common sense practices and to be more prudent with local, cultural characteristics. Comparatively, among the 50 policies studied, the current policy adopted by Apple is the most effective one against online guessing. However, it is at the cost of usability and leads to great user frustration and fatigue [29]. For example, the

"1+lower, 1+upper, 1+digit" rule highly hinders mobile users. This highlights the imperative needs for more academic efforts to guide the industrial practice.

## 4   Conclusion

In this work, we have conducted a large-scale empirical analysis of the current state of password creation policies imposed by 50 leading web services by using a systematic, evidence-supported approach. We find that the policies are highly diversified among the studied sites and largely fail to withstand online guessing attacks. Comparatively, password composition rules play a more important role in resisting online guessing than password strength meters, partly because most meters are merely suggestive, and partly because current meters are inaccurate in gauging the strength of passwords. Consistent with previous work [10], highly inconsistent outcomes are given for the same testing password by different meters, which may confuse users and undermine user trust in security advice, defeating the purpose of enforcing password policies in the first place.

As compared to Chinese sites, English sites generally enforce more stringent password polices. We also discuss the factors that may influence a site's choice of password policies. Our results show that, overall, security background or abundant capital, engineering resources do not correlate with noticeable advantages in password practice, as opposed to previous work [7]. A natural future work is to incorporate more sample sites (e.g., medium sites, and sites from other languages and services) and investigate more types of password policies (such as password change, lockout and expiration), gaining a more complete picture of the whole password ecosystem and proposing well-grounded policy recommendations.

**Acknowledgment.** We are grateful to the anonymous reviewers for their invaluable comments. We also thank Dr. Ye Bai, Zhecheng Sun, and Chen Zhu for helping collect the data. This research was supported by the National Natural Science Foundation of China (NSFC) program under Grant No. 61472016.

## References

1. Al-Ameen, M.N., Wright, M., Scielzo, S.: Towards making random passwords memorable: Leveraging users' cognitive ability through multiple cues. In: Proceedings of the ACM CHI 2015, Seoul, Republic of Korea, 18–23 April 2015, pp. 1–10 (2015)
2. Allan, C.: 32 million Rockyou passwords stolen, December 2009. http://www.hardwareheaven.com/news.php?newsid=526
3. Bauman, E., Lu, Y., Lin, Z.: Half a century of practice: who is still storing plaintext passwords? In: Lopez, J., Wu, Y. (eds.) ISPEC 2015. LNCS, vol. 9065, pp. 253–267. Springer, Heidelberg (2015)
4. Bishop, M., Klein, D.V.: Improving system security via proactive password checking. Comput. Secur. **14**(3), 233–249 (1995)
5. Bonneau, J.: The science of guessing: Analyzing an anonymized corpus of 70 million passwords. In: Proceedings of the IEEE S&P 2012, pp. 538–552 (2012)

6. Bonneau, J., Herley, C., van Oorschot, P., Stajano, F.: Passwords and the evolution of imperfect authentication. Commun. ACM **58**(7), 78–87 (2015)
7. Bonneau, J., Preibusch, S.: The password thicket: Technical and market failures in human authentication on the web. In: Proceedings of the WEIS 2010, Harvard University, USA, pp. 1–48. 7–8 June 2010
8. Burnett, M.: 10,000 top passwords, June 2011. https://xato.net/passwords/more-top-worst-passwords/
9. Burr, W., Dodson, D., Perlner, R., Polk, W., Gupta, S., Nabbus, E.: NIST SP800-63 – electronic authentication guideline. Technical report, Reston, VA, April 2006
10. Carnavalet, X., Mannan, M.: From very weak to very strong: Analyzing password-strength meters. In: Proceedings of the NDSS 2014, pp. 1–16 (2014)
11. Chiasson, S., van Oorschot, P.C.: Quantifying the security advantage of password expiration policies. Designs, Codes and Cryptography (2015, in press). http://dx.doi.org/10.1007/s10623-015-0071-9
12. CNNIC: CNNIC Released the 35th Statistical Report on Internet Development in China, February 2015. http://www.apira.org/news.php?id=1732
13. Das, A., Bonneau, J., Caesar, M., Borisov, N., Wang, X.: The tangled web of password reuse. In: Proceedings of the NDSS 2014, pp. 1–15 (2014)
14. DISA for DoD: Application security and development. Tech. rep., Defense Information Systems Agency (DISA), Reston, VA, July 2013. http://www.stigviewer.com/stig/application_security_and_development/
15. Egelman, S., Sotirakopoulos, A., Beznosov, K., Herley, C.: Does my password go up to eleven?: the impact of password meters on password selection. In: Proceedings of the CHI 2013, pp. 2379–2388. ACM (2013)
16. Florencio, D., Herley, C.: A large-scale study of web password habits. In: Proceedings of the WWW 2007, pp. 657–666. ACM (2007)
17. Florêncio, D., Herley, C.: Where do security policies come from? In: Proceedings of the ACM SOUPS 2010, 14–16 July 2010, pp. 1–14. ACM, Redmond (2010)
18. Furnell, S.: An assessment of website password practices. Comput. Secur. **26**(7), 445–451 (2007)
19. Furnell, S.: Assessing password guidance and enforcement on leading websites. Comput. Fraud Secur. **2011**(12), 10–18 (2011)
20. Furnell, S., Bär, N.: Essential lessons still not learned? examining the password practices of end-users and service providers. In: Marinos, L., Askoxylakis, I. (eds.) HAS 2013. LNCS, vol. 8030, pp. 217–225. Springer, Heidelberg (2013)
21. Goldman, J.: Chinese Hackers Publish 20 Million Hotel Reservations, December 2013. http://www.esecurityplanet.com/hackers/chinese-hackers-publish-20-million-hotel-reservations.html
22. Haikun, C.: Multiply the total to 3.647 million on chinese web sites, February 2015. http://www.changhaikun.com/index.php/2015/04/03/multiply-the-total-to-3-647-million-on-chinese-web-sites/
23. Herley, C., Van Oorschot, P.: A research agenda acknowledging the persistence of passwords. IEEE Secur. Priv. **10**(1), 28–36 (2012)
24. Huang, X., Xiang, Y., Chonka, A., Zhou, J., Deng, R.H.: A generic framework for three-factor authentication: Preserving security and privacy in distributed systems. IEEE Trans. Parallel Distrib. Syst. **22**(8), 1390–1397 (2011)
25. Huang, Z., Ayday, E., Fellay, J., Hubaux, J.P., Juels, A.: Genoguard: Protecting genomic data against brute-force attacks. In: Proceedings of the IEEE S&P 2015, San Jose, CA, USA, pp. 447–462. 17–21 May 2015
26. Ihm, S., Pai, V.S.: Towards understanding modern web traffic. In: Proceedings of the ACM SIGCOMM 2011, pp. 295–312. ACM (2011)

27. Jakobsson, M., Dhiman, M.: The benefits of understanding passwords. In: Proceedings of the HotSec 2012, pp. 1–6. USENIX Association (2012)

28. Jiang, Q., Tan, C.H., Phang, C.W., Sutanto, J., Wei, K.K.: Understanding chinese online users and their visits to websites: Application of zipf's law. Int. J. Inf. Manage. **33**(5), 752–763 (2013)

29. Johns, R.: Illogical apple id password rules, May 2012. https://discussions.apple.com/thread/3785494

30. Keith, M., Shao, B., Steinbart, P.: A behavioral analysis of passphrase design and effectiveness. J. Assoc. Inf. Syst. **10**(2), 2 (2009)

31. Kelley, P.G., Komanduri, S., Mazurek, M.L., Shay, R., Vidas, T., Bauer, L., Christin, N., Cranor, L.F., Lopez, J.: Guess again (and again and again): Measuring password strength by simulating password-cracking algorithms. In: Proceedings of the IEEE S&P 2012, pp. 523–537. IEEE (2012)

32. Ma, J., Yang, W., Luo, M., Li, N.: A study of probabilistic password models. In: Proceedings of the IEEE S&P 2014, pp. 538–552. IEEE (2014)

33. Martin, R.: Amid Widespread Data Breaches in China, December 2011. http://www.techinasia.com/alipay-hack/

34. Mathew, J.S.: 15,000 twitter credentials stolen and leaked, hacker promises more soon, August 2013. http://www.itcmt.com/2013/08/23/15000-twitter-credentials-stolen-and-leaked-hacker-promises-more-soon/

35. Mazurek, M.L., Komanduri, S., Vidas, T., Cranor, L.F., Kelley, P.G., Shay, R., Ur, B.: Measuring password guessability for an entire university. In: Proceedings of the CCS 2013, 4–8 November 2013, pp. 173–186. ACM (2013)

36. McDowell, M., Hernan, S., Rafail, J.: Security Tip (ST04-002): Choosing and Protecting Passwords (2013). https://www.us-cert.gov/ncas/tips/ST04-002

37. Millward, S.: Xiaomi now has 100 million users of its android-based mobile os, February 2015. https://www.techinasia.com/xiaomi-miui-100-million-users/

38. Morris, R., Thompson, K.: Password security: A case history. Commun. ACM **22**(11), 594–597 (1979)

39. Rhodan, M.: Nearly 5 million google passwords leaked on russian site, September 2014. http://time.com/3318853/google-user-logins-bitcoin/

40. Scarfone, K., Souppaya, M.: NIST SP800-118: Guide to enterprise password management. Technical report, NIST, Reston, VA, August 2013

41. Schechter, S., Herley, C., Mitzenmacher, M.: Popularity is everything: A new approach to protecting passwords from statistical-guessing attacks. In: Proceedings of the HotSec 2010, pp. 1–8 (2010)

42. Shay, R., Bauer, L., Christin, N., Cranor, L.F., Forget, A., Komanduri, S., Mazurek, M., Melicher, W., Segreti, S.M., Ur, B.: A spoonful of sugar? the impact of guidance and feedback on password-creation behavior. In: Proceedings of the CHI 2015, Seoul, Korea, pp. 2903–2912. 18–24 April 2015

43. Shay, R., Komanduri, S., Durity, A.L., Huh, P.S., Mazurek, M.L., Segreti, S.M., Ur, B., Bauer, L., Christin, N., Cranor, L.F.: Can long passwords be secure and usable? In: Proceedings of the ACM CHI 2014, pp. 2927–2936. ACM (2014)

44. Top 500 chinese pinyin names, January 2015. http://www.data.ac.cn/zrzy/g22.asp

45. Ur, B., Kelley, P.G., Komanduri, S., et al.: How does your password measure up? the effect of strength meters on password creation. In: Proceedings of the USENIX Security 2012, Bellevue, WA, USA, 8–10 August 2012, pp. 65–80 (2012)

46. Wang, D., Cheng, H., Wang, P.: Understanding Passwords of Chinese Users: Characteristics, Security and Implications, January 2015. http://t.cn/RzSlpDz

47. Wang, D., He, D., Wang, P., Chu, C.H.: Anonymous two-factor authentication in distributed systems: certain goals are beyond attainment. IEEE Trans. Depend. Secur. Comput. **12**(4), 428–442 (2015)
48. Weir, M., Aggarwal, S., Collins, M., Stern, H.: Testing metrics for password creation policies by attacking large sets of revealed passwords. In: Proceedings of the CCS 2010, 4–8 October 2010, pp. 162–175. ACM (2010)
49. Yan, J., Blackwell, A.F., Anderson, R.J., Grant, A.: Password memorability and security: Empirical results. IEEE Secur. Priv. **2**(5), 25–31 (2004)
50. Yap, J.: 450,000 user passwords leaked in Yahoo breach, July 2012. http://www.zdnet.com/article/450000-user-passwords-leaked-in-yahoo-breach/
51. Zhu, B., Yan, J., Bao, G., Mao, M., Xu, N.: Captcha as graphical passwords-a new security primitive based on hard AI problems. IEEE Trans. Inform. Forensics Secur. **9**(6), 891–904 (2014)

# Policies

# A Theory of Gray Security Policies

Donald Ray and Jay Ligatti[(✉)]

Department of Computer Science and Engineering,
University of South Florida, Tampa, USA
{dray3,ligatti}@cse.usf.edu

**Abstract.** This paper generalizes traditional models of security policies, from specifications of *whether* programs are secure, to specifications
of *how* secure programs are. This is a generalization from qualitative,
black-and-white policies to quantitative, gray policies. Included are generalizations from traditional definitions of safety and liveness policies
to definitions of gray-safety and gray-liveness policies. These generalizations preserve key properties of safety and liveness, including that the
intersection of safety and liveness is a unique allow-all policy and that
every policy can be written as the conjunction of a single safety and a
single liveness policy. It is argued that the generalization provides several
benefits, including that it serves as a unifying framework for disparate
approaches to security metrics, and that it separates—in a practically
useful way—specifications of how secure systems are from specifications
of how secure users require their systems to be.

## 1   Introduction

Computer-security policies have traditionally been modeled as predicates,
partitioning the secure from the insecure system behaviors. Policies partition
behaviors by specifying constraints like "only administrators may write to files",
"packets destined for port 120 must be logged", or "all array accesses must be
bounds-checked". These are qualitative, black-and-white constraints that can be
used to decide whether a given system is secure.

This paper generalizes the qualitative, black-and-white model of policies to
a quantitative, gray model. Instead of specifying *whether* systems are secure,
gray policies specify *how* secure systems are. For example, a gray policy for
array-bounds checking might consider that checking every array access makes
a program 100 % secure and that each unchecked access decimates a program's
current rating.

Gray policies are useful because users are often unwilling to pay the costs
required to achieve 100 % security according to some policy. As is well understood, enforcement costs can be high, typically in the form of:

- performance overhead (e.g., due to increased runtime checks),
- code-size overhead (e.g., due to inlined monitoring code),
- decreased usability (e.g., due to authentication procedures), and

© Springer International Publishing Switzerland 2015
G. Pernul et al. (Eds.): ESORICS 2015, Part II, LNCS 9327, pp. 481–499, 2015.
DOI: 10.1007/978-3-319-24177-7_24

– consumption of other system resources (e.g., due to security checks draining batteries or security logs draining file-system space).

To make an analogy with the physical world, safes are not rated as secure or insecure, but rather by the estimated amount of time needed to penetrate them with a given set of tools. Such a quantitative rating enables consumers to weigh the security metric against other metrics, such as size, weight, price, and availability, when choosing a safe to buy. Importantly, a choice made in one context may differ from a choice made in another context, depending on the priorities of the purchaser and resources available.

In this paper's framework, a gray policy specifies a system's security rating, while a *silhouette judge* specifies a user's security requirements. Returning to the safe analogy, a silhouette judge is like a consumer's purchasing-decision algorithm that inputs a safe's security rating and, combining it with the safe's other attributes, outputs a buy or don't-buy decision.

Thus, this paper's framework separates the intuitively distinct specifications of how secure systems are (gray policies) from how secure users require their systems to be (silhouette judges). This separation enables users with different security requirements to use the same gray policy in different ways, by specifying different silhouette judges. For example, in the context of high-performance systems research users might require 0 % security (e.g., no array-bounds checking), while in the context of flight-navigation software users might require 100 % security.

There are additional benefits of the gray model over the black-and-white model. Gray policies enable users to compare the security of different systems when choosing which to use. In the black-and-white model, a user who can't afford to run a "secure" web browser has to choose between other browsers only known to be "insecure"; in the gray model, the same user could choose the most secure of the affordable browsers. As another potential benefit, consumers often base purchasing decisions on measurable attributes, so quantifying security could drive demand for security improvements, even ones that degrade performance by 10–20 % or more, thus countering the arguments of some developers that such security overheads are intolerable [32].

### Overview of Related Work and Contributions

Of course, the idea to quantify security is not new (e.g., [3,14,18,31,35,48,49]).

However, the extensive research into general-purpose models of policies has considered them to be predicates and therefore black and white (e.g., [17,22,24, 29,41,54]). Many interesting results have come from these qualitative models of policies, including definitions of safety and liveness properties, which are tied to particular classes of enforcement mechanisms, and proofs that every black-and-white property is the conjunction of one safety property and one liveness property.

This paper contributes a more general, quantitative model of policies and properties (Sect. 2). This model generalizes existing definitions of policies, properties, safety, liveness, hypersafety, and hyperliveness. It is shown that the new model is indeed a generalization, in that every black-and-white policy is also a gray policy, every black-and-white safety property is also a gray safety property, etc.

It is also shown that the gray model preserves interesting properties of safety and liveness that were previously derived in black-and-white models (Sect. 3). Specifically, the intersection of gray safety and gray liveness properties is a unique allow-all property, every gray property can be written as the conjunction of a single gray-safety and a single gray-liveness property, and similarly for hypersafety and hyperliveness policies.

Section 4 shows how this paper's model of gray policies can serve as a unifying framework for many disparate approaches to security metrics, and how gray policies might be constructed from existing black-and-white policies.

Section 5 formalizes silhouette judges and shows how they work in tandem with gray policies, and Sect. 6 briefly discusses future work.

## 2    From Black-and-White to Gray Policies

Policies reason about systems, which execute *events*. Let $E$ be a non-empty, countable set of events, with metavariable $e$ ranging over individual events. Intuitively, $E$ is the system API and might contain instructions for manipulating system resources.

A system *trace*, or *execution*, $x$, is a possibly infinite sequence of pairs of events called *exchanges*. The events in an exchange $\langle e, e' \rangle$ indicate (1) an event $e$ the system attempts to execute and (2) an event $e'$ that actually executes. For example, the trace

$$\langle sti(0, 0x9ABC), sti(0, 0x1ABC) \rangle \langle rdr(4, 0x8FFF), rdr(4, 0x0FFF) \rangle$$

indicates that the *target system* being reasoned about, for example an application program, attempted to store the immediate value 0 at memory address 0x9ABC, but 0 was instead written at address 0x1ABC, due to the involvement of a runtime mechanism such as a virtual-memory manager. The second exchange in the trace also shows involvement of a runtime mechanism, again decreasing the memory address being accessed by $2^{15}$.

This model of traces as sequences of exchanges is general, in part because it clarifies the effects of runtime mechanisms; such clarification improves expressiveness [24,42]. In cases where policies require no runtime support, such as statically enforced policies, the first and second events in exchanges will be the same.

Some additional notation will be useful. A set of events $E$ determines the set of possible exchanges $\mathcal{E}$. Given exchange set $\mathcal{E}$, $\mathcal{E}^*$ denotes the set of all finite executions (i.e., finite sequences of exchanges), $\mathcal{E}^\omega$ denotes the set of all infinite executions, and $\mathcal{E}^\infty$ denotes the set of all finite and infinite executions. Also, $x \preceq y$ and $y \succeq x$ mean that execution $x \in \mathcal{E}^*$ is a *prefix* of execution $y \in \mathcal{E}^\infty$. Finally, shorthand quantifications will be used in formulae; for example, $\exists x \preceq y : F$ means $\exists x \in \mathcal{E}^* : (x \preceq y \wedge F)$, while $\forall x \succeq y : F$ means $\forall x \in \mathcal{E}^\infty : (x \succeq y \Rightarrow F)$.

## 2.1   Policies and Properties

The black-and-white model defines *policies* $P$ as predicates over target systems; the policy returns a yes-no response to a given target system, to indicate whether that system is secure [54]. A target system $X$ is modeled as the set of executions it can produce, for example, all possible runs of an application program. Hence, on a system with exchange set $\mathcal{E}$, $X$ is a subset of $\mathcal{E}^\infty$, so a *black-and-white policy* is a $P : 2^{\mathcal{E}^\infty} \to \{false, true\}$.

The gray model defines policies $G$ as functions mapping target systems not to false/true values, but to a real number between 0 and 1, with greater numbers indicating higher security. Gray policies generalize black-and-white policies because false/true values in the black-and-white model can always be encoded as 0/1 values in the gray model. A *gray policy* is simply a $G : 2^{\mathcal{E}^\infty} \to \mathbb{R}_{[0,1]}$.

In the black-and-white model, *properties* are policies that place no constraints on the relationships between executions [54]. It can be determined whether a target system satisfies a property by examining each possible trace in isolation; if every trace is valid in isolation (according to some predicate $p$ over individual traces), then the policy as a whole is satisfied. Formally, a policy $P$ is a *black-and-white property* iff

$$\exists (p : \mathcal{E}^\infty \to \{false, true\}) : \forall X \subseteq \mathcal{E}^\infty : P(X) = (\forall x \in X : p(x)).$$

The gray model also considers a policy to be a property when the policy's value for a given a set of executions can be determined by examining each execution in isolation. While the black-and-white model determines the policy's value $P(X)$ as the *conjunction* of the values of $p(x)$, for all $x \in X$, the gray model determines the policy's value $G(X)$ as the *infimum* (inf) of the values of $g(x)$, for all $x \in X$. Here $g$, like $p$, is a function over individual traces. Formally, a policy $G$ is a *gray property* iff

$$\exists (g : \mathcal{E}^\infty \to \mathbb{R}_{[0,1]}) : \forall X \subseteq \mathcal{E}^\infty : G(X) = \inf\{g(x) \mid x \in X\}.$$

Gray properties generalize black-and-white properties because the conjunction of a set of false/true values always equals the infimum of a set of corresponding 0/1 values.[1]

It is often convenient to identify a property by the individual-trace function ($p$ or $g$) it uses. There is no ambiguity in doing so, due to the one-to-one correspondence between a $p$ or $g$ function and the property it induces.

## 2.2   Safety and Liveness

Two subsets of black-and-white properties have been studied extensively: safety and liveness properties [1,38]. These sets are fundamentally intertwined with the sets of properties that can be enforced in practice [2,24,25,41,54].

---

[1] The use of the infimum precludes limiting the range of security values in the gray model to computable reals; computable reals are not closed under infimum operations [57].

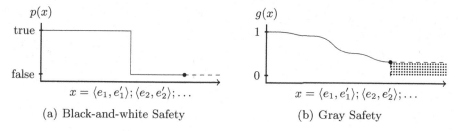

**Fig. 1.** The security of traces as they proceed. The security level is according to (a) a black-and-white safety property and (b) a gray safety property. The dotted lines and shaded area represent the possible security values of the executions' extensions. In all cases, security levels are nonincreasing.

*Safety.* Black-and-white safety properties partition "secure" from "insecure" traces in such a way that every insecure trace has a finite insecure prefix that can never become secure [38]. Formally, property $p$ is *black-and-white safety* iff

$$\forall x \in \mathcal{E}^\infty : (\neg p(x) \Rightarrow \exists x' \preceq x : \forall y \succeq x' : \neg p(y)).$$

An equivalent, perhaps more intuitive, definition of black-and-white safety is the set of properties that are both prefix- and omega-closed [24]. Prefix-closed means that all prefixes of secure traces are secure, while omega-closed means the converse, that if all prefixes of a trace $x$ are secure then so must be $x$. Formally, property $p$ is *black-and-white safety* iff

$$\forall x \in \mathcal{E}^\infty : p(x) = (\forall x' \preceq x : p(x')).$$

This formalization of black-and-white safety has an interesting similarity to the formalization of black-and-white properties; in both cases, an entity is secure exactly when all of its "simpler parts" are secure.

It can be seen from these definitions that black-and-white safety properties require traces to be as secure as their least-secure prefix; security cannot increase as traces proceed. Figure 1(a) plots the general shape of a trace's security as considered by a black-and-white safety property.

Gray safety properties also require traces to have nonincreasing security, as shown in Fig. 1(b). However, with gray safety, the requirement that traces be as secure as their least-secure prefix has to be modified—infinite traces may not have a least-secure prefix. To handle such cases the *infimum* is again used. Formally, property $g$ is *gray safety* iff

$$\forall x \in \mathcal{E}^\infty : g(x) = \inf\{g(x') \mid x' \preceq x\}.$$

This formalization of gray safety retains the similarity, present in the black-and-white model, between the definitions of properties and safety.

As an example, the gray property described earlier, specifying that a trace's security level gets decimated with each unchecked array access, is a gray safety

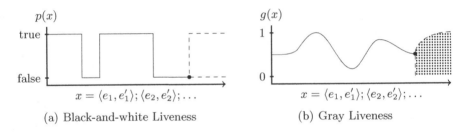

**Fig. 2.** The security of traces as they proceed. The security level is according to (a) a black-and-white liveness property and (b) a gray liveness property. The dotted lines and shaded area represent the possible security values of the executions' extensions. In all cases, less-than-fully-secure traces have more-secure extensions.

property. Traces according to this policy begin as 100 % secure (before any exchanges occur) and can only proceed to lower security. In the limit, a trace containing an infinite number of unchecked array accesses has 0 % security, because the infimum of $\{1, 0.9, 0.81, 0.729, \ldots\}$ is 0.

Gray safety is a proper generalization of black-and-white safety. To understand why, note that black-and-white policies (properties) can be trivially converted to gray policies (properties) by partitioning target systems (traces) not as insecure or secure but as having security levels of 0 or 1. Then because a black-and-white safety property $p$ is prefix- and omega-closed, traces are as secure as their least-secure prefix, so $p$ converts to a gray safety property. Conversely, a black-and-white nonsafety property $p'$ assigns the security of some trace to be different than its least-secure prefix, so $p'$ converts to a gray nonsafety property.

*Liveness.* Black-and-white liveness properties require every finite trace to have a secure extension [1], as shown in Fig. 2(a). A canonical example is the termination property, which requires traces to be finite (so every finite trace $x$ has a secure extension, namely $x$). Formally, property $p$ is *black-and-white liveness* iff

$$\forall x \in \mathcal{E}^* : \exists y \succeq x : p(y).$$

Analogously, gray liveness properties require every finite trace to have a more-secure extension, with traces that are already 100 % secure exempted (because a fully secure trace cannot have a more-secure extension). Figure 2(b) illustrates the requirement that, according to a gray liveness property, every imperfectly secure trace has a more-secure extension.

To formalize gray liveness, a new operator $\overset{>}{\phantom{.}}$ is defined that behaves exactly like a greater-than operator ($>$), except that $1 \overset{>}{\phantom{.}} 1$. Then property $g$ is *gray liveness* iff

$$\forall x \in \mathcal{E}^* : \exists y \succeq x : g(y) \overset{>}{\phantom{.}} g(x).$$

For example, a gray liveness property could map trace $x$ to a security value based on the number $n$ of resources acquired but unreleased in $x$; the security level might be $1 - 0.01n$ when $0 \leq n \leq 100$ and 0 when $n > 100$. This property gives traces a 1 % security penalty for every unreleased resource. It is a gray liveness property because every finite, imperfectly secure trace has a more-secure extension (in which acquired resources are released). It is interesting to compare the usefulness of, and information provided by, this gray property with its black-and-white version, which simply says that traces are secure iff all acquired resources eventually get released.

As with safety, gray liveness is a proper generalization of black-and-white liveness. A black-and-white liveness property $p$ requires every finite, insecure trace to have a secure extension, so $p$ converts to a gray liveness property. Conversely, a black-and-white nonliveness property $p'$ forbids some finite, insecure trace from becoming secure, causing $p'$ to convert to a gray nonliveness property.

## 2.3 Hypersafety and Hyperliveness

Just as black-and-white properties can be categorized as safety or liveness, the same can be done for black-and-white policies. Using the term "hyperproperty" to mean "policy", then, hyperproperties can be categorized as hypersafety or hyperliveness [17]. Intuitively, the definitions of hypersafety and hyperliveness raise the definitions of safety and liveness from the level of executions (properties) to the level of sets of executions (policies).

The definitions of safety and liveness rely on the the the $\preceq$ and $\succeq$ operators to indicate *executions* being prefixed or extended; definitions of hypersafety and hyperliveness will need to raise these operators to the level of *sets of executions*. This raising is accomplished by defining a *terminating target system* $X$—that is, a set of finite executions—to *prefix* another target system $Y$, written $X \sqsubseteq Y$, iff every execution in $X$ is a prefix of some execution in $Y$. Formally, given $X \subseteq \mathcal{E}^*$ and $Y \subseteq \mathcal{E}^\infty$, $X \sqsubseteq Y$ iff $\forall x \in X : \exists y \in Y : x \preceq y$ [17, Footnote 13]. The $Y \sqsupseteq X$ relation is defined symmetrically.

*Hypersafety.* Black-and-white hypersafety raises black-and-white safety from the level of traces (executions) to the level of target systems (sets of executions) by requiring that target systems are secure iff all their prefixes are secure. Hence, just as *property $p$* was defined to be black-and-white safety iff

$$\forall x \in \mathcal{E}^\infty : p(x) = (\forall x' \preceq x : p(x')),$$

*policy $P$* is *black-and-white hypersafety* iff

$$\forall X \subseteq \mathcal{E}^\infty : P(X) = (\forall X' \sqsubseteq X : P(X')).$$

Similarly, just as *property $g$* was defined to be gray safety iff

$$\forall x \in \mathcal{E}^\infty : g(x) = \inf\{g(x') \mid x' \preceq x\},$$

*policy $G$* is *gray hypersafety* iff

$$\forall X \subseteq \mathcal{E}^\infty : G(X) = \inf\{G(X') \mid X' \sqsubseteq X\}.$$

The reasoning that gray hypersafety is a proper generalization of black-and-white hypersafety follows the reasoning used to show that gray safety is a proper generalization of black-and-white safety.

Following [17], it is also possible to define (black-and-white and gray) $k$-hypersafety by restricting the set $X'$ to have at most $k$ elements. For example, policy $G$ is *gray $k$-hypersafety* iff

$$\forall X \subseteq \mathcal{E}^{\infty} : G(X) = \inf\{G(X') \mid X' \sqsubseteq X, |X'| \leq k\}.$$

*Hyperliveness.* Black-and-white hyperliveness requires that all terminating target systems have secure extensions. Just as *property p* was defined to be black-and-white liveness iff

$$\forall x \in \mathcal{E}^* : \exists y \succeq x : p(y),$$

*policy P* is *black-and-white hyperliveness* iff

$$\forall X \subseteq \mathcal{E}^* : \exists Y \sqsupseteq X : P(Y).$$

Similarly, just as *property g* was defined to be gray liveness iff

$$\forall x \in \mathcal{E}^* : \exists y \succeq x : g(y) \gtrless g(x),$$

*policy G* is *gray hyperliveness* iff

$$\forall X \subseteq \mathcal{E}^* : \exists Y \sqsupseteq X : G(Y) \gtrless G(X).$$

Gray hyperliveness is a proper generalization of black-and-white hyperliveness by the same reasoning used to show that gray liveness properly generalizes black-and-white liveness.

### 2.4  Summary

Table 1 summarizes the gray definitions and compares each with its black-and-white counterpart.

## 3  Further Analysis of the Model

The generalization of black-and-white to gray policies preserves key properties of the black-and-white model.

### 3.1  Singleton Intersection of Safety and Liveness

In the black-and-white models, exactly one property is both safety and liveness: the "allow-all" property that considers every trace secure [1]. Similarly, exactly one policy is both hypersafety and hyperliveness: the policy that considers every target system secure [17]. The following theorems show that, analogously, exactly one property (policy) is both gray (hyper)safety and gray (hyper)liveness: the property (policy) that considers every trace (target system) perfectly secure.

**Table 1.** Summary of the generalization from black-and-white to gray policies. The black-and-white definitions are taken from [1,17,24,54]. As a reminder, the $\tilde{>}$ operator behaves like greater-than ($>$), except that $1 \tilde{>} 1$.

| policy | ☑ | $P : 2^{\mathcal{E}^\infty} \to \{false, true\}$ |
|---|---|---|
| | ☐ | $G : 2^{\mathcal{E}^\infty} \to \mathbb{R}_{[0,1]}$ |
| property | ☑ | $\exists p : \forall X \subseteq \mathcal{E}^\infty : P(X) = (\forall x \in X : p(x))$ |
| | ☐ | $\exists g : \forall X \subseteq \mathcal{E}^\infty : G(X) = \inf\{g(x) \mid x \in X\}$ |
| safety | ☑ | $\forall x \in \mathcal{E}^\infty : p(x) = (\forall x' \preceq x : p(x'))$ |
| | ☐ | $\forall x \in \mathcal{E}^\infty : g(x) = \inf\{g(x') \mid x' \preceq x\}$ |
| liveness | ☑ | $\forall x \in \mathcal{E}^* : \exists y \succeq x : p(y)$ |
| | ☐ | $\forall x \in \mathcal{E}^* : \exists y \succeq x : g(y) \tilde{>} g(x)$ |
| hypersafety | ☑ | $\forall X \subseteq \mathcal{E}^\infty : P(X) = (\forall X' \sqsubseteq X : P(X'))$ |
| | ☐ | $\forall X \subseteq \mathcal{E}^\infty : G(X) = \inf\{G(X') \mid X' \sqsubseteq X\}$ |
| hyperliveness | ☑ | $\forall X \subseteq \mathcal{E}^* : \exists Y \sqsupseteq X : P(Y)$ |
| | ☐ | $\forall X \subseteq \mathcal{E}^* : \exists Y \sqsupseteq X : G(Y) \tilde{>} G(X)$ |

**Theorem 1.** *The gray property $g(x) = 1$ is the only gray property that is both gray safety and gray liveness.*

*Proof.* First note that $g(x) = 1$ is trivially both a gray safety and a gray liveness property.

Now let $g'$ be an arbitrary gray property that is both gray safety and gray liveness. For the sake of obtaining a contradiction, suppose there exists an execution $x$ such that $g'(x) < 1$. If $x$ is infinite, it must have a finite prefix whose security is also less than 1 because $g'$ is gray safety; let $x$ instead refer to that prefix. Because $g'$ is gray liveness, there exists $y \succeq x$ such that $g'(y) \tilde{>} g'(x)$, so because $g'(x) \neq 1$, it must be that $g'(y) > g'(x)$. Also, because $g'$ is gray safety, $g'(y)$ must equal $\inf\{g'(y') \mid y' \preceq y\}$. However, $x$ is a prefix of $y$, so by the definition of infimum, $g'(y) \leq g'(x)$, which contradicts the earlier result that $g'(y) > g'(x)$. Thus, for all $x$, $g'(x) = 1$, meaning that $g'$ must be $g$. $\qquad\square$

**Theorem 2.** *The gray policy $G(X) = 1$ is the only gray policy that is both gray hypersafety and gray hyperliveness.*

*Proof.* Analogous to that of Theorem 1. $\qquad\square$

Figure 3 depicts the relationships between gray properties, black-and-white properties, and their subsets of safety and liveness properties. Notably, the gray sets subsume the black-and-white sets, and the intersection of safety and liveness is the black-and-white allow-all property.

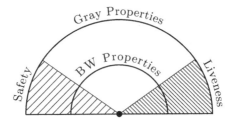

**Fig. 3.** Relationships between gray and black-and-white properties, and their subsets of safety and liveness properties. The central dot represents the intersection of safety and liveness, which only contains the property $g(x) = 1$.

## 3.2  Decomposition into Safety and Liveness

In the black-and-white models, every property $p$ can be decomposed into properties $p_s$ and $p_l$ such that:

- $p_s$ is a black-and-white safety property,
- $p_l$ is a black-and-white liveness property, and
- $p(x) = (p_s(x) \land p_l(x))$.

In other words, every black-and-white property is the conjunction of a single safety and a single liveness property. This result appeared in [1], with alternative proofs appearing in [41,53]. A similar result has been shown for decomposing policies into hypersafety and hyperliveness [17].

Theorem 3 shows that the gray model preserves this decomposition result.

**Theorem 3.** *Every gray property $g$ can be decomposed into $g_s$ and $g_l$ such that:*

- $g_s$ *is a gray safety property,*
- $g_l$ *is a gray liveness property, and*
- $g(x) = min(g_s(x), g_l(x))$.

*Proof.* Construct $g_s$ and $g_l$ as follows, where *sup* refers to the supremum function.

$$g_s(x) = \begin{cases} \inf\{g_s(x') \mid x' \preceq x\} & \text{if } x \in \mathcal{E}^\omega \\ g(x) & \text{if } x \in \mathcal{E}^* \text{ and } \forall x' \succeq x : g(x') \leq g(x) \\ \sup\{g(x') \mid x' \succeq x\} & \text{otherwise} \end{cases}$$

$$g_l(x) = \begin{cases} 1 & \text{if } x \in \mathcal{E}^* \text{ and } \forall x' \succeq x : g(x') \leq g(x) \\ g(x) & \text{otherwise} \end{cases}$$

To establish that $g_s$ is gray safety, it must be shown that for all $x \in \mathcal{E}^\infty$, $g_s(x) = \inf\{g_s(x') \mid x' \preceq x\}$. By construction, this constraint holds for all $x \in \mathcal{E}^\omega$. For finite executions, $g_s$ ensures that security never increases as traces proceed by giving every finite trace $x$ a security value that's greater than or equal to all of $x$'s extensions. Hence, the safety constraint holds for all finite executions as well.

To establish that $g_l$ is gray liveness, it must be shown that for all $x \in \mathcal{E}^*$, $\exists y \succeq x : g_l(y) \gtrless g_l(x)$. Let $x$ be a finite execution. If all extensions $x'$ of $x$ have security less than or equal to $x$ (according to $g$), then $g_l(x) = 1$ and the liveness constraint is satisfied by letting $y = x$. On the other hand, if some extension $x'$ of $x$ has security greater than $x$ (according to $g$), then $g_l(x) = g(x)$ and the liveness constraint is satisfied by letting $y = x'$ (where $g_l(x')$ must be at least $g(x')$, which is greater than $g(x) = g_l(x)$).

It remains to establish that $g(x) = min(g_s(x), g_l(x))$. If $x$ is a finite trace then this result immediately follows from the definitions of $g_s$ and $g_l$. If $x$ is an infinite trace, first observe that $g_s$ assigns every prefix $x'$ of $x$ a security level of at least $g(x)$. Hence, $g_s$ assigns $x \in \mathcal{E}^\omega$ a security level of at least $g(x)$, while $g_l$ assigns $x \in \mathcal{E}^\omega$ a security level of $g(x)$, which completes the proof. □

As in the black-and-white models, the decomposition result in the gray model extends to policies, hypersafety, and hyperliveness.

**Theorem 4.** *Every gray policy $G$ can be decomposed into $G_s$ and $G_\ell$ such that:*

- *$G_s$ is a gray hypersafety policy,*
- *$G_\ell$ is a gray hyperliveness policy, and*
- *$G(X) = min(G_s(X), G_\ell(X))$.*

*Proof.* Analogous to that of Theorem 3. □

# 4    Creating Gray Policies from Existing Metrics/Policies

Existing work on security metrics and on black-and-white policies can be used to create new gray policies.

## 4.1    Gray Policies Based on Security Metrics

The gray model serves as a unifying framework for disparate approaches to security metrics. The disparate approaches include:

- using greater values to indicate higher levels of security (e.g., [23]),
- using greater values to indicate lower levels of security (e.g., [46]),
- limiting security values to a bounded range (e.g., [14]),
- limiting security values to a range bounded only on the lower side (e.g., [40]), and
- placing no bounds on the range of security values (e.g., [9]).

In contrast to black and white models, all of these approaches can be encoded in the gray model.

Encoding these disparate approaches to security metrics in the gray model provides the benefit of consistency. In the gray model, security consistently ranges between 0 and 1, and for a fixed policy or property, greater security values consistently indicate higher security.

**Table 2.** Examples of functions that can be used to normalize security metrics to the gray model's range of $\mathbb{R}_{[0,1]}$. Variable $x$ denotes the output of the security metric, constants $A$ and $B$ denote the metric's minimum and maximum values (when applicable), and constant $C$ denotes a positive number ($C$ affects how quickly the functions converge to absolute security or insecurity).

|  | Bounded | Lower bounded | Unbounded |
|---|---|---|---|
| Higher values represent higher security | $y = \dfrac{x - A}{B - A}$ | $y = \dfrac{x - A}{x - A + C}$ | $y = 0.5 + \dfrac{\tan^{-1}(C * x)}{\pi}$ |
| Higher values represent lower security | $y = \dfrac{B - x}{B - A}$ | $y = \dfrac{C}{x - A + C}$ | $y = 0.5 + \dfrac{\tan^{-1}(-C * x)}{\pi}$ |

Table 2 shows several example functions that can be used to encode security metrics as gray policies. Every one of the more than forty metrics we've studied [3–10, 12–16, 18–21, 23, 27, 28, 30, 31, 33–37, 39, 40, 45–47, 49–52, 55, 56, 58–61], in domains as varied as access control, noninterference, privacy, integrity, and network security, can be encoded as a gray policy or property by using one of the functions shown in Table 2.

The arctangent functions shown in Table 2 can be used to normalize metrics having an unbounded range because the arctangent's domain is all real numbers, and its output monotonically increases over the range $(-\frac{\pi}{2}, \frac{\pi}{2})$. The arccotangent function ($\cot^{-1}$), and many others, could be used instead.

### 4.2   Graying Black-and-White Policies

Gray policies can also be created from existing black-and-white policies.

For example, a gray policy $G(X)$ could be created by quantifying how well the given target system $X$ obeys a particular black-and-white policy. This technique has already been used in this paper's examples: black-and-white policies might require all array accesses to be checked or all acquired resources to be released; these policies were grayed by penalizing target systems based on how far their traces deviate from ideal traces. A similar idea is used with cost-aware enforcement [25], where a cost, or penalty, can be assigned to certain exchanges.

Another approach to graying considers the overall security achieved by permitting some "insecure" executions to be run and/or denying some "secure" executions from being run [26].

Gray policies could be defined based on a similar idea: Given a black-and-white property of interest $p$, $G(X)$ might be defined as the product of:

– the probability that a randomly selected element of $X$ satisfies $p$—*such a probability measures the* soundness *of $X$ with respect to $p$*—and
– the probability that a randomly selected element of $\{x \mid p(x)\}$ is in $X$—*such a probability measures the* completeness *of $X$ with respect to $p$.*

Following [44], these probabilities could be weighted by the likelihood of traces to actually be observed (due to nonuniform input distributions and target-system functionality, some traces may be observed much more frequently than others). Therefore, when calculating $G(X)$ in terms of the soundness and completeness probabilities defined above, one might choose traces not from uniform distributions, but instead with the more-likely-to-be-observed traces more likely to be chosen.

## 5  Silhouettes and Their Judges

The gray model separates specifications of how secure target systems are (gray policies) from specifications of how secure users require their systems to be (silhouette judges). In the safe analogy of Sect. 1, silhouette judges input a safe's security rating and output a buy or don't-buy decision. In other words, silhouette judges input a *silhouette*—a distillation of a safe's characteristics into a security value—and output a no/yes decision to indicate whether that silhouette is acceptably secure.

### 5.1  Silhouettes

Thus, silhouette judges, as their name implies, judge silhouettes, by outputting a no/yes (or false/true) to indicate whether a given silhouette is acceptably secure.

In the gray model, a *silhouette* represents the shape of a trace's (or target system's) security. For example, the plots shown in Figs. 1 and 2 illustrate silhouettes of traces—the plots abstract from the events of the underlying traces to provide only the shape of the security values achieved as the traces proceed.

Silhouettes can be formalized in many ways. For generality, the key requirement is to encode a trace's (or target system's) evolution of security values.

For example, the silhouette of a trace $x$ according to property $g$ can be formalized as a function $s$ that takes a natural number $n$, or a special $\infty$ symbol, as input and returns the security (according to $g$) of $x$'s $n$-length prefix, or the security of $x$ itself if $s$'s input is $\infty$. With this formalization, silhouettes are partial functions; e.g., the silhouette of the empty trace is undefined for all inputs $n > 0$.

With this formalization, *the silhouette of trace $x$ according to gray property $g$* is the partial function $s_{x,g} : (\mathbb{N} \cup \{\infty\}) \to \mathbb{R}_{[0,1]}$, such that:

$$
s_{x,g}(n) = \begin{cases} g(x) & \text{if } n = \infty \\ g(x') & \text{if } x' \text{ is the } n\text{-length prefix of } x \end{cases}
$$

Because target systems may be infinite sets of infinite-length traces, silhouettes of target systems are more complicated than those of individual traces. Rather than mapping natural numbers to security values, target-system silhouettes could map real numbers to security values. In this case, the real number can encode which parts of the target system's traces to evaluate the security of.

For example, a silhouette for target system $X$ could interpret an input like 0.192939..969109119... as identifying the set of traces containing the 1-length prefix of $X$'s first execution (ordered lexicographically), the 2-length prefix of $X$'s second execution, and so on, with each prefix length delimited by a 9 and written in base-7. Under this encoding, the target-system silhouette could interpret a 7 (8) appearing before the $i^{th}$ 9 in an input real number as indicating exclusion of the (inclusion of the whole) $i^{th}$ execution in $X$.

With such a formalization, the *silhouette of target system $X$ according to gray policy $G$* is the partial function $S_{X,G} : \mathbb{R} \to \mathbb{R}_{[0,1]}$, such that:

$$S_{X,G}(r) = G(X'), \text{ where } r \text{ encodes } X' \text{ with respect to } X.$$

## 5.2   Silhouette Judges

Silhouette judges are simply predicates over silhouettes. A judge therefore acts as the final, black-and-white decision maker, determining whether a trace or target system is acceptably secure. Importantly, judges base their decisions on *silhouettes* of traces or target systems, not on the traces or target systems themselves, as is done in black-and-white models.

For example, a silhouette judge could forbid all trace silhouettes whose security ever drops below a certain minimum threshold. This sort of silhouette judge specifies a user's minimum security requirement, such as "traces must always be at least 80 % secure".

Another silhouette judge might forbid all silhouettes whose "final" security value (obtained by inputting $\infty$ to the given silhouette) is greater than 0. Such a judge might be used by high-performance systems researchers to require the complete insecurity of their executions.

More interesting judges can also be defined. For example, it may be reasonable to allow executions to occasionally behave less securely, provided they are usually more secure. Such a judge might be satisfied by exactly those silhouettes having a rolling average of security above a given threshold. Other judges could be satisfied by exactly those silhouettes that never dip below a desired threshold for more than $k$ consecutive exchanges.

Theorem 5 states that combining a gray property $g$ with a trace-silhouette judge $j$ produces a unique black-and-white property $p$, but, on the other hand, every black-and-white property can be decomposed into uncountably many different gray-property, trace-silhouette-judge pairs. Theorem 6 states a similar result for black-and-white policies and gray-policy, trace-system-silhouette-judge pairs.

**Theorem 5.** *There is a one-to-uncountably-many correspondence between black-and-white properties p and pairs of gray properties and trace-silhouette judges $(g, j)$ such that $\forall x \in \mathcal{E}^\infty : p(x) \Leftrightarrow j(s_{x,g})$.*

*Proof.* Every gray-property, trace-silhouette-judge pair $(g, j)$ is equivalent to exactly one black-and-white property $p$; otherwise, there must be some execution $x$ whose silhouette according to $g$, $s_{x,g}$, both satisfies and dissatisfies $j$, a contradiction.

It remains to show that every black-and-white property can be expressed by an uncountable number of gray-property, silhouette-judge pairs. Given black-and-white property $p$ and arbitrary $r \in \mathbb{R}_{[0,1]}$, construct a gray property $g_r$ and silhouette judge $j_r$ as follows:

$$g_r(x) = \begin{cases} r & \text{if } p(x) \\ 0 & \text{otherwise} \end{cases}$$

$$j_r(s) \Leftrightarrow (s(\infty) = r)$$

By construction, $p(x) \Leftrightarrow j_r(s_{x,g_r})$. Because there are uncountably many values of $r$, there are uncountably many pairs of $(g_r, j_r)$ equivalent to $p$. □

**Theorem 6.** *There is a one-to-uncountably-many correspondence between black-and-white policies P and pairs of gray policies and target-system-silhouette judges $(G, J)$ such that $\forall X \subseteq \mathcal{E}^\infty : P(X) \Leftrightarrow J(S_{X,G})$.*

*Proof.* Analogous to that of Theorem 5. □

These theorems demonstrate the increased expressiveness of gray policies, properties, and silhouette judges, compared to black-and-white policies and properties.

# 6   Future Work

Several directions exist for future work.

One would be to design and evaluate programming languages, or other tools, for specifying gray policies and silhouette judges. As a part of this direction, it would be interesting to consider case studies, to learn which sorts of gray policies and silhouette judges seem to be more common, or practically useful.

Another direction would investigate generalizations of existing program-verification techniques, to transition from determining whether programs obey black-and-white policies to determining how well programs obey gray policies.

It would also be interesting to consider ways in which the gray security model could benefit from results known in the area of fuzzy set theory. Intuitively, gray policies are to black-and-white policies what fuzzy sets are to sets: A fuzzy set is an ordered pair $(U, m)$, where $U$ is a set and $m : U \to \mathbb{R}_{[0,1]}$ is a membership function that describes the degree to which each element of $U$ is a member of the set [62]. Because of the similarity between gray policies and fuzzy sets, much of the work on fuzzy set theory is expected to translate to gray policies. For example, the "very" operator takes a fuzzy set $(U, m)$ and returns the fuzzy set $(U, m^2)$; such an operation is a simple way to make gray policies stricter.

Further generalizations of gray policies may also be possible. For example, rather than the totally ordered set of $\mathbb{R}_{[0,1]}$, gray policies could have complete lattices as their codomains. Some alterations would need to be made to the gray model to handle such codomains, including replacing infimum (supremum) operations with meet (join) operations.

Yet another direction is in the area of enforceability theory. As other work has delineated the black-and-white properties enforceable by various mechanisms (e.g., [11,24,25,41,43,54]), the same could be done for gray properties and/or silhouette judges. This direction of research would explore whether, and how well, different mechanisms (static code analyzers or runtime monitors, possibly constrained in various ways) can enforce classes of gray properties and/or silhouette judges.

# References

1. Alpern, B., Schneider, F.B.: Defining liveness. Inf. Process. Lett. **21**(4), 181–185 (1985)
2. Alpern, B., Schneider, F.B.: Recognizing safety and liveness. Distrib. Comput. **2**, 117–126 (1987)
3. Alvim, M.S., Chatzikokolakis, K., Palamidessi, C., Smith, G.: Measuring information leakage using generalized gain functions. In: Proceedings of the Computer Security Foundations Symposium, pp. 265–279, June 2012
4. An, X., Jutla, D., Cercone, N.: Privacy intrusion detection using dynamic bayesian networks. In: Proceedings of the International Conference on Electronic Commerce, pp. 208–215 (2006)
5. Andersson, C., Lundin, R.: On the fundamentals of anonymity metrics. In: Fischer-Hübner, S., Duquenoy, P., Zuccato, A., Martucci, L. (eds.) The Future of Identity in the Information Society. The International Federation for Information Processing, vol. 262, pp. 325–341. Springer, USA (2008)
6. Andrés, M.E., Palamidessi, C., van Rossum, P., Smith, G.: Computing the leakage of information-hiding systems. In: Esparza, J., Majumdar, R. (eds.) TACAS 2010. LNCS, vol. 6015, pp. 373–389. Springer, Heidelberg (2010)
7. Asnar, Y., Giorgini, P., Massacci, F., Zannone, N.: From trust to dependability through risk analysis. In: Proceedings of the Conference on Availability, Reliability and Security, pp. 19–26, April 2007
8. Au, M.H., Kapadia, A.: PERM: practical reputation-based blacklisting without TTPs. In: Proceedings of the Conference on Computer and Communications Security, pp. 929–940 (2012)
9. Au, M.H., Kapadia, A., Susilo, W.: BLACR: TTP-free blacklistable anonymous credentials with reputation. In: Proceedings of the Symposium on Network and Distributed System Security (2012)
10. Balzarotti, D., Monga, M., Sicari, S.: Assessing the risk of using vulnerable components. In: Proceedings of the Workshop on Quality of Protection, pp. 65–77 (2006)

11. Basin, D., Jugé, V., Klaedtke, F., Zălinescu, E.: Enforceable security policies revisited. ACM Trans. Inf. Syst. Secur. **16**(1), 3:1–3:26 (2013)
12. Braun, C., Chatzikokolakis, K., Palamidessi, C.: Quantitative notions of leakage for one-try attacks. Electron. Notes Theor. Comput. Sci. **249**, 75–91 (2009). Proceedings of the Conference on Mathematical Foundations of Programming Semantics
13. Chatzikokolakis, K., Palamidessi, C., Panangaden, P.: Anonymity protocols as noisy channels. In: Montanari, U., Sannella, D., Bruni, R. (eds.) TGC 2006. LNCS, vol. 4661, pp. 281–300. Springer, Heidelberg (2007)
14. Cheng, P.-C., Rohatgi, P., Keser, C., Karger, P.A., Wagner, G.M., Reninger, A.S.: Fuzzy multi-level security: an experiment on quantified risk-adaptive access control. In: Proceedings of the Symposium on Security and Privacy, pp. 222–230, May 2007
15. Clark, K., Singleton, E., Tyree, S., Hale, J.: Strata-Gem: risk assessment through mission modeling. In: Proceedings of the Workshop on Quality of Protection, pp. 51–58 (2008)
16. Clarkson, M.R., Myers, A.C., Schneider, F.B.: Quantifying information flow with beliefs. J. Comput. Secur. **17**(5), 655–701 (2009)
17. Clarkson, M.R., Schneider, F.B.: Hyperproperties. J. Comput. Secur. **18**(6), 1157–1210 (2010)
18. Clarkson, M.R., Schneider, F.B.: Quantification of integrity. Math. Struct. Comput. Sci. **25**(2), 207–258 (2015)
19. Clauß, S.: A framework for quantification of linkability within a privacy-enhancing identity management system. In: Müller, G. (ed.) ETRICS 2006. LNCS, vol. 3995, pp. 191–205. Springer, Heidelberg (2006)
20. Clauß, S., Schiffner, S.: Structuring anonymity metrics. In: Proceedings of the Workshop on Digital Identity Management, pp. 55–62 (2006)
21. Deng, Y., Pang, J., Wu, P.: Measuring anonymity with relative entropy. In: Dimitrakos, T., Martinelli, F., Ryan, P.Y.A., Schneider, S. (eds.) FAST 2006. LNCS, vol. 4691, pp. 65–79. Springer, Heidelberg (2007)
22. Devriese, D., Piessens, F.: Noninterference through secure multi-execution. In: Proceedings of the Symposium on Security and Privacy, pp. 109–124 (2010)
23. Díaz, C., Seys, S., Claessens, J., Preneel, B.: Towards measuring anonymity. In: Dingledine, R., Syverson, P.F. (eds.) PET 2002. LNCS, vol. 2482, pp. 54–68. Springer, Heidelberg (2003)
24. Dolzhenko, E., Ligatti, J., Reddy, S.: Modeling runtime enforcement with mandatory results automata. Int. J. Inf. Secur. **14**(1), 47–60 (2015)
25. Drábik, P., Martinelli, F., Morisset, C.: Cost-aware runtime enforcement of security policies. In: Jøsang, A., Samarati, P., Petrocchi, M. (eds.) STM 2012. LNCS, vol. 7783, pp. 1–16. Springer, Heidelberg (2013)
26. Drábik, P., Martinelli, F., Morisset, C.: A quantitative approach for inexact enforcement of security policies. In: Gollmann, D., Freiling, F.C. (eds.) ISC 2012. LNCS, vol. 7483, pp. 306–321. Springer, Heidelberg (2012)
27. Dwaikat, Z., Parisi-Presicce, F.: Risky trust: risk-based analysis of software systems. In: Proceedings of the Workshop on Software Engineering for Secure Systems, pp. 1–7 (2005)
28. Edman, M., Sivrikaya, F., Yener, B.: A combinatorial approach to measuring anonymity. In: Proceedings of the Conference on Intelligence and Security Informatics, pp. 356–363, May 2007
29. Fong, P.W.L.: Access control by tracking shallow execution history. In: Proceedings of the Symposium on Security and Privacy, pp. 43–55 (2004)

30. Frigault, M., Wang, L., Singhal, A., Jajodia, S.: Measuring network security using dynamic bayesian network. In: Proceedings of the Workshop on Quality of Protection, pp. 23–30 (2008)
31. Gervais, A., Shokri, R., Singla, A., Capkun, S., Lenders, V.: Quantifying web-search privacy. In: Proceedings of the Conference on Computer and Communications Security, pp. 966–977 (2014)
32. Göktas, E., Athanasopoulos, E., Bos, H., Portokalidis, G.: Out of control: overcoming control-flow integrity. In: Proceedings of the Symposium on Security and Privacy, pp. 575–589 (2014)
33. Goriac, I.: Measuring anonymity with plausibilistic entropy. In: Proceedings of the International Conference on Availability, Reliability and Security, pp. 151–160, September 2013
34. Gowadia, V., Farkas, C., Valtorta, M.: PAID: a probabilistic agent-based intrusion detection system. Comput. Secur. 24(27), 529–545 (2005)
35. Halpern, J.Y., O'Neill, K.R.: Anonymity and information hiding in multiagent systems. J. Comput. Secur. 13(3), 483–514 (2005)
36. Heumann, T., Trpe, S., Keller, J.: Quantifying the attack surface of a web application. In: Proceedings of Sicherheit, vol. 170, pp. 305–316 (2010)
37. Howard, M., Pincus, J., Wing, J.M.: Measuring relative attack surfaces. In: Lee, D.T., Shieh, S.P., Tygar, J.D. (eds.) Computer Security in the 21st Century, pp. 109–137. Springer, Heidelberg (2005)
38. Alford, M.W., Hommel, G., Schneider, F.B., Ansart, J.P., Lamport, L., Mullery, G.P., Zhou, T.H.: Distributed Systems: Methods and Tools for Specification. An Advanced Course. LNCS, vol. 190. Springer, Heidelberg (1985)
39. Lee, A.J., Yu, T.: Towards quantitative analysis of proofs of authorization: applications, framework, and techniques. In: Proceedings of the Computer Security Foundations Symposium, pp. 139–153, July 2010
40. Leversage, D.J., Byres, E.J.: Estimating a system's mean time-to-compromise. IEEE Secur. Priv. 6(1), 52–60 (2008)
41. Ligatti, J., Lujo, B., Walker, D.: Run-time enforcement of nonsafety policies. ACM Trans. Inf. Syst. Secur. 12(3), 1–41 (2009)
42. Ligatti, J., Reddy, S.: A theory of runtime enforcement, with results. In: Gritzalis, D., Preneel, B., Theoharidou, M. (eds.) ESORICS 2010. LNCS, vol. 6345, pp. 87–100. Springer, Heidelberg (2010)
43. Mallios, Y., Bauer, L., Kaynar, D., Ligatti, J.: Enforcing more with less: formalizing target-aware run-time monitors. In: Jøsang, A., Samarati, P., Petrocchi, M. (eds.) STM 2012. LNCS, vol. 7783, pp. 17–32. Springer, Heidelberg (2013)
44. Mallios, Y., Bauer, L., Kaynar, D., Martinelli, F., Morisset, C.: Probabilistic cost enforcement of security policies. In: Accorsi, R., Ranise, S. (eds.) STM 2013. LNCS, vol. 8203, pp. 144–159. Springer, Heidelberg (2013)
45. Manadhata, P.K., Wing, J.M.: An attack surface metric. IEEE Trans. Softw. Eng. 37(3), 371–386 (2011)
46. Manadhata, P., Wing, J., Flynn, M., McQueen, M.: Measuring the attack surfaces of two FTP daemons. In: Proceedings of the Workshop on Quality of Protection, pp. 3–10 (2006)
47. Mardziel, P., Alvim, M.S., Hicks, M., Clarkson, M.R.: Quantifying information flow for dynamic secrets. In: Proceedings of the Symposium on Security and Privacy, pp. 540–555 (2014)
48. Martinelli, F., Matteucci, I., Morisset, C.: From qualitative to quantitative enforcement of security policy. In: Kotenko, I., Skormin, V. (eds.) MMM-ACNS 2012. LNCS, vol. 7531, pp. 22–35. Springer, Heidelberg (2012)

49. McQueen, M.A., Boyer, W.F., Flynn, M.A., Beitel, G.A.: Time-to-compromise model for cyber risk reduction estimation. In: Gollmann, D., Massacci, F., Yautsiukhin, A. (eds.) Quality of Protection. Advances in Information Security, vol. 23, pp. 49–64. Springer, Heidelberg (2006)

50. Molloy, I., Dickens, L., Morisset, C., Cheng, P.-C., Lobo, J., Russo, A.: Risk-based security decisions under uncertainty. In: Proceedings of the Conference on Data and Application Security and Privacy, pp. 157–168 (2012)

51. Ngo, T.M., Huisman, M.: Quantitative security analysis for programs with low input and noisy output. In: Jürjens, J., Piessens, F., Bielova, N. (eds.) ESSoS. LNCS, vol. 8364, pp. 77–94. Springer, Heidelberg (2014)

52. Pamula, J., Jajodia, S., Ammann, P., Swarup, V.: A weakest-adversary security metric for network configuration security analysis. In: Proceedings of the Workshop on Quality of Protection, pp. 31–38 (2006)

53. Schneider, F.B.: Decomposing Properties into Safety and Liveness using Predicate Logic. Technical report 87–874, Cornell University, October 1987

54. Schneider, F.B.: Enforceable security policies. ACM Trans. Inf. Syst. Secur. 3(1), 30–50 (2000)

55. Serjantov, A., Danezis, G.: Towards an information theoretic metric for anonymity. In: Dingledine, R., Syverson, P.F. (eds.) PET 2002. LNCS, vol. 2482, pp. 41–53. Springer, Heidelberg (2003)

56. Smith, G.: On the foundations of quantitative information flow. In: de Alfaro, L. (ed.) FOSSACS 2009. LNCS, vol. 5504, pp. 288–302. Springer, Heidelberg (2009)

57. Specker, E.: Nicht konstruktiv beweisbare sätze der analysis. J. Symbolic Logic 14, 145–158 (1949)

58. Verslype, K., De Decker, B.: Measuring the user's anonymity when disclosing personal properties. In: Proceedings of the International Workshop on Security Measurements and Metrics, pp. 2:1–2:8 (2010)

59. Xi, L., Feng, D.: FARB: fast anonymous reputation-based blacklisting without TTPs. In: Proceedings of the Workshop on Privacy in the Electronic Society, pp. 139–148 (2014)

60. Xi, L., Shao, J., Yang, K., Feng, D.: ARBRA: anonymous reputation-based revocation with efficient authentication. In: Chow, S.S.M., Camenisch, J., Hui, L.C.K., Yiu, S.M. (eds.) ISC 2014. LNCS, vol. 8783, pp. 33–53. Springer, Heidelberg (2014)

61. Yu, K.Y., Yuen, T.H., Chow, S.S.M., Yiu, S.M., Hui, L.C.K.: PE(AR)$^2$: privacy-enhanced anonymous authentication with reputation and revocation. In: Foresti, S., Yung, M., Martinelli, F. (eds.) ESORICS 2012. LNCS, vol. 7459, pp. 679–696. Springer, Heidelberg (2012)

62. Zadeh, L.A.: Fuzzy sets. Inf. Control 8(3), 338–353 (1965)

# Factorization of Behavioral Integrity

Ximeng Li$^{(\boxtimes)}$, Flemming Nielson, and Hanne Riis Nielson

DTU Compute, Technical University of Denmark, Kongens Lyngby, Denmark
{ximl,fnie,hrni}@dtu.dk

**Abstract.** We develop a bisimulation-based nonintereference property that describes the allowed dependencies between communication behaviors of different integrity levels. The property is able to capture all possible combinations of integrity levels for the "presence" and "content" of actual communications. Channels of low presence integrity and high content integrity can be used to model the effect of Message Authentication Codes or the consequence of Denial of Service Attacks. In case the distinction between "presence" and "content" is deliberately blurred, the noninterference property specialises to a classical process-algebraic property (called SBNDC). A compositionality result is given to facilitate a structural approach to the analysis of concurrent systems.

## 1 Introduction

The semantic validation of information flow security [6,15] is achieved with *noninterference* properties [5,7]. Recent proposals of such properties for confidentiality in event-based systems distinguish between the "presence" and "content" of communication events (e.g. [13]).

Consider the simple process $c_1?x.c_2!d$, where some data is received from the confidential channel $c_1$, and forgotten immediately, with some data $d$ subsequently sent over the public channel $c_2$. Although the confidential input content is not leaked through the public channel $c_2$, this process is typically regarded as insecure [2,3,6,8,13,18], in case the input can be occasionally blocked by the environment. The reason is that the "presence" of the confidential input can be leaked through the "presence" of the public output.

When separate confidentiality levels can be assigned for the *presence* and *content* of communication, a more fine-grained analysis can be obtained. Supposing both the "presence" level and the "content" level of $c_2$ are public, then the content level of $c_1$ can still be confidential — only the presence level needs to be public, for the process to be secure. However, existing work introduces the constraint that "presence" can be no more confidential than "content" [13,14]: observing the content of a communication implies the knowledge that the communication is happening (present).

By the usually perceived duality [9] between confidentiality and integrity, separating "presence" and "content" applies for integrity as well. Still consider the process $c_1?x.c_2!d$. If both the "presence" and the "content" of communication over $c_2$ are of high integrity, then only the "presence" of communication

© Springer International Publishing Switzerland 2015
G. Pernul et al. (Eds.): ESORICS 2015, Part II, LNCS 9327, pp. 500–519, 2015.
DOI: 10.1007/978-3-319-24177-7_25

over $c_1$ needs to be of high integrity as well, the input content can still be of low integrity, for the process to be secure. However, the aforementioned constraint would preclude the use of channels with low presence integrity and high content integrity. Nevertheless, this combination is practically meaningful. When message authentication codes (MAC) are used, a MAC-checker can detect tampered (low integrity) content and choose to accept only high integrity content. As a result, the content, once received by an end user, can be used by her with confidence that no harm will arise. The worry, though, is that the communication allowing to receive that content may not be present. The suspension of this communication may be caused, for example, by message rejection in the MAC-checker due to content corruption. It is therefore sensible to regard the user channel as having low presence integrity and high content integrity.

*Our contribution* is a novel bisimulation-based noninterference property for integrity, where the *presence* and *content* of communication events are dealt with separately, and *all* combinations of integrity levels for these two dimensions are allowed. The property is shown to degenerate to the classical process-algebraic condition SBNDC (e.g., [6]), and a compositionality result is obtained to facilitate a structural approach to information flow analysis in a concurrent setting.

Our development will be performed in the Quality Calculus [12], a recent extension of the $\pi$-calculus. The distinguishing feature of the Quality Calculus is the use of composite binders $\&_q(b_1, ..., b_n)$ that describe the combinations of communications (at the basic input/output binders $b_1, ..., b_n$) that suffice for the computation to proceed. This makes system models more robust, since when faced with a computation environment that does not allow certain communications to be performed, their alternatives could still succeed. Take the composite binder $\&_{1\vee2}(c_1?x_1, c_2?x_2)$ as an example. This binder is passed immediately after the success of either input. If $x_1$ has received data $d$ when the binder is passed, then $x_1$ is bound to $\mathsf{some}(d)$; otherwise to $\mathsf{none}$, which resembles the optional data types used in languages like Standard ML. We can then use the "case construct" of the calculus to model branching decisions based on whether $x_1$ is bound to $\mathsf{some}(d)$ or $\mathsf{none}$. An example here is $\mathsf{case}\ x_1\ \mathsf{of}\ \mathsf{some}(y) : P_1\ \mathsf{else}\ P_2$ where $P_1$ and $P_2$ are two processes.

## 2  Motivating Examples

Let us give a few examples (in Fig. 1) to frame our mind in terms of *presence* integrity and *content* integrity, and further motivate the noninterference property to be proposed. Channels with two subscripts ($L$ or $H$, representing their integrity classification) will often be used. The first level describes the presence dimension and the second describes the content dimension. For each subscript, an $L$ (resp. $H$) will denote low (resp. high) integrity.

Processes 1 and 2 are intuitively secure. In process 1, given the low content integrity and high presence integrity of $c_{HL}$, the corruption of the input content by an attacker can be "passed on" to the output content, while the input cannot be blocked by the attacker, consequently blocking the output. Hence the low content integrity, high presence integrity of $c'_{HL}$ can be justified in accordance with the integrity classes of $c_{HL}$. In process 2, any influence on the presence of the input can in turn influence the presence of the output, but cannot by itself corrupt the output content, which also demonstrates the consistency of the integrity classes of $c_{LH}$ and $c'_{LH}$. On the other hand, process 3 is insecure: the classification of $c'_{LH}$ does not meet the intuition that both the presence of the final output, and its content, can be badly influenced.

One might think that the presence integrity can either be high for all channels, or low for all channels, hence at most one of the classes "high" and "low" is needed. This is not true, as illustrated by the insecurity of process 4, and the security of process 5. In process 4, the content integrity of the output channel cannot be $H$, since the presence of the input leads to more choices for the output content, some of which may not be possible with the input still blocked.

Given the insecure dependency of high integrity content on low integrity presence in process 4, it becomes interesting to see when certain source channels have the presence level $L$, which sink channels can still have the content level $H$ without being affected. Process 6 is coded in the Quality Calculus. It is a call to the procedure $M$ whose definition follows. This process is in fact a simple-minded "multiplexer" that directs incoming data from $c_{LH}$ to $c'_{LH}$, and from $c_{LL}$ to $c''_{LL}$. Note that if one of the four channels has low presence integrity, then all channels have low presence integrity, since the influence by the presence of communication over one of the channels on the control flow is global. However, $c'_{LH}$ preserves the high content integrity of $c_{LH}$, despite this pervasive corruption on the "presence" dimension.

1. $c_{HL}?x.c'_{HL}!x$
2. $c_{LH}?x.c'_{LH}!x$
3. $c_{LH}?x_1.c_{LL}?x_2.c'_{LH}!f(x_1,x_2)$,
   where $f(a,b) \neq f(c,d)$
   whenever $a \neq b$ or $c \neq d$
4. $c_{LH}?x_1.c'_{LH}!x_1 \mid c'_{LH}!d$
5. $c_{HH}?x_1.c'_{HH}!x_1 \mid c''_{HH}!d$
6. $M$ where
   $M \triangleq \&_{1\vee2}(c_{LH}?x_1, c_{LL}?x_2)$.
      case $x_1$ of some($y_1$) : $c'_{LH}!y_1.M$
      else case $x_2$ of some($y_2$) : $c''_{LL}!y_2.M$
      else 0
7. $A$ where
   $A \triangleq \&_{1\vee2}(c_{LL}?x_1, c'_{LL}?x_2)$.
      case $x_1$ of some($y_1$) : $c_{HL}!y_1.A$
      else case $x_2$ of some($y_2$) : $c_{HL}!y_2.A$
      else 0

**Fig. 1.** Some example processes

The process 7 is a call to procedure $A$ whose body uses the same predicate $1 \vee 2$, which enables it to source from alternative channels $c_{LL}$ and $c'_{LL}$. The input content, no matter from which source channel, will be output over the channel $c_{HL}$. The process is not secure if the environment can block the two inputs at the same time. However, $c_{LL}$ and $c'_{LL}$ might represent sources that are geographically distant or that fail with drastically different causes, which can be modeled by an *environment strategy* (e.g., [10, 13]) that always provides at least one of the inputs when the computation proceeds to the composite input binder. The procedure call will be secure under that strategy.

We end this section with a conceptualization of *presence integrity* and *content integrity*, although a more technical characterization comes along with our security property to be presented later.

- Presence integrity: for each $i$, whether the *existence* of the $i$-th output/input over channel $c$ in a finite sequence $\pi$ of communication actions can be influenced by the attacker
- Content integrity: for each $i$, whether the content of the $i$-th output/input over channel $c$ can be influenced by the attacker, *in case the input/output exists in a finite sequence $\pi$* of communication actions

Note that it is not only whether an input/output on a channel $c$ is eventually available, that matters, but how many times it occurs in each computation sequence, since we are concerned with nonterminating computation and looping behaviors: the processes 6 and 7 in Fig. 1 are such examples.

This paper is structured as follows. In Sect. 3, we present the syntax and semantics of the Quality Calculus. We then present our noninterference condition for behavioral integrity in Sect. 4. Two main theoretical properties of the noninterference condition, including its degeneration to SBNDC, and the compositionality result, are presented in Sect. 5. Further examples are given in Sect. 6, to illustrate the condition and its compositionality. We conclude in Sect. 7, with a few pointers to related work.

## 3 The Quality Calculus

**Syntax.** The Quality Calculus [12] has its roots in the $\pi$-calculus and CCS, but allows to specify criteria on which communications have to succeed for the computation to continue. This can be expressed by the construct $\&_q(b_1, ..., b_n)$ with predicate $q$ and communication binders $b_1,...,b_n$. The computation can then continue differently, depending on whether each of these communications has succeeded, using the construct case $e$ of some$(y)$ : $P_1$ else $P_2$. The predicate $q$ can refer to any specific binder among $b_1$, ..., $b_n$, by its index $(1,...,n)$, and can denote any boolean combination of their evaluation status. Since some previous inputs might be unsuccessful, we allow expressions that are missing data to be evaluated to none, or else to some$(c)$ with some constant $c$.

The complete syntax is given in Table 1. Terms $t$ and expressions $e$ are separate syntactical categories that capture the distinction between data and optional data. A constant $c$ is either a channel (**Chn**), or a datum (**Dt**), or both, as we allow **Chn** $\cap$ **Dt** $\neq \{\}$. For a constant in **Dt**, we also use $d$ ($d'$, etc.) for its denotation. Atomic input binders are of the form $t?x$. Atomic output binders are of the form $t!t'\{x\}$, where the variable $x$ is used as an indicator of whether the output has succeeded, the output content is also bound to $x$ in case it has. We abbreviate $t!t'\{x\}$ to $t!t'$ when such indication provided by $x$ is not needed. With a procedure call $A(\bar{e})$, the procedure $A$ needs to be defined as a process $P$, with $A(\bar{x}) \triangleq P$. Looping behavior is allowed via recursive procedure calls. The other features not mentioned so far are mostly standard. Although the Quality Calculus does not have a non-deterministic choice operator, an encoding of internal nondeterministic choice (in the style of Hoare's CSP) can be done using composite binders and case constructs, as presented in [12].

**Table 1.** The syntax of the quality calculus

| | |
|---|---|
| $t ::= c \mid y \mid f(t_1, \ldots, t_n)$ | |
| $e ::= x \mid \mathsf{some}(t) \mid \mathsf{none}$ | $P ::= (\nu c)P \mid P_1 \mid P_2 \mid b.P \mid \mathsf{A}(\bar{e}) \mid 0 \mid$ |
| | $\quad \mathsf{case}\ e\ \mathsf{of}\ \mathsf{some}(y) : \mathsf{P}_1\ \mathsf{else}\ \mathsf{P}_2$ |
| $b ::= t?x \mid t!t'\{x\} \mid \&_q(b_1, ..., b_n)$ | |

**Semantics.** To facilitate the specification of open systems, and the formulation of our security condition, we present a semantics that is parameterized on the computation environment. The tight correspondence of this semantics with the classical semantics [12] of the Quality Calculus is discussed in the appendix.

Processes and binders make transitions together with sequences $\pi \in \Pi$. Each such sequence contains a separator $\triangle$, which delimits the environment's past actions interacting with the process, and optionally a future communication attempt. Each communication action/attempt is represented by an "abstract binder" $\hat{b} \in AB$ given by the syntax $\hat{b} ::= c?x \mid c?c' \mid c!c' \mid \square$. The abstract binders $c?x$ and $c?c'$ represent a pending input and a completed input, respectively, *of the environment*; on the other hand, $c!c'$ represents either a pending output or a completed output, also *of the environment*. In addition, $\square$ represents the suspension of any communication by one step.

We write $[\pi]_\triangle$ for the prefix of $\pi$ up to the $\triangle$ in it, and $\Pi_\triangle$ for the set $\{[\pi]_\triangle \mid \pi \in \Pi\}$. Next introduce environment strategies $\delta : \Pi_\triangle \to 2^{AB} \setminus \{c?c' \mid c, c' \in \mathbf{Chn} \cup \mathbf{Dt}\}$ from the set **Strat**. For each $\pi \in \Pi_\triangle$, $\delta(\pi)$ gives the set of abstract binders that represent the environment's intended ways of "exercising" the specification for one more step. In case $\delta(\pi)$ is an input abstract binder, it will be of the form $c?x$ rather than $c?c'$, since it represents a pending input.

The transition relation for processes and binders is given in Table 2. We make use of an unspecified evaluation relation $\triangleright$ for terms and expressions. For binders, each transition rule is of the form $\langle b, \pi \rangle \xrightarrow{\beta} \langle b', \pi' \rangle$, representing that the binder $b$ performs the communication action $\beta$ ($\beta \neq \tau$) under the environment $\pi$ and becomes $b'$, turning the environment into $\pi'$. The intermediate binder $[c : \mathsf{some}(c')/x]$ is introduced (essentially extending the syntax for binders) to record the completion of the communication of some content $c'$ over channel $c$, subsequently binding $\mathsf{some}(c')$ to the variable $x$.

A $[c : \mathsf{some}(c')/x]$ is produced after a transition made by either $t!t'\{x\}$ or $t?x$, given that the content of the output/input is $c'$. In the case of $t!t'\{x\}$, $\pi_\triangle c?x'$ represents that the environment is expecting some data to be output over channel $c$ (from the process of $t!t'\{x\}$ where $t$ is evaluated to $c$), and the resulting $\pi.c?c'_\triangle$ represents the completion of this interaction, extending the environment's observational history by $c?c'$. In the case of $t?x$, $\pi_\triangle c!c'$ represents that the environment attempts to output $c'$ over channel $c$ (to the process of $t?x$ where $t$ is evaluated to $c$), and the resulting $\pi.c!c'_\triangle$ represents the completion of this interaction, growing the environment's observational history by $c!c'$. The transitions of composite binders $\&_q(b_1, ..., b_n)$ are simply built on top of those of their sub-binders.

**Table 2.** The transition relation for processes and binders

$$\frac{\langle b, \pi \rangle \xrightarrow{c!c'/c?c'} \langle b', \pi' \rangle}{\delta \vdash \langle b.P, \pi \rangle \xrightarrow{c!c'/c?c'} \langle P', \pi' \rangle} \quad \text{where } P' = \begin{cases} P\theta & (\text{if } b'::_{\mathsf{tt}}\theta) \\ b'.P & (\text{otherwise}) \end{cases}$$

$$\frac{\delta \vdash \langle P_1, {}_{\triangle}c?x \rangle \xrightarrow{c!c'} \langle P_1', \pi_1' \rangle \quad \delta \vdash \langle P_2, {}_{\triangle}c!c' \rangle \xrightarrow{c?c'} \langle P_2', \pi_2' \rangle}{\delta \vdash \langle P_1|P_2, \pi \rangle \xrightarrow{\tau} \langle P_1'|P_2', \pi \rangle}$$

$$\frac{e \triangleright \mathsf{some}(c) \quad \delta \vdash \langle P_1[c/y], \pi \rangle \xrightarrow{\beta} \langle P', \pi' \rangle}{\delta \vdash \langle CS(e,y,P_1,P_2), \pi \rangle \xrightarrow{\beta} \langle P', \pi' \rangle} \quad \frac{e \triangleright \mathsf{none} \quad \delta \vdash \langle P_2, \pi \rangle \xrightarrow{\beta} \langle P', \pi' \rangle}{\delta \vdash \langle CS(e,y,P_1,P_2), \pi \rangle \xrightarrow{\beta} \langle P', \pi' \rangle}$$

$$\frac{\bar{e} \triangleright \bar{w} \quad \delta \vdash \langle P[\bar{w}/\bar{x}], \pi \rangle \xrightarrow{\beta} \langle P', \pi' \rangle}{\delta \vdash \langle A(\bar{e}), \pi \rangle \xrightarrow{\beta} \langle P', \pi' \rangle} \text{ if } A(\bar{x}) \triangleq P \quad \frac{\delta \vdash \langle P_1, \pi \rangle \xrightarrow{\beta} \langle P_2, \pi' \rangle}{\delta \vdash \langle P_1|P, \pi \rangle \xrightarrow{\beta} \langle P_2|P, \pi' \rangle}$$

$$\frac{\delta \vdash \langle P, \pi \rangle \xrightarrow{\beta} \langle P', \pi' \rangle}{\delta \vdash \langle (\nu c)P, \pi \rangle \xrightarrow{\beta} \langle (\nu c)P', \pi' \rangle} \text{ if } c \notin \mathrm{Ch}(\beta) \quad \frac{P_1 \equiv P_2 \quad \delta \vdash \langle P_2, \pi \rangle \xrightarrow{\beta} \langle P_3, \pi' \rangle \quad P_3 \equiv P_4}{\delta \vdash \langle P_1, \pi \rangle \xrightarrow{\beta} \langle P_4, \pi' \rangle}$$

$$\frac{\neg(\exists c, c', \beta, P', \pi'' : (\beta = c!c' \vee \beta = c?c') \wedge \delta \vdash \langle P, \pi_{\triangle}\alpha.\pi' \rangle \xrightarrow{\beta} \langle P', \pi'' \rangle)}{\delta \vdash \langle P, \pi_{\triangle}\alpha.\pi' \rangle \xrightarrow{\square} \langle P, \pi.\square_{\triangle}\pi' \rangle}$$

$$\delta \vdash \langle P, \pi \rangle \xrightarrow{\mathsf{env}} \langle P, \pi.\alpha \rangle \text{ if } \pi = [\pi]_{\triangle} \wedge \alpha \in \delta(\pi)$$

$$\frac{t \triangleright c \quad t' \triangleright c'}{\langle t!t'\{x\}, \pi_{\triangle}c?x' \rangle \xrightarrow{c!c'} \langle [c : \mathsf{some}(c')/x], \pi.c?c'_{\triangle} \rangle} \quad t!t'\{x\}::_{\mathsf{ff}} [\mathsf{none}/x] \quad t?x::_{\mathsf{ff}} [\mathsf{none}/x]$$

$$\frac{t \triangleright c}{\langle t?x, \pi_{\triangle}c!c' \rangle \xrightarrow{c?c'} \langle [c : \mathsf{some}(c')/x], \pi.c!c'_{\triangle} \rangle} \quad [c : \mathsf{some}(c')/x]::_{\mathsf{tt}} [\mathsf{some}(c')/x]$$

$$\frac{\langle b_j, \pi \rangle \xrightarrow{\beta} \langle b_j', \pi' \rangle}{\langle \&_q(..., b_j, ...), \pi \rangle \xrightarrow{\beta} \langle \&_q(..., b_j', ...), \pi' \rangle} \quad \frac{\forall i : b_i ::_{v_i} \theta_i \quad v' = [\![q]\!](\bar{v})}{\&_q(b_1, ..., b_n) ::_{v'} \theta_n ... \theta_1}$$

The last couple of rules in Table 2 define the *evaluation* $b ::_v \theta$ of binders $b$, which is used by the transition rules for processes. Here $\theta$ is the substitution produced, recording the optional data bound to variables, and $v$ is a boolean value indicating whether the binder $b$ can already be passed. The basic binders $t!t'\{x\}$ and $t?x$ represent pending (incomplete) communications and hence for the evaluation of both binders, $v = \mathsf{ff}$, and the resulting substitution is $[\mathsf{none}/x]$, representing that no data is received into the variable $x$. For composite binders $\&_q(...)$, the last evaluation rule in Table 2 uses $[\![q]\!]$, the interpretation of the predicate $q$, to aggregate the evaluation statuses of the individual sub-binders. As examples, we have $[\![2]\!](v_1, v_2) = v_2$, and $[\![1 \vee 2]\!](v_1, v_2) = v_1 \vee v_2$. On the other hand, the resulting substitution is the composition of all the substitutions resulting from the evaluation of the sub-binders.

For processes, each transition rule of the form $\delta \vdash \langle P, \pi \rangle \xrightarrow{\beta} \langle P', \pi' \rangle$ governs the transition of process $P$ under environment $\pi$ into process $P'$, turning the environment into $\pi'$. On the other hand, each transition of the form $\delta \vdash \langle P, \pi \rangle \xrightarrow{\text{env}} \langle P, \pi' \rangle$ represents the advancement of the environment alone. This transition relation is defined assuming a standard structural congruence $\equiv$ (given in detail in Table 3 of the appendix).

For output and input, we start from a process of the form $b.P$. Suppose the binder $b$ makes a transition to the binder $b'$. In case $b'$ has the evaluation $b' ::_{\text{tt}} \theta$, the execution will embark on the process $P\theta$ — the process $P$ with the substitution $\theta$ applied to it. In case $b'$ has the evaluation $b' ::_{\text{ff}} \theta$, we stay with the process $b'.P$, waiting for further communication required by the binder $b'$ before it can be passed. The communication action (either an input or an output) performed by the process $b.P$ is the one performed by $b$. A synchronization between two processes does not rely on the environment $\pi$, and has no impact on it.

The next two rules use the abbreviation $CS(e, y, P_1, P_2)$ for the process case $e$ of some$(y)$ : $P_1$ else $P_2$, and describe the execution of the case construct. In case the expression $e$ is evaluated to some$(c)$, where $c$ is a constant, then the process $P_1[c/y]$ is executed, where the substitution records the binding of $y$ to $c$. In case $e$ is evaluated to none, then the process $P_2$ is executed, with no reference to $y$.

The rules for procedure calls, for parallel composition, for restriction, and for dealing with processes equivalent under $\equiv$, are self-explanatory. Notation-wise, $\text{Ch}(\beta)$ represents the set of channels occurring in $\beta$.

The second last transition rule for processes says that when a process $P$ cannot perform any communication action when the environment attempts to use the abstract binder $\alpha$ for the next interaction, we allow $P$ to do a $\square$-step, signaling that there is one step of delay. At the same time, the observational history of the environment is extended by a $\square$, recording the observation of this delay.

The last transition rule says that the environment can make its next interaction attempt when its observational history ends with a $\triangle$: it can only "prescribe" the most imminent interaction, without further predication of the future.

We illustrate the semantics in Example 1, where $\delta_{\text{ALL}} = \lambda\pi_\triangle.\{c!c'|c, c' \in \mathbf{Chn} \cup \mathbf{Dt}\} \cup \{c?x|c \in \mathbf{Chn}\} \cup \{\square\}$ is the strategy that allows the environment to produce any sensible abstract binder with any observation it has.

*Example 1.* The procedure call $M$ in Fig. 1 has the following transition sequence.

$$\delta_{\text{ALL}} \vdash \langle M, \triangle \rangle \xrightarrow{\text{env}} \langle M, \triangle c_{LL}!d \rangle$$
$$\xrightarrow{c_{LL}?d} \left\langle \begin{array}{l} \text{case none of some}(y_1) : c'_{LH}!y_1.M \\ \text{else case some}(d) \text{ of some}(y_2) : c''_{LL}!y_2.M \text{ else } 0 \end{array}, c_{LL}!d_\triangle \right\rangle$$
$$\xrightarrow{\text{env}} \left\langle \begin{array}{l} \text{case none of some}(y_1) : c'_{LH}!y_1.M \\ \text{else case some}(d) \text{ of some}(y_2) : c''_{LL}!y_2.M \text{ else } 0 \end{array}, c_{LL}!d_\triangle c''_{LL}?x \right\rangle$$
$$\xrightarrow{c''_{LL}!d} \langle M, c_{LL}!d.c''_{LL}?d_\triangle \rangle$$

We elaborate slightly on the second step above. According to the transition rules for binders, we have $\langle c_{LL}?x_2, \triangle c_{LL}!d \rangle \xrightarrow{c_{LL}?d} \langle [c_{LL} : \text{some}(d)/x_2], c_{LL}!d_\triangle \rangle$, which gives rise to $\langle \&_{1\vee 2}(c_{LH}?x_1, c_{LL}?x_2), \triangle c_{LL}!d \rangle \xrightarrow{c_{LL}?d} \langle \&_{1\vee 2}(c_{LH}?x_1, [c_{LL} : \text{some}(d)/x_2]), c_{LL}!d_\triangle \rangle$. Using the evaluation rules for binders, we have $\&_{1\vee 2}(c_{LH}?x_1, [c_{LL} : \text{some}(d)/x_2]) ::_{\text{tt}} [\text{none}/x_1][\text{some}(d)/x_2]$. Hence by the transition rule for $b.P$, with $b$ taken to be $\&_{1\vee 2}(c_{LH}?x_1, [c_{LL} : \text{some}(d)/x_2])$, the second transition is derived. $\square$

Hereafter, we will use the more compact $\delta \vdash \langle P, \pi \rangle \xrightarrow{\text{env},\beta} \langle P', \pi' \rangle$ to represent $\exists \pi_0 : \delta \vdash \langle P, \pi \rangle \xrightarrow{\text{env}} \langle P, \pi_0 \rangle \wedge \delta \vdash \langle P, \pi_0 \rangle \xrightarrow{\beta} \langle P', \pi' \rangle$. We will also use $\text{rch}(P)$ to represent the channel, polarity pairs of all possible communications that can be performed by a derivative of $\langle P, {}_\triangle \rangle$ under the strategy $\delta_{\text{ALL}}$, i.e., $\text{rch}(P) = \{(c, \rho) \mid \exists P', \pi', c' : \delta_{\text{ALL}} \vdash \langle P, {}_\triangle \rangle \rightarrow^* \langle P', \pi' \rangle \xrightarrow{c\rho c'}\}$.

# 4 Noninterference for Behavioral Integrity

In this section, we build up to our noninterference condition for behavioral integrity. We introduce the *classification mappings* $\mathcal{P}$ and $\mathcal{C}$ to keep track of the presence levels and content levels, respectively, for communication channels. In our definitions and propositions, we tacitly assume that all variables not explicitly quantified are in fact *universally* quantified.

We start by introducing a way of indexing into traces: $\pi @_i^{c,\rho}$ is $(n, c')$ if the $i$-th communication over channel $c$ with polarity $\rho$ in $\pi$ is the $n$-th communication overall in $\pi$, and the content of the communication is $c'$. All the indices start with 0. If the number of communications over $c$ with polarity $\rho$ in $\pi$ is less than or equal to $i$, then $\pi @_i^{c,\rho}$ is $\bot$. This is formalized in Definition 1 and illustrated in Example 2.

**Definition 1** $(\pi @_i^{c,\rho})$. $\pi @_i^{c,\rho} = \pi @_{i,0}^{c,\rho}$, where $i \geq 0$ and $\pi @_{i,0}^{c,\rho}$ is defined by

$$\pi @_{i,n}^{c,\rho} = \begin{cases} \bot & (\text{if } \pi = \epsilon) \\ (n, c') & (\text{if } \exists \pi' : \pi = c\rho c'.\pi' \wedge i = 0) \\ \pi' @_{i-1,n+1}^{c,\rho} & (\text{if } \exists c' : \pi = c\rho c'.\pi' \wedge i \neq 0) \\ \pi' @_{i,n+1}^{c,\rho} & (\text{if } \exists c'', \rho'', c''' : \pi = c''\rho''c'''.\pi' \wedge (c'' \neq c \vee \rho'' \neq \rho)) \end{cases}$$

*Example 2.* Consider the trace $\pi = c_{LL}!d.c_{LL}''?d_{\triangle}$ left by the environment from Example 1. We have $\pi @_0^{c_{LL}'',?} = (1, d)$ and $\pi @_i^{c_{LL}'',?} = \bot$ whenever $i \geq 1$.  □

We define the trace correspondence relation $W_{\mathcal{C}}^{\mathcal{P}}$ as follows, where $|\pi|$ stands for the length of $\pi$. The presence and content of communications in traces related by $W_{\mathcal{C}}^{\mathcal{P}}$ are supposed to reflect the integrity levels of their channels.

**Definition 2** $(W_{\mathcal{C}}^{\mathcal{P}})$. $\pi_1 \ W_{\mathcal{C}}^{\mathcal{P}} \ \pi_2$ if and only if $\pi_1$ and $\pi_2$ are finite, $|\pi_1| = |\pi_2|$, and $\forall i \geq 0 : \forall c, \rho : \pi_1 @_i^{c,\rho} \ W_{\mathcal{C}(c)}^{\mathcal{P}(c)} \ \pi_2 @_i^{c,\rho}$.

In Definition 2, two traces related by $W_{\mathcal{C}}^{\mathcal{P}}$ are required to have the same finite length, and the $i$-th occurrences of communication over channel $c$, with polarity $\rho$, are required to be related by $W_{\mathcal{C}(c)}^{\mathcal{P}(c)}$, for each $c$ and $\rho$. The latter relation is in turn defined as follows, where $c_1' \doteq c_2'$ if and only if $c_1' = c_2'$ or $c_2' \notin \mathbf{Chn} \cup \mathbf{Dt}$.

**Definition 3** $(W_{lc}^{l_{\mathcal{P}}})$. $(n_1, c_1') \ W_{lc}^{l_{\mathcal{P}}} \ (n_2, c_2')$ if and only if

$$
\begin{aligned}
(n_1, c_1') \ W_{lc}^{l_{\mathcal{P}}} \ (n_2, c_2') &\quad \text{iff} \quad (l_{\mathcal{P}} = H \Rightarrow n_1 = n_2) \wedge (l_c = H \Rightarrow c_1' \doteq c_2') \\
(n_1, c_1') \ W_{lc}^{l_{\mathcal{P}}} \ \bot &\quad \text{iff} \quad l_{\mathcal{P}} = L \\
\bot \ W_{lc}^{l_{\mathcal{P}}} \ (n_2, c_2') &\quad \text{iff} \quad l_{\mathcal{P}} = L \\
\bot \ W_{lc}^{l_{\mathcal{P}}} \ \bot &\quad \text{iff} \quad \text{true}
\end{aligned}
$$

It can be seen that for a channel $c$ with high presence integrity, the $i$-th occurrences of input/output over $c$ need to have the same overall index in their respective traces. On the other hand, for a channel $c$ with high content integrity, the $i$-th occurrences of input/output over $c$ need to have equivalent content. This corresponds tightly to our description of "presence integrity" and "content integrity" in Sect. 2. The reason that $\doteq$ is used for relating content, instead of $=$, is the potential existence of variables in traces of the form $\ldots_\triangle c?x$.

We will write $\stackrel{\widehat{\beta'}}{\Longrightarrow}$ for the weak transition used for standard observational equivalence, i.e., it stands for $(\stackrel{\tau}{\longrightarrow})^* \circ \stackrel{\beta'}{\longrightarrow} \circ (\stackrel{\tau}{\longrightarrow})^*$ when $\beta' \neq \tau$ and for $(\stackrel{\tau}{\longrightarrow})^*$ when $\beta' = \tau$. The weak transition will not be used directly in our noninterference property, but encapsulated within the transition $\stackrel{\widehat{\beta'}}{\underset{\beta}{\Longrightarrow}}$ introduced in Definition 4.

It boils down to the weak transition $\stackrel{\widehat{\beta'}}{\Longrightarrow}$ in case $\beta$ is a communication with high presence integrity; otherwise $\tau$'s are not allowed.

**Definition 4 ($\stackrel{\widehat{\beta'}}{\underset{\beta}{\Longrightarrow}}$).**     $\stackrel{\widehat{\beta'}}{\underset{\beta}{\Longrightarrow}} = \begin{cases} \stackrel{\beta'}{\longrightarrow} & (\text{if } \beta = \square \vee \exists c, \rho, c' : \beta = c\rho c' \wedge \mathcal{P}(c) = L) \\ \stackrel{\widehat{\beta'}}{\Longrightarrow} & (\text{otherwise}) \end{cases}$

We then define the notion of $\delta$-bisimulation, where $\delta \in \mathbf{Strat}$ is a strategy.

**Definition 5 ($\delta$-Bisimulation).** *A $\delta$-bisimulation is a symmetric relation $R$ on configurations such that if $\langle P_1, \pi_1 \rangle \; R \; \langle P_2, \pi_2 \rangle$, $\delta \vdash \langle P_1, \pi_1 \rangle \xrightarrow{\text{env},\beta} \langle P_1', \pi_1' \rangle$, $\delta \vdash \langle P_2, \pi_2 \rangle \xrightarrow{\text{env}} \langle P_2, \pi_{20} \rangle$, and $\pi_1' \, W_{\mathcal{C}}^{\mathcal{P}} \, \pi_{20}$, then we have*

$$\exists P_2', \pi_2', \beta' : \delta \vdash \langle P_2, \pi_{20} \rangle \stackrel{\widehat{\beta'}}{\underset{\beta}{\Longrightarrow}} \langle P_2', \pi_2' \rangle \wedge$$
$$[\pi_1']_\triangle \, W_{\mathcal{C}}^{\mathcal{P}} \, [\pi_2']_\triangle \wedge \langle P_1', [\pi_1']_\triangle \rangle \; R \; \langle P_2', [\pi_2']_\triangle \rangle.$$

If two configurations $\langle P_1, \pi_1 \rangle$ and $\langle P_2, \pi_2 \rangle$ are related by a $\delta$-bisimulation $R$, then after $\langle P_1, \pi_1 \rangle$ interacts with the environment $\delta$ for one step, and the environment makes an interaction attempt with $\langle P_2, \pi_2 \rangle$, such that the interaction and the attempt meet the integrity classes of their channels ($\pi_1' \, W_{\mathcal{C}}^{\mathcal{P}} \, \pi_{20}$), the configuration $\langle P_2, \pi_{20} \rangle$ can simulate the interaction made by $\langle P_1, \pi_1 \rangle$, in a way that meets the integrity classes of the channels involved ($[\pi_1']_\triangle \, W_{\mathcal{C}}^{\mathcal{P}} \, [\pi_2']_\triangle$).

The definition of $\delta$-Bisimulation introduces two universally quantified transitions, before simulating the first one with an existentially quantified transition. This pattern, previously adopted in [11], is rare in the literature.

We then define $\delta$-bisimilarity ($\underset{\delta}{\sim}$) as the union of all $\delta$-bisimulations (which is itself a $\delta$-bisimulation). Note that $\delta$-bisimilarity is *not* reflexive. In fact, our noninterference condition identifies the $\delta$-security of a process $P$ with the self-relatedness of $\langle P, \triangle \rangle$ in $\underset{\delta}{\sim}$, as stated in Definition 6.

**Definition 6 ($\delta$-Security).** *A process $P$ is $\delta$-secure, denoted by $\mathsf{Sec}_\delta(P)$, if and only if $\langle P, \triangle \rangle \underset{\delta}{\sim} \langle P, \triangle \rangle$.*

To arrive at a better understanding of $\delta$-security, we introduce in Definition 7 the notion of *kernel $\delta$-bisimulation*, which constrains the pairs of observational histories further than $\delta$-bisimulation does. Proposition 1 then says that kernel $\delta$-bisimulations, with a more complex formulation, can be used to characterize $\delta$-security equally well.

**Definition 7 (Kernel $\delta$-Bisimulation).** *A $\delta$-bisimulation $R$ is said to be a kernel $\delta$-bisimulation if and only if $\langle P_1, \pi_1 \rangle\, R\, \langle P_2, \pi_2 \rangle$ implies $knl(\pi_1, \pi_2)$, where $knl(\pi_1, \pi_2)$ represents $\pi_1\, W_C^P\, \pi_2$, $[\pi_1]_\triangle = \pi_1$, and $[\pi_2]_\triangle = \pi_2$.*

**Proposition 1.** *There is a $\delta$-bisimulation $R$ such that $\langle P, \triangle \rangle\, R\, \langle P, \triangle \rangle$, if and only if there is a kernel $\delta$-bisimulation $R'$ such that $\langle P, \triangle \rangle\, R'\, \langle P, \triangle \rangle$.*

For a $\delta$-secure process $P$, the implications of the existence of a kernel $\delta$-bisimulation $R$ such that $\langle P, \triangle \rangle\, R\, \langle P, \triangle \rangle$ are:

1. A communication $\beta$ with high presence integrity needs to be simulated by a communication over the *same* channel, possibly together with $\tau$'s. In case the channel also has high content integrity, the content of the simulating communication should be the same as that of $\beta$. If the channel has low content integrity, on the other hand, then the bisimulation should continue under all contents possibly attempted by the environment, that are not necessarily the same as that of $\beta$.
2. A communication $\beta$ with low presence integrity, or a $\square$-transition, is simulated by a communication over a channel also of low presence integrity, or by a $\square$-transition. If the channel of $\beta$, say $c$, has high content integrity, and it is being used for the $i$-th time with polarity $\rho$, then the content of $\beta$ needs to agree with the content of the communication occurring on $c$ with polarity $\rho$ for the $i$-th time in the second execution, *in case that communication exists*. A similar requirement is imposed on the simulating communication, when its channel has high content integrity.
3. A $\tau$ can only be simulated by a (possibly empty) sequence of $\tau$'s. This is because when a $\tau$-transition is made from a configuration $\langle P, \pi \rangle$, the $\triangle$ in $\pi$ does not move, which is not the case otherwise. By Proposition 1, it is obvious that $|\pi_1'| = |\pi_{20}|$. Hence $[\pi_1']_\triangle$ and $[\pi_2']_\triangle$ will not have the same length and $[\pi_1']_\triangle\, W_C^P\, [\pi_2']_\triangle$ will not hold, if a $\tau$ is not simulated only by $\tau$'s.

The $\delta_{\text{ALL}}$-security/insecurity of processes 1-6 in Fig. 1 of Sect. 2 agrees with the claims based on intuition in the same section, with an unconstrained environment. And process 7 is $\delta_{\text{ALT}}$-secure, where $\delta_{\text{ALT}}$ characterizes an environment that provides content over at least one of $c_{LL}$ and $c'_{LL}$ whenever the process is ready for input from these two alternative channels:

$$\delta_{\text{ALT}}(\pi) = \begin{cases} \{c_1!d \mid c_1 \in \{c_{LL}, c'_{LL}\} \wedge d \in \mathbf{Dt}\} & (\text{if } \pi = \triangle \vee \exists \pi', d' : \pi = \pi'.c_{HL}?d'_\triangle) \\ AB & (\text{otherwise}) \end{cases}$$

The construction of the underlying kernel $\delta_{\text{ALL}}$-bisimulation $R_*$ for the $\delta_{\text{ALL}}$-security of process 6 is given in the appendix. We demonstrate in Example 3 that some of the requirements of $\langle M, \triangle \rangle\, R_*\, \langle M, \triangle \rangle$ are fulfilled, to aid in the reader's intuition.

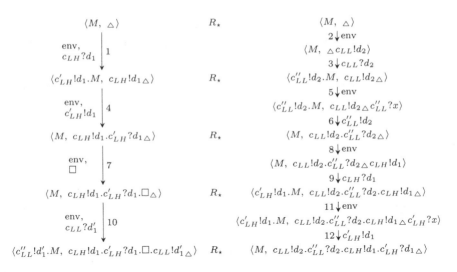

**Fig. 2.** Partial unfolding of the kernel bisimulation containing $(\langle M, \vartriangle \rangle, \langle M, \vartriangle \rangle)$

*Example 3.* Figure 2 contains a partial unfolding of $\langle M, \vartriangle \rangle \, R_* \, \langle M, \vartriangle \rangle$ where $R_*$ is a kernel $\delta_{\mathrm{ALL}}$-bisimulation. For each pair $\langle P_1, \pi_1 \rangle$ and $\langle P_2, \pi_2 \rangle$ related by $R_*$ in Fig. 2, $\pi_1 \, W_{\mathcal{C}}^{\mathcal{P}} \, \pi_2$ holds. After transitions 1 and 2, the environment has made the attempt to interact with the process on two different channels $c_{LH}$ and $c_{LL}$. This is allowed since $c_{LH}!d_1{}_\vartriangle \, W_{\mathcal{C}}^{\mathcal{P}} \, {}_\vartriangle c_{LL}!d_2$ holds. The process $M$ can indeed perform an input over $c_{LH}$, resulting in transition 1. This transition needs to be simulated by either an input over $c_{LL}$, or a $\square$-transition in case such an input cannot be performed. We are in the former situation and transition 1 is thus simulated by transition 3. Note that according to Definition 4, the simulation of low presence communications should be done without using $\tau$'s. This is because such simulation is actually used to introduce interference, rather than to demonstrate resilience to it. And $\tau$-transitions are conventionally used to weaken the requirement for a process to be resilient to interference. We then direct our attention to transitions 7, 8 and 9. The environment intentionally resists communication with the process in transition 7. On the other hand, it attempts to feed some content over $c_{LH}$ to the process through transition 8. That content is restricted to $d_1$ since only then it holds that $c_{LH}!d_1.c'_{LH}?d_1.\square_\vartriangle \, W_{\mathcal{C}}^{\mathcal{P}} \, c_{LL}!d_2.c''_{LL}?d_2{}_\vartriangle c_{LH}!d_1$. Intuitively, the input over $c_{LH}$ is blocked for a while in the second execution, but it needs to happen with the same content $d_1$ since the channel has high content integrity. For transitions 10, 11 and 12, the attempt of the environment to input from the process over channel $c'_{LH}$ in transition 11 is satisfied with the content $d_1$, resulting in transition 12. The latter transition is a legitimate simulation of transition 10 since the content $d_1$ is the same as that of transition 4 — the corresponding communication over $c'_{LH}$ in the first execution.    $\square$

A total order can be built on the set **Strat** of environment strategies, characterizing their relative aggressiveness (Definition 8), which has its impact on the strength of the security condition (Theorem 1).

**Definition 8 (Aggressiveness of Environments).** *Environment $\delta_2$ is said to be more aggressive than $\delta_1$, denoted $\delta_1 \leq \delta_2$, if $\forall \pi \in \Pi_\triangle : \delta_1(\pi) \subseteq \delta_2(\pi)$.*

**Theorem 1 (Monotonicity).** *$\delta$-bisimilarity is anti-monotonic in $\delta$, i.e., for all $\delta_1$, $\delta_2$ such that $\delta_1 \leq \delta_2$, it holds that $\underset{\delta_2}{\sim} \subseteq \underset{\delta_1}{\sim}$.*

This monotonicity result may look counter-intuitive since $\delta$ appears to be used both positively and negatively in Definition 5. However, $\delta \vdash \langle P_2, \pi_{20} \rangle \xADelta{\widehat{\beta'}}{\beta} \langle P_2', \pi_2' \rangle$ if and only if $\delta' \vdash \langle P_2, \pi_{20} \rangle \xADelta{\widehat{\beta'}}{\beta} \langle P_2', \pi_2' \rangle$ for all $\delta' \in \mathbf{Strat}$. In other words, $\delta$ is not actually used in the derivation of the transition sequence from $\langle P_2, \pi_{20} \rangle$.

**Corollary 1.** *The permissiveness of $\delta$-security is anti-monotonic in $\delta$, i.e.,*

$$\forall \delta_1, \delta_2 \in \mathbf{Strat} : \delta_1 \leq \delta_2 \wedge \mathsf{Sec}_{\delta_2}(P) \ \Rightarrow \ \mathsf{Sec}_{\delta_1}(P).$$

We will discuss deeper theoretical properties of our security condition in Sect. 5, focusing on $\delta_{\mathrm{ALL}}$-security. It will be seen that the most pessimistic assumption about the environment, captured by its most aggressive strategy $\delta_{\mathrm{ALL}}$, is in line with classical process-algebraic conditions like SBNDC, and also facilitates the compositional verification of the security property.

## 5   Theoretical Properties

**Connection with SBNDC.** We reformulate SBNDC [6] using the classical semantics of the Quality Calculus, and with respect to the environment $\mathcal{I}$ : $\mathsf{Chan} \to \{H, L\} \cup \{\bot\}$ that gives the presence level of a channel only when its presence level and content level are the same, i.e., $\mathcal{I}(c) = \begin{cases} \mathcal{P}(c) \ (\text{if } \mathcal{P}(c) = \mathcal{C}(c)) \\ \bot \quad (\text{otherwise}) \end{cases}$.
The aim of $\mathcal{I}$ is to obtain the integrity class of each channel when its presence integrity and content integrity are the same (using $\mathcal{C}(c)$ instead of $\mathcal{P}(c)$ in the definition of $\mathcal{I}(c)$ would have the same effect).

We also introduce the notation $\overline{loi}$ to represent the list of low integrity channels, i.e., $\overline{loi} = \{c \mid \mathcal{I}(c) = L\}$, and use $\mathsf{ch}(\beta)$ to denote the channel used by the (non-$\tau$) communication action $\beta$. The reformulation is then given in Definition 9, where $\approx$ is the standard observational equivalence. The intuitive interpretation is that before and after each low integrity communication, a process is required to have the same high integrity behaviors. Then the central result of this subsection, that $\delta_{\mathrm{ALL}}$-security coincides with SBNDC when the same integrity levels are always used for both "presence" and "content", is given in Theorem 2.

**Definition 9 (SBNDC).** *$P \in SBNDC$ if for all $P'$, $P''$, communication $\beta$, such that $P \to^* P'$, $P' \xrightarrow{\beta} P''$, and $\mathcal{I}(\mathsf{ch}(\beta)) = L$, we have $(\nu \overline{loi})P' \approx (\nu \overline{loi})P''$.*

**Theorem 2 (Degeneration).** *For all processes $P$, if $\forall c, \rho$ s.t. $(c, \rho) \in \mathsf{rch}(P)$ : $\mathcal{P}(c) = \mathcal{C}(c)$, then $\mathsf{Sec}_{\delta_{\mathrm{ALL}}}(P)$ if and only if $P \in SBNDC$.*

To build up to a proof of Theorem 2, we recast SBNDC in the form of *self-bisimilarity*. The underlying bisimulation is the $\triangleright$-bisimulation of Definition 10.

**Definition 10 ($\triangleright$-Bisimulation).** *A symmetric relation $R$ on processes qualifies as a $\triangleright$-bisimulation if $P_1 \; R \; P_2$ implies:*
*for all $P_1'$ and $\beta$ such that $P_1 \xrightarrow{\beta} P_1'$, there exists $P_2'$ such that*

- *if $\mathcal{I}(\mathsf{ch}(\beta)) = L$, then $P_2' \equiv P_2$ and $P_1' \; R \; P_2'$,*
- *if $\mathcal{I}(\mathsf{ch}(\beta)) = H$ or $\beta = \tau$, then $P_2 \xRightarrow{\hat{\beta}} P_2'$ and $P_1' \; R \; P_2'$.*

We define $\triangleright$-bisimilarity as the union of all $\triangleright$-bisimulations. The $\triangleright$ used here symbolizes the triangular structure created by the simulation of a low integrity communication by *inaction*, as required in Definition 10. It can be shown that self-$\triangleright$-bisimilarity coincides with self-$\delta_{\mathrm{ALL}}$-bisimilarity when the presence levels and content levels are the same for all channels whose uses are reachable.

**Lemma 1.** *Suppose $P$ is such that $\forall c, \rho$ s.t. $(c, \rho) \in \mathsf{rch}(P) : \mathcal{P}(c) = \mathcal{C}(c)$. Then $P \in SBNDC \iff P \sim_{\triangleright} P$, and $P \sim_{\triangleright} P \iff \langle P, \vartriangle \rangle \underset{\delta_{\mathrm{ALL}}}{\sim} \langle P, \vartriangle \rangle$.*

The degeneration result presented above demonstrates that the notion of $\delta$-security is in fact well-based on the classical process-algebraic noninterference properties, and SBNDC, as one of those properties, actually has the implicit assumption of the most aggressive environment.

**Compositionality.** Compositionality is a desirable property for the verification of noninterference properties. The security of a parallel composition can be directly obtained from that of its constituents, in case full compositionality is enjoyed by a noninterference condition. However, $\delta$-security is not fully compositional. Nevertheless, this is key to spotting the insecurity of the example process 4 given in Sect. 2, since the processes $c_{LH}?x_1.c_{LH}'!x_1$ and $c_{LH}'!d$ are themselves $\delta_{\mathrm{ALL}}$-secure. We then discuss the *sufficient conditions* required for $\delta_{\mathrm{ALL}}$-security to be compositional.

A process $P$ is *deterministic* with respect to output over a channel $c$, denoted by $\mathsf{det}(P, c)$, if

$$\delta_{\mathrm{ALL}} \vdash \langle P, \vartriangle \rangle \rightarrow^* \langle P', \pi' \rangle \wedge (\forall i \in \{1, 2\} : \delta_{\mathrm{ALL}} \vdash \langle P', \pi' \rangle \xrightarrow{c!c_i'} \langle P_i', \pi_i' \rangle) \; \Rightarrow \; c_1' = c_2'.$$

We then have the following theorem for the compositionality of $\delta_{\mathrm{ALL}}$-security.

**Theorem 3 (Compositionality).** *If $\mathsf{Sec}_{\delta_{\mathrm{ALL}}}(P_1)$, and $\mathsf{Sec}_{\delta_{\mathrm{ALL}}}(P_2)$, then we have $\mathsf{Sec}_{\delta_{\mathrm{ALL}}}((\nu \vec{c})(P_1 | P_2))$, provided that for all $i \in \{1, 2\}$ and channel $c$:*

$$\mathcal{P}(c) \not\sqsupseteq \mathcal{C}(c) \wedge (c, \rho_1) \in \mathsf{rch}(P_i) \wedge (c, \rho_2) \in \mathsf{rch}(P_{3-i}) \; \Rightarrow \; \rho_1 \neq \rho_2 \wedge \mathsf{det}(P_i, c) \wedge c \in \{\vec{c}\}.$$

In words, Theorem 3 says that given two processes $P_1$ and $P_2$ that are both $\delta_{\mathrm{ALL}}$-secure, the process $(\nu \vec{c})(P_1 | P_2)$ is $\delta_{\mathrm{ALL}}$-secure, provided that

1. No $LH$-channels are used by both $P_1$ and $P_2$ with the same polarity (note that the process 4 given in Sect. 2 does not meet this requirement), and

2. For each $LH$-channel $c$ used by $P_1$ and $P_2$ with different polarities, $P_1$ and $P_2$ must be deterministic with respect to output on $c$, and $c$ must be among the constants over which there is a top-level restriction; thus the input side always sources from the output side, never from the environment.

**Corollary 2.** *Suppose* $\forall c, \rho : (c, \rho) \in \mathsf{rch}(P) \Rightarrow \mathcal{P}(c) \sqsupseteq \mathcal{C}(c)$. *Then* $\mathsf{Sec}_{\delta_{\mathrm{ALL}}}(P_1 | P_2)$ *can be deduced from* $\mathsf{Sec}_{\delta_{\mathrm{ALL}}}(P_1)$ *and* $\mathsf{Sec}_{\delta_{\mathrm{ALL}}}(P_2)$.

The results presented above help elucidate the points below.

1. If $\delta$-security had been fully compositional, it would not have uncovered certain insecure dependencies of high integrity content on low integrity presence.
2. The notion of $\delta$-security is fully compositional for processes that do not make use of $LH$-channels.

## 6    Further Examples and Discussion

We have associated with $LH$-channels the meaning: communications over these channels can be blocked by the attacker, but with uninfluenced contents when they finally happen. So far the abstract environment has been assumed to be able to induce these channels. In this section, we present a concrete process in the Quality Calculus that can accomplish the same task. We then make the multiplexer process presented in Sect. 2 obtain its input from this process, to illustrate our compositionality result.

*On LH-Channels.* We illustrate that $LH$-channels can be induced from channels that are $LL$ and $HH$ by a concrete process. The procedure $SINK$ in Fig. 3 mimics the potential congestion of the high integrity data source $c_{HH}$ using a queue: output of the oldest element suspended in the queue is attempted through the sink channel $c_{LH}$ only when the low integrity switch $c_{LL}$ is on. Recall that the $\&_2(\_,\_)$ can be passed if and only if the second communication is successful.

The channels $c_i$, $c_d$, and $c_p$ are interfaces for the operations "insert" ("enque"), "delete" ("deque"), and "peek" (the non-destructive inspection of the oldest element) of the queue specified by the procedure $QUE$ (adapted from the priority queue in [17]) in the appendix. The procedure $SINK$ waits on the input over $c_{HH}$ for the composite binder on the first line to be passed. When

$$SINK \triangleq \&_2(c_{LL}?x_1, c_{HH}?x_2).$$
$$\text{case } x_2 \text{ of } \mathsf{some}(y_2):$$
$$(\nu c_f)(c_i!(y_2, c_f).c_f?x_f.$$
$$\text{case } x_1 \text{ of } \mathsf{some}(y_1):$$
$$(\nu c_e, c_r)(c_p!(c_e, c_r).c_r?x_3[y_3].$$
$$\&_2(c_{LH}!y_3\{x_3'\}, c_{HH}'?x_t).$$
$$\text{case } x_3' \text{ of } \mathsf{some}(y_3'):$$
$$(\nu c_e', c_r')(c_d!(c_e', c_r').c_r?x_4[y_4].SINK)$$
$$\text{else } SINK)$$
$$\text{else } c_{HH}'?x_t.SINK)$$
$$\text{else } 0$$

**Fig. 3.** The "Realization" of sink channels with low presence integrity and high content integrity

that happens, the input data over $c_{HH}$ is enqued, with the completion of the "enque" operation signaled on $c_f$. If the input over $c_{LL}$ was also successful, then outputting the head of the queue is attempted, with a high integrity timeout supposed to come over $c'_{HH}$. If the output is successful before the timeout, then the data item of the output is deleted from the queue. In the "peek" and "deque" operations, the channels $c_e$ and $c'_e$ are sent to the queue for the latter to signal back whether it is already an empty queue. In our case the non-emptiness of the queue is an invariant and hence neither $c_e$ nor $c'_e$ is subsequently used. The process $(\nu c_i, c_d, c_p)(SINK \mid QUE(\mathsf{some}(c_i), \mathsf{some}(c_d), \mathsf{some}(c_p)))$ is $\delta_{\mathrm{ALL}}$-secure.

*Compositionality.* We now consider making the multiplexer process (process 6 in Fig. 1) source from the channel $c_{LH}$ in Fig. 3. Let $SRC \triangleq (\nu c_i, c_d, c_p)\, (SINK \mid QUE(\mathsf{some}(c_i), \mathsf{some}(c_d), \mathsf{some}(c_p)))$. The process under consideration is $(\nu c_{LH})\, (SRC \mid M)$. It is not difficult to see that $\mathsf{det}(SRC, c_{LH})$ and $\mathsf{det}(M, c_{LH})$ hold. Hence we can deduce the validity of $\mathsf{Sec}_{\delta_{\mathrm{ALL}}}((\nu c_{LH})(SRC \mid M))$ by Theorem 3 and the $\delta_{\mathrm{ALL}}$-security of $SRC$ and $M$.

*Confidentiality.* We are in a position to further explain having developed our theory for integrity, rather than confidentiality. It has been illustrated by the example in Fig. 3 that a *concrete process* can influence the presence of communication over a sink channel of it, without influencing the communication content. For confidentiality, a channel $c_\star$ with high presence confidentiality and low content confidentiality would correspond to our channel with $LH$-integrity. Assuming the existence of $c_\star$ and developing the same theory would not be problematic. However, it is difficult to come up with a possibilistic process that leaks the content of $c_\star$ properly, without leaking the presence of communication over it, unless other channels also with confidential presence and public content are used. Hence the meaning of "confidential presence, public content" would be harder to justify as opposed to "low integrity presence, high integrity content".

# 7   Conclusion

We have studied the integrity of communication behaviors in process-algebraic systems from the viewpoint of information flow control. A fine-grained, bisimulation-based noninterference property is proposed: the *presence* and *content* of communications have separate integrity levels, and *all* combinations of integrity levels for both dimensions are allowed. When identical levels are always used for both dimensions, the property coincides with the classical process-algebraic property SBNDC (e.g., [6]), demonstrating faithful inheritance from known frameworks. A compositionality result is obtained, facilitating modular flow analysis of concurrent processes.

Our recasting of SBNDC as self-▷-bisimilarity may reflect the insights behind existing work [3] in bridging language-based and process-algebraic security, but may be the first direct reformulation of BNDC-like properties as self-bisimilarity. This gives another perspective on the secure semantics induced by SBNDC.

Clarkson et al. [4] dimensions *quantitative integrity* in terms of information *suppression* and *contamination*, where dissimilarity of integrity to confidentiality is also examined: information suppression has no confidentiality counterpart.

It would not be difficult to adapt $\delta$-security to support the use of *down-grading* [16], which relaxes information flow constraints. This can be done along the directions of [1]. Another interesting line of future work is the design of information flow type systems supporting $\delta$-security.

**Acknowledgement.** We would like to thank the ProSec research group at Chalmers University of Technology, especially Andrei Sabelfeld, Willard Rafnsson and David Sands, for useful feedback on this work at an earlier stage.

# A    Appendix

**Structural Congruence.** The structural congruence is the smallest congruence relation satisfying the rules in Table 3. In Table 3, the $\alpha$-equivalence of two processes is denoted by $\equiv_\alpha$, and $fc(P)$ gives the set of free constants of the process $P$ and can be defined in a straightforward manner.

**Table 3.** The structural congruence

| | |
|---|---|
| $P_1\|P_2 \equiv P_2\|P_1$ | $(\nu c_1)(\nu c_2)P \equiv$ |
| $P_1\|(P_2\|P_3) \equiv (P_1\|P_2)\|P_3$ | $(\nu c_2)(\nu c_1)P$ (if $c_1 \neq c_2$) |
| $P \mid 0 \equiv P$ | $(\nu c)(P_1\|P_2) \equiv ((\nu c)P_1)\|P_2$ |
| $(\nu c)P \equiv P$ (if $c \notin fc(P)$) | (if $c \notin fc(P_2)$) |
| $P \equiv_\alpha P' \Rightarrow P \equiv P'$ | $P_1 \equiv P_2 \Rightarrow (\nu c)P_1 \equiv (\nu c)P_2$ |

**Semantics Without Environment.** The "classical" semantics [11] of the Quality Calculus is given in Table 4. The transitions made by processes are of the form $P \xrightarrow{\beta} P'$, where $\beta$ is a communication action or a $\tau$. The correspondence between the two semantics is given in Lemma 2, where $\mathsf{ch}(\beta) = \begin{cases} c & (\text{if } \beta = c!c' \vee \beta = c?c') \\ \bot & (\text{if } \beta = \tau \vee \beta = \Box) \end{cases}$, $\rho(\beta) = \begin{cases} \rho_0 & (\text{if}\exists c, c' : \beta = c\rho_0 c') \\ \bot & (\text{otherwise}) \end{cases}$, $\widetilde{!} =?$ and $\widetilde{?} =!$.

**Lemma 2.** *For all processes* $P$, $P'$, *actions* $\beta_1$, $\beta_2$, ..., *and* $\beta_n$ *such that there is at most one* $i \in \{1,...,n\}$ *for which* $\beta_i \neq \tau$, *and* $\forall i \in \{1,...,n\} : \beta_i \neq \Box$, *histories* $\pi$ *such that* $\pi = [\pi]_\triangle$, *and* $\pi_0$ *such that* $\forall i \in \{1,...,n\} : \beta_i \neq \tau \Rightarrow \pi_0 = \pi.\widetilde{\mathsf{ch}(\beta_i)\rho(\beta_i)}c'$ *for some* $c'$, *the following are equivalent:*

1. $P \overset{\beta_1...\beta_n}{\Longrightarrow} P'$, *and*
2. $\delta_{\mathrm{ALL}} \vdash \langle P, \pi \rangle \xrightarrow{\mathrm{env}} \langle P, \pi_0 \rangle \wedge \exists \pi_0' : \delta_{\mathrm{ALL}} \vdash \langle P, \pi_0 \rangle \overset{\beta_1...\beta_n}{\Longrightarrow} \langle P', \pi_0' \rangle.$

*Proof.* Both directions can be shown by induction on the length of the corresponding sequences of semantic derivation. □

**Table 4.** The transition relation for processes

$$\frac{b \xrightarrow{c!c'} b'}{b.P \xrightarrow{c!c'} P'} \text{ where } P' = \begin{cases} P\theta & (\text{if } b'::_{\mathsf{tt}}\theta) \\ b'.P & (\text{if } b'::_{\mathsf{ff}}\theta) \end{cases} \qquad \frac{b \xrightarrow{c?c'} b'}{b.P \xrightarrow{c?c'} P'} \text{ where } P' = \begin{cases} P\theta & (\text{if } b'::_{\mathsf{tt}}\theta) \\ b'.P & (\text{if } b'::_{\mathsf{ff}}\theta) \end{cases}$$

$$\frac{P_1 \xrightarrow{c!c'} P_1' \quad P_2 \xrightarrow{c?c'} P_2'}{P_1|P_2 \xrightarrow{\tau} P_1'|P_2'}$$

$$\frac{e \triangleright \mathsf{some}(c) \quad P_1[c/y] \xrightarrow{\beta} P'}{\mathsf{case}\ e\ \mathsf{of}\ \mathsf{some}(y) : P_1\ \mathsf{else}\ P_2 \xrightarrow{\beta} P'} \qquad \frac{e \triangleright \mathsf{none} \quad P_2 \xrightarrow{\beta} P'}{\mathsf{case}\ e\ \mathsf{of}\ \mathsf{some}(y) : P_1\ \mathsf{else}\ P_2 \xrightarrow{\beta} P'}$$

$$\frac{\bar{e} \triangleright \bar{w} \quad P[\bar{w}/\bar{x}] \xrightarrow{\beta} P'}{A(\bar{e}) \xrightarrow{\beta} P'} \text{ if } A(\bar{x}) \triangleq P \qquad \frac{P \xrightarrow{\beta} P'}{(\nu c)P \xrightarrow{\beta} (\nu c)P'} \text{ if } c \notin \mathsf{Ch}(\beta)$$

$$\frac{P_1 \xrightarrow{\beta} P_2}{P_1|P \xrightarrow{\beta} P_2|P} \qquad \frac{P_1 \equiv P_2 \quad P_2 \xrightarrow{\beta} P_3 \quad P_3 \equiv P_4}{P_1 \xrightarrow{\beta} P_4}$$

$$\frac{t \triangleright c \quad t' \triangleright c'}{t!t'\{x\} \xrightarrow{c!c'} [c : \mathsf{some}(c')/x]} \qquad t!t'\{x\} ::_{\mathsf{ff}} [\mathsf{none}/x] \quad t?x ::_{\mathsf{ff}} [\mathsf{none}/x]$$

$$\frac{t \triangleright c}{t?x \xrightarrow{c?c'} [c : \mathsf{some}(c')/x]} \qquad [c : \mathsf{some}(c')/x] ::_{\mathsf{tt}} [\mathsf{some}(c')/x]$$

$$\frac{b_j \xrightarrow{\beta} b_j'}{\&_q(\ldots, b_j, \ldots) \xrightarrow{\beta} \&_q(\ldots, b_j', \ldots)} \qquad \frac{\forall i : b_i ::_{v_i} \theta_i \quad v' = \{\!\{q\}\!\}(\bar{v})}{\&_q(b_1, \ldots, b_n) ::_{v'} \theta_n \ldots \theta_1}$$

We introduce the notation $\pi \downarrow C$ for $\pi$ ending with $\triangle$, and $C$ a set of channels, to represent the order-preserving sequence of all communications on channels within $C$ in $\pi$, and abbreviate $\pi \downarrow \{c\}$ as $\pi \downarrow c$ where $c$ is a channel.

**$\delta_{\mathbf{ALL}}$-Security of Process 6.** We construct the binary relation $R_{\mathsf{sym}}$ that is the symmetric closure of the following relation $R$. Below, $\phi(\pi_1, \pi_2)$ stands for

$$knl(\pi_1, \pi_2) \land$$
$$\forall i \in \{1, 2\} : \forall c_a, c_b : c_{LH}!c_a \text{ is followed immediately by } c_{LH}'\rho c_b \text{ in } \pi_i \downarrow \{c_{LH}, c_{LH}'\}$$
$$\implies \rho = ? \land c_a = c_b.$$

In addition, $CSs(e_1, e_2)$ stands for

$$\mathsf{case}\ e_1\ \mathsf{of}\ \mathsf{some}(y_1) : c_{LH}'!y_1.M$$
$$\mathsf{else}\ \mathsf{case}\ e_2\ \mathsf{of}\ \mathsf{some}(y_2) : c_{LL}''!y_2.M\ \mathsf{else}\ 0$$

$$R = \{(\langle M,\ \pi_1\rangle, \langle M,\ \pi_2\rangle) \mid \phi(\pi_1, \pi_2)\} \cup$$
$$\{(\langle CSs(\mathsf{some}(c_a'), \mathsf{none}),\ \pi_1\rangle, \langle M,\ \pi_2\rangle) \mid \pi_1 = \ldots c_{LH}!c_a' \triangle \land \phi(\pi_1, \pi_2)\} \cup$$
$$\{(\langle CSs(\mathsf{none}, \mathsf{some}(c_a')),\ \pi_1\rangle, \langle M,\ \pi_2\rangle) \mid \pi_1 = \ldots c_{LL}!c_a' \triangle \land \phi(\pi_1, \pi_2)\} \cup$$
$$\{(\langle CSs(\mathsf{some}(c_a'), \mathsf{none}),\ \pi_1\rangle, \langle CSs(\mathsf{some}(c_b'), \mathsf{none}),\ \pi_2\rangle) \mid$$
$$\quad \pi_1 = \ldots c_{LH}!c_a' \triangle \land \pi_2 = \ldots c_{LH}!c_b' \triangle \land \phi(\pi_1, \pi_2)\} \cup$$
$$\{(\langle CSs(\mathsf{none}, \mathsf{some}(c_a')),\ \pi_1\rangle, \langle CSs(\mathsf{none}, \mathsf{some}(c_b')),\ \pi_2\rangle) \mid$$
$$\quad \pi_1 = \ldots c_{LL}!c_a' \triangle \land \pi_2 = \ldots c_{LL}!c_b' \triangle \land \phi(\pi_1, \pi_2)\} \cup$$
$$\{(\langle CSs(\mathsf{some}(c_a'), \mathsf{none}),\ \pi_1\rangle, \langle CSs(\mathsf{none}, \mathsf{some}(c_b')),\ \pi_2\rangle) \mid$$
$$\quad \pi_1 = \ldots c_{LH}!c_a' \triangle \land \pi_2 = \ldots c_{LL}!c_b' \triangle \land \phi(\pi_1, \pi_2)\}$$

It can be shown that $R_{\mathsf{sym}}$ is a $\delta_{\mathsf{ALL}}$-bisimulation relating $\langle M, \triangle\rangle$ to itself.

**Queue Specification.** We adapte the priority queue discussed in [17] to be a FIFO queue specified in Fig. 4. A peek operation that returns but does not remove the head of the queue is added.

$$QUE(x_i, x_d, x_p) \triangleq (\nu c_g)(E(x_i, x_d, x_p, \text{some}(c_g)) \mid G(\text{some}(c_g)))$$

$$G(x_g[c_g]) \triangleq c_g?(x_i, x_d, x_p).E(x_i, x_d, x_p, x_g) \mid G(x_g)$$

$$
\begin{aligned}
E(x_i[c_i], x_d[c_d], x_p[c_p], x_g[c_g]) \triangleq \\
c_i?(x, x_f)[\_, c_f]. \\
\quad (\nu c_i', c_d', c_p')(c_g!(c_i', c_d', c_p')).c_f! \checkmark .F(x_i, x_d, x_p, x, \text{some}(c_i'), \text{some}(c_d'), \text{some}(c_p'), x_g)) \\
+ \ c_d?(x_e, x_r)[c_e, \_].c_e! \checkmark .E(x_i, x_d, x_p, x_g) \\
+ \ c_p?(x_e', x_r')[c_e', \_].c_e'! \checkmark .E(x_i, x_d, x_p, x_g)
\end{aligned}
$$

$$
\begin{aligned}
F(x_i[c_i], x_d[c_d], x_p[c_p], x_k[c_k], x_i'[c_i'], x_d'[c_d'], x_p'[c_p'], x_g) \triangleq \\
c_i?(x, x_f)[y, c_f]. \\
\quad (\nu c_f')(c_i'!(y, c_f') \mid c_f'?x'.c_f! \checkmark .F(x_i, x_d, x_p, x_k, x_i', x_d', x_p', x_g)) + \\
c_d?(x_e, x_r)[\_, c_r]. \\
\quad (\nu c_e', c_r')(c_d'!(c_e', c_r') \mid \\
\quad (c_e'?x''.c_r!c_k.E(x_i, x_d, x_p, x_g) + c_r'?x'''.c_r!c_k.F(x_i, x_d, x_p, x''', x_i', x_d', x_p', x_g))) + \\
c_p?(x_e'', x_r'')[\_, c_r''].c_r''!c_k.F(x_i, x_d, x_p, x_k, x_i', x_d', x_p', x_g)
\end{aligned}
$$

**Fig. 4.** Specification of FIFO queue

**Sketch of Proof for Compositionality (Theorem 3).** Define $\tilde{\pi}$ to be the order-preserving sequence of all actions in $\pi$ with all the polarities $\rho$ changed to $\tilde{\rho}$. For convenience we rename the $P_1$ and $P_2$ in the precondition of Theorem 3 into $P_1^\circ$ and $P_2^\circ$, and the list $\bar{c}'$ into $\bar{c}^\circ$.

Construct the binary relation $R$ as:

$$
\begin{aligned}
R = \{(\langle P_1, \ \pi_1 \rangle, \langle P_2, \ \pi_2 \rangle) \mid \exists P_{11}, P_{12}, P_{21}, P_{22}, \pi_{11}, \pi_{12}, \pi_{21}, \pi_{22} : \\
\psi(P_1, P_2, P_{11}, P_{12}, P_{21}, P_{22}, \pi_1, \pi_2, \pi_{11}, \pi_{12}, \pi_{21}, \pi_{22})\},
\end{aligned}
$$

where $\psi(P_1, P_2, P_{11}, P_{12}, P_{21}, P_{22}, \pi_1, \pi_2, \pi_{11}, \pi_{12}, \pi_{21}, \pi_{22})$ is the conjunction of the following clauses:

$$\forall i \in \{1,2\} : P_i \equiv (\nu \bar{c}^\circ)(P_{1i} \mid P_{2i}) \tag{1}$$

$$\forall j, i \in \{1,2\} : \exists \pi' : \delta_{\text{ALL}} \vdash \langle P_j^\circ, \ \triangle \rangle \longrightarrow^* \langle P_{ji}, \ \pi' \rangle \tag{2}$$

$$\forall j \in \{1,2\} : \langle P_{j1}, \ \pi_{j1} \rangle \underset{\delta_{\text{ALL}}}{\sim} \langle P_{j2}, \ \pi_{j2} \rangle \tag{3}$$

$$knl(\pi_1, \pi_2) \tag{4}$$

$$\forall j \in \{1,2\} : knl(\pi_{j1}, \pi_{j2}) \tag{5}$$

$$\forall c \text{ s.t. } \mathcal{P}(c) = L \wedge \mathcal{C}(c) = H : \forall i \in \{1,2\} : \tag{6}$$
$$((\exists \rho : (c, \rho) \in \text{rch}(P_1) \wedge (c, \tilde{\rho}) \notin \text{rch}(P_2)) \Rightarrow \pi_i \downarrow c = \pi_{1i} \downarrow c \wedge \pi_{2i} \downarrow c = \epsilon) \wedge$$
$$((\exists \rho : (c, \rho) \in \text{rch}(P_2) \wedge (c, \tilde{\rho}) \notin \text{rch}(P_1)) \Rightarrow \pi_i \downarrow c = \pi_{2i} \downarrow c \wedge \pi_{1i} \downarrow c = \epsilon) \wedge$$
$$((\exists \rho : (c, \rho) \in \text{rch}(P_1) \wedge (c, \tilde{\rho}) \in \text{rch}(P_2)) \Rightarrow \pi_{2i} \downarrow c = \widetilde{\pi_{1i} \downarrow c} \wedge \pi_i \downarrow c = \epsilon)$$

We show that $R$ qualifies as a $\delta_{\mathrm{ALL}}$-bisimulation. Then $\mathsf{Sec}_{\delta_{\mathrm{ALL}}}((\nu\bar{c}^\circ)(P_1^\circ|P_2^\circ))$ will follow, since it holds that

$$\psi((\nu\bar{c}^\circ)(P_1^\circ|P_2^\circ), (\nu\bar{c}^\circ)(P_1^\circ|P_2^\circ), P_1^\circ, P_1^\circ, P_2^\circ, P_2^\circ, \triangle, \triangle, \triangle, \triangle, \triangle, \triangle),$$

and we thus have $\langle(\nu\bar{c}^\circ)(P_1^\circ|P_2^\circ), \triangle\rangle \, R \, \langle(\nu\bar{c}^\circ)(P_1^\circ|P_2^\circ), \triangle\rangle$.
We omit further details.  □

# References

1. Bossi, A., Piazza, C., Rossi, S.: Modelling downgrading in information flow security. In: 17th IEEE Computer Security Foundations Workshop, (CSFW-17 2004), 28–30 June 2004, Pacific Grove, CA, USA, p. 187 (2004)
2. Capecchi, S., Castellani, I., Dezani-Ciancaglini, M., Rezk, T.: Session types for access and information flow control. In: Gastin, P., Laroussinie, F. (eds.) CONCUR 2010. LNCS, vol. 6269, pp. 237–252. Springer, Heidelberg (2010)
3. Castellani, I.: State-oriented noninterference for CCS. Electron. Notes Theor. Comput. Sci. **194**(1), 39–60 (2007)
4. Clarkson, M.R., Schneider, F.B.: Quantification of integrity. In: Proceedings of the 23rd IEEE Computer Security Foundations Symposium, CSF (2010)
5. Cohen, E.S.: Information transmission in computational systems. In: SOSP, pp. 133–139 (1977)
6. Focardi, R., Gorrieri, R.: Classification of security properties. In: Focardi, R., Gorrieri, R. (eds.) FOSAD 2000. LNCS, vol. 2171, pp. 331–396. Springer, Heidelberg (2001)
7. Goguen, J.A, Meseguer, J.: Security policies and security models. In: IEEE Symposium on Security and Privacy, pp. 11–20 (1982)
8. Kobayashi, N.: Type-based information flow analysis for the pi-calculus. Acta Inf. **42**(4–5), 291–347 (2005)
9. Montagu, B., Pierce, B.C., Pollack, R.: A theory of information-flow labels. In: 2013 IEEE 26th Computer Security Foundations Symposium, New Orleans, LA, USA, 26–28 June 2013, pp. 3–17 (2013)
10. Muller, S., Chong, S.: Towards a practical secure concurrent language. In: Proceedings of the 27th Annual ACM SIGPLAN Conference on Object-Oriented Programming, Systems, Languages, and Applications, OOPSLA 2012, pp. 57–74 (2012)
11. Nielson, H.R., Nielson, F.: Safety versus security in the quality calculus. In: Liu, Z., Woodcock, J., Zhu, H. (eds.) Theories of Programming and Formal Methods. LNCS, vol. 8051, pp. 285–303. Springer, Heidelberg (2013)
12. Nielson, H.R., Nielson, F., Vigo, R.: A calculus for quality. In: Păsăreanu, C.S., Salaün, G. (eds.) FACS 2012. LNCS, vol. 7684, pp. 188–204. Springer, Heidelberg (2013)
13. Rafnsson, W., Hedin, D., Sabelfeld, A.: Securing interactive programs. In: 25th IEEE Computer Security Foundations Symposium, CSF 2012 (2012)
14. Sabelfeld, A., Mantel, H.: Static confidentiality enforcement for distributed programs. In: Hermenegildo, M.V., Puebla, G. (eds.) SAS 2002. LNCS, vol. 2477, pp. 376–394. Springer, Berlin Heidelberg (2002)
15. Sabelfeld, A., Myers, A.C.: Language-based information-flow security. IEEE J. Sel. Areas Commun. **21**(1), 5–19 (2003)

16. Sabelfeld, A., Sands, D.: Declassification: dimensions and principles. J. Comput. Secur. **17**(5), 517–548 (2009)
17. Sangiorgi, D., Walker, D.: The Pi-Calculus - A Theory of Mobile Processes. Cambridge University Press, UK (2001)
18. van Bakel, S., Vigliotti, M.G.: Note on a simple type system for non-interference. CoRR, abs/1109.4843 (2011)

# Checking Interaction-Based Declassification Policies for Android Using Symbolic Execution

Kristopher Micinski[1]([✉]), Jonathan Fetter-Degges[1], Jinseong Jeon[1], Jeffrey S. Foster[1], and Michael R. Clarkson[2]

[1] University of Maryland, College Park, USA
{micinski,jonfd,jsjeon,jfoster}@cs.umd.edu
[2] Cornell University, Ithaca, USA
clarkson@cs.cornell.edu

**Abstract.** Mobile apps can access a wide variety of secure information, such as contacts and location. However, current mobile platforms include only coarse access control mechanisms to protect such data. In this paper, we introduce *interaction-based declassification policies*, in which the user's interactions with the app constrain the release of sensitive information. Our policies are defined extensionally, so as to be independent of the app's implementation, based on sequences of security-relevant events that occur in app runs. Policies use LTL formulae to precisely specify which secret inputs, read at which times, may be released. We formalize a semantic security condition, *interaction-based noninterference*, to define our policies precisely. Finally, we describe a prototype tool that uses symbolic execution of Dalvik bytecode to check interaction-based declassification policies for Android, and we show that it enforces policies correctly on a set of apps.

**Keywords:** Information flow · Program analysis · Symbolic execution

## 1 Introduction

The Android platform includes a *permission* system that aims to prevent apps from abusing access to sensitive information, such as contacts and location. Unfortunately, once an app is installed, it has *carte blanche* to use any of its permissions in arbitrary ways at run time. For example, an app with location and Internet access could continuously broadcast the device's location, even if such behavior is not expected by the user.

To address this limitation, this paper presents a new framework for Android app security based on *information flow control* [8] and user interactions. The key idea behind our framework is that users naturally express their intentions about

This research was supported in part by NSF grants CNS-1064997 and CNS-1421373, AFOSR grants FA9550-12-1-0334 and FA9550-14-1-0334, the partnership between UMIACS and the Laboratory for Telecommunication Sciences, and the National Security Agency.

G. Pernul et al. (Eds.): ESORICS 2015, Part II, LNCS 9327, pp. 520–538, 2015.
DOI: 10.1007/978-3-319-24177-7_26

information release as they interact with an app. For example, clicking a button may permit an app to release a phone number over the Internet. Or, as another example, toggling a radio button from "coarse" to "fine" and back to "coarse" may temporarily permit an app to use fine-grained GPS location rather than a coarse-grained approximation.

To model these kinds of scenarios, we introduce *interaction-based declassification policies*, which extensionally specify what information flows may occur after which sequences of *events*. Events are GUI interactions (e.g., clicking a button), inputs (e.g., reading the phone number), or outputs (e.g., sending over the Internet). A policy is a set of *declassification conditions*, written $\phi \triangleright S$, where $\phi$ is a linear-time temporal logic (LTL) [20] formula over events, and $S$ is a sensitivity level. If $\phi$ holds at the time an input occurs, then that input is declassified to level $S$. We formalize a semantic security condition, *interaction-based noninterference* (IBNI), over sets of event *traces* generated by an app. Intuitively, IBNI holds of an app and policy if observational determinism [28] holds after all inputs have been declassified according to the policy. (Section 2 describes policies further, and Sect. 3 presents our formal definitions.)

We introduce ClickRelease, a static analysis tool to check whether an Android app and its declassification policy satisfy IBNI. ClickRelease generates event traces using SymDroid [11], a Dalvik bytecode symbolic executor. ClickRelease works by simulating user interactions with the app and recording the resulting execution traces. In practice, it is not feasible to enumerate all program traces, so ClickRelease generates traces up to some *input depth* of $n$ GUI events. ClickRelease then synthesizes a set of logical formulae that hold if and only if IBNI holds, and uses Z3 [17] to check their satisfiability. (Section 4 describes ClickRelease in detail.)

To validate ClickRelease, we used it to analyze four Android apps, including both secure and insecure variants of those apps. We ran each app variant under a range of input depths, and confirmed that, as expected, ClickRelease scales exponentially. However, we manually examined each app and its policy, and found that an input depth of at most 5 is sufficient to guarantee detection of a security policy violation (if any) for these cases. We ran ClickRelease at these minimum input depths and found that it correctly passes and fails the secure and insecure app variants, respectively. Moreover, at these depths, ClickRelease takes just a few seconds to run. (Section 5 describes our experiments.)

In summary, we believe that ClickRelease takes an important step forward in providing powerful new security mechanisms for mobile devices. We expect that our approach can also be used in other GUI-based, security-sensitive systems.

## 2    Example Apps and Policies

We begin with two example apps that show interesting aspects of interaction-based declassification policies.

*Bump App.* The boxed portion of Fig. 1 gives (simplified) source code for an Android app that releases a device's unique ID and/or phone number. This

```
1  public class BumpApp extends Activity {
2   protected void onCreate(...) {
3    Button sendBtn = (Button) findViewById(...);
4    CheckBox idBox = (CheckBox) findViewById(...);
5    CheckBox phBox = (CheckBox) findViewById(...);
6    TelephonyManager manager = TelephonyManager.getTelephonyManager();
7    final int id = manager.getDeviceId();
8    final int ph = manager.getPhoneNumber();
9    idBox.setChecked(false); phBox.setChecked(false);
10   sendBtn.setOnClickListener(
11     new OnClickListener() {
12      public void onClick(View v) {
13       if (idBox.isChecked())
14        Internet.sendInt(id); //Internet.sendInt(ph);
15       if (phBox.isChecked())
16        Internet.sendInt(ph); //Internet.sendInt(id);
17  }})}}
```

$$\text{id! } * \wedge (\mathcal{F}(\text{sendBtn!unit} \wedge \text{last}(\text{idBox}, \text{true}))) \triangleright Low,$$
$$\text{ph! } * \wedge (\mathcal{F}(\text{sendBtn!unit} \wedge \text{last}(\text{phBox}, \text{true}))) \triangleright Low$$

**Fig. 1.** "Bump" app and policy.

app is inspired by the Bump app, which let users tap phones to share selected information with each other. We have interspersed an insecure variant of the app in the red code on lines 14 and 16, which we will discuss in Sect. 3.1.

Each screen of an Android app is implemented using a class that extends Activity. When an app is launched, Android invokes the onCreate method for a designated main activity. (This is part of the *activity lifecycle* [10], which includes several methods called in a certain order. For this simple app, and the other apps used in this paper, we only need a single activity with this one lifecycle method.) That method retrieves (lines 3–5) the GUI IDs of a button (marked "send") and two checkboxes (marked "ID" and "phone"). The onCreate method next gets an instance of the TelephonyManager, uses it to retrieve the device's unique ID and phone number information, and unchecks the two checkboxes as a default. Then it creates a new callback (line 11) to be invoked when the "send" button is clicked. When called, that callback releases the user's ID and/or phone number, depending on the checkboxes.

This app is written to work with ClickRelease, a symbolic execution tool we built to check whether apps satisfy interaction-based declassification policies. As we discuss further in Sect. 4, ClickRelease uses an executable model of Android that abstracts away some details that are unimportant with respect to security. While a real app would release information by sending it to a web server, here we instead call a method Internet.sendInt. Additionally, while real apps include an XML file specifying the screen layout of buttons, checkboxes, and so on, ClickRelease creates those GUI elements on demand at calls to findViewById (since their screen locations are unimportant). Finally, we model the ID and phone number as integers to keep the analysis simpler.

ClickRelease symbolically executes paths through subject apps, recording a *trace* of *events* that correspond to certain method calls. For example, one path through this app generates a trace

id!42, ph!43, idBox!true, sendBtn!unit, netout!42

Each event has a *name* and a *value*. Here we have used names id and ph for secret inputs, idBox and sendBtn for GUI inputs, and netout for the network send. In particular, the trace above indicates 42 is read as the ID, 43 is read as the phone number, the ID checkbox is selected, the send button is clicked (carrying no value, indicated by unit), and then 42 is sent on the network. In ClickRelease, events are generated by calling certain methods that are specially recognized. For example, ClickRelease implements the manager.getDeviceId call as both returning a value and emitting an event.

Notice here that in the trace, callbacks to methods such as idBox and sendBtn correspond to user interactions. The key idea behind our framework is that these actions convey the user's intent as to which information should be released. Moreover, traces also contain actions relevant to information release—here the reads of the ID and phone number, and the network send. Thus, putting both user interactions and security-sensitive operations together in a single trace allows our policies to enforce the user's intent.

The policy for this example app is shown at the bottom of Fig. 1. Policies are comprised of a set of *declassification conditions* of the form $\phi \triangleright S$, where $\phi$ is an LTL formula describing event traces and $S$ is a security level. Such a condition is read, "At any input event, if $\phi$ holds at that position of the event trace, then that input is declassified at level $S$." For this app there are two declassification conditions. The top condition declassifies (to *Low*) an input that is a read of the ID at any value (indicated by $*$), if sometime in the future (indicated by the $\mathcal{F}$ modality) the send button is clicked and, when that button is clicked, the last value of the ID checkbox was true. (Note that *last* is not primitive, but is a macro that can be expanded into regular LTL.) The second declassification condition does the analogous thing for the phone number.

To check such a policy, ClickRelease symbolic executes the program, generating per-path traces; determines the classification level of every input; and checks that every pair of traces satisfies noninterference. Note that using LTL provides a very general and expressive way to describe the sequences of events that imply declassification. For example, here we precisely capture that only the last value of the checkbox matters for declassification. For example, if a user selects the ID checkbox but then unselects it and clicks send, the ID may not be released.

Although this example relies on a direct flow, ClickRelease can also detect implicit flows. Section 3.2 defines an appropriate version of noninterference, and the experiments in Sect. 5 include a subject program with an implicit flow.

Notice this policy depends on the app reading the ID and phone number when the app starts. If the app instead waited until after the send button were clicked, it would violate this policy. We could address this by replacing the $\mathcal{F}$ modality by $\mathcal{P}$ (past) in the policy, and we could form a disjunction of the two

```
18  public class ToggleRes extends Activity { ...
19  LocSharer mLocSharer = new LocSharer();
20  RadioManager mRadio = new RadioManager();
21  protected void onCreate(...) { ...}
22  private class LocSharer implements LocationListener { ...
23   public LocSharer(RadioManager rm) {
24    lm = (LocationManager) getSystemService(LOCATION_SERVICE);
25    lm.requestLocationUpdates(mCurrentProvider, SHARE_INTERVAL, distance, this);
26   }
27   public void onLocationChanged(Location l) {
28    if (mRadio.mFine) {
29      Internet . sendInt ( l . mLatitude);
30      Internet . sendInt ( l . mLongitude);
31    } else {
32      Internet . sendInt ( l . mLatitude & 0 xffffff00 );
33      Internet . sendInt ( l . mLongitude & 0 xffffff00 );
34  } } }
35   private class RadioManager
36    implements OnClickListener {
37     public boolean mFine = false;
38     public void onClick(View v) { mFine = !mFine; }
39  } }
```

$$longitude! * \wedge last(\text{mRadio}, true) \rhd Low,$$
$$longitude! * \wedge last(\text{mRadio}, false) \rhd MaskLower8$$

**Fig. 2.** Location sharing app and policy.

policies if we wanted to allow either implementation. More generally, we designed our framework to be sensitive to such choices to support reasoning about secret values that change over time. We will see an example next.

*Location Resolution Toggle App.* Figure 2 gives code for an app that shares location information, either at full or truncated resolution depending on a radio button setting. The app's onCreate method displays a radio button (code not shown) and then creates and registers a new instance of RadioManager to be called each time the radio button is changed. That class maintains field mFine as true when the radio button is set to full resolution and false when set to truncated resolution.

Separately, onCreate registers LocSharer to be called periodically with the current location. It requests location updates by registering a callback with the LocationManager system service. When called, LocSharer releases the location, either at full resolution or with the lower 8 bits masked, depending on mFine.

The declassification policy for longitude appears below the code; the policy for latitude is analogous. This policy allows the precise longitude to be released when mRadio is set to fine, but only the lower eight bits to be released if mRadio is set to coarse. Here ClickRelease knows that at the *MaskLower8* level, it should consider outputs to be equivalent up to differences in the lower 8 bits.

Primitives    $p ::= n \mid \mathsf{true} \mid \mathsf{false} \mid \mathsf{unit} \mid f(p_1, \ldots, p_i)$
Events        $\eta ::= name!p$
Traces        $t ::= \eta \ list$

(a) Event and Trace Definitions.

Policies         $P ::= C_1, C_2, \ldots$
Conditions       $C ::= \phi \triangleright S$
Security Levels  $S ::= High \mid Low \mid MaskLower8 \mid \ldots$
Atoms            $A ::= name!s \mid s \oplus s$
Messages         $s ::= x \mid p \mid *$
Formulae         $\phi ::= A \mid \neg\phi \mid \phi \wedge \phi \mid \phi \vee \phi \mid \phi \rightarrow \phi \mid \exists x.\phi \mid \forall x.\phi$
                 $\mid \mathcal{X}\phi \mid \phi \, \mathcal{U} \, \phi \mid \mathcal{G}\phi \mid \mathcal{F}\phi \mid \phi \, \mathcal{S} \, \phi \mid \mathcal{P}\phi$

(b) Interaction-based Declassification Policy Language.

**Fig. 3.** Formal definitions.

Finally, notice that this policy does not use the future modality. This is deliberate, because location may be read multiple times during the execution, at multiple values, and the security level of those locations should depend on the state of the radio button at that time. For example, consider a trace

$$\mathsf{mRadio!false, longitude!}v_1, \mathsf{mRadio!true, longitude!}v_2$$

The second declassification condition $(\mathsf{longitude!}* \wedge last(\mathsf{mRadio, false}))$ will match the event with $v_1$, since the last value of mRadio was false, and thus $v_1$ may be declassified only to $MaskLower8$. Whereas the first declassification condition will match the event with $v_2$, hence it may be declassified to $Low$.

# 3    Program Traces and Security Definition

Next, we formally define when a set of program traces satisfies an interaction-based declassification policy.

## 3.1    Program Traces

Figure 3(a) gives the formal syntax of events and traces. *Primitives* $p$ are terms that can be carried by events, e.g., values for GUI events, secret inputs, or network sends. In our formalism, primitives are integers, booleans, and terms constructed from primitives using uninterpreted constructors $f$. As programs execute, they produce a *trace* $t$ of *events* $\eta$, where each event $name!p$ pairs an event name $name$ with a primitive $p$. We assume event names are partitioned into those corresponding to inputs and those corresponding to outputs. For all the examples in this paper, all names are inputs except netout, which is an output.

Due to space limitations, we omit details of how traces are generated. These details, along with definition of our LTL formulas, can be found in a companion tech report [16]. Instead, we simply assume there exists some set $\mathcal{T}$ containing all possible traces a given program may generate. For example, consider the insecure variant bump app in Fig. 1, which replaces the black code with the red code on lines lines 14 and 16. This app sends the phone number when the email box is checked and vice-versa. Thus, its set $\mathcal{T}$ contains, among others, the following two traces:

$$\text{id!0, ph!0, idBox!true, sendBtn!unit, netout!0} \quad (1)$$
$$\text{id!0, ph!1, idBox!true, sendBtn!unit, netout!1} \quad (2)$$

In the first trace, ID and phone number are read as 0, the ID checkbox is selected, the button is clicked, and 0 is sent. The second trace is similar, except the phone number and sent value are 1. Below, we use these traces to show this program violates its security policy.

## 3.2 Interaction-Based Declassification Policies

We now define our policy language precisely. Figure 3(b) gives the formal syntax of declassification policies. A policy $P$ is a set of *declassification conditions* $C_i$ of the form $\phi_i \rhd S_i$, where $\phi_i$ is an LTL formula describing when an input is declassified, and $S_i$ is a *security level* at which the value in that event is declassified.

As is standard, security levels $S$ form a lattice. For our framework, we require that this lattice be finite. We include *High* and *Low* security levels, and we can generalize to arbitrary lattices in a straightforward way. Here we include the *MaskLower8* level from Fig. 2 as an example, where $Low \sqsubseteq MaskLower8 \sqsubseteq High$. Note that although we include *High* in the language, in practice there is no reason to declassify something to level *High*, since then it remains secret.

The *atomic predicates* $A$ of LTL formulae match events, e.g., atomic predicate *name!p* matches exactly that event. We include $*$ for matches to arbitrary primitives. We allow event values to be variables that are bound in an enclosing quantifier. The atomic predicates also include atomic arithmetic statements; here $\oplus$ ranges over standard operations such as $+$, $<$, etc. The combination of these lets us describe complex events. For example, we could write $\exists x.spinner!x \wedge x > 2$ to indicate the *spinner* was selected with a value greater than 2.

Atomic predicates are combined with the usual boolean connectives ($\neg$, $\wedge$, $\vee$, $\rightarrow$) and existential and universal quantification. Formulae include standard LTL modalities $\mathcal{X}$ (next), $\mathcal{U}$ (until), $\mathcal{G}$ (always), $\mathcal{F}$ (future), $\phi \, \mathcal{S} \, \psi$ (since), and $\mathcal{P}\phi$ (past). We include a wide range of modalities, rather than a minimal set, to make policies easier to write. Formulae also include *last*(*name, p*), which is syntactic sugar for $\neg(name!*) \, \mathcal{S} \, name!p$. We assume a standard interpretation of LTL formulae over traces [14]. We write $t, i \models \phi$ if trace $t$ is a model of $\phi$ at position $i$ in the trace.

Next consider a trace $t \in \mathcal{T}$ for an arbitrary program. We write $level(t, P, i)$ for the security level that policy $P$ assigns to the event $t[i]$:

$$level(t, P, i) = \begin{cases} \bigsqcap_{\phi_j \rhd S_j \in P}\{S_j \mid t, i \models \phi_j\} & t[i] = \mathsf{name}!p \\ Low & t[i] = \mathsf{netout}!p \end{cases}$$

In other words, for inputs, we take the greatest lower bound (the most declassified) of the levels from all declassification conditions that apply. We always consider network outputs to be declassified. Notice that if no policy applies, the level is $H$ by definition of greatest lower bound.

For example, consider trace (1) above with respect to the policy in Fig. 1. At position 0, the LTL formula holds because the ID box is eventually checked and then the send button is clicked, so $level((1), P, 0) = Low$. However, $level((1), P, 1) = High$ because no declassification condition applies for ph (phBox is never checked). And $level((1), P, 4) = Low$, because that position is a network send.

Next consider applying this definition to the GUI inputs. As written, we have $level((1), P, 2) = level((1), P, 3) = High$. However, our app is designed to leak these inputs. For example, an adversary will learn the state of idBox if they receive a message with an ID. Thus, for all the subject apps in this paper, we also declassify all GUI inputs as $Low$. For the example in Fig. 1, this means adding the conditions idBox! $* \rhd Low$, phBox! $* \rhd Low$, and sendBtn! $* \rhd Low$. In general, the security policy designer should decide the security level of GUI inputs.

Next, we can apply $level$ pointwise across a trace and discard any trace elements that are below a given level $S$. We define

$$level(t, P)^S[i] = \begin{cases} t[i] & level(t, P, i) \sqsubseteq S \\ \tau & \text{otherwise} \end{cases}$$

We write $level(t, P)^{S,in}$ for the same filtering, except output events (i.e., network sends) are removed as well. Considering the traces (1) and (2) again, we have

$$level((1), P)^{Low} = \mathsf{id}!0, \mathsf{idBox}!\mathsf{true}, \mathsf{sendBtn}!\mathsf{unit}, \mathsf{netout}!0$$
$$level((2), P)^{Low} = \mathsf{id}!0, \mathsf{idBox}!\mathsf{true}, \mathsf{sendBtn}!\mathsf{unit}, \mathsf{netout}!1$$
$$level((1), P)^{Low,in} = \mathsf{id}!0, \mathsf{idBox}!\mathsf{true}, \mathsf{sendBtn}!\mathsf{unit}$$
$$level((2), P)^{Low,in} = \mathsf{id}!0, \mathsf{idBox}!\mathsf{true}, \mathsf{sendBtn}!\mathsf{unit}$$

Finally, we can define a program to satisfy noninterference if, for every pair of traces such that the inputs at level $S$ are the same, the outputs at level $S$ are also the same. To account for generalized lattice levels such as $MaskLower8$, we also need to treat events that are equivalent at a certain level as the same. For example, at $MaskLower8$, outputs $\mathtt{0xffffffff}$ and $\mathtt{0xffffff00}$ are the same, since they do not differ in the upper 24 bits. Thus, we assume for each security level $S$ there is a appropriate equivalence relation $=_S$, e.g., for $MaskLower8$, it compares elements ignoring their lower 8 bits. Note that $x =_{Low} y$ is simply $x = y$ and $x =_{High} y$ is always true.

**Definition 1 (Interaction-based Noninterference (IBNI)).** *A program satisfies security policy P, if for all S and for all $t_1, t_2 \in T$ (the set of traces of the program) the following holds:*

$$level(t_1, P)^{S,in} =_S level(t_2, P)^{S,in} \implies level(t_1, P)^S =_S level(t_2, P)^S$$

Looking at traces for the insecure app, we see they violate non-interference, because $level((1), P)^{Low,in} = level((2), P)^{Low,in}$, but $level((1), P)^{Low} \neq level((2)P)^{Low}$ (they differ in the output). We note that our definition of noninterference makes it a 2-hypersafety property [6,7].

## 4   Implementation

We built a prototype tool, ClickRelease, to check whether Android apps obey the interaction-based declassification policies described in Sect. 3. ClickRelease is based on SymDroid [11], a symbolic executor for Dalvik bytecode, which is the bytecode format to which Android apps are compiled. As is standard, SymDroid computes with *symbolic expressions* that may contain *symbolic variables* representing sets of values. At conditional branches that depend on symbolic variables, SymDroid invokes Z3 [17] to determine whether one or both branches are feasible. As it follows branches, SymDroid extends the current *path condition*, which tracks branches taken so far, and forks execution when multiple paths are possible. Cadar and Sen [1] describe symbolic execution in more detail.

SymDroid uses the features of symbolic execution to implement nondeterministic event inputs (such as button clicks or spinner selections), up to a certain bound. Since we have symbolic variables available, we also use them to represent arbitrary secret inputs, as discussed below in Sect. 4.2. There are several issues that arise in applying SymDroid to checking our policies, as we discuss next.

### 4.1   Driving App Execution

Android apps use the Android framework's API, which includes classes for responding to events via callbacks. We could try to account for these callbacks by symbolically execution Android framework code directly, but past experience suggests this is intractable: the framework is large, complicated, and includes native code. Instead, we created an *executable model*, written in Java, that mimics key portions of Android needed by our subject apps. Our Android model includes facilities for generating clicks and other GUI events (such as the View, Button, and CheckBox classes, among others). It also includes code for LocationManager, TelephonyManager, and other basic Android classes.

In addition to code modeling Android, the model also includes simplified versions of Java library classes such as StringBuffer and StringBuilder. Our versions of these APIs implement unoptimized versions of methods in Java and escape to internal SymDroid functions to handle operations that would be unduly complex to symbolically execute. For instance, SymDroid represents Java String objects with OCaml strings instead of Java arrays of characters. It thus models methods such as String.concat with internal calls to OCaml string manipulation functions. Likewise, reflective methods such as Class.getName are handled internally.

For each app, we created a driver that uses our Android model to simulate user input to the GUI. The driver is specific to the app since it depends on the app's GUI. The driver begins by calling the app's onCreate method. Next it invokes special methods in the Android model to inject GUI events. There is one such method for each type of GUI element, e.g., buttons, checkboxes, etc. For example, Trace.addClick(id) generates a click event for the given id and then calls the appropriate event handler. The trace entry contains the event name for that kind of element, and a value if necessary. Event handlers are those that the app registered through standard Android framework mechanisms, e.g., in onCreate.

Let $m$ be the number of possible GUI events. To simulate one arbitrary GUI event, the driver uses a block that branches $m$ ways on a fresh symbolic variable, with a different GUI action in each branch. Typical Android apps never exit unless the framework kills them, and thus we explore sequences of events only up to a user-specified *input depth* $n$. Thus, in total, the driver will execute at least $m^n$ paths.

## 4.2   Symbolic Variables in Traces

In addition to GUI inputs, apps also use secret inputs. We could use SymDroid to generate concrete secret inputs, but instead we opt to use a fresh symbolic variable for each secret input. For example, the call to manager.getDeviceId in Fig. 1 returns a symbolic variable, and the same for the call to manager.getPhoneNumber. This choice makes checking policies using symbolic execution a bit more powerful, since, e.g., a symbolic integer variable represents an arbitrary 32-bit integer. Note that whenever ClickRelease generates a symbolic variable for a secret input, it also generates a trace event corresponding to the input.

Recall that secret inputs may appear in traces, and thus traces may now contain symbolic variables. For example, using $\alpha_i$'s as symbolic variables for the secret ID and phone number inputs, the traces (1) and (2) become

$$\text{id!}\alpha_1, \text{ph!}\alpha_2, \text{idBox!true}, \text{sendBtn!unit}, \text{netout!}\alpha_2 \quad (1')$$
$$\text{id!}\alpha_1, \text{ph!}\alpha_2, \text{idBox!true}, \text{sendBtn!unit}, \text{netout!}\alpha_2 \quad (2')$$

We must take care when symbolic variables are in traces. Recall *level* checks $t, i \models \phi$ and then assigns a security level to position $i$. If $\phi$ depends on symbolic variables in $t$, we may not be able to decide this. For example, if the third element in $(1')$ were idBox!$\alpha_3$, then we would need to reason with conditional security levels such as $level(t, P, 0) = \textbf{if } \alpha_3 \textbf{ then } Low \textbf{ else } High$. We avoid the need for such reasoning by only using symbolic variables for secret inputs, and by ensuring the level assigned by a policy does not depend on the value of a secret input. We leave supporting more complex reasoning to future work.

### 4.3  Checking Policies with Z3

Each path explored by SymDroid yields a pair $(t, \Phi)$, where $t$ is the trace and $\Phi$ is the path condition. ClickRelease uses Z3 to check whether a given set of such trace–path condition pairs satisfies a policy $P$. Recall that Definition 1 assumes for each $S$ there is an $=_S$ relation on traces. We use the same relation below, encoding it as an SMT formula. For our example lattice, $=_{High}$ produces true, $=_{Low}$ produces a conjunction of equality tests among corresponding trace elements, and $=_{MaskLower8}$ produces the conjunction of equality tests of the bitwise-and of every element with 0xffffff00.

Given a trace $t$, let $t'$ be $t$ with its symbolic variables primed, so that the symbolic variables of $t$ and $t'$ are disjoint. Given a path condition $\Phi$, define $\Phi'$ similarly. Now we can give the algorithm for checking a security policy.

**Algorithm 1.** *To check a set $T$ of trace–path condition pairs, do the following. Let $P$ be the app's security policy. Apply* level *across each trace to obtain the level of each event. For each $(t_1, \Phi_1)$ and $(t_2, \Phi_2)$ in $T \times T$, and for each $S$, ask Z3 whether the following formula (the negation of Definition 1) is unsatisfiable:*

$$level(t_1, P)^{S,in} =_S level(t'_2, P)^{S,in} \wedge level(t_1, P)^S \neq_S level(t'_2, P)^S \wedge \Phi_1 \wedge \Phi'_2$$

*If no such formula is unsatisfiable, then the program satisfies noninterference.*

We include $\Phi_1$ and $\Phi'_2$ to constrain the symbolic variables in the trace. More precisely, $t_1$ represents a *set* of concrete traces in which its symbolic variables are instantiated in all ways that satisfy $\Phi_1$, and analogously for $t'_2$.

If the above algorithm finds an unsatisfiable formula, then Z3 returns a counterexample, which SymDroid uses in turn to generate a pair of concrete traces as a counterexample. For example, consider traces (1') and (2') above, and prime symbolic variables in (2'). Those traces have the trivial path condition true, since neither branches on a symbolic input. Thus, the formula passed to Z3 will be:

$$\alpha_1 = \alpha'_1 \wedge \text{true} = \text{true} \wedge \text{unit} = \text{unit} \wedge (\alpha_1 \neq \alpha'_1 \vee \text{true} \neq \text{true} \vee \text{unit} \neq \text{unit} \vee \alpha_2 \neq \alpha'_2)$$

Thus we can see a satisfying assignment with $\alpha_1 = \alpha'_1$ and $\alpha_2 \neq \alpha'_2$, hence noninterference is violated.

### 4.4  Minimizing Calls to Z3

A naive implementation of the noninterference check generates $n^2$ equations, where $n$ is the number of traces produced by ClickRelease to be checked by Z3. However, we observed that many of these equations correspond to pairs of traces with different sequences of GUI events. Since GUI events are low inputs in all our policies, these pairs trivially satisfy noninterference (the left-hand side of the implication in Definition 1 is false). Thus, we need not send those equations to Z3 for an (expensive) noninterference check.

We exploit this observation by organizing SymDroid's output traces into a tree, where each node represents an event, with the initial state at the root.

Traces with common prefixes share the same ancestor traces in the tree. We systematically traverse this tree using a cursor $t_1$, starting from the root. When $t_1$ reaches a new input event, we then traverse the tree using another cursor $t_2$, also starting from the root. As $t_2$ visits the tree, we do not invoke Z3 on any traces with fewer input events than $t_1$ (since they are not low-equivalent to $t_1$). We also skip any subtrees where input events differ.

## 5  Experiments

To evaluate ClickRelease, we ran it on four apps, including the two described in Sect. 2. We also ran ClickRelease on several insecure variants of each app, to ensure it can detect the policy violations. The apps and their variants are:

- *Bump.* The bump app and its policy appear in Fig. 1. The first insecure variant counts clicks to the send button sends the value of the ID after three clicks, regardless of the state of the ID checkbox. The second (indicated in the comments in the program text) swaps the released information—if the ID box is checked, it releases the phone number, and vice-versa.
- *Location Toggle.* The location toggle app and its policy appear in Fig. 2. The first insecure variant always shares fine-grained location information, regardless of the radio button setting. The second checks if coarse-grain information is selected. If so, it stores the fine-grained location (but does not send it yet). If later the fine-grained radio button is selected, it sends the stored location. Recall this is forbidden by the app's security policy, which allows the release only of locations received while the fine-grained option is set.
- *Contact Picker.* We developed a contact picker app that asks the user to select a contact from a spinner and then click a send button to release the selected contact information over the network. The security policy for this app requires that no contact information leaks unless it is the last contact selected before the button click. (For example, if the user selects contact 1, selects contact 2, and then clicks the button, only contact 2 may be released.) Note that since an arbitrarily sized list of contacts would be difficult for symbolic execution (since then there would be an unbounded number of ways to select a contact), we limit the app to a fixed set of three contacts. The first insecure variant of this app scans the set of contacts for a specific one. If found, it sends a message revealing that contact exists before sending the actual selected contact. The second insecure variant sends a different contact than was selected.
- *WhereRU.* Lastly, we developed an app that takes push requests for the user's location and shares it depending on user-controlled settings. The app contains a radio group with three buttons, "Share Always," "Share Never," and "Share On Click." There is also a "Share Now" button that is enabled when the "Share On Click" radio button is selected. When a push request arrives, the security policy allows sharing if (1) the "Always" button is selected, or (2) the "On Click" button is selected and the user presses "Share Now." Note that, in the second case, the location may change between the time the request arrives and the time the user authorizes sharing; the location to be shared is

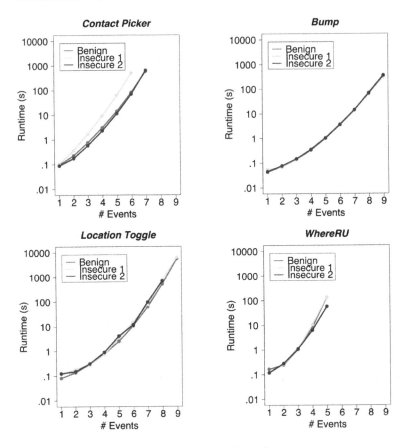

**Fig. 4.** Runtime vs. number of events.

the one in effect when the user authorized sharing, i.e., the one from the most recent location update before the button click. Also, rather than include the full Android push request API in our model, we simulated it using a basic callback. This app has two insecure variants. In the first one, when the user presses the "Share Now" button, the app begins continuously sharing (instead of simply sharing the single location captured on the button press). In the second, the app shares the location immediately in response to all requests.

*Scalability.* We ran our experiments on a 4-core i7 CPU @3.5 GHz with 16 GB RAM running Ubuntu 14. For each experiment we report the median of 10 runs.

In our first set of experiments, we measured how ClickRelease's performance varies with input depth. Figure 4 shows running time (log scale) versus input depth for all programs and variants. For each app, we ran to the highest input depth that completed in one hour.

For each app, we see that running time grows exponentially, as expected. The maximum input depth before timeout (i.e., where each curve ends) ranges

| App | Input Depth | Time (ms) | | |
|---|---|---|---|---|
| | | Exploration | Analysis | Total |
| Bump | 3 | 114 | 15 | 142 |
| Bump (insecure 1) | 5 | 2,100 | 1,577 | 3,690 |
| Bump (insecure 2) | 4 | 266 | 70 | 344 |
| Location toggle | 2 | 113 | 12 | 128 |
| Location toggle (insecure 1) | 2 | 143 | 12 | 163 |
| Location toggle (insecure 2) | 3 | 117 | 12 | 143 |
| Contact picker | 2 | 79 | 2 | 94 |
| Contact picker (insecure 1) | 2 | 325 | 27 | 361 |
| Contact picker (insecure 2) | 2 | 149 | 9 | 170 |
| WhereRU | 3 | 849 | 183 | 1,045 |
| WhereRU (insecure 1) | 3 | 860 | 234 | 1,108 |
| WhereRU (insecure 2) | 2 | 257 | 10 | 280 |

**Fig. 5.** Results at minimum input depth.

from five to nine. The differences have to do with the number of possible events at each input point. For example, WhereRU has seven possible input events, so it has the largest possible "fan out" and times out with an input depth of five. In contrast, Bump and Location Toggle have just three input events and time out with an input depth of nine. Notice also the first insecure variant of Contact Picker times out after fewer events than the other variants. Investigating further, this occurs due to that app's implicit flow (recall the app branches on the value of a secret input). Implicit flows cause symbolic execution to take additional branches depending on the (symbolic) secret value.

*Minimum Input Depth.* Next, for each variant, we manually calculated a *minimum* input depth guaranteed to find a policy violation. To do so, first we determined possible app GUI states. For example, in Bump (Fig. 1), there is a state with idBox and phBox both checked, a state with just idBox checked, etc. Then we examined the policy and recognized that certain input sequences lead to equivalent states modulo the policy. For example, input sequences that click idBox an even number of times and then click send are all equivalent. Full analysis reveals that an input depth of three (which allows the checkboxes to be set any possible way followed by a button click) is sufficient to reach all possible states for this policy. We performed similar analysis on other apps and variants.

Figure 5 summarizes the results of running with the minimum input depth for each variant, with the depths listed in the second column. We confirmed that, when run with this input depth, ClickRelease correctly reports the benign app variants as secure and the other app variants as insecure. The remaining columns of Fig. 5 report ClickRelease's running time (in milliseconds), broken down by the exploration phase (where SymDroid generates the set of symbolic traces) and the analysis phase (where SymDroid forms equations about this set and checks them using Z3). Looking at the breakdown between exploration and analysis, we see that the former dominates the running time, i.e., most of the time is spent simply exploring program executions. We see the total running time is typically around a second or less, while for the first insecure variant of Bump it is closer to 4 seconds, since it uses the highest input depth.

Our results show that while ClickRelease indeed scales exponentially, to actually find security policy violations we need only run it with a low input depth, which takes only a small amount of time.

## 6   Limitations and Future Work

There are several limitations of ClickRelease we plan to address in future work.

Thus far we have applied ClickRelease to a set of small apps that we developed. There are two main engineering challenges in applying ClickRelease to other apps. First, our model of Android (Sect. 4.1) only includes part of the framework. To run on other apps, it will need to be expanded with more Android APIs. Second, we speculate that larger apps may require longer input depths to go from app launch to interfering outputs. In these cases, we may be able to start symbolic execution "in the middle" of an app (e.g., as in the work of Ma et al. [15]) to skip uninteresting prefixes of input events.

ClickRelease also has several limitations related to its policy language. First, ClickRelease policies are fairly low level. Complex policies—e.g., in which clicking a certain button releases multiple pieces of information—can be expressed, but are not very concise. We expect as we gain more experience writing ClickRelease policies, we will discover useful idioms that should be incorporated into the policy language. Similarly, situations where several methods in sequence operate on and send information should be supported. Second, currently ClickRelease assumes there is a single adversary who watches netout. It should be straightforward to generalize to multiple output channels and multiple observers, e.g., to model inter-app communication. Third, we do not consider deception by apps, e.g., we assume the policy writer knows whether the sendBtn is labeled appropriately as "send" rather than as "exit." We leave looking for such deceptive practices to future work.

Finally, since ClickRelease explores a limited number of program paths it is not sound, i.e., it cannot guarantee the absence of policy violations in general. However, in our experiments we were able to manually analyze apps to show that exploration up to a certain input depth was sufficient for particular apps, and we plan to investigate generalizing this technique in future work.

## 7   Related Work

ClickRelease is the first system to enforce extensional declassification policies in Android apps. It builds on a rich history of research in usable security, information flow, and declassification.

One of the key ideas in ClickRelease is that GUI interactions indicate the security desires of users. Roesner et al. [22] similarly propose *access control gadgets* (ACGs), which are GUI elements that, when users interact with them, grant permissions. Thus, ACGs and ClickRelease both aim to better align security with usability [27]. ClickRelease addresses secure information flow, especially propagation of information after its release, whereas ACGs address only access control.

*Android-Based Systems.* TaintDroid [9] is a run-time information-flow tracking system for Android. It monitors the usage of sensitive information and detects when that information is sent over insecure channels. Unlike ClickRelease, TaintDroid does not detect implicit flows.

AppIntent [26] uses symbolic execution to derive the *context*, meaning inputs and GUI interactions, that causes sensitive information to be released in an Android app. A human analyst examines that context and makes an expert judgment as to whether the release is a security violation. ClickRelease instead uses human-written LTL formulae to specify whether declassifications are permitted. It is unclear from [26] whether AppIntent detects implicit flows.

Pegasus [2] combines static analysis, model checking, and run-time monitoring to check whether an app uses API calls and privileges consistently with users' expectations. Those expectations are expressed using LTL formulae, similarly to ClickRelease. Pegasus synthesizes a kind of automaton called a *permission event graph* from the app's bytecode then checks whether that automaton is a model for the formulae. Unlike ClickRelease, Pegasus does not address information flow.

Jia et al. [12] present a system, inspired by Flume [13], for run-time enforcement of information flow policies at the granularity of Android components and apps. Their system allows components and apps to perform trust declassification according to capabilities granted to them in security labels. In contrast, ClickRelease reasons about declassification in terms of user interactions.

*Security Type Systems.* Security type systems [25] statically disallow programs that would leak information. O'Neill et al. [19] and Clark and Hunt [5] define interactive variants of noninterference and present security type systems that are sound with respect to these definitions.

Integrating declassification with security type systems has been the focus of much research. Chong and Myers [3] introduce *declassification policies* that conditionally downgrade security labels. Their policies use classical propositional logic for the conditions. ClickRelease can be seen as providing a more expressive language for conditions by using LTL to express formulae over events. SIF (Servlet Information Flow) [4] is a framework for building Java servlets with information-flow control. Information managed by the servlet is annotated in the source code with security labels, and the compiler ensures that information propagates in ways that are consistent with those labels. The SIF compiler is based on Jif [18], an information-flow variant of Java.

All of these systems require adding type annotations to terms in the program code, e.g., method parameters, etc. In contrast, ClickRelease policies are described in terms of app inputs and outputs.

*Event Based Models and Declassification.* Vaughan and Chong [24] define expressive declassification policies that allow functions of secret information to be released after events occur, and extend the Jif compiler to infer events. ClickRelease instead ties events to user interactions.

Rafnsson et al. [21] investigate models, definitions, and enforcement techniques for secure information flow in interactive programs in a purely theoretical setting. Sabelfeld and Sands [23] survey approaches to secure declassification in a language-based setting. ClickRelease can be seen as addressing their "what" and "when" axes of declassification goals: users of Android apps interact with the GUI to control when information may be released, and the GUI is responsible for conveying to the user what information will be released.

## 8   Conclusion

We introduced interaction-based declassification policies, which describe *what* and *when* information can flow. Policies are defined using LTL formulae describing event traces, where events include GUI actions, secret inputs, and network sends. We formalized our policies using a trace-based model of apps based on security relevant events. Finally, we described ClickRelease, which uses symbolic execution to check interaction-based declassification policies on Android, and showed that ClickRelease correctly enforces policies on four apps, with one secure and two insecure variants each.

## References

1. Cadar, C., Sen, K.: Symbolic execution for software testing: three decades later. Commun. ACM **56**(2), 82–90 (2013). http://doi.acm.org/10.1145/2408776.2408795
2. Chen, K.Z., Johnson, N.M., D'Silva, V., Dai, S., MacNamara, K., Magrino, T., Wu, E.X., Rinard, M., Song, D.X.: Contextual policy enforcement in Android applications with permission event graphs. In: NDSS, The Internet Society (2013). http://dblp.uni-trier.de/db/conf/ndss/ndss2013.html#ChenJDDMMWRS13
3. Chong, S., Myers, A.C.: Security policies for downgrading. In: Proceedings of the 11th ACM Conference on Computer and Communications Security, pp. 189–209, October 2004
4. Chong, S., Vikram, K., Myers, A.C.: SIF: enforcing confidentiality and integrity in web applications. In: Proceedings of 16th USENIX Security Symposium on USENIX Security Symposium, SS 2007, pp. 1:1–1:16. USENIX Association, Berkeley (2007)
5. Clark, D., Hunt, S.: Non-interference for deterministic interactive programs. In: Degano, P., Guttman, J., Martinelli, F. (eds.) FAST 2008. LNCS, vol. 5491, pp. 50–66. Springer, Heidelberg (2009). http://dx.doi.org/10.1007/978-3-642-01465-9_4
6. Clarkson, M.R., Finkbeiner, B., Koleini, M., Micinski, K.K., Rabe, M.N., Sánchez, C.: Temporal logics for hyperproperties. In: Abadi, M., Kremer, S. (eds.) POST 2014 (ETAPS 2014). LNCS, vol. 8414, pp. 265–284. Springer, Heidelberg (2014). http://dx.doi.org/10.1007/978-3-642-54792-8_15

7. Clarkson, M.R., Schneider, F.B.: Hyperproperties. J. Comput. Secur. **18**(6), 1157–1210 (2010). http://dl.acm.org/citation.cfm?id=1891823.1891830

8. Denning, D.E.R.: Secure Information Flow in Computer Systems. Ph.D. thesis, West Lafayette, IN, USA (1975), aAI7600514

9. Enck, W., Gilbert, P., Chun, B.G., Cox, L.P., Jung, J., McDaniel, P., Sheth, A.N.: Taintdroid: An information-flow tracking system for realtime privacy monitoring on smartphones. In: Proceedings of the 9th USENIX Conference on Operating Systems Design and Implementation, OSDI 2010, pp. 1–6. USENIX Association, Berkeley (2010). http://dl.acm.org/citation.cfm?id=1924943.1924971

10. Google: Managing the Activity Lifecycle (2015). http://developer.android.com/training/basics/activity-lifecycle/index.html

11. Jeon, J., Micinski, K.K., Foster, J.S.: SymDroid: Symbolic Execution for Dalvik Bytecode. Technical report CS-TR-5022, Department of Computer Science, University of Maryland, College Park, July 2012

12. Jia, L., Aljuraidan, J., Fragkaki, E., Bauer, L., Stroucken, M., Fukushima, K., Kiyomoto, S., Miyake, Y.: Run-time enforcement of information-flow properties on android. In: Crampton, J., Jajodia, S., Mayes, K. (eds.) ESORICS 2013. LNCS, vol. 8134, pp. 775–792. Springer, Heidelberg (2013). http://dx.doi.org/10.1007/978-3-642-40203-6_43

13. Krohn, M., Yip, A., Brodsky, M., Cliffer, N., Kaashoek, M.F., Kohler, E., Morris, R.: Information flow control for standard OS abstractions. In: Proceedings of Twenty-first ACM SIGOPS Symposium on Operating Systems Principles, SOSP 2007, pp. 321–334. ACM, New York (2007)

14. Lichtenstein, O., Pnueli, A., Zuck, L.: The glory of the past. In: Parikh, R. (ed.) Logics of Programs. Lecture Notes in Computer Science, vol. 193, pp. 196–218. Springer, Berlin (1985). http://dx.doi.org/10.1007/3-540-15648-8_16

15. Ma, K.-K., Yit Phang, K., Foster, J.S., Hicks, M.: Directed symbolic execution. In: Yahav, E. (ed.) Static Analysis. LNCS, vol. 6887, pp. 95–111. Springer, Heidelberg (2011). http://dl.acm.org/citation.cfm?id=2041552.2041563

16. Micinski, K., Fetter-Degges, J., Jeon, J., Foster, J.S., Clarkson, M.R.: Checking interaction-based declassification policies for android using symbolic execution. Technical report CS-TR-5044, Department of Computer Science, University of Maryland, College Park, July 2015

17. de Moura, L., Bjørner, N.S.: Z3: an efficient SMT solver. In: Ramakrishnan, C.R., Rehof, J. (eds.) TACAS 2008. LNCS, vol. 4963, pp. 337–340. Springer, Heidelberg (2008). http://dx.doi.org/10.1007/978-3-540-78800-3_24

18. Myers, A.C.: Jflow: Practical mostly-static information flow control. In: Proceedings of the 26th ACM SIGPLAN-SIGACT Symposium on Principles of Programming Languages, POPL 1999, pp. 228–241. ACM, New York (1999). http://doi.acm.org/10.1145/292540.292561

19. O'Neill, K.R., Clarkson, M.R., Chong, S.: Information-flow security for interactive programs. In: Proceedings of the 19th IEEE Workshop on Computer Security Foundations, CSFW 2006, pp. 190–201. IEEE Computer Society, Washington (2006). http://dx.doi.org/10.1109/CSFW.2006.16

20. Pnueli, A.: The temporal logic of programs. In: Proceedings of the 18th Annual Symposium on Foundations of Computer Science, SFCS 1977, pp. 46–57. IEEE Computer Society, Washington (1977). http://dx.doi.org/10.1109/SFCS.1977.32

21. Rafnsson, W., Hedin, D., Sabelfeld, A.: Securing interactive programs. In: Proceedings of the 2012 IEEE 25th Computer Security Foundations Symposium, CSF 2012, pp. 293–307. IEEE Computer Society, Washington (2012). http://dx.doi.org/10.1109/CSF.2012.15

22. Roesner, F., Kohno, T., Moshchuk, A., Parno, B., Wang, H.J., Cowan, C.: User-driven access control: rethinking permission granting in modern operating systems. In: Proceedings of the 2012 IEEE Symposium on Security and Privacy, SP 2012, pp. 224–238. IEEE Computer Society, Washington (2012). http://dx.doi.org/10.1109/SP.2012.24

23. Sabelfeld, A., Sands, D.: Declassification: dimensions and principles. J. Comput. Secur. **17**(5), 517–548 (2009)

24. Vaughan, J.A., Chong, S.: Inference of expressive declassification policies. In: Proceedings of the 2011 IEEE Symposium on Security and Privacy SP 2011, pp. 180–195. IEEE Computer Society, Washington (2011). http://dx.doi.org/10.1109/SP.2011.20

25. Volpano, D., Irvine, C., Smith, G.: A sound type system for secure flow analysis. J. Comput. Secur. **4**(2–3), 167–187 (1996). http://dl.acm.org/citation.cfm?id=353629.353648

26. Yang, Z., Yang, M., Zhang, Y., Gu, G., Ning, P., Wang, X.S.: Appintent: analyzing sensitive data transmission in Android for privacy leakage detection. In: Proceedings of the 2013 ACM SIGSAC Conference on Computer and Communications Security, CCS 2013, pp. 1043–1054. ACM, New York (2013). http://doi.acm.org/10.1145/2508859.2516676

27. Yee, K.P.: Aligning security and usability. IEEE Secur. Priv. **2**(5), 48–55 (2004)

28. Zdancewic, S., Myers, A.: Observational determinism for concurrent program security. In: Proceedings of 16th IEEE Computer Security Foundations Workshop 2003, pp. 29–43 (2003)

# Applied Security

# Enhancing Java Runtime Environment for Smart Cards Against Runtime Attacks

Raja Naeem Akram[(⊠)], Konstantinos Markantonakis, and Keith Mayes

Information Security Group, Smart Card Centre,
Royal Holloway, University of London, Egham, Surrey, UK
{R.N.Akram,K.Markantonakis,Keith.Mayes}@rhul.ac.uk

**Abstract.** Smart cards are mostly deployed in security-critical environments in order to provide a secure and trusted access to the provisioned services. These services are delivered to a cardholder using the Service Provider's (SPs) applications on his or her smart card(s). These applications are at their most vulnerable state when they are executing. There exist a variety of runtime attacks that can circumvent the security checks implemented either by the respective application or the runtime environment to protect the smart card platform, user and/or application. In this paper, we discuss the Java Runtime Environment and a potential threat model based on runtime attacks. Subsequently, we discussed the counter-measures that can be deployed to provide a secure and reliable execution platform, along with an evaluation of their effectiveness, incurred performance-penalty and latency.

## 1 Introduction

An application on a smart card relies on the Smart Card Runtime Environment (SCRT) for secure and reliable execution. An SCRT contains a library of Application Programming Interfaces (APIs) that provide a secure and reliable interface between the installed applications and on-card services. An SCRT is used in order to:

1. Provide a secure and reliable program execution.
2. Enforce an execution isolation and access to memory locations.
3. Provide an interface to access cryptographic algorithms.
4. Protect the platform and applications from malicious or ill-formed applications.
5. Handle communication between applications and with external entities.

In early 2000, fault attacks became the modus operandi of adversaries to subvert the implemented cryptographic algorithms in the smart card industry. Since then the technology has evolved to counter these threats to some extent [3–5]. Althought, the full extent is not publically know, there has been a growing interest in fault injection and combined attacks [6–8] to subvert the protection mechanisms on a smart card. In combined attacks both the software (i.e. attacker's application) and fault injection are used to achieve the objectives. In this paper,

© Springer International Publishing Switzerland 2015
G. Pernul et al. (Eds.): ESORICS 2015, Part II, LNCS 9327, pp. 541–560, 2015.
DOI: 10.1007/978-3-319-24177-7_27

we analyse the attacks that target the SCRT and provide counter-measures. The attacks we have considered in this paper are fault and combined attacks targetted at the SCRT. In this paper, we focus on Java Cards; therefore, we will constantly refer to the Java Card Runtime Environment (JCRE) and it is used synonymously with SCRT. The rationale is that the JCRE has an open specification as compared to alternatives such as Multos, and new attacks mostly target Java Cards.

### 1.1    Contributions of the Paper

In this paper, we propose and evaluate the following:

1. A JCRE protection framework referred to as the "Runtime Protection Mechanism (RPM)".
2. Inclusion of the application developer's security requirements at the compilation of the application. If these requirements do not violate the security requirements of the JCRE, the runtime environment will try to enforce them.
3. A set of countermeasures that include:
   (a) Operand Stack Integrity: Safeguarding the JCRE's operand stack from any malicious modifications.
   (b) Permitted Execution Path Analysis: Evaluate the program flow and verify whether a particular execution path is allowed or not, based on the security requirements; defined by the application developer and/or JCRE.
   (c) Bytecode Integrity: To verify and validate whether the execution code of an application, in storage (persistent memory) and while in non-persistent memory during execution has not been modified.
4. Two variants of "Runtime Security Manager (RSM)" referred to as serial and parallel mode. The RSM enforces the security requirements defined by the application developers and JCRE as part of the RPM along with deploying the countermeasures. The variants are differentiated based on the architecture of the underlying hardware and the point at which the RSM verify and validate an application during its execution.
5. The proposed framework is implemented, and evaluated for security, incurred performance penalty and latency.

## 2    Smart Card Runtime Environment

In this section, we open the discussion with a brief description of the Java Card Virtual Machine (JCVM) followed by related work, and our motivation for the paper.

### 2.1    Java Card Virtual Machine

The JCRE consists of APIs, system classes, Java Card Virtual Machine (JCVM), and native methods. The most crucial component of the JCRE is the JCVM that actually interpret the application code to execute on the underlying hardware. The architecture of the JCVM is more or less similar between various Java Card versions.

An application is coded in a subset of the Java language that is supported by the JCVM, which is represented as a Java file. The application is then compiled into a class file, and it is packaged along with any resource files and supporting libraries into an installation package (e.g. CAP, or JAR file [9,10]) that can be downloaded to a Java Card. On the Java Card, the on-card bytecode verifier would analyse the downloaded application and validate that it conforms to the Java language semantics.

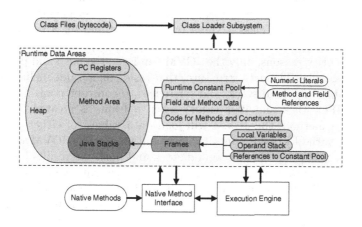

**Fig. 1.** Architecture of the Java card virtual machine

Figure 1 illustrates the architecture of a typical JCVM. Various components and their functions are described subsequently with emphasis on how they interact during the execution of an application.

The JCVM mainly deals with an abstract storage unit called *word* that is the smallest storage unit that it can process. The actual size of a *word* is left to the JCVM implementers. However, the JCVM specification [9] states that a word should be large enough to hold a value of `byte`, `short`, `reference`, or `returnAddress`.

When an application is initiated, the bytecode representation of an application is loaded into the JCVM memory by a "class loader subsystem". The class loader is responsible for locating and loading the class onto the memory areas used by the JCVM. This memory is divided into sub-areas, where each of them contains specific information regarding the application. The JCVM memory area is the heap, and all data/code related to an application is loaded onto it. The three main storage structures defined on the heap that are of relevance here are the Program Counter (PC) registers, method area, and Java stacks. These storage structures are briefly discussed here as they are referred to in the remaining paper (i.e., when we discuss our proposed counter-measures).

The PC registers store the memory address of the bytecode instruction currently executing. If the JCVM supports multiple threading then each thread will have its own PC register.

The method area is a memory space that consists of structures that include runtime constant pool, field and method data, and code related to methods and constructors. The runtime constant pool stores the constant field values (e.g. numeric literals) and references to the memory address related to methods and fields. The other two structures store the data and code related to fields and methods, etc.

A frame is created by the JCVM each time a method is invoked during the execution of an application. A frame is a construct that stores data, partial results, return values, and dynamically resolved links, associated with a single method (not the related class). These frames are stored on a last-in first-out (LIFO) stack called Java Stack. For each thread, there will be a different Java Stack. For security reasons, only the JCVM can issue the push and pop instructions to Java Stacks. The data structures that reside on a frame include an array of local variables, operand stack, and references to constant pool. The operand stack is a LIFO stack and it is empty when a frame is created. During the execution of a method, the JCVM will load data values (of either constant or non-constant variables/fields) onto the operand stack. The JCVM will operate on the values at the top of the operand stack and push the results back on it.

The JCVM provide well-defined interfaces to access native methods; however, contrary to traditional Java virtual machines they do not allow user-defined native methods. Each JCVM has an execution engine that is responsible for the execution of the individual instructions (opcodes) in an application code. The design of the execution engine is dependent on the underlying hardware platform and in a simple way, it can be considered as a software interface to the platform's processor.

This section does not exhaustively explain the JCRE and the rationale for covering the aforementioned topics is to make it easy to follow the subsequent discussion in the paper.

## 2.2    Related Work on JCRE Security

Earlier work on Java Cards was mainly related to the semantic and formal modelling of the JCVM [11,12], Java Card firewall mechanism [13,14], and applets [15–17]. The JCRE countermeasure against ill-formed applications was based on on-card bytecode verification [18–21], which became compulsory in the Java Card version 3 [9].

In the early 2000s, side channel analysis and fault attacks on smart card platforms were mainly focussed on the cryptographic algorithms [2,22–26]. However, in recent years, logical and fault attacks are combined to target the JCRE [27–29].

In 2008, Mostowski and Poll [30] loaded an ill-typed bytecode on various smart cards to test their security and reliability mechanisms. They also noted that smart cards that had an effective on-card bytecode verifier were less susceptible than others. In 2009, Hogenboom and Mostowski [31] managed to read arbitrary contents of the memory. They performed this attack even in the presence of the Java Card firewall mechanism. Similar results were also shown by Lanet and Iguchi-Cartigny [32]. Sere et al. [33] use the similar attack of modifying the bytecodes to gain unauthorised access or skip the security mechanism on a platform. However, Sere et al. relied on fault attacks to modify the bytecodes rather than modifying them off-card as done by [30]. This way, Sere et al. managed to bypass the on-card bytecode verification. A countermeasure to this attack provided by Sere et al. relied on tagging the bytecode instructions with integrity values (i.e. integrity bits) and during the execution, the JCVM checks these bits and if it fails, the execution terminates.

In 2010, Barbu et al. [7] along with Vétillard and Ferrari [6] used a similar attack methodology to Sere et al. [33] that later came to be known as combined attacks. Later, the combined attack technique was extended to target various components of JCVM in [34–36]. These attacks are significant; nevertheless, they require the loading of an application designed specifically to accomplish the attack goals.

Dubrile et al. [48] discussed the fault enabled mutants in the Java Cards and proposed a countermeasure based on the typed stack. In [49] Julien Lancia illustrated a combined attack on the memory references (object and variable references) and proposed a countermeasure based on a defensive virtual machine.

The discussion in this section is by no means exhaustive but it introduces the challenges faced by the JCRE.

## 2.3  Motivation

During an application's lifetime, the application's security is dependent on the security of the runtime environment. As discussed in Sect. 2.2, a smart card runtime environment is increasingly facing the convergence of various attack techniques (e.g. fault and logical attacks). Although, physical protection mechanisms regarding fault attacks are proposed [37], we consider that the necessary software protection for the runtime environment cannot be understated. The software protection can augment the hardware mechanism to protect against the combined attacks, as a similar approach has yielded successful results in the secure design of cryptographic algorithms for smart cards [38]. Therefore, in this paper, we will focus on the software protection mechanism.

In the literature, several methods are described for software protection mechanism, including application slicing in which an application is partitioned for performance [39] or to protect intellectual property [40]. Such partitioning can be used to tag individual segments of an application with adequate security requirements. The runtime environment can then take into account the security requirements, tagged with individual segments during the execution; thus providing configurable runtime security architecture. A similar approach is proposed by Java Card 3 [9] and as part of the counter-measures to combined attacks proposed by Sere et al. [36] and Bouffard et al. [41]. These proposals are based on using Java annotations to tag segments of an application with required security or reliability levels.

Developers can use Java annotations to provide information regarding an application (or its segment), which is used by either the compiler, or runtime environment (i.e. JCVM). Based on Java annotations, Bouffard et al. [41] and Sere et al. [36] proposed mechanisms to prevent control flow attacks. In addition, Loining et al. [42] used the Java annotations to ensure a secure and reliable development of applications for embedded devices (e.g. smart cards). Furthermore, Java Card 3 Connected Edition also makes provision for Java annotations [9]. The defined annotations by Java Card 3 are integrity, confidentiality, and full (which corresponds to both integrity and confidentiality). In addition, the specification also allows proprietary annotations that can be used to invoke specific protection mechanisms implemented by the respective card manufacturer. The Java Card 3 specification does not detail what operations a JCVM should perform when encountering a particular annotation, which are left to the discretion of the card manufacturers.

These proposals are useful but a malicious user can use the annotations to his advantage in order to accomplish malicious goals. To avoid this, in our proposal we have an on-card analyser that checks the security and reliability requirements of an application, validates the associated Java annotations (tags) with each segment of the application, and modifies the security annotations where adequate. In such a scenario, we may assume that tagging segments of an application with security annotations might be useful. Nevertheless, such an on-card analyser is not currently available on smart cards. In this paper, we solely focus on adequately hardening the runtime environment.

In our proposed framework, we tackle the problem from three aspects: application compilation, runtime protection, and trusted component. The Java annotations are used to tag properties of individual segments of an application. Runtime commands (opcodes) that might be subverted to gain unauthorised access are hardened with additional protection (security checks), and finally a trusted component is included to complement the runtime environment for security verification and validation of an application's execution.

## 3   Runtime Protection Mechanism

In this section, we describe the anticipated attacker's capability along with the security requirements for a reliable and safe JCRE. Subsequently, we discuss the proposed runtime protection mechanism and how it provides a secure and reliable framework for JCRE.

### 3.1   Attacker's Capability

Due to the advancement in chip technology and hardware protection mechanisms [43], we have taken a realistic approach in defining the attacker's capability, taking into consideration the current state-of-the-art in attack methodologies for smart cards. The attacker's capabilities are listed as below:

1. Has the knowledge of the underlying (hardware and software) architecture.
2. Has the ability to load a customised application onto a given smart card.

3. Has the capability to induce a fault attack at a precise clock cycle.
4. Has the limited capability of changing a byte value to either 0x00 or 0xFF, or a random value in between.
5. Has the potential to change values stored in a non-volatile memory permanently within the limits of the capability four.
6. Has the ability to inject multiple faults; however, only in serial fashion (i.e. after injecting a fault, the attacker waits for the results before injecting the next fault). The adversary cannot inject multiple faults in parallel — injecting two faults simultaneously.
7. Can overwrite the whole or part of a memory such as the Electrically Erasable Programmable Read-Only Memory (EEPROM) or off-card storage.

Capability four restricts an adversary to induce a precise byte error rather than the precise bit error. This restriction is based on the underlying smart card hardware architecture. This is not to say that precise bit errors are not possible in smart cards. On the contrary, they are technically possible but increasing the density of packaging (i.e. chip fabrication) makes it challenging to change a value of a bit in comparison to changing the value of a byte.

The rationale behind the choice of multiple fault attacks in serial fashion than parallel is to give precise control and reproducibility of the attack. In fault attacks where a malicious user injects multiple faults simultaneously (parallel), it is difficult to assess whether the first fault injection was successful; therefore, injecting the second fault may be less productive.

## 3.2  Security Requirements for a Runtime Protection Mechanism

In this section, we discuss the set of requirements appropriate for a runtime protection mechanism to defend against the attacker discussed in the previous section.

1. Customisable: Enables the application developers to define the security requirements (if preferred) for their applications, which will be enforced as long as they do not violate the platform's and/or other application's security requirements.
2. Developer Independent: Does not require the application developers to evaluate the security risks of their application and adequately tag it.
3. Code Integrity: Detect any unauthorised modification to the application code before it is executed.
4. Stack Integrity: Detect any modification to the values stored on the Java stacks (e.g. operand stack).
5. Execution Flow Evaluation: Detect any illegal jumps to either restricted areas (e.g. data or code locations for a different application) or violating the secure execution flow of the application.

These requirements are revisited in Sect. 4.5, when our proposal is compared with the existing proposals discussed in Sect. 2.2.

### 3.3   Overview of the Proposed Runtime Protection Mechanism

The proposed architecture of the runtime protection mechanism is involved at various stages of the application lifecycle - including the application compilation, on-card bytecode verification, and execution as shown in Fig. 2.

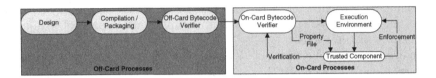

**Fig. 2.** Generic overview of the proposed runtime protection mechanism

During the compilation/packaging process additional information regarding individual methods, classes, and objects of an application is generated as part of the property file, discussed in Sect. 3.4. The property file assists the runtime environment to provide a security and reliability service during the execution of the application. The off-card bytecode verification checks whether the downloaded application conforms to the (given) language's semantics. The on-card bytecode verifier can also request the trusted component to validate the property file. The trusted component is the proposed Runtime Security Manager (RSM) discussed in Sect. 3.6 that actively enforces the security and reliability policy of the platform - taking into account the information included in the property file.

The proposed framework does not require that application developers perform security assessments of their application(s) to adequately tag application segments. The framework only requires at minimum that developers compile their applications in a way that they have property files that stores information related to the respective applications. The second requirement of the proposed framework is to adequately harden the runtime environment discussed in Sect. 3.5 along with introducing the RSM that will enforce the platform security policy (Sect. 3.6).

In subsequent sections, we will extend the generic architecture discussed in this section and explain how the different components come together.

### 3.4   Application Compilation

A Java compiler will take a Java file and convert it to a (bytecode) class file. The class file not only has opcodes, but it also includes information about various segments (e.g. methods, and classes) of an application that is necessary for the JCVM to execute the application. However, for our proposal we introduce a property file that includes additional information about an application. If a JCVM knows how to process property files then it will proceed with them; otherwise, it will ignore them. In our proposal a property file is stored and used by the RSM during the execution of the associated application. In order to integrate the RSM into the runtime environment, the JCVM is required to be modified so it can communicate with the RSM in order to safeguard the execution environment.

```
1  ApplicationInfo{
2        Application_Identifier  ApplicationIdentifier ;
3        ClassInformation  ClassInfo [ class_count ]; }
4  ClassInfo{
5        Class_Identifier  ClassIdentifier ;
6        MethodInformation  MethodInfo [ method_count ]; }
7  MethodInfo{
8        Method_Identifier  MethodIdentifier ;
9        MethodIntegrity  HashValue ;
10       PermittedExecutionPath  Path [ jumps_count ]}
```

**Listing 1.1.** Property file structure of a Java Card application.

The property file contains security and reliability information concerning an application that the runtime environment can utilise to execute an application. The structure of the property file is illustrated in Listing 1.1, which includes information regarding the permitted execution-paths, and integrity matrix (hash values of the non-mutable part of the individual methods in a class).

The ApplicationInfo data structure includes the application identifier (e.g. AID) and an array of classes that are part of the respective application. For each class in the application, we have a ClassInfo structure that contains the MethodInformation array that contains information regarding all methods associated with the given class. Each method is represented by the MethodInfo structure that includes the permitted execution-paths that are generated for each method. In the permitted execution-paths, child nodes represent jumps to other methods, irrespective of whether they are from the same application or from a different application. In a way, combining the method paths of all classes can give the complete permitted execution-path of the respective application. In addition to the permitted execution-paths, a MethodInfo also contains the hash value (of non-mutable code) of the respective method. This hash value can be generated at compile time and added to the property file, or at the time of the application installation: the RSM calculates the hash value and stores it in the property file.

### 3.5  Execution Environment

The runtime environment is modified to support the inclusion of the RSM that is shown in Fig. 3. At the time of application installation, the application bytecode is stored in the respective SP's domain along with the associated property file. The property file is sealed[1] so that neither the application nor an off-card entity (e.g. an SP or/and adversary) can modify it without detection. At the time of execution, the RSM will retrieve the file, verify the integrity of the file, and then decrypt it. If an SP wants to update its application then it will proceed with the

---

[1] Sealed: The data is encrypted (authenticated encryption) by the RSM storage key.

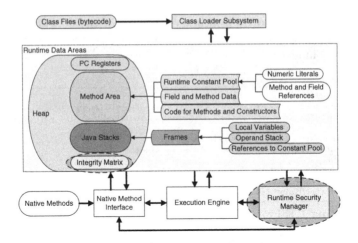

**Fig. 3.** Architecture of the proposed runtime environment for COM devices.

update command[2] that will notify the RSM of the update. At the completion of the update, the RSM will verify the application security certificate (if available), and update the property file – if required.

### 3.6   Runtime Security Manager

The purpose of the RSM is to enforce the security counter-measures (Sect. 3.7) defined by the respective platform. To enforce the security counter-measures, the RSM has access to the heap area (e.g. method area, Java stacks) and it can be implemented as either a serial or a parallel mode.

A serial RSM will rely on the execution engine of the JCVM (Fig. 1) to perform the required tasks. This means that when an execution engine encounters instructions that require an enforcement of the security policy, it will invoke the RSM that will then perform the checks. If successful the execution engine continues with execution, otherwise, it will terminate. A parallel RSM will have its own dedicated hardware (i.e. processor) support that enables it to perform checks simultaneously while the execution engine is executing an application. Note that having multiple processors on a smart card is technically possible [44]. The main question regarding the choice is not the hardware, but the balance between the performance and latency.

Performance, as the name suggests is concerned with the computational speed. Whereas, latency in this context deals with the number of instructions executed between an injected-error to the point it is detected. We will return to this discussion later in Sect. 4 where we provide test (simulated) implementation results.

---

[2] Update Command: We do not propose any update command in this paper but similar commands are defined as part of the GlobalPlatform card specification. The update command enables an authorised entity (e.g. SP) to modify an application.

## 3.7  Runtime Security Counter-Measures

The RSM along with the runtime environment would apply the required security counter-measures (as part of the runtime protection mechanism) that are discussed in subsequent sections.

**Operand Stack Integrity.** As discussed in Sect. 2.1, an operand stack is part of the Java stacks and they are associated with individual Java frames (methods). During the execution of an application, the runtime environment pushes and pops local variables, constant fields, and object references to the operand stack. The instructions specified in an application can then process the values at the top of the stack. Barbu et el. [34] showed that a fault injection that changes the values stored on the operand stack could have adverse effect on an application's security. Furthermore, they also provided three different counter-measures to the proposed attack.

The proposed countermeasure (second-refined method) of Barbu et al. [34] is based on the idea of operand stack integrity. They define a variable $\alpha$, and all values that are pushed on or popped from the operand stack are XORed with the $\alpha$. On every jump instruction beyond the scope of the current frame (method), the runtime environment XORs all the values stored on the operand and compares the result with $\alpha$. If they match then the integrity of the operand stack is verified. Their proposal does not measure the integrity of the operand stack on instructions like if-else or loops, which could be the target of the malicious user. In their proposed counter-measures they sacrificed security and (to some extent) performance for the sake of memory use, whereas our proposal focuses on security rather than saving the memory.

In our proposal, we use a Last In First Out (LIFO) stack referred to as integrity stack. One thing to note is that the JCVM knows the size of the operand stack when it loads a frame (Sect. 2.1); therefore, the RSM just creates an integrity stack of the size n where n is the size of the respective operand stack. We refer to the integrity stack as "InS" in Listing 1.2.

When a frame is loaded, the JCVM and the RSM will create an operand and integrity stack, respectively. Furthermore, the RSM will also generate a random number and stores it as $S_r$. The rationale for using the random number will become apparent in the subsequent discussion.

```
1  // Executed by RSM when a value is pushed onto an integrity stack.
2  On_Stack_Push(pushedValue){
3    push(InS[top] XOR pushedValue);}
4  // Executed by RSM when a value is popped from an operand stack.
5  On_Stack_Pop(poppedValue){
6    if(pop(InS) XOR poppedValue := InS[top]){
7    }else{
8      terminateExecution();
9    }}
```

**Listing 1.2.** Operand stack integrity operations.

When a value $V_i$ is pushed to the operand stack, if it is the first value on the stack then the value pushed on the InS will be $I_i = V_i \oplus S_r$. For all subsequent values (where $i > 1$) the values pushed on the Ins will be $I_i = V_i \oplus V_{i-1}$.

The rationale for using a random number is to avoid parallel fault injections that try to change the values on both operand and integrity stack simultaneously. Such a parallel fault injection will become difficult if an adversary cannot predict the values stored on the integrity stack, as each value on the integrity stack will be chained with the generated random number.

When a value is popped out of the operand stack, we also pop the integrity value from the integrity stack, XOR it with the popped value from the operand stack and compare it with the new top value on the integrity stack. If the values match then the integrity of the popped value from the operand stack is verified; otherwise, it has been corrupted and the RSM requests the JCVM to terminate the execution as shown in Listing 1.2.

The RSM will continuously monitor the integrity of the operand stack, in comparison to the Barbu's proposal. Furthermore, in this proposal the validation does not require the calculation of integrity value over the entire operand stack. If we take the Barbu's proposal then for an operand stack of length 'n', we have to perform "n-1" XOR operations every time we need to verify the state of the operand stack. However, in our proposal we only need to perform one XOR operation. We sacrifice the memory for the sake of performance in our proposal. We consider that operand stacks are not large data structures so even if we double the memory used by them, it will not have an adverse effect on the overall memory usage.

**Permitted Execution Path (PEP) Analysis.** In our proposal, we are concerned with jumps that refer to external resources. The term external resources in the context of PEP analysis means any jump that goes beyond the scope of the current Java frame (i.e. method) while it is still on the Java stack. Once a method completes its execution, the JCVM will remove the associated Java frame from the Java stacks (Fig. 1). Examples of such jumps defined in Java virtual machine specification [45] are **invokeinterface**, **invokestatic**, **invokevirtual**, **areturn**, etc.

```
1  byte B(byte inputValue){
2    byte a = 1;
3    if(inputValue != a){ C(inputValue);
4    }else{D(inputValue)}
5    return SG(inputValue);}
```

**Listing 1.3.** Code for an example method B.

To explain the Permitted Execution Path Analysis further, we consider an example method B that has three jumps before it reaches the return statement that completes the execution of the method. The method B's code is shown in Listing 1.3. Each invocation of a method (e.g. C, D, and SG) is represented by a symbolic method name (i.e. alphanumeric form that is easily readable/

recognisable by humans) that has an associated unique byte sequence referred as method identifier. For example, unique method identifier of methods B, C, D, and SG are 0xF122, 0xF123, 0xF124, and 0xF125, respectively. For explanation we have used method identifiers that consist of two bytes. Along with the method identifier the property file also includes `PermittedExecutionPath`, which is a set of PEPs sanctioned for the given method.

The `PermitedExecutionPath` in the property file (Listing 1.1) is simply constructed by taking into account every possible (legal) execution path of a method. Taking the example method B, the first jump can either be to method C or D depending upon the input. The construction of the `PermitedExecutionPath` (set of legal jumps) is constructed by XORing the method identifiers of individual jumps.

The PEP analysis requires that the RSM have a PEP variable "$cfa$" that stores the path taken by an application as $cfa = \Sigma_{j=1}^{n} C_j$. Where $C_j$ represents the jumps taken during execution of an application. During the execution of a method, when the JCVM encounters a jump to another method the RSM XORs the method identifier with the current value of "$cfa$" and lookup the `PermitedExecutionPath` of the given method in the associated property file. If it finds a matching value, the JCVM will proceed with the execution; if not it will terminate the execution. Our scheme also deals with the loop instructions that contain jumps to multiple methods depending upon the loop condition.

**Bytecode Integrity.** The property file associated with an application stores the hash values of individual methods. When the runtime environment fetches an application, the RSM will measure the integrity value of individual methods of the application and compare them with the hash values in the property file. Therefore, any method that is loaded to the heap goes through the integrity validation. This validation protects against the fault attacks on an application stored while it is stored on a non-volatile memory.

The hashes of the individual methods (code and constant local-data variables) along with the integrity values (hash values) generated on the global persistent data can create a whole application integrity matrix. During the execution of an application, when it jumps from one method to another, it can be assured that the execution path is going to a (potentially) trusted method or the integrity of the called method will be verified. The RSM also tracks the integrity of the global variables and update the hash values if any authorised changes are being performed by the application.

## 4    Analysis of the Runtime Protection Mechanism

In this section, we evaluate the suitability of countermeasures against the attacks discussed in Sect. 2.2 under the adversary's capability detailed in Sect. 3.1. Furthermore, we provide the latency and incurred overhead analysis for both serial and parallel RSMs.

## 4.1   Security Analysis

In this section, we discuss how the proposed counter-measures protect against the combined attacks under the attacker's capability detailed in Sect. 3.1.

**Operand Stack Integrity.** We proposed a more refined approach to Barbu et al. [34] and removed the need to perform integrity measurement of the entire operand stack on each validation. In addition, we made the validation process continuous thus checking the integrity of the operand stack on each pop and push operation. If a malicious user changes values on the operand stack, the RSM can not only detect the modification but can also provide error correction service by providing the correct value that was stored on the operand stand. Furthermore, by using a random number, our proposal makes it difficult for an adversary to know the values stored on the integrity stack, even if he has the knowledge of all values on the operand stack.

**PEP Analysis.** The PEP analysis performed by the RSM during the execution of an application effectively prevents execution path attacks. If an attacker has the capability of multiple fault injections simultaneously, (which is beyond the capability of our attacker as stated in Sect. 3.1) then he can in theory affect the RSM execution. Nevertheless, even with simultaneous injections the attacker may be able to skip a node in the execution tree but the RSM calculation on the subsequent nodes will reveal an illegal path of execution. Therefore, even in the parallel injection model the RSM will detect the erroneous execution path, unless the attacker keeps on injecting faults during the whole execution of an application.

**Bytecode Integrity.** Our countermeasure prevents an adversary from changing an application while it is stored on a non-volatile memory (capability four of an adversary discussed in Sect. 3.1). To avoid such modifications, the RSM generates a hash of individual methods that are requested by the JCVM. If the hash matches the stored value (`MethodIntegrity` in Listing 1.1) in the respective property file, the JCVM will proceed with the execution of the method; otherwise, the RSM will signal the termination of the application (and possibly mark it malicious and up for deletion). Furthermore, this protection mechanism can also safeguard the dynamic loading of applications/classes/routines as part of a simple web server or other applications, which are stored in off-card storage.

## 4.2   Evaluation Context

For evaluating the proposed counter-measures, we have selected four sample applications. Two of the applications selected are part of the Java Card development kit distribution: Wallet and Java Purse. The other two applications are the offline attestation algorithm [46] and the STCP$_{SP}$ protocol [47].

### 4.3   Latency Analysis

As discussed before, latency is the number of instructions executed after an adversary mounts an attack, before the system becomes aware of it. Therefore, in this section we analyse the latency of the proposed counter-measures under the concepts of serial and parallel RSMs that are listed in Table 1 and discussed subsequently.

**Table 1.** Latency measurement of individual countermeasure

| Counter-measures | Serial RSM | Parallel RSM |
|---|---|---|
| Operand Stack Integrity | 0 + i | 3 + i |
| Permitted Execution Path Analysis | 0 | $3(C_n)$ |
| Bytecode Integrity | 0 | 0 |

In case of the operand stack integrity, the serial RSM finds the occurrence of an error (e.g. fault injection) with latency "0+i", where 'i' is the number of instructions executed before the manipulated value reaches the top of the operand stack. Similarly, the latency value in case of the operand stack integrity for the parallel RSM is "3+i", where '3' is the number of instructions required to perform a comparison on pop operation (On_Stack_Pop(poppedValue) in Listing 1.2). The latency value of the parallel RSM is higher than the serial. This has to do with the fact that while the parallel RSM is applying the security checks the JCVM does not need to stop the execution of subsequent instructions.

Regarding the PEP analysis, the serial RSM has a latency of zero where the parallel RSM has latency value of "$3(C_n)$", where the value $C_n$ represents the number of legal jumps in the respective PermittedExecutionPath set. To explain this further, consider the example in Listing 1.3. The set method B has four possible values ($B_{cfa-Set}$ in Sect. 3.7). Thereby, the latency value for a jump in the method B in the worse case is "3(4) = 12". The value '3' represents the number of instructions required to execute individual comparison.

A notable point to mention here is that all latency measurements listed in Table 2 are based on the worst-case conditions. Furthermore, it is apparent that it might be difficult to implement a complete parallel RSM. To explain our point, consider two consecutive jump instructions in which the parallel RSM has to perform PEP analysis. In such a situation, there might be a possibility that while the RSM is still evaluating the first jump, the JCVM initiates the second jump instruction. Therefore, this might create a deadlock between the JCVM and parallel RSM, so we consider that either JCVM should wait for the RSM to complete the verification, or for the sake of performance the RSM might skip certain verifications. We opt for the parallel RSM that will switch to the serial RSM mode, restricting the JCVM to proceed with next instruction until the RSM can apply the security checks. This situation will be further explained during the discussion on the performance measurements in the next section.

### 4.4    Incurred Overhead Analysis

To evaluate the performance impact of the proposed counter-measures we developed an abstract virtual machine that takes the bytecode of each Java Card applet and then computes the computational overhead for individual counter-measure. When a Java application is compiled, the Java compiler (`javac`) produces a class file as discussed in Sect. 2.1. The class file is a Java bytecode representation, and we utilise the `javap` tool that comes with Java Development Kit (JDK) as it produces the bytecode representation of a class file in human-readable mnemonics as represented in the JVM specification [45]. The abstract virtual machine takes the mnemonic bytecode representation and searches for push, pop, and jump (e.g. method invocation) opcodes. Subsequently, we calculated the number of extra instructions required to be executed in order to implement the counter-measures discussed in previous sections.

**Table 2.** Performance measurement (percentage increase in computational cost)

| Applications | Serial RSM | Parallel RSM |
|---|---|---|
| Wallet | +29 % | +22 % |
| Java Purse | +30 % | +26 % |
| Offline Attestation [46] | +27 % | +23 % |
| STCP$_{SP}$ [47] | +39 % | +33 % |

We compute the incurred overhead as a number of instructions that are going to be executed by an application that our countermeasures verify/validate. After this measurement, we have associated costs based on additional instructions executed for each JCVM instruction and calculated as an (approximate) increase in the percentage of computational overhead and listed in Table 2. Furthermore, the computational cost of generating a hash is dependent on individual hardware configuration. The same is also true for the execution of each of the instructions. This is the reason why we opt for the evaluation based on the number of increased instructions rather then the performance as it provides us a hardware agnostic cost.

For each application, the counter-measures have different computational overhead values because they depend upon how many times certain instructions that invoke the counter-measures are executed. Therefore, the computational overhead measurements in Table 2 can only give us a measure of how the performance is affected in individual cases - without generalising for other applications.

### 4.5    Comparative Analysis

In this section, we will compare our proposed framework with the existing state-of-the-art discussed in Sect. 2.2 in the context of security requirements for a JCRE (listed in Sect. 3.2).

**Table 3.** Comparison between Proposed and Existing Proposals

| Requirement | Barbu et al. [7] | Sere et al. [36] | Dubreuil et al. [48] | Lancia [49] | RSM |
|---|---|---|---|---|---|
| Customisable | Limited | Yes | No | No | Yes |
| Developer Independent | Yes | No | Yes | Yes | Yes |
| Code Integrity | No | Yes | No | Yes | Yes |
| Stack Integrity | Yes | No | Yes | No | Yes |
| Execution Flow Evaluation | No | No | No | No | Yes |

Table 3 illustrates our proposed framework's results are better in comparison to other proposals, in the context of attacker capabilities and security requirements. One thing to note is that other proposals compared in Table 3 do not provide performance degradation matrix associated with their countermeasures, equivalent to one presented in Sects. 4.3 and 4.4

## 5 Conclusion

In this paper we discussed the smart card runtime environment by taking the Java Card as a practical example. The JCRE was described with its different data structures that it uses during the execution of an application. Subsequently, we discussed various attacks that target the smart card runtime environment and most of these attacks are based on perturbation of the values stored by the runtime environment. These perturbations are the result of fault injection, which was defined and mapped to an adversary's capability in this paper. Based on recent published attacks on the smart card runtime environment, we proposed an architecture that includes the provision of a RSM. We also proposed three counter-measures and provided the computational cost imposed by them. The overall protection framework is then compared with the existing frameworks and we showed that our proposal provides comparatively better protection. No doubt, counter-measures that do not change the core architecture the Java virtual machine, will almost always incur extra computational cost. Therefore, we concluded in this paper that a better way forward would be to change the architecture of the Java virtual machine. Finally, in the context of this paper we showed that the current architecture can be hardened at the expanse of a modest computational penalty.

## References

1. Anderson, R., Kuhn, M.: Low cost attacks on tamper resistant devices. In: Christianson, B., Lomas, M., Crispo, B., Roe, M. (eds.) Security Protocols 1997. LNCS, vol. 1361, pp. 125–136. Springer, Heidelberg (1998)
2. Kocher, P.C., Jaffe, J., Jun, B.: Differential power analysis. In: Wiener, M. (ed.) CRYPTO 1999. LNCS, vol. 1666, pp. 388–397. Springer, Heidelberg (1999)
3. Sauveron, D.: Multiapplication smart card: towards an open smart card? Inf. Secur. Tech. Rep. 14(2), 70–78 (2009)

4. Akram, R.N., Markantonakis, K.: Smart cards: state-of-the-art to future directions, invited paper. In: Douligeris, C., Serpanos, D. (eds.) IEEE International Symposium on Signal Processing and Information Technology (ISSPIT 2013). IEEE CS, Athens, Greece (2013)

5. Markantonakis, K., Mayes, K., Sauveron, D., Askoxylakis, I.: Overview of security threats for smart cards in the public transport industry. In: 2008 IEEE International Conference on e-Business Engineering. IEEE CS (2008)

6. Vétillard, E., Ferrari, A.: Combined attacks and countermeasures. In: Gollmann, D., Lanet, J.-L., Iguchi-Cartigny, J. (eds.) CARDIS 2010. LNCS, vol. 6035, pp. 133–147. Springer, Heidelberg (2010)

7. Barbu, G., Thiebeauld, H., Guerin, V.: Attacks on Java card 3.0 combining fault and logical attacks. In: Gollmann, D., Lanet, J.-L., Iguchi-Cartigny, J. (eds.) CARDIS 2010. LNCS, vol. 6035, pp. 148–163. Springer, Heidelberg (2010)

8. Chaumette, S., Sauveron, D.: An efficient and simple way to test the security of Java cards. In: Fernández-Medina, E., Castro, J.C.H., Castro, L.J.G. (eds.) Security in Information Systems, pp. 331–341. INSTICC Press, Miami (2005)

9. Java Card Platform Specification, Oracle Std. v3.0.1, May 2009

10. Java Card Platform Specification, Sun Microsystem Inc Std. v2.2.2, March 2006

11. Barthe, G., Dufay, G., Jakubiec, L., de Sousa, S.M.: A formal correspondence between offensive and defensive JavaCard virtual machines. In: Cortesi, A. (ed.) VMCAI 2002. LNCS, vol. 2294, pp. 32–45. Springer, Heidelberg (2002)

12. Barthe, G., Stratulat, S.: Validation of the JavaCard platform with implicit induction techniques. In: Nieuwenhuis, R. (ed.) RTA 2003. LNCS, vol. 2706, pp. 337–351. Springer, Heidelberg (2003)

13. Éluard, M., Jensen, T., Denne, E.: An operational semantics of the Java card firewall. In: Attali, S., Jensen, T. (eds.) E-smart 2001. LNCS, vol. 2140, pp. 95–110. Springer, Heidelberg (2001)

14. Éluard, M., Jensen, T.: Secure object flow analysis for Java card. In: Proceedings of the 5th Conference on Smart Card Research and Advanced Application Conference, CARDIS 2002, p. 11. USENIX Association, California (2002)

15. Lanet, J.L., Requet, A.: Formal proof of smart card applets correctness. In: Schneier, B., Quisquater, J.-J. (eds.) CARDIS 1998. LNCS, vol. 1820, pp. 85–97. Springer, Heidelberg (2000)

16. Meijer, H., Poll, E.: Towards a full formal specification of the JavaCard API. In: Attali, S., Jensen, T. (eds.) E-smart 2001. LNCS, vol. 2140, pp. 165–178. Springer, Heidelberg (2001)

17. Almaliotis, V., Loizidis, A., Katsaros, P., Louridas, P., Spinellis, D.D.: Static program analysis for Java card applets. In: Grimaud, G., Standaert, F.-X. (eds.) CARDIS 2008. LNCS, vol. 5189, pp. 17–31. Springer, Heidelberg (2008)

18. Basin, D., Friedrich, S., Posegga, J., Vogt, H.: Java bytecode verification by model checking. In: Halbwachs, N., Peled, D.A. (eds.) CAV 1999. LNCS, vol. 1633, pp. 491–494. Springer, Heidelberg (1999)

19. Leroy, X.: On-card bytecode verification for Java card. In: Attali, S., Jensen, T. (eds.) E-smart 2001. LNCS, vol. 2140, pp. 150–164. Springer, Heidelberg (2001)

20. Basin, D., Friedrich, S., Gawkowski, M.: Verified bytecode model checkers. In: Carreño, V.A., Muñoz, C.A., Tahar, S. (eds.) TPHOLs 2002. LNCS, vol. 2410, pp. 47–66. Springer, Heidelberg (2002)

21. Leroy, X.: Bytecode verification on Java smart cards. Softw. Pract. Exper. **32**(4), 319–340 (2002)

22. Biham, E., Shamir, A.: Differential fault analysis of secret key cryptosystems. In: Kaliski Jr, B.S. (ed.) CRYPTO 1997. LNCS, vol. 1294, pp. 513–525. Springer, Heidelberg (1997)

23. Messerges, T.S., Dabbish, E.A., Sloan, R.H.: Investigations of power analysis attacks on smartcards. In: Proceedings of the USENIX Workshop on Smartcard Technology on USENIX Workshop on Smartcard Technology, p. 17. USENIX Association, Berkeley (1999)

24. Skorobogatov, S.P., Anderson, R.J.: Optical fault induction attacks. In: Kaliski Jr, B.S., Koç, Ç.K., Paar, C. (eds.) CHES 2002. LNCS, vol. 2523, pp. 2–12. Springer, Heidelberg (2003)

25. Quisquater, J.-J., Samyde, D.: Eddy current for Magnetic Analysis with Active Sensor. Springer (2002)

26. Aumller, C., Bier, P., Fischer, W., Hofreiter, P., Seifert, J.-P.: Fault attacks on RSA with CRT: concrete results and practical countermeasures. In: Kaliski Jr, B.S., Koç, Ç.K., Paar, C. (eds.) CHES 2002. LNCS, vol. 2523, pp. 260–275. Springer, Heidelberg (2003)

27. Joint Interpretation Library - Application of Attack Potential to Smartcards, Online, Technical report, Apirl 2006

28. Vertanen, O.: Java type confusion and fault attacks. In: Breveglieri, L., Koren, I., Naccache, D., Seifert, J.-P. (eds.) FDTC 2006. LNCS, vol. 4236, pp. 237–251. Springer, Heidelberg (2006)

29. Lemarechal, A.: Introduction to fault attacks on smartcard. In: 11th IEEE International On-Line Testing Symposium, IOLTS 2005, p. 116, July 2005

30. Mostowski, W., Poll, E.: Malicious code on Java card smartcards: attacks and countermeasures. In: Grimaud, G., Standaert, F.-X. (eds.) CARDIS 2008. LNCS, vol. 5189, pp. 1–16. Springer, Heidelberg (2008)

31. Hogenboom, J., Mostowski, W.: Full memory read attack on a Java card. In: Pereira, O., Quisquater, J.-J., Standaert, F.-X. (eds.) 4th Benelux Workshop on Information and System Security. Springer, Belgium (2009)

32. Lanet, J.-L., Iguchi-Cartigny, J.: Developing a Trojan applet in a smart card. J. Comput. Virol. 6(1) (2009)

33. Sere, A.A., Iguchi-Cartigny, J., Lanet, J.-L.: Automatic detection of fault attack and countermeasures. In: Proceedings of the 4th Workshop on Embedded Systems Security, ser. WESS 2009, pp. 71–77. ACM, New York (2009)

34. Barbu, G., Duc, G., Hoogvorst, P.: Java card operand stack: fault attacks, combined attacks and countermeasures. In: Prouff, E. (ed.) CARDIS 2011. LNCS, vol. 7079, pp. 297–313. Springer, Heidelberg (2011)

35. Barbu, G., Thiebeauld, H.: Synchronized attacks on multithreaded systems - application to Java card 3.0 -. In: Prouff, E. (ed.) CARDIS 2011. LNCS, vol. 7079, pp. 18–33. Springer, Heidelberg (2011)

36. Sere, A.A., Iguchi-Cartigny, J., Lanet, J.-L.: Evaluation of countermeasures against fault attacks on smart cards. Int. J. Secur. Appl. 5(2), 49–61 (2011)

37. Derouet, O.: Secure smartcard design against laser fault. (Invited Speaker). In: 4th Workshop on Fault Diagnosis and Tolerance in Cryptography (FDRC 2007). IEEE-CS, Austria, Vienna, September 2007

38. Kim, S.-K., Kim, T.H., Han, D.-G., Hong, S.: An efficient CRT-RSA algorithm secure against power and fault attacks. J. Syst. Softw. 84(10), 1660–1669 (2011)

39. Zhang, T., Pande, S., Valverde, A.: Tamper-resistant whole program partitioning. In: LCTES 2003, the 2003 ACM SIGPLAN Conference on Language, Compiler, and Tool for Embedded Systems, pp. 209–219. ACM, New York (2003)

40. Zhuang, X., Zhang, T., Lee, H.-H.S., Pande, S.: Hardware assisted control flow obfuscation for embedded processors. In: CASES 2004. ACM, USA (2004)

41. Bouffard, G., Lanet, J.-L., Machemie, J.-B., Poichotte, J.-Y., Wary, J.-P.: Evaluation of the ability to transform SIM applications into hostile applications. In: Prouff, E. (ed.) CARDIS 2011. LNCS, vol. 7079, pp. 1–17. Springer, Heidelberg (2011)

42. Loinig, J., Steger, C., Weiss, R., Haselsteiner, E.: Identification and Verification of Security Relevant Functions in Embedded Systems Based on Source Code Annotations and Assertions. In: Samarati, P., Tunstall, M., Posegga, J., Markantonakis, K., Sauveron, D. (eds.) WISTP 2010. LNCS, vol. 6033, pp. 316–323. Springer, Heidelberg (2010)

43. Séré, A.A.K., Iguchi-Cartigny, J., Lanet, J.-L.: Checking the paths to identify mutant application on embedded systems. In: Kim, T., Lee, Y., Kang, B.-H., Slezak, D. (eds.) FGIT 2010. LNCS, vol. 6485, pp. 459–468. Springer, Heidelberg (2010)

44. Rankl, W., Effing, W.: Smart Card Handbook, 3rd edn. Wiley, New York (2003)

45. Lindholm, T., Yellin, F.: The Java Virtual Machine Specification, 2nd edn. Addison-Wesley Longman, Amsterdam (1999)

46. Akram, R.N., Markantonakis, K., Mayes, K.: Remote attestation mechanism for user centric smart cards using pseudorandom number generators. In: Qing, S., Zhou, J., Liu, D. (eds.) ICICS 2013. LNCS, vol. 8233, pp. 151–166. Springer, Heidelberg (2013)

47. Akram, R.N., Markantonakis, K., Mayes, K.: A secure and trusted channel protocol for the user centric smart card ownership model. In: 12th IEEE International Conference on Trust, Security and Privacy in Computing and Communications. IEEE CS, Australia, July 2013

48. Dubreuil, J., Bouffard, G., Lanet, J., Cartigny, J.: Type classification against fault enabled mutant in Java based smart card. In: 2012 Seventh International Conference on Availability, Reliability and Security (ARES), August 2012

49. Lancia, J.: Java card combined attacks with localization-agnostic fault injection. In: Mangard, S. (ed.) CARDIS 2012. LNCS, vol. 7771, pp. 31–45. Springer, Heidelberg (2013)

# Making Bitcoin Exchanges Transparent

Christian Decker[(✉)], James Guthrie, Jochen Seidel, and Roger Wattenhofer

Distributed Computing Group, ETH Zurich, Zürich, Switzerland
{cdecker,guthriej,seidelj,wattenhofer}@ethz.ch

**Abstract.** Bitcoin exchanges are a vital component of the Bitcoin ecosystem. They are a gateway from the classical economy to the cryptocurrency economy, facilitating the exchange between fiat currency and bitcoins. However, exchanges are also single points of failure, operating outside the Bitcoin blockchain, requiring users to entrust them with their funds in order to operate. In this work we present a solution, and a proof-of-concept implementation, that allows exchanges to prove their solvency, without publishing any information of strategic importance.

## 1 Introduction

Since the conceptual introduction of Bitcoin in 2008 by Satoshi Nakamoto [15] and the appearance of the first Bitcoin client in 2009, Bitcoin has seen massive growth on a multitude of fronts. Bitcoin currently has a market capitalisation of 3 billion US dollars and an average daily transaction volume of approximately 50 million US dollars.

One factor which has driven widespread adoption of Bitcoin is the emergence of Bitcoin exchanges: companies which allow trading bitcoins with fiat currency, such as Euros and US dollars. Bitcoin exchanges have helped the adoption of Bitcoin in two ways. Firstly, before the advent of Bitcoin exchanges, the only way to come by bitcoins was to *mine* them oneself or to informally trade bitcoins with other participants. Exchanges have opened the Bitcoin market to parties who might otherwise not have been able to participate. Secondly, exchanges publish their trade books which establishes an accepted exchange rate between fiat currencies and bitcoins. This in turn allowed vendors to value their goods and services in bitcoins in accordance to the market rates in fiat currency.

Although Bitcoin exchanges have had a positive contribution to the Bitcoin economy, they are not without risks. In Moore and Christin's analysis of the risks involved with Bitcoin exchanges [14] they analyse 40 Bitcoin exchanges, at the time of publication 18 of the 40 exchanges had ceased operation. Of those 18, 5 exchanges did not reimburse customers on closure, 6 exchanges claim that they did and for the remaining 7 there is no data available. Most of the collapsed Bitcoin exchanges were not long-lived, with their closure either being immediate or over a relatively short period of time.

Since the publication of that analysis the most high-profile exchange closure took place: the bankruptcy and closure of the Mt. Gox Bitcoin exchange, in which 650,000 bitcoins belonging to customers of the exchange were lost or stolen.

© Springer International Publishing Switzerland 2015
G. Pernul et al. (Eds.): ESORICS 2015, Part II, LNCS 9327, pp. 561–576, 2015.
DOI: 10.1007/978-3-319-24177-7_28

At the time, Mt. Gox claimed that a flaw in the Bitcoin protocol was to blame for the loss of its client's bitcoins, a claim which has since been refuted [7]. At the time of the event, Mt. Gox was one of the longest-running exchanges in the Bitcoin market with its cumulative number of transactions accounting for approximately 70 % of all Bitcoin transactions.

Bitcoin transactions are irreversible by design. Once a user has transferred her bitcoins to another user there is no way that she will get them back without the cooperation of the recipient. There is little recourse for the customer of an exchange: Bitcoin is new ground for insurers, regulators, and law enforcement who do not yet have any established methods for dealing with Bitcoin related legal issues.

In an effort to calm customers fears, some exchanges have taken to periodically publishing data proving their solvency: an anonymised list of their customers account balances and a list of Bitcoin addresses owned by the exchange along with a signature that proves the ownership. If the balance of the bitcoins available on the addresses is at least as large as the sum of the amounts owed by the exchange, the exchange is solvent. Although customers may be appreciative of this type of transparency, it may put the exchange at a disadvantage as it reveals information of strategic importance, such as the number of customers, the amounts the exchange's customers keep on hand and the total balance of bitcoins held by the exchange.

In conventional financial markets trust is placed in the financial statements made by institutions such as exchanges or investment funds through the process of auditing. An independent third party, which is perceived to be trustworthy by the customers of the institution, or a state mandated auditor inspects the financial records of the institution and publishes an audit result. Such an audit is an expensive and time-consuming process and is typically only performed in well-spaced intervals.

In this paper, we propose to perform a software-based audit of Bitcoin exchanges without revealing any information about the bitcoins that are possessed by either the exchange, or its customers to the public. This is achieved by replacing the human financial auditor by a piece of software. To ensure that the software is executed correctly we rely on Trusted Computing (TC) technology. In our scenario, the traditional limitations of financial auditing no longer apply. Software executes orders of magnitudes faster than humans, and the execution of a piece of software is generally not costly at all and it becomes feasible to provide daily audits of a Bitcoin exchange. Our contribution is twofold: we propose a system that uses Trusted Computing to prove the exchange's solvibility to its customers and we implement the proposed solution on consumer hardware minimizing obstacles to its deployment.

## 1.1  Related Work

Auditing Bitcoin exchanges has been previously discussed by Todd and Maxwell [10], and later by Maxwell and Wilcox [11]. Both approaches rely on modifying the merkle tree computation to defend against insertion of negative subtrees. Our use of TC for the merkle tree computation obviates any such modifications as the secure code would error out on negative sums.

Trusted Computing, and more specifically TPMs, have been proposed previously as a method to secure Bitcoin wallets by Hal Finney [8], storing sensitive keying material in the tamper proof storage. Since then several additional methods of securing funds have been proposed, including multisignature accounts [3], the creation of deterministic public keys that do not require private keys during the generation [4] and locking funds for a predetermined period of time [17]. The latter may also be used to extend the audit to guarantee the solvency for a certain period, by making the funds inaccessible until they are unlocked.

While regular audits may help detect fraud at an early stage, a regulatory framework is needed to prosecute perpetrators. Some initial work has been done in the field of regulation, examining the impact of Bitcoin on current anti-money laundering (AML) policies and on know-your-customer (KYC) policies [1,2,5,6,16].

## 2    Preliminaries

The software-based audit of a Bitcoin exchange relies on an understanding of both the Bitcoin project as well as Trusted Computing. This section introduces the fundamentals of Bitcoin and Trusted Computing, as needed in this paper.

### 2.1    Bitcoin

Bitcoin is a decentralized digital currency built on cryptographic protocols and a system of *proof of work*. Instead of relying on traditional, centralized financial institutions to administer transactions as well as other aspects concerning the economic valuation of the currency, peers within the Bitcoin network process transactions and control the creation of bitcoins. The major problems to be solved by a distributed currency are related to how consensus can be reached in a group of anonymous participants, some of whom may be behaving with malicious intent.

Transactions within the Bitcoin network are based on public key cryptography, users of Bitcoin generate an *address* which is used to receive funds. The Bitcoin address is derived, through cryptographic hash functions, from the public-key of an ECDSA key pair. A Bitcoin transaction records the transfer of bitcoins from some input address to output addresses. A transaction consists of one or more inputs and one or more outputs, each input to a transaction is the output of a previous transaction. The output of a transaction may only be used as the input to a single transaction. The outputs are associated with an address, whose private key is then used to sign transactions spending these outputs.

Transactions are generated by the sender and distributed amongst the peers in the Bitcoin network. Transactions are only valid once they have been accepted into the public history of transactions, the *blockchain*. As the blockchain contains Bitcoin's entire transaction history and is publicly distributed, any user can determine the bitcoin balance of every address at any time, by summing the value of unspent transaction outputs (UTXOs) associated with the address.

**Bitcoin Exchanges.** Bitcoin exchanges facilitate trade between fiat currency and bitcoins. In order to trade on the exchange, users create an account with the exchange and transfer fiat currency and/or bitcoins to the exchange. Should the user wish to retrieve their bitcoins, they must make a request that the exchange transfers the bitcoins to an address which the user controls. The exchange manages a balance of the bitcoins that the user has deposited with the exchange or traded for against fiat currency.

The user may place buy and sell orders for bitcoins or fiat currency which are executed for the user by the exchange, adjusting the balances of the user's Bitcoin or fiat currency accounts. The orders are executed internally within the exchange, that is they are not recorded in the blockchain. Given this model of operation, a Bitcoin exchange is not merely a marketplace but also acts as a fiduciary, administrating both fiat currency and bitcoin accounts for its clients.

## 2.2  Trusted Computing

When a third party, such as a Bitcoin exchange, is tasked with performing a computation, there is no method for the verification of the integrity of the result, short of performing the computation locally, which in some circumstances may not be feasible. Trusted Computing allows the creation of a *trusted platform* which provides the following features [18]:

**Protected Capabilities** are commands which may access *shielded locations*, areas in memory or registers which are only accessible to the trusted platform. These memory areas may contain sensitive data such as private keys or a digest of some aspect of the current system state.

**Integrity Measurement** is the process of *measuring* the software which is executing on the current platform. A measurement is the cryptographic hash of the software which is executing throughout each stage of execution.

**Integrity Reporting** is the process of delivering a platform measurement to a third party such that it can be verified to have originated from a trusted platform.

These features of the trusted platform are deployed on consumer hardware in a unit called the Trusted Platform Module (TPM), a secure cryptographic co-processor, which is usually incorporated on the mainboard of the hardware.

An important component in proving trust are the Platform Configuration Registers (PCRs), 20-byte registers which are only modifiable through the *extend* operation based on cryptographic hash digests. The properties of a cryptographic hash ensure that the value held in a PCR cannot be deliberately set.

Initially the TPM is equipped with a Storage Root Key (SRK) which may be used to sign and thus authenticate further keys which may be generated or loaded into the TPM. A number of different types of cryptographic keys may be present on the TPM, however we limit our description to Attestation Identity Keys (AIK). AIKs are signing keys that reside solely on the TPM, which are used to sign data, which originates from the TPM, in order to attest to the values originating from the TPM. In order to verify a TPM attestation, the verifying party requires the signed attestation, the AIK public key, and a valid SRK signature authenticating the AIK.

The TPM can be used to *seal* data which encrypts the data with a key which is loaded in the TPM and binds the data to the state of some of the PCRs. The encrypted data may only be decrypted or *unsealed* if PCRs are in the same state as when the data was sealed, thus binding the ability to decrypt to the measured state. TPMs provide two distinct paradigms:

**SRTM** (Static Root of Trust for Measurement): the system begins to boot in a piece of firmware which is trusted (the static root) and each component of the boot process is measured and verified against a known-good configuration before it is executed in order to assert that no component has been tampered with.

**DRTM** (Dynamic Root of Trust for Measurement): allows for a trusted platform to be established dynamically without requiring a system reboot. It even allows for a trusted platform to be established within a platform which is known to be compromised with malicious software.

DRTM is implemented in consumer general purpose processors from Intel and AMD under the names Intel Trusted eXecution Technology (TXT) and AMD Secure Virtual Machine (SVM). Intel TXT and AMD SVM provide additional security features when executing in the secure mode on top of the capabilities of the TPM. These include turning off system interrupts to prevent other execution paths, as well as memory protection for specific memory ranges which also prevents DMA access [9].

## 3    Auditing

The audit should determine the solvency of the exchange. In principle this is a binary result, either *solvent* in the case that the exchange's assets in bitcoins cover its liabilities in bitcoins, or *insolvent* otherwise. It is plausible that there are situations in which this binary result does not suffice, for instance an exchange which wishes to prove fractional reserves. In these cases a multiplicative factor can be applied to the liabilities of the exchange to show that the exchange can cover some percentage of its liabilities with its assets.

The auditing process can be broken into three individual steps: summing the user account balances (proof of liabilities), summing the assets, i.e., address balances, the exchange controls (proof of reserves), and proof that the reserves cover the liabilities (proof of solvency). Figure 1 illustrates the components of the audit, the inputs to each of the components of the calculation and the outputs of the audit.

The publicly available inputs are the address balance and the fraction factor, which determines the percentage of coverage that the exchange wishes to prove. The address balances can be computed by a third party by replaying transactions in the blockchain until the time of the audit. The non-public inputs consist of

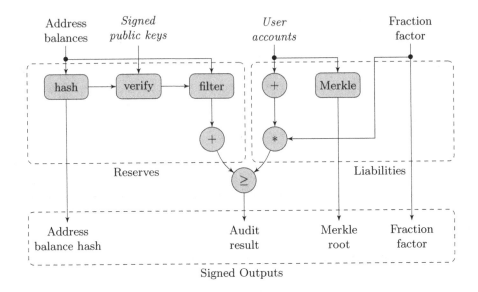

**Fig. 1.** An overview of the audit process. Italicised values are not published.

a list of signed public keys owned by the exchange and the list of user account information, including account balances and customer identifiers.

Unlike the inputs, the outputs of the auditing process should all be disclosed publicly. The address balance hash proves that the latest snapshot of the address balances was used in the audit and should match an independently computed hash. The audit result is the boolean result, either `true` if the exchanges assets are greater than the fraction of the liabilities or `false` otherwise. To prove that all liabilities have been considered a merkle tree is computed and its root is included in the outputs as well as the fraction which determines the coverage percentage. The output values are signed by the TPM, which also signs a hash digest of the binary which was executing at the time.

### 3.1   Proof of Reserves

The assets that the exchange possesses are in the form of bitcoins in the block-chain. The sum of assets is therefore calculated by determining which balances in the blockchain the exchange has access to and calculating the sum of those balances. In order for the exchange to access the bitcoins it needs to be in possession of the private keys belonging to the addresses.

To simplify the calculation, the audit program does not need to parse the entire blockchain to determine which balances should be summed. Instead, a preprocessor can be used to compute the address balances from the blockchain. This is secure as it is a deterministic aggregation over publicly available data.

The exchange can prove control of a Bitcoin address by providing the public key belonging to that Bitcoin address and signing it with the private key. For additional safety, the exchange should also sign a value which can be used to prove the freshness of the signature, a nonce. The hash of the last block added to the blockchain is an ideal candidate for the nonce, as it uniquely identifies the state of the blockchain and thus the address balances, it is not predictable and changes frequently. Thus, the second input to the audit process consists of a list of tuples of a public keys, and a signatures of the public key and the nonce:

$$\langle \text{PubKey}, \{\text{PubKey}, \text{Nonce}\}_\sigma \rangle$$

where $\{\text{data}\}_\sigma$ indicates that *data* is signed with the corresponding private key.

The overview of the steps of the calculation of reserves is shown in Fig. 1, internally it consists of four different stages. The first stage computes the hash of the address balances, which is required in the *verify* stage. The verify stage asserts that the signatures for the public keys are valid and that the provided nonce matches the hash of the provided address balances. It then passes the public keys to the *filter* stage, determines the Bitcoin address and filters for entries in the address balances which match the exchange's addresses. Finally, the balances of these entries are summed. The sum, as well as the hash of the address balances are produced as outputs of the proof of reserves.

## 3.2   Proof of Liabilities

The liabilities of the exchange are the balances in bitcoins owed to its customers. The audit process requires a list of tuples consisting of a customer identifier and a positive balance owed to the customer:

$$\langle \text{CustID}, \text{Balance} \rangle$$

An additional input to the proof of liabilities is the *fraction factor*, which is multiplied with the sum of client account balances to prove fractional reserves.

Using the above definition of liabilities, the total liabilities of the exchange are calculated as the sum of all customer account balances. The calculated sum is later compared against the sum of reserves to determine solvency. Additionally to the sum, the proof of liabilities component calculates the root of a merkle tree [13], as well as a hash of the fraction factor.

The basic schema is to construct a merkle tree with the user account information. That is, in order to compute a leaf in the tree one would take the cryptographic hash of the customer identifier and the balance owed to the customer. The leaves are then combined in a pairwise fashion and hashed, forming the nodes in the next layer of the tree. Nodes are combined and hashed until the root of the tree is constructed.

As the root of the merkle tree is dependent on all of the individual values within the tree, it serves as public record of the account balances which were counted in the summation of all account balances, without revealing individual customers account balances.

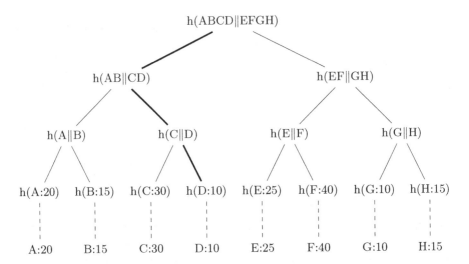

**Fig. 2.** An example merkle tree with the path from h(D:10) to the root highlighted

### 3.3    Proof of Solvency and Verification

The proof of the solvency of a bitcoin exchange consists of two components, one is the outputs of the audit, the other is an attestation which can be used to verify that the auditing software was executed in the trusted environment, and that it computed the outputs which are attested. The final output is the *Audit result*, which is a binary value, *true* if the reserves are greater than or equal to the liabilities, and *false* otherwise. The attestation is a signature for the outputs as well as the platform measurements, i.e., the hashes of the executed program.

Given the audit program, its public inputs and outputs and the attestation, a customer can independently verify the validity of the audit. By hashing the program and validating it against the attested measurements she can ensure that the TPM has executed the program. The validity of the program could be proven by publishing its source code. The customer can then proceed to validating the outputs, by checking the signatures, that the address balance hash matches the blockchain and that she is included in the merkle tree.

The customer can use the root of the merkle tree to verify that its account balance was included in the calculation. The merkle tree in Fig. 2 shows a potential scenario in which customer D wishes to determine whether it was accounted for in the hash h(ABCD‖EFGH). The nodes which D requires are the children of the nodes along the path from D's leaf node to the root excluding the nodes along that path. These are the nodes h(C:30), $h(A \| B)$, h(EF‖GH). With these node values, D can reconstruct the path from its leaf node to the root, calculating the same value of h(ABCD‖EFGH) that was provided by the exchange.

## 4    Implementation

The proof-of-concept presented in this work is built on the Flicker platform [12]. Flicker is a software platform which leverages DRTM to allow security sensitive components of software applications to execute in a secure, isolated environment. The developers of Flicker call such a component a Piece of Application Logic (PAL). The PAL comprises only the routines required to perform some security critical computation component of the application. Flicker consists of two components, the kernel module which prepares and launches the DRTM process, and the Secure Loader Block (SLB) core which performs bootstrapping of the secure execution environment for the PAL.

The execution scenario in which the PAL runs is made up of four distinct components: the user application, the Flicker kernel module, an Authenticated Code Module (ACM), and one or more PAL binaries, each consisting of the SLB core and PAL. The ACM is the root of dynamic trust for the DRTM in Intel TXT and is digitally signed by the chipset vendor. It functions as a secure bootloader for a lightweight piece of code which is to be executed on the processor in complete isolation from any other software or hardware access.

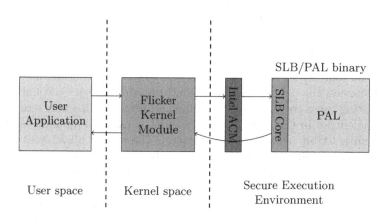

**Fig. 3.** Flicker PAL execution scenario.

The user application is a conventional application executing in userspace. The Flicker kernel module provides `data` and `control` file system entries with which the user application may interact in order to provide the Flicker kernel module with the SLB, PAL, and the inputs, as well as to read the outputs when execution of the PAL terminates.

Figure 3 illustrates the control flow when the user application needs to perform a security-critical task. First the application passes the PAL binary and inputs to the Flicker kernel module and instructs the kernel module to execute the PAL. The Flicker kernel module prepares the necessary data structures and memory protection to launch the DRTM and start the PAL, it then invokes the GETSEC[SENTER] CPU instruction which disables interrupts and triggers the start of the DRTM. These data structures are measured by the Intel ACM, which forms the root of the DRTM. The ACM hands control over to the Flicker SLB core which invokes the PAL and contains the necessary data structures to return the control flow directly to the Flicker kernel module when the PAL has finished executing.

During the execution of the SENTER operation, the dynamic TPM PCRs (17–23) are initialised to zero. PCR 17 is then extended with the hashes of the ACM and a number of configuration parameters. During the execution, PCR 18 is extended with the hash of the PAL. These PCR values are provided in the TPM's attestation, which can be used to prove to a third party that the PAL binary was executed and calculated the output values.

The Flicker platform was designed with lightweight, short-lived computations in mind, as such it imposes a number of restrictions which make a direct implementation of the audit as outlined in Sect. 3 unfeasible. The major restriction which poses problems for the automated software audit is memory. The Flicker environment has a stack size of 4KB, a heap size of 128KB, and a maximum input size of approximately 116KB. In addition each Flicker session has a significant overhead, between 0.2 and 1 second, depending on which TPM functionality is used during the invocation [12].

### 4.1   Architecture

Three of the four inputs to the audit process may be of considerable size: the address balances, the public keys and signatures, and the user accounts. At the time of writing there are a total of 3.7 million addresses with a non-zero balance. Each of the entries in the address balance input consists of an address of up to 35 byte and a 64 bit integer for the balance. The size of all address balances therefore is just under 160 MB. The size of the user accounts depends on the number of user accounts of the exchange. Generating a unique identifier from the account information by hashing results in a 32 byte identifier. Each account therefore has a 32 byte identifier with a 64 bit integer for the balance. Estimating the user base of the exchange at 1 million users this results in a total size for the user account input of 40 MB. While the number of addresses owned by the exchange is under control of the exchange, the prototype should support any number of addresses.

It is clear from the memory requirements posed by the input data and the available input sizes of the Flicker platform that the monolithic architecture of the audit as proposed in Fig. 1 must be broken into smaller components. The input data is split into input-sized chunks and processed in an incremental fashion. This does not change the result of the audit, however the calculation of the outputs which are required to verify the input data must change as a result of the components only having a view of a small subset of the input data in each iteration. The individual invocations of a component of the audit require a secure method of storing intermediate values, for instance a sum which is calculated over multiple iterations. The PAL can use the TPM to seal intermediate values

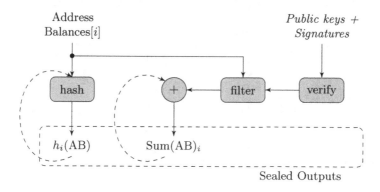

**Fig. 4.** An overview of the proof of reserves component. Italicised values are not published publicly. Dashed arrows indicate values which are passed from invocation to invocation

to the current PCR state, encrypting them such that they can only be decrypted by the TPM when it is executing the same PAL. The encrypted data is passed back to the user application which should provide it as an input to the next iteration of the component.

The process is driven by a user application, external to the trusted platform, which repeatedly invokes the computation in the trusted platform. As the encrypted data is passed back to the user application, which is executing in an untrusted and potentially malicious environment, there is the potential for a replay attack to be performed. However, the process of hashing the input ensures that replay attacks can be detected by the client when verifying the result of the audit.

We consider each component of the system individually and describe how it is implemented in order to support incremental invocations.

*Proof of Reserves.* The Proof of Reserves can be split into iterative invocations by splitting the address balance list, and the list of signatures and public keys into equal sized batches. Initially the address balance list is sorted lexicographically, in order to allow a verifier to compute the same hash. Each batch contains a list of address balances and a possibly empty set of signatures and public keys matching the address balances of the batch. This allows the system to verify the signatures and sum up the respective values. The hash of the address balances is computed by concatenating the hash from the previous round with the current hash and hashing the result: $h_0 = h(AB_0)$ and $h_i = h(h_{i-1} \| AB_i)$. The output includes the last considered address from the current batch. Due to the lexicographic ordering of addresses it is trivial for the proof of reserves to detect a replay attack, since it would require a lexicographically lower first address than the last address from the previous batch. Figure 4 shows an overview of the new POR component.

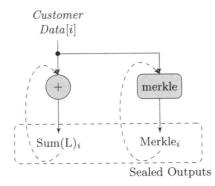

*Customer
Data[i]*

Sum(L)$_i$         Merkle$_i$

Sealed Outputs

**Fig. 5.** An overview of the proof of liabilities component. Italicised values are not published publicly. Dashed arrows indicate values which are passed from invocation to invocation

*Proof of Liabilities.* The Proof of Liabilities (POL) is invoked iteratively, similarly to the Proof of Reserves. Figure 5 shows an overview of the POL component. The merkle tree computation accepts a list of tuples consisting of merkle subtree root hashes, the root's height and the associated sum of the tree's value. It then iteratively computes the roots of the trees by combining the subtrees, summing the values and increasing the height. The resulting merkle root, height and value sum is then sealed for the next iteration or to be passed to the proof of solvency. In order to initiate the process, the proof of liabilities also accepts subtrees that are not sealed for height 0, i.e., the hashes of the account identifier and the account's value. Missing branches in the merkle tree are replaced with a single leaf with value 0.

Given that the merkle tree computation does not allow negative value sums for subtrees guarantees that, if an account was included in the computation, its value is included in the sum. A replay attack in this case does not benefit the exchange as it may only increase the sum that is to be covered.

*Proof of Solvency.* The Proof of Solvency (POS) component takes as inputs the sealed outputs from the Proof of Reserves (POR) and Proof of Liabilities (POS) components as well as the Fraction factor. As it handles only constant size inputs it is sufficient to call the proof of solvability once. Its main purpose is to compute the fraction that is to be covered and whether or not the assets are sufficient to cover the liabilities. A secondary purpose is to unseal the results from the other components and sign in order to publish them (Fig. 6).

The final step of the POS component is the attestation of the PAL binary. The audit no longer consists of an individual invocation of a PAL, instead the POR and POL components are invoked hundreds or thousands of times each of these invocations requires attestation. The solution to this problem is to put the separate logic for the POR, POL and POS components into a single binary. The initial invocations of both the POR and POL logic of the PAL produce a

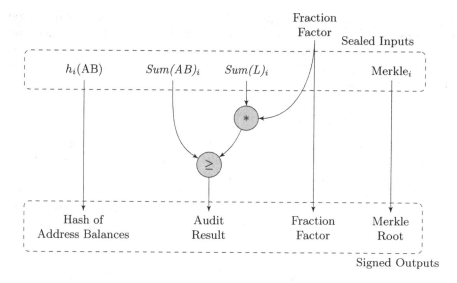

**Fig. 6.** An overview of the proof of solvency component.

sealed intermediate values which are tied to that PAL. The sealed blob is then unsealed by the next invocation, the intermediate values are modified and then resealed. When the POS is invoked, it unseals the intermediate results produced by the POR and POL.

The fact that the sealed blobs are unsealed and modified in each invocation of the POR and POL and that they can only be unsealed by the same PAL that initially created them means that the values in the sealed blob form a chain of trust from their respective first invocations until the invocation of the POS. An attestation of the POS is transitive to all previous PAL executions which were able to unseal the blobs that the POS unseals.

## 4.2  Execution Time

As previously mentioned, the Flicker invocation and some TPM operations pose a significant overhead of up to 1 s, when repeatedly entering and leaving the PAL. During the execution time of the PAL, the operating system on which the Flicker session is invoked does not process any interrupts. When the Flicker session ends, the operating system requires a small amount of time to process any interrupts and respond to system events. Tests showed that the operating system needs pauses of 500 ms to 1 s in order to continue processing without locking up or crashing. As the processing time for such a small number of inputs is quite low in comparison to the TPM overhead, we can safely assume that each Flicker invocation costs approximately two seconds.

For input sizes in the range previously discussed, 3.7 million address balances and 1 million customer accounts, the POR must be invoked approximately 1300 times if each invocation of the POR can process 3000 address balances, the

POL must be invoked approximately 500 times. This comes to a total of 1800 invocations, each of which requires 2 s to execute and wait for the operating system to recover. The overall execution time for an audit with inputs of this size is approximately one hour and scales linearly in the number of address balances and user accounts.

### 4.3   Additional Interfaces

Although the audit is the core component of proving solvency of a Bitcoin exchange, the signed audit output is not all that a customer requires in order to verify the audit. Customers must retrieve additional values from the exchange and perform some local computations in order to be able to verify the audit, and to have some form of recourse should the verification fail. The implementation of these interfaces is not in the scope of this work, what follows is an outline of the requirements of the peripheral software and interfaces.

**Audit Verification.** Most important for customers is the ability to verify the audit's result. This consists of the verification that the customer's balance was included in the calculation, verification of the address balances, and verification of the attestation. The customer of an exchange must be able to retrieve the nodes in the merkle tree which can be used to calculate the path from the customer's leaf node to the root of the merkle tree. If the customer is able to reproduce the merkle root using the nodes provided by the exchange and their own customer identifier and account balance at the time of the audit, then they can be assured that they were accounted for in the calculation. The interface for this purpose must take the hash of the tuple

$$\langle \text{Customer Identifier}, \text{Balance} \rangle$$

as an argument and deliver the set of nodes required to calculate the path from the customer's leaf node to the merkle root. Each node would consist of a tuple

$$\langle \text{Height}, \text{Hash} \rangle$$

where *Height* is the height of the node in the merkle tree and *Hash* is the hash digest stored at that node in the tree. The customer must also be able to verify that the hash of the address balances provided by the exchange represents the true account balances for a set blockchain height. For this purpose, the customer must be able to determine the blockchain height that was used to determine the address balances. The customer would require a software client which can determine the address balances for the blockchain at a given height. This consists of: extraction and aggregation of UTXOs, and sorting of the address balances. With the address balances calculated, the customer can calculate the hash and compare it with the hash provided by the audit. Finally, the customer must be able to verify the attestation. This consists of two components: verification that the attestation originates from a TPM, and verification of the binary which was executed in the trusted platform.

**Attestation Verification.** The customer needs to be able to verify that the attestation was indeed issued by a TPM, in other words, what the customer needs to know is that the Attestation Identity Key (AIK) used to sign the attestion was provided by a TPM. The method proposed by the TCG is Direct Anonymous Attestation (DAA) which allows for a customer to verify directly that an AIK belongs to a TPM. For this the exchange must provide an interface which performs DAA and the customer requires client software which can verify the DAA provided by the exchange.

**Binary Verication.** In order for the customer to verify that the PAL executed in the trusted environment actually calculates the audit, as opposed to always returning true, the customer must have access to the source code of the PAL and be able to reproduce the value of PCR 17 which is signed in the TPM's attestation. The exchange needs to provide a platform from which the PAL source code can be retrieved, as well as a method for compiling a reproducible binary, and instructions on how to transform the hash of the binary to the value of PCR 17 in the attestation.

**Signed Account Balance.** If a customer should determine that their account balance was not included in an audit, they require some form of proof that their account balances ought to have been taken into account in the audit. For this purpose the exchange should provide an interface which allows a customer to retrieve a signature of the hash of their $\langle$CustomrID, balance$\rangle$ tuple. With this signature, other customers or the community at large could verify that the exchange signed a value which is not included in the latest audit.

## 5    Conclusion

A string of Bitcoin exchange closures as well as various thefts from Bitcoin exchanges have left customers of exchange services somewhat hesitant as there has often been little transparency when such events took place. Exchanges have published customer account balances as well as proof of ownership of Bitcoin addressed which allow for customers and the public to determine the Bitcoin assets of the exchange.

In this work we propose using an automated software-based audit to determine the solvency of Bitcoin exchanges without revealing any private data. Methods are proposed, based on the Flicker Trusted Computing platform, with which the audit result can be verified and trusted to be correct. An architecture is proposed which allows for the computation to be split into individual pieces which iteratively compute a subset of the complete input to overcome the memory limitations posed by the Flicker platform. The verification methodology is expanded to cover the iterative execution scenario, allowing for customers of an exchange to verify the inputs to the audit. An analysis of the execution time showed that it is entirely feasible to conduct audits on a daily basis at the current estimate size of the Bitcoin ecosystem.

# References

1. Bitcoin virtual currency: Unique features present distinct challenges for deterring illicit activity. Technical report, Federal Bureau of Investigation (2012)
2. Application of fincen's regulations to persons administering: exchanging, or using virtual currencies. Technical report, Financial Crimes Enforcement Network, US Department of the Treasury (2013)
3. Andresen, G.: Bitcoin improvement proposal 11: M-of-N standard transactions (2011). https://github.com/bitcoin/bips/blob/master/bip-0011.mediawiki. Accessed February 2015
4. Araoz, M., Charles, R.X., Garcia, M.A.: Bip 45: Structure for deterministic P2SH multisignature wallets (2014). https://github.com/bitcoin/bips/blob/master/bip-0045.mediawiki. Accessed February 2015
5. Brito, J., Castillo, A.: Bitcoin: A Primer for Policymakers. Mercatus Center at George Mason University, Arlington (2013)
6. Bryans, D.: Bitcoin and money laundering: mining for an effective solution. Indiana Law J. **89**, 441–472 (2014)
7. Decker, C., Wattenhofer, R.: Bitcoin transaction malleability and MtGox. In: 19th European Symposium on Research in Computer Security (ESORICS), Wroclaw, Poland, September 2014
8. Finney, H.: bcflick - using TPM's and trusted computing to strengthen bitcoin wallets (2013). https://bitcointalk.org/index.php?topic=154290.msg1635481. Accessed February 2015
9. Intel Corporation: Intel Trusted Execution Technology Software Developers Guide, May 2014
10. Maxwell, G., Todd, P.: Fraud proof (2013). https://people.xiph.org/greg/bitcoin-wizards-fraud-proof.log.txt. Accessed March 2015
11. Maxwell, G., Wilcox, Z.: Proving your bitcoin reserves, February 2014. https://iwilcox.me.uk/2014/proving-bitcoin-reserves. Accessed 5th January 2015
12. McCune, J.M., Parno, B.J., Perrig, A., Reiter, M.K., Isozaki, H.: Flicker: An execution infrastructure for TCB minimization. In: ACM SIGOPS Operating Systems Review
13. Merkle, R.C.: A digital signature based on a conventional encryption function. In: Pomerance, C. (ed.) CRYPTO 1987. LNCS, vol. 293, pp. 369–378. Springer, Heidelberg (1988)
14. Moore, T., Christin, N.: Beware the middleman: empirical analysis of bitcoin-exchange risk. In: Sadeghi, A.-R. (ed.) FC 2013. LNCS, vol. 7859, pp. 25–33. Springer, Heidelberg (2013)
15. Nakamoto, S.: Bitcoin: A peer-to-peer electronic cash system (2008). https://bitcoin.org/bitcoin.pdf. Accessed February 2015
16. New York State Department of Financial Services: Virtual Currencies (2015). http://www.dfs.ny.gov/legal/regulations/revised_vc_regulation.pdf. Accessed February 2015
17. Todd, P.: BIP 65: OP_CHECKLOCKTIMEVERIFY (2014). https://github.com/bitcoin/bips. Accessed March 2014
18. Trusted Computing Group: TCG Specification Architecture Overview, rev. 1.4, August 2007

# Web-to-Application Injection Attacks on Android: Characterization and Detection

Behnaz Hassanshahi[(⊠)], Yaoqi Jia, Roland H.C. Yap, Prateek Saxena, and Zhenkai Liang

School of Computing, National University of Singapore, Singapore, Singapore
{behnaz,jiayaoqi,ryap,prateeks,liangzk}@comp.nus.edu.sg

**Abstract.** Vulnerable Android applications (or apps) are traditionally exploited via malicious apps. In this paper, we study an underexplored class of Android attacks which do not require the user to install malicious apps, but merely to visit a malicious website in an Android browser. We call them web-to-app injection (or W2AI) attacks, and distinguish between different categories of W2AI side-effects. To estimate their prevalence, we present an automated W2AIScanner to find and confirm W2AI vulnerabilities. We analyze real apps from the official Google Play store and found 286 confirmed vulnerabilities in 134 distinct applications. This findings suggest that these attacks are pervasive and developers do not adequately protect apps against them. Our tool employs a novel combination of static analysis, symbolic execution and dynamic testing. We show experimentally that this design significantly enhances the detection accuracy compared with an existing state-of-the-art analysis.

## 1 Introduction

In this paper, we present a detailed study of an underexplored class of application vulnerabilities on Android that allow a malicious web attacker to exploit app vulnerabilities. It can be a significant threat as the remote attacker has full control on the web-to-app communication channel and no malicious apps are needed on the device. A successful attack can exploit web APIs (WebView) and native APIs on Android.

The Android platform provides a *web-to-app communication bridge* which enables web-to-app interaction. The web-to-app bridge is used in Android to facilitate installed applications to be invoked directly via websites. This feature has many benign uses. It is used by many popular applications on the official Google App Store, e.g., the Google Maps app can seamlessly switch to the Phone app when phone numbers of businesses displayed on Google Maps are clicked, without explicitly starting the Phone app.

The web-to-app bridge exposes Android apps to unvetted websites when the user visits them in a browser. Without proper sanitization on the URI or "extra parameters" derived from the URI, a vulnerable app ends up using these values

This work has been supported in part by Huawei.

G. Pernul et al. (Eds.): ESORICS 2015, Part II, LNCS 9327, pp. 577–598, 2015.
DOI: 10.1007/978-3-319-24177-7_29

to start a malicious web page in a WebView or abuse Android native APIs. While it is known that the web-to-app bridge can lead to vulnerabilities [34], in this work, we study whether existing apps are susceptible to attacks from this channel in any significant way, and if so, to what extent. We systematically study and classify attacks which we call *Web-to-App Injection (W2AI)*. Web-to-App Injection attacks are different from other recently disclosed vulnerabilities. Such vulnerabilities arise either in the implementations of hybrid mobile application frameworks, or in application code written on top of such frameworks which access external device interfaces (e.g. camera) [9,14,17,26]. In contrast, attacks studied in this paper affect Android applications via the web-to-app bridge. Furthermore, W2AI attacks can be easily combined with existing app-to-app attacks.

**W2AIScanner.** To enable detection for W2AI on a large scale, we describe a tool that analyzes Android apps for W2AI vulnerabilities. Existing static analysis techniques alone are insufficient for conducting such analysis as the complexity and size of applications limits the precision of static analysis. Dynamic analysis, such as random testing and unguided symbolic execution, face the complementary problem of path space explosion, leading to expensive analysis. In this work, we employ a refinement-based static analysis combined with dynamic testing to overcome the challenges of these individual techniques. W2AIScanner can automatically analyze APK files and produce working (0-day) exploits. Thus, it shows a significant enhancement of the accuracy over the results generated by a purely static state-of-the-art analysis. It constructs a witness exploit, a URI, to be subsequently used by security analysts (or app store) to construct specific attack payloads for determining the severity of discovered vulnerabilities.

**Results.** First, to measure the prevalence of W2AI vulnerabilities, we present the first comprehensive study of web-to-app injection (W2AI) attacks in Android. We analyzed 12,240 applications from the official Google App Store where 1,729 of them expose browsable activities. Our tool, found 134 apps (7.75% of 1,729 apps) to have W2AI vulnerabilities by automatically constructing 286 attacks. Our results suggest that developers often neglect the risk posed by web-to-app vulnerabilities to Android users, taking insufficient countermeasures. We contacted the Android security team to disclose the vulnerabilities to the vulnerable apps. The Tencent security team has confirmed our reported vulnerabilities in the Tencent Android SDK (2.8) [3].

Second, we find that W2AI attacks introduce a broad range of possible exploits in installed Android applications which are analogous to vulnerabilities commonly known to occur in web applications — such as open redirect, database pollution, file inclusion, credential theft, and so on. Further, these vulnerabilities are not specific to implementations of certain application frameworks (or SDKs), as they can arise in application written in different SDKs. Third, we demonstrate that our analysis technique provides significantly higher precision than state-of-the-art static analysis techniques, at an acceptable analysis cost.

## 2   Overview

In Android, intents are the primary ways for an Android app to share data with other apps and to access system services [1]. An intent object carries information that Android uses to determine the component to start execution, plus information that the recipient component uses to properly perform the action. For example, the email app can be invoked to send an email via an intent by any other app.

A web page can invoke a component in an installed app if the target app declares one or more of its activities as being BROWSABLE in the app's manifest. When a user clicks a web hyperlink, in a certain format, Android translates it into an intent (object). We use *intent hyperlink* to refer to the hyperlink or its string and use *URI intent* to refer to the workings of the intent mechanism in Android. Intent hyperlinks carry parameters within the hyperlink – the fragment identifier, and information about the target activity specified as a tuple (*scheme, host, path*), etc.

### 2.1   Web-to-App Injection Attacks

URI intents expose a new channel of attacks targeting installed apps.

**Threat Model.** In a W2AI attack, we assume that the adversary is a standard web attacker [4], who controls a malicious website. To expand the coverage of victims, the attacker can disseminate the shortened URL of the malicious site through emails, social networks, ads, etc. We make the following conservative assumptions. We assume that the victim, Alice, only installs legitimate apps from Google Play on her Android device. We also assume that at least one app with adequate permissions on her device is benign but buggy, hence a W2AI vulnerability exists.

**W2AI Attacks.** Analogous to a conventional web attack, when Alice directly visits the malicious website or clicks a link redirected to the site, a W2AI attack occurs. A generic scenario for W2AI follows: (1) The attacker crafts and publishes a malicious intent hyperlink in a social network; (2) A user clicks the malicious link redirecting to the attacker's site in her mobile browser; (3) The site loads the malicious intent hyperlink in an iframe or a new tab; (4) The browser parses the hyperlink, generates the URI intent and launches the corresponding activity in the vulnerable app; and (5) Hence, the payloads derived from the URI intent running in the app can access the user's private information or perform privileged operations on behalf of the app.

W2AI vulnerabilities arise due to dataflows in the native Android code, rather than in application logic written in HTML5 code [9,14,17,26]. Unlike other vulnerabilities that exploit app-to-app communication interfaces [8,24,40,42], we emphasize that W2AI attacks do not need an installed malicious app on the device to launch attacks.

## 2.2   Categories of W2AI Vulnerabilities

Android applications typically use data derived from the intent hyperlink with Android API interfaces which can be divided into two categories, WebView and native interfaces. If the attacker-controlled data are used in these interfaces without any validation, the attacker can feed payloads to abuse them. We divide the W2AI vulnerabilities into: (i) abusing WebView; and (ii) abusing Android native app interfaces.

**Abusing WebView Interfaces.** WebView is a browser component provided by Android, which provides the basic functionalities of normal browsers (e.g., page rendering and JavaScript execution) and enables access to various interfaces (e.g., HTML5 APIs and JavaScript-to-native bridge). Certain applications take parameters in the intent hyperlink and treat them as web URLs, thereby loading them into WebView during execution. When this happens, the attacker's HTML code runs in the WebView. Furthermore, if the vulnerable application enables execution for JavaScript in the WebView, the attacker can run JavaScript in its HTML page, and can access all interfaces exposed to it by WebView. We further classify the vulnerabilities arising from unfettered access to the exposed interfaces into 4 sub-categories:

*(1) Abusing the JavaScript-to-Native Bridge.* JavaScript code loaded in the WebView can access native methods via the `android.webkit.JavascriptInterface`. The accessible native methods are specific to each application. In our experiments, we have found up to 29 distinct JavaScript-to-native interfaces accessible by a single app, e.g., many apps enable access to interfaces that retrieve the device's UUID, version and name, thereby opening up the threat of privacy-violating attacks. Furthermore, several interfaces allow reading and modifying the user's contact list and app-specific local files.

*(2) Abusing HTML5 APIs.* WebView enables access to standard HTML5 APIs, akin to normal web browsers, e.g., if the vulnerable app has the proper permissions and WebView settings, the attack web page running in the WebView can use JavaScript to call the HTML5 geolocation API. We found 29 apps with such tracking vulnerabilities.

*(3) Local File Inclusion.* When the user visits the malicious site, the site can trick the browser to automatically download an HTML file into the user's SD card by setting the HTML file as not viewable. When the site triggers the browser to parse the intent hyperlink that refers to the downloaded HTML file, e.g., `file:///sdcard/Downloads/attack.html`, it launches the vulnerable app to load the HTML file in its WebView. If the vulnerable app has certain WebView settings, the malicious JavaScript code in the HTML file can read any files under the app's directory or the readable system files (e.g., `/etc/hosts`) and send them to the attacker.

*(4) Phishing.* The attacker's web page can impersonate or phish the user interface of the original application. Since there is no address bar displayed by WebView that users can use to inspect the current page's URL, users cannot distinguish

the phishing page from the normal page. Such attacks via the web-to-app bridge are harder for users to discern than the conventional phishing attack on the web [12].

**Abusing Android Native App Interfaces.** Android Apps, even if WebView is not used, can expose native Android interfaces to URI intents if input is not properly sanitized. These lead to the further four categories of vulnerabilities:

*(1) App Database Pollution.* Android provides native interfaces for apps to execute SQL query statements to manage the app's database. Therefore, if the SQL queries are derived from the URI intent, it allows the web attacker to pollute (e.g., add or update the table's fields) the vulnerable app's database.

*(2) Persistent Storage Pollution.* Android native interfaces enable apps to store persistent states, e.g., authentication tokens, in the persistent storage (e.g., SharedPreferences and local files). Many vulnerable apps directly treat the parameters from the URI intent as the content to add or update the persistent storage. An attack URI intent can pollute the target app's persistent storage.

*(3) Open Re-delegation.* Android native interfaces provide the ability to launch specific activities addressed by name. If the name parameter is derived from URI intent, it allows the web attacker to invoke any in-app private activities directly, which are not required to be marked browsable. Moreover, the attacker might embed an additional intent hyperlink as a parameter to the original intent hyperlink and force the benign app to invoke another app. This leads to a broad range of problems such as permission redelegation [13]. Permission re-delegation is a confused deputy problem whereby a vulnerable app accesses critical resources under influence from an adversary. Though these attacks are previously known to be possible via the app-to-app [13], we show that they can be affected under influence of a website through the web-to-app bridge.

*(4) App-Specific Logic Flaws.* Android enables apps to perform various operations (e.g., popping up messages) via native interfaces. Due to the app-specific logic flaws, the vulnerable app directly uses the data from the URI intent as parameters to these operations. For example, we found that an attacker can exploit vulnerable apps to display a fabricated PayPal transaction status.

We use a real app as an example to explain how the W2AI attack works. The example app is WorkNet (3.1.0), a Korean information app with 1–5M downloads. It has a browsable activity, `kr.go.keis.worknet.WorknetActivity`, which loads arbitrary URLs in URI intents and is vulnerable to the following W2AI attacks: abusing JavaScript-to-native bridges, abusing HTML5 APIs, local file inclusion and phishing. The attack's life cycle is as follows: (1) The attacker hosts a malicious website, which loads an intent hyperlink (`"intent://#Intent;scheme=worknet;action=android.intent.action.VIEW;S.url=http://attacker.com;end;"`) into a new tab using `window.open`. The attacker posts the site's shortened link on social networks, e.g., Facebook. (2) When the user visits the attacker's site (by clicking the link on social networks, ads, and so on) in her Android browser, the site loads the hyperlink in a new tab. (3) The user's browser parses the hyperlink to the

URI intent which contains extra parameters and launches the `WorknetActivity` activity with the intent. (4) The activity loads the URL (http://attacker.com) derived from the malicious URI intent into the WebView without proper validation. Now the attacker's site is loaded with its JavaScript code running in the WebView. The attacker can utilize whatever is available to this activity, e.g., abusing JavaScript-to-native bridges.

We find that WorkNet has 21 such interfaces, e.g., accessing contacts, local files, device information, etc. Furthermore, being a WebView app, the attacker's site can mimic the UI of the original page. In the background, the scripts access the user's private data (e.g., device information and contacts), sending them to the attacker's server. In addition to abusing the JavaScript-to-native interfaces, the web attacker can also abuse HTML5 APIs to track Alice's geolocation and leak the content of local files via file inclusion in this app. From this example, we can see that the W2AI attacker can not only mount conventional web attacks (e.g., unvalidated redirect in the example), but can also hijack the vulnerable app to perform privileged operations on sensitive resources (e.g., local files and contacts) without any installation of malware in the user's device.

### 2.3  Detection Challenges

Our aim is to design a system that both *detects* and also *confirms* W2AI vulnerabilities. The target of W2AI attacks are *sinks* defined as sensitive/critical Android and Java APIs used to inject data which make the application vulnerable. The API calls which fetch intent objects containing data under the control of the attacker are called *sources*.

At the high level, detecting W2AI vulnerabilities can be considered a source to sink reachability analysis for Android apps. Existing analysis for Android apps [5,16,25]. employ static analysis techniques but this only gives potential reachability. Many of the potential source-sink flows detected may be false positives (i.e., potential vulnerability is signaled as a flow, even though it can never occur during execution) as we show in Sect. 4. We eliminate the false positives by generating intent hyperlinks which can be shown during execution to actually reach and affect a sink. In other words, we only report vulnerabilities when we can automatically generate a *0-day W2AI attack*. This makes the task of explaining and understanding a vulnerability significantly easier for security analysts or the app developers.

The complexity of the Android environment and apps also raises practical challenges. Figure 1 shows a simplification of the code of the WorkNet app, explained in Sect. 2.2, which has W2AI vulnerabilities. The browsable activity that is triggered by intent hyperlinks is `MainActivity`. When the user clicks on the malicious intent hyperlink in the default browser, the system generates an intent, launching `MainActivity`. Unlike Java programs, Android apps do not have a main method. When an intent invokes an activity, the Android runtime invokes the `onCreate()` or `onNewIntent()` callback methods. Next, the `getIntent()` and `onNewIntent()` methods obtain the intent messages. Once an intent is sent to an activity, any invocation of the `getIntent()` method throughout the activity

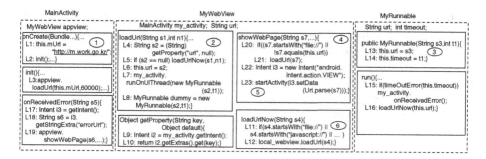

**Fig. 1.** An execution sequence which retrieves malicious parameters from an intent hyperlink. There are three classes separated by dashed lines: MainActivity, MyWebView and MyRunnable. MainActivity is the browsable activity, MyRunnable is an inner class of MainActivity implementing the Runnable interface. Methods are shown in boxes.

yields the same intent until setIntent(Intent) is called. Thus, the intent objects at lines L9 &L17 will refer to the same intent hyperlink.

We explain the possible execution paths in Fig. 1, where the browsable activity loads malicious parameters in a malicious intent hyperlink clicked by the user: (1) The MainActivity is launched and onCreate() is invoked storing the default URL in this.mUrl used by loadUrl() at L3. (2) However, the application does not load the default URL into the WebView immediately. Instead, getProperty() is called which invokes getIntent() at L9. This method looks for the "extra parameter" (i.e., the parameter returned by get[type]Extra() API with type string), having the key "url". If this parameter exists in the URI intent, runOnUiThread() at L7 is called which runs the MainActivity's UI thread. (3) Next, MyRunnable class is instantiated storing the malicious URL in this.url and run() method is invoked by the Android runtime. Line L15 in MyRunnable forks a thread (not shown) to check whether the network connection times out within timeout limit. In case of timeout, it calls onReceivedError() in the MainActivity which looks for another extra parameter with key "errorUrl" at line L18. (4) If the string conditions at line L20 are met, a string from the malicious URL is eventually loaded to the WebView (path 1 with sink 1, loadUrl(), at line L12). (5) Otherwise, the string will be incorporated into a new intent and attack suceeds to start another app (path 2 with sink 2, startActivity(), at line L23). (6) Alternatively, the malicious URL obtained at line L4 is loaded by the WebView (path 3 with sink 1, loadUrl() at line L12).

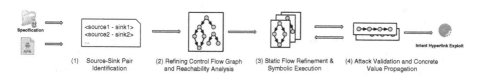

**Fig. 2.** Architecture of W2AIScanner

In this example, there are two vulnerable sinks at lines L12 and L23 with three paths to reach them. However, analyzing these vulnerabilities require dealing with challenges that are not currently dealt with satisfactorily in existing systems. The main reason is limitations in constructing the control flow graph (CFG) from the Dalvik code. We saw that paths one and two occur due to (nested) inner threads. The app also uses `runOnUiThread()` which changes execution to the main UI thread of the activity. Existing tools such as FlowDroid [5] do not report this path since the generated CFG lacks the edges necessary for the vulnerable paths. We remark that we have found 818 browsable apps using threads in our dataset. In this example, the `getIntent()` invocations happen to give the same intent message in all the code. The analysis needs to determine what intent `getIntent()` refers to. This example also shows that the analysis needs to be field-sensitive, since the malicious URL is stored in `this.url` field, and also object-sensitive to refer to the correct instance of `MyRunnable` class.

Our analysis not only aims for accuracy in finding the paths for the source-sink flow but also needs to generate instances of intent hyperlinks to confirm the vulnerability. We use symbolic reasoning on strings and other constraint solving in our analysis (lines L11, L20) to this end. In addition, the operations on intent parameters can be dependent on the intent filters in the app manifest. Hence, in addition to the bytecode analysis, intent filters from the app manifest need to be taken into account in the analysis.

# 3    Detecting and Confirming W2AI Vulnerabilities

We describe a tool, W2AIScanner, which can automatically detect and confirm W2AI vulnerabilities. In order to deal with the challenges described in Sect. 2.3, W2AIScanner works in four phases as shown in Fig. 2. We now describe each of these phases.

## 3.1    Source-Sink Pair Identification

Our design starts with a less precise analysis followed with an on-demand refinement of the analysis. The more efficient but less precise analysis identifies potentially vulnerable areas in the app that further benefit from a more precise and costly analysis which can reduce false alarms.

We start with a specification including a set of sources and sinks. The sources are the `getIntent()` and `onNewIntent()` methods that fetch the intent objects which start the activity and provide data inputs to the app. We choose a subset of the sinks provided by Susi [29] and also sinks relevant to the categories described in Sect. 2.2.

The initial CFG used by our analysis is the inter-procedural control flow graph in Soot [21] constructed based on the call graph created by SPARK [22]. In the first step, we generate pairs of source and sink program points for the given specification. We have two design choices: (i) locating all possible program points in the initial CFG by comparing the method signatures in the reachable methods;

and (ii) using an existing information flow analysis system like FlowDroid [5] to collect source-sink pairs with data dependency on inputs.[1]

We have observed that using FlowDroid, we need to perform the analysis for fewer source-sink pairs and remove some of the irrelevant pairs, thereby decreasing the analysis time. Hence, we use FlowDroid with a conservative setting. For instance, it is possible to choose the flow sensitivity of the backward alias search, we conservatively choose it to be flow-insensitive. Starting from the browsable activities,[2] FlowDroid finds pairs of source and sink program points using dataflow analysis. In the next step, we utilize these source-sink pairs for reachability testing and refining the initial CFG constructed by FlowDroid.

## 3.2   Refining the Control Flow Graph and Reachability Analysis

The less precise dataflow analysis in the previous step may introduce false alarms and the constructed CFG may also miss edges (informally, we call them as gaps). We compensate for this inaccuracy by a subsequent on-demand refinement and symbolic execution. We start with the initial CFG from the previous step. Given a source method, $S_c$, and a sink method $S_k$, W2AIScanner starts traversing and refining the CFG with $S_c$ being the starting node using depth-first search. We resolve virtual methods and interface calls using a backward variable type analysis, which considers assignments between callsites and class object instantiation program points. In our motivating example, a node for method `run()` in `MyRunnable` class is added because the CFG misses the edge from L7 to this method. In this example, the class implementation for the `Runnable` interface at L7 is resolved to `MyRunnable` class. Then, the `run()` method is loaded and its nodes are added to the CFG.

While refining the CFG, a reachability analysis is also performed to reduce the state explosion problems in the symbolic execution phase. When a branching node is visited, it examines whether $S_k$ is reachable from each of the branches and caches the reachability result. The CFG traversal stops in this step if $S_k$ is reached and continues for the next source-sink pair. If a new sink is detected, it will be added to the source-sink pairs to be examined later by the symbolic execution. In Sect. 4, we show that accurate thread handling helps in finding interesting vulnerabilities that are not detected by FlowDroid [5].

One problem is that $S_c$ can be invoked anywhere in the program. Therefore, the caller of the method where $S_c$ resides might not be known (e.g., line L9 in Fig. 1). Our analysis is conservative, thus, it returns to all possible callsites to continue the analysis. Note that a path may have more than one sink. In that case, the analysis continues until it reaches the other sinks.

In order to deal with backward edges caused by loops and recursive calls, a node in a specific calling context is visited within a bounded number of times.

---

[1]   FlowDroid [5] is a static state-of-art analyzer for Android built upon Soot [21] (based on the Interprocedural Finite Distributive Subset (IFDS) algorithm [30]) and incorporates the Android component lifecycle.

[2]   We have modified the entry point selection implementation to pick the browsable activities.

Later we unify all the reachability results for nodes visited in different calling contexts and use them in the symbolic execution. If a path does not include any backward edges but is too long, we enforce a depth limit for the depth first search.

### 3.3    Symbolic Execution and Static Flow Refinement

Static analysis is generally not sufficient to confirm vulnerabilities. However, confirmation with concrete execution needs concrete inputs in the form of an (attack) intent hyperlink. We employ symbolic execution [15,19] commonly used for automated test generation to help in generating the inputs. Our symbolic executor does not require any initial inputs and employs optimizations to reduce the number of paths that need to be explored using the sink reachability analysis conducted in the previous step. The final generated intent hyperlinks are produced by a combination of the symbolic execution and validation phases.

The initial dataflow analysis used for reachability analysis in the first step might produce a large number of flows, many of which may be false positives. Thus, a strategy is required to reduce the number of initial flows. W2AIScanner achieves an initial reduction by removing infeasible paths using symbolic execution. A path is feasible if there exists a program input for which the path is traversed during program execution, otherwise the path is infeasible [20]. So we immediately remove the infeasible paths.

The symbolic executor works on a worklist of statements. Our analysis picks a source-sink pair, $(S_c, S_k)$, starts from the source statement $S_c$ and symbolically executes the program until it reaches sink $S_k$. The reaching definition analysis starts simultaneously and the intent object returned by $S_c$ is marked as data dependent on input. From this point, any parameter extracted from the source intent object that has string, numeric, URI or boolean types is stored in a symbolic variable. A URI can be decomposed into many substrings. We model the URI class and convert it to string and integer compartments. We store symbolic variables in a symbolic variable pool which is updated when translating a definition statement. If a statement has a call invocation, we need to decide whether to enter the method or not. The symbolic execution enters a method if the sink reachability result shows that entering the method will lead to a program point where $S_k$ is invoked. If the method is available (i.e., it is not an external method) and the method callsite has a definition of a variable, the flow fact at the callsite is updated when the analysis returns from the method. Otherwise, the method call is considered dependent on inputs if any of its use variables (arguments or the instance variable) are dependent.

For IF statements, the sink reachability result is examined for each of the branches. If none of the branches are reachable to $S_k$, no new job will be added to the worklist and the next path will be traversed. If only one of the branches is reachable, that branch will be taken. Finally, if both branches are reachable to $S_k$, W2AIScanner will search for the immediate postdminator (ImPodm). Based on the CFG of a method, if W2AIScanner finds an ImPodm inside the method, a new pending merge state will be added to the merge stack.

An optimization arises during the analysis: if there is no ImPodm inside the method, we cannot merge the two branches which are reachable to the same sink $S_k$. If one of these branches does not contain input-dependent variables, forking it will produce spurious paths whose constraints will not be used for generating inputs. To avoid these paths, we introduce a dummy ImPodm: (1) We add a merge state to the merge stack when execution reaches an always feasible conditional statement and the mergepoint can be any of the exit statements of the method. An exit statement is a program point where execution exits a method; (2) When execution reaches any exit statement, it does not exit the method. Instead, if the method contains another distinct path, that path is added to the worklist; (3) Finally, when all paths inside the method are traversed and execution is exiting the method, the states at all of the exit statements which are data dependent on input and the constraints for class fields are merged and there will be only one merged state for all exit statements. In order to choose the program counter for this dummy ImPodm, we create a dummy exit statement. The data dependency results are also utilized to remove irrelevant constraints on the path formula if possible.

This step also involves a reaching definition analysis performed together with the symbolic execution. This analysis is field-sensitive and distinguishes objects originating at different allocation sites but reaching the same program point. We use symbolic values to point to a heap object. In an execution path, there may be variables whose values are used but not resolved, we employ an (on demand) backward copy constant search for more accuracy. The values are over-approximated in two ways: (i) The variable is a method parameter where we consider all possible callers of the method. Therefore, the result might be a set of possible values which will be considered one by one; (ii) The variable is a class field, so we do an over-approximation by considering all of the definition statements for this field variable in its declaring class.

In practice, symbolic execution on real world applications with large code-bases face some additional challenges. The backward edges due to loops and recursions or long paths may lead to scalability issues. In particular, loops pose many challenges in the analysis since even the Android activity lifecycle itself is a large loop. W2AIScanner employs a bounded symbolic execution and models iteration blocks of code (e.g., `Iterator` class in Java) to address these obstacles.

**Threads.** One challenge in supporting threads is passing arguments. Usually threads are initialized with arguments that are stored in class fields. Later, these class fields are queried in the body of the `run` methods and a field-sensitive analysis is required to keep track of them. Method arguments can also be passed to threads in specific ways (e.g., `AsyncTask`) which are more complicated than binding method arguments in the callsite for normal method invocations (where there exists a one-to-one mapping between actual parameters at callsite and formal parameters of the method). We model different ways provided by Android to use threads and also support binding arguments for them.

Once we get the abstract description for all the sinks and external methods in terms of formulas, we solve them and check the feasibility of each path. For feasible paths, a solution to the constraints is a witness which can be used to construct an intent hyperlink to drive the execution down this path. These intent hyperlinks are used at the last step to dynamically execute the program. We employ the CVC4 SMT solver [23] which deals with string, integer and boolean constraints. We provide intermediate formulas for string operations that are not directly supported by CVC4 such as (startsWith and split). Once the solver has instantiated some/all of the symbolic variables, we use them to instantiate an intent hyperlink. In order to incorporate the generated inputs to the intent hyperlink, our analysis resolves the key-value mappings (explained shortly) in the intent hyperlink syntax.

### 3.4    Attack Validation and Concrete Value Propagation

W2AIScanner automatically generates intent hyperlinks that can exploit the W2AI vulnerabilities. An intent hyperlink can be divided into two parts: (i) the scheme part which has to be matched with the intent filter for the activity defined in the manifest file; and (ii) the data inputs which are of key-value forms described below. The first part is collected by the manifest parser component which retrieves the intent filter specification for the source activity. It creates all possible schemes that will match the intent filter. Path is one of the elements in intent filters that will be checked for accepting an intent. It can be provided by developers in a special pattern (similar to regular expressions). We use the algorithms from the Android framework to find values that match these patterns.

The data inputs that make up an intent hyperlink are derived from the Intent class methods. In Sect. 2 we discussed that an intent hyperlink follows a specific syntax. Here is a simplified meta intent hyperlink:

```
intent://HOST/PATH?query=[string₁]#Intent;scheme=[string₂];action=[string₃];S.key
    =[string₄];end;
```

where data input can be sent through the [string] fields to the Android application code. There are several possible ways to send data via an intent hyperlink: (i) a data URI which references the data resources consisting of the scheme, host and path as well as query parameters which are the key-value mappings preceded by the "?"; (ii) intent extras, the key-value pairs whose type can also be specified in the intent hyperlink (e.g., the $S$ in $S.key = [string_4]$ refers to the string extra). Note that an intent hyperlink can have more parameters with other types, e.g., int; (iii) other intent parameters such as categories, actions, etc., that can be sent as string values.

As we explained in the previous step, there are intent APIs for each form of the inputs described above that can be utilized in the application code to get the data inputs. For instance, `Intent.getStringExtra(String key)` returns the extras in the intent whose type is string and is mapped to `key`. We infer such types and use them in generating intent hyperlinks. We define such methods as entry methods if they are invoked on an input intent object. These methods are considered as the input methods in the symbolic execution which generates test inputs for variables initialized by these entry methods. While constructing symbolic formulas in the previous step, we also correlate the entry methods with the intent filters in the manifest file to generate more accurate intent hyperlinks. The entry methods return string, integer and boolean types as well as the URI type.

We also need to find keys corresponding to each input parameter. We use constant propagation, explained in the previous step to find the values of the arguments of API calls such as `getStringExtra(String name)`. If it fails to resolve the key names, an arbitrary string value is generated.

Once we have the key-value pairs and other necessary inputs for the source-sink flows and the intent filter specifications for the target browsable activity, these can all be put together to form an intent hyperlink. Therefore a group of paths generated in the symbolic execution phase might contribute to a single intent hyperlink.

**Attack Validation.** The intent hyperlinks generated in the static phase are used by the dynamic executor explained below to validate whether they exploit the sink methods. The dynamic executor runs the generated inputs and inspects the results. Running the generated inputs, two possible scenarios might happen: (1) the sink method is invoked at runtime and the generated input is accurate enough to cause the exploit; (2) the sink method is invoked but it is not exploited. In this case, first we use the concrete values obtained from the runtime execution path and assign them to the unknown variables which symbolic executor has failed to resolve. The new path formula is passed to the solver again and we generate a new intent hyperlink. This procedure continues until intent hyperlinks do not change any more (i.e., analysis reaches a fixpoint).

In order to run the concrete generated inputs and obtain the execution trace, we chose to use a high-level but standard interface, Java Debug Wire Protocol (JDWP) [2] which is supported by the Android runtime (both Dalvik and Art) and independent of framework releases. One complexity is that the execution is run in Dalvik bytecode but the analysis is in Jimple (a 3-address intermediate instruction representation). We re-translate the generated execution trace back to Jimple. Dexpler [6] keeps a mapping between byte code instruction addresses and Jimple statements. We fetch the Jimple statements using these mappings. In order to assign the concrete value of a variable from execution trace to Jimple registers, for each method, we have to find the relation between variables on the execution stack and the Jimple registers in the method Body. After running the generated intent hyperlinks, we will use these register mappings to find out accurately which Jimple registers should be updated to be further processed during the analysis.

The validation component has to verify whether the generated intent hyperlink results in an exploit. This decision is based on the execution trace, concrete values and the attack policies provided by the security analyst. The attack policy consists of rules for each class of vulnerabilities. Depending on the category of the sink method reached on the execution trace, it applies different policy checks. There are two main classes of vulnerabilities: abusing WebView interfaces and abusing native app interfaces.

Table 1. Overall statistics of vulnerable apps in each W2AI Attack category

| Category | Sub-Category | # of Sinks | # of Vulnerable Apps | ID |
|---|---|---|---|---|
| Abusing WebView Interfaces | Abusing JavaScript-to-Native Bridge | 9 | 52 | 1 |
| | Abusing HTML5 APIs | 10 | 29 | 2 |
| | Local File Inclusion | 9 | 63 | 3 |
| | Phishing | 11 | 84 | 4 |
| Abusing Native App Interfaces | App Database Pollution | 14 | 10 | 5 |
| | Persistent Storage Pollution | 72 | 7 | 6 |
| | Open Re-delegation | 39 | 23 | 7 |
| | App-Specific Logic Flaws | 16 | 18 | 8 |

The first category is validated by sending a malicious URL through the intent hyperlink parameters. When a vulnerable application loads the malicious URL, the data retrieved from the device is sent to our server and we can confirm the attacks accordingly.[3] Attacks which abuse native app interfaces are more complex to validate. First we verify if the sink method is reached on the execution trace. But this is not sufficient. We should also check whether the concrete values of the sink method parameters are directly affected by the intent hyperlink fields. For this purpose, we compare the values resolved for the sink method parameters in the symbolic execution phase with the values observed after running the intent hyperlink. Then, according to the policy, we check for other methods (which we call category settings) on the path that should exist so that the exploit is not prevented from occurring. After confirming the sink method to be exploitable, the intent hyperlink will be reported as an exploit.

## 4   Evaluation

We assess the prevalence of web-to-app injection attacks on a large scale and also assess the detection capabilities of W2AIScanner. We choose the top 100 apps of all categories in Google Play plus the dataset used in [17][4] giving a total of 12,240

---

[3]  As an example, if the app has flows that reach the `WebView.loadUrl` sink and enables `setAllowFileAccess`, `setJavaScriptEnabled` and `setAllowFileAccessFromFileURLs` settings, the app is vulnerable to local file inclusion attacks.

[4]  Since numerous apps were out of the shelf (the dataset in [17] contains 15,510 apps), we could only download 9,877 apps in Google Play on April, 2014.

apps. We ran on Ubuntu 14.04 with an Intel Core i5-4570 CPU PC (3.20 GHz) with 16 GB of RAM. Apps are tested both on the Android 4.4 emulator as well as real Android devices, Galaxy Nexus and Nexus 7. W2AIScanner utilizes the `adb` command to launch the activity to validate the exploits that abuse WebView interfaces or native app interfaces and perform privileged operations (e.g., inserting data into the app's database) which is explained in Sect. 3.4.

**Prevalence of W2AI Vulnerabilities in Apps.** In the dataset, 1,729 apps have at least one `BROWSABLE` activity. W2AIScanner detected 286 W2AI vulnerabilities in those apps with `BROWSABLE` activities. This shows that our system is effective as a vulnerability detection tool for W2AI attacks.[5]

Table 1 gives a breakdown of the detected vulnerable apps into our 8 categories. The column, # of sinks, gives the number of sinks defined by our specification for that category. There can be overlaps among the different categories of sinks. For example, `WebView.loadUrl()` can be the sink for the first 4 categories. In total, we have 153 distinct sinks for 8 categories. An app may have vulnerabilities from more than one category. For instance, the WorkNet example has vulnerabilities from categories with ID 1 to 4. Thus, the sum of that column is greater than the number of vulnerable apps. The column, # of vulnerable apps, gives the number of apps for which we found a confirmed vulnerability for that class.

For each category, we have found at least one vulnerable application with more than 1 Million downloads. A popular application is Wikipedia (1.3.4) which is vulnerable to categories with ID 2 and 4. We have also detected and confirmed 14 Dropbox applications that are vulnerable to open-redelegation attacks where attacker can force them to invoke other apps hosting on the phone. One app-specific logic vulnerability appears in 587 apps, here we count it as *only one unique vulnerability* to avoid to skewing the results. Once this vulnerability is exploited, attacker can send fake Paypal payment notifications to the phone. The Tencent Android SDK (2.8) is also confirmed to be vulnerable to W2AI attacks. More details on representative applications in each attack category is given in Appendix A.

**Effectiveness of W2AIScanner in Detecting W2AI Vulnerabilities.** Our objective is effective detection of W2AI vulnerabilities with the following goals: (i) potential vulnerabilities found by the analyser should have only few false positives and the generated intent hyperlinks should be accurate; and (ii) it should find vulnerabilities which may be missed due to imprecision at the initial whole app-level analysis phase.

Figure 3(a) depicts the ratio of number of paths generated by W2AIScanner and those reported by vanilla FlowDroid. For most of the apps, there is a considerable reduction in the number of reported flows which means that either most of the false positive flows are rejected or the combination of symbolic execution and data-flow analysis has effectively reduced the number of generated paths. The ratio can also be greater than one as we detect flows not found by FlowDroid.

---

[5] We, in fact, process 12,240 apps, first rejecting those without browsable activities.

Figure 3(c) shows that W2AIScanner is able to effectively detect false positive sinks. Sometimes, our system is even able to find sinks which have been missed by vanilla FlowDroid. In Fig. 3(c), these sinks are shown as new_sinks. Note that if we do not find any new sinks for one app, we do not put 0 in the chart. In some cases, all of the sinks reported by FlowDroid are false positives while W2AIScanner finds the true positive ones. In total, we find 82 new true positive sinks in 69 applications after refining the CFG constructed by FlowDroid. The new sinks found in 39 applications are due to thread executions. Figure 3(b) shows the number of missing edges in FlowDroid CFG for each application in our dataset. In total, we find missing edges in 863 apps which are due to thread invocations.

The total execution time for static analysis phase can be found in Fig. 3(d). For most of the applications analysis takes less than 30 s. The execution time for dynamic analysis phase tends to be higher. We have measured the execution time per flow for 8 applications each representative for each attack category. The average execution time per flow is around 48 s. A large portion of the cost for the dynamic phase is due to operations such as networking.

In Fig. 3(a), it can be observed that for the first 200 apps, the number of paths reported by vanilla FlowDroid is much higher than W2AIScanner (the ratio is less than 0.2). Figure 3(c) also shows that FlowDroid has many false positive sinks for the same apps. This shows that our system can successfully reduce the number of generated paths for these apps by rejecting the false positive sinks. The high number of initial flows for these apps also results in more runtime execution in Fig. 3(d).

We successfully generate accurate intent hyperlinks that allow us to find 0-day vulnerabilities. The intent hyperlink parameters generated for many applications in our dataset follow complex patterns. For example, Letv is an Android app which only processes an intent hyperlink if it has a query parameter with `from` as the key and `baidu` as value. Another example is Kobobooks which requires that action parameter of the intent hyperlink that invokes the app be not equal to `android.intent.action.VIEW`. Thus, symbolic execution and validation is the key for finding confirmed paths. An alternative approach to symbolic execution is fuzzing but we believe that any fuzzing without some symbolic reasoning is unlikely to give good results.

## 5   Related Work

We discuss Android related work from two angles, attacks on apps and analysis of apps. Privilege escalation attacks have been shown in Android [8,10,13,24,31, 32,36,39,40]. These works all assume that the malicious apps are present on the victim's Android device, while our W2AI attacks work without any installation of malware.

Recently, WebView and hybrid apps have been shown to be vulnerable to new classes of attacks [9,14,17,26]. Luo et al. observe that malicious JavaScript code can access sensitive resources [26]. Georgiev et al. carry out an analysis on hybrid

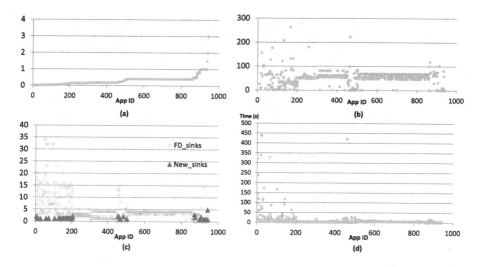

**Fig. 3.** (a) Ratio of number of paths generated by W2AIScanner and vanilla Flow-Droid; (b) Number of missing edges in the initial CFG which were found and added by W2AIScanner; (c) FD_sinks are number of FlowDroid false positive sinks and new_sinks are number of new true positive sinks found by W2AIScanner; (d) Total execution time for static analysis in seconds. Apps are sorted based on the ratio in figure (a). All apps have at least one potential vulnerable sink.

apps, and demonstrate vulnerabilities that affect bridge mechanisms [14]. Jin et al. introduce code injection attacks on HTML5-based mobile apps via internal and external channels [17]. These attacks require the user to visit the malicious page *directly* in the WebView of the hybrid apps. In contrast, our W2AI attacks utilize intent hyperlinks to convey the payload simply by clicking a link in the default browser, which is more probable.

Attacks have also been found through scheme mechanisms [18,33,34]. Wang et al. [34] reveal confused deputy attacks on Android and iOS applications which abuse channels provided by the OS. One of these channels is the scheme mechanism through which an attacker can invoke apps on the phone by crafting intent hyperlinks and publishing on web. They study the problem where the user surfs through the web in customized WebViews of benign applications and launch confused deputy attacks abusing the benign app's "origin". They present a CSRF attack on the Dropbox SDK in iPhone [34] launched through an intent hyperlink. However, our attacks differ because our attack model is more general – the user clicks on an intent hyperlink in the default browser which does not need to be started from the benign app and can leverage safer channels like default browsers. More importantly, we investigate which vulnerabilities can be exploited once the attacker can manage to start an application via an intent hyperlink. We present a detection and validation method which we show is able to scale for automatically detecting and generate exploits for vulnerabilities in real apps.

Another approach is static analysis of Android apps [5,25,35,41]. CHEX [25] finds component hijacking vulnerabilities in Android by approximating app execution as a sequential permutation of "splits". We try to reduce the over-approximation and show that precise detection is feasible. Additionally, our handling of threads is more precise than CHEX as our analysis is object-sensitive. FlowDroid [5] is a state-of-the-art information flow analyser tailored for Android applications which we leverage upon and improve in the context of W2AI. AppSealer can automatically generate patches for Android apps with component hijacking vulnerabilities [38]. This work can potentially be used as a solution for injection attacks like W2AI attacks.

There are also dynamic analysis approaches [11,27,37]. TaintDroid uses taint analysis to track the flow of privacy sensitive data through third-party apps [11]. However, it requires a proper set of inputs to begin with. Our analysis generates the requisite inputs for W2AI attacks. Symbolic execution has been used to generate test inputs for Android apps. Cadar et al. [7] generate event sequences based on concolic testing but does not address data inputs. Mirzaei et al. [28] perform symbolic execution for event sequences and data inputs by making an abstraction for modelling framework. However, their approach may not scale. Our refinement based approach is designed to reduce the state explosion problems inherent in symbolic execution.

## 6   Conclusion

We present a comprehensive study on an underexplored class of W2AI attacks in Android. These attacks can be significant threats as they open a web-to-app attack channel without needing malware and can perform privileged operations. Our work is also novel in that unlike most analysis papers which are about finding potential vulnerabilities, we show that it is possible to automatically both detect and confirm vulnerabilities with an attack intent hyperlink (0-day web input) at scale on real apps.

## A   Appendix

### Case Studies from Table 2

For each representative app in Table 2, we detail the exploitable sinks and the vulnerabilities with the attack settings in Table 3.

**Abusing JavaScript-to-Native Bridge.** WorkNet provides job information in Korea. This app enables settings for JavaScript and JavaScript-to-native interfaces in its configuration file (`config.xml`). We found vulnerabilities which exploit the `WebView.loadUrl` sink. This app enables the following settings:

    setJavaScriptEnabled, setGeolocationEnabled, setAllowFileAccess,

    setAllowFileAccessFromFileURLs

Hence, the web attacker can mount all the attacks in the WebView interfaces abuse category on WorkNet. As explained in Sect. 2, its WebView loads arbitrary

**Table 2.** Representative vulnerable apps for each W2AI vulnerability category

| ID | App | Version | Downloads |
|----|-----|---------|-----------|
| 1 | WorkNet (kr.go.keis.worknet) | 3.1.0 | 1 - 5 M |
| 2 | Wikipedia (org.wikipedia) | 1.3.4 | 10 - 50 M |
| 3 | WeCal Calendar (im.ecloud.ecalendar) | 3.0.8 | 1 - 5 M |
| 4 | IPharmacy (com.sigmaphone.topmedfree) | 1.0.92 | 1 - 5 M |
| 5 | i2X RDP (com.tux.client) | 11.0.1899 | 1 - 5 M |
| 6 | Moneycontrol (com.divum.MoneyControl) | 2.0 | 1 - 5 M |
| 7 | Caller ID (com.callapp.contacts) | 1.56 | 1 - 5 M |
| 8 | Sina Weibo (com.sina.weibo) | 4.3.0 | 5 - 10 M |

ID: Category ID
App: Representative App (Package Name)
Version: App's Version
Download: # of Downloads (Million)

URLs which exposes the Java native methods to the Javascript code. Once the user clicks the malicious link, WorkNet loads the URL from the intent hyperlink's parameters in the WebView. Therefore, the malicious page running in the WebView can invoke 21 JavaScript-to-native interfaces to access private user data (e.g., contacts) and perform privileged operations (e.g., modifying local files).

**Abusing HTML5 APIs.** Wikipedia is the free encyclopedia containing more than 32 M articles in 280 languages. It contains 2 paths that reaches the `WebView`. `loadUrl` sink and enables JavaScript and `geolocation` settings. The combination of this sink and setting enables the malicious site running in the WebView to access the GPS sensors and send out the user's current location to the attacker to track the user at any time.

**Local File Inclusion.** WeCal Calendar is a calendar assistant, which synchronizes with the Google calendar, takes notes, sets alarm and so on. W2AIScanner detects that the app has flows that reach the `WebView.loadUrl` sink and enables settings for JavaScript and the file's access. The settings are: `setAllowFileAccess`, `setAllowFileAccessFromFileURLs`. After validation, we find that when loading the local HTML file (whose URL comes from the URI intent) in the WebView, the file can utilize `XMLHttpRequest` to read the local files (e.g., `/etc/hosts`) and leak the content to the attacker.

**Phishing.** IPharmacy provides medical products. W2AIScanner detects that the `Webview.loadUrl` sink in this app is reachable and exploitable. Therefore, this app can be exploited to load a phishing page whose URL is derived from the intent hyperlink from the web attacker in the customized WebView.

**App Database Pollution.** 2X RDP Client is a popular remote desktop app. The exploitable sink reported by W2AIScanner is `SQLiteDatabase.insert`, which adds items to `farms` table. The web attacker can set sensitive attributes, e.g., credentials, in the URI intent to pollute the app's database.

**Table 3.** Sinks and policies/settings for representative apps from Table 2

| Category | Sub-category | Representative Sinks | Policies/Settings | ID |
|---|---|---|---|---|
| Abusing WebView Interfaces | Abusing Javascript-to-Native Bridge | `WebView.loadUrl` | JavaScript-to-native interfaces, `setJavaScriptEnabled` | 1 |
| | Abusing HTML5 APIs | `WebView.loadUrl` | `setGeolocationEnabled`,`set JavaScript Enabled` | 2 |
| | Local File Inclusion | `WebView.loadUrl` | `setAllowFileAccess`,`setJava ScriptEnabled`, `setAllowFileAccessFrom-FileURLs` | 3 |
| | Phishing | `WebView.loadUrl` | `setJavaScriptEnabled` | 4 |
| Abusing Native App Interfaces | App database pollution | `SQLiteDatabase.insert` | - | 5 |
| | Persistent Storage Pollution | `SharedPreferences.Editor.putString` | - | 6 |
| | Open Re-elegation | `Class.forName` | - | 7 |
| | App-Specific Logic Flaws | `TextView.setText` | - | 8 |

**Persistent Storage Pollution.** MoneyControl is a popular business and marketing app. W2AIScanner detects paths that inject data to the `SharedPreferences.Editor.putString` sink. Exploiting this vulnerability, the web attacker can make permanent changes to the storage.

**Open Re-delegation.** Caller ID - Call Blocker is a caller-ID app in Google Play that identifies unknown callers. The reached sink for this app is `Class.forName`. The attacker can set a private activity's name in the URI intent's parameters, this app will be launched and invoke the designated activity when the user clicks the malicious link.

**App-Specific Logic Flaws.** Sina Weibo is a microblogging client for Android phones. A W2AI vulnerability in this application allows the attacker to show arbitrary title messages to the victim user. The vulnerable sink in this application is `TextView.setText`. The attacker can launch an injection attack by putting an arbitrary title as query paramater in the malicious intent hyperlink.

# References

1. Intents and intent filters. http://developer.android.com/guide/components/intents-filters.html
2. Java debug wire protocol. http://developer.android.com/tools/debugging/index.html
3. Tencent Android SDK. http://wiki.open.qq.com/wiki/mobile/Android_SDK 使用说明
4. Akhawe, D., Barth, A., Lam, P.E., Mitchell, J., Song, D.: Towards a formal foundation of web security. In: CSF (2010)
5. Arzt, S., Rasthofer, S., Fritz, C., Bodden, E., Bartel, A., Klein, J., Traon, Y.L., Octeau, D., McDaniel, P.: FlowDroid: precise context, flow, field, object-sensitive and lifecycle-aware taint analysis for Android apps. In: PLDI (2014)
6. Bartel, A., Klein, J., Le Traon, Y., Monperrus, M.: Dexpler: converting Android dalvik bytecode to jimple for static analysis with Soot. In: SOAP (2012)
7. Cadar, C., Ganesh, V., Pawlowski, P.M., Dill, D.L., Engler, D.R.: Automated concolic testing of smartphone apps. In: FSE (2012)
8. Chen, Q.A., Qian, Z., Mao, Z.M.: Peeking into your app without actually seeing it: UI state inference and novel Android attacks. In: USENIX Security (2014)
9. Chin, E., Wagner, D.: Bifocals: analyzing webview vulnerabilities in Android applications. In: Kim, Y., Lee, H., Perrig, A. (eds.) WISA 2013. LNCS, vol. 8267, pp. 129–146. Springer, Heidelberg (2014)
10. Davi, L., Dmitrienko, A., Sadeghi, A.-R., Winandy, M.: Privilege escalation attacks on Android. In: Burmester, M., Tsudik, G., Magliveras, S., Ilić, I. (eds.) ISC 2010. LNCS, vol. 6531, pp. 346–360. Springer, Heidelberg (2011)
11. Enck, W., Gilbert, P., Chun, B., Cox, L.P., Jung, J., McDaniel, P., Sheth, A.: TaintDroid: an information-flow tracking system for realtime privacy monitoring on smartphones. In: USENIX Security (2010)
12. Felt, A.P., Wagner, D.: Phishing on mobile devices. In: W2SP (2011)
13. Felt, A.P., Wang, H.J., Moshchuk, A., Hanna, S., Chin, E.: Permission redelegation: attacks and defenses. In: USENIX Security (2011)
14. Georgiev, M., Jana, S., Shmatikov, V.: Breaking and fixing origin-based access control in hybrid web/mobile application frameworks. In: NDSS (2014)
15. Godefroid, P., Klarlund, N., Sen, K.: Dart: directed automated random testing. In: PLDI (2005)
16. Grace, M.C., Zhou, Y., Wang, Z., Jiang, X.: Systematic detection of capability leaks in stock android smartphones. In: NDSS (2012)
17. Jin, X., Hu, X., Ying, K., Du, W., Yin, H., Peri, G.N.: Code injection attacks on HTML5-based mobile apps: characterization, detection and mitigation. In: CCS (2014)
18. Kaplan, D.: (cve-2014-3500/1/2) Apache Cordova for Android - multiple vulnerabilities. http://seclists.org/fulldisclosure/2014/Aug/21
19. King, J.C.: Symbolic execution and program testing. Commun. ACM 19(7), 385–394 (1976)
20. Korel, B.: Automated software test data generation. IEEE Trans. Softw. Eng 16(8), 870–879 (1990)

21. Lam, P., Bodden, E., Hendren, L., Darmstadt, T.U.: The Soot framework for Java program analysis: a retrospective. In: CETUS (2011)
22. Lhoták, O., Hendren, L.: Scaling Java points-to analysis using SPARK. In: Hedin, G. (ed.) CC 2003. LNCS, vol. 2622, pp. 153–169. Springer, Heidelberg (2003)
23. Liang, T., Reynolds, A., Tinelli, C., Barrett, C., Deters, M.: A DPLL(T) theory solver for a theory of strings and regular expressions. In: CAV (2014)
24. Lin, C.C., Li, H., Zhou, X., Wang, X.: Screenmilker: how to milk your Android screen for secrets. In: NDSS (2014)
25. Lu, L., Li, Z., Wu, Z., Lee, W., Jiang, G.: Chex: statically vetting Android apps for component hijacking vulnerabilities. In: CCS (2012)
26. Luo, T., Hao, H., Du, W., Wang, Y., Yin, H.: Attacks on webview in the Android system. In: ACSAC (2011)
27. Machiry, A., Tahiliani, R., Naik, M.: Dynodroid: an input generation system for Android apps. In: FSE (2013)
28. Mirzaei, N., Malek, S., Păsăreanu, C.S., Esfahani, N., Mahmood, R.: Testing Android apps through symbolic execution. SIGSOFT Softw. Eng. Notes 37(6), 1–5 (2012)
29. Rasthofer, S., Arzt, S., Bodden, E.: A machine-learning approach for classifying and categorizing android sources and sinks. In: NDSS (2014)
30. Reps, T., Horwitz, S., Sagiv, M.: Precise interprocedural dataflow analysis via graph reachability. In: POPL (1995)
31. Schlegel, R., Zhang, K., Zhou, X.y., Intwala, M., Kapadia, A., Wang, X.: Soundcomber: a stealthy and context-aware sound trojan for smartphones. In: NDSS (2011)
32. Schrittwieser, S., Frühwirt, P., Kieseberg, P., Leithner, M., Mulazzani, M., Huber, M., Weippl, E.R.: Guess who's texting you? evaluating the security of smartphone messaging applications. In: NDSS (2012)
33. Terada, T.: Whitepaper attacking android browsers via intent scheme URLs. http://www.mbsd.jp/Whitepaper/IntentScheme.pdf
34. Wang, R., Xing, L., Wang, X., Chen, S.: Unauthorized origin crossing on mobile platforms: threats and mitigation. In: CCS (2013)
35. Wei, F., Roy, S., Ou, X., Robby: Amandroid: a precise and general inter-component data flow analysis framework for security vetting of Android apps. In: CCS (2014)
36. Xing, L., Pan, X., Wang, R., Yuan, K., Wang, X.: Upgrading your android, elevating my malware: privilege escalation through mobile OS updating. In: Security and Privacy (2014)
37. Yan, L.K., Yin, H.: DroidScope: seamlessly reconstructing the OS and Dalvik semantic views for dynamic Android malware analysis. In: USENIX Security (2012)
38. Zhang, M., Yin, H.: AppSealer: automatic generation of vulnerability-specific patches for preventing component hijacking attacks in Android applications. In: NDSS (2014)
39. Zhou, X., Lee, Y., Zhang, N., Naveed, M., Wang, X.: The peril of fragmentation: security hazards in android device driver customizations. In: Security and Privacy (2014)
40. Zhou, Y., Jiang, X.: Dissecting Android malware: characterization and evolution. In: Security and Privacy (2012)
41. Zhou, Y., Jiang, X.: Detecting passive content leaks and pollution in Android applications. In: NDSS (2013)
42. Zhou, Y., Wang, Z., Zhou, W., Jiang, X.: Hey, you, get off of my market: detecting malicious apps in official and alternative Android markets. In: NDSS (2012)

# All Your Voices are Belong to Us: Stealing Voices to Fool Humans and Machines

Dibya Mukhopadhyay, Maliheh Shirvanian[✉], and Nitesh Saxena

University of Alabama at Birmingham, Birmingham, AL, USA
{dibya,maliheh}@uab.edu, saxena@cis.uab.edu

**Abstract.** In this paper, we study voice impersonation attacks to defeat humans and machines. Equipped with the current advancement in automated speech synthesis, our attacker can build a very close model of a victim's voice after learning only a *very limited* number of samples in the victim's voice (e.g., mined through the Internet, or recorded via physical proximity). Specifically, the attacker uses *voice morphing* techniques to transform its voice – speaking any arbitrary message – into the victim's voice. We examine the aftermaths of such a voice impersonation capability against two important applications and contexts: (1) impersonating the victim in a *voice-based user authentication* system, and (2) mimicking the victim in *arbitrary speech* contexts (e.g., posting fake samples on the Internet or leaving fake voice messages).

We develop our voice impersonation attacks using an off-the-shelf voice morphing tool, and evaluate their feasibility against state-of-the-art *automated* speaker verification algorithms (application 1) as well as *human* verification (application 2). Our results show that the automated systems are largely ineffective to our attacks. The average rates for rejecting fake voices were under 10–20% for most victims. Even human verification is vulnerable to our attacks. Based on two online studies with about 100 users, we found that only about an average 50 % of the times people rejected the morphed voice samples of two *celebrities* as well as *briefly familiar users*.

## 1 Introduction

A person's voice is one of the most fundamental attributes that enables communication with others in physical proximity, or at remote locations using phones or radios, and the Internet using digital media. However, unbeknownst to them, people often leave traces of their voices in many different scenarios and contexts. To name a few, people talk out loud while socializing in cafés or restaurants, teaching, giving public presentations or interviews, making/receiving known and, sometimes unknown, phone calls, posting their voice snippets or audio(visual) clips on social networking sites like Facebook or YouTube, sending voice cards to their loved ones [11], or even donating their voices to help those with vocal impairments [14]. In other words, it is relatively easy for someone, potentially

---

The first two authors are equally contributing.

© Springer International Publishing Switzerland 2015
G. Pernul et al. (Eds.): ESORICS 2015, Part II, LNCS 9327, pp. 599–621, 2015.
DOI: 10.1007/978-3-319-24177-7_30

with malicious intentions, to "record" a person's voice by being in close physical proximity of the speaker (using, for example, a mobile phone), by social engineering trickeries such as making a spam call, by searching and mining for audiovisual clips online, or even by compromising servers in the cloud that store such audio information. The more popular a person is (e.g., a celebrity or a famous academician), the easier it is to obtain his/her voice samples.

We study the implications of such a commonplace leakage of people's voice snippets. Said differently, we investigate how an attacker, in possession of a certain number of audio samples in a victim's voice, could compromise the victim's security, safety, and privacy. Given the current advancement in automated speech synthesis, an attacker can build a very close model of a victim's voice after learning only a *very limited* number of previously eavesdropped sample(s) in the victim's voice. Specifically, *voice morphing* techniques can be used to transform the attacker's voice – speaking any arbitrary message – into the victim's voice based on this model. As a result, just a *few minutes worth of audio* in a victim's voice would lead to the *cloning of the victim's voice itself.*

We show that the consequences of imitating one's voice can be grave. Since voice is regarded as a unique characteristic of a person, it forms the basis of the authentication of the person. If voice could be imitated, it would compromise the authentication functionality itself, performed implicitly by a human in human-to-human communications, or explicitly by a machine in human-to-machine interactions. As our case study in this paper, we investigate the aftermaths of stealing voices in two important applications and contexts that rely upon voices as an authentication primitive. The *first application* is a voice-based biometric or speaker verification system that uses the potentially unique features of an individual's voice to authenticate that individual. Voice biometrics is the new buzzword among banks and credit card companies. Many banks and credit card companies are striving for giving their users a hassle-free experience in using their services in terms of accessing their accounts using voice biometrics [13, 15, 18, 22, 29, 31]. The technology has now also been deployed on smartphones as a replacement to traditional PIN locks, and is being used in many government organizations for building access control. Voice biometrics is based on the assumption that each person has a unique voice that depends not only on his or her physiological features of vocal cords but also on their entire body shapes, and on the way sound is formed and articulated. Once the attacker defeats voice biometrics using fake voices, he would gain unfettered access to the system (device or service) employing the authentication functionality.

Our *second application*, naturally, is human communications. If an attacker can imitate a victim's voice, the security of (remote) arbitrary conversations could be compromised. The attacker could make the morphing system speak literally anything that the attacker wants to, in victim's tone and style of speaking, and can launch an attack that can harm victim's reputation, his security/safety and the security/safety of people around the victim. For instance, the attacker could post the morphed voice samples on the Internet, leave fake voice messages to the victim's contacts, potentially create fake audio evidence in the court, and even impersonate the victim in a real-time phone conversations with someone the victim knows. The possibilities are endless. Such arbitrary conversations are usually (implicitly) verified by humans.

**Our Contributions:** In this paper, we study the security threat associated with stealing someone's voice (Fig. 1). We develop our voice impersonation attacks using an off-the-shelf voice morphing engine, and comprehensively evaluate their feasibility against state-of-the-art *automated* speaker verification algorithms (application 1 above) as well as *manual* verification (application 2). Our results show that the automated systems are largely ineffective to our voice impersonation attacks. The average rates for rejecting fake voices were under 10–20% for most of our victims. In addition, even human verification is vulnerable to our attacks. Based on an online study with 65 users, we found that only about an average 50 % of the times people rejected the morphed voice samples of two *celebrities*, while, as a baseline, they rejected *different speakers' voices* about 98 % of the times, and that 60–70% participants rated the morphed samples as being similar to original voices. We extended the same study for *briefly familiar voices* with 32 online participants, the results being slightly better than the previous study (rejection rates decrease and ambiguity of speaker verification increases).

Our work highlights a real threat of practical significance because obtaining audio samples can be very easy both in the physical and digital worlds, and the implications of our attacks are very serious. While it may seem very difficult to prevent "voice hacking," our work may help raise people's awareness to these attacks and motivate them to be careful while sharing and posting their audio-visuals online.

## 2   Background and Related Work

**Voice Conversion:** It has always been a challenge to get a machine to talk in a human's voice. Voice synthesis (artificial creation of human voice) has a growing number of applications most dominant one is text to speech systems. There are several instances of such voice synthesizers, whose qualities are judged based on their naturalness (similarity to human voice). Some of the recent synthesizers [2,5,10] significantly improved quality of the speech by reducing the robotic sound that was unavoidable in earlier synthesizer. However, still the synthesized speech is distinguishable from a human voice. Besides, such systems require a huge amount of data to learn phonemes.

The other technique to create a voice is voice morphing (also referred to as voice conversion and voice transformation). Voice morphing modifies a source speaker's voice to sound like a target speaker by mapping between spectral features of their voice. Similar to the voice synthesizers the major application of voice morphing is TTS that can speak in any desired voice. Usually such techniques require smaller amounts of training data and sound more natural and fluent compared to voice synthesizers [6]. Due to these advantageous properties, voice morphing becomes an excellent tool to attack someone's voice as studied in our paper.

We employed the CMU Festvox voice converter [6] (reviewed in Sect. 4) to attack machine-based and human-based speaker verification. We used Mel-Cepstral Distortion (MCD)[1] to measure the performance of conversion engine for different size of training dataset. The smaller the MCD, the better the quality of the conversion. MCD values between 5–8 dB are generally considered acceptable for voice conversions [9]. As a crucial component of our attacks, we found that the conversion quality is very good (within the desired range of 5–8 dB) even with very small amount of training data. Our MCD analysis is reported in Sects. 5.1 and 6.3.

**Machine-based Speaker Verification:** Speaker verification is the biometric task of authenticating a claimed identity by means of analyzing a spoken sample of the claimant's voice. It is a 2-class problem in which the claimant must be recognized as the true speaker or as an impostor [35]. To recognize a known target speaker, a speaker verification system goes through a prior speaker enrollment phase. In the speaker enrollment phase, the system creates a target model of a speaker from his/her speech samples so that they can be verified during the test phase in future.

A speaker verification system extracts certain spectral or prosodic features from a speech signal to enroll the model of the target speaker. After extracting the features from a speech signal, model enrollment or "voice print" generation of the target speaker is done using different modeling techniques.

With the emergence of advanced speech synthesis and voice conversion techniques, the automatic speaker verification systems may be at risk. De Leon et al. have studied the vulnerabilities of advanced speaker verification systems to synthetic speech [23–25], and proposed possible defenses for such attacks. In [16], the authors have demonstrated the vulnerabilities of speaker verification systems against artificial signals. The authors of [44] have studied the vulnerabilities of text-independent speaker verification systems against voice conversion based on telephonic speech.

In our paper, we pursue a detailed analysis of the vulnerabilities of a speaker verification system employing two advanced algorithms against voice conversion. Although some of the prior papers tested the same set of speaker verification algorithms we are testing in our paper, they did not evaluate the Festvox conversion system, which claims to require only few sentences for training [6]. Noticeably, a key difference between our work and previous studies lies in the number/length and type of samples required to build a good voice conversion model. We use very less amount of training samples (e.g., 50–100 sentences of length 5 s each) for voice conversion collected using unprofessional voice recording devices such as laptops and smartphones. Such short-size audio samples giving rise to a victim's voice, sets a fundamental premise of how easily a person's voice

---

[1] MCD is a metric used to measure the similarity of the converted voice and the original voice by calculating the different between the feature vectors of the original and converted voice [26,32,33].

can be attacked or misused. While the prior papers do not seem to clearly specify the sizes of their voice conversion training data sets, they employ spectral conversion approaches that typically require a large amount of high-quality training data [28,42].

**Human-based Speaker Verification:** Manual speech perception and recognition is a complex task, which depends on many parameters such as length/number of different samples, samples from familiar vs. famous people, and combinations thereof [38]. There exists a considerable volume of literature on how speech is recognized [20,21,38]. Linguistics researches show that the shorter the sentence, the more difficult it is to identify the source [27]. Based on the study conducted by Shirvanian et al. [39], it appears that the task of establishing the identity of a speaker is challenging for human users, especially in the context of short random strings (numbers or phrases). In our paper, we study the capability of human users in recognizing the speaker for an *arbitrary speech* of famous celebrities and briefly familiar speakers.

# 3   Our Attacks on Human Voices

## 3.1   Overview

In this paper, we study the attacks against human-based and machine-based speaker verification. Our attack system consists of three phases (visualized in Fig. 1). The *first phase* involves the collection of voice samples $O_T = (t_1, t_2, \cdots , t_n)$, previously spoken by the target victim. At this point, the audio (content) privacy may have been compromised as the victim gives away (willingly or unwillingly) his/her audio samples to the attacker. The *second phase* of our attack focuses on the creation of the victim's voice based on the audio samples collected in the first phase. The attacker (source) first speaks the same sentences $O_S = (s_1, s_2, \cdots , s_n)$ the victim (target) has spoken in the recorded audio, and then feeds $O_S$ and $O_T$ to the morphing engine to create a model $M = \mu(O_S, O_T)$ of the victim's voice. At this point, the attacker has at its disposal essentially the voice of the victim. The *third phase* involves the use of this voice imitation capability to compromise any application or context that utilizes the victim's voice. The target applications that we study in this paper are: machine-based and human-based speaker verification systems. The attacker can speak any new arbitrary sentence $A = (a_1, a_2, \cdots , a_m)$, as required by the attacked application, which the model built in the second phase will now convert into the victim's voice as $f_T = M(A) = (f_1, f_2, \cdots , f_m)$. The morphed samples will then be fed-back to the speaker verification systems (to authenticate the morphed voice as the target victim's voice), and to people (to attack them by fooling them into believing that the morphed attacker's voice is the voice of the benign victim). The third phase of our attack system serves to demonstrate the aftermaths of the breach of voice security.

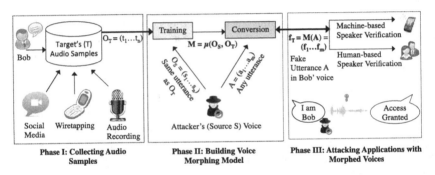

**Fig. 1.** An overview of our attack system

### 3.2 Threat Model

In our threat model, an attacker can collect a few of the victim's audio samples, for example, by recording the victim using a mobile audio recording device with or without the knowledge of the victim, or mining the previously posted samples on the web. As mentioned earlier, these samples are then used to train a morphing engine. In the training procedure, the attacker may use his own voice or could recruit other users (possibly those who can mimic the victim's voice very closely). Thus, the attacker has the ability to employ means to achieve favorable conditions for voice conversion so as to achieve the highest quality morphed samples.

Equipped with this voice morphing capability, the attacker then attempts to defeat the machine-based and human-based speaker verification systems/contexts. When attacking a machine-based speaker verification system, the attacker simply sends the morphed voices to impersonate himself as the legitimate user. In this case, we clearly assume that the attacker has permanent or temporary physical access to the terminal or device deploying voice authentication (e.g., a stolen mobile phone, a desktop left unattended during lunch-time, or a public ATM).

The attacker can defeat human-based speaker verification in many ways. Clearly in this context, faking face-to-face conversation would not be possible with voice morphing. However, the attacker can be remote and make spoofed phone calls, or leave voice messages impersonating the victim. He may even create real-time fake communication with a party with the help of a human attacker who provides meaningful conversations, which the morphing engine converts to the victim's voice on-the-fly. The attacker can also post the victim's morphed samples online on the public sites or disseminate via social networking sites, for example.

### 3.3 Attacking Machine-Based Speaker Verification

In this paper, we systematically test the advanced speaker verification algorithms that can be used for the purpose of user authentication, in the following scenarios:

**Different Speaker Attack:** This attack refers to the scenario in which, the speaker verification system trained with the voice of speaker A is attacked with another human speaker B's voice samples. If the system fails to detect this attack, then the system is not good enough to be used for the purpose of speaker verification. This is conceivably the simplest and the most naive attack that can be performed against an automatic speaker verification system. So, this attack might be used as a baseline to measure the security performance of the target speaker verification system.

**Conversion Attack:** This attack scenario refers to the one in which the speaker verification system is attacked by the morphed samples of an impostor replacing the legitimate user's samples. Such an attacker might have the capability to attack a speaker-verification system that gives a random challenge each time a victim user tries to login or authenticate to the system.

### 3.4   Attacking Human-based Speaker Verification

In this scenario, the attacker would simply create arbitrary morphed speech in the victim's voice and use it to communicate with others remotely. As mentioned earlier, some of the real life applications of this attack might include leaving fake voice-mails in the victim's voice to harm victim's family or friends, or broadcasting a morphed voice of a celebrity victim to defame him/her. While the attack itself is relatively straight-forward in many cases, the key aspect is whether the "human verifier" would fall prey to it or not. This is the primary aspect we study in our work via two user studies. Similar to our study on machine-based speaker verification, we evaluate the performance of the conversion attack contrasted with the different speaker attack as a baseline against human-based speaker verification.

## 4   Tools and Systems

**Festvox Voice Conversion System:** Voice conversion (as reviewed in Sect. 2) is an emerging technique to morph voices. For implementing our attacks, we have used Festvox [6], a speech conversion system developed at Carnegie Mellon University.

Festvox employs acoustic-to-articulatory inversion mapping that determines the positions of speech articulators of a speaker from the speech using some statistical models. Toda et al. proposed a method of acoustic-to-articulatory inversion mapping based on Gaussian Mixture Model in [41] that is independent of the phonetic information of the speech. The next phase in this system is spectral conversion between speakers for transforming the source speaker's to the target speaker's voice. The authors developed a spectral conversion technique [42], in which they have used maximum likelihood based estimation taking into account the converted parameter for each utterance. The evaluation results of this unique spectral conversion technique show that this technique has fared better than the conventional spectral conversion techniques [42]. For our experiment, we fed Festvox with recordings of some prompts spoken by the source (attacker) and the target (victim) speakers. Once the system is trained, any given arbitrary recording from the source speaker can generate the corresponding speech in the target's voice.

**Bob Spear Speaker Verification System:** In our experiment, we have used Spear verification toolbox developed by Khoury et al. [30] The Spear system is a open source speaker verification tools that has been evaluated with standard datasets like Voxforge [12], MOBIO [7] and NIST SRE [8]. Also, it represents the state-of-the-art in speaker verification systems having implemented the current well-known speaker verification algorithms, which makes it a representative system to evaluate our attack.

The input to this system, a set of clips spoken by a number of speakers, is split into 3 sets namely: *training set, development set* (Dev set) and *evaluation set* (Eval set). The training set is used for background modeling. The development and evaluation sets are further divided into two subsets, namely, Enroll set (Dev.Enroll, Eval.Enroll) and Test set (Dev.Test, Eval.Test). Speaker modeling can be done using any one of the given modeling techniques, namely, Universal Background Modeling in Gaussian Mixture Model (UBM-GMM) [37] and Inter-Session Variability (ISV) [43].

UBM-GMM is a modeling technique that uses the spectral features and then computes a log-likelihood of the Gaussian Mixture Models for background modeling and speaker verification [19,34,36]. ISV is an improvement to UBM-GMM, where a speaker's variability due to age, surroundings, emotional state, etc., are compensated for, and it gives better performance for the same user in different scenarios [40,43].

After the modeling phase, the system is then tuned and tested respectively using the Dev.Test and Eval.Test sets from Development and Evaluation sets. All the audio files in the Dev.Test and Eval.Test sets are compared with each of the speaker models for development and evaluation sets, respectively, and each file is given a similarity score with respect to each speaker in the corresponding set. The scores of the Dev.Test files are used to set a threshold value. The scores of the Eval.Test set are then normalized and compared with this threshold, depending on which each file is assigned to a speaker model. If the audio file actually belong to the speaker to whom it got assigned, then the verification is successful otherwise the verification is not successful.

## 5    Experiments: Attacking Machine-based Speaker Verification

We now present the experiments that we conducted to attack the well-known speaker verification algorithms using voice conversion techniques.

### 5.1    Setup

**Datasets:** We used MOBIO and Voxforge datasets, two open source speech databases that are widely used for testing different speech recognition tools.

Voxforge is a much more standard dataset in terms of the quality and the length of the speech compared to MOBIO. Voxforge samples are better quality samples of about 5 s each while MOBIO dataset is recorded using laptop microphones and also the length of the speech samples varies from 7 to 30 s. The reason behind choosing these two datasets was to test our attacks against both standard and sub-standard audio samples. We have chosen a set of 28 male speakers from Voxforge, and 152 (99 male and 53 female) speakers from the MOBIO. For the purpose of the experiment, this speaker set is divided into 3 subsets. These three subsets are used separately for background modeling (Train set), development (Dev set) and evaluation (Eval set) of the toolkit. The Dev and Eval sets contain both labeled and unlabeled voice samples. The labeled samples are used for target speaker modeling while the unlabeled samples are used for testing the system.

For the Voxforge dataset, the *development set* (Dev.Test) contains 30 unlabeled voice samples for each of the 10 speakers, i.e., a total of 300 voice samples. In contrast, for the MOBIO dataset, the Dev.Test subset contains 105 unlabeled samples of 24 male and 18 female speakers. The samples in the Dev.Test set are used for tuning the parameters of the system such that the system performs well on the evaluation set. The MOBIO dataset contains both male and female speakers and are modelled separately in two separate systems. Since we are using the speaker recognition tool specifically in a speaker verification scenario, our *evaluation* (Eval) set always contains a single speaker. For Voxforge, we test for 8 (male) speakers, and for MOBIO, we test for 38 male and 20 female speakers.

**Metrics Used:** The performance of a speaker verification system is evaluated based on the *False Rejection Rates (FRR)* and *False Acceptance Rates (FAR)*. A *benign setting* is defined as a scenario in which, the test samples are all genuine samples. That is, the samples fed to the system are spoken by the original speaker (the one whose samples were used during the training phase). If the system accepts a given test sample, then the system was successful in recognizing the speaker, while a rejection means that the system has wrongly rejected a genuine sample, and this is counted as a *false reject*.

An *attack setting* is defined as a scenario in which, the test samples are fake or morphed. That is, these samples are not spoken by the original legitimate speaker, but are either spoken by some other speaker (another user) or generated using voice conversion. For simulating an attack setting, we replaced the genuine test samples with our fake samples in the Eval.Test set. So, the success of our attacks is directly proportional to the number of accepts, i.e., *false accepts*, by the system.

**Different Speaker Attack Setup:** For testing Voxforge dataset in this scenario, we swapped the voice samples of the original speakers with that of 4 CMU Arctic speakers [4] that have spoken the same samples as the Voxforge speakers, and tested the performance of the system. For testing with the MOBIO dataset, we replaced each speaker with all the other speakers in the Test set to see if the system could determine that the original speaker has been swapped. As discussed in Sect. 3, this attack is a rather naive attack, and serves as a baseline for our conversion-based attacks.

**Conversion Attack Setup:** In this attack scenario, we tested how robust the Spear system is to voice conversion. For implementing this attack, we changed the genuine test samples with converted ones. The voice conversion was done by training the Festvox conversion system with a set of samples spoken by both an attacker and the victim speakers. In case of Voxforge, one CMU Arctic [4] speaker posed as attackers and the 8 speakers in the Test set were the victims. For the MOBIO dataset, we chose 6 male and 3 female speakers in the Test set as attackers, and the remaining 32 male and 17 female speakers were the victims.

In case of the Voxforge dataset, we used 100 samples of 5 s each (so approximately 8 min speech data), to train the conversion system. In the MOBIO dataset, the speakers have independently recorded free speech in response to some questions asked to them. However, there were some specific common text that all the speakers have recorded. We used 12 such samples of about 30 secs each (so approximately 6 min of speech data) to train the conversion system. The converted voices thus generated were swapped with the genuine samples of the victim test speakers.

The MCD value after conversion in case of MOBIO speakers was about 4.58 dB (for females) and about 4.9 dB (for males) for 12 training samples (of average length 30 s), which decreased by 0.16 dB (for females) and by 0.1 dB (for males) for about 100 training samples (of 15–30 s length). In case of Voxforge, the MCD values were on average 5.68 dB, 5.59 dB, 5.56 dB for 50, 100, 125 training samples (of average length 5 s each) respectively. The negligible improvement in MCD of about 3 % for MOBIO females, about 2 % for MOBIO males, about 0.53 % for Voxforge speakers led us to use 12 training samples for MOBIO and 100 training samples for Voxforge. Thus, its confirmed that voice conversion works well with only a small training dataset (a fundamental premise of our attack).

### 5.2   Results

**Benign Setting Results:** This experiment was done to set the baseline for the performance of the system being studied. The original clips of 8 Voxforge speakers, 38 male and 20 female MOBIO speakers, were used to evaluate the system. This test was done for both the algorithms: UBM-GMM and ISV. The results are summarized in the 2nd, 5th and 6th columns of Table 1. The results show that the rate of rejection of genuine (original speaker) samples (i.e., FRRs) is pretty low, less than 2 % in case of Voxforge speakers, and in the range of around 7 %–11 % in case of MOBIO speakers. The MOBIO speakers, both male and female, have a standard deviation of more than 10 % in case of UBM-GMM and that of about 8 %–9 % for ISV. The variation in the quality of speech across different speakers in the MOBIO dataset might be the reason behind this result.

**Different Speaker Attack Results:** The results for this attack is given in the 3rd, 7th and 8th columns of Table 1. From the results, we can see that the FAR

**Table 1.** Performance of machine-based speaker verification system against our attacks. Reported numbers represent error rates *mean (standard deviation)*.

| Algorithm | Voxforge Dataset | | | MOBIO Dataset | | | | | |
|---|---|---|---|---|---|---|---|---|---|
| | Original Speaker (FRR) | Different Speaker Attack (FAR) | Conversion Attack (FAR) | Original Speaker (FRR) | | Different Speaker Attack (FAR) | | Conversion Attack (FAR) | |
| | | | | Male | Female | Male | Female | Male | Female |
| UBM-GMM | 1.25% (2.48%) | 0.21% (0.60%) | 98.54% (2.07%) | 11.32% (15.31) | 11.71% (11.95%) | 11.78% (7.04%) | 16.70% (7.22%) | 86.60% (20.16%) | 64.42% (36.73%) |
| ISV | 1.67% (1.78%) | 0.73% (1.50%) | 98.29% (2.61%) | 9.12% (9.93%) | 7.85% (7.94%) | 10.79% (8.00%) | 16.10% (9.52%) | 73.54% (28.08%) | 62.24% (37.04%) |

(success rate of the attack) is less than 1 % for the Voxforge speakers, around 10 % for the male MOBIO speakers and around 16 % for the female MOBIO speakers. Both UBM-GMM and ISV algorithms seem to perform similarly in case of this attack. However, the FAR of female speakers, being higher, can be attributed to the level of similarity of their voices in the MOBIO dataset. The acceptance rate is significantly low for both the datasets, which proves that Spear is robust against the naive different speaker attack, and can successfully detect, with at least 94 % accuracy (for Voxforge) and with at least 84 % accuracy (for MOBIO), that the speaker has been changed. This makes Spear a worthwhile system to challenge with respect to more sophisticated attacks.

**Conversion Attack Results:** The results of this attack are shown in the 4th, 9th and 10th columns of Table 1. The FAR in this case is above 98 % for Voxforge, about 70–85% for male MOBIO speakers and about 60 % for female MOBIO speakers.

However, the standard deviation corresponding to the speakers in the MOBIO dataset seems to be pretty high (about 28 % in male and 36 % in females). Hence, we analyze the distribution of the FAR values across all the Test users in the MOBIO dataset (Fig. 3 of Appendix C). For MOBIO male speakers, we see that for 60 % of speakers with UBM-GMM and more than 30 % of speakers with ISV have 90 % FAR. Overall, about 88 % (for UBM-GMM) and about 85 % (for ISV) of the male speakers have more than 50 % FAR. For female speakers, about 52 % (for UBM-GMM) and about 47 % (for ISV) speakers have above 90 % success rate. Overall, around 70 % (for UBM-GMM) and 65 % (for ISV) of the speakers have above 50 % success rate. Thus, it is fair to say that the tested algorithms failed significantly against our voice conversion attacks.

**Conversion Attack vs. Different Speaker Attack:** We compared the mean FAR of the conversion attack with the mean FAR of the different speaker attack using the Wilcoxon Signed-Rank test, and found that the difference is statistically significant[2] with a p-value = 0 (for Males in case of both the algorithms), with a p-value = 0.0015 (for Females with UBM-GMM), with a p-value = 0.0019 (for Females with ISV) for MOBIO, and with a p-value = 0.0004 for Voxforge in case of both the algorithms. Thus, the conversion attack is significantly more successful than the different speaker attack.

---

[2] All significance results are reported at a 95 % confidence level.

**UBM-GMM vs. ISV:** In the two attacks, the ISV algorithm performs equally well, and in some cases, better than the GMM algorithm. We compared the two algorithms using the Wilcoxon Signed-Rank test, and noticed that the result is statistically significant for the conversion attack on male MOBIO speakers with a p-value = 0.0147, and in the benign setting for female MOBIO speakers with a p-value = 0.0466. This was an expected result since ISV has session variability parameters that makes it perform better than UBM-GMM and also the MOBIO dataset was recorded in various sessions.

The Voxforge dataset being a better and standard dataset has a higher attack success rate compared to MOBIO. The quality of voice conversion plays an important role here. The attacker (source) samples for voice conversion in case of the Voxforge dataset were from the CMU Arctic database that contains samples recorded in a professional recording environment. However, in case of MOBIO, attacker samples were chosen from the Test set of MOBIO itself and that affected the quality of conversion adversely. Moreover, the style of speaking among the speakers varied widely in case of MOBIO that can also be one of the factors affecting the voice conversion training.

# 6    Experiments: Attacking Human-based Speaker Verification

We now investigate the extent to which humans may be susceptible to the voice conversion attacks in arbitrary human-to-human communications.

## 6.1    Setup

To evaluate the performance of our voice impersonation attacks against human users, we conducted two web-based studies with 65 and 32 Amazon Mechanical Turk (M-Turk) online workers. In the first study, referred to as the *Famous Speaker Study*, we investigate a scenario, where the attacker mimics a popular celebrity, and posts, for example, the morphed fake samples of his/her speech on the Internet or broadcasts them on the radio. The primary reason for choosing celebrities in our case study was to leverage people's pre-existing familiarity with their voices. In our second study, called the *Briefly Familiar Speaker Study*, we consider a scenario, where humans are subject to a briefly familiar person's (fake) voice (e.g., someone who was introduced at a conference briefly). The failure of users in detecting such attacks would demonstrate a vulnerability of numerous real-world scenarios that rely (implicitly) on human speaker verification.

Our studies involved human subjects, who participated to provide their voice samples for building our morphing engine, and to evaluate the feasibility of our attacks (human verification of converted voices). Their participation in the study was strictly voluntary. The participants provided informed consent prior to the study and were given the option to withdraw from the study at any time. Standard best practices were followed to protect the confidentiality/privacy of participants' responses and audio samples acquired during the study as well as the morphed audio samples that were generated for in the study. Our study was approved by our University's Institutional Review Board.

The demographic information of the participants of our two studies is summarized in Appendix A Table 3. Most of the participants were young and well-educated native English speakers with no hearing impairments. For the first and second studies, each participant was paid \$1 and \$3, respectively, for his/her effort, which took about 30 min and 45 min, respectively, for completion.

## 6.2 Dataset

To build the dataset for our studies, we developed an application to collect audio samples from a group of American speakers, and posted the task on M-Turk. This job required mimicking two celebrities namely, *Oprah Winfrey* and *Morgan Freeman*.

We collected some audio samples of these celebrities available on the Internet, and, using our application, played back those samples to the speakers (who posed as attackers) and asked the male speakers to repeat and record the clips of Morgan Freeman and the female speakers to record the clips of Oprah Winfrey. While collecting these audio samples, speakers were categorically instructed to try their best to mimic the speaking style and emotion of the celebrity that they are listening to (our threat model allows the attack with such a leverage). There were around 100 samples for both the male (Morgan) and the female (Oprah) celebrities that took each user approximately an hour to record. Each participant was paid \$10 for this task. Over a period of two weeks, we collected samples from 20 speakers. Among these, we picked 5 male and 5 female speakers, who could record all clips successfully in a non-noisy environment and with a similar style and pace of the original speakers. The demographic information of the final 10 participants has been given in Appendix A Table 3.

## 6.3 Conversion Processes

The audio data collected from the M-Turk participants acted as the source voice to synthesize the voices of Oprah and Morgan (Famous Speaker Study). The same dataset was used to generate the voices of 4 briefly familiarized target speakers (Briefly Familiar Speaker Study).

We converted attacker's voice to target voice using the CMU Festvox voice converter, and observed that for 25, 50, 100 and 125 sentences, in the training dataset, the average MCD values are 7.52 dB, 7.45 dB, 7.01 dB, and 6.98 dB, respectively. This shows an improvement of only 1 %, 6 % and less that 1 % when increasing the training dataset size from 25 to 50, 50 to 100 and 100 to 125 sentences, respectively. This result confirms the suitability of the conversion system even with a small training dataset. Because of only a slight MCD improvement across different sample sizes, we fixed our training dataset size to only 100 sentences, each with an average duration of 4 s.

We converted the voice of each of the 5 female speakers to Oprah's voice and 5 male speakers to Morgan's voice (Famous Speaker Study). We also generated 2 female and 2 male voices by converting female attackers' voices to female targets' voices, and male attackers' voices to male targets' voices (Briefly Familiar Speaker Study).

## 6.4  Famous Speaker Study

In this study, we asked our participants to first listen to a two-minute speech of each of our victim celebrities (Oprah and Morgan) to get to recall their voices. After familiarization, the participants had to listen to several audio clips and complete two set of tasks, namely, "Speaker Verification" and "Voice Similarity", as defined below.

*Speaker Verification Test:* In the first set of questions, we played 22 audio clips of around 15 s each, and asked the participants to decide if the speaker is Oprah. In each question, they had the choice of selecting "Yes" if they could identify Oprah's voice, "No" if they could detect that the voice does not belong to Oprah, and "Not Sure" if they could not distinguish precisely whose voice is being played. 4 of the presented samples were Oprah's voice collected from different speeches, 8 samples were from a "different speaker" in our dataset described earlier, and 5 samples were from our converted voice dataset, generated by performing voice conversions on our dataset. Similar set of questions was asked about Morgan. Morgan's challenges, consisted of 4 voice of Morgan selected from different speeches and interviews, 6 samples of different speakers, and 6 converted voices picked from our voice conversion dataset.

*Voice Similarity Test:* In the second set of questions, we played several samples (original speaker, different speaker, and converted voice) and asked users to rate the similarity of the samples to the two target speakers' voices. We defined five ratings to capture the similarity/dissimilarity – "exactly similar", "very similar", "somehow similar", "not very similar" and "different". For each audio sample, participants could select one of the 5 options according to the similarity of the challenge voice to the celebrities' own voices. 4 original speaker, 5 converted voice and 6 different speaker samples were presented in Oprah's set of questions. Similarly, for Morgan's questions, 4 original speaker, 6 converted, and 7 different speaker samples were played.

In both tests, we categorized audio clips into three groups, namely, Original Speaker (benign setting), Different Speaker Attack and Conversion Attack.

**Results:** The results for the speaker verification test are summarized in Table 2. The success rate for users in answering original speaker challenges is shown in the first row (column 2 and 5) of Table 2, which is 89.23 % for Oprah and 91.54 % for Morgan (averaged across all samples across all participants). These results show that the participants were pretty much successful in detecting the original speaker's voice.

The second row (columns 3 and 6) of Table 2 depicts the accuracy of detecting the different speaker attack. The results show that a majority of participants were able to distinguish a different speaker's voice from the original speaker's voice. The rate of correctly identifying a different speaker was 95.19 % for Oprah and 97.95 % for Morgan (averaged across all different speaker samples across all participants). The results imply that the participants were somewhat more successful in detecting a different speaker than verifying the original speaker.

**Table 2.** Performance of human-based speaker verification against our attacks (Famous Speaker and Briefly Familiar Speaker studies). The accuracy of detecting the original as well as different speaker is around 90 %, but the accuracy of detecting the conversion attack is around 50 %.

| | Famous Speaker | | | | | | Briefly Familiar Speaker | | |
| | Oprah | | | Morgan | | | Averaged Over 4 Speakers | | |
| | Yes | No | Not Sure | Yes | No | Not Sure | Yes | No | Not Sure |
|---|---|---|---|---|---|---|---|---|---|
| Original Speaker | 89.23% | 9.62% | 1.15% | 91.54% | 8.46% | 0.00% | 74.69% | 22.81% | 2.50% |
| Different Speaker Attack | 4.04% | 95.19% | 0.77% | 1.28% | 97.95% | 0.77% | 14.06% | 82.81% | 3.13% |
| Conversion Attack | 45.85% | 45.85% | 8.31% | 29.33% | 54.10% | 16.67% | 27.81% | 47.81% | 24.38% |

However, the participants were not as successful in detecting the conversion attack (row three of Table 2; shaded cells). The rate of successfully detecting the presence of conversion attack was around 50 % (averaged across all morphed samples across all participants). Interestingly, ambiguity increased while detecting the conversion attack (which is inferred from the increase in "Not Sure" answers). This shows that participants got confused in identifying the converted voice compared to the original speaker's voice samples and different speaker's voice samples. In a real life setting, participants' confusion in recognizing the speaker might highly affect their accuracy of verifying the identity of a speaker. The reason is that, while in our experiment, participants had the choice of answering "Not Sure", in a real life application, where the users should either accept or discard a conversation (e.g., a voice message), they might rely on a random guess, possibly accept an illegitimate conversation or reject a legitimate conversation.

We compared the two attacks (different speaker and conversion attacks) using Wilcoxon Signed-Rank Test and noticed that the result is statistically significant for both of our familiar speakers (p-value = 0).

The results from the voice similarity test show that a majority of our participants found the original speaker samples as being "exactly similar" or "very similar" to the original speaker's voice. Only with negligible rates, participants found original samples different or not very similar to the original speaker. This is well-aligned with the speaker verification test results, and shows that people can successfully detect similarity of different samples of the same speaker. 88.08 % found samples of Oprah's voice exactly similar or very similar to her voice while 95.77 % found samples of Morgan's voice exactly similar or very similar to his voice.

As expected, the users could detect dissimilarity of a different speaker's voice to the original speaker. 86.81 % found different speaker's voices as "different" and "not very similar" to the Oprah's voice; this result was 94.36 % for Morgan's voice. Very few users considered a different speaker's voice similar to an original speaker's voice. In line with the speaker verification test, the voice similarity test shows the success of participants in detecting a different speaker.

Our study shows that most of the users rated converted voice as "somehow similar" or "very similar" to the original speaker. 74.10 % detected converted voice "very similar" and "some how similar" to Oprah's voice, while this result is 59.74 % for Morgan's voice. The voice conversion makes the attacker's voice sound similar to the original target voice. The conversion depends on many parameters, including similarity between source and target before the conversion, and the level of noise present in initial source and target recordings. Since we used same samples of the target voice (Oprah, Morgan) for all conversions, difference between the conversions is mainly due to the ambient noise present in source (attacker) recordings. The source recordings, being better in quality, worked better for conversion. The attacker is assumed to have the ability to improve quality of his recordings to improve the conversion. In our study, Oprah's converted voice was more similar to her original voice than Morgan's converted voice was to his voice. However, we cannot generalize this result to all speakers and all conversions. Figure 2 (Appendix B) summarizes the results of the voice similarity test.

### 6.5  Briefly Familiar Speaker Study

Similar to the Famous Speaker Study, we conducted a study evaluating the performance of human users in recognizing a briefly familiar speaker. For this study, we picked two female and two male speakers from our dataset as victims, and two female and two male speakers as the attackers from the same dataset mentioned in Sect. 6.2. We asked the participants to first listen to a 90 s recording of a victim's voice to get familiar with the voice, and then answer 15 speaker verification challenges and 15 voice similarity challenges about each speaker (each audio sample was about 15 s long). As in the previous study, in the speaker verification test, participants were asked to verify the speaker, and, in the voice similarity test, the participants were asked to rate the level of similarity of the audio clips to the original speaker's voice. Audio clips were categorized as 5 original speaker, 5 different speaker and 5 converted voice. Moreover, we asked the participants their opinion about the tasks, and the qualitative basis for their judgment. To discard possibly inattentive participants, we included dummy questions as part of the challenges that asked the user to pick the right most option from the answers.

**Results:** Table 2 includes the result of the Briefly Familiar Speaker study, and Fig. 2 (Appendix B) summarizes the result of the similarity test, averaged over all participants and all speakers. The participants show an average success rate of 74.68 % in recognizing the original speaker correctly averaged over the four speakers (row 1, column 8). Average success rate of users in distinguishing a different speaker is 82.81 % (row 2, column 9). These results show that, on an average, participants seem less successful in verifying a briefly familiar speaker compared to a famous speakers.

Importantly, the average success rate of detecting the conversion attack is 47.81 % (row 3, column 9). This shows that over 50 % of users could not detect the conversion attack. That is, they either misidentify the converted voice as the original speaker's voice or were not able to verify the speaker. We compared the two attacks (different speaker and conversion attacks) using the Wilcoxon Signed-Rank Test, and noticed that the result is statistically significant (p-value = 0.0038), which means the conversion attack works significantly better than the different speaker attack.

The results of the similarity test shows that majority of the participants found the samples in the benign settings exactly similar to the original speaker's voice, and majority of participants found the samples in the different speaker attack setting different from the original speaker's voice. The converted voice similarity is rated as somehow similar to the original speaker's voice, which stands between the different speaker's voice rate and original speaker's voice rate.

At the end of the survey we asked the participants how easy/difficult they found the task of recognizing a speaker, on what basis they made their decisions, and what would possibly improve the participant's accuracy. In general, they found speaker verification to be a challenging task, and quality of the voice to be a prominent factor in verifying the speaker. A summary of their answers is presented in Appendix D.

### 6.6  Briefly Familiar Speaker vs. Famous Speaker Verification

We compared the performance of the attacks between the two settings (Famous and Briefly Familiar Speaker). Although the result of the Mann-Whitney U test does not show statistical significance between the two settings in case of the conversion attack, the result is significant for the different speaker attack, for both Oprah and Morgan combined (p-value = 0). This shows that people can detect the different speaker attack better in the Famous Speaker setting compared to the Briefly Familiar Speaker setting.

The fraction of participants, who could not distinguish the speakers, seems to have increased compared to the Famous Speaker study (as reflected in the last column of Table 2). This suggests that the ambiguity in recognizing a speaker increases as the familiarity with the speaker decreases. The result of the Mann-Whitney U test confirms that this increase is significant for the conversion attack (p-value = 0.0076), but not significant for the other two type of settings (original speaker and different speaker) for both Oprah and Morgan combined.

## 7  Summary

We explored how human voice authenticity can be easily breached using voice conversion, and how such a breach can undermine the security of machine-based and human-based speaker verification. Our voice conversion attack against the state-of-the-art speaker verification algorithms has a very high success rate, about 80–90%. This suggests that current algorithms would not be able to prevent a malicious impostor with morphing capability from accessing the authentication terminal or remote services employing voice biometrics. In our attacks against human verification, the target victims were known users (celebrities) as well as briefly familiar users. The results corresponding to both types of victims highlight that even humans can be fooled into believing, in almost 50 % of the cases, that the morphed samples are from a genuine speaker. Naturally, people seem to detect attacks against celebrity voices better than briefly familiar voices. In light of this result, it seems that an attacker can compromise the authenticity of remote arbitrary human-to-human conversations with a relatively high chance.

Voice conversion sits right at the heart of all our attacks. Therefore, in order to achieve the best possible outcome, an attacker should strive to improve the voice conversion quality. This could be achieved by choosing high quality audio samples of the target (victim) when possible and by creating high quality audio samples for the source (attacker), ideally mimicking the victim's voice and verbal style as much as possible. Moreover, if required, the attacker may process the victim samples before and after performing the voice conversion to improve the voice quality (e.g., by filtering-out noise).

## 8   Conclusions, Limitations and Future Work

In this paper, we studied how human voices can be easily stolen and used against applications and contexts that rely upon these voices, specifically focusing on machine-based and human-based speaker verification. We showed that voice conversion poses a serious threat and our attacks can be successful for a majority of cases. Worryingly, the attacks against human-based speaker verification may become more effective in the future because voice conversion/synthesis quality will continue to improve, while it can be safely said that human ability will likely not.

Our current study has certain limitations that might affect the results when our attacks are implemented in real-life. First, we only used the known state-of-the-art biometric speaker verification system and an off-the-shelf voice conversion tool for conducting our attacks. There may be other systems, especially used in industry, that might give different (better or worse) results under our attacks. Second, our arbitrary speech attack was designed to imitate the scenario, in which an attacker posts fake audio samples of a victim over the Internet or even leaves fake voice messages to someone's phone. The current study does not tell us how the attacks might work in other scenarios such as faking real-time communication, or faking court evidences. Third, we asked the participants in our human verification study to pay close attention to the samples before responding. In real-life, however, if someone posts an audio snippet or leaves a voicemail, people may not pay as much attention. Thus, in this scenario, the possibility of accepting a morphed sample in real-life may actually increase (compared to our study). All these issues should be subject to further research, which we plan to explore.

Among these limitations, our study has certain strengths as well. The users who have participated in the study, in case of the arbitrary speech experiment, were all fairly young with no hearing problems. Older people, or those with hearing disabilities, might perform worse against our attacks. Moreover, our results may be much better if a trained mimicry artist serves the role of an attacker resulting in a better voice conversion model.

Although protecting against our attacks seems challenging, there can be ways to ensure that one's voice does not get stolen by an adversary in the first place.

Such measures may include people's awareness to these attacks, and people being wary about posting their audio-visuals online. Another line of defense lies in defeating audio monitoring in public places. For example, putting in place stricter policies for audio recording in public or actively preventing audio monitoring by using high frequency audio transmitters that cloak the audio recordings (without affecting human perception). There exist commercial equipment to jam audio and jeopardize audio surveillance systems [1,3].

Another natural defense strategy would be the development of speaker verification systems that can resist voice conversion attacks by using liveness tests for a speaker. A development in the field of speaker liveness detection is proposed by Baughman et al. [17]. In our future work, we plan to study these different defense strategies.

# A    Demographics Information

**Table 3.** Demographics information of (a) speakers of the arbitrary speech dataset (b) participants in the human-based famous speaker verification study (c) participants in the human-based briefly familiar speaker verification study

|  | (a) | (b) | (c) |
|---|---|---|---|
|  | N = 10 | N = 65 | N = 32 |
| **Gender** | | | |
| Male | 50% | 42% | 49% |
| Female | 50% | 58% | 51% |
| **Age** | | | |
| 18-24 years | 40% | 8% | 19% |
| 25-34 years | 60% | 61% | 46% |
| 35-44 years | 0% | 22% | 21% |
| 45-54 years | 0% | 6% | 8% |
| 55-64 years | 0% | 3% | 6% |
| **Education** | | | |
| High school degree or equivalent (e.g. GED) | 10% | 17% | 24% |
| Some college but no degree | 10% | 16% | 19% |
| Associate degree (e.g. AA, AS) | 0% | 8% | 19% |
| Bachelor's degree (e.g. BA, AB, BS) | 80% | 40% | 35% |
| Master's degree (e.g. MA, MS, MBA) | 0% | 13% | 3% |
| Professional degree (e.g. MD, DDS, JD) | 0% | 3% | 0% |
| Doctorate degree (e.g. PhD) | 0% | 2% | 0% |
| **English as First Language** | | | |
| Yes | 100% | 91% | 89% |
| No | 0% | 9% | 11% |
| **Hearing Impairment** | | | |
| Yes | 10% | 0% | 3% |
| No | 90% | 100% | 97% |

## B    Voice Similarity Test Results

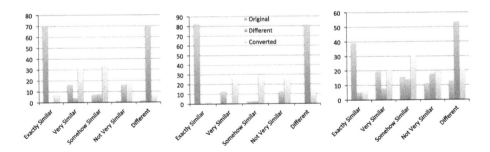

**Fig. 2.** The voice similarity test results for Oprah (left), Morgan (middle), and unfamiliar speakers (right)

## C    Voice Conversion Attack FAR Distribution (MOBIO Dataset)

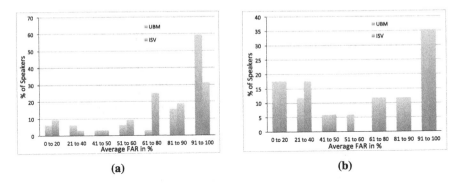

**Fig. 3.** Distribution of FAR for Voice Conversion Attack across the (a) Male, (b) Female users in the MOBIO dataset

## D    Open-Ended Feedback

At the end of the second study, we asked the participants as to how easy/difficult they find the task of recognizing a speaker. Majority of participants found the task to be "fairly difficult", some believed that it was easier for some recordings and more difficult for others, and a couple of participants found the female speakers more easy to distinguish. We also asked the participants what possibly can improve the accuracy of their answers. Most of the users reported that the quality of the recordings plays an important role, others believed that associating the voice to an image (i.e., a face) helps to recognize the speaker better. Some answered that listening to multiple topics spoken by the speaker or hear the speaker sing a song can help to understand his/her particular style of speaking. The last question polled the participants about the basis behind their decisions. Each user had distinct opinion, including quality, naturalness, genuineness, pitch, tone, style, pace, accent, volume, background noise, age, and race of the speaker.

# References

1. Atlassound – speech privacy/sound masking. http://www.atlassound.com/SpeechPrivacy-SoundMasking-376
2. AT&T Natural Voices Text-to-Speech. http://www2.research.att.com/~ttsweb/tts
3. Audio Jammers. http://www.brickhousesecurity.com/category/counter+surveillance/audio+jammers.do
4. CMU Arctic Databases. http://festvox.org/cmu_arctic/index.html
5. Festival. http://www.cstr.ed.ac.uk/projects/festival/
6. Festvox. http://festvox.org/
7. Mobio. https://www.idiap.ch/dataset/mobio
8. NIST SREs. http://www.itl.nist.gov/iad/mig//tests/spk/
9. Statistical Parametric Synthesis And Voice Conversion Techniques. http://festvox.org/11752/slides/lecture11a.pdf
10. The ModelTalker TTS system. https://www.modeltalker.org
11. Voice Cards. http://www.voicecards.com/index.html
12. Voxforge. http://www.voxforge.org/
13. Banking on the power of speech (2013). https://wealth.barclays.com/en_gb/internationalwealth/manage-your-money/banking-on-the-power-of-speech.html
14. VocaliD: Donating your voice to people with speech impairment (2014). http://www.assistivetechnologyblog.com/2014/03/vocalid-donating-your-voice-to-people.html
15. Wells Fargo tests mobile banking voice recognition (2014). http://www.mobilepaymentstoday.com/news/wells-fargo-tests-mobile-banking-voice-recognition
16. Alegre, F., Vipperla, R., Evans, N., Fauve, B.: On the vulnerability of automatic speaker recognition to spoofing attacks with artificial signals. In: 2012 Proceedings of the 20th European Signal Processing Conference (EUSIPCO) (2012)
17. Baughman, A.K., Pelecanos, J.W.: Speaker liveness detection, 19 November 2013. US Patent 8,589,167
18. Bjhorus, J.: Big banks edge into biometrics (2014)
19. Burget, L., Matejka, P., Schwarz, P., Glembek, O., Cernocky, J.: Analysis of feature extraction and channel compensation in a gmm speaker recognition system. IEEE Trans. Audio Speech Lang. Process. **15**, 1979–1986 (2007)
20. Campbell Jr., J.P.: Speaker recognition: a tutorial. In: Proceedings of the IEEE (1997)
21. Chevillet, M., Riesenhuber, M., Rauschecker, J.P.: Functional correlates of the anterolateral processing hierarchy in human auditory cortex. J. Neurosci. **31**, 9345–9352 (2011)

22. Crosman, P.: U.s. bank pushes voice biometrics to replace clunky passwords (2014)
23. De Leon, P.L., Apsingekar, V.R., Pucher, M., Yamagishi, J.: Revisiting the security of speaker verification systems against imposture using synthetic speech. In: 2010 IEEE International Conference on Acoustics Speech and Signal Processing (ICASSP) (2010)
24. De Leon, P.L., Pucher, M., Yamagishi, J.: Evaluation of the vulnerability of speaker verification to synthetic speech (2010)
25. De Leon, P.L., Pucher, M., Yamagishi, J., Hernaez, I., Saratxaga, I.: Evaluation of speaker verification security and detection of hmm-based synthetic speech. IEEE Trans. Audio Speech Lang. Process. **20**, 2280–2290 (2012)
26. Desai, S., Raghavendra, E.V., Yegnanarayana, B., Black, A.W., Prahallad, K.: Voice conversion using artificial neural networks. In: IEEE International Conference on Acoustics, Speech and Signal Processing, ICASSP 2009. IEEE (2009)
27. Hollien, H., Majewski, W., Doherty, E.T.: Perceptual identification of voices under normal, stress and disguise speaking conditions. J. Phonetics **10**, 139–148 (1982)
28. Kain, A., Macon, M.W.: Spectral voice conversion for text-to-speech synthesis. In: Proceedings of the 1998 IEEE International Conference on Acoustics, Speech and Signal Processing (1998)
29. Keiler, A.: Is voice-recognition the future of banking? wells fargo thinks so (2014). http://consumerist.com/2014/01/21/is-voice-recognition-the-future-of-banking-wells-fargo-thinks-so/
30. Khoury, E., El Shafey, L., Marcel, S.: Spear: an open source toolbox for speaker recognition based on bob. In: IEEE International Conference on Acoustics, Speech and Signal Processing (ICASSP) (2014)
31. Kinsbruner, E.: Key considerations for testing voice recognition in mobile banking applicaions (2013). http://www.banktech.com/channels/key-considerations-for-testing-voice-recognition-in-mobile-banking-applications/a/d-id/1296456?
32. Kominek, J., Schultz, T., Black, A.W.: Synthesizer voice quality of new languages calibrated with mean mel cepstral distortion. In: Proceedings of SLTU (2008)
33. Kubichek, R.F.: Mel-cepstral distance measure for objective speech quality assessment. In: IEEE Pacific Rim Conference on Communications, Computers and Signal Processing, vol. 1. IEEE (1993)
34. Suvarna Kumar, G., Prasad Raju, K.A., Mohan Rao, C.P.V.N.J., Satheesh, P.: Speaker recognition using gmm. Int. J. Eng. Sci. Technol. **2**, 2428–2436 (2010)
35. Melin, H.: Automatic speaker verification on site and by telephone: methods, applications and assessment (2006)
36. Reynolds, D.: An overview of automatic speaker recognition. In: Proceedings of the International Conference on Acoustics, Speech and Signal Processing (ICASSP) (2002)
37. Reynolds, D.A., Quatieri, T.F., Dunn, R.B.: Speaker verification using adapted gaussian mixture models. Digital Signal Process. **10**, 19–41 (2000)
38. Rose, P.: Forensic Speaker Identification. CRC Press, New York (2003)
39. Shirvanian, M., Saxena, N.: Wiretapping via mimicry: short voice imitation man-in-the-middle attacks on crypto phones. In: Proceedings of ACM CCS 2014 (2014)
40. Stolcke, A., Kajarekar, S.S., Ferrer, L., Shrinberg, E.: Speaker recognition with session variability normalization based on mllr adaptation transforms. IEEE Trans. Audio Speech Lang. Process. **15**, 1987–1998 (2007)
41. Toda, T., Alan W.B., Tokuda, K.: Acoustic-to-articulatory inversion mapping with gaussian mixture model. In: Proceedings of INTERSPEECH (2004)

42. Toda, T., Black, A.W., Tokuda, K.: Spectral conversion based on maximum likelihood estimation considering global variance of converted parameter. In: Proceedings of ICASSP, vol. 1 (2005)
43. Vogt, R., Sridharan, S.: Explicit modelling of session variability for speaker verification. Comput. Speech Lang. **22**, 17–38 (2008)
44. Wu, Z., Li, H.: Voice conversion and spoofing attack on speaker verification systems. In: Signal and Information Processing Association Annual Summit and Conference (APSIPA), 2013 Asia-Pacific (2013)

# Balloon: A Forward-Secure Append-Only Persistent Authenticated Data Structure

Tobias Pulls[1]([✉]) and Roel Peeters[2]

[1] Department of Mathematics and Computer Science,
Karlstad University, Karlstad, Sweden
`tobias.pulls@kau.se`
[2] ESAT/COSIC and iMinds, KU Leuven, Leuven, Belgium
`roel.peeters@esat.kuleuven.be`

**Abstract.** We present Balloon, a forward-secure append-only persistent authenticated data structure. Balloon is designed for an initially trusted author that generates events to be stored in a data structure (the Balloon) kept by an untrusted server, and clients that query this server for events intended for them based on keys and snapshots. The data structure is persistent such that clients can query keys for the current or past versions of the data structure based upon snapshots, which are generated by the author as new events are inserted. The data structure is authenticated in the sense that the server can verifiably prove all operations with respect to snapshots created by the author. No event inserted into the data structure prior to the compromise of the author can be modified or deleted without detection due to Balloon being publicly verifiable. Balloon supports efficient (non-)membership proofs and verifiable inserts by the author, enabling the author to verify the correctness of inserts without having to store a copy of the Balloon. We formally define and prove that Balloon is a secure authenticated data structure.

## 1 Introduction

This paper is motivated by the lack of an appropriate data structure that would enable the trust assumptions to be relaxed for privacy-preserving transparency logging. In the setting of transparency logging, an *author* logs messages intended for *clients* through a *server*: the author sends messages to the server, and clients poll the server for messages intended for it. Previous work [21] assumes a *forward security* model: *both* the author and the server are assumed to be initially trusted and may be compromised at some point in time. Any messages logged *before* this compromise remain secure and private. One can reduce the trust assumptions at the server by introducing a secure hardware extension at the server as in [25].

This paper proposes a novel *append-only authenticated data structure* that allows the server to be untrusted without the need for trusted hardware. Our data structure, which is named Balloon, allows for efficient proofs of both membership and non-membership. As such, the server is forced to provide a verifiable reply to all queries. Balloon also provides efficient (non-)membership proofs for past

© Springer International Publishing Switzerland 2015
G. Pernul et al. (Eds.): ESORICS 2015, Part II, LNCS 9327, pp. 622–641, 2015.
DOI: 10.1007/978-3-319-24177-7_31

versions of the data structure (making it *persistent*), which is a key property for providing proofs of time, when only some versions of the Balloon have been time-stamped. Since Balloon is append-only, we can greatly improve the efficiency in comparison with other authenticated data structures that provide the same properties as described above, such as persistent authenticated dictionaries [1].

Balloon is a key building block for privacy-preserving transparency logging to make data processing by service providers transparent to data subjects whose personal data are being processed. Balloon can also be used as part of a secure logging system, similar to the history tree system by Crosby and Wallach [6]. Another closely related application is as an extension to Certificate Transparency (CT) [12], where Balloon can be used to provide efficient non-membership proofs, which are highly relevant in relation to certificate revocation for CT [11,12,18].

For formally defining and proving the security of Balloon, we take a similar approach as Papamanthou *et al.* [19]. We view Balloon in the model of *authenticated data structures* (ADS), using the *three-party* setting [24]. The three party setting for ADS consists of the *source* (corresponding to our author), one or more *servers*, and one or more *clients*. The source is a trusted party that authors a data structure (the Balloon) that is copied to the untrusted servers together with some additional data that authenticates the data structure. The servers answer queries made by clients. The goal for an ADS is for clients to be able to verify the correctness of replies to queries based only on public information. The public information takes the form of a verification key, for verifying signatures made by the source, and some *digest* produced by the source to authenticate the data structure. The source can update the ADS, in the process producing new digests, to which is further referred to as *snapshots*. The reply we want to enable clients to verify is the outcome of a *membership query*, which proves *membership* or *non-membership* of an event with a provided key for a provided snapshot.

After we show that Balloon is a secure ADS in the three party setting, we extend Balloon to enable the author to discard the data structure and still perform verifiable inserts of new events to update the Balloon. Finally, we describe how *monitors* and a *perfect gossiping mechanism* would prevent the an author from undetectably modifying or deleting events once inserted into the Balloon, which lays the foundation for the forward-secure author setting.

We make the following contributions:

- A novel append-only authenticated data structure named Balloon that allows for both efficient membership and non-membership proofs, also for past versions of the Balloon, while keeping the storage and memory requirements minimal (Sect. 3).
- We formally prove that Balloon is a secure authenticated data structure (Sect. 4) according to the definition by Papamanthou *et al.* [19].
- Efficient verifiable inserts into our append-only authenticated data structure that enable the author to ensure consistency of the data structure without storing a copy of the entire (authenticated) data structure (Sect. 5).
- We define publicly verifiable consistency for an ADS scheme and show how it enables a forward-secure source (Sect. 6). Verifiable inserts can also have applications for monitors in, e.g., [3,10–12,22,27].

- In Sect. 7, we show that Balloon is practical, providing performance results for a proof-of-concept implementation.

The rest of the paper is structured as follows. Section 2 introduces the background of our idea. Section 8 presents related work and compares Balloon to prior work. Section 9 concludes the paper. Of independent interest, Appendix B shows why probabilistic proofs are insufficient for ensuring consistency of a Balloon without the burden on the prover increasing greatly.

## 2     Preliminaries

First, we introduce the used formalisation of an authenticated data structure scheme. Next, we give some background on the two data structures that make up Balloon: a history tree, for efficient membership proofs for any snapshot, and a hash treap, for efficient non-membership proofs. Finally we present our cryptographic building blocks.

### 2.1     An Authenticated Data Structure Scheme

Papamanthou *et al.* [19] define an authenticated data structure and its two main properties: correctness and security. We make use of these definitions and therefore present them here, be it with slight modifications to fit our terminology.

**Definition 1 (ADS scheme).** *Let $D$ be any data structure that supports queries $q$ and updates $u$. Let $auth(D)$ denote the resulting authenticated data structure and $s$ the snapshot of the authenticated data structure, i.e., a constant-size description of $D$. An ADS scheme $\mathcal{A}$ is a collection of the following six probabilistic polynomial-time algorithms:*

1. *$\{sk, pk\} \leftarrow genkey(1^\lambda)$: On input of the security parameter $\lambda$, it outputs a secret key $sk$ and public key $pk$;*
2. *$\{auth(D_0), s_0\} \leftarrow setup(D_0, sk, pk)$: On input of a (plain) data structure $D_0$, the secret key $sk$, and the public key $pk$, it computes the authenticated data structure $auth(D_0)$ and the corresponding snapshot $s_0$;*
3. *$\{D_{h+1}, auth(D_{h+1}), s_{h+1}, upd\} \leftarrow update(u, D_h, auth(D_h), s_h, sk, pk)$: On input of an update $u$ on the data structure $D_h$, the authenticated data structure $auth(D_h)$, the snapshot $s_h$, the secret key $sk$, and the public key $pk$, it outputs the updated data structure $D_{h+1}$ along with the updated authenticated data structure $auth(D_{h+1})$, the updated snapshot $s_{h+1}$ and some relative information $upd$;*
4. *$\{D_{h+1}, auth(D_{h+1}), s_{h+1}\} \leftarrow refresh(u, D_h, auth(D_h), s_h, upd, pk)$: On input of an update $u$ on the data structure $D_h$, the authenticated data structure $auth(D_h)$, the snapshot $s_h$, relative information $upd$ and the public key $pk$, it outputs the updated data structure $D_{h+1}$ along with the updated authenticated data structure $auth(D_{h+1})$ and the updated snapshot $s_{h+1}$;*

5. $\{\Pi(q), \alpha(q)\} \leftarrow query(q, D_h, auth(D_h), \text{pk})$: *On input of a query $q$ on data structure $D_h$, the authenticated data structure $auth(D_h)$ and the public key* pk, *it returns the answer $\alpha(q)$ to the query, along with proof $\Pi(q)$;*
6. $\{accept, reject\} \leftarrow verify(q, \alpha, \Pi, s_h, \text{pk})$: *On input of a query $q$, an answer $\alpha$, a proof $\Pi$, a snapshot $s_h$ and the public key* pk, *it outputs either* accept *or* reject.

Next to the definition of the ADS scheme, another algorithm was defined for deciding whether or not an answer $\alpha$ to query $q$ on data structure $D_h$ is correct: $\{accept, reject\} \leftarrow check(q, \alpha, D_h)$.

**Definition 2 (Correctness).** *Let $\mathcal{A}$ be an ADS scheme $\{genkey, setup, update, refresh, query, verify\}$. The ADS scheme $\mathcal{A}$ is correct if, for all $\lambda \in \mathbb{N}$, for all $\{\text{sk}, \text{pk}\}$ output by algorithm genkey, for all $D_h$, $auth(D_h)$, $s_h$ output by one invocation of setup followed by polynomially-many invocations of refresh, where $h \geq 0$, for all queries $q$ and for all $\Pi(q), \alpha(q)$ output by $query(q, D_h, auth(D_h), \text{pk})$ with all but negligible probability, whenever algorithm check $(q, \alpha(q), D_h)$ outputs accept, so does $verify(q, \alpha(q), \Pi(q), s_h, \text{pk})$.*

**Definition 3 (Security).** *Let $\mathcal{A}$ be an ADS scheme $\{genkey, setup, update, refresh, query, verify\}$, $\lambda$ be the security parameter, $\epsilon(\lambda)$ be a negligible function and $\{\text{sk}, \text{pk}\} \leftarrow genkey(1^\lambda)$. Let also $\mathbf{Adv}$ be a probabilistic polynomial-time adversary that is only given pk. The adversary has unlimited access to all algorithms of $\mathcal{A}$, except for algorithms setup and update to which he has only oracle access. The adversary picks an initial state of the data structure $D_0$ and computes $D_0, auth(D_0), s_0$ through oracle access to algorithm setup. Then, for $i = 0, ..., h = poly(\lambda)$, $\mathbf{Adv}$ issues an update $u_i$ in the data structure $D_i$ and computes $D_{i+1}, auth(D_{i+1})$ and $s_{i+1}$ through oracle access to algorithm update. Finally the adversary picks an index $0 \leq t \leq h + 1$, and computes a query $q$, answer $\alpha$ and proof $\Pi$. The ADS scheme $\mathcal{A}$ is secure if for all $\lambda \in \mathbb{N}$, for all $\{\text{sk}, \text{pk}\}$ output by algorithm genkey, and for any probabilistic polynomial-time adversary $\mathbf{Adv}$ it holds that*

$$Pr\left[ \begin{array}{c} \{q, \Pi, \alpha, t\} \leftarrow \mathbf{Adv}(1^\lambda, \text{pk}); accept \leftarrow verify(q, \alpha, \Pi, s_t, \text{pk}) \\ reject \leftarrow check(q, \alpha, D_t) \end{array} \right] \leq \epsilon(\lambda). \quad (1)$$

## 2.2 History Tree

A tamper-evident history system, as defined by Crosby and Wallach [6], consists of a *history tree* data structure and five algorithms. A history tree is in essence a *versioned* Merkle tree [15] (hash tree). Each leaf node in the tree is the hash of an event, while interior nodes are labeled with the hash of its children nodes in the subtree rooted at that node. The root of the tree fixes the content of the entire tree. Different versions of history trees, produced as events are added, can be proven to make consistent claims about the past. The five algorithms, adjusted to our terminology, are defined as follows:

- $c_i \leftarrow$ H.Add($e$): Given an event $e$ the system appends it to the history tree $H$ as the $i$:th event and then outputs a commitment[1] $c_i$.
- $\{P, e_i\} \leftarrow$ H.MembershipGen($i$, $c_j$): Generates a membership proof $P$ for the $i$:th event with respect to commitment $c_j$, where $i \leq j$, from the history tree $H$. The algorithm outputs $P$ and the event $e_i$.
- $P \leftarrow$ H.IncGen($c_i, c_j$): Generates an incremental proof $P$ between $c_i$ and $c_j$, where $i \leq j$, from the history tree $H$. Outputs $P$.
- $\{$accept, reject$\} \leftarrow$ P.MembershipVerify($i, c_j, e_i'$): Verifies that $P$ proves that $e_i'$ is the $i$:th event in the history defined by $c_j$ (where $i \leq j$). Outputs accept if true, otherwise reject.
- $\{$accept, reject$\} \leftarrow$ P.IncVerify($c_i', c_j$): Verifies that $P$ proves that $c_j$ fixes every event fixed by $c_i'$ (where $i \leq j$). Outputs accept if true, otherwise reject.

### 2.3　Hash Treap

A treap is a type of randomised binary search tree [2], where the binary search tree is balanced using heap priorities. Each node in a treap has a key, value, priority, left child and right child. A treap has three important properties:

1. Traversing the treap in order gives the sorted order of the keys;
2. Treaps are structured according to the nodes' priorities, where each node's children have lower priorities;
3. Given a deterministic attribution of priorities to nodes, a treap is *set unique* and *history independent*, i.e., its structure is unique for a given set of nodes, regardless of the order in which nodes were inserted, and the structure does not leak any information about the order in which nodes were inserted.

When a node is inserted in a treap, its position in the treap is first determined by a binary search. Once the position is found, the node is inserted in place, and then rotated upwards towards the root until its priority is consistent with the heap priority. When the priorities are assigned to nodes using a cryptographic hash function, the tree becomes probabilistically balanced with an expected depth of $\log n$, where $n$ is the number of nodes in the treap. Inserting a node takes expected $\mathcal{O}(\log n)$ operations and results in expected $\mathcal{O}(1)$ rotations to preserve the properties of the treap [9]. Given a treap, it is straightforward to build a hash treap: have each node calculate the hash of its own attributes[2] together with the hash of its children. Since the hash treap is a Merkle tree, its root fixes the entire hash treap. The concept of turning treaps into Merkle trees for authenticating the treap has been used for example in the context of persistent authenticated dictionaries [7] and authentication of certificate revocation lists [18].

We define the following algorithms on our hash treap, for which we assume that keys $k$ are unique and of predefined constant size $cst$:

---

[1] A commitment $c_i$ is the root of the history tree for the $i$:th event, signed by the system. For the purpose of this paper, we omit the signature from the commitments.

[2] The priority can safely be discarded since it is derived solely from the key and implicit in the structure of the treap.

- $r \leftarrow$ T.Add($k, v$): Given a unique key $k$ and value $v$, where $|k| = cst$ and $|v| > 0$, the system inserts them into the hash treap $T$ and then outputs the updated hash of the root $r$. The add is done with priority Hash($k$), which results in a deterministic treap. After the new node is in place, the hash of each node along the path from the root has its internal hash updated. The hash of a node is Hash($k||v||$left.hash$||$right.hash). In case there is no right (left) child node, the right.hash (left.hash) is set to a string of consecutive zeros of size equal to the output of the used hash function $0^{|\text{Hash}(\cdot)|}$.
- $\{P^T, v\} \leftarrow$ T.AuthPath($k$): Generates an authenticated path $P^T$ from the root of the treap $T$ to the key $k$ where $|k| = cst$. The algorithm outputs $P^T$ and, in case of when a node with key $k$ was found, the associated value $v$. For each node $i$ in $P^T$, $k_i$ and $v_i$ need to be provided to verify the hash in the authenticated path.
- $\{$accept, reject$\} \leftarrow$ $P^T$.AuthPathVerify(k,v): Verifies that $P^T$ proves that $k$ is a non-member if $v \stackrel{?}{=}$ null or otherwise a member. Verification checks that $|k| = cst$ and $|v| > 0$ (if $\neq$ null), calculates and compares the authenticator for each node in $P^T$, and checks that each node in $P^T$ adheres to the sorted order of keys and heap priority.

Additionally we define the following helper algorithms on our hash treap:

- pruned(T) $\leftarrow$ T.BuildPrunedTree($< P_j^T >$): Generates a pruned hash treap pruned(T) from the given authenticated paths $P_j^T$ in the hash treap $T$. This algorithm removes any redundancy between the authenticated paths, resulting in a more compact representation as a pruned hash treap. Note that evaluating pruned(T).AuthPathVerify($k, v$) is equivalent with evaluating $P^T$.AuthPath Verify($k, v$) on the authenticated path $P^T$ through $k$ contained in the pruned hash treap.
- $r \leftarrow$ $P^T$.root(): Outputs the root $r$ of an authenticated path. Note that pruned(T).root() and $P^T$.root() are equivalent for any authenticated path $P^T$ contained by the pruned tree.

## 2.4 Cryptographic Building Blocks

We assume idealised cryptographic building blocks in the form of a hash function Hash($\cdot$), and signature scheme that is used to sign a message $m$ and verify the resulting signature: $\{$accept, reject$\} \leftarrow$ Verify$_{vk}($Sign$_{sk}(m), m)$. The hash function should be collision and pre-image resistant. The signature scheme should be existentially unforgeable under known message attack. Furthermore, we rely on the following lemma for the correctness and security of a Balloon:

**Lemma 1.** *The security of an authenticated path in a Merkle (hash) tree reduces to the collision resistance of the underlying hash function.*

*Proof.* This follows from the work by Merkle [16] and Blum *et al.* [5]. $\square$

## 3    Construction and Algorithms

Our data structure is an append-only key-value store that stores events $e$ consisting of a key $k$ and a value $v$. Each key $k_i$ is assumed to be unique and of predefined constant size $cst$, where $cst \leftarrow |\mathtt{Hash}(\cdot)|$. Additionally, our data structure encodes some extra information in order to identify in which set (epoch) events were added. We define an algorithm $k \leftarrow \mathtt{key}(e)$ that returns the key $k$ of the event $e$.

Our authenticated data structure combines a hash treap and a history tree when adding an event an event $e$ as follows:

- First, the event is added to the history tree: $c_i \leftarrow H.add\big(\mathtt{Hash}(k\|v)\big)$. Let $i$ be the index where the hashed event was inserted at into the history tree.
- Next, the hash of the event key $\mathtt{Hash}(k)$ and the event position $i$ are added to the hash treap: $r \leftarrow \mathtt{T.Add}(\mathtt{Hash}(k), i)$.

Figure 1 visualises a simplified Balloon with a hash treap and a history tree. For the sake of readability, we omit the hash values and priority, replace hashed keys with integers, and replace hashed events with place-holder labels. For example, the root in the hash treap has key 42 and value 1. The value 1 refers to the leaf node in the history tree with index 1, whose value is p42, the place-holder label for the hash of the event which key, once hashed, is represented by integer 42.

By putting the hash of the event key, $\mathtt{Hash}(k)$, instead of the key into the hash treap, we avoid easy event enumeration by third parties: no valid event keys leak as part of authenticated paths in the treap for non-membership proofs. Note that when $\mathtt{H.MembershipGen}$ returns an event, as specified in Sect. 2.2, the actual event is retrieved from the data structure, not the hash of the event as stored in the history tree (authentication). We store the hash of the event in the history tree for sake of efficiency, since the event is already stored in the (non-authenticated) data structure.

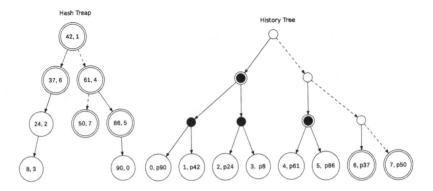

**Fig. 1.** A simplified example of a Balloon consisting of a hash treap and history tree. A membership proof for an event $e = (k, v)$ with $\mathtt{Hash}(k) = 50$ and $\mathtt{Hash}(e)$ denoted by p50 (place-holder label) consists of the circle nodes in both trees.

## 3.1  Setup

**Algorithm.** $\{\text{sk}, \text{pk}\} \leftarrow \text{genkey}(1^\lambda)$ : Generates a signature key-pair $\{\text{sk}, \text{vk}\}$ using the generation algorithm of a signature scheme with security level $\lambda$ and picks a function $\Omega$ that deterministically orders events. Outputs the signing key as the private key $\text{sk} = \text{sk}$, and the verification key and the ordering function $\Omega$ as the public key $\text{pk} = \{\text{vk}, \Omega\}$.

**Algorithm.** $\{\text{auth}(D_0), s_0\} \leftarrow \text{setup}(D_0, \text{sk}, \text{pk})$: Let $D_0$ be the initial data structure, containing the initial set of events $< e_j >$. The authenticated data structure, $\text{auth}(D_0)$, is then computed by adding each event from the set to the, yet empty, authenticated data structure in the order dictated by the function $\Omega \leftarrow \text{pk}$. The snapshot is defined as the root of the hash treap $r$ and commitment in the history tree $c_i$ for the event that was added last together with a digital signature over those: $s_0 = \{r, c_i, \sigma\}$, where $\sigma = \text{Sign}_{\text{sk}}(\{r, c_i\})$.

## 3.2  Update and Refresh

**Algorithm.** $\{D_{h+1}, \text{auth}(D_{h+1}), s_{h+1}, upd\} \leftarrow \text{update}(u, D_h, \text{auth}(D_h), s_h, \text{sk}, \text{pk})$: Let $u$ be a set of events to insert into $D_h$. The updated data structure $D_{h+1}$ is the result of appending the events in $u$ to $D_h$ and indicating that these belong the $(h+1)^{\text{th}}$ set. The updated authenticated data structure, $\text{auth}(D_{h+1})$, is then computed by adding each event from the set to the authenticated data structure $\text{auth}(D_h)$ in the order dictated by the function $\Omega \leftarrow \text{pk}$. The updated snapshot is the root of the hash treap $r$ and commitment in the history tree $c_i$ for the event that was added last together with a digital signature over those: $s_{h+1} = \{r, c_i, \sigma\}$, where $\sigma = \text{Sign}_{\text{sk}}(\{r, c_i\})$. The update information contains this snapshot $upd = s_{h+1}$.

**Algorithm.** $\{D_{h+1}, \text{auth}(D_{h+1}), s_{h+1}\} \leftarrow \text{refresh}(u, D_h, \text{auth}(D_h), s_h, upd, \text{pk})$: Let $u$ be a set of events to insert into $D_h$. The updated data structure $D_{h+1}$ is the result of appending the events in $u$ to $D_h$ and indicating that these belong the $(h+1)^{\text{th}}$ set. The updated authenticated data structure, $\text{auth}(D_{h+1})$, is then computed by adding each event from the set $u$ to the authenticated data structure $\text{auth}(D_h)$ in the order dictated by the function $\Omega \leftarrow \text{pk}$. Finally, the new snapshot is set to $s_{h+1} = upd$.

## 3.3  Query and Verify

**Algorithm.** $\{\Pi(q), \alpha(q)\} \leftarrow \text{query}(q, D_h, \text{auth}(D_h), \text{pk})$ (**Membership**): We consider the query $q$ to be "a membership query for an event with key $k$ in the data structure that is fixed by $s_{queried}$", where $queried \leq h$. The query has two possible answers $\alpha(q)$: $\{\text{true}, e\}$ in case an event $e$ with key $k$ exists in $D_{queried}$, otherwise $\text{false}$. The proof of correctness $\Pi(q)$ consists of up to three parts:

1. An authenticated path $P^T$ in the hash treap to $k' = \mathtt{Hash}(k)$;
2. The index $i$ of the event in the history tree;
3. A membership proof $P$ on index $i$ in the history tree.

The algorithm generates an authenticated path in the hash treap, which is part of $\mathtt{auth}(D_h)$, to $k'$: $\{P^T, v\} \leftarrow \mathtt{T.AuthPath}(\mathrm{k'})$. If $v \stackrel{?}{=} \mathtt{null}$, then there is no event with key $k$ in $D_h$ (and consequently in $D_{queried}$) and the algorithm outputs $\Pi(q) = P^T$ and $\alpha(q) = \mathtt{false}$.

Otherwise, the value $v$ in the hash treap indicates the index $i$ in the history tree of the event. Now the algorithm checks whether or not the index $i$ is contained in the history tree up till $\mathtt{auth}(D_{queried})$. If not, the algorithm outputs $\alpha(q) = \mathtt{false}$ and $\Pi(q) = \{P^T, i\}$. If it is, the algorithm outputs $\alpha(q) = \{\mathtt{true}, e_i\}$ and $\Pi(q) = \{P^T, i, P\}$, where $\{P, e_i\} \leftarrow \mathtt{H.MembershipGen}(i, c_{queried})$ and $c_{queried} \leftarrow s_{queried}$.

**Algorithm.** $\{\mathtt{accept}, \mathtt{reject}\} \leftarrow \mathtt{verify}(q, \alpha, \Pi, s_h, \mathtt{pk})$ (**Membership**): First, the algorithm extracts $\{k, s_{queried}\}$ from the query $q$ and $\{P^T, i, P\}$ from $\Pi$, where $i$ and $P$ can be $\mathtt{null}$. From the snapshot it extracts $r \leftarrow s_h$. Then the algorithm computes $x \leftarrow \mathtt{P^T.AuthPathVerify}(k, i)$. If $x \stackrel{?}{=} \mathtt{false} \vee P^T.\mathtt{root}() \neq r$, the algorithm outputs $\mathtt{reject}$. The algorithm outputs $\mathtt{accept}$ if any of the following three conditions hold, otherwise $\mathtt{reject}$:

- $\alpha \stackrel{?}{=} \mathtt{false} \wedge i \stackrel{?}{=} \mathtt{null}$;
- $\alpha \stackrel{?}{=} \mathtt{false} \wedge i > queried[-1]^3$ ;
- $\alpha \stackrel{?}{=} \{\mathtt{true}, e\} \wedge \mathtt{key}(e) \stackrel{?}{=} k \wedge y \stackrel{?}{=} \mathtt{true}$, \
  for $y \leftarrow P.\mathtt{MembershipVerify}(i, c_{queried}, \mathtt{Hash}(e))$ and $c_{queried} \leftarrow s_{queried}$.

## 4    Security

**Theorem 1.** *Balloon* $\{genkey, setup, update, refresh, query, verify\}$ *is a correct ADS scheme for a data structure $D$, that contains a list of sets of events, according to Definition 2, assuming the collision-resistance of the underlying hash function.*

The proof of correctness can be found in the full version of our paper [20].

**Theorem 2.** *Balloon* $\{genkey, setup, update, refresh, query, verify\}$ *is a secure ADS scheme for a data structure $D$, that contains a list of sets of events, according to Definition 3, assuming the collision-resistance of the underlying hash function.*

The full proof of security can be found in Appendix A.

---

[3] $queried[-1]$ denotes the index of the last inserted event in version $queried$ of the authenticated data structure.

*Proof (Sketch).* Given that the different versions of the authenticated data structure and corresponding snapshots are generated through oracle access, these are correct, i.e., the authenticated data structure contains all elements of the data structure for each version, the root and commitment in each snapshot correspond to that version of the ADS and the signature in each snapshot verifies.

For all cases where the check algorithm outputs reject, **Adv** has to forge an authenticated path in the hash treap and/or history tree in order to get the verify algorithm to output accept, which implies breaking Lemma 1.

## 5    Verifiable Insert

In practical three-party settings, the source typically has less storage capabilities than servers. As such, it would be desirable that the source does not need to keep a copy of the entire (authenticated) data structure for update, but instead can rely on its own (constant) storage combined with verifiable information from a server. We define new query and verify algorithms that enable the construction of a *pruned* authenticated data structure, containing only the nodes needed to be insert the new set of events with a modified update algorithm. The pruned authenticated data structure is denoted by $\mathtt{pruned}\big(\mathtt{auth}(D_h), u\big)$, where $\mathtt{auth}(D_h)$ denotes the version of the ADS being pruned, and $u$ the set of events where this ADS is pruned for.

**Algorithm.** $\{\Pi(q), \alpha(q)\} \leftarrow \mathtt{query}(q, D_h, \mathtt{auth}(D_h), \mathtt{pk})$ (**Prune**): We consider the query $q$ to be "a prune query for if a set of events $u$ can be inserted into $D_h$". The query has two possible answers: $\alpha(q)$: true in case no key for the events in $u$ already exist in $D_h$, otherwise false. The proof of correctness $\Pi(q)$ either proves that there already is an event with a key from an event in $u$, or provides proofs that enable the construction of a pruned $\mathtt{auth}(D_h)$, depending on the answer. For every $k_j \leftarrow \mathtt{key}(e_j)$ in the set $u$, the algorithm uses as a sub-algorithm $\{\Pi'_j(q), \alpha'_j(q)\} \leftarrow \mathtt{query}\,(q'_j, D_h, \mathtt{auth}(D_h), \mathtt{pk})$ (**Membership**) with $q = \{k_j, \mathsf{s}_h\}$, where $\mathsf{s}_h$ fixes $\mathtt{auth}(D_h)$. If any $\alpha'_j(q) \stackrel{?}{=}$ true, the algorithm outputs $\alpha(q) = $ false and $\Pi(q) = \{\Pi'_j(q), k_j\}$ and stops. If not, the algorithm takes $P^T_j$ from each $\Pi'_j(q)$ and creates the set $< P^T_j >$. Next, the algorithm extracts the latest event $e_i$ inserted into the history tree from $\mathtt{auth}(D_h)$ and uses as a sub-algorithm $\{\Pi'(q), \alpha'(q)\} \leftarrow \mathtt{query}(q', D_h, \mathtt{auth}(D_h), \mathtt{pk})$ (**Membership**) with q' $= \{\mathtt{key}(e_i), \mathsf{s}_h\}$. Finally, the algorithm outputs $\alpha(q) = $ true and $\Pi(q) = \{< P^T_j >, \Pi'(q)\}$.

**Algorithm.** $\{\mathtt{accept}, \mathtt{reject}\} \leftarrow \mathtt{verify}(q, \alpha, \Pi, \mathsf{s}_h, \mathtt{pk})$ (**Prune**): The algorithm starts by extracting $< e_j > \leftarrow u$ from the query $q$. If $\alpha \stackrel{?}{=}$ false, it gets $\{\Pi'_j(q), k_j\}$ from $\Pi$ and uses as a sub-algorithm $\mathtt{valid} \leftarrow \mathtt{verify}(q', \alpha', \Pi', \mathsf{s}_h, \mathtt{pk})$ (**Membership**), with q' $= \{k, \mathsf{s}_h\}$, $\alpha' = $ true and $\Pi' = \Pi'_j(q)$, where $k \leftarrow k_j$. If $\mathtt{valid} \stackrel{?}{=}$ accept and there exists an event with key $k$ in $u$, the algorithm outputs accept, otherwise reject.

If $\alpha \stackrel{?}{=}$ true, extract $\{< P_j^T >, \Pi'(q)\}$ from $\Pi$. For each event $e_j$ in $u$, the algorithm gets $k_j \leftarrow \text{key}(e_j)$, finds the corresponding $P_j^T$ for $k_j' = \text{Hash}(k_j)$, and uses as a sub-algorithm valid $\leftarrow$ verify$(q', \alpha', \Pi', s_h, \text{pk})$ (**Membership**), with $q' = \{k_j, s_h\}$, $\alpha' = $ false and $\Pi' = P_j^T$. If no corresponding $P_j^T$ to $k_j'$ is found in $< P_j^T >$ or valid $\stackrel{?}{=}$ reject, then the algorithm outputs reject and stops. Next, the algorithm uses as a sub-algorithm valid $\leftarrow$ verify$(q', \alpha, \Pi', s_h, \text{pk})$ (**Membership**), with $q' = \{\text{key}(e_i), s_h\}$ and $\Pi' = \Pi'(q)$, where $e_i \in \Pi'(q)$. If valid $\stackrel{?}{=}$ accept and $i \stackrel{?}{=} h[-1]$ the algorithm outputs accept, otherwise reject.

**Algorithm.** $\{s_{h+1}, upd\} \leftarrow$ update*$(u, \Pi, s_h, \text{sk}, \text{pk})$: Let $u$ be a set of events to insert into $D_h$ and $\Pi$ a proof that the sub-algorithm verify$(q, \alpha, \Pi, s_h, \text{pk})$ (**Prune**) outputs accept for, where $q = u$ and $\alpha = $ true. The algorithm extracts $\{< P_j^T >, \Pi'(q)\}$ from $\Pi$ and builds a pruned hash treap pruned$(T) \leftarrow$ T.Build PrunedTree$(< P_j^T >)$. Next, it extracts $P$ from $\Pi'(q)$ and constructs the pruned Balloon pruned$(\text{auth}(D_h), u) \leftarrow \{\text{pruned}(T), P\}$. Finally, the algorithm adds each event in $u$ to the pruned Balloon pruned$(\text{auth}(D_h), u)$ in the order dictated by $\Omega \leftarrow \text{pk}$. The updated snapshot is the digital signature over the root of the updated pruned hash treap $r$ and commitment in the updated pruned history tree $c_i$ for the event that was added last: $s_{h+1} = \{r, c_i\}, \text{Sign}_{\text{sk}}(\{r, c_i\})$. The update information contains this snapshot $upd = s_{h+1}$.

**Lemma 2.** *The output of* update *and* update* *is identical with respect to the root of the hash treap and the latests commitment in the history tree of* $s_{h+1}$ *and* $upd^4$.

The proof of Lemma 2 can be found in the full version of our paper [20]. As a result of Lemma 2, the update algorithm in Balloon can be replaced by update* without breaking the correctness and security of the Balloon as in Theorems 1 and 2. This means that the server can keep and refresh the (authenticated) data structure while the author only needs to store the last snapshot $s_h$ to be able to produce updates, resulting in a small constant size storage requirement for the author.

Note that, in order to reduce the size of the transmitted proof, verify (**Prune**) could output the pruned authenticated data structure directly. Since pruned$(T)$. AuthPathVerify$(k, v)$ and $P^T$.AuthPathVerify$(k, v)$ are equivalent, the correctness and security of verify (**Prune**) reduce to verify (**Membership**). Section 7 shows the reduction in the size of the proof with pruning.

## 6  Publicly Verifiable Consistency

While the server is untrusted, the author is trusted. A stronger adversarial model assumes forward security for the author: the author is only trusted up to a certain point in time, i.e., the time of compromise, and afterwards cannot change the

---

[4] Note that the signatures may differ since the signature scheme can be probabilistic.

past. In this stronger adversarial model, Balloon should still provide correctness and security for all events inserted by the author up till the time of author compromise.

Efficient incremental proofs, realised by the `IncGen` and `IncVerify` algorithms, are a key feature of history trees [9]. Anyone can challenge the server to provide a proof that one commitment as part of a snapshot is *consistent* with all previous commitments as part of snapshots. However, it appears to be an open problem to have an efficient algorithm for showing consistency between roots of different versions of a treap (or any lexicographically sorted data structure) [8]. In Appendix B, we show why one cannot efficiently use probabilistic proofs of consistency for a Balloon. In absence of efficient (both for the server and verifier in terms of computation, storage, and size) incremental proofs in hash treaps, we rely on a concept from Certificate Transparency [12]: monitors.

We assume that a subset of clients, or any third party, will take on a role referred to as a "monitor", "auditor", or "validator" in, e.g., [3,10–12,22,27]. A monitor continuously monitors all data stored at a server and ensures that all snapshots issued by an author are consistent. We assume that clients and monitors receive the snapshots through gossiping.

**Definition 4 (Publicly Verifiable Consistency).** *An ADS scheme is publicly verifiable consistent if anyone can verify that a set of events u has been correctly inserted in $D_h$ and $auth(D_h)$, fixed by $s_h$ to form $D_{h+1}$ and $auth(D_{h+1})$ fixed by $s_{h+1}$.*

**Algorithm.** $\{\alpha, D_{h+1}, auth(D_{h+1}), s_{h+1}\} \leftarrow$ `refreshVerify`$(u, D_h, auth(D_h),$ $s_h, upd, pk)$: First, the algorithm runs $\{D_{h+1}, auth(D_{h+1}), s_{h+1}\} \leftarrow$ `refresh`$(u,$ $D_h, auth(D_h), s_h, upd, pk)$ as a sub-algorithm. Then, the algorithm verifies the updated snapshot $\{r, c_i, \sigma\} \leftarrow s_{h+1} \leftarrow upd$:

- verify the signature: `true` $\overset{?}{=}$ `verify`$_{pk}(\sigma, \{r, c_i\})$; and
- match the root of the updated hash treap $r' \overset{?}{=} r$; and
- match the last commitment in the updated history tree $c'_i \overset{?}{=} c_i$.

If the verify succeeds, the algorithm outputs $\{\alpha = $ `true`$, D_{h+1}, auth(D_{h+1}),$ $s_{h+1}\}$. Otherwise, the algorithm outputs $\alpha = $ `false`.

**Theorem 3.** *With* `refreshVerify`*, Balloon is publicly verifiable consistent according to Definition 4, assuming perfect gossiping of the snapshots and the collision-resistance of the underlying hash function.*

The proof of publicly verifiable consistency can be found in the full version of our paper [20]. Note that for the purpose of verifying consistency between snapshots, it is not necessary to keep the data structure $D$. Moreover, the storage requirement for monitors can be further reduced by making use of pruned versions of the authenticated data structure, i.e., by using a `refresh*` sub-algorithm, similar to the `update*` algorithm. Finally, to preserve event privacy towards monitors, one can provide the monitors with $\tilde{u} = < \tilde{e}_j >$, where

$\tilde{e}_j = \big(\mathtt{Hash}(k_j), \mathtt{Hash}(e_j)\big)$, and not the actual set of events. However, in this case, one must ensure that the ordering function $\Omega \leftarrow \mathtt{pk}$ provides the same output for $u$ and $\tilde{u}$.

## 7   Performance

We implemented Balloon in the Go[5] programming language using SHA-512 as the hash function and Ed25519 for signatures [4]. The output of SHA-512 is truncated to 256-bits, with the goal of reaching a 128-bits security level. The source code and steps to reproduce our results are available at http://www.cs.kau.se/pulls/balloon/. Our performance evaluation focuses on verifiable inserts, which are composed of performing and verifying $|u|+1$ membership queries, since these algorithms presumably are the most common. Figure 2 shows the size of the proof from `query` (**Prune**) in KiB based on the number of events to insert ranging from 1–1000 for three different sizes of Balloon: $2^{10}$, $2^{15}$, and $2^{20}$ events. Figure 2a includes redundant nodes in the membership query proofs, and shows that the proof size is linear with the number of events to insert. Figure 2b excludes redundant nodes between proofs, showing that excluding redundant nodes roughly halves the proof size with bigger gains the more events are inserted. For large Balloons the probability that any two authenticated paths in the hash treap share nodes goes down, resulting in bigger proofs, until the number of events get closer to the total size of the Balloon, when eventually all nodes in the hash treap are included in the proof as for the $2^{10}$ Balloon.

Table 1 shows a micro-benchmark of the three algorithms that enable verifiable inserts: `query`(**Prune**), `verify`(**Prune**), and `update*`. The table shows the average insert time (ms) calculated by Go's built-in benchmarking tool that performed between 30–30000 samples per measurement. The `update*` algorithm performs the bulk of the work, with little difference between the different Balloon sizes, and linear scaling for all three algorithms based on the number of events to insert.

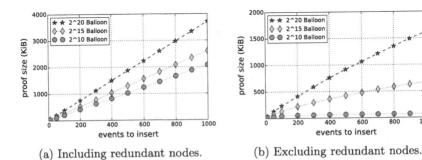

(a) Including redundant nodes.          (b) Excluding redundant nodes.

**Fig. 2.** The size of the proof from `query` (**Prune**) in KiB based on the number of events to insert $|u|$ for different sizes of Balloon.

---

[5] golang.org, accessed 2015-04-10.

**Table 1.** A micro-benchmark on Debian 7.8 (x64) using an Intel i5-3320M quad core 2.6 GHz CPU and 7.7 GB DDR3 RAM.

| Average time (ms) | Balloon $2^{10}$ | | | Balloon $2^{15}$ | | | Balloon $2^{20}$ | | |
|---|---|---|---|---|---|---|---|---|---|
| | # Events $\lvert u \rvert$ | | | # Events $\lvert u \rvert$ | | | # Events $\lvert u \rvert$ | | |
| | 10 | 100 | 1000 | 10 | 100 | 1000 | 10 | 100 | 1000 |
| query (**Prune**) | 0.04 | 0.37 | 3.64 | 0.04 | 0.37 | 3.64 | 0.06 | 0.37 | 3.62 |
| verify (**Prune**) | 0.07 | 0.72 | 6.83 | 0.07 | 0.73 | 6.84 | 0.07 | 0.72 | 6.85 |
| update* | 0.75 | 4.87 | 40.1 | 1.22 | 5.26 | 43.7 | 1.24 | 9.33 | 56.7 |

# 8 Related Work

Balloon is closely related to authenticated dictionaries [18] and persistent authenticated dictionaries (PADs) [1,7,8]. Balloon is not a PAD because it does not allow for the author to remove or update keys from the data structure, i.e., it is append-only. By allowing the removal of keys, the server needs to be able to construct past versions of the PAD to calculate proofs, which is relatively costly. In Table 2, Balloon is compared to the most efficient tree-based PAD construction according to Crosby & Wallach [8]: a red-black tree using Sarnak-Tarjan versioned nodes with a cache-everywhere strategy for calculated hash values. The table shows expected complexity. Note that red-black trees are more efficient than treaps due to their worst-case instead of expected logarithmic bounds on several important operations. We opted for using a treap due to its relative simplicity. For Balloon, the storage at the author is constant due to using verifiable inserts, while the PAD maintains a copy of the entire data structure. To query past versions, the PAD has to construct past versions of the data structure, while Balloon does not. When inserting new events, the PAD has to store a copy of the modified authenticated path in the red-black tree, while the storage for Balloon is constant. However, Balloon is less efficient when inserting new events with regard to the proof size due to verifiable inserts.

Miller et al. [17] present a generic method for authenticating operations on any data structure that can be defined by standard type constructors. The prover provides the authenticated path in the data structure that are traversed by the prover when performing an operation. The verifier can then perform the same operation, only needing the authenticated paths provided in the proof.

**Table 2.** Comparing Balloon and an efficient PAD construction [8]. The number of events in the data structure is $n$ and the size of the version cache is $v$.

| Expected complexity | Total storage size (A) | Query time (current) | Query time (past) | Insert storage size (S) | Insert time (A) | Insert time (S) | Insert proof size |
|---|---|---|---|---|---|---|---|
| Balloon | $\mathcal{O}(1)$ | $\mathcal{O}(\log n)$ | $\mathcal{O}(\log n)$ | $\mathcal{O}(1)$ | $\mathcal{O}(\log n)$ | $\mathcal{O}(\log n)$ | $\mathcal{O}(\log n)$ |
| Tree-based PAD | $\mathcal{O}(n)$ | $\mathcal{O}(\log n)$ | $\mathcal{O}(\log v \cdot \log n)$ | $\mathcal{O}(\log n)$ | $\mathcal{O}(\log n)$ | $\mathcal{O}(\log n)$ | $\mathcal{O}(1)$ |

The verifier only has to store the latest correct digest that fixes the content of the data structure. Our verifiable insert is based on the same principle.

Secure logging schemes, like the work by Schneier and Kelsey [23], Ma and Tsudik [13], and Yavuz et al. [26] can provide deletion detection and forward-integrity in a forward secure model for append-only data. Some schemes, like that of Yavuz et al., are publicly verifiable like Balloon. However, these schemes are insufficient in our setting, since clients cannot get efficient non-membership proofs, nor efficient membership-proofs for past versions of the data structure when only some versions (snapshots) are timestamped.

All the following related work operates in a setting that is fundamentally different to the one of Balloon. For Balloon, we assume a forward-secure author with an untrusted server, whereas the following related work assumes a (minimally) trusted server with untrusted authors.

Certificate Transparency [12] and the tamper-evident history system by Crosby & Wallach [6] use a nearly identical[6] data structure and operations. Even though in both Certificate Transparency and Crosby & Wallach's history system, a number of *minimally trusted* authors insert data into a history tree kept by a server, clients query the server for data and can act as auditors or monitors to challenge the server to prove consistency between commitments. Non-membership proofs require the entire data structure to be sent to the verifier.

In Revocation Transparency, Laurie and Kasper [11] present the use of a sparse Merkle tree for certificate revocation. Sparse Merkle trees create a Merkle tree with $2^N$ leafs, where $N$ is the bit output length of a hash algorithm. A leaf is set to 1 if the certificate with the hash value fixed by the path to the leaf from the root of the tree is revoked, and 0 if not. While the tree in general is too big to store or compute on its own, the observation that most leafs are zero (i.e., the tree is sparse) means that only paths including non-zero leafs need to be computed and/or stored. At first glance, sparse Merkle trees could replace the hash treap in a Balloon with similar size/time complexity operations.

Enhanced Certificate Transparency (ECT) by Ryan [22] extends CT by using two data structures: one chronologically sorted and one lexicographically sorted. Distributed Transparent Key Infrastructure (DTKI) [27] builds upon the same data structures as ECT. The chronologically sorted data structure corresponds to a history tree (like CT). The lexicographically sorted data structure is similar to our hash treap. For checking consistency between the two data structures, ECT and DTKI use probabilistic checks. The probabilistic checking verifies that a random operation recorded in the chronological data structure has been correctly performed in the lexicographical data structure. However, this requires the prover to generate past versions of the lexicographical data structure (or cache all proofs), with similar trade-offs as for PADs, which is relatively costly.

CONIKS [14] is a privacy-friendly key management system where minimally trusted clients manage their public keys in directories at untrusted key servers. A directory is built using an authenticated binary prefix tree, offering

---

[6] The difference is in how non-full trees are handled, as noted in Sect. 2.1 of [12].

similar properties as our hash treap. In CONIKS, user identities are presumably easy to brute-force, so they go further than Balloon in providing event privacy in proofs by using verifiable unpredictable functions and commitments to hide keys (identities) and values (user data). CONIKS stores every version of their (authenticated) data structure, introducing significant overhead compared to Balloon. On the other hand, CONIKS supports modifying and removing keys, similar to a PAD. Towards consistency, CONIKS additionally links snapshots together into a snapshot chain, together with a specified gossiping mechanism that greatly increases the probability that an attacker creating inconsistent snapshots is caught. This reduces the reliance on perfect gossiping, and could be used in Balloon. If the author ever wants to create a fork of snapshots for a subset of clients and monitors, it needs to maintain this fork forever for this subset or risk detection. Like CONIKS, we do not prevent an adversary compromising a server, or author, or both, from performing attacks: we provide means of detection after the fact.

## 9   Conclusions

This paper presented Balloon, an authenticated data structure composed of a history tree and a hash treap, that is tailored for privacy-preserving transparency logging. Balloon is a provably secure authenticated data structure, using a similar approach as Papamanthou et al. [19], under the modest assumption of a collision-resistant hash function. Balloon also supports efficiently verifiable inserts of new events and publicly verifiable consistency. Verifiable inserts enable the author to discard its copy of the (authenticated) data structure, only keeping constant storage, at the cost of transmitting and verifying proofs of a pruned version of the authenticated data structure. Publicly verifiable consistency enables anyone to verify the consistency of snapshots, laying the foundation for a forward-secure author, under the additional assumption of a perfect gossiping mechanism of snapshots. Balloon is practical, as shown in Sect. 7, and a more efficient solution in our setting than using a PAD, as summarised by Table 2.

**Acknowledgements.** We would like to thank Simone Fischer-Hübner, Stefan Lind-skog, Leonardo Martucci, Jenni Reuben, Philipp Winter, and Jiangshan Yu for their valuable feedback. Tobias Pulls has received funding from the Seventh Framework Pro-gramme for Research of the European Community under grant agreement no. 317550. This work was supported in part by the Research Council KU Leuven: GOA TENSE (GOA/11/007).

## A   Proof of Security

**Theorem 2.** *Balloon*  {*genkey,setup,update,refresh,query,verify*}  *is a secure ADS scheme for a data structure D, that contains a list of sets of events, according to Definition 3, assuming the collision-resistance of the underlying hash function.*

*Proof.* The adversary initially outputs the authenticated data structure $\mathtt{auth}(D_0)$ and the snapshot $\mathsf{s}_0$ through an oracle call to algorithm $\mathtt{setup}$. The adversary picks a polynomial number $i = 0, \ldots, h$ of updates with $u_i$ insertions of unique events and outputs the data structure $D_i$, the authenticated data structure $\mathtt{auth}(D_i)$, and the snapshot $\mathsf{s}_i$ through oracle access to $\mathtt{update}$. Then it picks a query $q = $ "a membership query for an event with key $k \in \{0,1\}^{|\mathtt{Hash}(\cdot)|}$ in the data structure that is fixed by $\mathsf{s}_j$, with $0 \le j \le h + 1$", a proof $\Pi(q)$, and an answer $\alpha(q)$ which is rejected by $\mathtt{check}(q, \alpha(q), D_j)$ as incorrect. An adversary breaks security if $\mathtt{verify}(q, \alpha(q), \Pi(q), \mathsf{s}_j, \mathtt{pk})$ outputs $\mathtt{accept}$ with non-negligible probability.

Assume a probabilistic polynomial time adversary **Adv** that breaks security with non-negligible probability. Given that the different versions of the authenticated data structure and corresponding snapshots are generated through oracle access, these are correct, i.e., the authenticated data structure contains all elements of the data structure for each version, the root and commitment in each snapshot correspond to that version of the ADS and the signature in each snapshot verifies.

The tuple $(q, \alpha(q), D_j)$ is rejected by $\mathtt{check}$ in only three cases:

**Case 1.** $\alpha(\mathsf{q}) = \mathtt{false}$ and there exists an event with key $k$ in $D_j$;
**Case 2.** $\alpha(\mathsf{q}) = \{\mathtt{true}, e\}$ and there does not exists an event with key $k$ in $D_j$;
**Case 3.** $\alpha(\mathsf{q}) = \{\mathtt{true}, e\}$ and the event $e^*$ with key $k$ in $D_j$ differs from $e$: $e = (k, v) \ne e^* = (k, v^*)$ or more specifically $v \ne v^*$;

For all three cases where the $\mathtt{check}$ algorithm outputs $\mathtt{reject}$, **Adv** has to forge an authenticated path in the hash treap and/or history tree in order to get the $\mathtt{verify}$ algorithm to output $\mathtt{accept}$:

**Case 1.** In the hash treap that is fixed by $\mathsf{s}_{h+1}$, there is a node with key $k' = \mathtt{Hash}(k)$ and the value $v' \le j[-1]$. However for the $\mathtt{verify}$ algorithm to output $\mathtt{accept}$ for $\alpha(q) = \mathtt{false}$, the authenticated path in the hash treap must go to either no node with key $k'$ or a node with key $k'$ for which the value $v'$ is greater than the index of the last inserted event in the history tree that is fixed by $\mathsf{s}_j$: $v' > j[-1]$.

**Case 2.** In the hash treap that is fixed by $\mathsf{s}_{h+1}$, there is either no node with key $k' = \mathtt{Hash}(k)$ or a node with key $k'$ for which the value $v'$ is greater than the index of the last inserted event in the history tree that is fixed by $\mathsf{s}_j$: $v' > j[-1]$. However for the $\mathtt{verify}$ algorithm to output $\mathtt{accept}$ for $\alpha(\mathsf{q}) = \{\mathtt{true}, e\}$, the authenticated path in the hash treap must go to a node with key $k'$, where the value $v' \le j[-1]$. Note that, in this case, $\mathcal{A}$ also needs to forge an authenticated path in the history tree to succeed.

**Case 3.** In the hash treap that is fixed by $\mathsf{s}_{h+1}$, there is a leaf with key $k' = \mathtt{Hash}(k)$ and the value $v' \le j[-1]$. In the history tree, the leaf with key $v'$ has the value $\mathtt{Hash}(e^*)$. However for the $\mathtt{verify}$ algorithm to output $\mathtt{accept}$ for $\alpha(\mathsf{q}) = \{\mathtt{true}, e\}$, the authenticated path in the hash treap must go to a leaf with key $k'$, where the value $v' \le j[-1]$, for which the authenticated path in the history tree must go to a leaf with key $v'$ and the value $\mathtt{Hash}(e)$.

From Lemma 1 it follows that we can construct a probabilistic polynomial time adversary $\mathbf{Adv}^*$, by using $\mathbf{Adv}$, that outputs a collision of the underlying hash function with non-negligible probability. $\qquad\Box$

# B  Negative Result on Probabilistic Consistency

Probabilistic proofs are compelling, because they may enable more resource-constrained clients en-mass to verify consistency, removing the need for monitors that perform the relatively expensive role of downloading all events at a server. Assume the following pair of algorithms:

- $P \leftarrow$ B.IncGen($s_i, s_j$, rand): Generates a probabilistic incremental proof $P$ using randomness rand between $s_i$ and $s_j$, where $i \leq j$, from the Balloon $B$. Outputs $P$.
- {accept, reject} $\leftarrow$ P.IncVerify($s_i, s_j$, rand): Verifies that $P$ probabilistically proves that $s_j$ fixes every event fixed by $s_i$, where $i \leq j$, using randomness rand.

## B.1  Our Attempt

Our envisioned B.IncGen algorithm shows consistency in two steps. First, it uses the H.IncGen algorithm from the history tree. This ensures that the snapshots are consistent for the history tree. Second, it selects deterministically and uniformly at random based on rand a number of events $E = < e_j >$ from the history tree. Which events to select from depend on the two snapshots. For each selected event, the algorithm performs a query (**Membership**) for the event key $k_j \leftarrow$ key($e_j$) to show that the event is part of the hash treap and points to the index of the event in the history tree.

The P.IncVerify algorithm checks the incremental proof in the history tree, verify (**Membership**) $\overset{?}{=}$ accept for each output of query (**Membership**), and that the events $E$ were selected correctly based on rand. Next, we explain an attack, why it works, and lessons learnt.

## B.2  Attack

The following attack allows an attacker to hide an arbitrary event that was inserted *before author compromise*. The attacker takes control over both the author and server just after snapshot $s_t$. Assume that the attacker wants to remove an event $e_j$ from Balloon, where $j \leq t[-1]$. The attacker does the following:

1. Remove the event key $k'_j = $ Hash($k_j$), where $k_j \leftarrow$ key($e_j$), from the hash treap, insert a random key, and rebalance the treap if needed. This results is a modified ADS auth($D_t$)$^*$.
2. Generate a set of new events $u$ and update the data structure: update($u, D_t$, auth($D_t$)$^*, s_t,$ sk, pk), resulting in a new snapshot $s_{t+1}$.

It is clear that the snapshot $s_{t+1}$ is inconsistent with all other prior snapshots, $s_p$, where $p \leq t$.

Now, we show how the attacker can avoid being detected by P.IncVerify in the case that the verifier challenges the server (and therefore the attacker) to probabilistically prove the consistency between $s_p$ and $s_{t+1}$, AND that the randomness rand provided by the verifier selects the event $e_j$ that was modified by the attacker. The attacker can provide a valid incremental proof in the history tree, using H.IncGen, since the history tree has not been modified. However, the attacker cannot create a valid membership proof for an event with key $k_j \leftarrow \text{key}(e_j)$ in the ADS, since the key $k'_j = \text{Hash}(k_j)$ was removed from the hash treap in $\text{auth}(D_{t+1})$. To avoid detection, the attacker puts back the event key $k'_j$ in the hash treap and rebalances the treap if needed. By inserting a set of events using update, a *new snapshot* $s_{t+2}$ is generated, which is then used to perform the membership query against that will now output a valid membership proof.

### B.3   Lessons Learnt

This attack succeeds because the attacker can, once having compromised the author and server, (a) create snapshots at will; and (b) membership queries are always performed on the current version of the hash treap.

In settings where snapshots are generated periodically, e.g., once a day, the probability of the attacker getting caught in this way is non-negligible given a sufficient number of queries. However, as long as the attacker can create snapshots at will, the probability that it will be detected with probabilistic incremental proofs is zero, as long as it cannot be challenged to generate past versions of the hash treap; and there are no monitors or another mechanism, that prevent the attacker from modifying or deleting events that were inserted into the ADS prior to compromise.

## References

1. Anagnostopoulos, A., Goodrich, M.T., Tamassia, R.: Persistent authenticated dictionaries and their applications. In: Davida, G.I., Frankel, Y. (eds.) ISC 2001. LNCS, vol. 2200, pp. 379–393. Springer, Heidelberg (2001)
2. Aragon, C.R., Seidel, R.: Randomized search trees. In: FOCS, pp. 540–545. IEEE Computer Society (1989)
3. Basin, D.A., Cremers, C.J.F., Kim, T.H., Perrig, A., Sasse, R., Szalachowski, P.: ARPKI: attack resilient public-key infrastructure. In: CCS. ACM (2014)
4. Bernstein, D.J., Duif, N., Lange, T., Schwabe, P., Yang, B.Y.: High-speed high-security signatures. J. Cryptographic Eng. **2**(2), 77–89 (2012)
5. Blum, M., Evans, W.S., Gemmell, P., Kannan, S., Naor, M.: Checking the correctness of memories. Algorithmica **12**(2/3), 225–244 (1994)
6. Crosby, S.A., Wallach, D.S.: Efficient data structures for tamper-evident logging. In: USENIX Security Symposium, pp. 317–334. USENIX (2009)

7. Crosby, S.A., Wallach, D.S.: Super-efficient aggregating history-independent persistent authenticated dictionaries. In: Backes, M., Ning, P. (eds.) ESORICS 2009. LNCS, vol. 5789, pp. 671–688. Springer, Heidelberg (2009)
8. Crosby, S.A., Wallach, D.S.: Authenticated dictionaries: Real-world costs and trade-offs. ACM Trans. Inf. Syst. Secur. 14(2), 17 (2011)
9. Crosby, S.A.: Efficient tamper-evident data structures for untrusted servers. Ph.D. thesis, Rice University (2010)
10. Kim, T.H., Huang, L., Perrig, A., Jackson, C., Gligor, V.D.: Accountable key infrastructure (AKI): a proposal for a public-key validation infrastructure. In: World Wide Web Conference, pp. 679–690. ACM (2013)
11. Laurie, B., Kasper, E.: Revocation transparency (2012). http://www.links.org/files/RevocationTransparency.pdf
12. Laurie, B., Langley, A., Kasper, E.: Certificate Transparency. RFC 6962 (2013). http://tools.ietf.org/html/rfc6962
13. Ma, D., Tsudik, G.: Extended abstract: Forward-secure sequential aggregate authentication. In: IEEE Symposium on Security and Privacy, pp. 86–91. IEEE Computer Society (2007)
14. Melara, M.S., Blankstein, A., Bonneau, J., Freedman, M.J., Felten, E.W.: CONIKS: A privacy-preserving consistent key service for secure end-to-end communication. Cryptology ePrint Archive, Report 2014/1004 (2014). https://eprint.iacr.org/2014/1004
15. Merkle, R.C.: A digital signature based on a conventional encryption function. In: Pomerance, C. (ed.) CRYPTO 1987. LNCS, vol. 293, pp. 369–378. Springer, Heidelberg (1988)
16. Merkle, R.C.: A certified digital signature. In: Brassard, G. (ed.) CRYPTO 1989. LNCS, vol. 435, pp. 218–238. Springer, Heidelberg (1990)
17. Miller, A., Hicks, M., Katz, J., Shi, E.: Authenticated data structures, generically. In: POPL, pp. 411–424. ACM (2014)
18. Nissim, K., Naor, M.: Certificate revocation and certificate update. In: USENIX, pp. 561–570. USENIX (1998)
19. Papamanthou, C., Tamassia, R., Triandopoulos, N.: Optimal verification of operations on dynamic sets. In: Rogaway, P. (ed.) CRYPTO 2011. LNCS, vol. 6841, pp. 91–110. Springer, Heidelberg (2011)
20. Pulls, T., Peeters, R.: Balloon: A forward-secure append-only persistent authenticated data structure. Cryptology ePrint Archive, Report 2015/007 (2015). https://eprint.iacr.org/2015/007
21. Pulls, T., Peeters, R., Wouters, K.: Distributed privacy-preserving transparency logging. In: WPES, pp. 83–94. ACM (2013)
22. Ryan, M.D.: Enhanced certificate transparency and end-to-end encrypted mail. In: NDSS. The Internet Society (2014)
23. Schneier, B., Kelsey, J.: Secure audit logs to support computer forensics. ACM Trans. Inf. Syst. Secur. 2(2), 159–176 (1999)
24. Tamassia, R.: Authenticated data structures. In: Di Battista, G., Zwick, U. (eds.) ESA 2003. LNCS, vol. 2832, pp. 2–5. Springer, Heidelberg (2003)
25. Vliegen, J., Wouters, K., Grahn, C., Pulls, T.: Hardware strengthening a distributed logging scheme. In: DSD, pp. 171–176. IEEE (2012)
26. Yavuz, A.A., Ning, P., Reiter, M.K.: BAF and FI-BAF: efficient and publicly verifiable cryptographic schemes for secure logging in resource-constrained systems. ACM Trans. Inf. Syst. Secur. 15(2), 9 (2012)
27. Yu, J., Cheval, V., Ryan, M.: DTKI: a new formalized PKI with no trusted parties. CoRR abs/1408.1023 (2014). http://arxiv.org/abs/1408.1023

# On the Fly Design and Co-simulation of Responses Against Simultaneous Attacks

Léa Samarji[1,2]([⊠]), Nora Cuppens-Boulahia[1], Frédéric Cuppens[1],
Serge Papillon[2], Waël Kanoun[2], and Samuel Dubus[2]

[1] Télécom Bretagne, rue de la Chataigneraie, 35510 Cesson-Sévigné, France
{layal.elsamarji,nora.cuppens,frederic.cuppens}@telecom-bretagne.eu
[2] Alcatel-Lucent Bell Labs, Villarceaux, route de Villejust, 91620 Nozay, France
{serge.papillon,wael.kanoun,samuel.dubus}@alcatel-lucent.com

**Abstract.** The growth of critical information systems in size and complexity has driven the research community to propose automated response systems. These systems must cope with the steady progress of the attacks' sophistication, coordination and effectiveness. Unfortunately, existing response systems still handle attacks independently, suffering thereby from (i) efficiency issues against coordinated attacks (e.g. DDoS), (ii) conflicts between parallel responses, and (iii) unexpected side effects of responses on the system. We, thus, propose in this paper a new response model against simultaneous threats. Our response is dynamically designed based on a new definition of capability-aware logic anti-correlation, and modeled using the Situation Calculus (SC) language. Even though a response can prevent or reduce an attack scenario, it may also have side effects on the system and unintentionally ease one of the attackers to progress on its scenario. We address this issue by proposing a response co-simulator based on SC planning capabilities. This co-simulator considers each response candidate apart and reasons, from the current system's and attackers' state, to assess the achieved risk mitigation on the protected system. Experimentations were led to highlight the benefits of our solution.

**Keywords:** Response system · Simultaneous attacks · Situation calculus

## 1 Introduction

Modern attack tools are rapidly evolving to become more powerful and sophisticated. Networks and information systems are frequently targeted by simultaneous attacks, which causes deterioration in system's performance and induce great damage to physical assets. Simultaneous attacks are those performed by different attack entities. Each of them may be a single individual attacker or composed of a Group of Coordinated Attackers (GCA), with a specific attack objective in the system. When the attack entity is a GCA, the system risks to suffer from coordinated attacks [20]. Unfortunately, existing response systems

© Springer International Publishing Switzerland 2015
G. Pernul et al. (Eds.): ESORICS 2015, Part II, LNCS 9327, pp. 642–661, 2015.
DOI: 10.1007/978-3-319-24177-7_32

proposals [7–9,17,19] still handle attacks as being independent actions, and each attack scenario is treated as if it is the only intrusion scenario in the system. Moreover, the majority of automated intrusion response systems rely on a predefined mapping of response actions to attacks. While this approach allows a system administrator to deal with intrusions faster, it lacks flexibility as "things do not always turn out the way we planned". Besides, when responding to simultaneous attacks by activating parallel response measures, unexpected conflicts between responses may occur, in addition to potential side effects on the system.

In this paper we propose a response system that overcomes these problems by dynamically designing and co-simulating response candidates for simultaneous attack threats. We first introduce a new response scheme. Our response is described as a sequence of non conflicting parallel actions, allowing thereby an execution in parallel or in sequence of different actions handling all the risky threats. Our response is dynamically designed based on a new definition of a capability-aware logic anticorrelation approach [2], and modeled through an efficient logic language, the Situation Calculus (SC) [11,14].

When a system is simultaneously threatened by different attack entities, multiple response candidates may be dynamically designed. In order to choose the most effective response, we also present in this paper a co-simulator based on the SC planning capabilities. This enables to have a real-time estimation of the total risk mitigation induced by each response candidate, and thus, the most optimal one can be chosen and deployed in the system.

The paper is organized as follows: Sect. 2 presents a Simultaneous Attacks Graph (SAG) which forecasts potential simultaneous attack scenarios. SAG is an input for our framework, since it allows us to identify risky threats for which we have to design a response. Section 3 introduces our new response scheme, and explains how responses can be dynamically designed based on a new definition of anticorrelation. Section 4 introduces the Situation Calculus language, and shows how to model our dynamic response with SC. Section 5 introduces our response co-simulator based on SC planning capabilities. In Sect. 6, we experiment our framework on an IP network threatened by simultaneous attacks. Then, Sect. 7 discusses related works, before we conclude on our proposals in Sect. 8.

## 2   Simultaneous Attacks Graphs

[15] differs from other works on attack modeling (e.g. [1,4,18], etc.), by proposing a formal description of actions that correspond to all types of attacks (individual, coordinated and simultaneous ones). An algorithm was also proposed to generate Attack Graphs (SAG) corresponding to Simultaneous attacks scenarios. Hence, given a system's state and a set of suspicious attackers, the algorithm is able to generate multiple SAGs each corresponding, to a combination of scenarios predicted for those attackers. Figures 1 and 2 are two examples of generated graphs for a telephony operator threatened by fourteen suspicious attackers at time $t0$. In each graph, attackers may be assembled differently into groups, and may

have a different end goal. Consequently, each graph represents only one combination of potential scenarios that can be simultaneously performed in the future by suspicious attackers. In the SAG of Fig. 1, the algorithm assembles attackers into 3 groups of coordinated attackers $\{a1, a2, a3, a4, a5, a6, a7, a8, a9, a10\}$, $\{a11, a12\}$, and $\{a13, a14\}$. For the first group, a scenario targeting the operator's reputation on its principal services (e.g. QoS) is predicted by performing a Distributed Denial of Service (DDoS) on one of its SIP servers. For the second group, a scenario that aims at inducing losses for an operator's client is predicted by hijacking its account and performing a toll fraud. For the third group, a scenario that aims at inducing losses for an operator's political client is predicted by recording its conversation and using it for black mailing. In another example, in Fig. 2, attackers $a11$ and $a12$ are not coordinated, and each one has it own end goal. Notice that an attack entity (e.g. $a11$) can block another one (e.g. $a12$) from progressing. This can occur due to a simultaneous access to unshareable resources in the system. Attackers in this case are called concurrent.

In [16], a new framework was proposed to properly assess the risk of Individual, Coordinated, and Concurrent Attack Scenarios. The method is based on a coordination aware-*Game Theoric* approach to derive an *Attack Likelihood* equation. An algorithm was also proposed to assess the *risk* of each attack scenario in a given SAG, considering the concurrency between attackers. Consequently, the SAG containing scenarios that are the most risky (i.e. scenarios with high likelihood and high impact) in the system is chosen. The most risky SAG is an input for our framework. Our framework will dynamically design and co-simulate a response efficient against attackers leading the risky scenarios within this SAG.

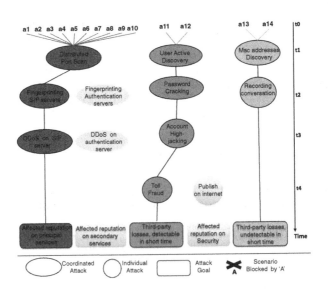

**Fig. 1.** Example 1 of a VoIP SAG.

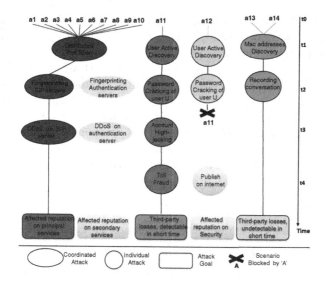

**Fig. 2.** Example 2 of a VoIP SAG.

## 3    New Scheme for a Complex Response

Let $[[a_1^1, a_2^1, ..., a_M^1]; [a_1^2, a_2^2, ..., a_M^2]; ...; [a_1^N, a_2^N, ..., a_M^N]]$ be the sequence of simultaneous attacks forecasted in the input SAG, where $M$ different attack entities are presented in the system, with $a_j^i$ being the action that is going to be executed in the $i^{th}$ place by the attack entity $j$. Symbol $','$ represents parallelism, and symbol $';'$ represents sequencing. Note that $a_j^i$ can also be no operation if no action is predicted for the entity. Consider that attack entities $1, 2, ..., K$ are considered as risky and attack entities $K + 1, ..., M$ are considered as not risky. Note that, in a given SAG, risky attack entities are those for which risky scenarios are forecasted. Hence, the following is the sequence of Risky Simultaneous Attacks ($RiskySAS$): $RiskySAS = [[a_1^1, ..., a_K^1]; [a_1^2, ..., a_K^2]; ...; [a_1^N, ..., a_K^N]]$.

R is considered a response against $RiskySAS$, if R is able, while maintaining the system in an operational state, to either prevent or delay entities $1, 2, ..., K$ from reaching their attack objectives. In order to respond to simultaneous threats, the response should not be limited to a single elementary action, we thus consider a response as a complex action, and we define it as a set of partially ordered elementary actions. In other words, a response may consist of non conflicting system's actions activated in parallel and of system's actions activated in sequence. Contrarily to an attack action, a system's action is an action triggered/executed by the system. $openSession(Src\_ip, Src\_port, Dest\_ip, Dest\_port)$, $restart(Server)$, $install(patchID, machineIP)$, $deploy(StrongAuthentication, Server)$, are examples of system's actions.

We introduce, in the following, a generic action scheme for a response R described as a sequence of length $x$ of parallel system's actions: $R = [[r_1^1, ..., r_{l1}^1]; [r_1^2, ..., r_{l2}^2]; ...; [r_1^x, ..., r_{lx}^x]]$ with $r_i^k$ being one of the $lk$ system's actions executed in the $k^{th}$ place (i.e. $k^{th}$ time step) , and $\forall k/\ 1 < k < x,\ \forall i \neq j\ /\ 1 < i,$ $j < lk,\ r_i^k$ and $r_j^k$ are not conflicting (i.e. meaning that parallel actions should be compatible together for a parallel execution).

In order to design such a response on the fly against a $RiskySAS$, a dynamic anticorrelation logic approach should be applied. Unfortunately, existing work on anticorrelation [2] is limited to an anticorrelation definition unaware of the applicability of actions, and is thereby inefficient for dynamic use. Moreover, the existing definition of anticorrelation is limited to responses consisting of a single elementary action. We thus propose in the following sections an applicability-aware anticorrelation definition adapted to our response scheme.

### 3.1    Applicability-Aware Anticorrelation

Anticorrelation in logic programming was defined in [2] as follows:

**Definition 1.** *Let $r$ and $a$ be respectively a system's action and an attack. postr is the set of predicates of post-condition of $r$ and prea is the set of predicates of pre-condition of $a$. Each of the post-condition and the pre-condition is a conjunction of predicates. $r$ and $a$ are anti-correlated if the following is satisfied: $anticorrelated(r, a) \leftrightarrow \exists Pr, Pa/(Pr \in postr \wedge \neg Pa \in prea) \wedge Pr, Pa$ are unifiable.*

Consider $passwordCrack(Attacker_1, U, Serv)$ a cracking of user $U$'s password through server $Serv$. A precondition of this attack is to have $Attacker_1$ having network access to $Serv$. Let $discard(Attacker_1, Serv)$ be a system's action consisting in disconnecting $Attacker_1$ from $Serv$'s network. Consequently, we have: $anticorrelated(discard(Attacker_1, Serv), passwordCrack(Attacker_1, U, Serv))$.

Unfortunately, Definition 1 does not consider the applicability of the system's action. Actually, if we reconsider the latest example, the $discard(Attacker_1, Serv)$ action, may not be possible for execution in the current state because the database containing allowed ip addresses for connection to $Serv$ is exclusively opened by another module in the system. Hence, response system should wait until the database is released, to be able to execute its action. Therefore, we propose an applicability-aware anticorrelation definition as follows:

**Definition 2.** *Let $r$ and $a$ be respectively a system's action and an attack. Let $S$ be the current system state, and $poss(r,S)$ a predicate meaning that it is possible to execute $r$ in $S$. $r$ and $a$ are anti-correlated in $S$ if the following is satisfied: $anticorrelated(r, a, S) \leftrightarrow poss(r, S) \wedge anticorrelated(r, a)$. $poss(r, S) \leftrightarrow \forall P \in prer, P$ holds in $S$.*

Definition 2 is limited to responses consisting of a single elementary action. However, a system may sometimes need to coordinate multiple elementary actions in order to react against an attack $a$, especially when $a$ is a coordinated attack [15]. As an example, consider that 25 users are registered to server $Serv$, that can handle up to 20 users deploying their entire bandwidth. Consider now that 22 users were infected by an external bot, and they are coordinately flooding $Serv$ (i.e. executing a DDoS). The set of compromised users is thus considered as a GCA. In order to respond to the DDoS attack, the system should discard in parallel at least two of the infected users to reduce the receiving flow below the threshold of $Serv$. Thus, it is the resulting effect of the three $discard$ actions which is opposite to the precondition of DDoS (which is $|\,GCA\,|> 20$). The following is a logic expression of the combined effect of the three elementary actions: $discarded(User_{21}) \wedge discarded(User_{22}) \rightarrow |\,GCA\,|< 20$.

In this case, it is the set of parallel actions $[discard(User_{21}), discard(User_{22})]$ which is anticorrelated with $DDoS(GCA, Serv)$. Therefore, we propose a definition of applicability-aware anticorrelation between a set of coordinated elementary system's actions and an attack, as follows:

**Definition 3.** *Let $rcoordinated = [r_1, r_2, ..., r_C]$ be a set of parallel system's actions, and a an attack. postrk is the set of predicates of post-conditions of $r_k$ and prea is the set of predicates of pre-condition of a. rcoordinated and a are anti-correlated if the following condition is satisfied:*

$anticorrelated([r_1, r_2, .., r_C], a, S) \leftrightarrow$

$poss([r_1, r_2, .., r_C], S) \wedge anticorrelated([r_1, r_2, .., r_C], a).$   *with:*

$anticorrelated([r_1, r_2, .., r_C], a) \leftrightarrow (Pr_1 \wedge Pr_2 \wedge .. \wedge Pr_C \rightarrow Pr) / Pr_k \in postr_k \wedge$
$\exists Pa /( \neg Pa \in prea \wedge Pr, Pa \text{ are unifiable}).$   *and*

$poss([r_1, r_2, ..., r_C], S) \leftrightarrow \forall i \in [1, C], poss(r_i, S) \wedge \forall j \neq i/1 < j < C,$
$\neg conflict(r_i, r_j).$

$\neg conflict(r_i, r_j)$ means that $r_i$ and $r_j$ are not conflicting (i.e. can be executed simultaneously). The semantic definition of *conflict* will be given in Sect. 4.3.

Definition 3 can be extended to the case of a complex system action (i.e. a sequence of parallel system's actions) as follows:

**Definition 4.** *Let $R* = [[r_1^1, ..., r_{l1}^1]; [r_1^2, ..., r_{l2}^2]; ...; [r_1^c, ..., r_{lc}^c]]$ be a complex action, and a an attack action. Let $S_{i+1}$ be the state of the system after the execution of $[r_1^i, ..., r_{li}^i]$ in state $S_i$. R* and a are anticorrelated in state $S_{c-1}$ if the following condition is satisfied:*

$anticorrelated([[r_1^1, ..., r_{l1}^1]; [r_1^2, ..., r_{l2}^2]; ...; [r_1^c, ..., r_{lc}^c]], a, S_{c-1})$
$\leftrightarrow anticorrelated([r_1^c, ..., r_{lc}^c], a) \wedge poss([r_1^1, ..., r_{l1}^1], S_0) \wedge$
$poss([r_1^2, ..., r_{l2}^2], S_1) \wedge .... \wedge poss([r_1^c, ..., r_{lc}^c], S_{c-1}).$

Based on Definition 4, we now propose a definition of applicability-aware anticorrelation between a complex action $R$, and a $RiskySAS$ as follows:

**Definition 5.** *Let $R = [[r_1^1, ..., r_{l1}^1]; [r_1^2, ..., r_{l2}^2]; ...; [r_1^x, ..., r_{lx}^x]]$ be a complex action, and RiskySAS a set of risky simultaneous attack scenarios, such that $RiskySAS = [[a_1^1, ..., a_K^1]; [a_1^2, ..., a_K^2]; ...; [a_1^N, ..., a_K^N]]$, with $a_j^i$ being an attack performed by attack entity j. R and RiskySAS are anti-correlated if the following condition is satisfied:*

$anticorrelated(R, RiskySAS, S) \leftrightarrow \forall entity(j), \exists R* \in R, \exists a \in [a_j^1; a_j^2; ...; a_j^N] /$
$anticorrelated(R*, a, S).$

Thus, $R$ is anticorrelated with $RiskySAS$ if for each attack sequence corresponding to an attack entity, we can find a complex action $R*$ within $R$ which is anticorrelated and applicable with at least one of the attacks that the entity will execute throughout its sequence.

### 3.2    Complex Response

A complex action $R$ is considered a dynamic response against $RiskySAS$ in a state $S$, if $R$ is applicable in $S$ and anticorrelated with $RiskySAS$, and no nominal constraint is violated at the end of $R$'s execution. Nominal constraints are those related to critical system assets that should not be violated, in order to guarantee a minimum operating state (i.e. service continuity) in the system. Consequently, $R$ should include 'operability' actions whenever nominal constraints risk to be violated by the system's actions composing $R$. We, thus, define a response $R$ against a $RiskySAS$ as follows:

**Definition 6.** *Let* $R = [[r_1^1, ..., r_{l1}^1]; [r_1^2, ..., r_{l2}^2]; ...; [r_1^x, ..., r_{lx}^x]]$ *be a complex action, and RiskySAS a set of risky simultaneous attack scenarios. And, let min_constraints be the set of nominal constraints. R is a response against RiskySAS in state S if the following condition is satisfied:*
$response(R, RiskySAS, S) \leftrightarrow anticorrelated(R, RiskySAS, S)$
$\wedge \forall Constraint \in min\_constraints, Constraint(S) = True.$

For example, consider a system threatened simultaneously by two risky threats T1 and T2. T1 aims at over-flooding server S1, and T2 aims at hijacking a legitimate user's account $U$ throughout a machine $M$ infected with a bot. The following sequence of parallel actions corresponds, thus, to a response against T1 and T2.

$$R = [\,[shareLoad(S1, S2), disconnect(M)]; [backupFiles(M, BackupServer)];$$
$$[reformatHarddrive(M)]; [install(SecurityPatch, M)]; [connect(M)]\,].$$

In a first step, sharing load is settled between $S1$ and another server $S2$ in order to prevent $S1$ from being overcharged by T1. In parallel, $M$ is disconnected from the network, and files on $M$ are backed up in order to reformat the machine and install a security patch in further steps. By this, the bot on $M$ is removed and the vulnerability is patched. In this example, $shareLoad(S1, S2)$, and $install(SecurityPatch, M)$ are two system's actions anticorrelated respectively with T1 and T2. $disconnect(M)$, $reformatHarddrive(M)$ and $backupFiles(M, BackupServer)$ are actions rendering the system capable to execute $install(SecurityPatch, M)$. We call them 'capability enabling' actions. Finally, $connect(M)$ is an 'operability' action. Note that without this latter, the response against T2 will not be effective.

In order to design our responses based on logic anticorrelation, system and attacks actions should be modeled using the same logic language. Additionally, the modeling language should follow a pre/post condition approach for actions description. In [15] different modeling languages were compared: LAMBDA [4],

STRIPS [1], JIGSAW [18], and Situation Calculus [11,14], and the latter turns
to be the most adapted language to describe all attack types. We, thus, investigate in the next section the adaptability of SC in modeling anticorrelation and
responses as defined in the previous section.

# 4    Modeling Responses with Situation Calculus (SC)

## 4.1    Basics of the Situation Calculus

Situation Calculus [11,14] is a dialect of first order logic, with second order-logic
terms for representing dynamic change. It basically consists of:

- Situations: a situation represents the system's state, and the action's history
  (i.e. sequence) from an initial empty action sequence $S0$.
- Fluents and Predicates: the world is described in terms of predicates and fluents. Whereas predicates are stateless, fluents are statefull, and thus take situations as arguments. For example, $Server(Serv)$ is a predicate meaning that
  $Serv$ is a server. While, $network\_access(M1, S2, s)$ is a fluent meaning that
  machine $M1$ has a network access to server $S2$ in situation $s$. Additionally, Fluents can be either relational, or functional. Relational fluents return boolean
  values, e.g. $is\_on(Serv, s)$, while functional fluents return a non boolean value,
  e.g. $received\_flow(Serv,s)=500$.
- Actions: consist of a function symbol and its arguments. For example,
  $reboot(Server1)$ is the action of rebooting $Server1$. In order to reason about
  the effects of an action, we refer to function $do(a,s)$. This latter denotes the
  situation that results from doing action $a$ in situation $s$.

SC also provides essential axioms to represent dynamic changes:

- Action precondition axioms: for each action $a$, there is a predicate $Poss(a, s)$
  that states if it is possible for action $a$ to be executed in situation $s$.
- Successor state axioms: there is one for each fluent $F$. It characterizes the
  conditions under which a fluent $F(x, do(a, s))$ changes from $s$ to $do(a, s)$.

## 4.2    Elementary System Actions

SC answers our need in (1) offering the possibility to dynamically design a
response whose requirements and effects depend on the system's state, and (2)
modeling system actions following a pre/post condition approach. The following
is an SC description of an operational action **shareLoad**$(S1, S2)$ which consists
in forcing a server $S1$ to share the load with another server $S2$ when overcharged.
**Poss**$(shareLoad(S1, S2), S) \leftrightarrow overcharged(S1, S) \wedge is\_on(S2)$
$\wedge runningService(S1, S) = runningService(S2, S).$
$overcharged(S1, \mathbf{do}(A, S)) \leftrightarrow A = ddos(GCA, S1) \vee (overcharged(S1, S) \wedge A \neq$
$shareLoad(S1, S2)).$

### 4.3 Concurrent System Actions

In [12,13], SC was expanded to handle concurrency. A new sort *concurrent* is added. Every *concurrent* variable $c$ is a set of concurrent simple actions $a$. The binary function $do(c,s)$ returns a situation term that results from the application of concurrent actions $c$ in situation $s$. $Poss(a,s)$ is thus extended to $Poss(c,s)$.

Additionally, in a simultaneous actions context, some actions can not be performed concurrently. This is due to incompatibility between actions in terms of resources that each action uses. As a solution, Pinto [12] proposed to add a finer level of granularity by appealing to the notion of resource: $xres(a,r)$ means that the action $a$ requires the exclusive use of the resource $r$, and $sres(a,r)$ means that the action $a$ requires the use of the resource $r$ for its execution, but $r$ can be shared. Finally, $poss(c,s)$ makes use of a conflict predicate *conflict* as a precondition in order to test compatibility between actions:

$$conflict(c) \leftrightarrow \exists a_1, a_2 \in c, \exists r \mid [(xres(a_1,r) \land$$
$$xres(a_2,r)) \lor (xres(a_1,r) \land sres(a_2,r)) \lor (sres(a_1,r) \land xres(a_2,r))]$$
$$Poss(c,s) \leftrightarrow [\forall a \in c, Poss(a,s)] \land \neg conflict(c)$$

Concurrent SC is thus efficient to avoid conflicts while designing a response.

### 4.4 Anticorrelation and Response in Situation Calculus

Let $r$ and $a$ be respectively a SC description of a system's action, and an attack action. Anticorrelation between $r$ and $a$ presented in Definition 2 is expressed in SC as follows: $anticorrelated(r,a,S) \leftrightarrow poss(r,S) \land \neg poss(a,do(r,S))$.

In SC, doing action $r$ renders action $a$ not possible for execution, this means that $r$ has rendered one of $a$'s precondition's predicates unfulfilled (i.e. false).

Let $C = [r_1, r_2, ..., r_L]$ be a set of parallel system's actions, and $a$ an attack action. Anticorrelation between $rconcurrent$ and $a$, as presented in Definition 3, can be expressed in concurrent SC as follows:
$anticorrelated(C,a,S) \leftrightarrow poss(C,S) \land \neg poss(a,do(C,S))$.

Now, let $R* = [C_0; C_1; ...; C_k]$ be a complex action with $C_i = [r_1^i, ..., r_{li}^i]$, and $a$ an attack action. Anticorrelation between $R*$ and $a$, as presented in Definition 4, can be expressed in concurrent SC as follows:
$anticorrelated(R*,a,S) \leftrightarrow poss(R*,S) \land \neg poss(a,do(R*,S))$.    with
$poss(R*,S) \leftrightarrow poss(C_0,S_0) \land poss(C_1,do(C_0,S_0)) \land ... \land$
$poss(C_k,do(C_{k-1},(..(do(C_0,S_0)..)))$.

Consequently, concurrent SC is adapted to model anticorrelation of a complex action against a *RiskySAS* as defined in Definition 5. And, a response (see Definition 6) can be modeled in SC as follows:
$response(R,RiskySAS,S) \leftrightarrow anticorrelated(R,RiskySAS,S) \land$
$\forall Ct \in min\_constraints, Ct(S).$  //*constraints can be modeled in SC as shown in* [5].

At this stage of the paper, we have proposed a mean to dynamically design a response against a set of simultaneous attacks scenarios. Since multiple response possibilities may exist, we introduce in the next section, the SC planning task that we use to propose a dynamic response co-simulator.

## 5    Planning in Situation Calculus

In [14], the author presented and implemented the world's simplest breadth-first planner ($wspbf$). $wspbf$ is a SC planner for an agent who can perform concurrent or sequential actions. It is supplied with a goal predicate $plannerGoal(s)$ to fulfill. Here is the Golog [10] program of the $wspbf$:

**proc** $wspbf(n)$
$plans(0, n)$
**endProc**

**proc** $plans(m, n)$
$m \leq n?; [actionSequence(m); plannerGoal? \mid plans(m{+}1,\ n)]$
**endProc**

**proc** $actionSequence(n)$
$n = 0? \mid n > 0?; (\pi c) [concurrent\_actions(c)?; c]\ ; actionSequence(n\text{-}1)$
**endProc**

The planner generates all sequences of concurrent actions $c$ fulfilling the goal. It terminates with failure if it does not find a sequence, which length is smaller or equal to $n$, that fulfills the goal.

### 5.1    Dynamic Response Co-simulator Based on SC Planning

We generalize the $wspbf$ to the case of a multi-agent system, where we have, on one hand, the system which can perform, concurrently or sequentially, a set of actions, and on the other hand, the attack entities present in the SAG, which can perform individual or coordinated attacks. First, we integrate all the attacks that have been specified to generate the SAGs. Second, a network and a security expert are needed to specify and describe in SC, all the elementary actions that the system can perform, considering the resource notion. Third, we integrate all the attack goals that have been specified to generate the SAGs. For instance, the following are two critical assets that may be considered attack goals in a system handling a voice over IP (VoIP) service.

$Attack\_Goal(Entity, S) \rightarrow in\_denial(Entity, VoIPserver, S) \lor is\_off(Entity, VoIPuser, S)$.
*//meaning that an attack entity can reach an attack goal in situation S, if in S, it has succeeded a denial of service over a VoIP server or a VoIP user.*

Forth, we describe more specifically the attack goal that each attack entity has reached in the considered SAG. For example, if $entity1$ has overflown a VoIP server then: $goalreached(entity1, S) \leftrightarrow in\_denial(entity1, VoIPserver, S)$.

Fifth, we specify in SC, for each attack entity appearing in SAG, if it is risky or not [16]. Besides, we specify for each risky entity, its attack scenario. For instance, $risky(entity1) \land riskySAS(entity1, scenario1)$, and $\neg risky(entityM)$.

Finally, we configure the co-simulator goal in a manner to reach a situation where a response is designed based on described system actions, and every risky entity is either (1) completely prevented from reaching her attack goal, or (2) forced to change her path and choose a more complex one before getting to her goal, thereby, reducing her risk. Concerning non risky entities, since they are not the prior concern of the system in the current situation, then no response will be intentionally designed for them. Note that if a response was able to additionally block or reduce the risk of a non risky entity, then this is also considered a solution for our co-simulator. We model our co-simulator's goal as follows:

$plannerGoal(S) \rightarrow$
$\forall risky(EntityA), [riskBlocked(EntityA, S) \vee riskReduced(EntityA, S)] \wedge$
$\forall \neg risky(EntityB), [riskBlocked(EntityB, S) \vee riskReduced(EntityB, S)$
$\vee Attack\_Goal(EntityB, S)]$.     with:

$riskBlocked(Entity, do(R*, S)) \rightarrow \exists Scenario/$
$riskySAS(Entity, Scenario) \wedge response(R*, Scenario, S) \vee riskBlocked(Entity, S)$.
*//meaning that: due to the response R\*, the attack entity was completely prevented from performing her attack scenario. Thus, the risk of this entity is totally blocked.*

$riskReduced(Entity, S) \rightarrow goalReached(Entity, S) \wedge privilegesLoss(Entity, S)$.
$privilegesLoss(Entity, do(C, S)) \rightarrow [\exists Predicate, \exists Object/Predicate(Entity, Object, S)$
$\wedge \neg Predicate(Entity, Object, do(C,S))] \vee privilegesLoss(Entity, S)$.
*//meaning that: due to some system actions C making part of the response, the attack entity has lost one of its privileges. Consequently, the entity will need to do more effort, thus, more time, to progress in its scenario Hence, the risk of this entity will decrease.*

Our response co-simulator generates an exhaustive list of all the response possibilities that can be designed against the risky threats, co-simulating, for each response, the potential behavior of the attackers face to this response, and the side effects that this latter can have on the system. Note that, each of the generated responses appears within a response plan. A response plan is a sequence of parallel actions. Each action can be either an attack or a system action. Actions in sequence are ordered in time, thereby, an administrator knows when to execute each system action making part of the response.

## 6   Experimentation

We implemented our response co-simulator using a prolog interpreter, SWI prolog (http://www.swi-prolog.org/). Then, we considered two different use cases for experimentation. In the first, we highlight the capability of our framework in generating responses handling sequencing and parallelism, and simulating the responses side effects. In the second experimentation, we highlight the efficiency of our framework in managing the conflict between actions.

### 6.1 Use Case 1

In Use case 1, we consider two simultaneous threats led by two attack entities (A1 and A2), as shown in the SAG of Fig. 3. In the initial system state, A1 has already infected machine M1 and actively scanned user U. In parallel, A2 has already infected machine M2 which belongs with M1 to the same Ethernet network (machines are reachable via $Switch12$). It is predicted for A1 to crack the password of U's account and highjack it in order to do a toll fraud which induces economic losses to U. Besides, a likely scenario for A2 is predicted starting by discovering M1 and then poisoning it with ARP messages, in order to spoof its address later on and make calls or inject packets as if they were sent by M1.

In a first experimentation, we consider that both threats are risky. Thus, our planner derives response plans for both of them. The following sequences are some of the response plans proposed by our planner:

Experimentation 1 - Response plan 1:

$t1:$    $[\ [passCrack(A1, server, u), discovermacaddress(A2, M2, M1)];$

$t2:$    **[notifychangepassword(u,server), deployAuthentication (Switch12)]**;

$t3:$    $[passCrack(A1, server, u)];$

$t4:$    $[highjack(A1, u, server)];$

$t5:$    $[tollFraud(A1, u)]\ ]$

Plan 1, presented in the graph of Fig. 4, designs a response R2 against both threats as parallel system actions. The first notifies U to change his password, and the second deploys an authentication on $Swith12$. Due to changing U's password, A1 is no more able to highjack U's account. Thus A1 should re-execute again a password cracking in order to continue its scenario. R2 is considered a response against A1, because it delays A1 from reaching its attack goal, thereby reducing its risk. Due to deploying authentication on switch12, A2 will not be able to poison M1 with ARP messages. Thus, it will not be able to reach its attack goal.

Experimentation 1 - Response plan 2:

$t1:$    $[\ $**[disconnect(M1)]**$;$

$t2:$    **[install(SecurityPatch,M1)]**;

$t3:$    **[connect(M1)]**;

$t4:$    $[discovermacaddress(A2, M2, M1)];$

$t5:$    $[arppoisoning(A2, M2, M1)];$

$t6:$    $[injectRTPpackets(A2, M2, M1)]\ ]$

Plan 2, presented in the graph of Fig. 5, designs a response R1 against both threats as a sequence of system actions. The response consists in patching the vulnerability in M1 and thereby prohibiting A1 from having a remote access to this machine. By disconnecting M1 in order to patch it, A2 will not be able to discover the mac address of M1. Consequently A2 will have to wait until M1 is reconnected to the network in order to continue its scenario. Hence, R1 blocks completely A1, and reduces the risk of A2.

In a second experimentation, we now consider that A1 is a risky threat, whereas A2 is not risky yet. Hence, we configure the planner's goal to respond against A1. The following is one of the solutions proposed by our planner:

Experimentation 2 - Response plan 1:

t1:     [ [passCrack(A1, server, u), discovermacaddress(A2, M2, M1)];
t2:     [**disconnect(M1)**];
t3:     [**install(SecurityPatch,M1)**, injectRTPpackets(A2, M2, M1)];
t4:     [**connect(M1)**] ]

The above sequence, presented in the graph of Fig. 6, designs a response R3 against threat A1. R3 consists in patching the vulnerability of M1, and blocking thereby A1. Note that, R3 is composed of the same actions as for R1. The only difference is that they do not have the same activation time. By launching R3, thus disconnecting M1, after that A2 discovers the address of M1, A2 does no more need to perform ARP poisoning. Indeed, disconnecting a machine is like inducing a denial of service on this machine. Consequently, A2 can directly spoof the address of M1 and fulfill its attack objective. Consequently, R3 has a side effect on the system, by increasing the risk of threat A2.

As you may notice, our framework is able to co-simulate the effects of each response on the system considering its activation time, allowing by this the system to choose the response plan bringing the highest risk mitigation.

## 6.2   Use Case 2

In Use case 2, we consider a system running a VoIP service, and a Trading service as shown in Fig. 7. For clients $\{cV1, cV2, ..., cV10\}$ subscribed to VoIP, a password based authentication using PAP (password authentication protocol) is considered and handled by a RADIUS server. While for clients $\{cT1, cT2, ..., cT8\}$

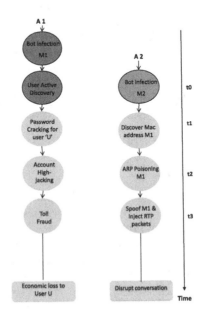

**Fig. 3.** SAG: System threatened by two attack entities A1 and A2.

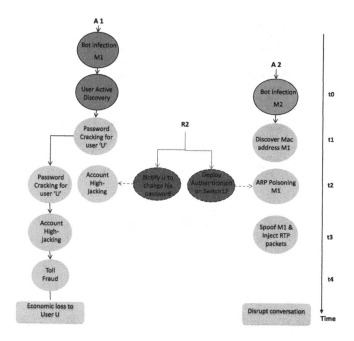

**Fig. 4.** Response against A1 and A2, designed as parallel actions.

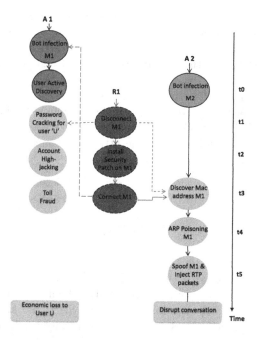

**Fig. 5.** Response against A1 and A2, designed as a sequence of actions.

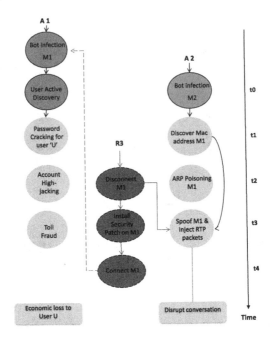

**Fig. 6.** Response against A1, having side effects on A2.

subscribed to Trading service, a strong authentication (e.g. multi-factor authentication, Digest access authentication, etc.) is adopted and handled by a Strong Authentication Server (SAS). SAS is suffering a Zero day vulnerability (e.g. Heart bleed[1]). Besides, in the initial system state, clients $\{cV1, ..., cV5\}$ and $cT1$ are compromised. The graph of Fig. 8 forecasts two different risky threats T1 and T2 led by these two attack entities. In T1, a coordinated password cracking attack scenario is predicted over $cV8$'s account. In T2, $cT1$ will try to exploit the vulnerability of SAS and prevent other traders from connecting to the trading service. The following is the attack sequence corresponding to the graph:

$t1$:    [ $[botinfect(a1,cV1),...,botinfect(a5,cV5),$ $scanVulnerability(cT1,fw2)]$;
$t2$:    $[cscanuser((cV1,...,cV5),cV8), modifyAccessRules(cT1,fw2)]$;
$t3$:    $[cpassCrack((cV1,..,cV5),sV1,cV8), scanserver(cT1,sas)]$;
$t4$:    [ $highjack(cV1,sV1,cV8),$ $exploitVulnerability(cT1,sas)]$ ]

In order to prevent T1, a solution would be to adapt the strong authentication to the VoIP service. To do so, the database containing information (passwords, accounts, etc.) about VoIP clients should be transferred to server SAS. Thus, $r_1 = transferData(sV1,SAS)$ is anticorrelated with $cpassCrack((cV1,...,cV5),sV1,cV8)$. Another solution would be to notify $cV8$

---

[1] http://www.zdnet.com/heartbleed-serious-openssl-zero-day-vulnerability-revealed-7000028166/.

to change his password before that $cV1$ highjacks his account. Thus, action $r_3 = changePassword(sV1, cV8)$ is anticorrelated with $highjack(cV1, cV8, sV1)$.

In order to prevent **T2**, a solution would be to disconnect SAS in order to install security patches or a new software version (e.g. OpenSSL 1.0.1g) to patch the vulnerability. Thus, action $r_2 = installPatch(sas)$ is anticorrelated with $exploitVulnerability(cT1, sas)$. Another solution would be to discard or blacklist the malicious trader for a while. Thus, $r_4 = discard(cT1)$ is anticorrelated with all actions executed by $cT1$.

A naive solution to respond to both threats would be to choose any combination $[r_i, r_j]$, with $i$ an even number and $j$ an odd number. However, $r_1$ and $r_2$ are in conflict. Actually, installing the security patch requires disconnecting $sas$ from the network, whereas transfering data to $sas$ requires this latter to stay online. Consequently, our framework prevents the execution of these two actions in parallel, by appealing the notion of resource: $xres(r_2, sas) \wedge sres(r_1, sas)$. Thus, $conflict([r_1, r_2])$ returns true, and $\boldsymbol{Poss}([r_1, r_2], S)$ returns false. Our planner avoids, thus, conflicting actions while designing the response plans:

Response Plan 1 presented in Fig. 9 integrates r3 and r2:

$t1$:   $[\,[botinfect(a1, cV1),.., botinfect(a5, cV5),\ scanVulnerability(cT1, fw2),$
        $\boldsymbol{diconnect(sas)}]$;

$t2$:   $[cscanuser((cV1,.., cV5), cV8),\ modifyAccessRules(cT1, fw2),$
        $\boldsymbol{installPatch(sas)}\ ]$;

$t3$:   $[cpassCrack((cV1,.., cV5), sV1, cV8), \boldsymbol{restart(sas)}]$;

$t4$:   $[\boldsymbol{changePassword(cV1, cV8)}, scanserver(cT1, sas)]$;

$t5$:   $[cpassCrack((cV1,.., cV5), sV1, cV8)]$;

$t6$:   $[highjack(cV1, cV8, sV1)]\,]$

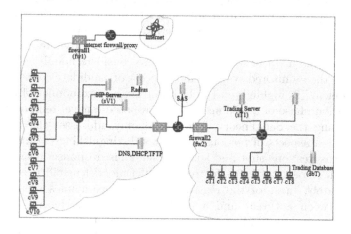

**Fig. 7.** Multi-services system topology.

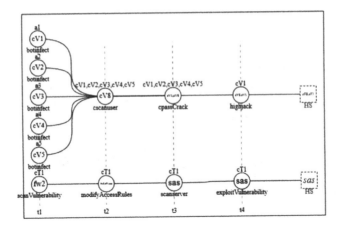

**Fig. 8.** SAG for the multi-services system.

Response Plan 2 presented in Fig. 10 integrates r1 and r4:

$t1$:  $[\,[botinfect(a1, cV1),...,botinfect(a5, cV5), scanVulnerability(cT1, fw2)];$
$t2$:  $[cscanuser((cV1,...,cV5), cV8), \mathbf{\textit{transferData(sV1, sas)}}, \mathbf{\textit{discard(cT1)}}]\,]$

## 7   Related Work

Stakhanova et al. [17] proposed a response selection mechanism that can be based on a (i) static mapping, (ii) dynamic mapping, or (iii) cost-sensitive mapping. As opposed to static mapping, in dynamic mapping, the countermeasure is determined in realtime by considering additional factors related to the attack occurrence (e.g. attack confidence, attack severity, past experience). Cost-sensitive response systems can be viewed as a particular form of dynamic mapping. In such response systems, the selection procedure considers mainly the impact of the attack on the monitored system, and the cost of candidate countermeasures.

Kanoun et al. [9] highlighted the lack in existing taxonomies of considering the deactivation phase of a response. They, proposed a novel temporal response taxonomy using the Set Theory. Their taxonomy addresses the lifetime and the deactivation aspects of response measures distinguishing two major classes of countermeasures: one-shot and sustainable. Thus, response measures can be classified with respect to their effectiveness, lifetime, defeasibility, etc.

Unfortunately, most of the existing response taxonomies are based on a matching between a threat and a predefined response. Hence, an expert is needed to, first, understand and reason about each threat, and then, specify the response policy, in advance, for every threat. Besides, the potential conflicts between simultaneous responses, and the potential side effect of responses on the system, are not considered.

In [3], different types of conflict between responses are described, and a solution to avoid the conflict was proposed. This latter consists in performing, offline,

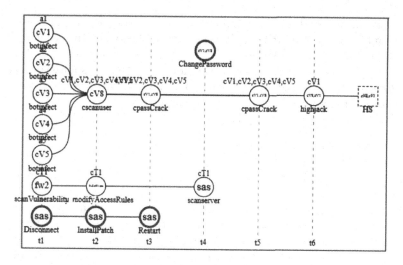

**Fig. 9.** Response Plan 1.

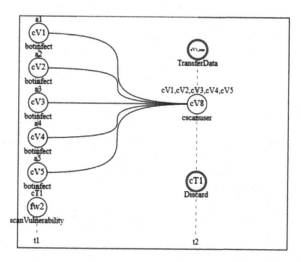

**Fig. 10.** Response Plan 2.

a static assignment of priorities over conflicting responses. However, conflicts between responses may depend on the current system's state and the dynamic resources' allocation. Thus, the conflict should be dynamically handled.

In [6], authors introduced a structured approach to evaluate a Return On Response Investment (RORI) index for all possible combinations of security measures that can be launched against simultaneous threats. In this work, security measures corresponding to each threat are designed by an expert in advance. Moreover, the risk mitigation for combined countermeasures is calculated by adding the effectiveness of countermeasures over the different surfaces they cover.

An attack surface is defined as the subset of the system's resources that an attacker may use to send/receive data into/from the system in order to attack the system. Thus, the effectiveness of a combination of responses, and thus its risk mitigation, is restricted to the threats for which these responses are considered. However, a proper risk mitigation should be calculated over the totality of the ongoing threats including not yet risky ones.

## 8    Conclusion

In this paper, we proposed a new response scheme for simultaneous threats, as a sequence of non conflicting parallel actions. Our response is dynamically designed based on a new definition of capability-aware logic anticorrelation, and modeled using the Situation Calculus language. This latter is efficient to describe conflicts between parallel actions by appealing the notion of resource. Moreover, in order to choose the most effective response, when multiple responses are possible, we presented a co-simulator based on SC planning capabilities. This latter co-simulates each response possibility apart, considering the system's state and the currently existing attack entities. Our framework is implemented in SWI-prolog, and experimentations were led to reveal the benefits of our solution.

In the future, we intend to assess the risk mitigation and the return on investment of each response plan in order to activate the most efficient one.

## References

1. Boutilier, C., Brafman, R.I.: Partial-order planning with concurrent interacting actions. J. Artif. Int. Res. **14**(1), 105–136 (2001)
2. Cuppens, F., Autrel, F., Bouzida, Y., Garcia, J., Gombault, S., Sans, T.: Anti-correlation as a criterion to select appropriate counter-measures in an intrusion detection network (2006)
3. Cuppens, F., Cuppens-Boulahia, N., Bouzida, Y., Kanoun, W., Croissant, A.: Expression and deployment of reaction policies. In: IEEE International Conference on Signal Image Technology and Internet Based Systems, SITIS 2008, pp. 118–127, November 2008
4. Cuppens, F., Ortalo, R.: LAMBDA: a language to model a database for detection of attacks. In: Debar, H., Mé, L., Wu, S.F. (eds.) RAID 2000. LNCS, vol. 1907, pp. 197–216. Springer, Heidelberg (2000)
5. Essaouini, N., Cuppens, F., Cuppens-Boulahia, N., Abou El Kalam, A.: Specifying and enforcing constraints in dynamic access control policies. In: 2014 Twelfth Annual International Conference on Privacy, Security and Trust (PST), pp. 290–297. IEEE (2014)
6. Gonzalez Granadillo, G., Belhaouane, M., Debar, H., Jacob, G.: Rori-based countermeasure selection using the OrBAC formalism. Int. J. Inf. Secur. **13**(1), 63–79 (2014)
7. Irvine, C., Levin, T.: Toward a taxonomy and costing method for security services. In: Proceedings of the 15th Annual Computer Security Applications Conference, ACSAC 1999, pp. 183–188. IEEE Computer Society, Washington, DC (1999)

8. Jr., C.C., Pooch, U.W.: An intrusion response taxonomy and its role in automatic intrusion response. In: The 2000 IEEE Workshop on Information Assurance and Security (2000)
9. Kanoun, W., Samarji, L., Cuppens-Boulahia, N., Dubus, S., Cuppens, F.: Towards a temporal response taxonomy. In: Di Pietro, R., Herranz, J., Damiani, E., State, R. (eds.) DPM 2012 and SETOP 2012. LNCS, vol. 7731, pp. 318–331. Springer, Heidelberg (2013)
10. Levesque, H.J., Reiter, R., Lespérance, Y., Lin, F., Scherl, R.B.: Golog: a logic programming language for dynamic domains (1994)
11. Mccarthy, J., Hayes, P.J.: Some philosophical problems from the standpoint of artificial intelligence. In: Machine Intelligence, vol. 4 (1969)
12. Pinto, J.A.: Temporal reasoning in the situation calculus (1994)
13. Reiter, R.: Natural actions, concurrency and continuous time in the situation calculus. In: Aiello, L.C., Doyle, J., Shapiro, S.C. (eds.) KR, pp. 2–13. Morgan Kaufmann, San Francisco (1996)
14. Reiter, R.: Knowledge in Action: Logical Foundations for Specifying and Implementing Dynamical Systems. The MIT Press, Massachusetts, Illustrated edition (2001)
15. Samarji, L., Cuppens, F., Cuppens-Boulahia, N., Kanoun, W., Dubus, S.: Situation calculus and graph based defensive modeling of simultaneous attacks. In: Wang, G., Ray, I., Feng, D., Rajarajan, M. (eds.) CSS 2013. LNCS, vol. 8300, pp. 132–150. Springer, Heidelberg (2013)
16. Samarji, L., Cuppens-Boulahia, N., Cuppens, F., Kanoun, W., Papillon, S., Dubus, S.: Liccas: assessing the likelihood of individual, coordinated, and concurrent attack scenarios. In: Security and Privacy in Communication Networks (2014)
17. Stakhanova, N., Basu, S., Wong, J.: A cost-sensitive model for preemptive intrusion response systems. In: Proceedings of the 21st International Conference on Advanced Networking and Applications, AINA 2007, pp. 428–435. IEEE Computer Society, Washington, DC (2007)
18. Templeton, S.J., Levitt, K.: A requires/provides model for computer attacks. In: Proceedings of the 2000 workshop on New security paradigms, NSPW 2000, pp. 31–38. ACM, New York (2000)
19. Wang, H., Wang, G., Lan, Y., Wang, K., Liu, D.: A new automatic intrusion response taxonomy and its application. In: Shen, H.T., Li, J., Li, M., Ni, J., Wang, W. (eds.) APWeb Workshops 2006. LNCS, vol. 3842, pp. 999–1003. Springer, Heidelberg (2006)
20. Zhou, C.V., Leckie, C., Karunasekera, S.: A survey of coordinated attacks and collaborative intrusion detection. Comput. Secur. 29(1), 124–140 (2010)

# Author Index

Printed in the United States
By Bookmasters